The Teacher's Encyclopedia of Behavior Management

100 Problems/ 500 Plans

Randall S. Sprick   •   Lisa M. Howard

Edited by Jami Leutheuser
Text layout and design by Sherri Rowe
Cover design by Londerville Design

ISBN #1-57035-031-0

Published and Distributed by:

Sopris West

1140 Boston Avenue • Longmont, CO 80501 • (303) 651-2829

CKNOWLEDGMENTS

This reference guide represents a collaborative effort by many people. First and foremost, we are indebted to the thousands of teachers who have, over the years, shared their concerns about and solutions for classroom problems. Many of these problems and plans have been included in this book.

We are particulary grateful to Marilyn Sprick and Mickey Garrison for reviewing portions of the manuscript, from early drafts to later revisions, and for providing invaluable suggestions that shaped the final product. Judy Shinn provided helpful assistance and feedback on the accuracy of bibliographic references.

Finally, we would like to thank the staff of Sopris West—Jami Leutheuser for her patient and highly competent editing, Sherri Rowe for text layout and design, and Stu Horsfall and Duane Webb for encouragement, feedback, and support.

Though this was a collaborative effort, any errors, omissions, or lack of clarity are our responsibility as authors—not the people who generously donated time and expertise to helping us with this project.

ACKNOWLEDGMENTS

ABOUT THE AUTHORS

Randall S. Sprick, Ph.D., is an educational consultant and teacher trainer in Eugene, Oregon. Each year, Dr. Sprick conducts workshops and classes for over 5,000 teachers and administrators throughout the United States and Canada. Much of his work involves helping teachers set up classrooms that encourage student responsibility and motivation, while humanely and effectively helping misbehaving students learn to behave in more responsible ways.

Dr. Sprick has developed numerous articles, books, audio tapes, and video-tapes that assist school personnel in dealing with the issues of discipline and classroom management. Dr. Sprick has been an assistant professor and currently is an adjunct faculty member of the University of Oregon and the Seattle Pacific University. He is a past president of the Association for Direct Instruction.

Lisa M. Howard, B.A., is a former special and general education teacher. She has worked on a number of school-based research projects in California, Oregon, and Washington.

OVERVIEW OF THE LIBRARY— MANAGEMENT, MOTIVATION & DISCIPLINE

. . . .

The Library—Management, Motivation & Discipline is a collection of practical materials designed to assist in creating productive, safe, and respectful learning environments. The materials are full of specific "how-to" information. Though each resource stands alone, all are designed around five basic concepts:

1. All students must be treated with dignity and respect.

2. Students can and should be taught skills for success.

3. Motivation and responsibility should be encouraged through positive interactions.

4. Misbehavior provides a teaching opportunity.

5. Collaboration is critical—staff must work together to meet student needs.

. . . .

Other Components of *The Library*

Foundations: Establishing Positive Discipline Policies assists staff in designing policies that create a calm, safe, and positive school climate. This site-based management approach to discipline allows staff to increase consistency, clarify expectations, increase positive interactions, improve student motivation, and reduce office referrals. Video and print materials provide step-by-step information on how to write, implement, and maintain a policy that actually guides daily practice.

Interventions: Collaborative Planning for Students At Risk is both a resource and a process for education professionals. Through consultation and collaboration, staff members learn to share their expertise in developing practical intervention plans. Booklets describe how to set up, implement, and fade 16 specific interventions. Interventions detailed include procedures such as *Managing Physically Dangerous Behavior, Managing Severely Disruptive Behavior, Self-Monitoring, Self-Control Training, Restructuring Self-Talk,* and *Academic Assistance.* An optional 20 cassette audio tape album is available to accompany this resource.

Substitutes: Planning for Productivity and Consistency provides information on how to manage the behavior of students when the teacher is absent. These video, software, and print materials teach substitute teachers the essentials of classroom and behavior management, including how to define expectations, how to deal with common discipline problems, and how to increase the cooperation and motivation of students. In addition, the building principal and teaching staff receive information about implementing a school-wide plan that sets the stage for success, as well as software that allows them to customize substitute plans. Among the issues addressed are teaching students how to treat substitute teachers with respect, ensuring that teachers leave adequate plans and information for the substitutes, and procedures for supporting substitute teachers. **(Available Winter '95)**

Although still in the planning stages, other critical topics in *The Library* will include resources on:

- Motivation in the classroom
- Building principals' guide to discipline and motivation
- Support staffs' guide to discipline and motivation
- Family involvement in discipline and motivation
- Special educators' role in discipline and motivation

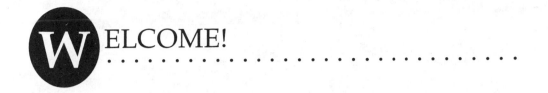

WELCOME!

It is our hope that this book will assist you in helping students learn to behave more responsibly. It addresses a number of common classroom problems (both individual and class-wide), and includes MODEL PLANS as well as suggestions for developing and implementing interventions. You may choose to either implement the MODEL PLANS as presented or to use them as prompts or guides for creating your own customized interventions.

When you use this book for the first time, begin by reading the INTRODUCTION section. The INTRODUCTION describes the organization of the book and explains how to use it most effectively. Once you are familiar with the procedures, you will be ready to look for information on the particular problem that concerns you.

Best of luck in your efforts to help your students learn to be increasingly responsible for their own behavior.

Randall S. Sprick
Lisa M. Howard

TABLE OF CONTENTS

. . . .

841 Additional Information

The
Teacher's
Encyclopedia of
Behavior Management:
100 Problems/500 Plans

• • • • • • • • • •

INTRODUCTION

INTRODUCTION

....
Purpose

Discipline and motivation problems are among the most frustrating aspects of any teacher's job. Inappropriate behavior disrupts learning—for the student or students who misbehave and often for their classmates. Such interference with learning is understandably upsetting and requires active problem solving.

Without a doubt, the keys to a well-run classroom are prevention and organization. Careful planning paired with systematically teaching students how to behave responsibly at the beginning of the year will prevent most behavior problems. *(NOTE: See the suggested references following.)*

Occasionally, however, problems occur in even the most organized and well-run classrooms. This book is intended for those situations. It is designed to be a reference guide to help you quickly develop and implement effective interventions for common classroom problems—those that are going on right now, *this week*!

Like most reference guides, this book is not meant to be read straight through from beginning to end. Think of it more like a collection of blueprints for you to consider. Maybe a metaphor will help. If you wanted to build a house, you could start by reading a text on architectural design, or you could look through a book of house plans. For most people, sitting down with a blank piece of paper and a textbook on architecture would be rather daunting. Skimming a book of house plans, however, is not intimidating and it allows you to evaluate many different options. You might find a plan that fits your specifications exactly (or with minimal modification), or you might combine aspects of different plans in order to meet your unique needs. This is a book of model intervention plans for responding to behavior, discipline, and motivation problems.

Following are some excellent references on overall behavior management and setting up a classroom at the beginning of the year:

Emmer, E.T., Evertson, C.M., Sanford, J.P., Clements, B.S., & Worsham, M.E. (1984). *Classroom management for secondary teachers*. Englewood Cliffs, NJ: Prentice Hall.

Evertson, C.M., Emmer, E.T., Clements, B.S., Sanford, J.P., & Worsham, M.E. (1984). *Classroom management for elementary teachers*. Englewood Cliffs, NJ: Prentice Hall.

Rhode, G., Jenson, W.R., & Reavis, H.K. (1992). *The tough kid book: Practical classroom management strategies*. Longmont, CO: Sopris West.

Sprick, R.S. (1981). *The solution book: A guide to classroom discipline*. Chicago: Science Research Associates.

Sprick, R.S. (1985). *Discipline in the secondary classroom: A problem by problem survival guide*. Englewood Cliffs, NJ: Prentice Hall.

Wong, H.K. & Wong, R.T. (1991). *The first days of school: How to start school successfully*. Sunnyvale, CA: Harry K. Wong Publications.

Philosophical Foundations and Beliefs

The main beliefs underlying *The Teacher's Encyclopedia of Behavior Management* are that: (1) teachers can make a difference in student behavior; and (2) what happens in the classroom can help any student learn to be more independent and responsible. While most of the recommended procedures rest on a behavioral research foundation, we also suggest techniques that are derived from counseling, Adlerian psychology, social learning theory, and cognitive/behavior modification approaches. Regardless of theoretical background, every procedure that has been included in this book meets two criteria:

1. It ensures that the student(s) are treated with dignity and respect.

2. It provides a reasonable chance of helping the student(s) learn to behave more responsibly.

We feel it is important to acknowledge from the outset that changing student behavior can be difficult. Irresponsible behavior often fulfills a specific need for a student (e.g., a way to gain adult attention or peer approval). Sometimes the misbehavior is a long-standing and/or deeply ingrained habit. In other instances, it represents a behavior that is modeled and reinforced in a student's home. Occasionally, a student may not know *how* to behave more responsibly. Thus, most interventions will have ups and downs, and require some time before long-term progress is achieved. Plan to be persistent and patient in your efforts to help students learn to behave responsibly.

Organization

This reference guide is divided into three main sections:

1. The INTRODUCTION, which describes the purpose, philosophical foundation, and organization of the book, and explains how to use it effectively.

2. The COMMON CLASSROOM PROBLEMS, which comprises the bulk of the book and contains approximately 100 entries arranged alphabetically by title. In most cases, the information presented within each problem includes GENERAL CONSIDERATIONS, up to six MODEL PLANS, and SUGGESTED STEPS FOR DEVELOPING AND IMPLEMENTING A PLAN.

3. The ADDITIONAL INFORMATION, which includes APPENDICES on the following three topics: reinforcing appropriate behavior; assigning responsibilities or jobs; and responding to inappropriate behavior.

Using the Book

A truly functional reference guide is designed so that the desired information is easily accessible. *The Teacher's Encyclopedia of Behavior Management* includes several features that we hope will make the book functional for you. What follows is a guide to using the book efficiently and effectively.

Finding the Appropriate Information

The classroom problems addressed in this reference guide are arranged alphabetically by title, so you can look up the particular issue that concerns you just as you would look for a topic in a standard encyclopedia. For example, you would find "**Disrespectful Behavior**" between "**Depression**" and "**Disruptive Behavior—Moderate**." Since most classroom problems can be referred to by a number of different titles, however, we have also provided a comprehensive INDEX. The INDEX, which contains more than 300 entries, includes *multiple* descriptive titles for each problem. If you are having a problem with a student who is disrespectful, for example, you might initially look in the TABLE OF CONTENTS under "Respect, Lack of." Although you would not find a problem with that title in the text, you would find this as an entry in the INDEX—

with a reference to the problem "**Disrespectful Behavior.**"

Once you have the problem located a specific problem in the text, you must then determine whether it is the most applicable/appropriate topic for your situation. To help you make this decision, each problem includes a title page on which you will find the following additional information:

- The DESCRIPTION—a general description of the type of situation that is addressed by the problem's plans.

- The GOAL—a statement of the result expected from the intervention.

- The OVERVIEW OF PLANS—brief explanations of the specific focus of each MODEL PLAN included for the problem.

If, after reviewing the title page, you do not think that particular problem is appropriate for your needs (or if you are still not sure), check for ALTERNATIVE PROBLEMS listed in the righthand column (the black bar). Whenever applicable, we have included a list of related problems. Thus, if you choose, you can examine the title pages of those problems to see whether one or more of them addresses your situation more directly. Once you have located an appropriate problem (or problems), you are ready to begin using the information to help you implement an effective intervention.

Using the Information

The first step is to skim all the information included with the problem (or problems) that you have identified as appropriate. Although, in most cases, the information will be presented in the following order, it is important to realize that the process of developing and implementing an intervention plan is not linear. The information in each of the sections relates to information in the others. After you have familiarized yourself with all the sections, you will be prepared to use the information effectively:

- GENERAL CONSIDERATIONS—This section will generally follow the OVERVIEW OF PLANS (discussed previously). This section describes possible factors related to the misbehavior that should be considered and, if necessary, addressed from the outset. For example, some misbehaviors may be affected by a student's inability to do the required academic work. In such cases, an intervention that only targets the inappropriate behavior—without concurrent efforts to assist the student academically—is not likely to succeed. When this is a possibility, it is suggested that before you begin your intervention, you determine the student's academic deficit(s) and a cross-reference to the problem **Academic Deficits, Determining** is provided.

Another example involves considering whether the apparent misbehavior reflects cultural differences (e.g., looking the teacher in the eye is an expected behavior in some cultures, but a sign of disrespect in others)—in which case it may be inappropriate to try to change the student's behavior.

- MODEL PLANS—In most of the problems, the next section will be the one to six sample plans that have been developed to address the particular problem behavior. Generally, the first plan provided is appropriate for a situation in which the problem is mild, while the remaining plans address circumstances in which the problem is more severe (i.e., the behavior is more disruptive/longer-standing), and/or the student's behavior is based on some specific underlying cause(s).

For example, in **Disrespectful Behavior,** PLAN A is appropriate when the student's misbehavior has just begun, occurs infrequently, or is only mildly disrespectful. The subsequent plans are appropriate when the disrespectful behavior is more severe, and address the following specific issues/conditions: a student who is disrespectful in order to gain adult attention or engage adults in one-to-one interactions (PLAN B); a student who is disrespectful to gain status with peers (PLAN C); a student for whom disrespectful behavior has become a habit (PLAN D); and a class-wide problem in which several students are disrespectful (PLAN E).

We encourage you to read through all the MODEL PLANS provided for the problem before deciding on one, for a couple of reasons. You may gain some new insights about what is actually going on in your situation (e.g., you may realize that the student is only disrespectful in front of peers). You will also get an idea of the range of techniques that might be useful in addressing the situation.

These MODEL PLANS have been included to save you time and/or to give you ideas; we hope that you use them creatively and flexibly to develop an intervention that is appropriate to your situation. While you might determine that one of the MODEL PLANS (as written) is appropriate, you may just as easily decide that your intervention will be more effective if you combine techniques from the different plans and/or with other procedures with which you are already more familiar/comfortable. The general rule is to use the least intrusive plan possible, however, to be successful, the intervention must be structured enough to address the conditions of the particular situation.

- SUGGESTED STEPS FOR DEVELOPING AND IMPLEMENTING A PLAN—The final section in most problems consists of procedures to help you develop an appropriate plan and implement it effectively. (As with the MODEL PLANS, the information presented in this section should be viewed as a recommendation rather than an absolute prescription.)

- Typically, the following procedures will be suggested:

   – Make sure you have enough information about the situation (data collection).

   – Identify a focus for the intervention and labels for referring to the appropriate and inappropriate behaviors.

   – Determine when and how to include parent(s).

   – Prepare for, then conduct, an initial meeting about the situation.

   – Give the student regular, ongoing feedback about his/her behavior.

   – Evaluate the situation (and the plan).

Keep in mind that, although the section as a whole follows all the MODEL PLANS, the procedures themselves may be referred to within the plans. For example, PLAN C of **Disrespectful Behavior** suggests that you " . . . use your notes (See SUGGESTED STEPS FOR DEVELOPING AND IMPLEMENTING A PLAN) to identify situations in which the student has been disrespectful . . . . " The "notes" refer to anecdotal notes, which are explained in Step 1 of the SUGGESTED STEPS FOR DEVELOPING AND IMPLEMENTING A PLAN provided at the end of that problem.

The procedures are presented as steps, however, they should not necessarily be followed sequentially. For example, it is generally recommended that you develop a plan *with the student* during an initial meeting. However, if the student is passive, he/she may not participate in the meeting. Thus, it is advisable to have a preliminary plan in mind before the meeting in order to avoid wasted time. On the other hand, if you present the preliminary plan as a given to a student who engages in power struggles, he/she is likely to rebel and/or sabotage the plan.

Why Some of the Problems Don't Have Plans

Several of the classroom problems included in this reference guide do not provide MODEL PLANS. In some cases, this is because the particular behavior being addressed involves complex issues that are beyond the scope of the book. For example, the problem of head banging and/or biting oneself (see **Self-Injurious Behavior**) is one that requires a formal analysis of the student's behavior and the conditions surrounding that behavior. Therefore, in lieu of MODEL PLANS, we have provided a reference for a more comprehensive text that deals specifically with conducting a functional analysis.

In other instances, MODEL PLANS have not been included because the problem does not involve a single behavior, but instead represents a broad label that encompasses a variety of behaviors. When this is the case, the most effective way to intervene is to help the student learn to manage one specific behavior at a time. Therefore, the information presented for these problems involves identification of the various behavior(s) that may be exhibited along with referrals to other specific problems within the text.

Conclusion

This book is intended to be a reference—much like a standard encyclopedia. When faced with a particular problem behavior, locate it in the text using the alphabetical listings in the TABLE OF CONTENTS and/or the INDEX. Next, review the cover page of that problem to see whether it seems appropriate for your situation. If necessary, check the cover pages of related problems (listed as ALTERNATIVE PROBLEMS) and/or look for other titles in the INDEX to find a problem listing that more closely matches your circumstances.

Once you have identified the most appropriate problem(s), read through all the information included (GENERAL CONSIDERATIONS, MODEL PLANS, and SUGGESTED STEPS FOR DEVELOPING AND IMPLEMENTING A PLAN) and begin your intervention to resolve the situation and help your student(s) learn to be more responsible. If your first attempt is not successful, modify the plan and try again. Remember—the most effective teacher is not the one who *knows* the most, but the one who, when faced with a problem situation, *tries* the hardest.

Best of luck in your efforts to teach your students to be successful and behave responsibly!

NOTE: Please give us feedback. If you encounter a problem behavior that is not addressed in this book, or if you develop a successful plan that is different from the MODEL PLANS that have been included, let us know. Your input will help us keep this reference guide current and more useful in future editions. You will find a GIVE US FEEDBACK form at the very end of the book that you can use for this purpose. Thanks.

The
Teacher's
Encyclopedia of
Behavior Management:
100 Problems/500 Plans

. . . .

COMMON CLASSROOM
PROBLEMS

ABSENTEEISM

Poor Attendance

DESCRIPTION

You have a student who has/is developing a pattern of chronic excused absences.

GOAL

The student will come to school consistently unless physically ill.

OVERVIEW OF PLANS

- PLAN A: For a situation in which the problem is relatively mild or has just begun.

- PLAN B: For a student who may be missing school because he does not feel any affiliation to school.

- PLAN C: For a student who may be missing school because of home factors.

- PLAN D: For a student who has no motivation to improve his attendance.

- PLAN E: For a situation in which the problem is class-wide (i.e., many students have a problem with absenteeism).

Alternative Problems

- **Hypochondria**
- **School Phobia**

. . . .
General Considerations

- If the student's absences stem from chronic health issues (i.e., a medically fragile student), you might consider referring the student for special education services; or if he is already special education identified, you should consult with his special education teacher. (See also **Allergies, Asthma, Disabilities, Seizures**).

- If the student's absences stem from academic issues (i.e., the student is unable to meet academic expectations and stays home to avoid having to do the work), concurrent efforts must be made to ensure his academic success. (See **Academic Deficits, Determining**).

- If the student's absences are unexcused, you should report them and follow through with school/district policies regarding truancy. Most schools have established consequences for unexcused absences—for example, after-school detention, lunch time detention, Saturday School, in-school suspension, and/or parentally imposed sanctions. Some states (e.g., Oregon)

even have monetary fines that truancy officials can impose on parents.

If possible, avoid assigning out-of-school suspension, as this is probably reinforcing for the student. If the formal consequences for truancy do not seem to be effective in motivating the student to come to school, you should certainly try the proactive approaches suggested in the MODEL PLANS provided for this problem. All of the plans can be modified for use with truancy, as long as the student realizes that he is still subject to mandated school consequences when his absences are unexcused.

NOTE: An excellent manual on attendance issues and procedures has been developed by the staff of Linn-Benton Educational Service District. For additional information, contact:

> *Royal Harger*
> *Linn-Benton ESD*
> *905 4th Avenue SE*
> *Albany, OR 97321*

. . . .
Model Plans

PLAN A

It is not always necessary, or even beneficial, to use an involved plan. If the problem has just begun (i.e., is occurring at the beginning of the school year), the following actions, along with making the student aware of your concerns, may resolve the situation.

Use reinforcement to encourage appropriate behavior.

Give the student increased praise for improved attendance. In addition, frequent teacher attention will help show the student that he has value in the classroom. Among the ways you might give extra attention:

- Say, "hello" whenever you see him outside of class;

- In the morning, ask him how he is doing;

- Ask him to join you and a couple of other students to redo a bulletin board; or

- Ask his opinion of a new room arrangement.

PLAN B

Sometimes a student is absent often because he does not feel a sense of affiliation with his classroom and/or school. For this type of student, the intervention should include encouraging and supporting the student's sense of belonging in the classroom so that he feels more emotionally secure about coming to school.

Make the student feel welcome at school.

a. Greet the student warmly after every absence. Regardless of whether the absence was valid, when the student returns to class let him know that you missed him. "Craig, it's nice to see you. We missed you in math the last two days." For the student who thinks, "Why bother going to school since no one notices that I am there?", this provides attention and demonstrates that people do miss him when he is gone. You may even want to suggest the procedure to other adults who work with this student.

b. Try to arrange for positive attention from other adults in the school. You might ask the principal, playground supervisors, and other teachers to give this student lots of attention. Having various adults making it a point to greet the student whenever they see him at school may increase his feelings of connection and affiliation.

c. You might also see about arranging an adult mentor for the student. Having a specific adult mentor (e.g., a volunteer such as a "foster grandparent" or any other adult with whom the student can have regular contact) may be very effective. A student like this can probably use all the help, support, and positive attention he can get.

 Encourage the student to become involved in school activities that he is likely to find rewarding.

The more involved the student gets in school activities, the more compelling it will be for him to come to school. Among the possibilities to consider are school clubs or scouting troops that meet at the school. Or you might see if he would like to try out for a part in the school play or help with the sets. If the library uses student assistants, see if he might be willing to apply for the job.

 Increase the student's academic success and involvement.

Make sure that the student is experiencing high rates of academic success and increase the student's level of academic engagement. For example, call on him frequently with questions that he has a high probability of answering correctly. During independent work, go to the student and ask

him if he has any questions. Later, when you talk with the student about his progress (see SUGGESTED STEPS FOR DEVELOPING AND IMPLEMENTING A PLAN), you might ask him for suggestions on making the lessons more interesting. When reports or projects are assigned, help the student pick a topic that may be of particular interest to him. (All of these suggestions are in addition to considering **Academic Deficits, Determining**.)

 Use reinforcement to encourage appropriate behavior.

Give the student increased praise and attention when he attends school (see PLAN A).

 Ensure a 3-1 ratio of positive to negative attention.

a. It is easy to fall into a pattern of interacting with a chronically absent student in negative ways (e.g., nagging him to finish things he is behind in because he has been absent). You need to make sure that the student is not getting more attention for being absent than for attending regularly.

To do so, record every interaction you have with the student for an entire day. Keep a card in your pocket and mark it each time during the day that you interact with the student. Mark a "+" if the interaction is in response to something positive the student has done and a "-" if the interaction has to do with negative behavior or being absent.

The goal is to have three interactions involving positive and responsible behavior for every one interaction involving his absences or irresponsible behavior.

b. If you find that you are not giving the student three times as much positive as negative attention, try to increase the number of positive interactions you have with him. Sometimes prompts can help. For example, you might decide that each time the student enters the classroom you will say "hello" to him; or that whenever you look at the clock you will find a time to praise the student; or that whenever a student uses the drinking fountain you will check the target student and, as soon as possible, praise some aspect of his behavior.

PLAN C

Some attendance problems stem from home factors (e.g., no one is available to wake the student up in the morning or make his lunch; the student does not have clean clothes to wear or is embarrassed about having to wear old clothes; the student does not have a reliable way to get to school). In this situation, the intervention plan should include ways to help the student assume responsibility for getting himself to school. *(NOTE: In some cases, this plan will need to be paired with PLAN D.)*

 Identify and address the factors that are contributing to the student's absenteeism.

Determine what kinds of things are hindering regular attendance. Then, together with the student, identify strategies that are both practical to implement and acceptable to the student that will help him deal with those circumstances. For example, if there is no one available to wake the student up, you might make arrangements for the student to get an alarm clock and teach him how to use it. Or you could have a classroom paraprofessional call the student immediately upon arriving at work each morning.

If the student does not have enough clothes, there might be charitable organizations that take students shopping at secondhand stores for decent clothes. If the student's clothes are often not washed, perhaps someone (e.g., the counselor) can teach the student to use a washing machine.

NOTE: Depending upon the parent(s)' willingness and ability to help, it is best to work with both the student and his parent(s). However, if the parent(s) are unavailable, for whatever reason, you need to be prepared to work with the student only. A student whose parent(s) do not live up to their responsibilities, yet are not so negligent that child abuse charges are warranted, deserves to be taught how to be responsible for himself. Obviously, this needs to be handled very carefully.

 Help the student set goals for improved attendance.

Give some thought to what *you hope* the student's attendance will be, and then, either by yourself or with the student, develop a contract that includes a broad-based attendance goal and at least three *specific* things the student can do to achieve the goal. Generally, when a student has been involved in the goal-setting process he is more likely to strive to achieve the goal.

A finished goal contract for excessive absenteeism might look like the sample following.

(Student Name)'s Goal Contract

My goal is:

> I will come to school every day unless I am physically ill (such as having a fever).

I can achieve my goal by:

> 1. Making sure I have clothes for the next day and washing some, if necessary.
>
> 2. Making sure my alarm clock is set each night before I go to bed.
>
> 3. If I think I am sick, calling Ms. Saltzman at school at 7:45 to discuss whether I should come to school or not.

Student Signature _____ Date _____

Teacher Signature _____ Date _____

Start Date _____ End Date _____ Goal Met? Y N

Use reinforcement to encourage appropriate behavior.

a. Give the student increased praise and attention when he attends school (see PLAN A).

b. Intermittently reward the student's efforts to meet his goal. When you know the student is making an effort to meet his goal, reward him specifically for assuming responsibility. "Craig, you have made it to school every day since our conference last week. You should be so proud of your ability to take on this responsibility."

Would you like to eat lunch with me in my office?"

Other rewards might include letting him help you with a job, tutoring a younger student, or even something as simple as letting him sit next to a friend during an assembly. *(NOTE: A list of additional reinforcement ideas can be found in APPENDIX 1.)* Only use rewards when the student is making a *significant* effort to follow through on the goal.

PLAN D

If the student's parent(s) are not willing to "make" him come to school, it may have become easier for the student to stay home. If your student has developed a habit of missing school and/or does not seem interested in improving his attendance, you may need to implement a system of external incentives (i.e., rewards) based on his attendance, to motivate him to attend school regularly.

 Have the student check-in daily with a counselor or administrator.

Arrange for the student to report to a responsible party each day and sign in on a calendar. This checking-in provides a way for the student to receive immediate attention when he comes to school and facilitates the implementation of the following reinforcement system. That is, the calendar will be the official record for determining points and graphically showing the student how many (or how few) days in a given month he has been at school.

 Establish a structured system for reinforcing the student's improved attendance.

a. With the student, identify rewards or privileges that he can earn for improved attendance, and structure the rewards as a system of reinforcement. For example, you might have the student earn a certain number of points for each day he comes to school and bonus points when he has perfect attendance for an extended period of time (e.g., two points each day he comes to school and four bonus points for five consecutive days with no absences; ten bonus points for ten consecutive days with no absences; and 20

bonus points for 20 consecutive days with no absences).

b. Have some of the reinforcement items be relatively "low cost," and others that require the student to save for a longer period of time. Periodically ask the student if he wants to spend some points or if he would like to keep saving.

Spent points are subtracted from the total, but do not affect the "consecutive days without an absence." For example, after 12 consecutive days of attendance the student would have 38 points (two points for each day, and 14 bonus points). If he spends 30 points to eat lunch with the teacher, he has eight points left over and is on day 13 of 20 consecutive days toward the 20 bonus points.

 Use reinforcement to encourage appropriate behavior.

a. Give the student increased praise and attention when he attends school (see PLAN A).

b. Show interest and enthusiasm in how the student is doing on the reinforcement system.

PLAN E

Sometimes, an entire classroom falls into a pattern of absenteeism. This can happen because the behavior has become habitual and/or because the majority of students are emulating a few influential students who choose not to come to school to look "cool" or "tough." In these cases it can be very difficult to change student behavior, and you may need to use a variety of techniques to create mild peer pressure to motivate the students to come to school.

 1. *Meet your students at the door and welcome them to the classroom.*

a. Being met at the door and receiving a friendly greeting such as, "Good morning Tamai. It's nice to see you," is a very pleasant way to start the day. If a student has been absent, let him know that you missed him. "Kamaal, we missed you yesterday. It's nice to have you back."

b. Begin class by thanking the students for being there and by giving them an overview of some the interesting and worthwhile things that will happen that day. (By the way, if you can't think of any, you need to reorganize your instructional priorities and/or methods.)

 2. *Publicly post the percentage of students in attendance each day.*

a. When you compile your attendance record for the day, calculate the percentage of students in attendance (i.e., divide the number of students present by the total number of students enrolled). If appropriate, have the students figure out the percentage for you. "I have just completed attendance and it appears we have 27 students here today, and two absent. Luke and Ella, please figure the percentage attending for us."

b. Record (or have a student record) this information on a large chart that is visible to the entire class. If you are a middle/junior high school teacher, use separate transparencies for each class, and only show any given class its own data.

c. As the data is being posted, talk to the class about trends—is attendance getting worse, staying the same, or getting better? When time permits, discuss the distinction between valid and invalid reasons for staying home. Note that in some cases, just having a parental excuse may not be a valid reason (e.g., for having a minor headache).

d. During this discussion (and periodically throughout the day), be a "coach" for good attendance. In sports, an effective coach rallies the team's energies to meet a challenge. In this case, you want to encourage your students to come to school each day that they are not physically ill.

Use actual situations to provide useful information to the entire class. For example, "Class, yesterday Stephanie told me that she had a slight headache in the morning, but that she and her mom decided she would try coming to school and see how things went. I am proud to report that Stephanie made it through the entire day and that her headache was gone by lunch. Nice job, Steph!" In addition, pump up student motivation for wanting to make theirs the best class in the school.

 3. *Encourage the class to set daily performance goals for class-wide attendance.*

Help the students set an attainable goal (e.g., increasing the percentage of students present daily from 70% to 80%). Some students may want to set an unrealistic goal (e.g., going from 70% to 100% present). Explain that if the goal is 80%, they can always get better than that, but they increase their chances of success.

As the class experiences success, progressively raise the goal until the percentage is acceptable to you (while still allowing for students to stay home when truly ill). Because the original problem is an excessive number of absences, success is *reducing* (not necessarily eliminating) absenteeism.

4. *Use reinforcement to encourage appropriate behavior.*

a. Praise individual students for regular attendance, especially those students who have had the greatest tendency to be absent. Whenever one of these students has been attending regularly, praise him/her. "Nice job, T.J, you have made it to school every day this week. Keep up the excellent attendance." If public praise would be embarrassing, praise the student(s) privately or even use notes.

b. Don't forget to occasionally praise those students who rarely or never have a problem with absenteeism. Because these students have already mastered the positive expectations, they do not need positive feedback as often as the students who have had difficulty. However, you do not want them to feel that you take their positive behavior for granted. "Janelle and Pat, you both have not missed a single day all year. That kind of attendance will really be appreciated by future employers who are lucky enough to have either of you working for them."

c. When there has been a significant overall improvement in class attendance, praise the entire class. Remember that any time attendance improves, you can give praise.

d. You may also wish to use intermittent rewards to acknowledge the class' success. Occasional, and unexpected, rewards can motivate the students to demonstrate responsible behavior more often. The idea is to provide a reward when the class has made significant improvements in overall attendance.

Appropriate rewards might include scheduling a fun field trip for the class, congratulating the class in front of the principal, or even providing the class with a food treat. *(NOTE: A list of additional reinforcement ideas can be found in APPENDIX 1).*

If you use intermittent rewards, do so more frequently at the beginning of the intervention to encourage the students, and then less often as the attendance improves.

5. *(OPTIONAL)*
Establish a group reinforcement system.

a. Have the students brainstorm a list of reinforcement ideas for the entire class, and then eliminate from the list any items that are not possible (i.e., the suggestion is too expensive or could not be provided to all the students in the class).

b. Assign "prices" (in points) to the remaining items on the list. The prices should be based on the instructional, personnel, and/or monetary costs of the items. Monetary cost is clear—the more expensive the item, the more points required to earn it. Instructional cost refers to the amount of instructional time lost or interfered with by a particular reward. Thus, an activity which causes the class to miss part of academic instruction should require more points than one the class can do during recess time. Personnel cost involves the time required by you and/or other staff to fulfill the reinforcer. For example, awarding an extra recess period which requires extra supervision would cost more than allowing music to play in class for 15 minutes.

c. Have the class vote on the reinforcers. The reinforcer that wins the most votes is the one they will work for first, and the items that come in second (and third) will be the next ones worked for.

d. On days that the group successfully meets or beats their goal, they earn a point toward their reward.

e. An alternative is to use a Mystery Motivator (Rhode, Jenson, & Reavis, 1992). In this system, you mark an "X" on certain days on a calendar, then cover every day's space with a paper dot. Each day the group meets their performance goal (i.e., percentage of attendance is at or above the goal), you uncover the space for that day to see if there is an "X." If there is, the group earns their reinforcer.

(NOTE: Even on days when the class is not successful, uncover the dot so they find out whether they would have received the reward if they had achieved their performance objective.)

· · · · · · · ·
Suggested Steps for Developing and Implementing a Plan

The following steps are designed to help you develop an appropriate intervention plan and implement it effectively, whether you choose to use one of the MODEL PLANS or create a customized plan of your own. The steps are, however, suggestions—they are not intended to be followed rigidly or in any particular order. Use your professional judgment and the knowledge of your particular situation to make them work for you.

 Make sure you have enough information about the situation.

a. With a problem like absenteeism, it is important to have accurate information about the student's actual attendance. Use your classroom records, if possible starting with the preceding month, and tally the number of times the student has been absent so you can determine a *"percentage of time present"* for each week. Simply divide the number of days the student was at school in a week by the number of days that school was in session that week. You will continue to calculate this attendance rate throughout the implementation of the plan.

Although you could calculate the "percentage of time absent" or "number of days present" (or absent), working to increase a behavior has more psychological (and aesthetic) "punch" than trying to decrease it; hence, making the focus on time "present" is preferable to time "absent." The advantage of using a percentage of time rather than a simple count is that you eliminate the potential problem of comparing unequal amounts of time (i.e., when different weeks have different numbers of school days because of holidays, etc.).

b. Displaying the student's attendance rate on a graph or a chart provides an effective way for the student to "see" his attendance record and a means of monitoring subsequent changes in his attendance.

2. Determine when and how to include the parent(s).

a. Absenteeism is the kind of problem in which it is important to include the parent(s) from the outset. If you are implementing a minimal plan (e.g., PLAN A), it may be enough to call the parent(s) or drop a note to share the attendance information you have collected and explain your concern. You might ask for parental input as to the reasons for the absences.

Whenever the student's absences are affecting his academic or social progress, you should invite the parent(s) to join you for the initial meeting with the student to develop a plan to help the student learn to "be responsible for coming to school." If the parent(s) are unable or unwilling to participate, let them know that you will keep them informed about the situation.

b. It is important to maintain contact with the parent(s) about the student's attendance rate and any efforts you are making to remedy the situation. *(NOTE: It is probably a good idea to document these contacts with the parent[s], as well as any actions you take with the student.)*

3. Prepare for, then conduct, an initial meeting about the situation.

a. Arrange for a meeting to discuss your concerns with the student (and if applicable, the parent[s]). Although the specifics of the meeting will vary depending upon the age of the student and the severity of the problem, there are some general guidelines to consider when you schedule the meeting. In general, you want to meet at a neutral time and in an appropriately private place. You also want to schedule enough time so that the meeting is not likely to be interrupted.

b. Construct a preliminary plan. Before you meet with the student decide (based on the information you have collected) whether you think you want to use one of the MODEL PLANS or create a customized plan using components from various plans and/or your own ideas.

Although you will invite and encourage the student to be an active partner in developing the plan, having a proposed plan in mind before you meet can alleviate frustration and wasted time if the student is unwilling or unable to participate.

c. Conduct the meeting in a atmosphere of collaboration. The following agenda is one way you might structure the meeting:

- **Share your concerns about the student's behavior.**

  Show the student the attendance graph and explain that missing this much school is likely to prevent him from being as successful in school as he could otherwise be. With older students, you might emphasize that school attendance habits often carry over to the workplace, and that bad habits are hard to break later.

- **Discuss how you can work together to improve the situation.**

  If you haven't already, try to get an idea of why the student is missing so much school. Then explain that you want to help the student learn to "be more responsible about attending school" and describe your preliminary plan.

  Invite the student to give you input on the plan and together work out any necessary details (e.g., the reinforcement system). You may have to brainstorm different possibilities if the student is uncomfortable with any aspect of the initial plan. Incorporating any of the student's suggestions that strengthen the plan is likely to increase his sense of "ownership" in the plan and his commitment to it.

- **Conclude the meeting.**

Always end the meeting with words of encouragement. Let the student know that you are confident that he can improve his attendance and that he might actually find that he likes school more when he is attending regularly. Be sure to reinforce him for participating in the meeting.

 4. *Give the student regular, ongoing feedback about his attendance.*

It is important to continue to meet periodically with the student to discuss his progress. A three to five minute meeting once per week should suffice. Review the week's percentage of time present and discuss whether or not the situation is improving. The meetings can be faded—to once every other week and then to once per month—as the student's attendance improves.

 5. *Evaluate the situation (and the plan).*

When evaluating the effectiveness of a plan for attendance problems, you must allow sufficient time for changes to occur—and yet not let a continuing problem go unaddressed for too long. A reasonable suggestion is to review the situation after four weeks.

The primary source for determining whether or not there has been improvement will be the attendance chart. Generally, if the student's rate of attendance has increased, stick with what you are doing. However, if the number of absences is staying the same or increasing, some kind of change is necessary. Discuss any changes in the plan with the student before you implement them.

ABUSE

DESCRIPTION

You have a student in your class who you know to be or suspect may be a victim of child abuse.

The issue of child abuse is beyond the scope of this reference guide and the authors' expertise, therefore there are no MODEL PLANS included with this problem. The purpose of the following information is to offer some basic considerations and suggestions for addressing a situation in which you know/believe child abuse is/may be a possibility.

· · · · · · · ·
General Information

- With an issue that has legal consequences, such as abuse, it is critical that you be aware of any building and/or district policies regarding appropriate responses. In most states, teachers are required by law to report any incidents of suspected abuse to state authorities. If you are not sure what the procedures are in your school, immediately check with your building administrator.

- When interacting with a student who has been abused, it is very important to make the student feel safe and welcome at school. Greet the student as she arrives at school each day and, whenever possible, chat with the student. For example, when you are walking the class down the hall, make a point of walking with the student and having a pleasant conversation. When correcting the student's work, be sure to point out the positive aspects of the student's work first and then explain the student's errors as diplomatically as possible.

- If the student exhibits a particular misbehavior (e.g., apathy, arguing), find the specific behavior in this reference guide and review the suggested MODEL PLANS for addressing that behavior. If you find a plan that seems appropriate, be sure that you implement it with an extra bit of care and compassion given the student's troubled situation.

ACADEMIC DEFICITS, DETERMINING

DESCRIPTION

You suspect a student is behavioral problem(s) (e.g., shyness, disruptive behavior, work completion problems) may be caused or compounded by academic difficulties.

GOAL

You will determine whether the student is capable of successfully meeting the academic expectations.

CONSIDERATIONS

The student who fails to thrive academically is often frustrated. When her performance fails to match her aspirations, the student may feel inadequate and engage in any number of inappropriate behaviors to mask her sense of incompetence. The student may become withdrawn, seem unmotivated, clown around, or act sarcastic, distractible, or hyperactive. Sometimes academic problems are a severe and obvious factor in behavioral problems. In other instances, academic problems may be contributing to the behavioral problems, but are so mild that they do not draw attention.

Meeting the academic needs of all students is an incredibly complex and difficult topic—well beyond the scope of this reference guide. The material presented here is designed to help you determine whether a student is *capable* of meeting the academic expectations, and includes suggestions for additional resources on how to adapt curricula and remediate skill deficits.

NOTE: *The following material is adapted with permission from* Intervention D: Academic Assistance, *which is one of 16 intervention booklets in:*

Sprick, R.S., Sprick, M.S., & Garrison, M. (1993). Interventions: Collaborative planning for students at risk. *Longmont, CO: Sopris West.*

. . . .

Conduct an Informal Academic Assessment

The following procedures are not intended to comprise a thorough diagnostic battery, but they can help determine whether a student has the skills and strategies required to complete academic tasks. Select procedures that are relevant for the age and needs of the student, as well as the requirements of your classroom.

 Analyze information from a teacher inventory.

Teacher perceptions are an invaluable part of an informal academic assessment. For example, how often does the student complete her work? Always? usually? sometimes? rarely? never? Is the quality of the work satisfactory? Does the student do well in one subject, but not in another? Gather enough information to develop a clear picture of the student's daily performance in different classes at the secondary level, or in different subjects or activities at the elementary level. A sample "Teacher Inventory" is shown on the next page.

The "Teacher Inventory" can be customized with different variables. For example, some schools may wish to include "cooperation," while others may want to stress "being respectful." Some may evaluate student performance in traditional subjects like "social studies," "science," and "P.E.," while others decide to evaluate "math center work," "project work," "writing," etc.

When a student has several teachers, a separate form should be given to each of the student's teachers in order to maintain student confidentiality and to avoid having teachers influenced by one another. Once you and the student's other teachers (if applicable) have responded, transcribe the individual teacher responses onto a single master form.

After all the information has been collected, analyze the responses. Pay attention to factors such as: Are there specific subjects that cause difficulty? Are there specific skills that present roadblocks for the student? Does the student have problems with homework? Does the student have difficulty with tests? Does the student fail to participate in class? Is attendance or tardiness a continual problem? Does the student have special difficulty in classes that require a lot of reading or writing? Does the degree of academic success seem to be related to behavior in class?

 Analyze student work samples.

Examine student work samples and ask the student's other teachers (if applicable) to attach a sample of the student's work to the inventory. (If you are unfamiliar with the course content or the degree of competency required by another teacher, ask the teacher to include work samples by an "excellent" student and an "average" student for comparison.)

Work samples can provide you with information that may not be obtainable from standardized tests. For example, the student may read and comprehend well enough to pass multiple choice reading tests, but lack the organizational skills to summarize a passage in writing. The student may have the skills to research and write a report, but lack the time management strategies that allow her to complete her work on schedule. Or the work samples may indicate that the student is lacking basic skills. For example, the student may do well verbally, but have trouble putting thoughts down on paper due to poor handwriting or fine motor skills.

3. ***Collect oral reading fluency data.***

Reading is a multidimensional skill that can be assessed in many ways and at many levels. It is beyond the scope of this intervention to provide information on how to conduct a detailed diagnostic battery; however, testing oral reading fluency is suggested as a preliminary tool for determining whether reading problems are contributing to an academic problem.

Oral reading fluency is a measure of both the rate and accuracy of a student's reading. Though somewhat narrow in scope, it is an extremely pow-

TEACHER INVENTORY								
Student			Grade	Date				
Please complete a student performance rating for this student. The information you provide will be used to help develop an individual plan of assistance.								

5 = Always 4 = Usually 3 = Sometimes 2 = Rarely 1 = Never NA = Not Applicable *NOTE: 3 or below indicates a problem.*	Periods or Subject Areas						
	1	2	3	4	5	6	7

	Student Performance	1	2	3	4	5	6	7
Please attach a representative sample of student work.	**Academic Standing** List the student's current grade using the values assigned on the student report card (i.e., letter grades, ✓ + -, etc.).							

Please identify student strengths and goals for improvement.

erful screener: "The most salient characteristic of skillful readers is the speed and effortlessness with which they seem able to breeze through text" (Adams, 1990, p. 409).

Although fluency alone is not sufficient for reading with understanding, it is clear that it is a *necessary prerequisite* for understanding, interpreting, and responding to print:

- Fluency allows, but does not guarantee, that readers can construct meaning. If students must search for appropriate words—self-correcting, inserting, omitting, misreading, and sounding out words—comprehension suffers. When mental energy is heavily invested in figuring out the words, readers have a difficult time understanding and responding to the text.

- Fluency allows, but does not guarantee, that readers will be motivated to read. If students read accurately but laboriously, it is difficult to grasp important concepts and ideas. If text moves slowly, it's much like watching a movie in slow motion; the message becomes distorted, and attention tends to wander. Students who lack fluency often become bored with reading.

- Fluency allows, but does not guarantee, that readers can read strategically (i.e., adjust the way they read, depending upon their purpose and the type of material being read). Fluent readers quickly skim through text when the material is familiar and read deeply when important or difficult information is presented. Students who haven't developed into fluent readers are unable to adjust their reading strategies to the materials and the purpose of their reading.

Thus, while fluency does not guarantee good comprehension, it certainly speeds and assists good comprehension, and allows the student to complete assignments within a reasonable amount of time.

Instructions

The following instructions outline curriculum-based oral reading fluency procedures.

Select two passages, each of which should be approximately 250 words long, from grade level reading. The passages may be taken from a basal reading text or from other reading material that will be used in the classroom. Choose passages that the student hasn't yet read and that represent the level of difficulty normally encountered by students in the class. Avoid passages with an unusual number of difficult words or hard to pronounce names. The passages should be cohesive—have a clear beginning point and a reasonable message.

The materials required for the assessment include a stopwatch and two copies of each passage—a clear copy for the student to read from and a scoring copy.

You will have the student read twice (for one minute on each passage). When assessing the student, follow the procedures listed below for each of the two passages.

Curriculum-Based Measurement Procedures for Assessing and Scoring Oral Reading Fluency

Say to the student: "When I say 'start,' begin reading aloud at the top of this page. Read across the page (demonstrate by pointing). Try to read each word. If you come to a word you don't know, I'll tell it to you. Be sure to do your best reading. Are there any questions?"

Say, "Start."

Follow along on your copy of the story, marking the words that are read incorrectly. If a student stops or struggles with a word for three seconds, tell the student the word and mark it as incorrect.

Place a vertical line after the last word read and thank the student.

The following guidelines determine which words are to be counted as correct or incorrect:

1. *Words read correctly.* Words read correctly are those words that are pronounced correctly, given the reading context. For example:

   a. The word "read" must be pronounced "reed" when presented in the context of "She will read the book," not as "red."

   b. Repetitions are not counted as incorrect.

   c. Self-corrections within three seconds are counted as correctly read words.

2. *Words read incorrectly.* The following types of errors are counted: (a) mispronunciations, (b) substitutions, and (c) omissions, as follows:

   a. Mispronunciations are words that are misread: "dog" for "dig."

   b. Substitutions are words that are substituted for the stimulus word; this is often inferred by a one-to-one correspondence between word orders: "dog" for "cat."

   c. Omissions are words skipped or not read; if a student skips an entire line, each word is counted as an error.

3. *Three-second rule.* If a student is struggling to pronounce a word or hesitates for three seconds, the student is told the word, and it is counted as an error.

Reprinted with permission from Shinn, M.R. (Ed.). (1989). *Curriculum-based measurement: Assessing special children* (pp. 239-240). New York: The Guilford Press.

Score each of the passages by counting only the words read correctly. Average the two scores.

After scoring the assessment, interpret the student performance scores. To do so, use the curriculum-based norms shown in the table below. These norms were derived from data collected between 1981 and 1990 with 7,000-9,000 students in grades two through five. Students sampled included general education students and students who were participating in compensatory, remedial, and special education programs.

The norms provide rough guidelines for determining adequate reading fluency. For example, a student who reads about 50 words correct per minute or better from beginning second grade materials in the fall of second grade is making adequate progress. However, a third grade student who reads about 50 words correct per minute from third grade materials has fairly severe reading difficulties.

Unfortunately, norms are not available for older students; however, some liberty can be taken in extrapolating from the norms that do exist. One can safely assume that sixth grade students should be approaching at least 120 words correct per minute in the fall and at least 150 words per minute by the end of sixth grade. In seventh grade, the fluency rate should be at least 150 words per minute or better, and by high school, students should read somewhere above 150 words per minute. (There is a point at which the rate of oral reading is no longer relevant. Due to the rate of speech, there is likely to be some variance in acceptable oral reading rates above 150 words per minute. More research is needed in this area.) If in doubt, it may be

Curriculum-Based Norms in Oral Reading Fluency for Grades 2-5 (Medians)

Grade	Percentile	Fall		Winter		Spring		SD*** of Raw Scores
		n*	WCPM**	n	WCPM	n	WCPM	
2	75	4	82	5	106	4	124	
	50	6	53	8	78	6	94	39
	25	4	23	5	46	4	65	
3	75	4	107	5	123	4	142	
	50	6	79	8	93	6	114	39
	25	4	65	5	70	4	87	
4	75	4	125	5	133	4	143	
	50	6	99	8	113	6	118	37
	25	4	72	5	89	4	92	
5	75	4	126	5	143	4	151	
	50	6	105	8	118	6	128	35
	25	4	77	5	93	4	100	

* n = number of median scores from percentile table of districts (maximum possible = 8).
** WCPM = words correct per minute.
*** SD = the average standard deviation of scores from fall, winter, and spring for each grade level.

Reprinted with permission from Hasbrouck, J.E. & Tindal, G. (1992). Curriculum-based oral reading fluency norms for students in grades 2 through 5. *Teaching Exceptional Children*, *24*(3), 41-44.

useful to assess two or three capable students for comparison with the target student.

In addition to determining the words read correctly per minute, include a descriptive or qualitative analysis of the student's reading. For example, "Susan appeared to read the passage with great confidence. She read with expression and understanding—sounding like a professional storyteller."

 4. **Conduct an informal reading inventory.**

If a more detailed assessment seems necessary, consider developing an informal reading inventory or administering one of the many published informal reading inventories available commercially. The *Analytic Reading Inventory (ARI)* by Woods and Moe (1989) is such a tool. It includes an array of subtests that examine general levels of word recognition, word recognition strategies, and comprehension strategies through retellings and questions. Oral and silent reading performance and listening comprehension are reported as "independent, instructional, and frustration levels" (p. 21).

The *ARI* helps ascertain whether the student can retain information that has been read, determine the meaning of vocabulary, and engage in higher order thinking about information presented in both narrative and expository passages. Used with an oral reading fluency measure, inventories like the *ARI* can provide valuable information.

5. **Work one-to-one with the student on an assignment.**

When a student has difficulty completing assignments or completing assignments satisfactorily, have the student work on an assignment one-to-one with you or another adult. It may be useful to have the student redo an assignment that was either incomplete or not completed satisfactorily.

Working one-to-one with a student makes it easier to identify the student's strengths and weaknesses. For example, when a student is unsure of how to proceed, behavior such as hesitation, task avoidance, unwillingness to persevere, etc. will be more apparent. One-to-one assistance provides the opportunity to observe closely and to ask the student to clarify her understanding of the expectations and how she will complete the task.

When working one-to-one with the student, keep the following questions in mind:

- Does the student understand the instructions?

On an assignment involving written instructions, try to determine whether the student understands the instructions without further clarification from an adult.

- Does the student have the prerequisite skills required to complete the assignment?

For example, if the assignment involves writing, consider whether the student has the necessary tool skills of handwriting and spelling to write fluently without losing her train of thought. If the assignment involves three-digit multiplication, determine whether the student is able to line the numbers up accurately, whether the student knows the multiplication facts, whether she accurately records numbers in the correct place, etc.

- Does the student have effective strategies for completing the assignment?

If the student is studying for a spelling test, for example, find out whether the student has a strategy for systematically learning how to spell words. If the assignment involves math story problems, determine whether the student has strategies for writing and solving equations. If the assignment includes essay questions, try to determine whether the student has the required knowledge, knows how to find the required knowledge, and can articulate and write a reasonable response.

- Is the student able to stay on task for extended periods of time?

When the student appears to have the required skills, but simply lacks the ability or motivation to stay on task, see **Distractibility/ Short Attention Span**.

 6. **Implement procedures to increase the student's academic success.**

If your informal assessment indicates that the student has academic difficulties, you will need to implement procedures to increase the student's academic success concurrent with (or in lieu of) behavioral interventions. Following is a list of resources that provide ideas for adapting curricula and remediating skill deficits:

Algozzine, B. & Ysseldyke, J. (1992). *Strategies and tactics for effective instruction (STEI)*. Longmont, CO: Sopris West.

Kameenui, E.J. & Simmons, D.C. (1990). *Designing instructional strategies: The prevention of academic learning problems*. Columbus, OH: Merrill/Macmillan.

Mercer, C.D. & Mercer, A.R. (1989). *Teaching students with learning problems* (3rd ed.). New York: Macmillan.

Sprick, R.S., Sprick, M.S., & Garrison, M. (1993). *Interventions: Collaborative planning for students at risk*. Longmont, CO: Sopris West.

7. *Address the academic difficulties of the class as a whole, if applicable.*

If a significant number of students in your class have academic difficulties, you might wish to explore the *Direct Instruction* curriculum materials developed by Seigfried Engelmann. These materials have been carefully field tested and revised to meet the needs of students who struggle academically.

For more information about the *Direct Instruction* programs, contact:

> Science Research Associates
> P.O. Box 543
> Blacklick, OH 43004-0543
> (800) 843-8855

Recommended titles include:

- **Math**

  – Connecting Math Concepts, Levels A-D (grades 1-4)

  – Corrective Mathematics (grades 3-12)

  – Distar Arithmetic I and II (preschool through grade 2)

  – Mathematics Modules (grade 4 through adult)

- **Reading**

  – Corrective Reading (grades 3-12)

  – Distar Language I-III (preschool through grade 3)

  – Reading Mastery I-VI (grades 1-6)

  – Reading Mastery: Fast Cycle (for faster learners in grades K-1, or "catch-up" in grades 2-3)

- **Spelling**

  – Corrective Spelling Through Morphographs (grade 4 through adult)

  – Spelling Master (grades 1-6)

- **Writing**

  – Basic Writing Skills (grades 4-8)

  – Cursive Writing Program (grades 3-4)

  – Expressive Writing I and II (grades 4-6)

AGGRESSION—VERBAL AND/OR PHYSICAL

DESCRIPTION

You have a student who is physically and/or verbally aggressive toward adults or peers.

GOAL

The student will learn to respect the physical and emotional safety of others.

OVERVIEW OF PLANS

- PLAN A: For a situation in which the problem has just begun and/or occurs sporadically.
- PLAN B: For a student who may not know how to interact with others in nonaggressive ways.
- PLAN C: For a student who is predatory and/or whose aggression is long-standing.
- PLAN D: For a situation in which several students are aggressive toward one another.

NOTE:

These plans are geared for a student who engages in a variety *of behaviors that might be described as aggressive. If any of the other behavior problems listed seem to more specifically describe the behavior exhibited by your student, you should review them. For example,* **Threatening Others (Staff or Students)** *has specific plans for dealing with a student who makes frequent verbal threats.*

Alternative Problems

- **Bothering/Tormenting Others**
- **Bullying Behavior/ Fighting**
- **Competitive, Overly**
- **Fighting**
- **Gang Involvement**
- **Physically Dangerous Behavior—to Self or Others**
- **Self-Control Issues**
- **Threatening Others (Staff or Students)**

· · · · · · · ·
General Considerations

- Aggression is a potentially very severe problem in which the more comprehensive and pervasive the plan, the greater its chances of success. You should not hesitate to involve a school administrator, school psychologist, or others in setting up an intervention plan, as this may lead to resources such as parent training classes or counseling being made available (if appropriate).

- If the behavior stems in any way from academic issues (e.g., the student behaves aggressively because he cannot do academic tasks), concurrent efforts must be made to ensure his academic success (see **Academic Deficits, Determining**).

- If the student lacks the basic social skills to interact with his peers appropriately, it may be necessary to begin by teaching him these skills. **Social Skills, Lack of** contains information on a variety of published social skills curricula.

- If you have any reason to suspect a physiological or neurological basis for the student's behavior (e.g., the student truly seems to be incapable of controlling his angry impulses), consult with your building administrator and/or school psychologist to get advice on district procedures for following up on this type of situation.

· · · · · · · ·
Model Plans

PLAN A

It is not always necessary or even beneficial to use an involved plan. If the inappropriate behavior has just begun, the following actions, along with making the student aware of your concerns, may resolve the situation.

 1. *Define "being aggressive."*

a. Review the information in your anecdotal notes (see SUGGESTED STEPS FOR DEVELOPING AND IMPLEMENTING A PLAN) and list all of the student's aggressive acts to date. Then decide upon a definition of what constitutes an aggressive act. You may want to establish two categories—mild and severe. Often a student will begin with mildly aggressive behaviors that

eventually lead to an aggressive act. If you are able to consistently intervene with the mild acts, you might reduce the probability that the student will engage in more aggressive acts.

b. Identify a corresponding "cooperative" behavior for each aggressive act you have identified, and create a chart, like the sample following.

Cooperative Acts	Mild Aggressive	Severe Aggressive
• Keeping hands and feet to self	• Teasing	• Pushing
• Stating opinions calmly	• Name calling	• Poking with pencil
• Stating requests calmly	• Knocking things off someone's desk	• Hitting
• Working independently	• Arguing with teacher	• Tripping
• Following playground rules	• Poking, tickling, getting in the way	• Grabbing
• Following classroom rules	• Making fun of someone's ideas	• Fighting

2. *Respond consistently to the inappropriate behavior.*

a. Determine a mild consequence to use when the student engages in a mild aggressive act. The consequence must be one that you will feel comfortable implementing every time. One possibility is time owed—for example, each time the student exhibits a mildly aggressive act, he loses (owes) one minute of recess. Or you might set up a response cost system in which the student begins the day with points (tickets or tokens for a younger student), and loses one for each infraction. Any points (tickets/tokens) remaining at the end of the day can be saved up to "purchase" a reinforcer of the student's choice.

b. Determine consequences for the more severe aggressive acts that reflect the nature/magnitude of the acts themself. For example, if the student hurts someone, he should have to go to the office where an administrator will contact his parent(s), and/or implement a consequence, and/or contact a law enforcement agency if necessary. If the student destroys or damages property, he should have to repair or replace the item or property. If the student engages in a behavior that *might* have hurt someone, but didn't (e.g., pulling a chair out from behind someone), an appropriate consequence might be 15 minutes of lunch time owed or after-school detention.

c. If the student argues with you when you assign a consequence, let him know that if he feels something is unfair he can make an appointment to talk to you about it at a later time. If he continues to argue, use the "broken record" technique—calmly restating the consequence and what the student should be doing. "The consequence for knocking Lou's book off the desk is owing one minute of recess, and now you need to take your seat and begin your math assignment."

d. Keep in mind that although consequences are necessary for aggressive acts, when they are implemented poorly they can backfire. If the consequence communicates the idea that adults are trying to use their power to "control" the student, there is a good chance that he will work hard to rebel and/or engage in power struggles. Thus, always use as mild a consequence as reasonably fits the infraction and be very calm in communicating the consequence to the student—avoid intensifying the consequence to "get back" at the student.

Additionally, while the student has to learn that there are consequences for his actions, reinforcing his appropriate "cooperative behavior" will actually have more impact on reducing his aggression.

3. *Use reinforcement to encourage appropriate behavior.*

a. Give the student increased praise. Be especially alert for situations in which the student is not acting aggressively and praise him specifically for demonstrating his ability to be cooperative. "Dan, for the last hour you have been cooperative. You've kept your hands to yourself and used a very respectful voice during our class discussion."

If the student would be embarrassed by public praise, praise the student privately or even give the student a note. Remember that any time the student is not being aggressive, you can praise him for being cooperative. Don't forget to praise the student for other positive behaviors he exhibits as well.

b. In addition, give the student frequent attention (e.g., say "hello" to him as he enters the classroom, call on him frequently during class activities, or occasionally ask him to assist you with a class job that needs to be done). You might also get to know the student's interests and talk to him about these subjects (unless they involve fighting, guns, etc.—in which case, try to find other topics which you can talk to him about).

PLAN B

Some students actually do not know how to interact with others in nonaggressive ways. If your student does not seem to possess the necessary skills to interact more cooperatively, the intervention must include a way to teach him those skills.

1. *Respond consistently to the inappropriate behavior.*

a. Define "being aggressive" and "being cooperative" for the student (see PLAN A).

b. Identify and implement appropriate consequences for both mild and severe aggressive acts (see PLAN A).

2. *Conduct lessons to teach the student how to be more cooperative.*

a. Decide what the student needs to learn and who will teach the lessons. Because teaching new behaviors can be time-consuming and difficult, you might want to determine whether there are other students who would benefit from this type of instruction and have the school counselor or psychologist conduct the lessons.

Any of the following social skills curricula may be appropriate for your needs:

Walker, H.M., McConnel, S., Holmes, D., Todis, B., Walker, J., & Golden, N. (1983). *The ACCEPTS program: A curriculum for children's effective peer and teacher skills* (Videotape No. 0371 and Curriculum Guide No. 0370). Austin, TX: Pro-Ed.

Walker, H.M., Todis, B., Holmes, D., & Horton, G. (1988). *The ACCESS program: Adolescent coping curriculum for communication and effective social skills* (Curriculum Manual and Student Study Guide No. 0365). Austin, TX: Pro-Ed.

Goldstein, A.P., Sprafkin, R.P., Gershaw, N.J., & Klein, P. (1980). *Skill-streaming the adolescent: A structured learning approach to teaching prosocial skills.* Champaign, IL: Research Press.

McGinnis, E., Goldstein, A.P., Sprafkin, R.P., & Gershaw, N.J. (1984). *Skillstreaming the elementary school child: A guide for teaching prosocial skills.* Champaign, IL: Research Press.

b. During the lessons, use your anecdotal notes to present either actual situations that have occurred or scenarios that are similar to actual events, and have the student role play more cooperative ways of interacting. If you are not teaching the student or group of students, give this information to whomever is. "Mrs. Lee, Dan seems to be having trouble stating requests in a nondemanding way. For example, ... Perhaps that situation could be used in some of the role plays you do during the lessons."

The lessons should also be a time for reviewing successes, as well as discussing and practicing problem situations. "Mrs. Lee, I noticed that Dan is getting much more consistent about stating his opinions in firm, but nonaggressive ways. One example is yesterday when we were having a class discussion about . . . ."

c. Use "homework" in conjunction with the lessons. That is, give the student a specific assignment to practice a skill taught during a lesson, and then have him report during the next lesson what he tried, how it worked, and any difficulties or problems encountered.

d. Conduct the lessons daily if possible, but at least twice per week, and involve just you and the student or group of students learning the skills (perhaps while the rest of the class is at recess). The lessons needn't last more than five to ten minutes, and it is important that they be handled in a matter-of-fact manner so the student does not feel that he is being ridiculed. (You want to be very clear that you are not trying to embarrass him, but that you *do* want him to see the behavior the way others do.)

Continue the lessons until the student is consistently behaving more cooperatively and/or no longer exhibiting the aggressive behaviors.

3. *Use reinforcement to encourage appropriate behavior.*

a. Give the student increased praise and attention when he is being cooperative (see PLAN A).

b. Make a special point of letting the student know that you notice his efforts to use the skills he has been learning/practicing. Give the student specific information on the benefits of using a particular skill. "Dan, that was a great example of stating your opinion respectfully. I know you and Mrs. Lee have been practicing being assertive about opinions without being aggressive, and when you use that skill I really like to listen to your ideas. Tell me more about why you think . . . ."

c. Provide intermittent rewards when the student is cooperative for especially long periods of time. For example, if the student typically has three or four mild aggressive acts in a morning and he makes it to 11:00 A.M. without any, you can acknowledge his success by giving him a special job or privilege. "Dan, you have been so cooperative all morning. Would you please take these papers to Mrs. Lee for me? Oh, and let me write her a note to tell her about your success."

Or, when you see the student use the skills in a situation that would have previously been difficult for him to handle, highlight his accomplishment in some way. "Dan and Lewis, I saw that you two were having a difference of opinion about who was going to use the computer first, but you were each stating your opinion in a respectful way. Did you get a plan worked out that both of you are satisfied with? Great, Luke gets to go for ten minutes and then Dan gets ten. Sounds good. In fact, working out a way to take turns is such a great plan that I am writing each of you a certificate that can be used for 15 minutes of additional computer time. You can use this any afternoon this week or next."

Also use intermittent rewards if the number of daily aggressive acts has decreased. Each day, when you and the student review his daily total (see SUGGESTED STEPS FOR DEVELOPING AND IMPLEMENTING A PLAN), celebrate improvements. "Dan, look at this chart. Today you have had only seven aggressive acts. This is your best day yet. I would like to write a note that you could give to your mom to let her know how much progress you are making. Would that be alright with you?"

4. *Ensure a 3-1 ratio of positive to negative attention.*

a. If the student has learned that aggression leads to a great deal of adult and peer attention, he may have become very skilled at "sucking people into negative exchanges." If this is the case, you want to be sure that you are giving the

student *three times as much* positive as negative attention.

One way to do this is to monitor your interactions with the student at least one day per week. Keep a card on a clipboard or in your pocket and record each interaction you have with the student as either positive or negative by marking a "+" or a "-", respectively, on the card. To determine whether an interaction is positive or negative, ask yourself whether the student was being aggressive (or otherwise misbehaving) at the time of the interaction.

Any interaction that stems from inappropriate behavior is negative, while all interactions that occur while the student is meeting classroom expectations are positive. Thus, providing a consequence is a negative interaction, while praising the student is positive. Greeting the student as he enters the room or asking him if he has any questions during independent work are also considered positive interactions.

b. If you find that you are not giving the student three times as much positive as negative attention, try to increase the number of positive interactions you have with the student. Sometimes prompts can help. For example, you might decide that each time the student enters the classroom you will say "hello" to him, or that whenever you look at the clock you will find a time to praise the student, or that whenever a student uses the drinking fountain you will check the target student and as soon as possible praise some aspect of his behavior.

PLAN C

When a student seems to deliberately plan aggressive acts and/or has been acting aggressively for a long time, ask for help from the school counselor, school psychologist, lead teacher, or a special educator. Collaborating on an intervention will increase the chances that you can obtain additional services—such as parent training or counseling—that a classroom teacher cannot realistically provide.

1. *Conduct lessons to teach the student how to be more cooperative (see PLAN B).*

2. *Respond consistently to the inappropriate behavior.*

a. Define being aggressive and being cooperative for the student (see PLAN A).

b. Identify and implement appropriate consequences for both mild and severe acts of aggression (see PLAN A).

3. *Modify the student's day to reduce the probability that severe aggressive acts will occur.*

a. Examine your anecdotal notes (see SUGGESTED STEPS FOR DEVELOPING AND IMPLEMENTING A PLAN) to see if you can identify particular situations that seem to cause the student the most problems. Then develop strategies for dealing with those situations. For example, if the student consistently has trouble on the playground, he may need to be assigned a "modified recess," in which he has a limited choice of activities and has to stay close to the playground supervisors.

Other examples: If the student has trouble during passing periods between classes, an adult may need to escort him from class to class (e.g., first period teacher escorts him to second period, second period teacher to third period, and so on). If the student has been aggressive when he is supposed to be going to the restroom, you may need to restrict him from using the restroom during class time unless there is an adult to accompany him. If the student has trouble during his lunch period, he may need to eat in an assigned place near a cafeteria supervisor.

b. If any one of the above (or similar) options is implemented, train the adult(s) who will be supervising the student to be pleasant and friendly with him. The goal is to set the student up for success and for positive interactions with adults—not to create autocratic and punitive supervision. In addition, when presenting the procedure to the student and his parent(s) (if applicable), emphasize that the purpose is to increase the probability that the student will behave successfully rather than to punish him.

4. *Develop procedures for periodically evaluating the student's behavior.*

a. Divide the day into time intervals, at the end of which the student's behavior will be rated for cooperation level during that period. The intervals, which should never be longer than an hour, should be short enough that the student has a good chance of being successful. For a middle/junior high school student, this might mean a whole class period, whereas for a student with a severe problem or an elementary age student, the interval might be 15-30 minutes.

b. At the end of each interval, discuss his behavior with the student and record the rating on a form like the sample shown. Gradually transfer the responsibility of making the evaluation from yourself to the student. That is, in the early stages, you should determine the rating and explain why you rated his behavior as you did. Then, as the student's behavior improves, have him self-evaluate, with your role being to agree or disagree. As long as the student is reasonably accurate in his assessments, allow him to do more and more self-evaluation and self-reinforcement.

	Aggression Self-Evaluation			
Name _____			Date _____	
For each time period, check one category.	**Two** or more minor aggressive acts and/or **one** major = 0 points	**One** minor aggressive act = 1 point	**No** aggressive acts = 2 points	**No** aggressive acts/ **respectful** and **cooperative** = 4 points
8:30 - 8:45		✓		
8:45 - 9:00				✓
9:00 - 9:15		✓		
9:15 - 9:30			✓	
(Etc.)			✓	
			✓	
			✓	
				✓
				✓
Total points for the day **22**		2	8	12

The Teacher's Encyclopedia of Behavior Management: 100 Problems/500 Plans

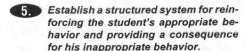

5. *Establish a structured system for reinforcing the student's appropriate behavior and providing a consequence for his inappropriate behavior.*

a. With the student, create a list of reinforcers that he can earn. Although you might want to have some suggestions in mind, the system will be more effective if the student identifies most of the items or activities himself. *(NOTE: A list of additional reinforcement ideas can be found in APPENDIX 1.)*

b. Assign "prices" (in points) for each of the rewards on the list and have the student pick the reward he wants to earn first.

The prices should be based on the instructional, personnel, and/or monetary costs of the items. Monetary cost is clear—the more expensive the item, the more points required to earn it. Instructional cost refers to the amount of instructional time lost or interfered with by a particular reward. Thus, an activity which causes the student to miss part of academic instruction should require more points than an activity the student can do on his own recess time. Personnel cost involves the time required by you and/or other staff to fulfill the reinforcer. Having lunch with the principal, therefore, would cost more points than spending five minutes of free time with a friend.

c. Apply the points from the self-evaluation ratings toward the reward. That is, at the end of each day, determine the total daily points and add them to the points the student has earned on previous days.

d. When the student has accumulated enough points to earn the reward he has chosen, he "spends" the points necessary and the system begins again. That is, he picks a new reward to earn and begins with zero points.

However, if the student is immature, and needs more frequent encouragement, you might consider letting him earn several "less expensive" rewards (e.g., 5 minutes of computer time after 20 points) on the way to a bigger reward (e.g.,

one hour helping you after school for 200 points). That is, the student receives the small rewards without spending his points; the points continue to accumulate toward the selected reward.

6. *Use reinforcement to encourage appropriate behavior.*

a. Give the student increased praise and attention when he is being cooperative (see PLAN A).

b. Show interest and enthusiasm about how the student is doing on the system.

NOTE:

The following resources may be useful in planning a comprehensive intervention for an aggressive student:

Goldstein, A.P. & Glick, B. (1987). Aggression replacement training. Champaign, IL: Research Press.

Long, N.J. & Brendtro, L.K. (Eds.). (1993). Rage and aggression. Journal of Emotional and Behavioral Problems, 2(1).

Morgan, D.P. & Jenson, W.R. (1988). Teaching behaviorally disturbed students. Columbus, OH: Merrill.

Rhode, G., Jenson, W.R., & Reavis, H.K. (1992). The tough kid book: Practical classroom management strategies. Longmont, CO: Sopris West.

Sprick, R.S., Sprick, M.S., & Garrison, M. (1993). Interventions: Collaborative planning for students at risk. Longmont, CO: Sopris West.

Walker, H. (in press). The acting-out child: Coping with classroom disruption (2nd ed.). Longmont, CO: Sopris West.

PLAN D

O ccasionally you may have a situation in which several students in the class are aggressive toward each other. This plan adapts components from PLANS A-C to be used with a group of students.

1. *Respond consistently to all instances of inappropriate behavior.*

a. Have a class meeting during which you define being aggressive and being cooperative, and identify consequences for mild and severe aggressive acts (see PLAN A).

b. Implement appropriate consequences for each mild and severe aggressive act, as necessary (see PLAN A).

2. *Develop procedures for publicly monitoring the frequency of aggressive acts.*

a. Identify a place—the chalkboard or a wall chart—on which you can record a daily count of aggressive acts.

b. Once you have defined what constitutes an aggressive act, make a tally mark on the chart each time there is an incident. *(NOTE: You will not be identifying the individuals responsible for the acts, simply recording the frequency.)* At the end of the day, compare that day's total to that of previous days. Discuss with the class whether things are getting better, worse, or staying about the same. If things are better, have the students reflect on the climate of the classroom—does it feel better? if so, how? if not, why not?

3. *Encourage the class to set performance goals for the next day.*

You may have to help the students identify a reasonable goal, as the students may have the tendency to say they want to reduce the number of

incidents from 15 on one day to zero on the next day, for example. You might tell the students that if they set a more realistic goal, such as 12, they significantly increase their chances of success and they can always reduce the number more than that. As the class successfully meets their goal, the number should become progressively lower.

4. *Use reinforcement to encourage appropriate behavior.*

a. When the class has demonstrated reductions in the total number of aggressive acts, provide class praise. "Class, everyone in the room should be proud of how cooperative they were today. According to our count, we have had a significant reduction in the number of minor aggressive acts, and no major aggression. Excellent work."

b. Occasionally, provide a class-wide reward to celebrate their success. "Class, you've done such a good job of being cooperative today—how about if we take the last five minutes of class to have choice time with some music playing?"

c. Alternately, establish a group reinforcement system in which you identify a goal for the whole class. On days when the class is successful in keeping their number of aggressive acts under the goal, the group earns a point toward a reward that they determined beforehand. An alternative is to use a technique like the Mystery Motivator (Rhode, Jenson, & Reavis, 1992), with which on days the group successfully meets their goal, they find out what they win by uncovering the Mystery Motivator space for that day.

. . . .

Suggested Steps for Developing and Implementing a Plan

The following steps are designed to help you develop an appropriate intervention plan and implement it effectively, whether you choose to use one of the MODEL PLANS or create a customized plan of your own. The steps are, however, suggestions—they are not intended to be followed rigidly or in any particular order. Use your professional judgment and the knowledge of your particular situation to make them work for you.

 1. *Make sure you have enough information about the situation.*

a. You need to be able to describe the types of things the student is doing in various instructional and noninstructional settings. Anecdotal notes on actual incidents can provide the details

to help you define the problem clearly and explain it specifically to the student, the parent(s), and any other school or mental health personnel that may participate in the intervention.

To collect this information, simply keep a card in your pocket or on a clipboard and make brief notes about each behavior you observe of the student's that might be considered aggressive—even fairly little things. For each entry, describe where and when it occurred, what was said and done, and any other relevant observations you may have (e.g., what prompted the behavior).

You should also take some notes on times the student is cooperative—this will make it clear that you are not only aware of his problem behavior, but also of when he behaves appropriately. When you meet with the student, these examples can also help you clarify how you want the student to behave.

b. In addition to formulating a description of what the student's inappropriate behavior looks like, it can also be useful to document how often it occurs (i.e., a frequency count). This information provides both a more objective measure of the problem and an objective way to monitor the student's progress. In this case, if you are making notes on each incident, they will also serve as a record of frequency.

c. If the student notices what you are doing and asks about it, be straightforward—tell him that you are collecting information to see whether his aggression is a problem that needs to be worked on.

Following is an example of anecdotal notes that have been collected on a student's aggressive behavior.

d. The frequency information is fairly easy to summarize on a chart or graph, and seeing how often he engages in aggressive acts may help the student and his parent(s) better understand your concern.

e. Once you implement an intervention plan, you will be delivering a consequence for each aggressive act. Keeping a record of these consequences will generate continuing frequency information, and allow you to monitor the effectiveness of your intervention. You might also want to continue to make occasional anecdotal notes on any aggressive acts that persist.

2. _Identify a focus for the intervention and labels for referring to the appropriate and inappropriate behaviors._

a. To be effective, the intervention must address more than just reducing the student's aggressive behavior—there must be a concurrent emphasis on _increasing_ some positive behavior or trait (e.g., being cooperative). Having a specific positive behavior in mind will make it easier to "catch" and reinforce the student for behaving appropriately, and a positive focus will allow you to discuss the situation in a more productive manner.

For example, if you describe the situation simply as, "the student has a problem with being aggressive," you provide the student and his parent(s) little in the way of useful information, and may put them on the defensive. However, when you explain that you want to "help the student learn to be more cooperative," you present an important, and reasonable, goal for the student to work toward and identify what the student needs to do to be successful.

b. Specifying labels for the appropriate and inappropriate behaviors (e.g., "being cooperative" and "being aggressive," respectively) will help you to use consistent vocabulary when discussing the situation with the student. If you some-

---

Dan's Aggressive Acts—2/4

8:28—On his way into the classroom, he and Shawn were horsing around, then Dan pushed Shawn so hard that he fell.

9:42—Walking by Sarah's desk, he swept all her books and papers onto the floor.

10:30—During the math lesson, he began to argue with me about whether or not he had to do the assignment.

12:15—Report from the playground supervisors that Dan was frequently tormenting others on the playground. They requested that he lose recess tomorrow.

1:25—Tripped Alexandria as she walked by his desk. Said, "Ohh, so sorry!" in a way that got others to laugh.

2:00—Used his pencil to write on the wall. I told him he had to clean it up. He refused, so I sent him to the office.

---

times refer to the inappropriate behavior as "hassling others" and other times tell the student that he is "being aggressive," he may not realize that you are talking about the same thing.

3. Determine when and how to include the parent(s).

a. The parent(s) need to be contacted immediately with this type of problem. Share any information you have collected about the behavior (i.e., anecdotal notes, frequency count), and explain why you are concerned. You might ask if the parent(s) have any insight into the behavior and/or whether they have noticed similar behavior at home.

Whether or not the parent(s) perceive a problem, invite them to join you for an initial meeting with the student and/or to assist you in developing a plan to help the student learn to "be more cooperative." If the parents are unable or unwilling to participate, let them know that you will keep them informed of the student's progress.

b. Once the parent(s) have been involved in any way, you should give them updates at least once per week while the plan is being implemented.

4. Prepare for, then conduct, an initial meeting about the situation.

a. Arrange for a meeting to discuss your concerns with the student and anyone else who will be involved in the plan (e.g., the parent[s], the school psychologist). Although the specifics will vary depending upon the age of the student and the severity of the problem, there are some general guidelines to consider when scheduling the meeting.

First, meet at a neutral time (i.e., not immediately after a problem has occurred), when emotions are less likely to hamper communication. In general, a day's notice is appropriate, however, a primary age student may worry excessively and/or forget what the meeting is about if it is scheduled more than an hour before it takes place.

Second, make the meeting appropriately private. With a primary student who has a mild problem, you might meet in the classroom while the other students are working independently. However, when dealing with a middle/junior high school student and the student's parent(s), you will want to use a private room (e.g., the counselor's office) to ensure that the discussion will not be overheard.

Third, try to make sure that the meeting is scheduled for a time and place that it is not likely to be interrupted. And finally, if the parent(s) will be participating, they should be the ones to tell the student about the meeting.

b. Construct a preliminary plan. Decide whether you can use one of the MODEL PLANS or if you need to create a customized plan using components from various plans and/or your own ideas. You will invite and encourage the student to help develop the plan during the initial meeting, however, having a proposed plan in mind before you meet can alleviate frustration and wasted time if the student is unwilling or unable to participate.

c. After reviewing the information you have collected and thinking about how you want the student to behave, prepare thorough descriptions of the inappropriate behavior and the positive behavior/trait on which the student will be working. The more specific you are and the more concrete examples you have, the easier it will be for you to clarify, and for the student to understand, your expectations. Be sure to consider the student's behavior in all relevant activities (e.g., independent work, teacher directed instruction, unstructured class times, recess and lunch, etc.).

d. Conduct the meeting in an atmosphere of collaboration. The following agenda is one way you might structure the meeting:

• **Share your concerns about the student's behavior.**

Briefly describe the problem behavior and, when appropriate, show the student a chart of how often he engages in it. Then explain why you consider the behavior to be a problem. You might include the concept that some acts of aggression are considered assault and are illegal.

If the student's behavior is severe and he does not seem to take this information very seriously, it may be appropriate to arrange for a police officer to meet with the student to discuss the legal ramifications and consequences of severe aggressive acts. In addition, the student should be informed about any school or district policies regarding aggression.

• **Discuss how you can work together to improve the situation.**

Tell the student that you would like to help him learn to "be more cooperative" and describe your preliminary plan. Invite the student to give you input on the various aspects of the plan, and together work out any necessary details (e.g., the evaluation system, reinforcers, and consequences). You may have to brainstorm different possibilities if the student is uncomfortable with the initial plan. Incorporating any of the student's suggestions that strengthen the plan is likely to increase his sense of "ownership" in and commitment to it.

- **Make sure the student understands what you mean by appropriate and inappropriate behavior.**

Use the descriptions you have prepared to define and clarify the problem behavior and the positive (desired) behavior as specifically and thoroughly as you can. In this case, be sure to make the distinction between mild and severe aggressive acts. You may even want to model examples of each of these categories.

To ensure that you and the student are in agreement about the expectations, you might present hypothetical scenarios and have him identify whether each is an example of mild aggression, severe aggression, or being cooperative. Or you might describe an actual situation that has occurred and ask him to explain how he would demonstrate being more cooperative in that situation.

- **Conclude the meeting.**

Always end the meeting with words of encouragement. Let the student know that you are confident that he can be successful. Be sure to reinforce him for participating in the meeting.

5. *Give the student regular, ongoing feedback about his behavior.*

It is important to meet with the student periodically to discuss his progress. With this problem, try to have a short meeting (i.e., three to five minutes) at the end of each day. Review any information that has been collected and discuss whether or not the situation is improving. As much as possible, focus on the student's improvements, however, also address any new or continuing problems. As the situation improves, the meetings can be faded—to once every other week and then to once per month.

6. *Evaluate the situation (and the plan).*

Implement any plan for at least two weeks before deciding whether to change plans, to continue, modify, or fade the plan you are using, or to cease the intervention. Generally, if the student's behavior is clearly improving (based on the objective information that's been collected and/or the subjective perceptions of yourself, the student, and possibly the parent[s]), stick with what you are doing. If the situation has remained the same or worsened, some kind of change will be necessary. Always discuss any changes to the plan with the student first.

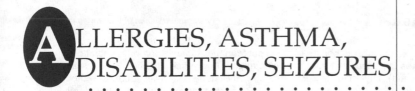

ALLERGIES, ASTHMA, DISABILITIES, SEIZURES

Chronic Health Problems

DESCRIPTION

You have a student with a diagnosed disability or health impairment, who has behavior problems intertwined with the disability or impairment.

Although all necessary accommodations should be made to ensure the physical safety and academic success of a student with a disability or health impairment, addressing these issues is beyond the scope of this reference guide. Therefore, there are no MODEL PLANS included with this problem. The purpose of the following information is to suggest an overall approach and some basic considerations for addressing the inappropriate behavior of a student who has a diagnosed disability or a health impairment.

Alternative Problems

- **Absenteeism**

- **Clinginess/ Dependency**

- **Helplessness**

- **Hypochondria**

- **Victim—Student Who Is Always Picked On**

. . . .
General Information

- Whenever a student has a diagnosed health impairment or disability, it is important that you include the student's parent(s), physician, psychologist, and/or special education teacher in the development of any intervention plan. That is, you should always coordinate any intervention efforts with these individuals.

- The key to effectively addressing the inappropriate behavior of a student who has a disability or health impairment is to identify one specific behavior the student exhibits (or fails to exhibit) that you can address. Then you can look for that particular problem in this reference and review the MODEL PLANS that accompany it. If one or more of the plans seems appropriate, begin implementation.

If the student exhibits a number of different inappropriate behaviors, and you are not sure which poses the biggest problem, record anecdotal information about the student's behavior for a week or so. This type of documentation is fairly easy to compile—simply keep a card in your pocket or on a clipboard and whenever the student does something (or doesn't do something) that creates a problem for herself or interferes with the smooth running of the class, make notes on the incident.

Briefly describe the circumstances—where and when the misbehavior occurred, what was said and/or done, and any other relevant observations you may have about the situation (e.g., what prompted the behavior). After about a week, use the information you have collected to choose one specific behavior to intervene with. This might be the misbehavior that occurs most often or that creates the biggest disruption for the class. Whatever your criteria, the important thing is to focus your intervention efforts on one problem behavior at a time. Often, as you work on one problem behavior, others seem to improve without specific intervention.

- Be cautious about paying too much attention to the disability or illness—this can, in fact, perpetuate the problem. For example, too much attention paid to asthmatic behavior can increase the frequency of asthmatic attacks. This does not mean that the student *fakes* asthma attacks, but rather that the excess attention is so reinforcing that the attacks occur more often than they would otherwise.

Find out from the student's parent(s) and/or physician exactly how much attention is necessary to insure the student's physical safety without giving so much attention that you inadvertently reinforce the student for being ill.

- You want to ensure a 3-1 ratio of positive to disability/illness-related attention for the student. Given that you have to pay attention to the student's disability/illness (e.g., making sure the student is safe during an asthma attack), it is important to make sure that you are also giving the student plenty of attention for her positive classroom behaviors.

You can do this by monitoring your interactions with the student at least one day per week. Simply keep a card on a clipboard or in your pocket and record each interaction you have with the student as either positive or disability/illness related by marking a "+" or a "-," respectively, on the card.

To determine if an interaction is positive or negative, ask yourself whether it occurred when the student was exhibiting the disability/illness or if the interaction was related to the disability/illness (e.g., reminding the student to take an inhalator out to recess). These interactions would be marked with "-." However, any interaction that occurs while the student is meeting classroom expectations is positive—so greeting the student as she enters the room or asking her if she has any questions during independent work are positive interactions.

If you find that you are not giving the student *three times as much* positive attention as disability/illness-related attention, try to increase the number of positive interactions you have with the student. Sometimes prompts can help. For example, you might decide that each time the student enters the classroom you will say "hello" to her, or that whenever you look at the clock you will find a time to praise the student, or that whenever there is an announcement over the intercom you will look at the student and, as soon as possible, praise some aspect of her behavior.

This suggestion in no way implies that you should ignore the student's disability or illness. Without a doubt, the student needs to feel physically safe and know that there is nothing wrong with having allergies (or whatever). The issue is one of ratio—you want to acknowledge the student more for her positive and productive behaviors than for her disability/illness.

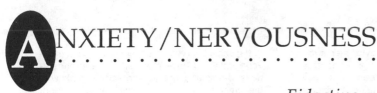

ANXIETY/NERVOUSNESS

Fidgeting

Worrying

Tension

DESCRIPTION

You have a student who often seems nervous, worried, or anxious—for no immediately identifiable reason. The problem is interfering with the student's ability to succeed in the classroom.

GOAL

The student will learn to be more relaxed and will improve his ability to function in the classroom.

OVERVIEW OF PLANS

- PLAN A: For a situation in which the problem has just begun or occurs infrequently.
- PLAN B: For a student who acts nervous or anxious because he does not know how to relax.
- PLAN C: For a student whose nervousness may stem from a lack of self-esteem.
- PLAN D: For a student who exhibits nervousness primarily by rapid hand movements—tapping or wringing his hands, cracking his knuckles, etc.

NOTE:

PLANS B and D involve procedures that some people consider to be slightly controversial. Be sure to obtain parental permission before using these techniques.

Alternative Problems

- **Daydreaming**
- **Hypochondria**
- **Perfectionism**
- **School Phobia**
- **Suicide Threats**
- **Tourette Syndrome**

· · · · · · · ·
General Considerations

- If the student's problem behavior stems in any way from academic issues (e.g., If the student engages in nervous behavior because he is worried or upset about academic failure), concurrent efforts must be made to ensure his academic success (see **Academic Deficits, Determining**).

- If you suspect that the student's nervousness could be related to the student being depressed, see **Depression**. This problem includes a set of questions to help you decide whether the student should be referred for counseling or psychological services.

- If the student's family or cultural background could be a factor in the behavior, (e.g., the parent[s] exhibit nervous mannerisms), do not intervene until you have checked the appropriateness of any intervention plan and its goals with the student's parent(s). If the behavior is not interfering with the student's academic or social success, it may be both unnecessary and inappropriate to intervene.

- If you have any reason to suspect a physiological or neurological basis for the student's behavior (e.g., the student could be suffering from a muscular disorder), consult with your building administrator and/or school psychologist to get advice on district procedures for following up on this type of situation.

· · · · · · · ·
Model Plans

PLAN A

It is not always necessary, or even beneficial, to use an involved plan. If the inappropriate behavior has just begun and/or occurs relatively infrequently, the following actions, along with making the student aware of your concerns, may resolve the problem.

 1. *Make sure the student has someone to whom he can turn to talk about problems.*

If there is a specific circumstance or problem that is causing the student to be tense, teaching him to act more relaxed might just mask the problem. Even if the student doesn't identify any particular problem, and the parent(s) are not aware of anything specific, make it clear to the student that he is welcome to come to talk to you (and/or the school counselor or nurse) if there is anything troubling him.

 2. *Respond consistently to the student's nervous behavior.*

After ensuring that the student has someone to talk to about his problems, it is not unreasonable to gently correct him when he is acting anxious. Therefore, occasionally when you notice the student being nervous, gently correct him and/or use redirection. That is, calmly provide information about what he should be doing. "Carlos, you need to keep your hands still on your desk. That tapping is distracting to others around you." Avoid being emotional or talking too much—you always want to make sure the student gets more attention for behaving appropriately than for acting nervous.

 3. *Use reinforcement to encourage appropriate behavior.*

Give the student increased praise. Be especially alert for situations in which the student is acting relaxed, and privately praise him by specifically describing what he was doing. "Carlos, you were very relaxed while participating in today's lesson. When I am teaching it is much easier to keep my attention focused when your hands are still and relaxed." Or, "Carlos, good morning. You look relaxed and ready for the school day. How was your baseball game last night? Did your team win?"

PLAN B

Some students simply do not know how to relax. If you are not certain that your student is aware of ways that he can relax, the intervention should include giving him strategies for knowing when he is getting tense, ways to calm himself down quickly, and possibly instruction in life-long stress management skills. *(NOTE: This plan involves procedures that some people consider to be slightly controversial. Be sure to obtain parental permission before using these techniques.)*

1. *Make sure the student has someone to whom he can go to talk about his problems (see PLAN A).*

2. *Arrange for the student to have lessons in learning to deal with stress and tension as well as relaxation techniques.*

a. Determine who will conduct the lessons. Because teaching new behaviors can be time-consuming and difficult, it may not be something you have time for. You might check with your school counselor or psychologist about whether there are any current groups working on stress reduction that the student can join. If there is nothing in place, it might be worthwhile to see whether there are other students in the school who could benefit from instruction of this type, and then organize a class to be taught by the counselor or a highly skilled paraprofessional.

b. Choose or develop the type of skills/information that will be taught. There are published curricula on relaxation. If you will be designing your own lessons, the following may give you some ideas for conducting the class:

• Teach the student to identify when he is getting tense. Help the student learn what his body does as he is getting progressively more tense. What does he do with his hands? does he make a fist? do his hands move rapidly? What does he feel in his neck? What does his voice sound like? Does he start moving faster? The goal is for the student to learn to recognize the signs that he is becoming tense.

• Identify and have the student practice strategies for relaxing quickly. For example, you might teach the student to count backwards from ten, or to concentrate on one hand, making it go completely limp, or to gently tell himself to breathe slowly and evenly and/or that he can stay relaxed.

• Give the student training in life-long stress management habits (e.g., learning to use deep muscle relaxation). Learning to physically relax is like learning any other physical activity; just as hitting better in baseball requires practice, so does being able to relax more easily. Therefore, the goal is to teach the student a skill that he can practice daily. The following script, reprinted with permission from *Interventions* (Sprick, Sprick, & Garrison, 1993), can be used with a student in third grade or above. *(NOTE: For a younger student, the script would need to be modified so that the practice is shorter and more game-like.)*

Script 1—Muscle Relaxation

Think about the muscles in your feet. Slowly tense those muscles.
Hold for five seconds. 1, 2, 3, 4, 5.
Now slowly let those muscles relax. 1, 2, 3, 4, 5.
Let the muscles go until they are more relaxed than when you started.
Focus your attention on how those muscles feel now.

Now, do the same thing with your calves. Slowly tense those muscles.
Hold for five seconds. 1, 2, 3, 4, 5.
Now slowly let those muscles relax. 1, 2, 3, 4, 5.
Feel how relaxed your calves and feet are.

Script 1—Muscle Relaxation (cont'd)

Focus on your thighs. Slowly tense those muscles.
Hold for five seconds. 1, 2, 3, 4, 5.
Gradually let go of the tension.

_____

Take ten seconds. Feel how relaxed your legs and feet are.
1, 2, 3, 4, 5, 6, 7, 8, 9, 10.

_____

Now concentrate on your lower torso—stomach, lower back, and seat. Slowly tense those muscles.
Hold for five seconds. 1, 2, 3, 4, 5.
Gradually let go of the tension until there's no more tension in your lower torso.
Feel how relaxed your lower body is. Pay special attention to you lower back. Let those muscles
    relase.

_____

Now concentrate on your hands and arms. Make fists. Tighten your biceps and triceps.
Hold for five seconds. 1, 2, 3, 4, 5.
Gradually release. Let the tension go.
Let the muscles go until they are more relaxed than when you started.

_____

Focus on your neck, shoulders, and chest.
Gradually tense up.
Hold for five seconds. 1, 2, 3, 4, 5.
Release.

_____

Concentrate on the muscles in your face.
Close your eyes as tightly as possible.
Scrunch up your face.
Hold for five seconds. 1, 2, 3, 4, 5.
Now let go. Relax those muscles.
Don't frown. Don't smile.
Simply relax those muscles.

_____

Now take a few moments to concentrate on your breathing.
Breathe easy and evenly.
Each time you exhale, think about letting the tension in your muscles dissolve away.

_____

Take ten seconds. Think about how relaxed your body feels.
1, 2, 3, 4, 5, 6, 7, 8, 9, 10.
Take a moment to enjoy this sensation and be aware that you can recreate this relaxed state at any
time.
Now, begin the rest of your day.

Other examples of life-long stress management techniques include getting regular physical exercise, balancing career (school) with one's personal life, and knowing when and how to take relaxation breaks.

c. The lessons should be scheduled for anywhere from five to 15 minutes daily, if possible. You can use the information from your anecdotal notes to create scenarios that reflect actual situations in which the student has been tense. (If you are not teaching the lessons, pass this information on to the person who is).

The lessons themselves should consist of modeling and structured practice opportunities, and should include "homework" assignments in which the student has to practice the skills that have been taught. For example, you might tell the student that the next day he has to write down three times that he notices he is tense, what strategies he tries, and whether or not the strategies help him become more relaxed. Have him bring his homework to the next lesson.

3. *Respond consistently to the nervous behavior.*

a. Gently correct or redirect the nervous behavior (see PLAN A).

b. During the initial meeting with the student, set up an unobtrusive signal that you can use to cue the student that he is acting nervous. Tell the student that you will use the signal to remind him that he needs to practice the strategies he has been learning in the lessons. Examples of signals include tugging your ear or putting your hand to your cheek.

c. Whenever the student is acting nervous, give the signal. If he responds to the signal by becoming more relaxed, praise him privately. If he has trouble responding to the signal, include practice with the signal as part of the daily lessons.

4. *Use reinforcement to encourage appropriate behavior.*

a. Give the student increased praise and attention when he is acting relaxed (see PLAN A).

b. Look for opportunities to reinforce the student for exhibiting the specific skills that have been taught during the lessons. Praise the student in a way that gives information on the benefits of his using that skill. "Carlos, when you came in this morning you seemed a little tense. I saw you go to your desk and although no one else would notice it, I could tell that you worked on breathing slowly and evenly and that you calmed yourself down. I could almost see the tension drain out of you. Then after that, your participation in class provided such a valuable contribution to our discussion! How do you feel it is going?" Or, "Carlos, when you were talking with the group, your hands were so still and relaxed. I know that people heard your ideas because they were not distracted." (If someone else, for example the counselor, is teaching the lessons, share examples of the student's success with that person so that he/she can use it during the lessons.)

c. You may also wish to use intermittent rewards to acknowledge the student's success. Occasional, and unexpected, rewards can motivate a student to demonstrate responsible behavior more often. The idea is to provide a reward when the student makes a significant effort to use the skills he is learning. For example, if the student typically becomes tense during cooperative groups, but makes an effort to relax, highlight that success by giving him a reward, a special job, or a privilege. "Carlos, you have been so relaxed during group. I would like to offer you a choice of an activity. You can either have five minutes of time to work on the computer by yourself, or you can take a quiet break at your seat and read. Which would you rather do?"

Use intermittent rewards more frequently at the beginning of the intervention to encourage the student, and less often as his behavior improves. *(NOTE: A list of additional reinforcement ideas can be found in APPENDIX 1.)*

PLAN C

Sometimes a student will have become so discouraged that he would rather not even try to improve a behavior. In this case, the intervention may need to be somewhat indirect. Rather than addressing the student's nervousness or fidgeting specifically, your efforts should focus on helping the student to feel more confident—which, in turn, may help him become more relaxed or at least more amenable to lessons in learning to relax.

1. **Make sure the student has someone to whom he can go to talk about his problems (see PLAN A).**

2. **Give the student increased praise and attention when he is acting relaxed (see PLAN A).**

3. **Consistently ignore the student's nervous behavior.**

If the student lacks confidence, constant reminders about being relaxed are likely to decrease his confidence even more. Therefore, whenever possible, try to ignore the student's nervous or fidgety behavior.

4. **Capitalize on strengths or interests that the student has.**

A potentially powerful way to build up a student's confidence is to build upon strengths or interests that already exist. The idea is that by building up the student's confidence about things he already does well, he will become more confident and relaxed as a result. The following are ideas on how you might do this:

- Check out a library book (or bring one of your own that you enjoyed when you were his age) on a subject the student is interested in (e.g., dogs).

- If the student is always at school on time, you might want to ask him to help with some aspect of the morning routine (e.g., passing out papers).

- If the student has artistic abilities, you can ask him to draw a cover for a class book that will be presented to the principal.

(NOTE: A list of additional ideas for jobs/responsibilities can be found in APPENDIX 2.)

5. **Help the student learn to use positive self-talk.**

a. Determine whether the student "puts himself down" with comments like:

- "I am so stupid."

- "I can't do that sort of thing."

- "I knew I would blow it."

Making these types of statements continually reinforces the student's negative beliefs about himself. The more often he says them, the more he will come to believe them to be true and, potentially, the more nervous he will become.

b. Use examples to teach the student how to replace the negative comments with more positive and hopeful statements. For example, model for the student how to reframe a negative comment into a positive one, and then have him repeat the positive statement.

Don't worry if the student acts like he does not believe the positive statements at first—with repetition, we all learn to believe what we say about ourselves. The following examples may help you get started.

Negative Statement	Positive Statement
• "I am so stupid."	• "I am smart and capable."
• "I can't do that sort of thing."	• "I can do that. Even if I have trouble, I'll get it eventually."
• "I knew I would blow it."	• "I had trouble with that assignment, but I am smart, so I can learn from my mistakes."

*(NOTE: For more information on positive self-talk, see **Self-Concept Problems**.)*

6. **Structure academic success.**

Make sure that the student is experiencing frequent success in the tasks he is being asked to do. All your other efforts to help the student to feel more self-confident will not be powerful enough to counteract daily academic failure (see **Academic Deficits, Determining**).

PLAN D

If the student exhibits nervous behavior primarily with fidgety hand mannerisms (e.g., tapping or wringing his hands, cracking his knuckles, etc.), the focus of the intervention should be on teaching the student to reduce and eventually eliminate the specific behavior(s). *(NOTE: This plan involves procedures that some people consider to be slightly controversial. Be sure to obtain parental permission before using these techniques.)*

1. *Make sure the student has someone to whom he can go to talk about his problems (see PLAN A).*

2. *Give the student increased praise and attention when he is acting relaxed (see PLAN A).*

3. *Schedule frequent lessons (focusing specifically on keeping hands still) for the student at least twice per week.*

Arrange for five to 15 minute lessons at least twice per week. During the lessons, provide modeling of and structured practice in how to keep one's hands still in a variety of activities. The lessons can be taught in three stages, each of which may take anywhere from a few minutes to a few weeks for the student to master. Once the student has mastered one stage, move on to the next—until the student has demonstrated mastery of all three stages.

a. **Stage 1:** Teach the student to relax the muscles in his hands and arms:

- Teach the student to distinguish between hands that are relaxed and hands that are tense (in the way his are) in several different activities. For example, model both ways for the student while reading a book, talking to a friend, sitting and listening to a lesson, etc., and have the student observe and note the differences. *(NOTE: Be careful not to make fun of the student's behavior. Do not do a parody of his hand movements, but rather show him what they look like so he will be able to discriminate relaxed hands from tense hands.)*

- Teach the student how to relax one arm and hand. Sit across from the student at a student-sized desk or table. Lay one of your hands on the table and relax your whole arm. (Practice this before the lesson so that you can do it easily.) Explain to the student that you are telling the muscles in your hand and arm to stop working. Then pick up the relaxed hand with your other hand and demonstrate how

the relaxed hand has no muscle tension—it is almost like a dead weight or a wet rag. The fingers are neither straight nor bunched into a fist.

Have the student then pick up your arm by the wrist, move your fingers, and/or drop your hand on the table. If your hand becomes tense, use this as a teaching opportunity. "Carlos, did you notice that when you dropped my hand it didn't fall on the desk? It kind of hung there for a second. That is because I tensed the muscles. It should just drop to the desk like a rag. Let me try it again. Learning to keep your hands relaxed is a skill that requires practice for any of us to do well."

- Have the student try this exercise. Instruct him to lay one hand on the desk. Have him do his best to keep it still and relaxed. Ask him if you may pick up his hand, gently by the wrist. If he gives you permission, pick it up and see if it is relaxed. If so, praise him. If not, demonstrate how his fingers are rigid and his arm is pushing or pulling you as you move the hand.

Alternate between modeling and having the student practice until he can consistently keep one hand and arm relaxed. Then practice with the other hand, and eventually with both hands at the same time.

- For some students, this first stage will be difficult and may require weeks of gradual improvement. Do not get discouraged and do not let the student get discouraged. Think of this like learning to ride a bike for the first time. Some people take to it easily, but for most of us it requires patience, persistence, and lots of practice.

b. **Stage 2:** Teach the student to keep his hands and arms relaxed in various positions and during various activities:

- Begin each lesson by having the student practice "relaxed hands," from Stage 1.

- Demonstrate to the student how one could keep one's hands relaxed on the desk while listening to a lesson or while participating in a cooperative group. Have the student practice in the pretend context.

- Show the student how one can keep one's hands partially relaxed and partially tense during different types of seated classroom activities. For example, holding a book open—with hands just tense enough to keep the book from closing. Have the student practice. When the student masters this, switch to writing activities. Show the student how one can have a relaxed grip on a pencil with one hand while the other hand is completely relaxed.

  Continue through a variety of activities (e.g., watching a performance or an assembly; standing and talking to someone in the hall; waiting in line; raising one's hand to be called on; working at the computer; playing a board game). For each activity, demonstrate how to keep one's hands relaxed and have the student practice.

c. **Stage 3**: Generalize the lessons to actual situations:

- With the student, identify a half-hour period of the school day during which the student will actively work on keeping his hands relaxed. Have it be a time when you are able to observe the student fairly frequently (e.g., an independent work period in which you are moving around and interacting with the students).

- With the student, identify signals that you can use to cue him that: (1) his hands are relaxed, or (2) he needs to relax his hands. The signals are to give the student nonverbal feedback on how he is doing. You might, for example, make eye contact with the student and gently fold your hands to indicate that he is doing great. To signal that he needs to relax his hands, you might make eye contact, and then make a fist that you slowly open to a relaxed hand.

- Give the student frequent feedback (using the signals) during the half-hour period. Then at the end of the period, have the student self-evaluate the degree to which he was able to keep his hands relaxed. You might use a form like the one following.

Self-Evaluation Form

Name _____

Date _____

Time Period _____

Rating—Each day, rate the time period and record in the boxes below.

0 = Hands tense and moving the entire time

1 = Hands still and relaxed a little bit of the time

2 = Hands still and relaxed some of the time

3 = Hands still and relaxed most of the time

4 = Hands still and relaxed the entire time

M	T	W	TH	F

As the student prepares to rate his behavior, you should also mentally identify the rating you would give. If the student's evaluation matches yours, praise him (even if the rating was low). "Carlos, I agree. Today is probably a 1, but what is important is that you are aware of that. Since you know today was not one of your better days, you can think about what you might do differently tomorrow."

(NOTE: You might consider using a structured reinforcement system to motivate the student to achieve a high rating. Have the student identify some rewards he might wish to earn and set prices [in terms of points] for them. Then let the student accumulate the points from the self-evaluation form to "buy" a reward.)

- Do not worry about (or address) the issue of the student's hands during the rest of the day. If he brings it up and/or asks how he is doing, give him honest feedback. However, it is important to remind him that learning this new skill can be very difficult and that you do not want him thinking that he has to concentrate on it throughout the entire day.

- As the student becomes increasingly more successful during the half-hour period (i.e., ratings of 3 or 4 for at least five to ten days), expand the time period to one hour, then to one and a half hours, then to half a day, then to a full day.

. . . .
Suggested Steps for Developing and Implementing a Plan

The following steps are designed to help you develop an appropriate intervention plan and implement it effectively, whether you choose to use one of the MODEL PLANS or create a customized plan of your own. The steps are, however, suggestions—they are not intended to be followed rigidly or in any particular order. Use your professional judgment and the knowledge of your particular situation to make them work for you.

1. *Make sure you have enough information about the situation.*

a. If you think a minimal intervention like PLAN A will be sufficient, you may already have enough information to proceed. However, when a more involved plan seems necessary, you should consider collecting additional descriptive and/or objective information for a couple of days.

b. You need to be able to explain what the student does that has led you to conclude that he "is inordinately nervous." Anecdotal notes on actual incidents should provide enough details to help you define the problem behavior thoroughly.

To collect anecdotal notes, simply keep a card in your pocket or on a clipboard and occasionally make notes on specific instances when the student does something that you believe demonstrates nervousness. For each entry, briefly describe where and when it occurred, what the student did or said, and any other relevant observations (e.g., any aspects of the behavior that seem to interfere with the student's academic or social success).

You do not need to make an entry every time the student exhibits nervousness; the idea is to capture a range of examples so you will be able to describe the behavior clearly and completely.

Also include some notes on times when the student acts in a more relaxed manner—this will make it clear that you are not only aware of his problem behavior, but also recognize when he behaves appropriately. These positive examples will help you clarify for the student how it is that you want him to behave.

c. If the student notices what you are doing and asks about it, be straightforward—tell him that you are collecting information to see whether his nervous behavior is a problem that needs to be worked on.

Following is an example of anecdotal notes that have been collected on a student's nervousness behavior.

Carlos' Nervousness—10/13

8:10—Coming into the room, Carlos' brow is furrowed. He walks rapidly to his seat and begins playing with his pencils in his hands. Throughout the opening of class, his hands never seem to stop.

10:35—His hands still going a mile a minute, Carlos is working with a cooperative group. He participates, but his speech is tentative and he makes frequent excuses: "This is only what I think, but . . . "; "Either way. I don't really have an opinion."; "This is a sort of dumb idea, but . . . ."

10:45—Sue, in Carlos' group, says, "Carlos, quit fidgeting all over, you're driving me crazy."

2:20—Carlos is working independently writing in his journal. Despite the fact that his nonwriting hand seems to move all about, he consistently gets his work completed and it is of high quality.

---

d. Continuing to collect this type of information while you implement a plan will help you monitor whether the situation is getting worse, staying the same, or getting better.

2. *Identify a focus for the intervention and labels for referring to the appropriate and inappropriate behaviors.*

a. To be effective, the intervention must address something other than reducing the student's nervousness—there must be a concurrent emphasis on *increasing* some positive behavior or trait (e.g., being more relaxed) for which the student can be reinforced. If you frequently refer to the student's problem as nervousness, it may increase his belief that he is nervous. Plus, you don't want to reinforce the student for "not being nervous."

Having identified a positive behavior will make it easier for you to "catch" and reinforce the student for behaving appropriately, and will allow you to frame the situation to the student more productively. If you explain that you want to "help the student learn to be more relaxed," you present an important, and reasonable, goal for the student to work toward and clearly identify what the student needs to do to be successful.

b. Specifying labels for the appropriate and inappropriate behaviors (e.g., "being relaxed" and "being tense," respectively) will help you to use consistent vocabulary when discussing the situation with the student. If you sometimes refer to the inappropriate behavior as "tenseness" and other times tell the student that "he is acting anxious," he may not realize that you are talking about the same thing.

3. *Determine when and how to include the parent(s).*

a. It is not necessary to contact the student's parent(s) if the problem has just begun, however, it might be a good idea to take advantage of any scheduled activities (e.g., conferences, weekly notes home) to let them know of your concern.

b. The parent(s) should be contacted whenever:

- You may be using procedures which they might find controversial.

- You suspect the student's anxiety is related to a specific problem.

- The student's behavior is affecting his academic performance or alienating him from his peers.

Share any information you have collected about the behavior (e.g., anecdotal notes), and explain why you are concerned. Focus in particular on how the behavior is hindering the student academically and/or socially.

You might ask if the parent(s) have any insight into the situation and/or whether they have noticed similar behavior at home, or if the problem is specific to school. Whether or not the parent(s) perceive a problem, explain that you want to help the student "learn to be more relaxed" and invite them to join you for an initial meeting with the student to develop a plan. If the parent(s) are unable or unwilling to participate, let them know that you will keep them informed of the student's progress.

c. Once the parent(s) have been involved in any way, you should give them updates at least

once per week while the plan is being implemented.

4. *Prepare for, then conduct, an initial meeting about the situation.*

a. Arrange a meeting to discuss your concerns with the student and anyone else who will be involved (e.g., the parent[s], the school psychologist). Although the specifics will vary depending upon the age of the student and the severity of the problem, there are some general guidelines to consider when scheduling the meeting.

First, meet at a neutral time (i.e., not immediately after a problem has occurred), when emotions are less likely to hamper communication. In general, a day's notice is appropriate, however a primary age student may worry excessively and/or forget what the meeting is about if it is scheduled more than an hour before it takes place.

Second, make the meeting appropriately private. With a primary student with a mild problem, you might meet in the classroom while the other students are working independently. However, when dealing with a middle/junior high school student and the student's parent(s), you will need some place private (e.g., the counselor's office) to ensure that the discussion will not be overheard.

Third, try to make sure the meeting is scheduled for a time and place that it is not likely to be interrupted. And finally, if the parent(s) will be participating, they should be the ones to tell the student about the meeting.

b. Construct a preliminary plan. Decide whether you think you can use one of the MODEL PLANS or if you need to create a customized plan using components from various plans and/or of your own design. Although you will invite and encourage the student to help develop the plan during the initial meeting, having a proposed plan in mind before you meet can alleviate frustration and wasted time if the student is unwilling or unable to participate.

c. After reviewing the information you have collected and thinking about how you want the student to behave, prepare thorough descriptions of the behavior that is getting in the way of the student's success and/or enjoyment of school, and what it would look like if the student were acting more relaxed.

The more specific you can be and the more concrete examples you have, the easier it will be to clarify (and for the student to understand) your expectations. Be sure to consider the student's behavior in all relevant activities (e.g., independent work, teacher directed instruction, unstructured class times, recess and lunch, etc.).

d. Conduct the meeting in an atmosphere of collaboration. The following agenda is one way you might structure the meeting:

* **Share your concerns about the student's behavior.**

    Briefly describe the problem behavior and explain why you consider it to be a problem. In this case, you might tell the student that, "We all do better at the things we do when we are relaxed." Use age-appropriate examples and capitalize on the student's interests, if possible. For example, if the student like sports you might explain that a great athlete only brings as much tension to a task as is necessary—if he/she gets too tense, he/she can get "psyched out" and make a mistake.

* **Discuss how you can work together to improve the situation.**

    Tell the student that you would like to help him "learn to be more relaxed," and describe your preliminary plan. Invite the student to give you input on the various aspects of the plan, and together work out any necessary details. You may have to brainstorm different possibilities if the student is uncomfortable with the initial plan. Incorporating any of the student's suggestions that strengthen the plan is likely to increase his sense of "ownership" in and commitment to it.

* **Make sure the student understands what you mean by appropriate and inappropriate behavior.**

    Use the descriptions you have prepared to define and clarify the problem behavior and the positive (desired) behavior as specifically and thoroughly as you can. To ensure that

you and the student are in agreement about the expectations, you might want to have the student demonstrate examples of relaxed behavior (this is probably not necessary with middle/junior high school students).

* **Conclude the meeting.**

    Always end the meeting with words of encouragement. Let the student know that you are confident that he can be successful. Be sure to reinforce him for participating in the meeting.

5. *Give the student regular, ongoing feedback about his behavior.*

It is important to meet with the student periodically to discuss his progress. In most cases, three to five minutes once per week should suffice. Review any information that has been collected and discuss whether or not the situation is getting better. As much as possible, focus on the student's improvements, however, also address any new or continuing problems. As the situation improves, the meetings can be faded to once every other week and then to once per month.

6. *Evaluate the situation (and the plan).*

Implement any plan for at least two weeks before deciding whether to change plans; to continue, modify, or fade the plan you are using; or to cease the intervention. Generally, if the student's behavior is clearly improving (based on the objective information that's been collected and/or the subjective perceptions of yourself, the student, and possibly the parent[s]), stick with what you are doing. If the situation has remained the same, some kind of change will be necessary. Always discuss any changes to the plan with the student first. *(NOTE: If the student seems to become more tensed or depressed at any point, consider a referral to the school psychologist or counselor.)*

APATHETIC BEHAVIOR

Student Does Just Enough to Get By

Student Does Nothing

Student is Unmotivated

DESCRIPTION

You have a student who acts apathetic and unmotivated. At her worst, the student does nothing and at her best, she does just enough to get by.

GOAL

The student will demonstrate increased motivation.

OVERVIEW OF PLANS

- PLAN A: For a situation in which the problem is relatively mild or has just begun.
- PLAN B: For a student who uses apathetic behavior to gain adult attention.
- PLAN C: For a student who does not seem to realize when and/or how frequently her behavior is apathetic. *(NOTE: This plan can be easily adapted for a small group or whole class.)*
- PLAN D: For a student who is not motivated to stop acting apathetic.
- PLAN E: For a student who acts apathetic because she has experienced so little success that she is not confident of her abilities, and therefore is unwilling to try.

Alternative Problems

- **Attention Deficit Hyperactivity Disorder (ADHD)**
- **Bored Behavior**
- **Complaining**
- **Compliance/Direction Following, Lack of**
- **Helplessness**
- **Out of Seat**
- **Shyness/Withdrawn Behavior**
- **Work Completion— Daily Work**

General Considerations

- If the student's family or cultural background could be a factor in the behavior (e.g., the parent[s] are very reserved), do not intervene unless you talk the parent(s) about the appropriateness of the proposed plan(s) and/or goals. If the behavior is not interfering with the student's academic or social success, it may be unnecessary, and potentially inappropriate, to intervene.

- If the student's problem behavior stems in any way from academic issues (e.g., the student is unable to do the work and uses apathetic behavior as a cover), concurrent efforts must be made to ensure her academic success (see **Academic Deficits, Determining**).

- If you suspect that the inappropriate behavior could be related to the student being depressed, see **Depression**. That problem includes a set of questions to help you decide whether the student should be referred for counseling or psychological services.

- If the inappropriate behavior is resulting in the student avoiding or not completing her schoolwork, start with a plan to increase the student's work completion (see **Work Completion—Daily Work**). Once the student is turning in completed work on a regular basis, you can reconsider an intervention for the apathetic behavior, if the problem still exists.

- If you have any reason to suspect a physiological or neurological basis for the student's behavior (e.g., the student acts extremely lethargic), consult with your building administrator and/or school psychologist to get advice on district procedures for following up on this type of situation.

Model Plans

P L A N   A

It is not always necessary, or even beneficial, to use an involved plan. If the apathetic behavior has just begun and/or is not interfering with the student's academic or social progress, the following actions, along with making the student aware of your concerns, may resolve the situation.

1. **Respond consistently to the inappropriate behavior.**

a. When the student manifests the apathetic behavior as not working or not following directions, try praising a student who is working or following directions. If the target student then begins acting more motivated, wait approximately 30-60 seconds and then praise her. If she does not begin to act motivated when you praise someone else, gently correct her by calmly providing information on what she needs to be doing. "Caryn, you need to stay motivated by (describe the expectation)." Avoid being emotional or talking too much—the student should get more attention for being on task than being off task.

b. If the student's apathy does not involve a specific behavior that affects her academic work, but seems to be a general attitude or demeanor (e.g., passiveness, boredom, or isolation), ignore the behavior, but keep anecdotal notes on the incidents so that you will be able to talk to the student about the behavior in a specific manner.

 2. **Use reinforcement to encourage appropriate behavior.**

a. Give the student increased praise. Be especially alert for situations in which the student acts in a motivated manner and praise her specifically for these. "Caryn, you are staying motivated about your work. This is a great demonstration of the goal we talked about." If the public praise would be embarrassing, praise the student privately or even use a note. Remember that any time the student is not acting apathetic, you can praise her.

b. Occasionally praise the entire class. "Everyone is the room is on task right now. What a pleasure to see 100% of the class on task and using this work time so effectively."

c. Praise the target student for other positive behaviors she exhibits, and give her frequent attention (e.g., say "hello" to her as she enters the classroom, call on her frequently during class activities, and occasionally ask her to assist you with a class job that needs to be done). For example, you might ask her what she did over the weekend. This demonstrates to the student that you are interested in many things she does, not just whether or not she is acting apathetic.

PLAN B

Some students are very skilled at getting attention through negative behavior. If you find yourself frequently nagging, reminding, or coaxing the student to act more motivated, it is possible she is trying to gain adult attention. Whether or not the student overtly seems to like the attention, you should make sure that she receives more frequent and more satisfying attention for behaving appropriately than for her apathetic behavior.

1. **Respond consistently when the student acts apathetic.**

a. You do not want to give undue attention to the student if she is using apathetic behavior to gain attention, however, you can't really ignore apathetic behavior if the student is wasting time or not following directions—she needs to be on task. Therefore, whenever the student is acting apathetic by being off task or noncompliant, gently correct her with a reminder about what she should be doing instead.

Keeping the interaction as short and unemotional as possible will make it less satisfying for the student. For example, if she is apathetic during an independent work period, you might say the student's name and state what she should be doing in a way that almost sounds like shorthand. "Caryn, looking at your book," or "Caryn, writing your story."

b. When the student's apathy manifests as passiveness, boredom, or isolation, and it is not interfering with the student's academic work, ignore the behavior.

2. **Use reinforcement to encourage appropriate behavior.**

a. Frequent praise and attention comprise the core of this plan. The student must see that she receives more attention (and more satisfying attention) when she behaves appropriately than when she acts apathetic. Thus, whenever the student is acting motivated, make an effort to praise and spend time with her: "Caryn, would it be okay if I sat with you a moment and watched as you and your group do the next step on this assignment?"

b. You may also wish to use intermittent rewards to acknowledge the student's success. Occasional, and unexpected, rewards can motivate a student to demonstrate responsible behavior more often.

The idea is to provide a reward when the student has acted motivated during a typically difficult activity or for a longer stretch of time than she has before. "Caryn, you have been staying motivated so well, would you like to take a break to do me a favor? I need this note taken to Mrs. Olin. Would you mind doing that for me?"

A list of additional reinforcement ideas can be found in APPENDIX 1. Use intermittent rewards more frequently at the beginning of the intervention to encourage the student, and less often as the student's behavior improves.

3. **Ensure a 3-1 ratio of positive to negative attention.**

a. Given that attention is a motivating force for this student, you want to be sure that you are giving the student *three times as much* positive as negative attention. One way to do this is to monitor your interactions with the student at least one day per week. Just keep a card on a clipboard or in your pocket and record each interaction you have with the student as either positive or negative by putting a "+" or a "-", respectively, on the card.

To determine whether an interaction is positive or negative, ask yourself whether the student was acting apathetic (or otherwise misbehaving) at the time of the interaction. Any interaction that stems from inappropriate behavior is negative, while all interactions that occur while the student is meeting classroom expectations are positive.

Thus, gently correcting the student is a negative interaction and praising the student for acting more motivated is positive. Greeting the student as she enters the room or asking her if she has any questions during independent work are also considered positive interactions. *(NOTE: Ignoring the student's inappropriate behavior is not recorded at all, because it is not an interaction.)*

b. If you find that you are not giving the student three times as much positive as negative attention, try to increase the number of positive interactions you have with the student. Sometimes prompts can help. For example, you might decide that each time the student enters the classroom you will say "hello" to her, that whenever you look at the clock you will find a time to praise the student, or that whenever a student uses the drinking fountain you will check the target student and as soon as possible praise some aspect of her behavior. You can also increase the ratio of positive to negative attention by ignoring more of the student's inappropriate behavior.

P L A N   C

Some students do not seem to realize how their behavior is perceived by others. When a student doesn't recognize that she is acting apathetic, the intervention should include some way of helping her to learn to identify when she is acting apathetic and when she is acting motivated.

 Teach the student to distinguish between when she is acting apathetic and when she is acting motivated.

For at least two days, preface any praise comments and/or corrections to the student with the question, "Caryn, are you acting motivated or apathetic?" If the student accurately identifies her behavior, even if she was acting apathetic, praise her for accurate self-assessment. "Right Caryn, I agree. You were sitting and playing with your pencil rather than working on your project, but I am glad that you can identify that as apathetic behavior. Let's see you get motivated."

Although the student needs to learn to identify both states, be sure to ask this question more frequently when she is motivated than when she is apathetic. If you only ask the question when she is apathetic, she will quickly learn that the correct answer is always "apathetic." Continue this procedure until the student is accurately assessing her behavior at least 95% of the time.

 Develop procedures for having the student periodically evaluate her own behavior.

a. Give the student an evaluation form similar to the following and explain that, at irregular intervals (when a beeper or timer goes off), she will be recording whether she was acting motivated or apathetic at the time.

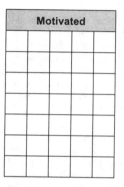

Motivated			Apathetic		

NOTE: Beeper tapes are audio tapes that play intermittent beeps in between periods of silence. You can make your own or purchase them. For example, The Practice Skill Mastery Program contains a set of six beeper tapes and step-by-step instructions for their use for a variety of objectives. The Program is available at the following address:

Mastery Programs, Ltd.
P.O. Box 90
Logan, Utah 84231

If you use a timer instead of beeper tapes, you will have to reset the timer each time it goes off, being careful to set it for varying amounts of time (e.g., one minute, then ten minutes, then 15 minutes). When the timer sounds, the student will mark if she was "Motivated" or "Apathetic" at the time.

b. At the end of each work period, review the form and discuss the results with the student. If appropriate, you might have the student chart the number of times she was acting motivated and the number of times her behavior was apathetic.

c. If necessary, help the student identify strategies she can use to increase her time on task. Or, give the student gentle reminders in between the beeps. "Caryn, you never know when that beep is going to happen; better get motivated on that science assignment."

d. Occasionally you should monitor the accuracy of the student's evaluations. For one period each week, keep your own evaluation record. When the beep sounds or the timer goes off, occurs, record whether you think the student was acting motivated or apathetic. At the end of the work period, compare your results to the student's. If the student has been accurate in her evaluations, praise her and provide intermittent rewards for accuracy.

NOTE: Some students might be embarrassed using a beeper system that peers would notice. It may be more appropriate for an older student (e.g., above fourth grade), for example, to use a self-evaluation form like the one following to self-evaluate her behavior for an entire class period at the end of the period. The two of you could then discuss the results, both for accuracy and/or to identify strategies for staying on task, during the passing period.

3. **Respond consistently to the inappropriate behavior.**

When the student is acting in an apathetic manner, either gently correct her or ignore the behavior, depending upon whether or not the behavior is affecting her academic performance (see PLAN A).

4. **Use reinforcement to encourage appropriate behavior.**

a. Give the student increased praise and attention for acting motivated (see PLAN A).

b. Praise the student for accurate recording (if applicable) during the meeting times to review the self-evaluation form. Even on a bad day, if the student is willing to chart the data and discuss why it was a bad day, praise her. "Caryn, you are really handling this responsibly. Even though it was a rough day, you are willing to talk to me about things you might do differently tomorrow. That is a real sign that you are growing up." Regardless of how the day went, try to make the meeting upbeat and encouraging.

Self-Evaluation Form for Motivated/Apathetic Behavior
(for a student in fourth grade or above)

Name _____   Class Period _____

Directions:

At the end of the period use the scale to rate the quality of motivation during the period. Record the rating in the boxes below.

RATING	DESCRIPTION
0	Apathetic through the entire period
1	Motivated a little bit of the period
2	Motivated about half of the period
3	Motivated for most of the period
4	Motivated the entire period

M	T	W	TH	F

5. **Encourage the student to use self-reinforcement.**

Whenever things are going well, prompt the student to mentally reinforce herself. "Caryn, this has been a very successful morning. I want you to silently tell yourself that you are doing a great job of staying motivated." Prompt the student in this manner intermittently throughout the day, when appropriate.

PLAN D

Whenever a student's problem behavior has become habitual and/or she does not seem to care whether or not she reduces it, you may need to use a structured system of external incentives (i.e., rewards and consequences) based on her behavior to encourage her to stop acting apathetic and to start acting motivated.

 1. **Respond consistently to the inappropriate behavior.**

When the student is acting in an apathetic manner, either gently correct her or ignore the behavior, depending upon whether or not the behavior is affecting her academic performance (see PLAN A).

 2. **Establish a structured system for reinforcing the student's appropriate behavior and providing a consequence for the inappropriate behavior.**

a. With the student, create a list of reinforcers that she can earn. Although you might want to have some suggestions in mind, the system will be more effective if the student identifies most of the items or activities herself. *(NOTE: A list of reinforcement ideas can be found in APPENDIX 1.)*

b. Assign "prices" (in points) for each of the rewards on the list and have the student choose the reward she wants to earn first.

The prices should be based on the instructional, personnel, and/or monetary costs of the items. Monetary cost is clear—the more expensive the item, the more points required to earn it. Instructional cost refers to the amount of instructional time lost or interfered with by a particular reward. Thus, an activity which causes the student to miss part of math instruction should require more points than one the student can do on her own recess time. Personnel cost involves the time required by you and/or other staff to fulfill the reinforcer. Having lunch with the principal, therefore, would cost more points than spending five minutes of free time with a friend.

If the student is immature, and needs more frequent encouragement, you might consider letting her earn several "less expensive" rewards (e.g., five minutes of computer time after 20 points) on the way to a bigger reward (e.g., one hour helping you after school for 200 points). That is, the student earns the small rewards without spending her points; they continue to accumulate toward the selected reward.

c. Design a response cost system in which the student begins each day with a set amount of points (equal to the average number of times you are reminding the student to act motivated per day, plus two). Thus, if you are reminding the student five times per day, she would begin each day with seven points. Each time you have to remind the student to stay motivated, she loses a point. The points remaining at the end of each day are added together to be applied toward the reinforcer the student is striving to earn.

(NOTE: A lottery system might be more effective with a primary level student. The student would begin each day with tickets in a jar instead of points. All the tickets have prizes written on them—one has a big prize, a couple have moderate prizes, and the majority have small prizes. Each time you have to remind the student about her apathetic behavior you would remove one ticket from the jar—but neither you nor the student would be allowed to see what is written on it. At the end of each day, the student draws one ticket from those remaining in the jar, and receives that prize.)

d. Whenever the student is making a special effort to exhibit more motivated behavior, give the student an extra point (or ticket). You might give one point or, if what the student did was very significant, several points. In addition to giving the student the point(s), describe exactly what the student did that prompted you to reward her. "Caryn, for the last hour you have demonstrated a model of motivated behavior. You participated and got a great deal accomplished. Five points are being added to your total for the day."

If you add a ticket rather than point(s), base the value of the reinforcer that is written on it on how difficult the behavior was or how highly motivated the student was in exhibiting the behavior. Keep in mind that you want to tell the student exactly what she did as you give the ticket so that the primary focus is on what the student did, and to a lesser extent on what she might earn.

e. When the student has accumulated enough points to earn the reward she has chosen, she "spends" the points necessary and the system begins again. That is, she begins accumulating points for the next reward she chooses to earn. For example, if the student had 38 points and spent 30 on her first reinforcer, she would carry over eight points as she began working for the next reinforcer.

f. Determine a *consequence* (e.g., time owed from recess or in detention) for any reminder that you have to give after the student has already lost her points (or tickets) for the day. If the student runs out of points (or tickets), implement the consequence for each subsequent reminder. The consequence should not involve taking away a previous day's points (or tickets). If the student can lose already-earned points, she might develop an attitude of, "I am losing so many points, why should I even bother to try?"

 Use reinforcement to encourage appropriate behavior.

a. Give the student increased praise and attention for acting motivated (see PLAN A).

b. In addition, show interest and enthusiasm about how the student is doing on the system. "Caryn, you have really stayed motivated for the last few days. Good job!"

PLAN E

Sometimes a student will have become so discouraged that she feels safer doing nothing and caring about nothing rather than risking further failure or rejection. For this type of student, the intervention plan should be somewhat indirect—instead of working specifically on the student's apathetic behavior, you want to try to help the student to feel more confident about herself as a way to encourage her to act more motivated.

 Make sure the student has an adult with whom she feels comfortable talking about personal problems.

During your initial meeting with the student (see SUGGESTED STEPS FOR DEVELOPING AND IMPLEMENTING A PLAN) you should try to determine whether there is a specific circumstance or problem that is causing the student to feel apathetic or discouraged. If the student does not identify anything specific and her parent(s) cannot pinpoint a specific cause, simply invite the student to feel free to talk to you (or the school counselor or school nurse) if she ever does want help or need to talk about a problem.

Identify the student's strengths or interests and structure activities or interactions to capitalize on them.

a. One potentially powerful way to boost a student's confidence is to build upon strengths and interests that already exist. Enhancing the student's confidence in things she already does well may help her develop more confidence overall and become more motivated as a result.

b. Following are some possible ways to do this:

- If the student has a particular interest, you might check out a book on the subject from the library or loan her one of your own that you enjoyed when you were her age.

- If the student is good on the computer, you might ask her to help set up a database to keep track of classroom supplies.

- If the student has artistic abilities, you might ask her to make a drawing that can be used to demonstrate a particular technique (e.g., shading a background) to the class.

Help the student learn to use positive self-talk.

a. Listen to the student's overt statements and try to determine whether she may be putting herself down. For example, watch for such comments as:

- "I never get anything done."

- "I am so ugly."

- "I can't do that sort of thing."

- "I always make that mistake."

Whenever the student makes this type of statement, she reinforces her negative beliefs about herself. The more often she makes such comments, the more she will come to believe them to be true and, potentially, the more discouraged and/or apathetic she will become.

b. Teach the student how to develop more positive and hopeful self-talk. Have the student reframe negative belief statements into more positive and hopeful statements. If the student can't do this, model it for her and have her repeat the positive statement after you. Don't worry if the student acts like she doesn't believe the positive statements at first—with repetition she will come to believe these positive statements about herself.

The following examples may help you get started.

- **Negative Statements**

  - "I never get anything done."

  - "I am so ugly."

  - "I can't do that sort of thing."

  - "I always make that mistake."

- **Positive Statements**

  - "I am smart and capable."

  - "I like the way I look."

  - "I can do that. Even if I have trouble, I'll get it eventually."

  - "I had trouble with that assignment, but I am smart so I can learn from my mistakes."

*(NOTE: For more information, see **Self-Concept Problems**.)*

 Structure academic success for the student.

Make sure that the student is experiencing frequent success in the tasks that she is being asked to do. If the student fails at academics frequently, your efforts to encourage her to use more positive self-talk and to see her strengths in other areas will not be powerful enough to counteract the daily failures. *(NOTE: For more information, see **Academic Deficits, Determining**.)*

 Respond consistently to the inappropriate behavior.

Plan to ignore the student's apathetic behavior. Given that the student lacks confidence, constant reminders about being motivated are likely to decrease her confidence even more.

. . . .

Suggested Steps for Developing and Implementing a Plan

The following steps are designed to help you develop an appropriate intervention plan and implement it effectively, whether you choose to use one of the MODEL PLANS or create a customized plan of your own. The steps are, however, suggestions—they are not intended to be followed rigidly or in any particular order. Use your professional judgment and the knowledge of your particular situation to make them work for you.

1. **Make sure you have enough information about the situation.**

a. If you think a minimal intervention like PLAN A will be sufficient, you may already have enough information to proceed. However, when a more involved plan seems necessary, you should consider collecting additional descriptive and/or objective information for a couple of days.

b. You want to be able to describe what it is about the student's behavior that has led you to conclude that she is apathetic. Anecdotal notes on actual incidents should provide enough details

to help you define the problem clearly and explain it specifically to the student and her parent(s).

To collect anecdotal notes, simply keep a card in your pocket or on a clipboard and occasionally make notes on specific incidents in which you thought the student was acting apathetic. For each entry, briefly describe where and when the behavior occurred, what was said and done, and any other relevant observations you may have (e.g., what prompted the behavior). You do not need to take notes *every* time the student acts apathetic; the idea is to capture a range of examples of the behavior so that you will be able to describe it completely.

You should also make notes on times when the student is acting motivated; this will make it clear that you are not only aware of her inappropriate behavior, but also recognize when she behaves appropriately. When you meet with the student, the positive examples will help you clarify how you want the student to behave.

c. In addition to recording information about what the student's inappropriate behavior looks like, it can also be useful to document how often it occurs (i.e., a frequency count). This provides a more objective measure of the problem (and an objective way to monitor progress).

You can use the same card on which you are recording anecdotal notes to keep a frequency count. Simply write a tally mark each time the student acts apathetic. Coding these tallies will allow you to discern whether the behavior occurs more frequently during certain times, subjects, or activities (e.g., using "A" or "P" to indicate whether the behavior occurred in the morning or afternoon; or clustering the tallies by math or reading, or teacher directed instruction or independent work, etc.).

d. If the student notices what you are doing and asks about it, be straightforward—tell her that you are collecting information to see whether her apathetic behavior is a problem that needs to be worked on.

Following is an example of anecdotal notes that have been collected on a student's apathetic behavior.

e. The frequency information can be easily summarized on a chart or graph. Seeing how often the student acts apathetic may help the student and her parent(s) better understand your concern.

f. Continuing to collect this type of information (and keeping the chart up-to-date) while you implement the plan will allow you to monitor whether the situation is getting worse, staying the same, or getting better over time.

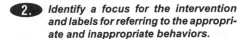 **Identify a focus for the intervention and labels for referring to the appropriate and inappropriate behaviors.**

a. To be effective, the intervention must address more than just reducing the student's apathy—there must be a concurrent emphasis on increasing some positive behavior or trait (e.g., being motivated, making an effort). Having a specific positive behavior in mind will make it easier to "catch" and reinforce the student for acting appropriately, and a positive focus will allow you to frame the situation productively.

For example, if you simply say, "the student has a problem with being apathetic," you offer little in the way of useful information, and may put the student and the parent(s) on the defensive. However, if you explain your concern by saying that you want to "help the student learn to act more motivated," you present an important, and reasonable, goal for the student to work toward and clearly identify what the student needs to do to be successful.

Caryn's Apathetic Behavior—December

Dec. 16th

10:15—From the moment she came into class, Caryn never smiled, never interacted with anyone unless they talked to her, and basically did very little. When I asked or told her to do something, she did it, but I can tell that it is not what she is capable of—just enough to keep me off her back.

2:45—The rest of the day went much like the morning. I did ask her if anything was bothering her or if she had a problem I could help with, and she just shrugged and said "no." There isn't anything in particular she is doing wrong—she just does so little.

Dec. 17th

12:15—I counted the times I needed to remind Caryn to get to work or to follow a direction, and it was only twice. It seems like a lot more because she acts so unmotivated, but she really gets done most of what she "has" to do. I guess the problem has to do with my sense that she is only doing things because she has to. I didn't observe a time that she volunteered or made an effort to do anything on her own, including even talking to another student.

---

b. Specifying labels for the appropriate and inappropriate behaviors (e.g., "being motivated" and "being apathetic," respectively) will help you to use consistent vocabulary when discussing the situation with the student. If you sometimes refer to the inappropriate behavior as "being apathetic" and other times tell the student that she "is not doing enough," she may not realize that you are talking about the same thing.

3. Determine when and how to include the parent(s).

a. You probably do not need to contact the student's parent(s) if the problem has just begun and is not interfering with the student's academic or social progress. You might, however, take advantage of any scheduled activities (e.g., conferences, weekly notes home) to let the parent(s) know of your concern.

b. The parent(s) should be contacted whenever the student's apathy is affecting her academic performance or is alienating her from her peers. Share with them any information you have collected about the behavior (i.e., anecdotal notes, frequency count), and explain why you are concerned. Focus in particular on how the apathy is hindering the student academically and/or socially.

   You might ask if the parent(s) have any insight into the behavior and/or whether they have noticed similar behavior at home. Whether or not the parent(s) perceive a problem, invite them to join you for an initial meeting with the student to develop a plan to help the student learn to "act more motivated." If the parent(s) are unable or unwilling to participate, let them know that you will keep them informed of the student's progress.

c. Once the parent(s) have been involved in any way, you should give them updates at least once per week while the plan is being implemented.

4. Prepare for, then conduct, an initial meeting about the situation.

a. Schedule a meeting to discuss your concerns with the student and anyone else who will be involved in the plan (e.g., the parent[s], the school psychologist). Although the specifics of the meeting will vary depending upon the age of the student and the severity of the problem, there are some general guidelines to consider when scheduling the meeting.

First, meet at a neutral time (i.e., not immediately after a problem has occurred), when emotions are less likely to hamper communication. In general, a day's notice is appropriate, however a primary age student may worry excessively and/or forget what the meeting is about if it is scheduled more than an hour before it takes place.

Second, make the meeting appropriately private. For example, with a primary student who has a mild problem, you might meet in the classroom while the other students are working independently. However, when dealing with a middle/junior high school student and the student's parent(s), you will want to use a private room (e.g., the counselor's office) to ensure that the discussion will not be overheard.

Third, try to make sure that the meeting is scheduled for a time and place that it is not likely to be interrupted. Finally, if the parent(s) will be participating, they should be the ones to tell the student about the meeting.

b. Construct a preliminary plan. Decide whether you can use one of the MODEL PLANS or if you need to create a customized plan using components from various plans and/or your own ideas. You will invite and encourage the student to help develop the plan during the initial meeting, however, having a plan in mind before you meet can alleviate frustration and wasted time if the student is unwilling or unable to participate.

c. After reviewing the information you have collected and thinking about how you want the student to behave, prepare thorough descriptions of the inappropriate behavior and the positive behavior/trait on which the student will be working. The more specific you are and the more concrete examples you have, the easier it will be to clarify (and for the student to understand) your expectations.

   Also be sure to consider the student's behavior in all relevant activities (e.g., independent work, teacher directed instruction, unstructured class times, recess and lunch, etc.).

d. Conduct the meeting in an atmosphere of collaboration. The following agenda is one way you might structure the meeting:

   • **Share your concerns about the student's behavior.**

   Briefly describe the problem behavior and, when appropriate, show the student a chart or graph of how often she engages in the behavior. Then, explain why you consider the behavior to be a problem. In this case, you might tell the student that while everyone acts apathetic now and then, being successful in school, work, sports, the arts, or just about anything else requires motivated attention.

- **Discuss how you can work together to improve the situation.**

    Explain that you would like to help the student learn to "act more motivated" and describe your preliminary plan. Invite the student's input on the plan, and together work out any necessary details (e.g., reinforcers, consequences). You may have to brainstorm different possibilities if the student is uncomfortable with the initial plan. Incorporating any of the student's suggestions that strengthen the plan is likely to increase her sense of "ownership" in and commitment to the plan.

- **Make sure the student understands what you mean by appropriate and inappropriate behavior.**

    Use the descriptions you have prepared to define and clarify the problem behavior and the positive (desired) behavior as specifically and thoroughly as you can. To ensure that you and the student are in agreement about the expectations, you might present hypothetical scenarios and have her identify whether each is an example of motivated or apathetic behavior. Or you might present an actual situation that has occurred and ask her to describe how she would demonstrate acting more motivated in that situation.

- **Conclude the meeting.**

    Always end the meeting with words of encouragement. Let the student know that it may be difficult, but that you are confident that she can be successful. Be sure to reinforce her for participating in the meeting.

5. *Give the student regular, ongoing feedback about her behavior.*

It is important to meet with the student periodically to discuss her progress. In most cases, a short meeting every day is optimum. During the meeting, review any information that has been collected and discuss whether the day went better, worse, or about the same as previous days. As much as possible, focus on the student's improvements, however, also use the time to address any new or continuing problems. As the situation improves, the meetings can be faded to once every other week and then to once per month.

6. *Evaluate the situation (and the plan).*

Implement any plan for at least two weeks before deciding whether to change plans; to continue, modify, or fade the plan you are using; or to cease the intervention. Generally, if the student's behavior is clearly improving (based on the objective information that's been collected and/or the subjective perceptions of yourself, the student, and possibly the parent[s]), stick with what you are doing. If the situation has remained the same or worsened, some kind of change will be necessary. Always discuss any changes to the plan with the student first.

ARGUING—STUDENTS WITH EACH OTHER

· ·

DESCRIPTION

There are students in your class who frequently argue with each other.

GOAL

The students will learn to interact with each other without arguing.

OVERVIEW OF PLANS

- PLAN A: For a situation in which the problem is relatively mild or has just begun.

- PLAN B: For a problem that may stem from students not knowing how to resolve conflicts without arguing.

- PLAN C: For a situation in which the problem seems to be that the students lack the motivation to resolve conflicts in peaceful ways.

NOTE:

These three MODEL PLANS assume the problem is class-wide (i.e., several students are involved). They can easily be modified to use with one to three students only.

Alternative Problems

- **Arguing—Student(s) With the Teacher**

- **Bossiness**

- **Bothering/Tormenting Others**

- **Bullying Behavior/ Fighting**

- **Cliques/Ganging Up**

- **Complaining**

- **Fighting**

- **Name Calling/Put-Downs**

- **Spoiled Behavior**

General Considerations

- If the problem behavior stems in any way from academic issues (e.g., several students are experiencing academic failure and the arguing is an outlet for frustration), concurrent efforts must be made to remediate any academic deficits (see **Academic Deficits, Determining**).

- If a number of the students lack the basic social skills to interact appropriately, it may be necessary to begin by teaching these skills. **Social Skills, Lack of** contains information on a variety of published social skills curricula.

- Given that a significant number of arguments may be occurring on the playground, coordinate your plan with the playground supervisors. If the playground is highly problematic, consider implementing a school-wide approach to managing the playground (see Sprick [1990] in the REFERENCES/ RESOURCES).

Model Plans

PLAN A

If the behavior has just begun and/or occurs only two to three times per week, it may not be necessary, or even beneficial, to use an involved plan. The following actions, along with making the students aware of your concerns, may resolve the situation.

1. Respond consistently to each instance of arguing.

a. Whenever you notice students arguing, give a gentle correction. Let the students know that their behavior is an example of arguing and provide information on what they should be doing instead. "Ron and Toby, this is an example of arguing. You need to lower your voices and take turns talking. If you need help solving the problem, let me know." Be emotionally neutral and avoid talking too much while giving the correction—your goal is to impart information.

b. If the students do not cease arguing, implement a brief, but immediate, time-out. "Ron, you need to stand over here. Toby, stand over here. Each of you think about the problem and try to come up with a plan. I will check on you in two minutes."

2. Use reinforcement to encourage appropriate behavior.

a. Praise individual students for meeting your expectations about interacting without arguing. Keep a special eye on those students who have had the greatest tendency to argue. Whenever one of these students is interacting without arguing, praise him/her for demonstrating the ability to solve conflicts peacefully. "Terri, I noticed that you and Crystal had a conflict but you talked about it peacefully and worked out a plan. Tell me about how you worked it out."

If the student(s) would be embarrassed by public praise, praise the student(s) privately or even use a note.

b. Occasionally praise those students who rarely or never have a problem with arguing. Because these students have already mastered the positive expectations, they do not need positive feedback as often as the students who have difficulty with them. However, you do not want them to feel that you take their positive behavior for granted. "Oleta, you are really a leader in this class. You are influential and often have strong opinions, yet you never resort to arguing. You will find the ability to influence without arguing to be a very useful skill."

c. When there has been a significant reduction in classroom arguing, praise the entire class. Remember that any time the students refrain from arguing, you can praise them for settling their conflicts peacefully.

PLAN B

If the students do not really know how to settle their disputes without arguing (i.e., how to "settle conflicts peacefully"), the intervention must include some way of teaching them how to do so.

 Conduct lessons to teach the students how to resolve conflicts peacefully and, if necessary, how to manage their anger.

a. Before the lessons, decide whether the whole class should participate or if the lessons should involve only a small group of students. In most cases, conducting the lessons with the entire class is advisable.

The lessons should include teaching the students to recognize conflict situations and what constitutes an argument, helping the students brainstorm strategies for resolving conflicts without arguing, and teaching them an alternative conflict resolution strategy, as follows:

- First, determine how you can teach students to identify conflict and realize that it is okay. Using the information from your anecdotal notes (see SUGGESTED STEPS FOR DEVELOPING AND IMPLEMENTING A PLAN) develop a list of typical conflict situations from the classroom. These examples will be useful for showing that conflict itself is not bad or wrong—the important thing is to resolve conflicts peacefully.

- Next, devise procedures for helping the students to identify what constitutes an argumentative way of resolving a conflict. The idea is to have the class develop a list of behaviors that involve arguing (e.g., raised voices, name calling, fighting, etc.).

- Then decide how the students will go about brainstorming different strategies for handling the hypothetical conflict situations you will present. Be sure you have some rules for this brainstorming phase in mind before you present the activity to the class. For example:

  1. Any idea is okay (but no obscenity).

  2. Ideas will not be evaluated initially (i.e., no approval—"Good idea" or disapproval—"What a stupid idea" or "We couldn't do that" should be expressed during brainstorming).

  3. All ideas will be written down and discussed at the conclusion of brainstorming.

- Finally, identify an overall strategy that the students can use to prevent conflicts from accelerating into arguments or fights. One is STP (Stop, Think, Plan). With this strategy, you teach the students that when they realize they are in a conflict situation, someone says: "Stop. We are in a conflict and need to develop a plan. Let's think." Then each of the parties involved thinks for a few moments and attempts to come up with a proposal for resolving the conflict. At that point, the students choose one of the techniques to try to resolve the conflict.

b. During the lessons, begin by presenting a type of conflict situation common in the class. Develop a scenario using hypothetical students. Then have the group brainstorm possible strategies for resolving that conflict. Have the class follow the rules for brainstorming, and write down everything anyone says. When the group is unable to produce any more ideas, go back through the list and evaluate the merits of the ideas identified—crossing out any that the group believes to be ineffective.

c. Repeat this process with at least two more scenarios involving different types of conflict. Make sure that one involves a conflict consisting of differences of opinion where there is no need for resolution. An adult example might be two friends—one who has strongly held Republican political beliefs and one who is a loyal Democrat. An analogous age-appropriate situation for fifth grade students could be two students who would like to be friends, but one loves baseball and the other thinks baseball is really stupid.

The purpose of having this type of example is for the students to realize that there are some conflicts with no clear resolution. Each person has a right to his/her own beliefs, however, if two people are going to be friends, they will need to work out ways to get along despite their different beliefs.

d. Take all of the strategies brainstormed that are potentially useful for resolving a conflict and have some student volunteers make a "Conflict Wheel." This is a large pie chart with a spinner (the chart should be large, but the spinner can be from a board game) on which the different

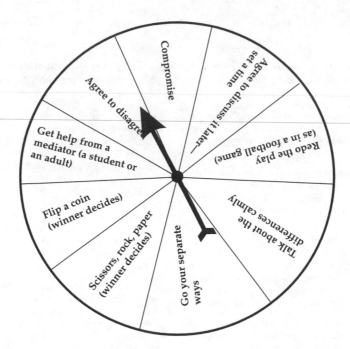

conflict resolution strategies are written in bold letters in each piece of the pie. You can use the following sample as a model, although the specific strategies should be those developed by your students during brainstorming.

e. In subsequent lessons, teach the students to use STP (or some other conflict resolution strategy). Explain that before a conflict can be resolved, the individuals involved need to realize that there is a conflict. Therefore, as soon as one person is aware that an argument has begun, that person has a responsibility to say something like, "Hey, let's not argue. Let's figure out a plan." This is the "Stop" phase. Then each party should think about how to resolve the conflict—thinking about the ideas on the Conflict Wheel, for example. This, obviously, is the "Think" phase, and during this phase the parties should try to come up with suggestions for a possible "Plan." When one of the parties has an idea, he/she should propose it as a possible plan. If the other person agrees, the conflict is solved. If not, they think some more.

If the students cannot agree on a plan, they might choose to go to the Conflict Wheel, give it a spin, and follow the first strategy that fits the problem. However, before spinning the spinner, the students should agree on which strategies are not applicable to their situation (e.g., "Redo the play" only applies to game situations) and

to abide by the first strategy that was not previously ruled out.

f. Use hypothetical scenarios and have students volunteer to role play different characters. Prompt the students to argue back and forth, and then have one employ STP. Let the students try to act out possible resolutions. After each role play, have the class discuss the situation. You may want to have the "actors" redo the role play, but with different conditions. "That was excellent. They came up with a plan they both agreed to. Let's do that again, but this time Chris, the character you are playing—'Darla' feels much more strongly that she is right. When 'Gail' proposes 'Go your separate ways,' 'Darla' feels that would not be fair. Let's give it a try, but this time let 'Gail' know that you do not agree with her plan and see what happens."

Repeat this process with different scenarios, making sure to vary the gender of the hypothetical students involved in the scenarios.

g. Conduct the lessons daily if possible, but at least twice per week. You should allow between 15-30 minutes per lesson, but realize that it may not be possible to complete all of the activities in one lesson. Continue the lessons until the students are consistently resolving their own conflicts without arguing.

(NOTE: Some students may need lessons in managing their anger. These can be conducted with individuals, small groups, or the entire class. See Self-Control Issues for more information.)

2. **Prompt appropriate behavior by using precorrections.**

Watch for circumstances in which the students are likely to have arguments and remind them to employ the strategies from the lessons. "Class, we are going to be working in groups on developing project plans. This is the type of activity where you may have differences of opinion. I will be watching to see if you remember to do what we practiced this morning. I'll bet you can."

3. **Respond consistently to all instances of arguing.**

a. Whenever you notice students arguing, gently correct them by employing STP. That is, stop the students, inform them that this seems like a conflict and prompt them to think, then come up with a plan. "Jacob, Ellen, that sounds like an argument because I hear raised voices and name calling. One of you should have done the 'Stop' step, but I am doing it now. Now each of you needs to think and come up with a plan. I will be right over here if you need help."

b. If the students continue arguing, assign each of them to a short time-out, then guide them through a conflict resolution process.

c. Watch for situations in which particular individuals are too willing to compromise (i.e., subjugate their own opinions too soon in an effort to prevent an argument). Meet with any such student(s) privately and encourage them to be assertive sometimes—let them know they have a right to stick up for themselves and have their opinions heard. If this seems especially difficult for any student, use role playing to teach him/her how to be assertive.

4. **Use reinforcement to encourage appropriate behavior.**

a. Praise individual students for meeting expectations regarding conflict resolution without arguing, and praise the entire class when improvement occurs (see PLAN A).

b. Make a special point of letting the students know (both individually and as a class) that you notice their efforts to use the skills they have been learning/practicing. "Class, Mary Ellen and Gary had a conflict, but they talked calmly about their opinions, and without needing help they worked out a compromise. Nice job of doing what we have been practicing."

c. You may also wish to use intermittent rewards to acknowledge the class' success. Occasional, and unexpected, rewards can motivate the students to demonstrate responsible behavior more often. The idea is to provide a reward when the class has had a particularly good period of resolving conflicts without arguing.

For this particular situation, appropriate rewards might include earning an extra recess, preparing a lesson for a younger class on conflict resolution, or having a city official or someone from an organization such as the NAACP come and congratulate them on what they are learning. *(NOTE: A list of additional reinforcement ideas can be found in APPENDIX 1.)*

When you use intermittent rewards, do so more frequently at the beginning of the intervention to encourage the students, and then less often as then behavior improves.

5. *(OPTIONAL)*
If the students seem to have trouble listening to each other, establish a procedure wherein the students are required to listen.

With primary students, you might use Talking/Listening Chairs. Teach the students that when they are instructed to go to the Talking/Listening Chairs the rule is that the person in the Listening Chair cannot say a word until the person in the Talking Chair is all finished. Then they switch places. This continues until the problem is resolved.

With older students, a similar technique can be employed using an object that is handed back and forth (e.g., a bean bag). The person holding the shell is the only one who can talk.

If it appears that some students use the technique as a way to avoid their work, assign them to conduct their discussions on their own time, such as after class or at the beginning of a recess period. Both methods require teaching the students how to use the procedure and assisting the students the first several times it is used.

PLAN C

Sometimes, an entire classroom falls into a pattern of arguing. This can happen when the behavior has become habitual. In these cases it can be very difficult to change student behavior, and you may need to use some kind of structured reinforcement system that creates mild peer pressure to motivate the students to behave appropriately.

 Proactively work to prevent arguing.

Examine the schedule of class activities and your records (see SUGGESTED STEPS FOR DEVELOPING AND IMPLEMENTING A PLAN) to identify times or activities in which arguing is frequent. Modify the structure of these times/activities so that the students are more actively engaged with relevant tasks. For example, if you notice that the students tend to argue in the last half of a 30-minute work period, reduce the amount of independent work time by half. The other half of the time, have the students work in cooperative groups. Conversely, if cooperative groups are a problem, increase the amount of teacher directed instruction.

For each problematic activity, increase the amount of active student engagement during that activity. For example, rather than simply lecturing, intersperse frequent questions, ungraded quizzes, and "You and you neighbor figure out the answer to . . . " scenarios.

Pay particular attention to activities like attendance taking when you are very busy, but the students have little to do. Taking attendance in a traditional manner (i.e., you call names or look at a seating chart) can require two or three minutes. This time goes by quickly for you because you are busy. However, for students expected to sit and do nothing, two or three minutes is an extremely long time—which increases the probability of their getting into arguments.

Consider giving the students a challenging problem to work on while you take attendance or having a student take attendance while you begin class. This way, you keep the students actively engaged and decrease the opportunities for arguing.

If arguing tends to occur when the class shifts from one activity to another, it may be that the students have too much time with too little to do during these transition periods. For example, it is not uncommon for it to take about a minute between giving an instruction such as, "Get your textbooks out and open to page 134," and the time instruction resumes. During this time, you may be very busy repeating the instruction, dealing with students who do not have their books, writing hall passes for students who need to get their books from their lockers, and so on. However, for individual students this leaves one minute with nothing to do, which can lead to interactions and arguments. Then while you deal with an argument, more students are left with nothing to do (and more arguments may start).

Devise a routine for problematic transitions and teach the students the new expectations. Then follow through consistently. If necessary, have the students practice particular transitions until they can handle the routine(s) efficiently. For additional information, see **Transitions, Problems With**.

 Publicly monitor how often you need to intervene with arguing.

a. To help the class become more aware of their behavior, create a space on the board or a wall chart on which you can record the number of daily arguments. When an incident occurs, simply correct the individuals involved and write a tally mark on the designated space. It is not necessary to note who was arguing—you do not want to put undue peer pressure on specific individuals. The idea is to have a class-wide total each day, not a record of which students had how many arguments.

b. Each day, conduct a short class meeting to review that day's record. Have a student total the tally on the chart (or do it yourself), and discuss whether the day was better, worse, or about the same as previous days. If the day did not go well, encourage the students to talk about why and have them identify what they can do the next day to remember to resolve conflicts peacefully rather than argue.

If the students act inappropriately during the review meeting, keep the session very short. Just let the class know that you are sure tomorrow will be a better day.

 Establish a group reinforcement system.

a. Have the students brainstorm a list of reinforcement ideas for the entire class. Then, eliminate any items from the list that are not possible (i.e., the suggestion is too expensive or could not be provided to all the students in the class).

b. Assign "prices" (in points) to the remaining items on the list.

The prices should be based on the instructional, personnel, and/or monetary costs of the items. Monetary cost is clear—the more expensive the item, the more points required to earn it. Instructional cost refers to the amount of instructional time lost or interfered with by a particular reward. Thus, an activity which causes the class to miss part of academic instruction should require more points than one the class can do during recess time. Personnel cost involves the time required by you and/or other staff to fulfill the reinforcer. Earning an extra recess period in which extra supervision would need to be arranged would cost more than having music playing in class for 15 minutes, for example.

c. Have the class vote on the reinforcers. The reinforcer that receives the most votes is the one they will work for first, and the items that come in second (and third) will be the next ones worked for.

d. Develop a scale for awarding points based on the number of arguments within the class per day. For example:

9 arguments or more	= 0 points for the day
5-8 arguments	= 1 point for the day
1-4 arguments	= 3 points for the day
0 arguments	= 4 points for the day

e. At the end of the day when the total is posted, determine how many points are accumulated toward the agreed-upon reward.

 (OPTIONAL)
If a class-wide system seems unlikely to be effective, set up a team competition and response cost lottery.

Identify or have students identify a moderate reward that would be reasonable to award a group of students each day. Then divide the class into four to six teams (made as equitable as possible). Each team begins the day with an equal number of tickets, on which they write the name of their team.

Whenever any students are arguing, their team(s) lose a ticket. For example, if two students from different teams were arguing, their teams would each lose a ticket. If two students from the same team were arguing, that team would lose two tickets.

At the end of the day, each team puts all their remaining tickets in a hat for a drawing. The team whose name is on the winning ticket receives the reward for that day (e.g., turning in a group assignment rather than five individual assignments).

(NOTE: Set up an additional consequence for individuals who argue after all their teams' tickets are gone. Time owed can sometimes be effective. Any time an individual student argues and his/her team's tickets are gone, that individual owes time off recess or after school.)

 While implementing any reinforcement system, keep student attention focused on the importance of resolving conflict peacefully.

Tell the class, for example: "Class, you earned five points for the day, but more importantly, you are all helping this class to be a place that we all will enjoy. Room 14 is a place we can all be proud of."

 Use reinforcement to encourage appropriate behavior.

Praise individual students for meeting expectations regarding arguing and praise the entire class when improvement occurs (see PLAN A).

....
Suggested Steps for Developing and Implementing a Plan

The following steps are designed to help develop an appropriate intervention plan and implement it effectively, whether you choose to use one of the MODEL PLANS or create a customized plan of your own. The steps are, however, suggestions—they are not intended to be followed rigidly or in any particular order. Use your professional judgment and the knowledge of your particular situation to make them work for you.

1. *Make sure you have enough information about the situation.*

a. You want to be able to explain what you mean when you say that the class has a problem with arguing. Since disagreements, in and of themselves, are not a problem, you will have to identify what it is about these students' disagreements that make them a problem. It is it how loud they are? What they say to each other? How long they go on?

(NOTE: Documentation of the problem is probably not necessary if the problem is relatively mild [i.e., if PLAN A is appropriate].)

Anecdotal notes from actual incidents can help you define the problem behavior thoroughly. Simply keep a card in your pocket or on a clipboard and occasionally, when you see students arguing, make notes. For each entry, briefly describe the circumstances—where and when it occurred, what was said and/or done, and any other relevant observations (e.g., what prompted the argument). You do not need to take notes every time students argue; the idea is to capture a range of examples so that you will be able to describe the behavior clearly and completely.

Also include notes on times when the students resolve their conflicts peacefully. This way, the students will realize that you are not only aware of their inappropriate behavior, but also notice their appropriate behavior. In addition, the positive examples will help you to clarify how you want the students to behave.

b. It may also be useful to document how often the arguing occurs (i.e., a frequency count). This will provide a more objective measure of the problem and an objective way to monitor progress. You can use the same card on which you are making anecdotal notes to keep a frequency count—simply make a tally mark on the card each time you have to intervene in an argument.

You might want to code the tallies to discern whether the behavior occurs more often during certain times, subjects, or activities (e.g., using

an "A" or "P" to indicate that the incident happened in the morning or afternoon; or clustering the tallies by math or reading, teacher directed instruction or independent work, etc.).

c. If a student notices what you are doing and asks about it, be straightforward—say that you are collecting information to see whether arguing is a problem that the class needs to work on.

Following is an example of anecdotal notes and a frequency count that has been collected on arguing.

Notes on Arguing—9/5

Classroom Count	Playground Count
AAPP	AAPPP PPPPP PPPP

10:00—In the classroom, Mike and Rob argued about who got to take out the soccer ball. I intervened but they couldn't resolve it. I finally just said that no one could take out the ball. I would rather they handle this sort of thing without my telling them what to do.

12:15—Lunch time recess was awful. I broke up arguments about rules, problems with students running through games, and many other seemingly trivial disputes.

---

d. The frequency information is fairly easy to summarize on a chart or graph. Seeing how often arguing occurs and/or how much time is involved may help the students better understand your concern.

e. Continuing to collect this type of information (and keeping the chart up-to-date) while you implement a plan will help you monitor whether the situation is getting worse, staying the same, or getting better.

2. *Identify a focus for the intervention and labels for referring to the appropriate and inappropriate behaviors.*

With this particular problem, the intervention should address more than just reducing the students' arguing—to be effective, there must be a concurrent emphasis on increasing some positive behavior or trait (e.g., resolving conflicts peacefully). Identifying a specific positive behavior will make it easier for you to "catch" and reinforce the students for behaving appropriately, and will help your explain your concerns more productively.

Simply saying that "the class has a problem with arguing," for example, doesn't really give the students any useful information (and may imply that conflict is bad—when in fact, conflict is unavoidable). However, telling the students that you want them "to learn to resolve conflicts peacefully" gives them an important, and reasonable, goal to work toward and clarifies what they need to do to be successful.

3. *Prepare for, then conduct, an initial presentation about the situation.*

a. Depending upon your personal philosophy, and whether or not you think a basic intervention like PLAN A is appropriate, you may simply choose to have an informal discussion with the students.

b. When you intend to use one of the other MODEL PLANS, you might want to schedule a class meeting. Wait for a time when you are calm (i.e., not right after an argument has occurred) and inform the students that you are finding the amount of arguing in the class to be a problem. Then specifically define your expectations regarding resolving conflicts appropriately and the procedures you will be implementing. Give the students the opportunity to ask questions and make comments. End the session by thanking the students for listening and letting them know that you are confident they will make an effort to treat each other more respectfully.

c. If you want the students to assume some ownership of the problem, you might want to hold a class meeting in which the students participate in analyzing the situation and developing an action plan. In this case, before the meeting you will need to have clarified the nature/extent of the problem and your expectations for the students' behavior. You will also need to identify any aspects of the problem/plan that you do not feel comfortable opening up to a group decision.

For example, you must decide ahead of time whether or not to give the class the opportunity to determine *if* there will be a consequence for arguing and/or what the consequence should be. If you firmly believe that there must be a consequence, then you should not seek student input on that particular issue. (The sample agenda following is a guide to helping the class generate a plan; although you may wish to suggest one or more procedures from the MODEL PLANS.)

d. Schedule the meeting for a neutral time and allow enough time for a reasonable discussion. Inform the students in advance that the meeting will take place; this will give them time to think about the problem. "Class, this afternoon we are going to have a class meeting on the problem of arguing. Please give some thought to this problem and what we might do as a class to solve it."

e. Use an agenda to structure the meeting. Shortly before the meeting, write the agenda on the chalkboard. Following is one possibility.

Agenda

1. Arguing—Define the magnitude of the problem (share data).

2. Review expectations regarding resolving conflicts peacefully.

3. Brainstorm ideas for improving the situation.

4. Select strategies that everyone agrees to.

5. Establish what the teacher will do when students argue.

---

f. Establish clear rules for both you and the students regarding the brainstorming phase of the meeting beforehand. For example:

- Any idea is okay (but no obscenity).

- Ideas will not be evaluated initially (i.e., no approval—"Good idea" or disapproval—"What a stupid idea" or "We couldn't do that" should be expressed during brainstorming).

- All ideas will be written down and discussed at the conclusion of brainstorming.

g. At the conclusion of brainstorming, evaluate the ideas, and lead the class to consensus on any decisions that need to be made. Use voting as a decision-making process when appropriate.

4. *Determine when and how to include the parent(s).*

a. When the situation is class-wide, contacting the parent(s) of all the students who have been arguing is probably neither appropriate nor realistic (e.g., you wouldn't want to call five to ten parents every night). However, after discussing the problem with the students, it may be useful to send a memo to all the parents (or include an item in the classroom newsletter, if you have one) explaining that you will be working with the students to learn how to resolve their conflicts peacefully.

b. If the situation involves one or two students who have or continue to have a problem with arguing, you should contact the parent(s) of those individuals. Let the parent(s) know that their child is having a problem with arguing and what steps you are taking to correct the situation.

Frequent contact is not required, but whenever you intend to implement an individualized plan, the parent(s) should be informed prior to its implementation and should be given feedback about the student's progress every two to four weeks.

 Give the class regular, ongoing feedback about their behavior.

Periodically meet with the class to discuss the situation. In most cases, three to five minutes once per week should suffice. *(NOTE: PLAN C requires daily meetings to record the data or to determine points.)* During the meetings, review any information that has been collected and discuss whether or not things are getting better. As much as possible, focus on improvements, however, also address any new or continuing problems.

As you discuss the problems, be sure to also acknowledge (without singling out individuals) that there are students in the class who consistently resolve conflicts peacefully. As the situation improves, the meetings can be faded to once every other week and then to once per month.

 Evaluate the situation (and the plan).

Any plan should be implemented for at least two weeks before deciding whether or not it is effective. Generally, if the situation has improved (based on the objective information that's been collected and/or the subjective perceptions of yourself and the students), continue with what you have been doing. (Eventually you will want to fade, then eliminate, the plan.) If the problem has remained the same or worsened, some kind of change (e.g., modifying the current plan or switching to another plan) will be necessary. Always discuss any change in the intervention with the class first.

ARGUING—STUDENT(S) WITH THE TEACHER

DESCRIPTION

You have a student who challenges every direction or request you make. You spend an inordinate amount of time explaining, justifying, or repeating requests and directions to this student.

GOAL

The student will stop arguing with you and will learn to be more cooperative by expressing her views and needs without arguing.

OVERVIEW OF PLANS

- PLAN A: For a situation in which the problem is relatively mild or has just begun.

- PLAN B: For a student who argues to gain adult attention.

- PLAN C: For a student who argues because it makes her feel powerful to make an adult angry.

- PLAN D: For a student who may not realize how much she argues.

- Plan E: For a student who has developed a habit of arguing to get her own way and/or is not motivated to change her arguing behavior.

Alternative Problems

- **Arguing—Students With Each Other**

- **Complaining**

- **Disrespectful Behavior**

· · · · · · · ·
General Considerations

- If the student's problem behavior stems in any way from academic issues (e.g., the student is unable to meet academic expectations and argues because she feels frustrated or discouraged), concurrent efforts must be made to ensure her academic success (see **Academic Deficits, Determining**).

· · · · · · · ·
Model Plans

PLAN A

It is not always necessary, or even beneficial, to use an involved plan. If the problem has just begun, the following actions, along with making the student aware of the problem, may resolve the situation.

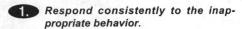 **Respond consistently to the inappropriate behavior.**

a. Whenever the student begins to argue, gently correct her. Let her know that this is an example of "arguing," and inform her of what she needs to do next. You might give her an instruction (e.g., "Alexa, you need to take your seat and begin your assignment.") or tell her different ways she can say what she needs to say (e.g., "Alexa, you can tell me your opinion, but you need to use a quiet and respectful voice."). Because your goal is to impart information, you want to be emotionally neutral while giving the correction.

b. If the student complies, praise her for being cooperative and following directions. If the student does not comply, implement a consequence such as time owed. For example, the student might owe one minute off of recess or after school for every minute that elapses between when you gave her a direction and when she finally did what you asked.

2. **Use reinforcement to encourage appropriate behavior.**

a. Give the student increased praise when she is being cooperative. Be especially alert for those times when the student interacts appropriately with you, and praise the student specifically for what she is doing. "Alexa, that was a cooperative way of letting me know that you want me to recheck that problem. When you make a request in such a cooperative way, I can really listen to what you are communicating."

Remember that any time the student is not arguing with an adult you can praise her for acting mature. If public praise would be embarrassing, praise the student privately or even use a note.

b. Praise the student for other positive behaviors she exhibits and give her frequent attention (e.g., say "hello" to her as she enters the classroom, call on her frequently during class activities, and occasionally ask her to assist you with a class job that needs to be done). For example, you might comment about the accuracy of her work or how consistent she is about making entries in her journal. This demonstrates to the student that you notice many positive things she does, not just the fact that she is refraining from arguing with adults.

PLAN B

Arguing can be an excellent means of gaining and securing adult attention—the longer the argument lasts, the more attention the student receives. If your student argues frequently about little things, the intervention should include making sure that the student receives more frequent and more satisfying attention for behaving appropriately than for arguing with you.

Respond consistently to the inappropriate behavior.

a. Establish procedures that allow the student to express complaints and concerns at a prearranged time. This will help her learn that while you respect her feelings and thoughts, you are not willing to participate in arguments during class. Identify a meeting schedule on the student's own time (e.g., before or after school, or at the beginning of recess), and establish ground rules for the allotted discussion time (e.g., "Calm voices. No more than five minutes. We may need to agree to disagree.").

Do not be concerned if the student overuses the time for a couple of weeks. Channeling her need for attention into a more appropriate time is an important step forward. After a couple of weeks, you may wish to work with the student to set goals for reducing how often she needs to discuss issues with you.

b. Establish a consequence to use if the student continues to argue after a reminder. With younger students (e.g., kindergarten or first grade), an appropriate consequence may be time-out. "Alexa, that is arguing. You need to go to time-out and think about this." For students in grades two and above, it may be more appropriate to use some form of response cost, such as time owed. "Alexa, that is arguing. You owe one minute off recess plus however long it takes until you are in your seat working on your math."

c Do not give the student undue attention during class for arguing. If she starts to argue, simply gently correct her and remind her of when she can discuss the issue. Keep the interaction short and your manner neutral. "If you want to discuss your concern with me, you can see me after class."

If the student continues to argue, inform her of the consequence, cease all interactions with her, and begin interacting positively with other students. This will show the student that to get your attention she needs to behave in a nonargumentative way. If you find yourself getting angry and/or arguing, stop and take a deep breath. Then inform the student that if she wishes to talk about the matter she can do so later.

 Use reinforcement to encourage appropriate behavior.

a. Frequent praise and attention is the core of this plan. Because the student must learn that she gains more frequent and more satisfying attention when she behaves appropriately than when she argues, whenever she is not arguing (or otherwise misbehaving) make an effort to praise and spend time with her. "Alexa, would it be okay if I sat with you a moment and watched as you and your group do the next step on this assignment?"

b. You may also wish to use intermittent rewards to acknowledge the student's success. Occasional, and unexpected, rewards can motivate the student to demonstrate responsible behavior more often. The idea is to provide a reward when the student has had a particularly good period of not arguing.

An appropriate reward might be helping you with a job that needs to be done (e.g., collating and stapling papers). A list of additional reinforcement ideas can be found in APPENDIX 1. Use intermittent rewards more frequently at the beginning of the intervention to encourage the student, and then less often as her behavior improves.

3. **Ensure a 3-1 ratio of positive to negative attention.**

a. If attention is the motivating force for this student, it is important to be sure that you are giving her *three times as much* positive as negative attention. One way to do this is to monitor your interactions with the student at least one day per week. Keep a card on a clipboard or in your pocket and record each interaction you have with the student as either "positive" or "negative" by writing a "+" or "-", respectively, on the card.

To determine whether an interaction is positive or negative, ask yourself whether the student was arguing with you (or otherwise misbehaving) at the time of the interaction. Any interaction that stems from inappropriate behavior is negative, while all interactions that occur while the student is meeting classroom expectations are positive. Thus, gently correcting the student and implementing time owed are both negative interactions, but praising the student for being cooperative is positive. Greeting the student as she enters the room and asking her if she has any questions during independent work are also considered positive interactions. *(NOTE: Ignoring the student's inappropriate behavior is not recorded at all because it is not an interaction.)*

b. If you find that you are not giving the student three times as much positive as negative attention, try to increase the number of positive interactions you have with her. Sometimes prompts can help. For example, you might use the hourly beep on your digital watch as a reminder to praise the student the very next time you see her behaving appropriately. Or you may decide that each time you look at the clock you will also look for a reason to praise the student. You can also increase the ratio of positive to negative attention by ignoring more of the student's inappropriate behavior.

PLAN C

Some students thrive on emotional reactions from adults. When a student can use an argument to make the teacher or other adult angry, she may feel a sense of power and influence. If your student seems to use arguing to control situations and influence your emotions and actions, you will need to reduce the feelings of power the student gains from arguing and provide alternative, positive opportunities for the student to achieve a sense of power.

 1. Respond consistently to the inappropriate behavior.

a. Establish procedures that allow the student to express her complaints and concerns appropriately (see PLAN B).

b. Establish a consequence to use when the student argues after a reminder (see PLAN B).

c. Be aware that if the student is trying to gain power, any emotional reaction on your part—frustration, irritation, anger, helplessness—will fuel the student's tendency to argue. To prevent this, mentally rehearse situations in which the student is likely to argue. Imagine yourself being a robot with preprogrammed responses that never vary. When the student argues, give a reminder. If she continues, you calmly and consistently apply a consequence (e.g., time owed).

The key is to remove the satisfaction the student has learned to receive from engaging adults in arguing. In all probability that satisfaction lies in both getting away with it sometimes, and/or getting an emotional reaction. Calm and consistent responses on your part give the student no satisfaction when she argues.

2. Provide the student with appropriate and positive experiences of power to reduce her need to argue.

One of the most effective ways of reducing a student's need to argue to gain power is to give her other ways of feeling powerful. The following suggestions are just a few of the ideas you might try:

• If the student is good on the computer, ask her to evaluate a piece of software that you are considering for the class.

• If the student has a nice voice, have her read a story into a tape recorder for students in a younger grade to listen to on their free time. (If appropriate, you may want to ask the student if she would like to go to a younger class and read aloud to a small group.)

• If the student is almost always at school on time, ask her to help with some aspect of the morning routine (e.g., getting the Lunch Count form from your desk and giving it to you as you take attendance.) *(NOTE: A list of additional ideas for jobs/responsibilities can be found in APPENDIX 2.)*

3. Use reinforcement to encourage appropriate behavior.

a. Give the student increased praise and attention when she is being cooperative (see PLAN A).

b. Look for opportunities to praise the student for using power in positive ways. The goal is to acknowledge that the student is a powerful individual and that she can use that power to benefit herself and the class. "Alexa, during the field trip you demonstrated some very important leadership qualities. I was very impressed with the way you represented our class while talking to the person who was guiding us. Have you ever thought of running for the student council?"

PLAN D

Sometimes a student is not really aware of when and/or how often she argues with adults. In this case, the intervention plan must include some way of helping the student become more aware of her own behavior.

1. Respond consistently to the inappropriate behavior.

a. During your initial meeting with the student (see SUGGESTED STEPS FOR DEVELOPING AND IMPLEMENTING A PLAN) establish a nonembarrassing signal that you can use to cue her that she is arguing. You want it to be a fairly subtle signal that only the student will recognize and understand, and one that is nonconfrontational.

A nonconfrontational gesture such as raising your hand close to your chest with the palm facing front (like a stop sign) while leaning slightly back serves as an assertive, but gentle, reminder that you are unwilling to participate in an argument. (A confrontational gesture such as leaning forward and thrusting your palm toward the student might actually encourage the student to argue even more.)

b. Whenever the student begins to argue, give her the signal and make sure the incident is recorded (see Step 2). If the student does not cease arguing, but she is not disrupting the class or refusing to participate, ignore the arguing. However, if the student is arguing and not participating, gently correct the lack of participation and ignore the arguing.

Be prepared to use the signal frequently and for a fairly long time, especially if the behavior has become an unconscious habit for the student.

2. Implement a system for monitoring the frequency of the student's arguing.

a. Determine who will do the recording. Since the point is for the student to become aware of her own behavior, having her do the recording (self-monitoring) will be more effective than if you record her behavior. However, if the student cannot or will not be accurate (or if she would be embarrassed to be seen recording), you should do the recording.

Remember, the idea is for the student to be aware of each time she argues, and for her to know that each incident is being recorded. *(NOTE: Even when the student self-monitors, you should keep your own record approximately* one day per week to verify the student's accuracy.)

b. If the student is recording her own behavior, you can have her keep a form like the sample following on her desk or in her notebook. Tell the student that each time she sees you give the signal, she should circle a number on the monitoring form. You might put a note on the form to remind the student that her goal is to reduce the overall number of arguments to a reasonable number (e.g., one per day).

Name _____

Date _____

Behavior to be monitored _____

_____

Monday

  1 2 3 4 5 6 7 8 9 10

11 12 13 14 15 16 17 18 19 20

21 22 23 24 25 26 27 28 29 30

Tuesday

  1 2 3 4 5 6 7 8 9 10

11 12 13 14 15 16 17 18 19 20

21 22 23 24 25 26 27 28 29 30

Wednesday

  1 2 3 4 5 6 7 8 9 10

11 12 13 14 15 16 17 18 19 20

21 22 23 24 25 26 27 28 29 30

Thursday

  1 2 3 4 5 6 7 8 9 10

11 12 13 14 15 16 17 18 19 20

21 22 23 24 25 26 27 28 29 30

Friday

  1 2 3 4 5 6 7 8 9 10

11 12 13 14 15 16 17 18 19 20

21 22 23 24 25 26 27 28 29 30

---

c. Each day, meet with the student for a few minutes to review that day's record. Have the student chart the information on a graph (or do it yourself), and talk with her about whether the day was better, worse, or about the same as previous days. If the day did not go well, encourage the student to talk about why and have her identify what she can do the next day to help herself remember to be cooperative rather than argumentative.

If the student behaves inappropriately during the meeting, keep the interaction very short. Just let the student know that you are sure tomorrow will be a better day.

3. **Use reinforcement to encourage appropriate behavior.**

a. Give the student increased praise and attention when she is being cooperative (see PLAN A).

b. Also praise the student for accurate recording (if applicable) during the daily review meetings, and for being willing to examine her cumulative record for the day. "Alexa, you are really handling this responsibly. Even though it was a rough day, you are willing to talk to me about things you might do differently tomorrow. That is a real sign that you are growing up." Regardless of how the day went, try to make these meetings upbeat and encouraging—you want the student to look forward to the review sessions at the end of the day.

4. **Encourage the student to use self-reinforcement.**

Whenever things are going well (i.e., less arguing than usual), prompt the student to mentally reinforce herself. "Alexa, this has been a very successful morning. Silently tell yourself that you are really good at being cooperative." Prompt the student intermittently throughout the day and during the review meetings.

PLAN E

Some students have learned (which has been inadvertently reinforced by their parents and teachers) that they can get their own way by arguing. If this happens often enough, arguing can become a habit that the student does not care to reduce. If it seems that your student has developed a habit of arguing and/or does not seem interested in reducing the behavior, you may need to implement a system of external incentives (i.e., rewards and/or consequences) to motivate her to stop arguing with adults and start being more cooperative.

1. **Use a signal to cue the student when she is arguing (see PLAN D).**

2. **Implement a system for monitoring the student's argumentative behavior (see PLAN D).**

3. **Establish a structured system for reinforcing the student's appropriate behavior and providing a consequence for the inappropriate behavior.**

a. With the student, create a list of reinforcers that she can earn. Although you might want to have some suggestions in mind, the system will be more effective if the student identifies most of the items or activities herself. *(NOTE: A list of additional reinforcement ideas can be found in APPENDIX 1.)*

b. Assign "prices" (in points) for each of the rewards on the list and have the student choose the reward she would like to earn first.

The prices should be based on how many points the student can earn and the instructional, personnel, and/or monetary cost of the items. Monetary cost is clear—the more expensive the item, the more points required to earn it. Instructional cost refers to the amount of instructional time lost or interfered with by a particular reward. Thus, an activity which causes the student to miss part of academic instruction should cost more points than one the student can do on her own recess time. Personnel cost involves the time required by you and/or other staff to fulfill the reinforcer. Having lunch with the principal, therefore, would cost more points than spending five minutes of free time with a friend.

c. Translate the information from the monitoring form into points the student can use to earn the rewards. Identify how many times the student tends to argue in a typical day and devise a system of daily points for arguing less than that number. For example, if the student generally argues ten times per day, a sliding scale like the sample following could be implemented:

10 or more arguments	= 0 points
7-9 arguments	= 1 point
4-6 arguments	= 2 points
1-3 arguments	= 3 points
0 arguments	= 5 points

d. When the student has accumulated enough points to earn the reward she has chosen, she "spends" the necessary points and the system begins again. That is, she selects another reward to earn and begins with zero points.

A young (or immature) student may need more frequent encouragement and/or reinforcement. For this type of student, it may be appropriate to let her earn several "less expensive" rewards (e.g., five minutes of computer time after 20 points) on the way to the bigger reward (e.g., having lunch with a favorite teacher for 200 points). The student earns the smaller rewards but doesn't have to spend her points to get them—the points continue to accumulate toward the selected reward.

e. Determine a consequence (e.g., time owed from recess or after school) for each incident of arguing that occurs at the top end of the scale. Thus in the previous example, the student might owe two minutes off of recess for each argument beyond nine in a single day. However, the consequence should not involve taking away a previous day's points. If the student can lose already-earned points, she might develop an attitude of, "I am losing so many points, why should I even bother to try?"

4. *Use reinforcement to encourage appropriate behavior.*

a. Give the student increased praise and attention when she is being cooperative (see PLAN A).

b. Show interest and enthusiasm about how the student is doing on the system. "Alexa, this is the best day you have had. Only one argument and therefore you earn three points today."

. . . .
Suggested Steps for Developing and Implementing a Plan

The following steps are designed to help you develop an appropriate intervention plan and implement it effectively, whether you choose to use one of the MODEL PLANS or create a customized plan of your own. The steps are, however, suggestions—they are not intended to be followed rigidly or in any particular order. Use your professional judgment and the knowledge of your particular situation to make them work for you.

1. *Make sure you have enough information about the situation.*

a. If you think a minimal intervention like PLAN A will be sufficient, you may already have enough information to proceed. However, when a more involved plan seems necessary, you should consider collecting additional descriptive and/or objective information for a couple of days.

b. You need to be able to explain what you mean when you say that "the student has a problem with arguing." Anecdotal notes on actual incidents should provide enough detail to help you define the problem behavior clearly and completely. To collect anecdotal notes, simply keep a card in your pocket or on a clipboard and occasionally make notes on specific instances when the student argues with you.

For each entry, briefly describe where and when it occurred, what the student did or said, and any other relevant observations (e.g., what prompted the argument). You do not need to make a note every time the student argues with you; the idea is to capture a range of examples of the behavior so you will be able to describe it completely.

Also include some notes on times when the student interacts with adults appropriately—this will make it clear that you are not only aware of her problem behavior, but also recognize when she is being cooperative. When you meet with the student, the positive examples will help you clarify how you want the student to behave.

c. In addition to information on what the student's inappropriate behavior looks like, it can also be useful to document how often it occurs (i.e., a frequency count). This will provide both a more objective measure of the problem and an objective way to monitor the student's progress. You can use the same card on which you are collecting anecdotal notes to keep a frequency count—simply write a tally mark on the card each time the student argues with or challenges you.

You might want to code the tallies to discern whether the behavior occurs more frequently during certain times, subjects, or activities (e.g., using an "A" or "P" to indicate that the incident happened in the morning or afternoon; or clustering the tallies by math or reading, teacher directed instruction or independent work, etc.).

d. If the student notices what you are doing and asks about it, be straightforward—tell her that you are collecting information to see whether her arguing is a problem that needs to be worked on.

Following is an example of anecdotal notes and frequency information that have been collected on a student's arguing behavior.

Alexa's Arguing—11/4

Frequency

w/Assistant	w/Teacher
AA PPPP	APAA PPPPP PPPPP

Notes:

9:05—Mr. Yarborough (assistant) told Alexa that she needed to clean up the Science Center when she finished. Alexa argued that it was a mess before she got there. They went back and forth several times until Alexa was almost shouting. I went over to find out what was going on, and Alexa told me to stay out of it and then started to argue with me.

9:50—When I was collecting the science papers, Alexa told me that I did not give her enough time to finish. I reminded her that she could take the work home as homework just like anyone else, but she kept demanding that I explain why I never give enough time to finish assignments.

1:00—I told the class that they needed to hand in their long-term project proposals. Alexa asked why I didn't remind them yesterday. I told her that I did, but she kept insisting that I hadn't. After a few back and forth exchanges, several other students told her that I had. That silenced her.

3:15—This afternoon was typical. Alexa didn't think she should have to do the art project, she didn't want Mr. Y to correct her work, she didn't know that we had given out book order forms, and on and on.

---

e. Frequency information is fairly easy to summarize on a chart or graph. Seeing how often the student argues with or challenges you may help the student and her parent(s) better understand your concern.

f. Continuing to collect this type of information (and keeping the chart up-to-date) while you implement a plan will help you monitor whether the situation is getting worse, staying the same, or getting better. After the initial meeting, anecdotal notes can be limited to new kinds of argumentative behavior or a specific type of arguing that continues to be problematic.

2. *Identify a focus for the intervention and labels for referring to the appropriate and inappropriate behaviors.*

a. To be effective, the intervention must address more than just reducing the student's arguing/challenging behavior—there must be a concurrent emphasis on *increasing* some positive behavior or trait (e.g., being cooperative, being respectful, being helpful). Having a specific positive behavior in mind will make it easier for you to "catch" and reinforce the student for behaving appropriately, and the positive focus will help you to frame the situation more productively.

For example, if you simply say that "the student has a problem with arguing," you don't really provide any useful information, and may put the student and her parent(s) on the defensive. However, when you explain that you want to "help the student learn to be more cooperative," you are presenting an important, and reasonable, goal for the student to work toward and clearly identifying what the student needs to do to be successful.

b. Specifying labels for the appropriate and inappropriate behaviors (e.g., "being cooperative" and "arguing," respectively) will help you to use consistent vocabulary when discussing the situation with the student. For example, if you sometimes refer to the inappropriate behavior as "arguing" and other times tell the student that "he is creating a hassle," she may not realize that you are talking about the same thing.

3. *Determine when and how to include the parent(s).*

a. It is not necessary to contact the student's parent(s) if the problem has just begun and is not interfering with the student's academic or social progress. However, it might be a good idea to take advantage of any scheduled activities (e.g., conferences, weekly notes home) to let them know of your concern.

b. The parent(s) should be contacted whenever the student's argumentative behavior is affecting her academic performance or is alienating her from her peers. Share any information you have collected about the behavior (i.e., anecdotal notes, frequency count), and explain why you are concerned. Focus in particular on how the behavior is hindering the student academically and/or socially (e.g., peers are avoiding the student).

You might ask if the parent(s) have any insight into the situation and/or whether they have noticed similar behavior at home. Whether or not the parent(s) perceive a problem, explain that you want to help the student "learn to be more cooperative," and invite them to join you for an initial meeting with the student to develop a plan.

If the parent(s) deny there is a problem and/or if they seem argumentative, ask the building administrator or school counselor to attend the planning meeting to serve as observer and mediator. If the parent(s) are unable or unwilling to participate, let them know that you will keep them informed of the student's progress.

c. Once the parent(s) have been involved in any way, you should give them updates at least once per week while the plan is being implemented.

4. *Prepare for, then conduct, an initial meeting about the situation.*

a. Arrange a meeting to discuss your concerns with the student and anyone else who will be involved in the plan (e.g., the parent[s], the building administrator). Although the specifics will vary depending upon the age of the student and the severity of the problem, there are some general guidelines to consider when scheduling the meeting.

First, meet at a neutral time (i.e., not immediately after a problem has occurred), when emotions are less likely to hamper communication. In general, a day's notice is appropriate, however a primary age student may worry excessively and/or forget what the meeting is about if it is scheduled more than an hour before it takes place.

Second, make the meeting appropriately private. With a primary student who has a mild problem, you might meet in the classroom while the other students are working independently. However, when dealing with a middle/junior high school student and the student's parent(s), you will need a private place (e.g., the counselor's office) to ensure that the discussion will not be overheard.

Third, try to make sure the meeting is scheduled for a time and place that it is not likely to be interrupted. Finally, if the parent(s) will be participating, they should be the ones to tell the student about the meeting.

b. Construct a preliminary plan. Decide whether you think you can use one of the MODEL PLANS or if you need to create a customized plan using components from various plans and/or your own ideas. Although you will invite and encourage the student to help develop the plan during the initial meeting, having a plan in mind before you meet can alleviate frustration and wasted time if the student is unwilling or unable to participate.

c. After reviewing the information you have collected and thinking about how you want the student to behave, prepare thorough descriptions of the inappropriate behavior and the positive behavior/trait on which the student will be working. The more specific you can be and the more concrete examples you have, the easier it will be to clarify (and for the student to understand) your expectations. Be sure to consider the student's behavior in all relevant activities and with a variety of adults (e.g., independent work, teacher directed instruction, unstructured classtimes, recess and lunch, etc.).

d. Conduct the meeting in an atmosphere of collaboration. The following agenda is one way you might structure the meeting:

• **Share your concerns about the student's behavior.**

Briefly describe the problem behavior and, when appropriate, show the student a chart of how often she engages in it. Then explain why you consider the behavior to be a problem. In this case, you might tell the student that argumentative behavior is not respectful to you and/or other adults, that it takes up valuable class time, and that it will cause her problems in subsequent grades in school.

• **Discuss how you can work together to improve the situation.**

Tell the student that you would like to help her "learn to be more cooperative," and describe your preliminary plan. Invite the student to give you input on the various aspects of the plan, and together work out any necessary details (e.g., use of a self-monitoring system). You may have to brainstorm different possibilities if the student is uncomfortable with the initial plan. Incorporating any of the student's suggestions that strengthen the plan is likely to increase her sense of "ownership" in and commitment to it.

- **Make sure the student understands what you mean by appropriate and inappropriate behavior.**

Use the descriptions you have prepared to define and clarify the problem behavior and the positive (desired) behavior as specifically and thoroughly as you can. To ensure that you and the student are in agreement about the expectations, you might present hypothetical scenarios and have her identify whether each is an example of being argumentative or of being cooperative. Or you might describe an actual situation that has occurred and ask her to explain how she would demonstrate being more cooperative in that situation.

- **Conclude the meeting.**

Always end the meeting with words of encouragement. Let the student know that you are confident that she can be successful. Be sure to reinforce her for participating in the meeting.

 Give the student regular, ongoing feedback about her behavior.

It is important to meet with the student periodically to discuss her progress. In most cases, three to five minutes once per week should suffice. *(NOTE: Plans D and E require daily meetings.)* During the meetings, review with the student any information that has been collected and discuss whether or not the situation is getting better. As much as possible, focus on the student's improvements, however, also address any new or continuing problems. As the situation improves, the meetings can be faded to once every other week and then to once per month.

 Evaluate the situation (and the plan).

Implement any plan for at least two weeks before deciding whether to change plans; to continue, modify, or fade the plan you are using, or to cease the intervention. Generally, if the student's behavior is clearly improving (based on the objective information that's been collected and/or the subjective perceptions of yourself, the student, and possibly the parent[s]), stick with what you are doing. If the situation has remained the same or worsened, some kind of change will be necessary. Always discuss any changes to the plan with the student first.

ATTENTION DEFICIT HYPERACTIVITY DISORDER (ADHD)

DESCRIPTION

You have a student in your class who has been identified as having Attention Deficit Hyperactivity Disorder (ADHD), and who exhibits inappropriate behaviors.

Because ADHD is not a discrete behavior, but a label that encompasses several different types or categories of behavior, there are no MODEL PLANS included with this problem. The purpose of the following information is to suggest an overall approach, and some basic considerations, for addressing the inappropriate behavior of a student who has ADHD.

Alternative Problems

- Aggression—Verbal and/or Physical
- Anxiety/ Nervousness
- Blurting Out/Not Raising Hand
- Bothering/Tormenting Others
- Bullying Behavior/ Fighting
- Compliance/Direction Following, Lack of
- Daydreaming
- Disruptive Behavior—Moderate
- Disruptive Behavior—Severe
- Distractibility/Short Attention Span
- Forgetting Materials
- Out of Seat
- Participation In Class, Lack of
- Physically Dangerous Behavior—to Self or Others
- Self-Control Issues
- Work Completion— Daily Work

....
General Information

- Attention Deficit Hyperactivity Disorder (ADHD)* is a psychiatric description used by the American Psychiatric Association in its *Diagnostic and Statistical Manual, Fourth Edition (DSM IV—1994)*. A student with this diagnosis may be predominantly hyperactive and impulsive (e.g., fidgets often, leaves seat, has difficulty playing quietly, talks excessively, blurts out, etc.), or predominantly inattentive (e.g., does not follow instructions, has trouble sustaining attention, does not seem to listen, is not organized, etc.), or may show combined symptoms.

- Many students diagnosed as ADHD receive medication. Whether or not your student's physician has prescribed medication, you, the parent(s), and the student can work together to develop positive behavioral interventions (like the MODEL PLANS that accompany various problems in this reference guide) to help the student learn to behave more responsibly. For students diagnosed as ADHD, it is especially important to work closely with the student's parent(s) and/or physician when developing and implementing any intervention.

- The key to helping a student diagnosed as ADHD learn to behave more responsibly is to focus the intervention on something that is manageable for you and for the student. That is, you want to identify one specific behavior the student exhibits (or fails to exhibit) that causes problems. Then, look up that particular problem in this reference and review the MODEL PLANS that accompany it. If one or more of the plans seems appropriate for your student, begin implementation.

  If the student exhibits so many different inappropriate behaviors that you cannot distinguish among them or you are not sure which creates the biggest problem for the student, record anecdotal information about the student's behavior for a week or so. Documentation of this type is fairly easy to compile—simply keep a card in your pocket or on a clipboard, and whenever the student does something that causes trouble for himself (or interrupts the smooth operation of the class), make notes on the incident. Briefly describe the circumstances—where and when the misbehavior occurred, what was said and/or done, and any other relevant observations you may have about the situation (e.g., what prompted the behavior).

  After about a week, use the information you have collected to select one specific behavior to intervene with. This might be the misbehavior that occurs most often or the one that creates the biggest disruption for the class. Whatever your criteria, the important thing is to focus your intervention efforts on one problem behavior at a time. Often, as you work on one behavior (e.g., out of seat behavior) other problem behaviors (e.g., bothering others) seem to improve without specific intervention.

- Perhaps the most important thing to keep in mind while working with a student who has been diagnosed with ADHD is that these students can make excellent progress when proactive and positive interventions are established.

- As an educator, you should not attempt to diagnose ADHD, any more than you should attempt to diagnose diabetes, clinical depression, or any other medical/psychological disorder. If you have a student who exhibits behaviors that suggest ADHD, discuss your concerns with your building administrator, school psychologist, and/or school nurse. Then, depending upon the circumstances and your district's policies for this type of situation, it may be appropriate to arrange for a meeting with the student's parent(s), and/or suggest that the student be evaluated by a physician. However, it is probably wise to first try the sort of behavioral interventions suggested in this (and other) behavior management resources. Any time you can help a student improve his behavior without labeling and/or medicating the student, everyone is better off.

- **CAUTION**: While ADHD is a formal diagnostic category of the American Psychiatric Association, there are some who question the assumptions that ADHD has a biologic etiology, the reliability of the rating scales used to diagnose ADHD, and even its utility as a diagnostic category. For an overview of these concerns, see:

  Reid, R., Maag, J.W., & Vasa, S.F. (1994). Attention deficit hyperactivity disorder as a disability category: A critique. *Exceptional Children, 60*(3), 198-214.

---

* In *DSM III* (1989), the labels for this disorder were separated as Attention Deficit Disorder (ADD) and Attention Deficit Hyperactivity Disorder (ADHD). The new label in *DSM IV* (1994), is ADHD, with the subcategories "Predominantly Hyperactive-Impulsive Type," "Predominantly Inattentive Type," and "Combined Type."

BABYISH BEHAVIOR

Baby Talk

DESCRIPTION

You have a student who uses immature speech or babyish mannerisms (e.g., thumbsucking, rocking, immature and "cutsey" behavior) to excess.

GOAL

The student will reduce and eventually eliminate the babyish behavior, and will learn to talk and act in an age-appropriate manner.

OVERVIEW OF PLANS

- PLAN A: For a situation in which the problem is relatively mild or has just begun.

- PLAN B: For a student who does not know how to consistently use age-appropriate mannerisms and/or who reverts to babyish behavior in times of stress.

- PLAN C: For a student who uses babyish behavior to gain attention and/or to prompt others to "mother" her.

- PLAN D: For a student who is unaware of how frequently she acts in a babyish manner.

- PLAN E: For a student whose babyish behavior is habitual.

Alternative Problems

- **Crying, Chronic**
- **Dawdling**
- **Helplessness**
- **Whining**

. . . .
General Considerations

- If the student's problem behavior stems in any way from academic issues (e.g., the student reverts to babyish behavior to hide the fact that she cannot be academically successful), concurrent efforts must be made to ensure her academic success (see **Academic Deficits, Determining**).

- If the student lacks the basic social skills to interact with her peers appropriately, it may be necessary to begin by teaching her those skills. The problem **Social Skills, Lack of** contains information on a variety of published social skills curricula.

- If the inappropriate behavior is resulting in the student avoiding or not completing her schoolwork, begin with a plan to increase the student's work completion (see **Work Completion—Daily Work**). Once the student is turning in completed work on a regular basis, you can consider an intervention for the babyish behavior, if the problem still exists.

- If you think the student might have a language or articulation problem, or speech patterns that may be related to maturation (e.g., "w" sound instead or the "r" sound), discuss the situation with a speech therapist before proceeding with any intervention plan(s).

. . . .
Model Plans

PLAN A

It is not always necessary, or even beneficial, to use an involved plan. If the inappropriate behavior has just begun and/or is relatively mild (i.e., not interfering with the student's academic or social progress), the following actions, along with making the student aware of your concerns, may resolve the situation.

1. *Respond consistently to the inappropriate behavior.*

a. During your initial meeting with the student (see SUGGESTED STEPS FOR DEVELOPING AND IMPLEMENTING A PLAN), establish a nonembarrassing signal that you can use to cue her that she is "not acting/sounding grown up." You want the signal to be fairly subtle, one that only the student will recognize and understand to minimize the chance that she will be teased by her peers. Possibilities include raising your eyebrows, rubbing your neck, or even just direct eye contact and a head nod. Let the student know that you may also need to quietly say her name to get her attention before you give the signal.

You should be prepared to use the signal frequently and for a fairly long time, since it is likely that the babyish behavior is, at least in part, an unconscious habit for the student.

b. Whenever the student is acting or speaking in a babyish manner, give the signal. If the student does not stop the babyish behavior and no other

students are around, gently correct her. Let her know that this is an example of "not acting/sounding grown up" and give her direct information about what she should be doing instead. "Lilly, you need to slow down and use a grown up voice."

Because your goal is to impart information, you should be emotionally neutral while giving the correction. If other students are around and the student does not cease acting babyish when you give the signal, ignore the behavior. You do not want to embarrass the student in front of her peers by correcting the babyish behavior.

2. *Use reinforcement to encourage appropriate behavior.*

a. Give the student increased praise and attention. Be especially alert for situations in which the student might have, but didn't, act babyish and praise her for these demonstrations of her ability to act/speak in a grown up manner. "Lilly, you used a nice deep voice, and you spoke clearly and slowly. This was a great example of speaking in a grown up manner. When you talk like that, it is much easier to realize that you have very important things to say."

If the student would be embarrassed by public praise, praise the student privately or even give the student a note. Remember that any time the student is not acting babyish, you can praise her for acting/speaking in a grown up way.

b. Praise the student privately for responding to the signal. "Lilly, twice during our discussion I gave you the signal. Both times you thought about what you were doing, you took a slow, deep breath and then switched to a grown up

way of acting. You should be very proud of yourself."

c. Give the student frequent attention (e.g., say "hello" to her as she enters the classroom, call on her frequently during class activities, and occasionally ask her to assist you with a class job that needs to be done) and praise her for other positive behaviors she exhibits. For example, you might comment about her performance on a test or praise her ability to listen and follow directions. This demonstrates to the student that you notice many positive things she does, not just the fact that she is refraining from acting babyish.

PLAN B

Some students might actually not know how to "act/speak in a grown up manner" on a consistent basis. If your student acts babyish in times of stress, or in certain settings, your intervention must include a way to teach her to act/speak in a grown up manner under those conditions.

 1. Respond consistently to the inappropriate behavior.

When the student acts/speaks in a babyish manner use a signal, then ignore or gently correct the behavior, as appropriate (see PLAN A).

 2. Try to identify possible patterns to the student's behavior.

Analyze the information in your anecdotal notes (see SUGGESTED STEPS FOR DEVELOPING AND IMPLEMENTING A PLAN) and answer the following questions: Does the student seem to act more babyish when she is nervous? around certain people? only in certain locations or during certain times of the day? Also find out if the student's parent(s) have noticed similar behavior at home.

 3. (OPTIONAL) Audio or video tape a range of the student's behavior.

The goal is to tape samples of both the student's babyish behavior and grown up behavior so that she can see/hear the difference. These tapes can be used during the lessons (see Step 4) both to show the student the difference and to have her identify the difference between her grown up behavior and her "not grown up" behavior. *(NOTE: Be sure to obtain administrative and parental approval for this step, should you choose to use it.)*

 4. Conduct lessons to teach the student how to act/speak in a more grown up manner.

a. Think about what behaviors the student needs to learn. Identify how the student tends to behave, and what she should do differently to act/speak in a more grown up fashion. If possible, identify specific strategies the student can use. For example, if the student uses a very high pitched and rapid speech pattern, she could be taught to "speak lower and slower." If the student tends to put her fingers in and around her mouth, she could be taught to have her hands at her sides or in her lap when she speaks.

b. During the lessons, use the information you have gathered to teach the student to identify the difference between "grown up" and "not grown up" behavior. Then conduct role plays using various scenarios (try to incorporate times, activities, locations, and/or situations that are most likely to be problematic), and have the student act out those situations using grown up behavior. Use verbal prompts to help the student remember how to act in a grown up manner (e.g., "Remember to speak low and slow.").

If you use audio or videotapes, present a variety of samples of the student's behavior and have her categorize each sample as "grown up" or "not grown up" behavior. Be sure to present more instances of "grown up" examples so that the student does not become discouraged and so that she sees mainly positive models of herself.

c. Conduct the lessons daily if possible, but at least twice per week. It is important to handle the lessons in a matter-of-fact manner so that the student does not feel that she is being ridiculed. You want to be very clear that you are not trying to embarrass her, but that you do want her to see her behavior the way others do.

Continue the lessons until the student is consistently responding to the signal and/or no longer acting in a babyish manner. *(NOTE: Because these lessons will probably last between ten to 15 minutes, it may not be possible for you [the classroom teacher] to conduct the lessons. In this case, ask for assistance from the counselor, school psychologist, or a highly skilled paraprofessional.)*

5. *Prompt the student to behave appropriately by using precorrections.*

Watch for those circumstances in which the student is likely to act babyish and remind her that she will need to remember to act in a grown up manner.

"Lilly, we are about to start our reading period. As you know, this is the time that it is especially hard to remember to act/speak in a grown up manner. I will be watching to see if you remember to do what we practiced this morning. I'll bet you can."

If time permits, you might have the student identify what she needs to do in order to help her remember. "Lilly, keep remembering what we have worked on in the lessons. What might you try? Excellent, give it a try." If this conversation would embarrass the student, conduct it privately.

6. *Use reinforcement to encourage appropriate behavior.*

a. Give the student increased praise and attention for acting in a grown up manner (see PLAN A).

b. In addition, make a special point of letting the student know that you notice her efforts to use the skills she has been learning/practicing. "Lilly, I saw you take a slow, deep breath and you remembered to speak low and slow. Nice job of doing what we have been practicing."

PLAN C

Some students are very skilled at gaining attention through their negative behavior—in this case, acting babyish. If you find yourself frequently nagging, reminding, or coaxing the student to stop acting babyish, it is possible that she is trying to gain adult attention. If other students tend to "mother" her, it is possible that she is trying to gain peer attention as well. Whether or not the student overtly seems to like the attention, you should make sure that she receives more frequent and more satisfying attention when she behaves appropriately than when she acts babyish.

1. *Respond consistently to the inappropriate behavior.*

a. Give the signal whenever the student acts babyish (see PLAN A).

b. If the student does not respond to the signal by changing her behavior immediately, ignore the behavior. While ignoring, do not look at the student or talk to her. Do not act disgusted or impatient with her behavior. Simply interact in positive ways with students who are behaving appropriately and meeting classroom expectations. As soon as the target student is no longer acting babyish, pay attention to her, but make no reference to her inappropriate behavior.

c. If other students give the target student attention when she is acting babyish (e.g., catering to her, carrying her around, getting things for her), gently correct them. "Nathan and Elissa,

Lilly can take care of herself. If she needs her pencil sharpened, she is fully capable of doing it herself. It would be best to let her work it out on her own."

2. *Use reinforcement to encourage appropriate behavior.*

a. Frequent praise and attention is the core of this plan. The student must see that she receives more frequent and more satisfying attention when she behaves appropriately than when she acts babyish. Thus, whenever the student is not acting babyish (or otherwise misbehaving), make an effort to praise and spend time with her. "Lilly, you are working so hard and acting in a very grown up manner. Would it be okay if I sat with you a moment and watched as you continue working on that project?"

b. You may also wish to use intermittent rewards to acknowledge the student's success. Occasional, and unexpected, rewards can motivate the student to demonstrate responsible behavior more often. The idea is to provide a reward when the student has had a particularly good period of acting in a grown up manner.

Appropriate rewards might include reading to students in a younger class, playing a game with you, or a compliment of the student's grown up behavior in front of the principal. *(NOTE: A list of additional reinforcement ideas can be found in APPENDIX 1.)*

Use intermittent rewards more frequently at the beginning of the intervention to encourage the student, and then less often as her behavior improves.

3. Ensure a 3-1 ratio of positive to negative attention.

a. Given that attention is a motivating force for this student, you want to be sure that you are giving the student *three times as much* positive as negative attention. One way to do this is to monitor your interactions with the student at least one day per week. Keep a card on a clipboard or in your pocket and record each interaction you have with the student as either positive or negative by marking a "+" or a "-", respectively, on the card.

To determine whether an interaction is positive or negative, ask yourself whether the student was acting babyish (or otherwise misbehaving) at the time of the interaction. Any interaction that stems from inappropriate behavior is negative, and all interactions that occur while the student is meeting classroom expectations are positive. Thus, giving the signal to remind her that she is not acting grown up is a negative interaction, but praising the student for not needing the signal is positive. Greeting the student as she enters the room or asking her if she has any questions during independent work are also considered positive interactions. *(NOTE: Ignoring the student's babyish behavior is not recorded at all, because it is not an interaction.)*

b. If you find that you are not giving the student three times as much positive as negative attention, try to increase the number of positive interactions you have with the student. Sometimes prompts can help. For example, you might decide that each time the student enters the classroom you will say "hello" to her, or that right after any recess you will find a time to praise the student, or that whenever a student sharpens his/her pencil you will check the target student and as soon as possible praise some aspect of her behavior. You can also increase the ratio of positive to negative attention by ignoring more of the student's inappropriate behavior.

PLAN D

Some students do not seem to know when they behave inappropriately. If your student doesn't realize when and/or how often she acts babyish, the intervention must include some way of helping the student become more aware of her own behavior.

1. Respond consistently to the inappropriate behavior.

a. When the student acts babyish, use the signal, then ignore or gently correct the behavior, as necessary (see PLAN A).

b. In addition, whenever you give the signal make sure the incident is recorded by either the student or yourself (see Step 2).

2. Implement a system for monitoring the frequency of the student's babyish behavior.

a. Determine who will do the recording. Since the point is for the student to become more aware of her own behavior, having her do the recording (i.e., self-monitoring) will be more effective

than if you record her behavior. However, if the student cannot or will not be accurate (or if she would be embarrassed to self-monitor), you should do the recording. Remember that the idea is for the student to be aware of each time she acts in a babyish manner, and for her to know that each incident is being recorded. *(NOTE: Even when the student self-monitors, you should keep your own record approximately one day per week to verify the student's accuracy.)*

b. If the student is self-monitoring her own behavior, you can have her keep a form on her desk or in her notebook like the sample following. Tell the student that each time she sees you give the signal, she should circle the next number on the form.

Name _____   Date _____

Behavior to be Counted: <u>*Each time I need to be reminded to act in a grown up manner.*</u>

MONDAY

  1 2 3 4 5 6 7 8 9 10 11 12 13 14 15 16 17 18 19 20 21 22 23 24 25

TUESDAY

  1 2 3 4 5 6 7 8 9 10 11 12 13 14 15 16 17 18 19 20 21 22 23 24 25

WEDNESDAY

  1 2 3 4 5 6 7 8 9 10 11 12 13 14 15 16 17 18 19 20 21 22 23 24 25

THURSDAY

  1 2 3 4 5 6 7 8 9 10 11 12 13 14 15 16 17 18 19 20 21 22 23 24 25

FRIDAY

  1 2 3 4 5 6 7 8 9 10 11 12 13 14 15 16 17 18 19 20 21 22 23 24 25

c. Each day, meet with the student for a few minutes to review that day's record. Have the student chart the information on a graph (or do it yourself), and talk with her about whether the day was better, worse, or about the same as previous days.

If the day did not go well, encourage the student to talk about why and have her identify what she can do the next day to help herself remember to act more grown up. If the student acts babyish during the meeting, keep the interaction very short. Just let the student know that you are sure tomorrow will be a better day.

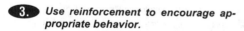 **Use reinforcement to encourage appropriate behavior.**

a. Give the student increased praise and attention for acting in a grown up manner (see PLAN A).

b. In addition, praise the student during the review meetings for accurate recording (if applicable) and for being willing to look at her daily record.

Even on a bad day, if the student is willing to chart the data and discuss why it was a bad day, praise her. "Lilly, you are really handling this responsibly. Even though it was a rough day, you are willing to talk to me about things you might do differently tomorrow. That is a real sign that you are making progress."

Regardless of how the day went, try to make the end of day meeting upbeat and encouraging—you want the student to look forward to this daily review.

4. **Encourage the student to use self-reinforcement.**

Whenever things are going well (i.e., less babyish behavior than usual), prompt the student to mentally reinforce herself. "Lilly, this has been a very successful morning. Silently tell yourself that you are really good at behaving in a grown up way." Prompt the student in this way intermittently throughout the day and during the review meeting.

PLAN E

Whenever a student's problem behavior has become habitual and/or she does not seem to have a desire to reduce it, you may need to use a structured system of external incentives (i.e., rewards and consequences) based on her behavior to motivate her to cease the babyish behavior and to begin acting more grown up.

1. **Respond consistently to the inappropriate behavior.**

When the student acts babyish, use the signal, then ignore or gently correct the inappropriate behavior, as necessary (see PLAN A).

2. *Implement a system for monitoring the frequency of the student's babyish behavior (see PLAN D).*

3. *Establish a structured system for reinforcing the appropriate behavior.*

a. With the student, create a list of reinforcers that she can earn. Although you might want to have some suggestions in mind, the system will be more effective if the student identifies most of the items or activities herself. *(NOTE: A list of reinforcement ideas can be found in APPENDIX 1.)*

b. Each day, have the student begin with a certain number of tickets in a bowl or jar. The number should equal the daily average of her inappropriate behavior, plus two. Thus, if she acts babyish an average of 13 times per day, she would begin each day with 15 tickets. All the tickets should have prizes written on them—one would have a big prize, a couple would have

moderate prizes, and the majority would have little prizes.

Each time you have to use the signal, the student records the incident on her monitoring form, and you remove one ticket from the jar—but neither you nor the student gets to see what is written on it. At the end of the day, the student draws one ticket from those remaining in the jar, and receives that prize.

4. *Use reinforcement to encourage appropriate behavior.*

a. Give the student increased praise and attention for acting in a grown up manner (see PLAN A).

b. In addition, show interest and enthusiasm about how the student is doing on the reinforcement system. "Lilly, we are half way through the day and we have only had to take out one ticket. I'll bet that big prize is still in the jar."

. . . .

Suggested Steps for Developing and Implementing a Plan

The following steps are designed to help you develop an appropriate intervention plan and implement it effectively, whether you choose to use one of the MODEL PLANS or create a customized plan of your own. The steps are, however, suggestions—they are not intended to be followed rigidly or in any particular order. Use your professional judgment and the knowledge of your particular situation to make them work for you.

 1. *Make sure you have enough information about the situation.*

a. If you think a minimal intervention like PLAN A will be sufficient, you may already have enough information to proceed. However, when a more involved plan seems necessary, you should consider collecting additional descriptive and/or objective information for a couple of days.

b. You need to be able to explain what you mean when you say "the student has a problem with not acting/speaking in a grown up manner." Anecdotal notes on actual incidents can help you define the problem behavior clearly and completely. To collect anecdotal notes, simply keep a card in your pocket or on a clipboard and occasionally make notes on specific instances when the student acts in a babyish way.

For each entry, briefly describe where and when the behavior occurred, what the student did or said, and any other relevant observations (e.g., what prompted the behavior). You do not need

to do this every time babyish behavior occurs, as the idea is to capture a range of examples of the behavior so that you can describe the problem thoroughly.

Also include some notes on times when the student behaves in a grown up manner. This will make it clear that you are not only aware of her problem behavior, but also recognize when she behaves appropriately. When you meet with the student, the positive examples will help you clarify how you want the student to behave.

c. If the student notices what you are doing and asks about it, be straightforward—tell her that you are collecting information to see whether her "not grown-up" behavior is a problem that needs to be worked on.

d. If you implement a more complex intervention such as PLAN D, it may be useful to summarize the information from the self-monitoring form on a chart or graph. Seeing how often she is signaled for not acting grown up may increase the student's motivation to improve, and charting the information will also help you to monitor whether the situation is getting worse, staying the same, or getting better.

2. *Identify a focus for the intervention and labels for referring to the appropriate and inappropriate behaviors.*

a. To be effective, the intervention must address more than just reducing the student's babyish behavior—there must be a concurrent emphasis on increasing some positive behavior or trait (e.g., acting/speaking more grown up). Having a specific positive behavior in mind will make it easier for you to "catch" and reinforce the student for acting appropriately, and the positive focus will frame the situation more productively.

b. Specifying labels for the appropriate and inappropriate behaviors (e.g., "acting/speaking in a grown up manner" and "not acting/speaking in a grown up manner," respectively) will help you to use consistent vocabulary when discussing the situation with the student. In this case, it's a good idea not to refer to the student's problem behavior as "being babyish" as you do not want to embarrass, belittle, or humiliate the student.

3. *Determine when and how to include the parent(s).*

a. It is not necessary to contact the student's parent(s) if the problem has just begun and/or is not interfering with the student's academic or social progress. However, it might be a good idea to take advantage of any scheduled activities (e.g., conferences, weekly notes home) to let the parent(s) know of your concern.

b. If the problem continues and you decide to involve the parent(s), share any information you have collected about the behavior (i.e., anecdotal notes, frequency count), and explain why you are concerned. Focus in particular on how the behavior is hindering the student socially (e.g., other students are treating her like a younger sibling, not a peer). You might want to ask if the parent(s) have any insight into the situation and/or whether they have noticed similar behavior at home.

Whether or not the parent(s) perceive a problem, explain that you want to help the student "learn to act/speak in a more grown up manner," and invite them to join you for an initial meeting with the student to develop a plan. If the parent(s) are unable or unwilling to participate, let

them know that you will keep them informed of the student's progress.

c. Once the parent(s) have been involved in any way, you should give them updates at least once per week while the plan is being implemented.

4. *Prepare for, then conduct, an initial meeting about the situation.*

a. Arrange a meeting to discuss your concerns with the student and anyone else who will be involved (e.g., the parent[s]). Although the specifics will vary depending upon the age of the student and the severity of the problem, there are some general guidelines to consider when scheduling the meeting.

First, meet at a neutral time (i.e., not immediately after a problem has occurred), when emotions are less likely to hamper communication. In general, a day's notice is appropriate, however a primary age student may worry excessively and/or forget what the meeting is about if it is scheduled more than an hour before it takes place.

Second, make the meeting appropriately private. With a primary age student who has a mild problem, you might meet in the classroom while the other students are working independently. However, when dealing with a middle/junior high school student and the student's parent(s), you will need some place private (e.g., the counselor's office) to ensure that the discussion will not be overheard.

Third, try to make sure the meeting is scheduled for a time and place that it is not likely to be interrupted. And finally, if the parent(s) will be participating, they should be the ones to tell the student about the meeting.

b. Construct a preliminary plan. Decide whether you think you can use one of the MODEL PLANS or if you need to create a customized plan using components from various plans and/or of your own design. Although you will invite and encourage the student to help develop the plan during the initial meeting, having a proposed plan in mind before you meet can alleviate frustration and wasted time if the student is unwilling or unable to participate.

c. After reviewing the information you have collected and thinking about how you want the student to behave, prepare thorough descriptions of the inappropriate behavior and the positive behavior/trait on which the student will be working. The more specific you can be and the more concrete examples you have, the easier it will be to clarify (and for the student to understand) your expectations. Be sure to consider the student's behavior in all relevant activities (e.g., independent work, teacher directed instruction, unstructured class times, recess and lunch, etc.).

d. Conduct the meeting in an atmosphere of collaboration. The following agenda is one way you might structure the meeting:

• **Share your concerns about the student's behavior.**

Briefly describe the problem behavior. Then explain why you consider the behavior to be a problem. In this case, you might tell the student that other people will not take her or her ideas seriously when she does not act/speak in a reasonably grown up manner.

• **Discuss how you can work together to improve the situation.**

Tell the student that you would like to help her learn to "act/speak in a more grown up way," and describe your preliminary plan. Invite the student to give you input on the various aspects of the plan, and together work out any necessary details (e.g., the signal, use of the self-monitoring form).

You may have to brainstorm different possibilities if the student is uncomfortable with the initial plan. Incorporating any of the student's suggestions that strengthen the plan is likely to increase her sense of "ownership" in and commitment to it.

• **Make sure the student understands what you mean by appropriate and inappropriate behavior.**

Use the descriptions you have prepared to define and clarify the problem behavior and the positive (desired) behavior as specifically and thoroughly as you can. To ensure that you and the student are in agreement about the expectations, you might present hypo-

thetical scenarios and have her identify whether each is an example of "grown up" or "not grown up" behavior. Or you might describe an actual situation that has occurred and ask her to demonstrate how she could act/speak in a grown up manner in that situation.

• **Conclude the meeting.**

Always end the meeting with words of encouragement. Let the student know that you are confident that she can be successful. Be sure to reinforce her for participating in the meeting.

 Give the student regular, ongoing feedback about her behavior.

It is important to meet with the student periodically to discuss her progress. In most cases, three to five minutes once per week should suffice. *(NOTE: PLANS D and E require daily meetings.)* Review any information that has been collected and discuss whether or not the situation is getting better. As much as possible, focus on the student's improvements, however, also address any new or continuing problems. As the situation improves, the meetings can be faded to once every other week and then to once per month.

6. *Evaluate the situation (and the plan).*

Implement any plan for at least two weeks before deciding whether to change plans; to continue, modify, or fade the plan you are using; or to cease the intervention. Generally, if the student's behavior is clearly improving (based on the objective information that's been collected and/or the subjective perceptions of yourself, the student, and possibly the parent[s]), stick with what you are doing. If the situation has remained the same or worsened, some kind of change will be necessary. Always discuss any changes to the plan with the student first.

BEGINNING CLASS— GETTING STUDENTS SETTLED DOWN

DESCRIPTION

There are students in your class who wander around, talk, roughhouse, or otherwise misbehave when class should begin (e.g., at the beginning of the day, after recess, etc.).

GOAL

The students will be in their seats and ready for instruction when it is time for class to begin.

OVERVIEW OF PLANS

- PLAN A: For a situation in which the problem is relatively mild or has just begun.

- PLAN B: For a problem that may stem from the students not knowing how to come into the room and get settled down.

- PLAN C: For a situation in which the students lack the motivation to come into the room and get ready for instruction.

NOTE:

These three plans are geared for a situation in which quite a few students in the class have a problem getting settled down and ready for instruction. However, each can easily be modified to intervene with only a few (one to three) students who have/continue to have this problem.

Alternative Problems

- **Chaos/Classroom Out of Control**

- **Dawdling**

- **Tardiness**

- **Transitions, Problems With**

. . . .
Model Plans

PLAN A

If this problem has just begun and/or occurs only one to two times per week, it may not be necessary, or even beneficial, to use an involved plan. The following actions, along with making the students aware of your concerns, may resolve the situation.

1. **Develop a signal to indicate that class is about to begin.**

a. When there is a bell to mark the beginning of a period or class (either in the morning or at the beginning of instructional periods), the bell can serve as the signal. When the bell rings, pick up a clipboard or notepad (see Step 2) and begin instruction.

b. When there is no bell (e.g., when the students return from recess or music class) use a hand signal, such as holding your hand high in the air. During the initial discussion with the students about the problem (see SUGGESTED STEPS FOR DEVELOPING AND IMPLEMENTING A PLAN), inform the class that your upraised hand will serve as a 30 second warning. Once you put your hand in the air, it is time for everyone to be in their seats and ready for instruction. At the end of the 30 seconds, put your hand down, pick up a clipboard or notepad (see Step 2), and begin class.

2. **Respond consistently to each instance of students not being ready for class to begin.**

a. When there are individual students who are not ready (e.g., two students are standing in the back of the room talking) do not wait for them—begin class immediately after the signal. At the same time write these students' names on the clipboard or notepad. Also make note of how long it takes for them to get in their seats and ready for instruction, writing the amount of time next to the students' names.

b. When it is time for the class to leave your room (e.g., for recess, lunch, end of the day), excuse all but the students whose names you've recorded. Tell these students how long it took them to get settled down after you began class and provide a gentle verbal correction. Let the students know that from now on you expect them to be in their seats and ready for instruction when it is time for class to begin—when the bell rings and/or within 30 seconds of the signal.

c. If there are many students (e.g., more than four students are out of their seats and engaged in talking or horse play) who are not ready for instruction when it is time for class to begin, raise the clipboard/notepad in the air. During the initial meeting about the problem, explain to the class that this signal indicates that class should have begun and that the students are now interfering with instructional time.

Keep the clipboard/notepad in the air until all the students are in their seats and ready for instruction. This is likely to result in gentle peer pressure: "Hey, sit down, you are wasting time."

Keep track of how much time is wasted, and record it for "the class," not particular individuals. Tell the class how much time was wasted, and give a gentle correction. Finally, let the class know that you expect them to be able to be ready for class to begin so you do not have to give the signal of raising the clipboard/notepad.

d. If, within two or three days, the students are not taking the signals seriously (i.e., they do not seem to be making more of an effort to be ready for class to begin), inform the class that for any subsequent incidents, the amount of time that has been wasted will need to be paid back.

When you have to raise the clipboard/notepad because many students are not ready and you cannot begin instruction, the entire class will owe time off the next recess. If one to four individual students are not ready, you will begin class and record the names of those students. In this case, those particular students will owe time, but the rest of the class will not.

(NOTE: At the middle/junior high school level, this consequence may not be possible if your students do not have a recess to use for time owed. Consider the possibility of keeping students for one or two minutes after class so they miss socializing time during the next passing period. If this is not possible, consider implementing PLAN C.)

. . . .

e. Keep in mind that when implementing any of these procedures, you should not nag, coax, remind, or yell at the students to get ready. Your goal is to give clear signals, but it is the students' job to get ready for class to begin.

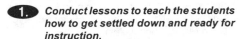 **Use reinforcement to encourage appropriate behavior.**

a. Praise individual students for meeting your expectations about being ready for class to begin. Pay particular attention to those students who have had the greatest tendency to dawdle or to otherwise waste time. Whenever one or more of these students are ready for instruction when the signal is given, praise them for demonstrating the ability to be ready at the beginning of class. "Jared, Paul, and Hanna, thank you for being ready."

If the students would be embarrassed by public praise, praise them privately, praise them nonverbally by simply making eye contact and giving a head nod as you begin instruction, or even give them a positive note.

b. In addition, occasionally praise those students who rarely or never have a problem with being ready. Because these students have already mastered the positive expectations, they do not need positive feedback as often as the students who have had difficulty. However, you do not want them to feel that you take their positive behavior for granted. "You people seated at this table consistently are ready when it is time for class to begin. I appreciate that I never need to give you reminders."

c. Finally, when there has been a significant overall improvement in the number of students being ready for instruction, praise the entire class. Remember that any time the students are ready when instruction is scheduled to begin you can praise them for their cooperation and their efficiency.

PLAN B

If the students are not clear about how to get settled down and ready for instruction, the intervention must include some way of teaching them how to do so.

1. **Conduct lessons to teach the students how to get settled down and ready for instruction.**

a. Before the lessons, decide whether the whole class should participate or if the lessons should involve only a select group of students. The next task is to identify the specific nature of the students' problem behavior(s) and strategies for dealing with those particular behaviors. The following questions may help you with this process:

• Are the students so wound up and excited that they are keeping each other "hyped"?

You might teach the class some physical relaxation exercises. *(NOTE: Anxiety/Nervousness includes a script for relaxation exercises that could be adapted for whole class instruction.)* Once the students have been taught these techniques, the first step to getting started after recess, lunch, etc. should be to conduct a short physical relaxation exercise.

• Are the students trying to do last minute things before sitting down (getting drinks, sharpening pencils, etc.)?

Identify the specific things the students are doing and develop an alternative for each. For sharpening pencils and getting materials ready, you could prompt the students to sharpen their pencils and get all their materials ready before they go out to recess (and provide an extra minute or two prior to recess if necessary). For getting drinks, suggest that the students remember to get a drink while on recess or on their way back into the classroom.

• Are the students carrying over problems from other settings (e.g., continuing minor disputes from the playground or wanting to tell you about situations that happened on the playground)?

Design a strategy for students to "leave the hassles at the door" and/or set up a complaint box. Tell the students that they are expected to come in and take their seats after recess or lunch, and then at a later time they can write a description of their problem and put it in the "Complaint Box." Explain that you will monitor the Complaint Box periodically and check with any student(s) who wrote a complaint to see if they are still concerned.

(NOTE: If the students simply seem to be unmotivated to get ready for class to begin, PLAN C may be more appropriate.)

b. Use the lessons to present the skills or strategies and have the students practice them. Provide opportunities for students to rehearse in as realistic a manner as possible. That is, send the students out in the hall and have them come into the room. Then give the signal and have the students get ready for class to begin.

Provide feedback. If they did well, let them know. If they took too long, tell them how much time they need to save on the next practice. If they made it in time but some students acted frantic (e.g., running, pushing, acting extremely rushed), give them feedback. Let them know that there is plenty of time, if they are calm and efficient. Continue this practice until the class can demonstrate mastery.

c. Conduct short (three to five minute) lessons immediately before the students are to leave the room. In other words, conduct the lessons on entering the room and getting settled down from recess just before the class goes out to recess. Conduct the lessons on coming into the room in the morning right before the students are excused to go home. Continue the lessons until the students are consistently being successful in meeting your expectations.

2. **Prompt appropriate behavior by using precorrections.**

As you phase out the lessons, substitute using a prompt to precorrect the students' behavior. For example, before excusing the students to go to lunch you could say, "Class, we don't need to have a lesson on how to come in after lunch because everyone is doing great in the practice. However, do remember that you only have two minutes from when you come in the room to get your pencils sharpened, get drinks, get out your materials, and get your papers numbered from 1-20 for our practice spelling test. Any questions?"

3. **Respond consistently to students who are not ready for instruction.**

a. Give clear signals. Whenever a student or students are taking too long, record the information on your clipboard/notepad and provide a gentle correction (see PLAN A).

b. Once you have conducted the lessons for a few days, inform the class that now that they know how to come in and get settled down correctly, if any individuals forget and take too long, those individuals will owe time (see PLAN A).

4. **Use reinforcement to encourage appropriate behavior.**

a. Praise individual students for meeting expectations regarding being ready for instruction, and praise the entire class when improvement occurs (see PLAN A). "Willie and Emma, you were very efficient in getting into the room and ready for the spelling test. Nice job of doing what we have been practicing."

b. You may also wish to use intermittent rewards to acknowledge the students' success. Occasional, and unexpected, rewards can motivate the class to demonstrate responsible behavior more often. The idea is to provide a reward when the students have had a particularly good period (e.g., morning, day, week) of being ready for instruction.

For this particular situation, appropriate rewards could be any class-wide activity (e.g., playing a game, extra recess, free time in class). "Class, you have all been so efficient about coming into the room and getting ready for instruction that we have saved a lot of time this week. Because you have all helped save time, let's take some time now to go out to recess early. I'll be with you until the other students and the playground supervisors arrive."

A list of additional reinforcement ideas can be found in APPENDIX 1. Use intermittent rewards more frequently at the beginning of the intervention to encourage the students, and then less often as their behavior improves.

PLAN C

Sometimes, an entire class falls into a pattern of wasting time and not being ready for instruction to begin. This can happen when a particular behavior becomes habitual and/or when a majority of students try to emulate a few influential students who use not being ready to look "cool" or "tough." In these cases it can be very difficult to change the class' behavior, and you may need to implement a system of structured reinforcement (i.e., rewards and consequences) which creates mild peer pressure to motivates the students to behave appropriately.

1. *Develop a clear signal to indicate the beginning of class, keep information on individual students or the class for taking too long, and implement time owed as a consequence (see PLAN A).*

2. *Publicly monitor how much time is wasted while the students get settled down.*

a. To help the students become more aware of their own behavior, create a space on the chalkboard or a wall chart on which to record the amount of time wasted daily. Each day, add together the minutes that all the individual students owed to obtain a total number of minutes that have been wasted. In addition, if the class as a whole owed time, multiply those minutes by the number of students in the class, and add that amount to the total minutes (see the sample below).

Beginning of Day:

Marcus	2 min
Jim	2 min

After Recess:

Tefin	1 min
Rosa	3 min
Dawn	2 min

After Lunch:

Class	2 min

(x 26 class members = 52 minutes)

Total minutes wasted today = 62 minutes

---

b. Be sure that you have clarified the criteria for what constitutes a class-wide problem rather than an individual problem. In PLAN A this was "more than four students not being ready." When one to four students were not ready, you would begin class, and record the names and amount of time wasted of just those individuals on the clipboard/notepad. However, when more than four students were not ready, you would raise your clipboard/notepad to indicate that it is now a class-wide problem. Your criteria may be different, the important thing is for the criteria to be clear and reasonably objective.

c. Each day, conduct a short class meeting to review that day's record. Have a student record the information on a publicly displayed chart (or do it yourself), and discuss whether the day was better, worse, or about the same as previous days.

d. Chart the data for at least a couple of days prior to implementing the performance goals and reinforcement system described in Steps 3 and 4.

3. *Respond consistently to students who are not ready for instruction.*

a. Give a clear signal. Whenever a student or students are taking too long to get ready for class to begin, record the information on your clipboard/notepad and provide a gentle correction (see PLAN A).

b. Use time owed as a consequence for both individual students and the group (see PLAN A). However, if this is not possible (e.g., you are a middle/junior high school teacher and cannot keep students after class), you might modify the system so that, for example, any individual who accumulates more than 20 minutes owed during a grading period must spend an hour in after-school detention. The drawback to this procedure is that it requires you to keep a cumulative record of time owed for an entire grading period.

4. *Establish a group reinforcement system.*

a. Have the students brainstorm reinforcement ideas for the entire class, and then eliminate any items from the list that are not possible (i.e., the suggestions are too expensive or could not be provided to all the students in the class).

b. Assign "prices" (in points) to the remaining items on the list. The prices should be based on the instructional, personnel, and/or monetary costs of the items. Monetary cost is clear—the more expensive the item, the more points required to earn it. Instructional cost refers to the amount of instructional time lost or interfered with by a particular reward. Thus, an activity which causes the class to miss part of academic instruction should require more points than one the class can do during recess time. Personnel cost involves the time required by you and/or other staff to fulfill the reinforcer. Thus, earning an extra recess period in which extra supervision would need to be arranged would cost more than having music playing in class for 15 minutes, for example.

c. Have the class vote on the reinforcers. The reinforcer that receives the most votes is the one they will work for first, and the items that come in second (and third) will be the next ones worked for.

d. Work with the class to establish a sliding scale that pairs total minutes wasted with points earned. For an elementary classroom this would involve the use of a daily total. For middle/junior high classes where there is only one time each day that this problem will occur (e.g., the beginning of class), a weekly scale would be more appropriate. The following scale demonstrates this concept; obviously, the numbers should be tailored to fit your unique class situation.

over 100 total minutes wasted	= 0 points
50-99 minutes wasted	= 1 point
25-49 minutes wasted	= 2 points
10-24 minutes wasted	= 3 points
4-9 minutes wasted	= 4 points
1-3 minutes wasted	= 6 points
0 minutes wasted	= 8 points

e. Record a cumulative total of points, and when the class has accumulated enough points, they earn the privilege and the system begins again.

f. Alternately, if a class-wide system seems unlikely to be effective, set up a team competition and response cost lottery. In this type of system, the class is divided into four to six teams (designed to be as equitable as possible). Each team begins the day with a certain number of tickets (e.g., six) on which they write the name of their team. Whenever a student is not ready for instruction, that student's team loses a ticket. At the end of the day, each team puts all their remaining tickets in a hat or basket for a lottery drawing. The team whose name is on the winning ticket earns the reward for that day.

g. When implementing any of these reinforcement systems, focus student attention on the fact that being ready for class means more time for class activities. "Class, you earned eight points for the day, but more importantly, there has been no instructional time wasted. I appreciate your cooperation and efficiency."

. . . .

Suggested Steps for Developing and Implementing a Plan

The following steps are designed to help you develop an appropriate intervention plan and implement it effectively, whether you choose to use one of the MODEL PLANS or create a customized plan of your own. These steps are, however, suggestions—they are not intended to be followed rigidly or in any particular order. Use your professional judgment and the knowledge of your particular situation to make them work for you.

 1. *Decide how to present the situation to the class.*

a. Depending upon your personal philosophy, and whether or not you think a simple intervention like PLAN A is appropriate, you may choose to

have an informal discussion about the problem with the students. Wait for a time that you are calm (not right after an incident of wasting time has occurred) and inform the students that you are finding the time required for people to get settled down and ready for instruction to be a problem. Then specifically define your expectations for each time the class comes into the room. If the expectation is different first thing in the morning than it is after recess, clarify these differences (e.g., there is a bell to signal the beginning of class in the morning, and you will use the raised hand and 30 second warning after recess).

Give the students an opportunity to ask questions or make comments and end the session by thanking the students for listening and letting them know that you are confident they will make an effort get settled down and ready for instruction whenever they enter the room.

b. If you prefer to implement one of the more structured MODEL PLANS, schedule a class meeting for the purpose of clarifying all aspects of the plan and giving the students an opportunity to ask questions or make comments.

c. If you want the students to assume some ownership of the problem, you might wish to hold a class meeting in which the students participate in analyzing the situation and developing an action plan. In this case, before the meeting you will need to have clarified the nature/extent of the problem and your expectations for the students' behavior.

You will also need to identify any aspects of the problem/plan that you do not feel comfortable opening up to a group decision. For example, you must decide ahead of time whether or not to give the class the opportunity to determine if there will be a consequence for the problems with getting ready for instruction and/or what the consequence should be. If you firmly believe that there should be a consequence, then you should not seek student input on that particular issue.

2. *Schedule and conduct a class meeting about the situation.*

a. The purpose of this meeting will be to either present your proposed plan or have the students help you generate a plan.

Schedule the meeting for a neutral time and allow enough time for a reasonable discussion. Inform the students in advance that the meeting will take place; this will give them time to think about the problem. "Class, this afternoon we are going to have a class meeting on the problem of time wasted when the class comes into the room. Please give some thought to this problem and what we might do as a class to solve this problem."

b. Use an agenda to structure the meeting. Shortly before the meeting, write the agenda on the chalkboard. Following is one possible agenda you may wish to use.

Agenda

1. Wasted time—Define the magnitude of the problem. (Share data on cumulative time wasted.)

2. Review of expectations regarding different times the class comes in and needs to get settled down.

3. Brainstorm ideas for improving the situation.

4. Select strategies that everyone agrees to.

5. Establish what the teacher will do if a student is wasting time and what the teacher will do if lots of students are wasting time.

---

c. It is important to establish clear rules (for both you and the students) regarding the brainstorming phase(s) of the meeting. For example:

- Any idea is okay (but no obscenity).

- Ideas will not be evaluated initially (i.e., no approval—"Good idea," or disapproval—"What a stupid idea," or "We couldn't do that" should be expressed during brainstorming).

- All ideas will be written down and discussed at the conclusion of brainstorming.

d. At the conclusion of brainstorming, evaluate the ideas, and lead the class to consensus on any decisions that need to be made. Use voting as a decision-making process when appropriate.

3. *Determine when and how to include the parent(s).*

a. Because this problem is more of a procedural than behavioral or motivational problem, involving the students' parent(s) is not critical if the situation is class-wide.

b. If the situation involves only one or two students who have or continue to have a problem with getting settled down, you should contact the parent(s) of those individual students. Let them know that their child is wasting time when coming into the classroom and what steps you are taking to correct the situation.

Frequent contact is not required, but whenever you intend to implement an individualized plan (e.g., the student will owe the time off recess or in detention), the parent(s) should be informed prior to its implementation and should be given feedback about the student's progress every two to four weeks.

4. Give the class regular, ongoing feedback about their behavior.

Periodically meet with the students to discuss the situation. In most cases, three to five minutes once per week should suffice. *(NOTE: PLAN C suggests daily meetings to record the data or to determine points.)* During the meetings, review any information that has been collected and discuss whether or not things are getting better. As much as possible, focus on improvements, however, also address any new or continuing problems.

As you discuss problems, acknowledge that there are individuals in the class who consistently be-

have appropriately. However, do not single out individuals when discussing problems or progress with the entire group. As the situation improves, the meetings can be faded to once every other week and then to once per month.

5. Evaluate the situation (and the plan).

Any plan should be implemented for at least two weeks before deciding whether or not it is effective. Generally, if the situation has improved (based on the objective information that's been collected and/or the subjective perceptions of yourself and the students), continue with what you have been doing. (Eventually you want to fade, then eliminate, the plan.) If the problem remains the same or worsens, some kind of change (i.e., modifying the current plan or switching to another plan) will be necessary. Always discuss any change in the intervention with the class first.

B LAMING OTHERS/ EXCUSES FOR EVERYTHING

· ·

Lack of Responsibility for Own Behavior

DESCRIPTION

You have a student who blames others for things he has done wrong (e.g., getting in a fight, not finishing an assignment, etc.).

GOAL

The student will learn to accept responsibility for his own actions.

OVERVIEW OF PLANS

- PLAN A: For a situation in which the problem is relatively mild or has just begun.

- PLAN B: For a student who seems to lack the skills of honestly accepting responsibility for his own actions.

NOTE:

PLAN B may also be appropriate for the student who is afraid of the consequences of his misbehavior.

- PLAN C: For a student who has learned to escape accountability for things he does wrong (i.e., his excuses actually work).

Alternative Problems

- **Cheating**

- **Corrected, Student Gets Upset When**

- **Lying**

- **Perfectionism**

General Considerations

- If the student's problem behavior stems in any way from academic issues (e.g., the student makes excuses about not getting his work done because he is not able to successfully meet academic demands, concurrent efforts must be made to ensure his academic success (see **Academic Deficits, Determining**).

- If the student lacks the basic social skills to interact with peers appropriately, it may be necessary to begin by teaching him those skills. The problem **Social Skills, Lack of** contains information on a variety of published social skills curricula.

Model Plans

PLAN A

It is not always necessary, or even beneficial, to use an involved plan. If the inappropriate behavior has just begun and/or is relatively mild (i.e., not interfering with the student's academic or social progress), the following actions, along with making the student aware of your concerns, may resolve the situation.

 Establish a set time when the student can talk to you about anything he feels is unfair.

This "contact time" should be scheduled so that it requires the student to use some of his free time (e.g., during recess, after school, etc.). Having such a time allows you to be unengaged with the student at a time that he makes excuses or claims something is unfair. For example, if he says, "I didn't do it. It wasn't my fault. Avery was the one who . . . " you can respond by saying, "If you want to discuss this, come see me during recess." If the student *does* come to see you at the established time, listen to what the student has to say.

 Respond consistently to the inappropriate behavior.

a. Do not accuse the student of engaging in any inappropriate behavior unless you know that the student was involved. If you are not absolutely sure that the student was involved, asking him just invites denial or the blaming of someone else. Then, when he denies involvement (with this student denial is quite predictable), you must take his word for it since you do not know for sure. If he actually *was* involved, this process reinforces his denial—he gets away with something again.

b. When you know the student was involved, pre-correct the denial. "David, we need to talk about

a problem. Do not claim you were not involved, and do not blame someone else." State the misbehavior and the consequences. If the student does deny involvement and/or blame someone else, ignore the denial or blaming (invite the student to come to talk to you at the prearranged time), but follow through with the consequence. "If you want to talk about this, come see me at recess; but it doesn't matter why you do not have your homework. The fact is you do not have it, and the consequence for not having it is . . . ."

 Use reinforcement to encourage appropriate behavior.

a. Give the student increased praise. Be especially alert for situations in which the student might, but does not, engage in blaming or denial and praise him for these demonstrations of his ability to "accept responsibility for his own behavior." "Deidre, you should be proud of yourself. You did something wrong, but you are accepting responsibility for your own behavior."

If the student would be embarrassed by public praise, praise the student privately or even give the student a note. Remember that any time the student has done something wrong and does not engage in blame or denial, you can praise him for "accepting responsibility for his own behavior."

b. Give the student frequent attention (e.g., say "hello" to him as he enters the classroom, call on him frequently during class activities, and talk to him in settings outside the classroom) and praise him for other positive behaviors he exhibits. For example, you might comment about the accuracy of his work or how polite and helpful he was to a guest speaker. This demonstrates to the student that you notice many positive things he does, not just the fact that he is refraining from engaging in blame or denial.

PLAN B

Some students actually may not know how to accept responsibility. If your student does not seem to possess the skills to honestly accept responsibility for his own actions, the intervention must include a way to teach him to do so.

NOTE: This plan can be modified for the student who is afraid of the consequences associated with misbehavior. The theme that should run through your discussions and lessons with this type of student is that the consequences are often less severe than the guilt and worry associated with trying to avoid the consequences. Emphasize that making a mistake and facing the consequence is better (i.e., more honest, more ethical) than lying to avoid the consequence.

*If the student is afraid of his parent(s) finding out that he did something wrong, and abuse is highly unlikely, contact the parent(s) and ask for their assistance in teaching the student that it is alright to make a mistake now and again, as long as one is willing to accept the consequences (see **Perfectionism** for more information on this type of problem). If you have reason to believe that there is any possibility of physical or emotional abuse of the student by his parent(s), discuss the situation with your building administrator.*

1. **Set up a time that the student can come to talk to you about anything he feels is unfair (see PLAN A).**

2. **Respond consistently to the inappropriate behavior.**

a. Do not accuse the student of engaging in any inappropriate behavior unless you *know* that the student was involved (see PLAN A).

b. When you are certain that the student was involved in a misbehavior, question him about it. If the student admits involvement, reinforce his honesty (see Step 4 for a rationale). While it is important to hold him accountable for the consequences of his original actions, he should be reinforced for being honest and accepting responsibility.

If the student denies involvement, tell him that you know he was involved and that he must pay the consequences.

3. **Conduct lessons to teach the student how to accept responsibility for his own actions.**

a. Before the lessons, think about how you would like to see the student behave. In other words, what responses would be acceptable from the student in place of blaming or denial? You might use the notes you have collected (see SUGGESTED STEPS FOR DEVELOPING AND IMPLEMENTING A PLAN) to identify situations in which the student has engaged in denial or blaming, and then try to specify responses a more responsible student would have in the same situations. For example, ways of "accepting responsibility for one's own behavior" might include:

- Saying nothing, but nodding affirmatively when the misbehavior is stated and the consequence is described.

- Saying, "I'm sorry."

- Saying, "It won't happen again."

- Saying, "Yes, I did it." when asked if you did something wrong and you did do it.

- Saying, "I didn't do it and I would like to come and talk to you about this when you have time." when asked if you did something wrong and you did not do it.

b. During the lessons, review a recent situation in which the student engaged in blaming or denial. Help the student identify what he could have done or said that would have been "accepting responsibility for his own behavior." Then role play the whole sequence. Repeat this process for other situations from your notes.

Also have the student help you generate different scenarios involving other minor misbehaviors, and role play those situations demonstrating how he would "accept responsibility." Occasionally, switch roles—you play the student and he plays the teacher (playground assistant, principal, etc.). During these role plays, you should sometimes accept responsibility and sometimes engage in blame or denial. Have the student identify when you behave correctly and when you engage in blame or denial. Any time you behave incorrectly, have the student tell you what you could have done that would have been an example of accepting responsibility.

c. Tell the student that you will be coming to him and asking if he was involved with a problem. Sometimes it will be when you know he was involved, and you hope he will accept responsibility in the manner you have been practicing. Other times, however, it will be when you know he was not involved in the problem. Review with the student how to respond responsibly when he truly was not involved.

d. Conduct the lessons at least twice per week, in a private atmosphere (e.g., perhaps while the other students are at recess). These lessons needn't last more than three to five minutes, but it is important that they be handled in a matter-of-fact manner so the student does not feel that he is being ridiculed. You want to be very clear that you are not trying to embarrass him, but that you do want him to see the difference between engaging in blame/denial as opposed to accepting responsibility. Continue the lessons until the student is no longer engaging in blame/ denial.

 Periodically ask the student if he was involved in a problem.

For example, ask, "David, did you leave a mess in the Science Center?" Do this both when you know he was involved in a problem and, occasionally, for a hypothetical problem that did not involve him. If you only go to the student when you know he was involved, he may learn that any time someone asks if he was involved he must admit involvement (even though sometimes he may not have been). It is important that the student learn how to responsibly deny involvement when he has not been involved.

(NOTE: For the hypothetical problems, use only minor problems, not something like asking if the student stole money from someone as you do not want to imply that you expect the student to be involved with serious incidents.)

 Use reinforcement to encourage appropriate behavior.

a. Give the student increased praise and attention for accepting responsibility for his own behavior (see PLAN A).

b. In addition, make a special point of letting the student know that you notice his efforts to use the skills he has been learning/practicing. "David, you were involved in that misbehavior, but you accepted responsibility. Nice job of doing what we have been practicing," or "David, you were not involved, and you said you were not involved and told me that you wanted to talk to me about it when I had time. That is a great way to handle it if you are ever accused of something you did not do."

c. Praise the student for participating in the lessons. "David, I know these lessons may seem sort of silly, but I appreciate your willingness to practice how to accept responsibility for your own behavior."

P L A N   C

Some students are very skilled at using blame or denial to actually escape the consequences for their own actions. If the student seems to negotiate and "weasel" out of accountability for his behavior, the intervention plan must include additional monitoring of the student's behavior, reducing the possibility that his attempts at negotiation will work, and increasing the student's motivation to accept responsibility for his own behavior.

 Set up a time that the student can come to talk to you about anything he feels is unfair (see PLAN A).

Respond consistently to the inappropriate behavior.

a. Do not accuse the student of engaging in any inappropriate behavior unless you know that the student was involved. Then follow through with consequences for the actual problems (see PLAN A).

b. When the student is responsible for the misbehavior but denies or blames, use a mild consequence, such as five minutes of time owed off recess or in lunch time detention, for engaging in denial or blame. Precorrect the student regarding denial/blame before confronting him about something he has done and the corresponding consequence. For example, "David, I am about to talk to you about something you have done and the consequence. I want you to know that if you deny or blame someone else, you will have an additional consequence of five minutes of time owed. So think carefully about what you say. Now the problem was that you . . . ."

 Supervise the student more closely during times or activities that are most likely to pose a problem.

a. The goal is to observe the student more frequently and more carefully to increase your confidence in confronting the student with things he has done wrong. Given that you will no longer negotiate and allow the student to make excuses, you must have confidence that any and all consequences you deliver are accurately applied.

b. If the student has a *severe problem with denial*, it may be necessary to document some of the student's misbehavior by video or audio taping him. This can be especially useful for a student who engages in frequent misbehavior on the playground but denies it. Someone can video tape the student from inside the classroom, and the tape can be used to "prove" to the student that he was engaged in misbehavior that he has denied. Be sure to arrange for administrative and parental approval for this step, should it be necessary.

 Conduct a goal-setting conference with the student.

A goal contract might be helpful in clarifying expectations and increasing the student's motivation for accepting responsibility for his own behavior.

The following sample goal contract can be modified for your use.

Goal Contract

Date _____

David:

A goal for me to work on is to learn to accept responsibility for my own behavior and to learn from my mistakes. I can show that I am working on this goal by:

1. Not negotiating (blaming someone else or denying that I did something). Instead I could say, "It was my mistake. I'll accept the consequence."

2. Telling myself that I am a trustworthy person.

_____

Student Signature

Mr. Neuman:

Some ways that I can help David achieve his goal are to:

1. Never accuse him of something unless I am sure he was involved.

2. Treat David as a trustworthy person, but not accept negotiating or blaming.

3. Talk to David during recess about anything he feels is unfair.

_____

Teacher Signature

Use reinforcement to encourage appropriate behavior.

a. Give the student increased praise and attention for accepting responsibility for his own behavior (see PLAN A).

b. In addition, praise the student for making an effort to achieve the goal. For example, if you must talk to the student about a missing homework assignment and he does not make excuses, reinforce him for accepting responsibility for his own behavior.

 6. Encourage the student to use self-reinforcement.

Whenever things are going well (i.e., less blaming or denial than usual), prompt the student to mentally reinforce himself. "David, you have been doing a great job of accepting responsibility for your own behavior. This has been a very successful morning. Silently tell yourself that you are trustworthy." Prompt the student in this manner intermittently throughout the day.

Suggested Steps for Developing and Implementing a Plan

The following steps are designed to help you develop an appropriate intervention plan and implement it effectively, whether you choose to use one of the MODEL PLANS or create a customized plan of your own. The steps are, however, suggestions—they are not intended to be followed rigidly or in any particular order. Use your professional judgment and the knowledge of your particular situation to make them work for you.

 1. Make sure you have enough information about the situation.

a. If you think a minimal intervention like PLAN A will be sufficient, you may already have enough information to proceed. However, when a more involved plan seems necessary, you should consider collecting additional descriptive information for a couple of days.

b. You need to be able to explain what has led you to conclude that the student has a problem with blame or denial. Anecdotal notes on actual incidents should provide enough details to help you define the problem behavior clearly and completely.

To collect anecdotal notes, simply keep a card in your pocket or on a clipboard and *occasionally* make notes on specific instances when the student engages in blaming or denying. For each entry, briefly describe where and when the incident occurred, what the student did or said, and any other relevant observations (e.g., what prompted the behavior). Keep a brief record of each incident that might provide useful information when talking to the student.

c. If the student notices what you are doing and asks about it, be straightforward—tell him that you are collecting information to see whether his blaming and denial is a problem that needs to be worked on.

d. Continuing to collect this type of information while you implement a plan will help you monitor whether the situation is getting worse, staying the same, or getting better.

 2. Identify a focus for the intervention and labels for referring to the appropriate and inappropriate behaviors.

To be effective, the intervention must address more than just reducing the student's use of blame or denial—there must be a concurrent emphasis on increasing some positive behavior or trait (e.g., accepting responsibility for his own behavior). Having a specific positive behavior in mind will make it easier for you to "catch" and reinforce the student for behaving appropriately, and the positive focus will help you frame the situation more productively.

For example, if you simply say that "the student has a problem with making excuses" you don't really provide any useful information, and may put the student and his parent(s) on the defensive. However, when you explain that you want to "help the student learn to accept responsibility for his own behavior," you present an important, and reasonable, goal for the student to work toward and clearly identify what the student needs to do to be successful.

3. Determine when and how to include the parent(s).

a. With this type of problem, the parent(s) should be contacted immediately. Given that the student is likely to tell his parent(s) his side ("The teacher accused me of doing something I did not do."), you should plan on reviewing each major situation or problem with the parent(s). If the parent(s) seem upset or defensive, plan to ask the building principal to join you for the meeting.

Focus in particular on how the student's use of denial/blame will affect how others perceive the student—either honest and ethical or dishonest and untrustworthy. You might want to ask if the parent(s) have any insight into the situation and/or whether they have noticed similar behavior at home.

Whether or not the parent(s) perceive a problem, explain that you want to help the student "learn to accept responsibility for his own behavior" and invite them to join you for an initial meeting with the student to develop a plan. If the parents are unable or unwilling to participate, let them know that you will keep them informed of the student's progress.

b. Once the parent(s) have been involved in any way, you should give them updates at least once per week while the plan is being implemented.

4. **Prepare for, then conduct, an initial meeting about the situation.**

a. Arrange a meeting to discuss your concerns with the student and anyone else who will be involved (e.g., the parent[s] building principal, etc.). Although the specifics will vary depending upon the age of the student and the severity of the problem, there are some general guidelines to consider when scheduling the meeting.

First, meet at a neutral time (i.e., not immediately after a problem has occurred), when emotions are less likely to hamper communication. In general, a day's notice is appropriate, however a primary age student may worry excessively and/or forget what the meeting is about if it is scheduled more than hour before it takes place.

Second, make the meeting appropriately private. With a primary student who has a mild problem, you might meet in the classroom while the other students are working independently. However, when dealing with a middle/junior high school student and the student's parent(s), you will need someplace private (e.g., the counselor's office) to ensure that the discussion will not be overheard.

Third, try to make sure that the meeting is scheduled for a time and place that it is not likely to be interrupted. And finally, when the parent(s)

will be participating, they should be the ones to tell the student about the meeting.

b. Construct a preliminary plan. Decide whether you think you can use one of the MODEL PLANS or if you need to create a customized plan using components from various plans and/or of your own design. Although you will invite and encourage the student to help develop the plan during the initial meeting, having a proposed plan in mind before you meet can alleviate frustration and wasted time if the student is unwilling or unable to participate.

c. After reviewing the information you have collected and thinking about how you want the student to behave, prepare thorough descriptions of the inappropriate behavior and the positive behavior/trait on which the student will be working. The more specific you can be and the more concrete examples you have, the easier it will be to clarify (and for the student to understand) your expectations. Be sure to consider the student's behavior in all relevant activities (e.g., independent work, teacher directed instruction, unstructured class times, recess and lunch, etc.).

d. Conduct the meeting in an atmosphere of collaboration. The following agenda is one way you might structure the meeting:

- **Share your concerns about the student's behavior.**

  Briefly describe the problem behavior and explain why you consider the behavior to be a problem. In this case, you might tell the student that the more he blames or denies, the harder it becomes to trust him. If appropriate, use the metaphor of "the little boy who cried wolf," and adapt it to the situation of blaming/denial. Let the student know that a student who is trustworthy can make the rare excuse and be believed by teachers or bosses, but someone who has made lots of excuses (or blaming), loses their credibility.

- **Discuss how you can work together to improve the situation.**

  Tell the student that you would like to help him learn to accept responsibility for his own behavior and describe your preliminary plan. Invite the student to give you input on the various aspects of the plan, and together work out any necessary details (e.g., goal contract or time owed).

  You may have to brainstorm different possibilities if the student is uncomfortable with the initial plan. Incorporating any of the student's suggestions that strengthen the plan is likely to increase his sense of "ownership" in and commitment to it.

- **Make sure the student understands what you mean by appropriate and inappropriate behavior.**

Use the descriptions you have prepared to define and clarify the problem behavior and the positive (desired) behavior as specifically and thoroughly as you can. To ensure that you and the student are in agreement about the expectations, you might present hypothetical scenarios and have his identify whether each is an example of accepting responsibility or blaming. Or you might describe an actual situation that has occurred and ask him to explain how he would demonstrate that he is accepting responsibility in that situation.

- **Conclude the meeting.**

Always end the meeting with words of encouragement. Let the student know that you are confident that he can be successful. Be sure to reinforce him for participating in the meeting.

 Give the student regular, ongoing feedback about his behavior.

It is important to meet with the student periodically to discuss his progress. In most cases, three to five minutes once per week should suffice. Review any information that has been collected (i.e., your anecdotal notes) and discuss whether or not the situation is getting better. As much as possible, focus on the student's improvements, however, also address any new or continuing problems. As the situation improves, the meetings can be faded to once every other week and then to once per month.

 Evaluate the situation (and the plan).

Implement any plan for at least two weeks before deciding whether to change plans; to continue, modify, or fade the plan you are using; or to cease the intervention. Generally, if the student's behavior is clearly improving (based on the objective information that's been collected and/or the subjective perceptions of yourself, the student, and possibly the parent[s]), stick with what you are doing. If the situation has remained the same or worsened, some kind of change will be necessary. Always discuss any changes to the plan with the student first.

B LURTING OUT/NOT RAISING HAND

DESCRIPTION

There are students in your class who don't follow designated classroom communication procedures (i.e., they
tend to blurt out answers to questions and/or requests for
assistance, rather than raising their hands and waiting to
be called on).

GOAL

The students will learn and consistently use the communication procedures that have been designated for various classroom activities.

OVERVIEW OF PLANS

- PLAN A: For a situation in which the problem is relatively mild or has just begun.

- PLAN B: For a situation in which the students are not
  clear about classroom communication procedures
  (e.g., when to raise their hands, when to wait, and when
  to speak without waiting).

- PLAN C: For a situation in which the students do not
  realize how frequently they fail to follow classroom
  communication procedures.

- PLAN D: For a situation in which the students lack the
  motivation to follow designated classroom communication procedures.

- PLAN E: For a situation in which the problem occurs/
  continues to occur with only one or two students.

Alternative Problems

- **Disruptive
  Behavior—Moderate**

- **Questions, Excessive**

- **Talking/Excessive
  Noise in Class**

· · · · · · · ·
General Considerations

Sometimes this type of problem occurs when students are excited about a lesson. Although you may be hesitant about intervening (after all, who wants to squelch enthusiastic responses), if the behavior is resulting in reduced opportunities for some students to participate (i.e., some students blurt out responses before others even have a chance to think), then it is probably necessary to take action. The focus of any intervention to deal with this problem should be to channel the enthusiasm in a way that permits equal opportunities for all students to participate.

· · · · · · · ·
Model Plans

PLAN A

If the problem has just begun and/or occurs infrequently, it may not be necessary, or even beneficial, to use an involved plan. The following actions, along with making the students aware of your concerns, may be sufficient to resolve the situation.

 1. *Respond consistently to all instances of students not following classroom communication procedures.*

a. Whenever one or more students have raised their hands, ignore any blurting out and call on a student with his/her hand up. Do this even if the correct answer has already been blurted out. "Rachael, you have your hand up. What is your answer?"

b. If necessary (e.g., a student is being especially insistent), gently correct individual students when they blurt out without raising their hands. Calmly provide information about what the student needs to be doing. "Sara, you need to quietly raise your hand and wait to be called on. Then we can listen to your idea." Wait for the corrected student to raise her hand, then call on her. Avoid being emotional and talking too much when giving the correction—you want the students to gain more attention from you and from each other when they raise their hands than when they blurt out.

2. *Use reinforcement to encourage appropriate behavior.*

a. During teacher directed instruction, praise students who raise their hands and wait to be called on. "I can see that Allison, Javar, Layne, and Michael have their hands up and have an idea for our list. Thanks. Javar, let's hear your idea first. The rest keep your hands in the air and I will get to you."

When you cannot call on all the students, acknowledge that even though they were not called on, those students were doing the correct thing. "All of you with your hands up quietly, thanks for letting me know in such a helpful way that you would be willing to volunteer to take this note to the office. Shizuko, thanks for volunteering. The rest of you may put your hands down."

b. During student directed activities, seatwork, labs, and so on, praise students who request assistance in appropriate ways, and let the students know that you will get to them quickly. "Joey, thanks for signaling that you want me to come over. I am helping Leslie first and then I will get right over to you."

c. Occasionally praise the entire class and explain why this behavior is important. "Everyone in the room has been remembering to raise their hands during our discussion. That is very respectful of your classmates because everyone has a chance to think about what they might want to contribute to our discussion."

PLAN B

Students may be blurting out answers and/or questions because the expectations for how to communicate appropriately are not clear to them. If your students are inconsistent about following classroom routines, it may be useful to clarify (and/or re-teach) those routines.

 1. Develop classroom communication procedures for the various classroom activities.

(NOTE: If you already have such procedures in place already, review and clarify them for yourself.)

Think about precisely what your expectations are for communication in the classroom. Use these expectations to specify communication procedures for all the different activities. The following examples review communication considerations for three typical classroom activities. You may prefer/need different procedures and/or have other activities that require clarification. The important point is to have in place consistent and clear procedures for each main type of classroom activity:

- **Teacher Direct Instruction/Class Discussion**

When determining communication procedures for responding to teacher questions, it is important to remember that different response forms are appropriate depending upon how a question is structured. You need to ask each classroom question in such a way that the students know the type of response you expect. The more clear and consistent you are, the less students will tend to blurt out when they should not. If frequent blurting out continues, strive for greater clarity:

– When asking higher order types of questions (e.g., analysis, synthesis, evaluation, etc.):

1. Ask the question and indicate that you want the students to delay answering;

2. Provide enough thinking time for every student in the class to formulate a response to the question; and

3. Assign the question to an individual student—do not have the students raise their hands.

"I am going to ask a question. Do not raise your hands and do not shout out your answer. Get your answer ready in your head and wait to be called on. Okay, here's the question: 'Identify one of the contributing causes of the Civil War.' Everyone get your answer ready. I can see that Jolene is really

thinking. Thomas is looking through yesterday's notes—that is an excellent strategy. Ahmud, what is your answer?"

– When asking lower order questions (e.g., reading vocabulary words, reviewing basic facts, group practice on math problems, etc.):

1. Ask the question of the entire class; and

2. Signal for a group response much like a symphony conductor.

"I am pointing to a continent. Everyone, tell me which continent. Get ready." (Signal by touching the continent.)

– When asking for volunteers to answer a question:

1. Ask any students who have an answer to quietly raise their hands and wait for you to call on someone; and

2. Choose a student who is waiting patiently with his/her hand raised.

"Quietly raise your hand when you have an idea we could add to this list."

- **Independent Seatwork Activities**

First, decide whether the students will be allowed to ask questions of their neighbor(s). There is no right or wrong standard for this— what is important is that you decide and be consistent. If you do not mind students talking to each other, you might teach them to ask their neighbor their questions first, and then ask you only if they are still stuck. If you prefer that students not talk during independent work periods, you must let them know that they have to direct all their questions to you.

Next, clarify how a student should let you know that he/she needs your assistance. Hand raising tends to be very inefficient for independent work periods since it might take you a long time to get to the student (and he/she might be off task while waiting for your help).

Having the students use some other kind of signal is probably a better idea. For example, middle/junior high school students might be taught to stand a book upright on their desks. For elementary level students, you might tape little "flags" to the front edge of their desks and teach them to flip the flag up when they need your assistance. Whatever signal you choose, you also need to teach the students that after signaling for assistance, they should mark the problem or question and continue working on the remainder of the task.

- **Lab Activities, Learning Center Projects, Cooperative Groups, Etc.**

When there is a lot of activity and movement occurring it is easy to overlook hands raised, flags, or other signals. During these types of activities, the students might indicate their need for assistance by writing their names on the chalkboard. Section off part of the chalkboard and use a heading such as "Next in Line for Teacher Time." When there are already names on the chalkboard, a student writes his/her name below the last name listed. As you move about the room, periodically look at the list and go to the next student listed. In this way, you are always helping the student who has been waiting the longest.

Again, the students should be taught to stay on task while they are waiting for assistance. Once a student has been helped, he/she should go to the chalkboard and draw a line through his/her name.

2. *Conduct mini-lessons to teach these procedures to the students.*

For a few days, immediately prior to each particular activity, teach (review) the communication expectations for that particular activity. Recognize that even procedures such as those described here can be relatively complicated for many students. To verify that the students understand the expectations, question individual students about the procedures. "Class, before you get started, let's review what you will do if you need my help in the next 20 minutes. Vera, what would you do if you need my attention while you are working on your map?" Continue these lessons daily until the students are consistently using the communication procedures correctly.

3. *Respond consistently to each instance of a student not following the designated classroom communication procedures.*

Whenever a student blurts out a question or an answer, ignore the behavior or gently correct the student as appropriate (see PLAN A).

4. *Use reinforcement to encourage appropriate behavior.*

a. Praise individual students for using the designated communication procedures (see PLAN A).

b. Praise the class as a whole after activities in which all the students used appropriate communication procedures. Let the students know how following the procedures helped make the activity a better learning experience. "Everyone remembered to put their name on the chalkboard when they wanted help. This is so much more pleasant and efficient than having some people raise their hands and other people shouting my name. Besides, it is much more fair, because I get to you in the order you need the help."

PLAN C

Sometimes students do not seem to realize when and/or just how often they fail to follow the classroom communication procedures. In this case, the intervention should include some way of helping the students become more aware of their own behavior.

1. *Develop (or clarify) communication procedures for the various classroom activities (see PLAN B).*

2. *Publicly monitor the number of "communication errors" made by the class.*

a. Create space on the chalkboard or a large chart, on which to record the number of "Communication Errors" that take place each day. Keep a frequency count of the communication errors— your goal is to obtain a class-wide total, so it is not important to track which individuals are making the errors (at least at this point).

b. At the end of each day, determine the total number of times that a communication error occurred and have a student fill in the appropriate space on the chart. Have a short meeting (three to five minutes) to talk about how the day went. If the number of communication errors is lower than on previous days, praise the class. If there were more communication errors than before, discuss the types of errors that occurred and have the class identify strategies for reducing the number the next day. Prompt them to be specific about what they might do to help each other remember to follow the communication procedures.

3. *Respond consistently when the students do not follow the classroom communication procedures.*

a. Whenever an individual student blurts out (or otherwise violates a communication procedure), ignore or gently correct the behavior, as appropriate (see PLAN A).

b. Make sure the incident is recorded (see Step 2).

4. *Use reinforcement to encourage appropriate behavior.*

a. Praise individual students who follow appropriate communication procedures (see PLAN A).

b. You may also wish to use intermittent rewards to acknowledge the class' success. Occasional, and unexpected, rewards can motivate the class to demonstrate responsible behavior more often. The idea is to provide a reward when the entire class has been particularly good at following our the communication expectations (i.e., the chart shows a significant reduction in errors). "Class, everyone has been doing such a nice job of following our procedures for raising hands/using flags/putting names on the chalkboard, let's have our health lesson outside on the lawn."

A list of additional class-wide reinforcement ideas can be found in APPENDIX 1. If you do use intermittent rewards, do so more frequently at the beginning of an intervention, and less often as the students' behavior improves.

PLAN D

If you are fairly certain that your students know the appropriate communication procedures, but choose not to follow them, you may need to implement a structured system of external incentives (i.e., rewards and consequences) to motivate the students to change their behavior.

1. *Develop (or clarify) communication procedures for the various classroom activities (see PLAN B).*

2. *Publicly monitor the number of "communication errors" made by the class (see PLAN C).*

3. *Use reinforcement to encourage the students to use the designated communication procedures.*

a. Praise individual students who follow the designated communication procedures (see PLAN A).

b. Establish a team competition using a response cost lottery as follows:.

- Divide the class into teams of four to six students (each with an equitable number of students who do and do not have problems with blurting out). Seat each team together (at the same table or with their desks in clusters) and have each team give itself a name.

- Have the students brainstorm reinforcers that they might like their teams to earn. Possibilities include each team member earning a free

homework pass or a ticket for a free ice cream in the cafeteria, or going to lunch a few minutes earlier than the rest of the class.

List at least six or seven different ideas and rank them in terms of value. Then write the different reinforcers on pieces of paper and put them in a grab bag or box. The most valuable items should be written on only one piece of paper, moderate reinforcers on two or three slips of paper, and the least valuable reinforcers on several (e.g., ten) pieces of paper. This procedure stacks the odds in favor of the smaller rewards.

After a couple of weeks, if the system has been successful, you will want to begin putting in an increasing number of slips that read, "You did great! But no prize today." This way you can fade the system, but the students still have a chance of earning the big prize.

- Give each team a certain number of blank tickets at the beginning of each day. Base the number of tickets on the formula of the average number of daily class communication errors divided by the number of teams, plus one.

Thus, if there are five teams and the class has typically averaged 30 blurting out incidents per day, each team would begin each day with seven tickets.

- Whenever an individual student makes a communication error, that student's team loses one ticket. At the end of the day, each team writes their team name on any of their remaining tickets and those tickets are placed in a bowl for a drawing. The team whose name is on the ticket drawn is that day's winner. Then, that team gets to draw a slip from the grab bag to see what reward they have won.

4. *Respond consistently when the students do not follow classroom communication procedures.*

a. Whenever an individual student blurts out (or otherwise violates a communication procedure), ignore or gently correct the behavior, as appropriate (see PLAN A).

b. Alternately, if the reinforcement system does not seem to be as effective as you would like, you can implement an additional consequence (e.g., time owed) for each communication infraction. Thus when a student blurts out, not only does his/her team lose a ticket, but that individual owes one minute off of recess or after school for each infraction, for example. Do not have the whole team owe time—losing the ticket is consequence enough.

PLAN E

Sometimes this behavior is/continues to be a problem for only one or two students. In this case, the intervention should focus specifically on those students, not the entire class.

1. *Develop (or clarify) communication procedures for the various classroom activities (see PLAN B).*

2. *Establish a structured system for reinforcing the appropriate behavior and providing a consequence for the inappropriate behavior.*

a. With the student(s), create a list of reinforcers that can be earned. Although you might want to have some suggestions in mind, the system will be more effective if the student(s) identify most of the items or activities themselves. *(NOTE: A list of reinforcement ideas can be found in APPENDIX 1.)*

b. Assign "prices" (in points) for each of the rewards on the list and have the student(s) pick the reward they would like to earn first.

The prices should be based on the instructional, personnel, and/or monetary costs of the items. Monetary cost is clear—the more expensive the item, the more points required to earn it. Instructional cost refers to the amount of instructional time lost or interfered with by a particular reward. Thus, an activity which causes the student(s) to miss part of academic instruction should require more points than one the student(s) can do on their own recess time. Personnel cost involves the time required by you and/or other staff to fulfill the reinforcer. Spend-

ing time with a favorite teacher, therefore, would cost more points than spending five minutes of free time on the computer.

c. Establish a system to monitor and record the number of times each day the student(s) blurt out. Have the student(s) each keep a card on his/her desk. Each time the student(s) blurt(s) out, instruct them to mark the card. If the student(s) would be unable or unwilling to keep an accurate record, keep the tally yourself. At the end of the day, record the total on a chart.

Make sure the student(s) know that the goal is for this number to go down. Each week, set a target number that the student(s) will try not to exceed. This number should be a slight reduction (approximately 10%) from the previous week's average.

d. Each day that the student(s) meet the goal, they earn a certain number of points (i.e., the daily goal for that day minus the number of infractions). For example, if a student's goal is to have less than 12 infractions and she had only seven, she would earn five points for that day. If she had no infractions, she would earn 12 points.

e. When the student(s) have accumulated enough points to earn the rewards they have chosen, they "spend" the points necessary and the system begins again. That is, they select another reward to earn and begin with zero points.

If the student(s) are immature, and need more frequent encouragement, you might consider letting them earn several "less expensive" rewards (e.g., five minutes of playing the piano after 20 points) on the way to a bigger reward (e.g., having their pictures posted in a prominent place for 200 points). That is, the student(s) receive the small rewards without spending points; they continue to accumulate toward the selected reward.

f. Implement a consequence (e.g., one minute of time owed) for each infraction that exceeds the daily goal. For example, if a student's goal is no more than 12 infractions, and she blurts out 15 times, she would earn no points and would owe three minutes of time off recess or after school.

3. *Use reinforcement to encourage appropriate behavior.*

a. Give the student(s) increased praise and attention for following appropriate communication procedures (see PLAN A).

b. In addition, show interest and enthusiasm about how the student(s) are doing on the system. For example, you could tell a student, "Patty, you have done a great job today. Look at your chart. The goal is 12 and you only had two incidents. You should be very proud of how well you did today."

· · · · · · · ·
Suggested Steps for Developing and Implementing a Plan

The following steps are designed to help you develop an appropriate intervention plan and implement it effectively, whether you choose to use one of the MODEL PLANS or create a customized plan of your own. The steps are, however, suggestions—they are not intended to be followed rigidly or in any particular order. Use your professional judgment and the knowledge of your particular situation to make them work for you.

 1. *Make sure you have enough information about the situation.*

(NOTE: Documentation of the problem is probably not necessary if the problem is relatively mild [i.e., if PLAN A is appropriate].)

a. You want to be able to explain what you mean when you say that "the class has a problem with not following classroom communication procedures/blurting out." Anecdotal notes from actual incidents can help you define the problem behavior thoroughly. Simply keep a card in your pocket or on a clipboard and occasionally, whenever a student fails to follow a designated communication procedure, make a note. For each entry, briefly describe the circumstances—where and when it occurred, what was said and/or done, and any other relevant observations (e.g., how it affected the other students). You do not need to make note of every time a student blurts out; the idea is to capture a range of examples so that you will be able to describe the behavior clearly and completely.

Also include notes on times when the students do follow classroom communication procedures. This way, the students will realize that you are not only aware of their inappropriate behavior, but also notice their appropriate behavior. The positive examples will also help you clarify how it is you want the students to behave.

b. It may also be useful to document how often the blurting out occurs (i.e., a frequency count). This will provide both a more objective measure of the problem and an objective way to monitor progress. You can use the same card on which you are collecting anecdotal notes to keep a frequency count—just write a tally mark on the card each time a student blurts out.

You might want to code the tallies to discern whether the behavior occurs more often during certain times, subjects, or activities. Use an "A" or "P" to indicate that the incident happened in the morning or afternoon, or cluster the tallies by subject, teacher directed instruction or independent work, etc.

c. If a student notices what you are doing and asks about it, be straightforward—say that you are collecting information to see whether the students' failure to use designated communication procedures is a problem that the class needs to work on.

Following is an example of frequency information collected on classroom communication errors.

Frequency of Blurting Out—11/27

Teacher Directed Instruction

JHT JHT JHT JHT III

Cooperative Groups/Labs

II JHT III

Independent Seatwork

I

---

d. The frequency information is fairly easy to summarize on a chart or graph. Seeing how often the behavior occurs may help the students better understand your concern.

e. Continuing to collect this type of information (and keeping the chart up-to-date) while you implement a plan will also help you monitor whether the situation is getting worse, staying the same, or getting better.

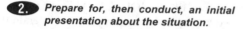

2. *Prepare for, then conduct, an initial presentation about the situation.*

a. Depending upon your personal philosophy, and whether or not you think a basic intervention like PLAN A is appropriate, you may simply choose to have an informal discussion with the students.

b. When you intend to use one of the other MODEL PLANS, you might want to schedule a class meeting. Wait for a time when you are calm (i.e., not right after an incident has occurred) and inform the students that you are finding their failure to follow classroom communication procedures/blurting out to be a problem. Explain that when students blurt out answers and/or questions instead of following the designated classroom communication procedures, it makes the classroom atmosphere more chaotic and is often unfair to other students.

Then specifically define your expectations regarding classroom communication procedures for various activities that will be implemented. Give the students the opportunity to ask questions/make comments, and end the session by thanking the students for listening and letting them know that you are confident they will make an effort to follow appropriate procedures.

c. If you want the students to assume some ownership of the problem, you might want to hold a class meeting in which the students participate in analyzing the situation and developing an action plan. In this case, before the meeting you will need to have clarified the nature/extent of the problem and your expectations for the students' behavior. You will also need to identify any aspects of the problem/plan that you do not feel comfortable opening up to a group decision.

For example, you must decide ahead of time whether or not to give the class the opportunity to determine if there will be a consequence for blurting out and/or what the consequence should be. If you firmly believe that there must be a consequence, then you should not seek student input on that particular issue.

d. Schedule the meeting for a neutral time and allow enough time for a reasonable discussion. Inform the students in advance that the meeting will take place; this will give them time to think about the problem. "Class, this afternoon we are going to have a class meeting on the problem of not following classroom communication procedures. Please give some thought to this problem and what we might do as a class to solve it."

e. Use an agenda to structure the meeting. Shortly before the meeting, write the agenda on the chalkboard. Following is a sample agenda that may be modified for your use.

Agenda

1. Not following classroom communication procedures—Define how much blurting out is occurring (share data).

2. Review the communication expectations for the various classroom activities.

3. Brainstorm ideas for improving the situation.

4. Select strategies that everyone agrees to.

5. Establish what teacher will do if a student does blurt out.

---

f. It is important to establish beforehand clear rules (for both you and the students) regarding the brainstorming phase of the meeting. For example:

• Any idea is okay (but no obscenity).

• Ideas will not be evaluated initially (i.e., no approval—"Good idea" or disapproval—"What a stupid idea" or "We couldn't do that" should be expressed during brainstorming).

- All ideas will be written down and discussed at the conclusion of brainstorming.

g. At the conclusion of brainstorming, evaluate the ideas, and lead the class to consensus on any decisions that need to be made. Use voting as a decision-making process when appropriate.

3. Determine when and how to include the parent(s).

a. Because blurting out is more of a procedural than behavioral or motivational problem, involving the students' parents is not critical if the situation is class-wide.

b. If the situation involves one or two students who have or continue to have a problem with blurting out, you should contact the parent(s) of those individuals. Let the parent(s) know that their child is not following the designated classroom communication procedures and what steps you are taking to correct the situation.

Frequent contact is not required, but whenever you intend to implement an individualized plan, the parent(s) should be informed prior to its implementation and should be given feedback about the student's progress every two to four weeks.

4. Give the class regular, ongoing feedback about their behavior.

Periodically meet with the class to discuss the situation. In most cases, three to five minutes once per week should suffice. *(NOTE: PLANS C, D, and E suggest daily meetings to record the data or to determine points.)* During the meetings, review any information that has been collected and discuss whether or not things are getting better. As much as possible, focus on improvements, however, also address any new or continuing problems. As the situation improves, the meetings can be faded to once every other week and then to once per month.

5. Evaluate the situation (and the plan).

Any plan should be implemented for at least two weeks before deciding whether or not it is effective. Generally, if the situation has improved (based on the objective information that's been collected and/or the subjective perceptions of yourself and the students), continue with what you have been doing. (Eventually you will want to fade, then eliminate, the plan.) If the problem remains the same or worsens, some kind of change (i.e., modifying the current plan or switching to another plan) will be necessary. Always discuss any change in the intervention with the class first.

B ORED BEHAVIOR

Apathy

DESCRIPTION

You have a student who acts bored and expresses an "I don't care" or "this is so stupid" attitude.

GOAL

The student will show increased interest, motivation, and excitement toward school and classroom activities.

OVERVIEW OF PLANS

- PLAN A: For a situation in which the problem is relatively mild or has just begun.

- PLAN B: For a student who may have learned that acting bored is an effective way to gain adult attention.

- PLAN C: For a student whose bored behavior may be a result of a lack of self-confidence.

- PLAN D: For a student who is unaware of when and/or how often he acts bored.

- PLAN E: For a student who lacks the motivation to act more interested or enthusiastic.

Alternative Problems

- **Apathetic Behavior**
- **Complaining**
- **Passive Resistance**
- **Self-Concept Problems**

· · · · · · · ·
General Considerations

- If the student's problem behavior stems in any way from academic issues (e.g., the student acts like things are too boring to bother with in order to cover up the fact that he is unable to do the work), concurrent efforts must be made to ensure his academic success (see **Academic Deficits, Determining**).

- If the student lacks the basic social skills to interact with his peers appropriately, it may be necessary to begin by teaching him these skills. **Social Skills, Lack of** contains information on a variety of published social skills curricula.

- If you suspect that the student's bored behavior could be related to the student being depressed, see **Depression**. This problem includes a set of questions to help you decide whether the student should be referred for counseling or psychological services.

- If the inappropriate behavior is resulting in the student avoiding or not completing his schoolwork, begin with a plan to increase the student's work completion (see **Work Completion—Daily Work**). Once the student is turning in completed work on a regular basis, you can consider an intervention for the bored behavior, if the problem still exists.

· · · · · · · ·
Model Plans

P L A N   A

It is not always necessary, or even beneficial, to use an involved plan. If the inappropriate behavior has just begun and/or is relatively mild (i.e., not interfering with the student's academic or social progress), the following actions, along with making the student aware of your concerns, may resolve the situation.

1. *Respond consistently to the inappropriate behavior.*

a. During your initial meeting with the student (see SUGGESTED STEPS FOR DEVELOPING AND IMPLEMENTING A PLAN) establish a nonembarrassing signal that you can use to cue him that he is "acting bored." You want the signal to be fairly subtle so that only the student will recognize and understand it, in order to minimize the chance that he will be teased by his peers. Possibilities include waving your hand, rubbing your neck, or even just direct eye contact and a head nod. Let the student know that you may also need to quietly say his name to gain his attention before you give the signal.

You should be prepared to use the signal frequently and for a fairly long time, since it is likely that the bored behavior is, at least in part, an unconscious habit for the student.

b. Whenever the student is acting bored, give the signal. If the student does not cease acting bored and other students are around, ignore the behavior. (However, make note of the incident so the information can be used in a follow-up

discussions with the student.) If you are interacting directly with the student and no other students are around, give the student feedback. "Alan, that tone of voice is an example of what we have been talking about. Can you say that again in a slightly more enthusiastic way?"

2. *Use reinforcement to encourage appropriate behavior.*

a. Give the student increased praise and attention. Be especially alert for situations in which the student shows interest or enthusiasm, and praise him for these demonstrations. If public praise would be embarrassing, praise the student privately, or even give the student a note. Remember that any time the student shows interest in something or acts in an enthusiastic manner, you can praise him. "Alan, I noticed that during your work with the group you let others know that you thought they came up with some good ideas. That is one excellent way to show interest and enthusiasm."

You can also praise the student for demonstrating a neutral response, or even a negative response handled in a tactful manner. "Alan, I noticed that when Ben suggested developing a mural as your groups' project, you did not act like it was a stupid or boring idea, but you did state that you disagreed with him. You handled that in a very mature way. You did not show enthusiasm—and you shouldn't when you are not in favor of something—but you did not imply that Ben's idea was stupid or boring."

b. Praise the student privately for responding to the signal. "Alan, twice this morning I gave you the signal that you were beginning to act bored and both times you stopped acting that way."

c. Give the student frequent attention (e.g., talk to him on the playground) and praise him for other positive behaviors he exhibits. For example, you might comment about the accuracy of his work or how consistent he is in completing his assigned work. This demonstrates to the student that you notice many positive things he does, not just the fact that he is refraining from acting bored.

P L A N   B

Some students are very skilled at gaining attention through their negative behavior. If you find yourself frequently nagging, reminding, or coaxing the student to cease acting bored, it is possible he is trying to gain adult attention. Whether or not the student overtly seems to like the attention, you should make sure that he gets more frequent and more satisfying attention when he behaves appropriately than when he is acting bored.

1. Respond consistently when the student acts bored.

Because it is important for the student to learn that he will not be able to prompt people to nag and pay attention to him by acting bored, you need to ignore the bored behavior. While ignoring the behavior, do not look at the student or talk to him. Do not act disgusted or impatient with his behavior. Simply interact in positive ways with students who are behaving appropriately and meeting classroom expectations. As soon as the target student is no longer acting bored, pay attention to him, but make no reference to his inappropriate behavior.

2. Use reinforcement to encourage appropriate behavior.

a. Frequent praise and attention is the core of this plan. The student must see that he receives more frequent and more satisfying attention when he behaves appropriately than when he acts bored. Thus, whenever the student is not acting bored (or otherwise misbehaving), make an effort to praise and spend time with him. "Alan, you have been so enthusiastic about the books you have read, would you help me develop a list of books that my own son might enjoy reading?"

b. You may also wish to use intermittent rewards to acknowledge the student's success. Occasional, and unexpected, rewards can motivate the student to demonstrate responsible behavior more often. The idea is to provide a reward when the student has had a particularly good period of showing interest or enthusiasm.

For this particular situation, appropriate rewards might include giving the student a responsibility, allowing the student to conduct a presentation to the class on a topic of interest to him, or allowing the student to show the principal an assignment or project he is especially proud of.

A list of additional reinforcement ideas can be found in APPENDIX 1. Use intermittent rewards more frequently at the beginning of the intervention to encourage the student, and then less often as the student's behavior improves.

3. Ensure a 3-1 ratio of positive to negative attention.

a. Given that attention is a motivating force for this student, you want to be sure that you are giving the student *three times as much* positive as negative attention. One way to do this is to monitor your interactions with the student at least one day per week. Keep a card on a clipboard or in your pocket and record each interaction you have with the student as either positive or negative by marking a "+" or a "-", respectively, on the card.

To determine whether an interaction is positive or negative, ask yourself whether the student was acting bored (or otherwise misbehaving) at the time the interaction occurred. Any interaction that stems from inappropriate behavior is negative, while all interactions that occur while the student is meeting classroom expectations are positive. Thus, any attention given to the student while he is acting bored is negative, but praising the student for showing interest in something is positive. Saying "good-bye" to the student as he leaves the room or asking him if he has any questions during independent work are also considered positive interactions. *(NOTE: Ignoring the student's bored behavior is not recorded at all, because it is not an interaction.)*

b. If you find that you are not giving the student three times as much positive as negative attention, try to increase the number of positive interactions you have with the student. Sometimes

prompts can help. For example, you might decide that each time the student enters the classroom you will say "hello" to him, that whenever a visitor enters the classroom you will find a time to praise the student, or that whenever you switch classroom activities you will check the target student and, as soon as possible, praise some aspect of his behavior. You can also increase the ratio of positive to negative attention by ignoring more of the student's bored behavior.

P L A N   C

Some students act bored because they lack self-confidence, and the bored demeanor is a strategy for looking "cool." If your student seems insecure or defensive (i.e., the bored behavior is masking his insecurity), the intervention must help the student become more self-confident.

1. *Respond consistently to the student's bored behavior by using a signal to cue the student (see PLAN A).*

2. *Provide frequent praise and attention when the student is showing interest or enthusiasm (see PLAN A).*

In addition to frequently praising the student, provide lots of noncontingent attention. Call on the student frequently in class, ask him what he plans to do over the weekend, etc. Demonstrate to the student that he has value, regardless of what he does. Interact with him as frequently as possible.

3. *Identify a student interest or strength on which to focus.*

The idea is that if you can capitalize on the student's strengths or interests, he may be more likely to show a spark of enthusiasm and, as a result, you will have more opportunities to give him positive feedback. For example, if the student is good at sports, he could demonstrate to the class some aspect of fitness. Or, if he likes antique cars, perhaps he could do a research project on them which you could then discuss. "Alan, it does my old teacher's heart good to see you enjoying doing a report. What have you learned that you have found the most interesting?"

4. *Give the student a responsibility.*

One of the best ways to help a student improve his self-concept is to have him do an important job around the school or in the classroom. If possible, find a job that the student will be expected to perform on a regular basis—not a one-time event. Examples include helping in the office, being a messenger, helping the teacher with attendance, or helping the principal sort his/her mail. If the student is a good reader, he can be assigned to tutor a less able, younger student. *(NOTE: A list of additional ideas for jobs/responsibilities can be found in APPENDIX 2.)*

5. *Have the student set goals.*

Be direct with the student about improving the amount of enthusiasm he exhibits throughout the day. Goal setting is one way to make your expectations for the student's behavior very clear and overt. Determine a goal for the student's behavior, either by yourself or with the student. Generally, when the student is involved in the process he will be more likely to strive to achieve the goal. In either case, you want to identify both a broad-based goal and at least three specific things the student can do to achieve that goal. Following is a sample goal-setting form that could be developed jointly by you and the student.

Goal-Setting Form

I, ___Alan___ , am willing to work on the goal of ___acting bored less frequently and occasionally showing interest or enthusiasm___ . I can show I am working on this goal by:

1. Not rolling my eyes and saying, "This is really boring" when the teacher or a student suggests an activity.

2. Stating my own opinions in ways that do not put other people's ideas down as being stupid or boring.

3. Sometimes showing enthusiasm by saying things like, "Good idea," "I would like to do that," or "Sure, that sounds fun."

I, ___Mr. Harlan___ , will support ___Alan___ 's goal by ___giving him the signal when he acts bored, giving him a note about times he shows enthusiasm, and by meeting with him once per week to discuss progress___ .

_____   _____
Student Signature   Teacher Signature

PLAN D

Some students do not seem to know when they are behaving inappropriately. If your student doesn't realize when and/or how frequently he acts bored, the intervention must include some way of helping the student become more aware of his own behavior.

1. Respond consistently to the inappropriate behavior.

a. When the student is acting bored, give him the signal then gently correct or ignore the behavior, as appropriate (see PLAN A).

b. In addition, whenever you give the signal make sure the incident is recorded by either the student or yourself (see Step 2).

c. Alternately, use humor to cue student when he acts bored. If the student seems unaware of how frequently or intensely he expresses boredom and you think he is relatively secure, you may occasionally wish to use a gentle, supportive joke in place of the signal. For example, after asking him to do something, but before he says anything, you could give a gentle imitation of what he is likely to say. "Wait. Don't tell me. 'This is soooooooo boring.' Am I right? Didn't know I could predict the future, did you?"

You need to be careful about using this procedure, though. This suggestion can be easily misused and abused—you think you are being funny, but the student feels ridiculed. If you do use humor, check to see if the student minds.

"Alan, for a couple of days, I have done some teasing about your 'boring' line. Would you prefer that I didn't do that?" Even if the student says he does not mind, do not overuse the procedure—remember that humor used poorly or too often can be destructive and cruel. _Do not_ use humor if the student suffers from a poor self-concept.

2. Implement a system for monitoring the frequency of the student's bored behavior.

a. Determine who will do the recording. Since the point is for the student to become more aware of his own behavior, having him do the recording (i.e., self-monitoring) will be more effective than if you record the behavior. However, if the student cannot or will not be accurate (or if he would be embarrassed to self-monitor) you should do the recording. Remember that the idea is for the student to be aware of each time he acts bored, and for him to know that each incident is being recorded. _(NOTE: Even when the student self-monitors, you should keep your own record approximately one day per week to verify the student's accuracy.)_

b. If the student is self-monitoring his own behavior, you can have him keep a form like the one shown below on his desk or in his notebook. Tell the student that each time he sees you give the signal, he should circle the next number on the form.

> Each time you act or sound bored, circle the next number.
>
> Date _____
>
> 1   2   3   4   5   6   7   8   9   10   11   12
> 13 14 15 16 17 18 19 20 21 22 23 24

(NOTE: Repeat this form four more times so it can be used for a week.)

c. Each day, meet with the student for a few minutes to review that day's record. Have the student chart the information on a graph (or do it yourself), and talk with him about whether the day was better, worse, or about the same as previous days.

If the day did not go well, encourage the student to talk about why and have him identify things he can do the next day to help himself remember to show interest rather than acting bored. If the student acts inappropriately during the meeting, keep the interaction very short. Just let the student know that you are sure tomorrow will be a better day.

 Use reinforcement to encourage appropriate behavior.

a. Give the student increased praise and attention for showing enthusiasm (see PLAN A).

b. In addition, praise the student during the self-monitoring review meetings for accurate recording (if applicable), and for being willing to look at his cumulative record for the day. Even on a bad day, if the student is willing to chart the data and discuss why it was a bad day, praise him. "Alan, you are really handling this responsibly. Even though it was a rough day, you are willing to talk to me about things you might do differently tomorrow. That is a real sign that you are growing up." Regardless of how the day went, try to make the end-of-the-day meeting upbeat and encouraging—you want the student to look forward to the review at the end-of-the-day.

4. **Encourage the student to use self-reinforcement.**

Whenever things are going well (i.e., less bored behavior than usual), prompt the student to mentally reinforce himself. "Alan, this has been a very successful morning. Silently tell yourself that you are really good at showing interest and enthusiasm." Prompt the student in this manner intermittently throughout the day and during the end-of-the-day meeting.

5. **(OPTIONAL)**
Identify peer models for the student to observe.

If you think the student may not know different ways to interact, you might suggest two or three other students for him to observe. "Alan, you might consider watching how Roger and Bill respond to assignments, requests to join in, and some of the other things we have talked about. I don't expect you to try to be like them—you're terrific just the way you are—but watching them may give you some ideas of how to be enthusiastic without overdoing it. You know, I do the same thing. For example, I just learned some new teaching ideas when I observed Mr. Carmody yesterday."

This procedure must be handled with sensitivity to avoid hurting the student's feelings or implying that he should be more like someone else.

PLAN E

Whenever a student's problem behavior has become habitual and/or he does not seem to have a desire to reduce it, you may need to implement a structured system of external incentives (i.e., rewards and consequences) based on his behavior to motivate him to stop acting bored and to start showing more enthusiasm.

1. **Use a signal to cue the student when he is acting bored (see PLAN A).**

2. **Implement a system for monitoring the frequency of the student's bored behavior (see PLAN D).**

Establish a structured system for reinforcing the student's appropriate behavior and providing a consequence for his inappropriate behavior.

a. With the student, create a list of reinforcers that he can earn. Although you might want to have some suggestions in mind, the system will be more effective if the student identifies most of the items or activities himself. *(NOTE: A list of reinforcement ideas can be found in APPENDIX 1.)*

b. Assign "prices" (in points) for each of the rewards on the list and have the student choose the reward he would like to earn first.

   The prices should be based on how many points the student can earn and the instructional, personnel, and/or monetary costs of the items. Monetary cost is clear—the more expensive the item, the more points required to earn it. Instructional cost refers to the amount of instructional time lost or interfered with by a particular reward. Thus, an activity which causes the student to miss part of academic instruction should require more points than one the student can do on his own free time. Personnel cost involves the time required by you and/or other staff to fulfill the reinforcer. Having lunch with the principal, therefore, would cost more points than spending five minutes of free time with a friend.

c. Have the student begin each day with a certain number of points. This number should equal the average number of times the student acts bored per day, plus two. Thus, if he acts bored an average of ten times per day, he would begin each day with 12 points. Throughout the day, each time you have to signal the student that he is acting bored, he loses a point. The points remaining at the end of each day are then added together to be applied toward the reinforcer the student is striving to earn.

   With a primary level student, a lottery system might be more effective. With a lottery system, the student would begin each day with tickets in a jar instead of points. All the tickets would have prizes written on them—one would have a big prize, a couple would have moderate prizes, and the majority would have small prizes. Each

time you would have to use the signal, you would remove one ticket from the jar—but neither you nor the student would be allowed to see what is written on it. At the end of each day, the student would draw one ticket from those remaining in the jar, and receive that prize.

d. When the student has accumulated enough points to earn the reward he has chosen, he "spends" the points necessary and the system begins again. That is, he selects another reward to earn and begins again with zero points.

   If the student is immature, and needs more frequent encouragement, you might consider letting him earn several "less expensive" rewards (e.g., being first in line for the day after 20 points) on the way to a bigger reward (e.g., earning extra recess time for the whole class for 200 points). That is, the student receives the small rewards without spending his points; they continue to accumulate toward the selected reward.

e. You will also need to determine a consequence (e.g., time owed from recess or in detention) for each incident of acting bored that occurs after the student has already lost his points (or tickets) for the day. If the student runs out of points (or tickets), implement the consequence for each subsequent incident of acting bored. The consequence should not involve taking away a previous day's points, because if the student can lose already-earned points, he might develop an attitude of, "I am losing so many points, why should I even bother to try?"

 Use reinforcement to encourage appropriate behavior.

a. Give the student increased praise and attention when he is showing interest or enthusiasm (see PLAN A).

b. In addition, show interest and enthusiasm yourself about how the student is doing on the system. "Alan, you have been doing a great job today. It is lunch time and you still have 12 points. This is the best day you have had yet!"

. . . .
Suggested Steps for Developing and Implementing a Plan

The following steps are designed to help you develop an appropriate intervention plan and implement it effectively, whether you choose to use one of the MODEL PLANS or create a customized plan of your own. The steps are, however, suggestions—they are not intended to be followed rigidly or in any particular order. Use your professional judgment and the knowledge of your particular situation to make them work for you.

1. **Make sure you have enough informa-tion about the situation.**

a. If you think a minimal intervention like PLAN A will be sufficient, you may already have enough information to proceed. However, when a more involved plan seems necessary, you should consider collecting additional descriptive and/or objective information for a couple of days.

b. You need to be able to explain what you mean when you say that the student "acts bored." What does the student do that has lead you to this conclusion? Is it things he says? tone of voice? body language? Anecdotal notes on ac-tual incidents should provide enough details to help you define the problem behavior clearly and completely.

To collect anecdotal notes, simply keep a card in your pocket or on a clipboard and occasion-ally make notes on specific instances when the student acted bored. For each entry, briefly describe where and when the incident occurred, what the student did or said, and any other relevant observations (e.g., what prompted the behavior). You do not need to make a note every time the student acts bored; the idea is to capture a range of examples of the behavior so that you will be able to describe it completely.

Also include some notes on times when the student acted enthusiastic—this will make it clear that you are not only aware of his problem behavior, but also recognize when he behaves appropriately. When you meet with the student, the positive examples will also help you to clarify how you want the student to behave.

c. In addition to information on what the student's inappropriate behavior looks like, it can also be useful to document how often it occurs using a frequency count. This will provide a more objec-tive measure of the problem and an objective way to monitor progress. You can use the same card on which you are making anecdotal notes to keep a frequency count—just write a tally mark on the card each time the student acts bored.

You might also want to code the tallies to dis-cern whether the behavior occurs more during certain times, subjects, or activities (e.g., using an "A" or "P" to indicate that the incident hap-pened in the morning or afternoon; or clustering the tallies by subject, teacher directed instruc-tion or independent work, etc.).

d. If the student notices what you are doing and asks about it, be straightforward—tell him that you are collecting information to see whether his bored behavior is a problem that needs to be worked on.

Following is an example of anecdotal notes and a frequency count that have been collected on the student's bored behavior.

Alan's Bored Behavior—1/19

AAAAA   AAAPP PPPP

Notes:

10:20—When I described the math homework, Alan sighed loudly, rolled his eyes, and said, "This will be a big thrill."

11:50—On the way to lunch, I asked Alan if there was anything he liked about school. He responded, "No. It's all really boring."

1:35—During cooperative group work, Alan was pulled back from his group, slouched down in his chair, sighed repeatedly, and never par-ticipated unless asked a direct question by a teammate.

---

e. Frequency is fairly easy to summarize on a chart or graph. Seeing how often he acts bored may help the student and his parent(s) better under-stand your concern.

f. Continuing to collect this type of information and keeping the chart up-to-date while you imple-ment a plan will help you monitor whether the situation is getting worse, staying the same, or getting better.

. . . .

2. *Identify a focus for the intervention and labels for referring to the appropriate and inappropriate behaviors.*

a. To be effective, the intervention must address more than just reducing the student's bored behavior—there must be a concurrent emphasis on increasing some positive behavior or trait (e.g., showing interest or enthusiasm). Having a specific positive behavior in mind will make it easier for you to "catch" and reinforce the student for acting appropriately, and the positive focus will frame the situation more productively.

For example, if you simply say that "the student has a problem with acting bored," you don't really provide any useful information, and may put the student and the parent(s) on the defensive. However, when you explain that you want to "help the student learn to show interest and enthusiasm," you are presenting an important, and reasonable, goal for the student to work toward and clearly identifying what the student needs to do to be successful.

b. Specifying labels for the appropriate and inappropriate behaviors (e.g., "showing interest or enthusiasm" and "acting bored," respectively) will help you to use consistent vocabulary when discussing the situation with the student. If you sometimes refer to the inappropriate behavior as "acting bored" and other times tell the student that he is "looking disgusted," he may not realize that you are talking about the same thing.

3. *Determine when and how to include the parent(s).*

a. It is not necessary to contact the student's parent(s) if the problem has just begun and is not interfering with the student's academic or social progress. However, it might be a good idea to take advantage of any scheduled activities (e.g., conferences, weekly notes home) to let them know of your concern.

b. The parent(s) should be contacted whenever the student's bored behavior is affecting his academic performance or is alienating him from his peers.

Share any information you have collected about the behavior (i.e., anecdotal notes, frequency count), and explain why you are concerned. Focus in particular on how the behavior is hindering the student academically and/or socially (e.g., adults and peers are interacting with him less frequently because he acts so bored with anything anyone suggests). You might want to ask if the parent(s) have any insight into the situation and/or whether they have noticed similar behavior at home.

Whether or not the parent(s) perceive a problem, explain that you want to help the student "learn to show interest and enthusiasm," and invite them to join you for an initial meeting with the student to develop a plan. If the parent(s) are unable or unwilling to participate, let them know that you will keep them informed of the student's progress.

c. Once the parent(s) have been involved in any way, you should give them updates at least once per week while the plan is being implemented.

4. *Prepare for, then conduct, an initial meeting about the situation.*

a. Arrange a meeting to discuss your concerns with the student and anyone else who will be involved (e.g., the parent[s], the school psychologist). Although the specifics will vary depending upon the age of the student and the severity of the problem, there are some general guidelines to consider when scheduling the meeting.

First, meet at a neutral time (i.e., not immediately after a problem has occurred), when emotions are less likely to hamper communication. In general, a day's notice is appropriate, however a primary age student may worry excessively and/or forget what the meeting is about if it is scheduled more than an hour before it takes place.

Second, make the meeting appropriately private. With a primary student who has a mild problem, you might meet in the classroom while the other students are working independently. However, when dealing with a middle/junior high school student and the student's parent(s), you will need some place private (e.g., the counselor's office) to ensure that the discussion will not be overheard.

Third, try to make sure that the meeting is scheduled for a time and place that it is not likely to be interrupted. Finally, if the parent(s) will be participating, they should be the ones to tell the student about the meeting.

b. Construct a preliminary plan. Decide whether you think you can use one of the MODEL PLANS or if you need to create a customized plan using components from various plans and/or of your own design. Although you will invite and encourage the student to help develop the plan during the initial meeting, having a proposed plan in mind before you meet can alleviate frustration and wasted time if the student is unwilling or unable to participate.

c. After reviewing the information you have collected and thinking about how you want the student to behave, prepare thorough descriptions of the inappropriate behavior and the positive behavior/trait on which the student will be working. The more specific you can be and the more concrete examples you have, the easier it will be to clarify (and for the student to understand) your expectations. Be sure to consider the student's behavior in all relevant activities (e.g., independent work, teacher directed instruction, unstructured class times, recess and lunch, etc.).

d. Conduct the meeting in an atmosphere of collaboration. The following agenda is one way you might structure the meeting:

- **Share your concerns about the student's behavior.**

  Briefly describe the problem behavior and, when appropriate, show the student a chart of how often he engages in the behavior. Then explain why you consider the behavior to be a problem. In this case, you might tell the student that his bored behavior leads others to feel defensive because he implies that their ideas or suggestions are stupid or boring.

- **Discuss how you can work together to improve the situation.**

  Tell the student that you would like to help him learn to "show interest and enthusiasm some of the time," and describe your preliminary plan. Invite the student to give you input on the various aspects of the plan, and together work out any necessary details (e.g., the signal, self-monitoring and reinforcement systems). You may have to brainstorm different possibilities if the student is uncomfortable with the initial plan. Incorporating any of the student's suggestions that strengthen the plan is likely to increase his sense of "ownership" in and commitment to it.

- **Make sure the student understands what you mean by appropriate and inappropriate behavior.**

Use the descriptions you have prepared to define and clarify the problem behavior and the positive (desired) behavior as specifically and thoroughly as you can. To ensure that you and the student are in agreement about the expectations, you might present hypothetical scenarios and have his identify whether each is an example of acting bored or showing interest or enthusiasm. Or you might describe an actual situation that has occurred and ask him to explain how he would demonstrate interest or enthusiasm in that situation.

- **Conclude the meeting.**

  Always end the meeting with words of encouragement. Let the student know that you are confident that he can be successful. Be sure to reinforce him for participating in the meeting.

5. *Give the student regular, ongoing feedback about his behavior.*

It is important to meet with the student periodically to discuss his progress. In most cases, three to five minutes once per week should suffice. *(NOTE: PLANS D and E suggest daily meetings.)* During the meetings, review any information that has been collected and discuss whether or not the situation is getting better. As much as possible, focus on the student's improvements, however, also address any new or continuing problems. As the situation improves, the meetings can be faded to once every other week and then to once per month.

6. *Evaluate the situation (and the plan).*

Implement any plan for at least two weeks before deciding whether to change plans; to continue, modify, or fade the plan you are using; or to cease the intervention. Generally, if the student's behavior is clearly improving (based on the objective information that's been collected and/or the subjective perceptions of yourself, the student, and possibly the parent[s]), stick with what you are doing. If the situation has remained the same or worsened, some kind of change will be necessary. Always discuss any changes to the plan with the student first.

BOSSINESS

Controlling

DESCRIPTION

You have a student who tends to tell you and/or her classmates what to do. Everyone is getting tired of her bossiness and seeming inability to compromise.

GOAL

The student will stop acting so bossy, and will learn to show respect for others' ideas. She will learn to balance being assertive with being able to compromise.

OVERVIEW OF PLANS

- PLAN A: For a situation in which the problem is relatively mild or has just begun.

- PLAN B: For a student who acts bossy because she lacks the skills to interact more appropriately and/or is unaware of how often she acts bossy.

- PLAN C: For a student who may be insecure and acts bossy to increase her sense of power and/or status.

- PLAN D: For a student who has developed the habit of acting bossy.

Alternative Problems

- **Aggression—Verbal and/or Physical**

- **Arguing—Student(s) With the Teacher**

- **Self-Concept Problems**

- **Smart-Aleck Behavior/Inappropriate Humor**

General Considerations

- If the student's problem behavior stems in any way from academic issues (e.g., the student is frustrated or angry about repeatedly being assigned work that she cannot do successfully), concurrent efforts must be made to ensure her academic success (see **Academic Deficits, Determining**).

- If the student lacks the basic social skills to interact with her peers appropriately, it may be necessary to begin by teaching her these skills.

Social Skills, Lack of contains information on a variety of published social skills curricula.

- If the inappropriate behavior is resulting in the student avoiding or not completing her schoolwork, begin with a plan to increase the student's work completion (see **Work Completion—Daily Work**). Once the student is turning in completed work on a regular basis, you can consider an intervention for the bossy behavior, if the problem still exists.

Model Plans

PLAN A

It is not always necessary, or even beneficial, to use an involved plan. If the bossiness has just begun and/or is relatively mild, the following actions, along with making the student aware of your concerns, may resolve the situation.

1. *Respond consistently to the inappropriate behavior.*

a. When the student starts to act bossy, gently correct her. Let her know that this is an example of being bossy, and give her direct information about what she should be doing instead. "Maija, this is an example of what we discussed. You need to let others have a chance to express their opinions." Because your goal is to impart information, you want to remain emotionally neutral while giving the correction.

b. If the student continues to act bossy, *privately* provide a gentle correction and a warning. Tell the student that if she continues to act bossy you will remove her from the situation she is in, and have the student identify what she needs to do differently when she goes back to interact with the other students. "Maija, if I have to speak to you again about being bossy with your group, you will need to work on your own for the remainder of the work period. What do you need to differently when you interact with your group?"

If the student goes back to the group and continues to act bossy, eliminate her opportunity to interact in a bossy way for the remainder of that activity by removing her from the group.

2. *Use reinforcement to encourage appropriate behavior.*

a. Give the student increased praise. Be especially alert for those times when the student is being cooperative with you and/or her classmates and praise her specifically for demonstrating her ability to be cooperative. "Maija, today was an excellent example of how well you can respect the views of others. You listened to the ideas that Megan and Ronda suggested and supported their suggestion about how the project should be organized. You then added some ideas to fine tune the plan."

b. Give the student frequent attention (e.g., say "hello" to her as she enters the classroom, call on her during class activities, and occasionally ask her to help you with a class job that needs to be done), and praise her for other positive behaviors that she exhibits. For example, you might comment about the accuracy of her work or how neat her assignments have been. This demonstrates to the student that you notice many positive things she does, not just the fact that she is refraining from acting bossy.

PLAN   B

Sometimes a student may not realize when she is acting bossy and/or may not know how to interact with others in a more cooperative way. For this type of student, your intervention must include some way of letting her know when she is acting bossy and teaching her how to behave instead.

1. *Respond consistently to the inappropriate behavior.*

a. During your initial meeting with the student (see SUGGESTED STEPS FOR DEVELOPING AND IMPLEMENTING A PLAN), establish a nonembarrassing signal that you can use to cue her when she is being bossy. You want the signal to be fairly subtle, one that only the student will recognize and understand in order to minimize the chance that she will be teased by her peers. Possibilities include making eye contact with the student and rubbing your shoulder in a slightly exaggerated manner, or making eye contact and putting your hand to your cheek.

Let the student know that you may need to quietly say her name to get her attention before you give the signal. You should be prepared to use the signal frequently and for a fairly long time, especially if the behavior is a somewhat unconscious habit on the part of the student.

b. Whenever the student begins to act bossy, give her the signal. If the student continues to act bossy, privately provide a gentle correction and a warning. Then if the bossiness continues, remove her from the situation in which she is being bossy (see PLAN A).

2. *Conduct lessons to teach the student how to interact in a less bossy manner.*

a. Teach the student how to handle situations without resorting to either being bossy or being a "doormat" (i.e., overly compromising). Use discussion, modeling, and role playing in the lessons. One easy way to structure the lessons is to play a board game the student knows—for example, "Checkers," "Sorry," or "Monopoly." Within the context of the game, give the student feedback on her behavior. You can even have the student practice different strategies. "Maija, how do you think it makes me feel when you say, 'Buying Baltic Avenue is stupid—you should buy a railroad'? Why don't we try that again, but see if you can say something that would be less likely to hurt the feelings of your opponent."

Be sure to also let the student know when she behaves appropriately—it is easier to accept constructive criticism if it is embedded within a discussion that includes one's successes and progress.

b. Conduct lessons at least twice per week until the student is consistently demonstrating less bossy behavior. Given that these lessons may require 15-20 minutes of one-to-one contact, it may be necessary to have someone other than yourself (e.g., the counselor) conduct them.

3. *Prompt the student to behave appropriately by using precorrections.*

Watch for circumstances in which the student is likely to act bossy, and speak to her before those activities begin. Remind her that her goal is to "respect the views of others," and give her suggestions about how to do this. While providing this precorrection, emulate a good coach. That is, you should not imply that you are expecting the student to fail, but rather that you are reviewing the "game plan" prior to a challenging situation. State that you know the student will be able to successfully meet these expectations.

4. *Use reinforcement to encourage appropriate behavior.*

a. Give the student increased praise and attention for respecting the views of others (see PLAN A).

b. Praise the student privately for responding to the signal. "Maija, twice during the time you were working with your partner, I gave you the signal. Both times, you thought about what you were doing and made an effort to listen to and respect your partner's ideas. How do you feel about the way things went working with Reiko this morning?"

c. Make a special point of letting the student know that you notice her efforts to use the skills that she has been practicing during the lessons. "Maija, nice job of doing what we've been practicing."

PLAN C

Occasionally a student will use bossy behavior to mask feelings of insecurity. In this case, the intervention must include some effort to help the student increase her sense of self-esteem as well as dealing with the bossy behavior itself.

1. Respond consistently to the inappropriate behavior.

a. Develop and use a signal to cue the student that she is acting bossy (see PLAN B).

b. When the student is being bossy, as soon as possible go to her and have her identify how she might have handled the situation differently. If she cannot do so, tell her how you think she might have been more respectful of the views of those around her. Try to do this in a nonembarrassing manner.

2. Help the student increase her feelings of self-worth and self-esteem.

a. Help the student learn to use positive self-talk. Identify one or more statements to teach the student to help bolster her confidence. The statements should be age-appropriate and tailored to fit the needs of the particular situation. The following examples can help get you started:

- Appropriate for a younger (e.g., grade K-3) student:

  - "I am good at what I do."

  - "I can let others learn."

- Appropriate for an older (e.g., grade 3-8) student:

  - "I am confident and secure."

  - "I can respect the ideas and beliefs of others."

  - "I can allow others to learn through experience."

b. When presenting this information to the student, have her modify your phrasing into statements that she would be willing to say to herself. Have her repeat each of the statements several times. Then help her identify different contexts in which repeating the statements to herself might reduce the probability of her being bossy. For example, if the student tends to try to direct other students' moves during board games, help her learn that whenever a student makes his/her own move—even a bad move—he/she can learn from it.

c. Give the student extra responsibility. Since the student likes to control situations, you might increase her confidence and reduce her need to control situations when it is inappropriate by giving her a responsibility which includes an element of control. There are two main ways to do this:

- Giving the student a job over which she has complete control. For example, the student could be asked to take responsibility for making a bulletin board.

- Giving the student a job in which the expectations and parameters are established. For example, you might ask the student to tutor a younger student who is struggling with math. If you used this idea, you would need to teach the student how to tutor (e.g., what lessons to cover, how to interact with the younger student in encouraging and motivating ways). You might also explain to the target student that if she treats the younger student in a controlling, bossy way, the younger student is likely to become even more discouraged.

  When using a responsibility like tutoring, provide enough supervision to ensure that the younger student is getting his/her needs met in the tutorial sessions.

  (NOTE: A list of additional ideas for jobs/responsibilities can be found in APPENDIX 2.)

3. Use reinforcement to encourage appropriate behavior.

a. Give the student increased praise and attention for respecting the views of others (see PLAN A).

b. You may also wish to use intermittent rewards to acknowledge the student's success. Occasional, and unexpected, rewards can motivate the student to demonstrate responsible behavior more often. The idea is to provide a reward when the student has had a particularly good period of being respectful of the views of others, and to let her know why she is receiving the reward.

For this situation, you might use privileges or activities that allow the student to demonstrate her strengths and abilities. "Maija, that was a very respectful way to state your opinion to the rest of the group. Would you like to read the next paragraph?" Use intermittent rewards more frequently at the beginning of the intervention to encourage the student, and then less often as her behavior improves.

PLAN D

If the student's problem behavior has become habitual and/or she does not seem to have a desire to reduce it, you may need to implement a system of external incentives (i.e., rewards and consequences) based on her behavior to motivate her to stop acting bossy and to start respecting the views of others.

1. Respond consistently to the inappropriate behavior.

a. Whenever the student is acting bossy, give her the signal (see PLAN B).

b. If the student does not cease engaging in the bossy behavior, remove the student from the situation she is in for the remainder of that class period. Note that the *signal* acts as the warning, and if she does not respond to that warning, she is no longer allowed to participate. If you are using this plan, be sure the student understands that there will be no verbal warning. When given the signal, if she ceases being bossy she will be allowed to continue to participate. If she continues to act bossy, she will be removed. *(NOTE: Also make sure that the student is still accountable for completing any assignments if she is removed from the problematic situation.)*

2. Establish a structured system for reinforcing the student's appropriate behavior and providing a consequence for the inappropriate behavior.

a. With the student, create a list of reinforcers that she can earn. Although you might want to have some suggestions in mind, the system will be more effective if the student identifies most of the items or activities herself. *(NOTE: A list of reinforcement ideas can be found in APPENDIX 1).*

b. Assign "prices" (in points) for each of the rewards on the list and have the student choose the reward she would like to earn first.

The prices should be based on the number of points the student can earn and the instructional, personnel, and/or monetary costs of the items. Monetary cost is clear—the more expensive the item, the more points required to earn it. Instructional cost refers to the amount of instructional time lost or interfered with by a particular reward. Thus, an activity which causes the student to miss part of academic instruction should cost more points than one the student can do on her own recess time. Personnel cost involves the time required by you and/or other staff to fulfill the reinforcer. Having lunch with the principal, therefore, would cost more points than spending five minutes of free time with a friend.

c. Award the student points for not exhibiting bossy behavior within a specified periods of time. For example, the student might earn one point for each hour in which she does not behave in a bossy manner. A form similar to the following example can be used.

Name Maija
Week of 3/15
Menu of Rewards and Costs

5 points	=	5 minutes of "game time" with a friend
10 points	=	15 minutes on computer
10 points	=	time after school helping the teacher
20 points	=	lead a class activity
30 points	=	ice cream treat

For each hour that Maija does not "act bossy," Ms. Jacobson will initial the space below and Maija will earn 1 point.

8:30-9:30 _____	11:30-12:30 _____
9:30-10:30 _____	12:30-1:30 _____
10:30-11:30 _____	1:30-2:30 _____

When using this type of system, modify the time periods and points to correspond to how frequently the problem behavior occurs. That is, if the behavior happens frequently, the time period might be half an hour or one hour. If the behavior occurs infrequently, the time period might be half the day. In any case, as the student's behavior improves, increase the time interval of appropriate behavior required to earn one point.

d. Initially, the student should earn her point for a given time period even if you have to give her the signal, but she ceases being bossy when signaled. As the student is consistently successful, let her know that beginning about a week later, she will only earn the point for a given time period if you do not even have to give her the signal.

e. At the end of each day, meet with the student for a few minutes to review how the day went and to record her daily points. Keep the meeting

positive, but, when necessary, discuss what she might do the following day to remember to act less bossy.

 Use reinforcement to encourage appropriate behavior.

a. Give the student increased praise and attention for respecting the views of others (see PLAN A).

b. In addition, show interest and enthusiasm about how the student is doing on the system. "Maija This is the third hour in row that you have gotten a point. This is a real indication of what a respectful person you are."

. . . .

Suggested Steps for Developing and Implementing a Plan

The following steps are designed to help you develop an appropriate intervention plan and implement it effectively, whether you choose to use one of the MODEL PLANS or create a customized plan of your own. The steps are, however, suggestions—they are not intended to be followed rigidly or in any particular order. Use your professional judgment and the knowledge of your particular situation to make them work for you.

 Make sure you have enough information about the situation.

a. If you think a minimal intervention like PLAN A will be sufficient, you may already have enough information to proceed. However, when a more involved plan seems necessary, you should consider collecting additional descriptive and/or objective information for a couple of days.

b. You need to be able to explain what you mean when you say "the student has a problem with being bossy." That is, what does the student do that has led you to conclude that she acts bossy? Anecdotal notes on actual incidents should provide enough details to help you define the problem behavior clearly and completely.

To collect anecdotal notes, simply keep a card in your pocket or on a clipboard and occasionally take notes on specific instances when the student acts in a way that you perceive to be bossy. For each entry, briefly describe where and when the behavior occurred, the circumstances—what the student did or said, and any other relevant observations (e.g., what prompted the behavior).

You do not need to take notes every time the student acts bossy; the idea is to capture a range of examples of the behavior so you will be able to describe it completely.

Also include some notes on times when the student is cooperative—this will make it clear that you are not only aware of her problem behavior, but also recognize when she behaves appropriately. When you meet with the student, the positive examples will help you clarify how you want her to behave.

c. If the student is bossy often, in addition to information on what the student's inappropriate behavior looks like, it can also be useful to document how often it occurs (i.e., frequency count). This will provide a more objective measure of the problem (and an objective way to monitor progress). You can use the same card on which you are collecting anecdotal notes to keep a frequency count—just write a tally mark on the card each time the student acts bossy.

You might also want to code the tallies to discern whether the behavior occurs more frequently during certain times, subjects, or activities (e.g., using an "A" or "P" to indicate that the incident happened in the morning or afternoon; or clustering the tallies by subject, teacher directed instruction, or independent work, etc.).

d. If the student notices what you are doing and asks about it, be straightforward—tell her that you are collecting information to see whether her bossy behavior is a problem that needs to be worked on.

Following is an example of anecdotal notes and frequency count collected on a student's bossy behavior.

Maija's Bossy Behavior—3/15

Frequency:

Teacher Directed Instruction
   AAAAA PP

Independent Work
   PP

Cooperative Groups
   AAA PPPPP

Notes:

10:45—Maija let Kendra be the group leader during science lab. Was very respectful of Kendra's suggestions and leadership.

1:30—While working in a cooperative group during language arts, Maija demanded in a loud and angry voice that the group use her answer to a question. Her answer was different from the one that the other members of the group agreed upon.

(Etc.)

---

e. The frequency information is fairly easy to summarize on a chart or graph. Seeing how often she acts bossy may help the student and her parent(s) better understand your concern.

f. Continuing to collect this type of information (and keeping the chart up-to-date) while you implement a plan will help you to monitor whether the situation is getting worse, staying the same, or getting better.

2. *Identify a focus for the intervention and labels for referring to the appropriate and inappropriate behaviors.*

a. To be effective, the intervention must address more than just reducing the student's bossy behavior—there must be a concurrent emphasis on increasing some positive behavior or trait (e.g., being cooperative, respecting others' views). Having a specific positive behavior in mind will make it easier for you to "catch" and reinforce the student for acting appropriately, and the positive focus will frame the situation more productively.

For example, if you simply say that "the student has a problem with being bossy" you don't really provide any useful information, and may put the student and her parent(s) on the defensive. However, when you explain that you want to "help the student learn to respect the views of others," you present an important, and reasonable, goal for the student to work toward and clearly identify what she needs to do to be successful.

b. Specifying labels for the appropriate and inappropriate behaviors (e.g., "respecting the views of others " and "being bossy," respectively) will help you to use consistent vocabulary when discussing the situation with the student. For example, if you sometimes refer to the inappropriate behavior as "not being cooperative" and other times tell the student that she is "being bossy," she may not realize that you are talking about the same thing.

3. *Determine when and how to include the parent(s).*

a. It is not necessary to contact the student's parent(s) if the problem has just begun or is not interfering with the student's academic or social progress. However, it might be a good idea to take advantage of any scheduled activities (e.g., conferences, weekly notes home) to let them know of your concern.

b. The parent(s) should be contacted whenever the student's bossiness is affecting her academic performance or is alienating her from her peers. Share any information you have collected about the behavior (i.e., anecdotal notes, frequency count), and explain why you are concerned. Focus in particular on how the behavior is hindering the student academically and/or socially (e.g., other students are getting so annoyed that they are beginning to avoid interacting with her).

You might ask if the parent(s) have any insight into the situation and/or whether they have noticed similar behavior at home. Whether or not the parent(s) perceive a problem, explain that you want to help the student "learn to respect the views of others" and invite them to join you for an initial meeting with the student to develop a plan. If the parent(s) are unable or unwilling to participate, let them know that you will keep them informed of the student's progress.

c. Once the parent(s) have been involved in any way, you should give them updates at least once per week while the plan is being implemented.

4. Prepare for, then conduct, an initial meeting about the situation.

a. Arrange a meeting to discuss your concerns with the student and anyone else who will be involved (e.g., the parent[s], the school psychologist). Although the specifics will vary depending upon the age of the student and the severity of the problem, there are some general guidelines to consider when scheduling the meeting.

First, meet at a neutral time (i.e., not immediately after a problem has occurred), when emotions are less likely to hamper communication. In general, a day's notice is appropriate, however a primary age student may worry excessively and/or forget what the meeting is about if it is scheduled more than an hour before it takes place.

Second, make the meeting appropriately private. With a primary age student who has a mild problem, you might meet in the classroom while the other students are working independently. However, when dealing with a middle/junior high school student and the student's parent(s), you will want some place private (e.g., the counselor's office) to ensure that the discussion will not be overheard.

Third, try to make sure the meeting is scheduled for a time and place that it is not likely to be interrupted. Finally, if the parent(s) will be participating, they should be the ones to tell the student about the meeting.

b. Construct a preliminary plan. Decide whether you think you can use one of the MODEL PLANS or if you need to create a customized plan using components from various plans and/or of your own design. Although you will invite and encourage the student to help develop the plan during the initial meeting, having a proposed plan in mind before you meet can alleviate frustration and wasted time if the student is unwilling or unable to participate.

c. After reviewing the information you have collected and thinking about how you want the student to behave, prepare thorough descriptions of the inappropriate behavior and the positive behavior/trait on which the student will be working. The more specific you can be and the more concrete examples you have, the easier

it will be to clarify (and for the student to understand) your expectations. Be sure to consider the student's behavior in all relevant activities (e.g., independent work, teacher directed instruction, unstructured class times, recess and lunch, etc.).

d. Conduct the meeting in an atmosphere of collaboration. The following agenda is one way you might structure the meeting:

• **Share your concerns about the student's behavior.**

Briefly describe the problem behavior and, when appropriate, show the student a chart of how often she engages in it. Then explain why you consider the behavior to be a problem. In this case, you might tell the student that most people don't particularly like it when someone bosses them, and that it seems like the other students are beginning to not want to be around her.

• **Discuss how you can work together to improve the situation.**

Tell the student that you would like to help her learn to "respect the views of others," and describe your preliminary plan. Invite the student's input on the various aspects of the plan, and together work out any necessary details (e.g., where and when the lessons will take place). You may have to brainstorm different possibilities if the student is uncomfortable with the initial plan. Incorporating any of the student's suggestions that strengthen the plan is likely to increase her sense of "ownership" in and commitment to it.

• **Make sure the student understands what you mean by appropriate and inappropriate behavior.**

Use the descriptions you have prepared to define and clarify the problem behavior and the positive (desired) behavior as specifically and thoroughly as you can. To ensure that you and the student are in agreement about the expectations, you might present hypothetical scenarios and have her identify whether each is an example of "being bossy" or "respecting the views of others." Or you might describe an actual situation that has occurred and ask the student to explain how she could demonstrate respecting the views of others in that situation.

- **Conclude the meeting.**

  Always end the meeting with words of encouragement. Let the student know that you are confident that she can be successful. Be sure to reinforce her for participating in the meeting, as well.

 Give the student regular, ongoing feedback about her behavior.

It is important to meet with the student periodically to discuss her progress. In most cases, three to five minutes once per week should suffice. *(NOTE: PLAN D suggests daily meetings.)* During the meetings, review any information that has been collected and discuss whether or not the situation is getting better. As much as possible, focus on the student's improvements, however, also address any new or continuing problems. As the situation improves, the meetings can be faded to once every other week and then to once per month.

 Evaluate the situation (and the plan).

Implement any plan for at least two weeks before deciding whether to change plans; to continue, modify, or fade the plan you are using; or to cease the intervention. Generally, if the student's behavior is clearly improving (based on the objective information that's been collected and/or the subjective perceptions of yourself, the student, and possibly the parent[s]), stick with what you are doing. If the situation has remained the same or worsened, some kind of change will be necessary. Always discuss any changes to the plan with the student first.

BOTHERING/ TORMENTING OTHERS

Hands and Feet Everywhere

DESCRIPTION

You have a student who bothers others students (e.g., poking, tripping, pulling hair, pushing, grabbing, etc.).

GOAL

The student will stop bothering other students and will learn to keep his hands and feet to himself.

OVERVIEW OF PLANS

- PLAN A: For a situation in which the problem is relatively mild or has just begun.

- PLAN B: For a student who bothers other students because he lacks the skills to interact more appropriately.

- PLAN C: For a student who bothers other students to gain attention.

- PLAN D: For a student who may be unaware that he bothers other students and/or is not motivated to stop doing so.

Alternative Problems

- **Aggression—Verbal and/or Physical**

- **Bullying Behavior/ Fighting**

- **Disruptive Behavior—Moderate**

- **Out of Seat**

- **Physically Dangerous Behavior—to Self or Others**

. . . .
General Considerations

- If the student's problem behavior stems in any way from academic issues (e.g., the student is unable to meet academic expectations and bothers others as a way to fill his time), concurrent efforts must be made to ensure his academic success (see **Academic Deficits, Determining**).

- If the student lacks the basic social skills to interact with his peers appropriately, it may be necessary to begin by teaching him those skills. **Social Skills, Lack of** contains information on a variety of published social skills curricula.

. . . .
Model Plans

PLAN A

It is not always necessary, or even beneficial to use an involved plan. If the problem has just begun and/or is relatively mild (i.e., the student bothers others less than three times per day), the following actions, along with making the student aware of your concerns, may resolve the situation.

1. Respond consistently to the inappropriate behavior.

Whenever the student is bothering another student, gently correct him. Label what the student is doing as an example of bothersome behavior and provide specific information about what he should be doing instead that would be more respectful of others. "Colin, tapping people on the head on your way to get a drink is an example of bothering others. You need to keep your hands to yourself any time you are going from one place to another."

If the student ceases the bothersome behavior, wait a few minutes and praise the student for demonstrating that he can treat other students with respect. If public praise would be embarrassing, praise the student privately or even use a note.

2. Use reinforcement to encourage appropriate behavior.

Give the student increased praise and attention. Be especially alert for situations in which the student might bother others, but does not—acknowledge the student for demonstrating respect toward others. "Colin, on your way to the pencil sharpener, you kept your hands to yourself. This was a good example of treating others with respect."

Also look for opportunities in which the student is interacting with other students in a way that is not bothersome. "Colin, during your time with your group today you treated everyone in the group with respect. You kept your hands and ruler to yourself. You listened to the other students' ideas, and you stayed with the group the entire time."

Be aware that any time the student is not engaged in bothering others, you can reinforce him for treating others with respect. Even if all the student is doing is entering the classroom without bothering someone else, this is an opportunity to provide praise and attention.

PLAN B

In some cases, the student may lack strategies or techniques that could help him refrain from bothering others. If the student does not seem to be able to help himself, or does not know what to do instead, this plan may be appropriate.

1. *Conduct lessons to teach the student how he can treat others with respect.*

a. Identify specific times/activities in which the student tends to have the most trouble with being bothersome. For example, is it when the student should be staying in his seat? when there is a lot of movement going on in the room (e.g., during transitions and unstructured times)? when he is working in close proximity to other students (e.g., during cooperative group activities)? If you can pinpoint one main problem area, make it the initial focus of the intervention plan and then, as the student's behavior improves during that time/activity, add others one at a time.

b. Develop some techniques and/or expectations for helping the student avoid bothering others, thus increasing the probability that the student will be successful during that time/activity. The following suggestions are provided to prompt ideas; you can adapt them and/or develop others to fit the unique needs of the student and of your classroom:

- If the student moves about the room when he should be at his desk, you might make a masking tape square around his desk. Explain that this is his "office," and that he cannot leave his office without your permission. For more details on this technique, including how to fade the plan so the student is operating under a more normalized classroom expectation, see **Out of Seat**.

- If the bothersome behavior tends to occur when the student moves about the room, you might teach him to keep his hands in his pockets. For example, when he is carrying something, he needs to hold the item in one of his hands near his abdomen, and keep his other hand in his pocket. Or you might establish that talking to anyone who is seated while he moves about the room is an example of "bothering someone," and that " treating others with respect" when moving from one place to another means keeping one's mouth closed—no talking.

- If the student has trouble working in close proximity with other students (e.g., peer tutoring, cooperative groups, etc.), the lessons might involve teaching the student how to keep his hands on his own desk or in his own personal space. You can use a masking tape line to show him the limits of his own physical space on a table, and teach him that going

beyond that space is an example of bothering others by not respecting their physical space.

c. During the lessons, use the techniques/expectations you have developed (see Step 1b) as a basis for explaining to the student how he can treat others with respect, asking the student questions, and providing structured practice opportunities. There are many ways to do this, depending upon the situation. For example, you might define the expectations for treating others with respect and then ask the student questions to verify that he understands the expectations. Or, you might set up a hypothetical situation and have the student model what treating others with respect would look like in that context.

Provide feedback and have the student practice until he is successful. You can also model different behaviors and have the student identify what you are doing as either treating others with respect or bothering others.

d. The lessons should last between five and ten minutes. Once the student demonstrates—both in the lessons and the actual situation—that he knows how to behave appropriately in one time/activity, add another time/activity. Continue this process until all appropriate times/activities have been covered.

2. *Respond consistently to the inappropriate behavior.*

a. Whenever the student bothers someone in a way that has been covered in the lessons, implement a consequence such as time owed off of recess or after school. Whenever consequences will be part of the plan, the student should be informed ahead of time—then if a situation arises, keep the interaction short, unemotional, and specific. "Colin, you need to remember to keep your hands to yourself when moving from one place to another. You owe one minute from recess."

b. When the student is bothering someone in a way that has not been covered in the lessons, gently correct him. Let the student know that although the behavior is an example of bothering someone, he will not owe time. "Colin, bumping into someone's desk with your leg is an example of bothering others. You don't owe a minute for doing that this time because we have not discussed it in the lessons."

Do not respond with exasperation or any emotion that implies that the student should know better, but make note of the incident and, when appropriate, include that type of situation in the daily lessons. Once it has been included in the lessons, subsequent infractions of that nature will result in a consequence. "Colin, from this point forward, any time you bump into someone's desk, what will happen? Right, you will owe one minute."

3. Use reinforcement to encourage appropriate behavior.

a. Give the student increased praise and attention for being respectful of others (see PLAN A).

b. Try to "catch" the student demonstrating respect (i.e., not bothering others) in any of the activities/times on which the lessons have fo-

cused. "Colin, you are remembering to move from place to place with your hands in your pockets and your mouth closed. You're doing exactly what we practiced in our lessons this morning. It is a great demonstration of respecting other students who are working on their projects."

If the student demonstrates respect in a category that is not yet the focus of the lessons, highlight the significance of going beyond the lessons. "Colin, we haven't even talked about it in the lessons, but you were very respectful in the way you worked with your group today. "

PLAN C

In some cases a student has learned that being bothersome leads to people getting annoyed and giving him attention. If the student's misbehavior seems to be fueled by the reactions of others (e.g., the student thinks it's funny if other students get angry with him), it may be the interaction itself that has become a motivating force in the student's bothersome behavior.

1. Respond consistently to the inappropriate behavior.

a. If the target student bothers another student, implement a consequence such as time owed off of recess or after school (see PLAN B).

b. Let the other students know that when the target student bothers them, they should tell him once to stop. If he does not stop, they should raise their hand or otherwise get your attention. If you see the misbehavior, you will have the target student owe a minute. Additionally, if you see the target student bug someone else, intervene and tell the target student that he owes a minute, even if the other student handles it well by telling the target student to cease.

The goal is to reduce the amount of peer engagement the student receives via his misbehavior. If another student argues with or nags the target student, let the other student know that he/she may actually be giving the target student what he wants. "Nikita, when you argue and get mad at Colin, he actually likes it. Remember that if he bugs you tell him one time to stop, and if he does not, get my attention."

If another student reports that the target student did something, but you did not see it, do not implement a consequence. You must operate under the "innocent until proven guilty" concept—even though there may be a 95% chance that the target student actually did what the other student says he did. "Emma, I am sorry that happened. Did you tell him to stop? Great.

Since I didn't see it, I cannot have him owe time, but I will watch more closely when he is in your group, so that if he does it again, I will be more likely to see it."

2. Use reinforcement to encourage appropriate behavior.

a. Frequent praise and attention is the core of this plan. You want the student to learn that he will receive more frequent and more satisfying attention when he behaves appropriately than when he bothers others. This may be especially difficult because the positive behavior in this particular situation (i.e., treating others with respect) is actually the *absence* of bothersome behavior, and therefore may not be very noticeable. On the other hand, the inappropriate behavior (i.e., bothering others) tends to elicit attention.

Thus, whenever the student is treating others with respect—that is, not engaging in bothersome behavior—it is very important that you make an effort to praise and spend time with him. "Colin, you have been doing such a fine job this morning of keeping your hands to yourself and treating others with respect. Would you walk with me as we go the cafeteria today? I would love to hear how your soccer game turned out yesterday."

b. You may also wish to use intermittent reinforcement. Occasional, and unexpected, rewards that acknowledge the student's success may motivate him to demonstrate responsible behavior more often. The idea is to provide a reward when the student has done especially well with treating others with respect. Given that the student may thrive on adult attention, use adult attention as a reward. "Colin, you have been treating others with respect all day. Would you like to eat lunch with me in the classroom today? If you would like, you could invite one other student to join us."

A list of additional reinforcement ideas can be found in APPENDIX 1. If you use intermittent reinforcement, do so more frequently at the beginning of the intervention to encourage the student, and less often as the student's behavior improves over time.

3. *Ensure a 3-1 ratio of positive to negative attention.*

a. Given that attention is a motivating force for this student, you want to be sure that you are giving the student *three times as much* positive as negative attention. One way to do this is to monitor your interactions with the student at least one day per week. Keep a card on a clipboard or in your pocket and record each interaction you have with the student as either positive or negative by writing a "+" or a "-," respectively, on the card.

To determine whether an interaction is positive or negative, ask yourself whether the student was bothering someone (or otherwise misbehaving) at the time the interaction occurred. Any interaction that stems from inappropriate behavior is negative, while all interactions that occur while the student is meeting classroom expectations are positive. Thus, gently correcting the student or assigning time owed are both negative interactions, but praising the student for keeping his hands to himself and respecting the physical space of another student is positive. Greeting the student as he enters the room and asking him if he has questions during independent work are also considered positive interactions.

b. If you find that you are not giving the student three times as much positive as negative attention, try to increase the number of positive interactions you have with him. Sometimes prompts can help. For example, each time there is a transition, you could look at the target student and praise him early in the transition. If you praise him for respecting others as he begins the transition there is an increased chance that he will be successful with the rest of that transition. Or, tell yourself that whenever you look at the clock you will find a time to praise the student, or any time a student uses the drinking fountain, you will look at the target student and, as soon as possible, praise some aspect of his behavior.

PLAN D

Some students do not recognize how frequently they bother others, their behavior has become habitual, and/or they do not have any desire to reduce it. If your student fits any of these categories, you may need to help the student become more aware of his own behavior and/or structure external incentives (i.e., rewards and consequences) based on his behavior to motivate him to stop bothering others and to begin treating others with respect.

1. *Monitor how frequently the student bothers others by recording each incident.*

a. Determine who will do the recording. Because the point of this step is to make the student more aware of his own behavior, having him record the frequency will be more effective than if you do the recording. However, if the student balks at self-monitoring, you should keep the frequency count of his behavior.

If you do the recording, remember that the idea is for the student to be made aware of each time he bothers someone, and for him to know that each incident is being recorded.

b. If the student will be recording his own frequency count, he can tape a card to his desk (or the front flyleaf of his notebook to be less obtrusive). Each time the student bothers someone, make sure he marks his card. Prompt the student to do so for a few days in order to establish an average of how many times per day the student bothers others.

2. *Establish a system of rewarding appropriate behavior and providing a consequence for inappropriate behavior.*

a. With the student, create a list of several reinforcers that he can earn. Although you might wish to have some suggestions in mind, the system will be more effective if the student identifies most of the items or activities himself. *(NOTE: A list of reinforcement ideas can be found in APPENDIX 1.)*

b. Assign a "price" (in points) for each of the reinforcers on the list, and have the student choose the one he would like to work for first.

The prices should be based on the number of points the student can earn and the cost—instructional, personnel, and/or monetary—of the items. Monetary cost is simple—the more expensive the item, the more points required to earn it. Instructional cost refers to the amount of instructional time lost or interfered with by a particular reward. Thus, an activity that causes the student to miss academic instruction would require more points than one the student can do on his own during lunch. Personnel cost involves the time required by you and/or other staff to fulfill the reinforcer. Earning extra recess time for the class, therefore, would cost more points than spending five minutes of free time on the computer.

c. Set up a response cost system in which the student begins each day with a certain number of points (equal to the average number of times per day the student has been bothering others, plus two). For example, if he has bothered others an average of 14 times per day, he would begin each day with 16 points. Then each time you have to give him the signal for bothering someone, he loses one point. The points remaining at the end of each day are added together and applied toward the reward the student is trying to earn.

A lottery system might be more effective with a primary level student. With a lottery system, the student would begin each day with tickets in a jar instead of points. All the tickets would have prizes written on them—one with a big prize, a couple with moderate prizes, and the majority with small prizes. Each time you have to use the signal, you would remove one ticket from the jar—but neither you nor the student would be allowed to see what is written on it. At the end of each day, the student would draw one ticket from those remaining in the jar, and earn that prize.

d. Determine a consequence (e.g., time owed from recess or in detention) for any incident that occurs when the student has lost all his points for the day. Do not take away any previously earned points. Once the student has earned the points, he should not be at risk of losing them or it may jeopardize the system. The student could develop an attitude of, "I am losing so many points, why should I even bother to try?"

3. *Prompt the student to behave appropriately with precorrections.*

Watch for times/activities that have been especially problematic for the student, and remind the student that the next activity may be a tough one in which to treat others with respect, but that you know that the student can do it. Then give a very quick reminder to the student about what successful behavior would look like in that situation. "Colin, we are about to get into our cooperative groups, and this is a time that is often a problem. I think today you will be able to remember the importance of keeping your hands to yourself and moving your desk and chair in a way that nothing of yours bumps into another student. I am looking forward to watching your success."

4. *Use reinforcement to encourage appropriate behavior.*

a. Give the student increased praise and attention for respecting others (see PLAN A).

b. In addition, show interest and enthusiasm about how the student is doing on the system. "Colin you are doing a great job of remembering to be respectful by keeping your hands and feet to yourself. You still have all your points so far today, and that means you'll be able to buy your reward tomorrow."

c. If the student is having a bad day, but then begins to improve his behavior, consider giving back some of the points that he has lost. "Colin, even though you lost a lot of points this morning, you have had a great first hour this afternoon. I am going to add back three of the points you lost." Do not do this very often—only as a special celebration of the student's efforts to be successful.

. . . .
Suggested Steps for Developing and Implementing a Plan

The following steps are designed to help you develop an appropriate intervention plan and implement it effectively, whether you choose to use one of the MODEL PLANS or create a customized plan of your own. The steps are, however, suggestions—they are not intended to be followed rigidly or in any particular order. Use your professional judgment and the knowledge of your particular situation to make them work for you.

1. *Make sure you have enough information about the situation.*

a. If you think a minimal intervention like PLAN A will be sufficient, you probably already have enough information to proceed. However, when a more involved plan seems necessary, you should consider collecting additional descriptive and/or objective information for a couple of days so that you can thoroughly describe the problem behavior and monitor any changes in the situation.

b. With this type of situation, descriptive information, from anecdotal notes, can be especially useful for developing a clear explanation of the problem behavior. That is, you should be able to describe exactly (and completely) what the student does that has lead you to conclude that his bothersome behavior is a problem. Recording details from actual incidents will help you clarify the situation for the student and his parent(s).

To collect anecdotal notes, simply keep a card in your pocket or on a clipboard and occasionally make notes on specific incidents when the student bothers someone. For each entry, include a brief description of the setting (where and when it occurred), what the student did or said, and any other relevant observations (e.g., what prompted the behavior). You do not need to make notes *every* time the student is bothersome; the idea is to capture a range of examples of the behavior so you will be able to describe it clearly.

You should also make some notes on times when the student is treating others with respect; this will help him realize that you are aware not only of his inappropriate behavior, but also when he behaves responsibly. In addition, when you meet with the student, these positive examples will help you clarify how you want the student to behave.

c. In addition to being able to describe what the student's bothersome behavior looks like, it can also be useful to document how often it occurs.

This frequency count provides both a more objective measure of the problem and an objective way to monitor the student's progress. Keeping a frequency count is not difficult. On the same card you use to keep anecdotal notes, simply write a tally mark each time the student interacts with another student in a way that seems bothersome.

Additionally, coding the tallies will allow you to discern whether the behavior occurs more frequently during certain times, subjects, or activities (e.g., in the morning [A] or afternoon [P]; during art or social studies, during class discussions or independent work, etc.).

d. If the student notices what you are doing and asks about it, be straightforward—tell him that you are collecting information to see whether his bothering others is a problem that needs to be worked on.

Following is an example of anecdotal notes and a frequency count that have been collected on a student's bothersome behavior.

Colin's Bothersome Behavior—4/3

Independent Work
    AAAAA AAAPP PPPPP PP

Teacher Directed Instruction
    PP

Cooperative Groups
    PPPPP PPPPP

Transitions
    AAAAA PPP PPPPP PPPP

Notes:

8:40, Transition—As Colin is moving to join his cooperative group, he pokes Blaine in the arm, knocks Belinda's books off her desk, and pulls Maria's hair.

(continued)

> **(cont'd)**
>
> 10:00, Independent Work—Colin takes away Sam's pencils and will not give them back. I have to intervene.
>
> 1:30, Cooperative Group—Colin uses his ruler to try to slap the hand of anyone is his group who points to any part of the map.
>
> 2:00, Class Discussion—Colin kept his hands to himself and participated well. I complimented him and he seemed proud.

e. The objective information can be easily summarized on a chart or graph. Seeing a visual representation of how often he bothers others may help the student (and his parent[s], if applicable) better understand your concern. In addition, by keeping the chart or graph up-to-date while you implement the plan (i.e., continuing to collect frequency information), you can easily monitor whether the situation is getting worse, staying the same, or getting better.

 Identify the focus for the intervention and labels for referring to the appropriate and inappropriate behaviors.

a. To be effective, the intervention must address more than just reducing the student's bothersome behavior—there must be a concurrent emphasis on increasing some positive behavior or trait (e.g., treating others with respect). Not only will having a specific positive behavior in mind make it easier to "catch" and reinforce the student for behaving appropriately, but a positive focus will allow you to frame the situation productively.

For example, if you describe the situation simply as "the student has a problem with bothering others," you offer little in the way of useful information, and may put the student and his parent(s) on the defensive. However, if you explain your concern by saying that you want to "help the student learn to treat others with respect," you present an important, and reasonable, goal for the student to work toward and clearly identify what the student needs to do to be successful.

b. Specifying labels for the appropriate and inappropriate behaviors (e.g., "treating others with respect" and "bothering others," respectively) will help you to use consistent vocabulary when discussing the situation with the student. For example, if you sometimes refer to the inappropriate behavior as "bothering others" and other times tell the student that he "is being annoying," he may not realize that you are talking about the same thing.

 Determine when and how to include the parent(s).

a. You probably do not need to contact the student's parent(s) if the problem has just begun and is not interfering with the student's academic or social progress. You might, however, take advantage of any scheduled activities (e.g., conferences, weekly notes home) to let the parent(s) know of your concern.

b. The parent(s) should be contacted whenever the student's inappropriate behavior is affecting his academic performance or is alienating him from his peers. Share any information you have collected about the behavior (i.e., anecdotal notes and frequency count), and explain why you are concerned. Focus in particular on how the student's behavior is hindering him academically and/or socially (e.g., other students are beginning to avoid him on the playground).

You might ask if the parent(s) have any insight into the situation and/or whether they have noticed similar behavior at home. Whether or not the parent(s) perceive a problem, invite them to join you for an initial meeting with the student to develop a plan to help the student learn to "treat others with respect." If the parent(s) are unable or unwilling to participate, let them know that you will keep them informed of the student's progress.

c. Once the parent(s) have been involved in any way, you should give them updates at least once per week while the plan is being implemented.

 Prepare for, then conduct, an initial meeting about the situation.

a. Schedule a meeting to discuss your concerns with the student and anyone else who will be involved with the plan (e.g., the parent[s], the school psychologist). Although the specifics of the meeting will vary depending upon the age of the student and the severity of the problem, there are some general guidelines to consider when scheduling the meeting.

First, meet at a neutral time (i.e., not immediately after a problem has occurred), when emotions are less likely to hamper communication. In general, a day's notice is appropriate, however a primary age student may worry excessively and/or forget what the meeting is about if it is scheduled more than an hour before it takes place.

Second, make the meeting appropriately private. For a primary student with a mild problem, you might meet in the classroom while the other students are working independently. However, when dealing with a middle/junior high school student and the student's parent(s), you will want a private room (e.g., the counselor's office) to ensure that the discussion will not be overheard.

Third, try to make sure the meeting is scheduled for a time and place that it is not likely to be interrupted. Finally, if the parent(s) will be participating, they should be the ones to tell the student about the meeting.

b. Construct a preliminary plan. Based upon the information you have collected and the focus of the intervention, you may decide to use one of the MODEL PLANS, or you might choose to create a customized plan using components from various plans and/or of your own design.

Also, although it is important to invite and encourage the student to be an active partner in developing the plan during the initial meeting, having a proposed plan in mind before you meet can alleviate frustration and wasted time if the student is unwilling or unable to participate.

c. Using your anecdotal notes, prepare thorough descriptions of the inappropriate behavior and the positive behavior/trait on which the student will be working. The more specific you are and the more concrete examples you have, the easier it will be for you to clarify (and for the student to understand) the expectations. Additionally, be sure to identify appropriate and inappropriate behaviors in all relevant activities (e.g., independent work, teacher directed instruction, unstructured class times, recess and lunch, etc.).

d. Conduct the meeting in an atmosphere of collaboration. The following agenda is one way you might structure the meeting:

*   **Share your concerns about the student's behavior.**

    Briefly describe the problem behavior itself and, when applicable, show him the chart of how often he engages in it. Then explain why you consider the behavior to be a problem. In this case, you might tell the student that when he bothers others it disrupts the class and even makes other students not want him

around because his behavior interrupts their work or makes them uncomfortable. You might also tell him that being successful at most things he may want to do in life will require that he treat others with respect.

*   **Discuss how you can work together to improve the situation.**

    Explain that you would like to help the student learn to "treat others with respect" and describe your preliminary plan. Invite the student to give you input on the plan and together work out any necessary details (e.g., the signal, reinforcers, consequences, etc.). You may have to brainstorm different possibilities if the student is uncomfortable with the initial plan. Incorporating any of the student's suggestions that strengthen the plan is likely to increase his sense of "ownership" in and commitment to it.

*   **Make sure the student understands what you mean by appropriate and inappropriate behavior.**

    Use the descriptions you have prepared to define and clarify the problem behavior and the positive (desired) behavior as specifically and thoroughly as you can. To ensure that you and the student are in agreement about the expectations, you might present hypothetical scenarios and have him identify whether each is an example of bothering others or treating others with respect. Or you might present an actual situation that has occurred and ask him to explain how he could demonstrate treating others with respect in that situation.

*   **Conclude the meeting.**

    Always end the meeting with words of encouragement. Let the student know that you are confident that he can be successful, and that he may actually find that he likes school more when he is treating others with respect. Be sure to reinforce him for participating in the meeting.

5. *Give the student regular, ongoing feedback about his behavior.*

It is important to periodically discuss his progress with the student. A three to five minute meeting once per week should suffice. Review any information that has been collected and discuss whether or not the situation is improving. As much as possible, focus on the student's improvements, however, also address any new or continuing problems. As the situation improves, the meetings can be faded to once every other week and then to once per month.

 6. *Evaluate the situation (and the plan).*

Implement any plan for at least two weeks before deciding whether to change plans; to continue, modify, or fade the plan you are using; or to cease the intervention. Generally, if the student's behavior is clearly improving (based on the objective information that's been collected and/or the subjective perceptions of yourself, the student, and possibly the parent[s]), stick with what you are doing. If the situation has remained the same or worsened, some kind of change will be necessary. Always discuss any changes to the plan with the student first.

BULLYING BEHAVIOR/ FIGHTING

Intimidation

DESCRIPTION

You have a student who intimidates others physically and/or psychologically.

GOAL

The student will stop the "bullying," and will learn to interact with other students in more positive and socially acceptable ways.

OVERVIEW OF PLANS

- PLAN A: For a situation in which the problem has just begun.
- PLAN B: For a student who does not know how to interact with others in more respectful (i.e., not bullying) ways.
- PLAN C: For a student who has trouble managing anger and engages in bullying when angry or frustrated.
- PLAN D: For a student who bullies because he enjoys exerting power over others.

NOTE:

- *For information on breaking up any physical fighting that does occur, see **Fighting**.*

- *If these four plans do not help you resolve the problem and/or bullying and intimidation is a school-wide problem, extensive information is provided in the publication:*

  Garrity, C., Jens, K., Porter, W., Sager, N., & Short-Camilli, C. (1994). Bully-proofing your school: A comprehensive approach for elementary schools. Longmont, CO: Sopris West.

Many of the ideas and suggestions following are adapted and condensed from this excellent resource.

Alternative Problems

- **Arguing—Students With Each Other**
- **Bossiness**
- **Cliques/Ganging Up**
- **Gang Involvement**
- **Physically Dangerous Behavior—to Self or Others**
- **Self-Control Issues**
- **Threatening Others (Staff or Students)**
- **Victim—Student Who Is Always Picked On**

········
General Considerations

- If the student's problem behavior stems in any way from academic issues (e.g., the student bullies out of academic frustration and/or to create an image to compensate for his beliefs about his intelligence—"I may be dumb, but I am tougher than anyone else here"), concurrent efforts must be made to ensure his academic success (see **Academic Deficits, Determining**).

- If the student lacks the basic social skills to interact with his peers appropriately, it may be necessary to begin by teaching him those skills. **Social Skills, Lack of** contains information on a variety of published social skills curricula.

- If there is a particular student whom the target student is consistently tormenting, concurrent efforts must be made to deal directly with the bully *and* to help the victim. See **Victim—Student Who Is Always Picked On** for ideas on assisting the student who is the brunt of the bullying.

········
Model Plans

PLAN A

It is not always necessary, or even beneficial, to use an involved plan. If the inappropriate behavior has just begun, the following actions, along with making the student aware of your concerns, may resolve the situation.

1. *Respond consistently to the student's bullying behavior.*

a. If the student's bullying behavior involves fighting (i.e., physical aggression), make sure that preestablished school policies and consequences (e.g., suspension) are enforced. *(NOTE: You may also wish to refer to the problem **Fighting** in this reference guide for suggestions on how to break up any fights that do occur.)*

b. For bullying behavior that does not involve fighting, establish a procedure of using a verbal warning initially, and implementing a consequence if it continues. For example, you might assign mild in-class consequences for the student such as time-out, followed by time owed, if necessary. "Jeff, if I see you bullying to get your own way in your cooperative group, I will give you a reminder that you need to respect the rights of others. However, if you keep going with the bullying, I will remove you from the group and you will work on your own. If there are repeated incidents, you will owe two minutes off of recess for each time I need to remind you about this."

c. If other students are present when you give the student a warning or implement a conse-quence, describe the inappropriate behavior as "not respecting the rights of others." Although you can refer to the behavior as bullying when discussing the situation privately with the student, using that term publicly might brand the student as a bully in front of his peers—which actually may be reinforcing for the student.

2. *Use reinforcement to encourage appropriate behavior.*

a. Give the student increased praise. Be especially alert for situations in which the student interacts with other students without bullying or fighting and praise him for these demonstrations of his ability to respect the rights of others. "Jeff, I noticed that you and Dana had a minor disagreement about who would be responsible for the football out at recess. You two worked out a good plan, Dana takes it today and you are responsible for it tomorrow. This is a great example of compromise, and being willing to compromise is one of the ways you can respect the rights of others. You should be very proud of yourself."

If the student would be embarrassed by public praise, praise the student privately or even give the student a note. Remember that any time the student is interacting with others and is not bullying, you can praise him for respecting the rights of others.

b. Praise the student privately for responding to the verbal warning. "Jeff, twice this morning I gave you the warning that you were bullying, and both times, you changed your behavior and began cooperating and treating the others with respect. You are learning some very important lessons about maturity."

c. Give the student frequent attention (e.g., say "hello" to him as he enters the classroom, call on him frequently during class activities, and occasionally seek him out during unstructured times to talk to him about his interests) and praise him for other positive behaviors he exhibits. For example, you might comment about the creativity of his art work or the insights he shared during a class discussion. This demonstrates to the student that you notice many positive things he does, not just the fact that he is refraining from bullying.

PLAN B

Some students may not actually know how to respect the rights of others. If you don't think your student possesses the necessary skills to interact without bullying, the intervention must include a way to teach him these social skills.

(NOTE: If the student lacks many social skills, a formal, sequenced social skills program would probably be more appropriate than this plan.)

 Respond consistently to the student's bullying behavior.

a. If the student's bullying behavior involves fighting (i.e., physical aggression), make sure that preestablished school policies and consequences are implemented. For bullying behavior that does not involve fighting, give the student a verbal warning, followed by time-out and/or time owed, as necessary (see PLAN A).

b. Place restrictions on the student if he has trouble with bullying in a particular location or during a particular time of the day. For example, if the student tends to have more trouble on a distant playing field at recess time, assign him location restrictions during recess. "Jeff, since you seem to get in fights on the soccer field, for two weeks you will not be allowed to go on the upper playground."

c. In addition to consequences for specific incidents of bullying behavior, it may be appropriate to assign the student a week of structured recess (or after-school detention) during which the student spends time practicing skills related to treating others with respect. (Suggestions for the content of these lessons follow in Step 2).

If you do implement these lessons, let the student know that you are not doing this to punish him, but because his behavior shows that he needs the lessons and practice sessions. A sports example may be meaningful. If the student likes football, for example, tell him that

when the kicking team for the Dallas Cowboys are having trouble with field goals, they get extra coaching and have to spend extra time practicing their field goals.

2. **Conduct one-on-one lessons with the student to teach him how to respect the rights of others.**

a. The lessons will probably require a minimum of 15 minutes each, and should occur daily for a minimum of one week. Since this is a significant amount of time, you may need the assistance of the counselor (or another skilled professional in the school) to plan and/or conduct the lessons. *(NOTE: The information in Steps 2b-2c is geared specifically for the person who will be conducting the lessons with the student.)*

b. Analyze any information you have collected on the student's bullying (see SUGGESTED STEPS FOR DEVELOPING AND IMPLEMENTING A PLAN) to see if there are certain times, places, and/or students involved. In addition, you might consider having the student complete the following "Thinking Style Rating" form, adapted with permission from *Bully-Proofing Your School* (Garrity et al., 1994).

The "Thinking Style Rating" form is based on Dr. Stan Samenow's work on antisocial personality development, which suggests that bullying behavior often stems from one or more of the following "thinking errors" (Garrity et al., p. 272):

• "Life is a one-way street—my way."; "If I want to do it, it is right, but if you want to do it, it is wrong."; entitled; unfair

- Disregard of injury to others; failure to empathize or make amends

- Unrealistic expectations and pretensions; "I should be number one overnight."; winning is everything; "If someone disagrees with me, they are putting me down."

- Taking the easy way; using shortcuts; quitting if not immediately successful; doing as little work as one can get away with

- Lying as a way of life; secretive; withholding information gives a sense of power; no concept of trust

- "It's not my fault."; refusing to held accountable; always has an excuse; blaming others

- An island unto oneself; feeling superior to peers; appearing sociable, but in actuality using others; not a team player; not loyal; no sense of mutuality in relationships

If you are able to identify patterns in and possible causes for the student's bullying behavior, you can customize the content of the lessons so that they are more likely to be productive. For example, you might design lessons that target some or all of the student's identified "thinking errors."

c. Use this sample lesson plan as a template for creating the lessons to use with the student:

- Explain to the student the nature of his particular thinking error. For example, suppose the student usually seems to operate from a belief that if he wants to do something, it is right, but if someone else wants to do it, it is wrong. You might use a visual aid such as the following Calvin and Hobbes cartoon to introduce the concept. (NOTE: Calvin and Hobbes cartoons provide a wealth of examples of various types of erroneous thinking.) Review the cartoon itself and then use a single statement that summarizes the thinking error that it depicts (i.e., "Life is a one-way street—my way.").

- Describe a hypothetical bullying situation (if possible, based on an actual situation in which the student has been involved), then help the student understand the erroneous thinking that led to the bullying actions, and how someone who was trying to "respect the rights of others" might have responded instead. You might, for example, ask the student to think about how he would feel if an older/bigger student treated (bullied) him that way, and/or to identify different ways the "bully" could have handled the situation. The primary goal is to help the student learn how he can meet his needs while still respecting the rights of others.

Thinking Style Rating

Student Directions:

For each question, check the circle by the thought that represents how you usually think.

1.	○ Everything should always go my way.	○ To be fair, things should go my way half the time and the other person's way the other half of the time.
2.	○ I don't care if I hurt other people.	○ I feel bad if I hurt other people because I know how it feels to be hurt.
3.	○ Success should come easy and quickly or I'll quit.	○ I know that success takes hard work and a lot of time.
4.	○ I shouldn't have to follow rules or do boring things.	○ I have to follow the rules and do my chores like everyone else.
5.	○ Lying can keep you out of trouble.	○ Lying is a wrong thing to do.
6.	○ I never make mistakes and things are never my fault.	○ Everyone makes mistakes and things are probably my fault about half the time.
7.	○ Most kids my age are boring and always pleasing adults.	○ I have a lot in common with kids my age.

• You might also have the student engage in some role playing. Identify a number of hypothetical situations (some of which can be based on actual incidents) and have the student act them out. Some of the time, have the student play the part of the bully, and some of the time have him play the part of the victim. *(NOTE: Be sure that you structure the role plays so that the student plays the victim at least three times more than he plays the bully; you don't want to provide excessive practice in bullying.)*

3. Prompt the student to behave appropriately by using precorrections.

Watch for circumstances in which the student is likely to bully and remind him that he will need to remember to respect the rights of others. "Jeff, remember that at recess part of respecting the rights of others is respecting their right to be safe. I have asked the playground supervisors to keep a close eye on you to see if you remember to do what you have been practicing with Mr. Wong. I'll bet you can."

If time permits, you might have the student identify what appropriate behavior would be and/or strategies he can use to avoid bullying others. "Jeff, before you go out, tell me a few things you have to remember about playing safely. Remember what you and Mr. Wong have worked on during the lessons. What might you try? Excellent, have a nice recess." If this will embarrass the student, question the student privately.

4. Use reinforcement to encourage appropriate behavior.

a. Give the student increased praise and attention for respecting the rights of others (see PLAN A).

b. In addition, make a special point of letting the student know that you notice his efforts to use the skills he has been learning/practicing. "Jeff, excellent job of treating others with respect. I heard from the supervisors that you had a great recess. This was a nice example of doing what you have been practicing with Mr. Wong."

P L A N   C

Sometimes a student engages in fighting and bullying mainly when something or someone makes him frustrated or angry. If the student usually seems upset when he is bullying (as opposed to calm and calculating), the intervention should include procedures to help the student learn to manage his anger or frustration more productively.

1. Respond consistently to the student's bullying behavior.

a. If the student's bullying behavior involves fighting (i.e., physical aggression), make sure that preestablished school policies and consequences are implemented. For bullying behavior that does not involve fighting, give the student a verbal warning, followed by time-out and/or time owed, as necessary (see PLAN A).

b. Place restrictions on the student if he has trouble in a particular location or during a particular time of the day (see PLAN B).

c. Identify a place (e.g., the counselor's office or the principal's office) where the student can go for self-imposed time-outs when he feels himself starting to become angry or when he is about to lose control. It is important for the student to understand that going to this place is not a punishment, but rather provides a way he can receive support by having someone talk to him/praise him for having exited a situation in

which he might have engaged in bullying or fighting.

d. Be sure to invite the person who works in this time-out place to the initial meeting with the student (see SUGGESTED STEPS FOR DEVELOPING AND IMPLEMENTING A PLAN). All parties involved should be clear about the circumstances under which the student should use this option, as well as what will happen (i.e., talk and support) when he is there.

2. Involve the student in a goal-setting process.

a. With the student and perhaps his parent(s), either during the initial meeting (see SUGGESTED STEPS FOR DEVELOPING AND IMPLEMENTING A PLAN) or at another scheduled meeting, help the student identify a goal that he can work toward regarding managing his anger and/or not bullying/fighting. Although you might want to have a fairly good idea about what the goal should entail prior to meeting with the student, remember that if the student feels that he has participated in deciding what his goal will be, he will be more likely to strive to achieve that goal.

b. Either way, identify one broad-based goal, such as "learn to manage anger while respecting the rights of others," and three specific ways that the student can demonstrate that he is working on the goal. Also include ways that you can help the student achieve his goal. A completed goal contract might look like the sample following:

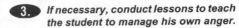 **3.** *If necessary, conduct lessons to teach the student to manage his own anger.*

For information on how to conduct such lessons, see PLAN B and/or **Self-Control Issues**.

If the student seems to have a low tolerance for *frustration* (i.e., he gets easily frustrated when things do not go his way, then he gets angry and fights or bullies), see **Spoiled Behavior** for information on conducting lessons to teach the student strategies for dealing with his own frustration.

Jeff

A goal for me to work on is _____ *to manage my anger while respecting the rights of others* _____. I can show that I am working on this goal by:

1. When angry at someone, keeping my hands in your pockets and telling that person what I need or want without threatening or fighting.

2. By being powerful and confident enough to sometimes let the other person have his/her way.

3. If I feel really angry, going to the counselor's office to cool down.

Ms. Bender

I will support you in this goal by:

1. Allowing you to go to Mr. Wong's office whenever you need to.

2. Giving a verbal warning if I see you start to have trouble.

3. Noticing your efforts to respect the rights of others.

Mr. Wong:

I will support you in this goal by:

1. Allowing you to come to my office whenever you need to.

2. Talking with you about the problem and what you might do to solve it. (If I am with another student, you may have to wait for a little while.)

3. Talking with you about how responsible you were to come to my office rather than bullying or fighting.

_____   _____
Student Signature   Teacher Signature

_____   _____
Date   Counselor Signature

---

4. Use reinforcement to encourage appropriate behavior.

a. Give the student increased praise and attention for respecting the rights of others (see PLAN A).

b. In addition, make a special point of letting the student know that you notice his efforts to use the skills he has been learning/practicing. "Jeff, I saw that you were disagreeing with Ty and you put your hands in your pockets and spoke to him in a quiet, respectful way. Did you notice that you convinced him to do it your way without threatening or bullying? You used your brain and words to convince him your idea was better. Nice job of doing what you agreed to on your goal contract!"

c. Provide intermittent reinforcers when you see the student making an effort to follow through on any part of the goal. For example, you might tell the student, "Jeff you showed a great deal of maturity in dealing with the situation on the playground. Going to the counselor's office to cool down showed your ability to manage your own anger. I think the other students are learning to have more respect for you, now that they see you using your power wisely. This afternoon, I could arrange some extra time for you in the computer lab, if you would like."

Other reinforcement ideas might involve helping you with a classroom job, tutoring a younger student, or even something as simple as spending some time in the gym shooting baskets or using gymnastics equipment. *(NOTE: A list of additional reinforcement ideas can be found in APPENDIX 1.)*

Use intermittent rewards more frequently at the beginning of the intervention to encourage the student, and then less often as his behavior improves.

PLAN D

Some students experience a sense of power through bullying or intimidation. If your student has a reputation for being "tough" and/or seems to enjoy influencing others, the intervention must include reducing the power the student feels from bullying and increasing his sense of power for behaving responsibly.

 1. Respond consistently to the student's bullying behavior.

a. If the student's bullying behavior involves fighting (i.e., physical aggression), make sure that preestablished school policies and consequences are implemented. For bullying behavior that does not involve fighting, give the student a verbal warning, followed by time-out and/or time owed, as necessary (see PLAN A).

b. Place restrictions on the student if he has trouble in a particular location or during a particular time of the day (see PLAN B).

c. In addition to consequences for specific incidents, consider assigning the student a week of structured recess (or after-school detention) during which he spends time practicing skills related to treating others with respect (see PLAN B).

d. Remain emotionally neutral when you give a verbal warning and/or implement a consequence. That is, communicate calmly—do not lecture or scold. You goal is to react as if the behavior is simply something to be dealt with—not a big deal. If the student senses that his bullying elicits any kind of emotionalism (e.g., frustration, anger, helplessness, etc.) on the part of adults, it will increase his sense of power.

 2. Use reinforcement to encourage the student's appropriate use of power.

Frequent praise and attention are at the core of this plan. The student must see that he receives more frequent and more satisfying acknowledgment for behaving appropriately than for bullying. Whenever the student is not bullying (or otherwise misbehaving), make an effort to praise and to acknowledge the power and influence the student has. "Jeff, during today's lesson you brought up a point that I had never thought of before. I appreciate the point you made and I am going to reread that chapter with your idea in mind. I would like to talk you more about it tomorrow. Would that be all right with you?" However, be cautious of praising "good behavior" in front of the student's peers. This student does not want to be good—he wants to be powerful.

 3. Ensure a 3-1 ratio of positive to negative attention.

a. In case adult attention is a motivating force for this student, you need to be sure that you are giving the student *three times as much* positive as negative attention. One way to do this is to monitor your interactions with the student at least one day per week. Keep a card on a clipboard or in your pocket and record each interaction you have with the student as either positive or negative by writing a "+" or a "-", respectively, on the card.

b. To determine whether an interaction is positive or negative, ask yourself whether the student was bullying (or otherwise misbehaving) at the time of the interaction. Any interaction that stems from inappropriate behavior is negative, and all interactions that occur while the student is meeting school-wide expectations are positive. Thus, giving a verbal warning, sending the student to time-out, and assigning time owed are all negative interactions, but praising the student for demonstrating a positive influence on the class is positive. Greeting the student as he enters the room or asking him if he has any questions during independent work are also considered positive interactions.

c. If you find that you are not giving the student three times as much positive as negative attention, try to increase the number of positive interactions you have with the student. Sometimes prompts can help. For example, you might decide that each time the student enters the classroom you will say "hello" to him, or that twice each day you will find a time to talk to the student for a minute or two about one of his interests, or that you will observe the student at athletic practice or a game and comment about his performance (positively) the next day.

4. **Set up a mentoring relationship for the student.**

a. Arrange for an adult (other than yourself) that the student likes/respects to spend time with the student. The intent here is to provide the student with extra adult attention and a positive role model (i.e., someone who demonstrates that a person can be powerful without resorting to intimidation or violence). Whenever possible, this person should be someone within the school, and of the same gender and racial background as the student.

b. The mentor should plan on meeting with the student at least once per week. The meetings need not be formal, but should be scheduled consistently enough that the student knows he can count on them. The meetings needn't focus solely on the student's bullying behavior (e.g., the student and mentor can talk about sports or other mutual interests), however, you want to encourage the mentor to occasionally talk with the student about the student's use of power and to discuss his progress in learning to respect the rights of others. If the student enjoys his time with his mentor, knowing that the mentor is likely to ask something like, "Jeff, let's talk about how you have done this week with respecting the rights of others" may provide extra incentive for the student to try harder.

5. **Conduct (or arrange for the mentor to conduct) at least one lesson on the societal consequences of bullying and fighting.**

a. It is important to teach the student about some potential long-term consequences of continued fighting and bullying. Identify how his peers may tend to avoid interacting with him for fear of being bullied, and provide examples. Then create an imaginary situation in which the student is being bullied by someone more powerful than he is, and have him identify how it feels to be put in that position. Ask the student if he would seek this person out as a friend. Have the student identify how someone he has bullied might have felt the same way.

b. A second major concept to teach the student concerns the legal ramifications of fighting and intimidation. Some students do not realize that what may be called "hitting" in school can be considered assault later in life, or that what is called "bullying" in school may legally be considered harassment, stalking, attempted assault, or another illegal behavior.

c. You might consider having a police officer attend this meeting with the student. If the student's problem with bullying is especially severe, you may even want to explore the possibility of arranging a field trip to a prison or juvenile detention center so that the student can see where his aggressive behavior may be leading him.

. . . .
Suggested Steps for Developing and Implementing a Plan

The following steps are designed to help you develop an appropriate intervention plan and implement it effectively, whether you choose to use one of the MODEL PLANS or create a customized plan of your own. The steps are, however, suggestions—they are not intended to be followed rigidly or in any particular order. Use your professional judgment and the knowledge of your particular situation to make them work for you.

1. *Make sure you have enough information about the situation.*

a. With this type of problem behavior, you should collect information from the outset. You not only need to be able to explain what you mean by "bullying," but complete records of all incidents could be crucial if the situation ever requires outside authorities (e.g., law enforcement officials, attorneys). Keeping anecdotal notes on every incident will give you an accurate record of frequency as well as providing enough details to help you define the problem behavior clearly and completely.

b. To collect anecdotal notes, simply keep a card in your pocket or on a clipboard and take notes each time the student engages in an act of bullying behavior. It may be necessary to ask the playground supervisors to keep anecdotal records for the playground as well.

Sometimes with bullying, any single event is not a horrible or significant problem, rather it is the accumulation of problems that is severe. For each entry, briefly describe where and when the bullying occurred, what the student did or said, and any other relevant observations (e.g., what prompted the behavior).

Also include some notes on times when the student interacts appropriately with other students—this will make it clear to the student that you are not only aware of his problem behavior, but also recognize when he behaves appropriately. When you meet with the student, the positive examples will help you to clarify how you want the student to behave.

c. Keeping these types of anecdotal records also provides you with a daily count of bullying incidents. Continuing to collect this type of information while you implement a plan will also help you to monitor whether the situation is getting worse, staying the same, or getting better.

d. If the student notices what you are doing and asks about it, be straightforward—tell him that you are collecting information to see whether his bullying is a problem that needs to be worked on.

Following is an example of anecdotal notes that have been collected on the student's bullying.

2. *Identify a focus for the intervention and labels for referring to the appropriate and inappropriate behaviors.*

a. To be effective, the intervention must address more than just reducing the student's bullying

---

Jeff's Behavior—5/22

9:20—Jeff grabbed Melissa by the muscle above the shoulder (like a pincer) and lead her away from the pencil sharpener back to her seat. He said with a big grin, "Now Melissa, you know I am always first to the pencil sharpener." By the time I intervened, she was crying and Jeff was smirking. I told him I was calling his parents tonight.

10:30—The recess supervisors reported that Jeff had been sent in from recess for repeatedly pushing and shoving and other aggressive acts. When Jeff came into the classroom he sauntered in saying, "I'm bad. I'm bad. Uh huh, I'm bad."

2:15—As we were cleaning up at the end of art, Jeff told Su Yen that he needed to clean up his things or he would "make his life miserable after school." I just happened to overhear. When Su Yen started to put away Jeff's things, I told Jeff he needed to do it himself. I reported the incident to the principal. When I asked Su Yen about it later, he denied it. I think he is afraid of what Jeff would do if he told.

---

behavior—there must be a concurrent emphasis on increasing some positive behavior or trait (e.g., respecting the rights of others). Having a specific positive behavior in mind will make it easier for you to "catch" and reinforce the student for behaving appropriately, and the positive focus will help you to frame the situation more productively.

For example, if you simply say that "the student has a problem with bullying," you don't really provide any useful information, and may put the student and his parent(s) on the defensive. However, when you explain that you want to "help the student learn to respect the rights of others," you present an important, and reasonable, goal for the student to work toward and clearly identify what the student needs to do to be successful.

b. Specifying labels for the appropriate and inappropriate behaviors (e.g., "respecting the rights of others" and "not respecting the rights of others," respectively) will help you to use consistent vocabulary when discussing the situation with the student. If you sometimes refer to the inappropriate behavior as "intimidating others" and other times tell the student that he is "not respecting the rights of others," he may not realize that you are talking about the same thing.

3. Determine when and how to include the parent(s).

a. With this type of problem, the parent(s) should be contacted immediately. Share any information you have collected about the student's behavior (i.e., your anecdotal notes), and explain why you are concerned. Focus in particular on how the behavior is hindering the student academically and/or socially (e.g., other students avoid him because they are afraid to interact with him). Also emphasize the disruptive influence this sort of intimidation has on the smooth running of the class (e.g., other students cannot focus on learning if they are afraid of what might happen next).

You might ask if the parent(s) have any insight into the situation and/or whether they have noticed similar behavior at home. Whether or not the parent(s) perceive a problem, explain that you want to help the student "learn to respect the rights of others" and invite them to join you for an initial meeting with the student to develop a plan.

If the parent(s) are unable or unwilling to participate, let them know that you will keep them informed of the student's progress. If the par-

ent(s) seem antagonistic (e.g., "I tell my son to punch the lights out of anybody who looks at him cross-eyed."), ask the building administrator or other appropriate school personnel to join you when you meet with the student and his parent(s).

b. Once the parent(s) have been involved in any way, you should give them updates at least once per week while the plan is being implemented.

4. Prepare for, then conduct, an initial meeting about the situation.

a. Arrange a meeting to discuss your concerns with the student and anyone else who will be involved in the plan (e.g., the parent[s], the building administrator). Although the specifics will vary depending upon the age of the student and the severity of the problem, there are some general guidelines to consider when scheduling the meeting.

First, meet at a neutral time (i.e., not immediately after a problem has occurred), when emotions are less likely to hamper communication. In general, a day's notice is appropriate, however a primary age student may worry excessively and/or forget what the meeting is about if it is scheduled more than an hour before it takes place. Second, make the meeting appropriately private. Third, try to make sure the meeting is scheduled for a time and place that it is not likely to be interrupted. Finally, if the parent(s) will be participating, they should be the ones to tell the student about the meeting.

b. Construct a preliminary plan. Decide whether you think you can use one of the MODEL PLANS or if you need to create a customized plan using components from various plans and/or of your own design. Although you will invite and encourage the student to help develop the plan during the initial meeting, having a proposed plan in mind before you meet can alleviate frustration and wasted time if the student is unwilling or unable to participate.

c. Review the information you have collected and think about how you want the student to behave. Then prepare thorough descriptions of the inappropriate behavior and the positive behavior/trait on which the student will be working. The more specific you can be and the more concrete examples you have, the easier it will be to clarify (and for the student to understand) your expectations. Be sure to consider the student's behavior in all relevant activities (e.g., independent work, teacher directed instruction, unstructured class times, recess and lunch, etc.).

d. Conduct the meeting in an atmosphere of collaboration. The following agenda is one way you might structure the meeting:

- **Share your concerns about the student's behavior.**

  Briefly describe the problem behavior and explain why you consider it to be a problem. In this case, you might tell the student that his behavior violates the right of other students to feel safe at school. Tell him that he and every other student have an equal right to feel safe and free from being intimidated or injured at school, but his behavior is interfering with that right for other students.

- **Discuss how you can work together to improve the situation.**

  Tell the student that you would like to help him learn to "respect the rights of others" and describe your preliminary plan. Invite the student to give you input on the various aspects of the plan, and together work out any necessary details (e.g., the verbal warning, use of time-out, time owed, self-imposed time-out in the counselor's office, etc.). You may have to brainstorm different possibilities if the student is uncomfortable with the initial plan. Incorporating any of the student's suggestions that strengthen the plan is likely to increase his sense of "ownership" in and commitment to it.

- **Make sure the student understands what you mean by appropriate and inappropriate behavior.**

  Use the descriptions you have prepared to define and clarify the problem behavior and the positive (desired) behavior as specifically and thoroughly as you can. To ensure that you and the student are in agreement about the expectations, you might present hypothetical scenarios and have the student iden-

tify whether each is an example of respecting the rights of others or not respecting the rights of others. Or you might describe an actual situation that has occurred and ask him to explain how he might demonstrate that he is respecting the rights of others, while still getting his needs met in that situation.

- Conclude the meeting.

  Always end the meeting with words of encouragement. Let the student know that you are confident that he can be successful. Also be sure to reinforce him for participating in the meeting.

5. *Give the student regular, ongoing feedback about his behavior.*

It is important to meet with the student periodically to discuss his progress. In most cases, three to five minutes once per week should suffice, although for the first week, a brief daily meeting may be useful. Review any information that has been collected and discuss whether or not the situation is getting better. As much as possible, focus on the student's improvements, however, also address any new or continuing problems. As the situation improves, the meetings can be faded to once every other week and then to once per month.

6. *Evaluate the situation (and the plan).*

Implement any plan for at least one week before deciding whether to change plans; to continue, modify, or fade the plan you are using; or to cease the intervention. However, since this is a severe problem, do not let the problem continue as students could be hurt by the bully. Generally, if the student's behavior is clearly improving (based on the objective information that's been collected via anecdotal records and/or the subjective perceptions of yourself, the student, and possibly the parent[s]), stick with what you are doing. If the situation has remained the same or worsened, some kind of change will be necessary. Always discuss any changes to the plan with the student first.

CHAIR TIPPING
. . . .

Leaning Back in Chair

DESCRIPTION

There are students in your class who lean back in their chairs (i.e., sit so that only two legs of the chair are on the floor).

GOAL

The students will sit properly in their chairs at all times (i.e., they will keep all four chair legs on the floor).

OVERVIEW OF PLANS

- PLAN A—For a situation in which the problem has just begun or occurs infrequently.

- PLAN B—For a situation in which the students may be unaware of the extent of their inappropriate behavior.

- PLAN C—For a situation in which the students lack the motivation to behave appropriately.

NOTE:

These three MODEL PLANS assume that the chair tipping problem is class-wide. All three can easily be modified to use with only one or a few students.

· · · · · · · · ·
Model Plans

PLAN A

It is not always necessary, or even beneficial, to use an involved plan. If the chair tipping has just begun and/or occurs infrequently (e.g., two to five times per week), the following actions, along with making the students aware of your concerns, may resolve the situation.

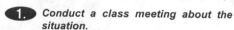 **Conduct a class meeting about the situation.**

Discuss with the class your concerns and explain your expectations (see SUGGESTED STEPS FOR DEVELOPING AND IMPLEMENTING A PLAN).

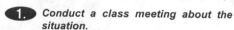 **Respond consistently to all instances of chair tipping.**

Whenever a student is tipping back in a chair, gently correct the student by stating your expectations about chair sitting. "Nathaniel, remember, you need all four feet of the chair on the floor." Avoid being emotional or talking too much when correcting the student. Your goal is simply to impart information.

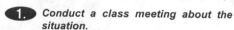 **Use reinforcement to encourage appropriate behavior.**

a. Praise individual students who are meeting your expectations regarding sitting in chairs properly (i.e., not tipping back). Keep an eye on those students who have had the greatest tendency to lean back in their chairs and acknowledge them for treating school property with care.

b. Also praise those students who have had little or no problem with chair tipping. These students do not need positive feedback as often as the students for whom chair tipping is a problem, however you do not want them to feel that you take their appropriate behavior for granted. "You people seated at this table consistently use the furniture the right way. Thanks." If public praise might be embarrassing for the students, praise them privately or even give the students a note.

c. When applicable, praise the class as a whole for treating school property with respect. Whenever the students are sitting correctly in their chairs, you can praise them for their responsible behavior.

PLAN B

Occasionally students are not really aware of when and/or how frequently they are leaning back in their chairs. In these cases, the intervention must include a way of helping them become more aware of their own behavior.

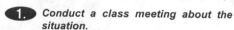 **Conduct a class meeting about the situation (see PLAN A).**

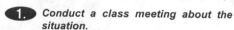 **Respond consistently to all instances of chair tipping.**

a. Whenever a student is leaning back in his/her chair, gently correct the student (see PLAN A).

b. In addition, make sure each incident is recorded (see Step 3).

 Publicly document the frequency of chair tipping in the classroom.

a. Because the goal is to obtain a total count of chair tipping incidents each day (i.e., a frequency count), as opposed to putting undue peer pressure on individual students, it is not necessary to identify which students are leaning back in their chairs. Simply keep a card in your pocket or on a clipboard, and write a tally mark for each incident of chair tipping.

b. Each day, hold a short class meeting to publicly record the information and review the day's record. If appropriate, have a student chart the information on a graph (or do it yourself). Then briefly discuss whether the number of incidents was more, less, or about the same as on previous days.

If the day did not go well, encourage the students to talk about why. Help them to identify what they can do the next day to help them remember to keep their chairs flat on the floor. If the students behave inappropriately during the meeting, keep the review session very short. Simply let the class know that you are sure tomorrow will be a better day.

4. *Use reinforcement to encourage appropriate behavior.*

a. Praise individual students and, when applicable, the entire class for treating school property with care and respect (see PLAN A).

b. When applicable, praise the students during the end-of-the-day review meetings for their willingness to look seriously at the day's results. Even on a bad day, if the students discuss why it was a bad day, praise them. "Class, you are really handling this responsibly. Even though it was a rough day, you are willing to talk to about things you might do differently tomorrow. That is a real sign that we are making progress."

Always try to make these meetings upbeat and encouraging (regardless of how the day went), as you want the students to look forward to the review at the end of the day.

PLAN C

Sometimes students who have fallen into the habit of chair tipping are simply not motivated to behave appropriately. In this case, the intervention should include a structured system of reinforcement (i.e., rewards and consequences) to encourage the students to change their behavior.

1. *Conduct a class meeting about the situation (see PLAN A).*

2. *Respond consistently to all instances of chair tipping.*

a. Establish a consequence that is logically associated with chair tipping, but that is mild enough that you will be willing to follow through on implementing it each time an incident occurs. For example, you might take away the student's chair for the remainder of that instructional activity and return it at the beginning of the next activity. Thus, if the tipping occurred at the beginning of a math lesson, for example, the chair would be returned to the student when the math lesson is completed.

b. Before you begin implementing the consequence for chair tipping, be sure that the students understand exactly what will happen when they are leaning back in their chairs. "Class, from now on, if I have to give a reminder to someone about chair tipping, that person will lose the privilege of having the chair for the remainder of the activity."

c. Whenever a student is leaning back in his/her chair, implement the consequence. Do not worry if, at first, the students act like it is great fun to be without a chair. If you simply ignore this behavior, the students will tire of the game within a few days. In addition to the consequence, make sure the incident is recorded (see Step 3).

3. *Publicly document the frequency of chair tipping in the classroom (see PLAN B).*

4. *Have the class establish a performance objective for reducing their number of daily chair tipping incidents.*

Because the students may be inclined to set an unrealistic goal (e.g., reducing the number of incidents per day from 15 to zero), you may have to help them set a more attainable goal. It is reasonable to aim for a reduction of about 30% each week (e.g., from 15 to 11 incidents per day). Explain to the students that if they have a goal of 11, they can always have less incidents than that, but by making their goal attainable, they increase their chances of success. Then, as the class consistently experiences success, continue lowering the goal by 30% each week until their objective is zero incidents.

5. *Implement a system for rewarding the class for appropriate behavior.*

a. During the initial meeting to discuss this situation with the class (See SUGGESTED STEPS FOR DEVELOPING AND IMPLEMENTING A PLAN), have the students brainstorm a number of class-wide rewards they might want to earn. Review the students' list and eliminate any items that are not possible (i.e., the suggestions are too expensive or could not be provided to all the students in the class), then assign "prices" (in points) to the remaining items on the list.

The prices should be based on the instructional, personnel, and/or monetary costs of the items. Monetary cost is clear—the more expensive the item, the more points required to earn it. Instructional cost refers to the amount of instructional time lost or interfered with by a particular reward. Thus, an activity which causes the class to miss part of academic instruction should require more points than one the class can do during recess time. Personnel cost involves the time required by you and/or other staff to fulfill the reinforcer. Thus, receiving an extra recess period during which extra supervision would need to be arranged, for example, would cost more than having music playing in class for 15 minutes.

b. Have the class vote on the reinforcer they would like to earn first. To save time, let them know that the item that receives the second most votes will be the one they will work for next.

c. On days when the class keeps the number of chair tipping incidents under their identified goal, award them a point (or points). They will continue to accumulate points until they can "pay for" their reward.

d. An alternative reinforcement system is the use of a Mystery Motivator (Rhode, Jenson, & Reavis, 1992). In this system, you mark random days on a class calendar with an "X," then cover all the daily spaces with a slip of paper. On the days when the class attains their goal, uncover the space for that day to see if there is an X. If there is, the class earns a predetermined rein-

forcer. *(NOTE: Also uncover the spaces for days on which the class was unsuccessful to show them whether they would have received a reward if they had achieved their performance objective.)*

e. If you don't think that a class-wide system is likely to be effective, consider using a team competition and response cost lottery. Divide the class into four to six equitable teams (i.e., each time would have an equal number of typical chair tippers). Give each team a certain number of tickets at the beginning of each day and have them write the name of their team on their tickets.

Whenever a student is tipping back in his/her chair, that student's team loses a ticket. At the end of the day, each team puts their remaining tickets in a hat for a lottery drawing. The name of the team on the ticket that is drawn earns the predetermined reward for that day.

Because with this system you will be giving daily rewards, the reinforcers should be moderate and reasonable (e.g., a pass for five minutes of extra time on a computer given to each team member).

f. Regardless of which reinforcement system you use, keep student attention focused on the fact that they are treating school property with care and respect. "Class, you earned your point for the day, but more importantly, you are treating school property with care and respect. Our class is a place we can all be proud of."

. . . .

Suggested Steps for Developing and Implementing a Plan

The following steps are designed to help you develop an appropriate intervention plan and implement it effectively, whether you choose to use one of the MODEL PLANS or create a customized plan of your own. The steps are, however, only suggestions—they are not intended to be followed rigidly or in any particular order. Use your professional judgment and knowledge of your particular situation to make them work for you.

 Make sure you have enough information about the situation.

With a behavior like chair tipping, the most useful information involves tracking how often it occurs (i.e., a frequency count). For about a week, simply keep a note card in your pocket or on a clipboard and write a tally mark whenever you notice a student leaning back in his/her chair. *(NOTE: When the problem has just begun and/or occurs infrequently [i.e., when a minimal intervention such*

as PLAN A is appropriate], you may not need this level of objective information.)*

 Present the situation to the class.

a. Depending upon your personal philosophy and the extent (severity/longevity) of the problem, you might want to either have an informal discussion with the students or conduct a more formal class meeting. In either case, wait until you are calm (i.e., not right after an incident has occurred) and make sure there will be enough time to adequately present the issue.

b. When the problem has just begun and/or occurs infrequently, an informal discussion may suffice. Tell the class that you are finding their chair tipping to be a problem and explain why. Inform them that there are both safety and economic reasons why you cannot allow this behavior to continue. That is, explain that chair tipping can result in severe injuries (e.g., a skull fracture) as well as putting undue stress on the chair and undue wear and tear on the floor.

Then clarify your expectations. Tell the students that the chairs were designed so that when someone is seated, all four feet of the chair would remain completely on the floor. Give the students the opportunity to ask questions/make comments. End the session by thanking the students for listening and telling them that you are confident that they will make an effort follow appropriate procedures in the future.

c. When the chair tipping problem is more serious (e.g., PLAN B or C is appropriate) and/or you want the students to assume some ownership of the problem, consider scheduling a class meeting. Inform the students about the meeting in advance so that they will have time to think about the problem. "Class, this afternoon we are going to have a class meeting on the problem of chair tipping. Please give some thought to this situation and how, as a class, we might solve it."

Share the frequency count with the students. Also, make sure that you are clear about your expectations for the students' behavior and that you have identified before the meeting any aspects of the plan that you do not feel comfortable opening up to a group decision (e.g., whether or not there will be a consequence for chair tipping and/or what the consequence will be). If you firmly believe that there should be a consequence for chair tipping, then you should not seek student input on that particular issue.

d. Use an agenda, such as the following, to provide a structure for the meeting. Write the agenda on the chalkboard shortly before the meeting.

3. *Determine when and how to include the parent(s).*

a. With a procedural issue such as chair tipping, it is not necessary to involve parents when the problem is class-wide. However, when the situ-

---

Agenda

1. Chair tipping—Define the problem.

   Share any information you have collected and explain why the chair tipping is a problem.

2. Clarify the expectations for the class.

   Clarify specifically how you want the students to behave with regard to chair tipping in your classroom. Be thorough.

3. Brainstorm ideas for improving the situation

   For brainstorming to be effective, you need to establish clear rules, both for yourself and the students. For example:

   • Any idea is okay (but no obscenity).

   • Ideas will not be evaluated initially (i.e., no approval—"Good idea" or disapproval— "What a stupid idea" or "We couldn't do that" should be expressed during brainstorming).

   • All ideas will be written down and discussed at the conclusion of brainstorming.

4. Select ideas that are agreeable to everyone in the class.

   Lead the class to consensus on any decisions that need to be made. Use voting as a decision-making process when appropriate.

5. Identify consequences—What will happen when there is chair tipping?

---

ation involves only one or a few students who continue to lean back in their chairs, contact the parents of those individual students. Explain that their student is not using the classroom chairs properly and what steps you are taking to correct the situation.

b. Although frequent contact is not required, whenever you are going to implement an individualized plan, the student's parent(s) should be informed beforehand and given updates on the situation approximately every two to four weeks.

4. *Give the class regular, ongoing feedback about their behavior.*

Periodically meet with the class (or the individual students) to evaluate how the situation is going. In most cases, three to five minutes once per week should suffice. During the meetings, review any information that has been collected and discuss whether or not things are getting better. As much as possible, focus on improvements, however, it is important to address any new or continuing problems. *(NOTE: In PLANS B and C, these review meetings have been included as part of the intervention.)* As the situation improves, the meetings can be faded to once every other week and then to once per month.

5. *Evaluate the situation (and the plan).*

After implementing an intervention plan for at least two weeks, determine whether or not it is effective using any objective information that has been collected (e.g., a frequency count) and/or the subjective perceptions of yourself and the students. If the problem behavior has remained the same or worsened, make some kind of change (e.g., modify the current plan or switch to another plan).

If the situation has improved, continue implementation of the plan for another two to four weeks. After a month or more of appropriate/acceptable behavior, gradually fade and then eliminate the intervention plan. Always inform the class (or appropriate individual students) before changing, fading, or eliminating the intervention plan.

CHAOS/CLASSROOM OUT OF CONTROL

DESCRIPTION

There are many students in your class who frequently engage in a variety of misbehaviors.

GOAL

The students will behave responsibly and follow the rules when in the classroom.

OVERVIEW OF PLANS

- PRE-INTERVENTION STEPS: For a situation in which improvements in the overall classroom management may prompt more responsible student behavior.

- PLAN A: For a problem that may stem from students not knowing how to behave responsibly and meet classroom expectations or not taking the rules seriously.

- PLAN B: For a problem that may stem from students not realizing how often they engage in irresponsible behavior.

- PLAN C: For a situation in which the students seem to lack the motivation to behave responsibly and follow the rules.

> ### NOTE:
>
> *Depending upon the severity of your particular problem, suggestions for dealing with this type of chaotic situation may be beyond the scope of this reference guide. If the following plans do not seem sufficient or if they have been ineffective in your classroom, ask for assistance from a colleague whom you respect. This may seem somewhat threatening, but any teacher who is skilled at managing behavior will not think less of you for seeking help. It may also be worthwhile for you and your colleague to jointly study one or more of the following books on behavior management:*
>
> *Emmer, E.T., Evertson, C.M., Sanford, J.P., Clements, B.S., & Worsham, M.E. (1984). Classroom management for secondary teachers. Englewood Cliffs, NJ: Prentice Hall.*
>
> *Evertson, C.M., Emmer, E.T., Clements, B.S., Sanford, J.P., & Worsham, M.E. (1984). Classroom management for elementary teachers. Englewood Cliffs, NJ: Prentice Hall.*
>
> *Jones, V.F. & Jones, L.S. (1986). Comprehensive classroom management. Boston: Allyn and Bacon.*
>
> *Morgan, D.P. & Jenson, W.R. (1988). Teaching behaviorally disordered students. Columbus, OH: Merrill.*
>
> *Paine, S.C., Radicchi, J., Deutchman, L., Rosellini, L.C., & Darch, C.B. (1983). Structuring your classroom for academic success. Champaign, IL: Research Press.*
>
> *Sprick, R.S. (1981). The solution book: A guide to classroom discipline. Chicago: Science Research Associates.*
>
> *Sprick, R.S. (1985). Discipline in the secondary classroom: A problem by problem survival guide. Englewood Cliffs, NJ: Prentice Hall.*
>
> *Sprick, R.S., Sprick, M.S., & Garrison, M. (1993). Interventions: Collaborative planning for students at risk. Longmont, CO: Sopris West.*

. . . .

General Considerations

- If there is a specific misbehavior that stands out as being more severe than others or occurring more often (e.g., **Disruptive Behavior—Severe** or **Name Calling/Put-Downs**), consider intervening with a plan to address that specific problem. A narrow focus on a specific problem may be more successful than the broad-based approaches suggested following.

- If a number of students lack the basic social skills to interact appropriately, it may be necessary to begin by teaching them those skills. Or, if most of the students in the class lack social skills, conduct lessons with the entire class. **Social Skills, Lack of** contains information on a variety of published social skills curricula.

- If the inappropriate behavior is resulting in the students avoiding or not completing their schoolwork, consider starting with a plan to increase the students' work completion (see **Work Completion—Daily Work**). Once the students are turning in completed work on a regular basis, you can consider an intervention for the chaotic behavior, if the problem still exists.

. . . .
Model Plans

PRE-INTERVENTION STEPS

If it is early in the school year and/or it has been some time since you reviewed and revised (if necessary) your classroom management and organization procedures, the following actions may resolve the situation. Whether or not the following steps alone are effective, "preventative management" is a prerequisite for the success of any of the other plans.

1. *Post three to six positively stated classroom rules.*

Clear, concise, posted classroom rules should be the basis of everything you do with regard to behavior management and discipline. Whenever you have discussions with the class or with individuals about behavior or motivation issues, the posted rules should be a focal point. When you correct misbehavior, the corrections and consequences should be based upon your rules. Even the positive feedback you provide to the students should be related to the rules. "Hally, you consistently arrive on time with all of your materials. Nice job of following Rule #2." *(NOTE: PLAN A provides suggestions for involving the students in the process of developing or revising the classroom rules, if this seems necessary.)*

2. *Keep your attention focused on positive behavior.*

a. Whatever you attend to most will occur most frequently. Teachers often inadvertently reinforce inappropriate behavior by giving it too much attention. Interact frequently with students behaving well. Call on them. Praise them. Comment on their work. "Catch" the students who have had the greatest tendency to misbehave when they are *not* misbehaving and let them know how responsible they are being. With each student, try to interact more frequently when he/she is behaving well than when he/she is misbehaving. Your goal should be *three positive interactions for every negative* interaction.

b. You can monitor your interactions by periodically audio taping yourself teaching. Later, listen to the tape and tally both positive and negative interactions by writing a "+" or a "-", respectively, on a sheet of paper.

To determine whether an interaction is positive or negative, ask yourself whether the interaction occurred because a student was breaking a rule (or otherwise misbehaving) at the time the interaction occurred. If so, the interaction would be considered negative. Those interactions that occurred while the students were meeting classroom expectations are positive. So, for example, stating warnings or assigning consequences would be negative interactions, but praising an individual or the group is positive. Greeting the students as they enter the room or asking a student if he/she has any questions during independent work are also considered positive interactions.

c. If you find that you are not giving three times as much positive as negative attention, try to increase the number of positive interactions you have with the students. Sometimes prompts can help. For example, you might decide that each time any student enters the classroom you will say "hello" to him/her, that you will try to praise at least ten different students each half hour, or that whenever a student uses the drinking fountain you will check the class and praise an individual/group who is/are following the rules. You can also increase the ratio of positive to negative attention by ignoring more of the students' mild inappropriate behavior (e.g., a student makes a smar-aleck remark).

3. *Adjust your instructional techniques.*

Try to determine whether student behavior is worse during particular instructional activities. If so, modify those activities. For example, if you tend to lecture a lot, you might modify your instructional style to keep the students more actively involved in the lessons. If you often use cooperative groups, but the students are frequently off task or argue during group work, reduce the amount of time spent each day in cooperative learning until the students demonstrate that they have the skills to work cooperatively. If the students tend to have the most problems during independent work, increase the amount of interactive teacher directed instruction. **Work Completion—Daily Work** provides additional suggestions for adaptations of instructional delivery.

Examine your schedule of activities for a typical day and revise it to ensure a fast pace that keeps the students academically engaged.

If the students are given long periods of time for independent seatwork, revise the schedule so there is greater variety. For example, if the students are typically given 30 minutes to work on their math assignments, consider breaking the time up by first having five minutes of guided practice, five minutes of independent work, five minutes of teacher directed time in order to correct what they have done so far and guide them through more of the assignment, and then 15 minutes to complete the assignment on their own. An effective schedule has daily consistency, but a wide variety of activities.

 Make transition times more efficient.

Define exactly how long the most common transitions should take, give the students feedback on their efficiency, and, if necessary, practice problematic transitions until the students are able to handle those transitions efficiently. "Class, I need your attention. It is time to switch from math to spelling. We will be doing our weekly spelling test, so take out a sheet of lined paper, put on the heading, and number the paper from one to 20. In one minute I will begin the test, so get ready quickly and quietly." For more information, see **Transitions, Problems With**.

 Increase your classroom supervision.

You need to be both out among the students as much as possible and increase your visual scans of the room. To use an adult example, on a freeway numerous, visible police cars will encourage more people to drive at the legal speed limit than on a freeway with no police presence. Whether the activity is teacher directed instruction, small group work, or independent work, your presence will prompt more responsible behavior, so move around the room in unpredictable patterns.

Regardless of what you are doing, frequently scan all parts of the classroom. You should know what is going on at all times. So even if you are sitting in with a cooperative learning group, for example, you should periodically stand up and scan what is taking place in the other groups.

 Modify the physical setting of the classroom to prompt more appropriate behavior.

Make sure that student desks are arranged so you can move throughout the classroom easily. Separate students who have trouble if they sit together. Recognize that with very social groups of children, a U-shaped arrangement (or even a double U-shape as long as you can easily walk back to the second tier) will be less conducive to off-task behavior (e.g., talking) than arranging students in rows. However, rows will be less conducive to off-task behavior than using groups or clusters. If you do cluster your students, avoid having more than four students in a single cluster—groups of six or eight will be more problematic.

PLAN A

Sometimes students misbehave because they are unclear about the expectations for their behavior and/or are rebelling against procedures to which they feel no allegiance. In either of these circumstances, the intervention must involve the collaborative development of clear classroom rules, expectations for student behavior, consequences for infractions, and rewards and incentives.

 Have the students help you revise the classroom rules and develop a realistic list of corresponding consequences.

a. Examine your classroom rules. If you do not have clearcut rules or have rules that the students do not take seriously, schedule a class discussion to develop new rules. Have the class brainstorm a set of possible rules. Before doing

so, establish some rules for brainstorming. For example:

- Any idea is okay (but no obscenity).

- Ideas will not be evaluated initially (i.e., no approval—"Good idea," or disapproval—"What a stupid idea" or "We couldn't do that" should be expressed during brainstorming).

- All ideas will be written down and discussed at the conclusion of brainstorming.

b. After brainstorming, lead the class through a discussion. Evaluate each idea and guide the group to narrow the list to three to six statements of positive expectations. *(NOTE: After selection, you will consistently use these expectations as a basis for correcting irresponsible behavior and for providing positive feedback.)*

c. If you anticipate that the students may be out of control during a discussion of this type, ask a building administrator to attend and assist you in conducting this discussion. This will not only help you maintain control of the class but also demonstrate to the students that you and the administrator are equally concerned about the problem and want them to take ownership of defining rules for the classroom.

d. Have the class brainstorm consequences for rule violations. Again, after the brainstorming, lead the class through a discussion to evaluate the ideas. Have the class choose (voting is one strategy that could be used to select) several consequences ranging from mild (e.g., one minute owed off of recess or a short time-out) to more structured (e.g., parental contact, after-school detention, office referral).

e. Lead the class through a discussion to link consequences with common rule infractions. Structure the discussion with questions such as, "If a student breaks Rule #2, what should I implement as a consequence? And what if he/she argues about it?" If the students suggest something unrealistic, have them identify another possible consequence and tell them why. "No, I don't think that would work. If I had to call parents whenever someone blurted out without raising his/her hand, I would have to spend all evening on the phone. What is something milder and more immediate?"

Continue this process until you have a written list that indicates a reasonable consequence for each type of common rule infraction.

2. Respond calmly and consistently to each instance of misbehavior.

Whenever a student misbehaves, follow through with the consequences that have been established. When a rule violation happens, do not argue or negotiate. Be emotionally neutral and avoid talking too much while giving the correction—just let the student know the consequence for his/her action. "Mohamed, that was disrespectful. As you know, the consequence for disrespect is to write an apology. It needs to be done before you can go out to recess."

3. Teach the students how the new rules relate to each type of classroom activity.

a. After school on the day that the new rules are developed, spend some time thinking about and visualizing *exactly how*, given the new rules, the students should behave during each different classroom activity. Think through the entire school day, taking one activity at a time—beginning with the students entering the room before school starts. For each particular activity, answer the following questions:

- What are common misbehaviors that occur at this time?

- What should the students be doing?

- Where should the students be?

- Should they be talking to each other? If so, about what? how loud? for how long?

- Should they be talking to me (the teacher)?

- How will I get the attention of the class, if necessary?

Note your answers, then proceed to the next activity—beginning class, taking attendance, and other "housekeeping" tasks. Then think about the next activity (e.g., a teacher directed lesson). Continue this process for every activity throughout the day. Don't forget times like going down the hall to the cafeteria.

b. The day after completing this exercise, share your information in a succinct manner with the students. Then immediately before each activity, tell the students your expectations. "Class, I am about to take attendance, and while I am taking attendance what you should be doing is . . . ." Do not begin any activity until all the students understand your expectations.

With primary students, you might want to demonstrate what you mean. Then ask a few students to demonstrate, and ask the students questions to verify that they understand the expectations. With intermediate students, explain how the expectations correlate with the rules the class developed.

Give the students an opportunity to ask questions, express their concerns, and even suggest alternative expectations. Incorporate any reasonable student suggestions. Respond to unreasonable suggestions (e.g., "Let us sleep instead of answering questions and taking notes.") by informing the students that you care too much about their education to allow that. If possible, use the class rules to explain why you cannot accept a particular suggestion. "Linda, I can't let you sleep. One of rules the class developed is 'Do your best—participate!' I care too much about the rules the class developed and too much about everyone's education to allow sleeping when you need to be participating."

c. Continue the practice of telling the students your expectations before each activity for about a week or until they demonstrate that they have mastered the expectations for the various activities. This may mean that you will review the expectations for beginning class for only five days, but the expectations for going to lunch for two weeks.

However, by day two or three, do not allow the students to negotiate alternative expectations, and do not continue to provide a rationale for procedures you have previously explained. If any students continue to make the same suggestions or ask the same questions, simply state that you will ignore that suggestion in the future. "Linda, you know why I can't let you sleep and from now on, I am not going to respond to that suggestion. However, if you want to talk to me after school about your suggestion, feel free to come see me."

With any activity that is not yet going well, continue to review the expectations for responsible behavior when you introduce the activity.

d. End each activity by telling the group how well the activity went. If it went perfectly, tell the students enthusiastically. "During our cooperative learning groups, *every* group used the time wisely and stayed on task. The noise level in each group was very respectful of the other groups. And each group that I listened to was doing a great job of giving each person a chance to participate!"

If the activity did not go so well, set goals for the next day. "During our cooperative learning groups, every group used the time wisely and stayed on task. However, tomorrow let's work harder on managing the noise level. Several of the groups got so into the lesson that people got too loud and I had to come over and remind them to be more quiet. Let's see if tomorrow each group can mange their own noise level without needing me to give them reminders."

4. **Use reinforcement to encourage appropriate behavior.**

a. Praise individual students for following the agreed upon classroom rules and procedures. Keep a watchful eye on those students who have had the greatest tendency to misbehave. Whenever one of these students is behaving appropriately, praise him/her for demonstrating the ability to follow the rules the class developed. If the student would be embarrassed by public praise, praise the student privately or even give the student a note.

b. In addition, occasionally praise those students who rarely or never have a problem with misbehavior. Because these students have already mastered the positive expectations, they do not need positive feedback as often as the students who have had difficulty. However, you do not want them to feel that you take their appropriate behavior for granted. "Libby, Greg, and Akeem, you are all very responsible. I didn't want to embarrass you in front of the others, but you should each be very proud. I appreciate the effort you put into making this a good class."

c. Finally, when there has been a significant improvement in the behavior of the entire group, praise the class. Remember that any time the students are refraining from misbehaving, you can praise them for being responsible and following the rules.

PLAN B

Sometimes students do not seem to realize when and/or how frequently they misbehave. In this case, the intervention should include some way of helping the students become more aware of their own behavior.

1. **Have the students help you revise the classroom rules and develop a realistic list of corresponding consequences (see PLAN A).**

2. **Respond consistently to each instance of misbehavior.**

a. Whenever an individual student engages in a misbehavior, follow through with the procedures you and the class developed (see PLAN A).

b. In addition, whenever you correct any student's behavior make sure the incident is recorded. (see Step 3).

3. Publicly monitor how often incidents of misbehavior occur.

a. To help the student become more aware of their own behavior, create some kind of a wall chart on which a daily class-wide total of rule violations can be recorded. Post the chart in a visible spot in the room.

b. Because the purpose of the wall chart is help the class as a whole become more aware of their own behavior, it is not necessary to publicly note which individual students had how many infractions (i.e., you do not want to put undue peer attention on individual students who misbehave). However, for your purposes, it can be useful to monitor the behavior of individual students (e.g., to ensure proper implementation of consequences and/or if it is necessary to meet with the parent[s] of a particular student who continues to have ongoing problems). Thus, your private tally of rule violations should indicate who committed each violation. The following sample "Tally of Rule Violations" form can be a very efficient way of collecting this information (including coding the various rule violations by type of infraction).

Notice that this level of information provides the kind of documentation that makes it easier to explain to a particular student's parent(s) how much more frequently that student misbehaves than his/her classmates. In addition, if you want to, you can also mark a "+" next to students'

names when you praise them, which could be useful for monitoring your own ratio of positive to negative interactions with both the class as a whole and with individual students (see PRE-INTERVENTION STEPS).

c. Each day, conduct a short class meeting to review that day's record. Have a student record the information on the chart (or do it yourself), and discuss whether the day was better, worse, or about the same as previous days. If the day did not go well, encourage the students to talk about why and have them identify what they can do the next day to help them remember to follow the classroom rules. If the students act inappropriately during the meeting, keep the review session very short. Just let the class know that you are sure tomorrow will be a better day.

4. Use reinforcement to encourage appropriate behavior.

a. Praise individual students for meeting classroom expectations and praise the entire class when improvement takes place (see PLAN A).

b. During the review meetings, praise the students for being willing to look seriously at the cumulative record for the day. Even on a bad day, if the students are willing to discuss *why* it was a bad day, praise them. "Class, you are really handling this responsibly. Even though it was a rough day, you are willing to talk to about things you might do differently tomorrow. That is a real sign that we are making progress." Regardless of how the day went, try to make the end-of-the-day meeting upbeat and encouraging—you

---

Tally of Rule Violations

Week of _____

Name	Mon.	Tues.	Wed.	Thurs.	Fri.	TOTAL
Akayima, Lisa						
Bessom, Jamal						
Carter, Todd						
. . .						
Ziminski, Brett						

Code

A = Arguing   D = Disruptive   O = Off Task

---

want the students to look forward to the review at the end of each day.

c. You may also wish to use intermittent rewards to acknowledge the class' success. Occasional, and unexpected, rewards can motivate the students to demonstrate responsible behavior more often. The idea is to provide a reward when the entire class has had a particularly good period of following the rules. For this situation, appropriate rewards might include earning an extra recess, a special treat for all the students at lunch (e.g., an ice cream), or having

the principal come to congratulate the class and lead the class in a fun activity. *(NOTE: A list of additional reinforcement ideas can be found in APPENDIX 1.)*

If you use intermittent rewards, do so more frequently at the beginning of the intervention to encourage the class, and then less often as the students' behavior improves. Do not give the rewards indiscriminately—there should be a significant improvement before you provide a reward.

PLAN C

Sometimes, when an entire classroom has fallen into a pattern of misbehaving, it's because their behavior has become habitual and/or the majority of students are trying to emulate a few influential students who misbehave to look "cool" or "tough." In these cases it can be very difficult to change student behavior, and you may need to implement a structured system of reinforcement (i.e., rewards and consequences) based on their behavior that creates mild peer pressure to motivate the students to behave appropriately. This plan includes a basic reinforcement system and several alternatives. You might wish to combine two or more of the alternatives to create even stronger incentive for encouraging appropriate behavior.

 Publicly monitor the frequency of classroom misbehavior (see PLAN B).

 Encourage the class to set daily performance goals for themselves.

Help the students set a realistic daily goal for reducing the number of incidents of classroom misbehavior (e.g., from 40 to 32). If there are students who want to set too challenging a goal (e.g., reducing the number immediately to zero per day), explain that with a goal of 32, they can always get less than that, but they increase their chances of being successful. Then as the class experiences success, the goal should become progressively lower until there are zero incidents of misbehavior on most days.

 Establish a group reinforcement system.

a. Have the students brainstorm a list of various reinforcement ideas for the entire class, then eliminate any items that are not possible (i.e., the suggestions are too expensive or could not be provided to all the students in the class).

b. Assign "prices" (in points) to the remaining items on the list. The prices should be based on the instructional, personnel, and/or monetary costs of the items. Monetary cost is clear—the more expensive the item, the more points required to

earn it. Instructional cost refers to the amount of instructional time lost or interfered with by a particular reward. Thus, an activity which causes the class to miss part of academic instruction should require more points than one the class can do on their own time. Personnel cost involves the time required by you and/or other staff to fulfill the reinforcer. Thus, earning an extra recess period in which extra supervision would need to be arranged would cost more than having music playing in the classroom for 15 minutes.

c. Have the class vote on the reinforcers. The reinforcer that earns the most votes is the one they will work for first, and the items that come in second (and third) will be the next ones worked for.

d. On days the group successfully keeps the number of misbehavior incidents under the identified goal, they earn prespecified points toward the agreed-upon reward. Establish a sliding point scale such as the sample shown following.

 ALTERNATIVE SYSTEMS

a. **Team Competition**

If a simple class-wide reinforcement system seems unlikely to be effective, consider implementing a team competition and response cost lottery. Divide the class into four to six teams

More than 32 incidents	= 0 points
22-32 incidents	= 1 point
15-21 incidents	= 2 points
7-14 incidents	= 3 points
3-6 incidents	= 4 points
1-2 incidents	= 5 points
0 incidents	= 6 points

(made as equitable as possible). Each team would begin each day with a certain number of tickets on which they would write the name of their team. Whenever a student misbehaves, his/her team loses a ticket. At the end of the day, each team would put all their remaining tickets in a hat for a lottery drawing. The team whose name is on the winning ticket would earn the reward for that day. (A list of possible rewards can be generated in the manner suggested in Steps 3a and 3b.)

b. **Lottery Tickets**

Reward individuals for responsible behavior. A relatively simple, yet highly effective, method is to use lottery tickets like the sample shown below.

Date _____

_____ has been especially responsible today. This ticket is worth one chance in the lottery drawing on Friday.

On an intermittent and unpredictable basis give a ticket to any individual student for an instance of following the rules. Have the student write his/her name on the ticket and put it in a box for a drawing at the end of the week. (The lottery prizes can be selected from those listed in APPENDIX 1 or brainstormed by the class.) Use the tickets to encourage the particular positive behavior(s) you want to see more of in your classroom.

With this type of system, it is important to be careful not to be discriminatory. For example, with individual students who have been especially troublesome in the past, you may inadver-

tently harbor a grudge and tend not to notice their positive behavior. Or, you may be so inclined to notice the small improvements of the "trouble" students and the great leaps of the high achievers, that you fail to notice the ongoing, sustained effort of the "average" students.

c. **Intermittent Spot Checks**

Let the students know that you will be setting a timer for anywhere from 10-120 minutes. If, when at the instant the timer goes off, everyone in the class is behaving responsibly someone will get to roll a pair of dice. The number thrown will determine the reward given as indicated on a chart posted in the room. The chart might look something like the sample shown.

Chance Rewards		
1	=	(Something must be wrong with these dice!)
2, 3, or 4	=	Better luck next time. (But nice job anyway!)
5 or 6	=	Five minutes at the end of the day for choice time
7 or 8	=	Reduce math homework by half
9 or 10	=	Music playing during study time
11 or 12	=	Extra ten minutes of recess

Once the timer goes off, determine if everyone in the class was behaving responsibly. If so, ask a student to roll the dice. Once the reward has been determined, reset the timer. Early on in the intervention, reset the timer 15-25 times per day. As the students' behavior improves, reduce the number of times the timer goes off (i.e., increase the length of time between "beeps"). Eventually, you should be resetting the timer only three to five times per day.

d. The idea behind using a combination of two or three of the above systems is that they will encourage gentle peer pressure to behave appropriately. Tell the students that when they see someone forgetting to behave responsibly, a quiet reminder might help. Be sure to note, however, that yelling at another student to "behave" would be irresponsible and just as much of a violation as any other misbehavior.

While implementing any reinforcement system, keep student attention focused on the fact that they are behaving responsibly, not the reward.

Tell the class, for example: "Class, you earned seven points for the day, but more importantly, you are all helping this class be a place that we will all enjoy. Our room is a place we can all be proud of."

Suggested Steps for Developing and Implementing a Plan

The following steps are designed to help you develop an appropriate intervention plan and implement it effectively, whether you choose to use one of the MODEL PLANS or create a customized plan of your own. The steps are, however, suggestions—they are not intended to be followed rigidly or in any particular order. Use your professional judgment and the knowledge of your particular situation to make them work for you.

1. **Make sure you have enough information about the situation.**

a. Anecdotal information from actual incidents will help you explain what has led you to conclude that "the class is out of control." This type of documentation is easy to collect—simply keep a card in your pocket or on a clipboard and, occasionally, when you see a student misbehaving, make notes.

For each entry, briefly describe the circumstances—where and when the misbehavior occurred, what was said and/or done, and any other relevant observations (e.g., what prompted the behavior). You do not need to take notes every time a students misbehaves; the idea is to capture a range of examples so that you will be able to describe the behaviors clearly and completely.

Also include notes on times when the class has behaved appropriately. This way, the students will realize that you are not only aware of their inappropriate behavior, but also notice their appropriate behavior. The positive examples will also help you clarify how you want the students to behave.

b. It may also be useful to document how often the inappropriate behavior occurs (i.e., a frequency count). Use the "Tally of Rule Violations" form described in PLAN B to obtain a daily class-wide total, and a record of which students are misbehaving how often and in what ways. The daily frequency count can be recorded on a posted chart.

c. If a student notices what you are doing and asks about it, be straightforward—say that you are collecting information on the amount and type of misbehavior in the class so you and the class can develop a plan.

d. Continuing to collect this type of information and keeping the chart up-to-date while you implement a plan will help you monitor whether the situation is getting worse, staying the same, or getting better.

2. **Discuss the situation with the class.**

a. Schedule a class meeting for a time when you are calm (i.e., not right after an incident has occurred). Inform the students that you are finding the amount of misbehavior in the class to be a problem. Then have the students develop or revise specific classroom rules and consequences for rule infractions (see PLAN A).

b. Next, present the logistics of the intervention plan you propose (e.g., MODEL PLAN B or C, or your own plan), and give the students the opportunity to ask questions and make comments. End the session by thanking the students for listening and letting them know that you are confident they will make more of an effort to behave responsibly and follow the rules in the classroom.

3. **Determine when and how to include the parent(s).**

a. When the situation is class-wide, contacting the parents of all the students who have misbehaved is probably neither appropriate nor realistic (you wouldn't want to call five to 15 parents every night). However, after discussing the problem with the students, it may be useful to send a memo to all the parents (or include an item in the classroom newsletter, if you have one) explaining that the class will be working on following new classroom rules.

b. If the students brainstorm certain behaviors that should result in parental contacts and you agreed to do this (see PLAN A), follow through on this procedure when appropriate.

4. *Give the class regular, ongoing feedback about their behavior.*

Periodically meet with the students to discuss the situation. In most cases, three to five minutes once per day should suffice. Review any information that has been collected (e.g., anecdotal notes, frequency count) and discuss whether or not the situation is getting better. As much as possible, focus on improvements, however, also address any new or continuing problems. As you discuss the problems, acknowledge that there are students in the class who consistently behave appropriately. (Do not single out individual students, as this may be embarrassing to them and/or set them up for accusations of being a "teacher's pet.") As the overall situation improves, the meetings can be faded to twice per week, once per week, once every other week, and then to once per month.

5. *Evaluate the situation (and the plan).*

Any plan should be implemented for at least two weeks before deciding whether or not it is effective. Generally, if the situation has improved (based on the objective information that's been collected and/or the subjective perceptions of yourself and the students), continue with what you have been doing. (Eventually you will want to fade, then eliminate, the plan.) If the problem has remained the same or worsened, some kind of change (i.e., modifying the current plan or switching to another plan) will be necessary. Always discuss any change in the intervention with the class first.

CHEATING

Plagiarism

Copying Others' Answers

DESCRIPTION

You have a student who has cheated on tests or plagiarized written materials.

GOAL

The student will stop cheating/plagiarizing, and will learn to take pride in doing her best.

OVERVIEW OF PLANS

- PLAN A: For a situation in which no previous interventions have been attempted.
- PLAN B: For a student who seems to be unaware that her actions might be viewed as cheating.

  (NOTE: This plan can easily be adapted for a small group or a whole class.)

- PLAN C: For a student who feels so much pressure to succeed that she cheats to avoid failure.

NOTE:

The problem behavior is referred to as cheating in these three MODEL PLANS, however, all the information can be just as easily applied to the problem of plagiarism.

Alternative Problems

- Lying
- Perfectionism

General Considerations

- If there is a building or district policy regarding cheating, be sure to modify the information suggested here to comply with the letter and the spirit of that policy. If you are unsure whether intervening is appropriate or within the bounds of that policy, check with your building administrator before you implement an intervention plan.

- If you believe the student's problem behavior could stem in any way from academic issues (e.g., the student cheats to cover up the fact that she cannot meet academic expectations), concurrent efforts must be made to ensure her aca-

demic success (see **Academic Deficits, Determining**).

- The MODEL PLANS included with this problem address the issue of simple, in-class cheating. If your situation involves cheating of a more serious nature (e.g., a test has been stolen or test answers have been distributed), you should coordinate intervention efforts with your building administrator.

Model Plans

PLAN A

This plan is the foundation for PLANS B and C (and any other type of plan you may choose to implement). If no previous interventions have been attempted, the following actions, along with making the student aware of your concerns, may resolve the situation.

 Reduce opportunities for cheating. (This is the most important step!)

Be sure to directly supervise student behavior (of all the students, not just the target student) during tests, quizzes, and assignments that require individual accountability. Wander around the room in an unpredictable manner, and be unpredictable in your visual scanning. This may sound pessimistic about human nature, but try to think of it like this: If you do not adequately supervise, a student may cheat and find out that she never gets caught doing so. Her grades go up, so she begins to study less. Lack of adequate supervision could contribute to the student learning that cheating is a wonderful way to get through school.

As much as we might like students to refrain from cheating out of a sense of honor, it is human nature—some people are likely to cheat if there is no fear of getting caught. This is not just true for children. Imagine if the IRS said that there was no longer a threat of tax audits, or if the state police said that they were no longer going to patrol interstate highways. The threat of being caught breaking the rules increases people's motivation to follow those rules.

 Respond consistently to the inappropriate behavior.

Whenever you notice the student cheating, implement a consequence. If the student is younger (e.g., in grades K-3), you might just have the student move to a more isolated location for the remainder of the test. "Karen, for the rest of the spelling test, please move to this desk." With an older student (e.g., in grades 4-8), let her know during the initial meeting (see SUGGESTED STEPS FOR DEVELOPING AND IMPLEMENTING A PLAN) that any assignments or tests she cheats on will immediately receive an "F" grade.

You will need to decide whether the student should be allowed to redo the assignment or retake the test (or otherwise make up the points). If there is a school policy, follow it. If there is no policy, it is generally recommended that you give the student the opportunity to retake the test or redo the assignment. Too harsh a stance may lead the student to give up altogether. If the problem continues however, a more stringent policy may be necessary.

3. *Use reinforcement to encourage appropriate behavior.*

a. Provide praise and attention at a variety of times to help the student learn to take pride in her own effort. When the student is working independently, praise the student. "Karen, you are on task and staying focused. Those are very important components of taking pride in your own effort."

b. In addition, "catch" the student whenever she is engaged in any other positive classroom behav-ior. Comment to the student about her partici-pation in a class discussion or how consistent she is in turning in her homework on time.

c. In addition to praise, give the student frequent attention (e.g., say "hello" to her as she enters the classroom, call on her frequently during class activities, and occasionally ask her to assist you with a class job that needs to be done). This demonstrates to the student that you notice many positive things she does, not just the absence of cheating.

PLAN B

Some students may not be aware that looking at another student's paper is inappropriate. This is not as silly as it may sound—if there has never been any instruction regarding what constitutes cheating, some students may not understand the distinctions. In addition, some-times primary teachers make such an effort to emphasize working in cooperative groups, that it is possible the student(s) in your class have never been held individually accountable for doing their own work completely independently. When there is a possibility that one or more of your students do not understand the nature of cheating, this plan may be appropriate.

 1. *Clarify the expectations for the vari-ous activities that comprise your daily lessons.*

Examine your lesson plans for the next week, and for every assignment or test, identify how you expect the students to behave while working on that task. Will the students be encouraged to work cooperatively? to work independently, but be al-lowed to ask their neighbor for assistance if they have difficulty? to be entirely accountable for their own work? Once you have identified your behav-ioral expectations for each activity or task, decide what behaviors might be considered cheating. For each activity or task, answer the question: Would it be considered cheating to . . .

- Look at someone else's paper?

- Look at one's own book?

- Talk to a neighbor about the questions or tasks?

- Look at one's own notes?

- Ask a neighbor for help?

- Ask the teacher for help?

Notice that the expected behaviors will vary depending upon the nature of the activity or task. In cooperative groups, talking to one's neighbor is an essential part of the expectation. However, for most tests this would not be ac-ceptable. Looking at one's notes may not only be acceptable, but encouraged, on some tests, but would be considered cheating on others.

 2. *Conduct daily lessons on taking pride in one's own effort and on what behav-ior(s) constitute cheating.*

a. Use the information generated in Step 1 as a basis for introducing the daily assignments. De-scribe each task or assignment, clarify the ex-pectations for student behavior, and clearly identify any behavior(s) that might be consid-ered cheating. Then:

- Ask questions to ensure that the students understand the expectations (e.g., "Can you work together on this test?").

- Think of a hypothetical situation and have the students identify if the example illustrates a student who was meeting expectations or a student who was cheating. Provide feedback and continue to provide examples until the students demonstrate understanding.

- Model different behaviors and have the stu-dents identify if you are "taking pride in your own effort" or if you are "cheating."

b. Follow these procedures for every activity or task for at least a week. Because expectations vary from task to task, in most classrooms the complexity level of expectations is quite high. The more information you give the students about how to be successful and exactly which behavior(s) they should avoid, the greater the chances the students will strive to meet your expectations.

Implement a consequence for each and every incident of cheating (see PLAN A).

3. *Reduce opportunities for cheating (see PLAN A).*

5. *Use reinforcement to encourage appropriate behavior.*

Give the students increased praise and attention for taking pride in their own effort (see PLAN A).

4. *Respond consistently to the inappropriate behavior.*

PLAN C

Some students have such poor self-images that they need to "succeed" in order to feel they have worth. For these students, any failure (even something as minor as doing poorly on a spelling test, for example) may lead to the feeling of, "I am a loser." Thus good scores or grades prove to these students, "I am a winner and I have worth." Of course, the feeling of worth lasts only until the next task, at which point the students must "succeed" again to feel worthwhile. The focus of this plan will be to build a student's self-confidence as a way of increasing her willingness to accept and like herself, regardless of whether she succeeds or fails at a particular task.

1. *Structure activities or interactions that capitalize on the student's identified strengths and interests—particularly those that require no grading or evaluation.*

Building a student's confidence through activities she already does well is a potentially powerful way to help her develop the confidence to be comfortable with who she is, regardless of whether she is "the best." Example of ways you can do this include:

- A student who is good at math could be trained to help a younger student who is struggling. The student could be trained to emphasize that the child she tutors needs to be encouraged to improve her performance—not necessarily do great on every test.

- A student who is a good singer might like to work with a couple of other students to learn a song that was popular during the Civil War (current history topic) that they can demonstrate for the class.

- Check out a record, tape, or computer program from the media center that the student might enjoy or be interested in. "Karen, I know you have an interest in astronomy and I came upon this computer program that might be neat. If you want to try it, let me know if it is any good. We might be able to use some of it for our science lessons."

(NOTE: A list of additional ideas for jobs/responsibilities can be found in APPENDIX 2.)

2. *Help the student learn to use positive self-talk.*

(NOTE: Some people may consider the following procedures to be slightly controversial. Be sure to obtain parental permission before using these techniques.)

a. A student who cheats to boost her feelings of self-worth may engage in self-talk that irrationally emphasizes the importance of always being successful: "I've got to get a good grade!" or "If I don't get 100%, it will be terrible." In addition, the student may use very negative self-talk any time she does not "succeed": "I am so stupid." or "I am such a loser." To compound the problem, the student may irrationally reinforce herself when she does "succeed": "I won, so I am the best." or "I had the highest score, so I must be important."

At the initial meeting with the student, try to determine the type of self-talk and explanations the student uses: (1) before doing a task, (2) after a task which was not done as well as she had hoped, and (3) after a task in which she was successful. Use this information to determine the focus for lessons on replacing the negative self-talk with more productive, alternative statements.

b. Teach the student the difference between positive and negative self-talk, and whenever you hear her make a negative belief statement, have her reframe it into a more positive and hopeful statement. If the student can't do this, you can model a positive statement and have the student repeat it. Don't worry if the student acts like she does not believe the positive statements at first. With enough repetition, we all learn to believe the things we say about ourselves. (For more detailed information on this procedure, see **Self-Concept Problems**.)

To get you started, some examples of negative self-talk statements, with positive alternatives, follow.

3. *Reduce opportunities for cheating (see PLAN A).*

4. *Respond consistently to the inappropriate behavior.*

Implement a consequence for each and every incident of cheating (see PLAN A).

5. *Use reinforcement to encourage appropriate behavior.*

Give the student increased praise and attention for taking pride in her own effort (see PLAN A).

Negative Statements	Positive Alternatives
• I've got to pass.	• I'll do my best and take pride in my effort.
• If I don't get an "A," it will be terrible.	• If I succeed, I like myself. If I fail the test, I like myself. I take pride in my effort.
• I'm such a loser.	• I did not do as well as I would like. I'll study more next time.
• I am so stupid.	• Some people got A's. I got a B, which is still a good grade. Besides, I take pride in doing my best.
• I won, so I am the best.	• I take pride in my best effort, and this time it resulted in my winning the spelling contest.
• I had the highest score.	• I'm so great! I did my best and got a high score.

. . . .
Suggested Steps for Developing and Implementing a Plan

The following steps are designed to help you develop an appropriate intervention plan and implement it effectively, whether you choose to use one of the MODEL PLANS or create a customized plan of your own. The steps are, however, suggestions—they are not intended to be followed rigidly or in any particular order. Use your professional judgment and the knowledge of your particular situation to make them work for you.

1. *Make sure you have enough information about the situation.*

a. If you think a minimal intervention like PLAN A will be sufficient, you may already have enough information to proceed. However, when a more involved plan seems necessary, you should consider collecting additional descriptive and/or objective information for a couple of days.

b. You need to be able to explain exactly what you mean when you say that the student "has a problem with cheating." Anecdotal notes on actual incidents should provide enough details to help you define the problem behavior clearly and completely, and will be important documentation should it become necessary to follow through with any official disciplinary action.

Be sure to retain these records for as long as you have the student in your class, then ask your administrator if you should keep the records longer or destroy them. The information is not difficult to collect. Simply keep a file folder in a confidential file cabinet. Each and every time there is an incident of cheating, write a brief narrative of the situation and any actions taken by you in response to the cheating incident.

Following is an example of the kinds of anecdotal notes that should be kept.

Karen's Cheating—January

1/18—Karen was copying off of Francie's spelling test. At first I was not sure, so instead of having the students correct each other's papers, I collected them all and corrected them myself. Francie missed two, and Karen's paper had exactly the same errors. I plan to talk to talk to Karen privately tomorrow morning. I am going to give her a zero on this test, but I will allow her to stay in from recess tomorrow to retake it.

1/19—In talking with Karen, she vehemently denied that she was cheating. She even went on to say that she thought that Francie was probably cheating off of her test. I told her that we probably needed to ask her parents to come to school to talk about this. At that point, she modified what she wanted and said that she would like to be able to retake the test.

---

c. Continue to collect information on the student's behavior throughout the intervention. *Every* incident of cheating (or suspected cheating) should be included in your records, and specifics are important. If referral to the school counselor or school psychologist becomes necessary, comprehensive records will be essential.

2. *Identify a focus for the intervention and labels for referring to the appropriate and inappropriate behaviors.*

a. To be effective, the intervention must address more than just reducing the student's cheating—there must be a concurrent emphasis on increasing some positive behavior or trait (e.g., taking pride in one's own effort). Having specific positive behavior(s) in mind will make it easier for you to "catch" and reinforce the student for acting appropriately, and the positive focus will frame the situation more productively.

For example, if you simply say that "the student has a problem with cheating," you don't really provide any useful information, and you may put the student and her parent(s) on the defensive. However, when you explain that you want to help the student "learn to take pride in her own effort," you are presenting an important, and reasonable, goal for the student to work toward and clearly identifying what the student needs to do to be successful.

b. Specifying labels for the appropriate and inappropriate behaviors (e.g., "taking pride in one's own effort" and "cheating," respectively) will help you to use consistent vocabulary when discussing the situation with the student. If you sometimes refer to the inappropriate behavior as "cheating" and other times tell the student not to "look" at someone else's paper," she may not realize that you are talking about the same thing.

3. *Determine when and how to include the parent(s).*

a. With this type of problem, the parent(s) should be contacted immediately. Share any information you have collected about the behavior (e.g., anecdotal notes) and explain why you are concerned. Focus on how serious the behavior is, particularly if it should continue as the student grows older.

You might ask if the parent(s) have any insight into the situation and/or whether there have been similar incidents in the past. (If there is a history of cheating, PLAN A alone is probably not appropriate.) Whether or not the parent(s) perceive a problem, explain that you want to help the student "learn to take pride in her own efforts," and invite them to join you for an initial meeting with the student to develop a plan. If the parent(s) are unable or unwilling to participate, let them know that you will keep them informed of the student's progress.

b. Once the parent(s) have been involved in any way, you should give them updates at least once per week while the plan is being implemented.

4. *Prepare for, then conduct, an initial meeting about the situation.*

a. Arrange a meeting to discuss your concerns with the student and anyone else who will be involved (e.g., the parent[s], the school psychologist). Although the specifics will vary depending upon the age of the student and the severity of the problem, there are some general guidelines to consider when scheduling the meeting.

First, meet at a neutral time (i.e., not immediately after a problem has occurred) when emotions are less likely to hamper communication. In general, a day's notice is appropriate, however a primary age student may worry excessively and/or forget what the meeting is about if it is scheduled more than an hour before it takes place.

Second, make the meeting appropriately private. With a primary age student who has a mild problem, you might meet in the classroom while the other students are working independently. However, when dealing with a middle/junior high school student and the student's parent(s), you will need someplace private (e.g., the counselor's office) to ensure that the discussion will not be overheard.

Third, try to make sure the meeting is scheduled for a time and place that it is not likely to be interrupted. And finally, if the parent(s) will be participating, they should be the ones to tell the student about the meeting.

b. Construct a preliminary plan. Decide whether you think you can use one of the MODEL PLANS or if you need to create a customized plan using components from various plans and/or of your own design. Although you will invite and encourage the student to help develop the plan during the initial meeting, having a proposed plan in mind before you meet can alleviate frustration and wasted time if the student is unwilling or unable to participate.

c. It is important to have clearly established in your own mind what it is that the student does that could be called "cheating." After reviewing the information you have collected (e.g., anecdotal notes) and thinking about how you want the student to behave, prepare thorough descriptions of the inappropriate behavior and the positive behavior/trait on which the student will be working. The more specific you can be and the more concrete examples you have, the easier it will be to clarify (and for the student to understand) your expectations. Be sure to consider the student's behavior in all relevant activities (e.g., independent work, teacher directed instruction, homework, tests, etc.).

d. Conduct the meeting in an atmosphere of collaboration. The following agenda is one way you might structure the meeting:

• **Share your concerns about the student's behavior.**

Briefly describe the problem behavior and explain why you consider the cheating to be a problem. Tell the student that cheating is a serious offense. Explain that as she gets older (into high school), she could fail an entire class if she is caught cheating—even on a small quiz.

• **Discuss how you can work together to improve the situation.**

Tell the student that you would like to help her learn to "take pride in her own effort," and describe your preliminary plan. Invite the student to give you input on the various aspects of the plan, and together work out any necessary details. You may have to brainstorm different possibilities if the student is uncomfortable with the plan. Incorporating any of the student's suggestions that strengthen the plan is likely to increase her sense of "ownership" in and commitment to it.

• **Make sure the student understands what you mean by appropriate and inappropriate behavior.**

Use the descriptions you have prepared to define and clarify the problem behavior and the positive (desired) behavior as specifically and thoroughly as you can. To ensure that you and the student are in agreement about the expectations, you might present hypothetical scenarios and have her identify whether each is an example of cheating or of taking pride in one's own efforts.

• **Conclude the meeting.**

Always end the meeting with words of encouragement. Let the student know that you are confident that she can be successful. Be sure to reinforce her for participating in the meeting.

5. *Give the student regular, ongoing feedback about her behavior.*

It is important to meet with the student periodically to discuss her progress. In most cases, three to five minutes once per week should suffice. Review any information that has been collected and discuss whether or not the situation is getting better. As much as possible, focus on the student's improvements, however, also address any new or continuing problems. As the situation improves, the meetings can be faded to once every other week and then to once per month.

6. *Evaluate the situation (and the plan).*

Implement any plan for at least two weeks before deciding whether to change plans; to continue, modify, or fade the plan you are using; or to cease the intervention. Generally, if the student's behavior is clearly improving (based on the objective information that's been collected and/or the subjective perceptions of yourself, the student, and possibly the parent[s]), stick with what you are doing. If the situation has remained the same or worsened, some kind of change will be necessary. Always discuss any changes to the plan with the student first.

CLEANING UP, PROBLEMS WITH

- -

Not Cleaning Up After Projects

Not Cleaning Up Learning Centers

DESCRIPTION

There are students in your class who do not adequately participate in clean-up activities.

GOAL

The students will participate in clean-up activities and restore the room (or center) to neatness and order.

OVERVIEW OF PLANS

- PLAN A: For a situation in which the problem has just begun or occurs infrequently.
- PLAN B: For a situation in which the students may not know how to meet the expectations for cleaning up.
- PLAN C: For a situation in which the students lack the motivation to participate in clean-up activities.

NOTE:

These three plans are geared for a situation in which quite a few students in the class have a problem with participating in classroom clean-up activities. However, each can easily be modified to intervene with only a few (one to three) students who have/continue to have a problem with cleaning up.

Alternative Problems

- **Transitions, Problems With**
- **Messy Desks**

General Considerations

- This information focuses on class-wide clean-up activities (e.g., cleaning up after an art project or cleaning and organizing learning centers). If you are concerned about students managing their personal space or materials, see **Messy Desks** or **Forgetting Materials**.

- If one or more individual students overtly refuse to participate in clean-up activities, implement one or more of the plans outlined in **Compliance/Direction Following, Lack of**.

Model Plans

PLAN A

If this problem has just started and/or occurs only infrequently, it may not be necessary, or even beneficial, to use an involved plan. The following actions, along with making the students aware of your concerns, may resolve the situation.

1. Respond consistently to each instance of cleaning-up problems.

a. Whenever you notice some students not participating adequately in clean-up activities, give a gentle correction. Call the students by name and provide information on what the students should be doing. Be emotionally neutral and avoid talking too much while giving the correction—your goal is to impart clear information. "Kerry, Meg, Raymond, and Traci, you need to help pick up papers and put away the brushes and glue."

b. Assign any student(s) who do not begin participating one minute of time owed (from recess or after school), plus however much additional time the students waste while the others are cleaning up and putting things away. "Meg and Raymond, you both owe one minute from recess, plus however much more time you choose to waste while the others are cleaning." Then pointedly look at your watch or the clock.

Make note of how much time each individual owes. For example, if Meg got right to work after this second reminder, she would owe one minute. If Raymond continued to play for an additional two minutes while his classmates finished cleaning, he would owe three minutes—one for the second warning and two minutes for the additional minutes wasted."

c. At the beginning of the next recess, excuse the class but keep in any students who owe time. These students should spend the minutes they owe engaged in cleaning the room while the others are at recess.

d. If the procedure of recording which students are not participating is unrealistic because so many students are not participating, reverse the process and announce and record the names of those students who are participating and who will not spend recess time doing additional cleaning.

2. Use reinforcement to encourage appropriate behavior.

a. Praise individual students for meeting your expectations about cleaning up. Keep a watchful eye on those students who have had the greatest tendency to not participate in cleaning. Whenever one or more of these students *is* participating, praise them for demonstrating the ability to be responsible for classroom chores. "Doyle and Mary Jo, nice job of being responsible for classroom chores." If the students would be embarrassed by public praise, praise the students privately or even give them a note.

b. In addition, occasionally praise those students who consistently assist with cleaning tasks. Because these students have already mastered the expectations, they do not need positive feedback as often as the students who have had difficulty. However, you do not want them to feel that you take their positive behavior for granted. "Everyone at this work station is consistently responsible about cleaning up after projects. I appreciate that I never need to give you reminders."

c. Finally, when there has been a significant improvement in the level of participation in cleaning-up tasks, praise the entire class. Remember that any time the class is actively participating in cleaning up, you can praise them for being responsible about classroom chores.

PLAN B

If the students do not know how to meet the expectations for cleaning up, the intervention must include some way of teaching them the procedures.

1. *Conduct lessons to teach the students how to meet your expectations for cleaning up.*

a. Identify three key times or three specific locations in the room (such as learning centers) to be the focus of the intervention. Narrowing the focus to three times or three locations is much more manageable. Trying to do too much at once may be overwhelming, and both you and the students could end up very frustrated. Simply continue handling the times and locations that are *not* part of the focus as you always have. If/when the three identified times or locations improve, you can add more times and locations later.

b. For each of the identified times or locations, first analyze the complexity of the clean-up tasks and the skill level of the students. If necessary, make modifications so that the students will be capable (after systematic instruction) to clean up for themselves. For example, some learning center areas may have materials with many small parts that need to be returned to different bins. However, students in primary grades, whose ability to sort and categorize may be limited, may tend to take out far more than they are capable of putting back. Thus, although you may like having these wonderful materials available for the students, if they are not yet capable of managing the materials independently, you are better off eliminating those particular materials and substituting something with fewer small parts that need to be categorized when put away.

c. During the lessons, provide instruction and practice opportunities for the entire class on how to clean up. Break the task down into three or four steps. "First, you . . . , then you . . . ." For each step describe, then demonstrate, what you expect. Then have a few students demonstrate the particular step. End by modeling examples of the step (some examples done in "right ways" and some in "wrong ways") and having the students evaluate your performance.

"Watch me and tell me if I do this the right way (demonstrate). Was that the right way? Good Tyrone, why wasn't that the right way?"

Repeat these procedures for each step—describe, demonstrate, have the students demonstrate, teacher models/asks "right or wrong way."

d. Begin with one of the identified times/locations (see Step 1a) and conduct lessons daily or as frequently as the clean-up task is required (e.g., art projects scheduled twice per week). Schedule the first few lessons for approximately three times as long as you think should be necessary for the actual clean up task. That is, if you think the clean up will take about three minutes, schedule a nine-minute lesson, which allows for six minutes of instruction and three minutes for the actual task.

Continue the lessons until the students are consistently successful with the clean-up task within the allotted time. Then begin lessons on the next identified time/location.

2. *Prompt appropriate behavior by using precorrections.*

Watch for those circumstances in which the students are likely to have trouble with clean-up activities, and remind the students about specific things they need to keep in mind. "Class, I am going to give the instruction to put away the supplies and wash off the desk tops. The most important thing for everyone to keep in mind is to . . . . I will be watching to see if you remember to do what we practiced yesterday. I'll bet you can."

If time permits, you might have individual students identify the specific task components. "Emery, what will you do while you are waiting for someone to get a sponge to you? Donna, what will you do when you are finished with the sponge? Keep remembering what we have worked on in the lessons. Let's give it a try."

3. *Respond consistently to students not meeting your expectations for clean up.*

Whenever you notice an individual student not meeting the expectations, gently correct the student. Use time owed for repeated infractions or nonparticipation (see PLAN A).

4. *Use reinforcement to encourage appropriate behavior.*

a. Praise individual students for meeting the expectations regarding clean up, and praise the

entire class when improvement occurs (see PLAN A).

b Make a special point of letting the students know (both individually and as a class) that you notice their efforts to use the skills they have been learning/practicing. "Mark and Kelly, you are being very efficient in passing out the sponges. Nice job of doing what we have been practicing. Tamara, Jesse, and Lashonda—great job remembering to put all of the pieces back in the right places in the science center."

PLAN C

Sometimes, a group of students will fall into a pattern of actively or passively resisting participation in a chore such as cleaning up. In these cases it can be very difficult to change student behavior, and you may need to implement a structured reinforcement system (i.e., rewards and consequences) that creates mild peer pressure to motivate the students to behave appropriately.

1. *Identify three key times or specific locations that will be the focus of the intervention and, if necessary, provide instruction on how to clean up (see PLAN B).*

2. *For each of the key times or locations, develop a checklist that identifies the important criteria that must be accomplished for meeting your clean-up expectations.*

Following is a sample checklist for cleaning up after an art project.

3. *Establish a group reinforcement system.*

a. Have the class brainstorm group reinforcement ideas/rewards that this would like to earn. After brainstorming, eliminate any items from the list that are not possible (i.e., the suggestions are too expensive or could not be provided to all the students in the class).

b. Assign "prices" (in points) to the remaining items on the list. The prices should be based on the instructional, personnel, and/or monetary costs of the items. Monetary cost is clear—the more expensive the item, the more points required to earn it. Instructional cost refers to the amount of instructional time lost or interfered with by a particular reward. Thus, an activity which causes the class to miss part of academic instruction should require more points than one

the class can do during recess time. Personnel cost involves the time required by you and/or other staff to fulfill the reinforcer. Thus, earning an extra recess period in which extra supervision would need to be arranged would cost

---

Checklist for Art Clean Up

_____ All students put away their own scissors, glue, scrap paper, etc.

_____ All students wash their own desk top with a sponge. Desk tops are clean (no pencil marks, glue smudges, or tape) and dry.

_____ Each table/group appoints one person to get a sponge, soap, and paper towels to be shared by the table/group.

_____ All water is wiped up from desktops and floor (each table/group should choose one person to check).

_____ Each table/group appoints one person to put away sponge and soap, and throw away used paper towels.

_____ **5 Bonus Points** if the entire class can cooperate (no arguments about who does what) and complete the clean up within 5 minutes (in a reasonably quiet manner and with no running).

_____ **TOTAL**

---

more than having music playing in class for 15 minutes.

c. Have the class vote on the reinforcers. The reinforcer that earns the most votes is the one they will work for first, and the items that come in second (and third) will be the next ones worked for.

d. Prior to a targeted clean-up activity, put the checklist on the overhead and review the important criteria with the class.

e. At the end of the clean-up activity, award the points—one point for each item successfully completed, and five bonus points if everything went smoothly. (For the example activity outlined in Step 2 the class could earn from zero to ten points.) Repeat this process for the other two key times or specific locations identified.

f. After awarding points for a clean-up activity, record the points on a chart so the students can see the current status and how far they have to go to reach the goal. "Class, we just earned five more points. Everybody do the math. Five more added to the 34 we already had. We need 60 to be able to have the extra 15 minutes of recess. How many more do we need? Raise your hand when you have it figured out."

g. Alternatively, if a class-wide system seems unlikely to be effective, set up a team competition. In this type of system, the class would be divided into four to six teams (made as equitable as possible). Then using the checklists developed for each of the three times/locations, you would evaluate the performance of each team.

The points each team earns could be awarded as "chance tickets"—pieces of paper on which the team writes its name. Then, each team would put their earned chance tickets (zero to ten in the sample checklist discussed previously) into a hat. At the end of the day, one chance ticket would be drawn from the hat, and every member of the team whose name is on that ticket would receive one of the identified rewards.

The idea is that any team can win, even with only one ticket earned, but the more tickets a team has earned the better the members' odds of winning.

4. **Respond consistently to any student not meeting your expectations for clean up.**

a. Whenever you notice an individual student not meeting the expectations, gently correct the student. Use time owed for repeated infractions or nonparticipation (see PLAN A).

b. If one or two individual students consistently continue to have problems with clean up, remove them from the group system. That is, their behavior does not cost any group points, but they are also not able to participate in the group's rewards. However, the student(s) could still owe time for nonparticipation.

When the students begin to cooperate, invite them to become part of the group system again.

5. **While implementing any reinforcement system, keep the students' attention focused on being responsible for classroom chores as the situation improves.**

For example, tell them: "Class, you earned ten points for the day—the full amount possible, but more importantly, you are all helping this class be a place where we all contribute and take responsibility. Room 8 is a place we can all be proud of."

· · · · · · · ·
Suggested Steps for Developing and Implementing a Plan

The following information is designed to help you implement an appropriate and effective intervention plan, whether you choose to use one of the MODEL PLANS or create a customized plan of your own. The steps are, however, suggestions—they are not intended to be followed rigidly or in any particular order. Use your professional judgment and the knowledge of your particular situation to make them work for you.

 Make sure you have enough information about the situation.

NOTE: Documentation is probably not necessary if the problem is relatively mild (i.e., PLAN A is appropriate).

a. You want to be able to explain what you mean when you say that "the class has a problem with clean up." Anecdotal notes from actual incidents can help you define the problem behavior thoroughly. To take anecdotal notes, simply keep a card in your pocket or on a clipboard and occasionally, when you see the students having trouble with cleaning up, record the incident. For each entry, briefly describe the circumstances—where and when the incident occurred, what the specific problem was, who was having trouble, and any other relevant observations.

You do not need to make notes on every time someone has trouble with clean up; the idea is to capture a range of examples so that you will be able to describe the behavior clearly and completely.

Also include notes on times when the students have been successful with clean-up tasks, so the students will realize that you are not only aware of their inappropriate behavior, but also notice their appropriate behavior. The positive examples will also help you clarify specifically how you want the students to behave.

b. It may also be useful to document how long particular clean-up activities require. This record of duration will provide both a more objective measure of the problem and an objective way to monitor progress. To keep a duration record, use the same card on which you are taking anecdotal notes to record the duration time. Each time the students are taking too long in cleaning up, mentally note the time the students should have completed the task and the time the task is actually completed. Write the difference (in number of minutes) with a note about the activity. At the end of the day, you will be able to calculate the "total number of minutes spent cleaning up over and above the time it should have required."

c. If a student notices what you are doing and asks about it, be straightforward—say that you are collecting information to see whether cleaning up is a problem that the class needs to work on.

The following example shows typical anecdotal notes and a duration time record that have been collected on clean-up problems for a class.

d. The duration information is fairly easy to summarize on a chart or graph. Seeing how much time is wasted each day may help the students better understand your concern about the problem.

Notes on Cleaning Up—10/14

- Gave the class an instruction to clean up after art. Had to nag and remind. Took 5 minutes longer than it should have taken.

- Gave the instruction to clean up centers. Took 10 minutes longer than it should have.

- Gave the instruction to put up chairs and get floor cleaned up at end of day. Took 2 minutes extra—was still not done so I had to let them go to the buses and had to pick up the scraps myself.

Total Extra Minutes—12

---

e. Continuing to collect this type of information and keeping the chart or graph up-to-date while you implement a plan will help you to monitor whether the situation is staying the same, getting worse, or getting better.

2. *Decide how to present the situation to the class.*

a. Depending upon your personal philosophy and whether or not you think a simple intervention like PLAN A is appropriate, you may choose to have an informal discussion with the class, taking a few minutes to make them aware of your concerns.

b. If the problem is more serious and you envision implementing a more structured plan, schedule a class meeting to present the plan. Wait for a time when you are calm (i.e., not right after an incident has occurred) and inform the students that you are finding cleaning up to be a problem. Use any anecdotal notes you have taken to describe the situation(s) that represent the biggest problems. Then specifically define your expectations regarding those clean-up activities and/or the procedures that will be implemented (e.g., checklists and rewards).

Give the students the opportunity to ask questions/make comments, and end the session by thanking the students for listening. Let them know that you are confident that they will make an effort to be responsible about clean-up activities in the future.

c. If you want the students to assume more ownership of the problem, you might want to have a class meeting in which the students participate in analyzing the situation and developing an action plan. In this case, before the meeting you will need to have clarified the nature/extent of the problem and your expectations for the students' behavior. You will also need to identify any aspect(s) of the plan that you do not feel comfortable opening up to a group decision.

For example, you must decide ahead of time whether or not to allow the class to determine if there will be a consequence for a problem with cleaning up and/or what the consequence should be. If you firmly believe that there must be a consequence, then you should not seek student input on that particular issue.

d. If you prefer to implement one of the MODEL PLANS rather than having the students generate a plan, the class meeting will be for the purpose of clarifying all aspects of the plan and giving the students the opportunity to ask questions or make comments about the plan.

3. **Conduct the class meeting to either present your proposed plan or have the students generate a plan.**

(NOTE: The following steps are a guide to helping the class generate a plan, although you may wish to additionally present one or more procedures from the MODEL PLANS.)

a. Schedule the meeting for a neutral time and allow enough time for a reasonable discussion. Inform the students in advance that the meeting will take place; this will give them time to think about the problem. "Class, this afternoon we are going to have a class meeting about the problem of cleaning up the classroom. Please give some thought to this problem and what we might do as a class to solve it."

b. Use an agenda to structure the meeting. Shortly before the meeting, write the agenda on the chalkboard. Following is a sample you may consider using.

Agenda

1. Cleaning up—Define the magnitude of the problem. (Share data such as time wasted each day.)

2. Review expectations regarding cleaning up.

3. Brainstorm solutions for improving the situation.

4. Select strategies that everyone agrees to.

5. Establish the consequences for a student not participating in clean up.

---

c. Establish clear rules for both you and the students regarding the brainstorming phase of the meeting. For example:

1. Any idea is okay (but no obscenity).

2. Ideas will not be evaluated initially (i.e., no approval "Good idea"—or disapproval—"What a stupid idea" or "We couldn't do that" should be expressed during brainstorming).

3. All ideas will be written down and discussed at the conclusion of brainstorming.

d. At the conclusion of brainstorming, evaluate the ideas and lead the class to consensus on any decisions that need to be made. Use voting as a decision-making process when appropriate.

4. **Determine when and how to include the parent(s).**

a. Because trouble with cleaning up is more of a procedural than behavioral or motivational problem, involving parents is not critical with a class-wide problem.

b. If the situation involves only one or two students who have or continue to have a problem with participating in clean-up activities, you should contact the parent(s) of those individuals. Let them know that their student is not being responsible for helping with clean up and is losing recess time as a result. Share any other steps you are taking to correct the situation.

Frequent contact is not required, but whenever you intend to implement an individualized plan, the parent(s) should be informed prior to its implementation and should be given feedback about the student's progress every two to four weeks.

5. **Give the class regular, ongoing feedback about their behavior.**

Periodically meet with the students to discuss the situation. In most cases, three to five minutes once per week should suffice. Review any information that has been collected (e.g., anecdotal notes, duration records) and discuss whether or not things are getting better. As much as possible, focus on improvements, however, also address any new or continuing problems.

As you discuss any problems, acknowledge that there are individuals in the class who consistently behave appropriately. However, do not single out individuals when discussing problems or progress with the entire group. As the situation improves, the meetings can be faded to once every other week and then to once per month.

 6. *Evaluate the situation (and the plan).*

Any plan should be implemented for at least two weeks before deciding whether or not it is effective. Generally, if the situation has improved (based on the objective information that's been collected and/or the subjective perceptions of yourself and the students), continue with what you have been doing. (Eventually you will want to fade, then eliminate, the plan.) If the problem remains the same or worsens, some kind of change (i.e., modifying the current plan or switching to another plan) will be necessary. Always discuss any change in the intervention with the class first.

CLINGINESS/ DEPENDENCY

DESCRIPTION

You have a student who seeks excessive attention, contact, and/or reassurance from you.

GOAL

The student will reduce and eventually eliminate the dependent and clingy behavior, and will be more independent and self-reliant.

OVERVIEW OF PLANS

- PLAN A: For a situation in which the problem is relatively mild or has just begun.

- PLAN B: For a student who acts clingy and/or dependent to gain adult attention.

- PLAN C: For a student who is unaware of how frequently he acts clingy and/or dependent.

- PLAN D: For a student whose clingy/dependent behavior has become habitual.

Alternative Problems

- **Babyish Behavior**

- **Crying, Chronic**

- **Helplessness**

- **Hypochondria**

- **Self-Concept Problems**

General Considerations

- If the student's problem behavior stems in any way from academic issues (e.g., because the student is experiencing academic failure he is compensating by demanding additional reassurance and attention from you), concurrent efforts must be made to ensure his academic success (see **Academic Deficits, Determining**).

- If the student lacks the basic social skills to interact with his peers appropriately, it may be necessary to begin by teaching him those skills. **Social Skills, Lack of** contains information on a variety of published social skills curricula.

Model Plans

PLAN A

It is not always necessary, or even beneficial, to use an involved plan. If the inappropriate behavior has just begun and/or is relatively mild (i.e., not interfering with the student's academic or social progress), the following actions, along with making the student aware of your concerns, may resolve the situation.

1. **Respond consistently to the inappropriate behavior.**

a. During your initial meeting with the student (see SUGGESTED STEPS FOR DEVELOPING AND IMPLEMENTING A PLAN), establish a nonembarrassing signal that you can use to cue the student that he needs to "be more independent." You want the signal to be a fairly subtle one that only the student will recognize and understand in order to minimize the chance that he will be teased by his peers. Possibilities include a subtle wave of your hand, placing your hand on your cheek, or even just direct eye contact and a head nod.

Let the student know that you may also need to quietly say his name to get his attention before you give the signal. You should be prepared to use the signal frequently and for a fairly long time, especially if the behavior is, at least in part, an unconscious habit for the student.

b. Whenever the student is acting overly dependent or clingy, give the signal. If the student does not stop the behavior, gently correct him. Let the student know that his behavior is an example of clinginess, and give him direct information about what he should be doing instead. "Dewel, this is an example of clinginess. You can show that you are independent by going to your seat and doing your work." Because your goal is to impart information, you should be emotionally neutral while giving the correction.

2. **Use reinforcement to encourage appropriate behavior.**

a. Give the student increased praise. Be especially alert for situations in which the student might have acted clingy but did not and praise him for these demonstrations of his ability to behave independently. "Dewel, for the last half hour you worked with the other students in the group. You didn't come over to me once. That was a great example of independence."

Remember that any time the student is not clingy or otherwise demanding your attention, you can praise him for demonstrating independence. Demonstrations of independence can even include behaviors as simple as coming into the room, hanging up his coat, and taking his seat.

b. Praise the student privately for responding to the signal. "Dewel, I gave the signal that you needed to be independent and you let go of my leg, went to your seat, and began working on your project. I appreciate it when you are so independent."

c. Give the student frequent attention (e.g., say "hello" to him as he enters the classroom, call on him frequently during class activities, and occasionally ask him to assist you with a class job that needs to be done) and praise him for other positive behaviors he exhibits. For example, you might comment about the accuracy of his work or how well he reads. This demonstrates to the student that you notice many positive things he does. By interacting with the student prior to the time when he would typically be clingy or dependent, your attention actually reinforces his independence.

 (OPTIONAL)
Arrange for positive attention from other adults.

If the student seems especially starved for attention, you might ask the principal, playground supervisors, and other teachers to give this student lots of attention. If several adults make a point to greet the student whenever they see him, and to "catch" and praise him when he is not being clingy, it may help reduce the student's dependent and clingy behavior in other school settings.

P L A N   B

Some students are very skilled at gaining attention through dependent and/or clingy behavior. If you find yourself interacting frequently with the student when he is dependent and/or clingy (e.g., comforting, reassuring, or even nagging and reminding the student to be more self-reliant), the focus of the intervention should be on ensuring that the student receives more frequent and more satisfying attention when he behaves independently than when he is being clingy or dependent.

 Respond consistently to the inappropriate behavior.

a. When the student is dependent and/or clingy, give the student the signal, and gently correct him if necessary (see PLAN A).

b. If the student does not respond to the signal or a gentle correction, ignore the student's clingy and/or dependent behavior. While ignoring, do not look at the student or talk to him. Do not act disgusted or impatient with his behavior. Simply interact in positive ways with other students who are behaving appropriately and meeting classroom expectations. This may sound silly, but ignore the behavior even if the student is clinging to your leg! As soon as the target student is no longer acting dependent and/or clingy, pay attention to him, but make no reference to his inappropriate behavior.

c. If other students give the target student attention when he is acting dependent and/or clingy (e.g., telling him that he needs to quit bothering you and go sit down), gently correct them. "Naomi and Edwardo, Dewel can take care of himself and he will be independent when he is ready. It would be best to let him work it out on his own."

 *Use reinforcement to encourage appropriate behavior.*

a. Frequent praise and attention is the core of this plan. The student must see that he receives more frequent and more satisfying attention when he behaves independently than when he is dependent and/or clingy. Thus, whenever the student is not demanding your attention or otherwise being dependent, make an effort to praise and spend time with him. "Dewel, you are being so independent as you work on that project. Would it be okay if I sat with you a moment and watched as you do the next step?"

b. You may also wish to use intermittent rewards to acknowledge the student's success. Occasional, and unexpected, rewards can motivate the student to demonstrate independent behavior more often. The idea is to provide a reward when the student has demonstrated independence for a longer period of time than he typically does.

Appropriate rewards might include sitting right next to you during an activity, walking next to you as you escort the class down the hallway, or playing a game with you. *(NOTE: A list of additional reinforcement ideas can be found in APPENDIX 1.)*

Use intermittent rewards more frequently at the beginning of the intervention to encourage the student, and then less often as his behavior improves.

 Ensure a 3-1 ratio of positive to negative attention.

a. Given that attention is a motivating force for this student, you want to be sure that you are giving the student *three times as much* positive as negative attention. One way to do this is to monitor your interactions with the student at least one day per week. Keep a card on a clipboard or in your pocket and record each interaction you have with the student as either positive or negative by writing a "+" or a "-", respectively, on the card.

To determine whether an interaction is positive or negative, ask yourself whether the student was acting dependent and/or clingy at the time the interaction occurred. Any interactions that stem from dependent and/or clingy behavior are negative, while all interactions that occur while the student is independent or otherwise meeting classroom expectations are positive. Thus, giving the signal and/or giving a gentle correction are both negative interactions, but praising the student for not needing the signal is positive. Greeting the student as he enters the room or asking him if he has any questions during independent work are also considered positive interactions. *(NOTE: Ignoring the student's dependent and/or clingy behavior is not recorded at all, because it is not an interaction.)*

b. If you find that you are not giving the student three times as much positive as negative attention, try to increase the number of positive interactions you have with the student. Sometimes prompts can help. For example, you might decide that each time the student enters the classroom you will say "hello" to him, or during each instructional period you will find a time to praise the student. You can also increase the ratio of positive to negative attention by ignoring more of the student's inappropriate behavior.

P L A N   C

Some students do not seem to know when they are behaving inappropriately. If your student doesn't realize when he is acting overly dependent and/or clingy, the intervention must include some way of helping the student become more aware of his own behavior.

 Conduct a goal-setting conference with the student.

Meet with the student, and perhaps the student's parent(s), to help him set a goal for being more independent. The goal can either be determined with the student or prepared in advance. Generally, when a student is involved in the process, he is more likely to strive to achieve the goal. In either case, identify a broad-based goal such as, "to be more independent" and three specific ways the student can demonstrate that he is working on the goal.

You can explain to the student that there are innumerable ways to demonstrate independence, but that the student can start with these three. A finished goal contract might look like the sample following.

2. **Respond consistently to the inappropriate behavior.**

a. When the student is dependent and/or clingy, give the student the signal, gently correct him if necessary, then ignore the behavior if it continues (see PLAN B).

b. In addition, whenever you give the signal make sure the incident is recorded by the student (see Step 3).

Goal Contract

Dewel

A goal for me to work on is _to be more independent_ . I can show that I am working on this goal by:

1. Keeping my hands to myself, not on Mrs. Tate (except for a couple of hugs a day that Mrs. Tate will give me).

2. Doing my own work and allowing Mrs. Tate to do hers (not following Mrs. Tate around the room).

3. Telling myself that I'm doing my best and waiting for Mrs. Tate to look at my work (instead of going up and asking her to look at it).

Mrs. Tate

I will help Dewel meet his goal by _giving him the signal when he needs to be more independent_ _and by praising him and giving him an occasional hug when he is being independent._

Student Signature _____   Date _____

Teacher Signature _____

---

3. **Devise a way to give the student feedback about how dependent and clingy he is being.**

a. Have the student keep a form on his desk like the sample shown and tell him that any time you give him the signal, he should circle a number in the Dependent section of the form.

Dewel's Independence Card

Date _____

Independent

1	2	3	4	5	6	7	8	9	10
11	12	13	14	15	16	17	18	19	20

Dependent

1	2	3	4	5	6	7	8	9	10
11	12	13	14	15	16	17	18	19	20

---

b. At various times throughout the day when the student is being independent, ask him if he is being independent. If the student says "yes," have him circle the next number in the Independent section. If the student says "no," but you think he was independent, explain why you think what he was doing was a good example of independence, have him circle a number in the "Independent" section, and then praise him for being independent.

Make sure the student understands that his goal is to have more Independent than Dependent numbers circled at the end of the day.

c. This procedure should not be implemented unless you are willing and able to "catch" the student more often when he is independent than when he is being dependent and/or clingy—even when the student is having a bad day. In other words, it is up to you to structure student success by asking the question, "Dewel, are you being independent?" more frequently than you signal him that he is being dependent. Eventually, the goal will be for the student to reduce his Dependent numbers circled to zero.

d. At the end of each day, review the chart with the student. If the number of Dependent numbers circled exceeds the Independent, you will need to make a more concerted effort to "catch" the student when he is behaving independently.

4. **Use reinforcement to encourage appropriate behavior.**

a. Give the student increased praise and attention for being independent (see PLAN A).

b. In addition, praise the student during the end-of-the-day review meetings for accurate recording and for being willing to look at his daily totals.

c. Chart the number of Dependent numbers circled and encourage the student to have the chart go down. Also chart the Independent numbers using a different color or symbol. Each day should have more Independent numbers than Dependent charted. Then, even if the number of Dependent numbers circled is up on a particular day, you can still reinforce the student for the Independent numbers that have been recorded.

 5. Encourage the student to use self-reinforcement.

Whenever things are going well (i.e., less dependent behavior than usual), prompt the student to mentally reinforce himself. "Dewel, this has been a very successful morning. Silently tell yourself that you are really good at being independent." Prompt the student this way intermittently throughout the day and during the end-of-the-day review meeting.

PLAN D

Whenever a student's dependent and/or clingy behavior has become habitual and/or he does not seem to have a desire to reduce it, you may need to implement a structured system of external incentives (i.e., rewards and consequences) based on his behavior to motivate him to reduce his dependent and/or clingy behavior.

1. Use a signal to cue the student when he is dependent and/or clingy (see PLAN A).

2. Implement a system for monitoring the student's dependent/clingy and independent behavior (see PLAN C).

3. Establish a structured system for reinforcing the appropriate behavior and providing a consequence for the inappropriate behavior.

a. With the student, create a list of reinforcers that he can earn. Although you might want to have some suggestions in mind, the system will be more effective if the student identifies most of the items or activities himself. *(NOTE: A list of reinforcement ideas can be found in APPENDIX 1.)*

b. Determine the number of dependent and/or clingy incidents (how many times you have to give the student the signal) that occur in a typical day. Let's say the number is 15. Make 15 tickets (1" x 3" slips of paper), each of which has a prize written on it. One ticket should have a big prize, a couple should have moderate prizes, and the majority should have little prizes.

Each day, the student begins with all the tickets in a jar. Then each time you have to give the student the signal, the student records the incident on his monitoring form and you remove one ticket from the jar—but neither you nor the student is allowed to see what is written on it. At the end of each day, the student draws one ticket from those remaining in the jar, and receives that reward.)

c. Determine a consequence (e.g., time owed from recess or in detention) that you can implement for each incident of dependent and/or clingy behavior that occurs after the student has already lost his tickets for the day.

4. Use reinforcement to encourage appropriate behavior.

a. Give the student increased praise and attention for being independent (see PLAN A).

b. Praise the student at the end of the day for the numbers circled on the Independent section of his monitoring form.

c. In addition, show interest and enthusiasm about how the student is doing on the system. "Dewel, this is a great day. It is now lunch time and you still have almost all your tickets left in the jar."

········
Suggested Steps for Developing and Implementing a Plan

The following steps are designed to help you develop an appropriate intervention plan and implement it effectively, whether you choose to use one of the MODEL PLANS or create a customized plan of your own. The steps are, however, suggestions—they are not intended to be followed rigidly or in any particular order. Use your professional judgment and the knowledge of your particular situation to make them work for you.

1. Make sure you have enough information about the situation.

a. If you think a minimal intervention like PLAN A will be sufficient, you may already have enough information to proceed. However, when a more involved plan seems necessary, you should consider collecting additional descriptive and/or objective information for a couple of days.

b. You need to be able to explain what you mean when you say that the student "has a problem with dependent and/or clingy behavior." Anecdotal notes on actual incidents should provide enough detail to help you define the problem behavior clearly and completely. To collect anecdotal notes, simply keep a card in your pocket or on a clipboard and occasionally make notes on specific instances when the student is engaged in behavior that you think is overly dependent and/or clingy.

For each entry, briefly describe where and when it occurred, what the student did or said, and any other relevant observations (e.g., what prompted the behavior). You do not need to take notes every time the student exhibits dependent and/or clingy behavior; the idea is to capture a range of examples so that you can describe the behavior thoroughly.

Also include some notes on times when the student is being independent—this will make it clear that you are not only aware of his problem behavior, but also recognize when he behaves appropriately. When you meet with the student, the positive examples will help you clarify how you want the student to act behave.

c. In addition to information on what the student's inappropriate behavior looks like, it can also be useful to document how often it occurs (i.e., a frequency count). This information will provide both a more objective measure of the problem and an objective way to monitor the student's progress. You can use the same card on which you are taking anecdotal notes to keep a frequency count—simply write a tally mark on the card each time the student is being overly dependent and/or clingy.

You might also want to code the tallies to identify particular types of behavior. For example, you could write a "C" on the card each time the student comes up and physically *clings* to you and an "R" on the card each time he seeks *reinforcement* or approval for something he has done.

d. If the student notices what you are doing and asks about it, be straightforward—tell him that you are collecting information to see whether his dependent and/or clingy behavior is a problem that needs to be worked on.

e. The frequency information is fairly easy to summarize on a chart or graph. Seeing how often he needs to be reminded about being dependent and/or clingy may help the student and his parent(s) better understand your concern. *(NOTE: If you are using PLAN C or D, you will automatically compile this information daily.)*

f. Continuing to collect this type of information (and with PLAN C or D, keeping the chart up-to-date) while you implement a plan will help you monitor whether the situation is getting worse, staying the same, or getting better.

2. Identify a focus for the intervention and labels for referring to the appropriate and inappropriate behaviors.

a. To be effective, the intervention must address more than just reducing the student's dependent and/or clingy behavior—there must be a concurrent emphasis on increasing some positive behavior or trait (e.g., independence). Having a specific positive behavior in mind will make it easier for you to "catch" and reinforce the student for behaving appropriately, and the positive focus will help you to frame the situation more productively.

For example, if you simply say that "the student has a problem with clinginess," you don't really provide any useful information, and may put the student and his parent(s) on the defensive. However, when you explain that you want to "help the student learn to be more independent and self-reliant," you present an important, and reasonable, goal for the student to work toward and clearly identify what the student needs to do to be successful.

b. Specifying labels for the appropriate and inappropriate behaviors (e.g., "dependent" or "clingy," and "independent", respectively) will help you to use consistent vocabulary when discussing the situation with the student. If you sometimes refer to the inappropriate behavior as "clinginess" and other times tell the student to stop "demanding attention," he may not realize that you are talking about the same thing.

3. *Determine when and how to include the parent(s).*

a. It is not necessary to contact the student's parent(s) if the problem has just begun and is not interfering with the student's academic or social progress. However, it might be a good idea to take advantage of any scheduled activities (e.g., conferences, weekly notes home) to let them know of your concern.

b. If the problem has continued for more than a few weeks, contact the student's parent(s). Share with them any information you have collected about the behavior (e.g., anecdotal notes, frequency count) and explain why you are concerned. Focus in particular on how the behavior is hindering the student academically and/or socially (e.g., the student is becoming so dependent on you that he is reticent to try doing things himself).

You might ask if the parent(s) have any insight into the situation and/or whether they have noticed similar behavior at home. Whether or not the parent(s) perceive a problem, explain that you want to help the student "learn to be more independent and self-reliant" and invite them to join you for an initial meeting with the student to develop a plan. If the parent(s) are unable or unwilling to participate, let them know that you will keep them informed of the student's progress.

c. Once the parent(s) have been involved in any way, you should give them updates at least once per week while the plan is being implemented.

4. *Prepare for, then conduct, an initial meeting about the situation.*

a. Arrange a meeting to discuss your concerns with the student and anyone else who will be involved in the plan (e.g., the parent[s]). Although the specifics will vary depending upon the age of the student and the severity of the problem, there are some general guidelines to consider when scheduling the meeting.

First, meet at a neutral time (i.e., not immediately after a problem has occurred) when emotions are less likely to hamper communication. With a primary student who has a mild problem, you might meet in the classroom while the other students are working independently. However, if the student's parent(s) will be involved, you will need some place private (e.g., the counselor's office or your room when other students are not present) to ensure that the discussion will not be overheard. Also, try to make sure the meeting is scheduled for a time and place that it is not likely to be interrupted.

b. Construct a preliminary plan. Decide whether you think you can use one of the MODEL PLANS or if you need to create a customized plan using components from various plans and/or of your own design. Although you will invite and encourage the student to help develop the plan during the initial meeting, having a proposed plan in mind before you meet can alleviate frustration and wasted time if the student is unwilling or unable to participate.

c. After reviewing the information you have collected and thinking about how you want the student to behave, prepare thorough descriptions of the inappropriate behavior and the positive behavior/trait on which the student will be working. The more specific you can be and the more concrete examples you have, the easier it will be to clarify (and for the student to understand) your expectations. Be sure to consider the student's behavior in all relevant activities (e.g., independent work, teacher directed instruction, unstructured class times, recess and lunch, etc.).

d. Conduct the meeting in an atmosphere of collaboration. The following agenda is one way you might structure the meeting:

- **Share your concerns about the student's behavior.**

    Briefly describe the problem behavior and explain why you consider the behavior to be a problem. You might tell the student that he is growing up now and as he gets older, success in school requires that he become more independent.

- **Discuss how you can work together to improve the situation.**

  Tell the student that you would like to help him "learn to be more independent and self-reliant," and describe your preliminary plan. Invite the student to give you input on the various aspects of the plan, and together work out any necessary details (e.g., the signal, the goal contract, the monitoring form). You may have to brainstorm different possibilities if the student is uncomfortable with the plan. Incorporating any of the student's suggestions that strengthen the plan is likely to increase his sense of "ownership" in and commitment to it.

- **Make sure the student understands what you mean by dependent/clingy and independent behavior.**

  Use the descriptions you have prepared to define and clarify the problem behavior and the positive (desired) behavior as specifically and thoroughly as you can. To ensure that you and the student are in agreement about the expectations, you might present hypothetical scenarios and have him identify whether each is an example of independent or dependent behavior. Or you might describe an actual situation that has occurred and ask the student to explain how he would demonstrate independence in that situation.

- **Conclude the meeting.**

  Always end the meeting with words of encouragement. Let the student know that you are confident that he can be successful. Be sure to reinforce him for participating in the meeting.

 5. *Give the student regular, ongoing feedback about his behavior.*

It is important to meet with the student periodically to discuss his progress. In most cases, three to five minutes once per week should suffice. *(NOTE: PLANS B and C require daily meetings.)* During the meetings, review any information that has been collected and discuss whether or not the situation is getting better. As much as possible, focus on the student's improvements, however, also address any new or continuing problems. As the situation improves, the meetings can be faded to once every other week and then to once per month.

6. *Evaluate the situation (and the plan).*

Implement any plan for at least two weeks before deciding whether to change plans; to continue, modify, or fade the plan you are using; or to cease the intervention. Generally, if the student's behavior is clearly improving (based on the objective information that's been collected and/or the subjective perceptions of yourself, the student, and possibly the parent[s]), stick with what you are doing. If the situation has remained the same or worsened, some kind of change will be necessary. Always discuss any changes to the plan with the student first.

CLIQUES/GANGING UP

Exclusion

Teasing/Taunting

DESCRIPTION

There are students in your class who form a subgroup and exclude and/or tease other students.

GOAL

The students will learn how, and why it is important, to form friendships and groups without making others feel excluded or bullied.

OVERVIEW OF PLANS

- PLAN A: For a situation in which the problem has just begun.

- PLAN B: For a situation in which students may not know how to deal with the ganging up.

Alternative Problems

- **Arguing—Students With Each Other**

- **Bossiness**

- **Bullying Behavior/Fighting**

- **Gang Involvement**

- **Harassment— Racial/Sexual**

- **Name Calling/ Put-Downs**

- **Physically Dangerous Behavior—to Self or Others**

- **Self-Control Issues**

- **Threatening Others (Staff or Students)**

- **Victim—Student Who Is Always Picked On**

General Considerations

- If there is a particular student whom the students (those in the clique) are tormenting, concurrent efforts must be made to deal directly with the students in the clique and to help the victim. See **Victim—Student Who Is Always Picked On** for ideas on assisting the student who is the target of the misbehavior.

- If a number of students lack the basic social skills to interact appropriately with their peers, it may be necessary to begin by teaching them those skills. **Social Skills, Lack of** contains information on a variety of published social skills curricula.

- You may want to discuss your plan with the playground supervisors. Consistency between playground procedures and classroom procedures will increase the effectiveness of any plan. In addition, ask the playground supervisors to keep a close eye on the students who have been doing most of the ganging up in order to increase the chance of adult intervention.

- In some cases, adults hesitate to intervene in the interactions between students because they want students to learn to solve their own prob-

lems. However, it is the responsibility of school personnel to make school a setting where every child feels safe, included, and welcome. Because ganging up can result in some students feeling alone and unsafe, it is important and appropriate to intervene when necessary.

- If this situation has resulted in (or has the potential to result in) physical confrontation, you may wish to review the problem **Fighting** for information on breaking up fights.

- If you are unable to resolve this problem with your students, and/or cliques/bullying/intimidation is a school-wide issue, you may wish to obtain a copy of the following publication:

  Garrity, C., Jens, K., Porter, W., Sager, N., & Short-Camilli, C. (1994). *Bully-proofing your school: A comprehensive approach for elementary schools.* Longmont, CO: Sopris West.

Many of the ideas and suggestions in these two MODEL PLANS have been adapted from this excellent resource.

Model Plans

PLAN A

If the problem with cliques has just begun, it may not be necessary, or even beneficial, to use an involved plan. The following actions, along with making the students aware of your concerns, may resolve the situation.

 Respond consistently each time the ganging up behavior excludes one or more students.

a. Whenever you notice a group of students deliberately excluding or teasing one particular individual student, give a gentle correction. Let the group of students know that what they are doing is an example of "ganging up," and provide information on what they need to do differently. "Suzanne, Kim, and Robin, come here please, I need to speak with you. Telling Eliza that she cannot join your group because she has red hair is an example of ganging up. If you three want to work together, fine, but not if you are going

to make others feel bad. You need to let others join in, or in a kind way tell the person that right now you are doing something that only three can do. Let the person know that you would like to have her join you another time

Be emotionally neutral and avoid discussion while giving the correction—your goal is simply to impart information.

b. If the students do not cease ganging up, implement a consequence. There is no one "correct" consequence, because every situation is slightly different. Below are a few possibilities from which you might choose:

- Do not let the group play/work together for the remainder of the period.

- Have the group identify how they are going to avoid the situation in the future (i.e., have the students develop a plan).

- Give each member of the group a brief time-out (in different locations).

- Keep the group in from recess or after class to discuss more inclusive ways they can be together.

- Have the group apologize to the student(s) who were being teased or excluded.

- Have the group stay after school for lessons on "compassion," or other appropriate topics.

- Have the group describe (or write, if appropriate) how they would feel if they were mistreated in the way they have been mistreating the other student(s).

- Contact the students' parents, or have the group contact them, so that they are aware of their childrens' behavior.

 Use reinforcement to encourage appropriate behavior.

a. Praise individual students for meeting your expectations about including and treating others them with respect. Keep a watchful eye on those students who have had the greatest tendency to form cliques. Whenever one of these students is playing with others or is inviting others to join her peer group, praise her for demonstrating the ability to include others. "Kim, it is a pleasure to see the way you have been including other students in the things you do. I noticed how you included Tina in the project you and Suzanne were working on, and I think it meant a lot to her to be invited to join you."

If the students would be embarrassed by public praise, praise the students privately or even give the students a note.

b. In addition, occasionally praise those students who rarely or never have a problem with ganging up. Because these students have already mastered the positive expectations, they do not need positive feedback as often as the students who have had difficulty. However, you do not want them to feel that you take their positive behavior for granted. "Wanda and Ursula, you two are such positive leaders. You are very sensitive to the feelings of others and when you notice someone feeling left out, you go out of your way to make that person feel included."

c. Finally, when there has been a significant reduction in the overall frequency of ganging up, praise the entire class. Remember that any time the students are refraining from ganging up, you can praise them for treating each other with respect and/or including others in class and playground activities.

PLAN B

Sometimes class members who are neither targeted by nor members of a clique can be effective in preventing ganging up behavior from starting and/or escalating. However, if the students do not know what to do about situations in which ganging up is occurring, the intervention must include some way of teaching them how to help address this problem.

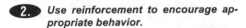 **Conduct lessons to teach the students how to identify situations in which ganging up is occurring and strategies for addressing the situation.**

a. Before the lessons, identify the specific ganging up behaviors that typically occur. That is, what do the students do when they gang up? When you conduct the lessons you want to present realistic situations, while being careful to avoid stigmatizing any individual students.

Typical "ganging up" behaviors might include (but are not limited to):

- Teasing/taunting;

- Making ethnic/racial slurs;

- Isolating/excluding one person from a group;

- Taking an individual's possessions;

- Arranging pranks/embarrassing situations directed at one person;

- Starting rumors about a person;

- Passing notes and writing graffiti about a person; and

- Threatening someone.

Identify the types of behaviors you have seen with your students. These should be the basis of your lessons.

b. Pick one of the situations that is a high probability event in your class (e.g., taking someone's possessions), and design a hypothetical scenario that includes a group of aggressors, a victim or victims, and bystanders. Change the names and the situation enough so that it has general applicability to many students (i.e., avoid a scenario so real that the students might think for example, "This does not apply to me. He is talking about what happened yesterday with Gina and Ruth.").

c. During the lessons, remind the class that the goal is to learn to include others and to treat everyone with respect. Describe your scenario using hypothetical names.

"We have four students who are good friends. Let's call them Joan, Adrienne, Samantha, and Talynda." (Write these names on the board under the heading "Aggressors" or "Bullies.") "We have another student, let's call her Jan." (Write her name under the heading "Victim.") "And we have five other students out there. Let's call them Travis, Hank, Rita, Ed, and Iris." (Write these names on the board under the heading "Bystanders.")

"They are all out in front of the school in the morning before school begins—the doors are locked. Joan, she is kind of the leader, decides to knock the things out of Jan's arms. Jan's lunch, her notebook, and her books all fall to the ground. Joan picks up Jan's lunch and starts going through the bag, making fun of the things in Jan's lunch. Adrienne and Samantha pick up the notebook and start doing the same thing with Jan's schoolwork. Jan asks them to stop, but they get louder and meaner."

d. After presenting the scenario, have the class brainstorm appropriate responses for each of the hypothetical students. Before doing so, establish some rules for brainstorming. For example:

• Any idea is okay (but no obscenity).

• Ideas will not be evaluated initially (i.e., no approval—"Good idea," or disapproval—"What a stupid idea" or "We couldn't do that" should be expressed during brainstorming).

• All ideas will be written down and discussed at the conclusion of brainstorming.

"Now, let's put ourselves in different places in this story. Let's start with what you could do if you were in Jan's place. Let's brainstorm all the different things that Jan might try to do."

Write down all the brainstormed suggestions under the heading "Victim." Repeat the brainstorming process for the "Bystanders," writing down the suggestions on that section of the chalkboard. Then have the group brainstorm things that "Talynda" might do to stop the ganging up. Note that in the scenario, Talynda is a friend of the "Aggressors" but is not yet involved in the aggressive acts. Tell the students that she feels bad for Jan, but is concerned that if she sticks up for Jan, that Joan might start excluding her, too.

If the group has trouble with brainstorming, provide prompts, questions, or suggestions to solicit additional ideas. Some responses that you might wish to prompt if they are not suggested by the students include: getting help from an adult, using "I messages," ignoring, making a joke, helping the victim by talking to her or getting her involved with something else, telling an adult at a later time, leaving the situation, etc.

e. After brainstorming, look over each list and guide the class in discussing the different options. "If Jan did _____, what do you think might happen?" Cross out any items from the lists that the group decides might make the situation worse. During this process, emphasize the power of the bystanders. Try to clearly communicate that ganging up will not continue if everyone in the class makes an effort to do something whenever they see ganging up occurring.

f. Then, have students volunteer to play the different parts in the scenario as a role play. "Okay, let's have Jan do _____, the bystander do _____, and Talynda do _____." For each blank, state one of the items from the brainstormed lists under each set of characters. Repeat this process using different students in different roles, trying different actions. After each role play, have the students, both the actors and the audience, talk about the actions performed. Would they help? would they make things worse?

g. After completing one scenario in this manner, develop a second. Be sure to vary the gender of the students who are victims, aggressors, and bystanders.

h. Conduct the lessons at least twice per week—daily, if possible. The lessons should involve the entire class and be scheduled for between 15-

30 minutes. It may not be possible to complete all of the activities in a single lesson. If not, consider treating the scenario like a soap opera. "Today we are out of time. But tomorrow you will see more of the continuing saga of Jan and Joan. Will Joan learn to be respectful? Will Jan learn to be assertive? Tune in tomorrow for more "Days of Our Bully."

Continue the lessons until there are no additional instances of ganging up on others and/or the students are empowered to respond to any ganging up that does happen.

2. *Respond consistently to all instances of ganging up with gentle corrections and appropriate consequences (see PLAN A).*

3. *Periodically meet individually with any students who have been the most frequent victims of ganging up.*

Find out if things are going better for these students by speaking with them privately. Make sure these students know that you are available to help them whenever they need it.

4. *Use reinforcement to encourage appropriate behavior.*

a. Praise individual students for meeting expectations regarding including others and treating others with respect, and praise the entire class when improvement takes place (see PLAN A).

b. Praise the students for participating in the lessons.

c. Make a special point of letting the students know (both individually and as a class) that you notice their efforts to use the skills they have

been learning/practicing. "Allie, I noticed what you did when Caitlin and Tony were making fun of Suvonn's glasses. That took a lot of courage and you handled it beautifully. Nice job of doing what we have been practicing."

d. You may also wish to use intermittent rewards to acknowledge the class' success. If the problem of ganging up is less prevalent (based on your observations, the observations of the playground supervisors, and the private reports of frequent victims), provide a class-wide reward. Occasional, and unexpected, rewards can motivate the students to demonstrate responsible behavior more often. The idea is to provide a reward when the class has had a particularly good period of refraining from ganging up.

Appropriate rewards might include giving the class an extra recess, giving the students a free half hour to play classroom games, or having the principal congratulate the class. *(NOTE: A list of additional reinforcement ideas can be found in APPENDIX 1.)*

If you use intermittent rewards, do so more frequently at the beginning of the intervention to encourage the class, and then less often as the students' behavior improves.

5. *Keep on the alert for possible instances of ganging up.*

One possible result of direct intervention with this problem is that the clique may not *stop* the behavior, just become more sneaky about it. Look for subtle signs (e.g., frequent glances between the students in the clique, arrogant attitudes, signs of stress or depression in students who may be victimized, etc.). If this is occurring, you may wish to implement the types of strategies suggested by Garrity et al. (1994).

· · · · · · · ·
Suggested Steps for Developing and Implementing a Plan

The following information is designed to help you implement an appropriate and effective intervention plan, whether you choose to use one of the MODEL PLANS or create a customized plan of your own. The steps are, however, suggestions—they are not intended to be followed rigidly or in any particular order. Use your professional judgment and the knowledge of your particular situation to make them work for you.

1. *Document the nature/extent of the problem.*

a. You need to be able to explain what you mean when you say "ganging up." Since having a

close peer group in and of itself is not a problem behavior, you will have to identify the aspects of the students' clique that make it inappropriate. Anecdotal notes from actual incidents can help you define the problem behavior thoroughly.

To take anecdotal notes, simply keep a card in your pocket or on a clipboard and occasionally, when you see an example of problematic clique behavior, make note of the incident. For each entry, briefly describe the circumstances—where and when it occurred, what was said and/or done, and any other relevant observations (e.g., what prompted the behavior).

b. Also include notes on times when these students include others and/or treat others respectfully. This way, the students will realize that you are not only aware of their inappropriate behavior, but also notice their appropriate behavior. The positive examples will also help you clarify how it is you want the students to behave.

 2. **Identify a focus for the intervention and labels for referring to the appropriate and inappropriate behaviors.**

To be effective, the intervention must address more than just reducing the students' involvement in a clique—there must be a concurrent emphasis on increasing some positive behavior or trait (e.g., "treating others with respect" and/or "including others"). Identifying some specific positive behavior(s) will make it easier for you to "catch" and reinforce the students for acting appropriately, and will help you explain your concerns more productively.

For example, simply saying that "the class has a problem with cliques," doesn't really give the students any useful information (and may put them on the defensive). However, telling the students that you want to help them learn "to include others and treat everyone with respect," gives them an important, and reasonable, goal to work toward and makes clear what they need to do to be successful.

3. **Decide how to present the situation to the class.**

a. Depending upon your personal philosophy, and whether or not you think a simple intervention like PLAN A is appropriate, you may choose to have an informal discussion with the class or with just the group of students involved in the clique.

b. When you intend to use PLAN B, you might want to schedule a class meeting. Wait for a time when you are calm (i.e., not right after an incident has occurred) and inform the students that you are finding the amount of ganging up to be a problem. Then specifically define your expectations regarding treating others with respect and including others.

Let the class know that they are going to have lessons and discussions on the problem, and give them the opportunity to ask questions and make comments. End the meeting by thanking the students for listening and letting them know that you are confident they will make an effort to treat each other more respectfully in the future.

c. If you want the students to assume some ownership of the problem, you might want to hold a class meeting in which the students participate in analyzing the situation and developing an action plan. In this case, before the meeting you need to clarify the nature/extent of the problem and your expectations for the students' behavior.

You also need to identify any aspects of the problem/plan that you do not feel comfortable opening up to a group decision. For example, you must decide ahead of time whether or not to allow the class to determine if there will be a consequence for ganging up and/or what the consequence should be. If you firmly believe that there should be a consequence, then you should not seek student input on that particular issue.

d. Schedule the meeting for a neutral time and allow enough time for a reasonable discussion. Inform the students in advance that the meeting will take place; this will give them time to think about the problem. "Class, this afternoon we are going to have a class meeting on the problem of ganging up—where a group of students excludes or teases one or two other students. Please give some thought to this problem and what we might do as a class to solve it."

e. Use an agenda to structure the meeting. Shortly before the meeting, write the agenda on the chalkboard. The following example is one possibility.

Agenda

1. Ganging up—Define the magnitude of the problem (share data from your anecdotal notes).

2. Review expectations regarding being respectful and including others.

3. Brainstorm ideas for improving the situation.

4. Select strategies that everyone agrees to.

5. Establish what the teacher will do if a group is ganging up on someone (i.e., consequences).

---

f. Establish clear rules for both you and the students regarding the brainstorming phase of the meeting (see PLAN B).

g. At the conclusion of brainstorming, evaluate the ideas and lead the class to consensus on any decisions that need to be made. Use voting as a decision-making process when appropriate.

4. *Determine when and how to include the parents.*

a. When the situation is class-wide, contacting the parents of all the students who have been ganging up is probably neither appropriate nor realistic (you wouldn't want to spend your time calling five to ten parents every night). However, after discussing the problem with the class, it may be useful to send a memo to all the parents (or include an item in the classroom newsletter, if you have one) explaining the focus of the plan the students will be working on—treating each other with respect and including others in activities.

b. If the situation involves the same group of students who have had or continue to have a problem with ganging up, or if the situation involves serious ganging up (e.g., threats of violence), you should contact the parents of the individuals involved in the situation. Let the parents know that their children have been involved in ganging up. Provide specific descriptions of the circumstances and identify what steps you are taking to correct the problem.

Frequent contact is not required, but whenever you intend to implement an individualized plan, the parents should be informed prior to its implementation and should be given feedback about the students' progress every two to four weeks.

5. *Give the class regular, ongoing feedback about their behavior.*

Periodically meet with the class to discuss the situation. In most cases, three to five minutes once per week should suffice. *(NOTE: If you are using PLAN B, this review can be incorporated into one of the daily lessons.)* During the meetings, review any information that has been collected (e.g., anecdotal notes) and discuss whether or not things are getting better. As much as possible, focus on improvements, however, also address any new or continuing problems.

As the situation improves, the meetings can be faded to once every other week and then to once per month.

6. *Evaluate the situation (and the plan).*

Any plan should be implemented for at least two weeks before deciding whether or not it is effective. However, if severe instances of ganging up are occurring, ask for assistance from your building administrator to identify additional ways to help the students who are being victimized feel safe and secure.

Generally, if the situation has improved (based on the objective information that's been collected and/or subjective perceptions of yourself and the class), continue with what you have been doing. (Eventually you will want to fade, then eliminate, the plan.)

If the problem stays the same or gets worse, some kind of change (i.e., modifying the current plan or switching to another plan) will be necessary. Always discuss any change in the intervention plan with the class first.

COMPETITIVE, OVERLY

DESCRIPTION

You have a student who tends to be excessively competitive—he always needs to be the best, the first, the highest (etc.) at anything he does.

GOAL

The student will become less concerned with how his performance compares to the performance of others, and will learn to take pride in his own best effort.

OVERVIEW OF PLANS

- PLAN A: For a situation in which the problem is relatively mild or has just begun.

- PLAN B: For a student who does not seem to realize when and/or how frequently he is overly competitive.

- PLAN C: For a student who is overly competitive because he is insecure and does not feel worthwhile unless he is first (the best, etc.).

- PLAN D: For a student who has developed a habit of being overly competitive.

- PLAN E: For a situation in which several students in the class are fiercely competitive.

Alternative Problems

- **Bossiness**
- **Name Calling/ Put-Downs**

General Considerations

- When addressing this problem, you must be careful not to imply that the student must change his personality—there are perfectly well-adjusted people who are quite competitive. The goal of the intervention should be to temper the student's competitiveness so that his assessment of himself and his worth does not depend solely upon how he compares to others, while still allowing the student to be highly competitive in some things (e.g., a favorite sport).

- If the student's family or cultural background could be a factor in his behavior (e.g., his father encourages high levels of competitiveness), do not intervene until you have checked the appropriateness of the intervention plan and its goals with the student's parent(s). If the behavior is not interfering with the student's academic or social success, it may be both unnecessary and inappropriate to intervene.

Model Plans

PLAN A

It is not always necessary, or even beneficial, to use an involved plan. If the problem has just begun or the behavior is relatively mild (e.g., doesn't occur all the time), the following actions, along with making the student aware of your concerns, may resolve the situation.

1. Respond consistently to the inappropriate behavior.

a. When the student's competitive behavior adversely impacts other students, intervene and gently correct him. "Stephan, you need to stop criticizing your teammates and be more cooperative. You are making everyone on your team feel like they cannot do anything right, but in fact everyone is trying their best."

b. If the student's behavior is not having an immediate adverse impact, ignore it. However, record some of these incidents in your anecdotal notes (see SUGGESTED STEPS FOR DEVELOPING AND IMPLEMENTING A PLAN) so you can discuss them with the student.

2. Use reinforcement to encourage appropriate behavior.

a. Give the student increased praise. Be especially alert for situations in which the student behaves in a way that is less competitive than he has in the past, and acknowledge these demonstrations of his ability to be cooperative. "Excellent example of cooperation, Stephan

and Sariah. You are both very proud of your projects and are not concerned about whose is the best. For what it's worth, I think they are both excellent."

b. In addition, privately praise the student for interacting cooperatively in situations that require a significant effort for him. "Stephan, during our scrimmages today you were really cooperative with your teammates. If anyone missed a shot you said things like 'Nice try,' or 'You'll get it next time.' I know that was hard because your team was behind, but your cooperative behavior helped your team to work well together."

c. Give the student frequent attention (e.g., say "hello" to him as he enters the classroom, call on him frequently during class activities, and occasionally ask him to help you with a class job that needs to be done), and praise him for other positive behaviors he exhibits. For example, you might comment about the accuracy of his work or how consistent he is about turning in his homework. This demonstrates to the student that you notice many positive things he does, not just the fact that he is refraining from being overly competitive.

PLAN B

In some cases, a student may be unaware of how frequently he is only competitive or unaware that a competitive nature is a good trait in some situations, but problematic in others. In this case, the intervention should focus on teaching the student to identify when it is appropriate to be competitive and when to avoid competitive behavior, as well as how to demonstrate responsible behavior in both competitive and noncompetitive pursuits.

 1. *Conduct lessons to teach the student how to discriminate between situations that call for competition and those that should be viewed as noncompetitive.*

a. Consider several different school-based situations and determine whether competitiveness contributes or interferes in those situations. Then try to categorize those situations in a way that defines productive or responsible ways of behaving. The following example represents such an analysis.

b. Teach the student to discriminate between types of tasks or situations that are individually competitive, that require teamwork, and that are noncompetitive. When the student can consistently discriminate between these different types of tasks, have him generate examples of cooperative ways of behaving within the different types of situations. For example, have the student identify noncompetitive ways of behaving when entering the classroom. What could he be doing other than turning it into a race? Ideas might include quietly talking to a friend, thinking about the good time he had at recess, or mentally preparing for the test that is coming up after recess.

c. If necessary and age-appropriate, have the student role play how to behave cooperatively in the various types of situations.

 2. *Respond consistently to the inappropriate behavior.*

When the student is overly competitive, gently correct him. As privately as possible, have the student identify the level of competitiveness that the current situation calls for, and have him describe what he did that was too competitive. Have him identify more responsible ways he could have handled the situation. For example, if the student was so competitive during a basketball scrimmage that he began ridiculing his teammates who were making errors, wait until the end of the period and talk to the student as you are going back to the classroom: "Stephan, is basketball a team sport or individual competition? What were some things

you did today that did not help your team? What could you do differently that would actually help the performance of your teammates?"

If it is not possible to correct the student without embarrassing him, ignore the behavior. However, make note of the situation in your anecdotal notes (see SUGGESTED STEPS FOR DEVELOPING AND IMPLEMENTING A PLAN), and use this example when you have a meeting with the student.

 3. *(OPTIONAL)*
Prompt student success by using pre-corrections.

If the problem persists, you might begin letting the student know when the next activity is one that may require extra effort on his part to be cooperative.

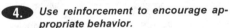 **4.** *Use reinforcement to encourage appropriate behavior.*

a. Praise the student for demonstrating cooperative behavior. When a task is individually competitive, praise him for having done his best—regardless of whether he won or lost. "Stephan, in that 100-yard dash you really gave it everything you had. Your concentration was focused on that finish line and you won!" or "Stephan, you really worked hard preparing for that district spelling competition. You tried to win and you represented our class well. Thank you for doing your best. I hope you know you are a great speller regardless of the outcome."

b. If a task requires teamwork, praise the student for being tolerant of others' mistakes, encouraging the effort of his teammates, and for demonstrating good sportsmanship. "Stephan, during that basketball scrimmage you were a great sport. You supported Matthew even though he was having trouble with his shots. You kept passing if someone else had a clearer shot than you did. And after winning you told the other team they played a great game. While being a good sport and teammate, you were a killer with those jump shots! Today was a great demonstration of cooperative competitive behavior in a team situation."

A.

- Situations in which individual competition is responsible and productive:
  - Individual sport (e.g., singles tennis, running races, swimming meets, etc.)
  - Spelling bees
  - Science fair competitions
- Cooperative ways of behaving:
  - Do your best.
  - Try to win.
  - Demonstrate that you can be a good sport—either a good winner or a good loser.
  - Enjoy the competition, regardless of the outcome.

B.

- Situations requiring teamwork, but in which team competition is responsible and productive:
  - Team sports (e.g., basketball, baseball, soccer, doubles tennis, etc.)
  - Class canned food drive (competing against other classes)
  - Cooperative groups working on an assignment (competing against other groups)
- Cooperative ways of behaving:
  - Do your best.
  - Support your teammates—give build-ups and no put-downs.
  - Try to beat the other team, but work with your own team.
  - Demonstrate that you can be a good sport—either a good winner or a good loser.
  - Enjoy the competition, regardless of the outcome

C.

- Situations in which everyone is a winner—being first or best is unimportant, but doing your own personal best is very important:
  - Spelling tests
  - Writing a report
  - Cooperative groups working on an assignment (and *not* competing against other groups)
  - Tutoring a younger student
  - Coming into the room after recess
  - Doing calisthenics in P.E. class
- Cooperative ways of behaving:
  - Do your best.
  - Don't worry about how anyone else is doing—it is not a competition.
  - Support other people's best efforts (who did better does not matter).
  - Enjoy putting forth your best effort.

c. If a task is noncompetitive, praise the student for doing his best and not worrying about how his performance stacked up against others in the class. "Stephan, you should be very proud of the cooperative way you conducted yourself when I handed back the book reports. You made no effort to find out if your score was the best. You looked at your score, saw it was very high, and quietly put the report in your notebook. Are you pleased with your report and the grade you received?"

PLAN C

Sometimes a student has such a poor self-image that he feels he needs to "beat" others and/or be the best to gain a sense of worth. For this type of student, if anyone else does better he thinks, "I am a loser," while being the best—even in noncompetitive activities such as a math test—proves that, "I am a winner and I have worth." Of course, the feeling of worth lasts only until the next task, at which point the student must "win" again to feel worthwhile. If this is the case with your student, the focus of intervention must be to build the student's self-confidence as a way of encouraging him to be less competitive and to help him learn to accept and like himself regardless of whether he "wins" or "loses" at a particular task.

1. **Structure activities or interactions that capitalize on the student's identified strengths and interests—particularly those that are noncompetitive in nature.**

Building a student's confidence through those activities he already does well is a potentially powerful way to help him feel comfortable with who he is, regardless of whether he is "the best." Ways to do this include:

- A student who is good at math could be trained to help a younger student who is struggling. The target student would be told to emphasize that the child he tutors needs to be encouraged to just improve her own performance—not to become the best in the class.

- A student who is a good singer might work with a couple of other students and learn a song that was popular during the Civil War (or other current history topic) and then demonstrate it for the class.

- Check out a record, tape, or computer program from the media center that the student might enjoy or find interesting. "Stephan, I know you have an interest in astronomy and I came upon this computer program that might be neat. If you want to, try it and let me know if it is any good. We might be able to use it for some of our science lessons." *(NOTE: A list of additional ideas for jobs/responsibilities can be found in APPENDIX 2.)*

2. **Conduct lessons to help the student learn to use positive self-talk.**

a. A student who is overly competitive may engage in self-talk that irrationally emphasizes the importance of winning (e.g., "I've got to win!" or "If I don't win it will be terrible."). Or, the student may use very negative self-talk any time he does not win (e.g., "I am so stupid." or "I am such a loser."). Or, the student may irrationally reinforce himself when he does win (e.g., "I won, so I am the best." or "I had the highest score so I must be important.").

During your initial meeting with the student (see SUGGESTED STEPS FOR DEVELOPING AND IMPLEMENTING A PLAN), try to determine the type of self-talk and explanations he uses: (1) before doing a task, (2) after a task in which he was not the best, and (3) after a task in which he was the best. You can then use this information to focus the lessons on replacing his negative self-talk with more productive, alternative statements.

b. Teach the student the difference between positive and negative self-talk, and whenever you hear him make a negative belief statement, have him reframe it into a more positive and hopeful statement. If the student can't do this, you can model a positive statement for the student and have the student repeat it. Don't worry if the student acts like he does not believe the positive statements at first. With enough repetition, we all learn to believe the things we say about ourselves (for more information, see **Self-Concept Problems**).

Following are some examples of negative belief statements, followed by corresponding positive alternatives, to illustrate this process.

3. Use reinforcement to encourage appropriate behavior.

a. Look for opportunities to praise the student for exhibiting cooperative behaviors. For example, if the class is having a competition with another class to collect canned food, and the student is encouraging other students, praise him. "Stephan, I know you have probably brought in more cans than anyone at this point, but as we were discussing this in class today, you said things like, 'We can do it. If everyone brings in a few more cans, we can beat Room 31, and we can help lots of needy people.' That was a very cooperative way of encouraging other members of the class to get with the program."

b. You might also wish to provide intermittent rewards on those occasions when the student makes a significant effort to use the positive self-talk. Occasional, and unexpected, rewards can motivate the student to demonstrate responsible behavior more often. "Stephan, today before the time test in spelling, you said, 'I am going to try to improve my score from yesterday.' That was a great example of a positive way to approach that task. I would like to write a note to your parents about the progress you are making with learning when to compete and when to be cooperative."

Use intermittent rewards more frequently at the beginning of the intervention to encourage the student, and then less often as his behavior improves.

4. Respond consistently to the inappropriate behavior.

a. When the student is overly competitive, gently correct him or ignore the behavior, as appropriate (see PLAN A).

b. If the student uses negative self-talk, prompt him to use a more positive statement. "Stephan, what might be a more positive way to describe how you did on that test?" If necessary, model positive self-talk for the student. "Well, one thing you could say instead of 'I lost' would be 'I did my best and I am proud of that.' Or you could say, 'I'll do better next time.'"

Negative Statements	Positive Alternatives
• I've got to win.	• I'll do my best.
• If I don't win, it will be terrible.	• If I win, I like myself. If I lose, I like myself.
• I'm such a loser.	• I was not first, and I still like myself.
• I am so stupid.	• Some people got A's. I got a B, which is still a good grade. Besides, I did my best.
• I won, so I am the best.	• I won and am proud of myself. Kevin ran a good race, too.
• I had the highest score. I'm so great!	• I did my best and got a high score.

PLAN D

Whenever a student's behavior has become habitual and/or he does not seem interested in trying to reduce it, you will need to implement a system of external incentives (i.e., rewards and consequences) based on his behavior to motivate him to stop being overly competitive and to start behaving more cooperatively.

1. Make sure the student knows how to be cooperative.

If the student does not know how to behave cooperatively, conduct lessons to teach him how to discriminate between situations that call for competition and those that should be viewed as noncompetitive (see PLAN B).

Respond consistently to the inappropriate behavior.

When the student is being overly competitive, gently correct him or ignore the behavior—depending upon whether the behavior is having an adverse affect on another student (see PLAN A).

 Develop procedures for periodically evaluating the student's behavior.

a. Divide the day into time intervals, at the end of which the student's behavior will be rated on how cooperative it was during that period. The intervals, which should never be longer than an hour, should be short enough so that the student has a good chance of being successful. For a middle/junior high school student this might mean a whole class period, whereas for a student with a severe problem or an elementary student, the interval might be 15-30 minutes.

b. At the end of each interval, discuss the student's behavior with him and record the rating on a form like the sample shown.

Self-Evaluation Form

Name: Stephan

Date: 1/16

Behavior being evaluated:

Excessive competitiveness

0 = Behaved in an excessively competitive way (0 points)

1 = Behaved in a cooperative manner (2 points)

2 = Behaved in an appropriately competitive way, and was supportive of others (2 points)

Time	Rating	Points
8:30 - 9:30		
9:30 - 10:30		
10:30 - 11:30		
11:30 - 12:30		
12:30 - 1:30		
1:30 - 2:30		

Gradually transfer the responsibility for making the evaluation from yourself to the student. That is, in the early stages, you should determine the rating and explain why you rated the student's behavior as you did. Then, as the student's behavior improves, have him self-evaluate his own behavior with your role being to simply agree or disagree with the evaluation. If you disagree with the student, discuss why. Try to reach agreement. If disagreements occur often, you may need to establish that you are the "umpire" (or "referee") and that the umpire has the final say. However, as long as the student is reasonably accurate in his assessment, allow him to do more and more self-evaluation and self-reinforcement.

 Establish a structured system for reinforcing the student's appropriate behavior and providing a consequence for his inappropriate behavior.

a. With the student, create a list of reinforcers that he can earn. Although you might want to have some suggestions in mind, the system will be more effective if the student identifies most of the items or activities himself. *(NOTE: A list of additional reinforcement ideas can be found in APPENDIX 1.)*

b. Assign "prices" (in points) for each of the rewards on the list and have the student select the reward he would like to earn first.

The prices should be based on the instructional, personnel, and/or monetary costs of the items. Monetary cost is clear—the more expensive the item, the more points required to earn it. Instructional cost refers to the amount of instructional time lost or interfered with by a particular reward. Thus, an activity which causes the student to miss part of academic instruction should require more points than one the student can do on his own recess time. Personnel cost involves the time required by you and/or other staff to fulfill the reinforcer. Having lunch with the principal, therefore, would cost more points than spending five minutes of free time with a friend.

c. Translate the self-evaluation ratings into points to be applied to earning the reward. For example, the two positive ratings on the form might be worth one and two points, respectively, and the negative rating worth zero points.

d. At the end of each day, determine the student's total points and add them to the points the student has earned on previous days.

e. When the student has accumulated enough points to earn the reward he has chosen, he "spends" the points necessary and the system begins again. That is, the student selects another reward to earn and begins with zero points.

If the student is immature, and needs more frequent encouragement, you might consider letting him earn several "less expensive" rewards (e.g., five minutes of computer time after 20 points) on the way to the bigger reward (e.g., one hour with you for 200 points). That is, the student receives the small rewards without spending points; they continue to accumulate toward the selected reward.

5. *Use reinforcement to encourage appropriate behavior.*

a. Give the student increased praise and attention for being cooperative (see PLAN A).

b. Show interest and enthusiasm about how the student is doing on the system. "Stephan, throughout the entire day you have been ap-

propriately competitive. You are really making progress."

6. *Encourage the student to use self-reinforcement.*

Each time the student has a high behavior rating, encourage him to mentally reinforce his performance. In the early stages, you might model specific statements that he could make. "Stephan, you should tell yourself, 'I am a very cooperative person. I helped my team work well together.'" As time goes on, prompt the student to reinforce himself, and ask him what he plans to say to himself. "Stephan, you should tell yourself that you are doing well with being cooperative. What could you say to yourself?" Then when the student can consistently think of an appropriate self-reinforcing statement, you can simply prompt him to reinforce himself. "Stephan, tell yourself something about how cooperative you are."

PLAN E

Occasionally you may have a class in which there are several students who are aggressive towards each other. This plan adapts components from PLANS A-D to be used with a class of overly competitive students.

1. *Hold a class meeting to discuss the problem.*

During the meeting, provide examples to teach the students to discriminate between situations that call for competition and those that should be viewed as noncompetitive (see PLAN B).

Then define "uncooperative competition" for the class. Uncooperative competition might be defined as any time an individual is competitive in a noncompetitive task or is overly competitive in a competitive task.

2. *Develop procedures for publicly monitoring the frequency of "uncooperative competition."*

a. Identify a place (e.g., the chalkboard or a wall chart) on which you can record a daily count of incidents of uncooperative competition.

b. Each day, write a tally mark on the chart each time there is an incident of uncooperative competition in the class. You should not identify the individuals responsible for the acts, simply record the occurrences.

At the end of the day, total the marks and compare the total to that of previous days. Discuss whether the situation is getting better,

worse, or staying about the same. If the situation has improved, have the students reflect on the climate of the classroom. Does it feel better? if so, how? if not, why not?

3. *Encourage the class to set a daily performance goal.*

After examining the daily totals of occurrences of uncooperative competition for a few days, the students should be instructed to set a performance goal to lower the number of daily occurrences. You may have to help the students identify a reasonable goal. They may say, for example, that they want to reduce the number of incidents from 15 on one day to zero on the next day. You might tell the students that if they set a more realistic goal, such as 12, they significantly increase their chances of success and they can always do better than their goal. Then as the class successfully meets their goals, the number of target incidents should become progressively lower.

4. *Use reinforcement to encourage appropriate behavior.*

a. When the class has demonstrated reductions in their total number of incidents of uncooperative competition, provide class praise. "Class, everyone in the room should be proud of how cooperative they were today. According to our count, we have had a significant reduction in the number of incidents of uncooperative competition. Excellent work."

b. Occasionally, provide a class-wide reward to celebrate their success. "Class, you've done such a good job of being cooperative today—how about if we take the last five minutes of

class to have free choice time with some music playing?"

c. Additionally, you may wish to establish a group reinforcement system in which you identify a daily performance goal for the class. On days when the students are successful in keeping their number of uncooperative competition incidents under the target number, the class earns a point toward a reward that they have chosen to earn.

. . . .
Suggested Steps for Developing and Implementing a Plan

The following steps are designed to help you develop an appropriate intervention plan and implement it effectively, whether you choose to use one of the MODEL PLANS or create a customized plan of your own. The steps are, however, suggestions—they are not intended to be followed rigidly or in any particular order. Use your professional judgment and the knowledge of your particular situation to make them work for you.

1. *Make sure you have enough information about the situation.*

a. If you think a minimal intervention like PLAN A will be sufficient, you may already have enough information to proceed. However, when a more involved plan seems necessary, you should consider collecting additional descriptive and/or objective information for a couple of days.

b. You need to be able to explain what has led you to conclude that "the student has a problem with being overly competitive." Anecdotal notes on actual incidents should provide enough detail to help you define the problem behavior clearly and completely. To collect anecdotal notes, simply keep a card in your pocket or on a clipboard and occasionally make notes on specific instances when the student does something that seems to you to be overly competitive.

For each entry, briefly describe where and when it occurred, what the student did or said, and any other relevant observations (e.g., what prompted the behavior). You do not need to take notes every time the student acts overly competitive; the idea is to capture a range of examples of the behavior so you will be able to describe it completely.

Also include some notes on times when the student is cooperative—this will make it clear that you are not only aware of his problem behavior, but also recognize when he behaves appropriately. When you meet with the student, these notes will also help you clarify how you want the student to behave.

c. If the student notices what you are doing and asks about it, be straightforward—tell him that you are collecting information to see whether his competitiveness is a problem that needs to be worked on.

Following is an example of anecdotal notes that have been collected on a student's competitiveness.

Notes on Stephan's Competitiveness—1/14

8:25—Stephan and two other students rushed into the room, quickly hung up their coats, and rushed to their seats. Stephan practically climbed over Jamal to get to his seat first, and then taunted several times, "I was first!"

9:15—As I handed back the spelling tests, Stephan publicly announced, "I got a 100%. Was I the only one or did anybody tie with me?"

1:00—During P.E. we were playing basketball and doing scrimmages. Stephan was yelling at his teammates, accusing them of "screwing up and costing us points." He didn't even stop talking about it when we were finished and had gone back to the classroom.

Don came to me later in the afternoon and asked if he could be on a different team than Stephan from now on because he was tired of having him "jump all over everybody, just because they make a mistake."

---

d. Continuing to collect this type of information while you implement a plan will allow you to monitor whether the situation is getting worse, staying the same, or getting better.

2. Identify a focus for the intervention and labels for referring to the appropriate and inappropriate behaviors.

a. To be effective, the intervention must address more than just reducing the student's competitiveness—there must be a concurrent emphasis on increasing some positive behavior or trait (e.g., cooperation, teamwork, respect for others). Having a specific positive behavior in mind will make it easier for you to "catch" and reinforce the student for behaving appropriately, and the positive focus will help you to frame the situation more productively.

For example, if you simply say that "the student has a problem with being overly competitive," you don't really provide any useful information, and may put the student and his parent(s) on the defensive. However, when you explain that you want to "help the student learn to be more cooperative," you are presenting an important, and reasonable, goal for the student to work toward and clearly identifying what the student needs to do to be successful.

b. Specifying labels for the appropriate and inappropriate behaviors (e.g., "being cooperative" and "being overly competitive," respectively) will help you to use consistent vocabulary when discussing the situation with the student. If you sometimes refer to the inappropriate behavior as "being overly competitive," for example, and other times tell the student that "he is being arrogant," he may not realize that you are talking about the same thing.

3. Determine when and how to include the parent(s).

a. It is not necessary to contact the student's parent(s) if the problem has just begun and is not interfering with the student's academic or social progress. However, it might be a good idea to take advantage of any scheduled activities (e.g., conferences, weekly notes home) to let them know of your concern.

b. The parent(s) should be contacted whenever the student's competitiveness is affecting his academic performance or is alienating him from his peers. Share any information you have collected about the student's behavior (e.g., anecdotal notes) with the parent(s), and explain why you are concerned. Focus in particular on how the behavior is hindering the student academically and/or socially (e.g., other students are beginning to avoid participating in activities with him).

You might ask if the parent(s) have any insight into the situation and/or whether they have noticed similar behavior at home. Whether or not the parent(s) perceive a problem, explain that you want to help the student "learn to be more cooperative," and invite them to join you for an initial meeting with the student to develop a plan. If the parent(s) are unable or unwilling to participate, let them know that you will keep them informed of the student's progress.

c. Once the parent(s) have been involved in any way, you should give them updates at least once per week while the plan is being implemented.

4. Prepare for, then conduct, an initial meeting about the situation.

a. Arrange a meeting to discuss your concerns with the student and anyone else who will be involved in the plan (e.g., the parent[s], the school psychologist). Although the specifics will vary depending upon the age of the student and the severity of the problem, there are some general guidelines to consider when scheduling the meeting. First, meet at a neutral time (i.e., not immediately after a problem has occurred), when emotions are less likely to hamper communication. In general, a day's notice is appropriate, however primary age students may worry excessively and/or forget what the meeting is about if it is scheduled more than an hour before it takes place.

Second, make the meeting appropriately private. With a primary student who has a mild problem, you might meet in the classroom while the other students are working independently. However, when dealing with a middle/junior high school student and the student's parent(s), you will need some place private (e.g., the counselor's office) to ensure that the discussion will not be overheard.

Third, try to make sure the meeting is scheduled for a time and place that it is not likely to be interrupted. Finally, if the parent(s) will be participating, they should be the ones to tell the student about the meeting.

b. Construct a preliminary plan. Decide whether you think you can use one of the MODEL PLANS or if you need to create a customized plan using components from various plans and/or of your own design. Although you will invite and encourage the student to help develop the plan during the initial meeting, having a proposed plan in mind before you meet can alleviate frustration and wasted time if the student is unwilling or unable to participate.

c. After reviewing the information you have collected and thinking about how you want the student to behave, prepare thorough descriptions of the inappropriate behavior and the positive behavior/trait on which the student will be working. The more specific you can be and the more concrete examples you have, the easier it will be to clarify (and for the student to understand) your expectations. Be sure to consider the student's behavior in all relevant activities (e.g., independent work, teacher directed instruction, unstructured class times, recess and lunch, etc.).

d. Conduct the meeting in an atmosphere of collaboration. The following agenda is one way you might structure the meeting:

- **Share your concerns about the student's behavior.**

    Briefly describe the problem behavior and explain why you consider it to be a problem. You will want to communicate to the student that there are settings in which a competitive spirit can be not only reasonable, but very helpful, but that there are other circumstances in which being overly competitive can be problematic. For example, being competitive with one's teammates may reduce the team's ability to win. Or, competing about whose paper is the best in a classroom can be very discouraging for some students, and even result in other students not wanting to be around the overly competitive person.

- **Discuss how you can work together to improve the situation.**

    Tell the student that you would like to help him "learn to be more cooperative" and describe your preliminary plan. (Remember, it is very important to be careful that you do not hurt the student's feelings or imply that he should change his personality.) Invite the student to give you input on the various aspects of the plan, and together work out any necessary details (e.g., when and where the lessons will take place).

You may have to brainstorm different possibilities if the student is uncomfortable with the initial plan. Incorporating any of the student's suggestions that strengthen the plan is likely to increase his sense of "ownership" in and commitment to it.

- **Make sure the student understands what you mean by appropriate and inappropriate behavior.**

    Use the descriptions you have prepared to define and clarify the problem behavior and the positive (desired) behavior as specifically and thoroughly as you can. To ensure that you and the student are in agreement about the expectations, you might present hypothetical scenarios and have the student identify whether each is an example of being overly competitive or of being cooperative. Or you might describe an actual situation that has occurred and ask the student to explain how he could demonstrate being more cooperative in that situation.

- **Conclude the meeting.**

    Always end the meeting with words of encouragement. Let the student know that you are confident that he can be successful. Be sure to reinforce him for participating in the meeting.

5. *Give the student regular, ongoing feedback about his behavior.*

It is important to meet with the student periodically to discuss his progress. In most cases, three to five minutes once per week should suffice. *(NOTE: PLANS D and E call for daily meetings.)* During the meetings, review any information that has been collected and discuss whether or not the situation is getting better. As much as possible, focus on the student's improvements, however, also address any new or continuing problems. As the situation improves, the meetings can be faded to once every other week and then to once per month.

6. *Evaluate the situation (and the plan).*

Implement any plan for at least two weeks before deciding whether to change plans; to continue, modify, or fade the plan you are using; or to cease the intervention. Generally, if the student's behavior is clearly improving (based on the objective information that's been collected and/or the subjective perceptions of yourself, the student, and possibly the parent[s]), stick with what you are doing. If the situation has remained the same or worsened, some kind of change will be necessary.

Always discuss any changes to the plan with the student first.

OMPLAINING

Negativity

DESCRIPTION

You have a student who tends to be negative and complains about almost everything.

GOAL

The student will reduce her complaining/negativity and will learn to use positive expressions of approval more often.

OVERVIEW OF PLANS

- PLAN A: For a situation in which the problem is relatively mild or has just begun.

- PLAN B: For a student who complains as a way of gaining attention from adults or peers.

- PLAN C: For a student who is not aware of how often she complains.

- PLAN D: For a student whose complaining is habitual.

- PLAN E: For a situation in which several students in your class tend to complain or be negative.

NOTE:

The information presented in these five plans refers to a student (or students) who complains, but can be easily adapted for a student who is generally negative.

Alternative Problems

- **Arguing—Student(s) With the Teacher**

- **Blaming Others/ Excuses for Everything**

- **Bored Behavior**

- **Disrespectful Behavior**

- **Tattling**

- **Whining**

....
General Considerations

- If the student's problem behavior could stem in any way from academic issues (e.g., she complains about academic tasks because they are beyond her ability), concurrent efforts must be made to ensure her academic success (see **Academic Deficits, Determining**).

....
Model Plans

PLAN A

It is not always necessary, or even beneficial, to use an involved plan. If the inappropriate behavior has just begun and/or is relatively mild (i.e., not interfering with the student's academic or social progress), the following actions, along with making the student aware of your concerns, may resolve the situation.

1. *Respond consistently to the inappropriate behavior.*

a. During your initial meeting with the student (see SUGGESTED STEPS FOR DEVELOPING AND IMPLEMENTING A PLAN), establish a nonembarrassing signal that you can use to cue her that she is complaining. You want the signal to be a fairly subtle one that only the student will recognize and understand in order to minimize the chance that she will be teased by her peers. Possibilities include an unobtrusive wave of your hand, rubbing your neck, or even just direct eye contact and a head nod.

Let the student know that you may also need to quietly say her name to get her attention before you give the signal. You should be prepared to use the signal frequently and for a fairly long time, especially if the behavior is in part an unconscious habit for the student.

b. Whenever the student is complaining, give her the signal. If the student does not cease the complaining and is with her peers, ignore the behavior. However, if other students are not around, gently correct her. Let the student know that her behavior is an example of complaining and give her direct information about what she should be doing instead. "Rochelle, I heard that you do not like the new playground equipment, now it is time to let go of that concern and talk about something else." Because your goal is to impart information, you want to be emotionally neutral while giving the correction.

2. *Use reinforcement to encourage appropriate behavior.*

a. Give the student increased praise. Be especially alert for situations in which the student expresses a positive or enthusiastic attitude toward something and praise her for these demonstrations of a positive attitude. "Rochelle, I can tell that you are making an effort to see the positive side of things." If the student would be embarrassed by this public praise, praise the student privately or even give the student a note.

b. Also praise the student privately for responding to the signal. "Rochelle, three times this morning I gave you the signal about complaining and you stopped. And there have been no complaints that I have heard the rest of the day. Good job of keeping a positive attitude."

c. Give the student frequent attention (e.g., say "hello" to her as she enters the classroom, call on her frequently during class activities, and occasionally ask her to assist you with a class job that needs to be done) and praise her for other positive behaviors she exhibits. For example, you might comment about the accuracy of her work or how consistent she is about making entries in her journal. This demonstrates to the student that you notice many positive things she does, not just the fact that she is refraining from complaining.

In addition, be sure to show an interest in anything that the student demonstrates a positive or enthusiastic attitude toward. "I am glad that you had a nice time. Tell me some more about your great weekend."

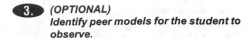 **(OPTIONAL)**
Identify peer models for the student to observe.

When you think the student may not fully understand different ways to interact, you might suggest two or three other students for her to observe. "Rochelle, you might consider watching how Alicia and Devan respond to assignments, requests to join in, and some of the other things we do through-out the day. I don't expect you to try to be like them—you're terrific just the way you are—but watching them may give you some ideas of how to be more positive about things. You know, I just learned some new teaching ideas when I observed Mr. Carmody yesterday." If used, this procedure needs to be handled well to avoid hurting the student's feelings or implying that she should be more like someone else.

PLAN B

Some students are very skilled at gaining attention through their negative behavior. If you find yourself feeling annoyed with and frequently nagging, reminding, or coaxing the student to stop complaining, it is possible that this is her motivation. Or, if the student complains more when her peers are around, the complaining may be her way of gaining attention from or looking "cool" in front of her peers. Whether or not the student overtly seems to like the attention, you should make sure that she receives more frequent and more satisfying attention when she is exhibiting productive behaviors and positive attitudes than when she is complaining.

1. Respond consistently to the inappropriate behavior.

a. Because it is important for the student to learn that she will not be able to prompt people to nag and/or pay attention to her by complaining, you need to avoid attending to her excessive complaints. Decide on a number of complaints each day that you are willing to respond to (e.g., two). Then let the student know during your initial planning meeting (see SUGGESTED STEPS FOR DEVELOPING AND IMPLEMENTING A PLAN) that you will listen and respond to only two complaints per day, but none after that.

b. For those first two complaints, show an active interest in what the student is saying. "Rochelle, tell me more about why you don't like the cafeteria food. Is there any way you can solve this problem?" If the student has already "used up" her two complaints for the day, politely interrupt the student's complaint or redirect her. "Rochelle, we have already heard about the things you do not like. Please give a specific suggestion on what we can do about the problem we are trying to solve."

c. When the student is engaging in subsequent complaints, do not look at the student or talk to her. Do not act disgusted or impatient with her behavior. Simply interact in positive ways with students who are behaving appropriately and meeting classroom expectations. As soon as the target student is no longer complaining, pay attention to her, but make no reference to her complaints.

(NOTE: For a student in kindergarten or first grade, redirection may be more appropriate than ignoring the complaint. Redirection involves gently moving the student off the topic she is complaining about and encouraging the student's interest in something else. "Tell me why you chose these colors for your picture.")

d. When other students give the target student attention when she is complaining, you will have to decide whether or not to intervene. If the other students seem to be involved by choice with the target student, it would probably be inappropriate to intervene and doing so could lead to a power struggle between you and the target student. That is, the student could begin competing with you to maintain the attention and involvement of the other students.

However, when the other students seem to be annoyed with the target student and/or are trying to get her to stop complaining, gently correct them. "Charli and Wyatt, you don't have to deal with these complaints. It would be best to let Rochelle deal with this concern on her own."

2. Use reinforcement to encourage appropriate behavior.

a. Frequent praise and attention are the core of this plan. The student must see that she receives more frequent and more satisfying attention when she behaves appropriately than when she complains. Thus, whenever the student is not complaining (or otherwise misbehaving), make an effort to praise and spend time with her. "Rochelle, you have been so involved in a positive way with this project, it is a pleasure to see. Would it be okay if I sat with you a moment and watched as you and your group do the next step?"

b. You may also wish to use intermittent rewards to acknowledge the student's success. Occasional, and unexpected, rewards can motivate the student to demonstrate responsible behavior more often. The idea is to provide a reward when the student has gone for a significant period of time without complaining (e.g., the student typically complains five to ten times before lunch, but goes all morning without complaining).

Appropriate rewards might include talking with you in an unstructured setting, walking with you as the class is going to lunch, or preparing a special project. *(NOTE: A list of additional reinforcement ideas can be found in APPENDIX 1.)*

Use intermittent rewards more frequently at the beginning of the intervention to encourage the student, and then less often as her behavior improves.

3. *Ensure a 3-1 ratio of positive to negative attention.*

a. Since attention is a motivating force for this student, you want to be sure that you are giving the student *three times as much* positive as negative attention. One way to do this is to monitor your interactions with the student at least one day per week. Simply keep a card on a clipboard or in your pocket and record each interaction you have with the student as either positive or negative by writing a "+" or a "-", respectively, on the card.

To determine whether an interaction is positive or negative, ask yourself whether the student was complaining (or otherwise misbehaving) at the time the interaction occurred. Any interactions that stem from inappropriate behavior are negative, while all interactions that occur while the student is meeting classroom expectations are positive. Thus, any gentle correction you give related to the student's complaining would be counted as a negative interaction, but praising the student for having a positive attitude would be positive. Greeting the student as she enters the room or asking her if she has any questions during independent work are also considered positive interactions. *(NOTE: Ignoring the student's inappropriate behavior is not recorded at all, because it is not an interaction.)*

b. If you find that you are not giving the student three times as much positive as negative attention, try to increase the number of positive interactions you have with the student. Sometimes prompts can help. For example, you might decide that each time the student enters the classroom you will say "hello" to her, that twice each morning will find a time to praise the student, or that whenever a student uses the drinking fountain you will check the target student and as soon as possible praise some aspect of her behavior. You can also increase the ratio of positive to negative attention by ignoring more of the student's complaints.

4. *Assign the student a responsibility.*

Giving the student an important/high status job at school may reduce the student's need to "act cool" and call attention to herself by complaining. With elementary level students, a public job, such as letting the student leave class for a short time each day to go read to the students in the kindergarten class, may be most effective. With middle/junior high school students, it may be better for the job to be something that the other students know about only if the target student chooses to tell them. For example, you might ask the student to stay after school two days per week to help set up special computer programs in a computer lab. *(NOTE: For a list of other possible jobs, see APPENDIX 2.)*

PLAN C

Some students do not seem to know when they are behaving inappropriately. If your student doesn't realize when and/or how often she complains, the intervention must include some way of helping the student become more aware of her own behavior.

1. *Respond consistently to the inappropriate behavior.*

a. When the student complains, use a signal, then ignore and/or gently correct the behavior, as necessary (see PLAN A).

b. In addition, whenever you give the student the signal, make sure the incident is recorded by either the student or yourself (see Step 2).

c. Explain to the student that a few complaints each day are fine; the problem is one of excess.

The student does not need to feel that she is doing something wrong every time you give her the signal. The point is for her to think about whether she is complaining unnecessarily or excessively.

2. Implement a system for monitoring the frequency of the student's complaints.

a. Determine who will record the student's complaints. Since the purpose of this procedure is for the student to become more aware of her own behavior, having her record the frequency (i.e., self-monitor) will be more effective than if you record the behavior. However, if the student cannot or will not be accurate (or if she would be too embarrassed to self-monitor) you should do the recording yourself. If you do the recording, the student should be made aware of each time that she complains, and know that each incident is being recorded. *(NOTE: Even when the student self-monitors, you should keep your own record approximately one day per week to verify the student's accuracy.)*

b. If the student is self-monitoring her complaints, she can keep a form like the sample shown on her desk or in her notebook. Tell the student that each time she sees you give her the signal, she should circle a number on the form.

Name   *Rochelle Dillon*

Behavior to be Counted: *Each time I*

complain or am negative.

Note: Zero to three each day is okay.

Date _____

1	2	3	4	5	6	7	8
9	10	11	12	13	14	15	16
17	18	19	20	21	22	23	24

(NOTE: The number list should be reproduced four more times so the form can be used for a week.)

c. Each day, meet with the student for a few minutes to review that day's record. Have the student chart the information on a graph (or do it yourself), and talk with her about whether the day was better, worse, or about the same as previous days. If the day did not go well, encourage the student to talk about why and have her identify things she can do the next day to help

herself remember to look at things more positively rather than complaining.

If the student behaves inappropriately during the meeting, keep the interaction very short. Just let the student know that you are sure tomorrow will be a better day.

d. Another idea is to use humor to cue the student when she complains. If you think the student is relatively secure, you may occasionally wish to use a gentle joke in place of the signal. For example, after asking her to get to work on her math assignment, but before she says anything, you could gently imitate what she is likely to say. "Wait. Don't tell me. 'Math really sucks.' Am I right? Didn't know I could predict the future, did you?"

You need to be careful, though. This suggestion can be easily misused and abused (i.e., you think you are being funny, but the student feels ridiculed). If you do use humor, check to see if the student minds. "Rochelle, for a couple of days, I have done some teasing about your complaining. Would you prefer that I didn't do that?" Even if the student says she does not mind, do not overuse the procedure—remember that humor used poorly or too often can be destructive and cruel. *(NOTE: Never use humor in this way if the student suffers from a poor self-concept.)*

3. Use reinforcement to encourage appropriate behavior.

a. Give the student increased praise and attention for demonstrating a positive attitude (see PLAN A).

b. In addition, praise the student during the end-of-the-day review meetings for accurate recording (if applicable) and for being willing to look at her daily total. Even on a bad day, if the student is willing to chart the data and discuss why it was a bad day, praise her. "Rochelle, you are really handling this responsibly. Even though it was a rough day, you are willing to talk to me about things you might do differently tomorrow. That is a real sign that you are growing up." Regardless of how the day went, try to make this meeting upbeat and encouraging—you want the student to look forward to the review meetings.

4. Encourage the student to use self-reinforcement.

Whenever things are going well (i.e., less complaining than usual), prompt the student to mentally reinforce herself. "Rochelle, this has been a very successful morning. Silently tell yourself that you are really good at looking at things positively.

"Prompt the student this way intermittently throughout the day and during the end-of-the-day review meetings.

PLAN D

Whenever a student's complaining has become habitual and/or she does not seem to have a desire to reduce it, you may need to implement a structured system of external incentives (i.e., rewards and consequences) based on her behavior to motivate her to reduce her complaining and to start having a more positive attitude.

 Respond consistently to the inappropriate behavior.

a. Use a signal to cue the student when she is complaining (see PLAN A).

b. Establish a mild consequence, such as one minute of time owed off of recess, for each incident of excessive complaining. Set a daily limit on the number of complaints or expressions of negative feelings that seem reasonable for any student—perhaps two or three per day in elementary classrooms. If you have the student for only one period per day, the number might be set at one complaint per day.

c. Each day, respond to any of the student's complaints within the limit exactly as you might for a student who does not chronically complain. "Rochelle, I am sorry that you don't like math. Tell me why, and perhaps we can do something to make math more pleasant for you." Then each complaint beyond the established number precipitates the mild consequence.

Responding to a limited number of complaints each day while assigning consequences for excessive complaining lets the student know that her opinions are of value, but there are limits on how frequently her negative opinions can be taken seriously. In explaining this concept to the student, you might share the story about the little boy who cried wolf.

 Define for the student the borderline between complaining and positive behavior/statements.

Since this plan involves rewards for reducing complaining and consequences for excessive complaints, consistency and clarity will be critical. That is, you will need to clearly define for the student the borderline between complaints (and/or negativity) and positive, cooperative behavior/statements. During your initial meeting with the student (see SUGGESTED STEPS FOR DEVELOPING AND IMPLEMENTING A PLAN), provide several examples to clarify the difference between complaints and statements that do not involve complaining. Work with the student until you are both absolutely clear regarding which behaviors/statements will be considered complaints and which will be considered positive and cooperative.

 Implement a system for monitoring the frequency of the student's complaints (see PLAN C).

 Establish a structured system for reinforcing the appropriate behavior.

a. With the student, create a list of reinforcers that she can earn. Although you might want to have some suggestions in mind, the system will be more effective if the student identifies most of the items or activities herself. *(NOTE: A list of reinforcement ideas can be found in APPENDIX 1.)*

b. Assign "prices" (in points) for each of the rewards on the list and have the student select the reward she would like to earn first. The prices should be based on the instructional, personnel, and/or monetary costs of the items. Monetary cost is clear—the more expensive the item, the more points required to earn it. Instructional cost refers to the amount of instructional time lost or interfered with by a particular reward. Thus, an activity which causes the student to miss part of academic instruction should require more points than one the student can do on her own recess time. Personnel cost involves the time required by you and/or other staff to fulfill the reinforcer. Having lunch with the principal, therefore, would cost more points than spending five minutes of free time with a friend.

c. Use the monitoring information to determine the number of points to be earned. Following is a sample point chart for a student who complains an average of 13-15 times per day.

15 or more complaints = 0 points

11-14 complaints = 1 point

7-10 complaints = 2 points

4-6 complaints = 3 points

0-3 complaints = 4 points

d. When the student has accumulated enough points to earn the reward she has chosen, she "spends" the points necessary and the system begins again. That is, she chooses another reward to earn and begins with zero points.

If the student is immature, and needs more frequent encouragement, you might consider letting her earn several "less expensive" rewards (e.g., five minutes of free time after 20

points) on the way to a bigger reward (e.g., one hour with you for 200 points). That is, the student receives the small rewards without spending points; they continue to accumulate toward the selected reward.

 5. *Use reinforcement to encourage appropriate behavior.*

a. Give the student increased praise and attention for demonstrating a positive attitude (see PLAN A).

b. In addition, show interest and enthusiasm about how the student is doing on the system. "Rochelle, you have earned either three or four points each day this week. What a wonderful job you are doing. You used to have trouble earning these points—now you make it seem easy!"

PLAN E

Sometimes a number of students in a classroom fall into a pattern of complaining and negativity. Often the students are not even aware of how frequently they are complaining. In other cases, the students may be indirectly encouraging each other to complain. This can occur when a few influential students are perceived to look "cool" or "tough" when they complain so other students try to emulate them. Soon, many students are complaining because their peers are doing so and/or because the "complainers" are popular. If you increase student awareness of when and how often complaining is occurring, this action may be enough to motivate the students to begin being more positive and cooperative. If not, you may need to implement a group reinforcement system to create mild peer pressure to change the behavior.

 1. *Hold a class discussion about the situation.*

Making the students aware of how frequently they complain may have a positive impact on their behavior. To make sure they completely understand which behavior/statements you feel are problematic, clearly define the borderline between complaints and positive statements (see PLAN D).

 2. *Record all occurrences of complaints in the classroom.*

a. Record the daily record on the chalkboard or a wall chart on which a space is filled in for every complaint. Do not attempt to record who does the complaining—the goal is to obtain a classwide total of complaints each day, not to identify individuals who are complaining.

b. At the end of each day, total the marks and compare the count to that of previous days. Discuss whether things are getting better, worse, or are about the same. If the situation is

getting better, have the students reflect on the climate of the classroom. Does it feel better? if so, how? if not, why not?

 3. *Encourage the class to set a daily performance goal.*

a. You may have to help the students set a realistic goal, as they may be likely to set a very challenging goal, such as reducing the number of complaints from 40 per day to zero per day. Let them know that if the goal is an attainable number, such as 32, they can always complain less than that, but they increase their chances of success.

b. As the class experiences success, the target number of complaints should become progressively lower until the goal is acceptable and comfortable. Do not have the students set zero as a goal. The students should feel that there is some latitude for occasionally complaining or expressing a negative opinion. As the original problem was the excessive number of complaints, success consists of reducing, but not eliminating, this behavior.

 Provide a way for the students to express honest concerns without them being considered complaints.

Set up a suggestion box, for example. Inform the class that the suggestions will be used to set the agenda for a weekly class meeting to discuss ideas for improving the class. If a student has a concern, he/she can write it in the form of a positive suggestion for change and put it in the box. These suggestions should not be included as part of the daily count of complaints.

 (OPTIONAL)
Establish a group reinforcement system.

a. If necessary, establish a group reinforcement system to motivate the students to strive to reduce their amount of complaining and negativity. For example, on days when the class successfully keeps the number of complaints below the identified goal, they earn a point toward a reward that they have agreed upon.

Or you could use a Mystery Motivator (Rhode, Jenson, & Reavis, 1992). In this system, you mark (with an "X," for example) random weekdays on a calendar, then cover every space with a slip of paper. On any day that the class is successful in attaining their goal, you uncover the space to see if there is an "X." If there is, the group earns a predetermined reinforcer.

b. If a class-wide reinforcement system doesn't seem likely to be effective, set up a team competition and response cost lottery. Divide the class into four to six teams, as equal as possible. Each team begins the day with a certain number of tickets on which they write the name of their team. Each time a student complains, that individual's team loses a ticket. Then at the end of the day, all the teams put their remaining tickets in a hat for a lottery drawing. The team whose ticket is drawn earns the predetermined reward for that day.

c. While implementing any group reinforcement system, keep student attention focused on how much more pleasant the classroom atmosphere is as the amount of complaining is reduced. "Class, you earned your point for the day, but more importantly, you are all helping this class be a place that we all will enjoy. This room is a place we can all be proud of."

· · · · · · · ·
Suggested Steps for Developing and Implementing a Plan

The following steps are designed to help you develop an appropriate intervention plan and implement it effectively, whether you choose to use one of the MODEL PLANS or create a customized plan of your own. The steps are, however, suggestions—they are not intended to be followed rigidly or in any particular order. Use your professional judgment and the knowledge of your particular situation to make them work for you.

 Make sure you have enough information about the situation.

a. If you think a minimal intervention like PLAN A will be sufficient, you may already have enough information to proceed. However, when a more involved plan seems necessary, you should consider collecting additional descriptive and/or objective information for a couple of days.

b. You need to be able to explain what has led you to conclude that "the student has a problem with complaining." Since complaining itself is not necessarily a misbehavior, there must be some aspect of this student's complaining that makes it inappropriate. Is it the frequency of the complaining? the vehemence with which the student

complains? Anecdotal notes on actual incidents can help you define the problem behavior clearly and completely.

To collect anecdotal notes, simply keep a card in your pocket or on a clipboard and occasionally make notes on specific instances when the student complains. For each entry, briefly describe where and when the complaining occurred, what the student did or said, and any other relevant observations (e.g., what prompted the complaint). You do not need to take notes every time the student complains; the idea is to capture a range of examples so that you will be able to describe the behavior thoroughly.

Also include some notes on times when the student responds positively, as this will make it clear that you are not only aware of her problem behavior, but also recognize when she behaves appropriately. When you meet with the student, the positive examples will also help you clarify how you want the student to behave.

c. In addition to information on what the student's inappropriate behavior looks like, it can also be useful to document how often it occurs (i.e., a frequency count). This information will provide both a more objective measure of the problem and an objective way to monitor the student's progress. You can use the same card on which you are collecting anecdotal notes to keep a frequency count—simply write a tally mark on the card each time the student complains.

You might also want to code the tallies to discern whether the complaining occurs more frequently during certain times, subjects, or activities (e.g., using an "A" or "P" to indicate that the complaint occurred in the morning or afternoon; or clustering the tallies by math or reading, teacher directed instruction or independent work, etc.).

d. If the student notices what you are doing and asks about it, be straightforward—tell her that you are collecting information to see whether her complaining is a problem that needs to be worked on.

Following is an example of anecdotal notes and a frequency count that have been collected on a student's complaining.

Rochelle's Complaining—1/12

AAAAA APPPP PPPPP P

9:39—During the time I was presenting on how the students should do their reports, Rochelle made at least three comments such as: "This is stupid. I don't see why we have to do a report." and "Why do we have to do a report on a person? I hate reports like this."

11:50—Before lunch Rochelle said, "I can hardly wait for my school barf—I mean lunch."

1:15—Coming in from lunch she said, "I get so bored during lunch. There is never anything to do. We just stand around and wait for the bell."

2:00—Rochelle was working with Suzy and complimented Suzy on the information she collected for their joint project.

---

e. The frequency information is fairly easy to summarize on a chart or graph. Seeing how often she complains may help the student and her parent(s) better understand your concern.

f. Continuing to collect this type of information (and keeping the chart up-to-date) while you implement a plan will help you to monitor whether the situation is getting worse, staying the same, or getting better.

2. *Identify a focus for the intervention and labels for referring to the appropriate and inappropriate behaviors.*

a. To be effective, the intervention must address more than just reducing the student's complaining—there must be a concurrent emphasis on increasing some positive behavior or trait (e.g., viewing some things more positively). Having a specific positive behavior in mind will make it easier for you to "catch" and reinforce the student for behaving appropriately, and the positive focus will help you to frame the situation more productively.

For example, if you simply say that "the student has a problem with complaining," you don't really provide any useful information, and may put the student and her parent(s) on the defensive. However, when you explain that you want to help the student view some things more positively," you are presenting an important, and reasonable, goal for the student to work toward and clearly identifying what the student needs to do to be successful.

b. Identifying labels for referring to the appropriate and inappropriate behaviors (e.g., "viewing things positively" and "viewing things negatively," respectively) will help you to use consistent vocabulary when discussing the situation with the student. If you sometimes refer to the negative behavior as "being whiny" and other times tell the student that she is "viewing things negatively," for example, she may not realize that you are talking about the same behavior.

3. *Determine when and how to include the parent(s).*

a. It is not necessary to contact the student's parent(s) if the problem has just begun and is not interfering with the student's academic or social progress. However, it might be a good idea to take advantage of any scheduled activities (e.g., conferences, weekly notes home) to let them know of your concern.

b. If the problem has been going on for more than a couple of weeks, contact the student's parent(s) to discuss your concern. Share with them any information you have collected about the behavior (e.g., anecdotal notes, frequency count), and explain why you are concerned. Focus in particular on how the behavior is hindering the student academically and/or socially (e.g., other students are tired of the student's negativity and are beginning to avoid her).

You might ask if the parent(s) have any insight into the situation and/or whether they have noticed similar behavior at home. Whether or not the parent(s) perceive a problem, explain that you want to help the student "learn to view some things more positively," and invite them to join you for an initial meeting with the student to develop a plan. If the parent(s) are unable or unwilling to participate, let them know that you will keep them informed of the student's progress.

c. Once the parent(s) have been involved in any way, you should give them updates at least once per week while the plan is being implemented.

4. **Prepare for, then conduct, an initial meeting about the situation.**

a. Arrange a meeting to discuss your concerns with the student and anyone else who will be involved in the plan (e.g., the parent[s], the school psychologist). Although the specifics will vary depending upon the age of the student and the severity of the problem, there are some general guidelines to consider when scheduling the meeting.

First, meet at a neutral time (i.e., not immediately after a problem has occurred) when emotions are less likely to hamper communication. In general, a day's notice is appropriate, however a primary age student may worry excessively and/or forget what the meeting is about if it is scheduled more than an hour before it takes place.

Second, make the meeting appropriately private. With a primary student who has a mild problem, you might meet in the classroom while the other students are working independently. However, when dealing with a middle/junior high school student and the student's parent(s), you will need some place private (e.g., the counselor's office) to ensure that the discussion will not be overheard.

Third, try to make sure the meeting is scheduled for a time and place that it is not likely to be interrupted. Finally, if the parent(s) will be participating, they should be the ones to tell the student about the meeting.

b. Construct a preliminary plan. Decide whether you think you can use one of the MODEL PLANS or if you need to create a customized plan using components from various plans and/or of your own design. Although you will invite and encourage the student to help develop the plan during the initial meeting, having a proposed plan in mind before you meet can alleviate frustration and wasted time if the student is unwilling or unable to participate.

c. After reviewing the information you have collected and thinking about how you want the student to behave, prepare thorough descriptions of the inappropriate behavior and the positive behavior/trait on which the student will be working. The more specific you can be and the more concrete examples you have, the easier it will be to clarify (and for the student to understand) your expectations. Be sure to consider the student's behavior in all relevant activities (e.g., independent work, teacher directed instruction, unstructured class times, recess and lunch, etc.).

d. Conduct the meeting in an atmosphere of collaboration. The following agenda is one way you might structure the meeting:

- **Share your concerns about the student's behavior.**

    Briefly describe the problem behavior and, when appropriate, show the student the chart of how often she engages in it. Then explain why you consider the complaining to be a problem. You might tell the student that complaining so much is likely to make her feel miserable in the long run. In addition, excessive complaining may alienate her teachers and other adults, create mistrust amongst her friends (e.g., if Rochelle complains to Anne about Inga, Anne may wonder if Rochelle complains about her when she is not there), and/or make it difficult to enjoy life if she views everything negatively.

- **Discuss how you can work together to improve the situation.**

    Tell the student that you would like to help her learn to "view some things more positively," and describe your preliminary plan. Invite the student to give you input on the various aspects of the plan, and together work out any necessary details (e.g., the signal, self-monitoring, rewards). You may have to brainstorm different possibilities if the student is uncomfortable with the initial plan. Incorporating any of the student's suggestions that strengthen the plan is likely to increase her sense of "ownership" in and commitment to it.

- **Make sure the student understands what you mean by appropriate and inappropriate behavior.**

Use the descriptions you have prepared to define and clarify the problem behavior and the positive (desired) behavior as specifically and thoroughly as you can. To ensure that you and the student are in agreement about the expectations, you might present hypothetical scenarios and have her identify whether each is an example of complaining or focusing on something positive. Or you might describe an actual situation that has occurred and ask her how she could express her opinion without complaining in that situation.

- **Conclude the meeting.**

Always end the meeting with words of encouragement. Let the student know that you are confident that she can be successful. Be sure to reinforce her for participating in the meeting.

 Give the student regular, ongoing feedback about her behavior.

It is important to meet with the student periodically to discuss her progress. In most cases, three to five minutes once per week should suffice. *(NOTE: MODEL PLANS C, D, and E suggest daily meetings.)* During the meetings, review any information that has been collected and discuss whether or not the situation is getting better. As much as possible, focus on the student's improvements, however, also address any new or continuing problems. As the situation improves, the meetings can be faded to once every other week and then to once per month.

 Evaluate the situation (and the plan).

Implement any plan for at least two weeks before deciding whether to change plans; to continue, modify, or fade the plan you are using; or to cease the intervention. Generally, if the student's behavior is clearly improving (based on the objective information that's been collected and/or the subjective perceptions of yourself, the student, and possibly the parent[s]), stick with what you are doing. If the situation has remained the same or worsened, some kind of change will be necessary. Always discuss any changes to the plan with the student first.

COMPLIANCE/ DIRECTION FOLLOWING, LACK OF

DESCRIPTION

You have a student who refuses to comply with directions given by you and/or other adults.

GOAL

The student will learn to comply with reasonable requests and directions given by adults in the school setting.

OVERVIEW OF PLANS

- PLAN A: For a situation in which the problem has just begun and/or occurs infrequently.

- PLAN B: For a student who tends to be noncompliant in an effort to exert his personal power.

- PLAN C: For a student who does not have the skills necessary for following directions and complying with requests.

- PLAN D: For a student whose noncompliance has become habitual.

Alternative Problems

- **Arguing— Student(s) With the Teacher**

- **Disruptive Behavior— Moderate**

- **Disruptive Behavior— Severe**

- **Participation In Class, Lack of**

········
General Considerations

- If the student's problem behavior stems in any way from academic issues (e.g., the student is noncompliant in order to cover up the fact that he is unable to complete the schoolwork he is assigned), concurrent efforts must be made to ensure his academic success (see **Academic Deficits, Determining**).

- If the student lacks the basic social skills to interact with adults and his peers appropriately, it may be necessary to begin by teaching him those skills. **Social Skills, Lack of** contains information on a variety of published social skills curricula.

- If the student is passively noncompliant and you suspect that the inappropriate behavior could be related to the student being depressed, see **Depression**. This problem includes a set of questions to help you decide whether the student should be referred for counseling or psychological services.

- If the student is receiving special education services for language processing problems, coordinate any intervention plan with the special education personnel and/or your school psychologist.

- Many of the ideas included within these four plans are adopted from and described in detail in the following two resources:

Rhode, G., Jenson, W.R., & Reavis, H.K. (1992). *The tough kid book: Practical classroom management strategies.* Longmont, CO: Sopris West.

Walker, H. & Walker, J. (1991). *Coping with noncompliance in the classroom: A positive approach for teachers.* Austin, TX: Pro-Ed.

········
Model Plans

PLAN A

If the inappropriate behavior has just begun or occurs infrequently, a complex plan may not be necessary to resolve the situation. However, because any refusal to comply with a reasonable adult request in a school setting should be viewed as a serious misbehavior, this basic plan is more involved than many. This intervention requires you to examine your own behavior (e.g., the clarity of the directions you give) as well as decide how to address the student's misbehavior.

 1. *Be sure that the directions you give (i.e., those that the students are expected to comply with) are clear and consistent.*

Good directions are simple, clear, direct, and businesslike. Following is a list of suggestions for giving clear and consistent directions that will increase the probability of compliance. Use the list to evaluate your own behavior and to identify any aspects that you may want to work on to make it easier for the students to comply with your directions:

- Give one direction at a time. Teachers often have a tendency to give a sequence of three, four, or five directions at the same time. "Stop talking to Kurt, go to your seat, pick up your pencil, and get started on your math. When you are finished, let me know so I can check that you did it." A better direction would be, "Please begin working on your math assignment at your seat."

- Avoid asking a question. "Wouldn't it be a good idea to sit down and get started on your math?" A question leaves room for the student to take an opposite position and begin a debate. "No, I don't think it would be a good idea. A better idea would be to . . . ."

- When possible, be physically close to the student when giving the direction. The optimum distance is about three feet—not right in the student's face, but not across the room. This isn't necessary for all students, but with a student who tends to be noncompliant, try to go over to him before giving the direction.

- Be polite but businesslike in tone. Avoid syrupy sweet directions—they imply that you can be walked on. Also avoid an autocratic or harsh tone, which sets up an adversial stance for some students (e.g., "You can't make me.").

- Use a voice that is semi-private. When you broadcast the direction to the entire class, the student may feel that he has to be defiant to save face. On the other hand, do not try to make the direction sound like a secret or the student may feel that everyone is looking at him to figure out what you said. The optimum voice level is a soft but firm conversational tone—remember the student is only three feet away.

- Avoid sarcasm. "Everyone with any sense has already put their things away. Kip, now it is your turn," or "Kip, I know that you have your selective hearing arranged so you won't hear this, but you need to . . . ."

- Avoid creating an ultimatum that implies that the student must "jump" or grovel. A direction that states that the student must *begin right now, this second* invites noncompliance.

- Use more "do" directions than "don't" directions. If the majority of your directions are to stop, cease, or avoid, they establish an adversial tone that invites further noncompliance. "Do" requests, on the other hand, imply that the student is expected to engage in activities necessary for his own success, not just to try to avoid "bugging" you.

- Only give important directions. When the student is participating in class, but wearing a sarcastic or smug facial expression, for example, you have to decide whether correcting the student is really worth a potential show-down. It may be better to just ignore the facial expression as, after all, the student *is* participating in the lesson. Giving a direction such as, "Wipe that expression off your face" invites a defiant or sarcastic response, or denial. "What was I doing? I am just sitting here!"

- Read the moment. When the student has just walked into the room and is upset about something that took place outside the classroom, a direction from you is likely to invite a noncompliant response. If the student is tormenting someone, you obviously must intervene. However, if the student simply took a circuitous route to his seat, for example, ignoring the behavior is probably wiser than correcting such a minor infraction.

- Don't give mixed messages. Teachers who have a close rapport and/or a fun relationship with their students may give mixed messages on directions. That is, the student thinks the teacher is still just joking around. If you tend to joke with your students a lot, you may want to introduce your directions with a consistent statement such as "Kip, this is important. Listen. Please . . . ."

2. *Develop a consistent pattern of responding to noncompliance using "precision requests."*

Having a predetermined sequence for responding to incidents of noncompliance will increase your consistency and clarity of directions. Rhode, Jenson, and Reavis (1992) have developed an effective set of steps that can be applied to most situations, a "Precision Request Sequence," illustrated following.

3. *Use reinforcement to encourage appropriate behavior.*

a. Give the student increased praise. Be especially alert for situations in which the student complies with directions and praise him for these demonstrations of his ability to follow directions. "Kip, you followed my direction the first time. I appreciate your cooperation." If the student would be embarrassed by public praise, praise the student privately or even give the student a note. Remember that any time the student complies with a "Please" request or a "Need" request, you can praise him.

b. Give the student frequent attention (e.g., say "hello" to him as he enters the classroom, call on him frequently during class activities, and occasionally ask him to assist you with a class job that needs to be done) and praise him for other positive behaviors he exhibits. For example, you might comment about the accuracy of his work or how creative his writing assignments have been. This demonstrates to the student that you notice many positive things he does, not just the fact that he is following directions immediately.

Precision Request Sequence

Following are the steps to using precision requests effectively:

1. Explain the precision request and its consequences to the whole class before the procedure is begun.

2. Make a quiet "Please" request (such as,
   "Please get your materials out and start working.") to the student in a nonquestion format,
   up close, with eye contact.

3. Wait five to ten seconds after making the request, and do not interact with the student
   during this time.

4. If the student starts to comply, verbally reinforce the student.

5. If the student does not comply within five to ten
   seconds, a second request is given with the
   signal word "need" (such as, "Now I *need* you
   to get your materials out and start working.").

6. If the student starts to comply, verbally reinforce the student.

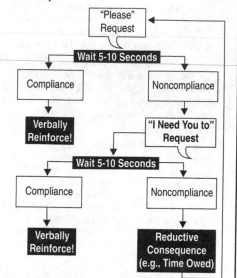

7. If the student still does not comply within five to ten seconds, implement time owed ("I will keep
   track of how many minutes it takes until you . . . ."). For elementary students, this time can be paid
   back by sitting and doing nothing during recess or after school. For middle/junior high school
   students, this time can be paid back during lunch or in after-school detention.

Adapted with permission from Rhode, G., Jenson, W.R., & Reavis, H.K. (1992). *The tough kid book:
Practical classroom management strategies*. Longmont, CO: Sopris West.

P L A N   B

Some students gain a feeling of power through noncompliance. If you often find yourself
getting angry and feeling like you need to *make* the student do what you tell him, it is possible
that he is trying to exert his personal power. Whether or not the student overtly seems to
thrive on the power struggle, the intervention should focus on giving the student a sense of
power while at the same time trying to enlist his cooperation in following directions.

1. *Be sure that the directions you give
(i.e., that the students are expected to
comply with) are clear and consistent
(see PLAN A).*

2. *Develop a consistent pattern of responding to noncompliance using
"precision commands" (see PLAN A).*

3. *Create opportunities for the student to
experience power in positive ways.*

a. Make an effort to acknowledge and channel the
student's personal power. One way to do this is
to examine what the student is trying to achieve
through his noncompliant behavior: Is he trying
to gain status in front of his peers? is he trying
to be funny? is he trying to gain your attention?

Use this information to identify how you could
give the student power in productive ways. For
example, could the student be put into a leadership role (e.g., leading a task force of students
whose goal is to solve a school problem such
as vandalism)? could the student be assigned

to be a tutor or mentor to a younger student? could the student be assigned a job in which he receives a lot of adult attention (e.g., delivering messages or papers to each teacher's classroom as an after-school job)? *(NOTE: APPENDIX 2 lists various jobs/ responsibilities that might be appropriate.)*

b. Do not make the student's assigned job/responsibility contingent upon appropriate behavior. Once the student has been assigned the job/responsibility, he should be allowed to perform it regardless of how other aspects of his day have gone. If the job/responsibility is made contingent upon his appropriate behavior, the student may misbehave just to demonstrate that this contingency does not have the power to shape his behavior.

4. *Ask the student what you might do differently to make it easier for him to comply with your directions.*

a. During the initial meeting with the student (see SUGGESTED STEPS FOR DEVELOPING AND IMPLEMENTING A PLAN), let the student know that you want him to make some changes in his behavior, but that you are willing to make some changes as well. If it seems comfortable, you might share with the student the suggestions for giving clear directions presented in PLAN A as a basis for enlisting feedback from the student.

b. The goal is to identify several things you will do differently in giving your directions and several things the student will do differently in complying with the directions. Pay particular attention to creating procedures that allow each of you to maintain dignity when interacting in front of the other students. Let the student know that you will ask for his feedback about how you are doing in the follow-up meetings (see SUGGESTED STEPS FOR DEVELOPING AND IMPLEMENTING A PLAN).

5. *Ensure a 3-1 ratio of positive to negative attention.*

a. The student is less likely to engage you in power struggles if he feels that you like him and are interested in him as a person—not just someone to be ordered around. To determine if you are giving the student *three times as much* positive as negative attention, monitor your interactions with the student at least one day per week. Simply keep a card on a clipboard or in your pocket and record each interaction you have with the student as either positive or nega-

tive by writing a "+" or a "-", respectively, on the card.

To determine whether an interaction is positive or negative, ask yourself whether the student was misbehaving at the time the interaction occurred. Any interactions that stem from inappropriate behavior are negative, while all interactions that occur while the student is meeting classroom expectations are positive. Thus, giving, an "I need you to" request or assigning time owed are both negative interactions, but praising the student for following directions is positive. Greeting the student as he enters the room or asking him if he has any questions during independent work are also considered positive interactions.

b. If you find that you are not giving the student three times as much positive as negative attention, try to increase the number of positive interactions you have with the student. Sometimes prompts can help. For example, you might decide that each time the student enters the classroom you will say "hello" to him, that during some of the classroom transitions you will interact with him, or that you will try to talk to the student enough that you can learn something new about him each week.

(NOTE: Be careful to avoid using praise too frequently with this student, however, as he may feel that you are trying to "control" him with the praise. The majority of the positive interactions should consist of simply showing an interest in the student, such as: "Kip, interesting color choices for this project. Could you tell me about how you did this?" or "Kip, I saw a book you might be interested in. Have you ever read . . . .")

You can also increase the ratio of positive to negative attention by decreasing the number of directions/commands you give the student, thus reducing the number of opportunities for the student to be noncompliant.

6. *(OPTIONAL)*
Establish procedures with your building administrator for addressing any continued noncompliance.

If the student refuses to comply, you might assign him the consequence of owing time off of recess or after school. However, if the student has still not complied by the end of the class period, you might write a description of what the student refused to do (see the sample following), have the student sign it, and send him to the office for administrative intervention of more severe consequences (e.g., in-school suspension). If the student refuses to sign the description, send him to the office and inform the administrator of both the original incident and of the student's refusal to sign the form.

I instructed Kip to put away his electronic game and begin work on his math. He refused, and continued to play the game. He already owes 20 minutes in after-school detention and still refuses to comply.

Teacher Signature _____   Student Signature _____

Date _____

PLAN C

Sometimes a student may not know how to respond in compliant ways. If the student seems to respond defiantly as a "knee-jerk" reaction to being given a direction, the intervention must teach the student appropriate ways of responding to and carrying out directions.

1. *Be sure that the directions you give (i.e., those that the students are expected to comply with) are clear and consistent (see PLAN A).*

2. *Develop a consistent pattern of responding to noncompliance using "precision commands" (see PLAN A).*

3. *Conduct lessons to teach the student how to respond appropriately to directions.*

a. Before the lessons, think about responses to directions that the student could make that would be acceptable to you. Morgan and Jensen (1988) found that teaching students to say "Sure I will," paired with precision commands, increases compliant behavior.

Other possible student responses might include:

• Okay, I'll do that.

• Sure.

• No problem.

• I can do that.

b. When you are developing the plan with the student (see SUGGESTED STEPS FOR DEVELOPING AND IMPLEMENTING A PLAN), have him select one of these responses, or together think of another response that is agreeable to both of you. This response will serve as the basis for practice sessions in following directions.

c. During the lessons, have the student practice responding to a variety of directions. When you give the direction, the student should make the agreed upon response, then carry out the direction.

Then for a few (but not all) of the directions, explore "What if" questions to ensure that the student fully understands how the "Sure I will" response (or other selected response) relates to your precision requests. "Kip, what would happen if you say 'Sure I will' but then don't follow the direction? Right. I would then say, 'Kip, I need you to . . . .' What if you still refused? Right, you would owe time in after-school detention. Now let's practice another one, where you do it the right way."

c. Conduct the lessons at least twice per week. The lessons should involve just you and the student (perhaps while the other students are at lunch), and needn't last more than three to five minutes apiece. It is important that the lessons be handled in a matter-of-fact manner so the student does not feel that he is being ridiculed. Continue the lessons until the student is consistently using the appropriate verbal response and then carrying out the directions.

4. *Prompt the student to behave appropriately by using precorrections.*

Watch for those circumstances in which the student is likely to resist following a direction and remind him that he will need to use the agreed upon response and then carry out the direction. "Kip, in just a few minutes I am going to ask you to pass out papers for me. I will be watching to see if you remember to do what we practiced yesterday. I'll bet you can. What are you going to say? Then what are you going to do? Great!" If this conversation would embarrass the student, you should have it privately.

5. *Use reinforcement to encourage appropriate behavior.*

a. Give the student increased praise and attention for complying with directions (see PLAN A).

b. In addition, make a special point of letting the student know that you notice his efforts to use the skills he has been learning/practicing. "Kip, all day you have been remembering your 'Sure I will' response. Nice job of doing what we have been practicing."

c. Praise the student for participating during the lessons. Let him know that you appreciate his willingness to cooperate and practice this skill.

PLAN D

Whenever a student's problem behavior has become habitual and/or he does not seem to have a desire to reduce it, you may need to implement a structured system of monitoring, and (optionally) of reinforcing, his behavior in order to motivate the student to stop being noncompliant and to start following directions.

1. *Be sure that the directions you give (i.e., those that the students are expected to comply with) are clear and consistent (see PLAN A).*

2. *Develop a consistent pattern of responding to noncompliance using "precision commands" (see PLAN A).*

3. *Implement a system for monitoring the frequency of the student's compliance.*

a. Let the student know that his level of compliance to directions/requests is going to be recorded. Tell him that each time a direction is given and he carries it out, a tally mark will be written in a column with the heading "Please." If he does not comply and you need to give the student an "I need you to" statement, but then he does comply, a tally mark will be recorded under a heading "Need." *(NOTE: If the student does not comply at all, you will keep track of the time owed.)*

Because the point of this procedure is to help the student become aware of his own behavior, it will be more effective if the student does the recording himself (i.e., self-monitors). However, if the student cannot or will not be accurate (or if he would be too embarrassed to self-monitor) you should record the student's compliance yourself.

Additionally, even when the student self-monitors his compliance, you should keep your own record approximately one day per week to verify the student's accuracy.

b. If the student is self-monitoring, he can keep a recording form on his desk or in his notebook each day like the sample shown.

Record of Kip's Following Directions
Date _____
_____ Please _____   _____ Need _____

c. Each day, meet with the student for a few minutes to review that day's record. *(NOTE: You can't really chart this information as the number of directions you give the student will vary from day to day, thus a chart could not give a good picture of progress.)* If the day did not go well, encourage the student to talk about why and have him identify what he could do the next day to help himself remember to follow directions. If the student behaves inappropriately during the meeting, keep the interaction very short. Just let the student know that you are sure tomorrow will be a better day.

4. *Use reinforcement to encourage appropriate behavior.*

a. Give the student increased praise and attention for complying with directions (see PLAN A).

b. In addition, praise the student during the end-of-the-day review meetings for accurate recording (if applicable) and for being willing to look at his daily record. Even on a bad day, if the student is willing to discuss why it was a bad day, praise him. "Kip, you are really handling this responsibly. Even though it was a rough day, you are willing to talk to me about things you might do differently tomorrow. That is a real sign that you are growing up."

Regardless of how the day went, try to make the meeting upbeat and encouraging—you want the student to look forward to the daily review meetings.

5. (OPTIONAL)
Establish a structured system for reinforcing the appropriate behavior.

a. With the student, create a list of reinforcers that he can earn. Although you might want to have some suggestions in mind, the system will be more effective if the student identifies most of the items or activities himself. (NOTE: A list of reinforcement ideas can be found in APPENDIX 1.)

b. Assign "prices" (in points) for each of the rewards on the list and have the student select the reward he would like to earn first. The prices should be based on the instructional, personnel, and/or monetary costs of the items. Monetary cost is clear—the more expensive the item, the more points required to earn it. Instructional cost refers to the amount of instructional time lost or interfered with by a particular reward.

Thus, an activity which causes the student to miss part of academic instruction should require more points than one the student can do on his own free time. Personnel cost involves the time required by you and/or other staff to fulfill the reinforcer. Having lunch with the principal, therefore, would cost more points than spending five minutes of free time with a friend.

c. Let the student know that he earns two points for each direction that he carries out at the "Please" stage and one point for each direction carried out at the "Need" stage. Make sure the student understands that he receives no points and owes time for any direction that is not carried out after the "Need" stage (i.e., after an "I need you to" request has been given).

d. When the student has accumulated enough points to earn the reward he has chosen, he "spends" the points necessary and the system begins again. That is, he chooses another reward to earn and begins with zero points.

If the student is immature or extremely defiant, and thus needs more frequent encouragement, you might consider letting him earn several "less expensive" rewards (e.g., 5 minutes of computer time after 20 points) on the way to a bigger reward (e.g., one hour of game time with a friend for 200 points). That is, the student receives the small rewards without spending points; they continue to accumulate toward the selected reward.

· · · · · · · ·

Suggested Steps for Developing and Implementing a Plan

The following steps are designed to help you develop an appropriate intervention plan and implement it effectively, whether you choose to use one of the MODEL PLANS or create a customized plan of your own. The steps are, however, suggestions—they are not intended to be followed rigidly or in any particular order. Use your professional judgment and the knowledge of your particular situation to make them work for you.

1. Make sure you have enough information about the situation.

a. Given the severity of this problem, you should consider collecting descriptive information both before and throughout the intervention. Maintaining anecdotal notes on actual incidents of noncompliance will help you describe the student's behavior clearly and completely. Simply keep a card in your pocket or on a clipboard and make brief notes each time the student does not comply with a direction. Making a brief note of

each incident also gives you a daily count of the frequency of noncompliance.

For each entry, indicate the direction that was given, where and when the noncompliance occurred, what the student did or said, and any other relevant observations (e.g., whether other students were around). Also include some notes on times when the student responds appropriately to directions. This will make it clear that you are not only aware of his problem behavior, but also recognize when he behaves appropriately. When you meet with the student, the positive examples will also help you clarify how you want the student to behave.

b. If the student notices what you are doing and asks about it, be straightforward—tell him that you are collecting information on the times he refuses to follow directions so you and his and his parent(s) can work out a plan.

c. Continuing to collect this type of information while you implement a plan will help you to monitor whether the situation is getting worse, staying the same, or getting better.

2. *Identify a focus for the intervention and labels for referring to the appropriate and inappropriate behaviors.*

a. To be effective, the intervention must address more than just reducing the student's noncompliance—there must be a concurrent emphasis on increasing some positive behavior or trait (e.g., following directions). Having a specific positive behavior in mind will make it easier for you to "catch" and reinforce the student for behaving appropriately, and the positive focus will help you to frame the situation more productively.

b. Specifying labels for the appropriate and inappropriate behaviors (e.g., "following directions" and "being noncompliant," respectively) will help you to use consistent vocabulary when discussing the situation with the student. If you sometimes refer to the inappropriate behavior as "being noncompliant," and other times tell the student that he is "acting stubborn," for example, he may not realize that you are talking about the same behavior.

3. *Determine when and how to include the parent(s).*

a. With a compliance problem, the student's parent(s) should be contacted immediately. Share with them any information you have collected about the behavior (e.g., anecdotal notes, daily frequency count), and explain why you are concerned. Focus in particular on how the behavior is hindering the student academically and/or socially (e.g., if the student doesn't learn to follow directions now he might not ever learn, which could affect his ability to hold a job).

You might ask if the parent(s) have any insight into the situation and/or whether they experience similar behavior at home. Whether or not the parent(s) perceive a problem, explain that you want to help the student "learn to follow directions" and invite them to join you for an initial meeting with the student to develop a plan. If the parent(s) are unable or unwilling to participate, let them know that you will keep them informed of the student's progress.

b. Once the parent(s) have been involved in any way, you should give them updates at least once per week while the plan is being implemented.

4. *Prepare for, then conduct, an initial meeting about the situation.*

a. Arrange a meeting to discuss your concerns with the student and anyone else who will be involved with the plan (e.g., the parent[s], the school psychologist). Although the specifics will vary depending upon the age of the student and the severity of the problem, there are some general guidelines to consider when scheduling the meeting.

First, meet at a neutral time (i.e., not immediately after a problem has occurred), when emotions are less likely to hamper communication. In general, a day's notice is appropriate, however a primary age student may worry excessively and/or forget what the meeting is about if it is scheduled more than an hour before it takes place.

Second, make the meeting appropriately private to ensure that the discussion will not be overheard. Third, try to make sure the meeting is scheduled for a time and place that it is not likely to be interrupted (e.g., the counselor's office). Finally, if the parent(s) will be participating, they should be the ones to tell the student about the meeting.

b. Construct a preliminary plan. Decide whether you think you can use one of the MODEL PLANS or if you need to create a customized plan using components from various plans and/or of your own design. Although you will invite and encourage the student to help develop the plan during the initial meeting, having a proposed plan in mind before you meet can alleviate frustration and wasted time if the student is unwilling or unable to participate. *(NOTE: If the student is largely motivated by power, involving him in the development of the plan is essential.)*

c. After reviewing the information you have collected and thinking about how you want the student to behave, prepare thorough descriptions of the student's inappropriate behavior and the positive behavior/trait on which the student will be working. The more specific you can be and the more concrete examples you have, the easier it will be to clarify (and for the student to understand) your expectations. Be sure to consider the student's behavior in all relevant activities (e.g., independent work, teacher directed instruction, etc.).

d. Conduct the meeting in an atmosphere of collaboration. The following agenda is one way you might structure the meeting:

• **Share your concerns about the student's behavior.**

Briefly describe the problem behavior and how often the student engages in it. Then explain why you consider the noncompliance to be a problem. You might tell the student that not following directions may affect his ability to be successful in many aspects of life—in school, sports, and especially on a job.

• **Discuss how you can work together to improve the situation.**

Tell the student that you would like to help him "learn to follow directions" and describe your preliminary plan. Invite the student to give you input on the various aspects of the plan, and together work out any necessary details (e.g., precision commands, use of time owed, the self-monitoring form, etc.).

You may have to brainstorm different possibilities if the student is uncomfortable with the initial plan. Incorporating any of the student's suggestions that strengthen the plan is likely to increase his sense of "ownership" in and commitment to it.

• **Make sure the student understands what you mean by compliance and noncompliance, and understands appropriate responses to precision commands.**

Use the descriptions you have prepared to define and clarify for the student the problem behavior and the positive (desired) behavior

as specifically and thoroughly as you can. Then discuss some hypothetical scenarios with the student in order to clarify different situations (e.g., "What would be some acceptable ways you might respond to an instruction such as 'Get started on your math assignment?'").

• **Conclude the meeting.**

Always end the meeting with words of encouragement. Let the student know that you are confident that he can be successful. Be sure to reinforce him for participating in the meeting.

5. *Give the student regular, ongoing feedback about his behavior.*

It is important to meet with the student periodically to discuss his progress. In most cases, three to five minutes once per week should suffice. *(NOTE: PLAN D calls for daily meetings.)* During the meetings, review any information that has been collected and discuss whether or not the situation is getting better. As much as possible, focus on the student's improvements, however, also address any new or continuing problems. As the situation improves, the meetings can be faded to once every other week and then to once per month.

6. *Evaluate the situation (and the plan).*

Implement any plan for at least two weeks before deciding whether to change plans; to continue, modify, or fade the plan you are using; or to cease the intervention. Generally, if the student's behavior is clearly improving (based on the objective information that's been collected and/or the subjective perceptions of yourself, the student, and possibly the parent[s]), stick with what you are doing. If the situation has remained the same or worsened, some kind of change will be necessary. Always discuss any changes to the plan with the student first.

CORRECTED, STUDENT GETS UPSET WHEN

. . . .

Defensiveness

Oversensitivity

DESCRIPTION

. . . .

You have a student who gets upset whenever he is corrected or given feedback.

> NOTE:
>
> *The negative reactions may stem from corrections that involve any or all of the following: (1) corrections to mistakes on written work; (2) feedback on academic performance (e.g., "Henri, you need to lay out the problem more neatly or you will not be able to tell what to do next."); or (3) behavioral feedback.*

GOAL

. . . .

The student will learn to calmly accept corrections and feedback, and will understand that one can learn from mistakes.

OVERVIEW OF PLANS

. . . .

- PLAN A: For a situation in which the problem is relatively mild or has just begun.

- PLAN B: For a student who gets upset when corrected in order to gain your attention and/or maintain lengthy interactions with you.

- PLAN C: For a student with self-concept problem who tends to view mistakes as examples of his incompetence and/or for a student who does not know how to react appropriately to being corrected.

- PLAN D: For a student who may not be aware of when and/or how often he reacts negatively to being corrected.

Alternative Problems

- **Arguing—Student(s) With the Teacher**

- **Blaming Others/Excuses for Everything**

- **Complaining**

- **Crying, Chronic**

- **Perfectionism**

- **Self-Concept Problems**

- **Spoiled Behavior**

- **Whining**

....
General Considerations

- If the student's problem behavior stems in any way from academic issues (e.g., the academic expectations are beyond the student's current ability and he is frustrated with continually having to correct his errors day after day), concurrent efforts must be made to ensure his academic success (see **Academic Deficits, Determining**).

- If the inappropriate behavior is resulting in the student avoiding or not completing his schoolwork, begin with a plan to increase the student's work completion (see **Work Completion—Daily Work**). Once the student is turning in completed work on a regular basis, you can consider an intervention to teach him appropriate responses to being corrected, if the problem still exists.

....
Model Plans

PLAN A

It is not always necessary, or even beneficial, to use an involved plan. If the inappropriate behavior has just begun and/or is not interfering with the student's academic or social progress, the following actions, along with making the student aware of your concerns, may resolve the situation.

1. Respond consistently to the inappropriate behavior.

Give a gentle correction when the student reacts inappropriately to being corrected. Calmly provide information about how the student should react differently. "Henri, when I tell you that you have some items to fix, you may ask me a question or you can say 'All right.' Getting upset does not help."

2. Use precorrections to help the student think about how he is going to react.

a. Immediately before giving any correction or feedback, prompt the student with a precorrection. Say to the student, for example, "Henri, I am about to give you some advice on the bibliography from your rough draft. Please remember our conversation about learning from mistakes. First, the number of references you have is great. But one thing you need to do differently is to . . . . "

Sometimes it is useful to state the precorrection in a way that gives the student a few seconds to prepare. "Henri, I have some feedback. Are you ready?" After a while, this type of precorrection can be shortened to a statement as concise as, "Some corrections—ready?"

A precorrection and pause gives the student an opportunity to mentally prepare for the feedback. Hopefully he will run through a quick mental process such as: "This is what Mr. Jameson and I have been talking about. This is one of those times when I should stay calm, listen to what I did right, listen to what I did wrong, and learn from what he tells me. Okay, I think I'm ready."

b. Begin the feedback by telling the student what he has done correctly. Always find some aspect of his effort to praise—even if it is only the heading of the paper or the fact that he turned it in on time. Hearing about what was done correctly makes it easier for the student to accept that mistakes were made and that it is okay that the mistakes were made.

3. Use reinforcement to encourage appropriate behavior.

a. Give the student praise for reacting calmly and responsibly to being corrected. Whenever the student reacts appropriately, inform him that he was successful. "Henri, your reaction to needing to make these corrections was very mature. You listened, you did the things I asked you to do, and when we were finished you said 'All right' and proceeded to do the things I suggested. That is a terrific example of the way your high school teachers will want you to react to their feedback."

After awhile, if the student is increasingly successful, the praise can be shorter. "Very calm reaction, Henri." As the student's success continues, praise him less frequently, but let the student know that you are still aware of his effort. "Henri, three or four times today I have made suggestions on corrections. Every time you have kept your cool and been able to learn from your mistakes. I know adults that cannot accept corrections as maturely as you."

Remember that any time the student does not react negatively to being correct, you can praise him for being willing to learn from his mistakes.

b. Give the student frequent attention (e.g., say "hello" to him as he enters the classroom, call on him frequently during class activities, and occasionally ask him to assist you with a class job that needs to be done) and praise him for other positive behaviors he exhibits. For example, you might comment about the quality of the questions he asked a guest speaker or how helpful he was in preparing the materials for a science experiment. This demonstrates to the student that you notice many positive things he does, not just the fact that he is reacting calmly to corrections.

PLAN B

Some students are very skilled at gaining attention through their negative behavior—in this case, by generating a lengthy interaction when being corrected. If you find yourself frequently reassuring, coaxing, or cajoling the student to react calmly to corrective feedback, it is possible that your interactions with him are reinforcing for the student. Whether or not the student overtly seems to like the attention, you need to make sure that he receives more frequent and more satisfying attention for appropriate behavior than for his negative reactions to being corrected.

1. *Use precorrections to help the student think about how he is going to react (see PLAN A).*

2. *Respond consistently to the inappropriate behavior.*

a. When the student reacts negatively to being corrected, implement a strategy of warning/withdrawing/ignoring/and re-engaging. First, give the student a warning. If the student continues to react inappropriately, withdraw from the interaction and ignore any further attempts to engage you with his misbehavior. Be sure you have established a way for the student to re-engage his interaction with you if he really needs help. That is, the student should know that you will be available when necessary.

b. To determine what the specific warning will be, you need to analyze how the student reacts negatively to being corrected. Does he argue? cry? pout and act sad? The goal is to provide the correction, but not become engaged in the student's misbehavior. For example, with a student who argues, the interaction might sound something like the example following.

With a student who whines or cries when corrected, give the warning and the reminder about how the student can request your help, then disengage. It

Mr. Jameson:	. . . now the thing you need to fix on these three questions is remembering to put your answer in complete sentences.
Henri:	I don't see why I should have to fix those. That's not fair. You never said we had to write in complete sentences.
Mr. Jameson:	This is the warning. I am not going to argue. Do you have any questions about what you need to do?
Henri:	It is not fair. I don't think I should have to . . .
Mr. Jameson:	(Gently interrupting) I am not going to argue. If you have any questions about how to do the work, simply raise your hand and I will come over. (The teacher then walks away.)

is not your job to sit with the student or to try to calm him down

c. If other students give the target student attention when he is upset about being corrected (e.g., trying to calm him down or reassure him that making the corrections is no big deal), gently correct them. "Calvin and Raul, Henri can take care of himself and he can make the corrections or ask for help when he is ready. It would be best to let him work it out on his own."

3. ***Use reinforcement to encourage appropriate behavior.***

a. Frequent praise and attention is the core of this plan. The student must see that he receives more frequent and more satisfying attention when he behaves appropriately than when he gets upset about being corrected. Thus, whenever the student does not reacting negatively (or otherwise misbehave), make an effort to praise and spend time with him. "Henri, you have done such a nice job of staying calm and listening. This is a great example of how you can learn from your mistakes. Would it be okay if I sat with you a moment and watched as you did those corrections?"

b. You may also wish to use intermittent rewards to acknowledge the student's success. Occasional, and unexpected, rewards can motivate the student to demonstrate responsible behavior more often. The idea is to provide a reward when the student has had a particularly good period of reacting calmly to being corrected.

Appropriate rewards would include any activity with you. Helping you during recess, sitting with you during an assembly, or even walking with you on the way to the cafeteria would probably be reinforcing to the student who thrives on adult attention. *(NOTE: A list of additional reinforcement ideas can be found in APPENDIX 1.)*

Use intermittent rewards more frequently at the beginning of the intervention to encourage the student, and then less often as his behavior improves.

4. ***Ensure a 3-1 ratio of positive to negative attention.***

a. Since attention is a motivating force for this student, you want to be sure that you are giving the student *three times as much* positive as negative attention. One way to do this is to monitor your interactions with the student at least one day per week. Simply keep a card on a clipboard or in your pocket and record each interaction you have with the student as either positive or negative by writing a "+" or a "-", respectively, on the card.

To determine whether an interaction is positive or negative, ask yourself whether the student was reacting negatively to being corrected (or otherwise misbehaving) at the time the interaction occurred. Any interactions that stem from inappropriate behavior are negative, and all interactions that occur while the student is meeting classroom expectations are positive. Thus, giving the warning is a negative interaction, but praising the student for reacting calmly is positive. Greeting the student as he enters the room or asking him if he has any questions during independent work are also considered positive interactions. *(NOTE: Ignoring the student's inappropriate behavior is not recorded at all, because it is not an interaction.)* Following is a chart that shows a sample of how some different interactions would be counted as either positive or negative.

b. If you find that you are not giving the student three times as much positive as negative attention, try to increase the number of positive interactions you have with the student. Sometimes prompts can help. For example, you might decide that each time the student enters the classroom you will say "hello" to him, that once during each instructional period you will try to have a positive interaction with the student, or that whenever there is an announcement over the intercom you will check the target student and as soon as possible praise some aspect of his behavior. You can also increase the ratio of positive to negative attention by ignoring more of the student's inappropriate behavior.

Interaction Between Teacher and Student	How Interaction is Counted
Mr. Jameson is handing back science tests.	
Mr. Jameson: Henri, I am about to give you some feedback on your science test. Are you ready?	One Positive
Henri: Sure, I'm ready.	
Mr. Jameson: Great! You are working on what we talked about yesterday.	
Mr. Jameson is welcoming students to class.	One Positive
Mr. Jameson: Good Morning, Henri.	
Mr. Jameson is checking with the students about their science projects.	
Mr. Jameson: Henri, any questions about what you need to do to fix the science project?	One Positive
Henri: No, I can get this done by the end of the period.	
Mr. Jameson: That is a very "can do!" attitude, and a very mature reaction to these corrections that need to be done.	
Mr. Jameson is giving Henri feedback on his math assignment. Henri begins to get upset.	One Negative
Mr. Jameson: This is a warning. Let's not argue.	
Henri: (Taking a deep breath) Okay.	One Positive
Mr. Jameson: Good job! You stopped yourself from engaging in an argument about this—big progress.	

PLAN C

Some students do not actually know how to react calmly when corrected and learn from their mistakes. If your student seems to have a very poor self-image and/or does not seem to possess the necessary skills to accept corrections calmly, the intervention must include procedures for teaching him appropriate reactions to corrective feedback.

1. *Conduct lessons to teach the student how to react calmly to corrections and to learn from his mistakes.*

a. Try to identify some strategies that might help the student to remain calm while being corrected. Possibilities include counting slowly backward from ten, remembering to breathe slowly and evenly, consciously remembering to keep one's hands relaxed rather than clenched in fists. In addition, think of one or more statements the student can use to help himself stay calm. For example, the student might learn to quietly say to himself, "I am capable and smart. Part of being smart is learning from my mistakes."

b. During the lessons, teach the student one or more of the strategies you have identified for reacting calmly while being corrected. Think of some hypothetical scenarios in which the student might be corrected by you, and have the student practice the new strategies in those situations.

Following is an example of how such a practice session might unfold.

c. Practice this procedure with a variety of hypothetical situations for a couple of lessons. Then, when the student has mastered the strategies with the hypothetical situations, have the student use the strategies with actual tasks. For example, if the student has some math prob-

Mr. Jameson: Let's pretend that I am about to tell you about some problems you need to fix on your math assignment. I will say, 'Henri, you have a few corrections. Are you ready?' So then what will you do?

Henri: I will tell myself, 'I am a smart person who can learn from my mistakes.' Then I will look at my hands and make sure that I am not making fists.

Mr. Jameson: Fabulous! If you are making fists, what will you do?

Henri: I'll work on relaxing my hands so they look more like this (student demonstrates).

Mr. Jameson: Yes, that is a very relaxed way to hold your hands. Then at that point, you can tell me if you are ready for the feedback. If you needed some more time to get relaxed before I started correcting, what could you do?

Henri: I don't know.

Mr. Jameson: You could always say something like, 'Can I have a minute to get ready?' and I will be glad to give you a bit of time to relax before we get to the corrections. Let's try it one time with this pretend math assignment.

lems that need to be corrected, present them during the lesson time as opposed to during the math period, if possible.

d. Conduct the lessons at least twice per week. The lessons should involve just you and the student (perhaps while the other students are at recess), and needn't last more than three to five minutes. It is important that they be handled in a matter-of-fact manner so the student does not feel that he is being ridiculed. Continue the lessons until the student is consistently reacting calmly to being corrected in the classroom setting.

2. *Prompt the student to behave appropriately by using precorrections.*

Each time you are about to correct some aspect of the student's work or behavior, let him know what you are about to do, prompt him to remember the strategies practiced in the lessons, then ask him if he is ready for the feedback. "Henri, I am about to tell you some things you need to fix on the rough draft of your report. I will be watching to see if you remember to do what we practiced this morning. I'll bet you can. Are you ready?"

If time permits, you might also have the student identify how he plans to react. "Henri, I want to show you some things to do differently on your science papers. Keep remembering what we have worked on in the lessons. What might you try? Excellent, give it a try." If this type of public interaction would embarrass the student, have this conversation with him privately.

3. *Respond consistently to the inappropriate behavior.*

When the student reacts negatively to being corrected, implement a strategy of warning/withdrawing/ignoring/and re-engaging (see PLAN B).

4. *Use reinforcement to encourage appropriate behavior.*

a. Give the student increased praise and attention for reacting calmly to being corrected (see PLAN A).

b. In addition, make a special point of letting the student know that you notice his efforts to use the strategies he has been learning/practicing. "Henri, when I gave you feedback about your math assignments, I saw you work on slow, even breathing and when you started to clench your hands into fists, you remembered to relax them. Nice job of doing what we have been practicing."

5. *Structure the student's academic work so that he experiences high rates of success.*

If the student is consistently making excessive errors (e.g., typically missing more than 20% of the problems presented), adjust the work so that the student is experiencing greater success. **Work Completion—Daily Work** includes ideas on adapting assignments to increase student success.

6. *Give the student a job or responsibility that he would enjoy, would be successful with, and that might bolster his self-confidence.*

A powerful way to help the student feel better about himself (and perhaps more calmly accept his mistakes) is to give him a job in the school which is perceived to be important. For example, the student might be put in charge of checking and maintaining the overhead projectors throughout the school, be made an office assistant, or even assigned to help the cafeteria staff develop a food waste reduction program (some schools weigh food waste daily and chart it to encourage the student body to reduce waste).

Do not make the student's job contingent upon calm reactions to being corrected—she should be allowed to perform the job regularly regardless of how well or how poorly he is reacting to being corrected.

*(NOTE: See APPENDIX 2 for additional jobs that the student might be assigned. Additionally, if the student has an extremely poor self-concept, see **Self-Concept Problems** for additional strategies that could be used to bolster the student's self-confidence.)*

PLAN D

Some students do not know when they behave inappropriately. If your student doesn't seem to realize when and/or how frequently he reacts negatively to corrections, the intervention must include some way of helping the student become more aware of his own behavior.

1. *Use precorrections to help the student think about how he is going to react (see PLAN A).*

2. *Respond consistently to the inappropriate behavior.*

a. When the student reacts negatively to being corrected, implement a strategy of warning/withdrawing/ignoring/and re-engaging (see PLAN B).

b. Additionally, each time the student reacts negatively to being corrected, make sure the incident is recorded on a self-monitoring form (see Step 3).

3. *Implement a system for monitoring the student's appropriate and inappropriate reactions to being corrected.*

a. Determine who will record the student's reactions. Since the point is for the student to become more aware of his own behavior, having him record his behavior (i.e., self-monitor) will be more effective than if you do the recording. However, if the student cannot or will not be accurate (or if he would be too embarrassed to self-monitor) you should record the student's reactions yourself.

If you do the recording, remember that the idea is for the student to be aware that each time he is given feedback, his reaction will be recorded as either appropriate or inappropriate.

(NOTE: Even when the student self-monitors, you should keep your own record approximately one day per week to verify the student's accuracy.)

b. When the student will be self-monitoring his reactions, you can give him a recording form like the following sample, and have him put it on his desk or in his notebook.

c. Whenever you are going to correct the student, give him a precorrection that includes a reminder that his reaction will be recorded as either appropriate or inappropriate. At the conclusion of correcting interaction, ask the student how he thinks his reaction should be recorded. Then decide how *you* think the reaction should be recorded.

(NOTE: When explaining this system to the student, tell him that when you and he disagree about how a reaction should be recorded, you will be willing to talk to him about it, but that your opinion will prevail. This may sound arbitrary, but it is necessary. It's similar to the situation in a baseball game—a player and the umpire may disagree, but the umpire's decision is final.)

Name Henri Auriette

Behavior to be counted: _appropriate and inappropriate reactions to being corrected_

Week of _4/26_

| Monday | | |
| Appropriate Reactions | | Inappropriate Reactions |

Monday
Appropriate Reactions

1 2 3 4 5 6 7 8 9 10 11 12 13 14
15 16 17 18 19 20 21 22 23 24 25 26

Inappropriate Reactions

1 2 3 4 5 6 7 8 9 10 11 12 13 14
15 16 17 18 19 20 21 22 23 24 25 26

Tuesday
Appropriate Reactions

1 2 3 4 5 6 7 8 9 10 11 12 13 14
15 16 17 18 19 20 21 22 23 24 25 26

Inappropriate Reactions

1 2 3 4 5 6 7 8 9 10 11 12 13 14
15 16 17 18 19 20 21 22 23 24 25 26

Wednesday
Appropriate Reactions

1 2 3 4 5 6 7 8 9 10 11 12 13 14
15 16 17 18 19 20 21 22 23 24 25 26

Inappropriate Reactions

1 2 3 4 5 6 7 8 9 10 11 12 13 14
15 16 17 18 19 20 21 22 23 24 25 26

Thursday
Appropriate Reactions

1 2 3 4 5 6 7 8 9 10 11 12 13 14
15 16 17 18 19 20 21 22 23 24 25 26

Inappropriate Reactions

1 2 3 4 5 6 7 8 9 10 11 12 13 14
15 16 17 18 19 20 21 22 23 24 25 26

Friday
Appropriate Reactions

1 2 3 4 5 6 7 8 9 10 11 12 13 14
15 16 17 18 19 20 21 22 23 24 25 26

Inappropriate Reactions

1 2 3 4 5 6 7 8 9 10 11 12 13 14
15 16 17 18 19 20 21 22 23 24 25 26

d. If the student assesses the interaction correctly, praise him. Even if he accurately identifies that he reacted inappropriately, praise his awareness and honesty. If you and the student disagree on the assignment, explain your reasons. If you still disagree, do not argue with the student. Simply mark (or have the student mark) the interaction on the form appropriately.

e. Each day, meet with the student for a few minutes to review that day's record. Help the student compute the percentage of "Appropriate Reactions" (by dividing the total number of appropriate by the combined total of both appropriate and inappropriate). Have the student chart the information on a graph (or do it yourself), and talk with him about whether the day was better, worse, or about the same as previous days.

If the day did not go well, encourage the student to talk about why and have him identify what he could do the next day to help himself remember to react responsibly to being corrected. If the student behaves inappropriately during the meeting, keep the interaction very short. Just let the student know that you are sure tomorrow will be a better day.

4. Use reinforcement to encourage appropriate behavior.

a. Give the student increased praise and attention for reacting calmly to being corrected (see PLAN A).

b. In addition, praise the student during the daily review meetings for accurate recording (if applicable), and for being willing to look at his daily totals/percentage. Even on a bad day, if the student is willing to chart the data and discuss why it was a bad day, praise him. "Henri, you are really handling this responsibly. Even though it was a rough day, you are willing to talk to me about things you might do differently tomorrow. That is a real sign that you are growing up."

Regardless of how the day went, try to make the meetings upbeat and encouraging—you want the student to look forward to the end-of-the-day review meetings.

5. **Encourage the student to use self-reinforcement.**

Whenever things are going well (i.e., more appropriate reactions to being corrected than usual), prompt the student to mentally reinforce himself. "Henri, this has been a very successful morning. Silently tell yourself that you are really good at being responsible in your reactions to being corrected." Prompt the student in this manner intermittently throughout the day and during the end-of-the-day review meetings.

6. **(OPTIONAL)**
Establish a structured system of reinforcement to motivate the student to react appropriately to corrections.

a. With the student, create a list of reinforcers that he can earn. Although you might want to have some suggestions in mind, the system will be more effective if the student identifies most of the items or activities himself. (NOTE: A list of reinforcement ideas can be found in APPENDIX 1.)

b. Assign "prices" (in points) for each of the rewards on the list and have the student select the reward that he would like to earn first.

The prices should be based on the instructional, personnel, and/or monetary costs of the items. Monetary cost is clear—the more expensive the item, the more points required to earn it. Instructional cost refers to the amount of instructional time lost or interfered with by a particular reward. Thus, an activity which causes the student to miss part of academic instruction should require more points than one the student can do on his own free time. Personnel cost involves the time required by you and/or other staff to fulfill the reinforcer. Having lunch with the principal, therefore, would cost more points than spending five minutes of free time with a friend.

c. Have the student begin each day with a certain number of points. This number should equal his average number of negative reactions per day, plus two. For example, if the student reacts inappropriately to corrections an average of eight times per day, he would begin each day with ten points. For every inappropriate reaction, he loses a point. The points remaining at the end of each day are added together and applied toward the reinforcer the student is striving to earn.

(NOTE: A lottery system might be more effective with a primary level student. In this system, the student would begin each day with tickets in a jar instead of points. All the tickets would have prizes written on them—one ticket with a big prize, a couple with moderate prizes, and the majority with small prizes. Each time the student reacts negatively to a correction, you remove one ticket from the jar—but neither you nor the student is allowed to see what is written on it. At the end of each day, the student draws one ticket from those remaining in the jar, and receives that prize.)

d. When the student has accumulated enough points to earn the reward he has chosen, he "spends" the points necessary and the system begins again. That is, he selects another reward to earn and begins with zero points.

If the student is immature, and needs more frequent encouragement, you might consider letting him earn several "less expensive" rewards (e.g., five minutes of computer time after ten points) on the way to a bigger reward (e.g., one hour with you for 100 points). That is, the student receives the small rewards without spending points; they continue to accumulate toward the selected reward.

e. Structure student success as necessary. For example:

- Sometimes give the student a very minor correction that will be very easy for the student to accept.

- Now and again, use bonus points. "You don't have any corrections you need to make, but let's mark three 'Appropriate Reactions' as a bonus for having done such a nice job on this assignment.

- Sometimes reward the student for reacting calmly to a precorrection. "Before I tell you about your corrections, let's mark an 'Appropriate Reaction' because of how calm you are right now. You can then earn another for staying calm after I tell you about the corrections that need to be made."

- Occasionally, give the student points for accurately assessing that his reaction was inappropriate. "Henri, I agree—that was not an appropriate way to respond so let's mark one 'Inappropriate Reaction.' However, I think we can also mark one 'Appropriate Reaction' because you are so calm right now."

. . . .

Suggested Steps for Developing and Implementing a Plan

The following steps are designed to help you develop an appropriate intervention plan and implement it effectively, whether you choose to use one of the MODEL PLANS or create a customized plan of your own. The steps are, however, suggestions—they are not intended to be followed rigidly or in any particular order. Use your professional judgment and the knowledge of your particular situation to make them work for you.

1. *Make sure you have enough information about the situation.*

a. If you think a minimal intervention like PLAN A will be sufficient, you may already have enough information to proceed. However, when a more involved plan seems necessary, you should consider collecting additional descriptive and/or objective information for a couple of days.

b. You need to be able to explain what has lead you to conclude that "the student has a problem with being corrected." Anecdotal notes on actual incidents should provide enough detail to help you define the problem behavior clearly and completely. To collect anecdotal notes, simply keep a card in your pocket or on a clipboard and occasionally make notes on specific instances in which the student reacts negatively to being corrected.

For each entry, briefly describe the nature of the correction, how the student reacted, and any other relevant observations. You do not need to take notes every time the student reacts negatively to being corrected; the idea is to capture a range of examples so you will be able to describe the behavior completely.

Also include some notes on times when the student reacts calmly to being corrected—this will make it clear that you are not only aware of his problem behavior, but also recognize when he behaves appropriately. When you meet with the student, the positive examples will also help you clarify how you want the student to behave.

c. In addition to information on what the student's inappropriate behavior looks like, it can also be useful to document how often it occurs (i.e., a frequency count). This information will provide both a more objective measure of the problem and an objective way to monitor progress. You can use the same card on which you are taking anecdotal notes to keep a frequency count—simply write a tally mark on the card each time the student reacts negatively to being corrected. Counting his appropriate reactions to being corrected may also be useful.

You might want to code these tallies to discern whether the behavior occurs more frequently during certain times, subjects, or activities (e.g., using an "A" or "P" to indicate that the incident happened in the morning or afternoon; or clustering the tallies by math or reading, teacher directed instruction or independent work, etc.).

d. If the student notices what you are doing and asks about it, be straightforward—tell him that you are collecting information to see whether his reactions to being corrected are a problem that needs to be worked on.

Following is an example of anecdotal notes and a positive and negative frequency count that have been collected on a student's reactions to being corrected.

e. The frequency information (or percentage of appropriate reactions) is fairly easy to summarize on a chart or graph. Seeing how often he reacts inappropriately to corrections or how little of the time he reacts calmly may help the student and his parent(s) better understand your concern.

f. Continuing to collect this type of information (and keeping the chart up-to-date) while you implement a plan will help you monitor whether the situation is getting worse, staying the same, or getting better.

Henri's Reactions to Being Corrected—4/23

Appropriate Reactions	Inappropriate Reactions
///	~~HHT~~ ////

Notes:

10:00—I gave Henri his math paper and tried to explain how he got mixed up on a couple of the problems. Before I could even finish, he started to whine about having to fix the problems and not having enough time. I tried to reassure him that he had plenty of time. We went back and forth for several minutes.

1:30—I suggested to Henri that he needed to write his lab report neat enough for me to read, and he argued with me that he was writing his neatest and trying his best. I tried to show him some of his other lab reports to provide a comparison of what he is capable of, but then he just argued about how I was "always picking on him."

2:00—When I handed back the reading papers, Henri began to complain about having to do his corrections. He got himself so upset that he stomped around for about five minutes complaining, then sat and pouted for 15 minutes, then complained that he did not have enough time for the corrections.

 Identify a focus for the intervention and labels for referring to the appropriate and inappropriate behaviors.

a. To be effective, the intervention must address more than just reducing the student's negative reactions to corrections—there must be a concurrent emphasis on increasing some positive behavior or trait (e.g., responding responsibly to being corrected). Having a specific positive behavior in mind will make it easier for you to "catch" and reinforce the student for behaving appropriately, and the positive focus will help you to frame the situation more productively.

For example, if you simply say that "the student has a problem with being corrected," you don't really provide any useful information, and may put the student and his parent(s) on the defensive. However, when you explain that you want to "help the student learn to respond responsibly to being corrected so he can learn from his mistakes" you present an important, and reasonable, goal for the student to work toward and clearly identify what the student needs to do to be successful.

b. Specifying labels for the appropriate and inappropriate behaviors (e.g., "responding responsibly" and "reacting negatively," respectively) will help you to use consistent vocabulary when discussing the situation with the student. If you sometimes refer to the inappropriate behavior as "arguing" or "pouting," for example, the student may not realize that you are talking about reacting negatively to being corrected.

 Determine when and how to include the parent(s).

a. It is not necessary to contact the student's parent(s) if the problem has just begun and is not interfering with the student's academic or social progress. However, it might be a good idea to take advantage of any scheduled activities (e.g., conferences, weekly notes home) to let them know of your concern.

b. When the student's problem with corrections is severe or frequent, you should contact the student's parent(s). Share with them any information you have collected about the behavior (e.g., anecdotal notes, frequency counts, percentages), and explain why you are concerned. Focus in particular on how the behavior is hindering the student academically and/or socially (e.g., if the student does not learn to react calmly to being corrected and to learn from his mistakes, he is going to find school and most jobs extremely difficult and unpleasant).

You might ask if the parent(s) have any insight into the situation and/or whether they have noticed similar behavior at home. Whether or not the parent(s) perceive a problem, explain that you want to help the student learn to "react responsibly to being corrected" and invite them to join you for an initial meeting with the student to develop a plan. If the parent(s) are unable or unwilling to participate, let them know that you will keep them informed of the student's progress.

c. Once the parent(s) have been involved in any way, you should give them updates at least once per week while the plan is being implemented.

 4. **Prepare for, then conduct, an initial meeting about the situation.**

a. Arrange a meeting to discuss your concerns with the student and anyone else who will be involved in the plan (e.g., the parent[s]). Although the specifics will vary depending upon the age of the student and the severity of the problem, there are some general guidelines to consider when scheduling the meeting.

First, meet at a neutral time (i.e., not immediately after a problem has occurred), when emotions are less likely to hamper communication. In general, a day's notice is appropriate, however a primary age student may worry excessively and/or forget what the meeting is about if it is scheduled more than an hour before it takes place.

Second, make the meeting appropriately private. With a primary student who has a mild problem, you might meet in the classroom while the other students are working independently. However, when dealing with a middle/junior high school student and his parent(s), you will need some place private (e.g., the counselor's office) to ensure that the discussion will not be overheard.

Third, try to make sure the meeting is scheduled for a time and place that is not likely to be interrupted. Finally, if the parent(s) will be participating, they should be the ones to tell the student about the meeting.

b. Construct a preliminary plan. Decide whether you think you can use one of the MODEL PLANS or if you need to create a customized plan using components from various plans and/or of your own design. Although you will invite and encourage the student to help develop the plan during the initial meeting, having a proposed plan in mind before you meet can alleviate frustration and wasted time if the student is unwilling or unable to participate.

c. Review the information you have collected and think carefully about how you want the student to behave. Then prepare thorough descriptions of both the inappropriate behavior and the positive behavior/trait on which the student will be working. The more specific you can be and the more concrete examples you have, the easier it will be to clarify (and for the student to under-

stand) your expectations. Be sure to consider the student's behavior in all relevant activities (e.g., independent work, teacher directed instruction, unstructured class times, etc.).

d. Conduct the meeting in an atmosphere of collaboration. The following agenda is one way you might structure the meeting:

- **Share your concerns about the student's behavior.**

  Briefly describe the problem behavior and, when appropriate, show the student a chart or graph of his reactions to being corrected. Then explain why you consider his negative reactions to be a problem. You might tell the student that to be a successful learner, he has to be able to learn from his errors.

- **Discuss how you can work together to improve the situation.**

  Tell the student that you would like to help him "learn to respond responsibly to corrections" and describe your preliminary plan. Invite the student to give you input on the various aspects of the plan, and together work out any necessary details (e.g., use of the self-monitoring form, etc.). You may have to brainstorm different possibilities if the student is uncomfortable with the initial plan. Incorporating any of the student's suggestions that strengthen the plan is likely to increase his sense of "ownership" in and commitment to it.

- **Make sure the student understands what you mean by appropriate and inappropriate behavior.**

  Use your descriptions of the problem behavior and the positive (desired) behavior to clarify your expectations. To ensure that you and the student are in agreement about the expectations, you might present hypothetical scenarios involving corrections and have him identify whether each is an example of responding responsibly or reacting negatively. Or you might describe an actual situation that has occurred and ask the student to explain how he could have responded responsibly in that situation.

- **Conclude the meeting.**

  Always end the meeting with words of encouragement. Let the student know that you are confident that he can be successful. Be sure to reinforce him for participating in the meeting.

Give the student regular, ongoing feedback about his behavior.

It is important to meet with the student periodically to discuss his progress. In most cases, three to five minutes once per week should suffice. *(NOTE: PLAN D suggests daily meetings.)* During the meetings, review any information that has been collected and discuss whether or not the situation is getting better. As much as possible, focus on the student's improvements, however, also address any new or continuing problems. As the situation improves, the meetings can be faded to once every other week and then to once per month.

 Evaluate the situation (and the plan).

Implement any plan for at least two weeks before deciding whether to change plans; to continue, modify, or fade the plan you are using; or to cease the intervention. Generally, if the student's behavior is clearly improving (based on the objective information that's been collected and/or the subjective perceptions of yourself, the student, and possibly the parent[s]), stick with what you are doing. If the situation has remained the same or worsened, some kind of change will be necessary. Always discuss any changes to the plan with the student first.

CRYING, CHRONIC

Emotional Turmoil

DESCRIPTION

You have a student who cries for no apparent reason (or for seemingly trivial reasons).

GOAL

The student will reduce and eventually eliminate her crying, and learn to express herself in more mature ways.

OVERVIEW OF PLANS

- PLAN A: For a situation in which the problem is relatively mild or has just begun.

- PLAN B: For a student whose crying is an overreaction to a minor incident or fear.

- PLAN C: For a student who cries to gain attention and/or sympathy from adults.

- PLAN D: For a student who is unaware of how frequently or how long she engages in crying.

- PLAN E: For a student whose crying has become habitual.

Alternative Problem

- Complaining
- Helplessness
- Hypochondria
- Perfectionism
- School Phobia
- Tantrumming (K or 1st Grader)
- Tattling
- Whining

General Considerations

- If the student's problem behavior stems in any way from academic issues (e.g., the student cries because she is frustrated with her inability to do her schoolwork, or cries to avoid doing the work), concurrent efforts must be made to ensure her academic success (see **Academic Deficits, Determining**).

- If the student lacks the basic social skills to interact with her peers appropriately, it may be necessary to begin by teaching her those skills. **Social Skills, Lack of** contains information on a variety of published social skills curricula.

- If you suspect that the student's crying could be related to the student being depressed, see **Depression**. This problem includes a set of questions to help you decide whether the student should be referred for counseling or psychological services.

- Remain open to the possibility that the student is demonstrating the presence of abuse or neglect through chronic crying. If you believe that there is any possibility that physical abuse, emotional abuse, or neglect could be at the root of the problem, refer the situation immediately to your building administrator or other district official.

- Chronic crying could also be a symptom of other deep problems, such as trouble at home. If there has been a death in the family or the student has just learned of a pending divorce, the student's crying should not be viewed as a problem. (Crying is a healthy response to sad or stressful situations.) However, if there is not an identifiable circumstance that you or the student's parent(s) can identify, and the problem has been going on for several weeks, consider implementing one of the following plans.

- Alternately, crying may be simply a symptom of temporary worry, distress, or even fatigue. If the problem has only occurred once or twice, then comfort the student, investigate if there is anything the student wants to talk about or needs help with, and do not even imply that the crying is a problem.

Model Plans

PLAN A

It is not always necessary, or even beneficial, to use an involved plan. If incidences of crying have just begun and/or the behavior is relatively mild (i.e., not interfering with the student's academic or social progress), the following actions, along with making the student aware of your concerns, may resolve the situation.

1. Respond consistently to the student's crying.

a. You need to know how to respond (or not respond) when the student does cry. The best strategy is to work out your plan with the student. During your initial meeting with the student (see SUGGESTED STEPS FOR DEVELOPING AND IMPLEMENTING A PLAN), let the student know that if she needs to cry, that that is okay, but that you need to know what she would like you to do when she does cry. If she does not know, offer her the following choices

- I could just pretend I don't notice. That way you could cry as long as you need to and then you could pull yourself together.

- I could let you go to a private corner of the classroom.

- I could ask you if you need anything, such as a tissue.

- I could pat you on the shoulder or give you a hug, and then let you pull yourself together.

Be cautious about responses such as letting the student sit on your lap until she is through crying. This may be too reinforcing and may not be reasonable given that you have other students in the room and a responsibility to interact with all the students.

b. Once a strategy has been chosen, decide whether the other students need to be informed about the plan. That is, if other students tend to hover and comfort when the student cries, that attention may either make the student feel self-conscious or reinforce the student's crying.

You can ask the student what she would like the other students to do if she cries. If she says she likes having them comfort her, and the student's crying diminishes when they do so, that is fine. If, however, attention from the other students is reinforcing the crying, implement PLAN C in addition to this plan.

b. Make sure the student is still accountable for completing her academic work. If the student finds that spending time crying results in not having to complete her schoolwork, she may begin spending more and more time crying. If the student does not have time to complete her work because of the time spent crying, arrange for the student to complete her work during recess or lunch time, after school, or at home.

2. *Use reinforcement to encourage appropriate behavior.*

a. Give the student increased praise. Although you want to avoid praising the student for not crying (as any reference to the crying may prompt the student to cry), you should watch for situations in which the student is not crying and praise her for what she *is* doing. "Tammy, you should be very proud of how much you have accomplished today on your report."

If the student would be embarrassed by public praise, praise the student privately or even give the student a note. Remember that any time the student is not crying or otherwise behaving inappropriately, you can praise her for some positive behavior.

b. Give the student frequent attention. Ways to do so include saying "hello" to her as she enters the classroom, calling on her frequently during class activities, and occasionally asking her to assist you with a class job that needs to be done.

PLAN B

Sometimes a specific event or circumstance precipitates a student's crying. For example, the student may have missed her stop for getting off the bus once. She may then become so worried about missing the stop again, that she ends up crying. If this goes on, this fear can become self-perpetuating. If this is the case, the intervention must teach the student to overcome the specific fear or distress.

1. *Respond consistently to the student's crying (see PLAN A).*

2. *Address the specific circumstance(s) that precipitate the student's crying.*

a. Talk to the student and/or her parent(s) to determine what has been making the child fearful or nervous. You might also be able to observe for yourself what events seem to set off the student's crying. It may be a specific event or setting (e.g., riding the school bus or going out to recess) or a more general problem (e.g., the student is afraid of making mistakes on her work because she thinks it would displease her teacher).

b. When possible, reduce or ameliorate the problematic situation. For example, if the student is afraid of missing her bus stop, develop a plan with her parent(s), the bus driver, and the student working together.

If the student is anxious about recess, you might arrange for her to meet a playground supervisor and, if she likes, to walk with the supervisor during recess for a week or so until she is more comfortable on the playground. Or, if the student is afraid of making mistakes, you and the student could talk about mistakes and how to learn from them. You could even share age appropriate stories about ways in which you have learned from mistakes in your personal life. Then you could have the student practice some math problems and have her make a few purposeful mistakes so that she can see that getting corrected is not a horrible experience.

3. *Use precorrections to help the student through problematic situations.*

Shortly before the student will face a problematic situation, remind her that a plan has been developed to help her deal with that situation. "Tammy, it is getting close to the time to get on the bus. Remember that you are going to watch for your stop. Mrs. Cox said that she will be sure to remind you of which stop is yours, and she will not let you get off at the wrong place. In addition, your mom will be at the stop and if she does not see you getting off, she will get on the bus to remind you. Everybody is working together to make sure you have a great ride home each day."

4. Use reinforcement to encourage responsible behavior.

a. Give the student increased praise and attention for any positive behavior she exhibits (see PLAN A).

b. Praise the student for facing the problematic situation, even if she still cries occasionally. Let the student know that she should be proud of her strength and her willingness to work through a tough situation. "Tammy, I know that the bus situation has been hard, but everyday you have gone and gotten on that bus. You are a very strong person to be able to face and learn to deal with a situation that has been scary. I think you will soon find that it no longer makes you afraid."

PLAN C

Some students are very skilled at gaining attention through their negative behavior. If you find yourself frequently comforting the student, it is possible that she is trying to gain adult attention through her crying. Whether or not the student overtly seems to like the attention, you should make sure that she receives more frequent and more satisfying attention for being positively engaged in classroom expectations than for crying.

1. Respond consistently to the student's crying.

a. Because it is important for the student to learn that she will not be able to prompt people to comfort her and give her lots of attention when she cries, you should identify a private place where she can go to cry when necessary. With a primary age student, this place might be a quiet corner of the classroom; with an older student a location such as the counselor's office might be more appropriate.

Work with the student in establishing this procedure, and make sure she knows that she should come back to the classroom setting as soon as she is finished crying.

b. Whenever the student cries, she should go to the designated location until she has stopped crying. If the student does not go there herself, give her one reminder. "Tammy, you can go to the reading corner until you are finished crying."

c. While the student is in the designated location, ignore all of her crying. If the student does not go to the designated location after the reminder, ignore the behavior. While ignoring, do not look at the student or talk to her. Do not act disgusted or impatient with her crying. Simply interact in positive ways with students who are behaving appropriately and meeting classroom expectations.

As soon as the target student is no longer crying, pay attention to her, but make no reference to her previous crying.

d. The only time you shouldn't ignore the crying is when it affects other students (e.g., if the student is crying and keeping the class waiting to go to lunch). On these occasions, you can use a consequence, such as time owed off of recess or after school.

If the need for consequences seems likely, the student should be told during the initial meeting (see SUGGESTED STEPS FOR DEVELOPING AND IMPLEMENTING A PLAN) what will happen when her crying affects the class. Then, if the student is crying and keeping the class waiting, you can simply state, for example, "Tammy, you need to line up or you will owe time off of your recess."

Use consequences only for situations in which a class activity cannot proceed unless the student complies with a direct request. In this way, you are still ignoring the crying, but are implementing a consequence for the student behaving in a way that affects other students negatively.

(NOTE: For a student in kindergarten or first grade, redirection may be more appropriate than time owed. Redirection involves gently leading the student through the task or direction without saying anything or making eye contact. For example, if the class is waiting because the student is crying and won't line up, you would just guide the student into line without saying anything to her.)

e. If other students give the target student attention when she is crying (e.g., trying to comfort her or find out what is upsetting her), gently correct them. "Stan and Theresa, Tammy can take care of herself and she will stop crying when she is ready. It would be best to let her work it out on her own."

2. *Use reinforcement to encourage appropriate behavior.*

a. Frequent praise and attention is the core of this plan. The student must see that she receives more frequent and more satisfying attention when she behaves appropriately than when she cries. Thus, whenever the student is not crying (or otherwise behaving inappropriately), make an effort to praise and spend time with her. "Tammy, you have such creative ideas. Would it be okay if I sat with you a moment and watched as you and your group do the next step on this project?"

b. You may also wish to use intermittent rewards to acknowledge the student's success. Occasional, and unexpected, rewards can motivate the student to demonstrate responsible behavior more often. The idea is to provide a reward when the student has had a particularly good period of demonstrating self-control.

Appropriate rewards might include playing a game with you, helping you with a bulletin board, or running an errand. *(NOTE: A list of additional reinforcement ideas can be found in APPENDIX 1.)* Use intermittent rewards more frequently at the beginning of the intervention to encourage the student, and less often as her behavior improves.

3. *Ensure a 3-1 ratio of positive to negative attention.*

a. Given that attention is a motivating force for this student, you want to be sure that you are giving the student *three times as much* positive as negative attention. One way to do this is to monitor your interactions with the student at least one day per week. Simply keep a card on a clipboard or in your pocket and record each interaction you have with the student as either positive or negative by writing a "+" or a "-", respectively, on the card.

To determine whether an interaction is positive or negative, ask yourself whether the student was crying (or otherwise behaving inappropriately) at the time the interaction occurred. Any interactions that stem from inappropriate behavior are negative, and all interactions that occur while the student is meeting classroom expectations are positive. Thus, giving the student a reminder to go to the designated area to cry and assigning time owed are both negative interactions, but praising the student for completing her work or for demonstrating self-control is positive. Greeting the student as she enters the room or asking her if she has any questions during independent work are also considered positive interactions. *(NOTE: Ignoring the student's crying is not recorded at all, because it is not an interaction.)*

b. If you find that you are not giving the student three times as much positive as negative attention, try to increase the number of positive interactions you have with the student. Sometimes prompts can help. For example, you might decide that each time the student enters the classroom you will say "hello" to her, that whenever you are handing out papers you will find a time to interact with the student, or that whenever a student uses the drinking fountain you will check the target student and as soon as possible praise some aspect of her behavior. You can also increase the ratio of positive to negative attention by ignoring more of the student's inappropriate behavior.

4. *(OPTIONAL)*
Arrange for positive attention from other adults.

If the student seems especially starved for attention, you might ask the principal, playground supervisors, and other teachers to give her lots of attention. If several adults make a point to greet the student whenever they see her, and if they make an effort to "catch" her when she is not crying, it may reduce her need to cry to gain attention in other school settings.

PLAN D

Some students do not seem to know how often they engage in crying. If your student doesn't realize how frequently and/or for how long she cries, the intervention must include some way of helping the student become more aware of her own behavior.

1. *Respond consistently to the student's crying (see PLAN A).*

2. *Implement a system to monitor the duration of the student's crying.*

a. Determine who will do the recording. Since the point is for the student to become more aware of her own behavior, having her record the duration (i.e., self-monitor) will be more effective than if you do it. However, if the student cannot or will not be accurate (or if she would be too embarrassed to self-monitor), you should re-cord the duration yourself. *(NOTE: Even when the student self-monitors, you should keep your own record approximately one day per week to verify the student's accuracy.)*

b. If the student is self-monitoring the duration of her crying, have her keep a piece of paper on her desk or in her notebook. Each time she cries, time in minutes how long it takes the student to stop crying and have her record that information on the paper. You can give her the time subtly by slipping her a piece of paper with the number of minutes written on it.

The student's recording sheet need not be com-plicated. Following is an example of the type of form you might use.

Tammy's Record of Minutes Spent Crying

Date	Minutes Per Incident	Total
1/15	5, 8, 13	26
1/16		
1/17		
1/18		
1/19		

c. Each day, meet with the student for a few minutes to review that day's record. Have the student calculate the total number of minutes she spent crying during the day, and chart this information on a graph (or do it yourself). Talk with her about whether the day was better, worse, or about the same as previous days.

If the day did not go well, encourage the student to talk about why and have her identify what she can do the next day to help herself remember to demonstrate more self-control. If the student behaves inappropriately during the meeting, keep the interaction very short. Just let the student know that you are sure tomorrow will be a better day.

3. *Conduct a goal-setting session with the student.*

Help the student to set a goal for demonstrating self-control. The goal can be determined with the student or prepared in advance. Generally, when the student is involved in the process, she is more likely to strive to achieve the goal.

In either case, identify a broad-based goal such as, "to show self-control by crying less," and three specific ways that the student can demonstrate that she is working on the goal. One of the ways should relate specifically to reducing the number of min-utes spent crying. A finished goal contract might look like the sample shown.

Goal Contract

I, ___Tammy___, am willing to make an effort to

show self-control by crying less _____.

I can show that I am working on this goal by:

1. Taking some deep breaths when I feel like crying.

2. Going to my "private spot" spot if I need to cry.

3. Recording the amount of time I spend crying and trying to cry less than 30 minutes each day.

I, __Mr. Handel__, will support this goal by

reminding Tammy to go to her private spot

and by helping her to record and chart the

number of minutes spent crying each day. .

_____

Student Signature

_____

Teacher Signature

---

4. Use reinforcement to encourage appropriate behavior.

a. Give the student increased praise and attention for any positive behavior she exhibits (see PLAN A).

b. In addition, praise the student during the end-of-the-day review meetings for accurate recording (if applicable) and for being willing to look at her daily total. Even on a bad day, if the student is willing to chart the data and discuss why it was a bad day, praise her. "Tammy, you are really handling this responsibly. Even though it was a rough day, you are willing to talk to me about things you might do differently tomorrow to demonstrate more self-control. That is a real sign that you are growing up."

Regardless of how the day went, try to make this meeting upbeat and encouraging—you want the student to look forward to the review each day.

5. Encourage the student to use self-reinforcement.

Whenever things are going well (i.e., less crying than usual), prompt the student to mentally reinforce herself. "Tammy, this has been a very successful morning. Silently tell yourself that you are really demonstrating a lot of self-control." Prompt the student this way intermittently throughout the day and during the end-of-the-day review meetings.

P L A N   E

If the student's behavior has become habitual and/or she does not seem to have a desire to reduce her crying, you may need to implement a system of external incentives (i.e., rewards and consequences) based on her behavior to motivate her to reduce her crying and to increasingly demonstrate self-control.

1. Respond consistently to the student's crying (see PLAN A).

2. Implement a system to monitor the duration of the student's crying (see PLAN D).

3. Establish a structured system for reinforcing the student's appropriate behavior.

a. With the student, create a list of reinforcers that she can earn. Although you might want to have some suggestions in mind, the system will be more effective if the student identifies most of the items or activities herself. *(NOTE: A list of reinforcement ideas can be found in APPENDIX 1.)*

b. Assign "prices" (in points) for each of the rewards on the list and have the student select the reward she would like to earn first. The prices should be based on the instructional, personnel, and/or monetary costs of the items. Monetary cost is clear—the more expensive the item, the more points required to earn it. Instructional cost refers to the amount of instructional time lost or interfered with by a particular reward. Thus, an activity which causes the student to miss part of academic instruction should require more points than one the student can do on her own recess time. Personnel cost involves the time required by you and/or other staff to fulfill the reinforcer. Having lunch with the principal, therefore, would cost more points than spending five minutes of free time with a friend.

c. Establish a system to award the student points on any day that the number of minutes spent crying is below identified levels. These levels should reflect the average number of minutes per day the student typically spends crying. The sample chart following is based on a student who cries 45-90 minutes each day, with an average of 60 "crying minutes."

> - If there are no more than **60** "crying minutes," Tammy earns **1** point.
>
> - If there are no more that **40** "crying minutes," Tammy earns **3** points.
>
> - If there are no more than **20** "crying minutes," Tammy earns **5** points.
>
> - If there are no more than **5** "crying minutes," Tammy earns **7** points.
>
> - If there are **no** "crying minutes," Tammy earns **10** points.

d. When the student has accumulated enough points to earn the reward she has chosen, she "spends" the points necessary and the system begins again. That is, she selects another reward to earn and begins with zero points.

If the student is immature, and needs more frequent encouragement, you might consider letting her earn several "less expensive" rewards (e.g., five minutes of free time after 20 points) on the way to a bigger reward (e.g., one hour with you for 200 points). That is, the student receives the small rewards without spending points; they continue to accumulate toward the selected reward.

e. If appropriate (and/or necessary), specify a consequence for excessive crying (per incident and/or per day). For example, you might decide that each minute spent crying over three min-

utes (at one time) and/or over 60 minutes (for the whole day) equals one minute of time owed off of recess or after school. Thus, if the student cries for 75 minutes in a single day, she receives no points and owes 15 minutes after school.

4. Use reinforcement to encourage appropriate behavior.

a. Give the student increased praise and attention for any positive behavior she exhibits (see PLAN A).

b. In addition, show interest and enthusiasm about how the student is doing on the system. "Tammy, you have made it through the entire day without crying. This is the first day that you have been this successful. You should be very proud of the fact that you earned ten points!"

. . . .
Suggested Steps for Developing and Implementing a Plan

The following steps are designed to help you develop an appropriate intervention plan and implement it effectively, whether you choose to use one of the MODEL PLANS or create a customized plan of your own. The steps are, however, suggestions—they are not intended to be followed rigidly or in any particular order. Use your professional judgment and the knowledge of your particular situation to make them work for you.

1. Make sure you have enough information about the situation.

a. If you think a minimal intervention like PLAN A will be sufficient, you may already have enough information to proceed. However, when a more involved plan seems necessary, you should consider collecting additional descriptive and/or objective information for a couple of days.

b. Anecdotal notes on actual incidents should provide enough detail to define the problem behavior clearly and completely. To collect anecdotal notes, simply keep a card in your pocket or on a clipboard and occasionally make notes on specific instances when the student cries.

For each entry, briefly describe where and when it occurred, what the student did (e.g., went to her "private spot"), and any other relevant observations (e.g., what prompted the behavior). You do not need to take notes every time the student cries; the idea is to capture a range of examples of the crying so that you can describe the behavior completely.

Also include some notes on times when the student demonstrates self-control. This will make it clear that you are not only aware of her crying, but also recognize when she behaves appropriately. When you meet with the student, the positive examples will also help you clarify how you want the student to behave.

c. In addition to information on what the student's inappropriate behavior looks like, it can also be useful to document for how much time she engages in it (i.e., a duration record). This information will provide both a more objective measure of the problem and an objective way to monitor the student's progress. You can use the same card on which you are making anecdotal notes to record the number of minutes spent crying. Each time the student cries, mentally note the time when she starts and the time when she stops. Write the difference (in number of minutes) on the card. At the end of the day, you will know how many times she cried and will be able to calculate the total number of minutes spent crying.

d. If the student notices what you are doing and asks about it, be straightforward—tell her that you are collecting information to see whether her crying is a problem that needs to be worked on.

e. Duration information is fairly easy to summarize on a chart or graph. Seeing how much time she spends crying each day may help the student and her parent(s) better understand your concern.

f. Continuing to collect this type of information (and keeping the chart up-to-date) while you implement a plan will help you monitor whether the situation is getting worse, staying the same, or getting better.

2. *Identify a focus for the intervention and labels for referring to the appropriate and inappropriate behaviors.*

a. To be effective, the intervention must address more than just reducing the student's crying—there must be a concurrent emphasis on increasing some positive behavior or trait (e.g., self-control), unless the problem has been precipitated by a specific circumstance or is in the early stages. With those circumstances (see PLANS A and B), it is advisable to avoid reinforcing the student for not crying. However, in most other cases, having a specific positive behavior in mind will make it easier for you to "catch" and reinforce the student for behaving appropriately, and a positive focus will help you to frame the situation more productively.

For example, if you simply say that "the student has a problem with crying," you don't really provide any useful information, and may put the student and her parent(s) on the defensive. However, if you explain that you want to "help the student learn to demonstrate increased self-control," you present an important, and reasonable, goal for the student to work toward and clearly identify what the student needs to do to be successful.

b. Specifying labels for the appropriate and inappropriate behaviors (e.g., "self-control" and "crying," respectively) will help you to use consistent vocabulary when discussing the situation with the student. If you sometimes refer to the inappropriate behavior as "crying" and other times tell the student that "she is getting upset," for example, she may not realize that you are talking about the same thing.

3. *Determine when and how to include the parent(s).*

a. With this type of problem, the parent(s) should be contacted immediately because they need to know that their child is very upset about something.

b. Share with them any information you have collected about the behavior (e.g., anecdotal notes, duration record), and explain why you are concerned. Focus in particular on how the behavior is hindering the student academically and/or socially (e.g., the student is crying instead of participating in class activities).

You might ask if the parent(s) have any insight into the situation and/or whether they have experienced similar behavior at home. Whether or not the parent(s) perceive a problem, explain that you want to help the student "demonstrate increased self-control," and invite them to join you for an initial meeting with the student to develop a plan. If the parent(s) are unable or unwilling to participate, let them know that you will keep them informed of the student's progress.

c. Once the parent(s) have been involved in any way, you should give them updates at least once per week while the plan is being implemented.

4. *Prepare for, then conduct, an initial meeting about the situation.*

a. Arrange a meeting to discuss your concerns with the student and anyone else who will be involved in the plan (e.g., the parent[s], the school psychologist). Although the specifics will vary depending upon the age of the student and the severity of the problem, there are some general guidelines to consider when scheduling the meeting.

First, meet at a neutral time (i.e., not immediately after a problem has occurred), when emotions are less likely to hamper communication. In general, a day's notice is appropriate, however primary age students may worry excessively and/or forget what the meeting is about if it is scheduled more than an hour before it takes place.

Second, make the meeting appropriately private. With a primary student who has a mild problem, you might meet in the classroom while the other students are working independently. However, when dealing with a middle/junior high school student and the student's parent(s), you will want to use a private room (e.g., the counselor's office) to ensure that the discussion will not be overheard.

Third, try to make sure the meeting is scheduled for a time and place that it is not likely to be interrupted. Finally, if the parent(s) will be participating, they should be the ones to tell the student about the meeting.

b. Construct a preliminary plan. Decide whether you think you can use one of the MODEL PLANS or if you need to create a customized plan using components from various plans and/or of your own design. Although you will invite and encourage the student to help develop the plan during the initial meeting, having a proposed plan in mind before you meet can alleviate frustration and wasted time if the student is unwilling or unable to participate.

c. After reviewing the information you have collected and thinking about how you want the student to behave, prepare thorough descriptions of the inappropriate behavior and the positive behavior/trait on which the student will be working. The more specific you can be and the more concrete examples you have, the easier it will be to clarify (and for the student to understand) your expectations. Be sure to consider the student's behavior in all relevant activities (e.g., independent work, teacher directed instruction, unstructured class times, recess and lunch, etc.).

d. Conduct the meeting in an atmosphere of collaboration. The following agenda is one way you might structure the meeting:

- **Share your concerns about the student's behavior.**

  Briefly describe the problem behavior and, when appropriate, show the student a chart of how much time per day she engages in crying. Then explain why you consider the crying to be a problem. You might tell the student that there is nothing wrong with crying unless it interferes with class participation, which hers does.

- **Find out if there is something specific that is bothering the student.**

  If there is a specific problem that the student can identify, explore ways of helping the student learn to better manage the fearful circumstance or event.

- **Discuss how you can work together to improve the situation.**

  Tell the student that you would like to help her learn to "demonstrate increased self-control" and describe your preliminary plan. Invite the student to give you input on the various aspects of the plan, and together work out any necessary details (e.g., how you will respond when the student cries, use of self-monitoring, a goal, etc.).

  You may have to brainstorm different possibilities if the student is uncomfortable with the initial plan. Incorporating any of the student's suggestions that strengthen the plan is likely to increase her sense of "ownership" in and commitment to it.

- **Make sure the student understands what you mean by appropriate and inappropriate behavior.**

  Use the descriptions you have prepared to define and clarify the problem behavior and the positive (desired) behavior as specifically and thoroughly as you can. To ensure that you and the student are in agreement about the expectations, you might present hypothetical scenarios and have her identify whether each is an example of demonstrating self-control or crying. Or you might describe an actual situation that has occurred and ask the student to explain how she could demonstrate increased self-control in that situation.

- **Conclude the meeting.**

  Always end the meeting with words of encouragement. Let the student know that you are confident that she can be successful. Be sure to reinforce her for participating in the meeting.

5. *Give the student regular, ongoing feedback about her behavior.*

It is important to meet with the student periodically to discuss her progress. In most cases, three to five minutes once per week should suffice. *(NOTE: PLANS D and E call for daily meetings.)* During the meetings, review any information that has been collected and discuss whether or not the situation is getting better. As much as possible, focus on the student's improvements, however, also address any new or continuing problems. As the situation improves, the meetings can be faded to once every other week and then to once per month.

6. *Evaluate the situation (and the plan).*

Implement any plan for at least two weeks before deciding whether to change plans; to continue, modify, or fade the plan you are using; or to cease the intervention. Generally, if the student's behavior is clearly improving (based on the objective information that's been collected and/or the sub- jective perceptions of yourself, the student, and possibly the parent[s]), stick with what you are doing. If the situation has remained the same or worsened, some kind of change will be necessary. Always discuss any changes to the plan with the student first.

DAWDLING

Being Inefficient
Wasting Time

DESCRIPTION

You have a student who dawdles (i.e., takes far longer than the other students to get out his materials, put things away, line up, etc.).

GOAL

The student will learn to be more efficient when performing tasks and making transitions.

OVERVIEW OF PLANS

- PLAN A: For a situation in which the problem is relatively mild (i.e., the student is just a little slower than his peers) or has just begun.

- PLAN B: For a student who dawdles because he does not know how to be more efficient.

- PLAN C: For a student who dawdles to gain adult attention.

- PLAN D: For a student who does not realize when and/or how often he dawdles.

- PLAN E: For a student whose dawdling has become habitual.

Alternative Problems

- **Bored Behavior**
- **Compliance/Direction Following, Lack of**
- **Helplessness**
- **Transitions, Problems With**
- **Work Completion— Daily Work**
- **Work Completion— Long-Term Projects**

········
General Considerations

- If there is any reason to suspect a physiological or neurological basis for the student's behavior (i.e., if it seems unusually severe), consult with your building administrator and/or school psychologist for advice on district procedures for following up on this type of situation.

- If you suspect that the problem behavior could be related to the student being depressed, see **Depression**. This problem includes a set of questions to help you decide whether the student should be referred for counseling or psychological services.

- If the student's problem behavior stems in any way from academic issues (e.g., the student is unable to meet the academic expectations and wastes time to avoid doing the work), concurrent efforts must be made to ensure his academic success (see **Academic Deficits, Determining**).

- If the dawdling is resulting in the student not completing his schoolwork, begin with a plan to increase the student's work completion (see **Work Completion—Daily Work**). Once the student is turning in completed work on a regular basis, you can consider an intervention for the dawdling, if the problem still exists.

········
Model Plans

PLAN A

It is not always necessary, or even beneficial, to use an involved plan. If the problem has just begun and/or the student is just a little slower than his peers, the following actions, along with making the student aware of your concerns, may resolve the situation.

 Respond consistently to the inappropriate behavior.

Whenever the student dawdles, gently correct him. "Damean, this is an example of dawdling. You need to get out your paper now and get ready for the spelling test." Your goal is to make the student aware that his behavior is a problem—that is, to impart information. Thus, you want to be emotionally neutral while giving the correction, rather than trying to use emotional power (e.g., guilt, humiliation, etc.) to make the student hurry or be more efficient.

 Use reinforcement to encourage appropriate behavior.

a. Give the student increased praise. Be especially alert for situations in which the student takes less time than usual to follow a direction or complete a transition, and praise him specifically for being efficient. "Damean, that was very efficient. You put your books away quickly and immediately lined up." If the student would be embarrassed by this public praise, praise the student privately or even give the student a note.

In addition, privately praise the student for making progress. "Jared, all morning you have been making an effort to be efficient. You have followed directions quickly and have not kept the class waiting once. This is a big change and you should be very proud of yourself."

b. Give the student frequent attention (e.g., say "hello" to him as he enters the classroom, call on him frequently during class activities, and occasionally ask him to assist you with a class job that needs to be done) and praise him for other positive behaviors he exhibits. For example, you might comment about the accuracy of his work or how well he is keeping his attention focused on his assignments during independent work periods. This demonstrates to the student that you notice many positive things he does, not just the fact that he is refraining from dawdling.

PLAN B

Some students may not actually know how to be efficient. If you are not sure that your student knows how to be more efficient, the intervention plan must include procedures for teaching him efficiency.

 1. *Respond consistently to the inap-propriate behavior.*

Gently correct the student when he dawdles (see PLAN A).

 2. *Conduct lessons to teach the student how to perform tasks or complete transitions more efficiently.*

a. Identify three to five activities or transitions during which the student typically dawdles (e.g., putting away one book and getting out another, putting materials away, and lining up at the door) to be the focus of the lessons. For each targeted activity, describe what the student does when he is dawdling and what he would be doing if he were being efficient.

b. During the lessons, share these descriptions with the student and teach him how to be more efficient. For example, you might simulate one or more of the target activities and have the student practice being more efficient. Or, you might model several examples for the student, and have the student identify whether they are examples of dawdling or being efficient. Whenever you can identify specific strategies that the student could use (e.g., how to put materials away efficiently), focus the training on those strategies.

c. Conduct the lessons daily if possible, but at least twice per week. They needn't last more than five to ten minutes. It is important to present these lessons in a matter-of-fact manner so the student does not feel that he is being ridiculed. Make it clear that you are trying to help

the student learn a skill that will help him throughout his school career. Continue the lessons until the student is consistently being more efficient in the targeted activities.

 3. *Prompt the student to behave appropriately by using precorrections.*

Watch for circumstances in which the student is likely to dawdle and remind him that the particular situation is a time when he needs to remember to be efficient. You might remind him to use the skills that he has been practicing in the lessons. "Damean, I am going to tell everyone to get out a paper and get ready for spelling. I will be watching to see if you remember to do what we practiced yesterday. I'll bet you can!" If this prompt would embarrass the student, have this conversation with him privately.

4. *Use reinforcement to encourage appropriate behavior.*

a. Give the student increased praise and attention for being efficient (see PLAN A).

b. Be especially attentive when the student is efficient in one or more of the targeted activities. Let the student know that you notice his efforts to use the skills he is learning/practicing. "Damean that was even better than when we practiced it. You got out your paper quickly and quietly. You put on the heading and the numbers at the same time everybody else did."

Primary age students often appreciate public praise. "Class, Damean is one of the first students to be ready for this test."

PLAN C

Some students are very skilled at gaining attention through their negative behavior. If you find yourself frequently nagging, reminding, or coaxing the student to hurry up, it is possible that he dawdles to gain adult attention. Whether or not the student overtly seems to like the attention, you should make sure that he receives more frequent and more satisfying attention for behaving appropriately than for dawdling.

1. **Respond consistently to the inappropriate behavior.**

a. Because the student needs to learn that he will not be able to prompt people to nag and pay attention to him by dawdling, it is important for you to ignore his behavior when the student dawdles. While ignoring, do not look at the student or talk to him. Do not act disgusted or impatient with the dawdling. Simply interact in positive ways with students who are behaving well and meeting classroom expectations. As soon as the target student stops dawdling, pay attention to him, but make no reference to the dawdling.

b. When the student's dawdling affects other students (e.g., the rest of the class has to wait while the student puts his books away), you may need to use a consequence such as time owed off of recess or after school. If consequences are going to be used, the student should know ahead of time.

During your initial meeting with the student (see SUGGESTED STEPS FOR DEVELOPING AND IMPLEMENTING A PLAN) explain what will happen when his dawdling affects the class. Then, if the student dawdles and does not line up for music, for example, and you cannot leave the student unsupervised or send the class without supervision, simply state, "Damean, each minute it takes until you join us in line will cost you five minutes from your next recess."

Only use a consequence for situations in which a class activity cannot proceed unless the student complies with a direct request—otherwise ignore the inappropriate behavior.

(NOTE: For a student in kindergarten or first grade, redirection may be more appropriate than time owed. Redirection involves gently leading the student through the task or direction without saying anything to him or making eye contact. For example, if the class has to wait because the student is not lining up, you would just guide him into line without saying a word.)

c. If other students give the target student attention when he is dawdling (i.e., trying to make him hurry), gently correct them. "Dale and Charles, Damean can take care of himself and it does not help him to have us trying to take care of something he can handle on his own. It would be best to mind our own business. Corky and Wanona, I appreciate how cooperative you are being while we are waiting."

2. **Use reinforcement to encourage appropriate behavior.**

a. Frequent praise and attention is the core of this plan. The student must see that he receives more frequent and more satisfying attention when he behaves responsibly than when he dawdles. Thus, whenever the student is being efficient, make an effort to praise and spend time with him. "Damean, you got started so quickly. Would it be okay if I sat with you a moment and watched you work on your assignment? It is such a pleasure to see you learning to be so efficient."

b. You may also wish to use intermittent reinforcement. Occasional, and unexpected, rewards that acknowledge the student's success may motivate him to demonstrate responsible behavior more often. The idea is to provide a reward when the student has had a particularly good period of being efficient.

For a student who dawdles, an appropriate reward might be taking a short break to relax and do something he wants to do. "Damean, you have been so efficient, would you like to take a break? You can have three minutes to get a drink, sit and relax, or do whatever you want to do." *(NOTE: A list of additional reinforcer ideas can be found in APPENDIX 1.)*

If you use intermittent reinforcement, do so more frequently at the beginning of the intervention to encourage the student, and less often as the student's behavior improves over time.

3. **Ensure a 3-1 ratio of positive to negative attention.**

a. Given that attention is a motivating force for this student, you want to be sure that you are giving the student *three times as much* positive as negative attention. One way to do this is to monitor your interactions with the student at least one day per week. Simply keep a card on a clipboard or in your pocket and record each interaction you have with the student as either positive or negative by writing a "+" or a "-", respectively, on the card.

To determine whether an interaction is positive or negative, ask yourself whether the student was dawdling (or otherwise behaving) at the time the interaction occurred. Any interaction that stems from inappropriate behavior is negative, while all interactions that occur while the student is meeting classroom expectations are positive. Thus, gently correcting or redirecting the student are both negative interactions, but praising the student for being efficient is positive. Greeting the student as he enters the room or asking him if he has any questions during independent work are also considered positive interactions. *(NOTE: Ignoring the student's dawdling is not recorded at all, because it is not an interaction.)*

b. If you find that you are not giving the student three times as much positive as negative attention, try to increase the number of positive interactions you have with the student. Sometimes

prompts can help. For example, you might decide that each time the student enters the classroom you will say "hello" to him, that whenever you look at the clock you will find a time to praise the student, or that whenever a student uses the drinking fountain you will check the target student and as soon as possible praise some aspect of his behavior. You can also increase the ratio of positive to negative attention by ignoring more of the student's inappropriate behavior.

PLAN D

$\mathbf{S}$ome students do not seem to realize when they dawdle and/or how often they dawdle. If your student dawdles a lot but doesn't seem to know it, the intervention should include some way of helping the student become more aware of his own behavior.

1. *Respond consistently to the inappropriate behavior.*

Gently correct the student when he dawdles (see PLAN A).

2. *Implement a system to have the student periodically evaluate his behavior.*

a. Identify five times (i.e., activities or transitions) when the student tends to dawdle. You may wish to focus on times when the student's dawdling affects other students or his own academic performance. Each day, directly following the identified times, have the student rate his behavior in terms of efficiency. He can use a simple rating form like the sample shown.

b. Before a student can use the self-evaluation form, you must be sure that he is able to distinguish between behavior that is dawdling and behavior that is being efficient. In addition, together you need to develop and agree upon common definitions for the different rating categories included on the form. If necessary, you should conduct lessons using modeling and role playing to teach the student this information (see PLAN B).

c. For about a week, prompt the student with a precorrection immediately prior to each of the five identified times. That is, privately let the student know that the next task or transition is one during which he will be evaluating his behavior. It may be useful, if time permits, to have him identify what he will need to do to be

---

Self-Evaluation Form

Name _____ Date _____

Directions:

Rate how efficient you were during the following times. Put a check (✓) in the most appropriate box.

	Dawdling a Lot	Dawdling Somewhat	Okay	Mostly Efficient	Extremely Efficient
(Activity 1)					
(Activity 2)					
(Activity 3)					
(Activity 4)					
(Activity 5)					

---

efficient. "Damean, I am about to have everyone get out their math books and get a paper headed. What will you need to do to be able to mark that you were extremely efficient?"

d. Each day, meet with the student for a few minutes to review that day's record. Talk with the student about whether the day was better, worse, or about the same as previous days. If the day did not go well, encourage the student to talk about why and have the student identify things he can do the next day that will help him remember to be efficient rather than dawdle.

 3. **Use reinforcement to encourage appropriate behavior.**

a. Give the student increased praise and attention for being efficient (see PLAN A).

b. In addition, praise the student during the end-of-the-day review meetings for accurately evaluating his own behavior (if applicable) and for being willing to look at his rating for the day. Even on a bad day, if the student has been

accurate in his self-evaluation, praise him. "Damean, you are really handling this responsibly. Even though it was a rough day, you were honest in your evaluation of your behavior and you are willing to talk to me about things you might do differently tomorrow. That is a real sign that you are growing up."

Regardless of how the day went, try to make the meeting upbeat and encouraging—you want the student to look forward to the review at the end of the day.

 4. **Encourage the student to use self-reinforcement.**

Whenever things are going well (i.e., less dawdling than usual), prompt the student to mentally reinforce himself. "Damean, this has been a very successful morning. Silently tell yourself that you are being really efficient." Encourage this sort of self-reinforcement intermittently throughout the day and during the end-of-the-day review meetings.

PLAN E

Some students are quite capable of being more efficient, but simply choose to dawdle. If your student's dawdling has become habitual and/or he does not seem to have a desire to reduce it, you may need to implement a system of external incentives (i.e., rewards and consequences) based on his behavior to motivate him to stop dawdling and to start being more efficient.

1. **Implement a system to have the student periodically self-evaluate his behavior (see PLAN D).**

2. **Establish a structured system for reinforcing the appropriate behavior and providing a consequence for the inappropriate behavior.**

a. With the student, create a list of reinforcers that he can earn. Although you might want to have some suggestions in mind, the system will be more effective if the student identifies most of the items or activities himself. (NOTE: A list of reinforcement ideas can be found in APPENDIX 1.)

b. Assign a "price" (in points) for each of the reinforcers on the list, and have the student select the one he would like to earn first.

The prices should be based on the number of points the student can earn and the cost—instructional, personnel, and/or monetary—of the items. Monetary cost is clear—the more expen-

sive the item, the more points required to earn it. Instructional cost refers to the amount of instructional time lost or interfered with by a particular reward. Thus, an activity that causes the student to miss academic instruction would require more points than one the student can do on his own recess time. Personnel cost involves the time required by you and/or other staff to fulfill the reinforcer. Having lunch with the principal, therefore, would cost more points than spending five minutes of free time with a friend.

A young and/or immature student may need more immediate and/or frequent reinforcement. In this case, it might be more effective to let the student earn several "less expensive" reinforcers (e.g., five minutes of free computer time after 20 points) on the way to a bigger reward (e.g., one hour with you for 200 points). That is, the student receives the small rewards without spending points; they continue to accumulate toward the selected reward.

c. Decide how the self-evaluation ratings will be translated into points that can be used to earn the reward. For example, each of the positive ratings could be given a point value. For example, in the sample form shown, each rating of "Okay" would equal one point; "Mostly Efficient," two points; and "Extremely Efficient," four points.

d. At the end of each day, determine the total points for that day and add them to the points the student has earned on previous days. When the student has accumulated enough points to earn the reinforcer, he "spends" the necessary points and the system begins again. That is, he begins with zero points and he selects another reinforcer to earn.

e. Determine a consequence (e.g., time owed off of recess or in after-school detention) for each of the negative ratings on the evaluation form. For example, "Dawdling a Lot" would result in the student owing two minutes off of recess, while "Dawdling Somewhat" would result in one minute owed. (NOTE: For the first week or two, "Dawdling Somewhat" could be worth zero points rather than the consequence of time owed in order to give the student a bit of leeway while learning the system.)

The consequence should not involve taking away points previously earned. If the student can lose already-earned points, he might develop an attitude of, "I am losing so many points, why should I even bother to try?"

f. If the student has a history of dawdling for inordinately long periods of time, also identify a consequence for any dawdling that lasts a long time. In this case, you should plan on timing each of the student's dawdling incidents (e.g., the difference in number of minutes between when you give a gentle correction and when the student stops dawdling). Then you can document how many minutes the student spends dawdling each day and have him owe that many minutes off of the next recess or after school in addition to the minutes owed from the "Self-Evaluation Form."

When you use this procedure, establish a way for the student to indicate to you that he is done dawdling and ready to resume meeting the classroom expectations. This lessens the possibility that you will begin timing the behavior, then get busy with other students and not notice that he has stopped dawdling.

3. *Use reinforcement to encourage appropriate behavior.*

a. Give the student increased praise and attention for being efficient (see PLAN A).

b. In addition, show interest and enthusiasm about how the student is doing on the system. "Damean, we are half way through the day and you have already earned ten points. You should be proud of how efficient you are being."

Self-Evaluation Form

Name _____ Date _____

Directions:

Rate how efficient you were during the following times. Put a check (✓) in the most appropriate box.

	Dawdling a Lot (2 min. owed)	Dawdling Somewhat (1 min. owed)	Okay (1 pt.)	Mostly Efficient (2 pts.)	Extremely Efficient (4 pts.)
(Activity 1)					
(Activity 2)					
(Activity 3)					
(Activity 4)					
(Activity 5)					

· · · · · · · ·
Suggested Steps for Developing and Implementing a Plan

The following steps are designed to help you develop an appropriate intervention plan and implement it effectively, whether you choose to use one of the MODEL PLANS or create a customized plan of your own. The steps are, however, suggestions—they are not intended to be followed rigidly or in any particular order. Use your professional judgment and the knowledge of your particular situation to make them work for you.

1. **Make sure you have enough information about the situation.**

a. If you think a minimal intervention like PLAN A will be sufficient, you probably already have enough information to proceed. However when a more involved plan seems necessary, you should consider collecting descriptive and/or objective information for a couple of days so you can thoroughly describe the problem behavior and monitor any changes in the situation.

b. Details on actual incidents in the form of anecdotal notes can be particularly useful for explaining the situation to the student and his parent(s). To collect anecdotal notes, simply keep a card in your pocket or on a clipboard and occasionally make notes on incidents of the student's dawdling.

For each entry, include a brief description of the setting (where and when the dawdling occurred), what the student said or did, and any other relevant observations you may have (e.g., what prompted the behavior). It is not necessary to take notes every time the student dawdles; the idea is to capture a range of examples of the behavior so you will be able to describe it completely.

You should also make notes on times when the student was efficient; this will help him realize that you are not only aware of his inappropriate behavior, but also when he behaves appropriately. In addition, when you meet with the student these examples will help you clarify how you want the student to behave.

c. In addition to this information on what the student's dawdling looks like, it can also be useful to quantify how often it occurs and/or how much time it involves. Both measurements provide more objective information about the problem and an objective way to monitor the student's progress. The easiest thing to do is to record how often the dawdling occurs (i.e., a frequency count). On the same card on which you are collecting anecdotal notes, simply write a tally mark each time the student dawdles.

Coding the tallies will allow you to discern whether the behavior occurs more frequently during certain times, subjects, or activities (e.g., in the morning or afternoon, during math or reading, during teacher directed instruction or independent work, etc.).

If you are concerned about how much time the student spends dawdling, you may wish to also (or instead of the frequency count) document how many minutes the student dawdles (i.e., duration time). To do this, each time the student dawdles, mentally note the time when the majority of the students are ready and the time when the target student is finally on task. Record the difference (in number of minutes) next to or in place of the tally mark. Then at the end of the day you will be able to calculate the total number of minutes spent dawdling.

d. If the student notices what you are doing and asks about it, be straightforward—tell him that you are collecting information to see whether his dawdling is a problem that needs to be worked on.

The following example shows anecdotal notes, a frequency count, and duration time information that has been collected on a student's dawdling.

e. It is fairly easy to summarize frequency and/or duration information on a chart or graph. Seeing how often and/or how much time he spends dawdling may help the student and his parent(s) understand your concern.

If you collect both frequency and duration information, chart them separately as one may improve faster than the other. For example, the number of times the student dawdles may stay about the same, while the number of minutes spent dawdling decreases dramatically. The distinction could be important when deciding whether the situation is improving, remaining the same, or worsening.

Damean's Dawdling—4/26

8:00—Entering the classroom—Damean entered before the bell but was slow to hang up his coat and get to his desk (4 minutes).

8:15—Getting ready for spelling (3 minutes).

8:45—Getting out journals and beginning to write (5 minutes).

9:30—Putting things away and lining up for the Computer Room—The whole class was kept waiting while he slowly put away his books, then looked for his pencil, then put away another book, then get out his notebook. Other students were nagging him to hurry. I could not leave him alone nor send the rest of the class unescorted (3 minutes).

10:30—In from recess (6 minutes).

11:15—Math, putting things away (2 minutes).

 Identify a focus for the intervention and labels for referring to the appropriate and inappropriate behaviors.

a. To be effective, the intervention must address more than just reducing the student's dawdling—there must be a concurrent emphasis on increasing some positive behavior or trait (e.g., being efficient, being more organized). Not only will having a specific positive behavior in mind make it easier for you to "catch" and reinforce the student for behaving appropriately, but a positive focus will allow you to frame the situation more productively.

For example, if you simply say that "the student has a problem with dawdling," you offer little in the way of useful information, and may put the student and his parent(s) on the defensive. However, if you explain your concern by saying that you want to "help the student learn to be more efficient," you present an important, and reasonable, goal for the student to work toward and clearly identify what the student needs to do to be successful.

b. Identifying labels for the appropriate and inappropriate behaviors (e.g., "being efficient" and "dawdling," respectively) will help you use consistent vocabulary when discussing the situation with the student. If you sometimes refer to the inappropriate behavior as "dawdling" and other times tell the student that he "is wasting time," for example, he may not realize that you are talking about the same thing.

 Determine when and how to include the parent(s).

a. You probably do not need to contact the student's parent(s) if the problem has just begun and is not interfering with the student's academic or social progress. You might, however, take advantage of any scheduled activities (e.g., conferences, weekly notes home) to let the parent(s) know of your concern.

b. The parent(s) should be contacted whenever the student's dawdling is affecting his academic performance or is alienating him from his peers. Share any information you have collected about the behavior (i.e., anecdotal notes, frequency count, duration time), and explain why you are concerned. Focus in particular on how the student's dawdling is hindering him academically and/or socially (e.g., the other students are becoming frustrated at having to always wait for him, and are beginning to resent the student).

You might ask if the parent(s) have any insight into the problem and/or whether they have noticed similar behavior at home. Whether or not the parent(s) perceive a problem, invite them to join you for an initial meeting with the student to develop a plan to help the student "learn to be more efficient." If the parent(s) are unable or unwilling to participate, let them know that you will keep them informed of the student's progress.

c. Once the parent(s) have been involved in any way, you should give them updates at least once per week while the plan is being implemented.

 Prepare for, then conduct, an initial meeting about the situation.

a. Arrange for a meeting to discuss your concerns with the student and anyone else who will be involved in the plan (e.g., the parent[s]). Although the specifics of the meeting will vary depending upon the age of the student and the severity of the problem, there are some general guidelines to consider when scheduling the meeting.

First, meet at a neutral time (i.e., not immediately after a problem has occurred) when emotions are less likely to hamper communication. In general, a day's notice is appropriate, however a primary age student may worry excessively and/or forget what the meeting is about if it is scheduled more than an hour before it takes place.

Second, make the meeting appropriately private. For example, if a primary student has a mild problem, you might meet in the classroom while the other students are working independently. However, if you are dealing with a middle/junior high school student and the student's parent(s), you will want to meet in a private room (e.g., the counselor's office) to ensure that the discussion will not be overheard.

Third, try to make sure the meeting is scheduled for a time and place that it is not likely to be interrupted. Finally, whenever the parent(s) will be participating, they should be the ones to tell the student about the meeting.

b. Construct a preliminary plan. Based on the information you have collected and the focus for the intervention that you have identified, you may decide to use one of the MODEL PLANS or you might choose to create a customized plan using components from various plans and/or of your own design.

Although you will invite and encourage the student to be an active partner in developing the plan during the meeting, having a proposed plan in mind before you meet can alleviate frustration and wasted time if the student is unwilling or unable to participate.

c. Using the information you have collected, prepare thorough descriptions of the inappropriate behavior and the positive behavior/trait on which the student will be working. Be as specific as you can and add concrete examples whenever possible. Doing so this will make it easier for you to clarify (and for the student to understand) the expectations. Be sure to identify appropriate and inappropriate behaviors in all relevant activities (e.g., independent work, teacher directed instruction, unstructured class times, recess and lunch, etc.).

d. Conduct the meeting in an atmosphere of collaboration. The following agenda is one way you might structure the meeting:

- **Share your concerns about the student's behavior.**

  Briefly describe the problem behavior and, if applicable, show him the chart(s) of how often/how much time he spends dawdling. Then explain why you consider the dawdling to be a problem. You might tell the student that his dawdling slows things down in the classroom and that it is affecting how others feel about him.

- **Discuss how you can work together to improve the situation.**

  Explain that you would like to help the student "learn to be more efficient," and describe your preliminary plan. Invite the student to give you input on the plan and together work out any necessary details (e.g., the monitoring system, reinforcers, consequences). You may have to brainstorm different possibilities if the student is uncomfortable with any aspects of the initial plan. Incorporating any of the student's suggestions that strengthen the plan is likely to increase his sense of "ownership" in and commitment to it.

- **Make sure the student understands what you mean by appropriate and inappropriate behavior.**

  Use the definitions you have prepared to explain and clarify the problem behavior and the positive (desired) behavior as specifically and thoroughly as you can. To ensure that you and the student are in agreement about the expectations, you might present several hypothetical scenarios and have him identify whether each is an example of being efficient or dawdling. Or you might describe an actual situation that has occurred and ask him to explain how he could be more efficient in that situation.

- **Conclude the meeting.**

  Always end the meeting with words of encouragement. Let the student know that you are confident that he can be successful, and that he may actually find that he likes school more when he is being efficient. Be sure to reinforce him for participating in the meeting.

5. *Give the student regular, ongoing feedback about his behavior.*

It is important to meet with the student periodically to discuss his progress. Unless the plan calls for daily meetings (e.g., PLANS D and E), a three to five minute meeting once per week should suffice. During the meetings, review any information that has been collected and discuss whether or not the situation is improving. As much as possible, focus on the student's improvements, however, also address any new or continuing problems. As the situation improves, the meetings can be faded to once every other week and then to once per month.

6. Evaluate the situation (and the plan).

Implement any plan for at least two weeks before deciding whether to change plans; to continue, modify, or fade the plan you are using; or to cease the intervention. Generally, if the student's behavior is clearly improving (based on the objective information that's been collected and/or the sub- jective perceptions of yourself, the student, and possibly the parent[s]), stick with what you are doing. If the situation has remained the same or worsened, some kind of change will be necessary. Any changes in the plan should be discussed with the student first.

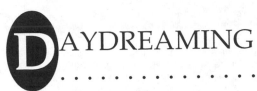

DAYDREAMING

Not Paying Attention

DESCRIPTION

You have a student who has trouble paying attention/ listening—her mind seems to wander instead of being focused on teacher presentations.

Although there are no MODEL PLANS included with this problem, the following information presents some considerations to help you determine whether the student's daydreaming behavior might either have a physiological cause or be the result of a skill deficit.

Alternative Problems

- **Compliance/Direction Following, Lack of**

- **Distractibility/Short Attention Span**

- **Participation In Class, Lack of**

· · · · · · · ·
General Considerations

- Because there are a variety of possible contributing factors to this problem, the student's parent(s) should be contacted immediately. Inform them of your concern and make them aware of the steps you are taking to investigate the nature of their child's problem. Work with the parent(s) during both the information-gathering process and when (if) an intervention plan is developed.

- If the student's hearing has not been recently evaluated, arrange for a hearing screening. If hearing impairment is a possibility, coordinate any intervention plan with a qualified professional who has experience working with children who have hearing impairments.

- If you believe the daydreaming may stem in any way from academic issues (e.g., academic expectations are beyond the student's abilities so she daydreams—when she tries to listen, it is "all Greek" to her), concurrent efforts must be made to ensure her academic success (see **Academic Deficits, Determining**).

- If you suspect that the student's daydreaming could be related to the student being depressed, see **Depression**. That problem includes a set of questions to help you decide whether the student should be referred for counseling or psychological services.

- If you have any reason to suspect a neurological basis for the student's behavior (e.g., the student cannot keep her attention focused even on tasks and activities she truly enjoys) or that the student's behavior could be a symptom of drug use, consult with your building administrator and/or school psychologist for advice on building/district procedures for following up on either type of situation.

- If the student's cultural background could be a factor in the behavior, do not intervene until you have checked the appropriateness of any intervention plan and its goals with someone who can give you accurate information on any relevant cultural issues (i.e., someone who is from that culture or has worked with people from that culture).

For example, you believe the student is not listening because she does not make eye contact with you when you are talking to the class. However, in some cultures, failure to make eye contact is a sign of respect. If the behavior is not interfering with the student's academic or social success, it may be both unnecessary and inappropriate to intervene if cultural factors are present.

· · · · · · · ·
Intervention Steps

One important subskill for listening and paying attention is the ability to keep spoken messages in one's short-term memory long enough that the information can be processed. A student who cannot hear and immediately repeat back a statement may lack this important subskill. To determine whether the student has the necessary prelistening skills, implement the following procedures.

 Ask the student to repeat statements.

First have the student repeat back simple statements to see whether she is able to engage in statement repetition. Tell the student that you are going to say something and that you want her to repeat it back exactly the way you say it. Make a statement and ask the student to repeat it. *(Do not let the student see any printed words.)* Begin with very short statements and proceed to longer and longer statements. Continue to progress in dif-

ficulty until the student makes an error on three consecutive statements. *(NOTE: The content is not the important issue—you are mainly interested in the number of words the student is able to repeat back.)*

Following are samples of 2-14 word statements that you might use. As an example, if the student made an error on Items 7, 8, and 9, you would say that she was able to successfully repeat back a seven-word sentence:

1. Go home.

2. She is tall.

3. The book is open.

4. Eight girls stayed after school.

5. Twelve boys arrived at school early.

6. A large plate fell off the table.

7. Follow the boy who is wearing black pants.

8. The girl began working with the computer this morning.

9. The heavy snow broke many branches from the fir tree.

10. October 17 is the day of the environmental clean up project.

11. Meteorologists study weather patterns to help predict the weather in the future.

12. In the United States, people get to vote to determine their congressional representatives.

13. Two large polar bears came from the glacier into the town of Barrow, Alaska.

 Ask the student comprehension questions.

Next, determine whether the student can answer simple comprehension questions. To do so, go back to the longest statement that the student successfully repeated. Present that statement again, have the student repeat the statement, and then ask a few basic comprehension questions (e.g., questions related to Item 6 could include "What fell? What did it fall off of? What size was it?"). This will help you determine if the student can retain the information long enough to use the information to answer the questions.

Conduct comparison diagnostic tests with other students.

For a point of comparison, conduct this same diagnostic procedure with two other students you believe to have average listening abilities. If the target student's performance on one or both of the two tasks is significantly lower than the other two students', discuss the situation with a district speech and language specialist. For example, if the target student is only able to successfully repeat a three word statement, while the other students can repeat a 12 word statement, it would be a good idea to include a specialist in the intervention design.

EPRESSION

DESCRIPTION

You have a student who is "acting depressed" (i.e., he is unusually sad and/or withdrawn).

Because "acting depressed" is not a discrete behavior, but a label that encompasses a variety of behaviors, and because these behaviors may represent a serious medical/psychological condition (which is beyond the scope of this reference guide and the authors' expertise), there are no MODEL PLANS included with this problem. The purpose of the following information is to suggest some basic procedures and considerations for assisting a student who "acts depressed."

Alternative Problems

- **Bored Behavior**
- **Crying, Chronic**
- **School Phobia**
- **Self-Concept Problems**
- **Shyness/Withdrawn Behavior**
- **Social Skills, Lack of**
- **Suicide Threats**

....
General Information

- When a student is "acting depressed," it is important not to minimize the possible seriousness of the situation. Some people mistakenly think that children and teenagers cannot actually be depressed. This is a myth—it is entirely possible that your student is experiencing severe depression. You do need to be careful, however, when you discuss your concerns with the student and/or his parent(s). You should not label the student as "depressed" (as such a diagnosis requires a trained mental health professional) or imply that the student should be examined by a psychologist or psychiatrist. Made in the wrong way, such a suggestion could result in the school district having to pay for an evaluation (and possibly subsequent treatment).

- Document the student's behavior using anecdotal notes. For about a week, keep a card in your pocket or on a clipboard, and record information on all instances in which the student behaves in a way that seems to suggest depression. Describe the circumstances of each instance briefly but thoroughly. That is, include where and when the incident took place, who else was involved, what the student said or did, or how he acted. The following example illustrates three sample entries.

5/22—Jed was mopey all day in class. He did not interact with anyone unless he was asked to participate.

5/23—Checked with the playground supervisors and they said that Jed just wanders around by himself during recess.

5/23—Jed responded to my compliment of his drawing by saying, "I hate my picture, it is boring just like everything else."

- Talk privately to the student to see if he is willing/able to tell you whether there is something specific bothering him. (You may want to share with him some of the information from your anecdotal notes.) You don't want to put the student on the spot or exacerbate the situation, however, if there is something specific that is bothering him, you want him to know that you might be able to help him yourself or refer him to someone else who might be able to help him with his concern.

- You should also consider whether the student may be depressed because he is continually asked to do things he cannot do. If this is the case, your attempts to deal with the depression will not be effective unless concurrent efforts are made to increase the student's academic success (see **Academic Deficits, Determining** for additional suggestions).

- You may wish to consider the possibility of clinical depression. The following checklist (reprinted with permission) may be useful in this regard. Read through the information and note any symptoms that apply to your student. If there seems to be a strong possibility that the student could be clinically depressed, immediately discuss the situation with your building administrator, school counselor, and/or school psychologist.

Is Your Child or Adolescent Depressed?
by Norman E. Alessi

One of the most frequent questions I'm asked is, "How can I tell if my student or child is depressed?" The following checklist is an attempt to provide a method by which you might determine if a youth is depressed. The first step in helping those with depression is its identification. The following is a checklist of general symptoms. If four or more symptoms are evident, the need for a professional assessment exists.

Difficulties they may experience:
- Expressed sadness or "emptiness."
- Expressed hopelessness or pessimism.
- Expressed unnecessary "guilt."
- Expressed worthlessness.
- Unable to make decisions.
- Loss of interest or pleasure in ordinary activities.
- Increased boredom.

Physical complaints:
- Complains of loss of energy—seems slowed down.
- Trouble going to sleep, staying asleep, or getting up.

(continued)

Is Your Child or Adolescent Depressed? (cont'd)

- Appetite problems—losing or gaining weight.
- Headaches, stomachaches, or back-aches.
- Chronic aches and pains.

Difficulties in school:

- More than usual problems with school-work, as well as difficulties at home.
- Unable to concentrate or remember.
- Wants to be alone.
- Avoiding social contact with friends.
- Cutting classes.

Dropping hobbies and other activities:

- Expression of irritability.
- Increased shouting and screaming.
- Increased intolerance of everyday events that would have been seen as nothing.
- Talked about death. Talked about suicide or attempted suicide.
- May be drinking or taking drugs.

Reprinted with permission from Alessi, N.E. (1993). Is your child or adolescent de-

---

- Contact the student's parent(s). Whenever you believe a student may be experiencing depression, that student's parent(s) should be contacted immediately. Let the parent(s) know that you are concerned because the student seems to be particularly "sad" or "withdrawn." *(NOTE: Do not use the term "depressed," as clinical depression is a condition that requires diagnosis by a trained mental health professional.)* Share with them any information you have collected (i.e., from your anecdotal notes or conversation with the student), and ask the parent(s) whether they have noticed similar behavior at home and/or are aware of anything specific that might

be troubling the student. You may, in fact, wish to suggest that the parent(s) review the Alessi checklist as well.

If the parent(s) identify a particular reason for the student's behavior (e.g., a death in the family), ask them what you might do to support the student while he is at school. Depression that arises from specific circumstances may simply require waiting and watching. If the student's behavior evens out after a few weeks, further action is probably unnecessary.

However, if the parent(s) know of nothing that could be causing the depressed behavior and/or the situation continues for more than a couple of weeks, ask the parent(s) to join you and the school counselor/psychologist for a conference.

- Whether or not the student is experiencing clinical depression, make sure he knows that he is a valued member of the school community and that adults are available to assist him. Try to increase your levels of praise of the student (both in terms of frequency and range of activities) and the amount of positive attention you give him (e.g., make a point of greeting the student when he enters the classroom, actively involve the student in class activities and discussions). In addition, let the student know where and when he can talk to you, the school counselor, and/or anyone else who might be available if he needs or wants assistance.

- For more information on depression, see:

Alessi, N.E. (Ed.). (1993). Depression in children and youth [Special Issue]. *Journal of Emotional and Behavioral Problems, 2*(2).

Walker, H.M. & Severson, H.H. (1990). *Systematic screening for behavior disorders (SSBD).* Longmont, CO: Sopris West. (This reference provides information on school-wide screening for early identification of students who are at risk of a variety of problems, including depression.)

DISRESPECTFUL BEHAVIOR

. . . .

DESCRIPTION

There is a student in your class who is overtly disrespectful to you and/or other adults.

GOAL

The student will treat all adults with respect.

OVERVIEW OF PLANS

- PLAN A: For a situation in which the problem is relatively infrequent or has just begun.

- PLAN B: For a student who is disrespectful to gain adult attention (i.e., engage adults in one-to-one interactions).

- PLAN C: For a student who behaves disrespectfully to demonstrate her personal power and/or to gain status with her peers.

- PLAN D: For a student whose disrespectful behavior has become habitual.

- PLAN E: For a situation in which several students in the class are disrespectful to you and/or other adults.

Alternative Problems

- **Arguing—Student(s) With the Teacher**

- **Complaining**

- **Compliance/Direction Following, Lack of**

- **Rude/Impolite Behavior**

- **Smart-Aleck Behavior/Inappropriate Humor**

General Considerations

- If the student's problem behavior stems in any way from academic issues (e.g., the student is experiencing academic failure and behaves disrespectfully to look "tough," rather than "stupid," in front of her peers), concurrent efforts must be made to ensure her academic success (see **Academic Deficits, Determining**).

- If the student lacks the basic social skills to interact with her peers and adults appropriately,

it may be necessary to begin by teaching her those skills. **Social Skills, Lack of** contains information on a variety of published social skills curricula.

- If the student's disrespectful behavior often takes the form or refusing to comply with instructions, **Compliance/Direction Following, Lack of** has plans that may be more appropriate.

Model Plans

PLAN A

It is not always necessary, or even beneficial, to use an involved plan. If the disrespectful behavior has just begun and/or occurs relatively infrequently (e.g., less than one in ten of the student's interactions with you could be considered disrespectful), the following actions, along with making the student aware of your concerns, may resolve the situation.

1. Respond consistently to the inappropriate behavior.

a. Use a gentle verbal correction to let the student know that what she did was disrespectful, and provide information about what she should do differently. "Lupe, that was not respectful. A more respectful way to let me know that you disagree would be to say something like, 'I think . . . .'" Because your goal is to impart information, you want to be emotionally neutral while giving the correction.

b. If gentle corrections do not seem sufficient, establish a consequence for being disrespectful (see PLAN B) and give the student plenty of warnings (i.e., for several days) before implementing the consequence. "Lupe, that was disrespectful, and beginning next Monday there will be consequences for making that choice."

2. Use reinforcement to encourage appropriate behavior.

a. Give the student increased praise. Be especially alert for situations in which the student interacts with you appropriately and praise her for these demonstrations of her ability to be

respectful. "Lupe, talking to me like you just did is a great example of respect." If the student would be embarrassed by public praise, praise the student privately or even give the student a note.

Remember that any time the student is not being disrespectful, you can praise her for being respectful: "Lupe, the way you listened quietly while I was giving directions to the class was very respectful," or "Lupe, when you state your opinion in such a respectful way, it makes me want to think about what you are saying."

b. Give the student frequent attention (e.g., say "hello" to her as she enters the classroom, call on her frequently during class activities, and occasionally ask her to assist you with a class job that needs to be done) and praise her for other positive behaviors she exhibits. For example, you might comment about the overall quality of her work or mention that you noticed the effort she gave to making maps for a report. This demonstrates to the student that you notice many positive things she does, not just the fact that she is refraining from being disrespectful.

PLAN B

Some students are very skilled at gaining attention through their negative behavior. If you find yourself frequently nagging, reminding, coaxing, or scolding the student when she is being disrespectful, it is possible that her motivation is to gain adult attention. Whether or not the student overtly seems to like the attention, you need to make sure that she receives more frequent and more satisfying attention for behaving appropriately than for being disrespectful.

1. Respond consistently to the inappropriate behavior.

a. Define the borderline between respectful and disrespectful interactions. One of the most difficult aspects of addressing this misbehavior is consistency. To be consistent, the borderline must be clearly defined. However, what is respectful and what is disrespectful is often unclear because there are several different aspects of an interaction that could make it either respectful or disrespectful, such as:

- What the student says;

- Tone of voice used;

- Volume level;

- Body language;

- Whether an instruction was complied with; and

- Whether an instruction was complied with in a reasonable amount of time.

Usually the most efficient and clear way to define the borderline is to identify common classroom situations and then generate examples of being both respectful and disrespectful in those situations. You might want to use the following examples as a basis for defining the borderline between respect and disrespect with your student.

b. Once enough examples have been generated, establish a consequence to be used for any and all of the unacceptable examples (or other disrespectful behavior). One particularly effective consequence is time owed. At the elementary level, the student might owe one minute off of recess for each disrespectful interaction. With a middle/junior high school student, the first and second infractions may result in 30 seconds owed after class, and each subsequent infraction would result in ten minutes of detention. When paying back the time owed, the student must sit and do nothing.

c. Do not set the fine for disrespect too high. For example, if the student is supposed to lose a recess for each disrespectful act, you have a problem if the student is disrespectful 15 times in one day. Furthermore, having too high a cost will make the consequence too severe for minor disrespectful acts. On the other hand, with a consequence like one minute owed off of recess, you are more likely to be consistent in

SITUATION: **The teacher says, "Good morning. How are you, Lupe?"**	
Disrespectful Behavior	Respectful Behavior
• Lupe says in a mocking voice, "Good morning, teacher." • Lupe turns her back on the teacher. • Lupe compares Mrs. Pollack to a TV character, with sarcasm.	• Lupe responds in a friendly or neutral voice, "Good morning," or "Fine, how are you?" • Lupe responds with a smile or nod. • Lupe says sincerely, "I am having a really lousy morning."

SITUATION: **The teacher asks Lupe to take her seat at the beginning of the period.**	
Disrespectful Behavior	Respectful Behavior
• Lupe asks, "Why should I?" • Lupe mimics the teacher. • Lupe walks in exaggerated slow motion.	• Sitting down without comment. • Saying, "I'm sharpening my pencil. Is it okay if I finish?"

(continued)

. . . .
The Teacher's Encyclopedia of Behavior Management: 100 Problems/500 Plans

---

(cont'd)

SITUATION: **The teacher announces an assignment to the class.**

Disrespectful Behavior	Respectful Behavior
• Lupe mimics, "Do problems 1-10." • Lupe says, "That's a joke." • Lupe asks, "Why should I do it?" • Lupe calls Mrs. Pollack a name. • Lupe sulks.	• Lupe gets busy on the assignment without comment. • Lupe asks a question to clarify what she needs to do on the assignment.

---

responding to each and every disrespectful act. "Lupe, that was disrespectful and costs a minute off your next recess."

(NOTE: If you do not previously define the borderline between respect and disrespect, each time the student engages in a disrespectful act you must take the time to explain why her action was disrespectful. Clearly define for the student the borderline between respect and disrespect. Then each time the student is disrespectful, do not lecture or explain, simply state the misbehavior and the consequence.)

d. If the student begins to argue about the consequence, give an instruction and let the student know that she will owe as much time as it takes her to begin to carry out the instruction. Then ignore additional attempts on the part of the student to engage you in disrespectful interactions. "Lupe, you need to quietly take your seat. I will keep track of how much time it takes you to do so, and you will owe that time off of your next recess."

2. **Use reinforcement to encourage appropriate behavior.**

a. Frequent praise and attention is the core of this plan. The student must see that she receives more frequent and more satisfying attention when she behaves appropriately than when she is disrespectful. Thus, whenever the student is not being disrespectfully (or otherwise misbehaving), make an effort to praise and spend time with her. "Lupe, you have been so respectful to me in the last few days, I really enjoy spending time with you. Would you be able to help me arrange the room for my next class? I will write you a slip so you won't be counted as tardy to your next class."

b. You may also wish to use intermittent rewards to acknowledge the student's success. Occasional, and unexpected, rewards can motivate the student to demonstrate re-

spectful behavior more often. The idea is to provide a reward when the student has been respectful for a longer period of time than she has been before or at times/in places that have been problematic for her in the past.

Appropriate rewards might include writing the student a note about how her respectful behavior will be viewed by her employers later in life, giving the student free time in the computer lab, or asking the student to help a younger student learn about the importance of treating adults with respect. *(NOTE: A list of additional reinforcement ideas can be found in APPENDIX 1.)* Use intermittent rewards more frequently at the beginning of the intervention to encourage the student, and less often as her behavior improves.

3. **Ensure a 3-1 ratio of positive to negative attention.**

a. If attention is a motivating force for this student, you want to be sure that you are giving the student *three times as much* positive as negative attention. One way to do this is to monitor your interactions with the student at least one day per week. Simply keep a card on a clipboard or in your pocket and record each interaction you have with the student as either positive or negative by writing a "+" or a "-", respectively, on the card.

To determine whether an interaction is positive or negative, ask yourself whether the student was being disrespectful (or otherwise misbehaving) at the time the interaction occurred. Any interaction that stems from inappropriate behavior is negative, and all interactions that occur while the student is meeting classroom expectations are positive. Following are some examples of interactions, with an indication of how each would be counted.

b. If you find that you are not giving the student three times as much positive as negative attention, try to increase the number of positive inter-actions you have with the student. Sometimes prompts can help. For example, you might decide that each time the student enters the class-room you will say "hello" to her, or that twice each class period you will approach her while she is on task and positively comment about her work.

Interaction Between Teacher and Student:		How it is Counted:
Mrs. Pollack:	Lupe, you have some corrections to do on this math paper.	
Lupe:	Oh great. I was hoping you would make my day.	
Mrs. Pollack:	That was disrespectful. You owe one minute off of recess.	One Negative
Mrs. Pollack:	Lupe, your assignment was done accurately and completely.	One Positive
Mrs. Pollack:	Class, time to get ready to go, the period is about over.	
Lupe:	Is there a spelling test tomorrow?	
Mrs. Pollack:	"Lupe, good question. No, the spelling test is not until next Monday.	One Positive
Lupe:	I need some help on these study questions.	
Mrs. Pollack:	Lupe, I'd be glad to help, let's take a look.	One Positive
(Lupe is out of her seat bothering another student.)		
Mrs. Pollack:	Lupe, you need to take your seat.	
Lupe:	Take it where? To your mama's house?	
Mrs. Pollack:	Lupe, that was disrespectful. You owe a minute.	One Negative
Lupe:	That wasn't disrespectful. You're not fair. All I was doing was trying to	
Mrs. Pollack:	(nonaggressively interrupting the student) Lupe, you will also owe the time it takes you to get to your seat. Now class, the first thing we are going to do	One Negative
Mrs. Pollack:	Lupe, do you have any questions about what you need to do?	One Positive
Lupe:	No, I can get this done by the end of the period.	
Mrs. Pollack:	Okay, great. (Then privately) I appreciate how respectful you are being today.	One Positive

PLAN C

Sometimes a student is disrespectful toward adults as a way of demonstrating power and/or to impress her peers. If your student seems motivated by the reactions she receives from her peers, the intervention must include ways of reducing the power the student achieves through disrespectful interactions and methods for helping her learn to wield her power in appropriate ways.

1. *Respond consistently to the inappropriate behavior.*

a. Define the borderline between respectful and disrespectful interactions, and establish time owed as a consequence for each disrespectful interaction (see PLAN B).

b. Demonstrate that the student's disrespectful behavior has no power to influence you. If power is an issue, the student is probably skilled at "pushing adults' buttons" (i.e., making adults angry, flustered, or otherwise upset). Your goal should be to remain perfectly calm whenever the student is trying to make you upset.

If necessary, mentally rehearse interactions in which the student is trying to "push your buttons," and imagine yourself calmly and consistently stating the consequence and resuming instruction. Tell yourself that any time the student sees that she has the power to hurt you or make you angry through her disrespect, you have done the equivalent of paying her $50.00 for having been disrespectful.

2. *Acknowledge the student's power with her peers.*

a. During the initial meeting with the student (see SUGGESTED STEPS FOR DEVELOPING AND IMPLEMENTING A PLAN), let her know that you are aware that she has a great deal of influence over other students, and that you do not want to take that away from her. If appropriate, tell her that she is a natural leader. Explain that you do not expect her to become a "goody-goody" type of student, but that she can maintain her powerful image with her peers and still be respectful to you and other adults.

b. Use your anecdotal notes (see SUGGESTED STEPS FOR DEVELOPING AND IMPLE-MENTING A PLAN) to identify situations in which the student has been disrespectful, and help her identify different ways she could respond that would allow her to exert her personal power, while still being respectful toward you. The goal is to help the student to realize that win/win situations are better than power struggles between the two of you that may create win/lose situations.

c. Optionally, if the student is not well-liked by her peers and is trying to use disrespect to gain status, suggest a peer model. Encourage the student to watch another student in the class that she respects—a student who uses her personal power skillfully. Suggest that the student observe the way this peer model handles her power, while still being respectful to you. "Lupe, one thing I would like to encourage you to do is to watch Jodi. Do you think Jodi is a 'goody-goody' type of person? No, I don't either. And yet, she is consistently very respectful of me. For the next few days, any time Jodi is interacting with me, watch what she does. I think you might get some good ideas about how to treat me respectfully without having to feel embarrassed or like a teacher's pet."

Avoid implying, however, that the peer model is somehow a better or more worthwhile person than the target student. The idea is simply to communicate that the model student has a particular skill that would be worth observing.

3. *Invite the student to give you feedback about how you could treat her more respectfully.*

By giving the student the opportunity to tell you about any times she feels that you have not treated her with respect, you demonstrate your commitment to the idea that *everyone* needs to be treated with respect—including her. "Lupe, we have been talking about ways for you to treat me more respectfully. Now let's talk about ways I can treat *you* more respectfully. Can you think of things I can do differently? Does anything I do embarrass you?"

4. *Give the student a high status job or responsibility.*

a. One of the most effective ways to teach a student to wield her personal power wisely is to put her in a position of power within the school. Try to think of a job or responsibility that the student would enjoy and at which she would be proficient. For example, could the student tutor a younger student in math? work in the school's computer lab? be a library assistant? The best job will be one that happens regularly (e.g., daily, or twice per week) and one in which the student's "job supervisor" will be someone other than yourself. When a job is assigned, be sure the student is provided specific training and that all expectations are defined clearly in the beginning.

b. If the student is assigned a job, she should be allowed to do the job regardless of how respectful or disrespectful she has been in the classroom. Just as you are expected to go to your job each day regardless of how well you are getting along with your spouse, the student should be expected to do her job each day (or whenever scheduled). If the job is made contingent upon her being respectful, it may become just another power issue. The student is likely to think, for example, "You can't make me be respectful by threatening that I will not get to tutor."

5. Use reinforcement to encourage appropriate behavior.

a. Give the student frequent praise and attention for being respectful (see PLAN A).

b. Ask the student for input on how to praise her without embarrassing her. One idea is to determine an acceptable signal that allows you to unobtrusively recognize her respectful behav-

ior. For example, you and the student may decide that when she behaves respectfully, you will say her name, pause, give a slight head nod, and then say something unrelated to the issue of respect.

If the student comes into class before the bell rings and says something respectful, for example, you could say, "Lupe, (pause and head nod) how did you do in the gymnastics meet last night?" It is also important to find private opportunities occasionally to specifically praise the student for behaving more respectfully.

PLAN D

Whenever a student's problem behavior has become habitual and/or she does not seem to have a desire to reduce it, you may need to implement a system of external incentives (i.e., rewards and consequences) based on her behavior to motivate her to stop being disrespectful and to start being more respectful to adults.

1. Respond consistently to the inappropriate behavior.

a. Define the borderline between respectful and disrespectful interactions, and establish time owed as a consequence for each disrespectful interaction (see PLAN A).

b. Meet with the student each day to chart the number of minutes the student was fined that day. (This is the total of the number of times the student was disrespectful, plus the number of minutes the student took to comply with instructions.)

2. Establish a structured system for reinforcing the reduction of disrespectful behavior.

a. With the student, create a list of reinforcers that she can earn. Although you might want to have some suggestions in mind, the system will be more effective if the student identifies most of the items or activities herself. (NOTE: A list of reinforcement ideas can be found in APPENDIX 1.)

b. Assign "prices" (in points) for each of the rewards on the list and have the student select the reward that she would like to earn first.

The prices should be based on the instructional, personnel, and/or monetary costs of the items. Monetary cost is clear—the more expensive the item, the more points required to earn it. Instructional cost refers to the amount of instructional time lost or interfered with by a particular re-

ward. Thus, an activity which causes the student to miss part of academic instruction should require more points than one the student can do on her own free time. Personnel cost involves the time required by you and/or other staff to fulfill the reinforcer. Having lunch with the principal, therefore, would cost more points than spending five minutes of free time with a friend.

c. Have the student begin each day with a certain number of points. This number should equal the average number of minutes the student has owed per day, plus two. Thus, if the student has owed an average of 13 minutes per day, she would begin each day with 15 points.

Each time you assign the consequence of time owed (e.g., a minute), the student loses a point. The points remaining at the end of each day are added together to be applied toward the reinforcer the student is striving to earn.

(NOTE: A lottery system might be more effective with a primary level student. With this system, the student would begin each day with tickets in a jar instead of points. All the tickets would have prizes written on them—one with a big prize, a couple with moderate prizes, and the majority with small prizes. Each time the student is disrespectful, you would remove one ticket from the jar—but neither you nor the student would be allowed to see what is written on it. At the end of each day, the student would draw one ticket from those remaining in the jar, and receive that prize.)

d. When the student has accumulated enough points to earn the reward she has chosen, she "spends" the points necessary and the system begins again. That is, she selects another reward to earn and begins with zero points.

If the student is immature, and needs more frequent encouragement, you might consider letting her earn several "less expensive" rewards (e.g., five minutes of computer time after 20 points) on the way to a bigger reward (e.g., having a pizza lunch with a friend of choice and the principal). That is, the student receives the small rewards without spending points; they continue to accumulate toward the selected reward.

e. When all the student's points (or tickets) are gone, the student will still owe one minute for each subsequent incident of disrespectful behavior, but will not lose any additional points (or tickets). That is, if the student runs out of points, do not begin to take away the previous day's points. If the student can lose already-earned points, she might develop an attitude of, "I am losing so many points, why should I even bother to try?"

f. If the student is frequently losing points, meet with the student to further clarify the borderline between respectful and disrespectful interactions (see PLAN A). Use more examples of hypothetical situations and respectful and disrespectful ways the student could respond in those situations. Focus in particular on what the student could do that would be respectful. "Lupe, what could you do or say in that situation that would be more respectful?"

If the student cannot identify respectful ways to respond, prompt the student or suggest some ideas yourself. However, be careful that your suggestions not be viewed as silly to the student. The student needs ideas that would be respectful, but still socially acceptable to her peer group.

3. *Use reinforcement to encourage appropriate behavior.*

a. Give the student frequent praise and attention for being respectful (see PLAN A).

b. In addition, show interest and enthusiasm about how the student is doing on the system. "Lupe, you have been doing such a nice job of remembering to be respectful, you have not lost any points all morning. As a special thank you from me, I am adding three bonus points to those that you have saved, plus however many you have left at the end of today."

4. *Use precorrections when you think the student has a high probability of being disrespectful.*

Prior to an interaction that may become disrespectful, giving the student advance notice may allow her time to think about how to respond respectfully. "Lupe, I need to point out some errors in your social studies assignment, but before I show you what they are, think carefully about how you will respond. I am hopeful that you will be respectful of me as I show you some things you need to fix. Are you ready?"

PLAN E

Sometimes an entire class of students will fall into a pattern of being disrespectful. Occasionally, the students are not even aware of how frequently they are being disrespectful. In other cases, they may be indirectly encouraging each other to be disrespectful (e.g., a few influential students look "cool" or "tough" when they are disrespectful, and other students try to emulate them to be popular). The intervention should involve increasing the students' awareness of when and how often they are being disrespectful and, optionally, using a reinforcement system to create mild peer pressure to reduce the disrespect.

 Decide if your plan should focus only on disrespect to you, or if you will include disrespectful interactions between students as part of the system.

Although it will probably be easier to gain student cooperation if *all* disrespectful acts are included in the plan, you will have to work with the class to define the borderline between respectful and dis-

respectful interactions between students. (See PLAN B for information on defining this borderline.)

 Design a procedure to count and chart the frequency of disrespectful acts.

a. One way to monitor the frequency of disrespect is to write the name of any student who is disrespectful on a card you keep in your pocket or on a clipboard. This way you will obtain both a class-wide total and a record of how many times individual students are being disrespectful per day. You also could use a code to differentiate whether the disrespect was student-to-teacher or student-to-student (e.g., by writing a "T" or an "S," respectively, next to the student's name).

b. Each time there is a disrespectful interaction, write the responsible student's name on the card. At the end of each day, total the number of names and compare the count to that of previous days. Use this information to make a chart on an overhead transparency to show to the class.

c. Each day, discuss with the class whether things are getting better, worse, or are about the same. If the situation is improving, have the students reflect on the climate of the classroom. Does it feel better? if so, how? if not, why not?

3. *Encourage the class to set a daily performance goal.*

You may need to help the students set a realistic goal, such as reducing the number of daily disrespectful acts from 20 to 15. The students may tend to set an overly ambitious goal, such as reducing the number of their disrespectful acts from 20 to zero per day. Let the class know that with a goal of 15, for example, they can always have less disrespectful interactions, but that they increase their chances of success by making the goal attainable. Then as the class consistently experiences success, the goal should become progressively lower until the disrespectful acts have been eliminated.

4. *Provide a way for the students to express honest concerns without them being considered disrespectful.*

For example, set up a class suggestion box. Inform the students that the suggestion box will be used to set agendas for weekly class meetings about improving the class. Any student who has a concern should be encouraged to write it down as a positive suggestion for change and put it in the box.

Also help the students generate alternative examples of how they can respectfully state an opinion or a request directly to you.

5. *Help the class identify an individual consequence that can be implemented whenever a student has more than a certain number of disrespectful acts.*

For example, once any individual student has more than two disrespectful acts in a day, a consequence would be imposed on that student for any subsequent incidents of disrespect. Possible consequences for the class to consider could include parental contact, time owed off of recess, in-class time-out, loss of a privilege, etc.

6. *(OPTIONAL)*
Establish a group reinforcement system.

a. If necessary, establish a group reinforcement system to motivate the students to reduce their number of disrespectful acts. On days when the class successfully keeps the number under an identified goal, they earn a point toward a reward that they, as a group, agreed to work toward. After earning the predetermined number of points, the class receives the reward.

b. If a class-wide system seems unlikely to be effective, you might consider a team competition and response cost lottery. In this type of system, the class is divided into four to six relatively equivalent teams (i.e., the students with the greatest tendency to be disrespectful are divided evenly amongst the teams). Each team begins the day with a certain number of tickets on which they write the name of their team. Whenever a student is disrespectful, that student's team loses a ticket. At the end of the day, all the teams put their remaining tickets in a hat for a drawing. The name of the team on the winning ticket receives the predetermined reward for that day.

c. While implementing either reinforcement system, keep student attention focused on how much more pleasant the classroom atmosphere is as the amount of disrespect is reduced. "Class, you earned your point for the day, but more importantly, you are all helping this class be a place that we all will enjoy. Our class is a place we can all be proud of."

• • • • • • • •
Suggested Steps for Developing and Implementing a Plan

The following steps are designed to help you develop an appropriate intervention plan and implement it effectively, whether you choose to use one of the MODEL PLANS or create a customized plan of their own. The steps are, however, suggestions—they are not intended to be followed rigidly or in any particular order. Use your professional judgment and the knowledge of your particular situation to make them work for you.

1. **Make sure you have enough information about the situation.**

a. If you think a minimal intervention like PLAN A will be sufficient, you may already have enough information to proceed. However, when a more involved plan seems necessary, you should consider collecting additional descriptive and/or objective information for a couple of days.

b. You need to be able to explain what you mean when you say that "the student is disrespectful." Anecdotal notes on actual incidents should provide enough detail to help you define the problem behavior clearly and completely. To collect anecdotal notes, simply keep a card in your pocket or on a clipboard and occasionally make notes on specific instances when the student does something you believe to be disrespectful.

For each entry, briefly describe where and when the disrespectful act occurred, what the student did or said, and any other relevant observations (e.g., what prompted the behavior). You do not need to take notes every time the student is disrespectful; the idea is to capture a range of examples so that you will be able to describe the behavior completely.

Also include some notes on times when the student interacts with you respectfully—this will make it clear that you are not only aware of her problem behavior, but also recognize when she behaves appropriately. When you meet with the student, the positive examples will also help you clarify how you want the student to behave.

c. In addition to information about what the student's inappropriate behavior looks like, it can also be useful to document how often it occurs (i.e., a frequency count). This information will provide both a more objective measure of the problem and an objective way to monitor student progress. You can use the same card on which you are making anecdotal notes to keep a frequency count—simply write a tally mark on the card each time the student is disrespectful.

You might also want to code these tallies to discern whether the behavior occurs more fre-quently during certain times, subjects, or activities (e.g., using an "A" or "P" to indicate that the incident happened in the morning or afternoon; or clustering the tallies by math or reading, teacher directed instruction or independent work, etc.).

d. If the student notices what you are doing and asks about it, be straightforward—tell her that you are collecting information to see whether her disrespect to you/adults is a problem that needs to be worked on.

Following is an example of anecdotal notes and a frequency count that have been collected on a student's disrespectful behavior. In this sample, the teacher wanted information about whether the student's disrespect occurred most frequently when she gave her a direction (D), asked her a question (?), or when simply interacting, such as greeting the student (I).

Lupe's Disrespect in Morning Block—9/16

Frequency:

D D D I ?   D ? D

Notes:

• I asked Lupe to please listen to my instructions and she responded by saying, "If you weren't so dull I would be able to."

• I asked the class if there were any questions. Lupe raised her hand and when I called on her, she asked me if I was Polish.

• There was noise in the hall, so I asked Lupe to close the door for me. She did a very exaggerated slow motion all the way to the door and back, then asked me, "Is there anything else I can do for you, oh Wise One?"

---

e. The frequency information is fairly easy to summarize on a chart or graph. Seeing how often she is disrespectful may help the student and her parent(s) better understand your concern.

f. Continuing to collect this type of information (and keeping the chart up-to-date) while you implement a plan will help you monitor whether the situation is getting worse, staying the same, or getting better.

2. Identify a focus for the intervention and labels for referring to the appropriate and inappropriate behaviors.

a. To be effective, the intervention must address more than just reducing the student's disrespectful acts—there must be a concurrent emphasis on increasing some positive behavior or trait (e.g., being respectful). Having a specific positive behavior in mind will make it easier for you to "catch" and reinforce the student for behaving appropriately, and the positive focus will help you to frame the situation more productively.

For example, if you simply say that "the student has a problem with disrespect," you don't really provide any useful information, and may put the student and her parent(s) on the defensive. However, when you explain that you want to help the student "learn to treat teachers (and later bosses) with respect," you are presenting an important, and reasonable, goal for the student to work toward and clearly identifying what the student needs to do to be successful.

b. Specifying labels for the appropriate and inappropriate behaviors (e.g., " respect" and "disrespect," respectively) will help you to use consistent vocabulary when discussing the situation with the student. For example, if you sometimes refer to the inappropriate behavior as "being rude" and other times tell the student that she "needs to stop being sarcastic toward you" she may not realize that you are talking about the same thing—the problem of being disrespectful.

3. Determine when and how to include the parent(s).

a. It is not necessary to contact the student's parent(s) if the problem has just begun and is not interfering with the student's academic or social progress. However, it might be a good idea to take advantage of any scheduled activities (e.g., conferences, weekly notes home) to let them know of your concern.

b. If the student is flagrantly disrespectful or exhibits disrespectful behavior consistently for more than a week, contact the student's parent(s) regarding the problem. Share with them any information you have collected about the behavior (e.g., anecdotal notes, frequency count), and explain why you are concerned. Focus in particular on how the behavior is hindering the student academically and/or socially (e.g., if the student treats other teachers the way she is treating you, she will eventually be kicked out of a class).

You might ask if the parent(s) have any insight into the situation and/or whether they have noticed similar behavior at home. Whether or not the parent(s) perceive a problem, explain that you want to help the student "learn to treat teachers with respect" and invite them to join you for an initial meeting with the student to develop a plan. If the parent(s) are unable or unwilling to participate, let them know that you will keep them informed of the student's progress.

(NOTE: If the parent[s] seem disrespectful or hostile toward you during this initial contact, invite your building principal or counselor to join you at the planning meeting with the student and her parent[s].)

c. Once the parent(s) have been involved in any way, you should give them updates at least once per week while the plan is being implemented.

4. Prepare for, then conduct, an initial meeting about the situation.

a. Arrange a meeting to discuss your concerns with the student and anyone else who will be involved in the plan (e.g., the parent[s], the building administrator). Although the specifics will vary depending upon the age of the student and the severity of the problem, there are some general guidelines to consider when scheduling the meeting.

First, meet at a neutral time (i.e., not immediately after a problem has occurred), when emotions are less likely to hamper communication. In general, a day's notice is appropriate, however a primary age student may worry excessively and/or forget what the meeting is about if it is scheduled more than an hour before it takes place.

Second, make the meeting appropriately private (e.g., the counselor's office) to ensure that the discussion will not be overheard. Third, try to make sure the meeting is scheduled for a time and place that it is not likely to be interrupted. Finally, if the parent(s) will be participating, they should be the ones to tell the student about the meeting.

b. Construct a preliminary plan. Decide whether you think you can use one of the MODEL PLANS or if you need to crate a customized plan using components from various plans and/or of your own design. Although you will invite and encourage the student to help develop the plan during the initial meeting, having a proposed plan in mind before you meet can alleviate frustration and wasted time if the student is unwilling or unable to participate.

c. After reviewing the information you have collected and thinking about how you want the student to behave, prepare thorough descriptions of the inappropriate behavior and the positive behavior/trait on which the student will be working. The more specific you can be and the more concrete examples you have, the easier it will be to clarify (and for the student to understand) your expectations. Be sure to consider the student's behavior in all relevant activities (e.g., independent work, teacher directed instruction, unstructured class times, recess and lunch, etc.).

d. Conduct the meeting in an atmosphere of collaboration. The following agenda is one way you might structure the meeting:

- **Share your concerns about the student's behavior.**

  Briefly describe the problem behavior and, when appropriate, show the student a chart of how often she engages in disrespectful acts. Then explain why you consider her disrespect to be a problem. You might tell the student how other teachers and future employers are likely to respond to these sorts of disrespectful acts. Communicate how, on most jobs, incidents like those in your anecdotal notes would result in the student being fired. Since school is, in part, preparation for the workplace, you want the student to learn to treat you with the same respect her employers will demand.

  Also find out from the student if she feels you treat her respectfully. If not, solicit suggestions on what you could do differently. Show respect for her opinions by making a commitment to incorporate any reasonable suggestions she has made into your future interactions with the student.

- **Discuss how you can work together to improve the situation.**

  Tell the student that you would like to help her learn to "treat teachers with respect," and describe your preliminary plan. Invite the student to give you input on the various aspects of the plan, and together work out any necessary details (e.g., use of time owed, a peer model, etc.). You may have to brainstorm different possibilities if the student is uncomfortable with the initial plan (this is especially critical if power is a major issue for the student). Incorporating any of the student's suggestions that strengthen the plan is likely to increase her sense of "ownership" in and commitment to it.

- **Make sure the student understands what you mean by appropriate and inappropriate behavior.**

  Use the descriptions you have prepared to define and clarify the difference between respect and disrespect as thoroughly as you can. To ensure that you and the student are in agreement about the expectations, you might present hypothetical scenarios and have the student identify whether each is an example of respect or disrespect. Or, you might describe an actual situation that has occurred and ask the student to explain how she could demonstrate respect in that situation.

- **Conclude the meeting.**

  Always end the meeting with words of encouragement. Let the student know that you are confident that she can be successful. Be sure to reinforce her for participating in the meeting.

5. *Give the student regular, ongoing feedback about her behavior.*

It is important to meet with the student periodically to discuss her progress. In most cases, three to five minutes once per week should suffice. *(NOTE: PLAN E suggests daily meetings.)* During the meetings, review any information that has been collected and discuss whether or not the situation is getting better. As much as possible, focus on the student's improvements, however, also address any new or continuing problems. As the situation improves, the meetings can be faded to once every other week and then to once per month.

6. *Evaluate the situation (and the plan).*

Implement any plan for at least two weeks before deciding whether to change plans; to continue, modify, or fade the plan you are using; or to cease the intervention. Generally, if the student's behavior is clearly improving (based on the objective information that's been collected and/or the sub-jective perceptions of yourself, the student, and possibly the parent[s]), stick with what you are doing. If the situation has remained the same or worsened, some kind of change will be necessary. Always discuss any changes to the plan with the student first.

DISRUPTIVE BEHAVIOR— MODERATE

DESCRIPTION

You have a student who engages in one or more types of disruptive behavior in the classroom.

GOAL

The student will reduce and eventually eliminate his disruptive behavior.

OVERVIEW OF PLANS

- PLAN A: For a situation in which the problem has just begun or occurs infrequently.
- PLAN B: For a student who engages in disruptive acts to gain attention from adults or his peers.
- PLAN C: For a student who engages in disruptive acts to gain power or status.
- PLAN D: For a student who is unaware of the magnitude or frequency of his disruptive acts.
- PLAN E: For a student whose disruptive behavior has become habitual.

NOTE:

These five plans are geared toward single student with a chronic problem. However, they can easily be implemented with two or three students who have the same problem. If more than three students in your class regularly engage in disruptive behavior, see **Chaos—Classroom Out of Control** *for suggestions on managing group behavior.*

Alternative Problems

- **Arguing—Student(s) With the Teacher**
- **Attention Deficit Hyperactivity Disorder (ADHD)**
- **Blurting Out/Not Raising Hand**
- **Chaos/Classroom Out of Control**
- **Disruptive Behavior—Severe**
- **Self-Control Issues**
- **Smart-Aleck Behavior/Inappropriate Humor**
- **Talking/Excessive Noise in Class**
- **Tourette Syndrome**

....
General Considerations

- If the student's problem behavior stems in any way from academic issues (e.g., the student is behaving in a disruptive manner to hide the fact that he is incapable of meeting the academic expectations), concurrent efforts must be made to ensure his academic success (see **Academic Deficits, Determining**).

- If the student lacks the basic social skills to interact with his peers appropriately, it may be necessary to begin by teaching him those skills.

Social Skills, Lack of contains information on a variety of published social skills curricula.

- If the disruptive behavior is resulting in the student not completing his schoolwork, begin with a plan to increase the student's work completion (see **Work Completion—Daily Work**). Once the student is turning in completed work on a regular basis, you can consider an intervention for the disruptive behavior if the problem still exists.

....
Model Plans

P L A N   A

It is not always necessary, or even beneficial, to use an involved plan. If the disruptive behavior has just begun and/or occurs infrequently, the following actions, along with making the student aware of your concerns, may resolve the situation.

 Respond consistently to the disruptive behavior.

a. Each time the student engages in disruptive behavior, provide a gentle verbal correction. Inform the student that his behavior is disruptive and provide information on what he should be doing differently. Whenever possible, move close to the student rather than providing the verbal correction from across the room. "Zeke, that tapping is disruptive. You need to keep your hands still and listen to Martin's report."

b. Record the frequency of these verbal corrections. This will not only provide essential information about whether or not the plan is working, but the fact that you are counting and recording each incident of the behavior (and sharing the results periodically with the student), will demonstrate to the student that the situation is serious.

 Use reinforcement to encourage appropriate behavior.

a. Give the student increased praise. Be especially alert for situations in which the student is not being disruptive and praise him for these demonstrations of his ability to "cooperate."

"Zeke, throughout the time the guest speaker was here you were cooperative. You listened, asked questions, and kept your hands and feet quiet. Thank you for your cooperation."

If the student would be embarrassed by public praise, praise the student privately or even give the student a note. Remember that any time the student is not being disruptive, you can praise him for cooperating.

b. Praise the student for reducing the number of disruptions as compared to previous days. "Zeke, today you only had five disruptions. This is the best day since I have been counting."

c. Give the student frequent attention (e.g., say "hello" to him as he enters the classroom, ask him questions about his work when he is on-task and focused, and occasionally ask him what he did the previous evening or how he is doing with a sport/activity that he participates in) and praise him for other positive behaviors he exhibits. For example, you might comment about the creativity of his writing or how consistent he is about completing his assignments on time. This demonstrates to the student that you notice many positive things he does, not just the fact that he is refraining from disruption.

PLAN B

Some students are very skilled at gaining attention through their negative behavior. If you find yourself frequently nagging, reminding, or coaxing the student to stop being disruptive, it is possible that he is trying to gain adult or peer attention. Whether or not the student overtly seems to like the attention, you should make sure that he receives more frequent and more satisfying attention when he behaves cooperatively than when he is disruptive.

1. Respond consistently to the disruptive behavior.

a. Because it is important for the student to learn that he will not be able to prompt people to nag and pay attention to him with this behavior, you need to ignore most of it. While ignoring, do not look at the student or talk to him. Do not act disgusted or impatient with his behavior. Simply interact in positive ways with students who are behaving appropriately and meeting classroom expectations. As soon as the target student is no longer being disruptive, pay attention to him, but make no reference to his inappropriate behavior.

b. The only time you shouldn't ignore the disruptive behavior is when it affects other students (e.g., the target student is poking another student or is so loudly disruptive that the others cannot hear your directions for an assignment). On these occasions, you may need to use a consequence, such as time owed off of recess or in after-school detention.

If the need for consequences seems likely, the student should be told during the initial meeting (see SUGGESTED STEPS FOR DEVELOPING AND IMPLEMENTING A PLAN) what will happen when his disruptive behavior affects the class. Then, when the student is disruptive in a way that intrudes upon other students you can simply state, "Zeke, you are interfering with student who are trying to complete their science experiment. You owe a minute off recess, plus however long it takes until you are at your desk and quiet."

Use consequences only for situations in which a class activity cannot proceed or when the student's behavior is directly interfering with another student—otherwise ignore the disruptive behavior.

(NOTE: For a student in kindergarten or first grade, redirection may be more appropriate than time owed. Redirection involves gently leading the student to an alternative activity without saying anything or making eye contact. For example, if the student is bothering others

in a science center, you would simply guide him back to his seat without saying a word.)

c. If other students give the target student attention when he is disruptive (e.g., trying to get him to stop making an annoying noise), gently correct them. "Shereen and Tim, Zeke can take care of himself and cooperate when he is ready. It would be best to let him work it out on his own."

2. Use reinforcement to encourage appropriate behavior.

a. Frequent praise and attention is the core of this plan. The student must see that he receives more frequent and more satisfying attention when he behaves cooperatively than when he is disruptive. Thus, whenever the student is not being disruptive (or otherwise misbehaving), make an effort to praise and spend time with him. "Zeke, you have been very positive and cooperative throughout the entire morning. Would it be okay if I joined you for lunch today?"

With a student in middle/junior high school, give this sort of attention privately as opposed to a public statement (e.g., call the student at home to tell him how well he is doing).

b. You may also wish to use intermittent rewards to acknowledge the student's success. Occasional, and unexpected, rewards can motivate the student to demonstrate responsible behavior more often. The idea is to provide a reward when the student has had a particularly good period of cooperation.

Appropriate rewards might include commenting on the student's progress to another adult when the student can overhear, asking the student to help you organize a learning center, or giving the student the opportunity to spend time with you after school. *(NOTE: A list of additional reinforcement ideas can be found in APPENDIX 1.)*

Use intermittent rewards more frequently at the beginning of the intervention to encourage the student, and less often as his behavior improves.

3. *Ensure a 3-1 ratio of positive to negative attention.*

a. Given that attention is a motivating force for this student, you want to be sure that you are giving the student *three times as much* positive as negative attention. One way to do this is to monitor your interactions with the student at least one day per week. Simply keep a card on a clipboard or in your pocket and record each interaction you have with the student as either positive or negative by writing a "+" or a "-", respectively, on the card.

To determine whether an interaction is positive or negative, ask yourself whether the student was being disruptive (or otherwise misbehaving) at the time the interaction occurred. Any interactions that stem from disruptive behavior are negative, while all interactions that occur while the student is meeting the classroom expectations are positive. Thus, assigning time owed is a negative interaction, but praising the student for cooperating is positive. Greeting the student as he enters the room or asking him if he has any questions during independent work are also considered positive interactions. *(NOTE: Ignoring the student's disruptive behavior is not recorded at all, because it is not an interaction.)*

b. If you find that you are not giving the student three times as much positive as negative attention, try to increase the number of positive interactions that you have with the student. Sometimes prompts can help. For example, you might decide that each time the student enters the classroom you will say "hello" to him, that each time he is disruptive you will try to find two things to praise after his behavior improves, or that each time there is an intercom announcement you will check the target student and as soon as possible praise some aspect of his behavior. You can also increase the ratio of positive to negative attention by ignoring more of the student's disruptive behavior (i.e., using time owed less frequently).

4. *Increase the frequency of your visual supervision in the portion of the room where the student is spending time.*

Making the student aware of your increased watchfulness can often prompt more responsible behavior. If the student is behaving well, try to make eye contact and give a nod of your head and a smile to let the student know that you see and are pleased with his cooperation. Increased scanning should also provide more opportunities to give the student attention for his positive behavior.

PLAN C

Some students use disruptive acts as a way to obtain power over an adult and/or to gain peer status. If your student is routinely making you angry and/or impressing other members of the class with how "bad" or "tough" he is, the intervention must include strategies for both reducing the power gained through the misbehavior and increasing the "power" that the student achieves through cooperation.

 1. *Respond consistently to the disruptive behavior.*

a. Calmly implement a consequence each and every time the student is disruptive. Prior to implementing this procedure, you and the student must have reached a clear understanding about what will occur whenever the student is disruptive. So that the consequence itself does not become a power issue. "Whenever you are disruptive, the consequence will be . . . . " Unless the consequences have been systematically designed in this manner, they can contribute to a power conflict with the student. "You have disrupted my class and made me mad, so what I will do to you is . . . . "

b. Make an extensive list of the types of disruptive acts the student engages in and a list of corresponding responsible behaviors. Be very specific. Following are a few examples:

* **Disruptive**

  – Talking to anyone or touching anyone or their materials when walking to the pencil sharpener is disruptive.

  – Walking to the pencil sharpener while the teacher is presenting a lesson is disruptive.

  – Blurting out without raising your hand is disruptive.

  – Making drumming noises on your desk is disruptive.

- **Not Disruptive**

  - Walking quietly to the pencil sharpener during a work period, sharpening the pencil, then going immediately back to your seat and beginning work would be responsible.

  - Waiting until the teacher directed section of the lesson is finished and then quietly going the pencil sharpener would be responsible.

  - Raising your hand and waiting to be called on would be responsible.

  - Keeping your hands quiet during class discussions would be responsible.

  Be sure the list captures all the disruptive acts the student tends to engage in. Identifying all the possibilities at the outset reduces the student's need to experiment with various misbehaviors to find out what you will do.

c. Determine a consequence that you will feel comfortable implementing every time the student engages in a disruptive act. During your initial meeting with the student (see SUGGESTED STEPS FOR DEVELOPING AND IMPLMENTING A PLAN), involve the student in identifying an appropriate consequence. One possibility is to have the student owe one minute off of recess for each disruptive act (or with a middle/junior high school student, to owe five minutes of his lunch break or in after-school detention).

  Another possibility is assigning a short (i.e., less than five-minute) in-class time-out. Regardless of the consequence chosen, the important point is to agree in advance what the consequence will be and to implement it without argument or negotiation when the student is disruptive.

d. When the student is disruptive, try not to get mad or show that you are frustrated—simply state the consequence and resume teaching. If the student disrupts five minutes later, again state the consequence (e.g., "Zeke, that is disruptive so you owe another minute.") and resume teaching. If you become emotional in response to his disruptions you will be giving the student exactly what he wants—*power!*

2. *Identify a positive trait for describing behavior that is nondisruptive.*

a. If the student is seeking power through his disruptive behavior, you need to label all positive alternatives to being disruptive with a description that implies maturity or power. "Cooperation" is a term that was utilized in

PLANS A and B, however, a student motivated by power may not be motivated by the goal of cooperation. Think of a label that would give the student a sense of power through appropriate behavior; for example, "positive leadership," "responsibility," or "self-control."

b. Praise the student when he is participating in nondisruptive ways using the positive label you have selected. "Zeke, you have exhibited positive leadership today. You listened and participated well." Also try to "catch" the student before he has a chance to misbehave and use the positive label to describe what the student is doing. The idea is to acknowledge that the student has a great deal of power—but in positive ways.

c. When discussing this plan during the initial meeting with the student, be very direct about what a powerful person he is and how you want to help him learn to channel that power in ways that will help him be increasingly successful in school.

3. *If possible, put the student in a position of positive power within the school as a way to reduce his need to engage in power struggles.*

The goal is to channel the student's misbehavior in productive directions. For example, if the student tends to misbehave in ways that make his classmates laugh, you might give the student a three-minute opportunity to tell jokes to the class. If the student likes control and influence, he may experience a sense of positive leadership by tutoring a younger student.

Whatever the activity, it should not be contingent upon the student's positive behavior. If the student is scheduled to read to a kindergarten class on Tuesday and Thursday afternoons, for example, he should be allowed to do this even if he had several disruptive incidents in the morning. When the activity is made contingent upon his appropriate behavior, the activity itself can become part of the power struggle between the teacher and the student. The goal is to give the student a taste of positive power as frequently as possible, regardless of how often he has misbehaved.

4. *Use reinforcement to encourage appropriate behavior.*

a. Give the student increased praise and attention for behaving responsibly (see PLAN A).

b. In addition, praise the student for any examples of behavior that demonstrate a positive use of power. "Zeke, I noticed that in your group a couple of students had a disagreement. You made some suggestions that helped them com-

promise—a great example of positive leadership."

PLAN D

Some students do not seem to know when they behave inappropriately. If your student doesn't seem to realize when and/or how frequently he is disruptive, the intervention must include some way of helping the student become more aware of his own behavior.

1. (OPTIONAL)
Use a video camera to record examples of both the student's disruptive and nondisruptive behaviors to serve as a basis for discussing the problem with the student.

a. In some cases, the student and/or his parent(s) may deny that a behavior problem exists. If so, a video recording of the behavior can be useful for verifying the severity and frequency of the student's disruptive acts. One potential difficulty is that having the camera in the room may temporarily squelch the problem behavior. However, even this occurrence can be useful, because then the student will be able to see himself exhibiting cooperative behavior.

Alternately, although it may not yield as much information, an audio recording may be less intrusive and give a better idea of the typical nature of the student's disruptive acts.

b. Check with your administrator about whether parental permission is required to tape the student. Let the administrator know that only yourself, the student, and possibly his parent(s) will be viewing (or listening to) the tape. Once any necessary authorization has been obtained, arrange for someone (e.g., a paraprofessional or the school counselor) to videotape the student's behavior in the classroom. Have the person tape footage of the student behaving appropriately as well as being disruptive.

Explain to the class that you are taping the class so that you can figure out ways to improve your teaching. Whoever is doing the taping should set up the video camera to get a wide shot of many students so that the target student is not aware of the camera being focused on him.

c. You can use the footage of the student behaving appropriately to show how well the student can do and to explain that the behavior the student is seeing on the tape is how you hope he will behave all the time. In essence, having the student watch his own behavior can help

him develop a more positive self-image that includes successful performance.

2. Respond consistently to the disruptive behavior.

a. During your initial meeting with the student (see SUGGESTED STEPS FOR DEVELOPING AND IMPLEMENTING A PLAN) establish a nonembarrassing signal that you can use to cue him that he is being disruptive. You want the signal to be a fairly subtle one that only the student will recognize in order to minimize the chance that he will be teased by his peers. Possibilities include a slight wave of your hand, scratching your nose, or even just direct eye contact and a head nod.

Let the student know that you may also need to quietly say his name to gain his attention before you give the signal. You should be prepared to use the signal frequently and for a fairly long time since it is likely that the behavior is, at least in part, an unconscious habit for the student.

b. Whenever the student is disruptive, give the student the signal. If the student does not cease the disruption when you give the signal, implement a consequence such as time owed (see PLAN C). Thus the signal acts as a warning—if the student responds to the warning, there is no consequence; if he does not, a consequence is immediately implemented.

3. Implement a system for monitoring the frequency (and/or duration) of the student's disruptive acts.

a. Determine what components will be monitored (i.e., the frequency and/or duration) and who will do the recording. If the disruptions last for long periods of time, you may wish to monitor the duration of each incident. Otherwise, a frequency count is generally sufficient. Since the point is for the student to become more aware of his own behavior, having him record his disruptive acts (i.e., self-monitoring) will be more effective than if you do the recording.

However, if the student cannot or will not be accurate (or if he would too be embarrassed to self-monitor) you should record the behavior yourself.

If you do the recording, remember that the idea is for the student to be aware of each time that he disrupts, and for him to know that each incident is being recorded. *(NOTE: Even when the student self-monitors, you should keep your own record approximately one day per week to verify the student's accuracy.)*

b. If the student is self-monitoring his behavior, he can keep a form like the sample shown on his desk or in his notebook. When the frequency is being monitored, tell the student that each time he sees you give the signal, he should circle a number on the form.

c. For duration monitoring, you need to time how long it takes the student to stop his disruption after you give him signal and have the student write that amount of time (in minutes) next to (or in place of) the circled number. You can give the student the time information subtly by slipping him a piece of paper on which the number of minutes is written. Of course, if the student stops the disruptive act when you give him the signal, the incident is recorded only for frequency, not duration time. *(NOTE: When you monitor both frequency and duration, chart them separately as one may improve faster than the other.)*

d. Each day, meet with the student for a few minutes to review that day's record. Have the student chart the information on a graph (or do it yourself), and talk with him about whether the day was better, worse, or about the same as previous days. If the day did not go well, encourage the student to talk about why and have him identify what he could do the next day to help himself remember to be more cooperative. If the student behaves inappropriately during the meeting, keep the interaction very short. Just let the student know that you are sure tomorrow will be a better day.

4. Use reinforcement to encourage appropriate behavior.

a. Give the student increased praise and attention for being cooperative (see PLAN A).

b. In addition, praise the student during the review meetings for accurate recording (if applicable)

Name _Zeke Turner_

Behavior to be Counted: _Each time you are given the signal for being disruptive, circle the next number._

MONDAY _3/2_

1 2 3 4 5 6 7 8 9 10 11 12
13 14 15 16 17 18 19 20 21 22 23 24

TUESDAY _3/3_

1 2 3 4 5 6 7 8 9 10 11 12
13 14 15 16 17 18 19 20 21 22 23 24

WEDNESDAY _3/4_

1 2 3 4 5 6 7 8 9 10 11 12
13 14 15 16 17 18 19 20 21 22 23 24

THURSDAY _3/5_

1 2 3 4 5 6 7 8 9 10 11 12
13 14 15 16 17 18 19 20 21 22 23 24

FRIDAY _3/6_

1 2 3 4 5 6 7 8 9 10 11 12
13 14 15 16 17 18 19 20 21 22 23 24

---

and for being willing to look at his total(s) for the day. Even on a bad day, if the student is willing to chart the data and discuss why it was a bad day, praise him. "Zeke, you are really handling this responsibly. Even though it was a rough day, you are willing to talk to me about things you might do differently tomorrow. That is a real sign that you are growing up."

Regardless of how the day went, try to make the meetings upbeat and encouraging—you want the student to look forward to the end-of-the-day review meetings.

5. Encourage the student to use self-reinforcement.

Whenever things are going well (i.e., less disruptions than usual), prompt the student to mentally reinforce himself. "Zeke, this has been a very successful morning. Silently tell yourself that you are really cooperative." Prompt the student this way intermittently throughout the day and during the end-of-the-day review meetings.

PLAN E

When a student's disruptive behavior has become habitual and/or he does not seem to have a desire to reduce it, you may need to implement a system of external incentives (i.e., rewards and consequences) based on his behavior to motivate him to stop being disruptive and to start behaving more cooperatively.

1. *Use a signal to cue the student when he is being disruptive (see PLAN D).*

2. *Implement a system for monitoring the frequency (and/or duration) of the student's disruptive acts (see PLAN D).*

3. *Establish a structured system for reinforcing the appropriate behavior and providing a consequence for the disruptive behavior.*

a. With the student, create a list of reinforcers that he can earn. Although you might want to have some suggestions in mind, the system will be more effective if the student identifies most of the items or activities himself. *(NOTE: A list of reinforcement ideas can be found in APPENDIX 1.)*

b. Assign "prices" (in points) for each of the rewards on the list and have the student select the reward that he would like to earn first.

The prices should be based on the instructional, personnel, and/or monetary costs of the items. Monetary cost is clear—the more expensive the item, the more points required to earn it. Instructional cost refers to the amount of instructional time lost or interfered with by a particular reward. Thus, an activity which causes the student to miss part of academic instruction should require more points than one the student can do on his own free time. Personnel cost involves the time required by you and/or other staff to fulfill the reinforcer. Having lunch with the principal, therefore, would cost more points than spending five minutes of free time with a friend.

c. Establish a response cost system in which the student begins each day with a certain number of points. This number should equal the average number of times the student disrupts per day, plus two. Thus, if the student disrupts the class an average of 13 times per day, he would begin each day with 15 points.

Each time you have to signal the student that he is being disruptive, he loses a point. The points remaining at the end of every day are added together to be applied toward the reinforcer the student is striving to earn.

d. When the student has accumulated enough points to earn the reward he has chosen, he "spends" the points necessary and the system begins again. That is, he selects another reward to earn and begins with zero points.

If the student is immature, and needs more frequent encouragement, you might consider letting him earn several "less expensive" rewards (e.g., five minutes of computer time after 20 points) on the way to a bigger reward (e.g., a pizza lunch with a friend and the principal for 200 points). That is, the student receives the small rewards without spending points; they continue to accumulate toward the selected reward.

e. Alternately, a lottery system might be more effective with a primary level student. With this system, the student begins each day with tickets in a jar instead of points. All the tickets have prizes written on them—one has a big prize, a couple have moderate prizes, and the majority have small prizes. Each time you have to give the student the signal, you remove one ticket from the jar—but neither you nor the student is allowed to see what is written on it. At the end of each day, the student draws one ticket from those remaining in the jar, and receives that prize.

f. When you are monitoring frequency, you need to determine a consequence (e.g., time owed off of recess or in after-school detention) for each incident of disruption that occurs if the student has already lost his points (or tickets) for the day. If the student runs out of points (or tickets), implement the consequence for each subsequent disruptive act. However, the consequence should *not* involve taking away a previous day's points. If the student can lose already-earned points, he might develop an attitude of, "I am losing so many points, why should I even bother to try?"

g. When you are monitoring duration, you need to establish a consequence for disruptions that last a long time. Time the length of every incident. If an incident is a very short outburst, count it as 30 seconds owed—even if the incident lasted only two seconds. For example, you might have the student owe the number of minutes spent disrupting the class off of the next recess or after school. If you use this procedure, establish a way for the student to indicate to you that he is finished being disruptive and is ready to meet classroom expectations. This lessens the possibility that you will get busy with other students after you begin timing and fail to notice that the student has stopped being disruptive.

 Use reinforcement to encourage appropriate behavior.

a. Give the student increased praise and attention for being cooperative (see PLAN A).

b. In addition, show interest and enthusiasm about how the student is doing on the system. "Zeke, you are really learning to cooperate. It is almost the end of the day and you still have 12 points. It won't be long until you have saved up enough for that free homework pass."

· · · · · · · ·
Suggested Steps for Developing and Implementing a Plan

The following steps are designed to help you develop an appropriate intervention plan and implement it effectively, whether you choose to use one of the MODEL PLANS or create a customized plan of your own. The steps are, however, suggestions—they are not intended to be followed rigidly or in any particular order. Use your professional judgment and the knowledge of your particular situation to make them work for you.

 Make sure you have enough information about the situation.

a. If you think a minimal intervention like PLAN A will be sufficient, you may already have enough information to proceed. However, when a more involved plan seems necessary, you should consider collecting additional descriptive and/or objective information for a couple of days.

b. You need to be able to explain what you mean when you say that "the student has a problem with disruptive behavior." Anecdotal notes on actual incidents should provide enough detail to define the problem behavior clearly and completely. To collect anecdotal notes, simply keep a card in your pocket or on a clipboard and occasionally make notes on specific instances when the student is disruptive.

For each entry, briefly describe where and when the disruptive behavior occurred, what the student did or said, and any other relevant observations (e.g., what prompted the behavior, or what about it made it disruptive). You do not need to take notes every time the student is disruptive; the idea is to capture a range of examples so that you will be able to describe the behavior thoroughly and completely.

Also include notes on times when the student behaves cooperatively—this will make it clear that you are not only aware of his disruptive behavior, but also recognize when he behaves appropriately. When you meet with the student,

the positive examples will also help you clarify how you want the student to behave.

c. In addition to information on what the student's disruptive behavior looks like, it can also be useful to document how often it occurs (i.e., a frequency count) and/or how long it lasts (i.e., the duration time). This information will provide both a more objective measure of the problem and an objective way to monitor the student's progress. You can use the same card on which you are making anecdotal notes to keep a frequency count—simply write a tally mark on the card each time the student is disruptive.

You might want to code these tallies to discern whether the behavior occurs more frequently during certain times, subjects, or activities (e.g., using an "A" or "P" to indicate that the incident happened in the morning or afternoon; or clustering the tallies by math or reading, teacher directed instruction or independent work., etc.).

d. If the student's disruptions last a long time and/or waste a lot of class time, you may want to record the duration time in addition to (or rather than) the frequency count. To record the duration time, mentally note the time when the student begins to be disruptive and the time when he stops. Each time, write the difference (in number of minutes) next to (or in place of) the tally mark. At the end of the day, you will be able to calculate the total number of minutes spent disrupting.

e. If the student notices what you are doing and asks about it, be straightforward—tell him that you are collecting information to see whether his disruptive behavior is a problem that needs to be worked on.

Following is an example of anecdotal notes and frequency count that have been collected on a student's disruptive behavior.

Zeke's Disruptive Behavior—9/10

AAAAA AAAPP PPPPP PPPPP

Notes:

8:40 (transition)—Zeke began pounding his hands on his desk pretending he was playing a drum.

10:00 (independent work)—Zeke was playing with a wad of paper and singing "Take Me Out to the Ball Game."

1:30 (cooperative group)—Zeke started making fun of a question Mica asked and then even went and interrupted other groups to tell them about it.

---

e. Both the frequency and the duration time are fairly easy to summarize on a chart or graph. Seeing how often and/or how much time he spends being disruptive may help the student and his parent(s) better understand your concern. (NOTE: If you collect both frequency and duration time information, chart them separately as one may improve faster than the other. For example, the number of incidents may stay about the same, while the number of minutes spent disrupting decreases dramatically.)

f. Continuing to collect this type of information (and keeping the chart[s] up-to-date) while you implement a plan will help you monitor whether the situation is getting worse, staying the same, or getting better.

2. *Identify a focus for the intervention and labels for referring to the appropriate and inappropriate behaviors.*

a. To be effective, the intervention must address more than just reducing the student's disruptions—there must be a concurrent emphasis on increasing some positive behavior or trait (e.g., cooperation or positive leadership). Having a specific positive behavior in mind will make it easier for you to "catch" and reinforce the student for behaving appropriately, and the posi-

tive focus will help you frame the situation more productively.

For example, if you simply say that "the student has a problem with disrupting," you don't really provide any useful information, and may put the student and his parent(s) on the defensive. However, when you explain that you want to "help the student learn to be more cooperative," you present an important, and reasonable, goal for the student to work toward and clearly identify what the student needs to do to be successful.

b. Specifying labels for the appropriate and inappropriate behaviors (e.g., "cooperative" and "disruptive," respectively) will help you to use consistent vocabulary when discussing the situation with the student. If you sometimes tell the student that he is "bothering others," and sometimes refer to the behavior as "being disruptive," he may not realize that you are talking about the same thing.

3. *Determine when and how to include the parent(s).*

a. Although it is not necessary to contact the student's parent(s) if the problem has just begun and is not interfering with the student's academic or social progress, you might want to take advantage of any scheduled activities (e.g., conferences, weekly notes home) to let them know of your concern.

b. If the problem has been going on for more than a week, however, you should discuss the problem with the student's parent(s). Share with them any information you have collected about the behavior (e.g., anecdotal notes, frequency count, duration time), and explain why you are concerned. Focus in particular on how the behavior is hindering the student academically and/or socially (e.g., the student is disrupting the class so frequently that he is interfering with other students getting their work done).

You might ask if the parent(s) have any insight into the situation and/or whether they have noticed similar behavior at home. Whether or not the parent(s) perceive a problem, explain that you want to help the student "learn to be more cooperative" and invite them to join you for an initial meeting with the student to develop a plan. If the parent(s) are unable or unwilling to participate, let them know that you will keep them informed of the student's progress.

c. Once the parent(s) have been involved in any way, you should give them updates at least

once per week while the plan is being implemented.

4. Prepare for, then conduct, an initial meeting about the situation.

a. Arrange a meeting to discuss your concerns with the student and anyone else who will be involved in the plan (e.g., the parent[s], the school psychologist). Although the specifics will vary depending upon the age of the student and the severity of the problem, there are some general guidelines to consider when scheduling the meeting.

First, meet at a neutral time (i.e., not immediately after a problem has occurred), when emotions are less likely to hamper communication. In general, a day's notice is appropriate, however a primary age student may worry excessively and/or forget what the meeting is about if it is scheduled more than an hour before it takes place.

Second, make the meeting appropriately private. With a primary student who has a mild problem, you might meet in the classroom while the other students are working independently. However, when dealing with a middle/junior high school student and the student's parent(s), you will need some place private (e.g., the counselor's office) to ensure that the discussion will not be overheard.

Third, try to make sure the meeting is scheduled for a time and place that it is not likely to be interrupted. Finally, when the parent(s) will be participating, they should be the ones to tell the student about the meeting.

b. Construct a preliminary plan. Decide whether you think you can use one of the MODEL PLANS or if you need to create a customized plan using components from various plans and/or of your own design. Although you will invite and encourage the student to help develop the plan during the initial meeting, having a proposed plan in mind before you meet can alleviate frustration and wasted time if the student is unwilling or unable to participate.

c. After reviewing the information you have collected and thinking about how you want the student to behave, prepare thorough descriptions of the disruptive behavior and the positive behavior/trait on which the student will be working. The more specific you can be and the more concrete examples you have, the easier it will be to clarify (and for the student to understand) your expectations. Be sure to consider the student's behavior in all relevant activities (e.g., independent work, teacher directed instruction, unstructured class times, recess and lunch, etc.).

d. Conduct the meeting in an atmosphere of collaboration. The following agenda is one way you might structure the meeting:

- **Share your concerns about the student's behavior.**

  Briefly describe the problem behavior and, when appropriate, show the student the chart(s) of how often/how long he engages in the behavior. Then explain why you consider the disruptive behavior to be a problem. You might tell the student that his behavior is interfering with his own learning and the learning of the other members of the class.

- **Discuss how you can work together to improve the situation.**

  Tell the student that you would like to help him "learn to be more cooperative," and describe your preliminary plan. Invite the student to give you input on the various aspects of the plan, and together work out any necessary details (e.g., the signal, the self-monitoring form, etc.). You may have to brainstorm different possibilities if the student is uncomfortable with the plan. Incorporating any of the student's suggestions that strengthen the plan is likely to increase his sense of "ownership" in and commitment to it.

- **Make sure the student understands what you mean by appropriate and inappropriate behavior.**

  Use the descriptions you have prepared to define and clarify the problem behavior and the positive (desired) behavior as specifically and thoroughly as you can. To ensure that you and the student are in agreement about the expectations, you might present hypothetical scenarios and have him identify whether each is an example of cooperative or disruptive behavior. Or you might describe an actual situation that has occurred and ask him to explain how he could demonstrate more cooperative behavior in that situation.

- **Conclude the meeting.**

  Always end the meeting with words of encouragement. Let the student know that you are confident that he can be successful. Be sure to reinforce him for participating in the meeting.

Give the student regular, ongoing feedback about his behavior.

It is important to meet with the student periodically to discuss his progress. In most cases, three to five minutes once per week should suffice. *(NOTE: PLANS D and E suggest daily meetings.)* During the meetings, review any information that has been collected and discuss whether or not the situation is getting better. As much as possible, focus on the student's improvements, however, also address any new or continuing problems. As the situation improves, the meetings can be faded to once every other week and then to once per month.

 Evaluate the situation (and the plan).

Implement any plan for at least two weeks before deciding whether to change plans; to continue, modify, or fade the plan you are using; or to cease the intervention. Generally, if the student's behavior is clearly improving (based on the objective information that's been collected and/or the subjective perceptions of yourself, the student, and possibly the parent[s]), stick with what you are doing. If the situation has remained the same or worsened, some kind of change will be necessary. Always discuss any changes to the plan with the student first.

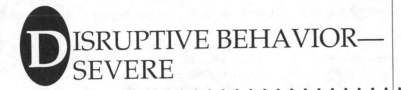

DISRUPTIVE BEHAVIOR— SEVERE

DESCRIPTION

You have a student whose behavior is so disruptive that you cannot teach and the other students cannot learn (e.g., she screams, tips over desks, or engages in direct defiance).

Although there are no MODEL PLANS included with this problem, the information provided is designed to help you establish smooth procedures for removing the student from the classroom when severe disruptions occur, and for later transitioning the student back into the classroom.

> **NOTE:**
>
> *The following material is adapted and condensed from Intervention B: Managing Severely Disruptive Behavior, which is one of 16 intervention booklets in:*
>
> *Sprick, R.S., Sprick, M.S., & Garrison, M. (1993). Interventions: Collaborative planning for students at risk. Longmont, CO: Sopris West.*

Alternative Problems

- **Aggression—Verbal and/or Physical**

- **Blurting Out/Not Raising Hand**

- **Bothering/ Tormenting Others**

- **Chaos/Classroom Out of Control**

- **Compliance/Direction Following, Lack of**

- **Disruptive Behavior— Moderate**

- **Out of Seat**

- **Physically Dangerous Behavior—to Self or Others**

- **Self-Control Issues**

- **Swearing/Obscene Language**

- **Tantrumming (K or 1st Grader)**

········
Intervention Steps

The following procedures will help you respond effectively and appropriately to a student's behavior that is highly disruptive *but not physically dangerous*. Keep in mind that these suggestions provide an immediate, but temporary, solution to what may be a fairly pervasive problem. Therefore, they should be implemented along with a proactive intervention plan that has been specifically designed to help the student learn more appropriate behaviors.

PROCEDURES

 1. Set up a record-keeping and evaluation system.

All instances of severe misbehavior should be recorded in an anecdotal log (i.e., from the onset of the problem). Include the following information for each entry:

- Date and time of day;

- Location;

- Adult(s) who were supervising at the time of the incident;

- A detailed description of the student's behavior during the incident, including the duration of the episode and student's specific behavior;

- Immediate action(s) taken;

- Consequences implemented (if any); and

- Action(s) taken to minimize future occurrences of the disruptive behavior.

By recording every incident, you will have detailed information for your reference in working with your building administrator, communicating with the student and her parent(s), and making judgments about the long-term effectiveness of your plan.

2. Contact the student's parent(s) or guardian.

a. The student's parent(s) *must* be involved whenever there is an incidence of seriously disruptive behavior. The initial contact can be limited to letting the parent(s) know there has been a problem; eventually, however, a conference should be held to begin the process of collaborative problem solving. The parent(s) can provide valuable input as you determine how to help the student.

Depending upon the severity of the situation, you may also wish to bring in a representative from other social agencies (e.g., police or mental health professionals) to help you develop a comprehensive plan.

b. As you work with the parent(s), you will need to make professional judgments about how to best involve them. You can start by letting the parent(s) know that you are truly committed to helping the student learn more successful behavior, and that you do not expect them to take full responsibility for problems that occur at school. (Parents of students with severe misbehavior often do not know what to do at home, much less how to get the students to behave at school.) Instead, make it clear that you hope to work proactively with them to develop ways of encouraging and supporting appropriate behavior, while teaching the student to avoid inappropriate behavior.

3. Establish procedures for removing the student from the classroom for each incident of _severe_ disruption.

a. There must be arrangements made to remove the student from the classroom whenever her misbehavior is so severe that you cannot teach. Since this will involve other personnel, these procedures should be developed in collaboration with and support from your building administrator.

Together with the building administrator, counselor, and/or other personnel who deal with severe misbehavior, clarify exactly what behaviors require that the student be removed from the classroom (see Step 4). Be sure to specify where the student will go, who will provide help in removing the student from the classroom (if necessary), and how the student will transition back into your classroom (see Step 5).

b. Once emergency procedures have been established, arrange another meeting to develop a proactive plan to help the student improve her behavior and for dealing with mildly disruptive behavior that does not warrant removal from the classroom (see Step 6). Be sure the parent(s) are involved in (or at least invited to) this planning meeting. If the parent(s) do not attend the meeting, inform them of what efforts are being made to assist the student.

4. *Clarify exactly which behaviors prevent you from teaching.*

a. For example, the list might include screaming, loud sustained banging on a desk, knocking books off shelves, etc. The purpose is for you and the building administrator to compile a list of all misbehaviors which warrant removal of the student from the classroom.

b. Disruptive behavior that is less severe should be dealt with using in-class consequences. For ideas, see **Disruptive Behavior—Moderate**. (For outright defiance, see the plans provided in the problem **Compliance/Direction Following, Lack of**.)

(NOTE: If the building administrator does not agree that a behavior is so severe that it warrants removal from the classroom, you will need to consider that particular behavior to be "moderate," and use the plans described in **Disruptive Behavior—Moderate** *to deal with that behavior.)*

5. *Arrange for out-of-class consequences for severe misbehavior, if necessary.*

a. The chart below shows a sample set of actions for responding to the student's severe misbehavior.

b. Develop procedures to first ensure that no one is in a physically dangerous situation. See **Physically Dangerous Behavior—to Self or Others** to prepare yourself ahead of time with procedures to use if such a situation exists.

c. Determine how you should initially respond to the student who is engaging in severely disruptive behavior. When a student is out of control or beginning to escalate into out of control behavior, calmly tell the student to "Stop and think!" and then direct her to do something else (e.g., "You need to stop and think about what you're doing. Then begin working on your assignment."). If the student does not stop the misbehavior, immediately summon help (e.g., from the office) and direct the attention of the other students elsewhere.

d. Establish an out-of-class location where the student can be sent for a time-out. When a student engages in severe behavior that is not physically dangerous, an out-of-class consequence is often necessary, but still not desirable. The student must not be allowed to unduly detract from the learning of the other students. On the other hand, removal of the disruptive

Severe Misbehavior	Actions to Take
Yells obscenities	• Intervene early, and assess the safety of everyone in the room.
	• Use "stop, think, redirect." (Tell the student to stop and think, then give her a direction.)
	• If necessary, call the office for an out-of-class time-out.
Will not stop arguing	• Intervene early, and assess the safety of everyone in the room.
	• Use "stop, think, redirect." (Tell the student that if she wishes to discuss the issue, she can talk to you during recess.)
	• Ignore subsequent arguing unless the student is loud or persistent.
	• If necessary, call the office for an out-of-class time-out.
Overtly defies the teacher by refusing to comply	• Intervene early, and assess the safety of everyone in the room.
	• Restate the direction the student refused to comply with.
	• If the student refuses again, call the office for an out-of-class time-out.

student may result in her increasing the frequency of her severely disruptive behavior.

If an out-of-class consequence *is* required, be sure to develop a long-term intervention plan to increase the probability that permanent improvement will occur. Remember that *removing the student from the classroom is a temporary measure that will not solve the problem in and of itself.*

When selecting a location for an out-of-class consequence, three criteria should be carefully weighed:

- The location should be supervised. Unsupervised locations create a risk of the student leaving the building, destroying property, or hurting herself.

- The location should be dull. A busy environment may provide a place that is more interesting to the student than the classroom.

- The location should allow a carefully orchestrated transition back into the classroom. Before the student returns, someone will need to help her identify what she did that was inappropriate, and what she might do differently in the future.

e. Evaluate the advantages and disadvantages of various out-of-class consequences. Advantages and disadvantages of some of the most common out-of-class consequences include:

- **Sending the student into the hallway**

  Moving a disruptive student into the hallway is a very weak option because the student is unsupervised. While out in the hall, who is responsible for the student? What are the liability issues if the student runs away and is injured, or hurts another student?

  Also, hallways are not boring enough. When other students are in the hallway, the misbehaving student is on display. This can result in the student being teased or ostracized, or result in the student being able to set herself up as a "negative heroine." (e.g., "Look how *bad* I am. I got sent to the hallway.").

  Finally, if the student who has engaged in severe misbehavior is placed in the hallway, the teacher will need to transition the student back into the classroom. If the misbehavior was upsetting, it may be very difficult for the teacher to calmly ask the student to clarify what she did and to identify how she might behave differently in the future.

- **Sending the student home**

  At first glance, sending the student home may seem like a logical consequence and the best possible option when a student engages in severe misbehavior. In an ideal situation, a parent is contacted and immediately comes to the school to pick up the student. The student is then taken directly home and not allowed to watch TV, listen to the radio or tapes, read, draw, or play, etc. The child is bored. Later that evening, the parent(s) and child have a serious conversation about the importance of school. The parent(s) let the child know the consequence for this and future problems. The child learns that her parent(s) are deeply disappointed with her behavior.

  Unfortunately, for a student with serious behavior problems, this scenario may be far from reality. For example, it may not be possible to reach a parent immediately. Some parents will not or cannot supervise a student who has been sent home. Some parents will sympathize with the student and talk about for example, "those *blankety-blank* teachers and that principal—she doesn't know what she's doing." Other students may be physically abused at home as a punishment for their misbehavior at school.

- **Sending the student to the office**

  The office meets the criterion of adequate supervision, but is hardly a dull place. A major drawback is that the office may be the most stimulating environment in the whole school. The student may thoroughly enjoy watching the secretary work, listening to the intercom, greeting the copy machine repairperson, and so on.

  These issues can sometimes be circumvented if a relatively quiet space within the office can be created. For example, it may be possible to position a study carrel in the quietest corner of the office so that the student is visually shielded from the high traffic areas.

- **Sending the student to another classroom**

  Other classrooms can serve as out-of-class placements. This is a reasonable option if the alternative classroom is composed of mature students who are not easily distracted, and who will ignore the student.

  If this option is selected, arrangements must be made in advance with another classroom teacher. The cooperating classroom teacher should tell his/her students that they may have another student join their class occasionally. If this occurs, their job will be to simply provide a quiet space. The class is expected to ignore the student and continue working. The teacher should explain that sometimes people need a place to get away and think. They will be helping others by providing that space.

When using this option, the student who engages in severe misbehavior is escorted to the alternative classroom and takes a preassigned seat in an unobtrusive location. The other classroom teacher should continue teaching his/her class without interruption.

Do not use this option to embarrass the student who has engaged in a severe misbehavior. Avoid sending an older student to a classroom of very young children.

- **Using a time-out room or in-school suspension**

  Time-out rooms can work very well if a school has both the space and the personnel to supervise the room. A time-out room is generally supervised by a trained assistant who does not interact with the student until she is ready to be transitioned back into the classroom.

  Though out-of-class placements have inherent problems, they may be necessary. When used, be aware that out-of-class placements are only temporary responses to misbehavior. It is highly unlikely that the consequence alone will change the student's behavior in the future.

f. Establish a plan for receiving adult assistance immediately. Develop a list of all staff members who could come quickly to the classroom and escort the student to the appropriate out-of-class location. The first person might be the principal. If the principal is out of the building, the next person might be the counselor. If the counselor is unavailable, it might be the teacher in the room next door whose own room could be covered briefly by a member of the office staff.

  Each person on the list should be trained to calmly gain the student's attention and tell her that they will go together to the out-of-class placement. If the student fails to comply, the staff member should quietly ask the student if she will need assistance. If the student fails to respond or comply, a gentle physical prompt (e.g., taking the student by the arm) can be

attempted if building and school board policy permit.

If the student still does not respond appropriately, there are only three options remaining:

- The student can be physically removed if the staff member is large enough and/or the student is small enough.

- Another adult can be called for assistance to physically remove the student.

- The other students can be removed from the room.

*(NOTE: Before any of these options is used, you should carefully study **Physically Dangerous Behavior—to Self or Others** to develop contingency plans.)*

g. Develop procedures for transitioning the student back into the classroom. To do so, develop answers to the following questions:

- **How long should the student stay in the out-of-class placement?**

  While the student is in the out-of-class placement, she should be directed to wait quietly. The length of time to be spent in the alternate setting should be predetermined. For example, from the time the student is calm, she may owe a certain number of minutes. Or, if the severe misbehavior occurs in the early morning, she may need to wait in the out-of-class placement until the end-of-the-morning recess. If the disruptive behavior occurs after morning recess, the student may need to eat her lunch in the out-of-class placement and remain there until lunch recess is over.

- **How will the student be returned to the classroom?**

  Determine who will discuss the severe misbehavior with the student and escort her back to class. At the designated time, the student should discuss with this adult what happened and how she can avoid future outbursts. This information should also be written down by the student if the student can write easily. If not, the adult should transcribe what happened and what the student thinks she could do differently in the future.

6. *Develop a plan for helping the student learn to be more responsible.*

At some time after the severely disruptive behavior is dealt with, you will need to attempt to determine any likely causes of the disruptive behavior and to establish a proactive intervention plan (or plans) to address the less severe misbehavior(s) the student exhibits within the classroom. For example, if you believe the student's problem behavior stems in any way from academic issues (i.e., the student is frustrated and disruptive because she cannot do academic tasks), concurrent efforts must be made to ensure her academic success (see **Academic Deficits, Determining**).

CONCLUSION

For severely disruptive behavior, a plan should be established for removing the student from the classroom whenever she engages in the severely disruptive acts. However, additional procedures must be established to: (1) facilitate the student's return to the classroom, (2) deal with moderately disruptive behavior within the classroom setting, and (3) help the student learn to behave in a more responsible manner overall.

Depending upon the severity and complexity of the student's behavior, the information in this reference guide may not be detailed enough. Below are several other references that deal with severe misbehavior in a more comprehensive fashion:

Kauffman J.M., Hallahan, D.P., Mostert, M.P., Trent, S.C., & Nuttycombe, D.G. (1993). *Managing classroom behavior: A reflective case-based approach*. Boston: Allyn and Bacon.

Kerr, M.M. & Nelson, C.M. (1989). *Strategies for managing behavior problems in the classroom* (2nd ed.). New York: Macmillan.

Morgan, D.P. & Jenson, W.R. (1988). *Teaching behaviorally disordered students*. Columbus, OH: Merril.

Rhode, G., Jenson, W.R., & Reavis, H.K. (1993). *The tough kid book: Practical classroom management strategies*. Longmont, CO: Sopris West.

Walker, H.M. (in press). *The acting-out child: Coping with classroom disruption*. Longmont, CO: Sopris West.

DISTRACTIBILITY/SHORT ATTENTION SPAN

Off-Task Behavior

DESCRIPTION

You have a student who has difficulty keeping his attention focused during independent work and/or teacher directed instruction.

GOAL

The student will learn to stay focused during instructional presentations and academic work periods.

OVERVIEW OF PLANS

- PLAN A: For a situation in which the problem is relatively mild or has just begun.
- PLAN B: For a student who becomes distracted because he does not know how to keep his attention focused.
- PLAN C: For a student who has learned that distractible behavior leads to frequent interactions with adults.
- PLAN D: For a student who is unaware of how frequently he becomes distracted.
- PLAN E: For a student whose distractible behavior has become habitual.
- PLAN F: For a situation in which several students in your class tend to be off task during independent work periods.

NOTE:

Throughout these six plans, the problem behavior is referred to as "distractible behavior," however, "off-task behavior" or "attention span problems" are both viable alternative descriptors.

Alternative Problems

- **Attention Deficit Hyperactivity Disorder (ADHD)**
- **Daydreaming**
- **Out of Seat**
- **Work Completion— Daily Work**

General Considerations

- If the student's problem behavior stems in any way from academic issues (e.g., the academic expectations are far above or below the student's abilities, and therefore staying focused is extremely difficult for the student), concurrent efforts must be made to ensure his academic success (see **Academic Deficits, Determining**).

- If you suspect that the student's distractible behavior could be related to the student being depressed, see **Depression**. This problem includes a set of questions to help you decide whether the student should be referred for counseling or psychological services.

- If the inappropriate behavior is resulting in the student avoiding or not completing his schoolwork, consider first implementing a plan to increase the student's work completion (see **Work Completion—Daily Work**). Once the student is

turning in completed work on a regular basis, you can consider an intervention for the distractible behavior, if the problem still exists.

- If you have any reason to suspect a physiological or neurological basis for the student's behavior (e.g., you have carefully implemented three or four of these intervention plans, and the student's behavior has not improved), consult with your building administrator and/or school psychologist for advice about district procedures for following up on this type of situation.

- If the student has been diagnosed with either Attention Deficit Disorder (ADD) or Attention Deficit Hyperactivity Disorder (ADHD), review any intervention plan with the student's parent(s) and/or physician. Staying on task is a reasonable expectation for all students, and even those diagnosed with ADD or ADHD can learn to be more focused.

Model Plans

PLAN A

It is not always necessary, or even beneficial, to use an involved plan. If the inappropriate behavior has just begun and/or is relatively mild (i.e., not interfering with the student's academic or social progress), the following actions, along with making the student aware of your concerns, may resolve the situation.

 Respond consistently to the inappropriate behavior.

Whenever the student is becoming distracted, give a gentle correction. That is, quietly say his name to get his attention and then state what he should be doing in a way that sounds almost like shorthand: "Kareem, reading your book."; or "Kareem, eyes on me."; or "Kareem, writing your story."

The purpose of this type of correction is to reduce the amount of attention the student receives and to save you time—thus you do not want to go into lengthy explanations. Because your goal is to impart information, you also want to be emotionally neutral while giving the correction. You should be prepared to correct the student frequently and for a fairly long time, since it is likely that the behavior is, at least in part, an unconscious habit for the student.

 Use reinforcement to encourage appropriate behavior.

a. Give the student increased praise. Be especially alert for situations in which the student is not distracted and praise him for these demonstrations of his ability to stay focused. "Kareem, you kept your attention focused the whole time I was demonstrating how to do the experiment. Staying focused is a very important skill for someone interested in science as a career."

If the student would be embarrassed by public praise, praise the student privately or even give the student a note. Remember that any time the student is not distracted (or is less distracted than usual), you can praise him for staying focused.

b. Praise the student privately for responding to the verbal correction. "Kareem, three times during Sustained Silent Reading I reminded you to read your book, and each time you went right back to the task. I appreciate your willingness to work on staying focused."

c. Give the student frequent attention (e.g., say "hello" to him as he enters the classroom, call on him frequently during class activities, and occasionally ask him to assist you with a class demonstration) and praise him for other positive behaviors he exhibits. For example, you might comment about the creativity of his story or how respectful the student is in the way he interacts with you. This demonstrates to the student that you notice many positive things he does, not just the fact that he is striving to stay focused.

PLAN B

Some students do not actually know how to stay focused. If your student does not seem to possess the necessary skills to keep his attention focused on a task, the intervention must include a way to teach the student on-task behavior.

 Respond consistently to the inappropriate behavior.

When the student is distracted, give a short verbal correction stating what the student should be doing instead (see PLAN A).

 Conduct lessons to teach the student how to stay focused.

a. Identify the types of classroom activities in which the student seems most distracted (e.g., teacher directed instruction, cooperative groups, or independent work periods). Begin the lessons with the one activity during which the student has the most difficulty staying focused. This way improvement is likely to be more dramatic and will help both you and the student. Eventually all the problematic classroom activities will be covered in the lessons.

b. Then, examine your anecdotal notes (see SUGGESTED STEPS FOR DEVELOPING AND IMPLEMENTING A PLAN) and, based on the types of things the student does when distracted, think of three to five "guidelines for staying focused" for each classroom activity that will be covered in the lessons. Following are some examples for three types of common classroom activities. (NOTE: Remember to start with only one as the focus of the lessons.)

- **Activity: Teacher directed instruction (e.g., lessons, stories, giving directions, etc.)**

   Guidelines:

   – Keep your eyes and your mind on the teacher.

   – Keep your hands on your desk.

   – Be ready to answer questions about what the teacher is saying.

   – Follow directions quickly and quietly (e.g., "Get out your books.").

- **Activity: Cooperative groups**

   Guidelines:

   – Listen to others in the group.

   – Look at the person talking.

   – Keep your hands on your desk or folded in your lap.

   – Tell others in the group your ideas about the question or task.

   – Follow directions (i.e., once the group has decided on something to work on, read, write, or think about the job to be done).

- **Activity: Independent work periods**

   Guidelines:

   – Keep your eyes on the work (i.e., sometimes the chalkboard, sometimes a book, sometimes your own paper).

   – Read, write, or think about the task.

   – Work until the job is done or the period is over.

c. Unless this would cause the student embarrassment, tape a copy of the appropriate guidelines to his desk. Then these guidelines can serve as a convenient way to provide quick reminders throughout the day about how to stay focused. (NOTE: If the student is a prereader, use pictorial representations of the expected behaviors.)

d. Also use the guidelines for staying focused as the basis for the lessons. The structure of the lessons can incorporate any or all of the following activities:

- Reviewing the guidelines.
- Modeling what staying focused looks like.
- Presenting a hypothetical situation and having the student model staying focused. (Provide feedback and have the student practice until he can demonstrate focused behavior consistently in that situation.)
- Modeling different behaviors and having the student identify whether you are staying focused or becoming distracted.
- Presenting a hypothetical situation or assignment and timing how long the student can stay focused. (Keep a chart of how many consecutive seconds the student can stay focused each lesson.)
- Having the student evaluate how well he stayed focused during the lesson. (Discuss your perceptions of his performance, then either praise the student or set goals for tomorrow's lesson.)

e. Conduct the lessons daily if possible, but at least twice per week. Schedule the lessons to last between ten to 15 minutes. Because this is such a time-consuming procedure, it may not be possible for you as the classroom teacher to conduct the lessons yourself. Talk to your building administrator about who else might be available to provide such lessons (e.g., the school counselor, a highly skilled paraprofessional). There may also be other students who could benefit from these lessons, and you may wish to consider conducting these lessons with a small group of students.

f. Once the student is consistently keeping his attention focused during the first type of classroom activity (e.g., teacher directed instruction),

introduce the second activity but continue to conduct a periodic review of the first activity. Eventually, present the activity during the lessons, and periodically review the first two activities as well.

 Prompt the student to behave appropriately by using precorrections.

Watch for circumstances in which the student is likely to become distracted and remind him that he will need to remember to apply what he has been learning in the lessons. "Kareem, our guest speaker is about to arrive. It is very important that you keep your attention focused on the speaker at all times. I will be watching to see if you remember to do what you practiced with Ms. Wachera this morning. I'll bet you can."

If time permits, you might have the student identify how he will demonstrate that he is staying focused. "Kareem, what will you do to show that you are focused while the speaker is talking to the class?" If this question would embarrass the student, have this conversation privately.

 Use reinforcement to encourage appropriate behavior.

a. Give the student increased praise and attention for staying focused (see PLAN A).

b. In addition, make a special point of letting the student know that you notice his efforts to use the skills he has been learning/practicing. "Kareem, you are keeping your eyes on your paper and writing. Great example of staying focused. You're doing exactly what we practiced in our lessons yesterday." If the guidelines for staying focused are taped to the student's desk, point to the specific guideline the student is following while you comment about it.

P L A N   C

Some students are very skilled at gaining attention through their negative behavior. If you find yourself frequently nagging, reminding, or coaxing the student to stay focused, it is possible that the student is trying to gain adult attention through his distractible behavior. Whether or not the student overtly seems to like the attention, you should make sure that he receives more frequent and more satisfying attention when he behaves appropriately than when he is distracted.

 Respond consistently to the inappropriate behavior.

a. When the student is distracted, give a short verbal reminder about what the student should be doing instead (see PLAN A). Be sure to keep the correction brief and emotionally neutral.

b. If the student does not respond to the verbal correction, ignore the distractible behavior. The student must learn that you will not constantly nag and remind him to stay focused. While ignoring, do not look at the student or talk to him. Do not act disgusted or impatient with his behavior. Simply interact in positive ways with students who are behaving appropriately and meeting classroom expectations. As soon as the target student is no longer distracted, pay attention to him, but make no reference to his inappropriate behavior.

c. If other students give the target student attention when he is distracted (e.g., reminding him to do what you stated in your correction), gently correct them. "Pedro and Emmett, Kareem can take care of himself and he will focus on his assignment when he's ready. It would be best to let him work it out on his own."

2. Use reinforcement to encourage appropriate behavior.

a. Frequent praise and attention is the core of this plan. The student must see that he receives more frequent and more satisfying attention when he behaves appropriately than when he is distracted. Thus, whenever the student is staying focused (or otherwise behaving responsibly), make an effort to praise and spend time with him. "Kareem, it is such a pleasure to see you focused so intently on this assignment. Would it be okay if I sat with you a moment as you continue to work?"

b. Praise the student for not needing a correction to stay focused. "Kareem, throughout the entire math period I did not have to remind you once about staying focused."

c. You may also wish to use intermittent rewards to acknowledge the student's success. Occasional, and unexpected, rewards can motivate the student to demonstrate responsible behavior more often. The idea is to provide a reward when the student has had a particularly good period of staying focused.

Appropriate rewards might include short breaks (e.g., letting the student get a drink of water, having him run an errand for you, having him staple some papers for a few minutes, etc.). *(NOTE: A list of additional reinforcement ideas can be found in APPENDIX 1.)* Use intermittent rewards more frequently at the beginning of the intervention to encourage the student, and then less often as his behavior improves.

3. Ensure a 3-1 ratio of positive to negative attention.

a. Given that attention is a motivating force for this student, you want to be sure that you are giving the student *three times as much* positive as negative attention. One way to do this is to monitor your interactions with the student at least one day per week. Simply keep a card on a clipboard or in your pocket and record each interaction you have with the student as either positive or negative by writing a "+" or a "-", respectively, on the card.

To determine whether an interaction is positive or negative, ask yourself whether the student was off task (or otherwise misbehaving) at the time the interaction occurred. Any interactions that stem from inappropriate behavior are negative, while all interactions that occur while the student is meeting classroom expectations are positive. Thus, giving a verbal correction is a negative interaction, but praising the student for staying focused is positive. Greeting the student as he enters the room or asking him if he has any questions during independent work are also considered positive interactions. *(NOTE: Ignoring the student's distractible behavior is not recorded at all, because it is not an interaction.)*

b. If you find that you are not giving the student three times as much positive as negative attention, try to increase the number of positive interactions you have with the student. Sometimes prompts can help. For example, you might decide that each time the student enters the classroom you will say "hello" to him, that at least once during each instructional period you will "catch" the student while he is focused, or that whenever there is an announcement over the intercom you will watch the target student and as soon as possible praise some aspect of his behavior.

PLAN D

Some students do not know when they behave inappropriately. If your student doesn't seem to realize when and/or how frequently he becomes distracted, the intervention must include some way of helping the student become more aware of his own behavior.

Help the student learn to recognize when he is distracted and when he is focused.

a. For a two to three day period, preface your interactions (both praise and corrections) with a question. "Kareem, are you focused or distracted?" Try to ask this question more frequently when the student is focused, to increase the amount of praise you give him. Alternately, if you only ask the question when the student is distracted, he will quickly learn that the correct answer is always "distracted." It is important to ask the question both when the student is focused and when he is distracted to help the student learn to identify both states.

b. Praise the student for correctly answering the questions. Even if the student was distracted, praise him for accurate self-assessment. "Right, Kareem, I agree. You were staring out the window, but I am glad you can identify that as distracted behavior. Let's see you get focused." Continue this procedure until the student is accurate in his assessment at least 95% of the time.

 Have the student self-monitor his behavior.

a. Identify one work period for the student to self-monitor each day. During this period, use beeper tapes or a timer to produce a sound at unpredictable intervals. Whenever the student hears the sound, he should evaluate whether he was focused or distracted and check the appropriate response on a form like the sample shown.

Focused				Distracted			

If you plan to use beeper tapes, discuss the procedure with the student and explain that, if he is willing to try the procedure, you will have to explain the situation to the class so that the other students know what the beep sound is about. You might also tell the student that if the procedure works well for him, you may ask him to help you make a class presentation on using beeper tapes and a focused/distracted card, so that occasionally all the students can self-monitor their behavior.

Beeper tapes may be easiest to use because they are prerecorded to beep intermittently, with silence in between. A timer, on the other hand, must be reset each time it goes off and you must remember to use varying intervals each time you set the timer.

NOTE: You can make your own beeper tapes or purchase them. The <u>Practice Skill Mastery Program</u> contains a set of six beeper tapes and step-by-step instructions for using the tapes for a variety of objectives. You can obtain the program by contacting:

> *Mastery Programs, Ltd.*
> *P.O. Box 90*
> *Logan, UT 84231*

b. Give the student gentle reminders in between the beeps to help him stay focused. "Kareem, the beep may go off any time; don't forget to stay focused on that experiment."

c. At the end of the work period, privately discuss the results with the student. If necessary, identify strategies that he could use to increase his on-task behavior. If appropriate, have the student chart the number of his focused checks and the number of distracted checks. An older student can calculate and chart their percentages.

NOTE: For more information on beeper tapes and ways they can be used, see:

> *Rhode, G., Jenson, W.R., & Reavis, H.K. (1993). <u>The tough kid book: Practical classroom management strategies</u>. Longmont, CO: Sopris West.*

3. **Occasionally assess the accuracy of the student's self-monitoring.**

Occasionally keep your own record of whether the student was focused or distracted at the time of the beeps. At the end of the work period, compare your results with the student's. If the student is accurate in his self-monitoring, praise him, and also provide intermittent rewards for accuracy. When the student is inaccurate, provide feedback and plan to monitor and compare your results more frequently until the student is accurate about 95% of the time.

Use reinforcement to encourage appropriate behavior.

a. Give the student increased praise and attention for staying focused (see PLAN A).

b. In addition, praise the student at the end of the monitored work period for accurate recording (if applicable) and for being willing to look at his record for the period. Even on a bad day, if the student is willing to chart the data and discuss why it was a bad work period, praise him. "Kareem, you are really handling this responsibly. Even though it was a rough day, you are willing to talk to me about things you might do differently tomorrow."

 Use a verbal correction to remind the student to stay focused (see PLAN A).

Use these brief verbal corrections especially to remind the student to keep his attention focused during work periods other than the one being monitored.

 Encourage the student to use self-reinforcement.

Whenever things are going well (i.e., the student is staying more focused than usual), prompt the student to mentally reinforce himself. "Kareem, this has been a very successful morning. Silently tell yourself that you are really good at staying focused." Prompt the student in this manner intermittently throughout the day.

PLAN E

Whenever a student's problem behavior has become habitual and/or he does not seem to have a desire to reduce it, you may need to implement a structured system of external reinforcement (i.e., rewards and consequences) based on his behavior to motivate the student to reduce his distractibility and to increase his focused behavior.

 Respond consistently to the inappropriate behavior.

When the student is distracted, give a brief verbal correction stating what the student should be doing instead (see PLAN A).

 Monitor the frequency of the verbal corrections you are providing the student about staying focused.

Either you or the student can keep a record of these verbal reminders (i.e., a frequency count). That is, whoever will be doing the recording can keep a notecard on his/her desk, and everytime you give a correction, the recorder simply writes a tally mark on the card.

 Establish a structured system for reinforcing the appropriate behavior and providing a consequence for the inappropriate behavior.

a. With the student, create a list of reinforcers that he can earn. Although you might want to have some suggestions in mind, the system will be more effective if the student identifies most of the items or activities himself. *(NOTE: A list of reinforcement ideas can be found in APPENDIX 1.)*

b. Assign "prices" (in points) for each of the rewards on the list and have the student select the reward he would like to earn first.

The prices should be based on the instructional, personnel, and/or monetary costs of the items. Monetary cost is clear—the more expensive the item, the more points required to earn it. Instructional cost refers to the amount of instructional time lost or interfered with by a particular reward. Thus, an activity which causes the student to miss part of academic instruction should require more points than one the student can do on his own free time. Personnel cost involves the time required by you and/or other staff to fulfill the reinforcer. Having lunch with the principal, therefore, would cost more points than spending five minutes of free time with a friend.

c. Have the student begin each day with a certain number of points. This number should equal the average number of reminders to stay focused you have been providing the student each day, plus two. Thus, if you have been reminding the student an average of 13 times per day, he would begin each day with 15 points.

Each time you have to correct the student for being distracted, he loses a point. The points remaining at the end of each day are added together to be applied toward the reinforcer the student is striving to earn.

(NOTE: A lottery system might be more effective with a primary level student. With this type of system, the student would begin each day with tickets in a jar instead of points. All the tickets would have prizes written on them—one would have a big prize, a couple would have moderate prizes, and the majority would have small prizes. Each time you correct the student for being distracted, you would remove one ticket from the jar—but neither you nor the student would be allowed to see what is written on the ticket. At the end of each day, the student would draw one ticket from those remaining in the jar, and receive that prize.)

d. When the student has accumulated enough points to earn the reward he has chosen, he "spends" the points necessary and the system begins again. That is, he selects another reward to earn and begins with zero points.

If the student is immature, and needs more frequent encouragement, you might consider letting him earn several "less expensive" rewards (e.g., five minutes of computer time after 20 points) on the way to a bigger reward (e.g., one hour with you for 200 points). That is, the

student receives the small rewards without spending points; they continue to accumulate toward the selected reward.

e. You should also determine a consequence (e.g., time owed off of recess or in after-school detention) to implement for each correction that you give the student after he has already lost his points (or tickets) for the day. However, the consequence should not involve taking away a previous day's points. If the student can lose already-earned points, he might develop an attitude of, "I am losing so many points, why should I even bother to try?"

4. Use reinforcement to encourage appropriate behavior.

a. Give the student increased praise and attention for staying focused (see PLAN A).

b. In addition, show interest and enthusiasm about how the student is doing on the system. "Kareem, you have not lost any points today. It is truly a pleasure to see how well you have stayed focused."

PLAN F

Sometimes several students in a class have a problem with off-task behavior. This may be the result of the students being unaware of the expectations for on-task behavior, or because they are unmotivated to remain on task. This intervention provides a number of suggestions for improving the on-task behavior of the entire class, some or all of which may be useful in your situation.

1. If the students are unable to stay on task and/or are unaware of how frequently they are off task, modify PLANS B and/or D to implement them with the entire class.

2. Respond consistently to any off-task behavior.

a. Whenever a student is off task, praise several other students who are on task. If the off-task student then gets back on task, wait a few minutes, then praise the student. If the student does not get back on task, give the student a warning.

b. In addition, keep records of the corrections you give on a class list that you keep near you at all times. Each time you correct a student who is off task, write a tally mark next to his/her name (see the sample shown).

c. Any individual student should owe time (e.g., one minute for each tally mark) off recess or in after-school detention for each infraction after the warning.

Off-Task Corrections					
Week of 10/2					
Name	Mon.	Tues.	Wed.	Thurs.	Fri.
Aarom, Linda	~~IIII~~	I	II	II	I
Benson, Jerry		II			II
Carthum, Todd	III	II	I		I
(Etc.)					
Total	8	5	3	2	4

3. Increase the class' awareness of the problem.

a. Post a chart that shows the total number of corrections for off-task behavior you give each day. This should be a class total, not a record of which students had how many offenses. *(NOTE: If you are a middle/junior high school teacher, keep the chart on a transparency that can be placed on the overhead during this particular class rather than posting it in the classroom.)*

b. Each day, conduct a short class meeting to review that day's record. Have a student record the information on the chart (or do it yourself), and discuss whether the day was better, worse, or about the same as previous days.

If the day did not go well, encourage the students to talk about why and have them identify what they could do the next day to help them remember to stay focused. If the students behave inappropriately during the meeting, keep the review session very short. Just let the class know that you are sure tomorrow will be a better day.

4. Use reinforcement to encourage appropriate behavior.

a. Praise individual students for meeting the expectations regarding staying on task (see PLAN A), and praise the entire class when overall improvement occurs.

b. During the review meetings, praise the class for being willing to look seriously at the daily total. Even on a bad day, if the students are willing to discuss why it was a bad day, praise them. "Class, you are really handling this responsibly. Even though it was a rough day, you are willing to talk to about things you might do differently tomorrow. That is a real sign that we are making progress."

Regardless of how the day went, try to make the daily meetings upbeat and encouraging—you want the students to look forward to the end-of-the-day review sessions.

c. Use intermittent rewards to acknowledge the class' success. Occasional, and unexpected, rewards can motivate the students to demonstrate on-task behavior more often. The idea is to provide a reward when the students have had a particularly good period of staying on task.

Appropriate rewards might include the opportunity to talk quietly during an activity that is usually a "no talking" time, going to recess a few minutes early, or reducing the length of a homework assignment. *(NOTE: A list of additional reinforcement ideas can be found in APPENDIX 1.)*

If you use intermittent rewards, do so more frequently at the beginning of the intervention to encourage the students, and less often as their behavior improves.

5. Encourage the class to set a daily performance goal.

You may have to help the students identify a realistic goal for reducing the number of daily corrections for off-task behavior (e.g., reducing the daily number of incidents from 40 to 32). If some students want to set a very challenging goal (e.g., reducing the number of incidents to zero per day), explain that with a more attainable goal (e.g., 32), they can always reduce the number even more, but they increase their chances of success. Then, as the class consistently experiences success, the target number should become progressively lower until there are only a few incidents of off-task behavior on most days.

6. (OPTIONAL) Establish a group reinforcement system.

a. Have the students brainstorm a list of reinforcement ideas for the entire class, and then eliminate any items from the list that are not possible (i.e., the suggestions are too expensive or could not be provided to all the students in the class).

b. Assign "prices" (in points) to the remaining items on the list. The prices should be based on the instructional, personnel and/or monetary costs of the items (see PLAN E).

c. Have the class vote on the reinforcers. The reinforcer that earns the most votes is the one they will work for first, and the items that come in second (and third) will be the next ones worked for.

d. Establish a sliding scale in which the class can earn points for attaining their daily goal, and can earn additional points if even fewer incidents of off-task behavior occur. For example, if the initial daily goal is 32 or less corrections, the following scale could be used.

32 or more corrections	= 0 points
25-31 corrections	= 1 point
18-24 corrections	= 2 points
10-17 corrections	= 3 points
4-9 corrections	= 5 points
0-3 corrections	= 7 points

e. If a class-wide system seems unlikely to be effective, set up a team competition and res-

ponse cost lottery. In this alternate system, the class would be divided into four to six teams (designed to be as equitable as possible). Each team would begin the day with a certain number of tickets on which they write the name of their team. Whenever you have to correct a student for being off-task, that student's team loses a ticket. At the end of the day, each team would put all of their remaining tickets in a hat for a lottery drawing. The team whose name is on the winning ticket would receive the reward for that day.

. . . .

Suggested Steps for Developing and Implementing a Plan

The following steps are designed to help you develop an appropriate intervention plan and implement it effectively, whether you choose to use one of the MODEL PLANS or create a customized plan of your own. The steps are, however, suggestions—they are not intended to be followed rigidly or in any particular order. Use your professional judgment and the knowledge of your particular situation to make them work for you.

1. *Make sure you have enough information about the situation.*

a. If you think a minimal intervention like PLAN A will be sufficient, you may already have enough information to proceed. However, when a more involved plan seems necessary, you should consider collecting additional descriptive and/or objective information for a couple of days.

b. You need to be able to explain what you mean when you say that "the student has a problem with distractibility." Anecdotal notes on actual incidents should provide enough detail to help you define the problem behavior clearly and completely. To collect anecdotal notes, simply keep a card in your pocket or on a clipboard and occasionally make notes on specific instances when the student is distracted.

For each entry, briefly describe when the distractible behavior occurred, what the student should have been doing instead, what he was actually doing, and any other relevant observations (e.g., what prompted the behavior). You do not need to take notes every time the student is distracted; the idea is to capture a range of examples so you will be able to describe the behavior thoroughly.

Also include some notes on times when the student is able to stay focused—this will make it clear that you are not only aware of his problem behavior, but also recognize when he be-

haves appropriately. When you meet with the student, these positive examples will also help you clarify how you want him to behave.

c. In addition to information on what the student's inappropriate behavior looks like, it can also be useful to document how often it occurs (i.e., a frequency count). This will provide both a more objective measure of the problem and an objective way to monitor the student's progress. You can use the same card on which you are collecting anecdotal notes to keep a frequency count—simply write a tally mark on the card each time you have to remind the student to stay focused.

You might want to code these tallies to discern whether the behavior occurs more frequently during certain times, subjects, or activities (e.g., using an "A" or "P" to indicate that the incident happened in the morning or afternoon; or clustering the tallies by math or reading, teacher directed instruction or independent work, etc.).

d. If the student notices what you are doing and asks about it, be straightforward—tell him that you are collecting information to see whether his distractibility is a problem that needs to be worked on.

Following is an example of anecdotal notes and frequency count that have been collected on a student's distractible behavior.

Kareem's Distractible Behavior—10/1

Teacher Directed Instruction	Independent Work Periods	Cooperative Groups/Labs
APP	AAAAP PPPPP P	AAAPP

Notes:

9:05—Kareem was tapping his desk and looking around when he should have been working on his math.

9:42—Kareem was talking with Larry when he should have been listening to my directions.

12:45—Kareem was reading a comic book when he should have been working with his science group.

2:15—Kareem was staring at students in the science center when he should have been writing in his journal.

---

e. The frequency information is fairly easy to summarize on a chart or graph. Seeing how often he needs to be reminded to stay focused may help the student and his parent(s) better understand your concern.

f. Continuing to collect this type of information (and keeping the chart up-to-date) while you implement a plan will help you monitor whether the situation is getting worse, staying the same, or getting better.

2. *Identify a focus for the intervention and labels for referring to the appropriate and inappropriate behaviors.*

a. To be effective, the intervention must address more than just reducing the student's distractible behavior—there must be a concurrent emphasis on increasing some positive behavior or trait (e.g., staying focused). Having a specific positive behavior in mind will make it easier for you to "catch" and reinforce the student for behaving appropriately, and the positive focus will frame the situation more productively.

For example, if you simply say that "the student has a problem with being distracted" you don't really provide any useful information, and may put the student and his parent(s) on the defensive. However, when you explain that you want to "help the student learn to stay focused" you present an important, and reasonable, goal for the student to work toward and clearly identify what the student needs to do to be successful.

b. Specifying labels for the appropriate and inappropriate behaviors (e.g., "staying focused" and "distractible behavior," respectively) will help you to use consistent vocabulary when discussing the situation with the student. If you sometimes refer to the inappropriate behavior as "being distracted" and other times tell the student that he "needs to concentrate better," for example, he may not realize that you are talking about the same thing.

3. *Determine when and how to include the parent(s).*

a. It is not necessary to contact the student's parent(s) if the problem has just begun and is not interfering with the student's academic or social progress. However, it might be a good idea to take advantage of any scheduled activities (e.g., conferences, weekly notes home) to let them know of your concern.

b. When the problem is severe or has continued for more than a couple of weeks, you should discuss the situation with the student's parent(s). Share any information you have collected about the behavior (e.g., anecdotal notes, frequency count), and explain why you are concerned. Focus in particular on how the behavior is hindering the student academically and/or socially (e.g., the student is not paying attention to directions and so is having trouble completing some of his assignments accurately).

You might ask if the parent(s) have any insight into the situation and/or whether they have noticed similar behavior at home. Whether or not the parent(s) perceive a problem, explain that you want to help the student "learn to stay focused" and invite them to join you for an initial meeting with the student to develop a plan. If the parent(s) are unable or unwilling to participate, let them know that you will keep them informed of the student's progress.

c. Once the parent(s) have been involved in any way, you should give them updates at least

once per week while the plan is being implemented.

 4. *Prepare for, then conduct, an initial meeting about the situation.*

a. Arrange a meeting to discuss your concerns with the student and anyone else who will be involved in the plan (e.g., the parent[s], the school psychologist). Although the specifics will vary depending upon the age of the student and the severity of the problem, there are some general guidelines to consider when scheduling the meeting.

First, meet at a neutral time (i.e., not immediately after a problem has occurred) when emotions are less likely to hamper communication. In general, a day's notice is appropriate, however a primary age student may worry excessively and/or forget what the meeting is about if it is scheduled more than an hour before it takes place.

Second, make the meeting appropriately private. With a primary student who has a mild problem, you might meet in the classroom while the other students are working independently. However, when dealing with a middle/junior high school student and the student's parent(s), you will need some place private (e.g., the counselor's office) to ensure that the discussion will not be overheard.

Third, try to make sure the meeting is scheduled for a time and place that it is not likely to be interrupted. Finally, if the parent(s) will be participating, they should be the ones to tell the student about the meeting.

b. Construct a preliminary plan. Decide whether you think you can use one of the MODEL PLANS or if you need to create a customized plan using components from various plans and/or of your own design. Although you will invite and encourage the student to help develop the plan during the initial meeting, having a proposed plan in mind before you meet can alleviate frustration and wasted time if the student is unwilling or unable to participate.

c. After reviewing the information you have collected and thinking about how you want the student to behave, prepare thorough descriptions of the inappropriate behavior and the positive behavior/trait on which the student will be working. The more specific you can be and the more concrete examples you have, the easier it will be to clarify (and for the student to understand) your expectations. Be sure to consider the student's behavior in all relevant activities (e.g., independent work, teacher directed instruction, unstructured class times, etc.).

d. Conduct the meeting in an atmosphere of collaboration. The following agenda is one way you might structure the meeting:

• **Share your concerns about the student's behavior.**

Briefly describe the problem behavior and, when appropriate, show the student the chart of how often he engages in it. Then explain why you consider the distractible behavior to be a problem. You might tell the student that success in school, in sports, on a job, and even in hobbies requires that one be able to keep one's attention focused.

• **Discuss how you can work together to improve the situation.**

Tell the student that you would like to help him "learn to stay focused" and describe your preliminary plan. Invite the student to give you input on the various aspects of the plan, and together work out any necessary details (e.g., use of beeper tapes, reinforcers). You may have to brainstorm different possibilities if the student is uncomfortable with the initial plan. Incorporating any of the student's suggestions that strengthen the plan is likely to increase his sense of "ownership" in and commitment to it.

• **Make sure the student understands what you mean by appropriate and inappropriate behavior.**

Use the descriptions you have prepared to define and clarify the problem behavior and the positive (desired) behavior/trait as specifically and thoroughly as you can. To ensure that you and the student are in agreement about the expectations, you might present hypothetical scenarios and have the student identify whether each is an example of distracted or focused behavior.

• **Conclude the meeting.**

Always end the meeting with words of encouragement. Let the student know that you are confident that he can be successful. Be sure to reinforce him for participating in the meeting.

Give the student regular, ongoing feedback about his behavior.

It is important to meet with the student periodically to discuss his progress. In most cases, three to five minutes once per week should suffice. *(NOTE: PLANS D, E, and F suggest daily review meetings.)* During the meetings, review any information that has been collected and discuss whether or not the situation is getting better. As much as possible, focus on the student's improvements, however, also address any new or continuing problems. As the situation improves, the meetings can be faded to once every other week and then to once per month.

 Evaluate the situation (and the plan).

Implement any plan for at least two weeks before deciding whether to change plans; to continue, modify, or fade the plan you are using; or to cease the intervention. Generally, if the student's behavior is clearly improving (based on the objective information that's been collected and/or the subjective perceptions of yourself, the student, and possibly the parent[s]), stick with what you are doing. If the situation has remained the same or worsened, some kind of change will be necessary. Always discuss any changes to the plan with the student first.

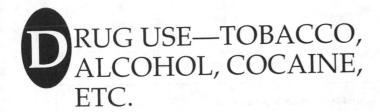

DRUG USE—TOBACCO, ALCOHOL, COCAINE, ETC.

. . . .

Substance Abuse

DESCRIPTION
. . . .

You have a student in your class whose behavior suggests the possibility of substance abuse.

Because substance abuse is such a complex and potentially
serious issue (and is thus beyond the scope of this reference
guide and the authors' expertise), there are no MODEL PLANS
included with this problem. The purpose of the following information is to suggest procedures and basic considerations for
recognizing and addressing medical emergencies that may
occur as the result of substance abuse.

> *NOTE:*
>
> *Much of the following information is adapted with permission from:*
>
> *Linn-Benton Educational Service District. (1993). A principal's handbook.
>   Albany, OR: Author.*

. . . .
General Information

- All schools should have a general health crisis management plan. If your school does not, you might consider suggesting something like the following to your administrator:

School Medical Emergency Plan

The following procedures should be followed in the case of a medical emergency. (These procedures are basically the same whether they are for responding to a substance use reaction or an illness.)

1. Immediately send for the school nurse, an administrator, and/or a health crisis manager.

2. Provide the student in crisis with as much privacy and comfort as possible.

3. Have a qualified individual follow standard medical procedures. These procedures should include, as necessary:

   - Administering first aid

   - Calling an ambulance

4. If at all possible, obtain information about any drug(s) involved and confiscate any drug(s) still in the student's possession. *(NOTE: A health emergency itself is sufficient grounds for reasonable search and seizure.)*

   If the student is unable or unwilling to identify the substance ingested, ask anyone else who might know (this applies to poison as well as illegal drugs).

5. Notify the student's parent(s) as soon as possible.

6. After the medical emergency itself has been addressed, take any necessary subsequent steps. These steps may include:

   - Referring the student for assessment and post-emergency planning.

   - Administering disciplinary measures (if the emergency involved a specific, verified violation of school policy).

   - Notifying law enforcement officials (if a law violation, such as possession/use of illegal substances, is suspected).

   - Developing and implementing a plan for communicating with the staff and other students about the incident.

- You should be aware of what constitutes a medical emergency. Symptoms and/or behaviors that may constitute a medical emergency include:

  - An anxiety or panic reaction, including hyper-excitability, hyperventilation, and/or expressions of extreme fearfulness.

  - Loss of consciousness.

  - Violent behavior.

  - Violent gastrointestinal upset (nausea, vomiting).

  - Shock (rapid pulse, pale complexion, clammy skin).

  - Severe lethargy and/or lack of responsiveness.

  - Extreme disorientation in time, space, location, or identity.

- When you have a nonemergency concern about the possibility of drug use, you should contact your building administrator or school counselor for information on how to proceed. Do not confront a student or the student's parent(s) about your suspicions without first having discussed the situation with a school official.

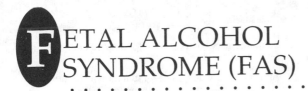FETAL ALCOHOL SYNDROME (FAS)

DESCRIPTION

You have a student who has been identified as having Fetal Alcohol Syndrome (FAS) who exhibits inappropriate behavior(s) in your classroom.

Because FAS is not a discrete behavior, but a label for a disorder that may encompass many different inappropriate behaviors, there are no MODEL PLANS included with this problem. The purpose of the following information is to suggest an overall approach and some basic considerations for addressing the inappropriate behavior of a student who has FAS.

Alternative Problems

- **Aggression—Verbal and/or Physical**

- **Anxiety/Nervousness**

- **Apathetic Behavior**

- **Babyish Behavior**

- **Bothering/ Tormenting Others**

- **Bullying Behavior/ Fighting**

- **Compliance/Direction Following, Lack of**

- **Distractibility/Short Attention Span**

- **Passive Resistance**

- **Physically Dangerous Behavior—to Self or Others**

- **Self-Concept Problems**

- **Shyness/Withdrawn Behavior**

- **Work Completion— Daily Work**

. . . .
General Information

- Fetal Alcohol Syndrome (FAS) is a disorder that may be characterized by one or more of the following: aggression, distractibility, self-concept problems, etc. Perhaps the most important thing to keep in mind while working with a student who has been diagnosed with FAS is that this student can make excellent progress when proactive and positive interventions are established.

- The key to dealing effectively with a student who has FAS and misbehaves is to begin by targeting one specific inappropriate behavior the student exhibits (or perhaps an appropriate behavior the student fails to exhibit). Then review the MODEL PLANS that accompany that particular problem behavior in this reference guide and develop an intervention to help the student learn to manage his behavior more responsibly.

- If the student exhibits a number of different inappropriate behaviors, and you are not sure which poses the biggest problem, record anecdotal information about the student's behavior for a week or so. This type of documentation is fairly easy to collect—simply keep a card in your pocket or on a clipboard and whenever the student does something (or doesn't do something) that creates a problem for himself or interferes with the smooth running of the class, make note of the incident. For each entry, briefly describe the circumstances—where and when the misbehavior occurred, what was said and/or done, and any other relevant observations you may have about the situation (e.g., what prompted the behavior).

After about a week, review the information you have collected and use it to choose one specific behavior to intervene with. This might be the misbehavior that occurs most often or the one that creates the biggest disruption for the class. Whatever your criteria, the important thing is to focus your intervention efforts on one problem behavior at a time. Often, as you work on one behavior (e.g., aggression), other problem behaviors (e.g., getting upset when corrected) seem to improve without specific intervention.

- Whenever you intend to intervene with a misbehaving student who has been diagnosed with FAS, it is important to work closely with the student's parent(s) and/or physician, if appropriate, when developing and implementing a plan.

- As an educator, you should not attempt to diagnose Fetal Alcohol Syndrome, any more than you should attempt to diagnose diabetes or any other medical/psychological disorder. If you have a student who exhibits behaviors that suggest the possibility of FAS, discuss your concerns with a building administrator, school psychologist, and/or school nurse. Then, depending upon the circumstances and your district's policy for addressing this type of situation, it may be appropriate to arrange for a meeting with the student's parent(s) and/or suggest that the student be evaluated by a physician.

FIGHTING

Physical Conflicts

DESCRIPTION

You have a student or students who engage in fighting.

The term "fighting" is actually a label that can refer to a variety of different behaviors (i.e., some people consider verbal arguments fighting, while for others fighting, by definition, must involve physical assault). Therefore, there are no MODEL PLANS included with this problem. The purpose of the following information is to suggest an overall approach for dealing with a student who you feel has a problem with fighting, as well as specific procedures for responding to situations that do involve physical confrontation.

Alternative Problems

- **Aggression—Verbal and/or Physical**

- **Arguing—Students With Each Other**

- **Bothering/ Tormenting Others**

- **Bullying Behavior/ Fighting**

- **Cliques/Ganging Up**

- **Physically Dangerous Behavior—to Self or Others**

- **Threatening Others (Staff or Students)**

- **Self-Control Issues**

········

Intervention Steps

 Define fighting, and identify the specific problem behavior(s).

a. To work with a student who fights, first identify specific behavior(s) the student engages in that have led you to conclude that he has a problem with fighting. Then look up those particular problem behaviors in this reference guide to see whether one or more of the suggested MODEL PLANS might be applicable. For example, if you have a student who attacks other students, you could review the plans in **Physically Dangerous Behavior—to Self or Others**. For a student who fights as a way to intimidate and control other students, the information in **Bullying Behavior/Fighting** will probably be most useful. Or, if the student fights because he cannot seem to control himself when he gets angry, see **Self-Control Issues**.

b. If the student exhibits several different problem behaviors, choose one to work on first. Often by working on one problem (e.g., self-control), other problems (e.g., bullying) seem to improve without specific interventions being implemented.

 Actively involve the student's parent(s) in your intervention efforts.

a. If the student's parent(s) are supportive of your concerns, work with them to set up appropriate consequences for each incident of fighting. For example, it may be that when the student fights, he is sent home for the remainder of the school day and grounded to his room through that evening by his parent(s). Make sure the parent(s) know that physical consequences, such as spanking, may actually make the fighting problem worse.

b. If the parent(s) are not supportive (e.g., "You'd better butt out, because I am teaching my child to fight and defend himself."), establish appropriate school-based consequences that do not require parental involvement. Possibilities include in-school suspension, assignment to structured recesses with the school counselor, restitution such as writing an apology letter, etc.

In addition, work with the building administrator to develop a plan for working with the parent(s) in the future. Among the questions you will need to answer are: Should the parent(s) be informed of future incidents? Should the parent(s) be

brought in for a meeting with school personnel (and/or police) to discuss the seriousness of the student's behavior?

 Establish procedures for dealing with physical fights if and when they occur.

(NOTE: The following information could serve as the basis for a short staff inservice on dealing with an immediate crisis involving two or more students fighting.)

a. **Call for assistance or break up the fight.**

Establish procedures so that any adult can call for assistance from any location in the school—in classrooms, on the playground, in the cafeteria, etc. These procedures should be discussed school-wide so that every staff member in the school knows his/her role. Staff should also rehearse the procedures in the same way they prepare for fire drills. Finally, all staff members should be aware of building and school district policy regarding police involvement: At what point should the police be called (e.g., only for a 911 emergency)? only if weapons are involved? when more than four students are involved?

If you know with 100% certainty that you can successfully break up the fight without risk of injury to yourself or the students, you may chose to intervene on your own. For example, if you are average size and two small first grade students are fighting, you can probably take each student by the collar, gently separate them, and hold them apart from one another until they are calm enough to release. However, the average sized person should not attempt to do this with average sized fifth graders, for example.

b. **Disperse the audience.**

The presence of an audience keeps a fight going more than any other factor. When there is an audience, neither student can back down or cease fighting without being branded "the loser" by his peers. Therefore, you should give firm and clear instructions about where the students comprising the audience are to go. "Everyone who is watching this needs to move over to the blacktop area NOW! Anyone left standing here will lose time off the next recess."

If there are students still standing around when the crisis passes, give their names to the building administrator. The administrator should then direct those students' classroom teachers to keep them in from some portion of the next recess. If there were many students, the building administrator should arrange for classroom discussions to educate the student body about the importance of moving away from any subsequent fights.

c. **Verbally intervene (i.e., give instructions to stop fighting).** *(NOTE: There is no guarantee this will work, but it should always be attempted.)*

Identify yourself by name and position. Tell the students to stop fighting. Then instruct one of the students to go to a specific location close by and the other student to come to you. "This is Mrs. Reynaldo, the playground supervisor. STOP NOW! Hans, go stand by the goal post. Wes, come over here to me."

When giving these instructions, use a firm and loud voice, but do not yell. If there is a pretty clear "winner" and "loser" in the fight, the student who was "losing" should be instructed to go to the specific location and the student who was "winning" should come over to you. The reason for this is that at that moment, the loser will probably be interested in stopping the fight and therefore more likely to follow your instructions. The winner, on the other hand, needs to be in closer proximity to authority.

d. **Physically intervene, if necessary and prudent.**

If you made the decision not to intervene until you had help, wait for that help to arrive. Intervening before that time may increase the chance that someone will be seriously injured. For example, if you go ahead and separate the students you may end up being able to pull only one student back, making him a perfect target for the other student.

When intervening with the assistance of another adult, coordinate your efforts so that you each pull off one student at approximately the same time.

Remember, however, that even with two adults, there is no requirement that you must physically intervene. If doing so would result in a high probability of injury to yourself, wait for more help, or even have someone call 911.

e. **Once the immediate crisis has passed, send the students to the office.**

The students should be sent to the office either at separate times, or with one or more adults escorting them.

f. **Document the incident immediately.**

Write down as much information as possible about the incident, and sign this document, including the date and time. Keep one copy in your files and give another copy to the building administrator.

Documentation of this sort is essential for this kind of crisis. In the unlikely event that someone is seriously injured (e.g., a concussion that is not diagnosed until later), or there is a lawsuit (e.g., a parent sues the school for negligence in dealing with the fight), thorough and accurate documentation will be the school's best defense. When such documentation is not completed within 24 hours, it can be very hard to complete accurately, and tends not to be as credible.

FORGETTING MATERIALS

DESCRIPTION

There are students in your class who are coming to class without the necessary materials (e.g., books, paper, pencils, etc.).

GOAL

The students will be responsible for bringing the necessary materials to class each day.

OVERVIEW OF PLANS

- PLAN A—For a situation in which the problem has just begun or is relatively mild (i.e., occurs infrequently).

- PLAN B—For a situation in which the students may be unaware of how often the problem is occurring.

- PLAN C—For a situation in which the students lack the motivation to improve their behavior.

> *NOTE:*
> *These three MODEL PLANS assume that the problem of students forgetting their materials is class-wide. They can easily be modified to use with one to three students.*

Alternative Problem

- **Homework Issues**

General Considerations

- If this problem stems in any way from academic issues (e.g,. one or more of the students are "forgetting" materials in order to avoid work that is too difficult) concurrent efforts must be made to ensure the students' academic success (see **Academic Deficits, Determining**).

Model Plans

PLAN A

It is not always necessary, or even beneficial, to use an involved plan. If the problem has just begun and/or there are only one to two class incidents per week, the following actions, along with making the students aware of your concerns, may resolve the situation.

1. *Develop a reasonable "back-up" system to use with any student who doesn't have the necessary materials.*

The best system is one in which, when the students occasionally forget something, it is not upsetting or time-consuming for you. There is no one "right" system—the important points are that the system not take a lot of your time or energy and that it works in your unique situation.

The following sample system is one that is easily taught to students:

- When you don't have the necessary materials, try to handle the problem without teacher assistance by borrowing or sharing with another student.

- If you are not able to do this, and what you need is:

  – A pencil; there are pencil stubs by the sharpener. (When a pencil is so short that you intend to throw it away, put it in my "stub can" so you or another student can use it in a pinch.)

  – A textbook; there are two extra books on my desk that can be checked out. You must sign and date the card in the book, leave the card on my desk, and return the book before you leave class.

- If you absolutely have to go to your locker, pick up a hall pass from my desk, fill it out, and bring it to me to sign.

Remember, think efficiency. If the system requires a lot of your time, modify it. Unless the system minimizes the time and effort required by you to address the problem, the system will be as unsettling as the problem behavior itself.

2. *Conduct a class meeting about the situation.*

Discuss with the class your concerns and explain your expectations (see SUGGESTED STEPS FOR DEVELOPING AND IMPLEMENTING A PLAN).

3. *Respond consistently whenever a student does not have the materials necessary for class.*

a. Whenever a student forgets to bring necessary materials, remind him/her about the back-up system.

b. When you do need to become involved (e.g., you need to sign a student's hall pass), gently correct the student. "Autumn, here is the pass, but I expect you to make a greater effort to remember your materials for this class so your time and my time is not wasted." Your goal is to impart information, therefore you want to be emotionally neutral while giving the correction.

4. *Conduct periodic spot checks at the beginning of class.*

a. Occasional "surprise inspections" will let the students know how important it is to have their materials, and will create an immediate and visible level of accountability.

b. When conducting a spot check, begin class by requiring the students to lay out all the necessary materials on their desks. Go around the room and determine which students have everything they need. Gently reprimand any student or students who are missing one or more required materials, and ask if they can use the back-up plan to obtain the missing material(s) without having to involve you (e.g., borrowing from a classmate). Praise students who have the necessary materials and students who can obtain the necessary materials through the back-up plan.

5. Use reinforcement to encourage appropriate behavior.

a. Praise individual students for remembering their materials. Keep an eye on the students with the greatest tendency to forget their materials. When these students are bringing the expected supplies on a regular basis, praise them for their responsibility. "Gray, earlier this term you had some trouble remembering class

supplies, but you have turned that problem around. I appreciate your making an effort to arrive at class prepared."

Occasionally, praise individual students who rarely or never have a problem with forgetting materials. Although these students have already mastered the positive expectations, you do not want them to feel that you take their positive behavior for granted. If public praise would be embarrassing for the students, praise them privately or even give them a note.

b. When there has been a significant overall improvement in remembering materials, praise the entire class. "Class, for the last two weeks, everyone has come prepared to class. It is a pleasure to be able to begin class without having to go through a rush of borrowing and going to lockers. I appreciate your organization and preparation."

PLAN B

Sometimes a classroom of students who have fallen into a pattern of forgetting their materials are not even aware of how often this problem is occurring. When this is the situation, the intervention must include some way of increasing student awareness, along with the use of mild consequences to encourage them to improve their behavior.

1. Develop a reasonable "back-up" system to use with any student who doesn't have the necessary materials (see PLAN A).

2. Conduct a class meeting about the situation (see PLAN A).

3. Respond consistently whenever a student does not have the materials necessary for class.

a. Whenever a student forgets to bring necessary materials, remind him/her about the back-up system (see PLAN A).

b. Decide on a reasonable consequence (e.g., time owed off of recess and in after-school detention) for situations that require your involvement (e.g., a student needs a hall pass signed).

c. When a student who has forgotten his/her materials is not able to use the back-up system, assign the consequence (e.g., one minute owed off of recess), have the student mark the incident on a classroom monitoring chart (see Step 4), and then help the student work out the

problem (e.g., "I'll sign your pass, but you will owe one minute off of your next recess.").

(NOTE: A student who doesn't have a pencil, for example, but who goes to the "stub can" on his/her own, would not owe time or mark the chart because he/she was able to solve the problem without involving you.)

4. Monitor how often you have to intervene because of forgotten materials.

Since you want the students to become more aware of the problem of forgotten materials, it will be most effective if you use a public means of charting the frequency of forgotten materials. For example, you might hang a wall chart with spaces to be filled in each time a student forgets materials (i.e., whenever an incident occurs, the student involved must write his/her name in one of the spaces).

5. Use class-wide performance goals to reduce the number of incidents of forgotten materials.

a. Each week, establish a goal for the maximum number of times you will have to get involved because of forgotten materials. Use the classroom monitoring wall charts' frequency information to determine the average number of incidents of forgetting materials each week, and then aim for about a 20% reduction each week. Thus, if there were ten incidents the first week, the performance objective for the next week would be eight. Continue lowering the goal by 20% each week until the target number of incidents is zero. *(NOTE: The students may want to set a more aggressive goal, such as reducing the number of incidents per week to zero. If so, explain to the students that if they have a more reasonable goal of eight, they can always have less incidents of forgotten materials, but they increase their chance of success.)*

b. Not meeting the weekly performance goal indicates that the class has a significant problem with forgetting materials and suggests that those students who are still forgetting their materials need additional instruction in organizational skills. Therefore, whenever the performance objective is not met, have the students whose names are on the chart stay in from a recess (or some other fun activity) for a brief review lesson on personal organization. *(NOTE: Middle/junior high school students should be kept after class for 30-60 seconds for this review.)*

The lesson itself can be as short as five to ten minutes, but each student present should be required to specify what he/she is planning to do differently next week. The students should all know in advance that this consequence will be implemented if the class exceeds their performance objective.

c. Each week, conduct a short class meeting to review the week's record. If the week did not go well, encourage the students to talk about why and have them identify what they can do the next week to help them remember their materials. If the students behave inappropriately during the meeting, keep the meeting very short. Just let the class know that you are sure that next week will be better.

6. *Use reinforcement to encourage appropriate behavior.*

a. Praise individual students and, when applicable, the whole class for being responsible about bringing the necessary materials to class (see PLAN A).

b. Use intermittent rewards with the entire class when significant improvement takes place. "Class, the performance objective was to have less than eight incidents of forgotten materials and we have had only three. I appreciate the effort people are making to improve this situation. Since we have saved time this week by not having to deal with this problem, why don't you take the last ten minutes of class we have left as free choice time. You can choose from the following activities: . . . ."

PLAN C

When the students habitually forget their materials, they may simply be unmotivated to behave appropriately. In this case, you may need to implement a system of structured reinforcement (i.e., rewards and consequences) to create mild peer pressure to encourage the students to change their behavior.

1. *Develop a reasonable "back-up" system to use with any student who doesn't have the necessary materials (see PLAN A).*

2. *Conduct a class meeting about the situation (see PLAN A).*

3. *Respond consistently whenever a student does not have the materials necessary for class (see PLAN B).*

4. *Monitor how often you have to intervene because of forgotten materials (see PLAN B).*

5. *Use class-wide performance goals to reduce the number of incidents of forgotten materials (see PLAN B).*

6. *Use reinforcement to encourage appropriate behavior.*

a. Praise individual students and, when applicable, the whole class for being responsible about bringing the necessary materials to class (see PLAN A).

b. Use a structured group reinforcement system to create mild peer pressure. First have the class brainstorm a list of class-wide rewards they would like to earn, then eliminate any items that are not possible (i.e., the suggestions are too expensive or could not be provided to all the students in the class).

Next, assign "prices" (in points) to the remaining items on the list and have the class vote on the reinforcer they would like to work for first. To save time, tell the class that the item that receives the second most votes will be the next reinforcer they will work for.

The prices should be based on the instructional, personnel, and/or monetary costs of the items. Monetary cost is clear—the more expensive the item, the more points required to earn it. Instructional cost refers to the amount of instructional time lost or interfered with by a particular reward. Thus, an activity which causes the class to miss part of academic instruction should require more points than one the class can do during their free time. Personnel cost involves the time required by you and/or other staff to fulfill the reinforcer. Thus, earning an extra recess period during which extra supervision would be required, for example, would cost more than having music playing in class for 15 minutes.

Each week that the students meet or beat their performance goal, the class earns points. De-termine how many points by subtracting the number of actual incidents of forgotten materials from the performance goal. If the goal was eight incidents and there were only four, the class would earn four points towards the predetermined reinforcer.

c. If a class-wide system is not likely to be effective, an alternative reinforcement method is the use of a team competition and response cost lottery. To implement this system, divide the class into four to six equitable teams (i.e., the same number of students who typically forget their materials on each team). Each week, each team receives a certain number of tickets on which they write their team name. Whenever a student forgets his/her materials, that person's team loses a ticket. At the end of the week, all the teams put their remaining tickets in a hat for a drawing. The name of the team on the ticket that is drawn receives that week's reward.

d. When using any structured reinforcement system, keep student attention focused on the fact that they are demonstrating increased organization and responsibility. "Class, you earned three points for the week, but more importantly, everyone is demonstrating that they are becoming more responsible."

Suggested Steps for Developing and Implementing a Plan

The following steps are designed to help you develop an appropriate intervention plan and implement it effectively, whether you choose to use one of the MODEL PLANS or to create a customized plan of your own. The steps are, however, suggestions—they are not intended to be followed rigidly or in any particular order. Use your professional judgment and the knowledge of your particular situation to make them work for you.

1. *Make sure you have enough information about the situation.*

With a behavior like forgetting materials, the most useful information is probably how often it occurs (i.e., a frequency count). For about a week, simply keep a note card in your pocket or on a clipboard and write a tally mark whenever you have to intervene because a student does not have the necessary materials for class. *(NOTE: When the problem is minor enough for a minimal intervention such as PLAN A, this level of documentation may not be necessary.)*

2. *Present the situation to the class.*

a. Depending upon you personal philosophy and the extent (severity/longevity) of the problem, you might want to have an informal discussion with the students or you might choose to conduct a more formal class meeting. In either case, wait until you are calm (i.e., not right after an incident has occurred) and make sure there will be enough time to adequately present the issue.

b. When the problem has just begun and/or occurs infrequently, an informal discussion may suffice. Tell the class that you are finding the number of times that they do not have the necessary classroom materials to be a problem and explain why. You might emphasize to them that class time is being wasted and/or the importance of the students developing organizational skills.

c. When the problem is more serious (i.e., a more involved plan is necessary) and/or you want the students to assume some ownership of the problem, consider scheduling a class meeting. Inform the students about the meeting in advance so that they will have time to think about the problem. "Class, this afternoon we are going to have a class meeting on the problem of students forgetting to bring their materials to class. Please give some thought to this situation and how, as individuals and as a class, we might solve it."

d. Before the meeting, you will need to clarify your expectations regarding bringing materials to class and identify any aspects of the plan that you do not feel comfortable opening up to a group decision. For example, if you firmly believe that there must be a consequence for not having the necessary materials, do not seek student input on that particular issue.

Using an agenda, such as the following, can provide an effective way to structure the meeting. Write an agenda on the chalkboard shortly before the meeting.

Agenda

1. Forgetting necessary materials—Define the problem.

   Share any information you have collected and explain why forgetting materials is a problem.

2. Clarify your expectations for the class.

   Specifically clarify what your expectations are regarding coming prepared to class. In addition, explain the back-up system the students should use when possible.

3. Brainstorm ideas for improving the situation.

   For a brainstorming session to work you need to establish clear rules, both for yourself and the students. For example:

   • Any idea is okay (but no obscenity).

   • Ideas will not be evaluated initially (i.e. no approval—"Good idea" or disapproval—"What a stupid idea" or "We couldn't do

   (continued)

(cont'd)

   that" should be expressed during brainstorming).

   • All ideas will be written down and evaluated at the conclusion of brainstorming.

4. Select strategies that are agreeable to everyone in the class.

   Lead the class to consensus on any decisions that need to be made. Use voting as a decision-making process when appropriate.

5. Explain the consequences for continuing to forget necessary class materials.

---

3. *Determine when and how to include parent(s).*

a. When the problem is class-wide, it is not realistic to contact the parent(s) of individual students who forget their materials (i.e., it isn't feasible to call numerous parents every night). However, once you have discussed the situation with the students, it can be useful to send a memo to all the parents (or to write an item in the classroom newsletter, if you have one) that explains the problem and the plan that is being implemented.

b. If only one or two students have or continue to have a problem with forgetting their materials, inform the parents of those individual students. Let them know that their student is forgetting materials and explain what steps you are taking to correct the situation. Frequent contact is not required, but whenever you intend to implement any kind of individualized plan, the parent(s) should be informed about the plan prior to implementation and should be given feedback about the student's progress every two to four weeks.

4. *Give the class regular, ongoing feedback about their behavior.*

Periodically review the situation with the class (or appropriate individual students). In most cases, three to five minutes once per week should suffice. Present any information that has been collected and discuss whether or not things are getting better. As much as possible, focus on improvements, however, also address any new or continuing problems. As the situation improves, the meetings can be faded to once every other week and then to once per month.

5. *Evaluate the situation (and the plan).*

After implementing an intervention plan for at least two weeks, determine whether or not it is effective using any objective information that has been collected (i.e., the frequency counts) and/or the subjective perceptions of yourself and the students. If the problem behavior has remained the same or worsened, make some kind of change (i.e., modify the current plan or switch to another plan). If the situation has improved, continue implementation for another two to four weeks. After a month or more of appropriate behavior, gradually fade and then eliminate the intervention plan. Always inform the class (or individual students) before changing, fading, or eliminating the intervention plan.

GANG INVOLVEMENT

DESCRIPTION

You have a student whose behavior suggests the possibility of gang involvement.

The problem of youth gangs is a serious and complex issue, which is beyond the scope of this reference guide and the authors' expertise. Therefore, there are no MODEL PLANS included with this problem. The purpose of the following information is to help you increase your awareness about the extent of gang activity in your community, and to provide a brief list of references and resources that might be useful in addressing this complex problem.

> *Although youth gangs have been a part of American life since the early 18th century, today's gangs pose a greater threat to public safety and order than at any time in recent history. Youth gangs, whose organization and existence at one time had primarily a social basis, now are motivated by violence, extortion, intimidation, and illegal trafficking in drugs and weapons. Today's gangs are better organized, remain active for longer periods, and are much more mobile; they also have access to sophisticated weaponry.*
> *— Ronald D. Stephens (Goldstein and Huff, 1993, p. 219)*

....
General Considerations

- One of the best ways to reduce an individual student's attraction to gangs is to structure success for that student within the school setting. You might consider developing an intervention plan that gives the student a greater sense of affiliation and success with school. For example, if the student is not doing his schoolwork, a proactive and positive plan, such as one provided in **Work Completion—Daily Work**, may reduce the student's need to gain affiliation through gang activity.

ASSESSMENT

The following assessment tool, which was developed by Ronald D. Stephens for Pepperdine University's National School Safety Center (Goldstein & Huff, 1993), can be used by school staff to determine the degree to which gangs and gang members are present in your school. Add up the point value for each question with a "Yes" answer.

1. **Do you have graffiti on or near your campus? (5 points)**

   Graffiti is one of the first warning signs of gang activity. If you have graffiti in your community or on your campus, you probably have gang activity.

2. **Do you have crossed-out graffiti on or near your campus? (10 points)**

   At an elementary school in Los Angeles, five different graffiti monikers were present on the schoolhouse door. Each of the previous ones had been crossed out. The principal apologized for the graffiti, stating that the painters had not been to the campus since the previous Friday; this was only Monday. Crossed-out graffiti indicates that more than one gang is in the community, and the likelihood of gang warfare is higher.

3. **Do your students wear colors, jewelry, or clothing; flash hand signals; or display other behaviors that may be gang-related? (10 points)**

   Dress styles, hand signs, jewelry, and other identifying marks reinforce members' affiliation with a particular gang. More and more school districts are establishing dress codes that prohibit the wearing of gang symbols, gang colors, or disruptive dress styles. Parents should be particularly aware of gang styles and colors and make certain their children do not wear them. It is all too easy to be mistaken for a gang member and to end up as another fatal statistic.

4. **Are drugs available at or near your school? (5 points)**

   Drugs and gangs are inseparably related. Some gangs are developing tremendous expertise in drug trafficking and sales. They have their own experts in money laundering, marketing, distribution, recruiting, and law. A gang will move into a community and provide the rent, utilities, telephone, and a starter kit of supplies to help members get the drug-trafficking operation going. Gangs are on the move and looking for new opportunities, perhaps in your community.

5. **Has there been a significant increase in the number of physical confrontations/stare-downs within the past 12 months in or near your school? (5 points)**

   Fights symbolize increasing conflict on many campuses. School violence and intimidation encourage gang formation and gang-related activity. Increasing violence may signal a growing tendency toward gang violence. It is important to clearly communicate, consistently enforce, and fairly apply reasonable behavior standards.

6. **Are weapons increasingly present in your community? (10 points)**

   Weapons are the tools of the trade for gangs. Wherever gangs are found, weapons will follow. Unfortunately, when a weapon is used, an irreversible consequence and a chain reaction often result. A fist fight is one thing, but

(continued)

....

(cont'd)

a gunfight can have a tragic outcome—and the violence usually only escalates.

7. **Do your students use beepers, pagers, or cellular phones? (10 points)**

The trend is for schools increasingly to outlaw the use of such devices by students. Most students are not doctors or lawyers and do not need beepers. Except in rare cases, beepers and pagers are inappropriate and unnecessary for students.

8. **Has there been a drive-by shooting at or near your school? (15 points)**

Drive-by shootings reflect more advanced gang-related problems. It is possible to have a gang presence in your community without drive-by shootings. Most shootings are the result of competition between rival gangs for drug turf or territorial control of a specific area. Once gang rivalry begins, it often escalates to increasing levels of violence. If you have had a drive-by shooting on or near your campus, conditions are grave and gang activity in your community has escalated to its most serious state.

9. **Have you had a "show-by" display of weapons at or near your school? (10 points)**

Before you have a drive-by shooting, a "show-by"—a flashing of weapons—will usually occur. About the best course of action when such an incident happens is to duck and look for cover.

The head football coach in a suburban Portland, Oregon community told of a recent incident in which a group of "Crips" (a powerful, nationally established gang), dressed in blue, came speeding through his school's field house parking lot. It was near the end of the day. His team was with him when he shouted, "Slow it down, fellas." They did, only to pull out a semiautomatic weapon and point it at the coach and his team. The coach had the good judgment to hit the deck and order his team to drop for cover. The coach said, "I thought I had bought the farm. Fortunately, they didn't pull the trigger. In my 20 years of teaching, I have never been afraid until this year."

A North Carolina teacher, a veteran of 18 years, related that her mother had offered to buy out her teaching contract if only she would leave the profession. School violence has motivated some of the nation's best teachers to pull out.

10. **Is your truancy rate increasing? (5 points)**

There is a high correlation between truancy and daytime burglary. Excellent examples of truancy prevention and intervention programs are in effect in Houston, Texas; Rohnert Park, California; and Honolulu, Hawaii. Students who are not in school are often terrorizing the community. Cooperation between schools and law enforcement to keep kids in school is important.

11. **Is an increasing number of racial incidents occurring in your community or school? (5 points)**

A high correlation exists between gang membership and racial conflict. We have often treated new immigrants and people from diverse cultural and ethnic backgrounds poorly, and thus have encouraged the formation of gangs. Many gangs are formed along racial and ethnic lines for purposes of protection and affiliation. Sometimes friendship and affiliation take a backseat to criminal acts of violence and intimidation. People want to be respected and appreciated. It is important to cultivate multicultural understanding and respect that embraces diversity.

12. **Does your community have a history of gangs? (10 points)**

Gangs are not a new phenomenon. They have been around for decades—in some cases, for several generations. Youth gangs are even mentioned in the Bible (2 Kings 2:23). If your community has a history of gangs, your children are much more likely to be influenced by them.

13. **Is there an increasing presence of informal social groups with unusual names like "the Woodland Heights Posse," "Rip Off a Rule," "Kappa Phi Nasty," "18th Street Crew," or "Females Simply Chillin"? (15 points)**

The development of hard core gang members often begins in groups with innocent and yet revealing names. Children in these groups often become primary recruiting targets for hard core gang members.

(continued)

(cont'd)

Scoring

- A score of 15 points or less indicates that the school or community does not have a significant gang problem and there is no need for alarm.

- A score of 20-40 points indicates an emerging gang problem. Gang factors and related incidents should be closely monitored, and a gang prevention plan should be developed.

- A score of 45-60 points indicates the need to immediately establish a comprehensive, systematic gang prevention and intervention plan.

- A score of 65 points or more indicates an acute gang problem that merits a total gang prevention, intervention, and suppression program.

OTHER RESOURCES

If it appears that gang involvement is a problem in your community or school, the following three excellent references might serve as beginning points in your exploration of possible interventions:

Goldstein, A.P. (1991). *Delinquent gangs: A psychological perspective*. Champaign, IL: Research Press.

Goldstein, A.P. & Huff, C.R. (Eds.). (1993). *The gang intervention handbook*. Champaign, IL: Research Press. (In particular, see Chapter 7 by R.D. Stephens—"School-Based Interventions: Safety and Security.")

The National School Safety Center, a program of the United States Departments of Justice and Education and Pepperdine University, works with law enforcement and education agencies nationwide in developing effective gang prevention and gang intervention strategies. In addition to publishing written resources, the center provides customized assessment, training, and technical assistance programs. For additional information, contact:

National School Safety Center
4165 Thousand Oaks Boulevard, Suite 290
West Lake Village, CA 91362
(805) 373-9977

GUM CHEWING

DESCRIPTION

There are students who are chewing gum in your class in violation of classroom/school policy.

GOAL

The students will consistently observe the gum chewing policy in your classroom.

OVERVIEW OF PLANS

- PLAN A—For a situation in which the problem has just begun or occurs infrequently.

- PLAN B—For a situation in which the students may be unaware of the extent of their inappropriate behavior and/or lack the motivation to behave appropriately.

NOTE:

These two MODEL PLANS assume that the gum chewing problem is class-wide. Either can easily be modified to use with only one or a few students.

. . . .
General Considerations

- Familiarize yourself with any school-wide policies related to gum chewing. If there is no school-wide policy (or the policy is not enforced by all staff), be prepared to explain to your students why you consider chewing gum to be a problem in your class. If some members of the school staff do allow students to chew gum, it will be more difficult for you to consistently enforce a "no gum chewing" policy in your classroom, and it may take longer for any intervention you implement to be successful.

- Decide whether you want/need a "no gum" policy or a "no mess from gum" policy. If you feel comfortable allowing gum chewing, but are concerned about the mess caused by gum (e.g., gum wrappers on the floor, used gum under chairs or desks, gum in the rug, etc.) modify the following MODEL PLANS accordingly. The key to an effective "no mess" policy is establishing procedures for you and the students to intermittently check the floors, under chairs and desks, etc. When there is a mess, require that all the students do a few minutes of clean up. Occasionally when there is no mess, you can provide a group reward.

. . . .
Model Plans

PLAN A

It is not always necessary, or even beneficial, to use an involved plan. If the problem with gum chewing has just begun and/or occurs infrequently (e.g., two to five times per week), the following actions, along with making the students aware o fyour concerns, may resolve the situation.

 Conduct a class meeting about the situation.

Discuss with the class your concerns and explain your expectations (see SUGGESTED STEPS FOR DEVELOPING AND IMPLEMENTING A PLAN).

 Respond consistently to all instances of gum chewing.

a. Whenever an individual student is chewing gum, gently correct him/her and instruct the student to throw the gum away. "Lad, we have discussed the damage gum causes, wrap it in paper and throw it away." It's important to be emotionally neutral when making the correction—your goal is to impart information.

b. Determine how you will address a situation in which the student claims (sometimes truthfully), "I'm not chewing gum." The key here is to respond in a way that does not necessitate/encourage a student response. You want to avoid letting the student's initial denial escalate into a power struggle, which can be both time-consuming and potentially embar-

rassing for you. Thus, you might say something like, "Fine, it appeared as if you were. Since I am required to remind any student who appears to be chewing gum, please try not to make it look as though you are."

c. If you have one or two students who "play games" with the gum chewing policy (e.g., they pretend to be chewing gum), meet with the students privately and inform them that for all subsequent corrections given (whether they are actually chewing gum or not), you will implement a consequence for the wasted time their behavior is causing. Time owed (off of recess, at lunch time, or in after-school detention) is a reasonable consequence for this type of behavior.

3. **Use reinforcement to encourage appropriate behavior.**

a. Praise individual students who are meeting your expectations regarding gum chewing in class. Keep an eye on those students who have had the greatest tendency to violate the policy and acknowledge their appropriate behavior frequently. "Reagan, I appreciate that you have been conscientious about remembering not to chew gum in my class."

You should also praise those students who have had little or no problem with gum chewing. Although such students do not need positive feedback as often as the students for whom gum chewing is a frequent problem, you do not want them to feel that you take their appropriate behavior for granted. If public praise might be embarrassing for the students, praise them privately or even give them a note.

b. When applicable, praise the class as a whole for being responsible about not chewing gum. Whenever the students are refraining from chewing gum in your class, you can acknowledge their cooperation and help in solving the gum chewing problem.

PLAN B

Sometimes a group of students that have fallen into a pattern of chewing gum in class may not even be aware of how often they do so and/or may not be motivated to change their behavior. In these cases, the intervention should include some way of increasing the students' awareness of their own behavior and the use of consequences when the gum chewing does occur.

1. Conduct a class meeting about the situation (see PLAN A).

2. Respond consistently to all instances of gum chewing.

a. Whenever an individual student is chewing gum, gently correct him/her and instruct the student to throw the gum away (see PLAN A).

b. In addition, have the student write his/her name on the chalkboard or on a designated wall chart.

c. Alternately, determine how you will address a situation in which the student claims (sometimes truthfully), "I'm not chewing gum" (see PLAN A).

3. Have the class establish a performance objective for reducing the number of weekly gum chewing incidents.

a. Identify the average number of gum chewing incidents that take place in a week. If you have collected a frequency count (see SUGGESTED STEPS FOR DEVELOPING AND IMPLEMENTING A PLAN), use that information. Otherwise, for about a week keep a simple tally of how often you correct the students for chewing gum.

b. Because the students may be inclined to set an unrealistic goal (e.g., reducing the number of incidents per week from 20 to zero), you may have to help them set a more attainable goal. It is reasonable to aim for a reduction of about 30% each week (e.g., from 20 to 14 incidents per week). Explain to the students that if they have a goal of 14, they can always have less incidents than that, but by making their goal attainable, they increase their chances of success. Then as the class consistently experiences success, continue lowering the goal by 30% each week until their objective is zero incidents.

4. Implement a consequence when the performance objective is not met.

a. When the number of gum chewing incidents in a given week exceeds the objective for that week, require those students whose names are listed to miss a recess (or some other fun activity) to clean the classroom. This is both an appropriate and reasonable consequence since gum chewing creates extra work for the building custodians. (NOTE: The students should know what the consequence will be ahead of time.)

b. If the problem occurs/continues to occur with only one or two students, implement a consequence for each incident of their gum chewing. Since having to correct the students wastes both your and the class' time, you might assign the students five minutes of time owed off of recess or in after-school detention for each incident of gum chewing.

During the time owed, have the students clean desks or do some other task to assist you in the classroom. However, if you suspect that the misbehavior was an attempt to gain your attention, the students should instead sit and do nothing during their time owed.

5. *Use reinforcement to encourage appropriate behavior.*

a. Praise individual students and, when applicable, the class as a whole for meeting your expectations regarding gum chewing in class (see PLAN A).

b. Occasionally, when significant improvement has occurred (e.g., the class meets its performance objective for two weeks in a row), provide a reward to the entire class." Class, the performance objective was to have less than ten incidents of gum chewing, but this week we had only four. I appreciate the effort people are making to improve this situation. Why don't we have class outside this afternoon as my way of thanking you for your help with this."

 6. *Conduct short weekly meetings to review the class' record.*

You want the students to remain aware of how the class as a whole is doing. Then, schedule some time each week to have the class examine how many gum chewing incidents have occurred. If it hasn't been a good week, encourage the students to talk about why and have them identify what they can do the next week to help themselves remember not to chew gum in class. If the students behave inappropriately during the meeting, keep it very short. Just let the class know that you are sure that next week will be better.

· · · · · · · ·
Suggested Steps for Developing and Implementing a Plan

The following steps are designed to help you develop an appropriate intervention plan and implement it effectively, whether you choose to use one of the MODEL PLANS or create a customized plan of your own. The steps are, however, suggestions—they are not intended to be followed rigidly or in any particular order. Use your professional judgment and knowledge of your particular situation to make them work for you.

 1. *Make sure you have enough information about the situation.*

With a behavior like gum chewing, the most useful information involves tracking how often it occurs (i.e., a frequency count). For about a week, simply keep a note card in your pocket or on a clipboard and write a tally mark whenever you correct a student chewing gum in class. (*NOTE: When the problem has just begun and/or occurs infrequently [i.e., a minimal intervention such as PLAN A is appropriate], you may not need this level of objective information.*)

 2. *Present the situation to the class.*

a. Depending upon your personal philosophy and the extent (severity/longevity) of the problem, you might want to either have an informal discussion with the students or conduct a more formal class meeting. In either case, wait until you are calm (i.e., not right after an incident has occurred) and make sure there will be enough time to adequately present the issue.

b. When the problem has just begun and/or occurs infrequently, an informal discussion may suffice. Tell the class that you are finding their gum chewing to be a problem and explain why. You might, for example, inform them that gum chewing is against class/school policy, that it creates a mess that the custodians must deal with, and/or that the noise of gum chewing is annoying and distracting to other students.

Then clarify your expectations regarding gum chewing in your classroom. Give the students the opportunity to ask questions/make comments. If, as they are likely to do, the students bring up the fact that other teachers let them chew gum in class, simply state that while that may be the choice of those teachers, you choose to allow no gum chewing. End the session by thanking the students for listening and telling them that you are confident they will make an effort to follow appropriate procedures in the future.

c. When the gum chewing problem is more serious (e.g., Plan B is appropriate) and/or you want the students to assume some ownership of the problem, consider scheduling a class meeting. Inform the students about the meeting in advance so that they will have time to think about the problem. "Class, this afternoon we are going to have a class meeting on the problem of chewing gum in class. Please give some thought to this situation and how, as a class, we might solve this problem."

Share the frequency count with the students. Also make sure that you are clear about your expectations for the students' behavior and that you have identified before the meeting any aspects of the plan that you do not feel comfortable opening up to a group decision (e.g., whether or not there will be a consequence for gum chewing and/or what the consequence will be). If you firmly believe that there should be a consequence for chewing gum in class, then you should not seek student input on that particular issue.

Using an agenda, such as the following, will provide a structure for the meeting. Write an agenda on the chalkboard shortly before the meeting.

Agenda

1. Gum chewing in class—Define the problem.

   Share any information you have collected and explain why the gum chewing is a problem.

2. Clarify the expectations for the class.

   Clarify specifically how you want the students to behave with regard to gum chewing in your classroom. Be thorough.

3. Brainstorm ideas for improving the situation.

   For brainstorming to be effective, you need to establish clear rules, both for yourself and the students. For example:

   • Any idea is okay (but no obscenity).

   • Ideas will not be evaluated initially (i.e., no approval—"Good idea" or disapproval—"What a stupid idea," or "We couldn't do that" should be expressed during brainstorming).

   • All ideas will be written down and discussed at the conclusion of brainstorming.

4. Select ideas that are agreeable to everyone in the class.

   Lead the class to consensus on any decisions that need to be made. Use voting as a decision-making process when appropriate.

5. Identify consequences—What will happen when there is gum chewing?

---

3. Determine when and how to include the parent(s).

With a procedural issue such as gum chewing, it is not critical to involve parents if the problem is class-wide. However, when the situation involves only one or a few students who continue to chew gum in class, contact the parents of those individual students. Explain that their student is not following the classroom/school policy regarding gum chewing in class and what steps you are taking to correct the situation.

Although frequent contact is not required, whenever you are going to implement an individualized plan, the student's parent(s) should be informed beforehand and given updates on the situation approximately every two to four weeks.

4. Evaluate the situation (and the plan).

After implementing an intervention plan for at least two weeks, determine whether or not it is effective using any objective information that has been collected (e.g., a frequency count) and/or the subjective perceptions of yourself and the students. If the problem behavior has remained the same or worsened, make some kind of change (i.e., modify the current plan or switch to another plan).

If the situation has improved, continue implementation of the plan for another two to four weeks. After a month or more of appropriate/acceptable behavior, gradually fade and then eliminate the intervention plan. Always inform the class (or appropriate individual students) before changing, fading, or eliminating the intervention plan.

HARASSMENT—RACIAL/SEXUAL

Racial Slurs

Gender-Based Put-Downs

DESCRIPTION

There are students in your class who engage in behavior(s) that could be considered racial or sexual harassment.

GOAL

The students in your class will refrain from engaging in any sort of harassment. In addition, you will encourage your building administrator to increase the awareness of school staff regarding the need for a school-wide effort to prevent harassment from occurring.

OVERVIEW OF THE PLAN

For a situation in which you wish to increase student awareness of the issue and have the class design a plan for dealing with the problem of racial/sexual harassment.

NOTE:

The information and suggestions included with this problem could easily be modified and applied to harassment based on any type of prejudice.

Alternative Problems

- **Bullying Behavior/Fighting**

- **Name Calling/ Put-Downs**

- **Victim—Student Who Is Always Picked On**

. . . .
General Considerations

- Harassment is a serious matter that can result in legal action being taken against individuals and/or the school district. If you have any doubt about what actions to take to address this problem, talk to your building administrator and/or the school district lawyer.

- All schools have a legally recognized official duty to prevent racial and sexual harassment. Therefore, the best approach is comprehensive and proactive—that is, school-wide actions taken to solve problems before they have a chance to balloon. Talk to your building administrator regarding what efforts are being made to:

  - Prevent harassment from occurring;

  - Catch any incidents of harassment early and intervene; and

  - Teach alternative behaviors to the student body.

- For information on a variety of high quality training materials on the topic of harassment, contact:

  Northwest Regional Educational Laboratories
  101 S.W. Main Street, Suite 500
  Portland, OR 97204
  (503) 275-9518

- For other plans that could be adapted to the problem of harassment, see **Name Calling/Put-Downs**.

. . . .
Model Plan

Along with the implementation of school-wide procedures for dealing with harassment, consider having a problem-solving session with the members of your class. Following are suggestions for doing so.

1. **Document the nature/extent of the problem.**

a. Keep anecdotal notes on every interaction that could possibly be construed as harassment. Even a statement like "You throw like a girl" may be considered harassment by the courts. For each entry, briefly describe the circumstances—where and when the harassment occurred, who was involved, what was said and/or done, any adult(s) who were supervising at the time, and any other relevant observations (e.g., what prompted the harassment). In addition, make notes on any discussions or lessons you conduct with your class or with individual students to address these problems.

This documentation is important for several reasons: actual examples can be very helpful in educating the class about the definition of harassment; thorough information is imperative when contacting the parent(s) of any students involved in a harassment incident; and such records could be critical if any legal action arises. Continuing to collect this type of information while you implement a plan can also help you determine if the situation is getting worse, staying the same, or improving.

b. If a student notices what you are doing and asks about it, be straightforward—say that you are documenting all instances of potential harassment so that you will have accurate information to present to the students, their parents, and the legal authorities, if necessary.

2. **Held a class meeting in which you and the students can analyze the situation, establish a classroom definition of harassment, and develop an action plan.**

a. Before the meeting you will need to clarify the nature/extent of the problem and your expectations for the students' behavior. (Use your anecdotal notes for examples.) You will also need to identify any aspects of the problem/plan that you do not feel comfortable opening up to a group decision. For example, you must decide ahead of time whether or not to give the class the opportunity to determine if there will be a consequence for harassment and/or what the consequence should be. If you firmly believe that there must be a consequence, then you should not seek student input on that particular issue.

. . . .
The Teacher's Encyclopedia of Behavior Management: 100 Problems/500 Plans

b. If you anticipate that the meeting could be volatile or that some students may take offense, invite the building administrator, school counselor, and perhaps some concerned parents to lend an air of seriousness and professionalism to the discussion.

c. Schedule the meeting for a neutral time, (i.e., not right after an incident has occurred) and allow enough time for a reasonable discussion to take place. Inform the students in advance of the meeting; this will give them time to think about the problem. "Class, this afternoon we are going to have a class meeting on the problem of racial/sexual harassment. You may think of this as teasing, but it is actually a legal issue, and we need to ensure that this kind of teasing does not take place. Please give some thought to this problem and what we might do as a class to solve it."

d. Use an agenda to structure the meeting. Shortly before the meeting, write the agenda on the chalkboard. The following sample is one possibility.

Harassment—What is it, and what are we going to do about it?

1. Define "respect" versus "harassment."

   (NOTE: If appropriate, have a discussion in which different forms of teasing, name calling, nicknames, joking, etc. are identified as either respectful or harassing. Make sure the students are aware that any teasing or put-downs that involve inherent characteristics [e.g., skin color, shape of lips, etc.] would be considered harassment.)

2. Review expectations regarding treating others with respect.

3. Brainstorm ways to improve the situation.

4. Select strategies that everyone agrees to.

5. Establish what will happen if a student engages in harassment.

---

e. Be sure to specify clear rules for both yourself and the students regarding the brainstorming phase of the class meeting. For example:

   1. Any idea is okay (but no obscenity).

   2. Ideas will not be evaluated initially (i.e., no approval—"Good idea" or disapproval—"What a stupid idea" or "We couldn't do that" should be expressed during brainstorming).

3. All ideas will be written down and discussed at the conclusion of brainstorming.

   At the conclusion of brainstorming, evaluate the ideas, and lead the class to consensus on any decisions that need to be made. Use voting as a decision-making process when appropriate.

3. *Determine whether to involve the parents.*

You should contact the parents of all individuals involved in any incident of possible harassment (i.e., both those who did the harassing and those who were harassed). Tell the parents what happened and what steps are being taken. If the parent(s) of the perpetrator(s) make light of the situation (e.g., "Boys will be boys."), you should explain that harassment is a serious legal matter and that you feel obligated to contact the parent(s) of the student who was harassed.

You can ask the parent(s) of the student who was harassed how they (and the student) would like the situation handled. As much as possible, try to honor these requests. For example, if the parent(s) and the student who was harassed do not want a big deal made of the incident, avoid procedures like public apologies—it might only make the recipient feel worse about what occurred.

4. *Follow up on the situation with the class.*

Periodically meet with the class to discuss the students' behavior. In most cases, three to five minutes once per week should suffice. Review any information you have collected (e.g., anecdotal notes) and discuss whether or not things are getting better. As much as possible, focus on improvements, however, also address any new or continuing problems. As you discuss any problems, acknowledge that there are individuals in the class who consistently behave appropriately. However, do not single out individuals when discussing problems or progress with the entire class. As the situation improves, the meetings can be faded to once every other week and then to once per month.

5. *Evaluate the situation (and the plan).*

Any plan should be implemented for at least two weeks before deciding whether or not it is effective. Generally, if the situation has improved (based on the objective information that's been collected and/or subjective perceptions of yourself and the students), continue with what you have been doing. (Eventually you will want to fade, then eliminate, the plan.) If the problem remains the same or worsens, some kind of change (e.g., modifying the current plan) will be necessary. Always discuss any change to the intervention with the class first.

 ELPLESSNESS

DESCRIPTION

You have a student who exhibits what seems to be "learned helplessness"—that is, the student acts unable to do things in order to encourage others to help her.

GOAL

The student will start being more self-sufficient and will learn to take pride in being increasingly independent.

> ### NOTE:
> *You do not want to imply to the student that asking for help is a problem, but to teach the student to ask for help only when she needs it—that is, to be as self-reliant as possible. Make sure the student understands that you will always be there to provide whatever assistance the student truly needs to experience school success.*

OVERVIEW OF PLANS

- PLAN A: For a situation in which the problem is relatively mild or has just begun.
- PLAN B: For a student who does not realize that she can be successful with certain tasks independently.
- PLAN C: For a student who acts helpless in order to gain attention from peers and/or adults.
- PLAN D: For a student who is unaware of when and/or how often she acts helpless and/or who is unmotivated to become more self-reliant.

Alternative Problems

- Clinginess/ Dependency
- Hypochondria
- Questions, Excessive
- Victim—Student Who Is Always Picked On
- Work Completion—Daily Work
- Work Completion—Long-Term Projects

········
General Considerations

- If the student's problem behavior stems in any way from academic issues (e.g., the student engages in helpless behavior because she is unable to meet the academic expectations), concurrent efforts must be made to ensure her academic success (see **Academic Deficits, Determining**).

- If the student lacks the basic social skills to interact with her peers appropriately, it may be necessary to begin by teaching her those skills. **Social Skills, Lack of** contains information on a variety of published social skills curricula.

- If the inappropriate behavior is resulting in the student avoiding or not completing her schoolwork, begin with a plan to increase the student's work completion (see **Work Completion—Daily Work**). Once the student is turning in completed work on a regular basis, you can consider an intervention for the helplessness, if the problem still exists.

- If the student has a disability, consult with the special education staff to determine reasonable expectations for the student's independent functioning and to identify those situations or skills for which the student may require accommodations or assistance. With a student who has a disability, there is a fine line between humane accommodation and enabling helplessness. Work directly with the student's parent(s) and special education personnel to adapt these plans to ensure that the student's needs are met, while maintaining high expectations for the student's independence.

········
Model Plans

P L A N   A

It is not always necessary, or even beneficial, to use an involved plan when a student is behaving in a helpless manner. If the problem has just begun or occurs infrequently (e.g., the student seeks unnecessary help less than five times per week), the following actions, along with making the student aware of your concerns, may resolve the situation.

1. **Respond consistently to the student's inappropriate behavior.**

a. When the student is acting helpless or asking for assistance in a situation that she should be able to handle on her own, gently correct her. Acknowledge the situation or problem the student is facing, but let her know that she should try to solve the problem by relying on herself. "Kara, you know where your coat is, you can rely on your own ability to get it yourself."

b. If you think the student can handle the task herself, but you are not *sure*, provide only as much help as the student needs, but require the student to rely on herself for some components of the task.

2. **Use reinforcement to encourage appropriate behavior.**

a. Give the student increased praise. Watch for situations in which the student might seek help, but does not. When this occurs, acknowledge the behavior as an example of self-reliance. "Kara, I saw that when you needed a pencil, you found one by yourself. That was a great example of being self-reliant. You didn't need anyone else to help you solve that problem."

In addition, watch for situations in which the student may need assistance and appropriately seeks help. "Kara, someone moved the basket where we put library books. Let me put it back where it should be. I am glad you asked for help. You tried to find it on your own—that is self-reliant, but when you couldn't find it you asked for help. I am always happy to help any time you are really stuck." If public praise would be embarrassing for the student, praise her privately or even give her a note.

b. Give the student frequent attention (e.g., say "hello" to her as she enters the classroom, call on her frequently during class activities, and occasionally ask her to help you with a class job that needs to be done), and praise her for other positive behaviors she exhibits. For example, you might comment on how consistent she is about making entries in her journal or how neat her work is. This demonstrates to the student that you notice many positive things she does, not just the fact that she is refraining from asking for help unnecessarily.

PLAN B

Sometimes a student may really believe that she cannot do the tasks for which she seeks help. In this situation, the intervention should involve teaching the student to distinguish between those tasks she can accomplish independently and those for which she actually does require assistance.

1. Conduct lessons to teach the student how to be more self-reliant.

a. Examine your anecdotal notes (see SUGGESTED STEPS FOR DEVELOPING AND IMPLEMENTING A PLAN) to see if it is possible to categorize the types of tasks or situations in which the student typically seeks assistance. For example, the categories might include:

- Help with academic tasks (e.g., how to do a particular type of math problem).

- Help with classroom procedures (e.g., where to turn in assignments).

- Help with routines (e.g., what she should do next).

- Help with locations outside of the classroom (e.g., the playground, the cafeteria, etc.).

- Help with interactions with other students (e.g., finding someone to talk to).

b. Choose the category in which the student is currently the most independent to be the focus of the initial lessons on self-reliance. Identify some questions that will determine what the student knows and does not know relative to this category. "Kara, what should you do after you finish your math? And if you did not remember what to do, how could you find out in a way that would still be relying on yourself? Right, you could look on the chalkboard, because it tells you the order of tasks to be completed."

Also identify practice tasks relating to the selected category that will require the student to demonstrate how to be self-reliant.

c. Schedule five to 15 minute lessons daily. During each lesson, provide activities like those suggested following:

- Ask the student questions about the expectations.

- Think of a hypothetical situation and have the student model what self-reliant behavior would look like in that situation. Provide feedback and have the student practice until she is successful.

- Model different behaviors and have the student identify if you are being self-reliant or if you are depending too much on the help of others.

d. As the student masters one category, both within and outside the lessons, begin working on another category during the lessons. As you progress to a new category within the lessons, create the expectation that the student will use the skills and information in the classroom. Continue the lessons until all the identified categories have been mastered.

2. Respond consistently to the student's inappropriate behavior.

a. If the student is acting helpless in a way that has been covered in a lesson, gently correct her by referring to the lesson, but without giving the student too much help. "Kara, remember what we have worked on in the lessons. Think about the three steps we talked about and see if you can figure out what you have to do next. I know you can be self-reliant."

b. If the student asks for help with a task that has not yet been the focus of a lesson, provide the information that the student needs. Keep the interaction short, unemotional, and specific. "Yes, Kara, you can sharpen your pencil now." Do not respond to the student's helpless behavior with exasperation or any emotion that implies that the student should know how to do the task without help.

c. If another student or students are helping the target student with something about which she should be self-reliant (and has been a focus of a lesson), inform the student offering the help that the target student can rely on herself for that. "Olive, thanks for trying to help, but Kara can rely on herself to find out what she should be doing next."

3. Use reinforcement to encourage appropriate behavior.

a. Give the student increased praise and attention for being self-reliant (see PLAN A).

b. "Catch" the student exhibiting independence in any aspect of the chosen category and privately praise her. "Kara, you finished your math, and then went right on to science without asking what to do next. You are relying on yourself and being very successful. You're doing exactly what we practiced in our lessons this morning."

If the student demonstrates self-reliance in a category that is not yet a focus of the lessons, praise the student's self-reliance in a way that highlights the significance of going beyond the lessons yet. "Kara, we haven't even talked about it in the lessons yet, but you were self-reliant in the way that you . . . ."

PLAN C

In some cases, a student who likes adult and/or peer attention learns that being helpless leads to people doing things for her (i.e., giving her attention). If the student seems to seek help with tasks that she already knows how to do herself, it may be the interaction itself that has become a motivating force in the student's helplessness, and you will need to make sure that the student receives more frequent and more satisfying attention when she is being self-reliant than when she is acting helpless.

1. Respond consistently to the student's inappropriate behavior.

a. You need to demonstrate to the student that helplessness is not an effective way of behaving—that people will expect her to be self-reliant. Therefore, when the student acts helpless with a task you know she can do, gently correct her by informing her that she should be able to do what needs to be done without assistance. If she continues to act helpless, ignore her behavior.

If the student has learned that she can prompt people to either nag and/or help her (i.e., pay attention to her) by being helpless, any assistance at this point gives her what she wants and reinforces her helplessness. While ignoring, do not look at the student or talk to her. Do not act disgusted or impatient with her behavior. Simply interact in positive ways with students who are meeting classroom expectations.

As soon as the target student is no longer acting helpless, pay attention to her, but make no reference to the previous helpless behavior. However, make note of activities that are problematic and discuss them with the student during follow-up meetings about the problem (see SUGGESTED STEPS FOR DEVELOPING AND IMPLEMENTING A PLAN).

b. If the student acts helpless with a task that she may actually need help with, provide the necessary information or assistance, but keep the interaction as short and emotionally neutral as possible. The goal is for the student to learn that she will receive help when she really needs it, but that the attention will not be satisfying—especially when contrasted with the amount and quality of attention she receives when being self-reliant.

c. If other students provide excessive help, remind them that the target student is just as capable of being self-reliant as anyone else in the class, and request that they allow the target student to be self-reliant.

2. Use reinforcement to encourage appropriate behavior.

a. Frequent praise and attention is the core of this plan. The student must see that she receives more frequent and more satisfying attention when she behaves appropriately than when she acts helpless. Thus, whenever the student is being self-reliant, praise and spend time with the student. "Kara, you are relying on yourself to move from one task to the next. You should be very proud of yourself. Would it be okay if sat with you a moment and watched as you begin working on this assignment?"

b. You may also wish to use intermittent rewards to acknowledge the student's success. Occasional, and unexpected, rewards can motivate the student to demonstrate responsible behavior more often. The idea is to provide a reward when the student has had a particularly good period of being self-reliant. Given that the student may thrive on adult attention, use adult attention as a reward. "Kara, you have been so self-reliant this morning, I would like to take you by the principal's office on the way to lunch today and we can fill her in on what a self-reliant individual you are."

Use intermittent rewards more frequently at the beginning of the intervention to encourage the student, and then less often as her behavior improves.

3. Ensure a 3-1 ratio of positive to negative attention.

a. Given that attention is a motivating force for this student, you want to be sure that you are giving the student *three times as much* positive as negative attention. One way to do this is to monitor your interactions with the student at least one day per week. Simply keep a card on a clipboard or in your pocket and record each interaction you have with the student as either positive or negative by writing a "+" or a "-", respectively, on the card.

To determine whether an interaction is positive or negative, ask yourself whether the student was acting unnecessarily helpless (or otherwise misbehaving) at the time the interaction occurred. Any interaction that stems from inappropriate behavior is negative, while all interactions that occur while the student is meeting classroom expectations are positive. Thus, gently correcting the student is negative, but praising her for being self-reliant is positive. Greeting the student as she enters the room or asking her if she has any questions during independent work are also considered positive interactions. *(NOTE: Ignoring the student's inappropriate behavior is not recorded at all, because it is not an interaction.)*

b. If you find that you are not giving the student three times as much positive as negative attention, try to increase the number of positive interactions that you have with the student. Sometimes prompts can help. For example, each time you interact with a particular student (e.g., Jeanine), look at the target student and praise her as soon as she is doing something self-reliant. Or, tell yourself that whenever you look at the clock you will then find a time to praise the student. Or, each time there is an announcement over the intercom, you will look at the target student to see if there is a self-reliant behavior you could praise.

In addition, you may need to periodically re-evaluate which behaviors you are ignoring. If the student is still receiving lots of help, you either need to ignore more of the helpless behavior, or begin the kinds of lessons outlined in PLAN B.

PLAN D

If the student does not realize how frequently she acts helpless, the intervention should include procedures for making the student more aware of her own behavior. In addition, if the student doesn't seem to care whether or not she is being unnecessarily helpless, you may need to implement a system of external incentives (i.e., rewards and consequences) based on her behavior to increase her motivation to be more self-reliant.

1. Implement a system for monitoring how often the student asks for help.

This system can be as simple as having the student keep a card on her desk (or taped to the front flyleaf of her notebook if she would like the procedure to be less obtrusive). Tell the student that each time she asks for help (from an adult or another student), she should write a mark on the card. Have the student do this for several days to give you an idea of how many times the student asks for help per day on average.

2. Set an initial goal for the student to reduce the overall number of times she requests help by approximately 10%.

a. From the monitoring cards, determine the average number of times per day that the student asks for help from an adult or another student. Then reduce this number by 10% to obtain the goal number (e.g., if the student is asking for help an average of 30 times per day, the goal should be 27).

b. At the end of each day, have a short discussion to review the goal with the student and have her identify some things she asked for help with that day that she thinks she can rely on herself for the next day. If there are particular skills or strategies the student is having difficulty with, also plan to review those skills/strategies with the student at the beginning of the next day. "Kara, remember that today you are going to be making a special effort to rely on yourself to have your books and papers ready at the beginning of each lesson." When the student has had at least three consecutive days of success with the initial goal, set a new goal that is another 10% less.

(NOTE: Make sure the student understands that asking for help in and of itself is not bad or wrong [i.e., the goal is not to reduce the number to zero], but that her problem is one of excess and her goal will be to reduce the number of requests for assistance to a manageable number.)

3. **Prompt the student to behave appropriately by using precorrections.**

a. Each time the student begins to ask for help, or behaves in a way that implies that she needs help (e.g., looking troubled or lost about what to do), ask her to evaluate whether she really needs the help or if she can rely on herself to figure out what to do. Remind her that if she really needs the help, you are glad to provide it, but the request will need to be marked on the card.

b. If the student turns down the help and says she can figure out what she needs to do herself, praise the student for self-reliance. If the student does need the help, provide the help, but do not act disappointed, exasperated, or in any other negative way that implies that the student should have been able to handle it on her own. Simply provide the help and check that the student records the incident on the card.

4. **Respond consistently to the inappropriate behavior.**

a. If the student persists in asking for help after you have given her a reminder (see Step 3), provide the help and make sure that the request is recorded.

b. When the number of requests for help exceeds the student's identified goal, implement a consequence (e.g., time owed off of recess or in after-school detention). For example, you may decide that each request for help that exceeds the goal number will result in one minute of time owed off of recess.

Be sure the student understands ahead of time how the consequence will work. "Kara, the initial goal will be to have 27 or less times each day that you ask for help. Each time after you reach 27 will equal one minute owed off of the next recess. The reason for this is that every student may have some questions or times they need help, but if a student asks for help for things she should be self-reliant about, it is a waste of the person's time who is giving the help."

5. **Use reinforcement to encourage appropriate behavior.**

a. Give the student increased praise and attention for being self-reliant (see PLAN A).

b. Also praise the student each day that her number of requests for help are under the targeted goal number.

6. **(OPTIONAL)**
Implement a structured system of reinforcement to give the student extra incentives to achieve her daily goal.

a. During your initial meeting with the student (see SUGGESTED STEPS FOR DEVELOPING AND IMPLEMENTING A PLAN), help the student brainstorm a variety of reinforcers. If the student is having difficulty generating ideas, you might read to the student the list of reinforcement ideas found in APPENDIX 1, and/or you can observe what the student likes to do in her free time to help generate ideas.

b. From the brainstormed list, have the student select one or two reinforcers that she would most like to earn.

c. Use a Mystery Motivator (Rhode, Jenson, & Reavis, 1992) to determine whether the student earns a reinforcer each day. On a calendar, mark some of the school days with an "X." This can be done with an invisible ink pen or with a regular pen (in which case you will need to cover each calendar space with a removable slip of paper so the student cannot see which days have "X"s. At the end of each day, review the student's record card. Then examine the calendar to see if there is an "X" on the square for that day, either by removing the paper slip or by having the student color in the square with the pen that reveals the invisible ink.

If the student was under the targeted goal number, and an "X" is on the calendar space for that day, the student receives the predetermined reward or privilege. If the student was under the targeted goal number, but the "X" is not on the calendar space for that day, the student should be praised for her success and encouraged to try again tomorrow. If the student was over her targeted goal number and the "X" is on the calendar, the student should understand that if she had asked for help a little less she would have received the reward. This type of system allows a daily ritual surrounding the reward, without having to actually give the student a reward for each day that she is successful. The "gimmicky" aspects of the system are also very intriguing to many students.

....
Suggested Steps for Developing and Implementing a Plan

The following steps are designed to help you develop an appropriate intervention plan and implement it effectively, whether you choose to use one of the MODEL PLANS or create a customized plan of your own. The steps are, however, suggestions—they are not intended to be followed rigidly or in any particular order. Use your professional judgment and the knowledge of your particular situation to make them work for you.

1. *Make sure you have enough information about the situation.*

a. If you think a minimal intervention like PLAN A will be sufficient, you may already have enough information to proceed. However, when a more involved plan seems necessary, you should consider collecting additional descriptive and/or objective information for a couple of days.

b. You need to be able to explain what you mean when you say that "the student has a problem with acting helpless." That is, you need to be able to explain what it is that the student does that has led you to conclude that her behavior is a problem. Anecdotal notes on actual incidents should provide enough detail to help you define the problem behavior clearly and completely. To collect anecdotal notes, simply keep a card in your pocket or on a clipboard and occasionally make notes on specific instances when the student engages in helpless behavior.

For each entry, briefly describe where and when the helpless behavior occurred, what the student did or said, and any other relevant observations (e.g., your perception of the student's ability to be more self-reliant in that circumstance). You do not need to take notes every time the student acts helpless; the idea is to capture a range of examples of the behavior so you will be able to describe it completely.

Also include some notes on times when the student demonstrates self-reliance—this will make it clear that you are not only aware of her problem behavior, but also recognize when she behaves appropriately. When you meet with the student, the positive examples will also help you clarify how you want her to behave.

c. In addition to information on what the student's inappropriate behavior looks like, it can also be useful to document how often it occurs (i.e., a frequency count). This information will provide both a more objective measure of the problem and an objective way to monitor the student's progress. You can use the same card on which you are collecting anecdotal notes to keep a frequency count—simply write a tally mark on the card each time the student acts helpless.

You might also want to code the tallies to indicate whether you think the student should have been able to do the task without assistance. Or, you could code the tallies to discern whether the behavior occurs more often during certain times, subjects, or activities (e.g., to indicate if the incident happened in the morning or afternoon, or clustering the tallies by math or reading, teacher directed instruction or independent work, etc.).

d. If the student notices what you are doing and asks about it, be straightforward—tell her that you are collecting information on how often she asks for help to determine if she is depending upon the help of others too much.

Following is an example of anecdotal notes and frequency information that have been collected on a blind student's helpless behavior.

Help Given to Kara—3/27

Morning	Afternoon
IIHII II?	III?I IHIII IIII? IIIII

(**Key:** I = should have been able to function independently; H = really needed help; ? = not sure if the student needed help or not)

Notes:

10:20—Kara asked the aide to help her get her coat so she could go out for recess. She knows where the coats are kept, and the students always get their own coats.

11:00—Kara couldn't find a pencil for spelling; after checking her desk, she went to the pencil can and got one herself.

11:30—Ms. Shinn (music teacher) reported that Kara kept asking for help with putting her flute together, even though she has done it herself many times before.

1:10—Kara said she couldn't find her math homework, and acted very upset. I helped her look in her notebook and it was right on top in the front pocket.

---

e. The frequency information is fairly easy to summarize on a chart or graph. Seeing how often the student asks for help may help the student's parent(s) better understand your concern.

f. Continuing to collect this type of information (and keeping the chart up-to-date) while you implement a plan will help you monitor whether the situation is getting worse, staying the same, or getting better.

2. *Identify a focus for the intervention and labels for referring to the appropriate and inappropriate behaviors.*

a. To be effective, the intervention must address more than just reducing the student's helpless behavior—there must be a concurrent emphasis on increasing some positive behavior or trait (e.g., self-reliance). Having a specific positive behavior in mind will make it easier for you to "catch" and reinforce the student for behaving appropriately, and the positive focus will help you to frame the situation more productively.

For example, if you simply say that "the student has a problem with acting helpless," you don't really provide any useful information, and may put the student and her parent(s) on the defensive. However, when you explain that you want to "help the student learn to be more self-reliant," you present an important, and reasonable, goal for the student to work toward and clearly identify what the student needs to do to be successful.

b. Specifying labels for the appropriate and inappropriate behaviors (e.g., "being self-reliant" and "acting helpless," respectively) will help you to use consistent vocabulary when discussing the situation with the student. If you sometimes refer to the inappropriate behavior as "acting helpless" and other times tell the student to "stop asking for unnecessary help," for example, she may not realize that you are talking about the same thing.

3. *Determine when and how to include the parent(s).*

a. It is not necessary to contact the student's parent(s) if the problem has just begun and is not interfering with the student's academic or social progress. However, it might be a good idea to take advantage of any scheduled activities (e.g., conferences, weekly notes home) to let them know of your concern.

b. The parent(s) should be contacted whenever the student's helpless behavior is affecting her academic performance and/or is alienating her from her peers. Share with them any information you have collected about the behavior (e.g., anecdotal notes, frequency count), and explain why you are concerned. Focus in particular on how the behavior is hindering the student academically and/or socially (e.g., the student isn't getting work completed because she spends so much time asking for help on simple tasks that she can do herself).

You might ask if the parent(s) have any insight into the situation and/or whether they have noticed similar behavior at home or in the past at school. Whether or not the parent(s) perceive a problem, explain that you want to help the student "learn to be more self-reliant" and invite them to join you for an initial meeting with the student to develop a plan. If the parent(s) are unable or unwilling to participate, let them know that you will keep them informed of the student's progress.

c. Once the parent(s) have been involved in any way, you should give them updates at least once per week while the plan is being implemented.

Prepare for, then conduct, an initial meeting about the situation.

a. Arrange a meeting to discuss your concerns with the student and anyone else who will be involved in the plan (e.g., the parent[s], a special education teacher). Although the specifics will vary depending upon the age of the student and the severity of the problem, there are some general guidelines to consider when scheduling the meeting.

First, meet at a neutral time (i.e., not immediately after a problem has occurred), when emotions are less likely to hamper communication. In general, a day's notice is appropriate, however a primary age student may worry excessively and/or forget what the meeting is about if it is scheduled more than an hour before it takes place.

Second, make the meeting appropriately private. With a primary student who has a mild problem, you might meet in the classroom while the other students are working independently. However, when dealing with a middle/junior high school student and the student's parent(s), you will need some place private (e.g., the counselor's office) to ensure that the discussion will not be overheard.

Third, try to make sure the meeting is scheduled for a time and place that it is not likely to be interrupted. Finally, if the parent(s) will be participating, they should be the ones to tell the student about the meeting.

b. Construct a preliminary plan. Decide whether you think you can use one of the MODEL PLANS or if you need to create a customized plan using components from various plans and/or of your own design. Although you will invite and encourage the student to help develop the plan during the initial meeting, having a proposed plan in mind before you meet can alleviate frustration and wasted time if the student is unwilling or unable to participate.

c. After reviewing the information you have collected and thinking about how you want the student to behave, prepare thorough descriptions of the inappropriate behavior and the positive behavior/trait on which the student will be working. The more specific you can be and the more concrete examples you have, the easier it will be to clarify (and for the student to understand) your expectations. Be sure to consider the student's behavior in all relevant activities (e.g., independent work, teacher directed instruction, unstructured class times, recess and lunch, etc.).

d. Conduct the meeting in an atmosphere of collaboration. The following agenda is one way you might structure the meeting:

• **Share your concerns about the student's behavior.**

Briefly describe the problem behavior. Then explain why you consider the helpless behavior to be a problem. You might tell the student that asking for unnecessary help wastes the time of others and can make her feel as if she cannot do things for herself. You should communicate to the student that everyone needs help or direction now and again, but that when someone asks for help on something they can do themselves, that is a problem.

• **Discuss how you can work together to improve the situation.**

Tell the student that you would like to help her "learn to be more self-reliant," and describe your preliminary plan. Invite the student to give you input on the various aspects of the plan, and together work out any necessary details (e.g., where and when the lessons will take place). You may have to brainstorm different possibilities if the student is uncomfortable with the initial plan. Incorporating any of the student's suggestions that strengthen the plan is likely to increase her sense of "ownership" in and commitment to it.

• **Make sure the student understands what you mean by appropriate and inappropriate behavior.**

Use the descriptions you have prepared to define and clarify the problem behavior and the positive (desired) behavior as specifically and thoroughly as you can. To ensure that you and the student are in agreement about the expectations, you might discuss hypothetical scenarios and have her identify whether each is an example of being self-reliant or asking for unnecessary help. Or you might describe an actual situation that has occurred and ask her to explain how she could demonstrate more self-reliance in that situation.

• **Conclude the meeting.**

Always end the meeting with words of encouragement. Let the student know that you are confident that she can be successful. Be sure to reinforce her for participating in the meeting.

5. Give the student regular, ongoing feedback about her behavior.

It is important to meet with the student periodically to discuss her progress. In most cases, three to five minutes once per week should suffice. *(NOTE: PLAN D suggests daily meetings.)* During the meetings, review any information that has been collected and discuss whether or not the situation is getting better. As much as possible, focus on the student's improvements, however, also address any new or continuing problems. As the situation improves, the meetings can be faded to once every other week and then to once per month.

6. Evaluate the situation (and the plan).

Implement any plan for at least two weeks before deciding whether to change plans; to continue, modify, or fade the plan you are using; or to cease the intervention. Generally, if the student's behavior is clearly improving (based on the objective information that's been collected and/or the subjective perceptions of yourself, the student, and possibly the parent[s]), stick with what you are doing. If the situation has remained the same or worsened, some kind of change will be necessary. Always discuss any changes to the plan with the student first.

HOMELESSNESS

DESCRIPTION

You have a student (or students) in your class whose family is homeless.

The issue of homelessness is beyond the scope of this reference guide and the authors' expertise, therefore there are no MODEL PLANS included with this problem. The purpose of the following information is to offer some basic considerations and suggestions for addressing a situation in which one or more of your students is homeless.

> *NOTE:*
>
> *Much of the following information was adapted with permission from:*
>
> *Staff. (1994, December). Homeless children: What can teachers do? CONNECT, 4(1), 4-5.*

. . . .
General Information

- Unfortunately, homelessness is affecting school age children with increasing frequency. It is estimated that over 40% of the homeless population in the United States are families. Students from homeless families may experience depression, have attendance problems, feel alienated from their peers, and have trouble completing assignments.

Schools and classrooms are often the best source of safety and stability for these children. Following are things that you, as a classroom teacher, might do to help a student whose family is homeless:

- Provide a stable environment at school.

- Provide structure in the classroom.

- Allow personal possessions or space and encourage rights to them.

- Expect and unobtrusively monitor regressions.

- Assign projects that can be broken into small components to ensure at least some successes.

- Allow the student to express his/her fears.

- Allow the student to express his/her frustrations and give him/her opportunities in which to do so in ways other than through verbalization (e.g., drawing).

- Make professional help (e.g., an informed school counselor) available quickly.

- Be open to the student's need to talk about his/her experiences, without prying.

- Do not assume that the student knows how to play; he/she may have to be taught.

- Be well-informed about homelessness issues.

- It is very important to make the student feel welcome and safe at school. Greet the student as she arrives at school each day and, whenever possible, chat with the student. For example, when you are walking the class down the hall, make a point of walking with the student and having a pleasant conversation. When correcting the student's work, be sure to point out the positive aspects of the student's work first and then explain the student's errors as diplomatically as possible.

- If the student exhibits a particular misbehavior (e.g., apathy, absenteeism), find the specific behavior in this reference guide and review the suggested MODEL PLANS for addressing that behavior. If you find a plan that seems appropriate, be sure that you implement it with an extra bit of care and compassion given the student's troubled situation.

HOMEWORK ISSUES

DESCRIPTION

You have a student who fails to complete and/or turn in required homework.

GOAL

The student will consistently turn in completed homework on time.

OVERVIEW OF PLANS

- PLAN A: For a situation in which the problem has just begun or occurs infrequently.

- PLAN B: For a student whose homework issues stem primarily from the lack of a place and/or time to study.

- PLAN C: For a student who, for one or more reasons, has become extremely discouraged about his ability to successfully turn in completed homework.

- PLAN D: For a student whose homework issues stem primarily from a lack of necessary organizational skills.

- PLAN E: For a student has no interest in improving his rate of completed homework turned in on time.

- PLAN F: For a situation in which many students in the class have problems with homework completion.

Alternative Problems

- **Work Completion—Daily Work**

- **Work Completion—Long-Term Projects**

········
General Considerations

- If the student's problem behavior stems in any way from academic issues (e.g., the student does not complete his homework because he is unable to do the work), concurrent efforts must be made to ensure his academic success (see **Academic Deficits, Determining**).

- If the student is receiving special education services, consult with his special education teacher(s) before developing an intervention plan to ascertain what expectations are reasonable for the student

and/or what assistance/ accommodations may be necessary to assist him in being successful.

- If the student is in middle/junior high school and has other teachers, you might want to find out whether he is having homework problems in their classes as well. Collaborating on the intervention may increase its chances of success. In addition, seeing his teachers working together to help him succeed may be very encouraging to the student.

········
Model Plans

PLAN A

It is not always necessary, or even beneficial, to use an involved plan. If the inappropriate behavior has just begun and/or occurs only sporadically, the following actions, along with making the student aware of your concerns, may resolve the situation.

1. **Respond consistently to the inappropriate behavior.**

a. Implement class-wide consequences (e.g., a 10% point reduction for any assignment turned in late) for any student who hands in homework late.

b. Whenever the target student fails to turn in and/or complete his homework, gently correct him as soon as possible. If there are already identified classroom consequences established, review them. "Salvador, homework is a very important part of this class. The consequence for not turning in the assignment is that you will have after-school detention until it is completed." Do not give the student a chance to make excuses, and do not give the student too much attention.

2. **Use reinforcement to encourage appropriate behavior.**

a. Give the student increased praise. Be especially alert for situations in which the student turns in completed homework on time and praise him for these demonstrations of his ability to be responsible. The more immediate the feedback, the greater the chance that it will motivate the student to continue being respon-

sible. Ideally, you want to praise the student as he is turning in the work. (NOTE: One way to accomplish this is to collect the work directly from the students on the day it is due. See PLAN E for suggestions on how to physically collect homework.)

If overt public praise would embarrass the student, praise the entire class, but look directly at the target student so that he realizes that you are pleased with him. "Lots of responsible people in this class have completed this homework assignment on time."

Later, praise the student privately. "Salvador, you have been responsible about getting in your homework everyday this week. You should be very proud of your effort and organizational ability."

b. Also, frequently praise the student for other positive behaviors he exhibits, such as his musical talent or how helpful he has been in preparing for a guest speaker. This lets the student know that you notice many positive things he does, not just his homework completion.

c. Finally, give the student frequent attention (e.g., say "hello" to him as he enters the class or ask him to help you prepare some materials for the next lesson you are going to teach).

PLAN B

Sometimes students have homework problems because their homes are not conducive to study. This plan is appropriate for the student who may not have an adequate place to study at home or whose family is in crisis. Remember that in addition to helping the student make alternative arrangements for study, you need to encourage him to use them.

 1. Talk with the student about his current homework situation (i.e., the time and place he has available to work).

You want to identify whether the student's home situation is such that it is interfering with his ability to complete assigned work at home. Be especially careful about the student's (and parent's) feelings if the circumstances are in any way sensitive.

 2. Respond consistently to the inappropriate behavior.

When the student fails to turn in completed homework on time, gently correct him and hold him accountable for any class-wide consequences (see PLAN A).

3. Help the student set up a plan for getting his homework done.

a. Explore school-based settings where the student might study. Options include the school library, your own classroom, the foyer to the counselor's office, the nurse's room, etc. Or if you know of other students in the school with the same type of problem, you might consider proposing that the staff set up a "Homework Room" supervised by a friendly teacher assistant and open at various times during the day (e.g., before/after school and during lunch) to students who wish to use it.

Keep in mind that a Homework Room should not be used as a punishment (i.e., a place where students have to go when they have not finished their homework). This room should be an invitational place that students want to use because it is quiet, pleasant, and has someone who can answer an occasional question.

You might also consider locations outside the school, such as the public library or a nearby business willing to offer desk space for an hour per day that the student might use to study.

b. During your initial meeting with the student (see SUGGESTED STEPS FOR DEVELOPING AND IMPLEMENTING A PLAN), ask the student for his suggestions on settings other than his home where he might study (e.g., a relative's or friend's house he could use). Then assist the student in making any necessary arrangements for use of this location.

Keep in mind, however, that with a location outside the school, the student's use of the location must be fairly regular. That is, if the student will be going to someone's house to study, he should go there every day regardless of whether or not he has homework. And when the student isn't able to make it, he needs to assume responsibility for letting the person know as it would not be fair to leave that person wondering (and worrying) about where he is.

c. With the student, consider a range of possible times when he might use the study place (e.g., before school, after school, during recesses or breaks, during lunch, etc.) and help him to set up a firm study schedule.

 4. Monitor the student's use of his plan.

If the student is using a school-based option, stop in and visit the student a couple of times per week during the first few weeks. Sit down with the student and see if he has any questions about his work. Praise the quality of his work and let him know how impressed you are that he is following through on his commitment. Gradually reduce your visits to once every couple of weeks.

If the student is using a study option outside the school, monitor the situation by periodically talking to the student at school about how the alternative plan is working.

5. Use reinforcement to encourage appropriate behavior.

a. Give the student increased praise and attention for turning in completed homework on time (see PLAN A).

b. Also praise the student for how well he is following through on his study plan.

PLAN C

For a variety of reasons, some students have become so discouraged about doing homework that it becomes easier for them to fail by doing nothing than to risk trying and failing again (i.e., they literally give up). This plan may be appropriate if your student seems passive or defeated about his homework.

1. *Respond consistently to the inappropriate behavior.*

When the student fails to turn in completed homework on time, gently correct him and hold him accountable for any class-wide consequences (see PLAN A).

2. *Make sure the student is capable of actually doing the homework before he leaves class.*

When introducing a homework task, lead all the students through the first part of the assignment to find out if they understand what they need to do (i.e., guided practice). As you do this, pay particular attention to the target student. Make frequent eye contact with him. Stand near his desk. Call on him frequently. Praise several students, but particularly the target student. "Salvador and Aaron, I can tell by how you did on these first problems that you know what to do on the rest."

If necessary, gently correct the student to keep him focused during the guided practice. "Salvador, you need to keep focused because we are going over what you need to do tonight."

3. *Be a "coach" to convince the student that doing his homework is worth the effort.*

a. Whenever possible, "sell" the student on the idea of his own success. Think of yourself as the coach of a sports team about to face their toughest opponent. The effective coach doesn't just say, "Here is the task. Go do it." Instead, the coach will work to "pump up" the team; convincing the team that it is a challenge that they are ready for, that they can do it.

b. If appropriate, consider making the coaching example a private joke between you and the student. You are the "coach," he is the "team," and "incomplete homework" is his opposition. You and the student could even keep score. "Salvador, the score is now Salvador—4, Incomplete Homework—0. What a game! What courage! However, there are two assignments due tomorrow. Incomplete Homework could

start catching up. Stay tuned tomorrow, sports fans, for the latest update."

4. *Structure activities or interactions that capitalize on the student's strengths or interests.*

Although not directly related to the homework problem, building the student's self-confidence and sense of self-worth may increase the likelihood that he will try to succeed at his homework. That is, focusing the student's attention on those things he already does well may help him feel more confident in general and more relaxed about his performance.

There are many ways to boost a student's self-confidence. For example, if the student is proficient on the computer, you might ask him to help you set up a database to keep track of classroom supplies. If the student has artistic abilities, you might ask him for a drawing that can be used to demonstrate a particular technique to the class. Or, if appropriate, ask the student if he would like to tutor a younger student. *(NOTE: A list of additional ideas for jobs/responsibilities can be found in APPENDIX 2.)*

5. *Use reinforcement to encourage appropriate behavior.*

Give the student increased praise and attention for turning in completed homework on time (see PLAN A).

6. *(OPTIONAL)*
Encourage the student to engage in more positive self-talk.

a. Try to find out (by asking the student directly and/or by listening closely) whether the student tends to make comments or think thoughts that put himself down, such as:

- "I never get anything done."

- "I am so dumb."

- "I can't do that sort of thing."

- "I always make that mistake."

b. Making self-statements like these continually will tend to reinforce the student's negative beliefs about himself. That is, the more he thinks or says them, the more he will believe them to be true, and the more discouraged he may become. One way to help the student is to teach him the difference between positive and negative self-talk and how to reframe his negative statements into more positive and hopeful statements. *(NOTE: Additional information on this procedure can be found in Self-Concept Problems).*

PLAN D

Sometimes a student with homework problems simply lacks organizational skills. If your student forgets to write down assignments, loses his assignment sheets, forgets his homework at home, and/or loses his homework, the intervention should focus on helping the student learn to be better organized.

 Help the student learn and use strategies for keeping track of assignments, due dates, and completed papers.

a. Ideas of strategies the student can use include:

- Storing papers in the proper sections of a three-ring binder with clearly labeled dividers for each academic subject.

- Determining which materials are necessary to successfully complete each assignment before beginning homework.

- Using a recording system such as the sample shown to keep track of assignments and due dates.

Homework Completion Self-Monitoring Form

Name _____   Date _____

DUE	ASSIGNMENT	MATERIALS	DONE

Before leaving school I will study from _____ to _____. I will also study from _____ to _____, if necessary.

❏ 1. I have logged any long-term assignments not yet finished on tomorrow's assignment sheet.

❏ 2. I have organized my assignments in my notebook.

❏ 3. I have packed all my books, materials, and notebook in my backpack.

❏ 4. I have put my backpack by the door.

Give the student a new form each day. Have him first transfer any assignments not yet completed (e.g., a term paper) from the previous day's form and then check off Item 1 at the bottom of the page. Items 2, 3, and 4 should be checked off by the student at home.

NOTE: Another excellent resource is the "Student Daily Planner." This is a detailed planning calendar complete with goal-setting activities and information on organizational and study skills that is most appropriate for middle/junior high school, and college students. Contact:

Elan Publishing Company
P.O. Box 683
Meridith, NH 03253
(800) 258-2000

b. If one student needs to be taught these strategies, it is likely that others in the school could also use some instruction in this area. You can teach the lessons yourself, or it may make more sense to arrange for someone else (e.g., the school counselor) to conduct a study skills class for a small group of students. An excellent resource for these lessons is:

Archer, A. & Gleason, M. (1990). *Skills for school success*. North Billerica, MA: Curriculum Associates.

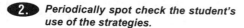 **Periodically spot check the student's use of the strategies.**

a. At least twice per week in the beginning, check the student's notebook and assignment sheet. This will give the student extra incentive to keep things organized and current. If the student is following through, provide praise.

b. Occasionally you might want to provide intermittent rewards. For example, when the student has had his notebook and assignment sheet current and up to date two spot checks in a row, you might cut one of his homework assignments in half. "Salvador, getting organized can really save time. I don't know whether you can tell yet, but this organizational effort will pay off. In fact, just to show you how it can save you time, I am going to cut your math assignment in half." *(NOTE: A list of additional reinforcement ideas can be found in APPENDIX 1.)*

c. If the student's notebook or assignment sheets do not meet the expectations that you and the student have discussed, arrange for the student to spend time during a break or after school getting his materials reorganized and up-to-date.

d. As the student demonstrates consistent success, fade the frequency of the spot checks to once per week (but not always on the same day), then to once every other week until the student has demonstrated acceptable homework behavior for one month.

3. **Respond consistently to the inappropriate behavior.**

When the student fails to turn in completed homework on time, implement the designated class-wide consequence and gently correct him (see PLAN A).

4. **Use reinforcement to encourage appropriate behavior.**

Give the student increased praise and attention for turning in completed homework on time (see PLAN A).

PLAN E

When a student is not concerned about the designated consequences of failing to turn in completed homework and/or does not value the sense of satisfaction that comes with completing and turning in required work, you may need to implement a system of external incentives (i.e., rewards and consequences) to motivate him to turn in completed homework on time.

1. **Establish a structured system for reinforcing the appropriate behavior and providing a consequence for the inappropriate behavior.**

a. With the student, create a list of rewards he would like to earn. The rewards may need to be relatively high in perceived value in order to

create a powerful incentive to motivate the student to get his homework completed on a regular basis. To get some ideas for the list, watch what the student does during less structured times in class—what does he do when he has choices? Or you can ask the student for his preferences. *(NOTE: A list of reinforcement ideas can be found in APPENDIX 1.)*

You might also have the student read through the list of your ideas and then together discuss the possibilities. If the student's parent(s) will be working with you and the student on the plan, maybe some of the reinforcers could be things the parent(s) provide at home (e.g., having a friend spend the night, a later curfew, additional money for clothing, etc.).

b. Assign "prices" (in points) for each of the rewards on the list and have the student select the reward he would like to earn first.

The prices should be based on the instructional, personnel, and/or monetary cost of the items. Monetary cost is clear—the more expensive the item, the more points required to earn it. Instructional cost refers to the amount of instructional time lost or interfered with by a particular reward. Thus, an activity which causes the student to miss part of academic instruction should require more points than one the student can do on his own free time. Personnel cost involves the time required by you and/or other staff to fulfill the reinforcer. Having lunch with the principal, therefore, would cost more points than spending five minutes of free time with a friend.

The prices must be low enough that the student will think, for example, "You mean all I have to do is _____, and I can earn _____!" If the desired reinforcers are priced too high and would take the student too long to earn (from his perspective), he may not be any more motivated to complete his homework than he was without the system.

c. Develop a homework completion self-monitoring form (like the sample shown in PLAN D), and establish a system to translate each successfully filled in space into points. For example, the student might earn one point each for accurately recording the assignment, the due date, and the necessary materials (three points total). When the assignment is completed and turned in, the student might earn another five points, making each homework assignment worth a total of eight points.

Larger assignments or projects, such as writing a report, could be broken down into steps, each with its own line and due date on the monitoring form. For example, the outline, the note cards, the rough draft, and the final draft could be treated as separate assignments, each worth eight points—making the whole report worth a possible 32 reinforcement points. (For additional ideas on long-term projects, see **Work Completion—Long-Term Projects**.)

d. When the student has accumulated enough points to earn the reward he has chosen, he "spends" the points necessary and the system begins again. That is, he selects another reward to earn and begins with zero points.

2. **Respond consistently to the inappropriate behavior.**

a. Gently correct the student when he fails to turn in his homework (see PLAN A).

b. Establish consequences (in addition to any predetermined class-wide consequences) for not being responsible for his homework. The most obvious consequence would be that if the student does not turn in the work, he fails that assignment. However, that consequence alone may be too abstract and delayed to affect the student's behavior in the short run. Another, and more immediate, consequence will probably be necessary (e.g., the student must stay in from recess/breaks and/or stay after school until the work is caught up).

If the parent(s) are working with you on the reinforcement portion of the plan, you can consider asking them to implement a consequence at home as well, such as grounding the student until he is caught up with his work. However, this is only appropriate if the parent(s) are also reinforcing the student—the parent(s)' role should *never* be only punitive.

c. When neither home-based nor school-based consequences are possible, for whatever reason, it puts more pressure on the positive aspects of the intervention to ensure that the plan is powerful enough to motivate the student to complete his homework—despite the lack of consequences for not turning it in.

3. **Use reinforcement to encourage appropriate behavior.**

a. Give the student increased praise and attention for turning in completed homework on time (see PLAN A).

b. In addition, show interest and enthusiasm about how the student is doing on the system. "Salvador, every day this week you have earned all eight points for every assignment. Congratulations! You should be very proud of your organizational skill."

PLAN F

Sometimes many students in a class will develop a pattern of not turning in homework. When this happens, it can be helpful to evaluate and possibly even revise the routines you use for designing, assigning, collecting, and returning homework. In addition, procedures for class-wide monitoring and the use of rewards and incentives may be a necessary part of the intervention.

(NOTE: This plan suggests many procedures. Pick and choose three to five that have the greatest applicability to your situation.)

1. ***Respond consistently to any student who does not have his/her homework completed on the due date.***

Whenever a student fails to turn in homework, gently correct the student and hold him/her accountable for any established class-wide consequences (see PLAN A).

2. ***Make sure that the amount of homework assigned is reasonable.***

Determine if your homework expectations are reasonable. There are several ways to do this: (1) check with your building or district curriculum administrators about policies concerning the amount of homework recommended at different grade levels; (2) check with other teachers of the same grade level or subject in other schools, and even other districts, about how much work they assign; and/or (3) check with the parents of your students about the amount of time the students are spending on homework. After gathering this information, you might need to revise your expectations.

3. ***Make sure that the homework assigned is both relevant and at an appropriate difficulty level.***

Remember that the purpose of homework is to give the students additional practice on skills that have been mastered in class. This means that the homework content should lag behind class content. Without sufficient class practice, homework assignments may be so difficult that the students become discouraged and cease to try completing them.

In addition, when the assigned homework has not been fully understood, students whose parents are unwilling, unavailable, or unable to help are at a disadvantage. A rough guideline is that students should not be assigned content as homework until it has been taught and reviewed in class for at least three days.

4. ***Make sure to provide guided practice on homework.***

a. As you design lessons, schedule time to guide your students through the first part of any homework task. This gets the students started on the assignment before they even leave school, and helps you to verify that the difficulty level is appropriate. This procedure also gives the students the opportunity to ask questions about anything on the assignment that they do not understand.

b. In addition, try to schedule a few minutes each day for the students to work on the homework in class. This allows one more opportunity for you to answer any questions about the directions or a particular concept. If you do provide this kind of time, it is important to let the students know that if they do not use the time appropriately, you will not continue to provide it.

5. ***Establish a routine for assigning homework.***

Preestablished homework routines can positively affect the amount of homework completed. While there is no one right way to schedule homework, a teacher with no routine (e.g., zero assignments one week, five the next week, and three the week after that) is more likely to have problems getting homework returned.

Routines eliminate student excuses that they did not know they had homework, and can help with parental support. When parents know the class routine, they know when their students are supposed to have homework. That is, they have a way of knowing if their students are telling the truth when they say that there is no homework.

In the following example, the students (and their parents) in the second grade class know that if it is Tuesday, there is math homework. Following are sample homework routines for 2nd, 6th, and 8th grades.

2nd Grade

Math—Homework every Monday, Tuesday, and Wednesday

Spelling—List home on Monday; test on Friday

6th Grade

Math—Homework every Monday, Tuesday, Wednesday, and Thursday.

Writing—Assigned on Monday; due on Friday

History—Study questions assigned on Friday, due Tuesday

8th Grade

Study Questions or Weekly Project—Assigned Wednesday, due Tuesday

History Test—Every Friday

Major Project—Progress sheets due on Friday

give them information about any missing assignments. If possible, provide this information to their parents as well. If you have access to a computer, you might use a computerized gradebook to do this. Many programs generate individualized printouts for each student, showing both work completed and work missing.

Even without a computer, you can devise an efficient method for giving the students feedback. You may, for example, carry your gradebook while monitoring an independent work period. Then you can share the information in your gradebook during brief conferences with individual students. Spending a few minutes with one-fifth of the students each day allows you to have a short conference with every student each week.

If there are several students who need to be more responsible for their homework, hold weekly small group sessions during lunch or after school with those students. Identify and/or review strategies (see PLANS C and D for ideas) that may help the students develop better habits and motivation related to homework. These sessions do not have to be lengthy—five minutes each may be sufficient.

 Establish routines for collecting homework.

Having the students place their homework in a box or basket may seem impersonal, and leave the students feeling let down. If you collect the work yourself the students are much more likely to feel acknowledged for having been responsible enough to get their homework done. Additionally, any student who hasn't done the work will face immediate consequences—not one, two, or three days later.

One way to personally collect homework is to meet your students at the door and have them give you their homework on the way into class. This can be a powerful technique, although it is not always feasible. Another method is to have the students leave their homework on their desks so you can pick it up while they work on an assignment or challenge problem. With either method, you can provide immediate feedback to the students—a key to getting them to improve. If a student (or students) does not have the homework, give a gentle reprimand and tell the student that you will talk later.

 Establish procedures for giving feedback on missing work.

Along with gently confronting students when they do not turn homework in on time, once per week

 As a class, have the students brainstorm ideas for remembering to do their homework.

After the brainstorming session, have each student create a list of the ideas that he/she will personally implement to become more responsible about handing in completed homework on time. Then have the students give you their lists. You can use these lists to review the strategies with individual students periodically if homework problems continue.

 Develop a "study buddy" plan.

Have all the students choose a partner. These pairs of students will be responsible for reminding each other about getting their homework done. Encourage the students to call their partners at a prearranged time to find out if they are done with their homework or if they have any questions.

A potential problem with this procedure is if there is an "untouchable" in class, a student that no other students want to work with. If such a situation exists in your class, this procedure should not be used because it is likely to cause that student a great deal of embarrassment and pain.

Design and post a chart that shows the percentage of homework turned in.

a. Review your gradebook for the last two or three weeks and calculate a daily percentage of homework turned in. Record this information on a chart.

b. Post this chart in a highly visible place in the classroom. If you are a middle/junior high school teacher, use a transparency for each class instead of a posted chart. Put the appropriate transparency on the overhead during times when you are assigning and collecting homework.

c. On each day that homework is due, even before the work has been corrected determine how many students handed in the work and calculate the percentage of the class this number represents. (Or, if age appropriate, have the students calculate the percentage themselves.) Be sure to adjust for students who are absent that day. Chart this percentage.

d. Each time you chart a percentage, discuss the chart with the students and give them feedback on their completion rates. Let the students know that the ultimate goal is to achieve 100% completion on every homework assignment, but that a more immediate goal is to improve past performance (e.g., perhaps 80%).

e. Try to increase student motivation for completing homework. When assigning homework, communicate the importance of the task. In some ways, try to emulate an effective coach. For example, let the students know that you think they can do it. Remind them of the goal of at least 80/% of the work turned in on time. Encourage the students to make a commitment to themselves to complete their homework and turn it in. Have the students identify the time of the afternoon or the evening that they plan to sit down and complete their homework. Call on a few students and have them state their time for doing homework. Most importantly, keep your enthusiasm high, and communicate that you know the students are mature and responsible enough to meet their homework goal.

 Use intermittent rewards to celebrate the student's improvements.

Highlight the importance of being responsible for homework by providing various rewards to individual students and to the class as a whole when they are responsible for their work. Occasional, and unexpected, rewards can motivate the class to demonstrate responsibility for their homework more often.

Appropriate rewards for the entire class might include a few minutes of extra recess or free time. For a middle/junior high school class, you might allow music to be played during an independent work period or give the class a few minutes for relaxed socializing at the end of the period.

When some students complete their homework and others do not, you could excuse the students who had their homework done on time first for lunch, or give all the students who had their homework done a certificate for an ice cream from the cafeteria. *(NOTE: A list of additional reinforcement ideas can be found in APPENDIX 1.)* If you use intermittent rewards, do so more frequently at the beginning of the intervention to encourage the students, and then less often as their behavior improves.

 (OPTIONAL)
Establish a group reinforcement system.

a. Have the students brainstorm reinforcement ideas for the entire class, and then eliminate any items from the list that are not possible (i.e., the suggestions are too expensive or could not be provided to all the students in the class).

b. Assign "prices" (in points) to the items remaining on the list. The prices should be based on the instructional, personnel, and/or monetary costs of the items. Monetary cost is clear—the more expensive the item, the more points required to earn it. Instructional cost refers to the amount of instructional time lost or interfered with by a particular reward. Thus, an activity which causes the class to miss part of academic instruction should require more points than one the class can do on their own free time. Personnel cost involves the time required by you and/or other staff to fulfill the reinforcer. Earning an extra recess period during which supervision would need to be arranged would cost more than having music playing in class for 15 minutes, for example.

c. Have the class vote on the reinforcers. The reinforcer that earns the most votes is the one they will strive to earn first, and the items that receive the second (and third) most votes will be the next ones worked for.

d. On days when the class successfully keeps their percentage of turned in homework above the percentage on the previous day, the class earns five points toward the selected reward.

For any record-breaking percentage, the class earns ten points. And, whenever 100% of the students turn in their completed homework on time, the class earns 15 points. Then when the class accumulates enough points to earn the agreed-upon reward, they "spend" the points necessary and the system begins again (i.e., they select another reward and begin with zero points).

· · · · · · · ·
Suggested Steps for Developing and Implementing a Plan

The following steps are designed to help you develop an appropriate intervention plan and implement it effectively, whether you choose to use one of the MODEL PLANS or create a customized plan of your own. The steps are, however, suggestions—they are not intended to be followed rigidly or in any particular order. Use your professional judgment and the knowledge of your particular situation to make them work for you.

1. *Make sure you have enough information about the situation.*

a. Use your gradebook to determine the student's weekly rate of homework completion, if possible from the beginning of the current grading period. For each week, simply divide the number of assignments the student turned in completed and on time by the total number of assignments given that week. While calculating these percentages, look for any possible patterns to the student's behavior (e.g., the student has the most difficulty turning in completed homework on Mondays, or has specific difficulty with turning in book reports). *(NOTE: If you are implementing PLAN F, you will use daily rather than weekly information.)*

b. These weekly percentages are fairly easy to summarize on a chart or graph. Seeing how infrequently the student turns in completed homework may help the student and his parent(s) better understand your concern.

c. Continuing to calculate weekly homework completion rates and keeping the chart up-to-date while you implement a plan will help you to monitor whether the situation is getting worse, staying the same, or getting better.

2. *Identify a focus for the intervention and labels for referring to the appropriate and inappropriate behaviors.*

a. Although your goal is to reduce the number of times the student fails to turn in completed homework on time, this is not a particularly effective way to frame the issue. On the other hand, emphasizing a positive behavior or trait such as "being responsible for homework" provides a reasonable and important goal on which the student can work, and is likely to be more motivating for the student. Having a positive focus in mind will also help you to be more aware the student's appropriate behavior and provide you more opportunities to praise and reinforce him.

b. Decide on labels to describe both the appropriate and inappropriate behaviors (e.g., "being responsible for homework" and "not being responsible for homework," respectively) so that you can use consistent vocabulary when discussing the situation with the student. "Salvador, every day for the last week you have demonstrated that you are being responsible for your homework. Great job!"

3. *Determine when and how to include the parent(s).*

a. If the student's homework problem is mild enough that it is not affecting the student's grades, it may not be necessary to make a special effort to contact the parent(s). However, you might take advantage of any scheduled activities (e.g., conferences, report cards) to share your concern.

b. Whenever the student's homework problem is affecting his grades, his parent(s) should be informed. Explain your concern and share with them the data on the (low) percentage of homework the student has turned in each week. Let the parent(s) know that the student's homework problem has begun to interfere with his academic performance and that, if left unchecked, it may become a habit that negatively affects his academic success in subsequent years.

Tell the student's parent(s) that you will be working to support the student's efforts in every way possible, and invite them to meet with you and the student to develop an intervention plan. You might also ask if they would like information on how they can help the student remember to be responsible for his homework and, if appropriate, find out whether the student has a place for study in the home and regular times during which he is supposed to complete his homework. If the parent(s) are unable or unwilling to participate, let them know that you will keep them informed of the student's progress.

c. Once the parent(s) have been involved in any way, you should give them updates at least once per week while the plan is being implemented.

4. *Prepare for, then conduct, an initial meeting about the situation.*

a. Arrange a meeting to discuss your concerns with the student and anyone else who will be involved in the plan (e.g., the parent[s]). Although the specifics will vary depending upon the age of the student and the severity of the problem, there are some general guidelines to consider when scheduling the meeting.

First, meet at a neutral time (i.e., not immediately after a homework problem has occurred), when emotions are less likely to hamper communication. In general, a day's notice is appropriate, however a primary age student may worry excessively and/or forget what the meeting is about if it is scheduled more than an hour before it takes place.

Second, make the meeting appropriately private. With a primary student who has a mild problem, you might meet in the classroom while the other students are working independently. However, when dealing with a middle/junior high school student and the student's parent(s), you will need some place private (e.g., the counselor's office) to ensure that the discussion will not be overheard.

Third, try to make sure the meeting is scheduled for a time and place that it is not likely to be interrupted. Finally, if the parent(s) will be participating, they should be the ones to tell the student about the meeting.

b. Construct a preliminary plan. Decide whether you think you can use one of the MODEL PLANS or if you need to create a customized plan using components from various plans and/or of your own design. Although you will invite and encourage the student to help develop the plan during the initial meeting, having a proposed plan in mind before you meet can

alleviate frustration and wasted time if the student is unwilling or unable to participate.

c. Before the meeting, you need to be clear about your expectations regarding the student's homework completion. For example, is it enough that he hands an assignment in? Or, does it also have to be correct? neat? If the student almost never hands in homework, the initial focus of the intervention should be on encouraging the student to hand in anything—with neatness and accuracy to come later. In other cases, it may be appropriate to emphasize homework that is neat, complete, and at least 70% correct.

Whatever the criteria, they need to be specified to the student during the meeting. You might also want to note specific homework assignments that the student is missing at that time.

d. Conduct the meeting in an atmosphere of collaboration. The following agenda is one way you might structure the meeting:

• **Share your concerns about the student's behavior.**

Briefly describe the problem behavior and show the student a chart of his homework completion rates for the term. Then explain why you consider his low homework completion rates to be a problem. You might tell the student that learning to be responsible for his homework is not only important in your class, but will be important in subsequent years of his schooling, and possibly even on a job. Make sure the student understands that there will not always be someone around to make him do his work, and part of the importance of homework is to help him learn to manage his own time.

• **Discuss how you can work together to improve the situation.**

Tell the student that you would like to help him "learn to be responsible for his homework," and describe your preliminary plan. Invite the student to give you input on the various aspects of the plan, and together work out any necessary details. You may have to brainstorm different possibilities if the student is uncomfortable with the initial plan. Incorporating any of the student's suggestions that strengthen the plan is likely to increase his sense of "ownership" in and commitment to it.

- **Conclude the meeting.**

Always end the meeting with words of encouragement. Let the student know that you are confident that he can be successful. Be sure to reinforce him for participating in the meeting.

 Give the student regular, ongoing feedback about his behavior.

It is important to meet with the student periodically to discuss his progress. In most cases, three to five minutes once per week should suffice. *(NOTE: PLANS E and F and suggest daily meetings.)* During the meetings, review any information that has been collected and discuss whether or not the situation is getting better. As much as possible, focus on the student's improvements, however, also address any new or continuing problems. As

the situation improves, the meetings can be faded to once every other week and then to once per month.

 Evaluate the situation (and the plan).

Implement any plan for at least two weeks before deciding whether to change plans; to continue, modify, or fade the plan you are using; or to cease the intervention. Generally, if the student's rate of homework completion is clearly improving (based on the objective information that's been collected), stick with what you are doing. If the situation has remained the same or worsened, some kind of change will be necessary. Always discuss any changes to the plan with the student first.

HYGIENE PROBLEMS

DESCRIPTION

You have a student who does not perform basic hygiene (e.g., she does not brush her teeth, shower/bathe, and/or wear clean clothes, etc.).

GOAL

The student will learn to take care of her basic hygiene needs prior to coming to school.

OVERVIEW OF PLANS

- PLAN A: For a problem that has just begun and/or is relatively mild.

- PLAN B: For a student who lacks the knowledge and/or skills to take care of her own basic hygiene needs.

- PLAN C: For a student who knows about good hygiene, but often forgets to address her basic hygiene needs.

NOTE:

PLANS B and C are time-intensive, and may not be feasible for a classroom teacher to implement. The school counselor or nurse may need to implement these plans.

Alternative Problems

- **Nose Picking/Oral Fetishes**

- **Wetting/Soiling Pants**

········
General Considerations

- If this problem has gone on for more than a couple of days (i.e., it is beyond the scope of PLAN A), ask for assistance from the school counselor, school nurse, or the school administrator as the problem is likely to be resistant to a simple intervention implemented only by the classroom teacher.

- If you know of a history of neglect or abuse in the student's home, immediately involve your building administrator to determine if social service agencies, such as protective services or mental health agencies, should be included in intervention planning from the beginning.

········
Model Plans

PLAN A

It is not always necessary, or even beneficial, to use an involved plan. If the problem has just begun and/or is relatively mild, the following actions, along with making the student aware of your concerns, may resolve the situation.

 Contact the student's parent(s).

Inform the parent(s) about the situation and ask them to help the student with her basic hygiene needs. Then if the problem is not resolved in a day or two, proceed with Steps 2 and 3 of this plan.

 Respond consistently to the inappropriate behavior.

When the student has not attended to her basic hygiene needs, gently correct her. "Tori, today is an example of not using good hygiene. Tomorrow, you need to remember to take a shower, put on clean clothes, brush your hair, and brush your teeth." The goal of this correction is to make the student aware that her current appearance is problematic. It is important to be emotionally neutral when correcting the student—your goal is to impart information, not to humiliate the student into performing good hygiene. Also avoid making statements to the student that imply that her parent(s) are not meeting their responsibilities. Statements such as, "Your mom really ought to be helping you remember to do this," will make the student feel as if she has to defend her mother. Instead, simply describe what the student must remember before coming to school.

 Use reinforcement to encourage appropriate behavior.

a. When it is clear that the student has made an effort to arrive at school with her basic hygiene

needs taken care of, praise her. As you greet the students entering the room, you might acknowledge the appearance of some of them, including the target student . "Lisa, don't you look nice today. Jacob, fine looking haircut. Did you just get it cut? Tori, you look very nice this morning."

b. In addition, as the student consistently improves, provide private praise that acknowledges the effort the student is making to address her basic hygiene needs. "Tori, I want you to know that your efforts to use good hygiene skills are really paying off. Each day for the last week you have arrived at school showered, with your hair brushed, and you really look ready to begin the day. You should be very proud of yourself."

c. Give the student frequent attention (e.g., say "hello" to her as she enters the classroom, call on her frequently during class activities, and occasionally ask her to assist you with a class job that needs to be done) and praise her for other positive behaviors she exhibits. For example, you might comment about the accuracy of her work or how consistent she is about turning in her assignments on time. This demonstrates to the student that you notice many positive things she does, not just the fact that her hygiene is improving.

PLAN B

Some students need to be taught hygiene skills that most of us take for granted: showering, brushing teeth, and brushing hair (and with an older student—shaving, using deodorant, etc.). If your student does not know how to perform good hygiene, does not have access to the tools of good hygiene, and/or is not receiving adequate support in these efforts from her parent(s), hygiene lessons may be the most effective intervention.

 Determine whether the student has the necessary hygiene skills.

Talk to the student and find out if she can tell you where she finds soap, shampoo, and towels in her home when she wants to shower; where she keeps her clean clothes; if she has access to a washer and dryer (and knows how to use them); and/or if she has a toothbrush and toothpaste and a comb or brush, etc.

 If the student does not have access to appropriate hygiene tools (soap, shampoo, clean clothes, etc.), arrange to provide them.

If your school does not have a discretionary budget for such items, you might check with a social service agency or service club in your community about paying for these items for the student. The student's parent(s) should do this, of course, but if they do not, the student should not have to come to school ungroomed while school personnel and/or authorities from Child Protective Services, for example, try to encourage them to meet their obligations.

 Identify an adult (of the same sex) who will monitor the student's hygiene on a daily basis, and who can conduct lessons if necessary.

(NOTE: The school nurse or counselor might be the most appropriate person.)

a. Each day before school starts, the monitor will check how well the student has performed her basic morning hygiene tasks. If any aspect of basic hygiene is undone or inadequately done, the monitor will conduct a lesson on that task then and there. The idea is to ensure that the student arrives in the classroom reasonably well-groomed each day. To avoid embarrassing the student, both the hygiene check and the lessons should take place outside the classroom (e.g., in the nurse's office, locker room, etc.).

b. If a lesson is necessary, it should consist of both a discussion about and practice in the particular task(s) that have been neglected. For example, the monitor might model correct and incorrect methods of brushing teeth, combing hair, etc., and then have the student practice those behaviors.

Although this procedure may seem silly for an older student, if she never learned appropriate hygiene skills as a young child, she needs the same sort of instruction that a parent would use with a very young child. In one case, with a middle school student, the school nurse conducted lessons on how to use the laundry facilities at the apartment complex where the student lived. This was done with the mother's permission ("Sure, I don't care. I don't have time to teach her myself, so go ahead, what do I care?") and a paraprofessional was also present to prevent any accusations of impropriety.

c. If the problem involves showering/bathing, the student should use the shower facilities in the school, if possible. If there are no showers at school, the lessons should focus on how the student should shower at home. In this case, the adult conducting the lessons should tell the student how to wash with soap, shampoo her hair, etc., and then encourage her to do so.

(NOTE: It is very important to avoid any possibility that the adult could be accused of impropriety as a result of the lessons. Thus, it may be necessary to have two adults conduct the lessons together. The should it ever be necessary, they will be able to verify that the student showered entirely in private while they waited for her to finish, for example.)

d. The lessons should also include "homework assignments." "Tori, tomorrow morning before you come to school, take a shower, brush your teeth, brush your hair, and put on clean clothes. Check in with me tomorrow morning first thing to show me the results." Any hygiene behavior the student did not perform at home should be the topic of that day's lesson.

4. **Use reinforcement to encourage appropriate behavior.**

a. Give the student increased praise and attention for taking care of her hygiene needs (see PLAN A).

b. Let the student know that you notice her efforts to perform good hygiene. Since this sort of public praise would likely be embarrassing for the student, praise the student privately or even give her a note. "Tori, I can really tell that those lessons with Mrs. Jimenez are making a big difference. You look so nice, and I can tell that you are very proud of your appearance."

Occasionally, praise the student publicly for her overall appearance, but be matter-of-fact when doing so. "Good morning Ellen. Hi Tori. Don't you both look nice this morning. Tori, how did your soccer game go last night?"

c. If the student works well during the hygiene lessons and/or has a particularly good period of remembering to perform her basic hygiene before coming to school, the adult conducting the lessons may wish to provide intermittent rewards to the student (or to ask the classroom teacher to do so). "Tori, this is the first day that you have remembered to do every part of the hygiene homework assignment. Great work, and I hope you're proud of the way you look, because to me you look like someone who really takes care of herself. In fact, since there is nothing we need to take care of, and since I don't see another student for 15 minutes, I would like to give you a choice. We could play a quick game of chess, you could use my computer, we could just talk, or you could go back to class a little early. What would you like to do?" (NOTE: A list of additional reinforcement ideas can be found in APPENDIX 1.)

PLAN C

In some cases, a student will need to be given incentives to perform basic hygiene. If the student has the skills and access to the necessary tools to perform basic hygiene, but fails to do so on a regular basis, the intervention should include a self-monitoring system (possibly paired with a structured reinforcement system).

(NOTE: This plan assumes that, despite being informed about the problem, the student's parent[s] are not monitoring or assisting with the student's basic hygiene needs.)

1. **Make sure the student has the skills and tools to perform basic hygiene.**

If you are not sure if this is the case, talk to the student. If the student can verbalize what she needs to do to maintain good hygiene (e.g., she knows where soap and towels are kept in her home, she has a toothbrush and toothpaste, she knows where her clean clothes are or knows how to use the laundry facilities at her home), then she probably has both the tools and the skills to perform her basic hygiene and this plan may be appropri-

ate. If she lacks the necessary tools and/or skills, PLAN B would be more appropriate.

2. **Identify an adult (of the same gender) with whom the student can check in each morning and who will monitor the student's hygiene performance (see PLAN B).**

3. **Develop a form that can be used to monitor the student's personal hygiene.**

A form like the example following, tailored to the student's age and vocabulary, could be used each day in conjunction with the daily lessons.

Tori's Self-Monitoring Hygiene Form

Date _____

Directions:

Check off the items that were completed successfully prior to coming to school.

○ Teeth brushed   ○ Showered   ○ Shampooed hair

○ Used deodorant   ○ Brushed hair   ○ Put on clean clothes

Total points for the day _____

To use the form, every morning the student and the adult can evaluate her hygiene together and fill out the form. The descriptor "successfully" means that the student and the adult agree that the student performed that item adequately. For example, if the student says she brushed her teeth, the nurse should check them. If the student did brush her teeth moderately well (they appear clean/free of food particles upon a cursory glance), the student checks off that item on the form. If she says she brushed her teeth, but was unsuccessful in doing so (i.e., the student's teeth do not appear to have been brushed), the student would not be allowed to check off that item, and the adult should give the student information about how to be more successful tomorrow. "Tori, you may have brushed your teeth this morning, but we cannot check it off because when you brush, you need to make sure that you brush up and down long enough to remove all the food from in between your teeth."

 Encourage the student to use self-reinforcement.

As more items are being checked off on the form each day, teach the student to think reinforcing statements to herself as a way of increasing the likelihood that she will be motivated to continue these skills as life-long habits. Examples of self-reinforcing statements related to hygiene include:

- I feel better and look better after I shower.

- Putting on clean clothes feels so good.

- I am proud of how I look and feel when I brush my hair.

- I am worth taking care of, so I'll take care of myself.

 Help the student devise strategies for addressing hygiene behavior(s) that are consistently not being checked off.

If the student claims she does not have time in the morning for a particular hygiene behavior, help her establish an evening routine for performing the behavior. If the student says she can't remember to brush her teeth in the morning, for example, suggest that she put her toothbrush on her bag or backpack to remind herself to brush before she leaves the house.

 (OPTIONAL)
Establish a structured system to reinforce the student for appropriate behavior.

a. Have the student identify rewards or privileges she would like to earn and assign "prices" (in points) for each of the reasonable suggestions. Decide which reinforcer the student will work for first, then have the student earn one point for each item that is checked off on the self-monitoring form. When the student has accumulated enough points to earn the identified reinforcer, the system begins again.

b. When implementing this type of a system, be sure to keep the focus on skills the student is learning rather than on the extrinsic rewards she is earning. "Tori, you are becoming so responsible about remembering to use good hygiene skills. You should be very proud of how well you are taking care of yourself. Looks like you are now up to 23 points."

. . . .
Suggested Steps for Developing and Implementing a Plan

The following steps are designed to help you develop an appropriate intervention plan and implement it effectively, whether you choose to use one of the MODEL PLANS or create a customized plan of your own. The steps are, however, suggestions—they are not intended to be followed rigidly or in any particular order. Use your professional judgment and the knowledge of your particular situation to make them work for you.

 Make sure you have enough information about the situation.

a. If you think a minimal intervention like PLAN A will be sufficient, you may already have enough information to proceed. However, when a more involved plan seems necessary, you should consider collecting additional descriptive and/or objective information about the behavior for a couple of days.

b. You need to be able to explain what you mean when you say that "the student has a problem with basic hygiene." For example, you should be able to specify whether the student has these problems every day or just on some days. Anecdotal notes can provide the detail you need to describe the situation clearly and completely. To collect anecdotal notes, simply keep a card or piece of notebook paper on which you can make daily notes about the student's appearance and any odor problems. Include information about whether other students are noticing the problem and reacting negatively to the target student, but avoid judgmental statements and/or conclusions such as, "I wish her parents would do their job."

Also keep detailed records of all the contacts you have with the student's parent(s) regarding this issue. If the problem continues, and the parent(s) do not follow through with helping the student resolve it, your anecdotal notes could be vital in efforts by authorities to make the parent(s) assume their responsibilities and/or should it become necessary to charge the parent(s) with neglect.

c. Following is an example of anecdotal notes that have been collected on a student's hygiene problem.

d. Keeping anecdotal notes throughout the implementation of the intervention will not only provide you with potentially valuable documentation of your efforts, but can also help you monitor whether the situation is getting worse, staying the same, or getting better.

 Identify a focus for the intervention and labels for referring to the appropriate and inappropriate behaviors.

One of the more difficult aspects of addressing this situation is finding a way to discuss the problem without insulting the student or her parent(s). Identifying a positive trait or label (e.g., cleanliness, good hygiene, or personal management) to use when talking about the problem can make the situation less awkward, and will allow you to use consistent vocabulary whenever you are discussing the problem with the student.

3. *Determine when and how to include the parent(s).*

a. As uncomfortable as it may be to make this contact, involve the parent(s) immediately with this problem. The parent(s) may not realize that their child's hygiene is so poor that it is noticeable to others and, once informed, may follow through on their parenting responsibilities.

If it seems clear from the contact that the parent(s) do not know how to help their child with basic hygiene or are unable to provide the necessary hygiene tools, it may be necessary to contact a social service agency to arrange help for this family. *(NOTE: Don't take this step without first checking with your building admin-*

Notes on Tori's Hygiene

9/16—Tori came to school today and her hair was not brushed, her teeth had not been brushed, and she had not showered or changed her clothes since yesterday. Several other students were teasing Tori today, holding their noses and pointing to her.

9/17—Last night, I contacted Mrs. Mayfair and told her that her daughter needed help remembering to get ready for school and that the problem was hurting Tori's relationship with the other students. She said she would take care of it.

Today, Tori had her hair combed and had on different clothes, but I don't think they were clean because she still smelled to the point that other students were reacting, and even I found it unpleasant to be too close to her. Her teeth had not been brushed either. I talked to her privately, asked her if she had showered, and she said no. I tried to be diplomatic, and explain to her that she was at the age where showering and teeth brushing are necessary daily. She said she would try to remember.

9/18—Same problems again today. I am going to call Mrs. M again tonight.

9/19—When I contacted Mrs. M last night and told her that the problem still existed, she became angry and verbally abusive, saying things like, "You f____ teachers should mind your own d____ business and let me raise my kid."

Tori seemed cleaner today, and her clothes were clean. There was no offensive odor.

---

istrator regarding district policies for these types of situations.)

Keep in mind that even if the parent(s) make it clear that they feel the problem is none of the school's business, when a hygiene problem is so blatant that others notice, it is school business because the problem is interfering with the student's social growth. Regardless of the parental perception, develop a plan and keep the parent(s) informed and as involved as possible.

b. When the parent(s) cannot or will not help the student take care of her basic hygiene needs, focus the intervention on assisting the student in being more responsible for her own hygiene by implementing one or more of the MODEL PLANS presented. Do this even when efforts are being made to inform authorities of the neglect possibly occurring in the student's home. Waiting for outside agencies to successfully work with the parent(s) may take too long.

c. Once the parent(s) have been involved in any way, you should give them updates at least once per week while the plan is being implemented.

4. *Prepare for, then conduct, an initial meeting about the situation.*

a. Arrange a meeting to discuss your concerns with the student and anyone else who will be involved in the plan (e.g., the parent[s], the school nurse). Although the specifics will vary depending upon the age of the student and the severity of the problem, there are some general guidelines to consider when scheduling the meeting.

First, meet at a neutral time. A day's notice is generally appropriate, however a primary age student may worry excessively and/or forget what the meeting is about if it is scheduled more than an hour before it takes place.

Second, make the meeting appropriately private. Third, try to make sure the meeting is scheduled for a time and place that it is not likely to be interrupted (e.g., the counselor's office). Finally, if the parent(s) will be participating, they should be the ones to tell the student about the meeting.

b. Construct a preliminary plan. Decide whether you think you can use one of the MODEL PLANS or if you need to create a customized plan using components from various plans and/or of your own design. Although you will invite and encourage the student to help develop the plan during the initial meeting, having

a proposed plan in mind before you meet can alleviate frustration and wasted time if the student is unwilling or unable to participate.

c. Carefully review your anecdotal notes and make sure you have identified the labels you plan to use for referring to both the problem and desired behaviors.

d. Conduct the meeting in an atmosphere of collaboration. The following agenda is one way you might structure the meeting:

- **Share your concerns about the student's behavior.**

  Briefly describe the problem behavior and explain that poor hygiene will affect how others interact with the student and how they think of her. Share your notes about how the other students have been reacting to her. Obviously this information must be presented diplomatically, but the student needs to know that her hygiene problem has become obvious enough that it could alienate her from her peers.

- **Discuss how you can work together to improve the situation.**

  Tell the student that you would like to help her learn to "be responsible for good hygiene," and describe your preliminary plan. Invite the student to give you input on the various aspects of the plan, and together work out any necessary details. You may have to brainstorm different possibilities if the student is uncomfortable with the initial plan. Incorporating any of the student's suggestions that strengthen the plan is likely to increase her sense of "ownership" in and commitment to it.

- **Conclude the meeting.**

  Always end the meeting with words of encouragement. Let the student know that you are confident that she can be successful. Be sure to reinforce her for participating in the meeting.

5. *Give the student regular, ongoing feedback about her behavior.*

It is important to meet with the student periodically to discuss her progress. With PLAN A, meeting for three to five minutes once per week should suffice. However, PLANS B and C require daily meetings. During the meetings, review any information that has been collected and ask for the student's perspective on whether or not the situation is improving. As much as possible, focus on any improvements, however, also address any new or continuing problems. As the situation improves, the meetings can be faded to once every other week and then to once per month.

6. *Evaluate the situation (and the plan).*

Implement any plan for at least two weeks before deciding whether to change plans; to continue, modify, or fade the plan you are using; or to cease the intervention. Generally, if the student's hygiene is clearly improving (based on the objective information that's been collected and/or the subjective perceptions of yourself, the student, and possibly the parent[s]), stick with what you are doing. If the situation has remained the same or worsened, some kind of change will be necessary. Always discuss any changes to the plan with the student first.

HYPOCHONDRIA

Chronic Health Complaints

DESCRIPTION

You have a student who frequently complains of feeling ill or having aches and pains.

GOAL

The student will learn to eliminate unnecessary complaints about his physical health.

OVERVIEW OF PLANS

- PLAN A: For a student who has just begun to have frequent health complaints.

- PLAN B: For a student who uses health complaints to gain attention and sympathy.

- PLAN C: For a student who uses health complaints to escape or avoid situations which he finds unpleasant.

- PLAN D: For a student who has developed a habit of complaining about his health.

Alternative Problems

- **Absenteeism**

- **Allergies, Asthma, Disabilities, Seizures**

- **Clinginess/ Dependency**

- **Crying, Chronic**

- **Helplessness**

- **School Phobia**

- **Tourette Syndrome**

- **Whining**

········
General Considerations

- If the student's problem behavior stems in any way from academic issues (e.g., he is unable to be successful with academic tasks and develops "aches and pains" due to stress or to escape his schoolwork), concurrent efforts must be made to ensure his academic success (see **Academic Deficits, Determining**).

- If the student lacks the basic social skills to interact with his peers appropriately and complains about his health to avoid interacting them, it may be necessary to begin by teaching the student those skills. **Social Skills, Lack of** contains information on a variety of published social skills curricula.

- If you suspect that the student's health complaints could be related to the student being depressed, see **Depression**. This problem includes a set of questions to help you decide whether the student should be referred for counseling or psychological services.

- If you have any reason to suspect a physiological or neurological basis for the student's health complaints (e.g., the student's symptoms might be caused by diabetes or another organic disorder), consult with your building administrator, school nurse, and/or school psychologist for advice on district procedures for following up on this type of concern.

········
Model Plans

PLAN A

It is not always necessary, or even beneficial, to use an involved plan. If the student's health complaints have just begun, the following actions, along with making the student aware of your concerns, may resolve the situation.

 Respond consistently to the student's health complaints.

a. With the student's parent(s) and the school nurse, develop steps to follow whenever the student complains of not feeling well. Because the goal is for school personnel to avoid being put in a position of wondering, "What am I supposed to do now?", the steps should be structured as a sequence of "if . . . , then . . . " statements that define how everyone should respond to all of the student's health complaints.

The following sample might help you develop a sequence that fits your unique situation.

When the student is in class and complains about feeling ill, check to see if he feels feverish.

- If the student does not feel feverish, he will stay in the classroom and lay his head on his desk for five minutes. Then:

  – If the student feels better after five minutes, he will resume class activities.

  – If the student still feels ill after five minutes, he will be sent to the nurse (or the secretary, if the nurse is not there).

- If the student does feel feverish, he will be sent to the nurse (or the office) to have his temperature taken:

  – If the student has a fever (or other observable signs of illness), his parent(s) will be contacted and the student will go home.

  – If the student does not have a fever, he will lay down for 30 minutes and then return to class.

Once the sequence is established, review it to determine if the most likely possibilities have been included. Modify the procedures if necessary so they are applicable for all relevant school settings (e.g., the playground, cafeteria, music class, etc.).

b. All adults interacting with the student when he reports feeling ill should be very businesslike. They should be courteous to the student, but the interactions should be as short and emotionally neutral as possible. The goal is for the student to realize that, while his health needs will be attended to, the quality and quantity of the attention he receives when complaining about his health will not be as satisfying as the attention received for participating without complaining.

The following examples demonstrate the contrast between a busineslike interaction and an overly sympathetic interaction:

- **Short and Neutral Interaction**

  "Good morning, Armondo. Take a seat on the bench and hold this thermometer under your tongue. I will be back in three minutes."

- **Lengthy and Overly Sympathetic Interaction**

  "Good morning, Armondo. I am so sorry that you are not feeling well. Let's take your temperature. Come over here and sit with me. Put this under your tongue. I hope you don't have a fever. You have been sick so much lately I would hate for you to have to miss even more school. It will just take a little bit longer now."

 Use reinforcement to encourage participation in class activities (i.e., the absence of health complaints).

a. Give the student increased praise. Be especially alert for situations in which the student is participating and not complaining about his health, and praise him for his participation. Do not mention the health issues directly, as you do not want to remind the student to think about how he feels. Instead, focus on what the student is doing. "Armondo, it is really a pleasure to watch the way you have been working on that project. You keep your attention focused so well that you have gotten a lot done in a short period of time."

Remember that any time the student is not complaining about his health (or misbehaving), you can praise him for his participation.

b. Give the student frequent attention (e.g., say "hello" to him as he enters the classroom, call on him frequently during class activities, and make eye contact with and smile at him occasionally while you are presenting to the class) and praise him for other positive behaviors he exhibits. For example, you might comment about the neatness of his penmanship or how responsible he is about doing his homework. This demonstrates to the student that you notice many positive things he does, not just the fact that he is refraining from complaining about his health.

PLAN B

Some students are very skilled at gaining attention through their negative behavior. If you find yourself paying a lot of attention to the student when he complains about his health (e.g., trying to comfort him, trying to find out if he is really sick, even nagging him to stop complaining), it is possible that this is his motivation. Whether or not the student overtly seems to like the attention, you should make sure that he receives more frequent and more satisfying attention for behaving appropriately than for complaining about his health.

 Respond consistently to the student's health complaints (see PLAN A).

In this type of situation, it is very important to make the response sequence as streamlined as possible. That is, while you need to ensure that any real illness (e.g., a fever) will be identified, the student should receive minimal attention for complaining about his health.

 Use reinforcement to encourage appropriate behavior.

a. Frequent praise and attention is the core of this plan. The student must see that he receives more frequent and more satisfying attention when he participates in school activities than when he complains about his health. Thus, whenever the student is not complaining about his health (or misbehaving), make an effort to praise and spend time with him.

These interactions should be warm, friendly, and satisfying to the student. The goal is to create an extreme contrast between the short and neutral attention paid to his health complaints and the warm, lengthy attention paid to him when participating without complaining. "Armondo, you have been participating so well this morning. Would it be okay if I sat with you a moment and talked as you put your things away to get ready for lunch?"

b. You may also wish to use intermittent rewards to acknowledge the student's participation. Occasional, and unexpected, rewards can motivate the student to demonstrate responsible behavior more often. The idea is to provide a reward when the student has had a particularly long period with no health complaints.

Appropriate rewards might include choosing a friend to play a game with him and the teacher during recess, sitting with you as you read the class a story, or helping you pass out papers. *(NOTE: A list of additional reinforcement ideas can be found in APPENDIX 1.)*

Use intermittent rewards more frequently at the beginning of the intervention to encourage the student, and then less often as the frequency of the student's health complaints diminishes.

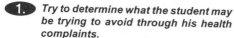 **3.** **Ensure a 3-1 ratio of positive to negative attention.**

a. Given that attention is a motivating force for this student, you want to be sure that you are giving the student *three times as much* positive as

negative attention. One way to do this is to monitor your interactions with the student at least one day per week. Keep a card on a clipboard or in your pocket and record each interaction you have with the student as either positive or negative by writing a "+" or a "-", respectively, on the card.

To determine whether an interaction is positive or negative, ask yourself whether the interaction was precipitated by a health complaint (or was a response to misbehavior). Any interactions that stem from health complaints or other inappropriate behavior are negative, while all interactions that occur while the student is meeting classroom expectations are positive.

Thus, each interaction that is part of the sequence for dealing with health complaints would be a negative interaction, but praising the student for participation is positive. Greeting the student as he enters the room or asking the student if he enjoyed an assembly are also considered positive interactions.

b. If you find that you are not giving the student three times as much positive as negative attention, try to increase the number of positive interactions you have with the student. Sometimes prompts can help. For example, you might decide that each time the student enters the classroom you will say "hello" to him, that once during each activity you will give the student some attention, or that each time you ask the students get out their books, you will look at the student and give him a warm smile.

PLAN C

Some students will use health complaints to avoid or escape situations which they find unpleasant. If there are patterns to the student's complaints (i.e., he always misses a particular activity due to his health complaints), the intervention should include modifying the activity and concurrently helping the student learn to participate in that activity.

1. **Try to determine what the student may be trying to avoid through his health complaints.**

a. Consult your anecdotal notes (see SUGGESTED STEPS FOR DEVELOPING AND IMPLEMENTING A PLAN) and use your knowledge of past events to identify the particular activity or location the student may be trying to escape. Possibilities include:

• Particular academic subjects;

• Tests;

• Work in cooperative groups with other students;

• Recess or other unstructured times;

• A particular student (e.g., a bully);

• Substitute teachers; or

• Other particular adults (e.g., P.E. teachers, the librarian, etc.).

(NOTE: It may be that you will need to obtain this information from the student and/or the student's parent[s].)

b. Try to identify what it is about the situation (activity, place, person) that the student fears, and try to find ways to reduce the student's fear. For example, if the student is afraid to go out to recess, meet with the student to find out why. If you find that the student is being victimized by a bully on the playground, deal directly with the bullying situation (see **Bullying Behavior/ Fighting**) and teach the target student strategies so he will feel safe on the playground (see **Victim—Student Who Is Always Picked On**).

If the student is fearful of a particular adult, you might make arrangements for you and the student to get together with that adult so the student has the opportunity to get to know the person better. If the student is fearful of substitutes in particular, you could have the student meet a substitute teacher (who is subbing for another teacher that day), so that he has advance contact with a friendly person who might be the sub on a day when you are not at school.

2. *Help the student deal with his anxiety about the situation.*

If the student is still anxious about the situation after reasonable modifications/attempts at addressing it have been made, teach the student strategies for dealing with his anxiety. One useful procedure is to teach the student to use self-reinforcing statements. For example, if the student is nervous about going to P.E., you might teach the student to keep take slow, even breaths and to repeat to himself a statement such as, "P.E. will be fun. I will do my best and that is fine."

3. *Respond consistently to the student's health complaints (see PLAN A).*

4. *Modify the procedures for responding to health complaints so that the student is not allowed to escape the setting or activity that he has been avoiding.*

For example, if the student complains about his health right before recess, instead of letting the student put his head down and checking him five minutes later, you could say, "Let me know how you feel after recess and we will see if you need to go to the nurse." Although this response may sound harsh or cruel, remember that efforts have already been made to reduce the frightening aspects of the situation (e.g., dealing with the bullying situation on the playground). If the student is allowed to successfully use his health complaints to avoid fearful circumstances, he will continually be reinforced for his hypochondria.

5. *Use reinforcement to encourage appropriate behavior.*

a. Give the student increased praise and attention for participating in school activities (see PLAN A).

b. In addition, praise the student privately for having the courage to face the difficult situation. "Armondo, I know you have been a bit nervous about going to P.E. but for the last two days you have gone. How did it go? You know that if you ever need to talk to me about something that is bothering you, you can feel free to come and see me."

PLAN D

Whenever a student's health complaints have become habitual and/or he does not seem to have a desire to reduce them, you may need to use a structured system of external incentives (i.e., rewards) based on his behavior to motivate him to stop complaining about his health and to begin participating more fully.

1. *Respond consistently to the student's health complaints (see PLAN A).*

2. *Have the student self-evaluate the quality of his behavior.*

a. Periodically throughout the day have the student rate his own behavior. The hope is that if he sees just how frequently he complains about

his health and/or misses out on school activities, the student may be motivated to reduce the complaints and increase his active participation. Each hour (or period) the student might use an evaluation form like the example (customized to the student's age and reading level) following.

Self-Evaluation Form for Complaining Behavior

Name _____ Date _____

Directions:

Circle the number that best describes your level of participation.

First Hour	0	1	2	3	4
	Went to the health room.	Complained about how I felt.	Acted sick or tired.	Was okay.	Was enthusiastic .
Second Hour	0	1	2	3	4
	Went to the health room.	Complained about how I felt.	Acted sick or tired.	Was okay.	Was enthusiastic.
(Etc.)					

Total points for the day _____

---

b. When you explain the system to the student, you will also need to agree on the definitions for each of the ratings on the form. Use the information you have collected in your anecdotal notes (see SUGGESTED STEPS FOR DEVELOPING AND IMPLEMENTING A PLAN) as the basis for the definitions. For example, you and the student might decide that a "2" rating means that during the hour the student participated in activities and did not complain about feeling ill, but acted sick and lethargic. A rating of "3" ("Was okay.") might mean that the student did not complain about his health and did not act sick or tired, but was not particularly enthusiastic about his participation, either.

Discuss each of the ratings with the student and then ask him questions to ensure his understanding. "Armondo, what would you rate your behavior if . . . ."

c. Check with the student each hour (or period) just before he completes his self-evaluation. Ask the student what rating he plans to mark and, if you don't agree with his evaluation, discuss why. If you do agree with the rating, reinforce the student for accuracy even if the rating is low. "Armondo, I agree that you acted kind of sick and tired. The important thing now, though, is that you are being aware of that and being honest with yourself."

3. **Pair a structured reinforcement system with the self-evaluations.**

a. With the student, create a list of reinforcers that he can earn. Although you might want to have some suggestions in mind, the system will be more effective if the student identifies most of the items or activities himself. (NOTE: A list of reinforcement ideas can be found in APPENDIX 1.)

b. Assign "prices" (in points) for each of the rewards on the list and have the student select the reward he would like to earn first.

The prices should be based on the instructional, personnel, and/or monetary costs of the items. Monetary cost is clear—the more expensive the item, the more points required to earn it. Instructional cost refers to the amount of instructional time lost or interfered with by a particular reward. Thus, an activity which causes the student to miss part of academic instruction should require more points than one the student can do on his own free time. Personnel cost involves the time required by you and/or other staff to fulfill the reinforcer. Having lunch with the principal, therefore, would cost more points than spending five minutes of free time with a friend.

c. Translate the self-evaluation ratings into points to be used in earning the reward. With the sample form shown previously, for example, each rating could indicate the number of points the student could earn for that hour (e.g., a rating of "4" would indicate the maximum number of points the student could earn in that hour: four). Then at the end of each day, determine the total points for that day and add them to the points the student has earned on previous days.

d. When the student has accumulated enough points to earn the reward he has chosen, he "spends" the points necessary and the system begins again. That is, he selects another reward to earn and begins with zero points.

If the student is immature, and needs more frequent encouragement, you might consider letting him earn several "less expensive" rewards (e.g., five minutes of computer time after 20 points) on the way to the selected reward (e.g., one hour with you for 200 points). That is, the student receives the small rewards without spending his points; they continue to accumulate toward the big reward.

 4. **Use reinforcement to encourage appropriate behavior.**

a. Give the student increased praise and attention for participating in school activities (see PLAN A).

b. In addition, show interest and enthusiasm about how the student is doing on the system. "Armondo, this is the third hour that you have gotten four points. It does my heart good to see you participating in such an enthusiastic way."

....
Suggested Steps for Developing and Implementing a Plan

The following steps are designed to help you develop an appropriate intervention plan and implement it effectively, whether you choose to use one of the MODEL PLANS or create a customized plan of your own. The steps are, however, suggestions—they are not intended to be followed rigidly or in any particular order. Use your professional judgment and the knowledge of your particular situation to make them work for you.

1. **Make sure you have enough information about the situation.**

a. If you think a minimal intervention like PLAN A will be sufficient, you may already have enough information to proceed. However, when a more involved plan seems necessary, you should consider collecting additional descriptive and/or objective information for a couple of days.

b. You need to be able to explain what you mean when you say the student "complains about his health." Anecdotal notes on actual incidents should provide enough detail to help you define the problem behavior clearly and completely. To collect anecdotal notes, simply keep a card in your pocket or on a clipboard and occasionally make notes on specific instances when the student claims he does not feel well.

For each entry, briefly describe the student's complaint, what you and/or other school personnel did, and any other relevant observations (e.g., exactly when the complaint occurred, where the student was, who was around the student, the next activity the student would be expected to participate in, etc.). You do not need to take notes every time the student has a health complaint; the idea is to capture a range of examples of the behavior so you will be able to describe it completely.

c. In addition to information on what the student's inappropriate behavior "looks like," it can also be useful to document how often it occurs (i.e., a frequency count). This information will provide both a more objective measure of the problem and an objective way to monitor the student's progress. You can use the same card on which you are making anecdotal notes to keep a frequency count—simply write a tally mark on the card each time the student complains that he does not feel well.

You might want to code the tallies to discern whether the behavior occurs more frequently during certain times, subjects, or activities (e.g., using an "A" or "P" to indicate that the incident happened in the morning or afternoon; or clustering the tallies by math or reading, teacher directed instruction or independent work, etc.).

d. If the student notices what you are doing and asks about it, be straightforward—tell him that you are collecting information to see whether his health complaints are a problem that needs to be worked on.

e. The frequency information is fairly easy to summarize on a chart or graph. Seeing how often he complains about his health may help the student and the student's parent(s) better understand your concern.

f. Continuing to collect this type of information (and keeping the chart up-to-date) while you implement a plan will help you monitor whether the situation is getting worse, staying the same, or getting better.

2. Determine when and how to include the parent(s).

a. With this type of problem, the parent(s) should be contacted immediately. Given that the student's health could truly be at risk, it is critical that the parent(s) be kept informed about the student's health complaints. When you contact the parent(s), share with them any information you have collected about the behavior (e.g., the anecdotal notes, frequency count), and explain why you are concerned. Focus in particular on how the behavior is hindering the student academically and/or socially (e.g., the student is spending so much time in the nurse's office that he is missing too much class).

You might ask if the parent(s) have any insight into the situation and/or whether they have noticed similar behavior at home. Whether or not the parent(s) perceive a problem, explain that you want to help the student "feel better and participate more actively," and invite them to join you for an initial meeting with the student to develop a plan. If the parent(s) are unable or unwilling to participate, let them know that you will keep them informed of the student's progress.

b. Once the parent(s) have been involved in any way, you should give them updates at least once per week while the plan is being implemented.

3. Prepare for, then conduct, an initial meeting about the situation.

a. Arrange a meeting to discuss your concerns with the student and anyone else who will be involved with the plan (e.g., the parent[s], the school nurse). Although the specifics will vary depending upon the age of the student and the severity of the problem, there are some general guidelines to consider when scheduling the meeting.

First, meet at a neutral time (i.e., not immediately after a complaint has occurred), when emotions are less likely to hamper communication. In general, a day's notice is appropriate, however a primary age student may worry excessively and/or forget what the meeting is

about if it is scheduled more than an hour before it takes place.

Second, make the meeting appropriately private. Third, try to make sure the meeting is scheduled for a time and place that it is not likely to be interrupted (e.g., the counselor's office). Finally, when the parent(s) will be participating, they should be the ones to tell the student about the meeting.

b. Construct a preliminary plan. Decide whether you think you can use one of the MODEL PLANS or if you need to create a customized plan using components from various plans and/or of your own design. Although you will invite and encourage the student to help develop the plan during the initial meeting, having a proposed plan in mind before you meet can alleviate frustration and wasted time if the student is unwilling or unable to participate.

c. After reviewing the information you have collected and thinking about how you want the student to behave, prepare thorough descriptions of the inappropriate behavior and the positive behavior/trait on which the student will be working. The more specific you can be and the more concrete examples you have, the easier it will be to clarify (and for the student to understand) your expectations. Be sure to consider the student's behavior in all relevant activities and settings (e.g., independent work, teacher directed instruction, unstructured class times, recess and lunch, etc.).

d. Conduct the meeting in an atmosphere of collaboration. The following agenda is one way you might structure the meeting:

- **Share your concerns about the student's behavior.**

  Briefly describe the problem behavior and explain why you consider it to be a problem. You might tell the student that his complaints about his health are resulting in his missing out on many useful and interesting learning opportunities. In addition, you might use the "little boy who cried wolf" fable to communicate that if he complains too often, people will not be able to tell when he is really sick.

- **Discuss how you can work together to improve the situation.**

  Tell the student that you would like to help him learn to "feel better and participate more actively," then describe your preliminary plan. Invite the student to give you input on the various aspects of the plan, and together work out any necessary details (e.g., use of the self-evaluation form, etc.).

You may have to brainstorm different possibilities if the student is uncomfortable with the initial plan. Incorporating any of the student's suggestions that strengthen the plan is likely to increase his sense of "ownership" in and commitment to it.

- **Conclude the plan.**

Always end the meeting with words of encouragement. Let the student know that you are confident that he can be successful. Be sure to reinforce him for participating in the meeting.

 Give the student regular, ongoing feedback about his behavior.

It is important to meet with the student periodically to discuss his progress. In most cases, three to five minutes once per week should suffice. *(NOTE: PLAN D may require a daily meeting as part of the reinforcement system.)* During the meetings, review any information that has been collected and discuss whether or not the situation is getting better. As much as possible, focus on the student's improvements, however, also address any new or continuing problems. As the situation improves, the meetings can be faded to once every other week and then to once per month.

5. *Evaluate the situation (and the plan).*

Implement any plan for at least two weeks before deciding whether to change plans; to continue, modify, or fade the plan you are using; or to cease the intervention. Generally, if the student's behavior is clearly improving (based on the objective information that's been collected and/or the subjective perceptions of yourself, the student, and possibly the parent[s]), stick with what you are doing. If the situation has remained the same or worsened, some kind of change will be necessary. Always discuss any changes to the plan with the student first.

INTIMACY, INAPPROPRIATE DISPLAYS OF

DESCRIPTION

There are students in your class who are displaying inappropriate intimacy for a school setting (i.e., they are kissing, hugging, and/or fondling each other in the classroom and/or other areas of the school).

GOAL

The students will refrain from inappropriate displays of intimacy and will interact with each other in ways that would be appropriate for a "workplace setting."

OVERVIEW OF PLANS

- PLAN A: For a situation in which the problem has just begun or occurs infrequently.

- PLAN B: For a situation in which the problem occurs/continues to occur with only one or two couples.

Alternative Problem

- **Sexual Comments**

········
General Considerations

- Sexual behavior is obviously a very sensitive topic, and personal values differ on what is right and wrong regarding adolescent sexual behavior. It is beyond the scope of this book and the authors' purpose to suggest the nature of moral or sexual education in your school. Therefore, the MODEL PLANS included here do not specifically address morality or sex education issues, but focus on the concept of "responsible behavior for a workplace setting." Since school is, at least in part, preparation for the workplace, it is appropriate for you to intervene when students behave in ways that would not be acceptable at work.

- When this behavior is occurring outside the classroom, solving the problem will require the efforts of the entire faculty. If other staff members are unwilling or unable to deal with this situation, the most you can do is address the behavior within your own classroom.

········
Model Plans

PLAN A

It is not always necessary, or even beneficial, to use an involved plan. If the inappropriate behavior has just begun and/or occurs infrequently, the following actions, along with making the students aware of your concerns, may resolve the situation.

1. *Respond consistently to each instance of inappropriate intimacy.*

a. Whenever two students are being inappropriately intimate, gently correct them. Go over to the students and quietly say, for example, "This is not responsible workplace behavior. Wendy, please go to your own seat." The quieter and more subtle you can be, the less likely that the students will become defensive and put on a show of defiance in front of their peers. Because your goal is to impart information, you want to be emotionally neutral while giving the correction.

b. Intervene consistently and calmly—and be prepared to do so frequently until the students learn that you will not tolerate this behavior in your class.

2. *Use reinforcement to encourage appropriate behavior.*

a. Privately praise individual students for meeting your expectations regarding responsible behavior for a workplace. Watch closely those students with the greatest tendency to engage in intimate behavior. Whenever one of these students refrains from inappropriate intimacy, praise the student for this demonstration of responsibility. "Wendy, I want to compliment you on your ability to demonstrate responsible workplace behavior. I know you and Carl care for each other, but you have been very responsible about how you interact in my class."

b. Praise the entire class when there has been a significant decrease in the inappropriately intimate behavior. Remember that any time the students are refraining from displaying intimacy, you can praise them for exhibiting responsible workplace behavior. "Class, everyone is doing a fine job of remembering the expectations about appropriate workplace behavior."

c. You may also wish to use intermittent rewards to acknowledge the class' success. Occasional, and unexpected, rewards can motivate the students to demonstrate responsible behavior more often. The idea is to provide a reward when the entire class has been behaving responsibly.

Appropriate rewards might include letting the class work outside, giving the class a five minute break, or reducing the length of a homework assignment. *(NOTE: A list of additional group reinforcement ideas can be found in APPENDIX 1.)* Use intermittent rewards more frequently at the beginning of the intervention to encourage the students, and then less often as their behavior improves.

········

PLAN B

If only one or two couples are (or continue to be) inappropriately intimate, a more direct intervention with these students may be necessary.

1. Meet privately with the couple(s) to discuss the problem.

a. Share any information you have collected (see SUGGESTED STEPS FOR DEVELOPING AND IMPLEMENTING A PLAN) and define for the students exactly what does (and does not) constitute appropriate "workplace" behavior.

b. Help the couple(s) identify things they might do to make it easier to avoid behavior that would be irresponsible in the workplace. For example, they might consider moving to different desks, keeping their desks separated by the aisle, or remember to avoid touching of any kind during class (if they wish to hold hands in the hallway or during lunch, that is their business).

You might also suggest a way they could remind each other not to hold hands (or other inappropriate displays of affection) in a way that would not offend the other person.

2. Respond consistently to each instance of inappropriate intimacy.

a. Determine a consequence for future incidents of the behavior and inform a students that you will implement a consequence whenever you see them being inappropriately intimate. Possible consequences include: being assigned seats; parental contact; or owing time in detention (one student during lunch and the other student after school).

If it seems appropriate (or necessary), you might also consider having one of the students moved to a different class if the inappropriate behavior continues.

b. If the intimate behavior is relatively innocuous (e.g., holding hands), you might set up a plan involving repeated corrections. That is, if you have to remind the couple four times (not four times per day—four times total) not to hold hands in class, then you will contact their parents.

c. Be sure the students know what you will do each time you have to intervene, and then follow through and be consistent in applying the predetermined consequences.

3. Use reinforcement to encourage appropriate behavior.

a. Give these students increased praise for refraining from inappropriate displays of affection (see PLAN A).

b. In addition, when they are participating responsibly in class, pay frequent attention to these students. Call on them frequently, make eye contact with them, and listen to their opinions. Demonstrate that you are interested in them and that you notice their efforts to engage in responsible behavior in the classroom.

. . . .

Suggested Steps for Developing and Implementing a Plan

The following information is designed to help you implement an appropriate and effective intervention plan, whether you choose to use one of the MODEL PLANS or create a customized plan of your own. The steps are, however, suggestions—they are not intended to be followed rigidly or in any particular order. Use your professional judgment and the knowledge of your particular situation to make them work for you.

1. Make sure you have enough information about the situation.

a. You need to be able to explain what you mean when you say that "the class has a problem with behavior that would not be responsible in the workplace." That is, you need to identify the

aspect(s) of their behavior that make it inappropriate. Is it what the students are actually doing? Is it that they are distracted from school tasks? Anecdotal notes from actual incidents can help you define the problem behavior thoroughly.

To take anecdotal notes, simply keep a card in your pocket or on a clipboard and occasionally, when you see students behaving in an inappropriately intimate manner, make notes. For each entry, briefly describe the circumstances—where and when it occurred, what was said and/or done, and any other relevant observations (e.g., how others reacted). You do not need to make notes every time an incident occurs; the idea is to capture a range of examples so that you will be able to describe the behavior clearly and completely.

b. It may also be useful to document how often the students are being inappropriately intimate (i.e., a frequency count). This will provide both an objective measure of the problem and an objective way to monitor the students' progress. You can use the same card on which you are taking anecdotal notes to keep a frequency count—just make a tally mark on the card each time you need to intervene with a gentle correction. "Morgan, Johanna, holding hands while you are working would not be responsible in the workplace. Please keep your hands to yourselves and focus on your work."

c. Continuing to collect this type of information while you implement a plan will help you monitor whether the situation is getting worse, staying the same, or getting better.

2. *Identify a focus for the intervention and labels for referring to the appropriate and inappropriate behaviors.*

a. The intervention should address more than just reducing the students' inappropriate intimacy—to be effective, there must be a concurrent emphasis on increasing some positive behavior or trait (e.g., "responsible workplace behavior"). Identifying some specific positive behavior(s) will make it easier for you to "catch" and reinforce the students for behaving appropriately, and will help you explain your concerns more productively.

For example, simply saying that "the class has a problem with inappropriate intimacy" doesn't really give the students any useful information (and may put them on the defensive). However, telling the students that you want to help them "to exhibit behavior that would be responsible on a job," provides an important, and reasonable, goal to work toward and clarifies what they need to do to be successful.

b. The purpose of specifying labels for both the appropriate and inappropriate behaviors (e.g.,

"responsible workplace behavior " and "not responsible workplace behavior," respectively) is so you will use consistent vocabulary whenever you talk about the situation. If you sometimes refer to the inappropriate behavior as "sexual activity" and other times say that "they are being lovey dovey," the students may think you are talking about different things and that one is more acceptable than the other. In addition, describing a problem situation as "not responsible workplace behavior" is very neutral and nontitillating.

3. *Decide how to present the situation to the class.*

a. You may choose to have an informal discussion with the students. Wait for a time that you are calm (i.e., not right after an incident has occurred) and inform the students that you are finding their displays of intimacy to be a problem. Explain that part of your job is to help them learn to behave in a manner that would be responsible for a work setting and that the kissing, hugging, and so on would not be acceptable at most workplaces. Then specifically define your expectations regarding physical intimacy and/or the procedures that will be implemented.

Give the students the opportunity to ask questions/make comments, and end the session by thanking the students for listening. Let them know that you are confident they will make an effort not to engage in inappropriate displays of intimacy.

b. If you want the students to assume some ownership of the problem, you might want to have a class meeting in which the students participate in analyzing the situation and developing an action plan. In this case, before the meeting you will need to have clarified the nature/extent of the problem and your expectations for the students' behavior.

You will also need to identify any aspects of the plan that you do not feel comfortable opening up to a group decision. For example, you must decide ahead of time whether or not to allow the class to determine if there will be a consequence for being inappropriately intimate and/or what the consequence should be. If you firmly believe that there needs to be a consequence, then you should not seek student input on that particular issue.

4. Schedule and conduct a class meeting (if applicable).

a. Schedule the meeting for a neutral time and allow enough time for a reasonable discussion. Inform the students in advance that the meeting will take place; this will give them time to think about the problem. "Class, this afternoon we are going to have a meeting on the problem of intimate behavior that would not be responsible in the workplace—kissing, holding hands, and so on. Please give some thought to this problem and what we might do as a class to solve it."

b. Use an agenda to structure the meeting. Shortly before the meeting, write the agenda on the chalkboard. The following sample is one possibility you might consider using.

Responsible Workplace Behavior

1. Is the class' behavior a problem? *(NOTE: Share the information you have collected, but do not use individual names or direct the discussion toward particular students.)*

2. Intimacy and the world of work—what's appropriate on the job?

3. Brainstorm ideas for creating a more professional atmosphere in the classroom.

4. Select strategies that everyone agrees to.

5. Decide what will happen if a couple exhibits behavior in the classroom that would not be responsible in the workplace.

---

c. Establish clear rules for both you and the students regarding the brainstorming phase of the class meeting. For example:

 1. Any idea is okay (but no obscenity).

 2. Ideas will not be evaluated initially (i.e., no approval—"Good idea," or disapproval—"What a stupid idea," or "We couldn't do that," should be expressed during the brainstorming).

 3. All ideas will be written down and discussed at the conclusion of brainstorming.

d. At the conclusion of brainstorming, evaluate the ideas, and lead the class to consensus on any decisions that need to be made. Use voting as a decision-making process when appropriate.

e. If the students challenge you about what is appropriate in the workplace, consider conducting the following activity.

Have the students phone or visit a number of employers and find out what "bosses" from several different fields would consider to be acceptable and unacceptable from two employees who cared about each other. *(NOTE: You might also consider inviting a personnel director from a local company to speak to the class about this issue.)* Following are some questions that the students might ask:

1. Would it be acceptable for two employees who cared about each other to be holding hands while they were working? What about an arm around a shoulder or waist?

 • What about during a break?

 • What about walking down the hallway?

2. What about kissing during a break? If a kiss would be okay, how much kissing?

3. Would it be appropriate for one employee to be sitting on another's lap?

4. What about hugging in a hallway during a break time?

5. What about in the cafeteria?

 • Holding hands?

 • Kissing?

 • Arm over a shoulder?

5. Determine when and how to include the parent(s).

a. Because intimate behavior is more of a personal problem than a behavioral or motivational one, involving parents is not critical when there is a class-wide problem.

b. If one or two couples have or continue to have a problem with this behavior, you should contact the parents of those individuals. Inform them that their student is engaging in inappropriately intimate behavior, and explain the steps you are taking to correct the situation. Share any information you have collected about the behavior (e.g., anecdotal notes, frequency count), and explain why you are concerned. Focus in particular on how the behavior is hindering the student academically (e.g., he is so busy holding hands and trying to get close, he is not getting his work done).

c. Once parents have been involved in any way, you should give them updates at least once per week while the plan is being implemented.

6. *Give the class regular, ongoing feed-back about their behavior.*

It is important to meet with the class (or the individual students, if the problem concerns just one or two couples) periodically to discuss their progress. In most cases, three to five minutes once per week should suffice. Review any information that has been collected and discuss whether or not the situation is getting better. As much as possible, focus on improvements, however, also address any new or continuing problems. As the situation improves, the meetings can be faded to once every other week and then to once per month.

7. *Evaluate the situation (and the plan).*

Implement any plan for at least two weeks before deciding whether to change plans; to continue, modify, or fade the plan you are using; or to cease the intervention. Generally, if the students' behavior is clearly improving (based on the objective information that's been collected and/or the subjective perceptions of yourself and the students), stick with what you are doing. If the situation has remained the same or worsened, some kind of change will be necessary. Always discuss any changes to the plan with the class first.

L ATE WORK

Procrastination

DESCRIPTION

There are students in your class who turn in their assignments after the due dates.

GOAL

The students will turn in their assignments on (or prior to) the deadline.

OVERVIEW OF PLANS

- PLAN A: For a situation in which the problem occurs infrequently or has just begun.

- PLAN B: For a situation in which the students lack the motivation to turn their assignments in on time.

NOTE:

These two plans have been designed for a situation in which there are a number of students who have a problem with late work. However, each can easily be modified to intervene with only a few (one to three) students who continue to have a problem with late work.

Alternative Problems

- **Homework Issues**

- **Work Completion— Daily Work**

- **Work Completion— Long-Term Projects**

· · · · · · · ·
General Considerations

• If the students' problem behavior stems in any way from academic issues (e.g., the students are unable to meet the academic expectations and cannot do the assigned work within allotted time limits), concurrent efforts must be made to ensure their academic success. PLAN B in **Work Completion—Daily Work** suggests accommodations for helping students complete assignments (but these accommodations will not remediate skill deficits). The problem **Academic Deficits, Determining** has information on determining if academic tasks represent reasonable expectations for students.

• If the problem stems primarily from students lacking the organizational skill to keep track of due dates, see **Homework Issues**. One of this problem's plans provides a form for students to write down assignments and check off their completed work.

If organization is a big problem for many students in the class, you might want to consult:

Archer, A. & Gleason, M. (1990). *Skills for school success*. North Billerica, MA: Curriculum Associates.

This is an excellent program that teaches study skills in a comprehensive and effective manner.

· · · · · · · ·
Model Plans

PLAN A

It is not always necessary, or even beneficial, to use an involved plan. If this problem has just begun and/or occurs only occasionally, the following actions, along with making the students aware of your concerns, may resolve the situation.

 Clearly define what constitutes a deadline.

There is no one correct way to structure deadlines for your students; what's important is for you to be clear and consistent. Consider the following questions: On due dates, does the work have to be turned in at the beginning of the period? at the end of the period? by the end of the day? before you (the teacher) leave school? Specifically teaching what constitutes the deadline to the students in advance eliminates the need to argue or negotiate with the student who says things like, "My mom will bring it by after school—we will get it to you before you leave school."

One method is to have the students put their completed assignments on their desks so you can pick them up while the students work on another assignment or a challenge problem. An alternative is for the students to put their completed assignments into a box or basket that has a place for them to initial that they have turned their assignment in (see the sample following).

Then at the time the work is due, you can look at the chart, flip through the assignments that have been turned in, and you will know who turned in the work on time and who did not. With either method, you can provide immediate feedback to the students—a key to their improvement.

 At the time an assignment is due, collect it from students in a way that creates immediate accountability.

NOTE: *If your concern is about a general tendency to procrastinate, the following reference provides specific information on analyzing the problem and developing strategies to overcome the problem:*

Ellis, A. & Knaus, W.J. (1977). *Overcoming procrastination*. New York: Signet.

 Mark your gradebook in a way that makes clear which assignments were late.

One simple way to do so is by writing a small "L" in the appropriate spaces. You want space to enter a score later, but this way you can see at a glance how many students were late turning in a particular assignment as well as how many times each individual has turned work in late. Such a cumulative record in your gradebook allows you to easily

```
┌─────────────────────────────────────────────────────────────────────────┐
│                         Completed Assignments                             │
│                                                                           │
│  Week of _____                               │
│                                                                           │
│  Directions:                                                              │
│                                                                           │
│  When you turn in an assignment, put your initials in the space next to   │
│  your name, under that assignment.                                        │
└─────────────────────────────────────────────────────────────────────────┘
```

Name	Lab 10—2/15	Lab 11—2/17	Notebook—2/18	Project—2/19				
Alder, Trisha	AT	AT	AT	AT				
Buck, Kyle	KB	KB	KB					
Cartozian, Judd	JC	JC	JC	JC				

absorb the magnitude and nature of the problem and to evaluate the effectiveness of any intervention plan.

4. *Respond consistently to each instance of late work.*

a. Provide a gentle verbal correction to any and all students who do not have their work in on time. "Kyle and Kathi, I see that you have not checked off that you turned in your science projects. I expect you to put more effort into getting your work turned in on time." If a student has turned in the work, but simply forgot to initial, he/she can let you know immediately. After completing this procedure, you should know exactly who has turned in assignments on time and who has not.

b. Later, meet privately with any student(s) who did not complete an assignment and explain that timely work completion is an important part of success. Help the students to identify strategies (e.g., being more consistent about writing down assignments, setting up a work schedule, or using work time efficiently) that they could use to meet deadlines in the future.

c. Next you will want to assign, and consistently apply, consequences for late work. Following are three suggestions which can be tailored to the structure of your classroom and the developmental level of your students:

• If you use academic grades, establish a point fine for late work. For example, you might specify a 5% reduction in possible points for each day late. The key to this strategy's effectiveness is for the fine to be large enough that

it is an incentive to get things in on time, but not so severe that when the work is late, students will feel that it's not even worth doing.

• Establish a policy that no work will be accepted beyond a certain date. For example, the policy might state that no assignment will be accepted more than one week past its assigned due date.

• Establish a plan so that if work is not completed by a certain time, the students are restricted from privileges until they are caught up on their work. *(NOTE: This procedure is most appropriate at the elementary level, and may or may not be combined with point fines for late work.)* For example, the students may be told that any of the day's work that is not completed by the end of the day will result in the students having to stay after school until the work is completed.

If this is not an option because of transportation or supervision issues, use check points during the day. That is, certain tasks must be completed by each check point or the student do not receive privileges. For example, a student who does not have three assignments completed by lunch time would have to work through the lunch break (the student would still eat his/her lunch, but would not have a break or recess until he/she completes the required number of tasks). Two more assignments would have to be completed by the afternoon break, or the student would work through that break time, as well.

Use reinforcement to encourage appropriate behavior.

a. Praise individual students for meeting your expectations about completing work on time. Watch closely those students who have had the greatest tendency to turn work in late. Whenever one of these students turns in an assignment on time, praise him/her for demonstrating the ability to be responsible. "John, it is nice to see you being responsible about getting your work in on time. You have handed in every assignment on or before the due date for the entire week." If the student would be embarrassed by public praise, praise the student privately, nonverbally (e.g., a nod and smile as the student turns in an assignment before the due date), or even give the student a note.

b. In addition, occasionally praise those students who rarely or never have a problem with late work. Because these students have already mastered the positive expectations, they do not need positive feedback as often as the students who have had difficulty. However, you do not want them to feel that you take their positive behavior for granted. "Melody, you consistently turn all of your work in on time. Meeting deadlines is one of many successful habits you demonstrate."

c. Finally, when there has been significant overall improvement in the amount of work being turned in on time, praise the entire class. Remember that any time all the students have their work turned in on or before the due date, you have an opportunity to praise the group.

PLAN B

Sometimes late work is a problem because students have not been taught to meet due dates and/or feel little incentive to do so. They may possess a "What's the big deal?" sort of attitude. If this is the case, the intervention may need to include a variety of procedures to increase student awareness and to motivate them to meet their deadlines.

 Clearly define what constitutes a deadline, collect work in a way that creates immediate accountability, and implement consistent consequences for late work (see PLAN A).

 Use direct teaching and guided practice for more of each assignment.

For example, if the science lesson consists of twenty study questions, lead the class as a whole through the first ten question—allowing students to complete the first half of the assignment together as a class. This gets the students started on the task and helps them identify questions or difficulties they may have with the assignment.

 Publicly post the percentage of students turning in work on time.

(NOTE: Only use this procedure if several students have a problem with late work. If only one or two students have this problem, set up an individualized plan to compute their individual weekly percentages of work turned in on time.)

a. At the deadline for each assignment, compute the percentage of the students who turned that assignment in on time by dividing the number of students with on time work by the number of students present that day.

b. Record (or have a student record) the information on a large chart that is visible to the entire class. (NOTE: If you are a middle/junior high school teacher, use a transparency for each class, and only show any given class their own data.) Recording the data immediately emphasizes to the entire class how strongly you feel about the importance of turning work in on time.

c. As the data is being posted, talk to the class about trends—are more, less, or about the same percentage of students turning their work in on time? If time permits, discuss strategies the students might use to help them complete their work on time (e.g., avoiding socializing during work periods, or working on other parts of an assignment while waiting for teacher assistance with a problem area).

d. During this discussion (and throughout the day, if appropriate) be a "coach" regarding timely work completion. In sports, an effective coach rallies the team's energies to meet a challenge. Frequently encourage the students to complete their work on time (or even early). Use examples from employment situations, sports, the arts, etc. to emphasize how punctuality and dependability are habits of successful people.

4. *Use reinforcement to encourage appropriate behavior.*

a. Praise individual students and the entire class for on time work completion (see PLAN A).

b. You may also wish to use intermittent rewards to acknowledge the class' success. Occasional, and unexpected, rewards may motivate the students to turn in their work on time more often. The idea is to provide a reward when the class as a whole has made significant improvements in timely work completion.

Appropriate rewards might include eliminating a homework assignment, congratulating the class in front of the principal, or even providing the class with an edible treat. *(NOTE: A list of additional group reinforcement ideas can be found in APPENDIX 1.)*

If you use intermittent rewards, do so more frequently at the beginning of the intervention to encourage the students, and then less often as the class' timely work completion rate improves.

5. *(OPTIONAL)*
Establish a group reinforcement system.

a. Have the students brainstorm a list of reinforcement ideas for the entire class, and then eliminate any items that are not possible (i.e., the suggestions are too expensive or could not be provided to all the students in the class).

b. Assign "prices" (in points) to the remaining items on the list. The prices should be based on the

instructional, personnel, and/or monetary costs of the items. Monetary cost is clear—the more expensive the item, the more points required to earn it. Instructional cost refers to the amount of instructional time lost or interfered with by a particular reward. Thus, an activity which causes the class to miss part of academic instruction should require more points than one the class can do during recess time. Personnel cost involves the time required by you and/or other staff to fulfill the reinforcer. Thus, earning an extra recess period in which extra supervision would need to be arranged would cost more than having music playing in class for 15 minutes.

c. Have the class vote on the list of reinforcers. The reinforcer that wins the most votes is the one they will work for first, and the items that come in second and third will be the next ones worked for.

d. On those days when the percentage of students turning in work on time is higher than the day before, the class earns five points toward the agreed upon reward. Any day the group has a record-breaking percentage (e.g., the highest percentage to date was 63% and today they had 67%) they earn ten points. And whenever 100% of the students turn in their work on time, the class earns 15 points. Once the class accumulates enough points, they earn the agreed upon reward and the system begins again.

. . . .
Suggested Steps for Developing and Implementing a Plan

The following information is designed to help you implement an appropriate and effective intervention plan, whether you choose to use one of the MODEL PLANS or create a customized plan of your own. The steps are, however, suggestions—they are not intended to be followed rigidly or in any particular order. Use your professional judgment and the knowledge of your particular situation to make them work for you.

1. *Discuss the situation with the class.*

a. If you plan to use one of the two MODEL PLANS as written, schedule a class meeting. Wait for a time when you are calm (i.e., not while you are angry or frustrated about a particular assignment on which many students were late) and inform the students that you are finding the late work to be a problem. Explain that timely work completion is important in school and on a job. Then, specifically define your expectations re-

garding deadlines and outline the procedures that will be implemented.

Give the students the opportunity to ask questions and make comments. End the session by thanking the students for listening and let them know that you are confident they will turn their work in on time in the future.

b. If you want the students to assume some ownership of the problem, you might wish to hold a class meeting in which the students participate in analyzing the situation and developing an action plan. In this case, before the meeting you will need to clarify the nature/extent of the problem (use the information from your gradebook) and your expectations for deadlines.

You will also need to identify any aspects of the plan that you do not feel comfortable opening up to a group decision. For example, you must decide ahead of time whether or not to allow the class to determine *if* there will be a consequence for late work and/or what the consequence should be. If you firmly believe that there should be a consequence, then you should not seek student input on that particular issue.

c. Schedule this class meeting for a neutral time and allow enough time for a reasonable discussion. Inform the students in advance that the meeting will take place; this will give them time to think about the problem. "Class, this afternoon we are going to have a class meeting on the problem of assignments being handed in late. Please give some thought to this problem and what we might do as a class to solve it."

d. Use an agenda to structure the meeting. Shortly before the meeting, write the agenda on the chalkboard. The following example is one possibility you may wish to use.

It is important to have clear rules (for both you and the students) regarding the brainstorming phase of the meeting. For example:

1. Any idea is okay (but no obscenity).

2. Ideas will not be evaluated initially (i.e., no approval—"Good idea" or disapproval—"What a stupid idea," or "We couldn't do that," should be expressed during brainstorming).

Agenda

1. Late work—Define the magnitude of the problem (share class-wide percentages from your gradebook).

2. Review of expectations regarding deadlines.

3. Brainstorm ideas for improving the situation.

4. Select strategies that everyone agrees to.

5. Establish what will happen if a student turns in work late.

---

3. All ideas will be written down and discussed at the conclusion of brainstorming.

e. At the conclusion of brainstorming, evaluate the ideas, and lead the class to consensus on any decisions that need to be made. Use voting as a decision-making process when appropriate.

2. Determine when and how to include the parent(s).

Any time an individual student has turned in late assignments two or three times in a grading period, you should contact the parent(s) of that individual. *(NOTE: If the problem is widespread, you will need to make several calls.)* Let them know that their student is having trouble turning assignments in on time and what steps you are taking to correct the situation. Frequent contact is not required, but as long as the problem continues you should keep the parent(s) informed of the behavior and the consequences that you are implementing at school.

3. Give the class regular, ongoing feedback about their behavior.

Periodically meet with the students to discuss the situation. In most cases, three to five minutes once per week should suffice (although with public posting of percentages, as in PLAN B, you will have a two to three minute meeting each time an assignment is due). During the meetings, review any information that has been collected and discuss whether or not the situation is improving. As much as possible, focus on improvements, however, also address any new or continuing problems.

As you discuss problems, acknowledge that there are individuals in the class who consistently turn their work in on time. Do not single out individuals when discussing problems or progress with the entire group. As the situation improves, the meetings can be faded to once every other week and then to once per month.

4. Evaluate the situation (and the plan).

Any plan should be implemented for at least two weeks before deciding whether or not it is effective. Generally, if the situation has improved (based on the objective information that's been collected and/or subjective perceptions of yourself and the students), continue with what you have been doing. (Eventually you will want to fade, then eliminate, the plan.) If the problem remains the same or worsens, some kind of change (e.g., modifying the current plan or switching to another plan) will be necessary. Always discuss any change in the intervention with the class first.

LAUGHING/GIGGLING, INAPPROPRIATE

DESCRIPTION

You have a student who laughs or giggles inappropriately (i.e., at inappropriate times or subjects, or in an inappropriate manner—too long or too often).

GOAL

The student will learn to laugh at appropriate times and in an appropriate manner (i.e., to eliminate the problematic aspects of her laughter while maintaining a sense of humor and enjoyment of life).

OVERVIEW OF PLANS

- PLAN A: For a situation in which the problem has just begun or occurs infrequently.

- PLAN B: For a student who uses inappropriate laughter to gain attention from adults and/or peers.

- PLAN C: For a student who does not realize when her laughter is inappropriate and/or how often she laughs inappropriately.

- PLAN D: For a student whose inappropriate laughter has become habitual.

Alternative Problem

- **Self-Control Issues**

········
General Considerations

- If the inappropriate behavior stems in any way from academic issues (e.g., the student is unable to meet the academic expectations and laughs because she is tense about her academic failure), concurrent efforts must be made to ensure her academic success (see **Academic Deficits, Determining**).

- If the student's laughter is inappropriate for physical reasons that may be beyond her control, you may wish to consult the information contained in the problem(s) **Allergies, Asthma, Disabilities, Seizures** and/or **Tourette Syndrome**.

········
Model Plans

PLAN A

It is not always necessary, or even beneficial, to use an involved plan. If the problem has just begun and/or occurs infrequently, the following actions, along with making the student aware of your concerns, may resolve the situation.

1. *Respond consistently to the inappropriate behavior.*

Whenever the student laughs inappropriately, gently correct her. Let her know that her behavior is an example of inappropriate laughter and give her direct information about what she should be doing instead. "Bonita, this laughter is inappropriate. What you need to be doing right now is listening quietly to other student's ideas, or sharing your own ideas." Because your goal is to impart information, you want to be emotionally neutral while giving the correction.

2. *Use reinforcement to encourage appropriate behavior.*

a. Give the student increased praise. Be especially alert for situations in which the student makes an effort to refrain from laughing at a time when she otherwise would have (e.g., when another student gives a wrong answer), and privately praise her for her ability to demonstrate self-control. "Bonita, I noticed that when Jarvis gave a wrong answer earlier, you kept from laughing. That is an excellent example of using self-control and treating a classmate with dignity and respect."

Also try to "catch" the student when her laughter is appropriate and interact with her in a way so that she knows that this type of laughter is fun and useful. This can be done with overt praise, or even by laughing along with the student.

You can also praise the student for making overall progress. "Bonita, all morning you have been making an effort to use self-control. This is a big change and you should be very proud of yourself."

b. Give the student frequent attention (e.g., say "hello" to her as she enters the classroom, call on her frequently during class activities, and occasionally ask her to assist you with a class job that needs to be done), and praise her for other positive behaviors she exhibits. For example, you might comment about the accuracy of her work or how well she is keeping her attention focused on her assignments during independent work periods. This demonstrates to the student that you notice many positive things she does, not just the fact that she is refraining from laughing inappropriately.

PLAN B

Some students are very skilled at gaining attention through their negative behavior. If you find yourself frequently nagging, reminding, or coaxing the student to stop laughing inappropriately, it is possible that this is her motivation. Whether or not the student overtly seems to like the attention, you should make sure that she receives more frequent and more satisfying attention for behaving responsibly than for laughing inappropriately.

1. Respond consistently to the inappropriate behavior.

a. Because it is important for the student to learn that she will not be able to prompt people to nag and pay attention to her by laughing inappropriately, you need to ignore the student's inappropriate laughter. While ignoring the behavior, do not look at the student or talk to her. Do not act disgusted or impatient with her laughter. Simply interact in positive ways with students who are behaving appropriately and meeting classroom expectations. As soon as the target student stops the inappropriate laughter, pay attention to her, but make no reference to her previous laughing.

b. If the student's inappropriate laughter affects other students (e.g., the laughter is cruel toward or at the expense of another student), you may need to use a consequence such as time-out. On these occasions, quietly tell the student to go to a time-out area until she can stop her laughter, at which time she can rejoin the class.

Whenever consequences will be used, the student needs to be told during the initial meeting (see SUGGESTED STEPS FOR DEVELOPING AND IMPLEMENTING A PLAN) what will happen when her laughter is hurtful toward others.

c. If other students give the target student attention when she is laughing inappropriately (i.e., trying to get her to stop), gently correct them. "Quella and Mary, Bonita can take care of herself and it does not help her to have us trying to take care of something she can handle on her own. It would be best to mind our own business. Corrin and Wes, I appreciate how well you are working on that lab activity."

2. Use reinforce to encourage appropriate behavior.

a. Frequent praise and attention is the core of this plan. The student must see that she receives more frequent and more satisfying attention when she behaves responsibly than when she laughs inappropriately. Thus, whenever the student is behaving appropriately, make an effort to praise and spend time with her. "Bonita, you have been such a pleasure to be around today. I enjoy seeing you work so hard while still having a good time. I am especially impressed with how you have been using self-control."

b. You may also wish to use intermittent reinforcement. Occasional, and unexpected, rewards that acknowledge the student's success may motivate her to demonstrate responsible behavior more often. The idea is to provide a reward when the student has had a particularly good period of not laughing inappropriately. "Bonita, you have been so responsible today, and your laughter has been so appropriate. Would you like to go to Ms. Williamson's room and read a joke from this book to her class?" (NOTE: A list of additional reinforcement ideas can be found in APPENDIX 1.)

If you use intermittent reinforcement, do so more frequently at the beginning of the intervention to encourage the student, and less often as the student's behavior improves over time.

3. Ensure a 3-1 ratio of positive to negative attention.

a. Given that attention is a motivating force for this student, you want to be sure that you are giving the student *three times as much* positive as negative attention. One way to do this is to monitor your interactions with the student at least one day per week. Keep a card on a clipboard or in your pocket and record each interaction you have with the student as either positive or negative by writing a "+" or a "-", respectively, on the card.

To determine whether an interaction is positive or negative, ask yourself whether the student was laughing inappropriately (or otherwise misbehaving) at the time the interaction occurred. Any interaction that stems from inappropriate behavior is negative, while all interactions that occur while the student is meeting classroom expectations are positive. Thus, gently correcting the student or sending her to time-out are both negative interactions, but praising the student for using self-control is positive. Greeting the student as she enters the room or asking her if she has any questions during independent work are also considered positive interactions. *(NOTE: Ignoring the student's inappropriate laughter is not recorded at all, because it is not an interaction.)*

b. If you find that you are not giving the student three times as much positive as negative attention, try to increase the number of positive interactions that you have with the student.

Sometimes prompts can help. For example, you might decide that each time the student enters the classroom you will say "hello" to her, that whenever you look at the clock you will find a time to praise the student, or that whenever a student uses the drinking fountain you will check the target student and as soon as possible praise some aspect of her behavior. You can also increase the ratio of positive to negative attention by ignoring more of the student's inappropriate behavior.

PLAN C

Some students are not really aware of when their laughter is inappropriate and/or how often they laugh inappropriately. If your student laughs inappropriately frequently but doesn't seem to know it or doesn't realize that others are bothered by her laughter, the intervention must include some way of helping the student become more aware of her own behavior.

1. **Respond consistently to the inappropriate behavior.**

a. During your initial meeting with the student (see SUGGESTED STEPS FOR DEVELOPING AND IMPLEMENTING A PLAN), agree upon a nonembarrassing signal that you can use to cue her that she is laughing inappropriately. You want the signal to be a fairly subtle one that only the student will recognize and understand in order to minimize the chance that she will be teased by her peers.

Possibilities include tugging your ear, an unobtrusive wave, softly saying the student's name with direct eye contact, or rubbing your neck. You may need to use the signal frequently and for a fairly long time if the behavior is, even in part, an unconscious habit for the student.

b. Whenever the student is laughing inappropriately, give the signal. If the student stops laughing when you give the signal, praise her privately for paying attention to the signal and for changing her behavior. If the student does not stop laughing, gently correct her (see PLAN A).

2. **Implement a system for monitoring the frequency (and/or duration) of the student's laughter.**

a. Determine which aspect(s) of the student's behavior will be monitored (i.e., frequency and/or duration time) and who will do the recording. In this case, if the student laughs for long periods of time you may wish to monitor how much time the student spends laughing (i.e., the duration time). Otherwise, a frequency count alone is

appropriate. Since the point of the intervention is for the student to become more aware of her own behavior, having her record the information (i.e., self-monitor) will be more effective than if you record the information. However, if the student cannot or will not be accurate (or if she would be too embarrassed to do the recording), you should do it yourself.

If you record the information, remember that the idea is for the student to be made aware of each time that she laughs, and for her to know that each incident is being recorded. *(NOTE: Even when the student self-monitors, you should keep your own record approximately one day per week to verify the student's accuracy.)*

b. If the student is self-monitoring, have her tape a card like the sample shown following to the inside cover of her notebook or in some other unobtrusive location. When the frequency of the student's inappropriate laughter is being monitored, explain that whenever she sees you give the signal, she should cross out one number on the card (starting with 1).

If duration time will be monitored (either by itself or along with a frequency count), each day give the student an index card to keep on her desk or in her notebook. Whenever the student laughs inappropriately, mentally note the time when you give the signal and the time when she stops laughing. Write the difference (in number of minutes) on a piece of paper and subtly give it to the student. She can then record the information on her index card. *(NOTE: This system also gives you a daily frequency count—simply total the number of entries on each card.)*

Name Bonita Martinez

Behavior to be counted: Each time you
laugh (**Note:** 10 times per day is okay)

MONDAY 4/3

1 2 3 4 5 6 7 8 9 10 11 12
13 14 15 16 17 18 19 20 21 22 23 24

TUESDAY 4/4

1 2 3 4 5 6 7 8 9 10 11 12
13 14 15 16 17 18 19 20 21 22 23 24

WEDNESDAY 4/5

1 2 3 4 5 6 7 8 9 10 11 12
13 14 15 16 17 18 19 20 21 22 23 24

THURSDAY 4/6

1 2 3 4 5 6 7 8 9 10 11 12
13 14 15 16 17 18 19 20 21 22 23 24

FRIDAY 4/7

1 2 3 4 5 6 7 8 9 10 11 12
13 14 15 16 17 18 19 20 21 22 23 24

c. Each day, meet with the student for a few minutes to review that day's record. Have the student chart the information on a graph (or do it yourself), and talk with her about whether the day was better, worse, or about the same as previous days. *(NOTE: If you monitor both a frequency count and the duration time, chart them separately as one may improve faster than the other.)*

If the day did not go well, encourage the student to talk about why and have her identify what she can do to help herself remember to use self-control the next day. If the student behaves inappropriately during the meeting, keep the interaction very short. Just let the student know that you are sure tomorrow will be a better day.

3. **Use reinforcement to encourage appropriate behavior.**

a. Give the student increased praise and attention for using self-control (see PLAN A).

b. In addition, during the end-of-the-day review meetings praise the student for responding to the signal (if applicable), for accurately monitoring her own behavior (if applicable), and/or for being willing to look at her record for the day. Thus, even on a bad day, if the student has recorded her behavior accurately, you can praise her. "Bonita, you are really handling this responsibly. Even though it was a rough day, you accurately recorded your behavior and you are willing to talk to me about things you might do differently tomorrow. That is a real sign that you are growing up."

Regardless of how the day went, try to make the end-of-the-day meeting upbeat and encouraging—you want the student to look forward to the review meetings.

4. **(OPTIONAL)**
Identify peer models for the student to observe.

If you think the student may not know what appropriate laughter is, you might suggest two or three other students for her to observe. However, you need to be very careful not to hurt the student's feelings or imply that she should be more like someone else. "Bonita, you might consider watching how Julia and Peg laugh—what they laugh at and what they don't. I don't expect you to try to be like them, you're terrific just the way you are, but watching them may give you some ideas of how long and when to laugh and when not to laugh. You know, I just learned some new golf techniques from watching someone I played with this weekend."

PLAN D

If your student's inappropriate laughter has become habitual and/or she does not seem to have a desire to reduce it, you may need to implement a system of external incentives (i.e., rewards and consequences) based on her behavior to motivate her to stop laughing inappropriately and to start using self-control.

1. **Use a signal to prompt the student that she is laughing inappropriately, then gently correct her if necessary (see PLAN C).**

2. **Implement a system for monitoring the frequency (and/or duration) of the student's laughter (see PLAN C).**

3. *Establish a structured system for reinforcing the appropriate behavior and providing a consequence for the inappropriate behavior.*

a. With the student, create a list of several reinforcers that she can earn. Although you might want to have some suggestions in mind, the system will be more effective if the student identifies most of the items or activities herself. *(NOTE: A list of reinforcement ideas can be found in APPENDIX 1.)*

b. Assign a "price" (in points) for each of the reinforcers on the list, and have the student select the reinforcer that she would like to earn first.

The prices should be based on the number of points the student can earn and the costs—instructional, personnel, and/or monetary —of the rewards. Monetary cost is clear—the more expensive the item, the more points required to earn it. Instructional cost refers to the amount of instructional time lost or interfered with by a particular reward. Thus, an activity that causes the student to miss part of academic instruction would require more points than one the student can do on her own time. Personnel cost involves the time required by you and/or other staff to fulfill the reinforcer. Having lunch with the principal, therefore, would cost more points than spending five minutes of free time with a friend.

A young or immature student may need more immediate and/or frequent reinforcement. In this case, it might be more effective for the student to earn several "less expensive" reinforcers (e.g., five minutes of computer time after 20 points) on the way to a bigger reward (e.g., one hour with you for 200 points). That is, the student receives the smaller rewards without spending points; they continue to accumulate toward the selected reward.

c. Decide how the monitoring information will be translated into points for earning the rewards. Generally, the average number of incidents per day plus two should equal zero points, and the rest of the points be determined from that standard. So, if the student averages 13 incidents per day, for example, the following scale would be established.

15 or more incidents	= 0 points
11-14 incidents	= 1 point
6-10 incidents	= 2 points
3-5 incidents	= 3 points
0-2 incidents	= 4 points

d. At the end of each day, calculate the student's total points for that day and add them to the points earned on previous days. When the student has accumulated enough points to earn the selected reinforcer, she "spends" the points necessary and the system begins again. That is, she begins again with zero points and selects another reinforcer to earn.

e. Determine a consequence (e.g., time owed off of recess or after-school detention) for laughter that exceeds an identified maximum. For example, if you are monitoring frequency, each incident of laughter that exceeds the number that results in zero points (in this example, 15) would result in a consequence.

If you are monitoring duration time, translate the time into points and consequences using a similar scale. For example, if the student keeps her total time of laughter to 0-2 minutes, she would earn 4 points; for 3-5 minutes she earns 3 points; etc. For each minute beyond 15, the student would owe a minute off of recess or in after-school detention.

4. *Use reinforcement to encourage appropriate behavior.*

a. Give the student increased praise and attention for using self-control (see PLAN A).

b. In addition, show interest and enthusiasm about how the student is doing on the system. "Bonita, we are half way through the day and you have only crossed off seven numbers. You are well on your way to earning two points today. Good job!"

....
Suggested Steps for Developing and Implementing a Plan

The following steps are designed to help you develop an appropriate intervention plan and implement it effectively, whether you choose to use one of the MODEL PLANS or create a customized plan of your own. The steps are, however, suggestions—they are not intended to be followed rigidly or in any particular order. Use your professional judgment and the knowledge of your particular situation to make them work for you.

1. Make sure you have enough information about the situation.

a. If you think a minimal intervention like PLAN A will be sufficient, you probably already have enough information to proceed. However, when a more involved plan seems necessary, you should consider collecting additional descriptive and/or objective information for a couple of days so that you can thoroughly describe the problem behavior and monitor any changes in the situation.

b. Details from actual incidents in the form of anecdotal notes may be especially important for generating a clear definition of the problem behavior. That is, since laughter in and of itself is not a misbehavior, you need to be able to specify what aspect(s) of the student's laughter makes it inappropriate. Is it that the student laughs for long periods of time? that she laughs in the wrong situations (e.g., inappropriate time or place)? that she laughs at the wrong type of things (e.g., another's mistakes)? Even if you are not sure what it is about the student's laughter that concerns you, anecdotal notes will help you clarify the problem for the student and her parent(s).

To collect anecdotal notes, simply keep a card in your pocket or on a clipboard and occasionally make notes on specific incidents when the student laughed inappropriately. For each entry, include a brief description of the setting (where and when), exactly how the student behaved, and any other relevant observations you have about the situation (e.g., what prompted the laughter). You do not need to make notes every time the student laughs inappropriately; the idea is to capture a range of examples of the behavior so you will be able to describe it clearly.

You should also make notes on times when the student's laughter is appropriate; this will help her realize that you are not only aware of her inappropriate behavior, but also when she behaves responsibly. In addition, when you meet with the student, these positive examples will help you clarify how you want the student to behave.

c. In addition to being able to describe what the inappropriate laughter looks like, it can also be useful to document how often it occurs and/or how much time is involved. Both measurements provide more objective information about the problem and an objective way to monitor the student's progress. The easiest measurement is to record how often the student laughs inappropriately (i.e., a frequency count). Using the same card on which you are collecting anecdotal notes, simply write a tally mark each time the student laughs inappropriately.

You might want to code these tallies as a way of discerning whether the behavior occurs more frequently during certain times, subjects, or activities (e.g., using an "A" or "P" to distinguish incidents that happened in the morning or afternoon; or clustering the tallies by math or reading, teacher directed instruction or independent work, etc.).

On the other hand, if you are concerned about the amount of time the student spends laughing inappropriately, you may wish to also (or instead of the frequency count) document how many minutes the student laughs inappropriately per day (i.e., the duration time). To do so, each time the student laughs inappropriately, mentally note the time when she starts and the time when she stops. Record the difference (in number of minutes) in place of the tally mark. At the end of the day, you will be able to calculate the total number of minutes spent laughing inappropriately. If you total the number of entries you made, you'll also have a frequency count.

d. If the student notices what you are doing and asks about it, be straightforward—tell her that you are collecting information to see whether her inappropriate laughter is a problem that needs to be worked on.

Following is an example of anecdotal notes, a frequency count, and the duration time that has been collected on a student's inappropriate laughter.

Bonita's Laughter—4/1

Frequency:

AAAAA AAAPP PPPPP PP

Notes:

9:15—Bonita began laughing when Summer asked a question she seemed to think was funny. She was very loud and rude.

9:30—I don't know what set Bonita off, but she began laughing and seemed almost out of control. This lasted for about five minutes, and she finally quit when I sternly told her, "Enough."

10:45—Same as above, but what set her off was a picture in our science book that she though was funny. Before beginning to laugh, she said, "What a dorky looking guy." Her giggling lasted ten minutes, but was not as loud or frantic as earlier.

---

e. Both the frequency count and the duration time are fairly easy to summarize on a chart or graph. Seeing how often and/or how much time she spends laughing inappropriately may help the student and her parent(s) better understand your concern.

If you collect both frequency and duration information, chart them separately as one may improve faster than the other. For example, the number of times the student laughs inappropriately may remain about the same while the number of minutes spent in inappropriate laughter decreases dramatically. The distinction could be important when deciding whether the situation is improving, remaining the same, or worsening.

 Identify a focus for the intervention and labels for referring to the appropriate and inappropriate behaviors.

a. To be effective, the intervention must address more than just reducing the student's inappropriate laughter—there must be a concurrent emphasis on increasing some positive behavior or trait (e.g., using self-control). Not only will having a specific positive behavior in mind make it easier to "catch" and reinforce the student for behaving appropriately, but a positive focus will allow you to frame the situation more productively.

For example, if you simply say that "the student has a problem with inappropriate laughter," you offer little in the way of useful information and may put the student and her parent(s) on the defensive. However, if you explain your concern by saying that you want to "help the student learn to use more self-control," you present an important, and reasonable, goal for the student to work toward and clearly identify what the student needs to do to be successful.

b. Identifying labels for referring to the appropriate and inappropriate behaviors (e.g., "using self-control" and "laughing inappropriately," respectively) will help you to use consistent vocabulary when discussing the situation with the student. If you sometimes refer to the inappropriate behavior as "laughing inappropriately" and other times tell the student that she "is out of control," she may not realize that you are talking about the same thing.

3. **Determine when and how to include the parent(s).**

a. You probably do not need to contact the student's parent(s) if the problem has just begun and is not interfering with her academic or social progress. You might, however, take advantage of any scheduled activities (e.g., conferences, weekly notes home) to let the parent(s) know of your concern.

b. The parent(s) should be contacted whenever the student's inappropriate laughter is affecting her academic performance or is alienating her from her peers. Share with them any information you have collected about the behavior (i.e., anecdotal notes, frequency count, and/or duration time), and explain why you are concerned. Focus in particular on how the behavior is hindering the student academically and/or socially (e.g., other students are avoiding her).

You might ask if the parent(s) have any insight into the situation and/or whether they have noticed similar behavior at home. Whether or not the parent(s) perceive a problem, tell them that you would like to help the student "learn to use more self-control" and invite them to join you for an initial meeting with the student to develop a plan. If the parent(s) are unable or unwilling to participate, let them know that you will keep them informed of the student's progress.

c. Once the parent(s) have been involved in any way, you should give them updates at least

once per week while the plan is being implemented.

4. Prepare for, then conduct, an initial meeting about the situation.

a. Schedule a meeting to discuss your concerns with the student and anyone else who will be involved in the plan (e.g., the parent[s], the school psychologist). Although the specifics of the meeting will vary depending upon the age of the student and the severity of the problem, there are some general guidelines to consider.

First, meet at a neutral time (i.e., not immediately after a problem has occurred), when emotions are less likely to hamper communication. In general, a day's notice is appropriate, however a primary age student may worry excessively and/or forget what the meeting is about if it is scheduled more than an hour before it takes place.

Second, make the meeting appropriately private. For a primary student with a mild problem, you might meet in the classroom while the other students are working independently. However, if you are dealing with a middle/junior high school student and the student's parent(s), you will want to meet in a private place (e.g., the counselor's office) to ensure that the discussion will not be overheard.

Third, try to make sure the meeting is scheduled for a time and place that it is not likely to be interrupted. Finally, if the parent(s) will be participating, they should be the ones to tell the student about the meeting.

b. Construct a preliminary plan. Based on the information you have collected and the focus for the intervention you have identified, you may decide to use one of the MODEL PLANS or you might choose to create a customized plan using components from various plans and/or of your own design. Although you will invite and encourage the student to be an active partner in developing the plan during the initial meeting, having a proposed plan in mind before you meet can alleviate frustration and wasted time if the student is unwilling or unable to participate.

c. Using the information you have collected, prepare thorough descriptions of the inappropriate behavior and the positive behavior/trait on which the student will be working. Be as specific as you can and add concrete examples whenever possible. This will make it easier for you to clarify (and for the student to understand) your expectations. Also be sure to identify appropri-

ate and inappropriate behaviors in all relevant activities (e.g., independent work, teacher directed instruction, unstructured class times, recess and lunch, etc.).

d. Conduct the meeting in an atmosphere of collaboration. The following agenda is one way you might structure the meeting:

• **Share your concerns about the student's behavior.**

Briefly describe the problem behavior and, if appropriate, show the chart(s) of how often/how long the student laughs inappropriately. Then explain why you consider the inappropriate laughter to be a problem. You might tell the student that her inappropriate laughter is negatively affecting how her peers feel about her.

• **Discuss how you can work together to improve the situation.**

Explain that you would like to help the student "learn to use more self-control" and describe your preliminary plan. Invite the student to give you input on the plan and together work out any necessary details (e.g., the monitoring system, reinforcers and consequences). You may have to brainstorm different possibilities if the student is uncomfortable with the initial plan. Incorporating any of the student's suggestions that strengthen the plan is likely to increase her sense of "ownership" in and commitment to it.

• **Make sure the student understands what you mean by appropriate and inappropriate behavior.**

Use the descriptions you have prepared to define and clarify the problem behavior and the positive (desired) behavior as specifically and thoroughly as you can. To ensure that you and the student are in agreement about the expectations, you might present hypothetical scenarios and have the student identify whether each is an example of appropriate or inappropriate laughter. Or you might describe an actual situation that has occurred and ask her to explain how she could use more self-control in that situation.

• **Conclude the meeting.**

Always end the meeting with words of encouragement. Let the student know that you are confident that she can be successful. Be sure to reinforce her for participating in the meeting.

5. *Give the student regular, ongoing feedback about her behavior.*

It is important to meet with the student periodically to discuss her progress. Unless the plan calls for daily meetings (I.e., MODEL PLANS C and D), three to five minutes once per week should suffice. During the meetings, review any information that has been collected and discuss whether or not the situation is improving. As much as possible, focus on the student's improvements, however, also address any new or continuing problems. As the situation improves, the meetings can be faded to once every other week and then to once per month.

6. *Evaluate the situation (and the plan).*

Implement any plan for at least two weeks before deciding whether to change plans; to continue, modify, or fade the plan you are using; or to cease the intervention. Generally, if the student's behavior is clearly improving (based on the objective information that's been collected and/or the subjective perceptions of yourself, the student, and possibly the parent[s]), stick with what you are doing. If the situation has remained the same or worsened, some kind of change will be necessary. Always discuss any changes to the plan with the student first.

L ISTENING, PROBLEMS WITH

P R O B L E M

You have a student whose behavior has lead you to conclude that he is a poor listener.

Because a listening problem is not a discrete behavior, but a label that encompasses many different types of behavior, this problem includes no MODEL PLANS. The purpose of the following information is to suggest an overall approach and some basic considerations for assisting a student you believe has a listening problem.

Alternative Problems

- **Daydreaming**

- **Compliance/Direction Following, Lack of**

- **Distractibility/Short Attention Span**

- **Participation In Class, Lack of**

· · · · · · · · ·
General Information

- It is important to be sure the student does not have a hearing problem. If it has been a long time since hearing screening has been done at school, talk to the school nurse about arranging for the student's hearing to be tested, and/or the need for a physical. Be sure to follow school procedures regarding parental consent for such actions.

- The key to dealing effectively with a student who is a poor listener is to identify one specific inappropriate behavior the student exhibits, and begin by working on that behavior. For example, if you decide to target the student's "difficulty in keeping his attention focused during independent work periods," you could review the information in the problem **Distractibility/Short Attention Span** to develop an intervention plan to help the student learn to manage that behavior more responsibly.

- If the student displays a number of different behaviors that indicate poor listening, and you are not sure where to start, keep anecdotal notes on the student's behavior for a week or so. This type of documentation is fairly easy to collect—simply keep a card in your pocket or on a clipboard and whenever the student behaves in a way that demonstrates poor listening, make notes on the incident.

- For each entry, briefly describe the circumstances—where and when the behavior occurred, what the student did (or didn't do), and any other information that seems relevant. After about a week, review your notes and see if you can determine whether the issue is mainly a lack of compliance, distractibility, or some other specific behavior that you can address.

- The important point is to focus your intervention efforts on one problem behavior at a time. Often, as you work on one behavior (e.g., distractibility), other problem behaviors (e.g., lack of compliance) seem to improve without specific intervention.

L YING

Exaggerating

Telling Fantasy As If Reality

DESCRIPTION

You have a student who tends to not tell the truth—whether by deliberately lying, chronically exaggerating events, or telling fantastic stories as if they were true.

GOAL

The student will learn to tell the truth (without squelching her imagination or creativity), and will learn the importance of telling the truth.

OVERVIEW OF PLANS

- PLAN A: For a problem that has just begun and/or occurs infrequently.
- PLAN B: For a student who tells fantasies as if they were reality.
- PLAN C: For a student who chronically exaggerates events or circumstances and insists that the exaggerated descriptions are true.
- PLAN D: For a student who uses lies to accomplish specific objectives (e.g., to avoid consequences for her behavior or to avoid her schoolwork).
- PLAN E: For a student who lacks the motivation to stop lying.

NOTE:

If the student truly does not seem to be able to distinguish between fantasy and reality, immediately request assistance from the school psychologist or school counselor. A student who is out of touch with reality has more serious problems than will be addressed in these five plans.

Alternative Problems

- **Blaming Others/ Excuses for Everything**
- **Cheating**
- **Stealing—Minor Problem, Culprit Known**

....
General Considerations

- If the student's problem behavior stems in any way from academic issues (e.g., the student lies to avoid doing schoolwork that she is unable to do), concurrent efforts must be made to ensure her academic success (see **Academic Deficits, Determining**).

- If the student lies because she lacks the basic social skills to interact with her peers appropriately (e.g., she frequently exaggerates in order to impress her peers), it may be necessary to begin by teaching her those skills. **Social Skills,**

Lack of contains information on a variety of published social skills curricula.

- If the inappropriate behavior is resulting in the student not completing her schoolwork, implement a plan to increase the student's work completion (see **Work Completion—Daily Work**) in conjunction with one of the following plans for lying.

- Never accuse the student of lying unless you have proof. Accusations without proof only lead to power struggles.

....
Model Plans

PLAN A

It is not always necessary, or even beneficial, to use an involved plan. If the student has lied only a few times or occasionally "stretches the truth," the following actions, along with making the student aware of your concerns, may resolve the situation.

1. *Respond consistently to the inappropriate behavior.*

a. Any time you know for a fact that the student is lying, gently correct her. Inform the student that you know what she is saying is untrue, and how you know. Then have the student make a more accurate statement. "Jin-Luen, I know that is a lie because I see the incomplete reading assignment sticking out of your book right here. You need to tell me the truth about whether you have turned in your reading assignment."

If the student tries to argue, withdraw from the situation—do not engage in an argument. "Jin-Luen, I am not going to discuss this. You have until the end of the day to complete the reading assignment and get it turned in."

b. When you are unsure about whether the student is lying or telling the truth, try to be neutral in your response. "Hmm, that is interesting. I'll need to look into that." Avoid implying that you do not know if you believe the student, because if she *is* telling the truth at that moment she may become discouraged and think, "She doesn't believe me whether I tell the truth or not."

2. *Use reinforcement to encourage appropriate behavior.*

a. Give the student increased praise and attention. Watch for situations in which you are certain the student is telling the truth (even if it is about something fairly minor) and praise the student. "Jin-Leun, I appreciate your honesty about not having turned in your science paper yet. It is really a pleasure to have you giving me accurate information about what's complete and what is not yet finished. Let me know if you need any help getting it completed by the end of the day, okay?"

If the student would be embarrassed by public praise, praise the student privately or even give the student a note. Remember that any time you know that the student is telling the truth, you can praise her for her honesty.

b. Give the student frequent attention (e.g., say "hello" to her as she enters the classroom, call on her frequently during class activities, and occasionally ask her to assist you with a class job that needs to be done) and praise her for other positive behaviors she exhibits. For example, you might comment about the accuracy of her work or how helpful she has been in preparing for a class play. This demonstrates to the student that you notice many positive things she does, not just the fact that she is refraining from lying.

PLAN B

Sometimes a primary age student will tell fantasies as if they were facts. That is, the student is not lying to accomplish some objective, simply reporting untrue events as if they actually happened. If your student reports her daydreams or fantasies as if they were factual events, the intervention must include procedures to teach the student the difference between fantasy and reality.

 1. ***Determine whether the student understands the difference between fiction and nonfiction.***

If the student does not, provide lessons on the difference between fantasy and reality. *(NOTE: If these concepts have not been previously taught, these lessons may be of use to the entire class.)* During the lessons, introduce the concepts and use lots of examples to give the student(s) practice in identifying whether different things (e.g., books, films, cartoons, etc.) are fiction or nonfiction. Be sure to communicate the idea that both fiction and nonfiction are important, fun, and useful. You do not want to imply that somehow nonfiction is better or worse than fiction; just that they are different.

2. ***Whenever the student tells you something that you know is either true or not true, have the student identify whether she is telling you fiction or nonfiction.***

a. For example, if the student tells you that on the way to school an eight-foot tall dog followed her, you might say, "Jin-Leun, that is very interesting. Are you telling me something that is fiction or nonfiction?" If the student says that her report is fiction, show an active interest in what she is telling you, and encourage the student to write a story or draw a picture. "Jin-Leun, this sounds like a wonderful fictional story. Tell me some more about this."

b. If the student identifies that what she is reporting is nonfiction (e.g., "The dog really *was* eight feet tall."), respond in a neutral fashion, gently correct her, and keep the interaction short. It is not necessary to confront the student with the fact that what she is reporting is untrue, however, you do not want to encourage the student to report fantastic events as facts. The best responses are those that neither confront nor encourage the student. "Hmm, that is interesting, but I'll bet it is fiction. Class, it is time to get ready to . . . ."

As long as these types of situations occur, continue to conduct short lessons on the difference between fiction and nonfiction.

c. Occasionally when the student tells you something you know to be factual (e.g., "We played soccer during P.E.), ask the student if she is telling you something that is fiction or nonfiction. If the student responds correctly, reinforce her for her understanding of the concept of fiction and nonfiction, and show an interest in what she is telling you.

If the student responds incorrectly, provide a gentle verbal correction. "Jin-Leun, that was an example of nonfiction. I know because Mrs. Bainbridge told me she was going to be working with the class on soccer for the next two weeks." This type of error indicates that the student needs more instruction on the concepts of fiction and nonfiction.

d. These procedures accomplish several objectives. First, you show an active interest in what the student has to say, which communicates that when the student wants to tell stories, you are there to listen—as long as she can identify the story as fiction. In addition, when the student insists that something fantastic is nonfiction, you are nonconfrontational, without giving her too much attention at that point in time.

3. ***If the student tells you something and you are not sure if it is true or not true, respond in a neutral manner.***

Neutral responses neither encourage nor discourage the student's statements. Do *not* ask whether the student is telling you fiction or nonfiction, because you have no way of verifying the student's assessment. Simply acknowledge the student's statement, then if possible, change the subject. "Oh, I see. How are you doing on your art project?"

Following is a flowchart that illustrates the responses to the student's statements outlined in Steps 1-3.

4. ***Use reinforcement to encourage appropriate behavior.***

a. Give the student increased praise and attention for telling the truth (see PLAN A).

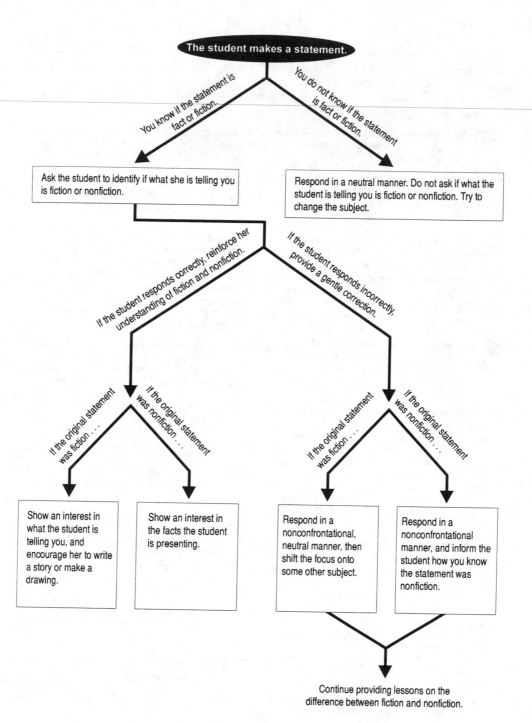

The student makes a statement.

You know if the statement is fact or fiction.

You do not know if the statement is fact or fiction.

Ask the student to identify if what she is telling you is fiction or nonfiction.

Respond in a neutral manner. Do not ask if what the student is telling you is fiction or nonfiction. Try to change the subject.

If the student responds correctly, reinforce her understanding of fiction and nonfiction.

If the student responds incorrectly, provide a gentle correction.

If the original statement was fiction . . .

If the original statement was nonfiction . . .

If the original statement was fiction . . .

If the original statement was nonfiction . . .

Show an interest in what the student is telling you, and encourage her to write a story or make a drawing.

Show an interest in the facts the student is presenting.

Respond in a nonconfrontational, neutral manner, then shift the focus onto some other subject.

Respond in a nonconfrontational manner, and inform the student how you know the statement was nonfiction.

Continue providing lessons on the difference between fiction and nonfiction.

b. In addition, make a special point of letting the student know that you notice her efforts to be accurate about what is fiction and what is non-fiction.

PLAN C

Sometimes a student will exaggerate events and circumstances in an effort to impress others or to make herself feel more important. If your student frequently exaggerates, the intervention should include procedures for improving the student's self-confidence and for reducing her need to inflate her own importance.

(NOTE: In this situation, there may be no need to make the student overtly aware of your concern about her exaggerating. You can begin to implement this plan without scheduling a planning meeting with the student [as described in the SUGGESTED STEPS FOR DEVELOPING AND IMPLEMENTING A PLAN]. If, after two weeks, the situation has not improved, then conduct an awareness discussion to explain your perception of the problem to the student and to ask for her input on the plan.)

 1. When the student tells you something that you know is an exaggeration (or is probably an exaggeration), respond in a neutral manner and keep the interaction short.

Accept what the student says, but shift the focus of the conversation as quickly as possible without hurting the student's feelings. For example, if the student tells you that her father took her camping over the weekend and they saw a fox, but you know or suspect the student is making this up because her father is rarely around, you might say something like, "Spending time with someone you like is always nice. Who else do you like spending time with?"

Do *not* ask the student if what she is telling you is true (or fiction/nonfiction), as this will box the student into a corner. She either has to admit that she is lying or stick to a story that is untrue.

 2. Whenever the student tells you something that you know is true, show an active and sincere interest.

Talk to the student about what she is telling you, paraphrase her statements, ask her leading questions, relate what she says to appropriate incidents in your own life, relate similar experiences from your childhood, etc. You want to make it clear to the student that you are more interested in her and her real life events than in any grossly exaggerated stories she may tell.

 3. Use reinforcement to encourage appropriate behavior.

a. Provide frequent praise when the student is meeting classroom expectations. For example, praise the student for being on task, for good attendance, for work completion, for participating in class, etc.

b. Avoid praising the student for honesty or for not exaggerating, because you do not want to make an issue of her tendency to exaggerate or lie. Besides, if you have not had a planning meeting with the student, you will not have even discussed her exaggerating and/or lying as a problem yet.

b. Give the student lots of attention. For example, make frequent eye contact with her and smile. Walk with and talk to the student as the class is going down the hallway. Call on the student frequently during class discussions. Etc.

4. Structure activities or interactions that capitalize on the student's strengths and interests.

The student may exaggerate because she is insecure or feels insignificant or unimportant. A potentially powerful way to increase the student's self-confidence is to build upon her strengths and interests that already exist. The hope is that helping the student feel more confident about things she already does well will result in less of a need for the student to exaggerate.

Following are some suggestions for building on the student's strengths and interests:

- If the student has a particular academic interest (e.g., American History), check out a library book or loan her one of your own that you read and enjoyed when you were her age.

- If the student is proficient on the computer, ask her to help you set up and maintain a database to keep track of classroom supplies.

- If the student has artistic abilities, ask her to draw a poster that can be used to demonstrate a particular technique/concept to the class.

- If the student reads well, ask her if she would be willing to tutor a younger student.

(NOTE: See APPENDIX 2 for additional ideas on jobs the student could be given to increase her sense of importance.)

PLAN D

Sometimes a student lies to accomplish a specific objective (e.g., avoiding consequences for her behavior or avoiding an undesirable task). The student may have learned that lying is a more effective means of getting one's needs met than telling the truth (e.g., "The truth is for suckers."). If the student seems devious and/or intentionally deceitful, the intervention must include ways to demonstrate that lying will not accomplish the student's objectives and will result in consequences.

1. **Prepare and conduct one or more lessons on the importance of trust.**

During the lesson(s), include concepts such as:

- Lying decreases one's future credibility (use a fable like the little boy who cried wolf or a story with a similar message).

- Trust is something that is created over time, and one lie can destroy the trust. You might use the following diagram, or even an actual scale, to show how trust and distrust cancel each other out.

  Explain that when you first meet someone, you neither trust nor distrust them. But each time that person is honest with you, you begin to trust that person. Each honest act is like a small block being placed on the scale—tipping the balance toward trust. One lie, however, can be like a huge block being placed on the other side with such force that it knocks all the "honest" blocks off the scale. The result is distrust.

  Then explain how once the lie is there it takes many "honest" blocks to tip the scale back to trust.

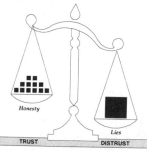

- Trust is important in friendships, on the job, etc.

2. **Establish consequence(s) for any overt lie.**

a. Let the student know that any time she tells you something that you know is not true, she will owe time off of recess or in after-school detention. If the student is in a primary grade, five minutes per infraction is appropriate. For an intermediate grade student, assign ten minutes of time owed for each infraction. In middle/junior high school, the student should owe 15 minutes per infraction.

b. In addition, it is very important that the student not be able to avoid whatever she was lying about. For example, if the student lied to avoid the calisthenics in P.E., she should owe the time, plus have to do the calisthenics. If the student's statement is identified as a lie after she has already avoided the calisthenics have her do the calisthenics during recess or in after-school detention, and *then* spend the 15 minutes of time owed, for example.

c. Be direct and assertive when you know the student has told you a lie. However, do not argue or engage in a debate. If other students are around, refer to the student's behavior as "saying something untrue." "Jin-Leun, that is not true. I saw you . . . , so you owe 15 minutes." If the student tries to debate or argue, tell her that she can see you after school or during recess if she wishes to speak to you more about the issue.

If other students are not around, label the student's behavior as lying. "Jin-Leun, that is an example of the problem we have been talking about, lying. I know that what you said is untrue because . . . . You owe 15 minutes after school."

3. *Use reinforcement to encourage appropriate behavior.*

Provide frequent praise and attention when the student is telling the truth and otherwise meeting classroom expectations (see PLAN A).

4. *Periodically test the student's honesty.*

a. Several times per day, ask the student about something she did, using the following two different types of questions:

- Type 1 Questions—those for which you are sure of the "honest" answer. "Jin-Luen, did you push past Joyce on your way out the door?" (This is a Type 1 Question as long as you know whether she did or not.) If the student lies, she receives the time owed consequence.

  If the student answers honestly, praise her. "Jin-Leun, I wish you hadn't pushed past her, but the more important issue right now is that you are being honest."

  Occasionally when the student answers honestly, you may wish to provide an intermittent reward. "Jin-Leun, I am so pleased about your honesty that I am going to give you a "Free Homework" pass. *(NOTE: Additional ideas for reinforcers can be found in APPENDIX 1.)*

- Type 2 Questions—those for which you are unsure of the "honest" answer. "Jin-Leun, did you push past Joyce on your way out the door?" If you do not know for sure whether she did or not, ask the question, accept the student's answer, and inform the student that you have no direct knowledge so you have no basis for making a judgment. "Joyce says you did, but I didn't see it, so I will believe you both—she thinks she was pushed, you think someone pushed you past her."

b. There are a few key elements to making this procedure work. First, the student should never know in advance whether a question is a Type 1 or a Type 2 Question. That is, when you ask the question, the student should be thinking something like, "I don't know if she knows or not. If she does and I lie I am in even bigger trouble. If I am honest, I may even get rewarded for my honesty."

Second, as much as possible, ask more Type 1 than Type 2 Questions. For example, if it is possible to covertly observe the student during a portion of her recess or lunch, you will observe situations that you can turn into Type 1 Questions.

Finally, ask a variety of questions. The following examples illustrate the variety of questions that you should ask:

- Questions about misbehavior when you know she is guilty.

  "Did you push past her?"

- Questions about misbehavior when you know she is innocent.

  "Did you push past her?"

- Questions about positive behavior when you know she is guilty.

  "Did you have a successful recess, or did Mr. Madden have to speak to you?"

- Questions about positive behavior when you know she is innocent.

  "Did you have a successful recess, or did Mr. Madden have to speak to you?"

If you only ask the student a Type 1 Question when you know she is guilty, she will soon learn that she should always admit guilt. By using a full range of questions, the student is forced to evaluate her behavior and decide whether it is in her best interest to lie or to tell the truth. By structuring a great number of Type 1 Questions in this manner, you will demonstrate that it is in her best interest to tell the truth.

PLAN E

In some cases, a student lies habitually. If the student's lying behavior has worked for her (i.e., helping accomplish her objectives and avoid undesirable events/tasks) for a long time, you may need to implement a structured system of external incentives (i.e., rewards and consequences) based on her behavior to motivate her to stop lying and to start telling the truth.

1. *Implement all aspects of PLAN D.*

2. *Establish a system for reinforcing the appropriate behavior and for providing a consequence for the inappropriate behavior.*

a. With the student, create a list of reinforcers that she can earn. Although you might want to have some suggestions in mind, the system will be more effective if the student identifies most of the items or activities herself. The rewards may need to be perceived as relatively high value (but not necessarily monetarily) in order to create a powerful enough incentive to motivate the student to strive for honesty. *(NOTE: A list of reinforcement ideas can be found in APPENDIX 1.)*

b. Assign "prices" (in points) for each of the reasonable rewards on the list and have the student select the reward that she would like to earn first.

The prices should be based on the instructional, personnel, and/or monetary costs of the items. Monetary cost is clear—the more expensive the item, the more points required to earn it. Instructional cost refers to the amount of instructional time lost or interfered with by a particular reward. Thus, an activity which causes the student to miss part of academic instruction should require more points than one the student can do on her own time. Personnel cost involves the time required by you and/or other staff to fulfill the reinforcer. Having lunch with the principal, therefore, would cost more points than spending five minutes of free time with a friend.

c. Each honest answer to a Type 1 Question will equal five points. Each untrue response to a Type 1 Question will equal 15 minutes of time owed. (Do not take away points the student has already earned when she lies, otherwise the student may lose so many points that she becomes discouraged from trying to earn them.)

Each answer to a Type 2 Question yields no points and no time owed because you cannot verify the student's response.

d. As the student becomes increasingly successful on the system, begin asking Type 1 Questions slightly less frequently so it takes the student longer to earn any given reinforcer.

e. If the student would be embarrassed about being on a system of this type, respect her need to keep the plan confidential (i.e., just between the two of you, and her parent[s], if applicable.)

f. When the student has accumulated enough points to earn the reward she has chosen, she "spends" the points necessary and the system begins again. That is, she selects another reward to earn and begins with zero points.

If the student is immature, and needs more frequent encouragement, you might consider letting her earn several "less expensive" rewards (e.g., five minutes of free time after 20 points) on the way to a bigger reward (e.g., one hour of supervised use of the gymnasium with a friend for 200 points). That is, the student receives the small rewards without spending points; they continue to accumulate toward the selected reward.

3. *Use reinforcement to encourage appropriate behavior.*

a. Give the student increased praise and attention for telling the truth (see PLAN A).

b. In addition, show interest and enthusiasm about how the student is doing on the system. "Jin-Leun, you are racking these points up so fast and have not owed any time for two days. It is a pleasure dealing with such an honest student."

· · · · · · · ·
Suggested Steps for Developing and Implementing a Plan

The following steps are designed to help you develop an appropriate intervention plan and implement it effectively, whether you choose to use one of the MODEL PLANS or create a customized plan of your own. The steps are, however, suggestions—they are not intended to be followed rigidly or in any particular order. Use your professional judgment and the knowledge of your particular situation to make them work for you.

 1. Make sure you have enough information about the situation.

a. If you think a minimal intervention like PLAN A will be sufficient, you may already have enough information to proceed. However, when a more involved plan seems necessary, you should consider collecting additional descriptive and/or objective information for a couple of days.

b. You need to document specific incidents to demonstrate that the student's problem is more than simply telling harmless little fibs. Anecdotal notes can provide enough detail to help you define the problem behavior clearly and completely. To collect anecdotal notes, simply keep a card in your pocket or on a clipboard and occasionally make notes on specific instances when the student lied/exaggerated. For each entry, briefly describe what the student claimed and how/why you know it is untrue. Record every instance of proven lying.

c. You may also wish to make notes on times when you suspect that the student is lying, but have no proof. These examples will be useful when talking with the student about trust. The record of known lies juxtaposed against the incidents of suspected lies will help you explain to the student and her parent(s) why you often suspect the student is lying when you have no proof. Also take some notes on times when the student tells the truth so she knows you're aware of her positive behavior as well.

d. If the student notices what you are doing and asks about it, be straightforward—tell her that you are collecting information on situations in which she lies/exaggerates so you can work with her and her parent(s) to set up an intervention plan.

Following is an example of anecdotal notes that have been collected on a student's lying and suspected lying.

Notes on Jin-Luen's Lying—10/2

8:25—Jin-Leun told the class that her father is a pilot in the Navy and that he is away on a secret mission.

Untrue—Her father is unemployed and lives out of state.

9:30—Jin-Leun told me that she did not have her homework because some boys stole it from her this morning. (True?)

12:30—Jin-Leun claimed that she could not participate in P.E. because she sprained her ankle at lunch. It was not swollen, but I sent her to the nurse to get it checked out. The nurse didn't know for sure, so we let her sit out. (True?)

2:15—When I was collecting the reading assignments, Jin-Luen said she already turned in the completed assignment. I asked her to find it in the stack and she couldn't. She claimed I lost it.

Untrue—I happened to see the incomplete assignment hanging out of her book. She then denied lying, and said she was just confused.

---

e. Continuing to collect this type of information while you implement a plan will help you to monitor whether the situation is getting worse, staying the same, or getting better.

2. Identify a focus for the intervention and labels for referring to the appropriate and inappropriate behaviors.

a. To be effective, the intervention must address more than just reducing the student's lying—there must be a concurrent emphasis on increasing some positive behavior or trait (e.g., "honesty").

b. Specifying labels for the appropriate and inappropriate behaviors (e.g., "honesty " and "lying," respectively) will help you to use consistent vocabulary when discussing the situation with the student. *(NOTE: If the student tends to exaggerate or tell fantasies as if reality, you might refer to her problem as "telling something that is not true" rather than labeling the problem behavior "lying.")*

3. ***Determine when and how to include the parent(s).***

a. It is not necessary to contact the student's parent(s) if the problem involves only mild exaggerations or the occasional telling of fantasies as reality. However, it might be a good idea to take advantage of any scheduled activities (e.g., conferences, weekly notes home) to let them know of your concern.

b. If the student engages in overt lying, her parent(s) should be informed. Share with them any information you have collected about the behavior (e.g., anecdotal notes), and explain why you are concerned. You might ask if the parent(s) have any insight into the situation and/or whether they have noticed similar behavior at home.

Whether or not the parent(s) perceive a problem, explain that you want to help the student "learn the importance of honesty" and invite them to join you for an initial meeting with the student to develop a plan. If the parent(s) are unable or unwilling to participate, let them know that you will keep them informed of the student's progress.

c. If the parent(s) respond antagonistically, include another professional (e.g., the principal or school counselor) during all further interactions with the parent(s).

d. Once the parent(s) have been involved in any way, you should give them updates at least once per week while the plan is being implemented.

4. ***Prepare for, then conduct, an initial meeting about the situation.***

a. Arrange a meeting to discuss your concerns with the student and anyone else who will be involved in the plan (e.g., the parent[s], the school psychologist). Although the specifics will vary depending upon the age of the student and the severity of the problem, there are some general guidelines to consider when scheduling the meeting.

First, meet at a neutral time (i.e., not immediately after a problem has occurred), when emotions are less likely to hamper communication. In general, a day's notice is appropriate, however a primary age student may worry excessively and/or forget what the meeting is about if it is scheduled more than an hour before it takes place.

Second, make the meeting appropriately private. Third, try to make sure the meeting is scheduled for a time and place that it is not likely to be interrupted (e.g., the counselor's office). Finally, if the parent(s) will be participating, they should be the ones to tell the student about the meeting.

b. Construct a preliminary plan. Decide whether you think you can use one of the MODEL PLANS or if you need to create a customized plan using components from various plans and/or of your own design. Although you will invite and encourage the student to help develop the plan during the initial meeting, having a proposed plan in mind before you meet can alleviate frustration and wasted time if the student is unwilling or unable to participate.

c. After reviewing the information you have collected and thinking about how you want the student to behave, prepare thorough descriptions of the inappropriate behavior and the positive behavior/trait on which the student will be working. The more specific you can be and the more concrete examples you have, the easier it will be to clarify (and for the student to understand) your expectations. Be sure to consider the student's behavior in all relevant activities (e.g., independent work, teacher directed instruction, unstructured class times, recess and lunch, etc.).

d. Conduct the meeting in an atmosphere of collaboration. The following agenda is one way you might structure the meeting:

• **Share your concerns about the student's behavior.**

Briefly describe the problem behavior and explain why you consider it to be a problem. You might tell the student how even one lie can affect her credability for a long time—not just with you, but with anyone she interacts with.

• **Discuss how you can work together to improve the situation.**

Tell the student that you would like to help her "learn the importance of honesty," and describe your preliminary plan. Invite the student to give you input on the various aspects of the plan, and together work out any necessary details (e.g., consequences, points, reinforcers, etc.). You may have to brainstorm different possibilities if the student is uncomfortable with the initial plan. Incorporating any of the student's suggestions that strengthen the plan is likely to increase her sense of "ownership" in and commitment to it.

- **Conclude the meeting.**

Always end the meeting with words of encouragement. Let the student know that you are confident that she can be successful. Be sure to reinforce her for participating in the meeting.

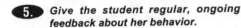 **5.** *Give the student regular, ongoing feedback about her behavior.*

It is important to meet with the student periodically to discuss her progress. In most cases, three to five minutes once per day should be sufficient. During the meetings, review any information that has been collected and discuss whether or not the situation is getting better. As much as possible, focus on the student's improvements, however, also address any new or continuing problems. As the situation improves, the meetings can be faded to once every other week and then to once per month.

6. *Evaluate the situation (and the plan).*

Implement any plan for at least two weeks before deciding whether to change plans; to continue, modify, or fade the plan you are using; or to cease the intervention. Generally, if the student's behavior is clearly improving (based on the objective information that's been collected and/or the subjective perceptions of yourself, the student, and possibly the parent[s]), stick with what you are doing. If the situation has remained the same or worsened, some kind of change will be necessary. Always discuss any changes to the plan with the student first.

 **M**ASTURBATION

Rubbing Genitals

DESCRIPTION

You have a student who rubs his genitals in the classroom and/or on the playground.

GOAL

The student will stop masturbating in public.

OVERVIEW OF PLANS

- PLAN A: For a problem that has just begun or occurs infrequently.
- PLAN B: For a situation in which the student masturbates in public to get attention or to shock others.

NOTE:

These plans are geared for a primary grade student or a naive special education student. If you are faced with a student in the fourth grade or above who masturbates in an exhibitionist manner—to gain attention or to shock adults or peers—immediately refer the situation to the building administrator or school counselor. Although one or both of these plans may be appropriate with an intermediate age student, this behavior should be viewed as more serious with an older student, and collaboration is warranted.

Alternative Problem

- **Sexual Comments**

....
General Considerations

- If the student's problem behavior stems in any way from academic issues (e.g., masturbating is the student's attempt to relieve the stress of frequent academic frustration and failure), concurrent efforts must be made to ensure his academic success (see **Academic Deficits, Determining**).

- If the student seems "high strung" or tense, pairing either or both of these plans with strategies to help the student learn to manage his anxiety may be helpful. See **Anxiety/Nervousness** for information on how to teach relaxation skills to students.

- If you have any reason to believe that the student could be a victim of sexual abuse, immediately discuss the situation with your building administrator. Every other aspect of the plan should be secondary to protecting the health and safety of the student. Follow your district and state guidelines for reporting suspected abuse.

....
Model Plans

PRE-INTERVENTION STEPS

- Since masturbation is such a sensitive issue, the student's parent(s) are the most appropriate adults to intervene. Therefore, you should immediately contact the student's parent(s) and ask them to discuss the situation with their child. In addition, ask them how/whether you should intervene in the school setting at this point.

- When you speak with the student's parent(s), do not imply that the behavior is shocking—many young children engage in it. You might suggest that the parent(s) teach the student the importance of "touching private parts of one's body only in private." Let them know that they may

have to use examples to teach the student which are the "private parts" of his body.

- Also let the parent(s) know that they may need to use examples to teach their child about private versus public settings. Ask the parent(s) to focus on helping the student understand that school is a public place and therefore not a place where he should be touching his private body parts.

- Any school-based intervention(s) should occur only if parental efforts have been ineffective. If it does become necessary to intervene at school, it is very important that the parent(s) be encouraged to attend any meetings where this issue will be discussed with the student.

PLAN A

If the parent(s) have intervened, but the student still occasionally masturbates at school, a simple school-based plan may be necessary.

1 **Respond consistently to the inappropriate behavior.**

a. During your initial meeting with the student (see SUGGESTED STEPS FOR DEVELOPING AND IMPLEMENTING A PLAN), establish a nonembarrassing signal that you can use to cue the student that he is "touching private body parts in a public place." You want the signal to be a fairly subtle one that only the student will recognize and understand in order to minimize the chance that he will be teased by his peers. Possibilities include folding your arms across

your chest, rubbing your neck, or even just direct eye contact and a head nod. Let the student know that you may also need to quietly say his name to get his attention before you give him the signal.

You should be prepared to use the signal frequently and for a fairly long time since it is likely that the behavior is, at least in part, an unconscious habit for the student.

b. In addition, work out how the student should respond to the signal. That is, you might suggest that when the student sees the signal he should either fold his arms across his chest or, if seated at his desk, place his hands on the desk.

c. Whenever you see the student masturbating, give him the signal. If the student does not stop masturbating, gently correct him. Quietly give the student a direction that specifies what he needs to do with his hands. "Les, put your hands on your desk." Because your goal is to impart information, you want to be emotionally neutral while giving the correction.

2. Use reinforcement to encourage appropriate behavior.

a. Give the student increased praise and attention. Be especially alert for situations in which the student has had a tendency to masturbate, but is not. For example, if independent seatwork periods have been a problem in the past, and the student has been successful for an entire work period, acknowledge this as an important demonstration of the student's success.

Praise the student privately so as not to embarrass him. "Len, today throughout the entire morning work period you kept your hands on your desk or on your paper. You should be proud of how quickly you are learning about how you should behave in a public place." Remember that any time the student is refraining from masturbating, you can praise him.

b. Privately praise the student for responding to the signal. "Len, twice today I gave the signal of folding my arms across my chest, and each time you stopped what you were doing and folded your own arms across your chest. You are working hard on learning about what to do in a public place."

c. Give the student frequent attention (e.g., say "hello" to him as he enters the classroom, call on him frequently during class activities, and occasionally ask him to assist you with a class job that needs to be done) and praise him for other positive behaviors he exhibits. For example, you might comment about the accuracy of his work or how well he is keeping his attention focused on his assignments. This demonstrates to the student that you notice many positive things he does, not just that he is refraining from masturbating.

PLAN B

Some students are very skilled at gaining attention through their negative behavior. Your student may have learned that he can elicit reactions (e.g., shock or laughter) from others by grabbing and/or rubbing his genitals. If you find yourself frequently reminding or coaxing the student to stop masturbating, or if he seems to enjoy the other students' reactions, it maybe that he is using the behavior to gain attention. Whether or not the student overtly seems to like the attention, you should make sure that he receives more frequent and more satisfying attention for behaving appropriately than for masturbating.

1. Respond consistently to the inappropriate behavior.

a. Whenever the student masturbates, use a nonverbal signal to cue the student that he is "touching private body parts in a public place" (see PLAN A).

b. In addition to the signal, implement a consequence for each incident of masturbation in public (e.g., he will owe one minute off of the next recess). Be sure that the student is aware that you are recording each incident and that he owes one minute for each infraction. During the minute(s) the student owes, he should have to sit with his hands on his desk, doing nothing.

c. When giving the signal and when following through with the consequence, be emotionally neutral. Never act disgusted, frustrated, or disappointed with his behavior. Any emotional reaction may fuel the student's inappropriate, attention-getting behavior.

Also, do not be distressed if the student acts like he enjoys the time owed. He will tire of the game within a week or two—unless he senses that he is "getting to you."

2. (OPTIONAL)
Teach the other students to ignore the target student's inappropriate behavior.

Whenever the target student is obtaining a reaction for his inappropriate behavior from another student, gently correct the student who is reacting. "Sheera, it would be best to pay no attention. He wants you to react. Just ignore." After doing this a few times with a few different students, switch your strategy. Praise one or more students who are ignoring. "Clifford, nice job of not reacting. You have a very powerful attention span to be able to keep focused on your work."

3. Use reinforcement to encourage appropriate behavior.

a. Frequent praise and attention is the core of this plan. The student must see that he receives more frequent and more satisfying attention when he behaves appropriately than when he masturbates. Thus, whenever the student is not masturbating (or otherwise misbehaving), make an effort to praise and spend time with him. "Les, you are sure intent on this experiment. Would it be okay if I sat with you a moment and watched as you do the next step?"

b. You may also wish to use intermittent rewards to acknowledge the student's success. Occasional, and unexpected, rewards can motivate the student to demonstrate responsible behavior more often. The idea is to provide a reward when the student has gone for a significant period of time without masturbating in public.

Appropriate rewards might include performing a skit for the class, taking an announcement or message into some other teachers' rooms, or having some of his work displayed in the office. *(NOTE: A list of additional reinforcement ideas can be found in APPENDIX 1.)*

Use intermittent rewards more frequently at the beginning of the intervention to encourage the student, and then less often as his behavior improves.

4. Ensure a 3-1 ratio of positive to negative attention.

a. If attention is the motivating force for the student, you want to be sure that you are giving him *three times as much* positive as negative attention.

One way to do this is to monitor your interactions with the student at least one day per week. Keep a card on a clipboard or in your pocket and record each interaction you have with the student as either positive or negative by writing a "+" or a "-", respectively, on the card.

To determine whether an interaction is positive or negative, ask yourself whether the student was masturbating (or otherwise misbehaving) at the time the interaction occurred. Any interaction that stems from inappropriate behavior is negative, and all interactions that occur while the student is meeting classroom expectations are positive. Thus, giving the signal and assigning time owed are both negative interactions, but praising the student for not needing the signal is positive. Talking to the student before he leaves the room or thanking him for contributing a comment during a class discussion are also considered positive interactions.

b. If you find that you are not giving the student three times as much positive as negative attention, try to increase the number of positive interactions you have with the student. Sometimes prompts can help. For example, you might decide that each time the student enters the classroom you will say "hello" to him, that whenever you look at the clock you will find a time to praise the student, or that whenever another student uses the drinking fountain you will check the target student and, as soon as possible, praise some aspect of his behavior.

. . . .

Suggested Steps for Developing and Implementing a Plan

The following steps are designed to help you develop an appropriate intervention plan and implement it effectively, whether you choose to use one of the MODEL PLANS or create a customized plan of your own. The steps are, however, suggestions--they are not intended to be followed rigidly or in any particular order. Use your professional judgment and the knowledge of your particular situation to make them work for you.

1. Make sure you have enough information about the situation.

a. If the masturbation is occurring more than a couple of times per day, or has been going on

for a long time, it can be useful to document how often it occurs (i.e., a frequency count). This information will provide both a more objective measure of the problem and an objective way to monitor the student's progress. To maintain a frequency count, simply keep a card on a clipboard or in your pocket and write a tally mark each time you see the student masturbating.

If the student is masturbating in settings other than the classroom (e.g., on the playground), ask the adult(s) supervising that setting to keep records also and to share the information with you. *(NOTE: PLAN C requires a frequency count of the number of times you signal the student about the behavior, as the student will owe this number of minutes off of recess.)*

b. Frequency is fairly easy to summarize on a chart or graph. Seeing how often you give him the signal may help the student and his parent(s) better understand your concern.

c. Continuing to collect this type of information (and keeping the chart up-to-date) while you implement a plan will also help you to monitor whether the situation is getting worse, staying the same, or getting better.

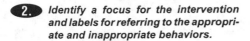

2. Identify a focus for the intervention and labels for referring to the appropriate and inappropriate behaviors.

To be effective, the intervention must address more than just reducing the student's masturbation—there must be a concurrent emphasis on increasing some positive behavior or trait (e.g., "learning to touch private parts of your body only in private"). This phrase also provides a way to refer to the problem in a relatively nonembarrassing way.

3. Determine when and how to include the parent(s).

a. With this type of problem, the student's parent(s) should be contacted immediately and asked to discuss the issue with the student at home.

b. If the problem continues, invite the student's parent(s) to join you for an initial meeting with the student to develop a plan. If the parent(s) are unable or unwilling to participate, let them know that you will keep them informed of the student's progress. If the parent(s) appear extremely uncomfortable or antagonistic about the problem, invite another school professional (e.g., the counselor, the principal) to assist you in the meeting.

c. Once the parent(s) have been involved in any way, you should give them updates at least once per week while the plan is being implemented.

4. Prepare for, then conduct, an initial meeting about the situation.

a. Arrange a meeting to discuss your concerns with the student and anyone else who will be involved in the plan (e.g., the parent[s], the school counselor). Make the meeting appropriately private, and schedule it for a time and place that it is not likely to be interrupted. If the parent(s) will be participating, they should be the ones to tell the student about the meeting.

b. Construct a preliminary plan. Decide whether you think you can use one of the MODEL PLANS or if you need to create a customized plan using components from various plans and/or of your own design. Although you will invite and encourage the student to help develop the plan during the initial meeting, having a proposed plan in mind before you meet can alleviate frustration and wasted time if the student is unwilling or unable to participate.

c. After reviewing the information you have collected (i.e., a frequency count) and thinking about how you want the student to behave, prepare descriptions of the inappropriate behavior (e.g., touching private body parts in public) and the positive behavior/trait on which the student will be working (e.g., touching private body parts only in private).

d. Conduct the meeting in an atmosphere of collaboration. The following agenda is one way you might structure the meeting:

- **Share your concerns about the student's behavior.**

  Briefly describe the problem behavior and explain why you consider it to be a problem. You might explain that seeing someone touching private body parts in public makes others feel uncomfortable. Depending upon the parent(s)' viewpoint, you may also wish to tell the student that although what he is doing is not necessarily bad or wrong, some body parts are private and should only be touched in private.

- **Discuss how you can work together to improve the situation.**

  Tell the student that you would like to help him learn to "touch private body parts only in private," and describe your preliminary plan. Invite the student to give you input on the various aspects of the plan, and together work out any necessary details (e.g., the signal, the appropriate/desired response to the signal, etc.).

You may have to brainstorm different possibilities if the student is uncomfortable with the initial plan. Incorporating any of the student's suggestions that strengthen the plan is likely to increase his sense of "ownership" in and commitment to it.

• **Conclude the meeting.**

Always end the meeting with words of encouragement. Let the student know that you are confident that he can be successful. Be sure to reinforce him for participating in the meeting.

5. *Give the student regular, ongoing feedback about his behavior.*

It is important to meet with the student periodically to discuss his progress. In most cases, two minutes once per day would be useful. During the meetings, review any frequency count information that has been collected and discuss whether or not the situation is getting better. As much as possible, focus on the student's improvements, however, also address any new or continuing problems. As the situation improves, the meetings can be faded to once every other week and then to once per month.

6. *Evaluate the situation (and the plan).*

Implement any plan for at least two weeks before deciding whether to change plans; to continue, modify, or fade the plan you are using; or to cease the intervention. If the situation has remained the same or worsened, some kind of change to the plan will be necessary. If so, discuss the problem with your school counselor or school psychologist.

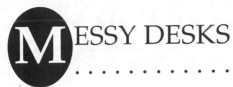

MESSY DESKS

Poor Organization of Materials

DESCRIPTION

There are students in your class whose work and/or storage areas (e.g., desks, cubbies) are so messy that time is wasted as they attempt to locate their papers, pencils, books, etc.

GOAL

The students will keep their work and/or storage areas neat enough that necessary materials can be found quickly.

OVERVIEW OF PLANS

- PLAN A: For a problem that has just begun.
- PLAN B: For a problem that may stem from the students having too many possessions.
- PLAN C: For a problem that may stem from the students not having the necessary organizational and cleaning skills.
- PLAN D: For a situation in which the students lack the motivation to keep their desks neat.

NOTE:

- *These four plans are geared for a situation in which quite a few students in the class have a problem keeping their work/storage areas neat. However, each can easily be adapted for intervening with only a few (one to three) individual students who have/continue to have a problem with messiness.*

- *Although these plans focus on messy desks, procedures could also be adapted for any personal storage areas used by students (e.g., cubbies, lockers, etc.).*

Alternative Problems

- **Beginning Class—Getting Students Settled Down**

- **Cleaning Up, Problems With**

- **Dawdling**

- **Forgetting Materials**

- **Sloppy Work**

- **Transitions, Problems With**

General Considerations

- If the issue goes beyond messy desks and in-cludes problems with overall organization (e.g., not keeping track of assignments, not managing time, not using effective study habits), you might consider implementing the following curriculum:

Archer, A. & Gleason, M. (1991). *Skills for school success*. North Billerica, MA: Curriculum Associates.

Model Plans

PLAN A

If this problem has just begun, it may not be necessary, or even beneficial, to use an involved plan. The following actions, along with making the students aware of your concerns, may resolve the situation.

 Schedule and conduct a class-wide discussion to clarify the problem, brainstorm possible solutions, and devise an action plan.

a. Let the students know one day in advance that there will be a class meeting to think of ideas for keeping their desks more neat and organized. Prior to the meeting, write an agenda similar to the sample following on the chalkboard.

Agenda

1. Define the problem—How messy are the desks? how much time is wasted each day because of the messiness?

2. Describe what a neat desk would look like.

3. Classroom pride—Let's have a room we can be proud of!

---

b. For agenda Item #2, record the students' sug-gestions on the chalkboard or on a wall chart. Do not fill in the examples beforehand; this chart should be developed jointly with the students. The following sample chart shows the kinds of ideas that you and the students might generate. When developing the chart, it is important that each item on the list have both a "Neat" example and a "Messy" example.

A Neat Desk	A Messy Desk
The top is clean.	The top has pencil marks or smudges and dried glue.
All papers are in a notebook or in the folder to take home.	There are loose papers (some done, some unfinished, some blank paper).
The books are in a neat stack and there are not too many.	There are books thrown in (many library books or books from home).
Pencils, scissors, erasers, and any other little things are in the pencil box.	Pencils and other little stuff is loose in the desk.
No toys are in the desk.	Toys and other little junk are cluttering the desk.

c. Once the chart has been developed, copy the "Neat" examples onto a poster (or you might want to have a group of students design this poster). Use the poster throughout the day to intermittently remind the students to keep their desks neat. The poster can also be used as a way to focus follow-up meetings on the problem (see SUGGESTED STEPS FOR DEVELOP-ING AND IMPLEMENTING A PLAN).

2. Respond consistently to all instances of messiness.

a. Whenever you notice that an individual student's desk is beginning to look messy, ask that student to review the chart and tell you what he/she needs to change to clean up the desk. If he/she can't tell you, prompt the student. Give the student a deadline (e.g., before he/she goes to recess) for getting the desk clean.

b. At the specified time, check the student's desk. If it does not meet the criteria for a neat desk (as summarized on the chart), have the student stay in from recess until the task is completed.

3. Use reinforcement to encourage appropriate behavior.

a. Praise individual students who keep their desks neat. In particular, if you see a student cleaning his/her desk, praise the student for demonstrating the ability to "keep his/her work space neat and organized." If the student would be embarrassed by public praise, praise the student privately, or even put a note in his/her desk.

b. When all of the students are making an effort to keep their desks neat, praise the entire class. "Class, everyone should be very proud of how well you are keeping your work spaces neat and organized. It is such a pleasure to work with a class that can quickly find their pencils, papers, and books."

PLAN B

Sometimes students have trouble keeping their work spaces neat because they just have too many things to keep organized. The more things that the students have to keep track of, the greater the skill and time necessary to stay organized and neat. If your students' problem with messy desks stems, even in part, from having too many things, the intervention should include strategies for reducing the amount of their possessions.

1. Require every student to have a pencil box or pouch.

Small objects like pencils, scissors, erasers, etc., tend to sift to the bottom of the students' desks. Without a pencil box or pouch, the students will end up pulling everything out of their desks whenever they need a pencil or other small item. If many of your students are from low-income families and thus requiring a pencil box is not reasonable, talk to your school administrator about whether the school could supply this critical organizational item. If the school's budget does not permit this, you might see if a local business would be willing to either donate the pencil boxes or purchase them for the students who need them.

2. Determine whether it is necessary for the students to keep all their books in their desks.

a. If having a large number of books in their desks is adding to the problem, identify those required books that are used infrequently. For example, if your third grade students have both a health book and a science book in their desks, but the schedule is such that the books are only used occasionally, you might consider keeping those books on a shelf and passing them out when they will be used.

b. If you have students who bring an excessive number of books for silent reading, let them know that while you are glad they love and are interested in books, nobody can read six books at a time, for example. Encourage the students to keep no more than two silent reading books in their desks at any given time.

3. Implement a routine in which the students take their graded papers home regularly.

This can be done on a daily or weekly basis. In either case, inform the parents of the routine and encourage them to look over their child's papers with the child. One way to send papers home systematically is to have each student keep a folder in his/her desk. Then, have the students put all their completed and graded papers into their folders until it is time to take them home (daily or weekly, depending upon your routine). "Class, it is Wednesday, so make sure you get the papers out of your Work Completed folder. I will come around and staple the papers together if you would like. Be sure to show these papers to your parents. They are interested in what you are doing."

Consider implementing a "no toys" or a "no more than one toy" policy.

Toys brought from home can contribute to clutter in desks. Let the students know that any toys in excess of the number allowed will be kept by you until the end of the day. The students can then pick their toys up before going home. If one or two students continue to bring toys (or too many toys), tell them that if you have to keep taking their toys away, you will start keeping them for a full week.

PLAN C

Some students are innately organized and neat, while others may not know how to keep their desk neat. If you suspect that many of your students lack the knowledge and/or skills for keeping their materials organized and personal space neat, the intervention must include some instruction in these areas.

 Conduct a lesson with the students to define the difference between neat and messy desks (see PLAN A).

(NOTE: In this plan, you will also take the time to discuss and model strategies for keeping desks neat.)

a. Put a chart similar to the sample shown on the chalkboard or a wall chart. Do not fill in the examples beforehand; this chart should be developed jointly with the students. When developing the chart, it is important that each item on the list have both a "Neat" example and a "Messy" example, as well as one or more strategies for

A Neat Desk	A Messy Desk	Strategies for Keeping Desks Neat
The top is clean.	The top has pencil marks or smudges and dried glue.	• A few pencil marks—Erase the marks. • Many marks or smudges—Wash the top with paper towel and a little cleanser. • Dried glue—Put a damp (no drips) paper towel over the glue and let sit for ten minutes. Then clean with cleanser.
All papers are in a notebook or in the folder to take home.	There are loose papers (some done, some unfinished, some blank paper).	• Put all papers away as soon as you are through with them (either in your notebook or Work Completed folder). • Once per week, sort through your notebook and get rid of scratch paper. Take your graded work home to show your parents.
There are books in a neat stack and there are not too many.	There are books thrown in (many library books or books from home).	• Put the smallest and lightest of your school books on top. • Keep no more than two books for silent reading in your desk at any time.
Pencils, scissors, erasers, and any other little things are in the pencil box.	Pencils and other little stuff is loose in the desk.	• Always put away small items in your pencil box as soon as you are finished with them. • Any little things you never use, throw away or take home.
No toys or other little junk are in the desk.	Toys and other little junk are cluttering the desk.	• Don't bring toys to school. • If you bring a toy for sharing, take it home on the same day you share.

preventing and/or correcting each "Messy" example.

b. Someone—either you or a student—should model each preventative/corrective strategy for the class. That is, don't just talk about the strategies, show the students how to implement them. Then have several students demonstrate each strategy to verify their understanding.

c. Once the chart has been developed, copy the "Neat" examples and the identified strategies onto a poster (or you might want to have a group of students design this poster). Use this poster throughout the day to intermittently remind the students to keep their desks neat. The poster can also be used as a way to focus follow-up meetings on the problem (see SUGGESTED STEPS FOR DEVELOPING AND IMPLEMENTING A PLAN).

 Schedule a time for all the students to clean their desks to the criteria for "A Neat Desk" using the strategies developed.

Try to do this immediately (or as soon as possible) after the chart is developed. Because some students will need very little time and others will take much longer, you should have a variety of "cushion" activities ready for the students to do when they have finished and had their desk checked by you. "When you think your desk is neat, stand by your desk with your hand in the air. I will come over and check. If your desk matches the definition of neat that we just developed, you can choose to go to one of our centers and enjoy yourself or I have some word searches I could give you to work on at your nice, neat desk."

 Use prompts to remind the students at those times when they have had a tendency to be messy.

Tell the class, for example: "Everyone, put away your math. If you are done, turn in your paper. If you are not done, neatly fold the paper in half and put it in your book. You will have more time to work on it this afternoon. Put any scratch paper in the recycling box. Put everything else neatly in your desk." As the students demonstrate mastery of these sorts of routines, reduce the amount of prompting.

 Schedule a weekly time for the students to clean their desks and have them checked by you.

Each week, briefly review the definitions of neat and messy desks, and give the students time to clean theirs. Provide positive feedback to the students whose desks are already neat. "We have seven students who do not need to clean their desks because they have kept them neat all week. You people can choose to (a desirable activity), while the rest of us, including me, take some time to clean our desks."

5. **Use reinforcement to encourage appropriate behavior.**

a. Praise individual students for meeting the expectations regarding neat desks, and praise the entire class when there has been a significant overall improvement (see PLAN A).

b. You may also wish to provide intermittent rewards and privileges. On some days when everyone is making an effort to keep their desks neat and organized, give some kind of reward or privilege to the entire class. "Class, we have been doing such a great job of keeping things neat, we are getting a lot more done. Any time I ask you to get out a pencil and a sheet of paper, everyone can quickly find those things. Let's all go out to recess five minutes early today."

6. **Respond consistently to all instances of messiness.**

a. Whenever an individual's desk is messy, ask that student to review the chart and give the student a deadline for getting the desk clean. "Andy, look at the chart and look at your desk. Tell me which of the strategies you need to use between now and recess time."

b. If it appears that many students' desks are messy between the weekly checks, occasionally conduct a "surprise check" a few minutes before a scheduled recess period. The criterion for being excused to recess is a clean desk. Therefore, students whose desks are neat can go out immediately, while students who need to clean their desks spend the first part of their recess period doing so. As soon as the students have adequately cleaned their desks, they should be excused to recess.

PLAN D

If the students know how to keep their desks neat, but just don't seem to want to bother, the intervention may need to include positive incentives and mild consequences to motivate the students to behave appropriately.

1. *Conduct a lesson with the students to define the difference between neat and messy desks, and develop a chart that summarizes this information (see PLAN A).*

2. *Use intermittent "spot checks" and have the students evaluate the neatness of their own desks.*

Convert the chart defining neat and messy desks into a self-evaluation form (see the sample provided) and give a copy to each student. Periodically, have the students rate how their desks look in relation to the definitions. Students who think their desks are neat should have you check to confirm that they really are neat. If you agree with their assessment, sign their form and allow them to choose from a variety of enjoyable activities. Students whose desks are not neat must continue cleaning them until you have approved their neatness.

3. *After one or two of these self-evaluations, inform the students that for future spot checks you will be giving mild consequences to students with messy desks, random rewards to individuals whose desks are neat, and a group reward if everyone has a neat desk.*

a. Schedule the spot check (using the self-monitoring form) of desk neatness right before recess or some other activity that most students enjoy. The students with neat desks will be allowed to participate in the activity. The others must miss the amount of time it requires to clean their desks as a mild consequence.

b. Students whose desks are neat without having to do any last minute cleaning at the time of a spot check should be allowed to put their signed self-monitoring form in a hat or box for a drawing. Draw two or three of the signed forms

---

Desk Neatness Self-Evaluation

Name _____   Date _____

Directions:

Check off how your desk rates against our definitions of "Neat" and "Messy."

A Neat Desk	A Messy Desk
○ The top is clean.	○ The top has pencil marks or smudges and dried glue.
○ All papers are in a notebook or in the folder to take home.	○ There are loose papers (some done, some unfinished, some blank paper).
○ There are books in a neat stack and there are not too many.	○ There are books thrown in (many library books or books from home).
○ Pencils, scissors, erasers, and any other little things and in the pencil box.	○ Pencils and other little stuff is loose in the desk.
○ No toys or other little junk are in the desk.	○ Toys and other little junk are cluttering the desk.

If your desk was neat with having to do any "last minute" cleaning, have the teacher sign here:

_____
Teacher Signature

randomly from the hat. Winning students receive a reward, such as a coupon for a free ice cream cone.

c. If everyone in the class has been keeping their desks neat, provide a group reward such as working outdoors for the afternoon. *(NOTE: For a list of ideas for group reinforcers, see APPENDIX 2.)*

. . . .
Suggested Steps for Developing and Implementing a Plan

The following information is designed to help you develop an appropriate intervention plan and implement it effectively, whether you choose to use one of the MODEL PLANS or create a customized plan of your own. The steps are, however, suggestions—they are not intended to be followed rigidly or in any particular order. Use your professional judgment and the knowledge of your particular situation to make them work for you.

1. *Make sure you have enough information about the situation.*

a. If you think a minimal intervention like PLAN A will be sufficient, you probably already have enough information to proceed. However, when a more involved plan seems necessary, you should consider collecting additional descriptive information for a couple of days.

b. You need to be able to explain what you mean when you say that "the class has a problem with messy desks." Anecdotal notes about actual circumstances should provide enough detail to help you define the problem behavior clearly and completely. To collect anecdotal notes, simply keep a card in your pocket or on a clipboard and occasionally make notes on specific instances of messy desks.

For each entry, briefly describe the situation, and make particular note of any class time that was wasted as a result. You do not need to take notes every time you notice a messy desk; the idea is to capture a range of examples of the behavior so you will be able to describe it completely.

c. If a student notices what you are doing and asks about it, be straightforward—tell the student, "I am concerned about how much time we waste because your desks are messy. I am making notes to see if this is a problem that needs to be worked on."

Following is an example of anecdotal notes that have been collected in a class with a problem of messy desks.

- When instructed to get out paper for a spelling quiz, Marissa, Forrest, Twyla, Jesus, and Molly all took too long rummaging through their messy desks (3 minutes wasted).

- Before recess, I had to instruct Arrielle to pick up her papers off the floor (that had spilled out of her desk) and either return them to her desk or put them in the recycling box (2 minutes wasted).

- Matt couldn't find his math book. I helped him find it in the mess in his desk (1 minute wasted).

d. Continuing to collect this type of information while you implement a plan will help you monitor whether the situation is getting worse, staying the same, or getting better.

2. *Identify a focus for the intervention and labels for referring to the appropriate and inappropriate behaviors.*

a. To be effective, the intervention must address more than just reducing the problem of messy desks—there must be a concurrent emphasis on increasing some positive behavior or trait (e.g., "keeping work spaces neat"). Identifying a specific positive behavior will make it easier for you to "catch" and reinforce the students for behaving appropriately, and will help you explain your concern more productively.

For example, simply saying that "the class has a problem with being messy" doesn't really give the students any useful information (and may put them on the defensive). However, telling the students that you want them "to learn to keep their work spaces neat" provides an important, and reasonable, goal for the students to work toward and clarifies what they need to do to be successful.

b. Identifying labels for referring to the appropriate and inappropriate behaviors (e.g., "keeping work spaces neat" and "being messy," respectively) will help you to use consistent vocabulary when discussing the situation with the students. If you sometimes refer to the inappropriate behavior as "being messy" and other times tell a student he/she doesn't "have a work space he can be proud of," for example, the students may not realize that you are talking about the same behavior.

3. **Determine when and how to include the parent(s).**

a. It is not necessary to contact individual parents about this sort of internal classroom issue. However, if you send out a class newsletter of some sort, it might be worth mentioning that the class is beginning to focus on "keeping their work space neat," and asking the parents to discuss with their children how this concept relates to their own work environments.

b. If the problem is occurring/continues to occur with only one or two students, you should contact the parent(s) of the those individuals. Let the parent(s) know that their student is having

a problem with being messy and explain what steps you are taking to resolve the situation.

If you do implement individualized plans with these students, continue to keep their parents informed about their progress—once per week should be sufficient.

4. **Give the class regular, ongoing feedback about their behavior.**

It is important to periodically to discuss progress with the class. In most cases, three to five minutes once per week should suffice. During the meetings, review any information that has been collected and discuss whether or not the situation is getting better. As much as possible, focus on improvements, however, also address any new or continuing problems. As the situation improves, the meetings can be faded to once every other week and then to once per month.

5. **Evaluate the situation (and the plan).**

Implement any plan for at least two weeks before deciding whether to change plans; to continue, modify, or fade the plan you are using; or to cease the intervention. Generally, if the situation is clearly improving (based on the subjective perceptions of yourself and the students), stick with what you are doing. If the situation has remained the same or worsened, some kind of change will be necessary. Always discuss any changes to the plan with the class first.

MISBEHAVIOR DURING SPECIAL EVENTS

DESCRIPTION

The students in your class tend to misbehave during special events such as class parties, assemblies, guest speakers, field trips, track and field days, etc.

Because the real key to solving the problem of students misbehaving during special events is to anticipate and prevent future occurrences, there are no MODEL PLANS included with this problem. The purpose of the following information is to suggest some procedures and basic considerations for developing and teaching your students positive expectations for individual special events.

Alternative Problem

- **Chaos/Classroom Out of Control**

· · · · · · · ·
General Information

- Identify your behavioral expectations for each type of special event (i.e., how the students should behave during each event). You may wish to do this for individual events as they arise (e.g., a field trip to the fire station) or for categories of events (e.g., assemblies). *(NOTE: When preparing for a specific event, be sure to allow yourself enough time to decide on expectations and teach them to the students—three or four days is generally sufficient.)*

  It is important for you to specify *exactly* how you expect the students to behave during each part of the individual activities. The more detail you can provide, the better. If necessary, contact other appropriate people (e.g., the director of the field day, tour director for the field trip, guest speaker, etc.) to discover details of which you may not be aware. This information will allow you to prepare the students for all aspects of a particular event and to discuss and rehearse with them all of your expectations.

- What follows are two general lists of questions—one pertaining to assembly behavior and one pertaining to field trip behavior. You should be able to answer all of these questions before you begin teaching your students the behavioral expectations for these types of activities. *(NOTE: You can use these lists as models for developing expectations for other special events.)*

- **Assemblies—How will/should the students:**

  - Be excused from class?

  - Proceed down to the assembly?

  - Enter the assembly and be seated?

  - Behave prior to the beginning of the program?
    Can they talk?
    To whom? How far away can that person be?
    How many people can be involved in a conversation—2, 3, 8 students?
    Can they change their seats (i.e., trade with others)?

  - Know that the program is about to begin?

  - End a conversation if the person that is talking does not see that the program is about to begin?

  - Behave during the program?
    Can they talk to anyone for any reason?
    Can they boo, hiss, or otherwise show displeasure?
    Can they laugh, applaud, or otherwise show approval?

  - Exit the assembly at the conclusion of the program?
    Do they wait to be excused by you?
    Do they go back to the classroom on their own?

- **Field Trips—How will/should the students:**

  - Be excused from the classroom?

  - Behave on the way to the bus?

  - Behave on the bus? (Recognize that some students may not ride the bus to and from school. Therefore, all bus rules should be taught or reviewed.)
    Can they sit wherever they want or will there be assigned seats?
    Can they talk? to whom and how far away?
    Can they get out of their seats?
    Can they open windows?

  - Get off the bus?

  - Give their attention to the tour guide?

  - Behave while the tour guide is speaking/while on the tour?

  - Politely let the tour guide know that they cannot see or hear?

  - Politely ask a question? (You may even want to identify in advance some of the types of questions the students might want to ask.)

  - Show appreciation at the end of the tour?

  - Return to and re-board the bus?

  - Go back to the classroom (if appropriate) after returning to the school?

• Establish a signal to use during an event to get the attention of all your students. During most special events (assemblies might be an exception), you should be able to give a signal that focuses all student attention on you within a relatively short period of time. This will be essential for ensuring some degree of teacher control over behavior during the event. One possible signal is an upraised hand. Teach your students that as soon as any student sees your upraised hand, he/she should raise his/her own hand to prompt the other students.

Also specify the amount of time that can elapse before all student attention must be focused on you. For activities where the group is physically all together (e.g., on the bus, in the classroom, waiting to get on the bus, etc.), 30 seconds or less is reasonable. For activities where the group may need to gather from different locations (e.g., at the conclusion of a field day, end of lunch at a park on a field trip, etc.), the length of time should be longer—perhaps five minutes.

• Identify the consequences that will be implemented for the various types of misbehavior (both group and individual) that could occur (i.e., have occurred in the past, or seem likely). Keep in mind that although, in most cases, the consequences will be assigned during the activity itself, they will be implemented after the fact. For ex-

ample, timed owed may be assigned for a misbehavior during a field trip, but it will be "paid back" during recess, lunch, or in after-school detention later that day or the next day. You may wish to develop a chart similar to the following sample, which identifies possible misbehaviors and their consequences.

• Prior to an actual special event, conduct several short lessons to prepare the students. First decide how many lessons will be necessary. The greater the chance of problems, the more lessons you should schedule. For example, in preparation for an assembly with a class that does well most of the time, one or two (one the day before and one immediately prior to the assembly) short (e.g., five minute) lessons are probably sufficient to teach or review expectations and preview the content of the assembly. For a group that may have lots of problems (e.g., it is the first assembly of the year, and this group of students has been a problem in years past), schedule five minute lessons every day for a week or even two weeks prior to the assembly.

During the lessons, first orient the students to what the experience will be like. Students often have a tendency to misbehave in new or unpredictable circumstances. Therefore, you want to prepare the students for what they are likely to encounter. "Class, the first thing that will happen

Common Problem	Consequence
Group does not respond within time limit to attention signal.	Group will owe time (equal to the amount of time required to get everyone's attention) off of next recess.
One individual student does not respond to attention signal.	Individual will owe time off of next recess.
Student is disrespectful to guest speaker or tour guide.	Student will have lunch time or after-school detention, and parent(s) will be contacted.
Student is in the wrong place (e.g., not staying with the group).	Student must stay by your side for remainder of activity.
Other misbehaviors are exhibited.	Time owed or detention will be implemented, as appropriate.
Group is too noisy.	Give attention signal. If group responds, no consequence. If group does not respond, time owed.
Group is exhibiting severe misbehavior (give examples).	Activity is concluded early (i.e., the field trip ends and class returns to school—"the party's over").
Individual student is exhibiting severe misbehavior (give examples).	Activity is concluded for that individual (i.e., student is returned to bus and waits there for remainder of field trip—note that he/she must have supervision).

when we get to the sawmill is that Mr. Torgeson will meet and speak to us while we are still on the bus. He will then take us to a classroom for a video presentation. After that, we will go into the main part of the mill. Because it will be really noisy, they are going to give us ear plugs. Here is what the ear plugs look like."

Then explain your expectations for each activity. Define exactly what the students will be expected to do. Ask questions to verify that the students thoroughly understand the expectations. "Ginny, what will you do if you have a question while we are in the main part of the mill? Right, you will remember your question until you get outside because it will be so noisy, Mr. Torgeson will not be able to hear or answer your question. Bobby, what will you do if . . . ."

Review all the potential misbehaviors and the corresponding consequence you will implement for each. The students must understand, in advance, the consequences for misbehavior during the event.

Let the students know that immediately following the event (or the next day, if necessary) there will be a class discussion to examine how well the group met the expectations.

• If you have any reason to expect that a particular student will have problems at an event (e.g., the student has a history of misbehaving during assemblies), make special arrangements in advance for that student. For example, if you have a student who has demonstrated a propensity to become out of control, his participation in the activity could be made contingent upon one of his parent(s) attending the special event with him. This must be handled sensitively, because procedures of this type could be used (consciously or unconsciously) to discriminate against a student. Talk to your administrator about any individualized plans regarding special events before implementing them.

• Respond consistently to any misbehavior that occurs during a special event. Follow through with the consequences that have been developed and discussed with the class before the event.

• Following each special event, conduct a class meeting to discuss how well the class met the expectations. Lead the class through a discussion about the quality of student behavior during the different activities that comprised the special event. "Class, without naming names or pointing fingers, let's talk about how the day went. I am interested in talking about problems, but I also want to hear what we did well. Let's start with the bus ride. Who has thoughts on that part of the trip?"

• Reinforce the students to encourage appropriate behavior. During an event, praise individual students for meeting your expectations. Be especially alert for students who have had the greatest tendency to engage in misbehavior who are behaving responsibly, and praise them for doing so. "Max, you have been very cooperative and respectful throughout our trip." If the student would be embarrassed by public praise, praise the student privately or even give the student a note.

Occasionally, praise individual students who rarely or never have a problem. Because these students have already mastered the positive expectations, they do not need positive feedback as often as the students who have difficulty with special events. However, you do not want them to feel that you take their positive behavior for granted. "Niko, Quint, Philip, you showed a lot of interest in what Mr. Torgeson was presenting. I know he appreciated how well you were paying attention."

When the entire group meets the positive expectations, praise the class. Remember that any time the students are not misbehaving, you can praise them for being responsible. Also share any positive feedback received from other adults. "This class is doing an excellent job of representing our school while we are here. Three different people have commented to me about what a polite and mature group of students you are. The president of the company even said we would be welcome again any time. How is that for a compliment?"

MISBEHAVIOR OUTSIDE OF CLASS— HALLWAYS/ PLAYGROUND/ CAFETERIA

· ·

DESCRIPTION

You have a student who misbehaves outside of the classroom.

GOAL

The student will learn to behave responsibly in all school settings, even when not directly supervised.

OVERVIEW OF PLANS

- PLAN A: For a problem that has just begun and/or that occurs infrequently.
- PLAN B: For a student who misbehaves in settings other than the classroom because she does not understand the expectations for those settings.
- PLAN C: For a student who misbehaves in settings other than the classroom to gain adult attention.
- PLAN D: For a student who lacks the motivation to behave responsibly in settings other than the classroom.
- PLAN E: For a student whose misbehavior in settings other than the classroom is so chronically unacceptable that, within the current structure, she is very unlikely to be successful.

NOTE:

Although these five plans are oriented for an individual student with behavior problems in settings other than the classroom, each could easily be adapted for use with two or three individual students who have the same problem.

Alternative Problems

- **Bullying Behavior/Fighting**

- **Misbehavior During Special Events**

- **Physically Dangerous Behavior—to Self or Others**

General Considerations

- If the student exhibits one specific misbehavior across settings (e.g., being disrespectful toward adults), consult that particular problem in this reference guide. If there are plans provided for that particular misbehavior, it may be useful to incorporate some of those ideas into these plans. In this way, the intervention will address features of both the specific misbehavior and the settings in which it occurs.

- If the student misbehaves in settings other than the classroom because she lacks the basic social skills to interact with her peers appropriately, it may be necessary to begin by teaching her those skills. **Social Skills, Lack of** contains information on a variety of published social skills curricula.

Model Plans

PLAN A

It is not always necessary, or even beneficial, to use an involved plan when a student has trouble managing herself outside the classroom. If the only problem has just begun and/or occurs infrequently (i.e., the student has a problem only once every couple of weeks), the following actions, along with making the student aware of your concerns, may resolve the situation.

 1. Periodically check in with supervisors of the cafeteria, playground, library, etc.

a. Ask each supervisor for a report on the student's behavior. The goal is to obtain information so that you can provide immediate feedback to the student on her behavior. Often when the student sees that her teacher is interested in how she does in settings outside of class, it is an incentive for her to demonstrate self-management.

You want to learn specifics—if it went well, what was the student doing? was she playing a game? was she by herself? did she interact with the supervisor? If the supervisor reports a problem, what exactly did the student do? how often? did she accept any consequences or corrections implemented by the supervisor? Even if there was a problem, find out whether any good things happened as well (e.g., Did the student manage herself for the first part of the library period?).

b. Focus on the setting that has been the biggest problem in the past. For example, if the student has had more problems on the playground than in the cafeteria, you might check with the play-

ground supervisor two to three times per week, and the cafeteria supervisors two to three times per month.

Try to check in with the supervisor immediately after the student has been in that setting. In this way, the feedback you provide to the student (in Steps 2 and 3) will occur while the student still remembers what her behavior was like in that setting. The younger and less sophisticated the student, the more critical it becomes that this feedback occur immediately.

 2. Respond consistently to the inappropriate behavior.

a. Whenever you receive a report that the student misbehaved, provide a gentle correction to the student. Describe the specific misbehavior that the supervisor reported to you. Let the student know that this behavior is not acceptable and that exhibiting this behavior demonstrates that the student is not managing herself well. Tell the student that the next time she is in that setting, you will expect her to manage herself appropriately and that you will expect a positive report from the supervisor.

b. The only exception to this procedure would be if the student's misbehavior violates a school-wide rule (e.g., fighting) for which there is a designated consequence. In this situation, implement the appropriate consequence.

3. Use reinforcement to encourage appropriate behavior.

a. If the supervisor provides a positive report, acknowledge the student's efforts to manage herself with praise. Let the student know that the supervisor reported that she managed herself well, and share the specific examples of positive behavior that the supervisor mentioned. Tell the student that you are pleased that she is able to manage herself even when you are not around.

If the student is older (i.e., fourth grade through middle/junior high school) it may be more effective to provide this feedback privately or through a written note to avoid embarrassing the student. With primary age students, public praise may be more effective.

b. Give the student frequent attention (e.g., say "hello" to her as she enters the classroom, call on her frequently during class activities, and occasionally ask her to assist you with a class job that needs to be done), and praise her for other positive behaviors she exhibits. For example, you might comment about how polite she is or what a good reader she is. This demonstrates to the student that you notice many positive things she does, not just the fact that she is behaving more responsibly outside the classroom.

PLAN B

Sometimes students misbehave because they do not fully understand the expectations for their behavior. If it seems possible that your student is unclear about what is expected of her (e.g., she is surprised if a supervisor thinks there is a problem), the intervention must include a way to teach her responsible behavior in settings outside the classroom.

(NOTE: This plan is more likely to be necessary with a primary age student than with an intermediate or middle/junior high school student.)

1. Periodically check in with supervisors of settings outside the classroom. (see PLAN A).

2. Conduct lessons to teach the student how to manage herself in different settings.

a. Begin with the setting in which the student is having the most trouble. Talk to the supervisor(s) of that setting to see if they would be willing to help you teach the student how to behave appropriately and follow the rules. Together with the supervisors, create a list of the specific infractions the student engages in and why each is a problem (e.g., it disrupts a game, it could be unsafe, it makes it difficult for the music teacher to teach the class, etc.). Then, for each problem behavior, identify a consequence the supervisors will implement (e.g., time-out, stay with the supervisor for two minutes). Finally, for each problem, identify one or more positive, alternative behaviors the student could do instead.

b. During the lessons, you and the supervisor(s) should teach or review the rules and behavioral expectations for that setting. Then, using the information about the types of misbehavior the student tends to exhibit as the basis, ask the student questions and provide structured practice opportunities for responsible behavior. Each lesson should include activities such as the following:

- Describe a problem behavior and have the student explain why that behavior is a problem. If the student cannot think of a reason, give the student an answer, and ask the question again a few minutes later. Continue with this procedure until the student can state the reasons why various misbehaviors are a problem.

- Construct a hypothetical situation and have the student model what appropriate behavior would look like in that context. Provide feedback and have the student practice until she is successful.

- Model different behaviors, some positive and some negative, and have the student identify whether you are managing yourself well or misbehaving. If the student correctly identifies a behavior as a misbehavior, have her describe or role play a more responsible alternative.

- Identify a misbehavior and have the student specify the consequence the supervisor(s) would be likely to implement.

c. Co-teaching the lessons accomplishes several things. First, it demonstrates to the student the level of concern—it is not just the cafeteria supervisors, for example, who think there is a problem. Second, it demonstrates to the student that you and the supervisors are in direct communication about her behavior. Third, it demonstrates to the student that two adults care enough about her and her success in this setting that they are taking the time to conduct these lessons.

d. Conduct the lessons as often as possible, but at least twice per week. They needn't last more than five to ten minutes each, however, it may be necessary to conduct repeated lessons across a period of several weeks. In this case, the supervisor(s) from the setting may only need to be directly involved for first couple of lessons.

Continue the lessons until the student is consistently following the rules and managing herself in that setting. *(NOTE: Because this procedure can be time-consuming, the lessons may need to be conducted by the school counselor [or other appropriate professional whose schedule permits one-to-one instruction] and the supervisor[s] from the problematic area.)*

e. Once the student is consistently behaving appropriately in the first setting, you can begin to focus the lessons on another setting. Invite the supervisor(s) of that new setting to assist with the first several lessons. When there is a switch to a new setting, spend a minute or two at the beginning of each lesson reviewing and practicing the expectations from previously covered settings.

3. *Prompt the student to behave appropriately by using precorrections.*

Immediately before the student goes to the problematic setting, remind her about the positive expectation for self-management. "Clarice, out on recess today you need to remember what we have been working on. I'll bet you can do a fine job of managing yourself." If time permits, you might have the student identify one or more of the things she needs to remember. "Clarice, what are some of the rules you need to keep in mind while you are out on recess today?" If this discussion would embarrass the student, conduct it privately.

4. *Respond consistently to the inappropriate behavior.*

a. Gently correct the student if a problem is reported (see PLAN A).

b. Support any consequences that are implemented by the supervisors in the different settings.

5. *Use reinforcement to encourage appropriate behavior.*

a. Give the student increased praise and attention, especially when a supervisor reports that she has been successful (see PLAN A).

b. In addition, make a special point of letting the student know that you notice her efforts to use the skills she has been learning/practicing. "Clarice, I heard that you have been doing a great job of remembering to stay within the boundaries of the playground. Nice job of doing what we have been practicing."

6. *(OPTIONAL)*
Identify peer models for the student to observe.

If you think the student could benefit from additional information on meeting the expectations of a given setting, you might suggest one or two other students for her to unobtrusively observe. "Clarice, you might want to watch Amy and Ti Lin to see how they behave in music. I don't think anyone in class thinks of them as nerds or teacher's pets, but they both participate very well in music class. I don't expect you to try to be like them—you're terrific just the way you are—but watching them may give you some ideas of how you can manage yourself in music and still be cool. You know, I just learned some piano techniques myself from watching a concert last week."

This procedure must be handled delicately to avoid hurting the student's feelings or implying that she should be more like someone else.

PLAN C

Some students are very skilled at gaining attention through their negative behavior. If you (and/or the supervisors from the problematic settings) seem to be frequently nagging, reminding, or coaxing the student to follow the rules, it is possible that this is her motivation. Whether or not the student overtly seems to like the attention, you should make sure that she receives more frequent and more satisfying attention when she behaves appropriately than when she misbehaves.

 1. **Set up a staffing with the supervisors from the problematic settings.**

This plan requires consistency and communication among yourself and all the supervisors. In addition, it may be advisable to include the building administrator as he/she should have input on the consequences for severe misbehavior. During the staffing, review the suggestions from this plan and from PLANS D and E.

2. **Respond consistently to the inappropriate behavior.**

a. Identify consequences for all common misbehaviors in each problematic setting. As much as possible, the consequences should be implemented immediately in the setting where the problem occurred. For example, playground problems should receive consequences immediately on the playground—not later in the classroom.

Possible consequences include a short (e.g., one to five minute) time-out in a low traffic area of that setting; staying with the supervisor for a short period (e.g., one to five minutes); describing to the supervisor the rule that was broken; writing and signing a brief description of the rule that was broken (the supervisors would need a clipboard with a pencil and blank paper); or apologizing to other student(s) (e.g., if she calls a name or runs through a game).

For most misbehaviors, the student should be given a warning first and then assigned the consequence if the behavior happens again that day. "Clarice, this is your warning. If you run through a game again you will have a two-minute time-out."

b. Identify any misbehaviors that are severe enough for the student to be sent to the administrator. Make this as small a list as possible—the majority of the misbehaviors should be handled immediately in the setting with mild consequences. As a general rule, the student should only be sent to the administrator for physically dangerous or illegal acts, or for overt and direct refusal to comply with a supervisor's instruction. All the responsible adults (i.e., the teacher, supervisors, building administrator) should agree on the behaviors that will require administrative involvement.

c. Because it is important for the student to learn that she will no longer receive satisfying attention for misbehaving, every implementation of a consequence should be as brief and emotionally neutral as possible. Do not argue with the student. Do not negotiate. Do not act disgusted or impatient with the student's behavior. If necessary, use the "broken record" technique of repeating the consequence.

d. If you think it is likely that the student will refuse to comply with a consequence (e.g., going to time-out for two minutes), review and incorporate suggestions from **Compliance/Direction Following, Lack of** in conjunction with this plan.

e. After a coordinated plan has been developed, a sample interaction between a supervisor on the playground and the student might look like the following.

Supervisor:	Clarice, that was name calling and I already gave you a warning. You need to go to the wall for a two-minute time-out.
Clarice:	That was not name calling. All I said was . . .
Supervisor:	You need to go to the wall for two minutes.
Clarice:	I don't see why I . . .
Supervisor:	You need to go to the wall for two minutes. If you refuse it is non-compliance, and I will have to send you Mr. Edlund's office. You have one minute to get there.

If the student goes to time-out, there is no additional consequence. If the student refuses, she is sent to the office for the overt refusal to comply. The main point is that *the supervisor shouldn't argue with or coax the student.*

f. Notice that as the classroom teacher, you are not involved in implementing consequences for the student's behavior in other settings. When you receive a report that the student has had trouble, it is appropriate to provide a gentle correction (i.e., talking to the student about the problem and encouraging her to do better tomorrow), but not to implement any consequences for the misbehavior. Playground consequences should be implemented by the playground supervisor, library consequences by the library supervisor, etc.

3. Use reinforcement to encourage appropriate behavior.

a. Frequent praise and attention is the core of this plan. The student must see that she receives more frequent and more satisfying attention when she behaves appropriately than when she misbehaves. Thus, whenever the student is not misbehaving, every adult who supervises her should make an effort to praise and spend time with her. "Clarice, you have been doing such a nice job of managing yourself on recess today."

b. You may also wish to use intermittent rewards to acknowledge the student's success. Occasional, and unexpected, rewards can motivate the student to demonstrate responsible behavior more often. The idea is to provide a reward when the student has had a particularly good period in a problematic setting. If a supervisor wants to provide an extra reward, he/she could write a brief note about the student's success to you (the classroom teacher) or to the building administrator, who could then provide a special reward.

Appropriate rewards might include playing a game with the teacher or a fun activity with the principal. For example, the principal (after receiving a note from the cafeteria supervisors) might contact the student after lunch and say, "Clarice, the cafeteria supervisors have given me such a positive report about your ability to be a self-manager, would you like to eat lunch with me in my office tomorrow? If you would like, you could invite one other student to join us." *(NOTE: A list of additional reinforcement ideas can be found in APPENDIX 1.)*

Use intermittent rewards more frequently at the beginning of the intervention to encourage the

student, and then less often as her behavior improves.

4. Ensure a 3-1 ratio of positive to negative attention.

a. If attention is a motivating force for this student, you want to be sure that the adults in the school are giving the student *three times as much* positive as negative attention. One way to do this is for you (and each supervisor, if possible) to monitor your interactions with the student at least one day per week. Each adult can keep a card on a clipboard or in their pocket and record each interaction they have with the student as either positive or negative by writing a "+" or a "-", respectively, on the card.

To decide whether an interaction is positive or negative, determine whether the student was misbehaving at the time the interaction occurred. Any interaction that stems from inappropriate behavior is negative, and all interactions that occur while the student is meeting expectations for her behavior are positive. Thus, a playground supervisor sending the student to time-out and you providing a gentle correction after the recess are both negative interactions, but praising the student for having a successful lunch period is a positive interaction. A lunch supervisor greeting the student as she enters the cafeteria, or the librarian asking if the student wants help in finding a book are also considered positive interactions.

b. If any of the adults find that they are not giving the student three times as much positive as negative attention, they should try to increase the number of positive interactions they have with the student. One way to do so is to set goals for the number of times they hope to interact with the student while she is managing herself. The goal can be established by multiplying the approximate number of times they have to interact with the student while misbehaving by three.

At first, this may seem impossible. "There are 170 students in the cafeteria and only two supervisors! How can I be expected to spend my entire time with this student?" However, let's say that the goal is to interact positively with the student nine times during lunch. Thus each of the two supervisors should have contact with the student four or five times when she is behaving appropriately. Following is an example of the types of contacts that could be made, with an estimate of the time required:

- Greet the student as she is standing in line for her lunch (3-10 seconds).

- Walk by the student's table (as part of your regular movement through the cafeteria) and make direct eye contact with her, nod your head, and smile (2 seconds).

- Some time during the lunch period, sit down next to the student and talk to her and several other students around her. Praise several students, including the target student, for their positive behaviors (10-30 seconds).

- Repeat the walk-by and smile (2 seconds).

- As you are excusing the student's table or the student is returning her lunch tray, comment to the student about her improved ability as a self-manager. Walk the same direction she is going for a few seconds and ask her how her day is going (5-10 seconds).

As can be seen, each supervisor would be spending between 22 and 54 seconds with the target student—some of which is time spent reinforcing other students as well. This is not an unreasonable expectation within a 20-minute lunch period.

PLAN D

When a student's misbehavior is habitual or long-standing, and/or the student seems to have an "I don't care" attitude about the consequences of her misbehavior, the intervention should include the use of external incentives (i.e., rewards and consequences) to motivate the student to behave appropriately.

1. Conduct a staffing with the supervisors from the problematic settings and the building administrator in which you establish consistent procedures for responding to the student's misbehavior (see PLAN C).

2. Establish a structured system for reinforcing appropriate behavior and providing a consequence for inappropriate behavior.

a. With the student, create a list of reinforcers that she can earn. Although you might want to have some suggestions in mind, the system will be more effective if the student identifies most of the items or activities herself. (NOTE: A list of reinforcement ideas can be found in APPENDIX 1.)

b. Assign "prices" (in points) for each of the rewards on the list and have the student choose the reward she would like to earn first.

The prices should be based on the instructional, personnel, and/or monetary costs of the items. Monetary cost is clear—the more expensive the item, the more points required to earn it. Instructional cost refers to the amount of instructional time lost or interfered with by a particular reward. Thus, an activity which causes the student to miss part of academic instruction should require more points than one the student can do on her own recess time. Personnel cost involves the time required by you and/or other

staff to fulfill the reinforcer. Having lunch with the principal, therefore, would cost more points than spending five minutes of free time with a friend.

c. Set up procedures for evaluating the student's self-management (i.e., the absence of misbehavior) in the various problematic settings. At the end of the time spent in each identified setting, the appropriate supervisors will rate the student's self-management for that period.

Following is a sample form that could be used by each supervisor. Note that the rating for each interval is based on the number of times the student's behavior required supervisor intervention.

At the end of each interval, a supervisor marks the appropriate rating and informs the student of the rating and why it was selected. The supervisor then gives card to the student to take to you (the classroom teacher). If the student cannot be trusted to bring the card to the classroom, some other method of returning the card to you should be devised. For example, you might have the supervisor put the card in your mailbox.

(NOTE: In the early stages of the intervention, the supervisors should determine the evaluation ratings, but as the system becomes increasingly successful, the student should be encouraged to conduct self-evaluations. Then the student is reasonably accurate in her assessment, the supervisors should allow the stu-

Evaluation of Clarice's Self-Management

Date: ___11/19_____   Setting: _Morning Recess_____

Directions:

Circle the number (i.e., the point value) in the scale below that best describes Clarice's self-management.

(+5) Self-managed the entire time

+3 Needed one warning

+1 Had to go to time-out once (but went without arguing)

 0 Had to go to time-out two or three times (or once, with arguing)

-3 Time owed (had to go to time-out more than three times or engaged in a severe misbehavior/direct noncompliance)

Total points earned (a *positive* value in the scale above)   _5____
Total minutes owed off next recess (a *negative* value in the scale above)   _____

---

dent to do more and more self-evaluations, and evaluate the student less themselves.)

d. Whenever the student has been in a setting outside the classroom, the two of you should review the student's rating and discuss whether it was better, about the same, or worse than the time before in that particular setting. Praise good or improved performance or, if the behavior was a problem, have the student identify things she could do differently to be more successful in that setting the next time.

e. Establish a system to translate the evaluations into points that can be applied toward the reward the student has selected. For example, the number (i.e., rating) circled on the self-evaluation sheet could equal the number of points earned during that time period. The minus number (i.e., negative point value) should not represent a loss of points, only the time the student owes off of recess or some other desirable noninstructional activity.

If you were to subtract points for poor ratings, you would run the risk of the student losing so many points that she becomes unmotivated to try. This way, when the student has problems, she simply does not earn positive points toward the reinforcer and receives an immediate consequence in the setting for each infraction (e.g., time-out). Additionally, if she is given more than three time-outs, she loses three minutes off of the next recess.

f. At the end of each day, the student's points should be totaled and added to the points from previous days. When the student has accumulated enough points to earn the reward she has chosen, she "spends" the points necessary and

the system begins again. That is, she selects another reward to earn and begins with zero points.

If the student is immature, or having a great deal of difficulty self-managing, and thus needs more frequent encouragement, you might consider letting her earn several "less expensive" rewards (e.g., five minutes of her free time after 20 points) on the way to a bigger reward (e.g., one hour with you for 200 points). That is, the student receives the small rewards without spending her points; they continue to accumulate toward the selected reward.

g. Plan to help the student chart the total number of points earned each day.

h. If the plan has been successful for three to four weeks, make the student's next reinforcer more expensive. For example, if the student had been required to earn 50 points for 15 minutes of time on the computer, require 70 points for the same privilege. Gradually making the reinforcers cost more and more—so the student has to demonstrate greater levels of self-management to earn them—is how the system will be faded.

3. *Use reinforcement to encourage appropriate behavior.*

a. Give the student increased praise and attention for managing herself well (see PLAN A).

b. In addition, show interest and enthusiasm about how the student is doing on the system. "Clarice, look at the ratings you received today. You have gotten five points from the playground, the cafeteria, and in music. You should be very proud of yourself!"

PLAN E

Unfortunately, there are some students who chronically misbehave, regardless of staff efforts to teach or motivate them to self-manage their behavior. This may be especially true in settings that are difficult to supervise (e.g., the playground or restrooms). If this is the case with your student, the intervention should involve limiting the student's opportunities to cause problems by reducing or restricting the student's access to unsupervised settings. However, since this plan is unlikely to help the student learn to manage herself, it should be implemented in conjunction with PLANS B, C, or D.

(NOTE: With a severe problem such as this, request assistance immediately. Ask for help from the school counselor, school psychologist, a lead teacher, or the special education department. Collaborating on an intervention will increase its chances of success. In addition, collaboration may increase access to additional services that a classroom teacher cannot realistically provide [e.g., counseling services].)

1. *Conduct a staffing with the supervisors from the problematic settings and the building administrator in which you establish consistent procedures for responding to the student's misbehavior (see PLAN C).*

2. *For any setting in which Step 1 has been/is likely to be inadequate, develop strategies to reduce the probability that severe problems will occur.*

a. Begin by examining your anecdotal notes (see SUGGESTED STEPS FOR DEVELOPING AND IMPLEMENTING A PLAN). If the student has consistently had trouble in the restrooms, for example, it may be necessary to restrict the student from unsupervised restroom use. If the student has trouble during passing periods between classes, you may need to arrange for her to be escorted from class to class by an adult (e.g., the first period teacher escorts her to the second period, the second period teacher escorts her to third period, etc.) If the student has trouble during the lunch period, she may need to be assigned to eat near a supervisor and/or be restricted from certain activities and locations after eating her lunch (i.e., limits on where she can be and what she can do).

b. A student who consistently has trouble on the playground may need to be assigned "modified recess," in which her choices of activities and locations are limited. There are different ways to structure modified recess. One way is to make the student stay in a limited physical area, an area in which one of the supervisors on duty spends his/her entire time.

Another modification involves having the counselor or a highly trained paraprofessional run small group classes (of one to six students) every day during recess. Based on her past problems, the student may be assigned to these classes for one to three weeks. In yet another form of modified recess, the student might be assigned to accompany a supervisor during the recess period for a predetermined number of days. During this time, the student would discuss the rules with the supervisor and help the supervisor identify students who are managing themselves versus those who are engaged in misbehavior.

c. If any or all of these options will be used, the adults responsible should understand that they are to be pleasant and friendly with the student. The goal is to set the student up for success and for positive interactions with adults, not to create autocratic and punitive supervision.

d. Any plan that involves a restriction on the student should also include predetermined criteria for earning the freedom back. One way to incorporate these criteria is to pair the restriction with the reinforcement system described in PLAN D. That is, the student could earn the freedom back by having a certain number of consecutive days with ratings of "3" or "5." For example, a student with chronic problems on the playground could be assigned a plan such as the one described following.

e. Any plan involving restricted freedom should be presented to the student and the student's parent(s) as a change that is designed to increase the probability that the student will behave successfully—not a punishment. As the student demonstrates an increased ability to manage herself, increased freedom will follow.

Any day with a fight or a rating of -3 begins the following sequence:

Step 1:   Daily lessons with the counselor on social skills and playground skills.

Criteria for exit—three consecutive days with ratings of "3" or "5" moves the student to Step 2.

Step 2:   Daily lessons with a playground supervisor (shadowing the supervisor).

Criteria for exit—three consecutive days with ratings of "3" or "5" moves the student to Step 3.

Step 3:   Restricted access—the student must remain in only one section of the playground, in proximity to a supervisor.

Criteria for exit—three consecutive days with ratings of "3" or "5" moves the student off of modified recess.

. . . .

Suggested Steps for Developing and Implementing a Plan

The following steps are designed to help you develop an appropriate intervention plan and implement it effectively, whether you choose to use one of the MODEL PLANS or create a customized plan of your own. The steps are, however, suggestions—they are not intended to be followed rigidly or in any particular order. Use your professional judgment and the knowledge of your particular situation to make them work for you.

1. *Make sure you have enough information about the situation.*

a. If you think a minimal intervention like PLAN A will be sufficient, you may already have enough information to proceed. However, when a more involved plan seems necessary, you should consider collecting additional descriptive and/or objective information for a couple of days.

b. You need to be able to explain the types of problems the student has in various settings outside the classroom. Anecdotal notes on actual incidents should provide enough detail to help you define the problem behavior clearly and completely. To collect anecdotal notes, ask the supervisors from the different settings to jot down notes on the types of problems that occur in those settings. For each entry, ask the supervisors to briefly describe where and when the problem occurred, what the student did or said, and any other relevant observations (e.g., what prompted the misbehavior).

The supervisors do not need to make notes every time the student misbehaves; the idea is to capture a range of examples in each setting so you will be able to describe the student's misbehavior completely and have enough information to set up a plan.

Also ask the supervisors to include some notes on times when the student behaves appropriately. This will make it clear that adults are not only aware of the student's problem behavior, but also recognize when she behaves appropriately. When you meet with the student, the positive examples will also help you clarify how you and the supervisors want the student to behave.

c. Maintain a file with all of these dated records.

d. If the student notices what a supervisor is doing and asks about it, encourage the supervisors to be straightforward with the student, and to tell her that information on her behavior is being collected so her teacher can see whether her misbehavior is a problem that needs to be worked on.

e. Having the supervisors continue to collect this type of information while you implement a plan will help you to monitor whether the situation is getting worse, staying the same, or getting better.

2. Identify a focus for the intervention and labels for referring to the appropriate and inappropriate behaviors.

To be effective, the intervention must address more than just reducing the student's misbehavior in different settings—there must be a concurrent emphasis on increasing some positive behavior or trait (e.g., self-management). Having a specific positive behavior in mind will make it easier for you to "catch" and reinforce the student for behaving appropriately, and the positive focus will help you to frame the situation more productively.

For example, if you simply say that "the student has a problem with misbehaving on the playground," you don't really provide any useful information, and may put the student and her parent(s) on the defensive. However, when you explain that you want to help the student "learn to manage her own behavior," you are presenting an important, and reasonable, goal for the student to work toward.

3. Determine when and how to include the parent(s).

a. It is not necessary to contact the student's parent(s) if the problem has just begun and is not interfering with the student's academic or social progress. However, it might be a good idea to take advantage of any scheduled activities (e.g., conferences, weekly notes home) to let them know of your concern.

b. Whenever a problem lasts for more than a couple of weeks, or if the misbehaviors are severe (e.g., fighting, defiance, etc.) you should contact the student's parent(s) immediately.

Share with them any information that has been collected about the student's behavior in the different settings (e.g., anecdotal notes, self-management evaluations), and explain why you are concerned. You might want to ask if the parent(s) have any insight into the situation and/or whether the student exhibits similar behavior at home.

Whether or not the parent(s) perceive a problem, explain that you want to help the student "learn to manage her own behavior," and invite them to join you for an initial meeting with the student to develop a plan. If the parent(s) are unable or unwilling to participate, let them know that you will keep them informed of the student's progress.

c. Once the parent(s) have been involved in any way, you should give them updates at least once per week while the plan is being implemented.

4. Prepare for, then conduct, an initial meeting about the situation.

a. Arrange a meeting to discuss your concerns with the student and anyone else who will be involved in the plan (e.g., the parent[s], supervisors from the various settings, the building administrator). Although the specifics will vary depending upon the age of the student and the severity of the problem, there are some general guidelines to consider when scheduling the meeting.

First, meet at a neutral time (i.e., not immediately after a problem has occurred), when emotions are less likely to hamper communication. In general, a day's notice is appropriate, however a primary age student may worry excessively and/or forget what the meeting is about if it is scheduled more than an hour before it takes place.

Second, make the meeting appropriately private. Third, try to make sure the meeting is scheduled for a time and place that it is not likely to be interrupted (e.g., the counselor's office). Finally, if the parent(s) will be participating, they should be the ones to tell the student about the meeting.

b. Construct a preliminary plan. (It may be necessary to conduct a staffing prior to meeting with the student.) Decide whether you think you can use one of the MODEL PLANS or if you need to create a customized plan using components from various plans and/or of your own design. Although you will invite and encourage the student to help develop the plan during the initial meeting, having a proposed plan in mind before you meet can alleviate frustration and wasted time if the student is unwilling or unable to participate.

c. After reviewing the collected information and thinking about how you want the student to behave, prepare thorough descriptions of the inappropriate behavior(s) and the positive behavior/trait on which the student will be working. The more specific you can be and the more concrete examples you have, the easier it will be to clarify (and for the student to understand) your expectations. Be sure to consider the student's behavior in all relevant settings.

d. Conduct the meeting in an atmosphere of collaboration. The following agenda is one way you might structure the meeting:

- **Share your concerns about the student's behavior.**

Briefly describe the problem behavior and explain why you consider it to be a problem. You might tell the student that her inability to use self-management worries you because there will not always be someone around to "make her behave." Let her know that you hope to help her learn to be a self-manager so that she can gain increased freedom and so that she can be trusted by teachers, supervisors, and, eventually, by employers.

- **Discuss how you can work together to improve the situation.**

Tell the student that you would like to help her "learn to be a self-manager," and describe your preliminary plan. Invite the student to give you input on the various aspects of the plan, and together work out any necessary details (e.g., the consequences for misbehavior, the evaluation form, etc.). You may have to brainstorm different possibilities if the student is uncomfortable with the plan. Incorporating any of the student's suggestions that strengthen the plan is likely to increase her sense of "ownership" in and commitment to it.

- **Make sure the student understands what you mean by appropriate and inappropriate behavior.**

Use the descriptions you have prepared to define and clarify the problem behavior and the positive (desired) behavior as specifically and thoroughly as you can. To ensure that you, the supervisors, and the student are in agreement about the expectations, you might present hypothetical scenarios and have the student identify whether each is an example of self-management or misbehavior. Or you might describe an actual situation that has occurred and ask the student to explain how she would demonstrate self-management in that situation.

- **Conclude the meeting.**

Always end the meeting with words of encouragement. Let the student know that you are confident that she can be successful. Be sure to reinforce her for participating in the meeting.

5. *Give the student regular, ongoing feedback about her behavior.*

It is important to meet with the student periodically to discuss her progress. In most cases, three to five minutes once per week should suffice. *(NOTE: PLAN D suggests daily meetings.)* During the meetings, review any information that has been collected and discuss whether or not the situation is getting better. As much as possible, focus on the student's improvements, however, also address any new or continuing problems. As the situation improves, the meetings can be faded to once every other week and then to once per month.

6. *Evaluate the situation (and the plan).*

Implement any plan for at least two weeks before deciding whether to change plans; to continue, modify, or fade the plan you are using; or to cease the intervention. Generally, if the student's behavior is clearly improving (based on the objective information that's been collected and/or the subjective perceptions of yourself, the supervisors of the various settings, the student, and possibly the parent[s]), stick with what you are doing. If the situation has remained the same or worsened, some kind of change will be necessary. Always discuss any changes to the plan with the student first.

OODINESS

Emotionalism

DESCRIPTION

You have a student who is "acting moody" to the point that his behavior is interfering with his academic or social progress.

Because "moodiness" is not a discrete behavior, but a label that encompasses many different types of behavior, there are no MODEL PLANS included with this problem. The purpose of the following information is to suggest an overall approach and some basic considerations for dealing with a student whose "moody" behavior is causing him problems.

Alternative Problems

- **Aggression—Verbal and/or Physical**
- **Anxiety/ Nervousness**
- **Complaining**
- **Crying, Chronic**
- **Depression**
- **Hypochondria**
- **Pouting**
- **Self-Concept Problems**
- **Shyness/Withdrawn Behavior**
- **Spoiled Behavior**
- **Victim—Student Who Is Always Picked On**
- **Whining**

....
General Information

- The key to effectively dealing with a student whose moody behavior is problematic is to target a specific behavior the student exhibits (e.g., pouting if he does not get his own way) that has led you to conclude that he has a problem with moodiness. Then find that problem behavior in this reference guide, review the MODEL PLANS that accompany it, and develop an intervention plan to help the student learn to manage his behavior more responsibly.

- If you are not sure exactly what it is that the student does or does not do that is problematic (i.e., you just have a vague sense that the student has a problem with moodiness), record anecdotal information about the student's behavior for a week or so. This is fairly easy to do—simply keep a card in your pocket or on a clipboard and whenever the student does something that you think demonstrates moodiness, make notes on the incident.

For each entry, briefly describe the circumstances—where and when the incident took place, what was said and/or done, and any other relevant observations you may have about the situation (e.g., what prompted the behavior). After about a week, review the information you have collected and use your notes to choose one specific behavior to address. This might the inappropriate behavior that occurs most often or an appropriate behavior that would most benefit the student. Whatever your criteria, the important thing is to focus your intervention efforts on one specific behavior at a time. often, as you work on one behavior, other aspects of the student's moodiness seem to improve without specific intervention.

- If you suspect that the student's moodiness indicates that the student is depressed, see **Depression** for additional information on how to proceed under those circumstances.

NAME CALLING/ PUT-DOWNS

Insults

Teasing

DESCRIPTION

There are students in your class who interact with each other in disrespectful ways.

GOAL

The students will interact with each other respectfully.

OVERVIEW OF PLANS

- PLAN A: For a situation in which the problem has just begun and/or occurs infrequently.

- PLAN B: For a problem that may stem from the students not knowing how to be respectful of each other and/or not being clear about the line between respectful and disrespectful interactions.

- PLAN C: For a problem that may stem from the students not realizing how often they engage is disrespectful interactions.

- PLAN D: For a situation in which the students seem to lack the motivation to be respectful to each other.

- PLAN E: For a situation in which the problem occurs/continues to occur with only one or two students.

NOTE:

Name calling, put-downs, insults, and teasing have been grouped together because each represents a disrespectful way students can interact with each other. Throughout these five MODEL PLANS, the problem behavior is referred to as "disrespect," using examples of each of these forms of disrespectful interactions. If, in your class, the problem is limited to one specific behavior, say name calling, focus only on that particular behavior during class discussions about the problem and when providing the students with feedback.

Alternative Problems

- **Arguing—Students With Each Other**

- **Disrespectful Behavior**

- **Harassment—Racial/ Sexual**

- **Victim—Student Who Is Always Picked On**

....
General Considerations

- If a number of students lack the basic social skills to interact appropriately, it may be necessary to begin by teaching them those skills. **Social Skills, Lack of** contains information on a variety of published social skills curricula.

- Be aware that a significant increase in the number of students using nicknames can be an indication of gang activity. **Gang Involvement** includes a questionnaire for identifying other signs of gang activity, and provides suggested references for addressing this problem.

....
Model Plans

PLAN A

If this problem has just begun and/or occurs only two to three times per week, it may not be necessary, or even beneficial, to use an involved plan. The following actions, along with making the students aware of your concerns, may resolve the situation.

1. **Respond consistently to each instance of a student being disrespectful toward another student.**

a. Whenever you notice an individual student being disrespectful, give a gentle correction. Let the student know that his/her behavior is an example of being disrespectful and provide information on what the student should do differently. Be emotionally neutral and avoid talking too much while giving the correction—your goal is simply to impart information.

b. If the student does not cease being disrespectful, assign a consequence, such as time owed off of recess or in detention. "Ned, if I have to talk to you again about being disrespectful by calling names, you will lose five minutes off recess for each time I need to talk to you."

2. **Use reinforcement to encourage appropriate behavior.**

a. Praise individual students for meeting your expectations about being respectful. Watch closely those students who have had the greatest tendency to be disrespectful. Whenever one of these students is interacting appropriately with other students, praise him/her for demonstrating the ability to treat others with respect. "Chanya, I have noticed that you have been respectful of other students all day. I know others enjoy interacting with you more when you treat them with respect." If the student would be embarrassed by public praise, praise the student privately or even give the student a note.

b. In addition, occasionally praise those students who rarely or never have a problem with being disrespectful. Because these students have already mastered the positive expectations, they do not need positive feedback as often as the students who have had difficulty. However, you do not want them to feel that you take their positive behavior for granted. "Lincoln, could I speak to you for a moment? I wanted to let you know that I appreciate how respectful you are with the other students. I think one of the reasons you are so well-liked is everyone trusts that you will never put them down. It is one of your many positive qualities."

c. Finally, when there has been a significant improvement in the students' treatment of each other, praise the entire class. Remember that any time the students are refraining from being disrespectful, you can praise them for treating each other respectfully. "Class, you are being much more respectful of each other. The feeling in the class is so much more pleasant, this is something we can all be proud of."

PLAN B

If the students are not clear about the borderline between respectful and disrespectful interactions, and/or do not know how to treat each other respectfully, the intervention must include some way of teaching them how to do so.

1. *Conduct lessons to teach the students how to be respectful and how to respond if someone is disrespectful to them.*

a. Before the lessons, first decide whether the whole class should participate or if the lessons should involve only a small group of students. Generally, if more than five students are at times disrespectful, conduct the lessons with the whole class. Then, prepare activities to teach the students the borderline between respectful and disrespectful interactions, and activities to teach them how to respond to situations in which someone treats them disrespectfully.

b. During the lessons, begin by working to clarify the line between respect and disrespect. Since this line is difficult to define, the most efficient procedure is to use examples. On the chalkboard or an overhead, draw a T chart like the sample shown and fill in a few examples that do not use real names or situations.

Respectful	Disrespectful
• Someone makes an error in a game and a teammate says, "Hey, no problem, we're doin' fine."	• Someone makes an error in a game and somebody yells, "Nice catch—NOT!"
• Using a nickname a person likes: *Nick for Nicholas*	• Using a nickname a person does not like: *Barf for Garth*
• Being tolerant of physical differences—saying nothing	• Being intolerant of physical differences—names about weight, height, hair color, etc.

c. Lead the students through the process of identifying a disrespectful interaction that they have the seen or heard happen in the classroom, on the playground, or anywhere else in the school. For each disrespectful interaction, have the students identify a respectful interaction that could have been used instead. Give the students assistance, as necessary. If the students begin to identify examples of extreme disrespect, lead them back to more subtle examples in which tone of voice or body language could turn respectful words into a disrespectful interaction.

Your goal is to help the students understand the line between respect and disrespect. The more examples generated the better; however, it is critical that for each disrespectful example, the class generate at least one corresponding respectful example.

d. Next, have the group identify procedures for responding to someone treating them disrespectfully (e.g., put-downs, name calling, etc.) Using the list of disrespectful interactions, help the students think of strategies to use when they are treated this way. "Class, the first example on our list of disrespectful interactions is a put-down when someone makes an error in a game ('Nice catch—NOT!'). Let's make a list of different ways you might handle it if someone said this to you." If the students have difficulty with this process, introduce concepts such as ignoring and using "I messages" (e.g., "I want you to call me by my real name, ___.").

Write all the suggestions on the chalkboard and have the students discuss whether or not each particular response would reduce or increase the chances that the person doing the insulting would do it again. Continue this process with all the different disrespectful examples from the list the students generated.

e. After discussing the possible responses to being teased or treated disrespectfully, have the students role play different situations. Ask two students to volunteer—one student to play the role of the "Teaser" and one to play the role of the "Target." Assign the roles yourself: cast a student with the tendency to tease in the role of "Target," and a student who often gets teased in the role of "Teaser."

Have the students role play a selected scenario and have the other students provide feedback. "Margot, this time respond to Josie's teasing, but sound angry. Class, if Margot responded like that, do you think Josie (remember she is playing the part of someone who likes to hurt others) would be more or less likely to tease Margot in the future?"

f. Conduct the lessons at least twice per week until the problem is largely solved. The lessons will probably require a minimum of 20 minutes apiece.

2. *Prompt appropriate behavior by using precorrections.*

Watch for circumstances in which the students are likely to be disrespectful toward each other and remind the class that they should be especially careful to think about what they do and say. "Class, we are about to have a brainstorming session on ___. This is an activity where in the past we have had some problems with disrespect—like calling other people's ideas 'lame' or 'stupid.' I will be watching to see if you can remember to do what we practiced this morning—saying nothing disrespectful. When we are evaluating the ideas, it is okay to disagree, but calmly state why you disagree. I'll bet you can all do this."

3. *Respond consistently to each instance of disrespect.*

Whenever you notice an individual student being disrespectful, give a gentle correction and, if the student does not cease the behavior, implement time owed (see PLAN A).

4. *Use reinforcement to encourage appropriate behavior.*

a. Praise individual students for meeting expectations regarding being respectful, and praise the entire class when improvement takes place (see PLAN A).

b. Make a special point of letting the students know (both individually and as a class) that you notice their efforts to use the skills they have been learning/practicing. "Elliot, I heard you tell Simon that it hurt your feelings when he made fun of your name. You handled that situation beautifully. I think you helped Simon learn not to do that. Let me know if it worked."

5. *If a student reports being teased (or otherwise treated disrespectfully), ask the student how he/she handled the situation.*

If the student handled the situation well, praise the student. If the student handled the situation poorly, prompt the student about different ways he/she could handle the same type of situation in the future. Do not involve the student who was accused, as this might lead to a "yes you did"/"no I didn't" kind of discussion. Respond only to the disrespectful interactions you observe directly.

PLAN C

Sometimes students do not seem to realize when and/or how often they are being disrespectful. In this case, the intervention should include some way of helping the students become more aware of their own behavior.

1. *Work with the class to define the borderline between respectful and disrespectful interactions (see PLAN B).*

2. *Publicly monitor the frequency of disrespectful interactions.*

a. Create a place on the chalkboard or a wall chart for recording the number of daily class-wide incidents of disrespect. Since you do not want to provide too much peer attention to an individual student who is disrespectful, do not make the entire class aware of who engaged in the behavior. Simply correct the individual privately and count the incident. The idea is to have a total count at the end of the day, not identification of how many incidents were committed by particular individuals.

b. Each day, conduct a short class meeting (of three to five minutes) to review that day's record. Have a student record the daily count on the chart (or do it yourself), and discuss whether the day was better, worse, or about the same as previous days. If the day did not go well, encourage the students to talk about why and have them identify what they can do the next day to help them remember to be more respectful. If the students act inappropriately during the meeting, keep the review session very short. Just let the class know that you are sure tomorrow will be a better day.

3. *Respond consistently to each instance of disrespect.*

a. Whenever an individual student engages in a disrespectful interaction, provide a gentle correction. If the student does not cease the behavior, implement time owed (see PLAN A).

b. In addition, whenever you correct an individual student, make sure the incident is recorded as part of the daily total count.

4. *Use reinforcement to encourage appropriate behavior.*

a. Praise individual students for meeting expectations regarding being respectful, and praise the entire class when improvement takes place (see PLAN A).

b. During the review meetings, praise the students for being willing to look seriously at the daily total count. Even on a bad day, if the students are willing to discuss why it was a bad day, praise them. "Class, you are really handling this responsibly. Even though it was a rough day, you are willing to talk about things you might do differently tomorrow. That is a real sign that we are making progress. In fact, this discussion has been very respectful."

Regardless of how the day went, try to make the end-of-the-day meeting upbeat and encouraging—you want the students to look forward to the daily review.

5. *If a student reports being teased (or otherwise treated disrespectfully), ask the student how he/she handled the situation (see PLAN B).*

PLAN D

Sometimes, an entire class falls into a pattern of being disrespectful. This can happen when a particular behavior becomes habitual and/or when a majority of the students try to emulate a few influential students who act disrespectful to look "cool" or "tough." In these cases, it can be very difficult to change student behavior, and you may need to implement a structured reinforcement system (i.e., rewards and consequences) that creates mild peer pressure to motivate the students to behave appropriately.

1. *Publicly monitor the frequency of disrespectful interactions (see PLAN C).*

2. *Encourage the class to set daily performance goals.*

Help the students to set a realistic goal (e.g., reducing the number of daily disrespectful incidents from 40 to 32). If the students want to set a very challenging goal, such as reducing the number of incidents from 40 per day to zero, explain that if the goal is no more than 32, they can always meet that goal, and by making the goal attainable, they increase their chances of success. Then as the class experiences success, the target number should become progressively lower until there are no disrespectful incidents on most days.

3. *Establish a group reinforcement system.*

a. Have the students brainstorm a number of reinforcement ideas for the entire class, and then eliminate from the list any items that are not possible (i.e., the suggestions are too expensive or could not be provided to all the students in the class).

b. Assign "prices" (in points) to the remaining items on the list. The prices should be based on the instructional, personnel, and/or monetary costs of the items. Monetary cost is clear—the more expensive the item, the more points required to earn it. Instructional cost refers to the amount of instructional time lost or interfered with by a particular reward. Thus, an activity which causes the class to miss part of academic instruction should require more points than one the class can do during recess time. Personnel cost involves the time required by you and/or other staff to fulfill the reinforcer. Therefore, earning an extra recess period in which extra supervision would need to be arranged would cost more than having music playing in class for 15 minutes.

c. Have the class vote on the reinforcers. The reinforcer that earns the most votes is the one they will work for first, and the items that come in second and third will be the next ones worked for.

d. On days when the class successfully keeps their number of disrespectful interactions under the identified goal, award the group a point towards their reward.

e. An alternative reinforcement system is the use of a Mystery Motivator (Rhode, Jenson, & Reavis, 1992). With this system, you would mark certain days of the calendar (with an "X," for example), then cover each space with a slip of paper. Each day, remove the slip of paper for that day. If there is an "X," the class would earn a small reinforcer (provided that they had been successful in meeting their goal that day). Even on days when the class has not been success-ful, remove the paper so the students can see whether they would have received the reward if they had achieved their behavior goal.

f. If a class-wide system seems unlikely to be effective, another option is to implement a team competition and response cost lottery. In this type of system, the class is divided into four to six teams, made as equitable as possible. Each team begins the day with a certain number of tickets on which they write the name of their team. Each time a student is disrespectful, that student's team loses a ticket. At the end of the day, the teams put all their remaining tickets in a hat for a lottery drawing. The team whose name is on the drawn ticket earns the reward for that day.

4. *While implementing any reinforce-ment system, focus student attention on the fact that everyone is being more respectful instead of on the rewards they are earning.*

Tell the class, for example: "Class, you earned your point for the day, but more importantly, you are all helping this class be a place that we will all enjoy. This class is a place we can all be proud of."

5. *Respond consistently to each in-stance of disrespect with a conse-quence of time owed.*

In MODEL PLANS A-C, the intervention specified a gentle correction followed by time owed for sub-sequent instances of disrespect. With this plan, there is no warning; each disrespectful interaction results in time owed off of recess (e.g., two minutes per infraction) or in after-school detention (e.g., five minutes per infraction).

6. *If a student reports being teased (or otherwise treated disrespectfully), ask the student how he/she handled the situation (see PLAN B).*

PLAN E

Sometimes disrespectful behavior is (or continues to be) a problem for only one or two students. In this case, the intervention should focus specifically on those students instead of the entire class.

1. *Work with the student to define the borderline between respectful and dis-respectful interactions (see PLAN B).*

2. *Respond consistently to each in-stance of disrespect with a conse-quence of time owed (see PLAN D).*

3. *Establish a structured system for rein-forcing the appropriate behavior and providing a consequence for the inap-propriate behavior.*

a. With the student, create a list of reinforcers that can be earned. Although you might want to have some suggestions in mind, the system will be more effective if the student identifies most of the items or activities himself/herself. *(NOTE: A*

list of reinforcement ideas can be found in AP-PENDIX 1.)

b. Assign "prices" (in points) for each of the re-wards on the list and have the student choose the reward he/she would like to earn first. The prices should be based on the instructional, personnel, and/or monetary costs of the items (see PLAN D).

c. Establish a system in which you record each instance of the student's disrespectful behavior (a simple tally will do). Meet with the student at the end of each day to tell the student what the day's total was. Have the student keep a daily chart of this number and make sure he/she understands that the idea is for this number to go down.

To assist the student, each week set a goal (i.e., a maximum number of times the student will be disrespectful each day) for the student to attain. Reduce this target number by approximately 10% each week. *(NOTE: The goal is a daily goal that the student works on each day for a week.)*

d. Each day that the student meets the goal, he/she earns a certain number of points (determined by subtracting the number of infractions from the target number for that day). For example, if the student's goal is to have less than 12 infractions and he/she had only seven, the student would earn five points for that day. If the student had no infractions, he/she would earn 12 points.

e. When the student has accumulated enough points to earn the selected reward, he/she "spends" the points necessary and the system begins again. That is, the student selects a new reward to earn and begins with zero points.

If the student is immature, and needs more frequent encouragement, you might consider letting him/her earn several "less expensive" rewards (e.g., five minutes of free time after 20 points) on the way to a bigger reward (e.g., one hour with you for 200 points). That is, the student earns the small rewards without spending points; they continue to accumulate toward the selected reward.

 Use reinforcement to encourage appropriate behavior.

a. Give the student increased praise and attention for being respectful (see PLAN A).

b. In addition, show interest and enthusiasm about how the student is doing on the system. "Priscilla, you have done a great job today. Look at your chart. The goal is 12 and you only had two incidents. You should be very proud of how well you did today."

· · · · · · · · ·
Suggested Steps for Developing and Implementing a Plan

The following steps are designed to help you develop an appropriate intervention plan and implement it effectively, whether you choose to use one of the MODEL PLANS or create a customized plan of your own. The steps are, however, suggestions—they are not intended to be followed rigidly or in any particular order. Use your professional judgment and the knowledge of your particular situation to make them work for you.

 Make sure you have enough information about the situation.

(NOTE: Documentation is probably not necessary if the problem is relatively mild [i.e., if PLAN A is appropriate].)

a. You want to be able to explain what you mean when you say that "the class has a problem with disrespect." Anecdotal notes from actual incidents can help you define the problem behavior thoroughly. To collect anecdotal notes, simply keep a card in your pocket or on a clipboard and occasionally, when you see a student treat another student in a way you consider to be disrespectful (e.g., calling a name, teasing, putting someone down), make notes.

For each entry, briefly describe the circumstances—where and when the incident occurred, what was said and/or done, and any other relevant observations (e.g., what prompted the behavior). You do not need to take notes every time a student treats another student disrespectfully; the idea is to capture a

range of examples so that you will be able to describe the behavior clearly and completely.

b. It may also be useful to document how often the disrespectful interactions occur (i.e., a frequency count). This will provide both a more objective measure of the problem and an objective way to monitor the student's progress. Use the same card on which you are taking anecdotal notes to keep a frequency count—simply write a tally mark on the card each time any student is disrespectful of another student.

You might also want to code the tallies to discern whether the behavior occurs more frequently during certain times, subjects, or activities (e.g., using an "A" or "P" to indicate that the incident happened in the morning or afternoon), or to code the tallies by category (e.g., by teasing, name calling, or insults).

c. If a student notices what you are doing and asks about it, be straightforward—say that you are collecting information to see whether the disres-

randomly from the hat. Winning students receive a reward, such as a coupon for a free ice
cream cone.

c. If everyone in the class has been keeping their
desks neat, provide a group reward such as
working outdoors for the afternoon. *(NOTE: For
a list of ideas for group reinforcers, see AP-
PENDIX 2.)*

....

Suggested Steps for Developing and Implementing a Plan

The following information is designed to help you develop an appropriate intervention plan
and implement it effectively, whether you choose to use one of the MODEL PLANS or create
a customized plan of your own. The steps are, however, suggestions—they are not intended
to be followed rigidly or in any particular order. Use your professional judgment and the
knowledge of your particular situation to make them work for you.

 **Make sure you have enough informa-
tion about the situation.**

a. If you think a minimal intervention like PLAN A
will be sufficient, you probably already have
enough information to proceed. However, when
a more involved plan seems necessary, you
should consider collecting additional descriptive
information for a couple of days.

b. You need to be able to explain what you mean
when you say that "the class has a problem with
messy desks." Anecdotal notes about actual
circumstances should provide enough detail to
help you define the problem behavior clearly
and completely. To collect anecdotal notes,
simply keep a card in your pocket or on a
clipboard and occasionally make notes on specific instances of messy desks.

For each entry, briefly describe the situation,
and make particular note of any class time that
was wasted as a result. You do not need to take
notes every time you notice a messy desk; the
idea is to capture a range of examples of the
behavior so you will be able to describe it completely.

c. If a student notices what you are doing and asks
about it, be straightforward—tell the student, "I
am concerned about how much time we waste
because your desks are messy. I am making
notes to see if this is a problem that needs to be
worked on."

Following is an example of anecdotal notes that
have been collected in a class with a problem
of messy desks.

- When instructed to get out paper for a spelling
  quiz, Marissa, Forrest, Twyla, Jesus, and
  Molly all took too long rummaging through
  their messy desks (3 minutes wasted).

- Before recess, I had to instruct Arrielle to pick
  up her papers off the floor (that had spilled
  out of her desk) and either return them to her
  desk or put them in the recycling box (2
  minutes wasted).

- Matt couldn't find his math book. I helped him
  find it in the mess in his desk (1 minute
  wasted).

d. Continuing to collect this type of information
while you implement a plan will help you monitor
whether the situation is getting worse, staying
the same, or getting better.

 **Identify a focus for the intervention
and labels for referring to the appropriate and inappropriate behaviors.**

a. To be effective, the intervention must address
more than just reducing the problem of messy
desks—there must be a concurrent emphasis
on increasing some positive behavior or trait
(e.g., "keeping work spaces neat"). Identifying
a specific positive behavior will make it easier
for you to "catch" and reinforce the students for
behaving appropriately, and will help you explain your concern more productively.

For example, simply saying that "the class has
a problem with being messy" doesn't really give
the students any useful information (and may
put them on the defensive). However, telling the
students that you want them "to learn to keep

Agenda

1. Disrespect—Define the magnitude of the problem. *(NOTE: Share your data.)*

2. Review the expectations regarding being respectful.

3. Brainstorm ideas for improving the situation.

4. Select strategies that everyone agrees to.

5. Establish what will happen if a student is disrespectful toward another student.

---

c. Establish clear rules for both you and the students regarding the brainstorming phase of the meeting. For example:

- Any idea is okay (but no obscenity).

- Ideas will not be evaluated initially (i.e., no approval—"Good idea," or disapproval—"What a stupid idea" or "We couldn't do that" should be expressed during brainstorming).

- All ideas will be written down and discussed at the conclusion of brainstorming.

d. At the conclusion of brainstorming, evaluate the ideas, and lead the class to consensus on any decisions that need to be made. Use voting as a decision-making process when appropriate.

5. *Determine when and how to include the parent(s).*

a. When the situation is class-wide, contacting the parents of all the students who have been disrespectful is probably neither appropriate nor realistic (it is not feasible for you to call five to ten parents each night). However, after discussing the problem with the students, it may be useful to send a memo to parents (or include an item in your classroom newsletter, if you have one) explaining the focus of the plan the students will be working on (i.e., treating each other with respect).

b. If the situation involves one or two students who have or continue to have a problem with being disrespectful, you should contact the parents of those individuals. Let them know that their student has been disrespectful toward other students and what steps you are taking to correct the situation.

Frequent contact is not required, but whenever you intend to implement an individualized plan, the parent(s) should be informed prior to its implementation and should be given feedback about the student's progress every two to four weeks.

6. *Give the class regular, ongoing feedback about their behavior.*

Periodically meet with the students to discuss the situation. In most cases, three to five minutes once per week should suffice. *(NOTE: PLANS D and PLAN E require daily meetings to record data or to determine points.)* During the meeting, review any information that has been collected and discuss whether or not things are getting better. As much as possible, focus on improvements, however, also address any new or continuing problems.

As you discuss problems, acknowledge (without singling out individuals) that there are students in the class who consistently behave appropriately. As the situation improves, the meetings can be faded to once every other week and then to once per month.

7. *Evaluate the situation (and the plan).*

Any plan should be implemented for at least two weeks before deciding whether or not it is effective. Generally, if the situation has improved (based on the objective information that's been collected and/or the subjective perceptions of yourself and the students), continue with what you have been doing. (Eventually you will want to fade, then eliminate, the plan.) If the problem remains the same or worsens, some kind of change (i.e., modifying the current plan or switching to another plan) will be necessary. Always discuss any change in the intervention with the class first.

NOSE PICKING/ORAL FETISHES

Mouth Habits (e.g., Chewing On Fingers)

DESCRIPTION

You have a student who picks his nose.

GOAL

The student will use a tissue to blow or clean his nose (and will not spend an excessive amount of time doing so).

OVERVIEW OF PLANS

- PLAN A: For a situation in which the problem is relatively mild or has just begun.
- PLAN B: For a student who is unaware of how unbecoming and/or unhygienic his behavior is.
- PLAN C: For a student who picks his nose to gain attention—either from adults or peers.

NOTE:

The information included in these three plans specifically addresses nose picking, but can be easily adapted for oral fetishes or other mildly compulsive behaviors.

· · · · · · · ·
General Considerations

• If the student's nasal problems are, in part, related to allergies, stay in close communication with the student's parent(s) to make sure the student is receiving appropriate medical treatment. It is still reasonable, however, to teach the student to use a tissue to blow or clean his nose.

· · · · · · · ·
Model Plans

PLAN A

It is not always necessary, or even beneficial, to use an involved plan. If the inappropriate behavior has just begun and/or is relatively mild (e.g., the student picks his nose once or twice per day for a few seconds each time, and stops when reminded), the following actions, along with making the student aware of your concerns, may resolve the situation.

1. **Respond consistently to the inappropriate behavior.**

a. During your initial meeting with the student (see SUGGESTED STEPS FOR DEVELOPING AND IMPLEMENTING A PLAN), establish a nonembarrassing signal that you can use to cue him that he "needs to use a tissue, and if he doesn't have one to get one off your desk." If the student is a slow learner, you may need to conduct multiple practice sessions to teach him to recognize the signal and to associate it with the need to use a tissue, and/or get a tissue if necessary.

The signal should be fairly subtle—one that only the student will recognize and understand in order to minimize the chance that he will be teased by his peers. Possibilities include putting the fingertips of your two hands together, rubbing your neck, or even just direct eye contact and a head nod. Let the student know that you may also need to quietly say his name to get his attention before you give the signal. Be prepared to use the signal frequently and for a long time initially, especially if the behavior is, at least in part, an unconscious habit for the student.

b. Whenever the student is picking his nose, give the signal. If the student does not stop, gently correct him by giving direct information about what he should be doing instead. "Ricardo, you need to get a tissue." Because your goal is to impart information, you want to be emotionally neutral while giving the correction.

2. **Use reinforcement to encourage appropriate behavior.**

a. Give the student increased praise. Be especially alert for situations in which the student remembers to use a tissue without being prompted and praise him for these demonstrations of his ability to use good hygiene skills. "Ricardo, I noticed that during math you went and got a tissue. You should be proud of your ability to remember good hygiene skills."

If the student would be embarrassed by public praise, praise the student privately or even give the student a note. Remember that any time the student uses a tissue, you can praise his use of good hygiene skills.

b. Praise the student privately for responding to the signal. "Ricardo, twice today I gave the signal of rubbing my neck, and each time you immediately got a tissue. You are working hard on learning good hygiene."

c. Give the student frequent attention (e.g., say "hello" to him as he enters the classroom, call on him frequently during class activities, and occasionally ask him to assist you with a class job that needs to be done) and praise him for other positive behaviors he exhibits. For example, you might comment about the creativity of his stories, how attentive he is during lessons, or how consistent he is about making entries in his journal. This demonstrates to the student that you notice many positive things he does, not just the fact that he is refraining from picking his nose.

PLAN B

Sometimes a student is not aware of how this behavior appears to others. If your student seems oblivious to how his actions are perceived, you should help him learn that using a tissue is much less offensive than picking his nose.

1. *Respond consistently to the inappropriate behavior.*

When the student picks his nose, give the signal, then gently correct him, if necessary (see PLAN A).

2. *Conduct lessons to teach the student how unbecoming nose picking is and/or how to use a tissue instead.*

a. Before the lessons, identify some way to show the student how unbecoming and unhygienic nose picking is. One possibility is a mirror, another is to use a video camera and playback equipment. The purpose will be for the student to see his behavior exactly as others do.

b. Begin the lesson by having the student pick his nose for a short time (e.g., 10-30 seconds) while observing himself in the mirror (or on the playback of the videotape). As he is doing this, emphasize how unhygienic the behavior seems. Ask the student to imagine an adult he respects doing that—how disgusting or silly it would seem. Then explain that everyone needs to blow their nose occasionally—especially if they have a cold or allergies—and that when a person uses a tissue, it is an example of good hygiene.

Then have the student observe himself using a tissue to blow or clean his nose, and again ask him to imagine the adult he respects using a tissue. Emphasize that this does not seem disgusting or silly.

c. Include additional practice in responding to the signal, if necessary. Have the student begin to pick his nose (or pretend, to if he prefers), then give the signal, and guide the student through the actions of getting a tissue, spending a few moments cleaning or blowing his nose, then throwing the tissue in the trash.

d. Conduct the lessons at least twice per week, until the student is no longer picking his nose. These lessons should involve just the two of you (perhaps while the other students are at recess). The lessons needn't last more than three to five minutes, and it is important to handle them in a matter-of-fact manner so the student does not feel that he is being ridiculed. You want to be very clear that you are not trying to embarrass the student, but that you do want him to see his behavior the way others do.

Continue the lessons until the student is consistently responding to the signal and/or no longer picking his nose.

3. *Use reinforcement to encourage appropriate behavior.*

a. Give the student increased praise and attention for using good hygiene skills (see PLAN A).

b. Praise the student for participating during the lesson. "Ricardo, you are cooperating so nicely while we are working together. It is fun to work with such a helpful student."

c. In addition, make a special point of letting the student know that you notice his efforts to use the skills he has been learning/practicing. "Ricardo, you have been doing very well at remembering to use good hygiene skills. Nice job of doing what we have been practicing."

PLAN C

Occasionally a student has learned that he can cause others to act disgusted or nag him by picking his nose. If the student seems intent on provoking reactions in others (e.g., he laughs when others act disgusted), this plan may be appropriate. Whether or not the student overtly seems to like the attention, you should make sure that he receives more frequent and more satisfying attention when he behaves appropriately than when he is picking his nose.

1. *Respond consistently to the inappropriate behavior.*

a. When the student picks his nose, give him the signal (see PLAN A).

b. Each time you have to give the student the signal, assign one minute of time owed off the next recess (or after school). It is important for the student to see you mark some sort of record sheet so that he knows that he owes one minute for the infraction that just occurred. During the time owed, you might have the student observe himself engaging in the behavior and practice hygienic alternatives (see PLAN B).

If the student makes any overt attempt to bother other students with the behavior, assign an additional minute of time owed. For example, if you give the signal, and on the way to get a tissue the student acts like he is going to wipe his finger on another student to cause that student to react, he would owe an additional minute. "Ricardo, you owe another minute for having bothered Barry in that way."

When giving the signal and reprimanding the student, be emotionally neutral. Never act disgusted, frustrated or disappointed—an emotional reaction from you may fuel the student's inappropriate, attention-getting behavior. Also, do not be distressed if during the lessons the student makes a show of enjoying the act of observing himself picking his nose. Unless he senses that he is "getting to you," he will tire of the game within a week or two.

c. If other students give the target student attention when he is picking his nose (e.g., acting like they are shocked or sickened), gently correct them. "Andrew and Lloyd, the best way to get him to stop doing that is to pay no attention. If you make a big deal about it, it may make Ricardo want to bother you even more. Just ignore it."

2. Use reinforcement to encourage appropriate behavior.

a. Frequent praise and attention is the core of this plan. The student must see that he receives more frequent and more satisfying attention when he behaves appropriately than when he picks his nose or tries to shock others. Thus, whenever the student is not picking his nose (or otherwise misbehaving), make an effort to praise and spend time with him. "Ricardo, you are working so hard on this project. Would you explain how you dot the colors to blend together like this?"

b. You may also wish to use intermittent rewards to acknowledge the student's success. Occasional, and unexpected, rewards can motivate the student to demonstrate responsible

behavior more often. The idea is to provide a reward when the student has had a particularly good period of not picking his nose.

Appropriate rewards might include letting the student perform in a skit, asking the principal to comment about a project the student has worked on, or letting the student read a story to some younger students. *(NOTE: A list of additional reinforcement ideas can be found in APPENDIX 1.)*

Use intermittent rewards more frequently at the beginning of the intervention to encourage the student, and then less often as his behavior improves.

3. Ensure a 3-1 ratio of positive to negative attention.

a. When attention is a motivating force for a student, you want to be sure that you are giving the student *three times as much* positive as negative attention. One way to do this is to monitor your interactions with the student at least one day per week. To do so, keep a card on a clipboard or in your pocket and record each interaction you have with the student as either positive or negative by writing a "+" or a "-", respectively, on the card.

To determine whether an interaction is positive or negative, ask yourself whether the student was picking his nose (or otherwise misbehaving) at the time the interaction occurred. Any interaction that stems from inappropriate behavior is negative, and all interactions that occur while the student is meeting classroom expectations are positive. Thus, giving the signal and assigning time owed are both negative interactions, but praising the student for not needing the signal is positive. Greeting the student as he enters the room or asking him if he has any questions during independent work are also considered positive interactions.

b. If you find that you are not giving the student three times as much positive as negative attention, try to increase the number of positive interactions you have with the student. Sometimes prompts can help. For example, you might decide that each time the student enters the classroom you will say "hello" to him, that you will praise him more frequently during small group instruction, or that you will identify a strength or interest of the student (e.g., he is interested in dogs) and look for times to compliment him on or engage him in conversation about that strength or interest.

Suggested Steps for Developing and Implementing a Plan

The following steps are designed to help you develop an appropriate intervention plan and implement it effectively, whether you choose to use one of the MODEL PLANS or create a customized plan of your own. The steps are, however, suggestions—they are not intended to be followed rigidly or in any particular order. Use your professional judgment and the knowledge of your particular situation to make them work for you.

1. Make sure you have enough information about the situation.

a. Unless this problem is chronic (e.g., the student picks his nose 20-30 times per day), formal methods of data collection are probably not necessary—your subjective perceptions of the student's progress will be sufficient. However, if the behavior is extremely frequent or has been resistant to other intervention attempts, keep a frequency count of the behavior.

To maintain a frequency count, simply keep a card in your pocket or on a clipboard and whenever you give the student the signal, write a tally mark on the card. If the student asks what you are doing, explain that you are trying to see how many times per day he picks his nose so you can decide whether it is problem that needs to be worked on. At the end of each day, total the number of times the student engaged in this behavior.

b. The frequency count information is fairly easy to summarize on a chart or graph. Seeing just how often he picks his nose may help the student and his parent(s) better understand your concern.

c. Continuing to collect this type of information and keeping the chart up-to-date while you implement a plan will help you monitor whether the situation is getting worse, staying the same, or getting better.

2. Identify a focus for the intervention and labels for referring to the appropriate and inappropriate behaviors.

To be effective, the intervention must address more than just reducing the student's nose picking—there must be a concurrent emphasis on increasing some positive behavior or trait (e.g., using good hygiene skills). Having a specific positive behavior in mind will make it easier for you to "catch" and reinforce the student for behaving appropriately, and the positive focus will frame the situation more productively. When you explain that you want to help the student learn to "use good hygiene skills" you present an important, and reasonable, goal for the student to work toward and clearly identify what the student needs to do to be successful.

3. Determine when and how to include the parent(s).

a. It is not necessary to contact the student's parent(s) if the problem has just begun and is not interfering with the student's academic or social progress. However, it might be a good idea to take advantage of any scheduled activities (e.g., conferences, weekly notes home) to let them know of your concern.

b. If you believe the problem could be related to allergies, if the behavior is happening 20-30 times per day, or if you tried a simple intervention such as PLAN A and it didn't work, contact the student's parent(s) and explain your intervention plan before implementation. Share with them any information you have collected about the behavior (e.g., the frequency count), and explain why you are concerned. For example, you might explain that the student's peers are avoiding him because of this behavior.

c. Once the parent(s) have been involved in any way, you should give them progress updates at least once per week while the plan is being implemented.

4. Prepare for, then conduct, an initial meeting about the situation.

a. Arrange a meeting to discuss your concerns with the student and anyone else who will be involved in the plan (e.g., the parent[s]). Make sure the meeting will be appropriately private (e.g., held in the counselor's office) to ensure that the discussion will not be overheard.

b. Construct a preliminary plan. Decide whether you think you can use one of the MODEL PLANS or if you need to create a customized plan using components from various plans and/or of your own design. Although you will invite and encourage the student to help develop the plan during the initial meeting, having a proposed plan in mind before you meet can alleviate frustration and wasted time if the student is unwilling or unable to participate.

c. Review any information you have collected and prepare a thorough description of both the inappropriate behavior (i.e., nose picking) and the positive behavior/trait on which the student will be working (i.e., use of good hygiene skills).

d. Conduct the meeting in an atmosphere of collaboration. The following agenda is one way you might structure the meeting:

- **Share your concerns about the student's behavior.**

    Briefly describe the problem behavior and, when appropriate, show the student a chart of how often he engages in it. Then explain why you consider the behavior to be a problem. For example, you might tell the student that the behavior is unhygienic and that most people find it offensive.

- **Discuss how you can work together to improve the situation.**

    Tell the student that you would like to help him learn to "use good hygiene skills," and describe your preliminary plan. Invite the student to give you input on the various aspects of the plan, and together work out any necessary details (e.g., location of tissues, use of the signals, time owed, etc.). You may have to brainstorm different possibilities if the student is uncomfortable with the initial plan. Incorporating any of the student's suggestions that strengthen the plan is likely to in-

crease his sense of "ownership" in and commitment to it.

- **Conclude the meeting.**

    Always end the meeting with words of encouragement. Let the student know that you are confident that he can be successful. Be sure to reinforce him for participating in the meeting.

5. *Give the student regular, ongoing feedback about his behavior.*

It is important to meet with the student periodically to discuss his progress. In most cases, three to five minutes once per week should suffice. Review any information that has been collected and discuss whether or not the situation is improving. As much as possible, focus on the student's improvements, however, also address any new or continuing problems. As the situation improves, the meetings can be faded to once every other week and then to once per month.

6. *Evaluate the situation (and the plan).*

Implement any plan for at least two weeks before deciding whether to change plans; to continue, modify, or fade the plan you are using; or to cease the intervention. Generally, if the student's behavior is clearly improving (based on the objective information that's been collected and/or the subjective perceptions of yourself, the student, and possibly the parent[s]), stick with what you are doing. If the situation has remained the same or worsened, some kind of change will be necessary. Always discuss any changes to the plan with the student first.

OUT OF SEAT

Wandering Around the Classroom

DESCRIPTION

You have a student who gets out of her seat and wanders around the classroom at inappropriate times.

GOAL

The student will stay in her seat and remain academically engaged as appropriate.

OVERVIEW OF PLANS

- PLAN A: For a situation in which the problem has just begun or is relatively mild (i.e., occurs infrequently).
- PLAN B: For a student who does not understand or has difficulty meeting the expectations of remaining in one place for any length of time.
- PLAN C: For a student who gets out of her seat in order to gain adult attention.
- PLAN D: For a student who is able to behave appropriately, but has developed a habit of getting out of her seat and wandering around.
- PLAN E: For a situation in which several students in the class get out of their seats inappropriately.

NOTE:

Although these five plans address the problem of a student who gets out of her seat, they could also be adapted for classroom situations in which the students do not spend much time at their desks. For example, in a class involving hands-on participation (e.g., middle/junior high school wood shop), the plans could be modified to use with a student who tends to wander from her work station or be in the wrong place at the wrong time.

Alternative Problems

- **Bothering/ Tormenting Others**

- **Chaos/Classroom Out of Control**

········
General Considerations

- If the student's problem behavior stems in any way from academic issues (e.g., the student wanders around the room trying to find something to do because she cannot do the assigned work), concurrent efforts must be made to ensure her academic success (see **Academic Deficits, Determining**).

- If the student is receiving special education services and/or has been diagnosed with an attention deficit disorder (i.e., ADD or ADHD), consult with the student's parent(s), special education teacher, and/or other professionals who may be involved with the student (e.g., psychologist or physician) before implementing any intervention.

- If the inappropriate behavior is resulting in the student avoiding or not completing her schoolwork, begin with a plan to increase the student's work completion (see **Work Completion—Daily Work**). Once the student is turning in completed work on a regular basis, you can consider an intervention for the out of seat behavior, if the problem still exists.

········
Model Plans

PLAN A

It is not always necessary, or even beneficial, to use an involved plan. If the inappropriate behavior has just begun or occurs infrequently, the following actions, along with making the student aware of your concerns, may resolve the situation.

1. Respond consistently to the inappropriate behavior.

a. During your initial meeting with the student (see SUGGESTED STEPS FOR DEVELOPING AND IMPLEMENTING A PLAN), establish a nonembarrassing signal that you can use to cue her that she is out of her seat. You want the signal to be a fairly subtle one that only the student will recognize and understand in order to minimize the chance that she will be teased by her peers. Possibilities include a unique hand gesture, rubbing your neck, or even just direct eye contact and a head nod.

Let the student know that you may also need to quietly say her name to get her attention before you give the signal. You should be prepared to use the signal frequently and for a fairly long time since it is likely that the behavior is, at least in part, an unconscious habit for the student.

b. Whenever the student is out of her seat, give her the signal and then gently correct her, if necessary, by providing a verbal reminder about where she needs to be. "Celine, right now you need to be in your seat working with your group on the project." If the student begins moving directly to where she needs to be, no further response is necessary.

c. If the student does not respond immediately to the verbal correction, implement a consequence such as time owed. Check the time (or start a stopwatch) when you give the verbal correction and have the student owe the number of minutes that elapse between the verbal correction and when she complies with that correction. For example, if the student takes two minutes to saunter slowly to her desk, she would owe two minutes off of the next recess or in after-school detention. If she takes three minutes, she would owe three minutes. However, if the student complies (even if it takes her ten seconds to get there) she would not owe any time.

Right before each recess (and/or the end of school day), total the number of owed minutes the student has accumulated. During the time owed, the student should just sit and do nothing. *(NOTE: If the necessity of implementing a consequence seems probable, be sure that the student knows what the consequence will be before you implement it.)*

2. Use reinforcement to encourage appropriate behavior.

a. Give the student increased praise. Be especially alert for situations in which the student remains in her seat when she is supposed to, and praise her for these demonstrations of her ability to stay in her assigned space. "Celine, throughout the time I was presenting the geography lesson, you remained in your seat and kept your attention on me. While I am teaching a lesson it is very helpful to have you stay in your own work space like that. Thank you."

If the student would be embarrassed by public praise, praise the student privately, use a positive nonverbal signal like a smile and a head nod, or even give the student a note. Remember that any time the student is in her seat, you can praise her for being in her assigned space.

b. Praise the student privately for responding to the signal. "Celine, three times this morning I gave you the signal that you were out of your seat, and three times you returned immediately to your work space. I did not even have to give you a reminder. Thanks for paying attention to the signal."

c. Give the student frequent attention (e.g., say "hello" to her as she enters the classroom, call on her frequently during class activities, and occasionally ask her to assist you with a class job that needs to be done) and praise her for other positive behaviors she exhibits. For example, you might comment about the accuracy of her work or how helpful she is with younger students during recess. This demonstrates to the student that you notice many positive things she does, not just the fact that she is staying in her seat.

PLAN B

Sometimes a student really may not know how to stay where she is supposed to be (e.g., an extremely restless primary level student who seems to need to move around and/or may be under the impression that it is all right to just get up and move about whenever she pleases). If this is the case with your student, this plan may be appropriate.

1. **Respond consistently to the inappropriate behavior.**

a. When the student is out of her seat inappropriately, give her a signal, then gently correct her and/or implement time owed as necessary (see PLAN A).

b. These responses may need to be modified if you modify your expectations for student behavior (several suggestions follow in Step 2).

2. **Conduct lessons to help the student learn when and how to stay in her seat and when it is appropriate to get out of her seat.**

a. Before the lessons, think about changes in the classroom expectations that might help the student successfully meet them.

Use one or more of the following ideas as the basis for a lesson or lessons to teach the student how to meet the revised expectations:

• If the student is unaware of how often/how long she is out of her seat, and she is old enough to tell time accurately, then establish a self-monitoring system in which the student records each time she gets out of her seat. The student should record the time when she gets out of her seat and the time when she gets back, and also indicate the reason why she was out of her seat. A form like the sample shown might be applicable.

A form such as this can also be used to specify goals for reducing the number of times and/or the number of minutes the student is out of her seat inappropriately. This

Time Left Seat	Time Back in Seat	# of Min. Out of Seat	Reason for Being Out of Seat

type of system is useful because, while it does not imply that being out of her seat is necessarily bad or wrong (i.e., there are perfectly valid reasons for being out of her seat), it does clarify any excesses that exist.

- If the target student seems unable to stay in her seat, and you want her to learn self-control strategies for staying in an assigned space, create a masking tape "office" that defines the borderlines of acceptable movement for the student. Place a masking tape square around the student's desk. Make the square about a chair's width larger than her desk all around so that the student can easily move around her desk and still stay in her office.

Teach the student that this office is her assigned space, and that although she does not have to stay in her seat, she does need to stay in her office. In this way, the student who has difficulty sitting can move about, yet receive teacher reinforcement for being in the right space. Thus, even when the student is not in her seat at all, she can be learning restraint and self-control. "Celine, throughout our math time you have stayed in your office. Excellent example of how to be in the right space. You should be very proud of yourself."

Also be sure to clarify the reasons and times that it is acceptable for the student to leave her office. You do not want to give the student the impression that she is imprisoned in her office. However, if the student leaves her office at the wrong time, there should be a minor consequence such as one minute of time owed off of recess for each infraction.

As the student is consistently successful with this system, make the office space progressively smaller. For example, limit the space on the right side so that the student is able to move only to the left side and the front and back of the desk. As she becomes more and more successful, reduce the space in front, then, eventually the left side. Once she is successful with these limitations, the expectation can be that she must be in contact with her chair, then in the seat of her chair. Keep in mind, however, that fading this type of system could take a very long time for a student who has a significant behavioral change to make.

- If the student moves about for valid reasons (e.g., sharpening her pencil, turning in an assignment, etc.), but just does so too frequently, create a ticket system wherein the student receives a certain number of tickets each day. Whenever the student moves out of her assigned space, it costs her a ticket. Once she is out of tickets, the student is not allowed to leave her assigned space. If she does so, she is assigned a minor consequence, such as one minute of time owed off of the next recess.

To implement this system, first identify how many times per day the student should be able to move about. If you are unsure, conduct a frequency count on the movement of two responsible students for a day or two. How many times per day on average do those two students get out of their seats? Compare this number to the number of times the target student gets out of her seat.

If the discrepancy is moderate (e.g., the target student 14 times per day; the responsible students an average of nine times per day), plan to give the target student a number of tickets equal to the number of times the responsible students move about.

If the discrepancy is large (e.g., the target student 31 times per day; the responsible students an average of nine times per day) plan to give the target student a number of tickets about 20% less than her typical number (e.g., 25 tickets). As she is consistently successful in meeting this expectation, reduce the number of tickets she receives at the beginning of each day to 20, then 16, 13, ten, and finally nine, for example.

- If the student would have trouble with a ticket system because she might make poor judgments (e.g., using up all her tickets by sharpening her pencil 25 times in the first hour of the day), create a self-monitoring chart and system in which the student can get out of her seat for certain reasons. However, when she does so, she must check the reason off on her chart and once checked off, she cannot get out of her seat for that reason again that day. Following is a sample chart. (NOTE: For young students, a pictorial representation of the chart may be more appealing and effective.)

Celine's Movement Chart

Date _____

Morning

___ Sharpen pencil

___ Get a drink of water

___ Turn in math assignment

___ Turn in reading assignment

___ Use the restroom

Afternoon

___ Sharpen pencil

___ Pick up papers

___ Turn in journal

___ Get supplies

___ Use the restroom

- If the problem is that the student takes too long each time she is out of her assigned space (e.g., she goes to sharpen her pencil, but wanders around for five minutes), arrange some form of timing. For example, the student could have a small digital timer taped to her desk. In addition, you and the student could create a chart showing the length of time different activities should reasonably take. Following is a sample chart, but the times specified should be verified by having your student actually perform these activities.

- Sharpening pencil—1 minute

- Turning in paper—1 minute

- Using the restroom—4 minutes

- Going from desk to group or a work center—1 minute

When the student is about to engage in one of the activities listed, she sets her timer for the correct number of minutes. If she makes it (without running or making a scene), praise the student. If she does not, she would owe one minute off the next recess or in after-school detention, plus any additional minutes it takes the student to return to her assigned space.

(NOTE: Any of these suggested systems can be implemented in conjunction with the subsequent PLANS C, D, or E.)

b. During the lessons, discuss the revised classroom expectations with the student, and have the student demonstrate that she understands and is capable of being successful with them. For example, have the student actually practice using the "Movement Chart" if that is part of the intervention plan.

c. Conduct the lessons daily if possible, but at least twice per week until the student fully understands and is successful with the revised classroom expectations. For some students, one lesson will be sufficient, whereas with other students daily lessons for a couple of weeks may be required. The lessons should involve just you and the student (perhaps while the other students are at recess), and they needn't last more than five minutes apiece. It is important that the lessons be handled in a matter-of-fact manner so that the student does not feel that she is being ridiculed.

3. *Prompt the student to behave appropriately by using precorrections.*

Watch for those circumstances in which the student is likely to have difficulty staying in her seat, and remind her that she will need to remember to use the strategies that you and she have been practicing. "Celine, we are about to start independent work in math. Remember to look at your chart before you get out of your seat to see if you have used up all your reasons. I will be watching to see if you remember to do what we practiced yesterday. I'll bet you can." If this conversation would embarrass the student, conduct it privately.

4. *Use reinforcement to encourage appropriate behavior.*

a. Give the student increased praise and attention for remaining in her seat (see PLAN A).

b. In addition, make a special point of letting the student know that you notice her efforts to use the skills she has been learning/practicing. "Celine, you checked your chart, saw that you could sharpen you pencil, came back to your seat, and checked off that space on the chart. Nice job of doing what we have been practicing."

5. **Make sure the student knows that if she has any questions about the system, she can always ask.**

Tell the student, for example: "Celine, if you are in your office and you are not sure whether it is okay to leave to do something, raise your hand, wait for me to call on you, and then ask."

PLAN C

Some students are very skilled at gaining attention through their negative behavior. If you find yourself frequently nagging, reminding, or coaxing the student to get back to her seat, it is possible that she is trying to gain adult attention. Whether or not the student overtly seems to like the attention, you should make sure that she receives more frequent and more satisfying attention when she behaves appropriately than when she is wandering around.

1. **Respond consistently to the inappropriate behavior.**

a. Because it is important for the student to learn that she will not be able to prompt people to nag and pay attention to her by getting out of her seat, you need to ignore her behavior whenever the student is out of her seat when she shouldn't be. While ignoring, do not look at the student or talk to her. Do not act disgusted or impatient with her behavior. Simply interact in positive ways with students who are behaving appropriately and meeting classroom expectations. As soon as the target student is back in her seat, pay attention to her, but make no reference to her wandering around.

b. The only time you shouldn't ignore the student's behavior is when it affects other students (e.g., she bothers other students when she is out of her seat). On these occasions, implement a consequence such as time owed off of recess or in after-school detention. If the need for consequences seems likely, the student should be told during your initial meeting (see SUGGESTED STEPS FOR DEVELOPING AND IMPLEMENTING A PLAN) what will happen when she is out of her seat and bothering someone. Then if that situation arises, simply state, for example, "Celine, stop bothering people who are working. You owe one minute off of recess." Only implement consequences when the student's wandering around directly interferes with another student, otherwise ignore the behavior.

(NOTE: For a student in kindergarten or first grade, redirection may be more appropriate than time owed. Redirection involves gently leading the student back to her seat without saying anything or making eye contact with her.)

c. If other students give the target student attention (e.g., reminding her that she needs to be in her seat) when she is out of her seat but not directly bothering others, gently correct them. "Veronica and Kendell, Celine can take care of herself and she knows she should be in her seat. It would be best to let her work it out on her own."

2. **Use reinforcement to encourage appropriate behavior.**

a. Frequent praise and attention is the core of this plan. The student must see that she receives more frequent and more satisfying attention for being in her seat than for wandering around. Make an effort to praise and spend time with the student whenever she is in her seat. "Celine, you have been working at your seat in such a responsible way this morning. Show me what you have been so busy working on."

b. You may also wish to use intermittent rewards to acknowledge the student's success. Occasional, and unexpected, rewards can motivate the student to demonstrate responsible behavior more often. Thus, when the student has gone for a particularly long time without wandering around, provide a small reward to celebrate.

Appropriate rewards might involve any form of movement (e.g., asking the student to take a note to the office or asking her to help you pass out papers), or a privilege such as keeping the class hamster on her desk during the next work period. "Celine, you have been so responsible about being in the right space, would you like to have the hamster cage on your desk for the next hour so he can watch what a responsible person you are?" *(NOTE: A list of additional reinforcement ideas can be found in APPENDIX 1.)*

If you use intermittent rewards, do so more frequently at the beginning of the intervention to encourage the student, and then less often as her behavior improves.

3. Ensure a 3-1 ratio of positive to negative attention.

a. When attention is the motivating force for a student, you need to be sure that you are giving the student *three times as much* positive as negative attention. One way to do this is to monitor your interactions with the student at least one day per week. Simply keep a card on a clipboard or in your pocket and record each interaction you have with the student as either positive or negative by writing a "+" or a "-", respectively, on the card.

To determine whether an interaction is positive or negative, ask yourself whether the student was out of her seat (or otherwise misbehaving) at the time the interaction occurred. Any interaction that stems from inappropriate behavior is negative, while all interactions that occur while the student is meeting classroom expectations are positive. Thus, assigning time owed is a negative interaction, but praising the student for being in her seat is positive. Greeting the student as she enters the room or asking her if she has any questions during independent work are also considered positive interactions. *(NOTE: Ignoring the student's wandering around is not recorded at all, because it is not an interaction.)*

b. If you find that you are not giving the student three times as much positive as negative attention, try to increase the number of positive interactions you have with the student. Sometimes prompts can help. For example, you might decide that each time the student enters the classroom you will say "hello" to her; tell yourself that whenever you have to ignore the student's wandering around, you will try to "catch" her as soon as she is in her seat and praise her; or you could decide that whenever another adult enters your class (e.g., a visitor, a parent, the principal, etc.) you will check the target student for a reinforcable behavior. You can also increase the ratio of positive to negative attention by ignoring more of the student's inappropriate behavior.

PLAN D

If the student's problem behavior has become habitual and/or she does not seem to have a desire to reduce it, you may need to implement a structured system of external incentives (i.e., rewards and consequences) to motivate her to change her behavior.

1. Respond consistently to the inappropriate behavior.

Use a signal to cue the student when she is out of her seat (see PLAN A).

2. Monitor the number of times you have to give the student the signal.

Keep a frequency count of the student's incidents of wandering around. Simply keep a card on a clipboard or in your pocket and write a tally mark on the card each time the student is out of her seat.

3. Implement a structured system for reinforcing the appropriate behavior and providing a consequence for the inappropriate behavior.

a. With the student, create a list of reinforcers that she can earn. Although you might want to have some suggestions in mind, the system will be more effective if the student identifies most of the items or activities herself. *(NOTE: A list of reinforcement ideas can be found in APPENDIX 1.)*

b. Assign "prices" (in points) for each of the rewards on the list and have the student select the reward she would like to work for first.

The prices should be based on the instructional, personnel, and/or monetary costs of the items. Monetary cost is clear—the more expensive the item, the more points required to earn it. Instructional cost refers to the amount of instructional time lost or interfered with by a particular reward. Thus, an activity which causes the student to miss part of academic instruction should require more points than one the student can do on her own recess time. Personnel cost involves the time required by you and/or other staff to fulfill the reinforcer. Having lunch with the principal, therefore, would cost more points than spending five minutes of free time with a friend.

c. Have the student begin each day with a certain number of points (equal to the average number of times per day the student is out of her seat, plus two). Thus, if she has averaged being out of her seat 13 times per day, she would begin each day with 15 points. Each time you have to signal the student that she is out of her seat, she loses a point. The points remaining at the end

of each day are applied toward the reinforcer the student is striving to earn.

d. A lottery system might be more effective with a primary level student. In this type of system, the student would begin each day with tickets in a jar instead of points. All the tickets would have prizes written on them—one would have a big prize, a couple would have moderate prizes, and the majority would have little prizes. Each time you have to give the student the signal, you would remove one ticket from the jar—but neither you nor the student would be allowed to see what is written on it. At the end of each day, the student would draw one ticket from those remaining in the jar, and receives that prize.

e. When the student has accumulated enough points to earn the reward she has chosen, she "spends" the points necessary and the system begins again. That is, she selects another reward to earn and begins with zero points.

If the student is immature, and needs more frequent encouragement, you might consider letting her earn several "less expensive" rewards (e.g., five minutes of computer time after 20 points) on the way to a bigger reward (e.g., one hour with you for 200 points). That is, the student receives the small rewards without spending points; they continue to accumulate toward the selected reward.

f. Determine a consequence (e.g., time owed off of recess or in after-school detention) for each incident of out of seat behavior that occurs after the student has already lost her points (or tickets) for the day. Once the student runs out of points (or tickets), implement the consequence for each subsequent infraction. However, the consequence should not involve taking away a previous day's points. If the student can lose already-earned points, she might develop an attitude of, "I am losing so many points, why should I even bother to try?"

Also implement time owed as a consequence when the student does not respond when you give her the signal (see PLAN A).

 Use reinforcement to encourage appropriate behavior.

a. Give the student increased praise and attention for remaining in her seat (see PLAN A).

b. In addition, show interest and enthusiasm about how the student is doing on the system. "Celine, it is 1:30 and you still have 13 tickets left. This is the best day you have had since we started the system two weeks ago. You should be very proud."

PLAN E

Sometimes there will be a number of students in a class who are frequently in the wrong place at the wrong time. If, at any given moment, several of your students tend to have "location" problems (e.g., being out of their seats, wandering away from the science demonstration), this plan may be appropriate.

 Regularly precorrect the students by prompting them about where they are supposed to be.

Right before each individual activity, clarify your location expectations for the students. This clarification must be specific enough that, if a photograph were taken at any point during the activity, you and the students would be able to easily (and with minimal or no disagreement) identify the total number of students who were not where they were supposed to be at that instant.

2. **Conduct random and objective spot checks to determine which students are in the right place and which are not.**

a. Use some type of system (e.g., beeps from a beeper tape, a timer set to go off periodically) to announce the spot checks throughout the day. Although you want to arrange for the same number of spot checks each day (e.g., 20), the key is for the checks to occur at random and unpredictable times.

(NOTE: Beeper tapes are audio tapes that contain no sounds other than an occasional beep. You can make your own tapes, or purchase them. The Practice Skill Mastery Program contains a set of six beeper tapes, each with a specific number of beeps per hour, and step-by-step instructions for using the tapes for a variety of objectives. Contact:

Mastery Programs, Ltd.
P.O. Box 90
Logan, Utah 94231

b. Explain to the students that whenever they hear the sound they are to freeze right where they are. Then, together, you and the students will identify how many students are not where they are supposed to be. Let the students know that you will be assigning a mild consequence, such as one minute owed off of recess, to any student who does not freeze at the sound of the beep/timer.

Keep a card in your pocket or on a clipboard and record the number of "in-the-wrong-location" students at the time of each spot check. Each day, add the results from all the spot checks to determine that day's total. If you choose, you can post a graph or chart on a chalkboard or on a bulletin board and publicly record each day's total at the end of the day.

3. *After two to three days of recording information from the spot checks, establish a structured reinforcement system.*

a. Have the class brainstorm a number of class-wide reinforcement ideas that they might like to earn. Eliminate any that are inappropriate, and assign "prices" (in points) for the remainder (see PLAN D). Then have the class select the reinforcer they would like to work for first.

b. Either by yourself, or with the class as a whole, set a goal for reducing the daily number of students inappropriately out of their seats. For example, if the class has been averaging 95

incidents per day, the daily goal might be to keep the number of incidents to under 80. Then if the daily total is less than 80, the class would earn five points plus however many less than 80 incidents occurred that day, for example. So, if the class total was 61 for the day, they would earn 24 points (80-61=19+5=24).

Each week, calculate the class' average and set a new goal for the following week. Once the class has earned its first reinforcer, have them select another item from their original list and begin the process over again.

c. Identify a consequence to be used with individual students who are out of their seats after the day's goal has already been exceeded. That is, if the class has a goal of 80, and there have been 81 incidents after only 16 of the 20 spot checks, the students have little incentive to try to be where they are supposed to be for the remaining four spot checks. A policy of assigning one minute of time owed off of recess to each student who is out of place in subsequent spot checks is reasonable.

4. *Use reinforcement to encourage appropriate behavior.*

Praise individual students who are where they are supposed to be at the time of the spot checks. Especially watch for opportunities to praise those students who have had problems with being inappropriately out of their seats. As the class-wide total of incidents decreases, praise the class as a whole. In addition, show enthusiasm about the reinforcement system and excitement about the group's progress.

· · · · · · · ·
Suggested Steps for Developing and Implementing a Plan

The following steps are designed to help you develop an appropriate intervention plan and implement it effectively, whether you choose to use one of the MODEL PLANS or create a customized plan of your own. The steps are, however, suggestions—they are not intended to be followed rigidly or in any particular order. Use your professional judgment and the knowledge of your particular situation to make them work for you.

1. *Make sure you have enough information about the situation.*

a. If a minimal intervention like PLAN A will be sufficient, you probably already have enough information to proceed. However, when a more involved plan seems necessary, you should

consider collecting additional descriptive and/or objective information for a couple of days.

b. Since students being out of their seats is not a problem in and of itself (all students get out of their seats several times per day), you must identify what aspects of the target student's behavior make it inappropriate. That is, does the problem involve when, how often, or how long the student is out of her seat and/or what the student does when she is out of her seat? Anecdotal notes on actual incidents can provide enough detail to help you define the problem behavior thoroughly.

To collect anecdotal notes, simply keep a card in your pocket or on a clipboard and occasionally make notes on specific instances when the student is inappropriately out of her seat. For each entry, briefly describe when the behavior occurred, what the student was doing when she was out of her seat, and any other relevant observations (e.g., what prompted the behavior). You do not need to take notes every time the student gets out of her seat inappropriately; the idea is to capture a range of examples of the misbehavior so that you will be able to describe it completely.

Also, include some notes on times when the student is out of her seat for legitimate reasons—this will make it clear that you are not only aware of her problem behavior, but also recognize when she behaves appropriately. When you meet with the student, the positive examples will also help you clarify how you want the student to behave.

c. In addition to information on what the student's inappropriate behavior looks like, it can also be useful to document how often it occurs (i.e., a frequency count) and/or how long it lasts (i.e., the duration time). Either or both measurements will provide a more complete picture of the problem and an objective way to monitor the student's progress. You can use the same card on which you are collecting anecdotal notes to keep a frequency count—simply write a tally mark on the card each time the student gets out of her seat inappropriately.

You might want to code these tallies to discern whether the behavior occurs more frequently during certain times, subjects, or activities (e.g., using an "A" or "P" to indicate that the incident happened in the morning or afternoon; or clustering the tallies by math or reading, teacher directed instruction or independent work, etc.).

If you are concerned because the student's behavior lasts a long time and/or wastes class time, you may wish to record duration time in addition to (or rather than) the frequency count. To record the duration time, mentally note the time whenever the student gets out of her seat inappropriately and also the time when she gets back to her seat. Write the difference (in the number of minutes) next to (or in place of) the tally mark on the card. At the end of the day, calculate the total number of minutes spent out of her seat.

d. If the student notices what you are doing and asks about it, be straightforward—tell her that you are collecting information to see whether her wandering around is a problem that needs to be worked on.

The following example shows anecdotal notes, as well as a frequency count and duration time information that have been collected on a student's out of seat behavior.

Celine's Out of Seat Behavior—10/13

(Time indicates number of minutes out of seat after I gave her the signal.)

Morning	Afternoon
1 minute	5 minutes
7 minutes	8 minutes
1 minute	6 minutes
a few seconds	4 minutes
5 minutes	

Total minutes for day: 37+

Number of times signal given: 9

Notes:

9:10—She should be working on her conservation assignment. Went to sharpen her pencil but visits, wanders, looks at the bulletin board on her way back to her seat (7 minutes).

2:15—Stayed working with her cooperative group for 20 minutes.

2:35—She leaves her group and goes to listen to another group, then wanders around and looks out the window, then browses through some books on the shelf. Returns to her seat when the group work is over (6 minutes).

---

e. The frequency and duration time information are fairly easy to summarize on a chart or graph. Seeing how often and/or how much time she is out of her seat may help the student and her parent(s) better understand your concern. (NOTE: If you collect both frequency and duration time information, chart them separately as one may improve faster than the other. For example, the number of incidents may remain *about the same, while the total number of minutes spent out of her seat decreases dramatically.)*

f. Continuing to collect this type of information and keeping the chart(s) up-to-date while you implement a plan will help you to monitor whether the situation is getting worse, staying the same, or getting better.

2. Identify a focus for the intervention and labels for referring to the appropriate and inappropriate behaviors.

a. To be effective, the intervention must address more than just reducing the inappropriate out of seat behavior—there must also be an emphasis on increasing some positive behavior or trait (e.g., staying in her assigned work space). Having a specific positive behavior in mind will make it easier for you to "catch" and reinforce the student for behaving appropriately.

In addition, a positive focus allows you to frame the situation more productively. If you say that "the student has a problem with wandering around," you don't provide the student or her parent(s) with any useful information, and may put them on the defensive. However, if you explain that you want to help the student "learn to stay in her assigned work space," you present an important, and reasonable, goal for the student to work toward and clearly identify what the student needs to do to be successful.

b. Specifying labels for the appropriate and inappropriate behaviors (e.g., "staying in her assigned work space" and "being out of her seat," respectively) will help you to use consistent vocabulary when discussing the situation with the student. If you sometimes refer to the inappropriate behavior as "wandering around" and other times tell the student that she "is not where she is supposed to be," she may not realize that you are talking about the same thing—inappropriately being out of her seat.

3. Determine when and how to include the parent(s).

a. If the problem has just begun and is not interfering with the student's academic or social progress, it is not necessary to contact the student's parent(s). However, it might be a good idea to take advantage of any scheduled activities (e.g., conferences, weekly notes home) to let them know of your concern.

b. If the problem is more severe and/or has lasted for a week or more, contact the student's parent(s). Share with them any information you have collected about the behavior (e.g., anecdotal notes, frequency count, duration time), and explain why you are concerned. Focus in particular on how the behavior is hindering the student academically and/or socially (e.g., she is out of her seat so often she is having trouble staying focused on her work).

You might ask if the parent(s) have any insight into the situation and/or whether they have noticed similar behavior at home. Whether or not the parent(s) perceive a problem, explain that you want to help the student "learn to stay in her assigned work space," and invite them to join you for an initial meeting with the student to develop a plan. If the parent(s) are unable or unwilling to participate, let them know that you will keep them informed of the student's progress.

c. Once the parent(s) have been involved in any way, you should give them updates at least once per week while the plan is being implemented.

4. Prepare for, then conduct, an initial meeting about the situation.

a. Arrange for a meeting to discuss your concerns with the student and anyone else who might be involved in the plan (e.g., the parent[s]). Although the specifics will vary depending upon the age of the student and the severity of the problem, there are some general guidelines to consider when scheduling the meeting.

First, conduct the meeting at a neutral time (i.e., not immediately after a problem has occurred), when emotions are less likely to hamper communication. In general, a day's notice is appropriate, however a primary age student may worry excessively and/or forget what the meeting is about if it is scheduled more than an hour before it takes place.

Second, make sure the meeting will be appropriately private. With a primary student who has a mild problem, you might meet in the classroom while the other students are working independently. However, when dealing with a middle/junior high school student and the student's parent(s), you will need some place private (e.g., the counselor's office) to ensure that the discussion will not be overheard.

Third, try to schedule the meeting for a time and place that it is not likely to be interrupted. Finally, when the parent(s) will be participating, they should be the ones to tell the student about the meeting.

b. Construct a preliminary plan. Decide whether you think you can use one of the MODEL PLANS or if you need to create a customized plan using components from various plans and/or of your own design. Although you will invite and encourage the student to help you develop the plan during the initial meeting, having a proposed plan in mind before you meet can alleviate frustration and wasted time if the student is unwilling or unable to participate.

c. Review the information you have collected and carefully consider how you would like the student to behave. Then prepare thorough descriptions of both the inappropriate behavior and the positive behavior/trait on which the student will be working. The more concrete you can be and the more specific examples you include, the easier it will be for you to clarify (and for the student to understand) your expectations. Be sure to identify the expected behaviors for all relevant activities (e.g., independent work periods, teacher directed instruction, unstructured class times, recess and lunch, etc.).

d. Conduct the meeting in an atmosphere of collaboration. The following agenda is one way you might structure the meeting:

- **Share your concerns about the student's behavior.**

  Describe the problem behavior and, if applicable, show the student the chart(s) of how often/how long she engages in it. Then explain why you consider the wandering around to be a problem. You might tell the student that an inability to stay in one's assigned space is a bad work habit that could cause problems later in school or on a job.

- **Discuss how you can work together to improve the situation.**

  Tell the student that you would like to help her "learn to stay in her assigned work space," and describe your preliminary plan. Invite the student to give you input on the various aspects of the plan, and together work out any necessary details (e.g., the signal, time owed, etc.). You may have to brainstorm different possibilities if the student is uncomfortable with the initial plan. Incorporating any of the student's suggestions that strengthen the plan is likely to increase her sense of "ownership" in and commitment to it.

- **Make sure the student understands what you mean by appropriate and inappropriate behavior.**

  Using the descriptions you have prepared, define and clarify what you mean by the appropriate and inappropriate behavior as specifically and thoroughly as you can. To ensure the student's understanding, you might present hypothetical scenarios and have her identify whether each is an example of staying in one's assigned work space or being out of one's seat. Or you might have the student describe the times when it would be okay for her to leave her assigned work space (e.g., getting out of her seat when you give the class an instruction to line up for recess).

- **Conclude the meeting.**

  Always end the meeting with words of encouragement. Let the student know that you are confident that she can be successful. Be sure to reinforce her for participating in the meeting.

 Give the student regular, ongoing feedback about her behavior.

It is important to meet with the student periodically to discuss her progress. In most cases, three to five minutes once per week should suffice. *(NOTE: PLANS B, D, and E suggest daily meetings.)* During the meetings, review any information that has been collected and discuss whether or not the situation is getting better. As much as possible, focus on the student's improvements, however, also address any new or continuing problems. As the situation improves, the meetings can be faded to once every other week and then to once per month.

 Evaluate the situation (and the plan).

Implement any plan for at least two weeks before deciding whether to change plans; to continue, modify, or fade the plan you are using; or to cease the intervention. Generally, if the student's behavior is clearly improving (based on the objective information that's been collected and/or the subjective perceptions of yourself, the student, and possibly the parent[s]), stick with what you are doing. If the situation has remained the same or worsened, some kind of change will be necessary. Always discuss any changes to the plan with the student first.

PARTICIPATION IN CLASS, LACK OF

Not Answering Questions

Not Joining in Discussions

DESCRIPTION

You have a student who avoids voluntarily participating in classroom activities (e.g., he does not volunteer during teacher directed instruction; he hardly ever joins in during cooperative group activities).

GOAL

The student will begin taking an appropriately active role in classroom activities.

OVERVIEW OF PLANS

- PLAN A: For a problem that has just begun or occurs infrequently.
- PLAN B: For a student whose problem may stem from being insecure or afraid of making mistakes.
- PLAN C: For a student who fails to participate in order to gain attention or exert power.
- PLAN D: For a student who does not realize how infrequently he participates.
- PLAN E: For a student who has developed a habit of not participating.
- PLAN F: For a class with several students who choose not to participate.

Alternative Problems

- **Apathetic Behavior**
- **Bored Behavior**
- **Compliance/Direction Following, Lack of**
- **Daydreaming**
- **Passive Resistance**
- **Shyness/Withdrawn Behavior**
- **Work Completion— Daily Work**

········

General Considerations

- The focus of this problem is a student who does not voluntarily participate in teacher directed instruction and/or class discussions. However, the six plans could be modified for a student (or students) who does not participate in cooperative groups or other type of classroom activity. *(NOTE: For a student who does not participate during independent work periods, also see* **Distractibility/Short Attention Span**.*)*

- You might also want to examine the INDEX of this reference guide. If you find a title (or titles) that more specifically describes what the student does when he is not participating, read through the plans for that specific problem. For example, if the student is being disruptive when he is not participating, **Disruptive Behavior—Moderate** may be appropriate. If the student refuses to follow direct instructions (e.g., "Everyone come over to the lab tables for a demonstration."), you might find more appropriate plans in **Compliance/ Direction Following, Lack of**.

- If the student's problem behavior stems in any way from academic issues (e.g., the student is unable to meet the academic expectations and thus chooses not to participate out of frustration), concurrent efforts must be made to ensure his academic success (see **Academic Deficits, Determining**).

- If you suspect that the lack of participation could be related to the student being depressed, see **Depression**. This problem includes a set of questions to help you decide whether the student should be referred for counseling or psychological services.

- If the inappropriate behavior is resulting in the student avoiding or not completing his schoolwork, consider beginning with a plan to increase the student's work completion (see **Work Completion—Daily Work**). Once the student is turning in completed work on a regular basis, you can consider an intervention for lack of participation in teacher directed activities, if the problem still exists.

- If the student is extremely shy, the intervention should involve little or no pressure—only gentle encouragement. Be very careful that the plan includes nothing that will traumatize a student who is fearful of speaking in public. (For additional suggestions, see **Shyness/Withdrawn Behavior**.)

- If the student seems to have extreme problems with self-confidence, consider implementing one or more of the plans for boosting the student's confidence (see **Self-Concept Problems**) along with the intervention for lack of participation.

········

Model Plans

PLAN A

It is not always necessary, or even beneficial, to use an involved plan. If the situation has just begun or occurs infrequently (e.g., has only been a problem for a week or two), the following actions, along with making the student aware of your concerns, may resolve the situation.

 Define exactly what aspect(s) of the student's behavior must be improved.

a. "Participation" is a broad and inclusive descriptor. Narrowing the focus to one or two observable behaviors will insure that you and the student have the same expectations about what aspect(s) of his behavior must be improved. Make the expectations realistic in order to avoid putting undue pressure on the student initially.

b. Review the expectations with the student during your initial meeting (see SUGGESTED STEPS FOR DEVELOPING AND IMPLEMENTING A PLAN), and also provide the expectations in writing for the student. You may wish to use the following sample as a model, although your actual definition should reflect your particular classroom expectations and the student's individual behavior.

Saul's Participation Expectations

1. During class discussions in social studies, Saul will raise his hand at least once, wait to be called on, then contribute his thought or opinion.

2. During teacher directed instruction in math, Mr. Ahlberg will call on Saul to answer a question or work a problem. Saul will *not* say, "I don't know," and will answer the question. (Mistakes are okay—that is how we all learn.)

3. At any other time during the day when Saul wants to contribute or answer a question, he is encouraged to do so.

---

2. *Respond consistently to the lack of participation.*

a. Whenever the student does not meet the identified expectations for voluntary participation, privately provide a gentle verbal correction at the end of the instructional period. "Saul, you did not raise your hand to contribute to our discussion in social studies. Was there a time when you thought you could have presented an idea or added to our discussion? That would have been an excellent contribution. Tomorrow, I expect you to raise your hand at least once."

b. If the student does not respond to a direct question or answers, "I don't know," tell him that you will come back to him with the same question in a minute or two and that he should have an answer prepared at that time. If, when you ask the student the question again, he still does not participate, do not make an issue of it—go on to another student. However, if this happens more than a few times, the problem should no longer be considered a mild one, and you should develop a more involved intervention plan to help the student learn to participate (see PLANS B through E).

3. *Use reinforcement to encourage participation.*

a. Give the student increased praise. In particular, watch closely during the specific time periods in which you have established minimum expectations for the student. When the student volunteers or answers a question, reinforce the student's participation. "Saul, thanks for contributing, I am going to put that down on our list of ideas."

However, avoid reacting too positively to the student's participation. An overreaction may draw the other students' attention to the fact that the student does not often participate. Simply thank the student for participating and then respond to the content of what the student said.

If the student's contribution was correct, particularly creative, or otherwise positive, let him know. If the student's response was incorrect, reinforce him for contributing, and correct the error or misconception in a way that does not embarrass or intimidate the student.

Also give the student immediate feedback about what he should do differently. "Saul, thanks for answering that question. When you are working a problem like this, you need to remember to . . . ." However, do not correct the error by asking the student the same question again (e.g., "Saul, try that problem one more time and see if you can get it right."), as this focuses everyone's attention on the student when he does not know how to do something.

b. After an instructional period in which the student has participated, privately praise the student for having contributed. This avoids making a public issue of the student's problem with participation. "Saul, could I speak to you over here for a minute? You should be proud of the contribution you made to our brainstorming session in social studies. You added a very creative idea to our list. If you hadn't contributed, that idea probably would not have been on the list. Thanks for sharing your idea with the class. We value your contribution."

c. Give the student frequent attention (e.g., say "hello" to him as he enters the classroom, walk next to him on the way to the cafeteria, and occasionally ask him to assist you with a class job that needs to be done) and praise him for other positive behaviors he exhibits (e.g., the accuracy of his work or the creativity of an art project). This will show the student that you notice many positive things he does, not just that he is making more of an effort to participate.

PLAN B

Sometimes a student does not participate in class because he does not know how to participate or is insecure and afraid of being embarrassed or making mistakes. This plan rests on your ability to create an unintimidating environment for participation, and on directly teaching the student that participation is not a threatening experience.

1. *Define exactly what aspect(s) of the student's behavior must be improved (see PLAN A).*

2. *Create a classroom atmosphere in which participation is not threatening.*

a. Speaking in front of their peers can be a very threatening experience for some students. In fact, there is a good chance that several of your students feel uncomfortable about speaking in front of the class. You can reduce your students' anxiety and possibly increase the participation of several of your more quiet or shy students by continually emphasizing the importance of participation.

The following concepts/phrases might serve as the basis for class-wide reminders to alleviate some of the threatening aspects of participation:

- If you don't practice, you can never improve. (Sports examples may be useful.)

- Class participation is one way to practice learning new skills and concepts. You can't learn if you don't try.

- Don't be afraid to make a mistake or give a wrong answer. Mistakes are okay. Making mistakes is a very important part of how everyone learns.

- There are no dumb questions. Whenever you have a question, ask!

- In this class, we never laugh at someone when they ask a question or contribute to a class lesson.

- Everyone has an obligation to the other members of this class to contribute ideas and to ask questions.

b. Another way to alleviate the pressure of class participation is to ask questions in nonthreatening ways. Directing a question to a single individual is potentially very intimidating. (e.g., "Saul, please tell us . . . .") as the student knows that everyone is looking at him as he tries to think of a response to the question. Two less

threatening ways of asking classroom questions follow:

- Ask questions in a manner that demands whole group responses. One way is to request choral responses (all the students respond verbally in unison); another way is to require written responses (e.g., "Everybody number a paper from one to three. Let's take a practice quiz.") which you could then check at a later time.

- When you are asking a manner for an individual student to answer, state the question, prompt everyone in the class to prepare an answer, then assign the question to a single student. With this type of question asking, everyone in the class develops a response, and the student selected is not singled out before he/she has had an opportunity to (hopefully) formulate a response.

3. *(OPTIONAL)*
If necessary and appropriate, conduct lessons to teach the student how to participate.

a. Review your expectations for student participation and ask yourself if the student has all the skills necessary to meet those expectations. If not, identify which skills are deficient and develop short, individual lessons in which the student can learn and practice the necessary skills. Skills you might want to address include: raising your hand and waiting to be called on; speaking loudly enough to be heard; speaking slowly and distinctly; staying calm when people are looking at you as you speak; and telling yourself that it is okay to make a mistake.

b. Begin each lesson by reviewing some or all of the participation concepts you have been teaching the whole class (see Step 2). Then, model the specific skill(s) you want the student to practice, such as speaking loudly enough to be heard. Have the student try the skill himself and give him feedback.

Once the student successfully demonstrates mastery of the skill during the lesson, practice with a specific question that you will present to him later that day (or the next day). Practice the entire sequence, from the signal (see Step 5), the question, and the student's response. Continue to practice with this question until the student has been successful at least three or four times.

c. These lessons should occur at least twice per week and should involve just you and the student (perhaps while the other students are at recess). The lessons needn't last more than three to five minutes, and it is important that they be handled in a matter-of-fact manner so the student does not feel undue pressure. Continue the lessons until the student is consistently using the practiced skills in class.

4. *Structure successful experiences for the student.*

a. Either during the lesson or during a short private conversation with the student, give him advance notice of the question(s) you plan to ask him that day (see Step 3), and make sure that he knows the answer(s). If necessary, provide the question(s) and the answer(s) on a card and let the student know that he can keep the card in his notebook or in his desk so that right before the lesson begins, he can review it to bolster his confidence.

b. Give the student advance notice of a discussion topic or question about which he might volunteer to contribute. For example, right before a career education lesson, inform the student that one activity that will occur during the lesson is a brainstorming session on what types of jobs require a college education. By giving the student advance notice, he has extra time to formulate possible responses. "Saul, what are some jobs that you think you could mention during the brainstorming? Excellent, teacher, doctor, and veterinarian all require a college education. As soon as we begin the brainstorming, raise your hand and when I call on you, share one or more of those ideas. Don't wait to raise your hand, though. If you wait too long, someone else might mention those things. By the way, if you think of others as we continue, raise your hand again and add some more to the list."

c. After a week or so of successful participation, modify the procedure so that you are giving the student advance notice of the question or topic, but not rehearsing the student's response. "Saul, today I am going to make it a little bit harder. A topic we are going to discuss is . . . ."

Think about possible things you could contribute to that discussion, but don't tell me now. I want to wait to hear your ideas until we get into the discussion. So get a few ideas ready for when we have that discussion later today."

5. *Use a signal to cue the student that you are going to ask the question or present the discussion topic that you informed him about earlier.*

During your initial meeting with the student (see SUGGESTED STEPS FOR DEVELOPING AND IMPLEMENTING A PLAN), agree upon a signal that only you and the student will understand for letting him know that now is the time to be ready to contribute or answer a question. Possible signals include tugging your ear, making eye contact with the student and nodding, or a specific phrase used to introduce the question. For example, you might use the phrase, "Class, this is very interesting question," to introduce a question presented to the whole class, give everyone thinking time, and then assign the target student to answer the question. Thus, during the time when you are stating the question and giving all the students in the class time to think, the target student knows that you will be assigning the question to him.

6. *Respond consistently to the lack of participation.*

If the student does not volunteer when he should have, provide a gentle verbal correction to the student privately at the end of the instructional period. If the student does not respond to a direct question, let him know you will come back to him with the same question in a moment (see PLAN A). Also use these nonparticipation situations as examples for the one-to-one lessons with the student the next day, if appropriate (see Step 4).

7. *Use reinforcement to encourage participation.*

a. Give the student frequent praise and attention for participation (see PLAN A).

b. Make sure the student realizes that you notice his efforts to use the skills he has been learning/practicing. "Saul, you did a beautiful job of participating in class. When I gave the signal, I saw you take a big, deep breath to calm yourself, you thought about the question, and when I called on you, you spoke in a clear and confident voice. Did you feel as confident as you sounded?"

PLAN C

Some students are very skilled at gaining attention through their negative behavior. Even a student who does not overtly seem to like the attention may be trying to satisfy a need for adult attention through his passivity. If you find yourself frequently nagging, reminding, or coaxing the student to participate in class, you will want to instead make sure that the student receives more frequent and more satisfying attention for participating in class than for passively doing nothing.

1. **Define exactly what aspect(s) of the student's behavior must be improved (see PLAN A).**

2. **Create a classroom atmosphere in which participation is not threatening (see PLAN B).**

3. **Respond consistently to the lack of participation.**

a. Because you need to teach the student that he will not be able to prompt people to nag and pay attention to him by not participating, most of the time you will want to ignore the student's behavior when he is not participating. Make sure the student is still responsible for getting his work done, but if he is not participating in class discussions or answering questions, ignore this passivity. While ignoring, do not look at the student or talk to him. Do not act disgusted or impatient with his behavior. Simply interact in positive ways with students who are behaving well and who are participating.

Try to conduct your lessons in a fast paced, reinforcing way so that the students who are participating are having fun. As soon as the target student begins to participate (even nonverbally, such as writing answers when you present a practice quiz to the class), pay attention to him. Make eye contact and let the student know that you are aware of his participation, but make no reference to his previous lack of participation.

b. If other students in the class give the target student attention when he is not participating (e.g., trying to get him to join in the lesson or expressing concern that the student should be made to participate), give them a gentle verbal correction. "Pablo and Russell, Saul can take care of himself and he will participate in the lesson when he is ready. It would be best to let him work it out on his own." In addition to the correction, also reinforce other students for their participation.

4. **Use reinforcement to encourage participation.**

a. Frequent praise and attention is the core of this plan. The student must see that he receives more frequent and more satisfying attention for behaving responsibly than for not participating. Therefore, whenever the student participates, make an effort to praise him. "Saul, you have an excellent point. Class I had not considered it, but Saul pointed out that . . . ."

In addition, praise the student for other responsible behaviors he exhibits. "Saul, thanks for taking care of organizing those shelves. You are very dependable. Whenever I ask you to help with something in class, I know it will get done."

b. You may also wish to use intermittent rewards to celebrate the student's success. Occasional, and unexpected, rewards can motivate the student to demonstrate responsible behavior more often. When the student has demonstrated improvements in participation, provide a reward.

Appropriate rewards may include a note home to his parent(s), a chance to tell a former teacher about his improved participation, or a note from you that the student finds in his desk. *(NOTE: A list of additional reinforcement ideas can be found in APPENDIX 1.)* If you do provide intermittent rewards, do so more frequently at the beginning of the intervention to encourage the student, and then less often as the student's behavior improves over time.

5. **Ensure a 3-1 ratio of positive to negative attention.**

a. When attention is a motivating force for the student, it is important to make sure that you are giving him *three times as much* positive as negative attention. You can do this by monitoring your interactions with the student at least one day per week. Simply keep a card on a clipboard or in your pocket and record each interaction you have with the student as either positive or negative by writing a "+" or a "-", respectively, on the card.

To determine whether an interaction is positive or negative, ask yourself whether the student was behaving responsibly or irresponsibly at the time the interaction occurred. Interactions that are the result of the student behaving inappropriately are negative, and any interaction that occurs while the student is meeting classroom expectations is positive. Thus, reprimanding the student (e.g., reminding him to get back to work on an assignment) is a negative interaction, while praising the student for his participation is positive. Greeting the student as he enters the room or asking him if he has any questions during independent work periods are also considered positive interactions. *(NOTE: Ignoring the student's lack of participation is not recorded at all, because it is not an interaction.)*

b. If you find that you are not giving the student three times as much positive as negative attention, try to increase the number of positive interactions you have with the student. Sometimes prompts can help. For example, you might decide that each time the student enters the classroom you will say "hello" to him that during each independent work period you will praise him for being on task, or that any time the student raises his hand to participate you will praise him. You can also increase the ratio of positive to nega-

tive attention by ignoring more of the student's inappropriate behavior.

6. *If the student seems to be defiant in his lack of participation (e.g., "Make me participate in class!"), ignore the power struggle, but arrange an opportunity for the student to experience a sense of power in a responsible way.*

The best way to do so is to give the student an important job or responsibility within the school that he would enjoy performing. For example, the student could be assigned the job of helping to do routine maintenance in the school's computer lab. *(NOTE: APPENDIX 2 contains a list of jobs that could be used to foster student responsibility.)*

The goal is for the student to experience the pleasure of holding a powerful (yet responsible) position—thus reducing his need to demonstrate his personal power through passivity. Being allowed to perform the job should not be made contingent upon class participation. Whether or not he participates in class, the student should be allowed to perform his job whenever regularly scheduled. If the job were to be made contingent on participation, the student would probably sabotage his own success as a way of demonstrating his personal power (e.g., "I don't care if I don't get to go to the computer lab. You can't make me participate.").

PLAN D

Sometimes a student does not even realize how seldom he participates in class. If this is the case, the objective of the intervention should focus on helping the student become more aware of his own behavior. This plan may also be appropriate if the student occasionally does participate, but not as frequently as you feel he can or should.

1. *Define exactly what aspect(s) of the student's behavior must be improved (see PLAN A).*

2. *Create a classroom atmosphere in which participation is not threatening (see PLAN B).*

3. *Help the student to monitor and evaluate his level of class participation.*

a. Decide whether the student will self-monitor his own participation or whether you will do the monitoring for him. When appropriate, it will be more effective to have the student keep a card on his desk or in his notebook and mark the card each time he meets the expectations for class

participation (e.g., voluntarily participating or answering a question posed by you). If the plan then goes so well that you cannot call on the student each time he raises his hand to contribute (i.e., because he is voluntarily contributing frequently), you may wish to have the student keep separate counts of the number of times he raises his hand to volunteer and the number of times he is actually called on or asked a question.

Following is a sample self-monitoring form that could be used by the student to record his level of participation.

Participation Record

Name Saul

Behavior to Be Counted: Each time you
your hand to volunteer, circle a number in
the top group. Each time you are called on,
circle a number in the bottom group.

Date _____

Times I raised my hand to volunteer:

    1 2 3 4 5 6 7 8

    9 10 11 12 13 14 15 16

    17 18 19 20 21 22 23 24

Times I was called on and I participated:

    1 2 3 4 5 6 7 8

    9 10 11 12 13 14 15 16

    17 18 19 20 21 22 23 24

*(NOTE: Repeat four more times so that this
form can be used for a week.)*

Participation Evaluation Record

Name _____

Date _____

Rating Scale

  0 Did not participate verbally and did not
      take notes

  3 Participated verbally at least once, but
      did not take notes

  6 Took notes, but did not participate ver-
      bally

  9 Participated verbally at least once and
      took notes

For each subject, circle the number that best
describes your level of participation.

    Subject: _____

          0   3   6   9

    Subject:_____

          0   3   6   9

If student self-monitoring is not appropriate (e.g., the student would be too embarrassed to self-monitor, or inaccurate), you should monitor the student's level of participation yourself. In either case, the key is for the student to be aware of each occurrence of participation during the day and to know that each instance of participation is being recorded. Even when the student self-monitors, you should keep your own record approximately one day per week to verify the student's accuracy.

b. If the nature of your participation expectations makes them difficult to count, establish an alternate system in which the student evaluates the quality of his participation at the end of each instructional period. For example, if the participation expectations include occasional verbal participation plus taking notes, the student could evaluate his performance at the conclusion of each instructional period with a scale like the sample shown.

(NOTE: Repeat as many times as necessary to rate all the relevant instructional periods.)

4. **Review the record with the student daily.**

a. Each day, meet with the student for a few minutes to examine his participation record.

Have the student chart the number of instances of participation (and, if appropriate, the number of times he raised his hand to volunteer but was not called on). Then discuss whether the day was better, worse, or about the same as previous days. If the student did not participate well that day, encourage the student to talk about why. Have the student identify things he can do the next day to help himself remember to participate more frequently.

If the student behaves passively during the meeting, keep the interaction very short. Just make sure the information is charted, and let the student know that you are sure tomorrow will be a better day. As much as possible, make these meetings upbeat and encouraging—you want the student to look forward to these daily review sessions.

b. If the student is rating the quality of his participation, rather than keeping a frequency count, discuss the rating for each instructional period at the end of that period, if possible. If this is not reasonable, arrange to discuss several instructional periods (or all of the periods at once) at the end of each day.

5. *Respond consistently to the lack of participation.*

Ignore the student's lack of participation during class (see PLAN C). Instead wait until the end-of-the-day review meetings to discuss with the student the lack of participation.

6. *Use reinforcement to encourage participation.*

a. Give the student frequent praise and attention for participation (see PLAN A).

b. Praise the student during the end-of-the-day review meetings for accurate self-monitoring/recording (if applicable) and for being willing to look at the cumulative record for the day. Even on a bad day, if the student is willing to chart the data and discuss why it was a bad day, praise

him. "Saul, you are really handling this responsibly. Even though it was not a very successful day, you are willing to talk to me about things you might do differently to increase your participation tomorrow. You should be proud of your participation during this meeting."

7. *Encourage the student to use self-reinforcement.*

Whenever things are going well (i.e., more participation than usual), prompt the student to silently reinforce himself. "Saul, this has been a very successful morning. Silently tell yourself that you have made important contributions to our class discussions today." Encourage the student to self-reinforce himself in this manner intermittently throughout the day and during the end-of-the-day review meetings.

PLAN E

Once a behavior (even a passive behavior) becomes a habit, it tends to be more difficult to change. If your student's lack of participation in class is long-standing, and/or the student does not seem to care about improving his behavior, you may need to implement a structured system of external incentives (i.e., rewards and consequences) based on his behavior to motivate the student to participate in class.

1. *Define exactly what aspect(s) of the student's behavior must be improved (see PLAN A).*

2. *Create a classroom atmosphere in which participation is not threatening (see PLAN B).*

3. *Help the student to monitor and evaluate his level of class participation or, if more appropriate, to rate the quality of his participation (see PLAN D).*

4. *Establish a structured system for reinforcing the appropriate behavior and providing a consequence for the inappropriate behavior.*

a. With the student, create a list of reinforcers that he can earn. Although you might want to have some suggestions in mind, the system will be more effective if the student identifies most of the items or activities himself. *(NOTE: A list of reinforcement ideas can be found in APPENDIX 1.)*

b. Assign "prices" (in points) for each of the rewards on the list and have the student select the reward he would like to earn first.

The prices should be based on the instructional, personnel, and/or monetary costs of the items. Monetary cost is clear—the more expensive the item, the more points required to earn it. Instructional cost refers to the amount of instructional time lost or interfered with by a particular reward. Thus, an activity which causes the student to miss part of academic instruction should require more points than one the student can do on his own free time. Personnel cost involves the time required by you and/or other staff to fulfill the reinforcer. Having lunch with the principal, therefore, would cost more points than spending five minutes of free time with a friend.

c. Design a system in which the student earns points for each instance of participation. One possibility is for the student to earn one point for each time he raises his hand to volunteer and three points for each time he is called on by you and contributes. At the end of each day, examine the student's self-monitoring form and assist him in figuring out how many points he earned that day.

Alternately, if the student is rating the quality of his participation rather than keeping a frequency count, you can translate the ratings into points. For example, the student could earn zero to nine points possible for each instructional period. At the end of each day, assist the student in determining the total points earned that day and add them to the points the student has earned on previous days.

d. When the student has accumulated enough points to earn the reward he has chosen, he "spends" the points necessary and the system begins again. That is, he selects another reward to earn and begins with zero points.

If the student is immature, and needs more frequent encouragement, you might consider letting him earn several "less expensive" rewards (e.g., five minutes of computer time after 20 points) on the way to a bigger reward (e.g., one hour with you for 200 points). That is, the student receives the small rewards without spending points; they continue to accumulate toward the big reward.

5. *Use reinforcement to encourage participation.*

a. Give the student increased praise and attention for participation (see PLAN A).

b. In addition, show interest and enthusiasm about how the student is doing on the system. "Saul, you have been volunteering so much and participating so well, you are accumulating points very rapidly. You should be proud of the improvements you are making."

PLAN F

Sometimes there are a number of students in your class who do not participate as frequently as you would like. This plan will be appropriate when more than a few students in your class have problems with participation.

1. *Clarify your expectations for participation as a whole class activity.*

Create a classroom atmosphere in which participation is not threatening, and conduct lessons to teach all the students how to participate in class. See PLAN B for instruction ideas, and adapt the suggestions for whole class instruction.

2. *Provide increased praise and attention to the students for participation (see PLAN A).*

3. *Establish a team competition using a response cost lottery.*

a. Divide the class into equal teams of four to six students. On each team, try to have an equitable number of students who do and do not have problems with participation. Seat each team together (i.e., teammates at the same table or with their desks in clusters). Have each team give themselves a name you can use to refer to them.

b. Have the class brainstorm ideas that they might like their team to be able to earn as a reinforcer. Ideas could include a free homework pass for all team members, leaving for lunch one minute earlier than the rest of the class, or a coupon for an ice cream in the cafeteria for each team member. Have the students develop a list of at least six or seven different ideas and rank them in order of perceived value.

c. Set up a grab bag system. Write the different reinforcers on individual pieces of paper and put these papers in a bag or box. The most valuable items should be written on only one piece of paper. Moderate reinforcers can each be written on two or three slips of paper. This reduces the students' odds of winning the "biggest" reward. After the system has been successful for a couple of weeks, begin adding an increasing number of slips with congratulatory messages only (e.g., "You did great! But no prize today."). This way you can fade the system, but students still have a chance of earning the big prize.

d. Decide how you can award points to the teams for their class participation. One possibility is to award each team a point for each time that everyone on the team raises their hands to volunteer to answer a classroom question. "Everyone on the Terrific Turtles, the Dragons, and the Cool Kids teams all have their hands up. Each of those teams gets a point. Okay, let's see. Deanna, please answer the question."

Another possibility is for you to award each team from zero to four points based on your evaluation of how well the members of that team participated during each instructional period.

e. At the end of the day, have each team write their team name on pieces of paper (tickets) corresponding to the number of participation points the teams earned that day. The more points a team has earned, the greater the odds that they will win the drawing, however, even a team that has only earned one point has a chance to win.

Place all of the tickets in a bowl for a drawing, and draw one ticket. The team whose name is

on the ticket drawn is that day's winner, and a student from that team then gets to draw a slip of paper from the grab bag to see what the team has won.

. . . .

Suggested Steps for Developing and Implementing a Plan

The following steps are designed to help you develop an appropriate intervention plan and implement it effectively, whether you choose to use one of the MODEL PLANS or create a customized plan of your own. The steps are, however, suggestions—they are not intended to be followed rigidly or in any particular order. Use your professional judgment and the knowledge of your particular situation to make them work for you.

 Make sure you have enough information about the situation.

a. If you think a minimal intervention like PLAN A will be sufficient, you may already have enough information to proceed. However, when a more involved plan seems necessary, you should consider collecting additional descriptive and/or objective information for a couple of days.

b. You need to be able to clarify what you mean when you say that "the student has a problem with participation." Anecdotal notes on actual instructional periods should provide enough detail to help you define the problem behavior clearly and completely. To collect anecdotal notes, simply keep a card in your pocket or on a clipboard and occasionally make notes on specific activities in which the student did not participate.

For each entry, briefly describe the activity and what the student actually did. You do not need to take notes every time the student is passive, the idea is to capture a range of examples of the problem so you will be able to describe it completely.

Also include some notes on times when the student does participate (if there are any instances). This will make it clear that you are not only aware of his passive behavior, but also recognize when he sometimes does participate. When you meet with the student, the positive examples will also help you to clarify how you want the student to behave.

c. If the student notices what you are doing and asks about it, be straightforward—tell him that you are collecting information to see whether

his lack of classroom participation is a problem that needs to be worked on.

Following is an example of anecdotal notes that have been collected on a student's lack of participation.

Saul's Lack of Participation—3/9
Notes:
• I had to remind Saul several times to get seated at his group's table for attendance and opening.
• During math, whenever I asked Saul a question, he did not respond. He just shrugged and refused to answer. (This may be my major concern.)
• During the first part of the cooperative group task in science, Saul actively participated with the other students in his group.
• Later in that same cooperative activity, I did have to remind Saul to participate with his cooperative group. When I corrected him, he said nothing and just put his head down on his desk.
• Three other times when I asked Saul a question during instruction or discussions, all he would say is, "I don't know."

d. Continuing to collect anecdotal notes while you implement a plan will help you to monitor whether the situation is getting worse, staying the same, or getting better.

Identify a focus for the intervention and labels for referring to the appropriate and inappropriate behaviors.

a. To be effective, the intervention must focus on increasing some specific aspect of the student's participation. The positive focus also offers a productive way to frame the problem. For example, when you describe the situation simply as "the student does not participate in class," you provide the student (and his parent[s]) with little useful information and may put them on the defensive. However, when you say that you want to help the student "learn to answer questions during lessons," or "contribute his ideas to class discussions," you identify a reasonable and important goal for the student to work toward and let the student know what he needs to do to be successful. Furthermore, having a specific positive behavior in mind will make it easier for you to "catch" and reinforce the student for behaving appropriately.

b. Specifying labels for the appropriate and inappropriate behaviors (e.g., "actively participating by answering questions or contributing ideas" and "not participating," respectively) will help you to use consistent vocabulary when discussing the situation with the student. If you sometimes refer to the inappropriate behavior as "being quiet," and other times tell the student that he is "acting shy," he may not realize that you are talking about the same thing—not participating.

3. **Determine when and how to include the parent(s).**

a. It is not necessary to contact the student's parent(s) if the problem has just begun. However, it might be a good idea to take advantage of any scheduled activities (e.g., conferences, weekly notes home) to let them know of your concern.

b. If the problem with participation has been going on for over a week, contact the student's parent(s). Share with them any information you have collected about the behavior (e.g., your anecdotal notes), and explain why you are concerned. Focus in particular on how the behavior is hindering the student academically (e.g., if the student never participates he may find it difficult to learn the concepts and could begin falling behind).

You might ask if the parent(s) have any insight into the situation and/or whether they have noticed similar behavior at home. Whether or not the parent(s) perceive a problem, explain that you want to help the student "learn to actively participate in class," and invite them to join you for an initial meeting with the student to develop a plan. If the parent(s) are unable or unwilling to participate, let them know that you will keep them informed of the student's progress.

c. Once the parent(s) have been involved in any way, you should give them updates at least once per week while the plan is being implemented.

4. **Prepare for, then conduct, an initial meeting about the situation.**

a. Arrange a meeting to discuss your concerns with the student and anyone else who will be involved in the plan (e.g., the parent[s]). Although the specifics will vary depending upon the age of the student and the severity of the problem, there are some general guidelines to consider when scheduling the meeting. For example, make the meeting appropriately private and make sure the meeting is scheduled for a time and place that it is not likely to be interrupted. Also, if the parent(s) will be participating, they should be the ones to tell the student about the meeting.

b. Construct a preliminary plan. Decide whether you think you can use one of the MODEL PLANS or if you need to create a customized plan using components from various plans and/or of your own design. Although you will invite and encourage the student to help develop the plan during the initial meeting, having a proposed plan in mind before you meet can alleviate frustration and wasted time if the student is unwilling or unable to participate.

c. After reviewing the information you have collected and thinking about how you want the student to behave, prepare thorough descriptions of the inappropriate behavior and the positive behavior/trait on which the student will be working. The more specific you can be and the more concrete examples you have, the easier it will be to clarify (and for the student to understand) your expectations.

d. Conduct the meeting in an atmosphere of collaboration. The following agenda is one way you might structure the meeting:

- **Share your concerns about the student's behavior.**

  Briefly describe the problem behavior and explain why you consider the lack of participation to be a problem. You might tell the student that when a student acts like he doesn't care and refuses to participate, teachers are likely to become frustrated and less inclined to help the student, for example, if he has problems on an assignment from a lesson in which he didn't ask questions or contribute.

- **Discuss how you can work together to improve the situation.**

   Describe your preliminary plan. Invite the student to give you input on the various aspects of the plan, and together work out any necessary details (e.g., the lessons, use of the self-monitoring form, the signal, etc.). You may have to brainstorm different possibilities if the student is uncomfortable with the initial plan. Incorporating any of the student's suggestions that strengthen the plan is likely to increase his sense of "ownership" in and commitment to it.

- **Make sure the student understands what you mean by appropriate and inappropriate behavior.**

   Using your anecdotal notes, make sure the student knows exactly what he does when you feel that he is not participating. Is he doing nothing? is he doodling? is he staring out the window? Then, as specifically as you can, describe the positive behavior the student will be working on or what he needs to do differently to be successful. Provide as much detail as necessary to make sure the student understands your expectations, and verify that the student understands the minimum expectations for participation by having him explain the expectations to you.

- **Conclude the meeting.**

   Always end the meeting with words of encouragement. Let the student know that you are confident that he can be successful, and that he may actually find that he likes school better and feels increasingly confident as he participates more and more. Be sure to reinforce him for participating in the meeting.

5. *Give the student regular, ongoing feedback about his behavior.*

It is important to meet with the student periodically to discuss his progress. In most cases, three to five minutes once per week should suffice. *(NOTE: PLANS D, E, and F suggest daily meetings.)* During the meetings, review any information that has been collected and discuss whether or not the situation is getting better. As much as possible, focus on the student's improvements, however, also address any new or continuing problems. As the situation improves, the meetings can be faded to once every other week and then to once per month.

6. *Evaluate the situation (and the plan).*

Implement any plan for at least two weeks before deciding whether to change plans; to continue, modify, or fade the plan you are using; or to cease the intervention. Generally, if the student's behavior is clearly improving (based on the objective information that's been collected and/or the subjective perceptions of yourself, the student, and possibly the parent[s]), stick with what you are doing. If the situation has remained the same or worsened, some kind of change will be necessary. Always discuss any changes to the plan with the student first.

PASSIVE RESISTANCE

Passive Aggressive Behavior

DESCRIPTION

You have a student whose behavior has lead you to conclude that she is passively resistant.

Because passive resistance is not a discrete behavior, but a label that encompasses many different types of behavior, this problem includes no MODEL PLANS. The purpose of the following information is to suggest an overall approach and some basic considerations for dealing with a student you believe to be exhibiting passive resistant behavior.

Alternative Problems

- **Work Completion—Daily work**
- **Apathetic Behavior**
- **Dawdling**
- **Compliance/Direction Following, Lack of**
- **Homework Issues**
- **Participation In Class, Lack of**

. . . .
General Information

- The key to dealing effectively with a student who engages in passive resistance is to identify one specific inappropriate behavior the student exhibits and begin working on that behavior. That is, once you identify a specific behavior, you can review the information that accompanies that problem in this reference guide and develop an intervention plan to help the student learn to manage that behavior more responsibly.

If you are not clear about what specific things the student does (or doesn't do)—that is, you just have a vague sense that the student is being passive resistant—keep anecdotal notes on the student's behavior for a week or so. This type of documentation is fairly easy to collect—simply keep a card in your pocket or on a clipboard, and whenever the student behaves in a way that you think demonstrates passive resistance, make notes on the incident. Briefly describe the circumstances (where and when the behavior occurred), what the student did (or didn't do), and any other information that seems relevant.

After about a week, review your notes to see if you can determine whether the problem involves mainly lack of compliance, low rates of work completion, or some other specific behavior.

The important thing is to focus your intervention efforts on one problem behavior at a time. Often, as you work on one behavior (e.g., lack of compliance), other problem behaviors (e.g., low rates of work completion) seem to improve without specific intervention.

- In general, a student who exhibits passive resistance is either trying to gain power or has become so discouraged that she has just given up. If the student's behavior tends to make you angry, there is probably a power issue occurring. Therefore, when developing and implementing your intervention, try to avoid power struggle situations. On the other hand, if the student's behavior often makes you feel sorry for her, she may be quite discouraged. Under these circumstances, you will want to ensure that your intervention is designed so that the student experiences frequent success.

PERFECTIONISM

Overachievement

Grade Anxiety

DESCRIPTION

You have a student who thinks that she must get everything right and/or must always receive a good grade.

GOAL

The student will learn to view her mistakes as learning opportunities and to take pride in her work regardless of her grade or how anyone else did.

OVERVIEW OF PLANS

- PLAN A: For a situation in which the problem is relatively mild or has just begun.

- PLAN B: For a student who has trouble accepting and learning from her mistakes.

- PLAN C: For a student who is obsessed with grades rather than doing her best.

- PLAN D: For a student who is unwilling to take risks or attempt challenges for fear of doing poorly or making mistakes.

Alternative Problems

- Competitive, Overly

- Corrected, Student Gets Upset When

General Considerations

- If the perfectionist behavior is resulting in the student avoiding or not completing her schoolwork, begin with a plan to increase the student's work completion (see **Work Completion—Daily Work**). Once the student is turning in completed work on a regular basis, you can consider an intervention for the perfectionism, if the problem still exists.

- If the student's perfectionism seems to be related to a poor self-image (i.e., she thinks she must not only receive good grades, but seems overly hard on herself in many different ways), see **Self-Concept Problems** for ideas that can be implemented in conjunction with one of these plans.

- Be sensitive to the possibility that the student's parent(s) are putting excessive pressure on the student to succeed. When this is the case, attempt to work with the student and her parent(s) to create a balance between perfectionism and more productive attitudes such as having the courage to attempt challenges or doing one's best.

Model Plans

PLAN A

It is not always necessary, or even beneficial, to use an involved plan. If the inappropriate behavior has just begun and/or is relatively mild (i.e., not interfering with the student's academic or social progress), the following actions, along with making the student aware of your concerns, may resolve the situation.

 Respond consistently to the inappropriate behavior.

Whenever the student engages in perfectionism (e.g., getting mad that she did not earn a perfect score on a science test), gently correct her. Let her know that her behavior is an example of perfectionism and give her direct information about what she should be doing instead. "Madeline, it is not useful to insult yourself because you did not get a perfect score. If you did your best, you have accomplished something important. Besides, you did a great job on the test and can learn something from the two mistakes you made." Because your goal is to impart information, you want to be emotionally neutral while giving the correction.

 Use reinforcement to encourage appropriate behavior.

a. Give the student increased praise. Be especially alert for situations in which the student might tend to be a perfectionist, but is not (e.g., when the student makes a few mistakes on a test, but accepts the errors without making a big production about them). Praise her for these demonstrations of her ability to do her best and learn from her mistakes. "Madeline, I was very impressed that when I handed back the tests you did not react to the fact that there were a few errors. Your reaction shows a great deal of maturity—accepting that you do not have to be perfect."

If the student would be embarrassed by this public praise, praise the student privately or even give the student a note. Remember that any time the student is not acting in a perfectionist manner, you can praise her for doing her best and learning from her mistakes.

b. However, avoid praising the student for getting 100% correct or for earning the highest score in the class. When she does get 100% correct and/or the highest score in the class, praise her for having done an excellent job and for doing her best work. Just be careful not to reinforce the student for being a perfectionist. "Madeline, the quality of your report indicates that you really understand the cause of the American Revolution. Nice work."

c. Give the student frequent attention (e.g., say "hello" to her as she enters the classroom, call on her frequently during class activities, and occasionally ask her to assist you with a class job that needs to be done) and praise her for other positive behaviors she exhibits. For example, you might comment about the creativity of her art project, how thoughtful she is of the feelings of others, or how well she explained a new math concept to a classmate. This demon-strates to the student that you notice many positive things she does, not just the fact that she is refraining from being a perfectionist.

PLAN B

Sometimes students have difficulty accepting and learning from their mistakes. If your student reacts emotionally to making errors, the intervention must focus on teaching the student that mistakes are an important part of the learning process.

1. *Respond consistently with a gentle verbal correction when the student engages in perfectionism (see PLAN A).*

2. *Help the student identify the positive aspects of making mistakes.*

a. During your initial meeting with the student (see SUGGESTED STEPS FOR DEVELOPING AND IMPLEMENTING A PLAN), discuss with the student the importance of being able to learn from her mistakes. Use examples that may have some relevance to the student. For example, if the student likes sports, you could talk about how each time a good soccer player misses a goal, she learns what to do differently. You could also use an example of a mistake that you made in the classroom that helped you learn to be a better teacher.

b. With the student, decide on a positive statement that she can use to help her keep her perspective on making mistakes, such as, "I can accept and learn from my mistakes." You might simply suggest this statement to a primary age student, but with an intermediate or middle/junior high school student, help her to develop a statement in her own words.

3. *Conduct lessons in which you have the student identify and practice responsible ways of handling mistakes.*

a. Schedule five-minute lessons for at least two times per week (daily lessons would be best). You may choose to conduct these lessons during recess or immediately after school.

b. During the lessons, first help the student identify strategies for responding to mistakes. "Madeline, let's pretend that I am returning your spelling paper that you made four mistakes on. Let's think about what you could do when I hand this paper back to you that would show both you and I that you can accept and learn from your mistakes."

If the student has difficulty thinking of ideas of her own, prompt her. Work together on this process until the student has identified at least two or three ways she can respond when she has made errors. Possibilities include:

- Saying nothing, not getting mad, and correcting the missed problems for her own knowledge.

- Saying, "I see what I did wrong."

- Saying, "I bet I won't make this mistake again."

c. Then, have the student practice the strategies she has identified. Discuss and role play different situations in which the student applies the identified strategies. If necessary, conduct these practice sessions for a few minutes a couple of times per week until the student begins using the strategies on her own in the classroom.

4. *Help the student stay focused on learning from her mistakes through precorrections.*

When handing a paper back to the student, remind her that she has agreed to learn from her mistakes. "Madeline, before I hand this back, what did you agree is important to keep in mind about mistakes? Right, there is nothing wrong with mistakes and you can learn something from any mistake that is made. Keep that in mind as I hand this test back to you." Prompt the student this way regardless of whether her work has any errors or not.

5. *Use reinforcement to encourage appropriate behavior.*

a. Give the student increased praise and attention for accepting her errors (see PLAN A).

b. In addition, make a special point of letting the student know that you notice her efforts to use the skills she has been learning/practicing. "Madeline, I saw the way you handled it when

Leo gave you back your corrected spelling test that had two errors. You stayed calm, said nothing, and looked at the original list to see how the words are correctly spelled. Do you think you could spell those words correctly now? Hey, you are learning from your mistakes. Nice job of doing what we have been practicing."

d. You might also wish to use intermittent rewards. Occasional, and unexpected, rewards can motivate the student to demonstrate responsible behavior more often. The idea is to provide a reward when the student has had a particularly

good period of avoiding perfectionism and/or using the strategies for responding to errors.

Appropriate rewards might include telling the principal about the effort she is making to do her best and to learn from her mistakes, tutoring a younger student, or choosing an assignment she is proud of to post on the class bulletin board. *(NOTE: A list of additional reinforcement ideas can be found in APPENDIX 1.)* Use intermittent rewards more frequently at the beginning of the intervention to encourage the student, and less often as her behavior improves.

PLAN C

In some cases a student's perfectionism manifests as excessive concern regarding grades. If this is the case with your student, the intervention should involve encouraging the student to realize that grades of "B" and "C" are perfectly adequate and that taking pride in doing one's best is more important than earning a superior grade.

1. *Respond consistently with a gentle verbal correction when the student engages in perfectionism (see PLAN A).*

2. *Explain to the student what different grades really mean, and emphasize that a "B" or "C" is not a bad grade.*

Some students have the mistaken notion that anything less than an "A" is a bad grade. Show the student the school/district definitions of "B" and "C" grades. Usually a grade of "C" means that the student mastered the essential course competencies. Even a "C" should be considered a good grade if the student learned something from the assignment or test.

3. *Help the student identify the positive aspects of doing one's best rather than trying only to earn a good grade.*

a. Use examples that are relevant for the student to explain the importance of being able to learn from tasks regardless of the grade. For example, if the student plays the piano, you might discuss preparing for a recital. The scores her piano teacher gives during the practice sessions don't matter as much as how well the student learns the skills in preparation for her recital performance. Or you could share a personal example of a time when you did not receive a good grade/high score, but learned some very useful skills or concepts.

Help the student see that one can learn more by focusing on "doing one's best" rather than trying to earn a good grade. Using tasks from your classroom, you could describe a hypothetical student who worked to get good grades and learned very little. "Madeline, let's imagine for a moment a pretend student name Cassie. Cassie focuses so much on getting good grades that she thinks more about her score than about learning from the assignment. On a social studies assignment, for example, she answers her questions using the study guide provided (since she thinks these are the "right" answers), rather than reading the chapter, learning more about the topic, and figuring the answers out for herself."

Also emphasize to the student that creative or innovative thinkers focus on the task to be learned or problem to be solved, rather than the grade to be earned. Be sure the student understands that grades are still important—just that they are less important than doing a job well and taking pride in one's best work.

b. With the student, decide on a positive statement that she can use to help keep her perspective on making mistakes, such as, "I'll do my best and learn all I can." With a primary age student, you might simply suggest that statement. With an intermediate or middle/junior high school student, assist her in developing a statement in her own words.

4. *Have the student monitor the degree to which she attempts to implement the chosen statement (e.g., "I'll do my best and learn all I can.").*

For each assignment that the student hands in, have her rate her effort to learn something from the material. She could use a scale like the sample following.

5. *Use reinforcement to encourage appropriate behavior.*

a. give the student increase praise and attention for accepting her errors (see PLAN A).

b. In addition, praise the student for focusing her energies on the quality of her effort, not the outcome (the grade). "Madeline, I see that you rated your efforts a "4"—that you focused on doing your best while working on this report. You should be proud of that, and I am looking forward to reading this report. Tell me a little bit about what you learned about Ireland."

Avoid praise that focuses on the grade. A statement like, "Nice work, you got an 'A' may be appropriate for some students, but not a student who has been overly focused on her grades.

c. Praise the student for accurately evaluating her own efforts on the rating form. Even with a poor rating, if the student has been honest in her self-assessment, praise her. "Madeline, you are really handling this responsibly. Even though you had a rough time focusing properly with this assignment, you were honest in you assessment. I'll bet next time you will be able to be less concerned about the grade and more concerned about how much effort you make to learn something."

d. Occasionally before handing a paper back to the student, prompt the student to focus on her effort rather than her grades. "Madeline, before I show you what you got, tell me which is more important—the grade on this paper or the fact that you did your best on this assignment! Great, I am glad you realize that!" Prompt the student in this manner sometimes when the student has earned an "A" and sometimes when her grade is less than an "A." When the grade is less than an "A" and the student does not become upset, praise her. "Madeline, you are becoming so much more mature. A couple of months ago a 'B' would have gotten you upset. Now, you know that a 'B' is a fine grade, as long as you did your best work."

6. *Encourage the student to use self-reinforcement.*

Whenever things are going well (i.e., less grade obsession than usual), prompt the student to mentally reinforce herself. "Madeline, this has been a very successful day. Silently tell yourself that you are really good at doing your best work." Give the student this encouragement intermittently throughout the day.

Effort Rating Scale

I, ___Madeline___ , agree to rate how well am remembering to ___focus on doing my best,___

___rather than just trying to get a good grade___ for each assignment.

Directions:

Circle the number that describes your focus while working on this assignment.

1	2	3	4	5
Focused only on my grade		Focused on my grade & on my effort		Focused only on "doing my best" and "learning as much as I can"

PLAN D

Some students may have developed such a pattern of perfectionism and/or obsession about good grades that they have become unwilling to try anything at which they risk being less than perfect. Over time, such students will tend to make less challenging choices for course work or career directions. The intervention plan must help your student learn to set goals for challenging activities.

1. *Respond consistently with a gentle verbal correction when the student engages in perfectionism (see PLAN A).*

2. *Conduct lessons to help the student realize that in order to excel, one must try new and difficult things.*

a. Use examples from your own life and/or from the classroom that show how one sometimes has to risk failure or poor performance in order to truly excel. For example, maybe in college you could have signed up for an easy elective course or a difficult art history course and you chose the difficult course. Even though you earned a "C" because the professor was not impressed with your final term paper, the course was very interesting and helped you appreciate the experience more fully when you visited famous art galleries on your trip to Europe after graduation.

b. Explain that it requires courage for a person to take on a challenge—something at which he/she might fail. If the student is mature enough, you might introduce the following quote from Eleanor Roosevelt as the basis for a discussion about courage:

> *You have never failed*
> *unless you have ceased to try.*

3. *Have the student set written goals for some "low risk" challenges that she is willing to undertake.*

Help the student identify a few challenges that she would not generally take on, but that interest her. For example, rather than preparing a written report to fulfill an assignment, she could design a set of visual displays to communicate the important information. Or, the student might set a goal of joining a choir or beginning some kind of community service.

If the student seems to go overboard—wanting to undertake too many challenges or challenges that are unrealistic or potentially dangerous, help her to temper or modify them.

4. *Use reinforcement to encourage appropriate behavior.*

a. Give the student increased praise and attention for accepting her errors (see PLAN A).

b. Additionally, praise the student for trying new or difficult things, regardless of the outcome. Praise her willingness to take a risk, but be cautious of praising the outcome. When a student's problem revolves around trying to please for some external evaluation, you must emphasize the positive aspects of doing these things for herself. "Madeline, you took a risk and should be very proud of the courage that required."

. . . .

Suggested Steps for Developing and Implementing a Plan

The following steps are designed to help you develop an appropriate intervention plan and implement it effectively, whether you choose to use one of the MODEL PLANS or create a customized plan of your own. The steps are, however, suggestions—they are not intended to be followed rigidly or in any particular order. Use your professional judgment and the knowledge of your particular situation to make them work for you.

1. Make sure you have enough information about the situation.

a. If you think a minimal intervention like PLAN A will be sufficient, you may already have enough information to proceed. However, when a more involved plan seems necessary, you should consider collecting additional descriptive information for a couple of days.

b. You need to be able to explain what has led you to conclude that "the student has a problem with perfectionism." Anecdotal notes on actual incidents should provide enough detail to define the problem behavior clearly and completely. To collect anecdotal notes, simply keep a card in your pocket or on a clipboard and occasionally make notes on specific instances when the student acts in a way that you believe demonstrates perfectionism.

For each entry, briefly describe where and when the incident occurred, what the student did or said, and any other relevant observations (e.g., what prompted the behavior). You do not need to take notes every time the student exhibits perfectionist behavior; the idea is to capture a range of examples so that you can describe the behavior thoroughly.

Also include some notes on times when the student is not behaving in a perfectionist manner—this will make it clear that you are not only aware of her problem behavior, but also recognize when she behaves appropriately. When you meet with the student, the positive examples will also help you clarify how you want the student to behave.

Following is a sample of anecdotal notes that have been collected on a student's perfectionism.

Notes on Madeline's Perfectionism

2/19 Math—Madeline chose not to do the optional challenge assignment, stating, "I might make a mistake if I try that."

2/21 Science—When I returned her test, Madeline made a big fuss about "only 98%."

2/21 Art—Madeline said, "I hate art—my pictures never come out the way I want them to look. I quit!"

---

c. If the student notices what you are doing and asks about it, be straightforward—tell her that you are collecting information to see whether

her need to be perfect is a problem that needs to be worked on.

d. Continuing to collect this type of information while you implement a plan will help you to monitor whether the situation is getting worse, staying the same, or getting better.

2. Identify a focus for the intervention and labels for referring to the appropriate and inappropriate behaviors.

a. To be effective, the intervention must address more than just reducing the student's perfectionism—there must be a concurrent emphasis on increasing some positive behavior or trait (e.g., "accepting and learning from mistakes," "doing your best and learning all you can," or "having the courage to accept a challenge"). Having a specific positive behavior in mind will make it easier for you to "catch" and reinforce the student for behaving appropriately, and the positive focus will help you frame the situation more productively.

For example, if you simply say that "the student has a problem with perfectionism," you don't really provide any useful information, and may put the student and her parent(s) on the defensive. However, when you explain that you want to help the student "learn to have the courage to accept challenges," you present an important, and reasonable, goal for the student to work toward and clearly identify what the student needs to do to be successful.

b. Identifying labels for referring to the appropriate and inappropriate behaviors (e.g., "accepting and learning from mistakes" and "not learning from mistakes," respectively) will help you to use consistent vocabulary when discussing the situation with the student. If you sometimes refer to the inappropriate behavior as "being too fussy," for example, and other times tell the student that she is "not learning from her mistakes," she may not realize that you are talking about the same behavior.

3. Determine when and how to include the parent(s).

a. It is not necessary to contact the student's parent(s) if the problem has just begun and is not interfering with the student's academic or social progress. However, you might want to take advantage of any scheduled activities (e.g., conferences, weekly notes home) to let them know of your concern.

b. If the problem has been going on for more than a couple of weeks, you should contact the student's parent(s) to discuss the problem. Share with them any information you have collected about the behavior (e.g., anecdotal notes) and explain why you are concerned. Focus in particular on how the behavior is hindering the student academically and/or socially (e.g., the student is so worried about earning good grades that she is unwilling to try a challenging activity).

You might ask if the parent(s) have any insight into the situation and/or whether they have noticed similar behavior at home. Whether or not the parent(s) perceive a problem, explain that you want to help the student learn to "have the courage to accept a challenge," and invite them to join you for an initial meeting with the student to develop a plan. If the parent(s) are unable or unwilling to participate, let them know that you will keep them informed of the student's progress.

c. Once the parent(s) have been involved in any way, you should give them updates at least once per week while the plan is being implemented.

4. *Prepare for, then conduct, an initial meeting about the situation.*

a. Arrange a meeting to discuss your concerns with the student and anyone else who will be involved in the plan (e.g., the parent[s]). Although the specifics will vary depending upon the age of the student and the severity of the problem, there are some general guidelines to consider when scheduling the meeting.

First, meet at a neutral time (i.e., not immediately after a problem has occurred), when emotions are less likely to hamper communication. In general, a day's notice is appropriate, however a primary age student may worry excessively and/or forget what the meeting is about if it is scheduled more than an hour before it takes place.

Second, make the meeting appropriately private. With a primary student who has a mild problem, you might meet in the classroom while the other students are working independently. However, when dealing with a middle/junior high school student and the student's parent(s), you will need some place private (e.g., the counselor's office) to ensure that the discussion will not be overheard.

Third, try to make sure the meeting is scheduled for a time and place that it is not likely to be interrupted. Finally, if the parent(s) will be participating, they should be the ones to tell the student about the meeting.

b. Construct a preliminary plan. Decide whether you think you can use one of the MODEL PLANS or if you need to create a customized plan using components from various plans and/or of your own design. Although you will invite and encourage the student to help develop the plan during the initial meeting, having a proposed plan in mind before you meet can alleviate frustration and/or wasted time if the student is unwilling or unable to participate.

c. After reviewing the information you have collected and thinking about how you want the student to behave, prepare thorough descriptions of the perfectionistic behavior and the positive behavior/trait on which the student will be working. The more specific you can be and the more concrete examples you have, the easier it will be to clarify (and for the student to understand) your expectations. Be sure to consider the student's behavior in all relevant activities (e.g., independent assignments, quizzes and tests, group projects, etc.).

d. Conduct the meeting in an atmosphere of collaboration. The following agenda is one way you might structure the meeting:

• **Share your concerns about the student's behavior.**

Briefly describe the problem behavior and share examples from your anecdotal notes. Then explain why you consider the perfectionist behavior to be a problem. You might tell the student that being overly concerned with being perfect or with good grades will eventually reduce how much she is able to learn. For example, the overly perfectionist person would not sign up for advanced placement classes, because it would be harder to earn good grades and perfect scores than if she signed up for easier classes.

• **Discuss how you can work together to improve the situation.**

Tell the student that you would like to help her learn to "have the courage to accept challenges," and describe your preliminary plan. Invite the student to give you input on the various aspects of the plan, and together work out any necessary details (e.g., the self-evaluation form). You may have to brainstorm different possibilities if the student is uncomfortable with the initial plan. Incorporating any of the student's suggestions that strengthen the plan is likely to increase her sense of "ownership" in and commitment to it.

- **Make sure the student understands what you mean by appropriate and inappropriate behavior.**

Use the descriptions you have prepared to define and clarify the problem behavior and the positive (desired) behavior as specifically and thoroughly as you can. To ensure that you and the student are in agreement about the expectations, you might present hypothetical scenarios and have her identify whether each is an example of perfectionism or of accepting a challenge. Or you might describe an actual situation that has occurred and ask her to explain how she could demonstrate courage to accept a challenge in that situation.

- **Conclude the meeting.**

Always end the meeting with words of encouragement. Let the student know that you are confident that she can be successful. Be sure to reinforce her for participating in the meeting.

 Give the student regular, ongoing feedback about her behavior.

It is important to meet with the student periodically to discuss her progress. In most cases, three to five minutes once per week should suffice. Review any information that has been collected and discuss whether or not the situation is getting better. As much as possible, focus on the student's improvements, however, also address any new or continuing problems. As the situation improves, the meetings can be faded to once every other week and then to once per month.

 Evaluate the situation (and the plan).

Implement any plan for at least two weeks before deciding whether to change plans; to continue, modify, or fade the plan you are using; or to cease the intervention. Generally, if the student's behavior is clearly improving (based on the objective information that's been collected and/or the subjective perceptions of yourself, the student, and possibly the parent[s]), stick with what you are doing. If the situation has remained the same or worsened, some kind of change will be necessary. Always discuss any changes to the plan with the student first.

PHYSICALLY DANGEROUS BEHAVIOR—TO SELF OR OTHERS

. . . .

Assaultive Behavior

Self-Destructive Behavior

DESCRIPTION

You have a student who engages in behavior that has a high risk that someone (the student himself or someone else) could be physically injured.

Although there are no MODEL PLANS included with this problem, the following suggested procedures have been designed to help you establish procedures to reduce the probability of physical injury resulting from misbehavior.

NOTE:

The following material is adapted and condensed with permission from Intervention A: Managing Physically Dangerous Behavior, which is one of 16 intervention booklets in:

> *Sprick, R.S., Sprick, M.S., & Garrison, M. (1993). Interventions: Collaborative planning for students at risk. Longmont, CO: Sopris West.*

Alternative Problems

- **Aggression—Verbal and/or Physical**

- **Bullying Behavior/Fighting**

- **Disruptive Behavior—Severe**

- **Self-Control Issues**

- **Weapons**

· · · · · · · ·
Intervention Information

The following procedures provide suggestions for responding to students when their behavior is physically dangerous to themselves or others around them (i.e., ways to effectively and appropriately respond to the emergency situation). These steps constitute an immediate but temporary solution to a severe problem, and should be implemented concurrently with another intervention or interventions designed to help the students learn more appropriate behaviors.

P R O C E D U R E S

If a student's behavior poses a threat to someone's physical safety—other students, adults, or the student himself, intervention must be immediate and intensive. Above all, safety must be the first consideration.

Effective intervention for physically dangerous behavior should include five major components, detailed following:

Component One:	Immediately implement procedures to ensure everyone's safety.
Component Two:	Involve and notify the student's parent(s).
Component Three:	Develop record-keeping and reporting procedures.
Component Four:	Determine whether the student should be referred for special education, and whether other agencies should be involved.
Component Five:	Teach the student to manage his own behavior.

All five components need to be implemented concurrently to increase the likelihood that every variable is being addressed and all possible resources explored. Each component is described in detail following.

Component One
Immediately implement procedures to ensure everyone's safety.

When a student's behavior escalates into physically violent or dangerous acts, staff members must act swiftly to ensure the safety of everyone involved. In every case, the first priority of the intervention is to ensure that no one is hurt, and the second priority is to respond in a way that the student is not reinforced for his out of control behavior. *(NOTE: This raises the issue of the importance of familiarity with district and/or building policy and training in dealing with physically dangerous behavior.)*

There are two immediate options when a physically threatening incident occurs: (1) get everyone out of the student's way; or (2) have an adult or adults physically restrain the student.

1. Use room clears whenever possible.

The preferred method for dealing with out of control behavior is to remove everyone else from the threat of violence. In a classroom situation, this procedure is referred to as a "room clear." *(NOTE: On a playground, all the other students would be moved away from the student who is out of control.)* Room clears are preferable to physical restraint for a number of reasons, the most important being that injuries (to the student, other students, or a staff member) are less likely to occur.

When a student begins exhibiting behavior that puts anyone in jeopardy, the teacher should follow a preestablished routine, such as the one following.

a. **Identify where the class will go and what students will do during a room clear.**

Routine provisions should be made so that if the students must clear the room, the disruption is minimized. Students should be taken into the hall until assistance can be summoned. As soon as another adult arrives, the class should be taken to a predetermined location. Relevant instructional tasks should be prepared in advance. For example, the students might be taken to the school stage where paper and pencils have been stored and given a writing assignment, asked to solve math problems, or run a spelling bee.

b. **Arrange for the supervision of the student who is engaged in physically dangerous behavior.**

• Establish procedures for summoning a trained staff member to the classroom immediately.

When a student begins engaging in physically dangerous behavior, the classroom teacher will need immediate assistance. Procedures should be established for receiving additional help rapidly. This should include a prearranged signal indicating that a crisis is occurring. Some schools use their intercom system for this purpose. Others use a specially designed "Red Card" that can be given to a student messenger. The messenger can take the crisis card to the office where an immediate response will be initiated.

Plans for providing an immediate response should include: (1) who will respond; (2) a chain of command in case the first person is unavailable; and (3) a communication process to ensure that everyone involved will be kept informed. These procedures should be carefully designed and occasionally rehearsed so that the procedures work smoothly and high probability contingencies (such as the principal being out of the building) have been addressed.

• Train all staff members who may be responsible for emergency duty.

This training should include identifying which of the student's behaviors the supervisor can safely ignore and which require intervention as dictated by building and/or district policy. Adults who will supervise an out of control student should be trained to stand at the door and to determine what actions to take if the situation escalates. If physical restraint is recommended under specified conditions, the adults should be trained in how to properly restrain a student.

c. **Determine in advance whether there will be consequences for out of control behavior.**

Consequences for out of control behavior tend to have little effect on preventing future incidents. Of far greater importance is teaching the student to control his own behavior. Nevertheless, consequences are generally part of a comprehensive plan and should thus be predetermined. Appropriate consequences might include owing time from a recess break or after school, restitution (i.e., repairing the damage or mess created), time-out, or suspension.

(NOTE: If the student is an identified special education student, a suspension may constitute a change of placement and cannot be instituted without due process. If a special education student engages in physically dangerous behavior, it is vital to work directly with the building and district special education personnel to avoid possible violation of federal law.)

2. **Use physical restraint only if necessary.**

Although a room clear is preferable to restraint, it is not always an appropriate procedure. If a student is about to stab someone with scissors, for example, there may not be time for a room clear. Or if a student is engaged in highly self-destructive behavior, such as head banging, some form of restraint or physical intervention may be necessary.

At other times, a room clear should be paired with some form of physical intervention. For example, if two students are involved in a violent fight, the teacher may need to send the other students out of the room, call for help, and when help arrives separate and restrain the two students until they calm down enough to be released.

(NOTE: All of the following information applies to two or more students fighting as well as to one individual student who is out of control.)

a. **Try to disperse the other students.**

In the classroom, use a room clear; outside, students may be sent to another part of the playground. Use a firm voice to direct the students to another location. "Everyone needs to move *immediately* to the other side of the blacktop. Jackson, Alissa, Sandra, Tad, move now!"

b. **Always try verbal interventions before resorting to any "hands-on" procedures.**

Avoid shouting, but use a firm and loud command. "Jeremy, stop pounding on that window and move to this side of the room, now!" Using the student's name increases the chance that he will respond to the verbal instruction. If more than one student is involved, direct each student to a different location. "Rico, move over to the doorway! Zach, move over to the lockers!"

c. **If at all possible, signal or call for help before beginning any sort of restraint.**

To avoid possible accusations regarding the use of undue force or even abuse during restraint, the adult involved should always summon assistance. The act of calling for help indicates that the presence of another adult was requested as quickly as possible, and that there has been no attempt to engage in inappropriate physical contact. *(NOTE: If the school staff does not currently have routines for signaling for adult assistance, such procedures should be devised for every school location, including all classrooms, hallways, playgrounds, the cafeteria, bus waiting areas, etc.—see Step 1.)*

d. Decide if restraint will be necessary and helpful.

If the student does not cease the dangerous behavior after the verbal instruction has been given, the staff member must use professional judgment regarding whether to physically intervene before assistance arrives, or to wait until help comes. There is no set rule for making a decision of this type.

It is important that staff understand that they are not required to put themselves in direct physical jeopardy. Staff members may mistakenly believe that they will be negligent if they do not intervene physically in a fight or other out of control situation. However, their responsibility is to behave in a reasonably prudent manner to keep everyone physically safe, including themselves. What is reasonable and prudent may depend upon several factors, such as the:

- Number of students involved;

- Size of the student or students involved;

- Size and strength of the adult;

- Degree of violence taking place;

- Presence of any weapons or potential weapons; and

- Amount of training provided for staff in the use of nonviolent restraint methods.

For example, if a small student is pounding on a window, it would be reasonable and prudent for the teacher to remove him. However, if the student is large and strong, and the teacher is small, it would be neither reasonable nor prudent for the teacher to physically intervene. The teacher should wait for help to arrive so the student can be safely restrained.

Also, staff are not required to try to disarm any student who has a weapon. The police should be called, and all adults and children should be kept as far from the crisis situation as possible.

When two or more students are involved in a fight, staff should take into account that attempt-

ing to break up the fight may actually increase the risk of injury to one of the students. If an adult grabs the arms of one of the combatants, it can make that student more vulnerable to direct blows from the other student. Unless both students are very small, a single staff member should probably wait for assistance before physically trying to break up an altercation.

Component Two
Involve and notify the student's parent(s).

The student's parent(s) must be involved whenever there is a problem involving physically dangerous behavior. After the first incident, the parent(s) should be requested to attend a conference to: (1) communicate the staff's willingness to help the student; (2) determine the severity of the problem; and (3) begin joint problem solving. Depending upon the severity of the situation, representatives from other social agencies should possibly be invited to the conference in order to assist in developing a comprehensive plan.

Alienation of the parent(s) from the school can often be avoided if staff communicate their desire to work collaboratively. Staff members should consciously avoid implying that a parent should be able to control a student's behavior at school. Then if a severe problem exists, the initial contact with the parent(s) may be the beginning of a successful cooperative effort to help a troubled student.

Preplanning for the possibility of a "next time" will also let the student, his parent(s), and staff know exactly what the consequences will be for any subsequent incidents of physically dangerous behavior.

Component Three
Develop record-keeping and reporting procedures.

Given the severe nature of behavior that poses a physical threat, systematic and detailed records must be kept.

 Set up an anecdotal log to record all incidents in which a student's behavior is physically dangerous.

An anecdotal log can be used in designing effective interventions and to help determine whether an immediate referral to special education or social services should be initiated. In addition, the anecdotal log provides the information necessary for keeping summary records of out of control behavior (see Step 2). The log should detail all past and current incidents of violent or physically dangerous behavior.

The following information should be included for each entry in the log:

- Date and time of day;

- Location of incident;

- Adult(s) supervising at the time of the incident;

- Events that occurred prior to the incident;

- A detailed description of the student's behavior during the incident, including duration of the incident and specific behavior observed;

- Action(s) staff took to prevent physical injury;

- Consequences given to the student (if any); and

- Action(s) taken to minimize future occurrences of the behavior.

2. *Keep summary records.*

Summary records indicate the number of incidents per week, or the number of minutes per week, during which the student was out of control. Because the intensity of out of control behavior is emotionally draining to participants, it is frequently difficult to determine objectively whether an intervention plan is helping a student. For example, if a first grade student reduces the number of tantrums from four or five times per week to once per week, progress is clearly being made. However, if that single incident is sufficiently distressing, staff may not be aware that progress is being made. Similarly, if the restraint procedures go smoothly, staff may feel that the procedure is working well when in fact the number of incidents has not been reduced. With summary data, the effectiveness of the intervention plan will be easier to judge.

Component Four
Determine whether the student should be referred for special education, and whether other agencies should be involved.

If the student is not currently identified as eligible for special education services, data collected as a part of the formal record-keeping system (see Component Three) should assist in determining whether a referral for evaluation should be initiated.

Staff should also begin immediately identifying whether other agencies should be brought into the planning process. If the student's behavior has been severe enough to be considered assault, for instance, the police or juvenile authorities should be contacted to determine whether interagency planning would be appropriate.

Component Five
Teach the student to manage his own behavior.

In addition to determining what to do in the event of another dangerous incident, methods should be developed to help the student learn to handle situations without losing control. This component is an essential part of your plan, as it will focus on helping the student develop strategies for *preventing* future violent or physically aggressive acts.

Examine the INDEX of this reference guide to locate plans for a specific behavior identified for the student to improve. Possibilities include **Self-Control Issues** and **Aggression—Verbal and/or Physical**. Then implement that behavior change plan, while implementing the procedures described here to ensure physical safety when an incident of physically dangerous behavior does occur.

POUTING

Sulking

Petulance

DESCRIPTION

You have a student who pouts or acts in a petulant manner when she wants something and/or doesn't get her way.

GOAL

The student will stop pouting and learn to communicate her wants, needs, and/or feelings in more responsible ways.

OVERVIEW OF PLANS

- PLAN A: For a situation in which the problem is relatively mild or has just begun.

- PLAN B: For a student who lacks the skills to communicate in more responsible ways.

- PLAN C: For a student who pouts to gain adult attention.

- PLAN D: For a student who does not realize when she pouts and/or how frequently she pouts.

- PLAN E: For a student whose pouting has become habitual.

Alternative Problems

- **Complaining**

- **Corrected, Student Gets Upset When**

- **Moodiness**

- **Spoiled Behavior**

- **Tantrumming (K or 1st Grader)**

General Considerations

- If the student's problem behavior stems in any way from academic issues (e.g., the student is unable to meet academic expectations and pouts or sulks out of frustration), concurrent efforts must be made to ensure her academic success (see **Academic Deficits, Determining**).

- If the student lacks the basic social skills to interact with her peers appropriately, it may be necessary to begin by teaching her those skills. **Social Skills, Lack of** contains information on a variety of published social skills curricula.

- If you suspect that the pouting could be related to the student being depressed, see **Depression**. This problem includes a set of questions to help you decide whether the student should be referred for counseling or psychological services.

- If the pouting is resulting in the student avoiding or not completing her schoolwork, begin with a plan to increase the student's work completion (see **Work Completion—Daily Work**). Once the student is turning in completed work on a regular basis, you can consider an intervention for the pouting, if the problem still exists.

Model Plans

PLAN A

It is not always necessary, or beneficial, to use an involved plan. If the pouting has just begun and/or is relatively mild (i.e., not interfering with the student's academic or social progress), the following actions, along with making the student aware of your concerns, may resolve the situation.

1. Respond consistently when the student pouts.

a. During your initial meeting with the student (see SUGGESTED STEPS FOR DEVELOPING AND IMPLEMENTING A PLAN) devise a nonembarrassing signal to cue her that she needs to stop pouting and communicate responsibly if there is something she needs. You want the signal to be a fairly subtle one that only the student will recognize and understand in order to minimize the chance that she will be teased by her peers. Possible signals include putting the fingertips of your hands together, rubbing your neck, or even just direct eye contact and a head nod.

Let the student know that you may also need to quietly say her name to gain her attention before you give the signal. You should be prepared to use the signal frequently and for a fairly long time, since it is likely that the behavior is, at least in part, an unconscious habit for the student.

b. Whenever the student is pouting, give the signal. If the student does not cease pouting, but is not disrupting the classroom or refusing to participate (e.g., the student pouts while you are giving directions for an assignment), ignore the behavior. However, if the pouting results in the student not participating (e.g., the student pouts at her desk when she should be observing a demonstration in the classroom's science center), gently correct the lack of participation, but ignore the pouting. "Kaleka, you need to join us in the science center."

2. Use reinforcement to encourage appropriate behavior.

a. Give the student increased praise. Be especially alert for situations in which the student communicates her wants, needs, or feelings in a responsible manner, and praise her for these demonstrations of her ability to communicate responsibly. "Kaleka, I noticed that you were disappointed that Isabelle chose not to join you at the computer, but you just decided to ask Reba if she wanted to work with you instead. You communicated responsibly and Reba chose to join you. Did the two of you find anything interesting about that new software program?"

If the student would be embarrassed by public praise, praise the student privately or even give the student a note. Remember that any time the student interacts with you or another student without pouting, you can praise her for communicating responsibly.

b. Praise the student privately for responding to the signal. "Kaleka, three times this morning I gave the signal that you were pouting, and all three times you pulled yourself out of it. Twice you just changed the way you acted—began acting much more grown up—and once you raised your hand and made a very responsible

request. If you hadn't told me, I wouldn't have even realized what you wanted."

c. Give the student frequent attention (e.g., say "hello" to her as she enters the classroom, call on her frequently during class activities, and occasionally ask her to assist you with a class job that needs to be done) and praise her for other positive behavior she exhibits. For example, you might comment about the accuracy of her work or how creative she is in art. This demonstrates to the student that you notice many positive things she does, not just the fact that she is refraining from pouting.

PLAN B

Sometimes a student may not actually know how to communicate responsibly. If the student does not seem to possess the social skills for communicating in ways other than pouting, you will need to teach her how to communicate her wants and needs in a responsible manner.

 Respond consistently when the student pouts.

When the student pouts, give her the signal, then ignore or gently correct the behavior, as necessary (see PLAN A).

 Conduct lessons to teach the student how to express her wants and needs in responsible ways.

a. Think about the types of situations in which the student is likely to pout, and identify some techniques or skills that might help the student in those situations. For example, you may teach the student to stay calm when she doesn't get her way by breathing deeply and counting backwards from ten, how to use "I messages" to tell how she feels, and/or how to use a calm voice to make a request or ask a question.

Next, decide on a way to help the student become aware of how she looks when she pouts (i.e., how others see her behavior). You could, for instance, have the student view herself in a mirror, or you might use a video camera and playback equipment.

b. Using your anecdotal notes (see SUGGESTED STEPS FOR DEVELOPING AND IMPLE- MENTING A PLAN), help the student to recall during the lessons an actual situation in which she pouted. Then have her role play this situation. If the student is unable to do this, you may need to model the pouting for her first. However, be very careful not to make the student feel that you are making fun of her.

Once the student can mimic her own pouting behavior, have her observe herself doing so in the mirror (or on videotape). As she is watching, emphasize how unlikely it is that anyone will understand (or even care about) what she wants or what is bothering her when she pouts like that. You might ask the student to imagine an adult she respects pouting like she does— how silly it would seem. Explain that everyone has things that frustrate them or make them upset, but the trick is to communicate in a responsible way.

c. Then explain and discuss the techniques or strategies you have previously identified (see Step 2a) that the student might use in that situation to help her react and/or communicate her feelings more responsibly. Next have the student observe herself practicing one of these techniques. You can also have her imagine the adult she respects behaving in this way. Em- phasize that this does not seem silly.

Use this process with several situations during each lesson. For all the situations, have the student role play one or more responsible ways to communicate, and for some (but not all) of the situations, have the student view herself role playing a pouting response.

You can also use the lessons to have the stu- dent practice responding to the signal. Tell the student to pretend to pout, then give the signal and have her practice replacing the pout with a more responsible way of communicating.

d. These lessons should occur at least twice per week and involve just you and the student (perhaps while the other students are at recess). The lessons needn't last more than three to five minutes. Also, it is important that they be handled in a matter-of-fact manner so the student does not feel that she is being ridiculed. That is, you want to be very clear that you are not trying to embarrass the student, but that you do want her to see her behavior the way others do. Continue the lessons until the student is consistently responding to the signal and/or no longer pouting in the classroom.

3. Prompt the student to behave appropriately by using precorrections.

Watch for those circumstances in which the student is likely to pout, and remind her that the particular situation is a time she needs to remember to communicate responsibly. You could also have her identify how she will communicate responsibly, and/or encourage the student to use the strategies she has learned. "Kaleka, could I see

you over here for a minute? In the situation that is going on right now, you may not get your way. Keep remembering what we have worked on in the lessons. What might you try? Excellent, let me know if it works." If this conversation would embarrass the student, conduct it privately.

4. Use reinforcement to encourage appropriate behavior.

a. Give the student increased praise and attention for communicating responsibly (see PLAN A).

b. In addition, make a special point of letting the student know that you notice her efforts to use the skills learned in the lessons. "Kaleka, I know that you found it somewhat frustrating that you didn't get to be first in line. You said you wanted to be first—very responsibly, by the way—but when I said someone else needed to get a turn, you calmly accepted that. Nice job of doing what we have been practicing."

PLAN C

Some students are very skilled at gaining attention through their negative behavior. If you find yourself frequently nagging, reminding, or coaxing the student to stop pouting, it is possible that she is pouting to gain adult attention. Whether or not the student overtly seems to like the attention, you should make sure that she receives more frequent and more satisfying attention when she behaves responsibly than when she pouts.

1. Respond consistently when the student pouts.

a. Because it is important for the student to learn that she will not be able to prompt people to nag and pay attention to her by pouting; that, in fact, she will receive no attention when she is pouting, you should ignore all instances of the student's pouting. While ignoring, do not look at the student or talk to her. Do not act disgusted or impatient with her behavior. Simply interact in positive ways with students who are behaving well and meeting classroom expectations. As soon as the target student is no longer pouting, pay attention to her, but make no reference to her pouting.

b. If the student's pouting affects other students you may need to use a consequence, such as time owed off of recess or in after-school detention. Whenever consequences will be used, the student should be made aware ahead of time, what will happen when her pouting affects the class. The consequences can be explained during the initial meeting with the student (see

SUGGESTED STEPS FOR DEVELOPING AND IMPLEMENTING A PLAN).

Then, for example, if the student is pouting and refuses to line up for music (and you cannot leave the student unsupervised or send the class without supervision), you can simply state, "Kaleka, each minute it takes until you join us in line will cost you five minutes from your next recess." Only use a consequence for situations in which a class activity cannot proceed unless the student complies with a direct request—otherwise ignore the pouting.

(NOTE: For a student in kindergarten or first grade, redirection may be more appropriate than time owed. Redirection involves gently leading the student through the task or direction without saying anything or making eye contact with the student. For example, if the class has to wait because the student is pouting and won't line up, you would simply guide her into line without saying a word.)

c. If other students give the target student attention when she is pouting (i.e., trying to get her to stop pouting), gently correct them. "Norma and Elaine, Kaleka, can take care of herself and she will communicate what she is feeling when she is ready. It would be best to let her work it out on her own."

2. Use reinforcement to encourage appropriate behavior.

a. Frequent praise and attention is the core of this plan. The student must see that she receives more frequent and more satisfying attention when she behaves responsibly than when she pouts. Therefore, whenever the student is not pouting (or otherwise misbehaving), make an effort to praise and spend time with her. "Kaleka, you handled that so responsibly. You stated your opinion and everyone listened to you. Would it be okay if I sat with you a moment and watched as you and your group do the next step of your project?"

b. You may also wish to use intermittent rewards to acknowledge the student's success. Occasional, and unexpected, rewards can motivate the student to demonstrate responsible behavior more often. The idea is to provide a reward when the student has had a particularly good period of behaving responsibly without pouting.

Appropriate rewards might include playing a game, helping you create a class bulletin board, being congratulated in front of the principal, or leading the class in a game of her choice. (NOTE: A list of additional ideas for reinforcers can be found in APPENDIX 1.) Use reinforcement more frequently at the beginning of the intervention to encourage the student, and then less often as her behavior improves.

3. Ensure a 3-1 ratio of positive to negative attention.

a. Given that attention is a motivating force for this student, you want to be sure that you are giving the student *three times as much* positive as negative attention. One way to do this is to monitor your interactions with the student at least one day per week. Simply keep a card on a clipboard or in your pocket and record each interaction you have with the student as either positive or negative by writing a "+" or a "-", respectively, on the card.

To determine whether an interaction is positive or negative, ask yourself whether the student was pouting (or otherwise misbehaving) at the time the interaction occurred. Interactions that are the result of the student behaving inappropriately are negative, while any interactions that occur while the student is meeting classroom expectations are positive. Thus, giving the signal and assigning time owed are both negative interactions, but praising the student for not needing the signal is positive. Greeting the student as she enters the room or asking her if she has any questions during independent work are also considered positive interactions. (NOTE: Ignoring the student's pouting is not recorded at all, because it is not an interaction.)

b. If you find that you are not giving the student three times as much positive as negative attention, try to increase the number of positive interactions you have with the student. Sometimes prompts can help. For example, you might decide that each time the student enters the classroom you will say "hello" to her, that whenever you look at the clock you will find a time to praise the student, or that whenever a student uses the drinking fountain you will check the target student and as soon as possible praise some aspect of her behavior. You can also increase the ratio of positive to negative attention by ignoring more of the student's inappropriate behavior.

PLAN D

Some students do not seem to realize when they pout and/or how frequently they pout. If your student pouts a lot but doesn't seem to be aware of it, the intervention should include some way of helping the student become more aware of her own behavior.

1. Respond consistently when the student pouts.

a. When the student pouts, give her the signal, then ignore or gently correct the behavior, as necessary (see PLAN A).

b. Whenever you give the signal, make sure the incident is recorded by either the student or yourself (see Step 2).

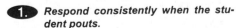

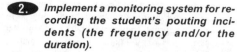

2. *Implement a monitoring system for recording the student's pouting incidents (the frequency and/or the duration).*

a. First, determine whether you or the student will record the behavior. Since the point of the monitoring system is for the student to become aware of each time she pouts during the day, having the student recording her own behavior (i.e., self-monitoring) is likely to be more effective than if you record the behavior yourself. However, do not have the student self-monitor her pouting behavior if you do not think that the student can and/or will be accurate. Or, if the student would be too embarrassed to self-monitor, you can do this for her. *(NOTE: Even when the student self-monitors, you should keep your own record approximately one day per week to verify the student's accuracy.)*

b. If the student is self-monitoring, have her keep a card on her desk or in her notebook. Each time you give the signal, the student should write a tally mark on the card.

If the student tends to pout for long periods of time, you may also want to monitor how much time she spends pouting. When the student continues to pout after you give the signal, time how long it takes her to stop pouting, and have the student record the number of minutes next to (or in place of) the tally mark. If the student is self-monitoring, you can subtly slip her a piece of paper on which the number of minutes is written. When you are timing the duration, interact with other students and check the target student every minute or so to see if she has ceased pouting. Of course, if the student stops pouting when you give her the signal, the incident would only be recorded for frequency, not duration.

3. *Discuss the student's behavior with her each day.*

Each day, meet with the student for a few minutes to review that day's record. If appropriate, have the student chart the number of incidents and/or the amount of time spent pouting on a graph (or do this

yourself). *(NOTE: If you do monitor both frequency and duration, chart them separately as one may improve faster than the other. For example, the number of incidents may stay about the same, but the number of minutes spent pouting may decrease dramatically.)*

Talk with the student about whether the day was better, worse, or about the same as previous days. If the day did not go well, encourage the student to talk about why. Also have the student identify things she can do the next day to help her remember to communicate responsibly rather than pout. If the student pouts during the meeting, keep the interaction very short. Just let the student know that you are sure tomorrow will be a better day.

4. *Use reinforcement to encourage appropriate behavior.*

a. Give the student increased praise and attention for communicating responsibly (see PLAN A).

b. In addition, praise the student during the daily review meetings for accurate recording (if applicable), and for being willing to look at her daily total. Even on a bad day, if the student is willing to chart the data and discuss why it was a bad day, praise her. "Kaleka, you are really handling this responsibly. Even though it was a rough day, you are willing to talk to me about things you might do differently tomorrow. That is a real sign that you are growing up."

Regardless of how the day went, try to make the end-of-the-day meeting upbeat and encouraging—you want the student to look forward to the daily review meetings.

5. *Encourage the student to use self-reinforcement.*

Whenever things are going well (i.e., less pouting than usual), prompt the student to mentally reinforce herself. "Kaleka, this has been a very successful morning. Silently tell yourself that you are really good at communicating in responsible ways." Encourage the student to reinforce herself in this manner intermittently throughout the day and during the end-of-the-day meeting.

PLAN E

Whenever a student's pouting has become habitual and/or she does not seem to have a desire to reduce it, you may need to implement a structured system of external incentives (i.e., rewards and consequences) based on her behavior to motivate her to stop pouting and to start communicating responsibly.

1. *Use a signal to cue the student when she is pouting (see PLAN A).*

2. *Implement a monitoring system to record the frequency and/or duration of the student's pouting incidents (see PLAN D).*

3. *Establish a structured system of providing a reward for appropriate behavior and a consequence for the inappropriate behavior.*

a. Identify several reinforcing items or activities that the student might want to earn. Although you may wish to think of some possibilities ahead of time, the system will be more effective if the student identifies most of the items or activities herself. *(NOTE: A list of ideas for reinforcers can be found in APPENDIX 1.)*

b. Set "prices" (in points) for the rewards the student identifies and have her select the one she would like to work for first.

The prices should be based on the instructional, personnel, and/or monetary costs of the items. Monetary cost is clear—the more expensive the item, the more points required to earn it. Instructional cost refers to the amount of instructional time lost or interfered with by the particular reward. Thus, an activity which causes the student to miss part of academic instruction should require more points than one the student can do on her own free time. Personnel cost involves the time required by you and/or other staff to fulfill the reinforcer. Having lunch with the principal, therefore, would cost more points than spending five minutes of free time with a friend.

c. Have the student begin each day with a certain number of points. This number should equal the average number of times the student pouts per day, plus two. Thus, if she pouts an average of 13 times per day, she would begin each day with 15 points. Each time you have to give the student the signal for pouting, she loses a point. The points remaining at the end of each day are then added together to be applied toward the reinforcer the student is striving to earn.

If the student is immature, it may be more effective to let her earn several small rewards (e.g., five minutes of computer time after 20 points) on the way to a bigger reward (e.g., one hour with you for 200 points). Thus, the student receives the small rewards, but does not spend points; instead they continue to accumulate toward the selected reward.

d. For a primary level student, a lottery system might be more effective. In this type of system, the student begins each day with tickets in a jar instead of points. All the tickets have prizes written on them—one has a big prize, a couple have moderate prizes, and the majority have small prizes. Each time you have to give the student the signal for pouting, you remove one ticket from the jar—but neither you nor the student is allowed to see what is written on it. At the end of each day, the student draws one ticket from those remaining in the jar, and receives that prize.

e. Determine a consequence (e.g., time owed off of recess or in after-school detention) for any pouting that occurs after the student has already lost her points (or tickets) for the day.

If the student runs out of points (or tickets), implement the consequence for each subsequent pouting incident. However, the consequence should not involve taking away a previous day's points. If the student can lose already-earned points, she might develop an attitude of, "I am losing so many points, why should I even bother to try?"

f. You may also wish to identify a consequence for pouting that lasts a long time. For example, you might record the number of minutes spent pouting and have the student owe that much time off of the next recess or after school. If you use this procedure, agree upon a way for the student to indicate to you that she is done pouting and ready to resume meeting classroom expectations. This lessens the possibility that you will start timing her pouting, then get busy with other students and not notice that she has stopped.

4. *Use reinforcement to encourage appropriate behavior.*

a. Give the student increased praise and attention for communicating responsibly (see PLAN A).

b. In addition, show interest and enthusiasm about how the student is doing on the system. "Kaleka, we are half way through the day and you still have 12 tickets in the jar. Your responsibility is increasing the chance that the 'hour on the computer' ticket is still in the jar."

. . . .
Suggested Steps for Developing and Implementing a Plan

The following steps are designed to help you develop an appropriate intervention plan and implement it effectively, whether you choose to use one of the MODEL PLANS or create a customized plan of your own. The steps are, however, suggestions—they are not intended to be followed rigidly or in any particular order. Use your professional judgment and the knowledge of your particular situation to make them work for you.

1. *Make sure you have enough information about the situation.*

a. If the behavior has just begun and is relatively mild (i.e., PLAN A is appropriate), you probably already have enough information to begin implementing your plan. However, if you are thinking about implementing any of the other plans, you should probably collect additional information for a couple of days. Descriptive information (e.g., anecdotal notes) can help you to develop a clear and comprehensive definition of the problem, and objective information (e.g., a frequency count and/or the duration time) can be used to delineate the magnitude of the initial problem and to monitor progress.

b. The easiest kind of objective information to collect involves recording how many times the student pouts each day (i.e., a frequency count). Simply keep a card in your pocket or on a clipboard, and any time the student pouts, write a tally mark on the card.

You may also wish to code these tallies to see whether the behavior occurs more frequently during certain times, subjects, or activities (e.g., in the morning or afternoon; during math or reading, during teacher directed instruction or independent work periods, etc.).

c. If the student pouts for long periods of time, you may also wish to know exactly how much time the student spends pouting (i.e., the duration time). For each incident, make a mental note of the time when the student begins and stops pouting, and record the difference (in number of minutes) next to (or in place of) the tally. At the end of the day, you can calculate the total number of minutes spent pouting.

d. It is fairly easy to summarize the objective information on a chart or graph. Being able to see how often and/or how much time the student pouts may help both the student and her parent(s) understand your concerns. Continuing to collect this type of information and keeping the chart or graph up-to-date while you implement the plan will also make it easier for you to monitor whether the situation is getting worse, staying the same, or getting better. *(NOTE: If you collect both frequency and duration information, chart them separately as one may improve faster than the other.)*

e. If the student notices what you are doing and asks about it, be straightforward. Explain that you are recording how many times/for how long she pouts so you can determine if her pouting is a problem that needs to be worked on.

f. Anecdotal notes can give you a clearer picture of the pouting behavior itself, including the circumstances surrounding it. For some of the occasions when the student pouts, jot down notes (on the same card that you are using to record frequency and/or duration information) that briefly describe the setting (i.e., where and when) of the pouting incident, what the student did or said, and any other observations about the situation you may have (e.g., what prompted the behavior). It is not necessary to take notes each time the student pouts; the idea is to capture a range of examples in order to describe the behavior clearly and completely.

g. The following example shows how you might record frequency and duration information, as well as anecdotal notes, on a student's pouting.

Kaleka's Pouting—11/30

Morning	Afternoon
1 minute	3 minutes
2 minutes	3 minutes
1 minute	8 minutes
a few seconds	1 minute
5 minutes	4 minutes

Notes:

8:30—Kaleka was trying to get Bridget to play with her before school started. Bridget wouldn't, so Kaleka pouted at her desk for one minute.

11:30—Someone bumped into Kaleka's desk on the way to the pencil sharpener and she started to get mad. I told her to calm down, and she pouted for five minutes.

2:30—Several times this afternoon Kaleka pouted about the fact that I would not let her use the clay that was set out. I told her the whole class would get to use it later in the afternoon, but each time she asked and I told her "no," she would pout for several minutes at her desk.

---

2. *Identify a focus for the intervention and labels for referring to the appropriate and inappropriate behaviors.*

a. To be effective, the intervention must emphasize more than just reducing the student's pouting—there should also be a concurrent emphasis on increasing some positive behavior or trait (e.g., communicating responsibly). Having a specific positive behavior in mind makes it easier for you to "catch" and reinforce the student for behaving appropriately.

This positive focus also provides a productive way to frame the problem. For example, describing the situation simply by saying that "the student has a problem with pouting" provides little useful information, and may, in fact, put the student and her parent(s) on the defensive.

However, explaining that you want to "help the student learn to communicate responsibly," presents an important, and reasonable, goal for the student to work toward and lets the student know what she needs to do to be successful.

b. Identifying labels for the appropriate and inappropriate behaviors (e.g., "communicating responsibly" and "pouting," respectively) will help you to use consistent vocabulary when discussing the situation with the student. If you sometimes refer to the inappropriate behavior as "pouting," and other times tell the student that she is being "sulky," for example, she may not realize that you are talking about the same thing.

3. *Determine when and how to include the parent(s).*

a. It is not necessary to contact the student's parent(s) if the problem has just begun and is not interfering with the student's academic or social progress. You might, however, take advantage of any scheduled activities (e.g., conferences, weekly notes home) to let them know of your concern.

b. The parent(s) should be contacted whenever the student's pouting is affecting her academic performance or is alienating her from her peers. Share with them any information you have collected (i.e., anecdotal notes, frequency count, duration time) about the behavior, and explain why you are concerned. Focus in particular on how the student's pouting is hindering her academic success and/or her interactions with her peers (e.g., other students are annoyed by her pouting and are beginning to avoid interacting with her).

You might ask if the parent(s) have any insight into the behavior and/or whether they have noticed similar behavior at home. Whether or not the parent(s) perceive a problem, invite them to join you for an initial meeting with the student to develop a plan. Even if the parent(s) are unable or unwilling to participate, let them know that you will keep them informed of the student's progress.

c. Once the parent(s) have been involved in any way, you should give them updates at least

once per week while the plan is being implemented.

 4. *Prepare for, then conduct, an initial meeting about the situation.*

a. Arrange for a meeting to discuss your concerns with the student (and, if applicable, the student's parent[s]). Although the specifics of the meeting will vary depending upon the age of the student and the severity of the problem, there are some general guidelines to consider when scheduling the meeting.

First, meet at a neutral time (i.e., not immediately after a problem has occurred), when emotions are less likely to hamper communication. In general, a day's notice is appropriate, however a primary age student may worry excessively and/or forget what the meeting is about if it is scheduled more than an hour before it takes place.

Second, make the meeting appropriately private. For example, if a primary student has a mild problem, you might meet in the classroom while the other students are working independently. However, if you are dealing with a middle/junior high school student and the student's parent(s), you will need a private room (e.g., the counselor's office) to ensure that the discussion will not be overheard.

Third, try to make sure the meeting is scheduled for a time and place that it is not likely to be interrupted. Finally, if the parent(s) will be participating, they should be the ones to tell the student about the meeting.

b. Construct a preliminary plan. Decide whether you think you can use one of the MODEL PLANS, or if you need to create a customized plan using components from various plans and/or of your own design. Although you will invite and encourage the student to be an active partner in developing the plan, having a proposed plan in mind before you meet can alleviate frustration and wasted time if the student is unwilling or unable to participate.

c. Prepare thorough definitions of both the inappropriate behavior and the positive behavior/trait on which the student will be working. Including specific information and concrete examples will make it easier for you to clarify (and for the student to understand) your expectations.

d. Conduct the meeting in an atmosphere of collaboration. The following agenda is one way you might structure the meeting:

• **Share your concerns about the student's behavior.**

Briefly describe the problem behavior, and, when appropriate, show the student a chart or graph of how often/how long she pouts. Then, explain why you consider the pouting to be a problem. You might tell the student that pouting is not an effective or appropriate way to express herself, and that it is negatively affecting how others feel about her.

• **Discuss how you can work together to improve the situation.**

Tell the student that you would like to help her "learn to communicate responsibly," and describe your preliminary plan. Invite the student to give you input on the plan, and together work out any necessary details (e.g., the signal, consequences, the monitoring system, reinforcers).

You may have to brainstorm different possibilities if the student is uncomfortable with any aspect of the initial plan. Incorporating any of the student's suggestions that strengthen the plan is likely to increase her sense of "ownership" in and commitment to it.

• **Make sure the student understands what you mean by appropriate and inappropriate behavior.**

Use the definitions you have prepared to explain and clarify the problem behavior and the desired (positive) behavior as specifically and thoroughly as you can.

There are several ways to ensure that you and the student are in agreement about the expectations. For example, you might present several hypothetical scenarios and have the student identify whether each is an example of responsible communication or pouting. Or, you might describe an actual situation that has occurred and ask the student to describe how she could have communicated responsibly in that situation.

• **Conclude the meeting.**

Always end the meeting with words of encouragement. Let the student know that you are confident that she can be successful, and that she may actually find that she is better able to obtain what she wants and needs by communicating responsibly. Be sure to reinforce the student for participating in the meeting.

5. *Give the student regular, ongoing feedback about her behavior.*

It is important to meet with the student periodically to discuss her progress. In most cases, three to five minutes once per week should suffice. *(NOTE: PLANS D and E suggest a brief meeting at the end of each day.)* Use the meetings to review any information that has been collected, and to discuss whether or not the situation is improving. As much as possible, focus on the student's improvements, however, also address any new or continuing problems. As the situation improves, the meetings can be faded to once every other week and then to once per month.

6. *Evaluate the situation (and the plan).*

Implement any plan for at least two weeks before deciding whether to change plans; to continue, modify, or fade the plan you are using; or to cease the intervention. If the situation has improved (based on the objective information that's been collected and/or the subjective perceptions of yourself, the student, and possibly the parent[s]), you should probably stick with what you are doing. If the situation has remained the same or worsened, some kind of change will be necessary. Any changes to the plan should be discussed with the student first.

QUESTIONS, EXCESSIVE

Unnecessary Questions

DESCRIPTION

You have a student who asks questions all the time, most of which he could answer on his own.

GOAL

The student will stop asking unnecessary questions and will learn to be increasingly independent of the teacher's assistance.

OVERVIEW OF PLANS

- PLAN A: For a situation in which the problem is relatively mild or has just begun.

- PLAN B: For a student who may not know the difference between necessary and unnecessary questions, and/or may not be aware of how often he asks questions.

- PLAN C: For a student who uses questions to gain adult attention and/or for the student whose question asking has become habitual.

- PLAN D: For a situation in which several students in your class ask unnecessary questions.

Alternative Problems

- **Clinginess/ Dependency**

- **Helplessness**

· · · · · · · ·
General Considerations

- If the student's problem behavior stems in any way from academic issues (e.g., the academic expectations exceed the student's capabilities and he asks frequent questions in order to meet the expectations), concurrent efforts must be made to ensure his academic success (see **Academic Deficits, Determining**).

· · · · · · · ·
Model Plans

PLAN A

It is not always necessary, or even beneficial, to use an involved plan. If the inappropriate behavior has just begun and/or is relatively mild (i.e., not interfering with the student's academic or social progress), the following actions, along with making the student aware of your concerns, may resolve the situation.

 Respond consistently to the inappropriate behavior.

Whenever the student asks an unnecessary question, provide a gentle verbal correction and repeat the question back to the student. "Kirk, I think you know, or can figure out, the answer to that question. What is the assignment? See if you can figure it out and I'll be back in a couple of minutes to check on you."

Deliver this correction in a neutral manner. Do not act angry or frustrated with the student's question, and do not be reinforcing or overly pleasant to the student. This will show the student that the attention he receives for asking necessary question is much more satisfying than the attention that comes with unnecessary questions.

After about one minute, check back with the student to verify whether he was able to answer the question independently. If so, praise the student. "Kirk, you were able to figure that out on your own. You should be proud of your ability." If the student was unable to answer the question, provide the information the student needs.

 Use reinforcement to encourage appropriate behavior.

a. Give the student increased praise. Be especially alert for situations in which the student has refrained from asking unnecessary questions and praise him for these demonstrations of his ability to be independent. "Kirk, you got started on this assignment and are doing a very fine job. This is a great example of how you can be independent and figure things out on you own." If the student would be embarrassed by public praise, praise the student privately or even give the student a note. Remember that any time the student does not ask unnecessary questions, you can praise his independence.

b. Praise the student for asking necessary questions. When the student asks an appropriate question or a question that he probably needed to ask, praise him. You do not want the student to get the impression that asking questions is bad or wrong, as it is an essential part of the learning process. "Kirk, thank you for that question. Class, Kirk's questions brings up some very interesting points about the Mayan culture that we have not discussed yet. One of the . . . ."

c. Give the student frequent attention (e.g., say "hello" to him as he enters the classroom, call on him frequently during class activities, and occasionally ask him to assist you with a demonstration to the class) and praise him for other positive behaviors he exhibits. For example, you might comment about his spelling ability or the enthusiasm he brings to science lessons. This demonstrates to the student that you notice many positive things he does, not just the fact that he is refraining from asking unnecessary questions.

PLAN B

Some students may not actually know the difference between a necessary and unnecessary question. If your student does not seem to realize the difference between them, it will be necessary to teach him this distinction. If the student does not seem to realize how frequently he is asking unnecessary questions, you might also want to have the student monitor his own behavior.

 1. Respond consistently to the inappropriate behavior.

a. Whenever the student asks an unnecessary question, provide a gentle verbal correction and repeat the question back to the student (see PLAN A).

b. Make note of the types of questions the student asks. You will use these notes during the lessons (see Step 2) to help the student learn to discriminate between necessary and unnecessary questions.

2. Conduct lessons to teach the student how to discriminate between necessary and unnecessary questions.

a. Examine your notes and think about the type of questions the student asks. Then, identify guidelines that the student can use (and/or that you can use when responding to the student) to help him decide before he asks a question whether it is necessary or unnecessary. Following is one example of possible guidelines (yours should be tailored to fit the unique aspects of your situation).

Before I ask a question, I need to consider the following:

1. **Do I know, or can I find, the answer to this question without asking?** If so, don't ask.

   If not, ask yourself . . .

2. **Do I need to know the answer to this question, at this moment, to be able to do my job?** If not, don't ask—although maybe you could ask at another time. If you need the information at another time, ask then.

Prepare a card that lists these guidelines to serve as a prompt for the student.

b. Develop a set of example questions that you can use to teach the student how to discriminate between necessary and unnecessary questions. Generate a wide variety of questions, both necessary and unnecessary, making sure to include actual questions that the student has asked in the past.

c. During the lessons, have the student use the guidelines to analyze one of your sample questions. For example, you could lead the student through an analysis such as the following:

"Kirk, one of the questions you asked yesterday was what the math assignment was. Let's use your card to figure out if that was a necessary question. Did you know what the math assignment was or could you have figured out what the assignment was without asking me? Right, you could have looked at your assignment sheet for the week, so that was an unnecessary question. You should be independent in figuring out the answer to that type of question.

"Let's look at another example. During our math work period you asked, 'Why is the sky blue?' First, do you have that information? Right, you don't—so that may be an okay question. Now let's look at the next thing to check to determine if it is a necessary question: Do you need to know the answer to that question, right now, to finish your job? Right, you don't. The question you asked is very interesting, and I would be glad to help you figure it out, but during math I need to help 29 other students. You need to help me by waiting with questions like your question about the sky."

Continue with several different examples so the student can practice discriminating between necessary and unnecessary questions.

c. Conduct the lessons at least twice per week. The lessons should involve just you and the student (perhaps while the other students are at recess). The lessons needn't last more than three to five minutes, but it is important that they be handled in a matter-of-fact manner so the student does not feel that he is being ridiculed. You want to be very clear that you are not trying to embarrass the student, but that you do want him to think before he asks a question.

Continue the lessons until the student is using better judgment about the type and amount of questions he is asking.

3. *Prompt the student to behave appropriately by using precorrections.*

Watch for those circumstances in which the student is likely to ask unnecessary questions and remind him that he will need to remember to use his card and to think before he asks questions. "Kirk, I am going to start our math lesson. I will be watching to see if you remember to do what we practiced this morning. I'll bet you can." If time permits, you might alternately have the student identify what he should remember to do. If this conversation would embarrass the student, conduct it privately.

4. *(OPTIONAL)*
Have the student monitor his own questions.

a. Explain that you want the student to keep track of how often he asks both necessary and unnecessary questions. Tell the student that each time he asks a question or asks for help his request will be recorded on a form (like the sample shown). Together you and the student will decide whether each question was really necessary. If the question was necessary, the student should mark the "Necessary Questions" section of the form. You should then answer the student's question and praise him for asking an important question.

If the question was unnecessary, the student should mark the "Unnecessary Questions" section of the form. If the question is unnecessary because he doesn't need the answer at that time, tell the student that you will answer the question later. "Kirk, when the math period is over I will be glad to go over the lunch menu, but right now I am helping people whose questions relate to the math assignment."

If the question is one that the student should be able to answer on his own, state this, and tell him that you will be back to check on him. After a minute or so, check back with the student. If he was able to answer his own question, praise him for his independence. If he was unable to

---

Name _____

Behavior to be Counted: <u>Necessary and</u>
<u>Unnecessary Questions</u>

Date _____

Necessary Questions

1	2	3	4	5	6	7	8
9	10	11	12	13	14	15	16
17	18	19	20	21	22	23	24

Unnecessary Questions

1	2	3	4	5	6	7	8
9	10	11	12	13	14	15	16
17	18	19	20	21	22	23	24

(NOTE: Repeat four more times so the form can be used for a week.)

---

answer the question, briefly and unemotionally provide the information the student needs to proceed.

b. With the student, examine this form at the end of each day and discuss progress. You and the student may also wish to chart the frequency of his unnecessary questions in order to monitor whether this number goes down over time.

5. *Use reinforcement to encourage appropriate behavior.*

a. Give the student increased praise and attention (see PLAN A).

b. Praise the student for his willingness to actively participate in the lessons.

c. In addition, make a special point of letting the student know that you notice his efforts to use the skills he has been learning/practicing. "Kirk, you thought through whether that was a necessary question, and I agree. Nice job of doing what we have been practicing. Now an interesting thing about your question is . . . . "

PLAN C

Some students are very skilled at gaining attention through their negative behavior. If you find yourself frequently nagging, reminding, or coaxing the student to ask fewer or different types of questions, it is possible that attention is the motivation for the student's behavior. Whether or not the student overtly seems to like the attention, you should make sure that he receives more frequent and more satisfying attention when he behaves appropriately than when he is asking unnecessary questions.

1. Respond consistently when the student asks unnecessary questions.

a. Establish a system in which the student has to "pay" for each question he asks. Use your notes on the problem (see PLAN B) to determine approximately how many necessary questions the student asks on a typical day. Increase this number slightly to determine the total number of questions the student will be allotted each day. For example, if the student typically asks eight necessary questions per day, his limit might be ten. Be sure that the number is reasonable and at least as many questions as most students ask you in a day. *(NOTE: If you are not sure what is reasonable, for a couple of days count the number of questions asked by two other students of approximately equal academic ability.)*

b. Next, determine how the student will "pay" for his questions. One possibility is to create tickets like the sample shown. Each time the student asks a question, necessary or not, he must relinquish a ticket.

```
┌─────────────────────────────────┐
│                                 │
│    Question to be Answered      │
│        by Mrs. Aikens           │
│                                 │
└─────────────────────────────────┘
```

If an older student would be embarrassed by the ticket system, give him the option of having you keep a tally on a card. That is, each time the student asks a question, you will write a tally mark on the card, keeping track of the number of questions asked.

c. Whether using tickets or keeping a tally, once the student has asked his allotted number of questions for the day, you should not answer any more of his questions unless it is an emergency. Instead, respond with a short, neutral reminder that the student has used his allotted questions for that day. "Sorry Kirk, you don't have any tickets left."

Be sure the student understands that when the daily allottment of questions has been reached, you will not answer any more questions, even necessary ones. This is because you are trying to teach the student that he needs to "budget" his questions.

2. Initially, help the student to consider whether his questions are or are not necessary.

For about a week, use a prompt when the student asks an unnecessary question. "Kirk, I will answer that question if you really want, but it will cost you a ticket and I think that you already know the answer I would give. Do you really want to ask that question?"

After a week, substitute a precorrection for this type of prompt. Whenever the student begins to ask a question say, "Before I listen to the question, think about if you really need this question answered now. Do you want to spend a ticket on this question?" Then after another week, fade this procedure and let the student know that from this point forward, he will have to use his own judgment about asking questions.

3. Use reinforcement to encourage appropriate behavior.

a. Frequent praise and attention is the core of this plan. The student must see that he receives more frequent and more satisfying attention when he behaves appropriately than when he asks unnecessary questions. Thus, whenever the student is not asking unnecessary questions (or otherwise misbehaving), make an effort to praise and spend time with him. "Kirk, you have been being so independent today, it is a pleasure to see. Let's talk on our way to the cafeteria today, okay?"

b. You may also wish to use intermittent rewards to acknowledge the student's success. Occasional, and unexpected, rewards can motivate a student to demonstrate responsible behavior more often. The idea is to provide a reward when the student has had a particularly good period of being independent (i.e., asking only necessary questions).

Appropriate rewards might include playing a game with you, calling the student at home to congratulate him on his progress, or asking the principal to write the student a congratulatory note. *(NOTE: A list of additional reinforcement ideas can be found in APPENDIX 1.)* Use intermittent rewards more frequently at the beginning of the intervention to encourage the student, and then less often as his behavior improves.

c. Optionally, you may wish to reinforce the student for not asking all of his allotted questions by letting him spend time with you. For example, if the student does not ride the bus, you might allow him to stay and help you after school— one minute for each ticket he has left at the end of the day. Or, the student could chart the number of leftover tickets on a graph in order to earn a reinforcer. For example, lunch with you in the classroom could be "priced" at 25 tickets, and you could make a chart with 25 spaces to be filled in. If the student had three tickets left over on the first day, three spaces would be filled in on the chart, with 22 left to go. Thus the fewer questions the student asks during the day, the faster he would earn the right to have lunch with you.

(NOTE: Be careful that the incentive for leftover tickets is not too strong, so that the student asks few or no questions—even those necessary to complete a task. Make the reward for leftover tickets only moderately compelling and tell the student that his work must be adequately completed before he can earn minutes or chart spaces for the tickets remaining at the end of the day.)

4. **Ensure a 3-1 ratio of positive to negative attention.**

a. Given that attention is a motivating force for this student, you want to be sure that you are giving the student *three times as much* positive as negative attention. One way to do this is to monitor your interactions with the student at least one day per week. Simply keep a card on a clipboard or in your pocket and record each interaction you have with the student as either positive or negative by writing a "+" or a "-", respectively, on the card.

To determine whether an interaction is positive or negative, ask yourself whether the student was asking an unnecessary question (or otherwise misbehaving) at the time the interaction occurred. Any interaction that stems from inappropriate behavior is negative, while all interactions that occur while the student is meeting classroom expectations are positive. Thus, taking a ticket for an unnecessary question is a negative interaction, while taking a ticket for a necessary question or praising the student for being independent are both positive interactions. Greeting the student as he enters the room or asking the student if he had a nice time at recess are also considered positive interactions.

b. If you find that you are not giving the student three times as much positive as negative attention, try to increase the number of positive interactions you have with the student. Sometimes prompts can help. For example, you might decide that each time the student enters the classroom you will say "hello" to him, that during transitions you will comment on his efficiency, or that whenever a student uses the drinking fountain you will check the target student and as soon as possible praise some aspect of his behavior.

PLAN D

Occasionally, a number of students in a class fall into a pattern of seeking too much teacher assistance. The students may not even realize how frequently they ask for help. In this case, the intervention plan must focus on increasing student awareness of their own behavior and, possibly, using incentives to motivate the students to reduce their unnecessary questions.

1. **Conduct a whole class lesson on the difference between necessary and unnecessary questions. (You might adapt the ideas in PLAN B for a whole class activity.)**

2. **Count and publicly chart the frequency of necessary and unnecessary questions.**

a. Chart the frequency of questions in a space on the chalkboard or on a wall chart, with a place to tally both types of questions. However, do not mark the tallies at the time of each question. Instead record them on a card kept in your pocket or on a clipboard during the work period, and at the end of the period, let the class know the results. "During this 30-minute work period, there were ten necessary questions, bringing the total to 27. And there were seven unnecessary questions, bringing the total to 19." Do not attempt to record or publicly state which students asked which questions. You simply need a class-wide total for each type of question.

b. Total each category of question at the end of the day, chart the results, and compare the daily totals to previous days. If the situation is getting better, let the students know that you appreciate their effort to respect your time. Make sure they understand that fewer unnecessary questions means that you have more time to answer their important questions.

 Have the class set a daily performance goal to reduce their unnecessary questions.

You may have to assist the students in setting a realistic goal (e.g., reducing their unnecessary questions from 40 to 32 per day). Let the students know that with a goal of 32, they can always ask less questions than that, but since this is an attainable goal, they increase their chances of success. Then as the class consistently experiences success, continue to lower the target number until there are no more than one or two unnecessary questions each day.

 Use reinforcement to encourage appropriate behavior.

a. Give the students increased praise and attention for being independent (see PLAN A).

b. Praise the class as a whole at the end of the day for any progress in reducing their number of unnecessary questions.

 (OPTIONAL)
Establish a group reinforcement system.

a. In some cases, it may be necessary to implement a group reinforcement system to motivate the students to reduce their unnecessary questions. In the simplest of such systems, when the number of unnecessary questions is under the identified goal, the class earns predetermined points toward agreed-upon rewards.

b. A somewhat more involved alternative is a team competition. With this type of system, you would group the students in teams of four or five, and give the students training and practice in asking their teammates questions instead of you. Then, begin the competition. Each day, each team would be given a certain number of tickets for questions. When a student has a question, he/she would first ask one of his/her teammates. If no one on the team can answer the question, the student's team must "pay" one of their tickets to ask the teacher. At the end of the day, each team puts their remaining tickets (with the name of the team written on them) in a hat for a lottery drawing. The team whose ticket is drawn earns a predetermined reward for the day, such as a reduction in the amount of homework for that night.

(NOTE: Be sure that the students feel comfortable talking to you privately if they are having trouble with their team. Occasionally team projects backfire, for example when a student is intimidated by his/her teammates or is on a team that does not care about earning the rewards. The students must know that they are not completely on their own to solve these problems, and that you are available to help.)

· · · · · · · ·
Suggested Steps for Developing and Implementing a Plan

The following steps are designed to help you develop an appropriate intervention plan and implement it effectively, whether you choose to use one of the MODEL PLANS or create a customized plan of your own. The steps are, however, suggestions—they are not intended to be followed rigidly or in any particular order. Use your professional judgment and the knowledge of your particular situation to make them work for you.

Make sure you have enough information about the situation.

a. If you think a minimal intervention like PLAN A will be sufficient, you may already have enough information to proceed. However, when a more involved plan seems necessary, you should consider collecting additional descriptive and/or objective information for a couple of days.

b. You need to be able to explain what you mean when you say that "the student has a problem with asking unnecessary questions." Since asking questions in and of itself is not a problem behavior, there must be something about the student's questions that make them inappropriate. For example, is it the type of questions, the amount of questions, and/or the timing of the questions? Anecdotal notes on actual incidents should provide enough detail to help you define the problem behavior clearly and completely.

To collect anecdotal notes, simply keep a card in your pocket or on a clipboard and occasionally make notes on instances when the student asks unnecessary questions. For each entry, briefly describe where and when the incident occurred, what the student asked, and any other relevant observations (e.g., whether the student was able to find the information any other way).

You do not need to take notes every time the student asks an unnecessary question; the idea is to capture a range of examples so that you can explain the problem thoroughly. Also include some notes on times when the student asks relevant and/or important questions. This will make it clear that you are not only aware of the student's problem behavior, but also recognize when he behaves appropriately. In addition, these positive examples will be especially important in helping you clarify the types of questions the student should continue to ask.

c. Along with information on what the student's inappropriate behavior looks like, it can also be useful to document how often it occurs (i.e., a frequency count). This will provide both a more objective measure of the problem and an objective way to monitor the student's progress. You can use the same card on which you are collecting anecdotal notes to keep a frequency count—simply write a tally mark on the card each time the student asks an unnecessary question.

You might want to code these tallies to discern whether the behavior occurs more frequently during certain times, subjects, or activities (e.g.,

using an "A" or "P" to indicate that the incident happened in the morning or afternoon; or clustering the tallies by math or reading, teacher directed instruction or independent work, etc.).

d. If the student notices what you are doing and asks about it, be straightforward—tell him that you are collecting information to see whether his asking unnecessary questions is a problem that needs to be worked on.

Following is an example of anecdotal notes and frequency count that have been collected on a student's questions.

Kirk's Questions—9/3

AAAAA AAAAA AAAPP PP

9:51—During math, Kirk asked what he was supposed to do. I reminded him to look at the chalkboard where the assignment is written every day. He could have answered this on his own.

9:55—During math, Kirk asked why we needed to learn long division. I explained that division was a necessary skill for things he would learn later in math such as fractions, ratios, decimals, etc. He has already asked me this question several times before.

10:02—During math, Kirk asked what he was supposed to do with the number left over. I reexplained remainders. he probably needed to ask this question.

---

e. The frequency information is fairly easy to summarize on a chart or graph. Seeing how often he asks unnecessary question may help the student and his parent(s) better understand your concern.

f. Continuing to collect this type of information and keeping the chart up-to-date while you implement a plan will help you monitor whether the situation is getting worse, staying the same, or getting better.

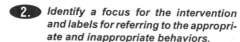 **Identify a focus for the intervention and labels for referring to the appropriate and inappropriate behaviors.**

a. To be effective, the intervention must address more than just reducing the student's unnecessary questions—there must be a concurrent emphasis on increasing some positive behavior or trait (e.g., independence, self-reliance, self-confidence). Having a specific positive behavior in mind will make it easier for you to "catch" and reinforce the student for behaving appropriately, and the positive focus will frame the situation more productively.

For example, if you simply say that "the student has a problem with asking unnecessary questions" you don't really provide any useful information, and may put the student and his parent(s) on the defensive. However, when you explain that you want to "help the student learn to be more independent," you present an important, and reasonable, goal for the student to work toward and clearly identify what the student needs to do to be successful.

b. Specifying labels for the appropriate and inappropriate behaviors (e.g., " independence" and "asking unnecessary questions," respectively) will help you to use consistent vocabulary when discussing the situation with the student. If you sometimes refer to the inappropriate behavior as "asking too many questions" and other times tell the student that "she should quit bothering you with nonsense questions," he may not realize that you are talking about the same thing.

3. Determine when and how to include the parent(s).

a. It is not necessary to contact the student's parent(s) if the problem has just begun and is not interfering with the student's academic or social progress. However, it might be a good idea to take advantage of any scheduled activities (e.g., conferences, weekly notes home) to let them know of your concern.

b. If you decide to involve the student's parent(s), share any information you have collected about the behavior (e.g., anecdotal notes, frequency count) and explain why you are concerned. Focus in particular on how the behavior is hindering the student academically and/or socially (e.g., he is becoming so dependent on interacting with you, he is not relying upon himself and his own abilities).

You might ask if the parent(s) have any insight into the situation and/or whether they have noticed similar behavior at home. Whether or not the parent(s) perceive a problem, explain that you want to help the student "learn to be more independent" and invite them to join you for an initial meeting with the student to develop a plan. If the parent(s) are unable or unwilling to participate, let them know that you will keep them informed of the student's progress.

c. Once the parent(s) have been involved in any way, you should give them updates at least once per week while the plan is being implemented.

4. Prepare for, then conduct, an initial meeting about the situation.

a. Arrange a meeting to discuss your concerns with the student and anyone else who will be involved in the plan (e.g., the parent[s], the school psychologist). Although the specifics will vary depending upon the age of the student and the severity of the problem, there are some general guidelines to consider when scheduling the meeting.

First, meet at a neutral time (i.e., not immediately after a problem has occurred), when emotions are less likely to hamper communication. In general, a day's notice is appropriate, however a primary age student may worry excessively and/or forget what the meeting is about if it is scheduled more than an hour before it takes place.

Second, make the meeting appropriately private. With a primary student who has a mild problem, you might meet in the classroom while the other students are working independently. However, when dealing with a middle/junior high school student and the student's parent(s), you will need some place private (e.g., the counselor's office) to ensure that the discussion will not be overheard.

Third, try to make sure the meeting is scheduled for a time and place that it is not likely to be interrupted. Finally, if the parent(s) will be participating, they should be the ones to tell the student about the meeting.

b. Construct a preliminary plan. Decide whether you think you can use one of the MODEL PLANS or if you need to create a customized plan using components from various plans and/or of your own design. Although you will invite and encourage the student to help develop the plan during the initial meeting, having a proposed plan in mind before you meet can alleviate frustration and wasted time if the student is unwilling or unable to participate.

c. After reviewing the information you have collected and thinking about how you want the student to behave, prepare thorough descriptions of the inappropriate behavior and the positive behavior/trait on which the student will be working. The more specific you can be and the more concrete examples you have, the easier it will be to clarify (and for the student to understand) your expectations. Be sure to consider the student's behavior in all relevant activities (e.g., independent work, teacher directed instruction, unstructured class times, recess and lunch, etc.).

d. Conduct the meeting in an atmosphere of collaboration. The following agenda is one way you might structure the meeting:

- **Share your concerns about the student's behavior.**

    Briefly describe the problem behavior and, when appropriate, show the student a chart of how frequently he asks unnecessary questions. Then explain why you consider asking unnecessary questions to be a problem. You might tell the student that he is not depending upon himself enough and that he is using your time for unnecessary questions that you should be spending with him and with other students providing help with necessary questions.

- **Discuss how you can work together to improve the situation.**

    Tell the student that you would like to help him "learn to be more independent" and describe your preliminary plan. Invite the student to give you input on the various aspects of the plan, and together work out any necessary details (e.g., the lessons, use of tickets, etc.). You may have to brainstorm different possibilities if the student is uncomfortable with the initial plan. Incorporating any of the student's suggestions that strengthen the plan is likely to increase his sense of "ownership" in and commitment to it.

- **Make sure the student understands what you mean by appropriate and inappropriate behavior.**

    Use the descriptions you have prepared to define and clarify the problem behavior and

the positive (desired) behavior as specifically and thoroughly as you can. To ensure that you and the student are in agreement about the expectations, you might present hypothetical scenarios and have the student identify whether each is an example of a necessary or a unnecessary question.

- **Conclude the meeting.**

    Always end the meeting with words of encouragement. Let the student know that you are confident that he can be successful. Be sure to reinforce him for participating in the meeting.

 Give the student regular, ongoing feedback about his behavior.

It is important to meet with the student periodically to discuss his progress. In most cases, three to five minutes once per week should suffice. *(NOTE: PLANS B, C, and D suggest daily meetings.)* During the meetings, review any information that has been collected and discuss whether or not the situation is getting better. As much as possible, focus on the student's improvements, however, also address any new or continuing problems. As the situation improves, the meetings can be faded to once every other week and then to once per month.

6. *Evaluate the situation (and the plan).*

Implement any plan for at least two weeks before deciding whether to change plans; to continue, modify, or fade the plan you are using; or to cease the intervention. Generally, if the student's behavior is clearly improving (based on the objective information that's been collected and/or subjective perceptions of yourself, the student, and possibly the parent[s]), stick with what you are doing. If the situation has remained the same or worsened, some kind of change will be necessary. Always discuss any changes to the plan with the student first.

REINFORCEMENT, MISBEHAVIOR AFTER RECEIVING

Student Unable to Handle Success

Negative Reactions to Positive Feedback

DESCRIPTION

You have a student who tends to misbehave immediately or shortly after receiving positive feedback about her behavior.

GOAL

The student will accept positive feedback without reacting inappropriately and will learn to be more comfortable with her own success.

OVERVIEW OF PLANS

- PLAN A: For a situation in which the problem is relatively mild or has just begun.

- PLAN B: For a student who misbehaves after reinforcement because she is embarrassed by positive feedback and/or wishes to impress her peers.

- PLAN C: For a student whose self-concept is so poor that experiencing success and teacher acknowledgment of that success is threatening.

NOTE:

- *If the type of misbehavior the student exhibits is consistent (e.g., she is almost always disrespectful after being reinforced) check the INDEX to see if there is a problem in this reference guide that directly addresses that specific misbehavior.*

- *Throughout the information presented in these three plans, the term "positive feedback" (rather than "reinforcement") refers to any procedure that is used to encourage responsible behavior (e.g., compliments, written notes, intermittent rewards, structured reinforcement systems, etc.).*

Alternative Problem

- **Self-Concept Problems**

General Considerations

- If the student's problem behavior stems in any way from academic issues (e.g., the student experiences academic success so infrequently that she has grown comfortable with failure), concurrent efforts must be made to ensure her academic success (see **Academic Deficits, Determining**).

- If you suspect that the student's inappropriate reactions to positive feedback could be related to the student being depressed, see **Depression**. This problem includes a set of questions to help you decide whether the student should be referred for counseling or psychological services.

- If the student's family or cultural background could be a factor in the behavior (e.g., the student is from a culture in which being publicly acknowledged as a successful individual is not a desirable experience), verify the appropriateness of any intervention plan with the student's parent(s) or someone else who is knowledgeable about the student's culture before implementing a plan. If the student is participating in class activities and assignments, and simply modifying how you provide positive feedback to the student could reduce the negative responses, it may be both unnecessary and inappropriate to intervene.

Model Plans

PLAN A

It is not always necessary, or even beneficial, to use an involved plan. If the inappropriate behavior has just begun and/or is relatively mild (i.e., not interfering with the student's academic or social progress), the following actions, along with making the student aware of your concerns, may resolve the situation.

 Respond consistently to the inappropriate behavior.

a. If the student misbehaves after reinforcement in a manner that has a prearranged consequence (e.g., hitting a classmate), calmly implement that consequence. "Sophie, the consequence for hitting is a lunch time detention."

b. If the student misbehaves in a way that has no prearranged consequence, provide a gentle verbal correction. Let the student know that her reaction is not inappropriate and give the student direct information about what she should be doing instead. "Sophie, it is not acceptable to tear up something that I hand back to you. You will need to pick up those paper scraps and put them in the recycling box before you go out to recess."

c. Do not react emotionally to the student's misbehavior and do not act disappointed. Simply address the misbehavior with a consequence or a gentle verbal correction.

 Prepare the student to accept positive feedback by using precorrections.

Prior to giving the student positive feedback, give her a choice about receiving the feedback now or at a later time. Let the student know that you would like to give her some positive feedback (or a structured reward if that is part of your overall classroom management plan). Ask the student if now is a time that she will be able to listen to and learn from the positive feedback you are about to provide. If the student says "yes," provide the positive feedback.

If the student says "no," ask her when would be a good time. If the student answers "never," quietly inform her that that is not an option. Let her know that part of a teacher's job is to let students know when they are being successful, therefore you need to inform her about something she has been successful with. Although she cannot avoid the positive feedback altogether, she can specify the time and place when she would like you to give her the feedback.

3. *Use reinforcement to encourage appropriate behavior.*

a. Give the student the positive feedback at the time and place she specified. Remember that any time the student is not engaged in misbehavior, you can provide the student attention or nonembarrassing praise for being responsible.

b. When you provide positive feedback to the student (at a time she has agreed to) and she does not react with misbehavior, praise her for her ability to accept positive feedback. In other words, the student will be receiving positive feedback both for her classroom success and for her ability to accept the positive feedback. "Sophie, I just told you what a fine job you did on your homework and you demonstrated that you can hear that, accept it, and learn from it. This shows a lot of growth—you are doing a good job of accepting positive feedback."

c. Give the student frequent attention (e.g., say "hello" to her as she enters the classroom, call on her frequently during class activities, and talk to her about her interests outside of school). This demonstrates to the student that you are interested in her as a person, not just how well she responds to your positive feedback in class.

PLAN B

Sometimes a student is embarrassed by positive feedback and reacts negatively because she is unsure of how to cope with her embarrassment. If the student seems self-conscious when positive feedback is given, and/or her reactions seem to be a performance for the benefit of her peers, this plan may be appropriate.

 1. *Respond consistently to the inappropriate behavior.*

If the student misbehaves after reinforcement in a manner that has a prearranged consequence (e.g., hitting a classmate), calmly implement that consequence. If the student misbehaves in a way that has no prearranged consequence, provide a gentle verbal correction (see PLAN A).

 2. *Modify your positive feedback so that it is less embarrassing for the student.*

During your initial meeting with the student (see SUGGESTED STEPS FOR DEVELOPING AND IMPLEMENTING A PLAN), ask the student to identify ways that you can provide positive feedback that are acceptable to her. There are no right or wrong ways to do this—the main point is for the two of you to identify them together. The following considerations might help you and the student decide what form of positive feedback she is most comfortable with, and what form of positive feedback she will be able to learn from:

- **Verbal Statements and Compliments**

  If verbal praise would be acceptable to the student, have her specify whether she would prefer that you behave emotionally neutral or pleased and excited when you give the compliment. Would she rather that you get close and whisper so that others in the class cannot hear, or that you stay more distant (and therefore, speak louder)? Does she want the compliments to be given publicly or privately?

- **Nonverbal Signals**

  Determine a signal that you could give the student that she would know means that she is being very responsible and successful, but that the other students would not understand. Possibilities include tugging on your ear, rubbing your neck, or even something as subtle as making eye contact and nodding your head. If the student prefers a nonverbal signal, decide how you can gain the student's attention if she is looking at something else, such as her work. Should you say her name and then give the signal? Should you walk over to the student's desk before giving the signal?

- **Written Notes**

  Determine whether you should write the student notes. If so, should they be given privately or is it all right with the student if other students see you giving her the note? Is it all right with the student if the note describes in detail what she did that was successful? Are there any shorthand tricks or codes that can be developed to reduce the amount of writing? For example, if the student is working on learning to stay more focused on her work, the note could be as simple as: "Sophie—Focused!"

Clarify appropriate ways the student can react to the agreed-upon forms of positive feedback.

a. Some students do not know how to accept a compliment. For example, they may not realize that it is okay to simply say nothing. If the student thinks she has to say "thank you" when given positive feedback, she might feel awkward in front of her peers. In this case, it is important to identify a variety of ways the student might respond to the positive feedback she has identified as acceptable. Possible responses include:

- Say nothing, just keep doing whatever you are doing (but don't misbehave).

- Nod your head so the teacher sees that you heard (saw, read) the positive feedback, and try to accept and learn from it.

- Smile in acknowledgment (this can be a very subtle smile that the other students will not even notice).

- Say, "Thank you."

- Acknowledge silently your own success (e.g., think, "I understand decimals better than I used to.").

- Use a predetermined nonverbal signal that will tell the teacher that you heard (saw, read) the positive feedback.

- Talk to the teacher privately to acknowledge the positive feedback and to discuss your success.

b. If necessary and appropriate, have the student practice one or more of these reactions with you privately. Role play with the student, giving her positive feedback in the agreed-upon form. Have the student practice reacting (or not reacting) in an appropriate manner.

 (OPTIONAL)
Identify peer models for the student to observe.

If you think the student could use some additional input on different ways to accept positive feedback, you might suggest two or three other students for her to observe. "Sophie, you might want to watch Orin and Goldie to see how they react when I am giving them positive feedback. I don't think anyone in class thinks of them as 'uncool,' but they both react very positively to hearing about their own success. I don't expect you to try to be like them—you're terrific just the way you are—but watching them may give you some ideas of how to react to positive feedback. You know, I just learned some new golf techniques from watching someone I played with this weekend."

If you do suggest peer models for the student to observe, this procedure must be handled with sensitivity to avoid hurting the student's feelings or implying that she should be more like someone else.

 Give the student praise and attention (in the agreed-upon form) for being able to accept positive feedback (see PLAN A).

PLAN C

There are students whose self-concept is so poor that success and adult acknowledgment of that success is frightening. If your student seems intent on proving (to you, to herself, and to her classmates) that she is really a failure, or if she seems to want to maintain an image of being very "tough" or "bad," it's possible that the student has experienced such a long history of failure that success causes her discomfort. If so, her misbehavior after receiving positive reinforcement may be a conscious, or unconscious, effort to return things to normal (i.e., everyone thinking of her as a failure). In this type of situation, the intervention must help the student learn to see herself as worthy of positive feedback.

 Critically evaluate your own beliefs about the student's capabilities and monitor "self-fulfilling prophecy" issues.

a. A student who has a very deeply ingrained negative image of herself will tend to behave in a manner that encourages others to adopt that same image of her. It is possible that, without your being aware of it, the student has convinced you that she is a failure (loser, trouble maker, or just plain mean). To test this theory, try to picture the student in your mind and visualize her being successful. If the image comes easily to you, and you have seen a great deal of successful behavior from the student, examining your reactions to the student may not be essential. However, if it was difficult to maintain an image of the student being successful, or if you can maintain the image but have rarely seen this kind of successful behavior from the student in actuality, then you should carefully review the following suggestions for critically evaluating your own beliefs about the student.

b. Examine your reactions to the student's success. The goal should be to have frequent interactions with the student that confirm her success as a person. If the student does not experience a great deal of success in the classroom, this may be difficult. You may need to reinforce the student more frequently, and for smaller steps towards successful behavior.

If the student has not experienced much positive feedback in class, she is probably uncomfortable with it. The less she receives, the less comfortable she is when it does happen. Thus, she misbehaves after being reinforced. Additionally, if you generally do not give the student positive feedback, there may be a tendency to react to her success as if it is an amazing phenomenon (i.e., making a big production out of the successful event). When a student's success is treated as a bizarre event—a momentary interruption in her typical failure—it can deepen her belief in herself as a failure.

Therefore, give the student mild, matter-of-fact positive feedback very frequently. Treat the student's small steps toward success as evidence of the success and responsibility that you know the student is capable of consistently achieving.

c. Examine your reactions to the student's misbehavior. Optimally, when the student misbehaves you should calmly and matter-of-factly give a gentle verbal correction (unless there is another preestablished consequence for that particular misbehavior) or implement the consequence (when the student knows ahead of time that a particular misbehavior leads to a given consequence) (see PLAN A).

Unfortunately, once a student has convinced you of her own image as a trouble maker or failure, you may have a tendency to react to her misbehavior with exasperation, frustration, or anger. For example, if there is a preestablished consequence for disruptive behavior, the most effective way to handle this type of situation with the student would be to state, "Sophie, that is disruptive, so you owe one minute off of the next recess" (or other appropriate consequence) in a very flat, unemotional tone.

On the other hand, making the same statement with an exasperated sigh and "I am fed up to here!" body language shifts the message from "This misbehavior equals this consequence" to "Here is one more bit of evidence regarding what a failure you are!" Remember that positive or destructive messages can be conveyed quite clearly in nonverbal ways.

d. Examine your reactions to the student's misbehavior after being reinforced. The goal should be to react no differently than you would if the misbehavior had occurred at any other time. That is, when the student misbehaves you calmly and matter-of-factly implement a gentle verbal correction or a predetermined consequences. However, there is a tendency to act very disappointed with the student in these instances—after all, she had just been successful and now she spoiled it.

Comments like, "Sophie, you were doing so well and I was so proud of you. Then you blow it by going around knocking people's books off their desks. It is beyond me why you do this sort of thing," may enhance the student's image of herself that she is most comfortable with—himself as a failure. Your disappointed reaction communicates to the student that her success was temporary and she is now back to normal, that is everyone thinking of her as a failure, including herself.

Remember, the best response is an emotionally neutral verbal correction or consequence. "Sophie, you need to pick up the books that you have knocked off." The lack of disappointment in your response communicates that you still think of the student as successful, and this event is a momentary interruption in the continued success you expect.

 2. **Help build the student's self-confidence by giving her an important job or responsibility.**

Nothing supports self-esteem like being entrusted with an important task. For example, you might arrange for the student to become an office assistant or a daily tutor for a younger student. *(NOTE: For additional ideas on other jobs and responsibilities, see APPENDIX 2.)* However, do not make the job contingent upon the student's successful behavior in the classroom. If you do, then the job is no longer a responsibility, but a reward to be earned. Since this student is uncomfortable with success, she will almost certainly behave in ways so that she does not earn the reward.

3. *(OPTIONAL, AND TIME-CONSUMING) Help the student learn to reduce her negative self-talk and replace it with positive self-talk instead.*

a. A student with an extremely negative image of herself may reinforce that image with the kinds of things she says to herself (either out loud or internally). To determine if the student is engaging in negative self-talk, describe one of the student's successes and ask her to explain why it happened. "Sophie, you got an 'A' on the spelling test last week. Why do you think that happened?" Listen for a tendency on the part of the student to explain successes as temporary situations, situations over which she has no influence, or even as "lucky" events. Common negative self-talk explanations might include:

- "The test was too easy."

- "I got real lucky."

- "Anette corrected my test and she probably didn't catch some of the mistakes."

Then, prompt the student to identify what she says to herself about "bad" events or failure situations. "Sophie, yesterday you knocked a bunch of books off of people's desks. Why did that happen?" The student may have a tendency to explain these sorts of events as permanent situations that are attributed to things about herself which are unchangeable. For example:

- "I guess I am just a bad person."

- "When I get frustrated, watch out because I am going to blow."

- "That's always the way I have been."

- "Hey—everybody is going to know that I'm tough and you don't mess with me."

b. For more information on how to help modify the student's negative self-talk, see **Self-Concept Problems**. Changing the way the student talks

to and thinks about herself can be a very time-consuming process. This may be something that will have to be undertaken by the school counselor or other appropriate adult who can work with the student individually (or in a small group with other students who could benefit from the same type of information).

c. Some people may find this type of technique controversial. Be sure to check with an administrator and/or obtain parental permission before implementing this particular suggestion with the student.

4. *Arrange for an adult mentor who will spend time with the student approximately once per week.*

The mentor could be a former teacher with whom the student has a positive relationship, or any adult in the school who shares a common interest with the student (e.g., love of books, a particular sport). The gender of the mentor should not matter, as long as the student (and the student's parent[s]) are comfortable with the person.

Try to arrange for the student to spend time doing something fun with the mentor one day each week after school or during the lunch break. There are two major advantages to this procedure. First, and most important, this adult will show unconditional interest in the student, and demonstrate that she has value independent of her performance in the classroom.

Second, once the relationship between the student and the mentor is well-established, you can occasionally ask the mentor to comment to the student about her successful classroom performance. "Ms. Fahd mentioned to me that your grades are going up in science and math. Tell me what you have been doing differently that is getting those grades up." However, do not use this procedure too frequently, and do not ask the mentor to talk to the student about any behavioral or academic problems occurring in your class.

. . . .

Suggested Steps for Developing and Implementing a Plan

The following steps are designed to help you develop an appropriate intervention plan and implement it effectively, whether you choose to use one of the MODEL PLANS or create a customized plan of your own. The steps are, however, suggestions—they are not intended to be followed rigidly or in any particular order. Use your professional judgment and the knowledge of your particular situation to make them work for you.

**Make sure you have enough informa-
tion about the situation.**

a. If you think a minimal intervention like PLAN A will be sufficient, you may already have enough information to proceed. However, when a more involved plan seems necessary, you should consider collecting additional descriptive information for a couple of days.

b. You need to be able to explain what has led you to conclude that "the student has a problem with accepting positive feedback." Anecdotal notes on actual incidents should provide enough detail to help you define the problem behavior clearly and completely. To collect anecdotal notes, simply keep a card in your pocket or on a clipboard and occasionally make notes on specific instances when the student misbehaves after you give her positive feedback.

For each entry, briefly describe the initial positive behavior, the feedback you provided, and the student's inappropriate reaction. You do not need to take notes every time the student reacts negatively to positive feedback; the idea is to capture a range of examples so you will be able to describe the behavior completely.

Also include some notes on times when the student accepts positive feedback in an appropriate manner. This will make it clear that you are not only aware of her problem behavior, but also recognize when she behaves appropriately. When you meet with the student, the positive examples will also help you clarify how you want the student to behave.

c. If the student notices what you are doing and asks about it, be straightforward—tell her that you are collecting information to see whether her reactions to positive feedback are a problem that need to be worked on.

Following is an example of anecdotal notes that have been collected on a student's difficulty with accepting positive feedback.

d. Continuing to collect this type of information while you implement a plan will help you monitor whether the situation is getting worse, staying the same, or getting better and will provide specific examples to use in discussing progress.

 **Identify a focus for the intervention
and labels for referring to the appropriate and inappropriate behaviors.**

a. To be effective, the intervention must address more than just reducing the student's negative

---

Sophie's Reactions to Positive Feedback—1/27

Notes:

8:50—I handed back spelling tests to the students and when I gave Sophie hers, I said that 85% showed that her hard work was really paying off. As soon as I said it, she tore up her paper and threw it on the floor.

11:00—I was walking around the room during an independent work period and I complimented Sophie on her on-task behavior. She responded sarcastically, "You're very on-task also, Ms. Fahd."

2:00—I privately commented to Sophie that she had worked hard and already completed her assignments for the day. She did not react positively or negatively.

---

reactions to positive feedback—there must be a concurrent emphasis on increasing some positive behavior or trait (e.g., "accepting positive feedback"). Having a specific positive behavior in mind will make it easier for you to "catch" and reinforce the student for behaving appropriately. This may sound somewhat nonsensical, but part of the plan must involve reinforcing the student for reacting responsibly to positive feedback.

In addition, the positive focus will help you frame the situation more productively. For example, if you simply say that "the student has a problem with accepting positive feedback," you don't really provide any useful information, and may put the student and her parent(s) on the defensive. However, when you explain that you want to help the student "learn to accept and learn from positive feedback," you present an important, and reasonable, goal for the student to work toward and clearly identify what the student needs to do to be successful.

b. Specifying labels for the appropriate and inappropriate behaviors (e.g., "accepting positive feedback" and "rejecting positive feedback," respectively) will help you to use consistent vocabulary when discussing the situation with the student.

3. *Determine when and how to include the parent(s).*

a. It is not necessary to contact the student's parent(s) if the problem has just begun and is not interfering with the student's academic or social progress. However, it might be a good idea to take advantage of any scheduled activities (e.g., conferences, weekly notes home) to let them know of your concern.

b. Whenever a student's reactions to positive feedback are severe (e.g., tantrumming, disrespect) or the problem has gone on for a couple of weeks, contact the student's parent(s). Share with them any information you have collected about the behavior (e.g., anecdotal notes), and explain why you are concerned. Focus in particular on how the behavior is hindering the student academically and/or socially (e.g., the student will have trouble knowing what she is doing well if she cannot accept positive feedback).

You might ask if the parent(s) have any insight into the situation and/or whether they have noticed similar behavior at home. Whether or not the parent(s) perceive a problem, explain that you want to help the student "learn to accept and learn from positive feedback" and invite them to join you for an initial meeting with the student to develop a plan. If the parent(s) are unable or unwilling to participate, let them know that you will keep them informed of the student's progress.

c. Once the parent(s) have been involved in any way, you should give them updates at least once per week while the plan is being implemented.

4. *Prepare for, then conduct, an initial meeting about the situation.*

a. Arrange a meeting to discuss your concerns with the student and anyone else who will be involved in the plan (e.g., the parent[s]). Although the specifics will vary depending upon the age of the student and the severity of the problem, there are some general guidelines to consider when scheduling the meeting. Make the meeting appropriately private and try to make sure the meeting is scheduled for a time and place that it is not likely to be interrupted. Additionally, if the parent(s) will be participating, they should be the ones to tell the student about the meeting.

b. Construct a preliminary plan. Decide whether you think you can use one of the MODEL PLANS or if you need to create a customized plan using components from various plans and/or of your own design. Although you will invite and encourage the student to help develop the plan during the initial meeting, having a proposed plan in mind before you meet can alleviate frustration and wasted time if the student is unwilling or unable to participate.

c. After reviewing the information you have collected and thinking about how you want the student to behave, prepare thorough descriptions of both the inappropriate behavior and the positive behavior/trait on which the student will be working. The more specific you can be and the more concrete examples you have, the easier it will be to clarify (and for the student to understand) your expectations. Be sure to consider the student's behavior in all relevant activities (e.g., independent work, teacher directed instruction, unstructured class times, recess and lunch, etc.).

d. Conduct the meeting in an atmosphere of collaboration. The following agenda is one way you might structure the meeting:

- **Share your concerns about the student's behavior.**

  Briefly describe the problem behavior and explain why you consider her negative reactions to positive feedback to be a problem. You might tell the student that being able to accept positive feedback is important in school and on a job. Positive feedback is how an employer and/or a teacher can communicate that things are going well, and that she should keep doing what she is doing. Communicate that her misbehavior following positive feedback might lead some teachers to stop giving her positive feedback, and would lead most bosses to fire her.

- **Discuss how you can work together to improve the situation.**

  Tell the student that you would like to help her learn to "accept and learn from positive feedback," and describe your preliminary plan. Invite the student to give you input on the various aspects of the plan, and together work out any necessary details (e.g., the use of a signal, a nonembarrassing procedure for praising the student, etc.).

  You may have to brainstorm different possibilities if the student is uncomfortable with the initial plan. Incorporating any of the student's suggestions that strengthen the plan is likely to increase her sense of "ownership" in and commitment to it.

- **Make sure the student understands what you mean by appropriate and inappropriate behavior.**

  Use the descriptions you have prepared to define and clarify the problem behavior and the positive (desired) behavior as specifically and thoroughly as you can. To ensure that you and the student are in agreement about the expectations, you might present hypothetical scenarios and have her identify whether each is an example of accepting or rejecting positive feedback. Or you might describe an actual situation that has occurred and ask the student to explain how she could demonstrate that she is accepting positive feedback in that situation.

- **Conclude the meeting.**

  Always end the meeting with words of encouragement. Let the student know that you are confident that she can be successful. Be sure to thank her for participating in the meeting.

 5. *Give the student regular, ongoing feedback about her behavior.*

It is important to meet with the student periodically to discuss her progress. In most cases, three to five minutes once per week should suffice. During the meetings, review any information that has been collected and discuss whether or not the situation is getting better. As much as possible, focus on the student's improvements, however, also address any new or continuing problems. As the situation improves, the meetings can be faded to once every other week and then to once per month.

6. *Evaluate the situation (and the plan).*

Implement any plan for at least two weeks before deciding whether to change plans; to continue, modify, or fade the plan you are using; or to cease the intervention. Generally, if the student's behavior is clearly improving (based on the objective information that's been collected and/or the subjective perceptions of yourself and/or the student), stick with what you are doing. If the situation has remained the same or worsened, some kind of change will be necessary. Always discuss any changes to the plan with the student first.

REINFORCEMENT, STUDENT WHO REQUESTS

DESCRIPTION

You have a student who requests reinforcement (e.g., he asks questions like, "What will I get if I . . . ?").

GOAL

The student's need for external reinforcers will lessen and he will learn to be increasingly motivated by intrinsic reinforcement.

OVERVIEW OF PLANS

- PLAN A: For a situation in which the problem has just begun or occurs infrequently.

- PLAN B: For a student who has not learned to take intrinsic pride in behaving responsibly and/or who asks for reinforcement to gain attention.

Alternative Problems

- **Participation In Class, Lack of**

- **Reinforcement, Misbehavior After Receiving**

- **Spoiled Behavior**

. . . .
General Considerations

- Keep in mind that it is human nature to want as much payment as possible for doing tasks—after all, most adults ask for a raise every year or two. For this to be a problem behavior the student must be immature or unreasonable in his requests. That is, he requests reinforcement too often or is too demanding in his requests.

- If the student has been motivated with extrinsic rewards for a long time, it's possible that he has not learned that motivated, responsible behavior can be its own reward. Changing this mindset can take time. If the student is on an extrinsic reward system that has been successful, do not jeopardize that system because of concerns about the student requesting reinforcement. Instead, plan to gradually fade the extrinsic reinforcement as the student's success continues.

- If the inappropriate behavior is resulting in the student avoiding or not completing his schoolwork, begin with a plan to increase the student's work completion (see **Work Completion—Daily Work**). Once the student is turning in completed work on a regular basis, you can reconsider an intervention for the overt request for reinforcement, if the problem still exists.

. . . .
Model Plans

PLAN A

It is not always necessary, or even beneficial, to use an involved plan. If the inappropriate behavior has just begun and/or occurs infrequently, the following actions, along with making the student aware of your concerns, may resolve the situation.

1. Respond consistently to the inappropriate behavior.

a. Whenever the student requests reinforcement or asks what he will get, gently correct him. Let the student know that it is better not to ask such a question directly.

If you wish to go into more detail with the student, consider the factors following:

- Identify any established rewards (e.g., points or grades) associated with the completion of the task. Tell the student, for example: "Well, Hal, every student who completes and turns in all their daily assignments earns ten points." or "Hal, by completing your math you will earn points that will be added up to determine your math grade."

- If there are no extrinsic rewards associated with the task, consider whether the task is one the student is required to do. If it is, tell the student that he will earn the sense of pride in meeting his responsibilities, *and*, if he chooses not to do it, he will not have that sense of satisfaction and he will receive whatever consequences are in place for not doing it. For example, if the student chooses not to clean up after an art project, he could be kept in from recess until it is finished.

- If the task is not required, let the student know that while he does not have to do the task, you hope that he will. Remind him that if he does the task, he can take pride in exceeding his responsibilities. "Hal, you do not have to help me take the books back to the library, but if you choose to, you can take pride in being responsible and cooperative. Besides, I would appreciate your help."

b. Never offer a reward or privilege when the student makes a request for reinforcement. In addition, never offer a reward for an immediate task that needs to be done. Statements like, "If you get all your work done today, I will give you . . ." may perpetuate the student's inappropriate requests for reinforcement. The next day he might wonder what his reward is, and if he doesn't get anything he might feel cheated.

However, with some students it may be appropriate to implement an ongoing reward (e.g., daily points for work completion to be saved up toward a reinforcer) to increase motivation. The former is akin to coercion, while the latter is more like an employment contract, and is an acceptable form of reinforcement.

2. *Use reinforcement to encourage appropriate behavior.*

a. Give the student increased praise. Be especially alert for situations in which the student might, but does not, ask for reinforcement and praise him for these demonstrations of his ability to take pride in being responsible. "Hal, I asked you to do me a favor and you did it without hesitation or asking what I would give you. That is a great example of how you can take pride in being responsible."

If the student would be embarrassed by public praise, praise the student privately or even give the student a note. Remember that any time the student is behaving responsibly and has not asked for reinforcement, you can praise him for taking pride in being responsible.

b. Give the student frequent attention (e.g., say "hello" to him as he enters the classroom, call on him frequently during class activities, and occasionally ask him about his interests outside of school), and praise him for other positive behaviors he exhibits. For example, you might comment about his participation in physical education or praise him for the effort he put into a geography report. This demonstrates to the student that you notice many positive things he does, not just the fact that he is refraining from asking for reinforcement.

PLAN B

Some students are very skilled at getting extra rewards and possibly attention by asking "What will I get if . . . ?" If you find yourself frequently nagging, reminding, or coaxing the student to stop asking for reinforcement, it is possible that he is trying to gain adult attention. Whether or not the student overtly seems to like the attention, you should make sure that he receives more frequent and more satisfying attention when he behaves appropriately than when he requests reinforcement and/or engages in other undesirable behaviors. Even if attention is not the main motivating force, the success of this plan rides on demonstrating to the student that better rewards come from not requesting reinforcement.

1. *Respond consistently when the student requests reinforcement.*

a. Never offer a reward or privilege when the student has made a request for reinforcement or for an immediate task that needs to be done (see PLAN A).

b. Whenever the student requests reinforcement, use a short statement that gives the student very little attention. For example, if the student asks what he will get for doing something, you could respond, "That's up to you, Hal." If the student asks what you will give him, you could reply, "Nothing Hal, but I hope you will give yourself something."

The purpose of these statements should be explained in the initial meeting with the student (see SUGGESTED STEPS FOR DEVELOPING AND IMPLEMENTING A PLAN). That is, you want the student to know ahead of time that when he makes such a request, you will not spend much time with him—but that you will spend time with him when he is taking pride in being responsible. Let him know that when he asks for reinforcement, you will tell him that it is up to him whether he learns anything from what he has to do and whether or not he will give himself a sense of pride.

c. If, after using your statement, the student immediately repeats his request or question, ignore the request. Do not let the student engage you in a discussion of what he might receive, or even a discussion about why he will not get anything. The goal is to interact with the student as little as possible when he is making a request for reinforcement.

2. *Use reinforcement to encourage appropriate behavior.*

a. Frequent praise and attention is the core of this plan. The student must see that he receives more frequent and more satisfying attention when he behaves appropriately than when he requests reinforcement. Thus, whenever the student engages in a responsible behavior without asking for reinforcement (or otherwise misbehaving), make an effort to praise and spend time with him. "Hal, you are working so diligently on these science labs. Would it be okay if I sat with you a moment and watched as you and your group do the next step?"

b. You may also wish to use intermittent rewards to acknowledge the student's success. Occasional, and unexpected, rewards can motivate the student to demonstrate responsible behavior more often. The idea is to provide a reward when the student has had a particularly good period of not having requested reinforcement. Appropriate rewards might include anything the student particularly likes to do. *(NOTE: A list of reinforcement ideas can be found in APPENDIX 1.)*

Use intermittent rewards more frequently at the beginning of the intervention to encourage the student, and then less often as his behavior improves.

(NOTE: Intermittent rewards should only be given occasionally—and not when the student has requested them. Never use intermittent reinforcement when the student has asked what he would get. Make it clear to the student that he is receiving the reward, in part, because he is being responsible and because he did not request it.)

3. **Ensure a 3-1 ratio of positive to negative attention.**

a. If attention is a motivating force for this student, you want to be sure that you are giving him *three times as much* positive as negative attention. One way to do so is to monitor your interactions with the student at least one day per week. Simply keep a card on a clipboard or in your pocket and record each interaction you have with the student as either positive or negative by putting a "+" or a "-", respectively, on the card.

To determine whether an interaction is positive or negative, ask yourself whether the student was requesting reinforcement (or otherwise misbehaving) at the time the interaction occurred. Any interaction that stems from inappropriate behavior is negative, and all interactions that occur while the student is meeting classroom expectations are positive. Thus, providing a gentle correction is a negative interaction, but praising the student for not requesting reinforcement is positive. Greeting the student as he enters the room or asking him if he tried out for the soccer team are also considered positive interactions. *(NOTE: Ignoring the student's requests for reinforcement is not recorded at all, because it is not an interaction.)*

b. If you find that you are not giving the student three times as much positive as negative attention, try to increase the number of positive interactions you have with the student. Sometimes prompts can help. For example, you might decide that each time the student enters the classroom you will say "hello" to him, or that you will interact with the student at least twice during his favorite part of the school day—during the activities in which he is least likely to ask, "What will I get if . . . ." You can also increase the ratio of positive to negative attention by ignoring more of the student's inappropriate behavior.

4. **Encourage the student to use self-reinforcement.**

During the initial meeting with the student (see SUGGESTED STEPS FOR DEVELOPING AND IMPLEMENTING A PLAN), introduce the concept that it can be very satisfying to tell oneself that you are doing a good job and behaving responsibly. Help the student identify statements he could use to reinforce himself in different situations. Then, prompt the student to use these statements when he is behaving responsibly. "Hal, what could you say to yourself right now that would help you take pride in what you are doing?"

. . . .
Suggested Steps for Developing and Implementing a Plan

The following steps are designed to help you develop an appropriate intervention plan and implement it effectively, whether you choose to use one of the MODEL PLANS or create a customized plan of your own. The steps are, however, suggestions—they are not intended to be followed rigidly or in any particular order. Use your professional judgment and the knowledge of your particular situation to make them work for you.

Make sure you have enough information about the situation.

a. If a simple plan like PLAN A seems sufficient, you may already have enough information to proceed. Otherwise, you should consider collecting additional descriptive information in the form of anecdotal notes for a couple of days.

b. If the student notices what you are doing and asks about it, be straightforward—tell him that you are collecting information to see whether his requesting reinforcement is a problem that needs to be worked on.

 Identify a focus for the intervention and labels for referring to the appropriate and inappropriate behaviors.

The intervention must focus on more than just reducing the student's requests for reinforcement—there must be a concurrent emphasis on increasing some positive behavior or trait (e.g., taking pride in being responsible). The positive focus will help you frame the situation in a more productive manner when discussing the situation with the student and his parent(s), and having a specific positive behavior in mind will make it easier for you to "catch" and reinforce the student for behaving appropriately.

3. **Determine when and how to include the parent(s).**

a. It is not necessary to contact the student's parent(s) if the problem has just begun or is not interfering with the student's academic or social progress, however it might be a good idea to take advantage of any scheduled activities (e.g., conferences, weekly notes home) to let them know of your concern.

b. If you do contact the student's parent(s), share any information you have collected about the behavior (e.g., anecdotal notes), and explain why you are concerned. Focus in particular on how asking for reinforcement tends to alienate teachers (and future employers). In addition, discuss how the student may learn to do only those things that have direct and immediate rewards, and yet much of success in life depends upon intrinsic motivation and delayed gratification.

You might ask if the parent(s) have any insight into the situation and/or whether they have noticed similar behavior at home. Whether or not the parent(s) perceive a problem, explain that you want to help the student "learn to take pride in being responsible," and invite them to join you

for an initial meeting with the student to develop a plan. If the parent(s) are unable or unwilling to participate, let them know that you will keep them informed of the student's progress.

c. Once the parent(s) have been involved in any way, you should give them updates at least once per week while the plan is being implemented.

4. **Prepare for, then conduct, an initial meeting about the situation.**

a. Arrange a meeting to discuss your concerns with the student and anyone else who will be involved (e.g., the parent[s]). Although the specifics will vary depending upon the age of the student and the severity of the problem, there are some general guidelines to consider when scheduling the meeting.

First, meet at a neutral time (i.e., not immediately after a problem has occurred) when emotions are less likely to hamper communication. In general, a day's notice is appropriate, however a primary age student may worry excessively and/or forget what the meeting is about if it is scheduled more than an hour before it takes place.

Second, make the meeting appropriately private. With a primary student who has a mild problem, you might meet in the classroom while the other students are working independently. However, when dealing with a middle/junior high school student and the student's parent(s), you will need some place private (e.g., the counselor's office) to ensure that the discussion will not be overheard.

Third, try to make sure the meeting is scheduled for a time and place that it is not likely to be interrupted. Finally, if the parent(s) will be participating, they should be the ones to tell the student about the meeting.

b. Construct a preliminary plan. Decide whether you think you can use one of the MODEL PLANS or if you need to create a customized plan using components from various plans and/or of your own design. Although you will invite and encourage the student to help develop the plan during the initial meeting, having a proposed plan in mind before you meet can alleviate frustration and wasted time if the student is unwilling or unable to participate.

c. Prepare a thorough description of the student's inappropriate behavior and a description of the positive behavior/trait on which the student will be working. The more specific you can be and the more concrete examples you have, the easier it will be to clarify (and for the student to understand) your expectations.

d. Conduct the meeting in an atmosphere of collaboration. The following agenda is one way you might structure the meeting:

• **Share your concerns about the student's behavior.**

Briefly describe the problem behavior and explain why you consider it to be a problem. For instance, you might tell the student that if he only does things that offer immediate rewards he will miss out on many exciting learning opportunities. You can also introduce the concept of taking pride in being responsible and give age-appropriate examples.

Provide some examples from your own life of things you do partially because of extrinsic rewards (e.g., coming to work every day) and some things you do even though there is no extrinsic reward (e.g., spending time talking to the student about this problem—you would get paid whether or not you have the discussion, or staying late to ensure that everything was prepared for the science lesson today). You might also wish to mention that questions such as, "What will I get for doing this assignment?" could be offensive to teachers who take pride in preparing worthwhile lessons for their students.

• **Discuss how you can work together to improve the situation.**

Tell the student that you would like to help him learn to " take pride in being responsible," and describe your preliminary plan. Invite the student to give you input on the various aspects of the plan, and together work out any necessary details (e.g., how you will respond if the student requests reinforcement).

You may have to brainstorm different possibilities if the student is uncomfortable with the plan. Incorporating any of the student's suggestions that strengthen the plan is likely to increase his sense of "ownership" in and commitment to it.

• **Make sure the student understands what you mean by appropriate and inappropriate behavior.**

Use the descriptions you have prepared to define and clarify the problem behavior and the positive (desired) behavior as specifically and thoroughly as you can. To ensure that you and the student are in agreement about the expectations, you might present hypothetical scenarios and have him identify whether each is an example of requesting reinforcement or of taking pride in being responsible. Or you might describe an actual situation that has occurred and ask him to explain how he could demonstrate taking pride in that situation.

• **Conclude the meeting.**

Always end the meeting with words of encouragement. Let the student know that you are confident that he can be successful. Be sure to reinforce him for participating in the meeting.

5. *Give the student regular, ongoing feedback about his behavior.*

It is important to meet with the student periodically to discuss his progress. In most cases, three to five minutes once per week should suffice. Discuss whether or not the situation is getting better. As much as possible, focus on the student's improvements, however, also address any new or continuing problems. As the situation improves, the meetings can be faded to once every other week and then to once per month.

6. *Evaluate the situation (and the plan).*

Implement any plan for at least two weeks before deciding whether to change plans; to continue, modify, or fade the plan you are using; or to cease the intervention. Generally, if the student's behavior is clearly improving (based on the objective information that's been collected and/or the subjective perceptions of yourself, the student, and possibly the parent[s]), stick with what you are doing. If the situation has remained the same or worsened, some kind of change will be necessary. Always discuss any changes to the plan with the student first.

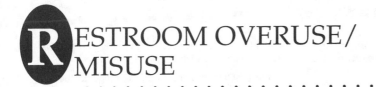RESTROOM OVERUSE/ MISUSE

DESCRIPTION

There are students in your class who overuse the restroom (i.e., in excess of what is physiologically necessary) and/or misuse the restroom (e.g., bothering other students, spraying water from sinks, plugging up toilets, etc.).

GOAL

The students will use the restrooms only when necessary and in responsible ways.

OVERVIEW OF PLANS

- PLAN A: For a situation in which the classroom policies for restroom use need to be revised or established.

- PLAN B: For a situation in which the students are overusing the restrooms and/or spending too much time in them.

- PLAN C: For a situation in which the students are misbehaving in the restrooms (bothering other students, making a mess, etc.).

NOTE:

- *These plans assume that the restrooms are "down the hall" rather than in each classroom.*

- *These three plans are geared for a situation in which quite a few students in the class have a problem with overusing and/or misusing the restrooms. However, each can easily be modified to intervene with only a few (one to three) students who have/continue to have a problem with restroom use.*

Alternative Problems

- **Misbehavior Outside of Class— Hallways/ Playground/Cafeteria**

- **Vandalism/Destruction of Property**

- **Wetting/Soiling Pants**

········

General Considerations

• If the problem behavior involves an individual student who seems to overuse the restroom, be sensitive to the possibility that the student has a physiological rather than a behavioral problem. Contact the student's parent(s) to discuss the behavior before attempting an intervention. If the student has not had a physical examination recently, it may be advisable. Consult with your building administrator concerning how to make such a recommendation.

• If the problem centers around damage to the restroom (e.g., spray paint, soap dispensers ripped from the walls, etc.) see **Vandalism/Destruction of Property** for additional ideas that may be coordinated with suggestions within these plans.

········

Model Plans

PLAN A

Procedures for proper use of restrooms must be taught to the students. This plan identifies decisions that need to be made, provides suggestions on some of the details that need to be addressed, and describes how to teach these procedures to students. If possible, coordinate the rules with the other teachers in your wing, or school-wide.

 Identify rules for responsible use of the restrooms.

Following is a sample set of rules:

• Use the restrooms on your way out to recess and during lunch.

• If the restrooms must be used during class or recess, you must have a hall pass.

• Use the restrooms responsibly (no playing with water, bothering others, etc.).

• Leave the restrooms as clean or cleaner than when you entered.

• Put toilet paper in the toilet. Put all other paper in the garbage.

• Flush the toilet (one time after use).

• Leave the stall unlocked after use.

• Wash your hands.

• Leave the restroom as soon as you finish.

Specifying this much detail may seem excessive, but it is better not to make assumptions. For example, one school staff assumed that the students were careless or negligent about flushing the toilets. However, when teaching the expectations, they realized that many students were recent immigrants from a country with water shortages and

had been specifically taught not to flush toilets after use.

 Decide whether the students will need your permission to use the restrooms.

This is largely an issue of teacher style. Some teachers want their students to ask permission so they can monitor who is going when and how often. Other teachers prefer to allow their students to simply use the restrooms whenever necessary. Regardless of your decision on this particular issue, you should implement specific procedures (see Steps 3 and 4) such as the use of hall passes and signing out of the classroom.

 Use some form of hall pass to ensure that no more than one boy and one girl have left the classroom for the restroom at any given time.

Some teachers use a small block of wood (approximately the size of an index card, and 1/4-1/2" thick) with a string so that the hall passes can be hung near the door to the classroom. Such a system has several advantages, the most important of which is that no more than one student from the class will be in the restroom at a time. The probability of mischief increases if two or more friends are in the bathroom at the same time unsupervised. Another advantage to the wood block system is that you do not have to write a hall pass whenever a student needs to go to the restroom.

Printed on the block is something like the following:

> # Hall Pass to the Girl's Restroom
> # Mr. Morgan's Classroom
> # Room 17

 Decide whether there should be some form of sign out whenever a student leaves your room.

Although this may not be possible for kindergarten students, when the students know how to write their names, a sign-out system helps you to monitor where every one of your students is at all times.

Keep a sheet near the hall passes and have the students sign out when they are leaving to use the restrooms. The sheet should have places to indicate the date, name of the student, the time when he/she leaves the classroom, the time when he/she returns (if your students are able to tell time), and the student's destination (if you plan to have the students sign out to other locations in addition to restrooms).

This sheet may seem like a lot of paperwork, but it allows you to monitor where your students are and whether any students are overusing their restroom privileges. It may be especially important for teachers who do not require permission to leave the room. When the students are allowed to go to the restrooms without permission, the teacher needs some way of knowing when an individual student has left the classroom for supervision and liability reasons.

5. **At the beginning of the year, after vacations, and at any other time when there have been significant problems, conduct lessons to teach (or reteach) the restroom expectations to the class.**

a. Before the lessons, think about the various issues and decide on restroom procedures for your class. In addition, identify any problems that have already occurred and exactly what you expect the students to do or not do in those situations. Include all this information in your lessons.

b. During the lessons, specify the expectations for student behavior and ask questions to verify that the students thoroughly understand the expectations for restroom use. Teachers in second grade and above can conduct the lessons in the classroom and simply talk about use of the restrooms. Kindergarten and first grade teachers should plan to hold at least part of the lessons in the restrooms. This may mean making arrangements for a female staff member to take the girls to the girls' restroom for that portion of the lesson (or vice versa).

c. Conduct the lessons until the student are consistently able to answer questions about the expectations correctly. With kindergarten and first grade students, plan ten-minute lessons daily for the first week of school. With older students, you may only need to conduct one or two ten-minute lessons total.

6. **Respond consistently to each instance of inappropriate restroom use.**

a. Whenever you learn of a restroom problem (e.g., the custodian has let you know that your students have been plugging toilets with paper towels), provide feedback to the class. Inform them of why the behavior is a problem (e.g., the custodian needs to spend time unplugging toilets when he/she should be engaged in other activities, it makes the restroom unusable by other students, etc.).

b. If you know (i.e., have proof), that a restroom problem was caused by specific students, those individuals should be responsible for reparations (see **Vandalism/Destruction of Property** for ideas).

7. **Use reinforcement to encourage appropriate behavior.**

a. Early in the year, and periodically throughout the year when there have been no problems with the restrooms, let the class know that you appreciate their ability to be responsible for taking care of the restrooms.

b. If there have been problems in the restrooms followed by improvement, provide feedback frequently. Help the students recognize that taking care of the restrooms is a way of demonstrating their independence, the ability to be a self-manager, and pride in the school.

PLAN B

If your concern is that the students seem to overuse or spend too long in the restroom during class time (do not count or monitor use of the restroom during regularly scheduled breaks), the intervention should involve first monitoring the behavior and then, if necessary, monitoring the students to reduce their excessive use of the restrooms.

 Monitor how often the students need to leave the classroom to use the restrooms.

a. Use the sign-out sheet (described in PLAN A) to determine how many times the students are going to the restrooms and how many minutes of class time are being missed each day. Do not calculate individual totals, only a class-wide total (i.e., the total number of trips to the restrooms and the total number of minutes spent outside the classroom).

b. Every day conduct a short class meeting to review that day's record. Have a student record the totals on a chart (or do it yourself). Discuss whether the day was better, worse, or about the same as previous days. If the day did not go well, encourage the students to talk about why and have them identify what they could do the next day to help them remember to use the restrooms at assigned break times rather than having to leave the classroom. In many cases, the act of charting the totals and having a short class discussion daily may be enough to improve student behavior.

 Encourage the class to set daily performance goals for the number of trips, the total number of minutes, or both.

Help the students to set a realistic goal (e.g., reducing the number of trips from 25 to 20). If some students want to set a very challenging goal (e.g., reducing the number from 25 per day to zero per day), explain that if the goal is "no more than 20," they can always reduce the number of trip even more, but they increase their chances of success.

As the class experiences success, the goal should become progressively lower until the number is acceptable to you. Do not worry about having zero as a goal. The students should feel that there is some latitude for occasionally needing to use the restroom other than at break times. Since the original problem was the *excessive* use of the restroom, success lies in reducing, but not necessarily eliminating, the behavior.

 Use reinforcement to encourage appropriate behavior.

a. Praise individual students for meeting your expectations regarding the appropriate use of the restroom and praise the entire class when improvement occurs (see PLAN A).

b. During the daily review meetings, praise the students for being willing to examine the cumulative record for the day. Even on a bad day, if the students are willing to discuss why it was a bad day, praise them. "Class, you are really handling this responsibly. Even though it was a rough day, you are willing to talk about things you might do differently tomorrow. That is a real sign that we are making progress." Regardless of how the day went, try to make the end-of-the-day meeting upbeat and encouraging—you want the students to look forward to this review.

c. On some occasions when the class meets their performance goal, provide an intermittent reward to the entire class. Occasional, and unexpected, rewards can motivate the students to demonstrate responsible behavior more often. The idea is to provide a reward when the class has made a concerted effort to reduce the number of trips to the restroom.

Appropriate rewards might include any class-wide activity—a game, extra recess time, free time, etc. *(NOTE: A list of additional reinforcement ideas can be found in APPENDIX 1.)* Use intermittent rewards more frequently at the beginning of the intervention to encourage the students, and then less often as their behavior improves.

PLAN C

If the problem is misuse of or misbehavior in the restrooms, it may be necessary to increase the monitoring and supervision of the restrooms to decrease the problems. In most cases, this will require coordinating your efforts with the custodial staff and other teachers whose students use the same restrooms. *(NOTE: You should discuss this plan with your building administrator before proposing it to other staff members.)*

 **1. Arrange for daily feedback from the custodians on the condition of the restrooms.**

a. Post a form similar to the following outside each restroom and ask the custodial staff to rate the neatness of the restrooms when they are cleaning them in the evening.

Yesterday _____ this restroom was:
              date

__ Great! Very neat and clean.

__ Pretty good.

__ Okay, but could be better.

__ Not very good. It needs to be cleaner.

__ Awful. The students need to be more responsible for taking care of this part of our school.

Notes:

---

b. Whenever they give a poor rating, have the custodial staff write a brief note on the form describing the specific problems (e.g., toilets plugged with paper towels, soap powder thrown around the room, toilet paper streamers on the floor, etc.). Distribute a copy of the form with the note to all the teachers whose students use that restroom.

c. Coordinate these procedures with the building administrator so that he/she can discuss the plan with the custodial staff.

2. Respond consistently to each instance of inappropriate use.

a. Any time there is a poor rating, give the class feedback on the problem. Conduct a class discussion in which you encourage the students to behave responsibly. Also, let them know that if the problem continues, additional action (such as more supervision in the restrooms, less freedom for students to use the restrooms independently, etc.) will be taken. You don't want this to sound threatening, but the students have to understand that the problem is serious enough that it cannot be allowed to continue.

b. If restroom problems continue, conduct a problem-solving discussion with the class (see SUGGESTED STEPS FOR DEVELOPING AND IMPLEMENTING A PLAN).

c. When those responsible for a restroom problem are known, assign a consequence involving cleaning the restrooms during recess or after school.

d. When those responsible are not known, invite the students to provide you with any information they have about who might be causing the problems. One way to do so is to make yourself accessible. Let the students know times and ways they can communicate to you in confidence. Make clear that you will keep the source of any information private. Since some students might prefer to remain anonymous, you might also invite them to leave a note, signed or unsigned, on your desk or to put a note in your box at the office.

Also let the students know of other adults to whom they can talk confidentially about the problem (e.g., the school counselor, principal, etc.). **Vandalism/Destruction of Property** includes suggested procedures for obtaining information from students about severe or costly damage that has been done.

3. If necessary, increase supervision of the restrooms.

Coordinate with the building administrator and other staff to establish spot checks of restrooms. The idea is for the students to realize that if they are playing in (and/or damaging) restrooms, it is likely that they will be caught. When all or almost all of the teachers in a particular wing of the building are the same sex (e.g., male), arrange for female staff members to make unannounced inspections of the girls' restrooms.

Increasing adult supervision of the restrooms and having each teacher use a classroom sign-out sheet should make it easier to identify those students who have been involved in any inappropriate restroom behavior.

 4. *Use reinforcement to encourage appropriate behavior.*

As the situation improves, the students should be given positive feedback from you, and occasionally from the custodial staff (either in person or via notes). Emphasize that responsible use of the restrooms is an example of school pride and of developing a sense of community.

········

Suggested Steps for Developing and Implementing a Plan

The following information is designed to help you implement an appropriate and effective intervention plan, whether you choose to use one of the MODEL PLANS or create a customized plan of your own. The steps are, however, suggestions—they are not intended to be followed rigidly or in any particular order. Use your professional judgment and the knowledge of your particular situation to make them work for you.

 1. *Decide how to present the situation to the class.*

a. If you decide to implement one of the MODEL PLANS, arrange a time to present your plan to the class. Wait for a time when you are calm (i.e., not right after an incident has occurred) and inform the students that you are finding their restroom behavior to be a problem. Then specifically define your expectations regarding restroom use and/or the procedures that will be implemented.

Give the students the opportunity to ask questions/make comments. End the session by thanking the students for listening and letting them know that you are confident that they will make an effort to follow the restroom rules in the future.

b. If you want the students to assume some ownership of the problem, you might want to hold a class meeting in which the students participate in analyzing the situation and developing an action plan. Before the meeting you will need to clarify the nature/extent of the problem and your expectations for the students' behavior.

You will also need to identify any aspects of the plan that you do not feel comfortable opening up to a group decision. For example, you must decide ahead of time whether or not to allow the class to determine *if* there will be a consequence for problems in the restrooms and/or what the consequence should be. If you firmly believe that there must be a consequence, then you should not seek student input on that particular issue.

 2. *Help the class generate a plan.*

(NOTE: You should feel free to suggest one or more procedures from the MODEL PLANS in addition to the guidelines following.)

a. Schedule the meeting for a neutral time and allow enough time for a reasonable discussion. Inform the students in advance that the meeting will take place; this will give them time to think about the problem. "Class, this afternoon we are going to have a class meeting on the problem of misuse (or overuse) of the restrooms. Please give some thought to this problem and what we might do as a class to solve it."

b. Use an agenda to structure the meeting. Shortly before the meeting, write the agenda on the chalkboard. Following is a sample you may consider using.

Agenda

1. Misuse (overuse) of the restrooms—Define the magnitude of the problem. *(NOTE: Share any relevant data.)*

2. Review expectations regarding restrooms.

3. Brainstorm ideas for improving the situation.

4. Select strategies that everyone agrees to.

5. Establish what will happen if there is future misuse (overuse) of the restrooms.

---

c. Be sure to establish clear rules (for both you and the students) regarding the brainstorming phase of the meeting. For example:

1. Any idea is okay (but no obscenity).

2. Ideas will not be evaluated initially (i.e., no approval—"Good idea" or disapproval—"What a stupid idea" or "We couldn't do that" should be expressed during brainstorming).

3. All ideas will be written down and discussed at the conclusion of brainstorming.

d. At the conclusion of brainstorming, evaluate the ideas and lead the class to consensus on any decisions that need to be made. Use voting as a decision-making process when appropriate.

3. *Determine when and how to include the parent(s).*

a. Because restroom misuse (or overuse) is more of a procedural than behavioral or motivational problem, involving the students' parents is not critical for a class-wide problem.

b. If the situation involves only one or two students who have or continue to have a problem with using the restroom responsibly, you should contact the parent(s) of those individuals. Let the parent(s) know that their student is having problems with restroom behavior and what steps you are taking to correct the situation.

Frequent contact is not required, but whenever you intend to implement an individualized plan, the parent(s) should be informed prior to its implementation and should be given feedback about the student's progress every two to four weeks.

4. *Give the class regular, ongoing feedback about their behavior.*

Periodically meet with the students to discuss the situation. In most cases, three to five minutes once per week should suffice. Review any information that has been collected and discuss whether or not the situation is getting better. As much as possible, focus on improvements, however, also address any new or continuing problems.

As you discuss problems, acknowledge that there are individuals in the class who consistently behave appropriately. Do not single out individuals when discussing problems or progress with the entire class. As the situation improves, the meetings can be faded to once every other week and then to once per month.

5. *Evaluate the situation (and the plan).*

Any plan should be implemented for at least two weeks before deciding whether or not it is effective. Generally, if the situation has improved (based on any objective information that's been collected and/or the subjective perceptions of yourself and the students), continue with what you have been doing. (Eventually you will want to fade, then eliminate, the plan.) If the problem remains the same or worsens, some kind of change (i.e., modifying the current plan or switching to another plan) will be necessary. Always discuss any change in the intervention with the class first.

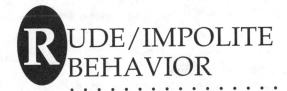

RUDE/IMPOLITE BEHAVIOR

Lack of Manners

Lack of Common Courtesy

Poor Social Amenities

DESCRIPTION

There are students in your class who fail to use good manners (e.g., "Please," "Thank you," etc.).

GOAL

The students will use good manners when interacting with you and each other.

OVERVIEW OF PLANS

- PLAN A: For a problem which may stem from the students not realizing that their behavior is impolite.

- PLAN B: For a problem which may stem from the students not having been taught how to be polite.

- PLAN C: For a situation in which the students lack the motivation to treat you and each other with common courtesy.

NOTE:

These three plans are designed for a situation in which a number of students in the classroom fail to use good manners. However, each can easily be modified to intervene with only one to three students who have or continue to have a problem with good manners.

Alternative Problems

- **Arguing—Students With Each Other**

- **Arguing—Student(s) With the Teacher**

- **Complaining**

- **Disrespectful Behavior**

- **Name Calling/ Put-Downs**

- **Smart-Aleck Behavior/ Inappropriate Humor**

- **Social Skills, Lack of**

. . . .
Model Plans

PLAN A

Because what constitutes common courtesy can differ from community to community and from family to family, some students who act rude may not even recognize that their behavior is inappropriate. For example, they may come from homes where simple requests consistently take the form of harsh demands (e.g., "Change the channel. That show is stupid.") and/or words like "please," "thank you," and "excuse me" are not part of the vocabulary. The purpose of this plan is to help the students become aware that they should act more politely.

1. **Respond consistently to instances of rude behavior.**

a. Whenever you observe a student being impolite, provide a gentle correction. State that what the student did was not polite and suggest an alternative way of interacting. "Dennis, grabbing the paper as Sharon is handing it to you is impolite. A more polite response would be to calmly take the paper from her and then tell her 'Thanks' or 'Thank you.'"

b. Whenever you observe a student who is not following through on the procedures for polite behavior that the class agreed to implement (see SUGGESTED STEPS FOR DEVELOPING AND IMPLEMENTING A PLAN), gently correct the student. "Shauna, we all agreed that . . . ."

2. **Model polite behavior.**

When interacting with the students, be sure to behave in ways that demonstrate to the students that one can be polite without being "syrupy" or

"wimpy." When giving directions or making requests, be sure to remember to include the words "please" and "thank you."

3. **Use reinforcement to encourage appropriate behavior.**

a. Praise individual students you observe being polite. With primary age students, reinforce them directly and publicly for being polite. "Amanda, you are doing a great job of remembering 'please' and 'thank you.'" With older students, public reinforcement of "politeness" may backfire—it might not seem "cool" or "macho" to them to be polite. If you wish to comment on an older student's polite behavior, do so privately or give the student a note.

b. When the class as a whole makes improvements, praise the entire class. With intermediate and middle/junior high school classes, reinforce the students' polite behavior by commenting upon how "respectful," "mature," or "responsible" they are being.

PLAN B

If the students are not polite because they have never been taught social amenities, the intervention must include some way of teaching them the basics of polite social interaction.

*(NOTE: If the problem is severe, you may need to consider systematic social skills training. **Social Skills, Lack of** contains information on a variety of published social skills curricula.)*

1. **Prepare and conduct a detailed lesson on rude and polite behavior.**

a. To teach the students to recognize the difference between rude/impolite behavior and polite/respectful behavior, first generate a list of sample situations, including some actual inci-

dents in which the students have been rude or impolite. (Be sure to change the names and details of the situation enough that no one student feels singled out.) Possible situations might include:

• A teacher (or boss) gives you a direction or task to do.

• A classmate makes a request of you.

• A new student asks if the desk next to you is taken.

- Someone you barely know says "Hello."

- You want to borrow some paper from the student next to you.

- That student gives you the paper.

- The principal asks, "How are you doing?"

- You're having a lousy day and the principal asks, "How are you doing?"

- You strongly disagree with a statement made in a class discussion.

- A teacher (or boss) tells you how to do something, but you think you have a better way of doing it.

b. During the lesson, present a situation and have the students identify one impolite response and at least two different polite responses. Then either move on to another situation or have the students generate additional examples of polite and impolite responses, if you feel that they need more practice. It is critical that the students think of polite examples. If there is too much focus on rudeness, the class is likely to get goofy and begin trying to "top" each other with the silliest or most obnoxious examples of impolite responses.

If a student raises the issue of polite responses being "wimpy" or what a "teacher's pet" would do, ask the students to generate responses that would allow them to both be polite and maintain their dignity in front of their peers. (Your purpose is not to turn fifth grade students, for example, into a group of "Little Lord Fauntleroys."

c. Have the students practice the polite/respectful behavior by role playing how various situations might be handled. The key to doing this well with older students is to help them see that they can be polite and still be "cool" (or whatever current term describes someone who is admired). The role playing sessions may need to be repeated periodically (perhaps twice per week) until most (or all) of the students consistently demonstrate polite behavior.

d. Then help the students develop strategies for responding to someone who is rude. You can ask the class to brainstorm how you (the teacher) should handle the situation if a student is rude to you. Decide which, if any, of their suggested responses you will use and inform them of your decision. Then ask the class for ideas on what you should do if you observe one student being rude to another. Again, choose one strategy you think is practical and inform the students. Next, ask for their ideas on what

one student can do if another student is rude to him/her. Lead the class to agree on two or three strategies for responding to rude treatment that provide feedback in a nonconfrontational manner.

Finally, have the class generate ideas on what a student can do if you (the teacher) are rude to him/her. Ending the lesson with this topic demonstrates that even the teacher can make a mistake and inadvertently be rude. If they have developed strategies for politely correcting the teacher, the students are not as likely to be angry when they are corrected by the teacher or another student for their own rude behavior.

2. *Respond consistently to each instance of rude/impolite behavior.*

Follow through with the strategies/procedures identified by the students in the lesson.

3. *Reduce the probability of rude behavior by using precorrections.*

Watch for situations in which a student (or students) is likely to be rude, and remind the student (or students) to be polite. "Aref, I am about to show you some corrections you need to make, but before I do, take a couple of seconds and think about how you can respond to me in a polite way (pause): Now the ones that you need to correct are . . . . "

4. *Use reinforcement to encourage appropriate behavior.*

a. Provide praise to individuals and the class as a whole for exhibiting polite behavior (see PLAN A).

b. Use intermittent rewards and incentives when the class makes significant progress. Occasionally, on a day when everyone is making an effort to be more polite, give some kind of reward or privilege to the entire class. "Class, we have been doing such a great job of being polite and respectful in the last couple of days, let's have music playing during our work periods this afternoon." *(NOTE: Additional ideas for group reinforcers can be found in APPENDIX 1.)*

5. *When you think your students have mastered basic politeness, arrange for the class to present to a younger class a lesson (including a skit on polite and impolite behavior) on the benefits of being polite.*

PLAN C

Sometimes the students know very well how to be polite, but simply choose not to behave that way (e.g., it's become a badge of honor or status to be rude). When this is the case, you might need to use a more structured system of reinforcement in which polite behavior is paired with occasional rewards and rude behavior results in a mild, but consistent, punitive consequence.

1. **Prepare and conduct a lesson to teach the students the difference between polite behavior and rude/impolite behavior (see PLAN B).**

2. **Respond consistently to each incident of rude behavior.**

a. If a student is rude to you or another student, provide a gentle correction (see PLAN A).

b. If the student responds rudely to your correction, implement time owed. With an elementary student, the student could lose one minute of recess time for each infraction that immediately follows a gentle correction. A middle/junior high school student might owe one minute after class the first time and ten minutes of detention for each subsequent infraction.

3. **Use reinforcement to encourage appropriate behavior.**

a. Provide intermittent rewards and incentives when the class makes progress (see PLAN B).

b. Use a lottery system to encourage individual students to be polite. Construct tickets (like lottery or movie tickets) to be used in a drawing, and tell the students that you will occasionally pass out tickets as a way of letting them know that their efforts in being polite are recognized

and appreciated. *(NOTE: Be sure they understand that this will not happen every time someone is polite—after all, being polite is the norm to be expected.)*

Some of the times that you observe a student being polite (to you or to another student), give that student a ticket and have that student write his/her name on it. You'll have to make an effort to acknowledge both the students who are usually polite and to "catch" those students who may have more of a tendency to be rude.

c. Identify a variety of reinforcers that the students might enjoy. The more that rudeness has become the norm with a group, the more powerful those reinforcers will need to be to turn around this behavior. Once per week (or daily, if the group initially needs greater and more immediate incentives) announce that it is time for the drawing. State the reinforcer and then draw a ticket. The student whose name is on the ticket earns that reward.

In the early stages, draw for two or three different reinforcers of different value. "The first name we will draw will receive a certificate from the cafeteria for a free cinnamon roll or ice cream. The second name will receive a 'Free Homework Pass,' and the third name will receive a certificate for a free tape or CD generously donated by Music World on 12th Street."

....

Suggested Steps for Developing and Implementing a Plan

The following steps are designed to help you develop an appropriate intervention plan and implement it effectively, whether you choose to use one of the MODEL PLANS or create a customized plan of your own. The steps are, however, suggestions—they are not intended to be followed rigidly or in any particular order. Use your professional judgment and the knowledge of your particular situation to make them work for you.

1. **Make sure you have enough information about the situation.**

a. For three to five days, keep a note card in your pocket or on a clipboard, and any time a student

acts in a way that you consider to be impolite, make a note of the incident. Be sure to specify those features of the student's behavior that led you to conclude that it was rude. For frequent rude behaviors, such as not saying "please,"

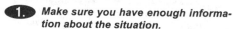

"thank you," and/or "excuse me," you might simply write tally marks on the card. Following is a sample of anecdotal notes that might typically be recorded on the card.

Rude Behavior—3/12

Please   / / / /

Thank You   _//////_

Excuse Me   / / /

Raul said, "Fine" sarcastically when I told him he had some corrections.

Saundra responded, "Well duh!" when Mary Louise asked her a question.

James asked Andi to borrow a pencil and Andi said, "Forget it, dork."

---

b. If a student asks what you are doing, simply say that you are trying to find out how often people in the class are rude to each other. Tell the student that the class will discuss the findings in a few days.

c. Keep a separate card for each day, and continue to collect this data one day per week after you begin the intervention.

2. **Schedule and conduct a class-wide discussion about the situation.**

a. Let the students know a day ahead of time that there will be a class meeting to discuss the problem of impolite behavior, and prepare an agenda to structure the meeting. Following is one sample agenda you may consider using.

Agenda

1. Define the nature of the problem—How much rudeness is there?

2. Provide examples of rude and polite behavior.

3. List benefits of treating each other more politely.

4. Brainstorm—What can be done?

---

b. During the meeting, invite participation from as many class members as possible. Begin the meeting by clarifying the nature of the problem. Share the information you have been collecting (i.e., the anecdotal notes). Then, work through the other steps on the suggested agenda. Fo-

cus the discussion on the "What can be done?" step, encouraging the students to brainstorm as many ideas as possible.

When a reasonable number of suggestions have been made, have the class select (by voting, when appropriate) a few of the suggestions that everyone agrees to implement.

c. Be sure to establish clear rules (for both you and the students) regarding the brainstorming phase of the meeting. For example:

1. Any idea is okay (but no obscenity).

2. Ideas will not be evaluated initially (i.e., no approval—"Good idea" or disapproval—"What a stupid idea" or "We couldn't do that" should be expressed during brainstorming).

3. All ideas will be written down and discussed at the conclusion of brainstorming.

3. **Determine when and how to include the parent(s).**

a. With a class-wide problem, parental involvement is probably not critical. However, you may wish to send a memo to parents (or put an announcement in your class newsletter, if you have one) explaining that you will be working with the students on polite behavior and encouraging them to work on the same behaviors at home.

b. If only one or two students have/continue to have a problem with rudeness, you should contact the parents of those individual students. Inform the parent(s) that their student is having problems with rude behavior and discuss any intended intervention plan.

c. Once the parent(s) have been involved in any way, you should continue to keep them informed of the students' progress. Once every other week is probably sufficient.

4. **Give the students regular, ongoing feedback about their behavior.**

Schedule periodic class meetings to discuss progress. In most cases, five minutes once per week should suffice. Share your findings from the one day per week that you have been continuing to keep anecdotal notes. When the situation has improved, ask the students if they have noticed that the class is a more pleasant place to be and congratulate them on their effort.

If there has not been improvement and/or the students do not feel that the class is more pleasant, discuss other things that could be done to improve the situation. Then as the situation improves, the meetings can be faded to once every other week and then to once per month.

 5. *Evaluate the situation (and the plan).*

Implement any plan for at least two weeks before evaluating its effectiveness. Generally, if the situation is clearly improving (based on the objective information that has been collected and/or the subjective perceptions of yourself and the students), stick with what you are doing for another two weeks. If the situation continues to improve, you can begin to fade the intervention. However, if the problem has remained the same or worsened, some kind of change will be necessary. Always discuss any changes in the plan with the class first.

SCHOOL PHOBIA

School Refusal

Frequent Absenteeism

Irrational Fear of School Activities

DESCRIPTION

You have a student who refuses to come to school or who acts extremely upset when she gets to school.

GOAL

The student will come to school each day that she is not physically ill and will learn to enjoy being at school.

OVERVIEW OF THE PLAN

For a situation in which the problem has just begun and/or there is an identifiable circumstance that is causing the student to be fearful of school.

NOTE:

Any subsequent intervention efforts should be done in collaboration with one or more of the following individuals:

- *School Psychologist*
- *Building Administrator*
- *Truant Officer*

Alternative Problems

- **Absenteeism**
- **Allergies, Asthma, Disabilities, Seizures**
- **Anxiety/ Nervousness**
- **Hypochondria**
- **Tantrumming (K or 1st Grader)**

....
General Considerations

- If the student's school phobia stems in any way from academic issues (e.g., the student is afraid to come to school because she is unable to meet academic expectations), concurrent efforts must be made to ensure her academic success (see **Academic Deficits, Determining**).

- If the student lacks the basic social skills to interact with her peers appropriately, it may be necessary to begin by teaching her those skills.

Social Skills, Lack of contains information on a variety of published social skills curricula.

- If you suspect that the student's fear of school could be related to the student being depressed, see **Depression**. It includes a set of questions to help you decide whether the student should be referred for counseling or psychological services.

....
Model Plan

If the student has missed only a couple of days of school and/or acted upset about being at school only one or two times, the following actions, along with making the student aware of your concerns, may resolve the situation.

 Determine if there is something specific that the student fears about being at school.

You may be able to obtain this information directly from the student or the student's parent(s). Do not dismiss or trivialize any specific fears the student identifies. Avoid statements like, "You're worried that you might miss your bus stop on the way home. That is nothing to worry about." Instead, let the student know that whatever concerns her is important and that together you can work out a plan to resolve the problem and/or to help the student learn to deal with it.

 Develop ways to specifically address the student's concerns.

Work with the student and the student's parent(s) on ways to allay the student's fear(s). For example, if the student is afraid of crying and embarrassing herself, you might suggest a private place in the school that the student could go any time she feels the need to cry. Or, if the student worries about missing her bus stop, you might decide to have the bus driver remind the student when it is time to get off and have her parent(s) there to meet her. If the student is concerned about being teased by another student, you could teach the student strategies for dealing with the teasing and talk to the student who is doing the teasing.

 Have an adult act as a "greeter" for the student as she arrives at school each day.

a. To help create an anxiety-free school arrival and transition to the classroom, identify someone who can meet the student when she gets to school every day—welcoming her, walking her to the classroom, getting her started on her day. This person could be you, or it might be an instructional assistant. If the greeter is someone other than yourself, make sure the student knows that once she gets to the classroom, you will be there to assist her.

b. Have the greeter participate in the initial discussion with the student (see SUGGESTED STEPS FOR DEVELOPING AND IMPLEMENTING THE PLAN), and arrange for the student and the greeter to practice the arrival routine. If the parent(s) bring the student to school, include them in the practice as well. You want the transition from parent to greeter to be smooth for the student (even when she gets upset), and for the parent(s) to feel comfortable leaving immediately. Everyone should understand that the idea is to avoid lengthy and dramatic good-byes. (NOTE: If the student rides the bus, you will need to establish procedures for the transition from parent(s) to bus driver and from bus driver to greeter.)

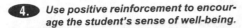

4. *Use positive reinforcement to encourage the student's sense of well-being.*

a. As soon as the greeter brings the student to the classroom, go over and give the student a warm welcome. Do not "gush" or go overboard, but help the student feel welcome. "Tricia, it's nice to see you this morning. Thanks for coming down with her, Mrs. Rodriguez. Tricia, let's get your things put away and get ready for the morning."

b. In addition, provide frequent praise and attention to the student throughout the day. "Tricia, you have been writing in your journal through

the entire period. You should be proud of what a hard worker you are."

NOTE: If this plan is ineffective, either because the student is still not coming to school or still gets upset when she is at school, you should refer the situation to your building administrator, school psychologist, and/or a truant officer. Or for more detailed information on dealing with school phobia, see:

Guevremont, D.C. (1991). Truancy and school absenteeism (pp. 581-591). In G. Stoner, M.R. Shinn, & H.M. Walker (Eds.). Interventions for achievement and behavior problems. Silver Spring, MD: National Association of School Psychologists.

. . . .
Suggested Steps for Developing and Implementing the Plan

The following steps are designed to help you develop an appropriate intervention plan and implement it effectively. The steps are, however, suggestions—they are not intended to be followed rigidly or in any particular order. Use your professional judgment and the knowledge of your particular situation to make them work for you.

 1. *Make sure you have enough information about the situation.*

a. Descriptive information, in the form on anecdotal notes, will be useful for generating a clear picture of the situation. Any time the student gets very upset when her parent(s) leave, jot down when the situation happened, what the student did, what you did, and what the parent(s) did.

Also, whenever the student does not come to school, record the reason given by the parent(s) for the student's absence. Your notes and up-to-date, accurate attendance records will be invaluable if it becomes necessary to involve other professionals or agencies in the problem.

b. If you think that additional objective information would be helpful, you can also document how long (i.e., the duration time) it takes the student to settle down when she gets upset. To collect this information, simply note the time when the student begins to get upset and the time when she becomes calm.

This record of "number of minutes spent being upset" can be summarized on a chart or graph which you can share with the student and her parent(s). Continuing to collect and graph this information while you are implementing a plan

will also make it easy to determine if progress is being made.

 2. *Identify a focus for the intervention and labels for referring to the appropriate and inappropriate behaviors.*

With a school phobia issue, the positive focus of the intervention is clear—coming to school. If you also wish to emphasize beginning classroom activities immediately (i.e., calmly beginning the day), a phrase or label that encompasses both of these objectives might be "participating in classroom activities."

3. *Determine when and how to include the parent(s).*

a. The student's parent(s) must be involved in this problem. Contact them immediately and arrange for them to come in for a conference with you and the student. Share whatever information you have collected (i.e., anecdotal notes, duration time records, and attendance records). During the conference, you might explain that if the student gets into bad attendance habits now, it will become more difficult for her to develop and maintain good attendance habits later. You can also ask if the student's parent(s) have any insight into the behavior (e.g., specific circumstances or events that are making the student fearful).

If the parent(s) are unable or unwilling to participate, it may be necessary to refer the problem immediately to your building administrator or school counselor or, if the situation warrants, a truant officer.

b. Continue to keep the parent(s) informed—giving them updates at least twice per week in the early stages. If you are documenting duration time and the number of minutes spent being upset per day is decreasing, reassure them that the plan is working. This may be especially important because they only see the child upset about school. It might be comforting for them to know that the student calms down and fits right in within a few minutes of coming into the classroom.

4. Prepare for, then conduct, an initial meeting about the situation.

a. Schedule a meeting to discuss your concerns with the student and her parent(s). *(NOTE: If you are planning on using a "greeter" other than yourself, invite this person to the meeting as well.)* Arrange the meeting for a neutral time and a private place. If the parent(s) would be more comfortable, you might even consider having the meeting at their home. In any case, schedule the meeting for a time and place that is unlikely to be interrupted.

b. Conduct the meeting in an atmosphere of collaboration. The following agenda is one way you might structure the meeting:

- **Share your concerns about the student's behavior.**

  Briefly describe what the problem behavior is and, if applicable, share the student's attendance record and/or the graph of how much time she spends being upset. Then explain *why* you consider the school phobia to be a problem. You might tell the student that you miss her when she is not at school, and that she is missing out on learning and fun.

- **Discuss how you can work together to improve the situation.**

  If you haven't already, try to find out if there is something specific that is bothering the student about being at school, and identify ways to address her concerns. Then explain about the greeter and invite the student to give you input on the plan.

  Privately—not in front of the student—let the parent(s) know that there is a good chance the student will not feel like coming to school the next day, but ask them not to give in to the student's requests. Help them see that they can provide lots of gentle reassurance while still holding firm to the fact that she must go to school.

  Finally, make sure that the parent(s) and the greeter both understand that when the student is upset they need to not make a big deal of it. The parent(s) should just guide the student out of the car to the greeter (or the bus driver), who will then gently but firmly guide the student to the classroom.

- **Conclude the meeting.**

  Always end the meeting with words of encouragement. Let the student know that you are confident that she can be successful, and that she will soon learn that school is often fun and almost always at least enjoyable. Be sure to reinforce her for participating in the meeting.

5. Evaluate the situation (and the plan).

If the student is coming to school each day, implement your intervention for at least two weeks before evaluating its effectiveness. In general, if the student's behavior is clearly improving, stick with the plan until the student no longer feels the need for the greeter. *(NOTE: You can check with the student on a weekly basis.)*

If the student's behavior does not improve (and/or the student is not even showing up for school), immediately refer the problem to your building administrator or district truancy officer.

SELF-CONCEPT PROBLEMS

. . . .

Lack of Self-Esteem

Poor Self-Image

Self-Deprecation

DESCRIPTION

You have a student whom you believe has a self-concept problem.

Because the term "self-concept problem" does not describe a discrete behavior, but is rather a label that encompasses many different types of behavior, this problem includes no MODEL PLANS. The purpose of the following information is to suggest some basic considerations for assisting a student you believe has a self-concept problem. In addition, information is provided on five categories of techniques—one or more of which may prove effective for helping a student who lacks self-esteem.

Alternative Problems

- **Apathetic Behavior**
- **Bored Behavior**
- **Depression**
- **Helplessness**
- **Hypochondria**
- **Participation In Class, Lack of**
- **Pouting**
- **Victim—Student Who Is Always Picked On**
- **Whining**

. . . .
General Information

- If the problem is serious enough that you are considering implementing one or more the techniques described following, inform the student's parent(s) of your concern and discuss your intentions with them. Be sensitive to the fact that some people may find some of the techniques (e.g., visualization practice, modifying self-talk) objectionable. If the student's parents(s) object to the specific technique(s) you have decided upon, suggest one or more of the others included here. If the parent(s) object to *any type* of intervention directed at improving their child's self-concept, respect their wishes and instead focus your efforts on specific and observable behavior (e.g., increasing the student's work completion, reducing the student's daydreaming, etc.).

- When a student is subjected to academic frustration and failure on a daily basis, no extraneous procedure will be powerful enough to have a lasting and positive effect on his self-concept. Therefore, if a student is struggling academically, part of the intervention plan *must* include procedures to increase the student's academic success. The problem **Academic Deficits, Determining** includes procedures for determining whether the student is experiencing academic difficulties. Another resource, *Interventions: Collaborative Planning for Students At Risk* by Sprick, Sprick, and Garrison (1993), includes specific suggestions for adapting instruction to remediate a student's skill deficits and increase his academic success.

- If you suspect that the student's moodiness may be related to the student being depressed, see **Depression**, which includes a set of questions to help you decide whether the student should be referred for counseling or psychological services.

- (NOTE: If the student does not engage in misbehavior, disregard this step.) If the student exhibits an overt misbehavior (e.g., babyish behavior, not completing assignments, hypochondria, apathy, etc.), use the INDEX of this reference guide to locate an appropriate plan for helping the student learn to behave more responsibly. As the student experiences greater success, emphasize how proud he should be of his level of responsibility.

- If you are not clear about the student's problem, but instead just have a vague sense that the student has a poor self-concept, keep anecdotal notes for a week or so. To do so, make a note of the incident or situation each time the student does something that you think is an indication of the student's poor self-concept. After a week, you should have collected a body of information that will assist you in implementing an intervention that best fits the nature of your student's particular problem.

- Most of the plans for specific problems included in this reference guide provide suggestions for increasing the amount of positive attention a student receives and for making sure that the student is receiving more frequent and more satisfying attention for positive (successful) behavior than for negative (unsuccessful) behavior. This can be especially critical for a student with poor self-esteem. See **Helplessness** for a MODEL PLAN that specifically focuses on giving the student attention in positive ways.

- The old adage "Nothing succeeds like success" is relevant for any issue involving self-concept. The more one experiences success, the more one expects to be successful in subsequent pursuits. Thus, in addition to helping the student make behavioral and academic progress, you should teach the student how to establish and achieve specific goals. Achieving a goal will not only improve how the student feels about himself, but will help him realize that he can control many aspects of his own life.

- Use the following procedures to establish and help the student achieve a goal relating to the management of one or more of his problematic behavior(s):

  1. Decide who should be involved in the process of setting the goal and negotiating a written agreement. Most of the time this process should include just you and the student. However, in some cases, you may also wish to involve the student's parent(s). If there is a high probability that the student and/or his parent(s) will be hostile during this meeting, invite the building administrator or school counselor to be an "unbiased" party who can mediate the discussion and keep communication from becoming adversarial.

  2. In the meeting, work with the parties present to set a written goal (i.e., a "contract"). Although you may want to have some predetermined ideas about what the goal contract should entail, the process is likely to be more effective if the student participates in the

actual writing of the contract and feels a sense of ownership of it.

Begin the meeting by reviewing its purpose. "The purpose of this meeting is to work together to set goals for Scott. Goal setting is a very useful skill to help you learn to be successful in whatever you wish to do."

Next, identify a broad, general goal that can help the student feel more powerful and in control of what happens to him at school. For example, if the student tends to be overly dependent on teacher support and help, the general goal might be for the student to be more independent and self-reliant. If the student is disorganized and messy, the general goal might be for the student to be organized and neat.

3. Once a general goal has been established, identify three very specific things the student can do to demonstrate that he is working toward that goal. Try to avoid general statements or behavior descriptions—these should be specific behaviors that the student is capable of achieving. The criteria should be both observable and specific enough so that two different observers would be likely to agree on what they saw. For example, "Turning in neat papers" is too broad. "Turning in papers that are whole, flat, and free from smudges and extra marks," is much more specific.

4. Discuss ways that you (the teacher) can assist the student in achieving his goal. Include on the goal contract information about one or more procedures that you and the student agree will be helpful to him in meeting his goal.

5. Discuss what should happen if the student does not work to meet the specified goal. Will there be consequences? If so, clarify what the consequences will be and include this information on the goal contract as well.

6. Decide whether the goal contract should be written as a structured reinforcement contract. If so, you will need to add a section on what the student will earn for successfully meeting the expectations of the goal contract. In addition, include a section on what the teacher (or other adults, if appropriate) will do to assist the student in achieving his goal.

If you aren't sure whether a structured reinforcement system will be necessary, first try the goal setting without the reinforcement. However, if you know that the student will not be motivated unless there are reinforcers tied to his improved performance, design a structured reinforcement system to supplement the goal-setting process right from the start.

7. Have each of the parties present sign the form to demonstrate their willingness to support the goal contract that has been established. If the student refuses to sign, ask why. Find out if there are specific changes that would make him willing to sign. If so, and if the changes are reasonable, make the requested modifications and have the student sign.

If the student still refuses to sign, and/or the changes he wants are not reasonable, tell him that the consequence(s) will be in place whether he signs or not. Do not turn signing the contract into a power struggle. Let the student know that you are still going to watch to see if he tries to achieve the goal and that you fully expect him to be successful because you know how capable he is.

Stick to the plan for a week, and if the student shows no sign of working on the goal, schedule another conference, set up a structured reinforcement system, and establish alternative and stronger consequence(s) for the problematic behavior.

8. After approximately one week, review the goal contract and make changes if necessary. At that time, look at whether the student is being successful in taking steps toward achieving the goal and determine whether or not to renew or revise the contract, or whether to establish an entirely different goal.

Continue this review process once per week whenever a goal contract is in place. Once the student is being consistently successful, fade the review meeting to once every two weeks, and then to once per month.

Following is a sample goal contract that is indicative of the types of goal-setting forms suggested in several of the plans within this reference guide.

Goal Contract

Scott:

A goal for me to work on is to be more independent.

I can show that I am working on this goal by:

1. Keeping my hands to myself, not on Miss Torrance (except for a couple of hugs per day that Miss Torrance will give me).

2. Doing my own work and allowing Miss Torrance to do hers—so I won't follow Miss Torrance around the room.

3. Telling myself that I'm doing my best and then waiting for Miss Torrance to look at my work (instead of going up and asking her to look at it).

_____

Student Signature

_____

Date

Consequences for Not Meeting the Goal:

1. Miss Torrance will give Scott reminders anytime he does not meet his goal. For example, if Scott begins to follow Miss Torrance around the room, Miss Torrance will say, "Scott, you need to be in your seat doing your own work."

2. If Scott continues to follow Miss Torrance, he will begin "owing time" off of recess—one minute of time owed for each minute it takes until he is following the instruction given by Miss Torrance.

Miss Torrance:

I will help Scott meet his goal by reminding him when he needs to be more independent, and by praising him and giving him an occasional hug when he is being independent.

_____

Teacher Signature

_____

Date

Date of Goal Evaluation: (Specify a date in approximately a week.) _____

9. Look for opportunities to reinforce the student for taking steps toward achieving the goal. Whenever the student exhibits one of the three specific behaviors, praise him by referring to the specific behavior and the broad goal. "Scott, you did that whole assignment without asking me for feedback. That is a great example of how independent you are becoming." If public praise would embarrass the student, praise him privately or even use a note.

• Help the student learn to make both positive statements and rational, negative statements, both out loud and to himself. In some cases this may involve monitoring and modifying negative statements. In almost all cases it will involve teaching and practicing more positive ways of talking about daily experiences.

Let's take a very specific example—a student who is very frightened about giving an oral report to the class. The student may be currently making statements such as, "I know I'll panic."; "I always freeze up in front of the group."; or "I can't ever talk in public." In addition to creating non-threatening opportunities for the student to speak to small groups and teaching the student skills for speaking to increasingly larger groups, the teacher and the student could work together on modifying the student's negative talk and increasing the amount of positive statements made.

The rationale for this procedure is that people tend to believe the things they frequently say—both out loud and internal verbalization, or self-talk. If what one says is negative, one perpetuates negative beliefs and can actually set oneself up for failure. On the other hand, making realistic, positive statements encourages positive beliefs and high expectations, and sets one up for success.

• Following are procedures for teaching and practicing positive self-talk. The steps can be either done together with the student or by the teacher alone and presented as a proposed plan to the student. If time permits and the student is likely to cooperate, it is better that the steps be planned together with the student, as the student will have more incentive to make a plan succeed if he has actively participated in developing it:

1. Identify two or three positive statements that will help the student feel better about himself. These statements should be realistic and achievable. Statements that are positive but unrealistic or untrue will have no affect. "I am the smartest person in the world" is unreal-

istic and unobtainable (for all but one person out of the billions on the planet). On the other hand, "I am capable and I work hard to succeed," is not only more realistic, but even if it has not been true in the past, it is certainly obtainable in the future.

The positive statements should be both *pervasive* and *permanent*. A pervasive statement is one that will include many different circumstances and settings. "I am independent and self-reliant" is positive and pervasive. "I can be successful in reading class" is positive but limited to one setting—reading class.

Permanent positive statements are those that remain constant across time. "I manage my anger to get what I need" is more permanent than "I stayed calm at recess." "I am a healthy person" is permanent, while "I have been healthy lately" is not.

The idea is that people can limit their success by limiting the permanence or pervasiveness of their positive statements. Developing and using a few permanent and pervasive positive statements will, hopefully, begin to change the way the student views himself. Then each positive experience and success will contribute to the student's belief in the pervasive and permanent positive statements he is making.

2. Identify whether the student makes frequent negative statements about himself that may be contributing to his poor self-concept. People with low self-esteem tend to take a limited bad experience and generate pervasive and permanent negative statements that are both destructive and blown out of proportion. For example, after having a bad experience while giving a speech, the student might say, "I am always so nervous. My voice always shakes and I think I will throw up all over my notes. I will never be able to talk in front of a group" instead of saying, "I was nervous while I was talking to the class."

If the student tends to make negative statements, analyze whether they are permanent and/or pervasive. Negative statements are not bad or wrong, but are often blown out of proportion. For example, of the following negative statements, those at the top are either permanent or pervasive (or both), and those on the bottom are neither permanent nor pervasive.

Permanent and /or Pervasive Negatives

- I am so stupid.
- I always blow tests.
- Nobody likes me.
- I'm so disorganized.

Nonpermanent and Nonpervasive Negatives

- I didn't understand that assignment.
- I had trouble with that test.
- Drew does not want to be with me right now.
- My desk is messy today.

---

3. Work with the student to modify his typical negative statements to be less permanent and less pervasive. Then have the student practice using rational negative statements that are nonpermanent and nonpervasive. To do so, think of a situation in which the student typically has difficulty or a problem, and have him generate some negative statements that would limit the impact of that experience. For example, present a situation in which the student performs poorly on a test. Help the student generate a realistic statement to himself such as, "I did badly on this test, so I should study longer and harder for the test next Friday."

4. Arrange for opportunities for the student to practice the skills:

   – Increasing the use of pervasive and permanent positive statements.

   – Decreasing the use of negative statements.

   – Modifying pervasive and permanent negative statements into limited negative statements.

   – Using a permanent and pervasive positive statement to conclude a limited negative statement (e.g., "I got a poor score on that test, but I am capable and work hard to succeed so I know I can do better.").

To encourage practice of the skills, you might arrange to meet with the student for a few minutes per day to review specific situations that frequently occur in the classroom and what the student has to say about those situations. Whenever necessary, work with the student to help him change the nature of his self-talk in explaining those events.

If you don't have time to do this, find out whether the school counselor or school psychologist does. If he/she does not have time, consider the possibility of using a skilled paraprofessional who is trained and supervised by the school counselor one day per week and works one-to-one with the student on the other four days.

5. Establish a system for monitoring the student's statements. You may wish to keep anecdotal notes, where you write down the student's statements, either positive or negative, to use in the daily lessons. Or, you may wish to count (or have the student count) the positive and negative statements being made by the student.

For example, you could give the student a card each day like the sample shown (reprinted with permission from Sprick, 1981). Whenever the student makes a positive or negative statement, you would have him write a number in one of the boxes on the card (so there is a running count of positive and negative comments). At the time of the daily lesson, if the student has more nega-

tives than positives, use the lesson time to have the student make positive statements until he has more positives that negatives. The goal is for the student to eventually make twice as many positive statements as negative.

6. Whenever you hear the student make a negative comment, ask him to modify it into a limited negative paired with a positive. "Scott, change that statement into one that only talks about what happened, and then use one of your positive statements to put everything in perspective."

NOTE: For detailed information on the subject of positive self-talk, both for adults and for children, see:

Seligman, E.P. (1990). _Learned optimism: How to change your mind and your life_. New York: Simon and Schuster (Pocket Books).

This book contains some easy-to-implement self-evaluation quizzes for identifying the type of negative and positive statements that children and adults tend to make, and specific recommendations for modifying destructive thinking by substituting more positive alternatives.

 SELF-CONTROL ISSUES

Problems With Anger Management

DESCRIPTION

You have a student who tends to lose emotional control and becomes angry or upset to the point that it interferes with her own success or the smooth running of the class.

Although there are no MODEL PLANS included with this problem, the following suggested procedures are designed to help you analyze the situation and teach the student how to handle emotional upsets responsibly.

(NOTE: Some people may consider some or all of these suggested procedures to be controversial. Be sure to check with your administrator and obtain parental permission before using the techniques.)

NOTE:

The following material is adapted and condensed with permission from Intervention H: Self-Control Training, *which is one of 16 intervention booklets in:*

Sprick, R.S., Sprick, M.S., & Garrison, M. (1993). Interventions: Collaborative planning for students at risk. Longmont, CO: Sopris West.

Alternative Problems

- **Anxiety/Nervousness**

- **Arguing—Students With Each Other**

- **Arguing—Student(s) With the Teacher**

- **Blaming Others/ Excuses for Everything**

- **Bullying Behavior/ Fighting**

- **Corrected, Student Gets Upset When**

- **Depression**

- **Disruptive Behavior—Severe**

- **Physically Dangerous Behavior—to Self or Others**

- **Tantrumming (K or 1st Grader)**

- **Whining**

· · · · · · · ·
Intervention Steps

Self-control training involves intensive daily lessons in which you teach the student to understand and recognize the events that trigger her out of control behavior, and how to anticipate and change behavior patterns that lead to out of control behavior. The goal is to empower the student with the ability to break the chain of accelerating behaviors so she can stay in control. Because the daily lessons are very time intensive, it may not be possible for a classroom teacher to conduct them. Therefore, you may need to coordinate with the school counselor, special education personnel, or other appropriate individual who has the time and expertise to conduct the daily lessons described in the following procedures.

PROCEDURES

 Establish a record-keeping and evaluation system.

All instances involving out of control behavior should be recorded in an anecdotal log (i.e., from the onset of the problem). In the log, be sure to include the following information:

- Date and time of day;

- Location;

- Situation (what set the student off?);

- A detailed description of the student's behavior during the incident, including the duration of the episode and the student's specific behavior;

- Action(s) taken; and

- Consequences implemented (if any).

By recording every incident, you will have detailed information for communicating with the student and her parent(s), and for making judgments about the long-term effectiveness of your plan.

 Contact the student's parent(s).

The student's parent(s) must be involved whenever there is an incidence of out of control behavior. The initial contact can be limited to letting the parent(s) know there has been a problem, however, eventually, a conference should be held to begin the process of collaborative problem solving. The parent(s) can provide valuable input as you determine how to help the student. Depending upon the severity of the situation, you may also wish to bring in representatives from other social agencies to help you develop a comprehensive plan.

As you work with the parent(s), you will need to make professional judgments about how to best involve them. You can start by letting the parent(s) know that you are truly committed to helping the student learn to control her own behavior, and that you do not expect them to take responsibility for problems that occur at school. (Parents of students with out of control behavior often do not know what to do about the behavior at home, much less how to get their students to control their behavior at school.) Instead, make it clear that you hope to work proactively and collaboratively with them to develop ways to teach the student how to handle her emotions responsibly.

 Identify the patterns of behavior that result in the student losing self-control.

Students who lose control usually engage in a "behavioral chain," or series of minor misbehaviors or agitated behaviors that culminate in out of control behavior. Colvin and Sugai (1989) describe this chain as a recognizable pattern of behavior that builds toward an emotional peak. A "trigger," something that sets the student off, begins the process. The student becomes agitated. The emotional intensity of the situation accelerates until finally, at the peak of the chain, the student "blows" (see the illustration following).

In many cases, the student is responding to a number of events, with anxiety increasing each time something else happens. Tolerance drops and frustration builds. The proverbial "straw that breaks the camel's back" may be a small, almost insignificant event. Some students gradually lose control over a period of several days, while others lose control within moments. If a trigger can be identified, it may be possible to help the student learn to deal with anxiety-producing events. If a

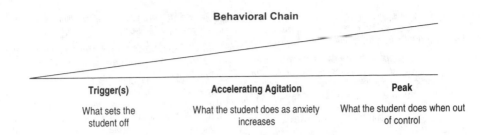

Behavioral Chain

Trigger(s)	Accelerating Agitation	Peak
What sets the student off	What the student does as anxiety increases	What the student does when out of control

trigger is not identifiable, the student can learn to recognize when she is beginning to become agitated and be taught to redirect herself before she loses control.

To identify behavioral chains, it may be helpful to begin by identifying what happens at the peak of out of control behavior. From there, trace backward to identify the pattern of behavior and events that seem to initiate and lead to the out of control behavior.

If the student frequently demonstrates out of control behavior, it may be useful for a specialist to schedule a series of observations. If this delays intervention because the outbursts are too infrequent or random to formally observe, information can be gathered by having staff keep anecdotal records of the dates, times, settings, who the student was interacting with, and activities she was engaged in prior to any out of control behavior. Information can also be obtained from interviews with staff, the student's parent(s), and the student herself. Ultimately this information will be used to plan self-control lessons for the student (see Step 5).

a. **Identify what the student does at the peak of out of control behavior.**

Avoid general statements such as "the student tantrums." List and describe observable behavior, such as: "Zoe lies down on the floor, pounds her fists, kicks her feet, and cries loudly." Precise descriptions of the behavior will help the student recognize the behavior she should be trying to avoid.

b. **Identify behaviors that accelerate toward the peak of out of control behavior.**

In most cases, students engage in a series, or chain, of behaviors between the event(s) that trigger the out of control behavior and the peak of the out of control behavior. As the student is accelerating, others will be able to notice a sense of agitation in her. The student may exhibit an increase in hand movements, fidgeting, tapping, rapid eye movements, picking things up and putting them down, or talking in short choppy speech—"Fine."; "Sure." On-task behavior is likely to decrease, and the student may have trouble keeping her attention focused. These and other similar behaviors indicate that the student is "winding herself up."

As the situation accelerates, the student is likely to engage in behavior that alienates others and yet pulls them into an intense emotional event. These behaviors might include arguments, defiance, name calling, sarcasm, excessive criticism, accusations, etc. For example:

Zoe:	Why should I have to do this?
Teacher:	Because it is the assignment. Everyone has to do it.
Zoe:	What If I don't?
Teacher:	Then you will fail this assignment.
Zoe:	I don't care. Why should I care about an 'F' in this stupid class?
Teacher:	I don't care whether you care or not. Stop this arguing and get to work.
Zoe:	You can't make me. Get out of my face.

The conclusion is predictable. The behavior will continue until either the teacher throws the student out of class or the student launches into out of control behavior, or both occur simultaneously. By identifying the sequence of behavior, a plan can be created to assist the student in recognizing the signs of stress or anger so she can learn to take an alternative course of action before it is too late.

c. **Identify "triggers"—settings, times, people, and/or events that seem to set the student off.**

Though triggers are highly personal, most students who lack self-control are responding to something that has increased their anxiety.

Common triggers include having work corrected by the teacher, being teased by other students, problems on the bus or at home, difficulty with an assignment, being laughed at by other students, or even small changes in established routines. Some students with extremely poor social skills may even have triggers as subtle and common as being talked to by another student or getting bumped in line.

The figure below shows a sample of an analysis of one student's out of control behavior. Once the trigger(s), accelerating behaviors, and peak behaviors have been defined, combine this information with any additional information you may have gotten from the student (e.g., she is often upset on Mondays because of a difficult home situation on the weekends). Use this information to develop daily lessons to teach the student self-control.

Triggers	• Teasing – Being called names – Students mimicking • Getting bumped into • Being touched • Doing poorly on an assignment or test
Accelerating Behavior (Signs of Stress or Anger)	• Pulls or backs away • Mumbles • Moves from foot to foot • Begins moving abruptly • Breathes rapidly • Turns red • Voice gets high
Peak Out of Control Behavior	• Inappropriate language • Yelling • Hysterical sobbing • Shouting • Chasing others

4. Identify strategies and signals to help the student control her behavior.

a. **Identify strategies that the student might use to break the acceleration pattern.**

Self-control strategies are procedures the student can use to redirect her behavior. Use of these strategies should result in the student calming down instead of accelerating into out of control behavior. These strategies include the following.

• *Counting to ten, then backwards to one*

Self-control strategies do not have to be fancy procedures. In fact, the simpler the better. Counting to ten is a time-tested strategy that many students learn from their parents. The procedure helps the student "buy time" before responding impulsively to a situation. If the student spins rapidly out of control, counting to ten and then backwards to one may provide her with the time needed to regain control.

• *Deep breathing*

As people become agitated, shortness of breath is often an accompanying sign of distress. Slow, deep breathing will help the student relax.

• *Positive self-talk*

Students with severe difficulties often talk themselves into out of control behavior. "I can't stand it. If she does that one more time, I'll . . . ." Negative self-talk tends to feed the process of spiraling out of control. On the other hand, positive self-talk helps the student redirect her thoughts and actions. (If learning positive self-talk may be a viable strategy for helping your student maintain self-control, see **Self-Concept Problems** for a detailed description of this procedure.)

• *Self-imposed time-out*

Students can avoid potentially volatile situations by physically removing themselves. Going to a private place in the school (e.g., the counselor's office, a quiet corner in the classroom, etc.) to calm down often allows the student the time and space necessary to redirect her energies.

• *Deep muscle relaxation*

Deep muscle relaxation can help students physically relax. Students who have self-control problems need to learn to remove their focus from the stressful situation and reduce the body's tendency to become tense. By learning to relax, the student can learn to maintain control. (For detailed information on deep muscle relaxation procedures, see **Anxiety/Nervousness**.)

- *Using Stop, Think, Plan (STP)*

With STP, students learn to follow these steps:

STOP:	When you feel mad, tell yourself to STOP.
THINK:	When you've stopped, THINK about your choices. What else could you do that won't get you in trouble?
PLAN:	PLAN what you are going to do next.

Each step in this strategy guides the student through actions that allow her to withdraw from a pattern of accelerating agitation, and to concurrently make purposeful decisions about what she wishes to do next.

- *Visualization*

Visualization is a form of positive self-talk. Many students cannot imagine themselves maintaining control. When scenarios are presented, their vision is limited to seeing behaviors of the past. "This is the way it is and the way it will always be." If the student has difficulty looking forward to behaving differently, visualization may be a worthwhile strategy to teach her. During instruction, the interventionist presents scenarios and verbally draws a picture of an appropriate response. The student may then draw a picture or close her eyes and try to "see" the scene presented.

- *Ignoring*

Learning to ignore events that trigger agitation may be the best strategy to avoid anger. When the student is taught strategies that require her to focus her attention elsewhere (such as deep breathing or positive self-talk), she also learns to ignore the events that trigger her emotional outbursts. It may also be worthwhile to directly teach the student to give no response to triggers such as teasing. (NOTE: See **Victim—Student Who Is Always Picked On** for suggestions on conducting lessons of this type.)

- *Using "I messages" to communicate feelings*

If the student must respond directly to difficult situations, it may be useful to teach her to use statements that begin with "I" rather than "you." For example, if another student tells the target student that she needs to do something, instead of saying, "You can't make me. Get out of my face," the student might calmly say, "I don't have to do that and I am not going to." Or rather than saying, "You're the fat pig, not me," the student might say, "I don't like to be called names. It hurts my feelings."

Following are some other "I messages" that the student could learn to say in place of arguing or name calling:

- "Please stop. I have a right to be treated with respect."

- "I know that is not true."

- "I don't let comments like that bother me."

When selecting possible self-control strategies, consider the age and ability of the student. If the student is not sophisticated, plan to help the student select a single self-control strategy. More mature students can be taught as many as four strategies that they can implement, depending upon the demands of the situation.

b. **Identify signals or cues that could be used by the teacher (and later the student) to prompt the use of a self-control strategy.**

Initially, the student may need a cue from an adult to break old patterns of agitation and acceleration. If the student typically becomes more and more agitated by engaging in a series of verbal exchanges with an adult, the teacher might simply put up a hand to signal the student that she needs to redirect her behavior. If the student often shows agitation by stuttering, blinking, or becoming short of breath, the teacher might prompt the student to redirect her behavior by asking, "How are you feeling?" The signal should be age-appropriate and unobtrusive so it will not be embarrassing to the student.

During the daily self-control lessons, the student will learn that adults can help her recognize the signs of agitation, and can signal her with a prearranged cue such as the question, "How are you feeling?" The student will learn that the cue is a prompt to begin engaging in alternative behavior.

Eventually, the student will need to prompt herself. As the student learns to recognize her own signs of agitation, she can be taught to provide herself with a self-cue. Self-cues might include short positive statements that the student can repeat. "I am in control. I can think positively. I am in control. I can think positively." Specific cues can be arranged with the student when the time comes.

5. Design and conduct daily lessons to help the student learn self-control.

Daily lessons will help the student become aware of the entire sequence of behaviors, from trigger(s) to the peak. Rather than engaging in behaviors that increase agitation, the student will learn to respond to the preselected signal or cue, and to use self-control strategies to calm down and control herself.

a. **Daily lessons should include opportunities for demonstrations and modeling, verbal practice, positive practice, and feedback.**

Through demonstrations and modeling, the adult simulates real situations and shows the student how to respond to the signal by shifting from agitation behaviors to alternative, calming behaviors. In verbal practice, the adult presents situations and has the student verbally explain what she would do to avoid accelerating into out of control behavior. In positive practice, the student practices responding to the signal and shifting from agitation to alternative behaviors. Positive practice, or role playing, also allows the adult to provide feedback and additional practice in a protected and nonthreatening situation.

As the student learns to successfully handle various scenarios, the daily lessons should address increasingly difficult situations. This can be accomplished by creating more and more volatile scenarios for practice, by moving practice sessions into real life contexts, and by gradually removing the use of the prompt. As the lessons progress, the student can also help generate her own scenarios for practice.

b. **Determine how much time will be needed for the lessons, where the lessons will take place, and who will conduct them.**

Teaching the student to use self-control strategies requires a great deal of learning. The student will need to practice the new behaviors in many different ways with many repetitions before she will be able to use them in real life situations. Therefore, short daily lessons will be more effective than long, infrequent lessons.

In most cases, the lessons will need to be conducted outside the classroom by someone other than the classroom teacher. The student must feel comfortable during these lessons so that any fear of failure is diminished and any sense of potential embarrassment in front of peers is eliminated. Also, the adult selected to work with the student must be patient. The student is likely to make many mistakes, and may become frustrated. This behavioral coach should be someone the student can trust, and who will convey ongoing support and encouragement despite difficulties that may be encountered.

6. Determine how to respond to out of control behavior.

Teaching students self-control takes time and patience. As the student learns to take control of events and her emotions, the intensity and frequency of her out of control behavior will gradually be reduced. In the meantime, procedures must be established for responding to any out of control behavior that does occur.

a. **Establish consequences to use if necessary.**

Consequences tend to have little effect on out of control behavior. When students are out of control, they are not thinking rationally about the consequences of their actions. Therefore, the threat of a consequence will generally have little effect. However, if the student damages property or has a significant disruptive effect on the class, a consequence will serve a dual purpose. The first purpose is to demonstrate that when someone disrupts learning or damages property, there is a consequence. The second purpose is to help the student see that self-control training will eventually empower her to make choices regarding what will happen to her.

Whenever possible, the consequence should have a logical association with the problem behavior. If the student damages property during out of control behavior, the student should be required to repair the damage or make some sort of restitution. If the student tears up papers and throws them around the room, she should be required to clean up the room. If the student destroys a book, she should be required to pay for the book, or work in the classroom to compensate for its value. If the student is verbally abusive, the consequence might be to write an apology to the person to whom she was abusive.

b. **Prepare a systematic plan for reengaging the student in class activities.**

Once students have "lost it," it is often difficult for them to come back into the classroom. Procedures must be developed that give the student very little attention, but allow the student and teacher to debrief so they can get on with the rest of the day. The "Behavior Improvement Form" shown on the following page (or something similar) works well when the student has the skills to read and complete the form. By filling out the form, the student acknowledges the problem and identifies what she will try to do differently in the future. Later, this form can be used in the daily lessons to role play and verbally rehearse alternative actions.

If the student does not have the skills to fill out the form, reengagement into the classroom will need to occur verbally. When the student has calmed down, the teacher should plan to have the student privately state what she did and how she might handle the situation differently in the future. The teacher should keep this discussion brief and businesslike. The more attention given to the student immediately following an incident, the greater the likelihood that the student will be reinforced for having lost control.

 Establish procedures to focus on appropriate behavior and student strengths.

It is often difficult to give a student with severe behavior problems any attention or recognition for appropriate behavior. Because the student usurps so much time and energy when she is misbehaving, it can feel uncomfortable giving her additional attention when she is being responsible. Unfortunately, this results in the student's learning again and again that adult attention is guaranteed during misbehavior but highly unlikely when she engages in appropriate behavior. When this occurs, misbehavior increases and responsible behavior decreases.

To emphasize the value of the student's appropriate behavior, identify the student's strengths and typical responsible behavior, and try to focus attention on what the student does well. Brainstorm a list of ways to focus attention on the student's appropriate behavior and then check those items that will be manageable.

 Watch for times when the student attempts to maintain self-control and provide encouragement.

Whenever the student employs strategies for maintaining self-control, adults should encourage her with verbal praise, a pat on the back, a note, or some other age-appropriate means of acknowledging her effort to maintain self-control.

Positive feedback should assist the student in recognizing that she is employing strategies that have been learned in the daily lessons. Students are sometimes not aware that they are making progress and may actually use these strategies without noticing.

Additionally, begin the next daily lesson by complimenting the student on her ability to successfully use self-control strategies. Work with the student to develop a sense of pride in her abilities to manage her own behavior.

CONCLUSION

Self-control training involves identifying the trigger(s) that set the student off and the behaviors the student engages in when accelerating toward out of control behavior. Lessons are then designed and conducted to teach the student strategies for staying calm in the presence of the trigger(s). This will probably be difficult for the student to learn and will require frequent practice, lots of patience on your part, and lots of encouragement given to the student.

Behavior Improvement Form

Room Clear: ○   Time-Out: ○

Followed Directions Appropriately: Yes ○   No ○

Name: _____

Date: _____

1. What was your behavior? _____

_____

_____

2. What did you want? (Check at least one.)

○ I wanted attention from others.

○ I wanted to be in control of the situation.

○ I wanted to challenge the teacher's authority.

○ I wanted to avoid doing my work.

○ I wanted to be sent home.

○ I wanted to cause problems because I am miserable inside.

○ I wanted to cause others problems because they don't like me.

○ I wanted revenge.

○ I wanted _____

3. Did you get what you wanted?   Yes ○   No ○
Why?

_____

4. What could you do differently? _____

_____

5. Will you be able to do it appropriately?   Yes ○   No ○
Why?

Given by:	Time Started:
Reviewed by:	Time Ended:
Class:	Number of Minutes:
Adapted with permission from Colvin, G. & Sugai, G. (1989). *Managing escalating behavior* (2nd ed.). Eugene, OR: Behavior Associates.	Time Added:
	Total Time Owed:

SELF-INJURIOUS BEHAVIOR

DESCRIPTION

You have a student who engages in self-injurious acts such as head banging, biting, or hitting himself.

Because self-injurious behavior is such a difficult and complex problem, it is beyond the scope of this reference guide. Therefore, there are no MODEL PLANS included with this problem. The purpose of the following information is to offer some basic suggestions for dealing with a situation in which a student engages in self-injurious acts.

Alternative Problems

- **Aggression—Verbal and/or Physical**

- **Physically Dangerous Behavior—to Self or Others**

- **Self-Control Issues**

- **Suicide Threats**

. . . .
General Information

- When a student exhibits self-destructive behavior, there are three main steps you should take:

  – **Get help.**

  If the student does not currently qualify for special services, immediately refer the problem to your building administrator and/or school psychologist. Self-destructive behavior requires a collaborative effort on the part of school personnel.

  – **Identify what to do when the student exhibits the behavior.**

  Work with the building administrator and the student's parent(s) to identify what you should do when the student engages in the self-injurious behavior. Should you restrain the student? should you call for someone else to restrain the student? when restraint is used, what are the criteria for releasing the student? after releasing the student, what should happen next?

The problem **Physically Dangerous Behavior—to Self or Others** has information on other questions and issues of this type that may require examination.

– **Help the student to learn alternative behavior(s).**

With the assistance of the building administrator, the school psychologist, and/or the student's parent(s), conduct a functional analysis to determine what is sustaining the student's self-destructive behavior. Then develop an intervention to address the problem. An excellent resource to consult during this process is:

O'Neill, R.E., Horner, R.H., Albin, R.W., Storey, K., & Sprague, J.R. (1990). *Functional analysis of problem behavior: A practical assessment guide.* Sycamore, IL: Sycamore Publishing.

SEXUAL COMMENTS

Off Color Jokes

Sexual Innuendoes

DESCRIPTION

You have a student who makes inappropriate comments, jokes, or innuendoes of a sexual nature.

GOAL

The student will stop making sexual comments, jokes, and/or innuendoes.

OVERVIEW OF PLANS

- PLAN A: For a problem that has just begun or occurs infrequently.

- PLAN B: For a situation involving a young student or a student receiving special education services who is naive and unaware of the significance of what she is saying.

- PLAN C: For a student who uses sexual comments to gain adult attention.

- PLAN D: For a student who uses sexual comments to shock or look sophisticated in front of her peers.

- PLAN E: For a student whose use of inappropriate sexual comments is long-standing and/or habitual.

- PLAN F: For a situation in which many students in the class engage in making sexual comments.

Alternative Problems

- **Disrespectful Behavior**

- **Harassment— Racial/Sexual**

- **Intimacy, Inappropriate Displays of**

- **Smart-Aleck Behavior/ Inappropriate Humor**

- **Swearing/Obscene Language**

· · · · · · · ·
General Considerations

- If the student's problem behavior stems in any way from academic issues (e.g., she is struggling academically and uses shocking comments as a way of deflecting attention from her academic failure), concurrent efforts must be made to ensure her academic success (see **Academic Deficits, Determining**).

- If the student lacks the basic social skills to interact with her peers appropriately, it may be necessary to begin by teaching her those skills. **Social Skills, Lack of** contains information on a variety of published social skills curricula.

- Carefully consider whether the inappropriate behavior might be a sign of abuse. If you have any reason to believe that the student may be a victim of abuse, immediately discuss the situation with your building administrator. Every other aspect of an intervention plan should be secondary to protecting the health and safety of the child involved. Follow district and state guidelines for reporting suspected abuse.

- Given the sensitive nature of this problem, keep the student's parent(s) informed throughout the intervention. Also, at any meeting with the student (and her parent[s]) pertaining to the student's use of sexual comments, arrange to have another education professional present. This reduces the chance of your ever being accused of impropriety, and provides a witness to the meeting in the event of such an accusation.

PRE-INTERVENTION STEPS

With this type of potentially sensitive issue, you should inform the student's parent(s) about the problem, and ask them to discuss the problem with the student, before you intervene. The use of any school-based intervention for this problem should occur only after parental efforts have been ineffective.

 Discuss the problem with the student's parent(s).

Immediately discuss this problem with the student's parent(s) and explain why you are concerned. Do not imply that the student's behavior is shocking or that it indicates promiscuity. Instead, focus on how the behavior is hindering the student academically and/or socially (e.g., other students are starting to view the student as an outcast).

You might ask if the parent(s) have any insight into the situation and/or whether they have noticed similar behavior at home.

2. *Ask the parent(s) to discuss the problem with the student.*

a. Ask the parent(s) to talk to the student about making sexual comments in public, and to tell her that part of being responsible about one's sexuality means refraining from making inappropriate comments, jokes, or innuendoes in public. If the parent(s) are comfortable with the idea, they might explain that an occasional "off color" joke between friends is no problem, but not too often and not in public so that others can hear.

b. If the student is young and/or naive, let the parent(s) know that they may have to use examples to teach the student what words she is saying that are inappropriate (provide the parent[s] with examples from the classroom to share with the student, if appropriate).

Ask the parent(s) to emphasize to the student that school is a public place, and so is not a place where she should be making sexual comments that others can hear.

c. After this initial request for the parent(s) to discuss the problem with the student, monitor the student's behavior carefully.

· · · · · · · ·
Model Plans

PLAN A

It is not always necessary, or even beneficial, to use an involved plan. If parental efforts have been ineffective but the problem occurs infrequently, the following actions, along with making the student aware of your concerns, may resolve the situation.

1. **Respond consistently to the inappropriate behavior.**

a. During your initial meeting with the student (see SUGGESTED STEPS FOR DEVELOPING AND IMPLEMENTING A PLAN), establish a nonembarrassing signal that you can use to cue her that she is making a sexual comment in public. You want the signal to be a fairly subtle one that only the student will recognize and understand in order to minimize the chance that she will be ridiculed by her peers.

Possibilities include a particular wave of your hand, rubbing your neck, or even just direct eye contact and a head nod. Let the student know that you may also need to quietly say her name to get her attention before you give her the signal.

b. If the student does not cease making the sexual comment when you give her the signal, provide a gentle verbal correction. Let the student know that what she is doing is an example of making a sexual comment in public. "Denise, that is not an appropriate comment in the classroom." Because your goal is to impart information, you want to be emotionally neutral while giving the correction.

c. In addition to identifying the comment as inappropriate, give the student a direction about what she should be doing instead. "Denise, stop. You are making a sexual comment at the expense of someone else. You need to participate in your group without commenting on other people."

d. Whether you use only the signal or the signal plus a verbal correction, record each sexual comment made by the student (i.e., anecdotal notes) and be sure the student knows that you are recording the comment. Making the student aware that you are keeping a written record of incidents will help communicate the idea that you view her behavior as a serious problem. If the student asks why you are writing the incident down, inform her that you want to have accurate information when you talk to her parent(s) about the situation. Do not make this sound like a threat hanging over the student, rather a piece of information about what you are doing and why.

2. **Use reinforcement to encourage appropriate behavior.**

a. Give the student increased praise. In situations in which the student makes comments that are appropriate, praise her positive contributions. "Denise, you added many useful ideas to our discussion." However, do not specifically praise the absence of sexual comments. The only time you should refer to the absence of sexual comments is during a follow-up meeting (see SUGGESTED STEPS FOR DEVELOPING AND IMPLEMENTING A PLAN) when the student's parent(s) and/or some other adult is present.

If the student would be embarrassed by public praise, praise the student privately or even give the student a note. Remember that any time the student is not making sexual comments (or otherwise misbehaving), you can praise her for some aspect of her responsible behavior.

b. Privately praise the student for responding to the signal. "Denise, twice today I gave the signal of folding my arms across my chest, and each time you stopped what you were saying and began using okay language. You are working hard on learning about what to do and say in a public place."

c. Give the student frequent attention (e.g., say "hello" to her as she enters the classroom, ask her opinion, and occasionally ask her to assist you with a class job that needs to be done) and praise her for other positive behaviors she exhibits. "Denise, you have done such a fine job of participating in class today. You have contributed some very useful ideas to the project." This demonstrates to the student that you notice many positive things she does, not just the fact that she is refraining from making sexual comments.

PLAN B

If the student is young or cognitively naive (e.g., a twelve-year old with developmental disabilities), she may not realize that her comments are inappropriate. In fact, she may not even understand some of what she is saying. If you believe your student may be unaware of the inappropriateness of her language, but just says things she has found make people laugh or act shocked, this plan will be appropriate.

 1. *Respond consistently to the inappropriate behavior.*

When the student makes sexual comments, give her the signal, then gently correct her, if necessary (see PLAN A).

2. *Conduct lessons to teach the student how to discriminate between topics that are "okay" to talk about at school and topics that are "not okay" to talk about at school.*

(NOTE: If the student's parent[s] are working with you on this plan, have them conduct these lessons at home using information provided by you about the types of inappropriate comments the student makes.)

a. Think about the types of inappropriate comments the student makes. It is important to identify whether or not the student understands the meaning of the vocabulary and concepts she is mentioning. If the student does not know the meaning of the words and/or phrases she is using, you must decide whether or not to teacher her those meanings in order to help illustrate their inappropriateness for the school setting. Discuss this issue with the student's parent(s) and your building administrator before proceeding.

The main objective of the lessons should be to teach the student to discriminate between words and topics that are "okay" to talk about at school and those that are "not okay" to talk about at school.

b. During the lessons, use actual comments the student has made as examples. Identify which of those comments are okay and which are not. Then present different topics and have the student specify whether each is a topic that is okay or not okay to talk about at school. Depending upon the age and sophistication of the student, you may need to include some relatively difficult discriminations (e.g., it is okay to use the word "penis" during a health class on reproduction, but not okay to use that word in other contexts).

c. Conduct the lessons at least twice per week. The lessons should be private (perhaps while the other students are at recess) and involve you, the student, the student's parent(s), and another adult to avoid any appearance of impropriety. The lessons needn't last more than three to five minutes, and it is important that they be handled in a matter-of-fact manner so the student does not feel that she is being ridiculed.

Continue the lessons until the student is consistently responding to the signal and/or no longer making inappropriate sexual comment in the classroom.

 3. *Prompt the student to behave appropriately by using precorrections.*

Watch for circumstances in which the student has the tendency to make sexual comments and remind her to only make comments that are appropriate to the school setting. "Denise, after recess we are going to be having a discussion about families. One thing we will talk about is young babies. I will be watching to see if you remember to do what we discussed this morning about comments that are okay and not okay." If this conversation would embarrass the student, conduct it privately.

5. *Use reinforcement to encourage appropriate behavior.*

a. Give the student increased praise and attention for making appropriate comments (see PLAN A).

b. Praise the student for participating with you in the lessons. "Denise, I know that it is probably a little uncomfortable for you to be talking about these things with us, but you should be very proud of how responsible you are being. I appreciate the way you have been participating."

c. In addition, make a special point of letting the student know that you notice her efforts to use the skills she has been learning/practicing. "Denise, you have made lots of comments today—and all of them were okay for school. Nice job of doing what we have been practicing."

PLAN C

Some students are very skilled at gaining attention through their negative behavior. If you find yourself frequently nagging, lecturing, or coaxing the student to stop making sexual comments, it is possible that she is trying to gain adult attention through the misbehavior. Whether or not the student overtly seems to like the attention, you should make sure that she receives more frequent and more satisfying attention for behaving appropriately than for making sexual comments.

 1. **Respond consistently to the inappropriate behavior.**

a. Conduct lessons to teach the student how to discriminate between topics that are "okay" to talk about at school and topics that are "not okay" to talk about at school (see PLAN B).

b. Establish time owed as a consequence for each sexual comment. That is, whenever the student makes an inappropriate (sexual) comment, she will owe one minute off of recess (if an elementary student). With a middle/junior high school student, the consequence should be one minute after class for the first incident and ten minutes in after-school or lunch time detention for each subsequent incident. During the time the student owes, she should sit and do nothing.

Alternately, the student could be required to write the inappropriate comment she said and sign the paper during the time she owes. This paper could be kept on file and shared with the building administrator and/or the student's parent(s) if the problem continues. Use professional judgment about whether sitting doing nothing or writing out the comment would be more effective with the student.

If a consequence such as time owed will be implemented, be sure to explain the use of consequences to the student beforehand, perhaps during the initial meeting to discuss a plan (see SUGGESTED STEPS FOR DEVELOPING AND IMPLEMENTING A PLAN).

c. Given that the student may be, at least in part, trying to gain your attention with the inappropriate comments, keep any interactions having to do with the sexual comments short and emotionally neutral. "Denise, that was inappropriate, you owe another minute." Resist the impulse to scold, lecture or explain—you have already explained "okay" and "not okay"—now take action.

d. If other students in the class pay attention to the inappropriate comments, provide a gentle correction to the student(s) who are reacting. "Darrel and Fern, would be helpful if you did not react at all to those sorts of comments. Please just pay attention to your own work." *(NOTE: If peer attention proves to be an ongoing problem, PLAN D may be a more useful approach.)*

2. **Use reinforcement to encourage appropriate behavior.**

a. Frequent praise and attention is the core of this plan. The student must see that she receives more frequent and more satisfying attention when she behaves appropriately than when she makes sexual comments. Thus, whenever the student is refraining from making sexual comments (or otherwise misbehaving), make an effort to praise and spend time with her. "Denise, you have been such a pleasure to have in class the last several days. Hey, let me know how your team does in the softball game tonight."

b. You may also wish to use intermittent rewards to acknowledge the student's success. Occasional, and unexpected, rewards can motivate the student to demonstrate responsible behavior more often. The idea is to provide a reward when the student has gone for a particularly long time without making sexual comments (e.g., a student who has generally been making four to five sexual comments before the morning recess makes it to lunch time without making one comment).

Appropriate rewards might include letting the student take the lead in a class activity, telling the student a good (clean) joke you recently heard, or commenting about the quality of the student's work in front of the principal. *(NOTE: A list of additional reinforcement ideas can be found in APPENDIX 1.)*

If you use intermittent rewards, do so more frequently at the beginning of the intervention to encourage the student, and then less often as the student's behavior improves.

3. Ensure a 3-1 ratio of positive to negative attention.

a. When attention is a motivating force for the student, you want to be sure that you are giving the student *three times as much* positive as negative attention. One way to do this is to monitor your interactions with the student at least one day per week. Simply keep a card on a clipboard or in your pocket and record each interaction you have with the student as either positive or negative by writing a "+" or a "-", respectively, on the card.

To determine whether an interaction is positive or negative, ask yourself whether the student was making a sexual comment (or otherwise misbehaving) at the time the interaction occurred. Any interaction that stems from inappropriate behavior is negative, and all interactions that occur while the student is meeting classroom expectations are positive. Thus, giving the signal and assigning time owed are both negative interactions, but praising the student for her positive contributions is positive. Strategies like smiling at the student as she comes in from recess or asking her if she has any questions during independent work are also considered positive interactions.

b. If you find that you are not giving the student three times as much positive as negative attention, try to increase the number of positive interactions you have with the student. Sometimes prompts can help. For example, you might decide that each time the student enters the classroom you will say "hello" to her, or that each day during the student's favorite subject you will praise her for her participation and enthusiasm.

4. Determine if the student would benefit from adult mentorship.

Some students are so starved for adult attention that being paired up with a responsible adult at the school who can spend one-to-one time with them in fun activities once or twice per week often reduces the need to gain attention via misbehavior. However, given the sexual nature of this problem, if you do arrange for an adult mentor, be sure the mentor is the same gender as the student and that she understands the importance of only being with the student in public (e.g., on the softball field during lunch).

PLAN D

Sometimes a student uses sexual comments as a way of demonstrating personal power and/or as an attempt to impress her peers. If your student seems encouraged by the reactions of her peers, the intervention must include ways of reducing the sense of power the student receives through inappropriate sexual comments and of helping the student wield her personal power in appropriate ways.

1. Respond consistently to the inappropriate behavior.

a. Conduct lessons to teach the student how to discriminate between topics that are "okay" to talk about at school and topics that are "not okay" to talk about at school (see PLAN B).

b. Establish time owed as a consequence for each sexual comment (see PLAN C).

c. Demonstrate that the student's sexual comments have no power to influence you. When power is the issue, the student is probably skilled at "pushing adults' buttons" (i.e., being able to make adults angry, embarrassed, flustered, or otherwise upset). Your goal should be to remain perfectly calm whenever the student is trying to prompt you to react.

If necessary, mentally rehearse interactions in which the student is trying to "push your buttons" with her comments, and imagine yourself calmly and consistently stating the consequence and resuming instruction. You might tell yourself that letting the student see that she has the power to embarrass you or make you angry is like paying her $50.00 for making the sexual comment.

2. Acknowledge the student's power with her peers.

a. During your initial meeting with the student (see SUGGESTED STEPS FOR DEVELOPING AND IMPLEMENTING A PLAN), tell the student that you know she has a great deal of influence with the other students and that you do not want to take that away from her. If appropriate, tell her she is a natural leader. Also let her know that you do not expect her to become a goody-goody type of student.

However, inform the student that making sexual comments in your class is a disrespectful thing to do. Be honest about her ability to prompt the other students to respond/react, and explain that because that is distracting to your instruction it is not respectful. Let the student know that you want to treat her with respect, and that you require the same level of respect from her.

b. Use your anecdotal notes (see SUGGESTED STEPS FOR DEVELOPING AND IMPLEMENTING A PLAN) to identify the kinds of situations in which the student typically makes inappropriate comments and help her think of alternatives that would allow her to exert her personal power, yet still be respectful. The goal is to help the student see that win/win situations are better than power struggles between the two of you.

3. *(OPTIONAL)*
If the student is not well-liked by her peers, and may be making sexual comments to gain status with them, you might suggest a peer model.

Encourage the student to watch another student she admires—one who is influential, but does not make inappropriate sexual comments. Have the student observe the way this peer model exerts her personal power without resorting to sexual comments. "Denise, I would like to encourage you to watch Grace. Do you think Grace is pretty influential with the other students? Do you think she is a goody-goody kind of person? No, I don't either. And yet, she is consistently very respectful and appropriate in class. For the next few days, watch Grace. I think you might get some good ideas about how to participate in class and use appropriate and respectful language without looking uncool."

However, care must be taken to avoid implying that the peer model is somehow better or more worthwhile than the target student. You should convey the idea that the peer model simply has a particular skill that would be worth observing.

4. **Give the student a high status job or responsibility.**

a. One of the most effective ways to help the student learn to wield her personal power wisely is to put her in a position of power. Think of a job or responsibility at school that the student would enjoy and at which she would be profi-

cient. For example, maybe the student could tutor a younger student in science, be an assistant in the library, or help the computer teacher maintain the computer lab. The best job will be one that occurs regularly (e.g., daily, twice per week, or at least once per week) and in which the student's "job supervisor" is someone other than yourself.

b. Be sure the student is given sufficient training and that all the expectations are defined at the beginning of the job, including the importance of refraining from sexual comments. The supervisor should stress the expectations which if violated could result in the student losing her job. "Denise, I know that you have had a tendency to use talk that is not okay at school. You need to know that if you are going to be a tutor for me here in the first grade, I will not tolerate any kind of sexual comments. My first graders will look up to you and try to imitate you. Therefore, if you are disrespectful toward me, or make a comment that uses bad language, you will lose your job. No warnings and no discussion, is that clear? Okay. I am very excited that you will be helping me. Several of my students can use extra help . . . ."

c. If a job is found that the student would like to do, she should be allowed to perform the job whenever scheduled, regardless of her behavior in your class. In the same way that you are expected to perform your job each day regardless of how you are getting along with your spouse, the student should be expected to perform her job each day (or whenever appropriate). If the job is made contingent on her not making sexual comments in your room, it is likely to become just one more power issue. The student may think, for example, "You can't make me stop by threatening that I will not get to tutor."

5. **Use reinforcement to encourage appropriate behavior.**

a. Give the student frequent praise and attention for making appropriate comments (see PLAN A).

b. Also praise the student for being responsible and successful with her new job/ responsibility. "Denise, Mrs. Johnson has told me that you have been very helpful to her in the first grade class. She said that her students really look forward to being tutored by you. Nice work!"

PLAN E

Whenever a student's problem behavior has become habitual and/or she does not seem to have a desire to reduce it, you may need to implement a structured system of external incentives (i.e., rewards and consequences) based on her behavior to motivate the student to stop making sexual comments and to start demonstrating restraint.

1. *Respond consistently to the inappropriate behavior.*

a. Conduct lessons to teach the student how to discriminate between topics that are "okay" to talk about at school and topics that are "not okay" to talk about at school (see PLAN B).

b. Establish time owed as a consequence for each sexual comment (see PLAN C).

c. Keep a record of the cumulative total of the number of minutes the student owes each day (regardless of whether or not they've been made up).

2. *Establish a system for reinforcing reductions in the inappropriate behavior.*

a. With the student, create a list of reinforcers that she can earn. Although you might want to have some suggestions in mind, the system will be more effective if the student identifies most of the items or activities herself. *(NOTE: A list of reinforcement ideas can be found in APPENDIX 1.)*

b. Assign "prices" (in points) for each of the rewards on the list and have the student select the reward she would like to earn first.

The prices should be based on the instructional, personnel, and/or monetary costs of the items. Monetary cost is clear—the more expensive the item, the more points required to earn it. Instructional cost refers to the amount of instructional time lost or interfered with by a particular reward. Thus, an activity which causes the student to miss part of academic instruction should require more points than one the student can do on her own free time. Personnel cost involves the time required by you and/or other staff to fulfill the reinforcer. Having lunch with the principal, therefore, would cost more points than spending five minutes of free time with a friend.

c. Establish a scale for awarding points based on how many inappropriate comments (and thus minutes owed) the student makes each day. If the student has averaged 15-20 inappropriate comments/minutes owed per day, the following scale might be appropriate.

15 or more inappropriate comments	= 0 points
11-14 inappropriate comments	= 1 point
6-10 inappropriate comments	= 2 points
3-5 inappropriate comments	= 3 points
1-2 inappropriate comments	= 5 points
0 inappropriate comments	= 7 points

In the example above, if the student makes six inappropriate comments, she would owe six minutes off of her recess (or in after-school detention, if a middle/junior high school student), but would still earn two points. If she made 17 comments, she would owe 17 minutes and earn no points.

d. When the student has accumulated enough points to earn the reward she has chosen, she "spends" the points necessary and the system begins again. That is, she selects another reward to earn and begins with zero points.

If the student is immature, and needs more frequent encouragement, you might consider letting her earn several "less expensive" rewards (e.g., five minutes of computer time after 20 points) on the way to a bigger reward (e.g., one hour with you for 200 points). That is, the student receives the small rewards without spending points; they continue to accumulate toward the selected reward.

3. *Use reinforcement to encourage appropriate behavior.*

a. Give the student increased praise and attention for making appropriate comments (see PLAN A).

b. In addition, show interest and enthusiasm about how the student is doing on the system. "Denise, this is the first day we have implemented this system and already you have reduced your number of inappropriate comments to five. Nice work. Three points today."

PLAN F

If there are more than a few students in your class who make inappropriate sexual comments, and/or if the students seem to encourage one another to make sexual comments, this intervention will be appropriate.

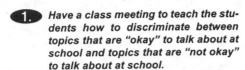 **1. Have a class meeting to teach the students how to discriminate between topics that are "okay" to talk about at school and topics that are "not okay" to talk about at school.**

Modify the suggestions in PLAN B for use with the entire class.

2. Establish a team competition and response cost lottery.

a. Divide the class into equal teams of four to six students, making sure they are equitable in terms of the number of students who do and do not have problems with making sexual comments. Seat the team members together at the same table or with their desks in clusters, and have each team give themselves a name you can use to refer to them.

b. Have the class brainstorm ideas of items or privileges for the teams to earn as reinforcers. Possibilities include a free homework pass for each team member, leaving for lunch a few minutes earlier than the rest of class, or a ticket for each team member for an ice cream in the cafeteria. Have the class identify at least six or seven different ideas and rank them in order of perceived value.

c. Set up a grab bag system. Write the different reinforcers on individual pieces of paper and put these in a bag or box. "Weight" the box so the most valuable items are included only once, while the more moderate reinforcers are each written on two or three slips of paper. This reduces the odds of winning the "biggest" reward—thus reducing how frequently you need to provide the big rewards.

After using the system successfully for a couple of weeks, increasingly add slips of paper with congratulatory messages only (e.g., "You did great! But no prize today."). This way you can fade the system, but the students will still have the chance to earn the big prize.

d. Each day, each team would begin with a set number of tickets, based on the following formula: The number of inappropriate comments made by the total class on a typical day, divided by the number of teams, plus one. For example, if the class has averaged 30 inappropriate sexual comments per day and there are five teams, each team would receive seven tickets.

e. Whenever a student makes an inappropriate sexual comment, that student's team loses one ticket. At the end of the day, each team writes their team name on their remaining tickets and places them in a bowl for a drawing. One ticket is drawn, and that team is allowed to draw a slip of paper from the grab bag. The team receives the prize written on the paper they've drawn.

**3. (OPTIONAL)
If this plan is ineffective, include time owed as an additional consequence.**

Whenever a student makes a sexual comment, his/her team would lose a ticket, plus the individual student would owe time off of recess or in after-school detention for each infraction. However, do not have the whole team owe time—losing the ticket is consequence enough for the student's teammates. (NOTE: See PLAN C for additional information on using time owed.)

4. Use reinforcement to encourage responsible behavior.

a. Give the students frequent praise and attention for making appropriate comments (see PLAN A).

b. In addition, praise entire teams and, when appropriate, the entire class for demonstrating restraint. If appropriate, you may wish to comment about how "professional" they are becoming about their classroom comments.

· · · · · · · · ·
Suggested Steps for Developing and Implementing a Plan

The following steps are designed to help you develop an appropriate intervention plan and implement it effectively, whether you choose to use one of the MODEL PLANS or create a customized plan of your own. The steps are, however, suggestions—they are not intended to be followed rigidly or in any particular order. Use your professional judgment and the knowledge of your particular situation to make them work for you.

1. *Make sure you have enough information about the situation.*

a. If you think a minimal intervention like PLAN A will be sufficient, you may already have enough information to proceed. However, when a more involved plan seems necessary, you should consider collecting additional descriptive and/or objective information for a couple of days.

b. You need to be able to explain what you mean when you say that "the student has a problem with making inappropriate sexual comments." Anecdotal notes on actual incidents should provide enough detail to help you define the problem behavior clearly and completely. To collect anecdotal notes, simply keep a card in your pocket or on a clipboard and occasionally make notes on specific times when the student says something that you consider to be an inappropriate sexual comment.

For each entry, briefly describe exactly what the student did or said, the setting, and any other relevant observations (e.g., what prompted the comment). You do not need to make notes every time the student says something inappropriate; the idea is to capture a range of examples so you will be able to describe the behavior completely.

Also include some notes on times when the student makes appropriate comments in class. This will make it clear that you are not only aware of the student's problem behavior, but also recognize when she behaves appropriately. When you meet with the student, the positive examples will also help you to clarify how you want the student to behave.

c. In addition to collecting information on what the student's inappropriate behavior sounds like, it can also be useful to document how often it occurs (i.e., a frequency count). This information will provide both a more objective measure of the problem and an objective way to monitor the student's progress. You can use the same card on which you are collecting anecdotal notes to keep a frequency count—simply write a tally mark on the card each time the student makes an inappropriate sexual comment. *(NOTE: You might also want to code the tallies to discern whether the behavior occurs more frequently during certain times, subjects, or activities.)*

d. If the student notices what you are doing and asks about it, be straightforward—tell her that you are collecting information to see whether her tendency to make sexual comments is a problem that needs to be worked on.

Following is an example of anecdotal notes and a frequency count that have been collected on a student's sexual comments.

Denise's Inappropriate Comments—2/20

Morning	Afternoon
////	~~LHT~~ ///

Notes:

8:40—During a discussion about nutrition, the book had a reference to German sausage and Denise said, "Yeah, I'd like to get my hands on a German sausage right now." The class laughed.

2:15—While getting ready to go to P.E., Denise said, "I hope we play basketball. I really like big balls." Everyone laughed.

---

e. The frequency information is fairly easy to summarize on a chart or graph. Seeing how often she makes inappropriate sexual comments may help the student and her parent(s) better understand your concern.

f. Continuing to collect this type of information and keeping the chart up-to-date while you implement a plan will help you monitor whether the situation is getting worse, staying the same, or getting better.

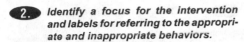 **Identify a focus for the intervention and labels for referring to the appropriate and inappropriate behaviors.**

a. To be effective, the intervention must address more than just reducing the student's inappropriate sexual comments—there must be a concurrent emphasis on increasing some positive behavior or trait (e.g., making appropriate comments). Having a specific positive behavior in mind will make it easier for you to "catch" and reinforce the student for behaving appropriately, and the positive focus will help you to frame the situation more productively.

For example, if you simply say that "the student has a problem with making inappropriate sexual comments," you don't really provide any useful information, and may put the student and her parent(s) on the defensive. Additionally, this may imply to the student that your concern stems from your simply being "uptight" about sexuality. However, when you explain that you want to "help the student learn to participate appropriately in school by making 'okay' comments" you present an important, and reasonable, goal for the student to work toward and clarify what the student needs to do to be successful.

b. Specifying labels for the appropriate and inappropriate behaviors (e.g., "okay comments" and "not okay comments," respectively) will help you to use consistent vocabulary when discussing the situation with the student.

Determine when and how to include the parent(s).

a. After your initial discussion with the student's parent(s) (see PRE-INTERVENTION STEPS), monitor the student's behavior carefully. If, after a couple of days, the situation does not appear to be improving, ask the student's parent(s) to join you for a meeting with the student to develop a plan.

Also plan to include another education professional (e.g., the principal, the school counselor) during all subsequent interactions related to this problem with either the student's parent(s) or the student. This provides for an objective third party who is a witness to all intervention steps in the unlikely event that there should be any claims of impropriety on your part.

b. Give the student's parent(s) updates at least once per week while the plan is being implemented.

Prepare for, then conduct, an initial meeting about the situation.

a. Arrange a meeting to discuss your concerns with the student, the student's parent(s), and the third party who will be involved in the plan (e.g., the school counselor). Make the meeting appropriately private and make sure the meeting is scheduled for a time and place that it is not likely to be interrupted (e.g., the counselor's office). The parent(s) should be the ones to tell the student about the meeting.

b. Construct a preliminary plan. Decide whether you think you can use one of the MODEL PLANS or if you need to create a customized plan using components from various plans and/or of your own design. Although you will invite and encourage the student to help develop the plan during the initial meeting, having a proposed plan in mind before you meet can alleviate frustration and wasted time if the student is unwilling or unable to participate.

c. After reviewing the information you have collected and thinking about how you want the student to behave, prepare thorough descriptions of the inappropriate behavior and the positive behavior/trait on which the student will be working. The more specific you can be and the more concrete examples you have, the easier it will be to clarify (and for the student and her parent[s] to understand) your expectations. Be sure to consider the student's behavior in all relevant activities (e.g., independent work periods, teacher directed instruction, unstructured class times, recess and lunch, etc.).

d. Conduct the meeting in an atmosphere of collaboration. The following agenda is one way you might structure the meeting:

- **Share your concerns about the student's behavior.**

  Describe the behavior and, if you have collected a frequency count, share that information as well. Then tell the student why you consider making sexual comments in class to be a problem. You might explain that what the student does or says privately is not your concern, but what she does and says in school is of concern to you because it affects how others think of her.

- **Discuss how you can work together to improve the situation.**

  Tell the student that you would like to help her "learn to participate appropriately in school by making okay comments" and describe your preliminary plan. Invite the student to give you input on the various aspects of the plan, and together work out any necessary details (e.g., the signal, timed owed, etc.).

You may have to brainstorm different possibilities if the student is uncomfortable with the initial plan. Incorporating any of the student's suggestions that strengthen the plan is likely to increase her sense of "ownership" in and commitment to it.

- **Make sure the student understands what you mean by appropriate and inappropriate behavior.**

Use the descriptions you have prepared to define and clarify the problem behavior and the positive (desired) behavior as specifically and thoroughly as you can (see PLAN B for suggestions). To ensure that you and the student are in agreement about the expectations, you might present hypothetical scenarios and have her identify whether each is an example of "okay" or "not okay" comments.

- **Conclude the meeting.**

Always end the meeting with words of encouragement. Let the student know that you are confident that she can be successful. Be sure to reinforce her for participating in the meeting.

 Give the student regular, ongoing feedback about her behavior.

It is important to meet with the student periodically to discuss her progress. In most cases, three to five minutes once per week should suffice. *(NOTE: PLANS E and F suggest daily meetings.)* During the meetings, review any information that has been collected and discuss whether or not the situation is getting better. As much as possible, focus on the student's improvements, however, also address any new or continuing problems. As the situation improves, the meetings can be faded to once every other week and then to once per month.

6. *Evaluate the situation (and the plan).*

Implement any plan for at least two weeks before deciding whether to change plans; to continue, modify, or fade the plan you are using; or to cease the intervention. Generally, if the student's behavior is clearly improving (based on the objective information that's been collected and/or the subjective perceptions of yourself, the student, and the student's parent[s]), stick with what you are doing. If the situation has remained the same or worsened, some kind of change will be necessary. Always discuss any changes to the plan with the student first.

SHYNESS/WITHDRAWN BEHAVIOR

DESCRIPTION

You have a student who spends most of her time alone, rarely interacting with others.

GOAL

The student will learn to interact more frequently with others and will not be fearful of those interactions.

OVERVIEW OF PLANS

- PLAN A: For a situation in which the problem has just begun or occurs infrequently.

- PLAN B: For a student who spends time by herself because she does not know how to interact with other students.

- PLAN C: For a student whose shyness may stem from a lack of self-confidence, and/or a student who has given up believing that others will like her.

- PLAN D: For a student who acts shy or lonely to gain attention from adults.

NOTE:

With this type of behavior, it is critical not to imply that the student has to change her personality. There are many perfectly well-adjusted people who are somewhat reserved. The goal of these four plans is not to make the student become extremely outgoing, but to increase her skills and comfort level in interacting with her peers and with adults.

Alternative Problems

- **Dawdling**

- **Depression**

- **Helplessness**

- **Moodiness**

- **Passive Resistance**

- **Social Skills, Lack of**

- **Suicide Threats**

- **Victim—Student Who Is Always Picked On**

· · · · · · · ·
General Considerations

- If the student's problem behavior stems in any way from academic issues (e.g., the student acts shy or lonely because she is discouraged about her academic performance), concurrent efforts must be made to ensure her academic success (see **Academic Deficits, Determining**).

- If you suspect that the student's shyness could be related to the student being depressed, see **Depression**. This problem includes a set of questions to help you decide whether the student should be referred for counseling or psychological services.

- If the student's family or cultural background could be a factor in the student's behavior (e.g., some Native American cultures emphasize quiet, reserved behavior as a sign of respect and/or strength), do not intervene until you have checked the appropriateness of any intervention plan and its goals with the student's parent(s). If the behavior is not interfering with the student's academic or social success, it may be both unnecessary and inappropriate to intervene.

- If the student lacks the basic social skills to interact with her peers appropriately, it may be necessary to begin by teaching her those skills. For additional information on conducting social skills lessons and published social skills curricula, see **Social Skills, Lack of**.

· · · · · · · ·
Model Plans

PLAN A

It is not always necessary, or even beneficial, to use an involved plan. If the inappropriate behavior has just begun and/or occurs infrequently, the following actions, along with making the student aware of your concerns, may resolve the situation.

1. **Respond consistently to the inappropriate behavior.**

a. Sometimes when you notice that the student is acting shy or withdrawn, praise other students who are interacting appropriately. "Oscar and Pamela, you are being very friendly in the way you are talking to each other as you are working on the computer." If the target student then begins to interact, wait about 30 seconds and then praise her for being friendly.

b. Occasionally, when the student does not join in appropriately, gently correct her by calmly providing information about what she should be doing instead. "Samira, we are working in cooperative groups and it is important that you stay with your group and add your own ideas. What is your opinion of . . . ?" Avoid being emotional or providing an overly lengthy correction. The idea is for the student to receive more frequent attention for being friendly than for acting shy or withdrawn.

(NOTE: It is neither necessary nor reasonable to respond every time the student is withdrawn, as everyone has the right to be quiet and alone some of the time.)

2. **Use reinforcement to encourage appropriate behavior.**

a. Give the student increased praise. Be especially alert for situations in which the student is interacting with others and praise both the target student and the student(s) with whom she is interacting. While praising, specifically describe their behavior. "Christian, Missy, and Samira, you people are having a friendly interaction. You are all working together on the lab report, talking, and it seems like you having a fun time."

b. Also privately praise the student for interacting in situations that require a significant effort on her part. "Samira, I noticed that when Dr. Uller came in the room you did not put your head on the desk. You looked at her and smiled as she greeted you. That was a great example of a friendly interaction and I know that she appreciated that smile."

· ·

c. Give the student frequent attention (e.g., say "hello" to her as she enters the classroom, call on her frequently during class activities, and occasionally ask her to assist you with a class job that needs to be done) and praise her for other positive behaviors she exhibits. For exam-ple, you might comment about the accuracy of her work or how consistent she is about making entries in her journal. This demonstrates to the student that you notice many positive things she does, not just the fact that she is refraining from acting shy.

PLAN B

Sometimes students act shy or withdrawn because they have not mastered some of the basic social skills most students take for granted (e.g., asking to join a game, responding to someone's attention, or even greeting another). If you suspect that your student lacks the necessary social skills to interact with her peers, the intervention must include a way to teach her those basic skills.

(NOTE: If you are uncertain about whether or not the student has mastered basic social skills, ask yourself the following question: Have you ever observed the student joining in with her peers unprompted and/or interacting in a friendly way? If you have, the student probably has the necessary skills in her behavioral repertoire and thus this plan would not be appropriate. If you haven't observed these behaviors, it is likely that the student lacks these basic social skills.)

1. **Respond consistently to the inappropriate behavior.**

Occasionally when the student is acting shy or withdrawn, gently correct her (see PLAN A).

2. **Conduct lessons to teach the student skills and strategies for being friendly and/or joining in activities with her peers.**

a. Decide who will teach the lessons. Because teaching new behaviors like these can be time-consuming and difficult, it may be worthwhile to see whether there are other students in the school who could also benefit from such instruction, and then arrange for the school counselor or school psychologist to conduct these lessons with a small group of students.

NOTE: For scripted social skills lessons appropriate for use with an entire class or a small group of students, you may wish to consult one or more of the following resources:

Huggins, P. (1994). Helping kids find their strengths. Longmont, CO: Sopris West.

Huggins, P. (1993). Teaching friendship skills: Intermediate version. Longmont, CO: Sopris West.

Huggins, P. (1993). Teaching friendship skills: Primary version. Longmont, CO: Sopris West.

b. Decide whether to develop the lessons yourself or to use a published social skills curriculum. Any of the following commercially available programs might be appropriate for your particular student/situation:

Goldstein, A.P., Sprafkin, R.P., Gershaw, N.J., & Klein, P. (1980). Skillstreaming the adolescent. Champaign, IL: Research Press.

McGinnis, E. & Goldstein, A.P. (1984). Skillstreaming the elementary school child. Champaign, IL: Research Press.

Walker, H.M., McConnel, S., Holmes, D., Todis, B., Walker, J., & Golden, N. (1983). The Walker social skills curriculum. The ACCEPTS program. Austin, TX: Pro-Ed.

Walker, H.M., Todis, B., Holmes, D., & Horton, D. (1988). Adolescent coping curriculum for effective social skills (ACCESS). Austin, TX: Pro-Ed.

c. If you do not have access to a published social skills curriculum and will be developing the lessons yourself, begin by listing the specific skills the student needs and prioritizing them. The lessons should begin with the most critical skill (e.g., teaching the student how and when to greet other students and how to respond when someone says "Hi" to her).

d. The lessons should be scheduled for five to 15 minutes daily. Teach (or have the school counselor or psychologist teach) one skill at a time until you have taught all the critical skills that you identified.

If you have only a few minutes per day for the lessons, you may have to spend about a week on each skill. Once a particular skill has been mastered (both in the lessons and within the classroom), address another skill. Whenever new skills are added, do not forget to include some review on those that have been mastered previously.

e. For the lessons themselves, you might present to the student scenarios featuring shy behavior similar to those that have actually occurred with the student, and include any or all of the following activities:

- Reviewing previously taught skills.

- Modeling what it looks like and sounds like to use the targeted social skill (e.g., say "Hi.").

- Using role play with hypothetical situations in order to have the student practice the skill while you provide feedback.

- Modeling different behaviors and having the student identify whether each is an example of being friendly/joining in or of being shy/withdrawn.

- Presenting hypothetical situations and having the student respond in a variety of friendly ways.

- Asking the student to evaluate how successful she has been during the lessons. (Then describe your perceptions of her performance and either praise her, or together set goals for the next lesson.)

- Giving the student "homework assignments" in which she must practice a skill that has been taught. (At the time of the next lesson, the student can report what she tried, how it worked, and any difficulties or problems she had implementing this new skill.)

f. Continue the lessons until the student is demonstrating mastery of all the identified critical skills and using them in contexts other than the lessons.

g. When someone else is teaching the lessons, share the information from your anecdotal notes (see SUGGESTED STEPS FOR DEVELOPING AND IMPLEMENTING A PLAN) and/or your perceptions of the student's behavior with that person: "Mr. Pratt, Samira is still having some trouble joining in games at recess. If someone invites her, she joins in, which is a huge step forward. But, if she's not directly invited, she is not using the skills you are teaching her. Perhaps she needs more practice in joining in?" or "Mr. Pratt, I've noticed that Samira is much more consistent about responding

when someone greets her. Lots of students and adults who never used to say anything to her are now saying 'hello' or 'good morning.'"

3. **Prompt the student to behave appropriately by using precorrections.**

a. Watch for circumstances in which the student is likely to be shy/withdrawn and remind her that she will need to remember to be friendly/join in. "Samira, I am going to introduce you to Mrs. McCormick. I will be watching to see if you remember to do what you have been practicing in your lessons. I'll bet you can."

b. If time permits, you might have the student identify what she will try to remember to do. "Samira, keep remembering what you have worked on in your lessons with Mr. Pratt. What might you try to say to Mrs. McCormick? Excellent, give it a try. " If this conversation would embarrass the student, conduct it privately.

4. **Use reinforcement to encourage appropriate behavior.**

a. Give the student increased praise and attention for being friendly (see PLAN A).

b. In addition, watch for instances when the student exhibits the specific skills that have been taught during the lessons. Praise in a way that gives the student information on the benefits of the particular skill(s): "Samira, as you came into class this morning, I noticed you using the 'Hi' strategy you have been working on in your lessons. You looked at the person you said 'Hi' to, and you smiled. Did you notice how Liam smiled back and asked, 'How are you doing?' You haven't even work on it yet, but you told her you were fine. That was very friendly!" or "Samira, when you went up to Dr. Uller and said 'Hi, Dr. Uller' she was so happy. I know that she is very proud of you and pleased that you like her well enough to go out of your way to say hello."

c. When you see the student interacting in a friendly way with another student, give both of the students a special privilege. "Samira and Polly, I saw that you two were having a good time working on the computer together—very friendly. I am writing each of you a certificate that can be used for 15 minutes of additional computer time. You can use the computer together any afternoon this week or next."

d. You may also wish to use intermittent rewards when the student makes a significant effort to use the skills taught in the lessons to behave in a friendly way. If the student is typically withdrawn during cooperative groups, for example, but makes an effort to participate, highlight that success by giving the student a reward, a special job, or a privilege. "Samira, you have been so friendly in sharing your ideas with your group. I would like to offer you a choice of activities.

You can either have five minutes of time to work on the computer by yourself, or you can go down to the office and say 'Hi' to Dr. Uller. If you choose to go to the office, I will write a note that you can give to her describing your friendly participation in your group. Which would you rather do?" *(NOTE: Additional ideas for reinforcement can be found in APPENDIX 1.)*

PLAN C

Sometimes a student will have become so discouraged or disheartened that she does not even want to try to change the situation or her shy behavior. If your student seems to lack self-confidence and/or to have given up on social interactions, the intervention may need to be somewhat indirect. Instead of working specifically on the student's shyness, you might want to focus instead on helping the student feel more confident with the hope that this will give her the courage to try harder at being friendly/joining in with her peers.

 Respond consistently to the inappropriate behavior.

Occasionally when the student is being shy or withdrawn, gently correct her (see PLAN A).

 Capitalize on the student's identified strengths or interests.

A potentially powerful way to increase a student's self-confidence is to determine what the student is interested in or does well and structure activities or interactions that build on those strengths. Increasing the student's confidence by focusing on what she already does well can help her develop the confidence to try things that are more threatening for her (e.g., interacting with others). Following are a few possible ways you might implement this step:

- If the student has a particular interest (e.g., space exploration), you might check out a library book on the topic that you think the student will find interesting. Put the book in her desk with a note stating that you thought she might like to look at the book during free reading time.

- If the student is proficient on the computer, ask her to evaluate a software program that you are considering for the classroom.

- If the student has neat penmanship, ask her to copy a note that will be included in the weekly class newsletter to parents.

- If the student has a nice voice, ask her to tape a story for students in a younger class to listen to on their free time. Or, ask the student if she would like to go to a younger class to read aloud to a small group.

- If the student is always at school on time, ask her to help with some aspect of the morning routines (e.g., getting the lunch count form from your desk and giving it to you as you take attendance.)

(NOTE: Additional ideas for jobs/responsibilities can be found in APPENDIX 2.)

 Encourage the student to use more positive self-talk.

a. Try to find out from the student whether she tends to "put herself down" with comments or thoughts such as:

- "I'm no good."

- "I can't do that sort of thing."

- "Nobody likes me."

- Etc.

These types of statements continually reinforce the student's negative beliefs about herself. The more she says or thinks them, the more she will come to believe them to be true.

b. Teach the student to engage in more positive and hopeful self-talk. You can use examples (like those following) to help the student learn to recognize the difference between positive and negative self-talk. Then have the student reframe her negative statements into positive ones.

This may be difficult for the student at first. If so, model the process for her and have her repeat the positive statement after you. Don't worry if the student acts like she does not believe the positive statements—with enough repetition,

Negative Statement	Positive and Hopeful Restatement
I'm no good.	I am a worthwhile person.
I can't do that sort of thing.	I can do this. Even if I have trouble, I'll get it eventually.
Nobody likes me.	I can get along with other students.

she will come to believe them. *(NOTE: For more information, see **Self-Concept Problems**.)*

 Structure academic success.

Make sure that the student is experiencing frequent success in the academic tasks she is being asked to do. When a student experiences a great deal of academic failure, simply using more positive self-talk and/or recognizing her strengths in other areas will not be powerful enough to counteract this daily failure. See **Work Completion—Daily Work** for ideas on adopting instruction to maximize student's success.

 Use reinforcement to encourage appropriate behavior.

Give the student increased praise and attention for being friendly (see PLAN A).

PLAN D

Some students have learned that they can prompt others to make lavish efforts to engage them in interactions by acting shy or withdrawn. If you think that your student may be using her shy behavior to gain attention, sympathy, and/or power, the intervention should focus on making sure that the student receives more frequent and more satisfying attention for behaving appropriately than for being shy or withdrawn.

1. Respond consistently to the inappropriate behavior.

a. For the most part, you should ignore the student's behavior when she is being shy or withdrawn. When the student has learned that people will comfort her and/or try to coax her into interacting when she is shy, such efforts may actually perpetuate her shy behavior. Giving the student no attention when she is being shy and frequent attention when she is not will help her learn that the way to receive attention is to participate and to act friendly. At first this may seem somewhat cruel. Remember though, you are not ignoring the student, merely refraining from interacting with her when she's being shy.

b. If ignoring is not appropriate in your particular situation (e.g., the student withdraws and will not participate in class activities), gently correct the student when she is being shy by providing information about what she should be doing instead (see PLAN A). However, keep the interaction short and your tone neutral. Don't beg or cajole, and don't act as if you feel sorry for the student. "Samira, you need to take a seat here on the rug while we read the story."

c. Gently correct other students who overdo efforts to include the target student. Be careful with this procedure, however. You do not want to give the impression that other students should stop inviting the target student to join them—just that they should refrain from making a big production of it if she refuses. That is, thank them for inviting the target student to participate, without fostering a "poor Samira" mentality. "Leah and Ted, thank you for inviting Samira to participate, but you don't need to beg her. Samira is a very bright young lady who can decide for herself if she wishes to respond to your invitation or not."

2. Use reinforcement to encourage appropriate behavior.

a. Give the student increased praise and attention for being friendly (see PLAN A). Use contingent praise for being friendly, and also frequent non-contingent interactions. For example, if the student is quietly working, it would not be appropriate to praise her for being friendly, but it would be appropriate to give her positive attention. "Samira, you are working hard. How are things going, do you have any questions?

Okay, great. If you do need anything, just raise your hand to let me know."

b. Use intermittent rewards to celebrate the student's success. For example, if the student typically acts withdrawn during recess, but you overhear her making arrangements to play with another student as the class is preparing to go outside, reward that behavior. You might meet with the student after recess, congratulate her on her efforts, and ask if she would like to choose a friend to work with her on changing the bulletin board during the next recess. *(NOTE: Additional ideas for reinforcement can be found in APPENDIX 1.)*

3. Ensure a 3-1 ratio of positive to negative attention.

a. If attention is a motivating force for the student, you need to be sure that you are giving the student *three times as much* positive as negative attention. One way to do this is to monitor your interactions with the student at least one day per week. To do so, keep a card on a clipboard or in your pocket and record each interaction you have with the student as either positive or negative by writing a "+" or a "-", respectively, on the card.

To determine whether an interaction is positive or negative, ask yourself whether the student was being shy (or otherwise misbehaving) at the time the interaction occurred. Any interaction that stems from inappropriate behavior is negative, and all interactions that occur while the student is meeting classroom expectations are positive. Thus, reminding the student to join in is a negative interaction (no matter how nice you sound), but praising her for working with another student is positive. Greeting the student as she enters the room or asking her if she has any questions during independent work are also considered positive interactions. *(NOTE: Ignoring the student's inappropriate behavior is not recorded at all, because it is not an interaction.)*

b. If you find that you are not giving the student three times as much positive as negative attention, try to increase the number of positive interactions you have with the student. Sometimes prompts can help. For example, you might decide that each time the student enters the classroom you will say "hello" to her, that whenever you look at the clock you will find a time to praise the student, or that whenever a student uses the drinking fountain you will check the target student and, as soon as possible, praise some aspect of her behavior. You can also increase the ratio of positive to negative attention by ignoring more of the student's inappropriate behavior.

. . . .
Suggested Steps for Developing and Implementing a Plan

The following steps are designed to help you develop an appropriate intervention plan and implement it effectively, whether you choose to use one of the MODEL PLANS or create a customized plan of your own. The steps are, however, suggestions—they are not intended to be followed rigidly or in any particular order. Use your professional judgment and the knowledge of your particular situation to make them work for you.

1. Make sure you have enough information about the situation.

a. If you think a minimal intervention like PLAN A will be sufficient, you may already have enough information to proceed. However, when a more involved plan seems necessary, you should consider collecting some descriptive information for a couple of days.

b. You need to be able to explain what has led you to conclude that "the student has a problem with being shy/withdrawn." Anecdotal notes on actual incidents can help you describe the situation clearly and completely. Simply keep a card in your pocket or on a clipboard and occasionally make notes on instances when the student is being shy.

For each entry, briefly describe where and when the incident occurred, what the student did or said, and any other relevant observations (e.g., who else was around). You do not need to make notes every time the student is shy or withdrawn; the idea is to capture a range of examples so that you will be able to describe the behavior thoroughly.

Also be sure to include some notes on times when the student is friendly/joins in. This will make it clear that you are not only aware of the student's problem behavior, but also recognize when she behaves appropriately. When you meet with the student, these positive examples will also help you clarify how you want the student to behave. *(NOTE: If there are no positive examples of the student joining in, disregard this step.)*

c. If the student notices what you are doing and asks about it, be straightforward—tell her that you are collecting information to see whether her shyness is a problem that needs to be worked on.

Following is an example of anecdotal notes that have been collected on a student's shy/withdrawn behavior.

Samira's Interactions—2/12

8:25—Coming into the room, Samira was hunched down into her coat and stayed close to the wall. Other students were talking and laughing as they hung up their coats. Samira watched them, but made no move to join in.

9:30 (cooperative group)—In Samira's group several students tried to solicit her ideas, but she just shrugged and said, "I don't know." After a couple of tries, the other students seemed to forget about her.

10:20—Watching the students at recess, Samira appeared to spend her whole recess wandering around with her hands in her pockets. She made no effort to join the others. When another student came up to her, she did not appear to respond. I asked the playground supervisors, and they said this was pretty typical of most days.

1:50—Dr. Uller (the principal) was in the room and was greeting and talking to the students and looking at their work. When she talked to Samira, she put her head down on her desk and would not look at Dr. Uller or respond to her greeting or questions.

---

d. Continuing to collect this type of information while you implement a plan will help you monitor whether the situation is getting worse, staying the same, or getting better.

2. *Identify a focus for the intervention and labels for referring to the appropriate and inappropriate behaviors.*

a. Along with reducing the student's shyness, there must be an emphasis on increasing some positive behavior or trait (e.g., being friendly, joining in, participating, interacting). Having a specific positive behavior in mind will make it easier for you to "catch" and reinforce the student for behaving appropriately, and the positive focus will help you to frame the situation more productively.

That is, if you address the issue by saying that "the student is shy," you might inadvertently reinforce her belief that she *is* shy. In addition, this doesn't really provide any useful information, and may put the student and her parent(s) on the defensive. However, if you explain that you want to "help the student learn to be more friendly with her peers," you present an important, and reasonable, goal for the student to work toward and clearly identify what the student needs to do to be successful.

b. Specifying labels for the appropriate and inappropriate behaviors (e.g., "acting shy" and "being friendly," respectively) will help you to use consistent vocabulary when discussing the situation with the student. If you sometimes refer to the inappropriate behavior as "acting shy" and other times tell the student that she is being "unfriendly," she may not realize that you are talking about the same thing.

3. *Determine when and how to include the parent(s).*

a. It is not necessary to contact the student's parent(s) if the problem has just begun and is not interfering with the student's academic or social progress. However, it might be a good idea to take advantage of any scheduled activities (e.g., conferences, weekly notes home) to let them know of your concern.

b. The parent(s) should be contacted whenever the problem has lasted longer than a couple of weeks and/or is affecting the student's academic performance or is alienating her from her peers. Share with them any information you have collected about the behavior (e.g., anecdotal notes), and explain why you are concerned. Focus in particular on how the behavior is hindering the student academically and/or socially.

You might ask if the parent(s) have any insight into the situation and/or whether they have noticed similar behavior at home. Whether or not the parent(s) perceive a problem, explain that you want to help the student "learn to be more friendly with her peers" and invite them to join you for an initial meeting with the student to develop a plan. If the parent(s) are unable or unwilling to participate, let them know that you will keep them informed of the student's progress.

c. Once the parent(s) have been involved in any way, you should give them updates at least once per week while the plan is being implemented.

4. Prepare for, then conduct, an initial meeting about the situation.

a. Arrange a meeting to discuss your concerns with the student and anyone else who will be involved in the plan (e.g., the parent[s], the school psychologist). Although the specifics will vary depending upon the age of the student and the severity of the problem, there are some general guidelines to consider when scheduling the meeting.

First, meet at a neutral time (i.e., not immediately after an incident of shyness has occurred), when emotions are less likely to hamper communication. In general, a day's notice is appropriate, however a primary age student may worry excessively and/or forget what the meeting is about if it is scheduled more than an hour before it takes place

Second, make the meeting appropriately private. With a primary student who has a mild problem, you might meet in the classroom while the other students are working independently. However, when dealing with a middle/junior high school student and the student's parent(s), you will need some place private (e.g., the counselor's office) to ensure that the discussion will not be overheard.

Third, try to make sure the meeting is scheduled for a time and place that it is not likely to be interrupted. Finally, when the parent(s) will be participating, they should be the ones to tell the student about the meeting.

b. Construct a preliminary plan. Decide whether you think you can use one of the MODEL PLANS or if you need to create a customized plan using components from various plans and/or of your own design. Although you will invite and encourage the student to help de-

velop the plan in mind during the initial meeting, having a proposed plan in mind before you meet can alleviate frustration and wasted time if the student is unwilling or unable to participate.

c. Review the information you have collected and think about how you want the student to behave. Then, prepare comprehensive descriptions of the student's shy behavior and the positive behavior/trait on which she will be working. The more specific you can be and the more concrete examples you have, the easier it will be to clarify (and for the student to understand) your expectations. Be sure to consider the student's behavior in all relevant activities (e.g., independent work, teacher directed instruction, unstructured class times, recess and lunch, etc.).

d. Conduct the meeting in an atmosphere of collaboration. The following agenda is one way you might structure the meeting:

- **Share your concerns about the student's behavior.**

  Briefly describe the problem behavior and explain why you consider shyness to be a problem. You might want to express the idea that human interactions can be fun and satisfying, but that they require give and take on the part of all persons involved. If appropriate, you can talk about the fact that people do not interact with inanimate objects (e.g., talk to chairs, play with doorknobs) because nothing is given back from those objects.

- **Discuss how you can work together to improve the situation.**

  Tell the student that you would like to help her "learn to be more friendly with her peers," and describe your preliminary plan. Invite the student to give you input on the various aspects of the plan, and together work out any necessary details (e.g., schedule of the lessons).

  You may have to brainstorm different possibilities if the student is uncomfortable with the initial plan. Incorporating any of the student's suggestions that strengthen the plan is likely to increase her sense of "ownership" in and commitment to it.

- **Make sure the student understands what you mean by appropriate and inappropriate behavior.**

  Use the descriptions you have prepared to clarify your expectations about the problem behavior and the positive (desired) behavior as specifically and thoroughly as you can. To ensure that you and the student are in agreement about the expectations, you might present hypothetical scenarios and have her identify whether each is an example of being shy/withdrawn or of being friendly. Or you might describe an actual situation that has occurred and ask the student to explain how she could be more friendly in that situation.

• **Conclude the meeting.**

Always end the meeting with words of encouragement. Let the student know that you are confident that she can be successful. Be sure to reinforce her for participating in the meeting.

5. *Give the student regular, ongoing feedback about her behavior.*

It is important to meet with the student periodically to discuss her progress. In most cases, 3-5 minutes once per week should suffice. *(NOTE: With PLAN B, these meetings can be incorporated into the lessons.)* During the meetings, review any informa-tion that has been collected and discuss whether or not the situation is getting better. As much as possible, focus on the student's improvements, however, also address any new or continuing problems. As the situation improves, the meetings can be faded to once every other week and then to once per month.

6. *Evaluate the situation (and the plan).*

Implement any plan for at least two weeks before deciding whether to change plans; to continue, modify, or fade the plan you are using; or to cease the intervention. Generally, if the student's behavior is clearly improving (based on the objective information that's been collected and/or the subjective perceptions of yourself, the student, and possibly the parent[s]), stick with what you are doing. If the situation has remained the same or worsened, some kind of change will be necessary. Always discuss any changes to the plan with the student first.

 **S**LOPPY WORK

Lack of Pride in Work
Penmanship Problems
Carelessness

DESCRIPTION

You have a student who turns in work that is torn, smudged, and/or sloppily written.

GOAL

The student will turn in work that is neater with each passing week.

OVERVIEW OF PLANS

- PLAN A: For a situation in which the problem is relatively mild or has just begun.

- PLAN B: For a student who lacks pride in his work.

- PLAN C: For a student who does not realize when and/or how frequently he turns in sloppy work.

- PLAN D: For a student whose sloppiness has become habitual.

- PLAN E: For a situation in which there are several students in the class who have a problem with sloppy work.

Alternative Problems

- **Cleaning Up, Problems With**

- **Corrected, Student Gets Upset When**

- **Messy Desks**

- **Work Completion— Daily Work**

General Considerations

- If the student's problem behavior stems in any way from academic issues (e.g., the student is unable to meet the academic expectations and makes his work messy to mask his academic deficits), concurrent efforts must be made to ensure his academic success (see **Academic Deficits, Determining**).

- If the student's work is sloppy because he lacks handwriting skills, begin by assigning the student a program designed to provide daily and sequential practice in handwriting. An excellent direct instruction program you may wish to consult is:

  Englemann, S. & Miller, S. (1980). *The cursive writing program*. Columbus, OH: Research Associates.

Model Plans

PLAN A

It is not always necessary, or even beneficial, to use an involved plan. If the problem has just begun and/or the sloppiness is not so severe that it is directly affecting the student's grades or other aspects of his academic success, the following actions, along with making the student aware of your concerns, may resolve the situation.

1. Respond consistently to the inappropriate behavior.

a. Whenever you notice that the student's work is beginning to get sloppy, gently correct him. Give the student specific information about what he should do to make the work neater, and what to keep in mind as he works toward completion. "Brad, don't press your pencil so hard. Look how much neater the first part of the paper looks before you started pressing so hard."

b. When handing back a paper that has been sloppily done, provide direct feedback on what the student should have done differently and, if possible, also point out what was neat about the paper. "Brad, you kept this paper whole and flat—that is an important part of taking pride in the neatness of your work. However, let's look at the spaces between words. Show me where one word stops and the next one begins . . . ."

2. Use reinforcement to encourage appropriate behavior.

a. Give the student increased praise. Be especially alert for situations in which the student is making an effort to be neat, and praise him for these demonstrations of his ability to take pride in the neatness of his work. "Brad, I see that you are taking pride in neatness. I can tell because your paper is whole and flat and there are no smudges." If the student would be embarrassed by this type of public praise, praise him privately or even give the student a note.

Remember that any time the student is working on a task and the paper is neat, you can praise him for taking pride in neatness—even if all he has done to this point is put his name of the paper. In fact, it's a good idea to "catch" him before the paper gets messy and praise his efforts—this may motivate the student to keep his paper neater than he might have done otherwise.

b. Give the student frequent attention (e.g., say "hello" to him as he enters the classroom, call on him frequently during class activities, and occasionally ask him to assist you with a class job that needs to be done) and praise him for other positive behaviors he exhibits. For example, you might comment about how respectful he is toward you or how proficient he is on the computer. This demonstrates to the student that you notice many positive things he does, not just the fact that he is making an effort to be neat.

PLAN B

Some students do not know how to take pride in neatness. If your student does not seem to possess the necessary skills to keep his work neat, the intervention must include a way to teach him pride in turning in neat work.

 Identify and define three levels of neatness for categoring the student's work.

a. Having three levels will allow you to hold the student accountable for minimal standards of neatness without being so rigid that the student becomes discouraged and gives up. The first level should consist of work that is so sloppy that it must be redone; the second, work that is somewhat sloppy but not enough to be done over; and third, work that is neat.

The following example shows how the levels might be defined for the student initially:

Too Sloppy
(Needs to Be Redone)

- The paper is torn.

- The paper is crumpled.

- The paper is crumpled.

- The paper has dark erasure smudges.

Okay
(But Could Be Neater)

- Some writing is not exactly on the line.

- There are some problems with spaces between words.

- There are some problems with the slant of the letters.

Neat

- The paper is whole and flat with no extra marks.

- The writing is appropriately on the lines.

- There are spaces between the words.

---

b. As the student progresses, the standards for each level can gradually become more demanding. For example, when the student is consistently turning in papers that do not have to be redone, give the student a couple of days' notice, and then add a new criterion to the "Too Sloppy" level. "Brad, starting on Wednesday I am going to have you redo any writing assignments with more than two mistakes of forgetting to leave a space between words. You are being so successful in working on neatness that you are ready for the next stage. This will be harder, but I know that you can do it because you are taking such pride in turning in neat work."

2. **Conduct one or more lessons to teach the student how to discriminate among the three levels of neatness, and to provide strategies for avoiding having to redo assignments.**

a. Create a chart of the three levels of neatness, which lists the definitions of each and includes a model of each. Then assemble several samples of the student's work representing each level.

b. During the lesson(s), use the chart and the student's work samples to teach the student how to discriminate between "too sloppy," "okay," and "neat." Make sure the student understands what criteria will be used to determine which papers need to be redone. "Brad, here are three papers you did last week. If you were to hand in a paper like these tomorrow, which one would have to be redone? Why? Right, if it is all crumpled up, you have to redo it."

Also have the student practice any particular skills that seem to be problematic. For example, one very basic skill that some students lack is knowing how to fold a paper neatly (i.e., only once, in half) and put it in a book to be finished later. Many students fold their papers several times or stuff unfolded papers in their desks, almost guaranteeing that the papers will be crumpled and/or torn. Another skill that you might need to teach is how to erase an answer without tearing the paper or leaving smudges.

c. The lessons should occur at least twice per week until the student is showing consistent progress with neat work. The lessons should involve just you and the student (perhaps while the other students are at recess), and needn't last more than three to five minutes. It is important that these lessons be handled in a matter-of-fact manner so that the student does not feel ridiculed. Be very clear that you are not trying to embarrass him, but that you do want him to see his work the way you do.

3. Respond consistently to the inappropriate behavior.

a. Have the student redo any work that is categorized as first level (i.e., "Too Sloppy").

b. Gently correct the student about any work that reflects the second level (i.e., "Okay"). "Brad, you do not have to redo this paper because there are no smudges and it is whole and flat. However, let's look at the spaces between words. On the next assignment you do, try to be a little more careful to . . . ."

4. Prompt the student to behave appropriately by using precorrections.

Watch for circumstances in which the student is likely to be sloppy or do something that will result in a messy paper, and remind him that he will need to remember to take pride in the neatness of his work. If time permits, you might also have the student identify how he will do this. "Brad, I am about to tell the class to put their things away and get ready for recess. If you are not finished with your paper when I give that instruction, what will you do? Excellent, you will fold the paper once, put it in your book, and work on it later this afternoon." If this conversation would embarrass the student, conduct it privately.

5. Use reinforcement to encourage appropriate behavior.

a. Give the student increased praise and attention for taking pride in the neatness of his work (see PLAN A) and for turning in work that falls in the "Neat" level.

b. In addition, make a special point of letting the student know that you notice his efforts to use the skills he has been learning/practicing. "Brad, this paper is a great example of one that is neat. Nice job of doing what we have been practicing. Let's take a close look at the things that make this paper neat. What is one of the things you remembered to do?"

c. You may also wish to use intermittent reinforcement. Occasional, and unexpected, rewards that acknowledge the student's success may motivate him to be neat more often. When the student turns in work that falls in the "neat" level you might provide a reward.

Appropriate rewards might include posting the student's work, commenting to another adult (so the student can overhear) about how neat the student's work has become, or letting the student show some of his neat work to the principal. "Brad, this work is so neat that not only does it not have to be redone, I would like to put this in your portfolio as a demonstration of a neat paper." *(NOTE: A list of additional ideas for reinforcers can be found in APPENDIX 1.)*

If you use intermittent reinforcement, do so more frequently at the beginning of the intervention to encourage the student, and less often as the student's work becomes neater over time.

PLAN C

Some students do not even know that their work is sloppy. If your student doesn't seem to realize when and/or how frequently he turns in sloppy work, the intervention must include some way of helping the student become more aware of his own performance.

1. Implement a system to have the student evaluate his work for neatness.

a. Use samples of the student's work to develop a "Neatness Evaluation Form," similar to the sample shown, and have the student attach a copy of the form to each assignment that he turns in.

Neatness Evaluation Form

Date: _____

Assignment: _____

Directions:

Circle the number that best describes the level of neatness of this assignment. If the assignment is rated "0" or "1," it will have to be cleaned up or redone. If the teacher agrees with your rating, there may be an occasional reward.

4 The paper is whole and flat with no extra marks. The writing sits appropriately on the line. There are spaces between the words. The capitals are big and the small letters are small. The writing is in all printing or all cursive. The writing is straight or at a uniform slant.

3 The paper is whole and flat with no extra marks. The writing sits appropriately on the line. There are spaces between the words. The capitals are big and the small letters are small. The writing is in all printing or all cursive.

2 The paper is whole and flat with no extra marks. The writing sit appropriately on the line. There are spaces between the words.

1 The paper is whole and flat, but has extra marks/smudges.

0 The paper is torn or crumpled.

(NOTE: For a student in grades 1-4, a visual sample of each rating may be more meaningful than these descriptions.)

b. Each day, meet with the student for a few minutes to examine his form or forms and each assignment the student has turned in that day. If the student's work was neater than on previous days, praise the student.

If the student's work was sloppy, have him identify how he could take pride in neatness rather than turning in messy papers the next day. Encourage the student to look at the rating sheet before he begins a task to decide what level he will strive to attain with that assignment.

2. *Respond consistently to the inappropriate behavior.*

a. When the student turns in work that you feel should be rated "0" or "1," return the work to him to be redone.

b. If the student turns in work that is appropriately marked with a "2" or "3," gently correct him and provide information on what he can do to make gradual improvements, but do not have him redo the work.

3. *Use reinforcement to encourage appropriate behavior.*

a. Give the student increased praise and attention for taking pride in the neatness of his work (see PLAN A) and for earning ratings of "4."

b. In addition, praise the student during the daily review meetings for accurate recording (if applicable), and for being willing to look at the neatness of his work that day. Even if the student's work was very sloppy, when the student is willing to discuss how he can take pride in neatness the next day, praise him. "Brad, you are really handling this responsibly. Even though you had a tough time with neatness today, you are willing to talk to me about things you might do differently tomorrow. That is a real sign that you are making progress."

Any time the student's rating is different from your own opinion of how the work should be rated, take a few minutes to discuss why. Over a period of several days, you and the student should begin to be quite consistent with each others' ratings. If this does not happen, try providing more frequent reinforcement when the student is accurate in his assessment, even if the assessment is low.

Regardless of the neatness of the work, try to make the end-of-the-day meeting upbeat and encouraging—you want the student to look forward to the daily review sessions.

4. *Encourage the student to use self-reinforcement.*

Whenever things are going well (i.e., the student is demonstrating an effort to turn in neat work), prompt the student to mentally reinforce himself. "Brad, this has been a very successful morning. Silently tell yourself that you are really taking pride in the neatness of your work." Prompt the student in this manner intermittently throughout the day and during the end-of-the-day meetings.

PLAN D

Whenever a student's problem behavior has become habitual and/or he does not seem to have a desire to reduce it, you may need to implement a structured system of external incentives (i.e., rewards and consequences) based on his behavior to motivate him to start taking pride in the neatness of his work.

 1. *Implement a system to have the student evaluate his work for neatness (see PLAN C).*

However, for this plan modify the "Neatness Evaluation Form" so that messy work equals zero points, neat work represents positive points, and agreement between the student's and your own ratings equals bonus points (see the sample).

In addition, you should adapt the form so that it addresses the specific issues you want the student to focus on. For example, you may wish to add criteria such as "all printing" or "all cursive," or "straight writing" or "uniform slant."

 2. *Establish a structured system for reinforcing the appropriate behavior and providing a consequence for the inappropriate behavior.*

a. With the student, create a list of reinforcers that he can earn. Although you might want to have some suggestions in mind, the system will be more effective if the student identifies most of the items or activities himself. *(NOTE: A list of reinforcement ideas can be found in APPENDIX 1.)*

b. Assign "prices" (in points) for each of the rewards on the list and have the student choose the reward he would like to earn first.

The prices should be based on the number of points the student can earn and the cost—instructional, personnel, and/or monetary—of the items. Monetary cost is clear—the more expensive the item, the more points required to earn it. Instructional cost refers to the amount of instructional time lost or interfered with by a particular reward. Thus, an activity which

---

Neatness Evaluation Form

Date: _____   Assignment: _____

Directions:

Circle the number that best describes the level of neatness of this assignment. If the assignment is rated "0" it will have to be cleaned up or redone, and then reassessed.

+5   The paper is whole and flat with no extra marks. The writing sits appropriately on the line. There are spaces between the words. The capitals are big and the small letters are small. The writing is in all printing or all cursive. The writing is straight or at a uniform slant.

+2   The paper is whole and flat with no extra marks. The writing sits appropriately on the line. There are spaces between the words. The capitals are big and the small letters are small. The writing is in all printing or all cursive.

+1   The paper is whole and flat with no extra marks. The writing sits appropriately on the line. There are spaces between the words.

 0   The writing does not sit appropriately on the line.

 0   The paper has unnecessary marks.

 0   There are no spaces between some of the words.

 0   The paper is torn or crumpled.

+3   **BONUS POINTS** if the teacher's rating matches yours.

_____   **TOTAL POINTS** for this assignment.

---

causes the student to miss part of academic instruction should require more points than one the student can do on his own recess time. Personnel cost involves the time required by you and/or other staff to fulfill the reinforcer. Having lunch with the principal, therefore, would cost more points than spending five minutes of free time with a friend.

c. A young and/or immature student may need more immediate and/or frequent reinforcement. It might be more effective to let such a student earn several "less expensive" reinforcers (e.g., five minutes of free time after 20 points) on the way to a bigger reward (e.g., one hour with you for 200 points). That is, the student receives the small rewards without spending points; they continue to accumulate toward the selected reward.

d. At the end of the day, calculate the total points the student has earned and add them to the points earned on previous days. When the student has accumulated enough points to earn the selected reward, he "spends" the points necessary and the system begins again. That

is, the student begins with zero points and selects another reinforcer to earn.

e. If the student is not accumulating points rapidly enough to maintain enthusiasm, use precorrections to help structure the student's success (see PLAN B).

f. Any rating of zero indicates that the work needs to be redone, then rated again so the student can earn points.

3. Use reinforcement to encourage appropriate behavior.

a. Give the student increased praise and attention for taking pride in the neatness of his work (see PLAN A).

b. In addition, show interest and enthusiasm about how the student is doing on the system. "Brad, we are half way through the day and you have already earned 15 points. Your effort and pride in doing things neatly is really making a big difference. I hope you are feeling very proud of yourself. "

PLAN E

If there are several students in your class who turn in sloppy work, you might consider establishing a group motivation system to encourage all your students to take pride in the neatness of their work.

 1. Develop a "Neatness Evaluation Form," similar to the sample shown in PLAN D.

 2. Teach the class how to use the rating form.

Schedule a whole class activity to teach all the students how to use the evaluation form to rate the neatness of their individual work.

2. Provide intermittent rewards to the students making an effort to be neat.

On certain assignments (i.e., approximately one per day in the earlier stages of the intervention and then less often over time), let the students know that each student who receives a certain rating or above can go to lunch a few minutes early (or some other desirable activity or reward). The students below the rating have to stay in the classroom for that time and redo their assignments. *(NOTE: If necessary, individualize this procedure for certain students. For example, a student who has motor skill problems might receive a reward for any rating*

above a "1," while the rest of the students must score at least a "2" to receive the reward.)

Sometimes give a reward to all the students who have a reasonably accurate self-evaluation. "Class, I am going to hand back your history papers. I have graded them and marked whether I agreed with your evaluation of neatness. Today, those of you whose evaluations matched mine, even if it was low, may take the next ten minutes and engage in free choice activities, including . . . . "

3. (OPTIONAL) Implement a team competition and response cost lottery.

a. Divide the class into equal teams of four to six students. Try to make the teams fairly equitable in terms of students who do and do not have difficulties with neatness. Seat each team together and have the teams assign themselves names.

(NOTE: If one team has a student with motor skill problems [e.g., a student who has Cerebral

Palsy], you should even the playing field a bit. For example, that student should be allowed to call any paper that he/she can keep whole and flat a five-point paper. This is not unfair. In fact, it is similar to the concept of giving a handicap in golf or bowling in which the less skilled players are given a point adjustment to make the game more even.)

b. At the end of each day, the teams will add together the positive points their team members earned that day for a daily team total.

c. Have the class brainstorm privileges or activities that they might like their team to earn as a reward. Ideas include a free homework pass for each team member, going to lunch a few minutes earlier than the rest of the class, a coupon for an ice cream in the cafeteria for each team member, etc. Have the class think of at least six

or seven different ideas, and then have the class rank them in terms of perceived value.

Write the most valuable rewards on a single piece of paper each, and each moderately valuable reward on two or three pieces of paper. (This reduces the odds of consistently receiving the more valuable rewards.) Put all of these pieces of paper in a grab bag of some kind. The team with the most total points each day gets to draw one piece of paper from the grab bag, and wins the reward that is written on it.

After the system has been successful for a couple of weeks, begin adding an increasing number of pieces of paper that have praise statements only written on them (e.g., "You did great! But no prize today."). In this way, you can fade the system while the students still have a chance of earning a big prize.

....
Suggested Steps for Developing and Implementing a Plan

The following steps are designed to help you develop an appropriate intervention plan and implement it effectively, whether you choose to use one of the MODEL PLANS or create a customized plan of your own. The steps are, however, suggestions—they are not intended to be followed rigidly or in any particular order. Use your professional judgment and the knowledge of your particular situation to make them work for you.

 Make sure you have enough information about the situation.

a. If you think a minimal intervention like PLAN A will be appropriate (i.e., the behavior has just begun and/or is relatively mild), you probably already have enough information to proceed. However, if it seems like a more involved plan will be necessary, you should consider collecting additional information.

b. Perhaps the most efficient and productive type of information to gather is to keep samples of or make copies of the student's work that cover the range of problems associated with his sloppiness. Keep these work samples in a folder to show the student and his parent(s). In addition, collect some samples of the student's neatest work. This will serve as an example of what the student is capable of, and will demonstrate that you are not only aware of his inappropriate performance.

c. You might also keep a simple record of the level of neatness of the work by making notations in your gradebook. For each assignment, record the score or grade the student received and

next to that write a small "+" if the paper was neat, a "/" if the paper was tolerable, and a "-" if the paper was sloppy. Use the neatness criteria outlined in PLAN B for this procedure, if you elect to use it.

 Identify a focus for the intervention and labels for referring to the appropriate and inappropriate behaviors.

a. To be effective, the intervention must address more than just reducing the student's sloppiness—there must be a concurrent emphasis on increasing some positive behavior or trait (e.g., taking pride in neatness, producing professional quality products, etc.). Not only will having a specific positive behavior in mind make it easier to "catch" and reinforce the student for being neat, but the positive focus will help you to frame the situation productively.

For example, if you describe the situation simply as, "the student has a problem with sloppiness" you offer little in the way of useful information, and may put the student and his parent(s) on the defensive. However, if you explain your concern by saying that you want to help the student "learn to take pride in neatness," you present an important, and reasonable, goal for the student to work toward and clearly identify what the student needs to do to be successful.

b. Specifying labels for the appropriate and inappropriate behaviors (e.g., "taking pride in neatness" and "sloppiness," respectively) will help you to use consistent vocabulary when discussing the situation with the student. If you sometimes refer to the inappropriate behavior as "sloppiness" and other times tell the student that he "is being careless," for example, he may not realize that you are talking about the same thing.

3. Determine when and how to include the parent(s).

a. You probably do not need to contact the student's parent(s) if the problem has just begun and is not interfering with his academic progress. You might, however, take advantage of any scheduled activities (e.g., conferences, weekly notes home) to let them know of your concern.

b. The student's parent(s) should be contacted whenever the student's sloppy work is hindering him from reaching his fullest academic potential. Share with them information on the work samples you have collected, and explain why you are concerned. Focus in particular on how many teachers (all the way through college) tend to unconsciously give better grades for neat papers and worse grades for sloppy ones.

You might ask if the parent(s) view the sloppy work as a problem. Whether or not the parent(s) perceive a problem, invite them to join you for an initial meeting with the student to develop a plan. If the parent(s) are unable or unwilling to participate, let them know that you will keep them informed of the student's progress.

c. Once the parent(s) have been involved in any way, you should give them updates at least once per week while the plan is being implemented.

4. Prepare for, then conduct, an initial meeting about the situation.

a. Schedule a meeting to discuss your concerns with the student and anyone else who will be involved in the plan (e.g., the parent[s], the school psychologist). Although the specifics of the meeting will vary depending upon the age of the student and the severity of the problem, there are some general guidelines to follow when scheduling the meeting.

First, meet at a neutral time (i.e., not immediately after the student has turned in sloppy work), when emotions are less likely to hamper communication. In general, a day's notice is appropriate, however a primary age student may worry excessively and/or forget what the meeting is about if it is scheduled more than an hour before it takes place.

Second, make the meeting appropriately private. For example, with a primary student who has a mild problem, you might meet in the classroom while the other students are working independently. However, if you are dealing with a middle/junior high school student and the student's parent(s), you will want a private room (e.g., the counselor's office) to ensure that the discussion will not be overheard.

Third, try to make sure the meeting is scheduled for a time and place that it is not likely to be interrupted. Finally, if the parent(s) will be participating, they should be the ones to tell the student about the meeting.

b. Construct a preliminary plan. Based on the information you have collected and the focus of the intervention, you may decide to use one of the MODEL PLANS or you might choose to create a customized plan using components from various plans and/or of your own design.

Although it is important to invite and encourage the student to be an active partner in developing the plan during the initial meeting, having a proposed plan in mind before you meet can alleviate frustration and wasted time if the student is unwilling or unable to participate.

c. Using the information you collected, prepare thorough descriptions of the levels of neatness for your student. Be as specific as you can and add concrete examples whenever possible. This will make it easier for you to clarify (and for the student to understand) your expectations.

d. Conduct the meeting in an atmosphere of collaboration. The following agenda is one way you might structure the meeting:

• **Share your concerns about the student's performance.**

Show the student the samples of his work that you have collected. Then, explain why you consider his sloppy work to be a problem. You might tell the student that as unfair as it might be, people will judge the content of his ideas and writing, at least in part, by the overall appearance of his papers. Let him know that in subsequent years of school, in college, and/or on a job, people will be less likely to take his ideas seriously if the paper he presents them in is sloppily done.

- **Discuss how you can work together to improve the neatness of his work.**

Explain that you would like to help the student "learn to take pride in neatness" and describe your preliminary plan. Invite the student to give you input on the plan and together work out any necessary details (e.g., use of the self-evaluation form). You may have to brainstorm different possibilities if the student is uncomfortable with the initial plan. Incorporating any of the student's suggestions that strengthen the plan is likely to increase his sense of "ownership" in and commitment to it.

- **Make sure that the student understands what you mean by the levels of neatness.**

Define and clarify the levels of neatness as specifically and thoroughly as you can. The best way to ensure that you and the student are in agreement about the expectations is to have him identify work samples as either "Too Sloppy," "Okay," or "Neat." *(NOTE: Be sure to use samples that you have not yet labeled.)* Continue examining and discussing his work samples until the student is accurate in categorizing the neatness of his work.

- **Conclude the meeting.**

Always end the meeting with words of encouragement. Let the student know that you are confident that he can be successful, and that he might actually find that he feels better about the work he does when he begins to take more pride in doing neat work. Be sure to reinforce the student for participating in the meeting.

5. *Give the student regular, ongoing feedback about his behavior.*

It is important to meet with the student periodically to discuss his progress. In most cases, three to five minutes once per week should suffice. *(NOTE: PLANS C and D suggest daily meetings.)* During the meetings, review the student's recent work. As the student is increasingly successful and the criteria for neatness become more difficult, keep the student's neatest work in a separate folder. Periodically have the student look at this neat work from the past so that he can see that he is making significant progress. As the student's performance improves, the meetings can be faded to once every other week and then to once per month.

6. *Evaluate the student's progress.*

Implement any plan for at least two weeks before deciding whether to change plans; to continue, modify, or fade the plan you are using; or to cease the intervention. In general, if the student's performance is clearly improving, stick with what you are doing. If the work samples show that the student's level of neatness has remained the same or worsened, some kind of change will be necessary. Always discuss any changes to the plan with the student first.

SMART-ALECK BEHAVIOR/ INAPPROPRIATE HUMOR

Wisecracks

Sarcasm

Cruel Humor

DESCRIPTION

You have a student who has a tendency to make inappropriate comments (e.g., she uses sarcasm, wisecracks, and/or cruel humor).

GOAL

The student will learn the difference between appropriate and inappropriate comments and will stop her smart-aleck behavior.

> *NOTE:*
>
> *Throughout these six plans, the problem behavior is referred to as "inappropriate comments," however, the plans could easily be adapted for the student whose "smart-aleck" behavior is inappropriate in other ways.*

OVERVIEW OF PLANS

- PLAN A: For a situation in which the problem is relatively mild or has just begun.
- PLAN B: For a student who makes inappropriate comments to gain adult attention.
- PLAN C: For a student who makes inappropriate comments to shock, entertain, or look sophisticated in front of her peers.
- PLAN D: For a student whose behavior is inappropriate because, although funny, she makes jokes so often that it is becoming disruptive.
- PLAN E: For a student who lacks the motivation to stop making inappropriate comments.
- PLAN F: For a situation in which several students in your class make inappropriate comments.

Alternative Problems

- **Arguing—Student(s) With the Teacher**
- **Blurting Out/Not Raising Hand**
- **Disrespectful Behavior**
- **Harassment—Racial/ Sexual**
- **Name Calling/ Put-Downs**
- **Rude/Impolite Behavior**
- **Sexual Comments**

General Considerations

- If the behavior stems in any way from academic issues (e.g., the student makes wisecracks to cover up the fact that she is unable to meet academic expectations), concurrent efforts must be made to ensure her academic success (see **Academic Deficits, Determining**).

- If the student lacks the basic social skills to interact with her peers appropriately, it may be necessary to begin by teaching her those skills. **Social Skills, Lack of** contains information on a variety of published social skills curricula.

Model Plans

PLAN A

It is not always necessary, or even beneficial, to use an involved plan. If the problem has just begun and/or occurs infrequently, the following actions, along with making the student aware of your concerns, may resolve the situation.

 1. Respond consistently to the inappropriate behavior.

a. Whenever the student makes an inappropriate comment (e.g., she says something that makes fun of another student), gently correct her. Let the student know that what she said was inappropriate, and tell her why. "Audrey, that was an inappropriate comment because talking about Mrs. Garfunkle like that is not respectful."; or "Audrey, that comment was inappropriate because you are repeating yourself. It was funny once, it was no big deal twice, and now it is distracting to the lesson." Because your goal is to impart information, you want to be emotionally neutral while giving the correction.

b. In addition to explaining why the comment was inappropriate, give the student information about what she needs to do instead. "Audrey, stop. That is an inappropriate comment because it is at the expense of someone else. You need to participate in your group without commenting on other people."

2. Use reinforcement to encourage appropriate behavior.

a. Give the student increased praise. Be especially alert for situations in which the student might have made an inappropriate comment, but didn't. Praise her for these demonstrations of her ability to use restraint. "Audrey, for the entire morning, you have not made a single inappropriate joke or wisecrack. That kind of

restraint will be very useful when you are in settings where joking could get you into trouble."

In addition, try to be aware of those times when the student's comments are funny and appropriate. If the student makes a funny joke, laugh with her and show her that you appreciate her sense of humor, when she uses it well. Later comment to the student about the incident. "Audrey, today in class the comment you made about General Grant was truly funny. Now that you are learning to refrain from making inappropriate comments, I really enjoy the jokes you do make."

If the student would be embarrassed by public praise, praise the student privately or even give the student a note. Remember that whenever the student refrains from making inappropriate comments and/or makes an appropriate joke, you can praise her responsible behavior.

b. Give the student frequent attention (e.g., say "hello" to her as she enters the classroom, call on her frequently during class activities, and occasionally ask her to assist you with a class job that needs to be done) and praise her for other positive behaviors she exhibits. "Audrey, you have done such a fine job of participating in class today. You have contributed some very useful ideas to the project." This demonstrates to the student that you notice many positive things she does, not just the fact that she is refraining from making inappropriate comments.

PLAN B

Some students are very skilled at gaining attention through their negative behavior. If you find yourself frequently nagging, reminding, or coaxing the student to stop making inappropriate comments, it is possible that she is trying to gain adult attention through the misbehavior. Whether or not the student overtly seems to like the attention, you should make sure that she receives more frequent and more satisfying attention when she behaves appropriately than when she makes inappropriate comments.

1. Define the borderline between appropriate and inappropriate comments.

a. Defining the borderline is the key to this plan, but can be very difficult because what is appropriate and what is inappropriate is not always clear. To help clarify the borderline for yourself and the student, consider the following questions: Is the problem one of *excess* (i.e., the student's comments are appropriate, but overdone); *timing* (i.e., the student makes comments at inappropriate times, such as during independent work periods or during lectures); or *content* (i.e., the student's comments are profane, cruel, or disrespectful)?

b. When the problem is one of excess (i.e., the number of comments, rather than their content is inappropriate), you need to make the student aware of how frequently she is making comments and what constitutes reasonable limits (see PLAN D).

c. When the problem is one of timing, use your daily schedule to identify for the student times and activities in which it is reasonable to make an appropriate joke or wisecrack and those times and activities in which it is not acceptable.

d. When the problem is that the content of the student's comments is inappropriate, you will need to specify the exact difference between appropriate and inappropriate content. The most efficient way to do this is to generate an explanation of what makes a comment inappropriate. For example, if a comment hurts another's feelings (i.e., a "cheap shot" at someone else's expense), or is profane or otherwise offensive.

Share your anecdotal notes with the student (see SUGGESTED STEPS FOR DEVELOPING AND IMPLEMENTING A PLAN), and together identify comments that are appropriate. Then talk about what aspects make a comment appropriate and what aspects make a comment inappropriate.

2. Respond consistently to the inappropriate behavior.

a. Establish time owed as a consequence for each inappropriate comment. For example, each time an elementary student's comment crossed the borderline to inappropriate, she would owe one minute off of the next recess. A middle/junior high school student should be assigned one minute after class for the first inappropriate comment and ten minutes in after-school or lunch time detention for each subsequent comment.

During the time that the student owes, she should sit and do nothing. Or, if the student has made an obscene or cruel comment, she could be required during the time owed to write down whatever she said and sign it. This statement could be kept on file and shared with the building administrator and/or the student's parent(s) if the problem continues. Use your professional judgment to determine whether this procedure would be more effective than having the student sitting and doing nothing during the time that she owes.

b. Given that the student may, at least in part, be trying to gain your attention through her inappropriate comments, keep the interactions you have with the student at the time the comments are made short and emotionally neutral. "Audrey, that was inappropriate, you owe another minute." Resist any impulse to scold or lecture the student. You have already explained appropriate and inappropriate comments to the student—now take action. *(NOTE: Be sure the student is made aware of the consequence for inappropriate comments during your initial meeting to set up the plan. See SUGGESTED STEPS FOR DEVELOPING AND IMPLEMENTING A PLAN.)*

Use reinforcement to encourage appropriate behavior.

a. Frequent praise and attention is the core of this plan. The student must see that she receives more frequent and more satisfying attention when she behaves appropriately than when she makes inappropriate comments. Thus, whenever the student refrains from making inappropriate comments (or otherwise misbehaving), or makes appropriate comments/jokes, make an effort to praise and spend time with her. "Audrey, you have been such a pleasure to have in class the last several days. Hey, let me know if you have a good joke, you could tell it to me right as the other students are heading out to recess."

b. You may also wish to use intermittent rewards to acknowledge the student's success. Occasional, and unexpected, rewards can motivate the student to demonstrate responsible behavior more often. The idea is to provide a reward when the student has gone for a particularly long period of time without making an inappropriate comment (e.g., a student who was making two to three inappropriate comments per day goes for three full days without one inappropriate comment).

Appropriate rewards might include letting the student take the lead in a class activity, telling the student a good (clean) joke you recently heard, or congratulating the student for her responsible behavior in front of the principal. *(NOTE: A list of additional reinforcement ideas can be found in APPENDIX 1.)* Use intermittent rewards more frequently at the beginning of the intervention to encourage the student, and then less often as her behavior improves over time.

Ensure a 3-1 ratio of positive to negative attention.

a. When attention is a motivating force for the student, you need to be sure that you are giving the student *three times as much* positive as negative attention. One way to do this is to monitor your interactions with the student at least one day per week. Keep a card on a clipboard or in your pocket and record each interaction you have with the student as either positive or negative by writing a "+" or a "-", respectively, on the card.

To determine whether an interaction is positive or negative, ask yourself whether the student was making an inappropriate comment (or otherwise misbehaving) at the time the interaction occurred. Any interaction that stems from inappropriate behavior is negative, and all interactions that occur while the student is meeting classroom expectations are positive. Thus, assigning time owed is a negative interaction, but praising the student for her restraint is positive. Greeting the student as she enters the room or asking her if she has any questions during independent work are also considered positive interactions. *(NOTE: Ignoring the student's inappropriate behavior is not recorded at all, because it is not an interaction.)*

b. If you find that you are not giving the student three times as much positive as negative attention, try to increase the number of positive interactions you have with the student. Sometimes prompts can help. For example, you might decide that each time the student enters the classroom you will say "hello" to her, or that twice each morning and afternoon you will try to have a positive interaction with the student.

PLAN C

Some students use inappropriate and/or smart-aleck comments to demonstrate their personal power and/or to try to impress their peers. If your student seems to enjoy the reactions she receives from her peers, the intervention must include ways of reducing the sense of power the student achieves with her inappropriate comments, and at the same time helping the student learn to wield her personal power in appropriate ways.

 Respond consistently to the inappropriate behavior.

a. Define the borderline between appropriate and inappropriate comments, and establish time owed as a consequence for each inappropriate comment (see PLAN B).

b. It will be important to demonstrate that the student's inappropriate comments have no power to influence you. If power is an issue in the student's behavior problem, she has probably become very skilled at "pushing adults' buttons" (i.e., being able to make adults angry, embarrassed, flustered, or otherwise upset). Your goal should be to remain perfectly calm whenever the student tries to prompt you to react.

If necessary, mentally rehearse interactions in which the student "pushes your buttons," and imagine yourself calmly and consistently stating the consequence and resuming instruction. Tell yourself that whenever the student sees that she has the power to embarrass you or make you angry, it's the same as having paid her $50.00 for making the inappropriate comment.

2. Acknowledge the student's power with her peers.

a. During your initial meeting with the student (see SUGGESTED STEPS FOR DEVELOPING AND IMPLEMENTING A PLAN), explain that you know that she has a great deal of influence over the other students, and that you do not want to take that away from her. If appropriate, tell her that she is a natural leader. Also let the student know that while you do not expect her to become a "goody-goody" type of student, you do expect her to be respectful and to refrain from making comments that are inappropriate.

b. Use your anecdotal notes (see SUGGESTED STEPS FOR DEVELOPING AND IMPLE-MENTING A PLAN), to describe situations in which the student made an inappropriate or smart-aleck comment, and work with the student to identify different ways she could have behaved that would have showed restraint and been respectful, yet still allowed her to exert her natural power with her peers. The goal is to help the student realize that win/win situations are better than power struggles between the two of you.

3. (OPTIONAL)
If the student is not well-liked by her peers, and is perhaps trying to use inappropriate and/or smart-aleck remarks to gain status with her peers, you might suggest a peer model.

Encourage the student to watch another student in the class—someone she looks up to and who is powerful among their peers, yet uses jokes and comments appropriately. Have the student observe the way this peer model manages to make comments/jokes in respectful ways. "Audrey, one thing I would like to encourage you to do is to watch Vida. Do you think Vida is funny? Do you think she is a goody-goody kind of person? No, I don't either. And yet, she is consistently very respectful in the way she interacts with me and the way she uses humor and restraint in class. For the next few days,

watch Vida. I think you might get some good ideas about how to be respectful without having to feel that you cannot be funny."

However, be very careful not to imply that the peer model is somehow a better or more worthwhile person than the target student. You should convey the idea that the peer model simply has a particular skill that would be worth observing.

4. Give the student a high status job or responsibility.

a. One of the most effective ways to help the student learn to wield her personal power wisely is to put her in a position of power. Try to think of a job or responsibility at school that the student would do well and enjoy. For example, maybe the student could tutor a younger student in reading, be an assistant in the library, or help the computer teacher to review some new software. The best job will be one that occurs regularly (e.g., daily, twice per week, or at least once per week) and in which the student's "job supervisor" is someone other than yourself.

b. Be sure the student has sufficient training for the job and that all the expectations are defined from the beginning, including what constitutes appropriate and inappropriate comments. The supervisor should stress the expectations which if violated could result in the student losing her job. "Audrey, I know that you have a tendency to sometimes put down adults or make what might be called smart-aleck remarks. You need to know that if you are going to be a tutor for me here in the second grade, I will not tolerate any kind of inappropriate humor. My second graders will look up to you and will try to imitate you. Therefore, if you are disrespectful toward me, or make an inappropriate comment, you will lose your job. No warnings and no discussion, is that clear? Okay. I am very excited that you will be helping me. Several of my students can use extra help . . . ."

c. If a job is found that the student would like to do, she should be allowed to perform the job whenever scheduled, regardless of how appropriate or inappropriate her comments have been in your class. Just as you are expected to perform your job each day regardless of how well you are getting along with your spouse, the student should be expected to go to her job each day (or whenever scheduled). If the job is made contingent on her being respectful in class, it is likely to become just one more power issue. The student might think, for example, "You can't make me be respectful by threatening that I will not get to tutor."

5. *Use reinforcement to encourage appropriate behavior.*

a. Give the student increased praise and attention for using restraint (see PLAN A).

b. Also praise the student for being responsible and successful with her new job/responsibility. "Audrey, Mr. Taylor informed me that your help in his class has made his job easier. He said he is really enjoying your company and your positive use of humor."

PLAN D

Some students do not seem to realize when they overdo humor. If your student generally makes funny comments that are appropriate, but she simply makes them too frequently, the intervention should include some way of helping the student become more aware of her behavior and the limits on that behavior in the classroom. Keep in mind that the purpose of the intervention should be to help the student learn the appropriate use of humor. That is, you do not want to prevent the student from trying to be funny—humor is a very useful and important skill that should be encouraged. However, you want the student to learn appropriate limits for the use of humor in the classroom.

1. *Respond consistently to the inappropriate behavior.*

a. During your initial meeting with the student (see SUGGESTED STEPS FOR DEVELOPING AND IMPLEMENTING A PLAN), establish a nonembarrassing signal that you can use to cue the student when she is overdoing her humor. You want the signal to be a fairly subtle one that only the student will recognize and understand in order to minimize the chance that she will be teased by her peers. Possibilities include a particular wave of your hand, rubbing your neck, or even just direct eye contact and a head nod.

Let the student know that you may also need to quietly say her name to get her attention before you give the signal. You should be prepared to use the signal frequently and for a fairly long time since it is likely that the behavior is, at least in part, an unconscious habit for the student.

b. In addition, whenever you give the student the signal make sure the incident is recorded by either the student or yourself (see Step 2).

c. If the student sometimes uses inappropriate humor (in addition to using appropriate humor too often), assign time owed as a consequence for each incidence of inappropriate humor/inappropriate comment (see PLAN B). However, these instances of inappropriate humor should not be recorded as part of the frequency monitoring of (see Step 2) the appropriate humor as these are separate issues.

2. *Monitor how often the student is using appropriate humor.*

a. Determine who will monitor the student's use of appropriate humor. Since the point is for the student to become more aware of her own behavior, having the student record the frequency (i.e., self-monitoring) will be more effective than if you record the behavior. However, if the student cannot or will not be accurate (or if she would be too embarrassed to self-monitor), you should do the recording yourself. *(NOTE: Even when the student self-monitors, you should keep your own record approximately one day per week to verify the student's accuracy.)*

b. If the student is self-monitoring the frequency of her use of appropriate humor, have her keep on her desk or in her notebook a form like the sample shown. Tell the student that each time she sees you give her the signal, she should circle the next number on the form.

c. Identify a reasonable limit on the number of times the student can use appropriate humor during class each day. This number should be comfortable for you, yet still allow the student to use her humorous ability. For example, in the sample form, the number of incidents specified is six.

When explaining this plan to the student, let her know that she can use appropriate humor as often as she wants to on the playground or in the cafeteria. This monitoring form is only for use in the classroom.

Name _____

Behavior to bo Counted: _Each time you use_
appropriate humor, circle the next number.
(Between zero to six times per day during
class is fine.)

Date _____

| 1 | 2 | 3 | 4 | 5 | 6 | 7 | 8 |

| 9 | 10 | 11 | 12 | 13 | 14 | 15 | 16 |

| 17 | 18 | 19 | 20 | 21 | 22 | 23 | 24 |

(NOTE: Repeat this form four more times so that it can be used for a week.)

d. Each day, meet with the student for a few minutes to review that day's record. Have the student chart the information on a graph (or do it yourself), and talk with her about whether the day was better, worse, or about the same as previous days.

If the day did not go well, encourage the student to talk about why and have her identify things she can do the next day to help herself remember to limit the frequency of her humor. If the student behaves inappropriately during the meeting, keep the interaction very short. Just let the student know that you are sure tomorrow will be a better day.

(NOTE: This system can be modified so that the behavior being monitored is the number of in-

appropriate [rather than appropriate] comments and used with PLANS E and F.)

 Use reinforcement to encourage appropriate behavior.

a. Give the student increased praise and attention for using restraint (see PLAN A).

b. In addition, praise the student during the end-of-the-day review meetings for accurate recording (if applicable), and for being willing to look at her cumulative record for the day. Even on a bad day, if the student is willing to chart the data and discuss why it was a bad day, praise her. "Audrey, you are really handling this responsibly. Even though it was a rough day, you are willing to talk to me about things you might do differently tomorrow. That is a real sign that you are growing up."

Regardless of how the day went, try to make the end-of-the-day meeting upbeat and encouraging—you want the student to look forward to the daily review sessions.

 When appropriate, laugh at the student's humor when the number of incidents is below the maximum allowed number.

When the student has reached her limit for the daily use of humor, ignore any additional attempts at humor. Then, if the problem continues and the student seems unmotivated to stay below the maximum allowed number of incidents, establish time owed as a consequence for each additional attempt at humor.

PLAN E

Whenever a student's problem behavior becomes habitual and/or she does not seem to have a desire to reduce it, you may need to implement a structured system of external incentives (i.e., rewards and consequences) based on her behavior to motivate the student to behave responsibly.

1 **Respond consistently to the inappropriate behavior.**

a. Define the borderline between appropriate and inappropriate comments, and establish time owed as a consequence for each inappropriate comment (see PLAN B).

b. Keep a record of the total number of minutes owed the student accrues each day, regardless of whether the time has been paid back. For example, the daily cumulative record might show that the student was assigned a total of

eight minutes owed for the day (five from the morning and three from the afternoon), even though she paid back five of the minutes during morning recess.

(NOTE: You may choose to use a monitoring system similar to that described in PLAN D—only you would track the frequency of the student's inappropriate comments rather than appropriate comments.)

Establish a structured system for reinforcing reductions in the inappropriate comments.

a. With the student, create a list of reinforcers that she can earn. Although you might want to have some suggestions in mind, the system will be more effective if the student identifies most of the items or activities herself. *(NOTE: A list of reinforcement ideas can be found in APPENDIX 1.)*

15 or more inappropriate comments	= 0 points
11-14 inappropriate comments	= 1 point
6-10 inappropriate comments	= 2 points
3-5 inappropriate comments	= 3 points
1-2 inappropriate comments	= 5 points
0 inappropriate comments	= 7 points

b. Assign "prices" (in points) for each of the rewards on the list and have the student select the reward she would like to earn first.

The prices should be based on the instructional, personnel, and/or monetary costs of the items. Monetary cost is clear—the more expensive the item, the more points required to earn it. Instructional cost refers to the amount of instructional time lost or interfered with by a particular reward. Thus, an activity which causes the student to miss part of academic instruction should require more points than one the student can do on her own free time. Personnel cost involves the time required by you and/or other staff to fulfill the reinforcer. Having lunch with the principal, therefore, would cost more points than spending five minutes of free time with a friend.

c. Devise a scale that awards points based on the number of inappropriate comments made (minutes owed) for the day. For example, if the student is averaging 15-20 inappropriate jokes or comments per day, the following scale might be used to determine the points the student earns toward the reward or privilege.

Using the sample scale, if the student made six inappropriate comments in a day, she would owe six minutes off of recess (or time in after-school detention if a middle/junior high school

student), but would still earn two points. If the student made 17 inappropriate comments, she would owe 17 minutes and earn no points.

d. When the student has accumulated enough points to earn the reward she has chosen, she "spends" the points necessary and the system begins again. That is, she selects another reward to earn and begins with zero points.

If the student is immature, and needs more frequent encouragement, you might consider letting her earn several "less expensive" rewards (e.g., five minutes of free time after 20 points) on the way to a bigger reward (e.g., one hour with you for 200 points). That is, the student receives the small rewards without spending points; they continue to accumulate toward the selected reward.

 Use reinforcement to encourage appropriate behavior.

a. Give the student increased praise and attention for using restraint (see PLAN A).

b. In addition, show interest and enthusiasm about how the student is doing on the system. "Audrey, this is the first day we implemented the system and already you have reduced your number of inappropriate comments to eight. Nice work. Two points today."

PLAN F

When there are several students in your class who make inappropriate comments/jokes, or when the students seem to encourage each other to use inappropriate humor, a class-wide intervention will be inappropriate.

 Have a class meeting to define the borderline between appropriate and inappropriate humor.

Modify the suggestions in PLAN B to be used with the entire class.

 Establish a team competition and response cost lottery.

a. Divide the class into equal teams of four to six students, making sure they are equitable in terms of the number of students who do and do not have problems with inappropriate humor. Seat the team members together (e.g., at the same table or with their desks in clusters), and have each team give themselves a name that you can use to refer to them. Encourage the teams to think of a funny, but appropriate, name if they wish.

b. Have the class brainstorm ideas for the teams to earn as reinforcers. Possibilities include a free homework pass for each team member, dismissing team members for lunch a few minutes earlier than the rest of the class, or giving team members a ticket for an ice cream in the cafeteria. Have the class identify at least six or seven different ideas, and rank them in order of perceived value.

c. Set up a grab bag system. Write the different reinforcers on individual pieces of paper and put these in a bag or box. "Weight" the box so the most valuable items are included only once, while the more moderate reinforcers are each written on two or three slips of paper. This reduces the students' odds of winning the "big" rewards—thus reducing how often you will have to provide the big rewards.

After using the system successfully for a couple of weeks, increasingly add slips with congratulatory messages only (e.g., "You did great! But no prize today."). This way you can fade the system, but the students still have a chance of earning the big prize.

d. Each day, each team would begin with a set number of tickets, based on the following formula: The number of inappropriate jokes made by the total class on a typical day, divided by the number of teams, plus one. For example, if the class has averaged 30 inappropriate jokes per day and there are five teams, each team would receive seven tickets.

e. Whenever a student makes an inappropriate joke, that student's team loses one ticket. At the end of the day, each team writes their team name on all their remaining tickets and places them in a bowl for a drawing. One ticket is drawn, and that team is allowed to draw a slip of paper from the grab bag. The team receives the prize written on the paper they've drawn.

(NOTE: To implement this plan you need to know [on average] how many inappropriate comments are made by the class per day. Therefore, for at least three or four days, keep a frequency count of the number of inappropriate comments. See SUGGESTED STEPS FOR DEVELOPING AND IMPLEMENTING A PLAN for ideas on how to keep a frequency count for an individual student; adapt the procedures for recording class-wide totals.)

 (OPTIONAL)
If this plan is ineffective, use time owed as an additional consequence.

Whenever an individual student makes an inappropriate comment, his/her team would lose a ticket, plus the individual student would owe time off of recess or in after-school detention for each infraction. However, do not make the whole team owe time—losing the ticket is consequence enough for the student's teammates. *(NOTE: See PLAN B for additional information on using time owed.)*

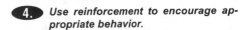 **Use reinforcement to encourage appropriate behavior.**

a. Provide praise and attention to students who use appropriate humor and who demonstrate restraint (see PLAN A).

b. In addition, praise the teams and, when appropriate, the entire class for demonstrating restraint and for using humor appropriately.

· · · · · · · ·
Suggested Steps for Developing and Implementing a Plan

The following steps are designed to help you develop an appropriate intervention plan and implement it effectively, whether you choose to use one of the MODEL PLANS or create a customized plan of your own. The steps are, however, suggestions—they are not intended to be followed rigidly or in any particular order. Use your professional judgment and the knowledge of your particular situation to make them work for you.

1. *Make sure you have enough informa-tion about the situation.*

a. If you think a minimal intervention like PLAN A will be sufficient, you may already have enough information to proceed. However, when a more involved plan seems necessary, you should consider collecting additional descriptive and/or objective information for a couple of days.

b. You need to be able to specify precisely how the student's comments are inappropriate. Is it the content of what the student says (e.g., she makes fun of others)? Step 1 in PLAN B pro-vides detailed information about how to clarify the exact nature of the problem.

Anecdotal notes on actual incidents should pro-vide enough detail to help you define the prob-lem behavior clearly and completely. To collect anecdotal notes, simply keep a card in your pocket or on a clipboard and occasionally make notes on specific instances when the student makes a comment that you consider to be inap-propriate. For each entry, briefly describe where and when the behavior occurred, what the stu-dent did or said, and any other relevant obser-vations (e.g., what prompted the behavior). You do not need to take notes every time the student says something inappropriate; the idea is to capture a range of examples so that you will be able to explain the problem thoroughly.

Also include some notes on times when the student uses appropriate humor—this will make it clear that you are not only aware of her problem behavior, but also recognize when she behaves appropriately. When you meet with the student, the positive examples will also help you to clarify how you want the student to behave.

c. In addition to being able to describe what the student's inappropriate comments sound like, it can also be useful to document how often the behavior occurs (i.e., a frequency count). This information will provide both a more objective measure of the problem and an objective way to monitor the student's progress. You can use the same card on which you are collecting anecdotal notes to keep a frequency count—simply write a tally mark on the card each time the student makes an inappropriate comment.

You might want to code these tallies to discern whether the behavior occurs more frequently during certain times, subjects, or activities. It might also be especially useful to differentiate between appropriately funny comments (by marking an "A") and those that are inappropriate (by marking an "I").

d. If the student notices what you are doing and asks about it, be straightforward—tell her that you are collecting information to see whether her use of inappropriate comments is a problem that needs to be worked on.

Following is an example of anecdotal notes and a frequency count that have been collected on a student's use of inappropriate comments.

Audrey's Comments—10/3

Morning	Afternoon
AAIII IIIII	IAAII II

Notes:

8:40—During the math lesson, I was present-ing information on decimals and Audrey kept imitating an Italian accent and saying things like, "Decimals, dis a smells, dis a smells fishy to me." By the fifth or sixth time, even the rest of the students were not laughing any more.

11:30—Right before lunch, Audrey referred to the cook Mrs. Garfunkle as 'Mrs. Barf Knuck-les.' Today she said this to her, and I think she was really offended.

Afternoon—Audrey made two comments dur-ing art that were honestly funny. The class and I all laughed.

---

e. The frequency information is fairly easy to sum-marize on a chart or graph. Seeing how often she makes inappropriate comments may help the student and her parent(s) better understand your concern.

f. Continuing to collect this type of information (and keeping the chart up-to-date) while you implement a plan will help you to monitor whether the situation is getting worse, staying the same, or getting better.

2. *Identify a focus for the intervention and labels for referring to the appropri-ate and inappropriate behaviors.*

a. To be effective, the intervention must address more than just reducing the student's use of inappropriate comments—there must be a con-current emphasis on increasing some positive behavior or trait (e.g., "restraint" or "appropriate humor"). Having a specific positive behavior in mind will make it easier for you to "catch" and reinforce the student for behaving appropri-ately, and the positive focus will help you to frame the situation more productively.

For example, if you simply say that "the student has a problem with being a smart-aleck," you don't really provide any useful information, and may put the student and her parent(s) on the defensive. However, when you explain that you want to "help the student learn restraint" you present an important, and reasonable, goal for the student to work toward and clarify what the student needs to do to be successful.

b. Specifying labels for the appropriate and inappropriate behaviors (e.g., "using restraint" and "inappropriate comments," respectively) will help you to use consistent vocabulary when discussing the situation with the student. If you sometimes refer to the inappropriate behavior as "being a smart-aleck," for example, and other times tell the student "to stop making wisecracks," she may not realize that you are talking about the same thing (i.e., "using restraint").

3. Determine when and how to include the parent(s).

a. It is not necessary to contact the student's parent(s) if the problem has just begun and is not interfering with the student's academic or social progress. However, it might be a good idea to take advantage of any scheduled activities (e.g., conferences, weekly notes home) to let them know of your concern.

b. If the problem has been going on for more than a week or two, contact the student's parent(s). Share with them any information you have collected (e.g., anecdotal notes, frequency count), and explain why you are concerned. Focus in particular on how the behavior is hindering the student academically and/or socially (e.g., she is spending so much time making jokes that she is not participating in the instruction).

You might ask if the parent(s) have any insight into the situation and/or whether they have noticed similar behavior at home. Whether or not the parent(s) perceive a problem, explain that you want to help the student "learn to use restraint," and invite them to join you for an initial meeting with the student to develop a plan. If the parent(s) are unable or unwilling to participate, let them know that you will keep them informed of the student's progress.

c. Once the parent(s) have been involved in any way, you should give them updates at least once per week while the plan is being implemented.

4. Prepare for, then conduct, an initial meeting about the situation.

a. Arrange a meeting to discuss your concerns with the student and anyone else who will be involved in the plan (e.g., the parent[s]). Although the specifics will vary depending upon the age of the student and the severity of the problem, there are some general guidelines to consider when scheduling the meeting.

First, meet at a neutral time (i.e., not immediately after a problem has occurred), when emotions are less likely to hamper communication. In general, a day's notice is appropriate, however a primary age student may worry excessively and/or forget what the meeting is about if it is scheduled more than an hour before it takes place.

Second, make the meeting appropriately private. Third, try to make sure the meeting is scheduled for a time and place that it is not likely to be interrupted (e.g., the counselor's office). Finally, if the parent(s) will be participating, they should be the ones to tell the student about the meeting.

b. Construct a preliminary plan. Decide whether you think you can use one of the MODEL PLANS or if you need to create a customized plan using components from various plans and/or of your own design. Although you will invite and encourage the student to help develop the plan during the initial meeting, having a proposed plan in mind before you meet can alleviate frustration and wasted time if the student is unwilling or unable to participate.

c. After reviewing the information you have collected and thinking about how you want the student to behave, prepare thorough descriptions of the inappropriate behavior and the positive behavior/trait on which the student will be working. The more specific you can be and the more concrete examples you have, the easier it will be to clarify (and for the student to understand) your expectations. Be sure to consider the student's behavior in all relevant activities (e.g., independent work periods, teacher directed instruction, unstructured class times, recess and lunch, etc.).

d. Conduct the meeting in an atmosphere of collaboration. The following agenda is one way you might structure the meeting:

- **Share your concerns about the student's behavior.**

  Briefly describe the problem behavior and explain why you consider the inappropriate comments to be a problem. You might tell the student that making inappropriate comments is a problem because she is cruel to others when she does so (if appropriate) and that this behavior is affecting how her peers feel about her. Or, focus on the academic effects and point out that if the student is too busy making inappropriate comments she won't be able to pay attention to your instruction, and her grades will surely begin to slip.

- **Discuss how you can work together to improve the situation.**

  Tell the student that you would like to help her "learn to use restraint," and describe your preliminary plan. Invite the student to give you input on the various aspects of the plan, and together work out any necessary details (e.g., defining the borderline, the use of time owed, the self-monitoring form, etc.). You may have to brainstorm different possibilities if the student is uncomfortable with the initial plan. Incorporating any of the student's suggestions that strengthen the plan is likely to increase her sense of "ownership" in and commitment to it.

- **Make sure the student understands what you mean by appropriate and inappropriate behavior.**

  Use the descriptions you have prepared to define and clarify the problem behavior and the positive (desired) behavior as specifically and thoroughly as you can. (NOTE: For details on defining the borderline, see PLAN B.) To ensure that you and the student are in agreement about the expectations, you might describe hypothetical scenarios and have her identify whether the behavior in each repre-

sents appropriate or inappropriate comments. Or you might describe an actual situation that has occurred and ask the student to explain how she could have demonstrated restraint in that situation.

- **Conclude the meeting.**

  Always end the meeting with words of encouragement. Let the student know that you are confident that she can be successful. Be sure to reinforce her for participating in the meeting.

5. *Give the student regular, ongoing feedback about her behavior.*

It is important to meet with the student periodically to discuss her progress. In most cases, three to five minutes once per week should suffice. (NOTE: PLANS D, E, and F suggest daily meetings.) During the meetings, review any information that has been collected and discuss whether or not the situation is getting better. As much as possible, focus on the student's improvements, however, also address any new or continuing problems. As the situation improves, the meetings can be faded to once every other week and then to once per month.

6. *Evaluate the situation (and the plan).*

Implement any plan for at least two weeks before deciding whether to change plans; to continue, modify, or fade the plan you are using; or to cease the intervention. Generally, if the student's behavior is clearly improving (based on the objective information that's been collected and/or subjective perceptions of yourself, the student, and possibly the parent[s]), stick with what you are doing. If the situation has remained the same or worsened, some kind of change will be necessary. Always discuss any changes to the plan with the student first.

SOCIAL SKILLS, LACK OF

DESCRIPTION

You have a student (or a group of students) who seems to lack the basic social skills to successfully interact with other students and/or with adults.

Because the term "social skills" encompasses such a broad and complex set of behaviors (making them beyond the scope of this reference guide), there are no MODEL PLANS included with this problem. The purpose of the following information is to suggest an overall approach and some basic considerations for addressing the lack of social skills—at an individual, small group, class-wide, and/or school-wide level. *(NOTE: A list of published social skills curricula is provided for your reference.)*

Alternative Problems

- **Arguing—Students With Each Other**
- **Arguing— Student(s) With the Teacher**
- **Bullying Behavior/Fighting**
- **Cliques/Ganging Up**
- **Disrespectful Behavior**
- **Name Calling/ Put-Downs**
- **Shyness/Withdrawn Behavior**
- **Smart-Aleck Behavior/ Inappropriate Humor**
- **Spoiled Behavior**
- **Victim—Student Who Is Always Picked On**

General Information

- If you are able to identify one specific social skill that your student lacks (e.g., treating adults with respect), look up that particular problem in this reference guide. However, if the student lacks many basic skills for interacting appropriately with his/her peers and/or adults, you should consider establishing regular and ongoing social skills training.

- When there are pervasive behavior problems throughout the entire school (e.g., disrespect for adults, name calling), you might consider encouraging the whole faculty to address the problem in a proactive way. One possibility is for a small group of faculty members to prepare a series of short lessons that all the teachers could use to teach the students positive behaviors that will replace the problem behaviors. If disrespect is a problem, for example, every classroom teacher could give lessons on how to respectfully gain adult attention, accept praise, accept criticism, and disagree with peers and/or teachers.

  The content of any school-wide lessons could be developed by having a staff brainstorming session to identify those contexts and situations in which the students tend to be disrespectful (or exhibit any other targeted social skill). The format of the lessons could consist of class discussions, teacher and student modeling, role playing, and feedback.

- If the lack of social skills seems to involve primarily the students in your class (and/or you are unable to generate school-wide involvement), you should plan to include scheduled social skills lessons in your class schedule. For example, if you know that the particular group of students who will be in your room in a given year have a reputation/history of challenging behaviors, you should spend a significant portion of time at the beginning of the year teaching the whole class the various social behaviors and routines that will be necessary for them to be successful in your classroom.

  (NOTE: The simplest teaching of these behaviors and routines is likely to benefit most classes, but if you have a group of students with a history

  of problems, be prepared to use very direct teaching and to provide lots of practice.)

- When only a few students are in need of social skills training, the most effective approach may be to have a counselor or skilled teaching assistant conduct the lessons in a small group setting. The lessons should be scheduled and conducted on a regular basis, and the group should include a mix of students (i.e., not just those with social skills problems) as appropriately behaving students may be needed to model the desired behavior(s), especially at the beginning. In addition, it is important that every classroom teacher who has a participating student is apprised of the skill(s) being taught so that they can provide positive and corrective feedback on their students' efforts.

  An example of when it might be appropriate to implement this kind of small group social skills instruction involves students who are having difficulty behaving themselves on the playground. The school counselor could implement structured recess with this group of students. For a couple of days, the students would be assigned to the counselor during recess, and the counselor would teach the social skills right there on the playground in the context of structured games rather than the students' usual free choice activities.

- The most difficult way to teach social skills is in a one-to-one context, as such an arrangement limits the variety of practice opportunities (in terms of situations and people) the student can experience. If one-to-one lessons seem necessary, consider inviting a range of different individuals to participate in the lessons whenever feasible. For example, you might ask another student to join you and the target student on one day, the principal on another day, and the custodian on yet another day.

- What follows are two lists of social skills curricula, one for elementary level students and one for secondary level students.

Social Skills Programs

Elementary Level

Huggins, P. (1990). *Teaching cooperation skills.* Longmont, CO: Sopris West.

Huggins, P. (1993). *Helping kids handle anger: Teaching self-control.* Longmont, CO: Sopris West.

Huggins, P. (1993). *Teaching friendship skills: Intermediate version.* Longmont, CO: Sopris West.

Huggins, P. (1993). *Teaching friendship skills: Primary version.* Longmont, CO: Sopris West.

Jackson, N.F., Jackson, D.A., & Monroe, C. (1983). *Getting along with others: Teaching social effectiveness to children.* Champaign, IL: Research Press.

McGinnis, E., Goldstein, A.P., Sprafkin, R.P., & Gershaw, N.J. (1984). *Skillstreaming the elementary school child: A guide for teaching prosocial skills.* Champaign, IL: Research Press.

Walker, H.M., McConnel, S., Holmes, D., Todis, B., Walker, J., & Golden, N. (1983). *The ACCEPTS program: A curriculum for children's effective peer and teacher skills.* Austin, TX: Pro-Ed.

Secondary Level

Goldstein, A.P. (1988). *The prepare curriculum.* Champaign, IL: Research Press.

Goldstein, A.P. & Glick, B. (1987). *Aggression replacement training.* Champaign, IL: Research Press.

Goldstein, A.P., Sprafkin, R.P., Gershaw, N.J., & Klein, P. (1980). *Skillstreaming the adolescent: A structured learning approach to teaching prosocial skills.* Champaign, IL: Research Press.

Walker, H.M., Todis, B., Holmes, D., & Horton, D. (1988). *The ACCESS Program: Adolescent coping curriculum for communication and effective social skills.* Austin, TX: Pro-Ed.

NOTE: For additional assistance in selecting the most appropriate social skills program for a student's individual needs, you may also wish to consult:

Alberg, J., Petry, C., & Eller, S. (1994). The social skills planning guide. Longmont, CO: Sopris West.

SPITTING

DESCRIPTION

You have a student who spits on property or people.

GOAL

The student will not spit at all while on school grounds.

OVERVIEW OF PLANS

- PLAN A: For a student who has either just begun to or infrequently spits on property.

- PLAN B: For a student who repeatedly spits on property (not people).

- PLAN C: For a student who spits on people.

> *NOTE:*
> *Each of these three plans can be adapted for use with several students, if necessary.*

Alternative Problem

- **Drug Use—Tobacco, Alcohol, Cocaine, Etc.**

....
General Considerations

- If the student's spitting behavior is a result of his chewing tobacco, implement a suggested intervention for spitting, but also refer the situation immediately to your school counselor, psychologist, or substance abuse coordinator.

- If the student must spit (e.g., a student with a deviated septum has a cold and must clear the phlegm or choke), any effort to deal with the student's spitting should be coordinated with his parent(s) and/or physician (if appropriate).

....
Model Plans

PLAN A

It is not always necessary, or even beneficial, to use an involved plan. If the spitting has just begun and/or occurs infrequently (i.e., the student has had single incidents of spitting a couple of months apart), the following actions, along with making the student aware of your concerns, may resolve the situation.

1. Respond consistently to the student's spitting.

a. Establish an "overcorrection" consequence in which the student has to clean up his spit *and* restore the area to a neater and more sanitary condition than before the spitting took place. This type of consequence is called an overcorrection because the student must do more than simply repair any damage directly associated with the misbehavior (i.e., clean up his saliva); additional compensation (e.g., cleaning and disinfecting the area) is also required. If the student spits on the classroom floor, for example, he would be required to get paper towels, wipe up the saliva, spray disinfectant on the area, and then wipe the area with towels again.

b. Be very calm when enforcing the consequence. If you or anyone else gets angry or upset about the spitting, it may inadvertently reinforce the student. Stay calm and speak in a neutral tone of voice, even if you have to remind the student about the clean-up process. "Frederick, you did not bring out the disinfectant. You need to go back to the office, get the disinfectant and more towels, then come back and wipe this area one more time." If the student tries to argue, simply restate what he needs to do.

c. If the student spits on the playground, the same type of consequence can be implemented, however, you should coordinate your efforts with the playground supervisors.

2. Use reinforcement to encourage the student to refrain from spitting.

a. When the student has gone for a significant period of time (e.g., one week) without spitting, praise him for demonstrating his ability to "treat school property with respect." If the student would be embarrassed by public praise, praise the student privately or even give the student a note.

b. Give the student frequent attention (e.g., say "hello" to him as he enters the classroom, call on him frequently during class activities, and occasionally talk to him about his interests outside the classroom) and praise him for positive behaviors he exhibits. For example, you might comment about how well he works in cooperative groups or discuss a paper on which he did a particularly nice job. This demonstrates to the student that you notice many positive things he does, not just the fact that he is refraining from spitting.

PLAN B

If the student repeatedly engages in spitting, a slightly more severe consequence may be required as part of the intervention.

 1. Respond consistently to each of the student's spitting incidents.

Use a more severe overcorrection procedure such as, in addition to having the student clean up his saliva and the immediate area, requiring him to spend time during recess or after school cleaning the entire room. For example, if the student spits on the classroom floor, he should immediately clean and disinfect that area. Then, during the next recess, he should have to disinfect the entire floor. If he spits on the playground, he could first clean and disinfect the area and then spend the next recess picking up the trash on the entire playground.

Let the student know in advance what the consequence will be for the next incident of spitting and explain the rationale—if the student does not know how to treat school property with respect, he will have to demonstrate through the consequence that he is learning to do so.

2. Use reinforcement to encourage appropriate behavior.

a. Give the student increased praise and attention for treating school property with respect (see PLAN A).

b. In addition, give the student a responsibility to increase his pride in himself and his affiliation with the school. Being assigned a daily job is a statement to the student that he is an important and contributing member of the school community. Possibilities for a job include raising the flag in the morning, making announcements over the intercom, etc.

The job or responsibility should be completely independent of his spitting behavior; one he gets to do every day regardless of whether or not he has been spitting. If the job is contingent upon the student "not spitting," it may lead to a power struggle (e.g., "I spit—now you won't let me do my job. So what? I'll spit any time I want to."). However, do not talk to the student about establishing the job until there have been a few days with no spitting. You do not want the student to get the idea that he has been assigned the job because he engaged in spitting.

PLAN C

If the student has spit on a person, even once, the student must learn the seriousness of this unacceptable behavior.

 1. Respond promptly the first time the student spits on a person.

a. Have the student write (or say) an apology to the person he spat on. Let the student know that he needs to apologize both for the spitting and for not treating the person he spit on with respect. Help the student generate an appropriate apology such as, "Frank, I am sorry that I treated you disrespectfully. I will not spit on you again or in any way treat you disrespectfully."

b. Contact the student's parent(s) and let them know about the incident.

c. Schedule a short lesson (three to five minutes) during which you will explain to the student the seriousness of this behavior. This lesson should take place during the student's recess or after

school. During the lesson, let the student know that if the behavior occurs again, his parent(s) will be called in for a conference.

(NOTE: If the student has spat on a person, discuss the situation with the school nurse to determine if there is any concern about the exchange of bodily fluids given issues related to AIDS. If so, and this is unlikely, the nurse and the building administrator should assist you in determining how to proceed.)

2. Respond promptly and decisively if the behavior occurs again.

a. Have the student write an apology to the person he spat on.

b. Call the parent(s) in for a conference with you and the student. Both the parent(s) and the student need to understand that spitting on another person is an extremely disrespectful act that will not be tolerated within the school. Let the student and his parent(s) know that if the behavior happens again, the consequence following will be implemented. *(NOTE: Be sure to clear this procedure with your building administrator before telling the student and his parent[s] about it.)*

c. This potentially effective consequence is somewhat disgusting, however, given the seriousness of this type of spitting behavior, it seems worth mentioning. If the student has a third incident of spitting on a person, he will report to the office or some other supervised setting that is out of view of his peers. There, since he seems to need to spit, he will spit into a paper cup until he fills it to a designated line. (When

the student has finished, he should be told that the next time the consequence will be even more severe [i.e., filling the cup higher]).

If implemented, do not allow the student to use the consequence to avoid his schoolwork; make sure he knows that he still has to finish all of his assignments.

If this consequence does not seem appropriate to the circumstances, implement another consequence such as requiring the student to sanitize the area where the spitting took place (see PLAN B) or spending time in after-school detention.

 Use reinforcement to encourage appropriate behavior.

Give the student increased praise and attention for treating others with respect (see PLAN A).

....
Suggested Steps for Developing and Implementing a Plan

The following steps are designed to help you develop an appropriate intervention plan and implement it effectively, whether you choose to use one of the MODEL PLANS or create a customized plan of your own. The steps are, however, suggestions—they are not intended to be followed rigidly or in any particular order. Use your professional judgment and the knowledge of your particular situation to make them work for you.

 Make sure you have enough information about the situation.

a. If the student is spitting on property (not people), additional record keeping is probably not necessary. However, it is important to document each time the student spits on another person. Such records will be essential if the problem continues to the point that legal action is taken (e.g., the parent[s] of the student who has been repeatedly spat on files harassment or assault charges).

To thoroughly document the problem, collect anecdotal notes, recording the details of every incident including the consequences that have been implemented to encourage the student to stop the behavior (e.g., parental contact, an apology letter, a session of spitting into the cup, etc.).

b. Continue to keep anecdotal notes while you implement a plan. This will help you monitor whether the situation is getting worse, staying the same, or getting better.

 Identify a focus for the intervention and labels for referring to the appropriate and inappropriate behaviors.

The intervention must address more than just reducing the student's spitting—there must be a concurrent emphasis on increasing some positive behavior or trait (e.g., respecting property, or respecting people). The positive focus will help you frame the situation in a more productive way when discussing the situation with the student and his parent(s), and having a specific positive behavior in mind will make it easier for you "catch" and reinforce the student for behaving appropriately.

3. **Determine when and how to include the parent(s).**

a. It is not necessary to contact the student's parent(s) if the problem has just begun and involves spitting on school property, however, it might be a good idea to take advantage of any scheduled activities (e.g., conferences, weekly notes home) to let them know of your concern.

If the problem involves spitting on people, contact the student's parent(s) after the first incident. If the behavior occurs a second time, the parent(s) should be called in for a conference.

b. Once the parent(s) have been involved in any way, let them know that you will report any future incidents to them and keep them apprised of the student's progress.

c. Depending upon the circumstances, you may wish to contact the parent(s) of the student who was spat on. For example, if the student who was spat on was upset about the incident or if he/she was embarrassed in front of peers, parental contact would be advisable. Inform the student's parent(s) of the incident and let them know that the "spitter" is receiving consequences for his actions.

4. Prepare for, then conduct, an initial meeting about the situation.

a. Arrange a meeting to discuss your concerns with the student and anyone else who will be involved in the plan (e.g., the student's parent[s], the principal). Although the specifics will vary depending upon the age of the student and the severity of the problem, there are some general guidelines to consider when scheduling the meeting.

First, meet at a neutral time (i.e., not immediately after a problem has occurred) when emotions are less likely to hamper communication. In general, a day's notice is appropriate, however a primary age student may worry excessively and/or forget what the meeting is about if it is scheduled more than an hour before it takes place. Second, make the meeting appropriately private. Third, try to make sure the meeting is scheduled for a time and place that it is not likely to be interrupted (e.g., the counselor's office). Finally, if the parent(s) will be participating, they should be the ones to tell the student about the meeting.

b. Construct a preliminary plan. Decide whether you think you can use one of the MODEL PLANS or if you need to create a customized plan using components from various plans and/or of your own design. Although you will invite and encourage the student to help develop the plan during the initial meeting, having a proposed plan in mind before you meet can alleviate frustration and wasted time if the student is unwilling or unable to participate.

c. Prepare a thorough description of the inappropriate behavior as well as a description of the positive behavior/trait on which the student will be working. The more specific you can be and the more concrete examples you have, the easier it will be to clarify (and for the student to understand) your expectations. Be sure to consider the student's behavior in all relevant locations (e.g., the classroom, hallways, the playground, the cafeteria, bus waiting areas, etc.).

d. Conduct the meeting in an atmosphere of collaboration. The following agenda is one way you might structure the meeting:

• **Share your concerns about the student's behavior.**

Briefly describe the misbehavior and explain why you consider it to be a problem. In the case of spitting on property, you might tell the student that his spitting is disrespectful of the school and the people within the school. You could point out how disgusting it would be if someone spit on the playground and another person fell in it. In the case of spitting on people, bring up the issues of disrespect, as discussed previously.

• **Discuss how you can work together to improve the situation.**

Tell the student that you would like to help him learn to "treat property /people with respect," and describe your preliminary plan. Invite the student to give you input on the various aspects of the plan, and together work out any necessary details (e.g., how the student will have to clean and disinfect after subsequent incidents).

You may have to brainstorm different possibilities if the student is uncomfortable with the plan. Incorporating any of the student's suggestions that strengthen the plan is likely to increase his sense of "ownership" in and commitment to it.

• **Conclude the meeting.**

Always end the meeting with words of encouragement. Let the student know that you are confident that he can be successful. Be sure to reinforce him for participating in the meeting.

5. Evaluate the situation (and the plan).

Implement any plan for at least two weeks before deciding whether to change plans; to continue, modify, or fade the plan you are using; or to cease the intervention. Generally, if the student's behavior is clearly improving, stick with what you are doing. If the situation has remained the same or worsened, some kind of change will be necessary. Always discuss any changes to the plan with the student first.

S POILED BEHAVIOR

Low Tolerance for Frustration

Student Must Get Own Way

DESCRIPTION

You have a student who reacts inappropriately when she does not get her own way and/or when she is frustrated.

GOAL

The student will learn to behave responsibly, despite not getting her own way and/or frustrating circumstances.

OVERVIEW OF PLANS

- PLAN A: For a situation in which the problem is relatively mild or has just begun.
- PLAN B: For a student who has not learned how to deal with frustrating circumstances appropriately.
- PLAN C: For a student who demands a lot of attention when she is frustrated or when she does not get her own way.
- PLAN D: For a student whose spoiled behavior has become habitual.

NOTE:

*These four plans assume that the student exhibits a variety of behaviors that might be considered "spoiled." You may wish to review the list of ALTERNATIVE PROBLEMS on this page and/or the INDEX to determine whether there is another behavior problem that more specifically describes your student's behavior when she doesn't get her own way and/or is frustrated. If another problem does seem more appropriate, read through the plans for that problem. For example, if your student becomes so angry that she loses control when frustrated, you may find that the plans in **Self-Control Issues** will be more effective in resolving the situation.*

Alternative Problems

- **Apathetic Behavior**
- **Arguing—Student(s) With the Teacher**
- **Babyish Behavior**
- **Bossiness**
- **Complaining**
- **Corrected, Student Gets Upset When**
- **Disrespectful Behavior**
- **Helplessness**
- **Moodiness**
- **Passive Resistance**
- **Perfectionism**
- **Pouting**
- **Self-Control Issues**
- **Smart-Aleck Behavior/ Inappropriate Humor**
- **Tantrumming (K or 1st Grader)**
- **Whining**

....
General Considerations

- If the student's problem behavior stems in any way from academic issues (e.g., the student feels frustrated much of the time because the academic expectations are beyond her current abilities), concurrent efforts must be made to ensure her academic success (see **Academic Deficits, Determining**).

- If the student lacks the basic social skills to interact with her peers appropriately, it may be necessary to begin by teaching her those skills. **Social Skills, Lack of** contains information on a variety of published social skills curricula.

....
Model Plans

PLAN A

It is not always necessary, or even beneficial, to use an involved plan. If the inappropriate behavior has just begun and/or occurs infrequently (e.g., the student behaves inappropriately only occasionally, when she doesn't get her own way), the following actions, along with making the student aware of your concerns, may resolve the situation.

1. Respond consistently to the inappropriate behavior.

a. During your initial meeting with the student (see SUGGESTED STEPS FOR DEVELOPING AND IMPLEMENTING A PLAN), establish a nonembarrassing signal that you can use to cue her that she is reacting irresponsibly. You want the signal to be a fairly subtle one that only the student will recognize and understand in order to minimize the chance that she will be teased by her peers. Possibilities include putting the fingertips of your hands together, rubbing your neck, or even just direct eye contact and a head nod.

Let the student know that you may also need to quietly say her name to get her attention before you give the signal. You should also be prepared to use the signal frequently and for a fairly long time, since it may be that the student's responses to frustration are, at least in part, an unconscious habit.

b. Whenever the student reacts inappropriately (i.e., acts spoiled), give her the signal. If the student does not stop reacting inappropriately, give her a gentle verbal correction. Let her know that this is an inappropriate way to handle frustration, and give her direct information about what she should be doing instead. "Doreen, you need to stop demanding that you be first in line. Go quietly to the back of the line." Because your goal is to impart information, you want to be emotionally neutral while giving the correction.

2. Use reinforcement to encourage appropriate behavior.

a. Give the student increased praise. Be especially alert for those times when the student has handled particularly trying situations without acting spoiled and praise her for demonstrating her ability to deal with frustration responsibly. "Doreen, I noticed that you didn't get the job of being group leader. You stayed very calm, and told the group that you would like to have the job the next time there is cooperative groups. This was a great example of dealing with frustration in a responsible way."

If the student would be embarrassed by public praise, praise her privately or even give the student a note. Remember that any time the student is not acting spoiled, you can praise her for handling frustration responsibly.

b. Praise the student privately for responding to the signal. "Doreen, earlier this morning I gave you the signal that you were reacting irresponsibly, and you changed your behavior. Good job."

c. Be careful not to inadvertently teach the student that she must always compromise or "roll over" when faced with frustrating circumstances that involve a difference of opinion. "Doreen, dealing with disagreements with other students can be very frustrating. Twice this morning I saw you deal with disagreements in a very responsible way. Once you compromised (you and Wayne worked out a plan to share the microscope) and once you stated a strong opinion (you told Miriam that it was your turn to be responsible for the soccer ball at recess), but you stayed calm and dealt with the problem. It is sometimes hard to know when to compromise and when to 'stick to your guns' but you did a great job today. You should be proud of yourself."

d. Give the student frequent attention (e.g., say "hello" to her as she enters the classroom, call on her frequently during class activities, and occasionally ask her to assist you with a class job that needs to be done) and praise her for other positive behaviors she exhibits. For example, you might comment about the accuracy of her work or how consistent she is about turning in her homework. This demonstrates to the student that you notice many positive things she does, not just the fact that she is not reacting inappropriately to frustration.

PLAN B

Some students may not have been taught how to responsibly deal with not getting their own way. If your student does not seem to have the necessary skills or strategies for handling frustration responsibly, the intervention must include a way to teach her these skills.

1. Respond consistently to the inappropriate behavior.

When the student reacts inappropriately (acts spoiled/frustrated), give her a signal, and if necessary, gently correct her (see PLAN A).

2. Prepare for lessons to teach the student how to deal with frustration more responsibly.

a. Use your anecdotal notes (see SUGGESTED STEPS FOR DEVELOPING AND IMPLEMENTING A PLAN) to identify the circumstances (i.e., settings, events, people, etc.) that are most likely to result in the student acting spoiled. This information will help you to think of hypothetical practice situations.

When possible, identify two different types of circumstances: (1) those in which responsible actions on the student's part could alleviate her frustration (e.g., responsible ways to ask for assistance when she does not understand some aspect of an assignment); and (2) situations that must simply be tolerated as part of responsibly meeting classroom expectations (e.g., the student doesn't like that she is expected to do her work rather than talk to her friend).

b. In addition, identify the types of things the student does when she is acting spoiled. Does she get angry? throw things? yell? cry? withdraw and refuse to participate? These details will be important for helping the student learn what behaviors she should strive to avoid.

c. Finally, think about how the student could respond to not getting her own way/frustrating events in more responsible ways. That is, what could the student do in place of the irresponsible actions you've identified. Although you will need to tailor this information for your student, following are some examples of appropriate responses:

- Quietly accepting that this is a situation that cannot be changed—and continuing to do what she should be doing.

- Calmly stating an opinion.

- Calmly accepting and respecting someone else's opinion.

- Seeking additional information.

- Calmly making a request.

- Withdrawing from a situation.

d. If the student tends to become angry and/or lose control when frustrated, identify some self-control techniques she could use to help her stay calm. Possibilities include deep and even breathing, positive self-talk, or deep muscle relaxation techniques. For other ideas and additional details, see **Self-Control Issues** and **Anxiety/Nervousness**.

3. Conduct the lessons.

a. During the lessons, use the information you've identified to:

- Teach the student how to discriminate between circumstances that might be solved through responsible actions and those that do not have a solution but must simply be tolerated. Use lots of examples, including some that are appropriate from your own life. "Doreen, one of the things that I find frustrating as a parent is . . . . Do you think that has a solution, or is that something I simply need to learn to live with?"

Once the student has become fairly skilled at identifying whether a situation has a clear-cut solution or not, introduce some examples in the "gray area." "Doreen, this next one is really tough. I don't know if there is a solution or if it just needs to be tolerated, but let's think about it together. One thing that often happens in class is . . . . "

- Teach the student to recognize the irresponsible ways she responds to not getting her own way/frustrating situations. Discuss and, if necessary, model the types of behavior the student engages in when she is acting spoiled. Help her see that when a situation can be resolved through responsible actions, an inappropriate response (e.g., crying, pouting, or whatever the student usually does) will reduce the probability that the student will achieve an outcome she desires. In addition, help her to understand that reacting inappropriately to a frustrating situation that must simply be tolerated (e.g., having to do her schoolwork instead of talking to her friend) will not remove the situation, just make her miserable.

- Teach the student the identified strategies for reacting responsibly to not getting her own way/frustrating situations. Be sure to include responsible strategies for: (1) coping with situations that cannot be changed, and (2) altering frustrating situations that have a solution. If necessary, include lessons on how to maintain emotional control.

b. Use many different examples. With some of the examples, talk through the previous steps. "Doreen, is there a solution through responsible action for this example, or is it a situation that cannot be changed? Excellent! What would be one responsible way to react to this situation? What would be an irresponsible way? Which way do you suppose will give you a better chance of getting what you want?"

Use role play some of the time. That is, have the student act out a responsible way of reacting to hypothetical frustrating situations. Occasionally, you might role play an inappropriate reaction so that the student can see that

irresponsible reactions to frustrating circumstances have a low probability of achieving a desirable outcome. As the lessons proceed, substitute more actual examples that have occurred during the school day for the hypothetical examples.

c. Tell the student that when she sees you give her the signal that she is reacting inappropriately, and that she should try to employ one or more of the strategies from the lessons.

d. Conduct the lessons at least twice per week. The lessons should involve just you and the student (perhaps while the other students are at recess), and needn't last more than three to five minutes. If more time seems necessary, consider arranging for the lessons to be conducted by the school counselor or a highly skilled paraprofessional who has time for such one-to-one instruction.

It is important that the lessons be handled in a matter-of-fact manner so that the student does not feel that she is being ridiculed. Continue the lessons until the student is consistently responding to the signal and/or no longer reacting to frustration irresponsibly in the classroom.

 Prompt the student to behave appropriately by using precorrections.

Watch for circumstances in which the student is likely to react inappropriately, and remind her that she will need to remember to handle the potentially frustrating situation responsibly. If time permits, you might also have her identify how she could implement the strategies she has learned.

If this conversation would embarrass the student, conduct it privately. "Doreen, could I see you over here for a minute? Think about this situation that is going on right now—does it have a solution or does it just need to be tolerated? Okay, so if this situation cannot be changed, what is a responsible way for you to handle it? Great, Doreen. Do you think you can do that? Excellent, give it a try."

5. Use reinforcement to encourage appropriate behavior.

a. Give the student increased praise and attention for dealing with frustration appropriately (see PLAN A).

b. In addition, make a special point of letting the student know that you notice her efforts to use the skills she has been learning/practicing. "Doreen, I know that you didn't like having to correct the mistakes on your geography paper, but you took a deep breath and just got started.

What a fine example of handling the situation responsibly."

PLAN C

Some students are very skilled at gaining attention through their negative behavior. If you find yourself frequently nagging, reminding, or coaxing the student to stop reacting inappropriately when she is frustrated, it is possible that she is trying to gain adult attention through her misbehavior. Whether or not the student overtly seems to like the attention, you should make sure that she receives more frequent and more satisfying attention for behaving appropriately than for acting spoiled.

1. Respond consistently to the inappropriate behavior.

a. When the student reacts to a situation inappropriately (i.e., acts spoiled), give her a signal (see PLAN A).

b. If the student does not respond to the signal, ignore her behavior. Because the student needs to learn that she cannot prompt people to nag and pay attention to her by reacting inappropriately to frustration, you must ignore the irresponsible behavior. While ignoring, do not look at the student or talk to her. Do not act disgusted or impatient with her behavior. Simply interact in positive ways with students who are behaving appropriately and meeting classroom expectations. As soon as the target student is no longer behaving inappropriately, pay attention to her, but make no reference to her inappropriate behavior.

c. The only time not to ignore the student's inappropriate reactions is when her behavior affects other students (e.g., she is insisting that other students do something her way). On these occasions, intervene by removing the other students from the situation. "Tristan and Frannie, come over here and talk to me about this. Doreen can join us in the discussion when she is ready to handle the situation in a responsible manner."

(NOTE: If ignoring does not seem appropriate for your particular circumstances, instead implement time-out when the student does not respond to the signal [see PLAN D]. Remember, however, that your goal will be to give the student minimal time and attention even when she is being sent to the time-out area.)

2. Use reinforcement to encourage appropriate behavior.

a. Frequent praise and attention is the core of this plan. The student must see that she receives more frequent and more satisfying attention when she behaves responsibly than when she reacts inappropriately. Thus, whenever the student is not acting spoiled (or otherwise misbehaving), make an effort to praise her. Following are some examples:

- The student graciously allows a decision to be influenced by someone else. "Doreen, I know that you really wanted your group's project to have a painted cover, but when the other members of the group expressed that they wanted a collage cover, you were willing to go along. You quietly accepted the majority opinion. That was a responsible way to handle not getting your own way."

- The student assertively expresses her own opinion when appropriate. "Doreen, I was very impressed with the calm way you tried to convince the group that your project needed a table of contents. You made your case in a clear and unemotional way, and convinced everyone in the group that it was a good idea. That was a very responsible way to handle a situation that might have frustrated you a month ago."

- The student responsibly accepts an undesirable circumstance. "Doreen, I know that you hoped we could change the day on which you were scheduled to give your report. I appreciate how maturely you accepted my decision that the schedule would not be changed. This shows me that you are learning that some things are just not worth getting upset about, and makes me much more willing to listen to the next request you might want to make."

b. You may also wish to use intermittent rewards to acknowledge the student's success. Occasional, and unexpected, rewards can motivate the student to demonstrate responsible behavior more often. The idea is to provide a reward when the student has handled a particularly difficult situation responsibly or has gone for a long period without acting spoiled.

Appropriate rewards might include any kind of activity that the student can do with you. "Doreen, we have never even discussed how to deal with a situation like . . . , but you reacted in a very responsible way and got the other students to listen to your position. In fact, your explanation was so logical and calm that you brought the whole group around to agree with you. Very persuasive. Doreen, I need some help preparing a report for a faculty meeting this afternoon. Would you help me make some copies for my presentation?" *(NOTE: A list of additional reinforcement ideas can be found in APPENDIX 1.)*

Use intermittent rewards more frequently at the beginning of the intervention to encourage the student, and then less often as her behavior improves.

3. *Ensure a 3-1 ratio of positive to negative attention.*

a. When attention is a motivating force for the student, you want to be sure that you are giving her *three times as much* positive as negative attention. One way to do this is to monitor your interactions with the student at least one day per week. Simply keep a card on a clipboard or in your pocket and record each interaction you have with the student as either positive or nega-

tive by writing a "+" or a "-", respectively, on the card.

To determine whether an interaction is positive or negative, ask yourself whether the student was acting spoiled (or otherwise misbehaving) at the time the interaction occurred. Any interaction that stems from inappropriate behavior is negative, and all interactions that occur while the student is meeting classroom expectations are positive. Thus, giving the signal is a negative interaction, but praising the student for not needing the signal is positive. Greeting the student as she enters the room or asking her if she has any questions during independent work are also considered positive interactions. *(NOTE: Ignoring the student's inappropriate behavior is not recorded at all, because it is not an interaction.)*

b. If you find that you are not giving the student three times as much positive as negative attention, try to increase the number of positive interactions you have with the student. Sometimes prompts can help. For example, you might decide that each time the student enters the classroom you will say "hello" to her, that whenever you look at the clock you will find a time to praise the student, or that whenever a student uses the pencil sharpener you will check the target student and as soon as possible praise some aspect of her behavior. You can also increase the ratio of positive to negative attention by ignoring more of the student's inappropriate behavior.

PLAN D

Whenever a student's problem behavior has become habitual and/or she does not seem to have a desire to reduce it, you may need to implement a system of external incentives (i.e., rewards and consequences) based on her behavior to motivate her to stop reacting inappropriately to frustration and to start handling occasions when she does not get her own way more responsibly.

1. *Respond consistently to the inappropriate behavior.*

a. When the student reacts to a situation inappropriately (i.e., acts spoiled), give her a signal (see PLAN A).

b. Establish a short in-class time-out to be used as a consequence when the student does not cease her irresponsible behavior after being given the signal. Establish a time-out area (this can be as simple as a chair placed in a low traffic area of the classroom), and decide how long the student must spend in time-out. Generally, with

an elementary student, the number of minutes in time-out should equal the grade level of the student. Thus a kindergarten or first grade student would be assigned one minute of time-out per infraction, while a fifth grade student would receive a five-minute time-out. With a middle/junior high school student, five minutes is appropriate. In all cases, the student should not be allowed to do anything during the time-out period.

c. During the initial planning meeting with the student (see SUGGESTED STEPS FOR DEVELOPING AND IMPLEMENTING A PLAN), make sure that the student understands that she will be sent to time-out whenever she does not respond to the signal. Then, whenever the student does not respond to your signal, tell her to go to the time-out area and think about how she might handle the current situation more responsibly. Do not start the timer until the student is in the time-out area and quiet.

When the time is up, ask the student if she has identified some responsible ways to deal with the situation. If she has, she can come out of the time-out area. If she has not, provide one or two suggestions yourself. If the student agrees to try one or more of the suggestions, she can come out of the time-out area and resume classroom participation.

d. If you anticipate that the student may refuse to go to the time-out area, specify that she will owe time off of recess (in after-school detention, if appropriate) when this occurs. The amount of time owed will equal the amount of time she wastes by refusing to go to the time-out area. So, if you instruct the student to go to time-out and she doesn't go for ten minutes, she must spend the first ten minutes of the next scheduled recess sitting and doing nothing.

(NOTE: For a student in kindergarten or first grade, redirection may be more appropriate than time owed. Redirection involves gently leading the student to the time-out area without saying anything or making eye contact with her.)

e. If other students give the target student attention when she is in time-out or when she is refusing to go to the time-out area, gently correct them. "Gloria and Khalid, Doreen can take care of herself. She knows that she is losing recess time by refusing to go to time-out. It would be best to let her work it out on her own."

 2. *Monitor how often the student needs to go to time-out each day.*

Write a mark on a card you keep on a clipboard or in your pocket (or for a K-3 student, a card taped to the student's desk) each time the student is sent to time-out. At the end of the day, calculate and chart the daily total. Tell the student that the goal is for the daily total to be reduced until eventually there are zero instances of her being sent to time-out.

3. *Establish a structured system for reinforcing the student for not needing the signal or for responding to the signal*

(so that she does not need to be sent to time-out).

a. With the student, create a list of reinforcers that she can earn. Although you might want to have some suggestions in mind, the system will be more effective if the student identifies most of the items or activities herself. *(NOTE: A list of reinforcement ideas can be found in APPENDIX 1.)*

b. Assign "prices" (in points) for each of the rewards on the list and have the student select the reward she would like to earn first.

The prices should be based on the instructional, personnel, and/or monetary costs of the items. Monetary cost is clear—the more expensive the item, the more points required to earn it. Instructional cost refers to the amount of instructional time lost or interfered with by a particular reward. Thus, an activity which causes the student to miss part of academic instruction should require more points than one the student can do on her own recess time. Personnel cost involves the time required by you and/or other staff to fulfill the reinforcer. Having lunch with the principal, therefore, would cost more points than spending five minutes of free time with a friend.

c. Have the student begin each day with a certain number of points. This number should equal the student's daily average of occurrences of being sent to time-out, plus two. Thus, if she has averaged five times a day in time-out, she would begin each day with seven points. Every time you send the student to time-out, she loses a point. The points remaining at the end of each day are added together to be applied toward the reinforcer the student is striving to earn.

d. A lottery system might be more effective with a primary level student. With this system, the student would begin each day with tickets in a jar instead of points. All the tickets would have prizes written on them—one would have a big prize, a couple would have moderate prizes, and the majority would have small prizes. Each time you have to send the student to time-out, you would remove one ticket from the jar—but neither you nor the student would be allowed to see what is written on it. At the end of each day, the student would draw one ticket from those remaining in the jar, and receive that prize.

e. When the student has accumulated enough points to earn the reward she has chosen, she "spends" the points necessary and the system begins again. That is, she selects another reward to earn and begins with zero points.

If the student is immature, and needs more frequent encouragement, you might consider letting her earn several "less expensive" rewards (e.g., five minutes of computer time after ten points) on the way to a bigger reward (e.g., one hour with you for 100 points). That is, the student receives the small rewards without spending points; they continue to accumulate toward the selected reward.

f. If the student loses all her points on a given day, she still has to go to time-out. However, there should be no additional consequence. That is, do not take away points the student has earned on previous days. If the student can lose already-earned points, she might develop the attitude that, "I am losing so many points, why should I even bother to try?"

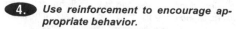 **Use reinforcement to encourage appropriate behavior.**

a. Give the student increased praise and attention for dealing with frustration appropriately (see PLAN A).

b. In addition, show interest and enthusiasm about how the student is doing on the system. "Doreen, you have not lost any points today. In fact, I don't even remember having to give you the signal. Today, you managed entirely on your own. I would like to award you four bonus points in addition to the seven that you earned today to thank you for your responsibility."

· · · · · · · ·

Suggested Steps for Developing and Implementing a Plan

The following steps are designed to help you develop an appropriate intervention plan and implement it effectively, whether you choose to use one of the MODEL PLANS or create a customized plan of your own. The steps are, however, suggestions—they are not intended to be followed rigidly or in any particular order. Use your professional judgment and the knowledge of your particular situation to make them work for you.

1. **Make sure you have enough information about the situation.**

a. If you think a minimal intervention like PLAN A will be sufficient, you may already have enough information to proceed. However, when a more involved plan seems necessary, you should consider collecting additional descriptive and/or objective information for a couple of days.

b. You need to be able to explain what you mean when you say that "the student has a problem with acting spoiled." That is, what specifically does the student do that has led you to conclude that her reactions are inappropriate? Is it the type of situation that provokes her? is it what she says or the way she says it? is it what else she does (e.g., cry, scream, pout)? Anecdotal notes on actual incidents can provide details to help you clarify the problem.

To collect anecdotal notes, simply keep a card in your pocket or on a clipboard and occasionally make notes on specific instances which you think demonstrate how the student acts spoiled. For each entry, briefly describe where and when the incident occurred, what the student did or said, and any other relevant observations (e.g., what prompted the behavior).

You do not need to take notes every time the student reacts inappropriately; the idea is to capture a range of examples so you will be able to describe the misbehavior completely. Also include some notes on times when the student responds to a frustrating situation in a responsible way—this will make it clear that you are not only aware of the student's problem behavior, but also recognize when she behaves appropriately. When you meet with the student, the positive examples will also help you to clarify how you want the student to behave.

c. In addition to information on what the student's inappropriate behavior looks like, it can also be useful to document how often it occurs (i.e., a frequency count). This information will provide both a more objective measure of the problem and an objective way to monitor the student's progress. You can use the same card on which you are collecting anecdotal notes to keep a frequency count—simply write a tally mark on the card each time the student reacts inappropriately (i.e., acts spoiled).

You might want to code these tallies to discern whether the behavior occurs more frequently during certain times, subjects, or activities (e.g., using an "A" or "P" to indicate that the incident happened in the morning or afternoon; or clustering the tallies by math or reading, teacher directed instruction or independent work, etc.).

d. If the student notices what you are doing and asks about it, be straightforward—tell her that you are collecting information to see whether her reactions to not getting her own way are a problem that need to be worked on.

Following is an example of anecdotal notes and a frequency count that have been collected on a student's spoiled behavior.

Doreen's Spoiled Behavior—11/2

Frequency:

AAAPP PPPPP PP

Notes:

8:50—During reading instruction, Doreen wanted to read the part of a particular character. Because she had a main part yesterday I assigned the main part to Eileen instead. Doreen started to get mad, then started to cry because she did not get the part.

10:10—Before recess Doreen was trying to talk some of the other girls into playing four-square with her, and when none of them seemed to want to, she then loudly proclaimed, "Okay, if none of you will play with me, I'll just be by myself!"

1:30—Doreen was sharpening her pencil and the sharpener would not turn. I told her that the container was full and asked her if she would empty it. A moment later she said loudly, "I can't get this stupid thing off. What is wrong with this? Why should I have to do this anyhow?" I then showed her how to get the container off, but she pouted and grumbled for several minutes about having had to empty it.

---

e. The frequency information is fairly easy to summarize on a chart or graph. Seeing how often she acts spoiled may help the student and her parent(s) better understand your concern.

f. Continuing to collect this type of information and keeping the chart up-to-date while you implement a plan will help you to monitor whether the situation is getting worse, staying the same, or getting better. (NOTE: In PLAN D, you will

instead be charting the number of times the student is sent to time-out each day.)

 Identify a focus for the intervention and labels for referring to the appropriate and inappropriate behaviors.

a. To be effective, the intervention must address more than just reducing the student's inappropriate reactions—there must be a concurrent emphasis on increasing some positive behavior or trait (e.g., handling frustrating situations responsibly). Having a specific positive behavior in mind will make it easier for you to "catch" and reinforce the student for behaving appropriately, and the positive focus will help you to frame the situation more productively.

For example, if you simply say that "the student has a problem with acting spoiled," you don't really provide any useful information, and may put the student and her parent(s) on the defensive. However, when you explain that you want to help the student "learn to handle frustrating situations responsibly," you present an important, and reasonable, goal for the student to work toward and clearly identify what the student needs to do to be successful.

b. Specifying labels for the appropriate and inappropriate behaviors (e.g., "handling frustrating situations responsibly" and "reacting inappropriately," respectively) will help you to use consistent vocabulary when discussing the situation with the student. If you sometimes tell the student that she is "pouting," for example, and other times chastise her for "always needing to get her own way," she may not realize that you are talking about the same problem—her inappropriate reaction to a frustrating situation.

Determine when and how to include the parent(s).

a. It is not necessary to contact the student's parent(s) if the problem has just begun and is not interfering with the student's academic or social progress. However, it might be a good idea to take advantage of any scheduled activities (e.g., conferences, weekly notes home) to let them know of your concern.

b. If the problem has continued for more than a week or two, you should notify the student's parent(s). Share with them any information you have collected about the student's behavior (e.g., anecdotal notes, frequency count), and explain why you are concerned. Focus in particular on how the behavior is hindering the student academically and/or socially (e.g., her actions are causing other students to avoid her).

You might ask if the parent(s) have any insight into the situation and/or whether they have noticed similar behavior at home. Whether or not the parent(s) perceive a problem, explain that you want to help the student "learn to handle frustrating situations responsibly" and invite them to join you for an initial meeting with the student to develop a plan. If the parent(s) are unable or unwilling to participate, let them know that you will keep them informed of the student's progress.

c. Once the parent(s) have been involved in any way, you should give them updates at least once per week while the plan is being implemented.

4. *Prepare for, then conduct, an initial meeting about the situation.*

a. Arrange a meeting to discuss your concerns with the student and anyone else who will be involved in the plan (e.g., the parent[s]). Although the specifics will vary depending upon the age of the student and the severity of the problem, there are some general guidelines to consider when scheduling the meeting.

First, meet at a neutral time (i.e., not immediately after a problem has occurred), when emotions are less likely to hamper communication. In general, a day's notice is appropriate, however a primary age student may worry excessively and/or forget what the meeting is about if it is scheduled more than an hour before it takes place.

Second, make the meeting appropriately private. Third, try to make sure the meeting is scheduled for a time and place that it is not likely to be interrupted (e.g., the counselor's office). Finally, if the parent(s) will be participating, they should be the ones to tell the student about the meeting.

b. Construct a preliminary plan. Decide whether you think you can use one of the MODEL PLANS or if you need to create a customized plan using components from various plans and/or of your own design. Although you will invite and encourage the student to help develop the plan during the initial meeting, having a proposed plan in mind before you meet can alleviate frustration and wasted time if the student is unwilling or unable to participate.

c. Review the information you have collected and think about how you want the student to behave.

Then prepare thorough descriptions of both the inappropriate behavior and the positive behavior/trait on which the student will be working. The more specific you can be and the more concrete examples you have, the easier it will be to clarify (and for the student to understand) your expectations. Be sure to consider the student's behavior in all relevant activities (e.g., independent work periods, teacher directed instruction, unstructured class times, recess and lunch, etc.).

d. Conduct the meeting in an atmosphere of collaboration. The following agenda is one way you might structure the meeting:

• **Share your concerns about the student's behavior.**

Briefly describe the problem behavior and, when appropriate, show the student the chart of how often she engages in it. Then explain why you consider her spoiled behavior to be a problem. You might tell the student that while no one likes it when things do not go their way, it is still not appropriate to react by acting spoiled.

Explain that sometimes she will be able to change things that are not going the way she wants, but that to do so she will need to behave responsibly (e.g., staying calm and talking, not crying or pouting). Remind her that there will be other times when a situation cannot be changed, and that she will need to accept the situation as it is—that is, to handle difficult situations responsibly.

• **Discuss how you can work together to improve the situation.**

Tell the student that you would like to help her "learn to handle frustrating situations responsibly" and describe your preliminary plan. Invite the student to give you input on the various aspects of the plan, and together work out any necessary details (e.g., the signal, the time-out area, etc.). You may have to brainstorm different possibilities if the student is uncomfortable with the initial plan. Incorporating any of the student's suggestions that strengthen the plan is likely to increase her sense of "ownership" in and commitment to it.

• **Make sure the student understands what you mean by appropriate and inappropriate behavior.**

Use the descriptions you have prepared to define and clarify the problem behavior and the positive (desired) behavior as specifically and thoroughly as you can. To ensure that you and the student are in agreement about the expectations, you might present hypothetical scenarios and have her identify whether each is an example of reacting inappropriately or of handling a frustrating situation responsibly. Or you might describe an actual situation that has occurred and ask her to explain how she could have handled that situation responsibly.

- **Conclude the meeting.**

Always end the meeting with words of encouragement. Let the student know that you are confident that she can be successful. Be sure to reinforce her for participating in the meeting.

5. *Give the student regular, ongoing feedback about her behavior.*

It is important to meet with the student periodically to discuss her progress. In most cases, three to five minutes once per week should suffice. *(NOTE:*

PLAN D suggests daily meetings.) During the meetings, review any information that has been collected and discuss whether or not the situation is getting better. As much as possible, focus on the student's improvements, however, also address any new or continuing problems. As the situation improves, the meetings can be faded to once every other week and then to once per month.

6. *Evaluate the situation (and the plan).*

Implement any plan for at least two weeks before deciding whether to change plans; to continue, modify, or fade the plan you are using; or to cease the intervention. Generally, if the student's behavior is clearly improving (based on the objective information that's been collected and/or the subjective perceptions of yourself, the student, and possibly the parent[s]), stick with what you are doing. If the situation has remained the same or worsened, some kind of change will be necessary. Always discuss any changes to the plan with the student first.

STEALING—MAJOR PROBLEM, CULPRIT KNOWN

DESCRIPTION

There is a student in your class who you know has stolen an expensive item or stolen expensive items on more than one occasion.

GOAL

The student will learn that there are consequences for stealing, and the probability of future theft will be reduced.

OVERVIEW OF PLANS

- PLAN A: Addresses issues and procedures that must be taken into account with any major theft, when the culprit is known.
- PLAN B: Includes additional suggestions for repeated incidents of theft, and/or the student who steals to:
  - Impress his peers (e.g., the student gives the stolen items to his friends and/or brags about the theft).
  - Retaliate against adults or peers with whom he is angry.
  - "Get a rush" (i.e., the student experiences anxiety or arousal when stealing).

NOTE:

For more detailed information on dealing with the student who steals, see:

Miller, G.E. & Prinz, R.J. (1991). Designing interventions for stealing. In G. Stoner, M.R. Shinn, & H.M. Walker (Eds.), <u>Interventions for achievement and behavior problems</u> (pp. 593-610). Silver Springs, MD: National Association of School Psychologists.

Alternative Problems

- **Stealing—Major Problem, Culprit Unknown**
- **Stealing—Minor Problem, Culprit Known**
- **Stealing—Minor Problem, Culprit Unknown**

General Considerations

- Look into your school's policy on searches. If you suspect theft, can you look through a student's desk? can you ask a student to empty his pockets? can you ask to look in a student's locker? Follow through on building and district policies as a part of any intervention.

- Remember, everyone is "presumed innocent until proven guilty." Never accuse a student and never implement consequences for stealing unless you have proof. You may ask questions and, within the bounds of building/district policy, find out whether a student possesses something that does not belong to him.

- If you believe a student's problem with theft could stem in any way from academic issues (e.g., the student is insecure about his academic failure and steals to create an image of power in front of his peers), concurrent efforts must be made to ensure his academic success (see **Academic Deficits, Determining**).

- If the student lacks the basic social skills to interact with his peers appropriately, it may be necessary to begin by teaching him these skills. **Social Skills, Lack of** contains information on a variety of published social skills curricula.

- Because theft is not just a behavioral problem, but also an illegal act, the school administration should be involved in all decisions concerning how and when to involve the law enforcement authorities, how to involve the student's parent(s), and how to provide additional security to reduce future incidents of theft.

Model Plans

PLAN A

This is the foundation for PLAN B (and any other type of plan you may choose to implement). This plan involves establishing appropriate consequences, analyzing the student's problem with theft, and reinforcing the student's responsible behavior.

 Establish and implement appropriate consequences for every occurrence of theft.

a. If the student has stolen something of high monetary value, consult with your school administrator about whether the consequence should involve contacting the police or juvenile department for possible legal action.

b. If bringing in outside authorities is not appropriate, implement a school-based consequence such as restitution. With restitution, the student must return or replace the exact item he took (e.g., he stole a tape recorder, so he has to return or replace the tape recorder). An alternative is "restitutional overcorrection." In this case, if the student stole a tape recorder he would not only have to replace the tape recorder, but also spend time cleaning the school to compensate for the inconvenience caused by the theft. This is most effective when established before the fact. "Kenton, if you steal something again, not only will you have to replace the item, but you

will have to spend time repaying the school for the trouble by washing windows."

c. If the student is unable to return or replace the original item, he should have to work at a school-based job to earn the money to pay for the item. This consequence is less effective if the student's parent(s) pay for the item. If they insist, however, encourage them to make the student work at home (over and above any regular chores) to reimburse them for the money they had to pay.

d. When you discuss this situation with the student initially, be sure he understands the likely consequences for any future incidents. Also let him know that since stealing is illegal, future incidents may require involving the police.

 Use reinforcement to encourage appropriate behavior and to demonstrate to the student that you are not holding a grudge for past incidents of stealing.

a. Give the student increased praise, especially when he is behaving responsibly. Part of your goal is to help the student view himself as able and responsible, thus reducing his need to steal. Thus, the more frequently you can "catch" the student behaving in responsible ways, the greater the chance that he will feel like an active and positive contributor to the school.

If the student would be embarrassed by public praise, praise the student privately or even give the student a note. Remember that any time the student is meeting classroom expectations, you can praise him for being responsible.

b. Give the student frequent attention (e.g., say "hello" to him as he enters the classroom, call on him frequently during class activities, and occasionally ask him to assist you with a class job that needs to be done). Providing lots of attention demonstrates to the student that you value him as a person—not just when he has done something responsible.

PLAN B

Occasionally there will be a student who steals repeatedly. If the student's problem appears to be chronic, a coordinated effort to help the student will be required. It will also be helpful to determine why the student steals and develop an intervention that addresses those reason(s).

1. *Involve the building administrator, the school counselor, and/or the school psychologist in all interventions to address a chronic theft problem.*

2. *Establish and implement appropriate consequences for every occurrence of theft (see PLAN A).*

3. *Frequently provide praise and attention when the student is behaving responsibly (see PLAN A).*

4. *Identify any preventative tactics that might be implemented to reduce the student's temptation to steal.*

If a student has a tendency to steal, the more that temptation can be removed, the more likely the student is to be successful. For example, you might analyze the school environment and see if there are rooms that can be locked that have not previously been kept locked. Or perhaps more comprehensive supervision can be provided during those times when stealing incidents have occurred.

5. *Determine whether there are any identifiable patterns to the problem.*

a. Use your anecdotal notes (see SUGGESTED STEPS FOR DEVELOPING AND IMPLEMENTING A PLAN) to attempt to answer the following (and similar) questions:

- What types of things does the student steal?

- Where does the stealing take place?

- Are there obvious reasons why the student steals?

b. You might also consider whether any of the possibilities listed following could describe the student's motivation to steal. Suggestions for intervention and/or sources for more detailed information are provided for each possible motivation identified, as follows:

- The student steals because he is trying to impress his peers (e.g., he gives the stolen items to his friends or brags to other students about the things he has stolen).

  – Help the student win peer recognition by giving him a job or responsibility he will enjoy and that will raise his social status amongst his peers. For example, the student could be asked to participate on a task force to solve a school problem such as vandalism. *(NOTE: APPENDIX 2 provides a list of jobs/responsibilities that may be appropriate.)*

  Do not give the student this privilege until a few days after the consequences for any stealing incidents have been implemented. You do not want the student to think that he is being given a job because he has stolen something.

  – Structure opportunities for the student to demonstrate that he is trusted and trustworthy by giving the student a job that demonstrates, to himself and his peers, that he can be trusted. For example, have the student take an envelope with some money to the office. Structure this activity to ensure success. Write the amount of money on the outside of the envelope to reduce the possibility that the student might think that some money will not be missed. Also let the office personnel know in advance that the student will be coming with the money and have them verify the amount immediately. A successful experience gives you the opportunity to reinforce the student for being responsible and trustworthy.

- The student steals because he is upset and is trying to retaliate against adults or peers with whom he is angry.

  - Identify any school-related events or conditions that may be contributing to the student's frustration or anger. Consider: When does the student get angry? what seems to set the student off? are there certain places the student is more likely to become angry? are there particular academic subjects that make the student angry? does the student get angry when interacting with peers? does being corrected make the student angry? does making academic mistakes make him mad? Make a list and prioritize the possibilities. Try to determine the events, people, places, etc. that make the student most angry.

  - Modify all those events or conditions possible in order to make success easier for the student. For example, if the student tends to become frustrated while waiting to get help from you during independent work periods, establish a system in which he can ask another student for help while he is waiting for you to get to him. If the student gets mad when he makes academic mistakes, evaluate whether the work can be modified so the student experiences less frustration. The goal is to reduce the amount of stress the student is experiencing.

  - Identify any events or conditions that cannot or should not be modified. For example, it would not be reasonable to stop correcting the student's work. However, it would be reasonable to have the student learn different strategies for handling the stress that results when his work *is* being corrected. See **Corrected, Student Gets Upset When** (or other applicable problem) for information on these strategies.

- Teach the student anger management skills to help him deal with the events and conditions that lead to anger, but that cannot be changed. Possibilities include relaxation training; counting backwards from ten; deep, even breathing; and affirming self-talk, among others. *(NOTE: Some people may consider some or all of these procedures to be controversial. Be sure to check with your administrator and/or obtain parental permission before using any of these techniques.)*

  Set up short daily lessons, from five to 15 minutes in length, depending upon the time available. For additional information, review the MODEL PLANS within **Self-Control Issues**, **Tantrumming (K or 1st Grader)**, and/or **Anxiety/Nervousness**.

- React unemotionally to any misbehavior, including stealing, exhibited by this student. If the stealing is in part an angry reaction toward others, getting upset or frustrated by the student's behavior will tend to give him exactly what he wants—for others to feel bad. When the student misbehaves, whether by stealing something or any other misbehavior, simply implement the prearranged consequence in a matter-of-fact manner. Then wait until the student is behaving responsibly again and reinforce him.

- The student steals to "get a rush" (i.e., the student experiences anxiety or arousal when stealing).

  - Talk to the school counselor or school psychologist about the possibility of having someone teach the student self-control strategies through lessons involving some or all of the techniques listed below. For each technique suggested, at least one recommended reference is provided.

Relaxation Training

Goldfried, M.R. (1971). Systematic desensitization as training in self-control. *Journal of Consulting and Clinical Psychology, 37,* 228-234.

Henderson, J. (1983). Follow-up of stealing behavior in 27 youths after a variety of treatment programs. *Journal of Behavior Therapy and Experimental Psychiatry, 14,* 331-337.

Self-Monitoring

Kanfer, F.H. (1970). Self-monitoring: Methodological limitations and clinical applications. *Journal of Consulting and
 Clinical Psychology, 35*, 143-152.

Self-Instruction

Meichenbaum, D.H. & Goodman, J. (1971).
 *Cognitive-behavior modification:
 An integrative approach.* New York:
 Plenum.

Token Reinforcement

Haines, A.T., Jackson, M.S., & Davidson,
 J. (1983). Children's resistance to the
 temptation to steal in real and hypothetical situations: A comparison of
 two treatment programs. *Australian
 Psychologist, 18*, 289-303.

· · · · · · · ·
Suggested Steps for Developing and Implementing a Plan

The following steps are designed to help you develop an appropriate intervention plan and implement it effectively, whether you choose to use one of the MODEL PLANS or create a customized plan of your own. The steps are, however, suggestions—they are not intended to be followed rigidly or in any particular order. Use your professional judgment and the knowledge of your particular situation to make them work for you.

 **Keep an anecdotal log of all incidents
 of stealing or suspected stealing.**

Begin by making anecdotal notes on any confirmed or suspected incidents from the past. For each incident, proven or unproved, describe the known facts and all actions taken by yourself and other school personnel. Thorough and accurate records will be useful for: (1) analyzing the problem; (2) keeping the student, the student's parent(s), and the school administration well-informed; (3) determining if progress is being made; (4) defending yourself from possible complaints by the student or his parent(s); and (5) providing sufficient information to law enforcement authorities, should it become necessary to involve them.

The sample below illustrates typical entries in an anecdotal log.

 **Determine when and how to include
 the parent(s).**

a. With a theft problem, the student's parent(s) should be contacted immediately. Given the seriousness of the infraction, discuss with your building administrator who should make the call to the parent(s). Whoever calls should share any information collected about the behavior (i.e., the anecdotal notes), and invite them to join school staff for an initial meeting with the student to develop a plan.

10/12—Last week, Rex accused Kenton of taking a CD from his gym locker. Kenton denied knowing anything about it. I sent them to the vice principal's office, where it was decided that nothing should be done since there was no proof of who took the CD.

10/14—Yesterday, a student reported to me in confidence that Kenton had been bragging about taking Rex's CD and also bragging about having stolen CDs from the local department store. When I quietly asked Kenton about this, he loudly proclaimed so others could hear, "Prove it. You can't touch me. I know my rights." I informed the vice principal, but without proof we took no further action.

10/17—Today, a tape recorder was missing from the classroom. A student reported to me that Kenton had been showing it around. When I confronted Kenton, he denied it, but seemed to be hiding something. I asked him to take off his coat and he had the tape recorder under the coat. A meeting has been set up for tomorrow with the VP, myself, Kenton, and his father.

In some cases, involving the parent(s) may be difficult. The parents may be suspicious or hostile. Regardless of how the parent(s) react, it is important for you (or whoever calls) to stay calm and explain that there will be consequences for stealing. Also make clear that every effort will be made to help the student be successful. If parental involvement is required, it may be necessary for the administrator to put the student on an in-school suspension until the parent(s) come in for a planning meeting.

b. Once the parent(s) have been involved in any way, you should give them updates regarding any subsequent incidents, and should provide occasional contacts to report responsible behavior being exhibited by the student.

c. If the stolen property belonged to another student, the parent(s) of that student must be informed and involved in decisions about restitution and/or whether the police should be involved.

3. *Prepare for, then conduct, an initial meeting about the situation.*

a. Arrange a meeting to discuss your concerns with the student and anyone else who will be involved in the plan (e.g., the parent[s], the school psychologist, the building administrator). Although the specifics will vary depending upon the age of the student and the severity of the problem, there are some general guidelines to consider when scheduling the meeting.

First, meet at a neutral time (i.e., not immediately after a theft has occurred), when emotions are less likely to hamper communication. In general, a day's notice is appropriate, however a primary age student may worry excessively and/or forget what the meeting is about if it is scheduled more than an hour before it takes place. Second, make the meeting appropriately private. Third, try to make sure the meeting is scheduled for a time and place that is not likely to be interrupted (e.g., the counselor's office). Finally, the parent(s) should be the ones to tell the student about the meeting.

b. Conduct the meeting in an atmosphere of collaboration. The following agenda is one way you might structure the meeting:

• **Share your concern's about the student's behavior and analyze the problem.**

Review your anecdotal notes and identify all those incidents in which the student was actually caught stealing. Then note the incidents in which the student was suspected of stealing (but not proved). Be honest with the student about how confirmed incidents of stealing lead people to be suspicious of him any time something is missing.

If the student denies stealing, try to determine whether he is unaware of what he is doing, defines his behavior differently (e.g., "I was just borrowing it"), or is trying to cover up what he has done.

If the student admits that he has stolen things, try to find out some of the following information:

– What types of things he steals;

– Where he steals;

– Why he steals;

– What he is feeling or thinking right before he steals;

– What he is feeling or thinking right after he steals;

– What happens to the stolen items; and

– What happens if he is caught (what other people usually do).

This information may be very useful in determining the student's motivation for stealing. For example, if the student talks about what a fuss angry adults make when he is caught, it may indicate that he is trying to make people angry and/or gain their attention. If he talks about liking to steal because he can give the stolen things to other students and they will like him, it may indicate that he lacks the social skills to get along with other students in more socially acceptable ways.

• **Discuss how you can work together to improve the situation.**

Let the student know that you hope to help him with a plan to eliminate stealing and to learn to behave more responsibly. Provide an overview of the plan you are considering, being very clear about the consequences that will take place for any future incidents of stealing. Give the student the opportunity to make suggestions about the plan.

• **Conclude the meeting.**

Always end the meeting with words of encouragement. Let the student know that you are confident that he can be successful. Be sure to reinforce him for participating in the meeting. Because you want to encourage the student to behave responsibly, you might end the discussion by letting the student know that you hope he will think about the benefits of not stealing and of learning to take pride in how responsible and trustworthy he can be.

4. Give the student regular, ongoing feedback about his behavior.

a. Give the student feedback about his responsible behavior. If there are no further incidents of stealing, a three to five minute meeting each week will probably suffice. During the meetings, identify specific positive things the student has done during the week. Encourage him to take pride in how responsible and trustworthy he is being.

b. Any time there is an incident of theft, schedule a meeting with the student, the student's par-ent(s), and the building administrator. Review the incident, establish appropriate consequences, and ask the student to identify how he could have avoided stealing.

5. Decide whether to continue, fade, or change intervention plans.

Continually evaluate the effectiveness of the intervention plan being implemented. If stealing incidents continue to occur, consider additional preventative tactics that might reduce the student's temptation to steal. Can a sign-in system be established so the student's whereabouts are constantly known? can the student's movements about the school be limited? If the behavior lasts longer than a month with intervention, consider implementing a coordinated plan involving law enforcement personnel.

STEALING—MAJOR PROBLEM, CULPRIT UNKNOWN

DESCRIPTION

There have been items of significant value (as opposed to pencils, erasers, etc.) stolen from the classroom and it is not clear who is doing the stealing.

GOAL

The stealing will stop and the stolen items will be returned. A secondary goal will be to identify the student(s) doing the stealing.

OVERVIEW OF PLANS

- PLAN A: Establishes basic procedures for helping the students report what they know without having to publicly "squeal."

> **NOTE:**
> This plan may also be appropriate when inexpensive items have been stolen and the plans described in **Stealing—Minor Problem, Culprit Unknown** have been ineffective.

- PLAN B: Includes procedures for reducing the probability of future theft.

Alternative Problems

- Stealing—Major Problem, Culprit Known

- Stealing—Minor Problem, Culprit Known

- Stealing—Minor Problem, Culprit Unknown

· · · · · · · ·
General Considerations

- Remember, everyone is "presumed innocent until proven guilty." Never accuse a student and never implement consequences for stealing unless you have proof. You may ask questions and, within the bounds of building/district policy, find out whether a student possesses something that does not belong to him/her.

- Given the sensitive nature of this issue, review any proposed actions with your building administrator prior to implementation. Investigate your school district policy for searches, and follow through on this policy.

- Because theft is not just a behavioral problem, but also an illegal act, the school administration should also be involved in all decisions concerning how and when to involve the law enforcement authorities, how to involve the student's parent(s), and how to provide additional security to reduce future incidents of theft.

· · · · · · · ·
Model Plans

P L A N   A

If only one valuable item has been stolen and the culprit is not known, the most effective intervention may be to create nonthreatening, anonymous procedures for students to report any knowledge of the situation.

 Arrange for the students to be able to report any information they may have about stealing incidents in a way that does not put them in jeopardy of being ostracized as a "squealer."

a. One way to do so is to make yourself accessible. Let the students know times and ways they can communicate with you in confidence. Make it clear that the source of any information shared with you will be kept confidential. Since some students might prefer to remain anonymous, you might also invite them to leave a note, signed or unsigned, on your desk or in your box in the office. Also let the students know about other adults to whom they can speak confidentially about the problem (e.g., the school counselor, the principal, etc.).

b. A slightly more assertive way to encourage the students to report any knowledge of the problem might involve implementing a procedure such as the following:

"Class, because the missing disk drive has not been returned as I requested, this matter must be investigated further. I have put the following statement up on the chalkboard:

I have reason to suspect that _____ may know something about the missing disk drive.

"When I tell you to, I want each of you to copy this statement on an index card that I will be passing out to you. You do not need to sign your name. Everyone in the class, whether or not they know anything, must write and turn in this statement. If you do not know anyone who might know something about the disk drive, write 'John Doe' in the blank. (NOTE: Write this name on the chalkboard.) I want you to understand that you are not accusing anyone of stealing, and that no one will be punished as a result of having their name written down. However, this will allow the principal and me to conduct a more thorough investigation of what really happened.

"For those of you who think that this is like 'ratting' on a classmates, I urge you to consider this: If you know something and do not report it, the person who stole the disk drive is likely to get away with it and may decide to continue stealing. Your silence could actually be putting this person's future in serious trouble. When we find out who did this, there will be consequences, of course, but we can also help this person learn to stop stealing. So if you know anyone who might know something about this, please write that person's name in the blank.

"Please take the index card I am now passing out. Cover it so that no one can see what you are writing and copy the statement on the board. If you can think of anyone who might know something about this, fill in the name or names. Remember, write 'John Doe' if you have no idea of anyone who might have direct knowledge."

c. Review the cards later, when the students are not present. If one or more names surface, share this information with your building administrator and get advice on how to proceed with

interviewing those student(s). Ask the administrator to join you for the interview(s) and coordinate with the administrator on when and how to involve the parent(s) and/or the juvenile authorities. *(NOTE: If a culprit has been identified, see **Stealing—Major Problem, Culprit Known** for ideas on how to intervene.)*

PLAN B

If there has been more than one major incident of theft, the intervention must include procedures for protecting school property and for teaching the students to protect their property.

 Reduce the probability that student possessions will be stolen in the future.

a. Have a class meeting about the problem, and ask the students to brainstorm strategies for protecting their own possessions.

First establish clear rules for brainstorming that would apply to both you and the students. For example:

1. Any idea is okay (but no obscenity).

2. Do not evaluate any idea during brainstorming (i.e., no approval—"Good idea" or disapproval—"What a stupid idea" or "We couldn't do that" should be expressed).

3. All ideas will be written down and discussed at the conclusion of brainstorming.

Begin the brainstorming by writing every suggestion made. Then lead the class in discussing the viability of each suggestion, and give the students the opportunity to ask questions about any of the ideas. For example, a student might say something like, "Never trust anybody." When discussing this suggestion, you might take the opportunity to talk about the value of trust, being trustworthy, what it feels like to have people you can trust, and what it feels like to have no one you can trust.

b. Encourage each student to set up a personal plan to protect his/her possessions. Consider including the brainstormed information in a

---

Dear Parents:

As you may already know, there has been a serious problem with theft in our classroom. Although efforts are being made to identify the culprit, thus far those steps have been unsuccessful. Therefore, I am asking all the students to be extra careful about protecting their own possessions.

During a class discussion, the students came up with the following ideas for doing so:

- "Don't bring valuable stuff to school."

- "Put things away in your desk or locker."

- "Keep money in your wallet or pocket at all times."

- "Don't bring any games (or electronics) from home."

Please review these suggestions with your child and discuss other things he/she might do to prevent the possibility of theft.

In addition, if your child has reported anything to you that might help us identify who has been involved in these thefts, please call me at school between 3:30 and 4:00, or call Mr. Tichner (the counselor) or Ms. Lennox (the principal) at any time.

Thank you.

memo to parents (see the sample memo following) to involve them in helping the students protect their possessions.

 Reduce the probability that school possessions will be at risk.

(NOTE: You may wish to combine this step with Step 1, however, they are really two separate topics.)

Have the class brainstorm ways to reduce the risk of school and classroom possessions being stolen. You might first have the class identify items that are most likely to be stolen (e.g., computers, calculators, etc.) and the times of greatest risk; then they can think of strategies that might help in these particular situations.

For example, the students may note that it is unwise for the room to be unlocked on Monday mornings while the teacher is in a staff meeting, and suggest that in the future they wait in the hall for the teacher to come and unlock the room as a way to eliminate this unsupervised opportunity to steal something.

· · · · · · · ·

Suggested Steps for Developing and Implementing a Plan

The following steps are designed to help you develop an appropriate intervention plan and implement it effectively, whether you choose to use one of the MODEL PLANS or create a customized plan of your own. The steps are, however, suggestions—they are not intended to be followed rigidly or in any particular order. Use your professional judgment and the knowledge of your particular situation to make them work for you.

 Make sure you have enough information about the situation.

To do so, keep an anecdotal log of all incidents of theft or suspected theft that have occurred in the current school year. For each incident, describe the known facts and all actions taken by yourself and/or other school staff. This information will be useful for: (1) analyzing the problem; (2) accumulating evidence that might help identify who is stealing; (3) defending yourself from possible complaints by the student suspected of theft and/or his/her parent(s); and (4) providing pertinent information to the law enforcement agencies, should that become necessary. The example log following contains typical entries.

4/21—About a week ago, I thought I had $20.00 stolen from my purse. I inadvertently left my purse on my desk during fourth period. I had no evidence of who might of taken it, and there was a small possibility (quite small) that I did not actually have the $20.00 in the purse. Therefore, I decided to do nothing.

4/21—Today, a computer disk drive is missing. There is no doubt that it was here this morning (I would have noticed it missing when I was arranging the computer center) and it was not here this afternoon. I told each of my afternoon classes about the problem, and said that if it was returned by noon on 4/23 there would be no consequences or investigation. I plan to make the same announcement to my morning classes tomorrow.

4/22—Talked to Ms. Lennox (the principal) about the problem and she encouraged me to continue with my plan and hope the disk drive is returned by the deadline. If not, I will meet with her after school tomorrow to map out a course of action. I also made the announcement to each of my morning classes.

4/23—The disk drive has not been returned and no one has come forward with any information. I told each class that Ms. Lennox and I would have to develop a plan after school. Many students seem curious about what we are going to do—so am I.

4/23—No news on the disk drive, but Adelle Villareale reported that she had a Walkman taken from her bag. She thinks it was taken during sixth period in my room, but is not sure. I told her that I was

(continued)

(cont'd)

4/23—No news on the disk drive, but Adelle Villareale reported that she had a Walkman taken from her bag. She thinks it was taken during sixth period in my room, but is not sure. I told her that I was meeting with Ms. Lennox this afternoon and that we would discuss it and talk to her tomorrow.

Notes from meeting with Ms. Lennox: Since this appears to be a serious problem, Ms. Lennox and I decided that we would conduct the "John Doe" card procedures to get any information possible. In addition, I will brainstorm with all of my classes on protecting personal and school possessions. As of now, we will not send a parent memo.

---

 2. *Determine when and how to include the parent(s).*

If you didn't do so initially, and the problem continues, be sure to make all the parents aware that their children's possessions are (or continue to be) at risk of being stolen. An updated memo or a notice in a classroom newsletter is probably sufficient.

 3. *Keep the students informed about the problem.*

a. Schedule a class meeting to discuss the situation with all the students. Meet at a neutral time (i.e., not immediately after a theft has occurred) when emotions are less likely to hamper communication. "Class, tomorrow we are going to have a class discussion about the problem we have regarding the computer disk drive being stolen."

b. Construct a preliminary plan. Decide whether you think you can use one of the MODEL PLANS or if you need to create a customized plan using components from the various plans and/or of your own design. Although you will invite and encourage the students to help develop the plan during the class meeting, having a proposed plan in mind before you meet can alleviate frustration and wasted time if the students are unwilling or unable to generate ideas themselves.

c. Conduct the class meeting in an atmosphere of collaboration. Remember that most of the students are not involved and should not be made to feel bad or guilty about a problem they did not create.

d. Give the students ongoing feedback about the problem. If no additional incidents of theft occur, regular follow-up meetings are not necessary, but occasionally mention to the class that it is a pleasure to teach a trustworthy group of students. However, have a follow-up meeting after any subsequent theft. Additional training should then be provided to the students on how to be vigilant of their own possessions, and additional efforts should be made to insure that school property is protected.

 4. *Evaluate the situation (and the plan).*

If, after intervention, there continue to be incidents of theft, ask for the assistance of a school administrator in deciding when and how to involve the police. If police involvement is not deemed prudent at this time, ask the administrator to help you implement another plan.

STEALING—MINOR PROBLEM, CULPRIT KNOWN

DESCRIPTION

There is a student in your class who you know has taken things that do not belong to her. The stolen items have been relatively inexpensive, and there have been no more than five incidents.

GOAL

The student will stop stealing and will learn that there are consequences for such behavior.

OVERVIEW OF PLANS

- PLAN A: For a situation in which there have been no more than five incidents.

- PLAN B: For a student who steals because she needs the items (e.g., a student who steals food because she is underfed), or *thinks* she needs the items.

- PLAN C: For a student who steals to gain adult attention.

NOTE:

*If more than five incidents of theft have occurred, the plans in **Stealing—Major Problem, Culprit Known** may be more appropriate to address the situation.*

Alternative Problems

- Stealing—Major Problem, Culprit Known

- Stealing—Major Problem, Culprit Unknown

- Stealing—Minor Problem, Culprit Unknown

....
General Considerations

- If the student's cultural background could be a factor in the behavior (e.g., some cultures operate within an "everything belongs to everyone" approach to life), do not intervene until you have checked the appropriateness of any intervention plan and its goals with the student's parent(s). You want to implement an intervention that teaches the student not to take others' things, but that does not belittle her family's beliefs.

- Look into your school's policy on searches. If you suspect theft, can you look through a student's desk? can you ask a student to empty her pockets? can you ask to look in a student's locker? Follow through on building and district policies as a part of any intervention.

- Remember, everyone is "presumed innocent until proven guilty." Never accuse a student and never implement consequences for stealing unless you have proof. You may ask questions and, within the bounds of building/district policy, find out whether a student possesses something that does not belong to her.

- If you believe a student's problem with theft could stem in any way from academic issues (e.g., the student is insecure about her academic failure

and steals to create an image of power in front of her peers), concurrent efforts must be made to ensure her academic success (see **Academic Deficits, Determining**).

- If the student lacks the basic social skills to interact with her peers appropriately, it may be necessary to begin by teaching her those skills. **Social Skills, Lack of** contains information on a variety of published social skills curricula.

- Because theft is not just a behavioral problem, but also an illegal act, the school administration should be involved in all decisions concerning how and when to involve the law enforcement authorities, how to involve the student's parent(s), and how to provide additional security to reduce future incidents of theft.

- For more detailed information on the topic of stealing, see:

  Miller, G.E. & Prinz, R.J. (1991). Designing interventions for stealing. In G. Stoner, M.R. Shinn, & H.M. Walker (Eds.), *Interventions for achievement and behavior problems* (pp. 593-610). Silver Springs, MD: National Association of School Psychologists.

....
Model Plans

PLAN A

It is not always necessary, or even beneficial, to use an involved plan. If there have been less than five incidents, the following actions, along with making the student and her parent(s) aware of your concerns, may resolve the situation.

 Establish and implement appropriate consequences for each incident of theft.

Choose one or more of the following consequences:

- **Restitution**

  If the student steals a pencil, she must replace that pencil. This technique is most logical as an after-the-fact consequence. "Danielle, because you took pencils from Renata and Jevon, you will need to bring two

brand new pencils tomorrow and give one to Jevon and one to Renata."

- **Restitutional Overcorrection**

  This technique is best used for occasions when restitution alone is not enough—when something additional is necessary to compensate the victim for the trouble the stealing caused. For example, if the student stole another student's notebook, she might have to both replace the notebook and its contents (the one that was stolen if it is available, or with a new notebook) *and* supply new pens and pencils—even though these items were not taken. This consequence is best used before the theft occurs. "Danielle, I don't think you will, but if you choose to steal something again you need to know that next time you will not only have to replace the stolen item, but will have to do even more. For example, ..."

If the student is unable to replace the original item and cannot afford a new one, the student should be made to work within the school to "pay" for the stolen item. This will be more effective if the student's parent(s) do not pay for the item. If they do pay, encourage them to make the student work at home (over and above any regular chores) to reimburse them.

- **Apology**

The student can be required to apologize (in person, in writing, or both) to the owner of the item that was stolen. If school property was stolen, the apology should be directed to the principal of the school.

- **Calling Parent(s) at Home or at Work**

For some students, having to call their own parents is more of a consequence than having the principal of the school call their parents.

When discussing the precipitating incident with the student, implement one or more of these consequences (e.g., restitution and calling her parent[s]). In addition, be sure the student knows the consequences of any future incidents. If appropriate, you can tell the student that since stealing is illegal, future incidents may require involving the police.

2. *Give the student praise and attention for responsible behavior.*

a. Praise the student frequently for actions which can be labeled responsible: "Danielle, it is so responsible of you to volunteer to make the chart for your group."; "Offering to help with the Cultural Fair is a very generous and responsible thing to do."; "Danielle, you have gotten every assignment turned in on time—another example of what a responsible student you are." The goal is to foster the student's belief that she is a responsible person, which may reduce her desire to steal.

When giving praise, avoid direct references to stealing. It is not a compliment to say, "Danielle, you have not stolen anything for three weeks." This only serves to remind the student that the teacher thinks of her as a thief. The focus of the positive attention should remain on specific, positive acts of responsible behavior.

b. Give the student frequent attention (e.g., say "hello" to her as she enters the classroom, call on her frequently during class activities, and occasionally ask her to assist you with a class job that needs to be done) and praise her for other positive behaviors she exhibits. For example, you might comment about the quality of the student's report or tell the student how well she behaved during a presentation by a guest speaker. This demonstrates to the student that you notice many positive things she does, not just the fact that she is refraining from stealing.

PLAN B

Sometimes a student steals things because she either needs or thinks she needs the items she is stealing. In such a case, the intervention must help the student learn both how to discriminate between what she wants and what she needs, and how to legally obtain the things she truly does need.

1. *Establish appropriate consequences for any current and future incidents of stealing, and provide frequent praise and attention to the student for responsible behavior (see PLAN A).*

2. *Analyze the types of things the student steals to determine what need the student is trying to fulfill, and establish a plan to meet that need without stealing.*

a. First determine if the student is stealing items she truly needs. For example, if the student steals food because her family cannot or is unwilling to provide breakfast and/or lunch for the student, you might look into a free breakfast and/or lunch program. If the student steals school items (e.g., pencils, paper, etc.), arrange for the student to have a before- or after-school job to earn these items.

Help the student brainstorm ideas about how she can legally obtain the things she needs. In addition, make sure the student understands that if she ever needs something for school, she can come to you, and you will work with her and her parent(s) to try to arrange some way for her to earn what she needs.

Finally, remind the student of the consequences of stealing (perhaps even referring to prison as the consequence for continued stealing) and help her see that stealing is not a viable way to obtain what one wants or needs.

b. Sometimes a student only thinks she needs the items she is taking. For example, it is not uncommon for a young child to think she needs a doll belonging to another student because she does not have one, and perhaps her family cannot afford one. In this case, use daily lessons to help the student learn the difference between what she *needs* and what she *wants*. For some students, a single lesson lasting a few minutes will suffice. Others may need short (three to five minute) lessons held twice per week for a few weeks to really understand the difference between wants and needs.

c. During the lessons, talk about items like the following and help the student analyze whether each is a want or a need: food for dinner, a video game, a special brand of sneakers for gym class (name a brand popular with the students), a certain toy, pencils for school, a place to sleep at night, etc. Try to help the student to understand that we can get by without things we want—you may even use examples from your own life (e.g., driving an economical compact car rather than a sports car).

(NOTE: Be sensitive to the possibility that some students may be in situations in which their families are going without a "need" item [e.g., homeless people with nowhere to sleep]. Avoid implying that there is something wrong with struggling to obtain a "need" item.)

d. The discrimination between wants and needs may be a useful lesson for all the students in the class. If you do conduct a class-wide lesson, be careful not to hurt the feelings of the student who did steal. Wait until there have been no stealing incidents for at least three to four weeks. This will reduce the probability of the student feeling like the focus of the discussion. You may even want to ask the student's permission to have this sort of class-wide lesson. "Danielle, about a month ago you and I spent some time learning about the difference between wanting things and needing things. I think maybe other students in our class confuse wants and needs as well. Would you be comfortable if I did some lessons with the whole class on this? I would not put you on the spot, but if you would like to help us generate some of the examples, I know that you really understand this concept. What do you think?"

3. **Use reinforcement to encourage appropriate behavior.**

a. Provide frequent praise when the student is behaving responsibly (see PLAN A).

b. Praise the student for participating with you in discussions/lessons on the issue of wants versus needs. "Danielle, you should be very proud of how hard you work and how quickly you are learning to tell the difference between wants and needs."

PLAN C

Some students are very skilled at gaining attention through their negative behavior. If you interact with this student frequently because she misbehaves (not just stealing, but other misbehaviors as well), it is possible that she is trying to gain adult attention through the misbehavior. Whether or not the student overtly seems to like the attention, you should make sure that she receives more frequent and more satisfying attention when she behaves appropriately than when she steals or engages in other misbehaviors.

 Establish appropriate consequences for any current and future incidents of stealing, and provide frequent praise and attention to the student for responsible behavior (see PLAN A).

With this type of student, it is important that when responding to stealing incidents, you are as un-

emotional and brief as possible. The goal is to show the student that the type of adult attention received for stealing is relatively boring. Throughout implementation of the consequences for stealing, use a very neutral voice that conveys no emotion. Try to sound as if you are on automatic pilot, and need to go through a consistent set of actions to implement the consequence. Keep the interaction short—avoid nagging and discussing.

2. Use reinforcement to encourage appropriate behavior.

a. Frequent praise and attention is the core of this plan. The student must see that she receives more frequent and more satisfying attention when she behaves appropriately than when she steals or engages in other misbehavior. Thus, whenever the student is not stealing (or otherwise misbehaving), make an effort to praise and spend time with her. "Danielle, you are being so responsible. Would you mind helping me take these things off the bulletin board?"

b. You may also wish to use intermittent rewards to acknowledge the student's success. Occasional, and unexpected, rewards can motivate the student to demonstrate responsible behavior more often. The idea is to provide a reward when the student has had a particularly good period of being responsible. Any activity the student could do with you will probably be effective (e.g., sitting with you at an assembly, eating lunch in the classroom with you, or helping you with a task while the others are at recess). *(NOTE: A list of additional reinforcement ideas can be found in APPENDIX 1.)*

Use intermittent rewards more frequently at the beginning of the intervention to encourage the student, and then less often as her behavior improves.

3. Ensure a 3-1 ratio of positive to negative attention.

a. When attention is a motivating force for the student, you want to be sure that you are giving the student *three times as much* positive as

negative attention. One way to do this is to monitor your interactions with the student at least one day per week. To do so, keep a card on a clipboard or in your pocket and record each interaction you have with the student as either positive or negative by writing a "+" or a "-", respectively, on the card.

To determine whether an interaction is positive or negative, ask yourself whether the interaction was related to stealing (or any other misbehavior). Any interaction that stems from inappropriate behavior is negative, and all interactions that occur while the student is meeting classroom expectations are positive. Thus, talking to the student about an item she has stolen is a negative interaction, but praising the student for completing her work is positive. Greeting the student as she enters the room or asking her if she has any questions during independent work are also considered positive interactions. *(NOTE: Ignoring some aspect of the student's inappropriate behavior [e.g., her blurting out without raising her hand] is not recorded at all, because it is not an interaction.)*

b. If you find that you are not giving the student three times as much positive as negative attention, try to increase the number of positive interactions you have with the student. Sometimes prompts can help. For example, you might decide that each time the student enters the classroom you will say "hello" to her, each time you see her handing in an assignment you will praise her diligence, or that whenever a student uses the drinking fountain you will check the target student and, as soon as possible, praise some aspect of her behavior. You can also increase the ratio of positive to negative attention by ignoring more of the student's inappropriate behavior.

. . . .
Suggested Steps for Developing and Implementing a Plan

The following steps are designed to help you develop an appropriate intervention plan and implement it effectively, whether you choose to use one of the MODEL PLANS or create a customized plan. The steps are, however, suggestions—they are not intended to be followed rigidly or in any particular order. Use your professional judgment and the knowledge of your particular situation to make them work for you.

1. Make sure you have enough information about the situation.

a. Keep an anecdotal log of all incidents of stealing or suspected stealing. Begin the records with

any confirmed or suspected stealing incidents from the past. For each incident (proven or unproven), describe the known facts and all actions taken by yourself and the other school

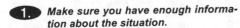

staff. This information will be useful for: (1) analyzing the problem; (2) keeping the student, her parent(s), and the school administration well-informed; (3) determining if progress is being made; and (4) defending yourself from possible complaints by the student accused of stealing or her parent(s). In addition, the information could be critical should it become necessary to involve law enforcement authorities at a later date. The sample log following contains typical entries.

> 9/12—While I was teaching a reading group, I saw Danielle take some of the rock samples from the science table. I asked her to come to my desk, and asked if she took something that was not hers. She denied it, so I asked her to empty her pockets. The rocks were there. I told her that she needed to write me a note describing the incident.
>
> 9/12—In the afternoon, Clevon accused Danielle of taking his pencil sharpener from his desk. During recess I privately asked Danielle if she knew anything about the pencil sharpener, and she said she did not. I asked her to empty her pockets and her desk, and did not find the pencil sharpener. I thanked her for her cooperation and sent her out to recess. I told Clevon that there was no proof that Danielle took the pencil sharpener and that I would continue to look. (I must say that I do still suspect that she took it.)

b. Continuing to collect this type of information while you implement a plan will also help you monitor whether the situation is getting worse, staying the same, or getting better.

2. *Identify a focus for the intervention and labels for referring to the appropriate and inappropriate behaviors.*

(NOTE: When a student is young and the value of the stolen items is small, there can be a tendency to avoid using the word "stealing"—it sounds so harsh. However, any time the student is in possession of items that do not belong to her, the situation should be referred to as "stealing" so the student learns the seriousness of her actions.)

a. To be effective, the intervention must address more than just reducing the student's stealing—there must be a concurrent emphasis on increasing some positive behavior or trait (e.g., taking pride in being responsible). Having a specific positive behavior in mind will make it

easier for you to "catch" and reinforce the student for acting appropriately, and the positive focus will frame the situation more productively.

b. Specifying labels for the appropriate and inappropriate behaviors (e.g., "taking pride in being responsible" and "stealing," respectively) will help you to use consistent vocabulary when discussing the situation with the student. If you sometimes refer to the inappropriate behavior as "borrowing things without permission," for example, and other times tell the student not to "take things that do not belong to her," she may not realize that you are really talking about stealing.

3. *Determine when and how to include the parent(s).*

a. Contact the student's parent(s) as soon as you have reasonable proof that the student is stealing, and keep them informed throughout the intervention. If the problem has just begun, simply keeping the parent(s) informed may be sufficient. However, if there have been more than three incidents of theft, have the parent(s) come in for a conference with you and the school administrator and/or counselor to design an intervention plan (see MODEL PLANS A-C for ideas).

If the student is also stealing at home or in the community, explore the possibility of obtaining help for the parent(s) in the form of parental training in communication and discipline skills.

b. In some cases, involving the parent(s) may be difficult, as they may be suspicious or hostile. Regardless of how the parent(s) react, stay calm and explain that there will be consequences for stealing, but that every effort will also be made to help the student be successful.

c. Once the parent(s) have been involved in any way, you should give them updates at least once per week while the plan is being implemented.

4. *Prepare for, then conduct, an initial meeting about the situation.*

a. Arrange a meeting to discuss your concerns with the student and anyone else who will be involved in the plan (e.g., the parent[s], the school administrator, the school counselor). Although the specifics will vary depending upon the age of the student and the severity of the problem, there are some general guidelines to consider when scheduling the meeting.

First, meet at a neutral time (i.e., not immediately after a theft has occurred), when emotions are less likely to hamper communication. In general, a day's notice is appropriate, however a primary age student may worry excessively and/or forget what the meeting is about if it is scheduled more than an hour before it takes place.

Second, make the meeting appropriately private. Third, try to make sure the meeting is scheduled for a time and place that is not likely to be interrupted (e.g., the counselor's office). Finally, if the parent(s) will be participating, they should be the ones to tell the student about the meeting.

b. Construct a preliminary plan. Decide whether you think you can use one of the MODEL PLANS, or if you need to create a customized plan using components from the various plans and/or of your own design. Although you will invite and encourage the student to help develop the plan during the initial meeting, having a proposed plan in mind before you meet can alleviate frustration and wasted time if the student is unwilling or unable to participate.

c. Conduct the meeting in an atmosphere of collaboration. The following agenda is one way you might structure the meeting:

- **Share your concerns about the student's behavior.**

  Briefly share your anecdotal notes about the problem behavior. When explaining why you consider the theft to be a problem, you might tell the student that not only is stealing illegal, but it is also a disrespectful way to treat the owners of the things she takes.

- **Discuss how you can work together to improve the situation.**

  Tell the student that you would like to help her learn to "take pride in being responsible" and describe your preliminary plan. Invite the student to give you input on the various aspects of the plan, and together work out any necessary details (e.g., what will happen if the student steals something again).

You may have to brainstorm different possibilities if the student is uncomfortable with the initial plan—although the final say on the nature of the consequences for future incidents of theft should be up to you, not the student. However, incorporating any of the student's suggestions that strengthen the plan is likely to increase her sense of "ownership" in and commitment to it.

- **Conclude the meeting.**

  Always end the meeting with words of encouragement. Let the student know that you are confident that she can be successful. Be sure to reinforce her for participating in the meeting.

5. *Give the student regular, ongoing feedback about her behavior.*

It is important to meet with the student periodically to discuss her progress. In most cases, three to five minutes once per week should suffice. Review any information that has been collected (i.e., anecdotal notes) and discuss whether or not the situation is improving. If there have been no stealing incidents, praise the student for demonstrating how she can take pride in being responsible.

If there have been incidents of theft, encourage the student to talk about what she can do next week to demonstrate responsible behavior. As much as possible, focus on the student's improvements, however, also address any new or continuing problems. As the situation improves, the meetings can be faded to once every other week and then to once per month.

6. *Evaluate the situation (and the plan).*

Generally, if the student's behavior is clearly improving, stick with what you are doing. However, if the student continues stealing and the total number of incidents reaches five, consider this to be a major problem and begin working collaboratively with your building administrator, school counselor, and/or school psychologist to design an additional intervention (see **Stealing—Major Problem, Culprit Known** for ideas).

STEALING—MINOR PROBLEM, CULPRIT UNKNOWN

DESCRIPTION

Inexpensive items have been stolen in the classroom and it is not clear who is doing the stealing.

GOAL

The stealing will cease and all the students will learn the benefits of respecting the possessions of others. If the stealing continues, a secondary goal will be to identify the student(s) doing the stealing.

OVERVIEW OF PLANS

- PLAN A: For a situation in which the stolen items have been relatively inexpensive (e.g., pencils, lunches, trinkets), and there have been only a couple of incidents.

- PLAN B: For a situation in which the stolen items have been relatively inexpensive, but there have been three or more incidents within a period of a few weeks.

NOTE:

These two plans are most appropriate for a problem at the primary level. For information on stealing at an intermediate or middle/junior high school level, see Stealing—Major Problem, Culprit Unknown.

Alternative Problems

- **Stealing—Major Problem, Culprit Known**

- **Stealing—Major Problem, Culprit Unknown**

- **Stealing—Minor Problem, Culprit Known**

· · · · · · · ·
General Considerations

- Because theft is not just a behavioral problem, but is also an illegal act, the school administration should be involved in all decisions concerning how and when to involve the law enforcement authorities, how to involve parent(s), and how to provide additional security to reduce future incidents of theft.

- Remember, everyone is "presumed innocent until proven guilty." Never accuse a student and never implement consequences for stealing unless you have proof. You may ask questions and, within the bounds of building/district policies, find out whether a student possesses something that does not belong to him/her.

- Look into your school's policy on searches. If you suspect theft, can you look through a student's desk? can you ask a student to empty his/her pockets? can you ask to look in a student's locker? Follow through on building and district policies as a part of any intervention.

- If a student's cultural background could be a factor in the behavior (e.g., some cultures operate within an "everything belongs to everyone" approach to life), do not intervene until you have checked out the appropriateness of any intervention plan and its goals with the student's parent(s). You want to implement an intervention that teaches the student not to take others' things, but that does not belittle his/her family's beliefs.

· · · · · · · ·
Model Plans

PLAN A

It is not always necessary, or even beneficial, to use an involved plan. When there have been no more than a couple of incidents of theft, an effective intervention may be as simple as teaching the class the importance of respecting the property of others.

1. **Respond promptly to all incidents of theft.**

a. Tell the class what is missing and ask their assistance in "keeping an eye out" for the item (or items).

b. Let the students know that, although there is no proof that the item was stolen, if it was taken by someone, it is stealing—not borrowing, not hiding, not a joke or a game. Don't hesitate to refer to the problem as stealing. The students need to know the seriousness of the behavior—even though only inexpensive items are involved.

c. Invite the students to talk to you privately if they know anything about the missing item. Let them know when and how they can approach you, giving them details about how they could contact you without the other students being aware of the discussion. For example, should they come before school, after school, or during lunch? should they leave you a note? if so, where?

d. Because the main goal is for the students to learn to respect the property of their classmates, the consequences for the theft of a small item do not need to be severe. However, 'the item does need to be replaced. Let the students know that if someone came to you and said that he/she took the item, you would help him/her to figure out a way to replace the item, and the student's privacy would be respected (i.e., the rest of the class wouldn't need to know anything about who stole the item).

You should also let the class know that stealing will be viewed much more seriously as they get older; as an illegal act, stealing is punishable by a prison sentence.

e. When speaking to the entire class, also invite the student who took the item (if in fact it was taken) to anonymously return it if he/she is uncomfortable coming in and talking to you directly. Give specific information about how the student could do this.

Conduct a discussion with the class on the importance of trust and respecting the property of others.

(NOTE: This discussion can be conducted in conjunction with the discussions described in Step 1, or separately.)

a. Begin the discussion by encouraging the students to talk about what it feels like to be able to trust someone and how it feels not to be able to trust someone. Let them know that if repeated problems with missing items occur, it will be difficult to trust their classmates.

b. Then shift the focus of the discussion to "respecting the property of others." Have the class generate positive and negative examples of respecting the property of others (e.g., finding a pencil on the floor, then determining the owner and returning it; and finding a pencil on the floor and taking it, respectively). The goal is to help the students conclude that taking something that belongs to someone else is an example of not respecting the property of others. Emphasize that you will be looking for examples of the students respecting the property of others.

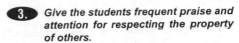 **Give the students frequent praise and attention for respecting the property of others.**

a. Throughout each day, if there are no incidents of stealing, give specific feedback to the group as a whole. "Class, I want you to know how proud I am that we are all learning to respect the property of others. We have not had any problems today with missing items. It is very nice to be with a group of people we can all trust."

b. Praise individual students that you see respecting others' property. Since you cannot see the absence of stealing, you will have to look for overt examples of other forms of respecting the property of others: "Ethan, thanks for closing the door rather than slamming it. That is an example of respecting the property of others—the school's property."; "Claire, I can tell that you respect the property of others by the way you were so careful to return that book you borrowed."

When praising individual students, do not make reference to stealing or the absence of stealing. Since you do not know who is responsible for the stealing that has occurred in the past, praising an individual student for not stealing could lead that student to fear that you think he/she may have been stealing in the past.

PLAN B

When there have been three or more stealing incidents, it may be necessary to use a more comprehensive and structured approach to teaching the students to "respect the property of others."

 Respond promptly to all incidents of theft (see PLAN A).

Be sure the students realize that if they know something about the theft and are not reporting it, they also are not respecting the property of others. Remind them that if they know something they must report it (continue to emphasize anonymity). Also emphasize that by not reporting whatever they know, they may even be hurting the student who is doing the stealing, because although there will be consequences for the stealing there will also be help provided to teach the student not to steal.

 Develop a sense of affiliation and class pride.

a. The purpose of cultivating class pride is to increase the degree to which all the students are proud to belong to the class, thus increasing the chance that each individual student might feel that stealing is taking something away from a place and people he/she cares about and where he/she feels a sense of belonging.

b. Schedule a discussion on the importance of creating a sense of group pride. Have the students identify groups or teams of which they have been extremely proud to be a part. Then encourage them to talk about how it feels to be part of such a group or team. Solicit ideas on ways that a sense of group pride might be established in the classroom. For example:

- Developing a class name and mascot/logo (e.g., The Room 9 Lions).

- Completing a service project together, such as:

  – Reading to students in a younger class.

– Raking leaves for residents of a nearby retirement community.

– Holding a canned food drive for a homeless shelter.

– Raising money to donate to an organization which helps preserve an endangered species.

• Inviting community members or school board members to observe the class in action.

• Setting class goals and working together to achieve those goals.

• Engaging in a daily self-evaluation (e.g., "Rate from 1 to 5 how well we worked together today.").

• Structuring opportunities for the entire class to reinforce student performance or behavior (e.g., everyone in the class writes "congratulations" notes to a classmate who has met an important goal).

• Making posters on "class pride" to decorate the classroom.

3. **Use reinforcement to encourage appropriate behavior.**

a. Give the students increased praise and attention for respecting the property of others (see PLAN A).

b. In addition, make a special point of commenting on any behaviors that contribute to a sense of class pride. "Troy and Bob both picked up some trash on the way in from recess—and they weren't even asked. This is a great example of what fabulous, responsible people we have here in Room 9, and a great example of respecting the property of others—because this school belongs to all of us."

4. **(OPTIONAL, FOR K-3 CLASSES)** **Use a group reinforcement system to monitor how class members are respecting the property of others.**

a. With the class, create a list of reinforcers that they can earn as a whole group. Although you might want to have some suggestions in mind, the system will be more effective if the students identify most of the items or activities themselves. *(NOTE: A list of reinforcement ideas can be found in APPENDIX 1.)*

b. Assign "prices" (in points) for each of the rewards on the list and have the class vote on the reward they would like to earn first.

c. Place items that might possibly be stolen in several prominent locations in the classroom. For example, a small hand-held pencil sharpener might be placed in the back of the room—Station 1; a small stuffed animal might be placed on the window sill—Station 2; and a small toy dinosaur might be placed near the sink—Station 3. At three or four random times throughout the day, have the students check each of the stations.

If the items are there, the group receives a point for each station that has not been tampered with. If any item is missing, issue a warning that if the item is not back within a half hour, the entire class will receive a fine. Initially the fine should be five points, but as the class accumulates points and the system is functioning successfully, raise the cost of the fine to ten and eventually 20 points. The system could be summarized with a visual representation on a bulletin board or poster, so the students can watch the points accumulating.

d. The station checks are best scheduled immediately before those times that the students have the greatest opportunity to take one of the items. For example, if the students move about the room a lot before and after recess, schedule one check just before the students are excused for recess. This gives you a chance to review in a positive and reinforcing way the importance of respecting the property of others. "Class, let's do our check to see if we have been respecting the school's property. Kristen, please check Station 1; Omar, Station 2; and Miguel, Station 3. Great, all of the items are in place; that is three more points toward our goal of a class party to celebrate. You should all be very proud of how well you are respecting the property of others."

(NOTE: If items other than those in the stations are reported missing, give the class points for the items in the stations and implement a point fine for each of the other missing items.)

e. When the class has accumulated enough points to earn the reward they have chosen, they "spend" the points necessary for the reward, identify another reward to earn, and the system begins again with zero points.

f. On the other hand, if this plan does not work quickly (e.g., after one week, items are still frequently missing) it may be that you have a student (or students) who views the station system as a challenge and/or an opportunity to steal and enjoy the reactions of classmates when the stations are checked. When you know who that student is, not only should the class not receive the point for each station not tampered with, but the culprit should receive an individual consequence (see **Stealing—Minor Problem, Culprit Known** *for possible consequences).*

. . . .

Suggested Steps for Developing and Implementing a Plan

The following steps are designed to help you develop an appropriate intervention plan and implement it effectively, whether you choose to use one of the MODEL PLANS or create a customized plan of your own. The steps are, however, suggestions—they are not intended to be followed rigidly or in any particular order. Use your professional judgment and the knowledge of your particular situation to make them work for you.

1. *Make sure you have enough information about the situation.*

a. Keep an anecdotal log of all incidents of stealing or suspected stealing. Begin the records with any confirmed or suspected stealing incidents from the past. For each incident (proven or unproved), describe the known facts and all actions taken by yourself and the other school staff. This information will be useful for: (1) analyzing the problem; (2) keeping the students, the parents, and the school administration well-informed; (3) determining if progress is being made; and (4) defending yourself from possible complaints by students or their parents. In addition, the information could be critical should it become necessary to involve law enforcement authorities at a later date. The sample log following contains typical entries.

1/30—In the past week we have had reports of missing scissors, crayons, and I am even missing a stapler. We are not sure of what things have simply been misplaced, but it is obvious there is a problem.

1/30—Breana reported that her file box for her note cards had been taken from her desk. She had the box yesterday. I had all the students search their desks to see if it had just been misplaced, and nothing turned up. I asked Breana to check at home tonight.

1/31—Breana did not find her box at home. This seems to be another item stolen.

2/1—Lunch money was reported stolen by Ira. I asked the class if anyone knew anything. Later his mother came to school with the money—she had forgotten to give it to him. Later (with Ira's permission), I will use this as an example of needing to be careful about saying something is stolen without proof.

b. Continuing to collect this type of information while you implement a plan will also help you monitor whether the situation is getting worse, staying the same, or getting better.

2. *Determine when and how to include the parent(s).*

When the culprit is not known, you need to be careful about how and when to involve the students' parents. If the problem has just begun and does not involve expensive or personal items, you can probably work on the problem in class without involving the parents directly. However, if there have been more than four or five different incidents of theft, and/or the stolen items have been personal possessions of the students, it is probably wise to inform all your students' parents about the problem.

You may want to ask the parents to talk to their children about the importance of respecting the property of others, as well as keeping their own possessions safe. Following is a sample memo that could be sent home to parents.

Dear Parents:

Recently we have had a problem with "missing items" in our class. It seems that there may be a problem with stealing. We are having class discussions on the importance of respecting the property of others. It might be a good time for you to discuss these values with your child at home, as well. I think if we emphasize honesty and respect for others' property we can solve this problem in the early stages.

Thanks for your help. I will keep you informed about what happens.

3. Give the class regular ongoing feedback about the situation.

a. If any more items turn up missing, let the students know that the problem still exists and schedule a follow-up meeting. Do not imply that you are disappointed in the class as a whole. After all, most of the students are not involved in the theft and should not be made to feel guilty because of the behavior of one or two students. "Class, I am sorry to report that we still have a problem of one or more students who are not respecting the property of others. We have had a pair of gloves and two lunches turn up missing. I know that most of you are very respectful of others' property, but since we still have this problem, we need to have another discussion about what we are going to do. This afternoon at 2:00 we will have another class meeting."

b. Unless more items are stolen, follow-up meetings are probably not necessary. However, periodically you should let the class know that they should be proud of how well they are all respecting the property of others.

4. Evaluate the situation (and the plan).

Implement any plan for at least two weeks before deciding whether to change plans; to continue, modify, or fade the plan you are using; or to cease the intervention. If no further incidents of theft occur, no further action is necessary. If there continue to be thefts, ask for the assistance of your school administrator in implementing a more stringent intervention plan.

SUICIDE THREATS

DESCRIPTION

You heard a student threaten (or heard about a student who has threatened) to commit suicide.

All suicide threats by students should be taken seriously and responded to immediately, however, any formal intervention should be undertaken by an appropriately qualified professional (e.g., a school psychologist or counselor). Therefore, there are no MODEL PLANS included for this problem. The purpose of the following information is to suggest procedures and basic considerations for appropriately and responsibly responding to an actual (or rumored) suicide threat.

Alternative Problems

- **Depression**
- **Self-Injurous Behavior**

. . . .
General Information

- Immediately inform a building administrator and/or school psychologist or counselor of any suicide threat. Given the potential consequences of this kind of comment, your actions should be guided by someone with training and experience in suicide ideation. Your objective is to make sure that the student receives appropriate support and counseling, and to follow district policies and state laws regarding suicide threats.

- As a teacher, you are not bound legally or ethically to keep a suicide threat secret. If a student asks you not to say anything about a suicide threat he made (or about a suicide threat he overheard), explain honestly that you cannot, and why you cannot. "Alonzo, I care too much about you to let this just be between you and me. I am not a counselor, and I don't know what to do to help you with what you just told me. I have to tell the school counselor about this incident. In fact, would you be willing to go with me right now to talk to Mr. Abrams? I also want you to know that either he or I will have to contact your parents."

  (NOTE: If you have any reason to suspect that the student's suicide threat is a result of abuse or that the student will be punished at home for making such a threat, this procedure may not be wise. In this case, discuss this situation with your administrator or the school counselor.)

- Keep a record of any suicide threats you hear (or hear of) and all subsequent action that was taken, including parental contact. Having notes on all actual (and rumored) suicide threats is very important. Information about what the student actually said and the circumstances (where, when, who else was involved) can be very useful to a mental health professional working with the student. In addition, such records are potentially critical should a liability issue arise. That is, it is important for both you personally and the school to be able to show that the student's threat was taken seriously and dealt with responsibly.

- For more information, see:

  Hicks, B.B. (1990). *Youth suicide: A comprehensive manual for prevention and intervention.* Bloomington, IN: National Education Service.

  Barrett, T. (1987). *Youth in crisis: Seeking solutions to self-destructive behavior.* Longmont, CO: Sopris West. (This is a step-by-step guide to implementing a whole community approach to intervention with self-destructive youth, as well as an overview of the legal and ethical implications of suicide intervention.)

SWEARING/OBSCENE LANGUAGE

· ·

Cussing

Foul Language

"Giving the Finger"

Profanity

DESCRIPTION
· ·

You have a student who uses obscene language.

GOAL
· ·

The student will cease swearing and learn to use language appropriate to the school setting.

OVERVIEW OF PLANS
· ·

- PLAN A: For a situation in which the problem occurs infrequently or has just begun.
- PLAN B: For a student who uses swearing to gain attention from or to shock adults.
- PLAN C: For a student who uses swearing to impress her peers.
- PLAN D: For a student whose swearing has become habitual.
- PLAN E: For a class with several students who swear (involves group problem solving).
- PLAN F: For a class with several students who swear (involves a structured monitoring and reinforcement system).

Alternative Problems

- Disrespectful Behavior
- Disruptive Behavior— Moderate
- Disruptive Behavior— Severe
- Harassment— Racial/Sexual
- Sexual Comments
- Smart-Aleck Behavior/Inappropriate Humor

········
General Considerations

- If the student lacks the basic social skills to interact with her peers appropriately (e.g., she swears because she does not know more appropriate ways of interacting with her peers), it may be necessary to begin by teaching her those skills. **Social Skills, Lack of** contains information on a variety of published social skills curricula.

- If you have any reason to suspect a physiological or neurological basis for the student's behavior (e.g., the student seems to swear or have other outbursts for no apparent reason and you suspect that this behavior may be caused by Tourette Syndrome), you may wish to consult that behavior problem in this reference guide in addition to consulting with your building administrator and/or school psychologist for advice on district procedures for following up on this type of situation.

- If the student swears at you, **Disrespectful Behavior** contains plans that may be more applicable to resolve the situation.

········
Model Plans

PLAN A

It is not always necessary, or even beneficial, to use an involved plan. If the swearing has just begun and/or is relatively infrequent (e.g., the student swears once every couple of weeks), the following actions, along with making the student aware of your concerns, may resolve the situation.

 Help the student identify replacement responses for her obscene language.

If, for example, the student tends to swear when she drops something or makes an error, during your initial meeting with the student (see SUGGESTED STEPS FOR DEVELOPING AND IMPLEMENTING A PLAN), you should work with the student to think of something else she could say that would also be an example of responsible language (e.g., "Oh shoot" instead of what she usually says).

Also discuss what types of language constitute swearing, so the student understands what words you consider to be inappropriate.

 Respond consistently to the inappropriate behavior.

a. Establish a mild consequence that will be implemented each time the student swears. For example, at the elementary school level, the student might lose one minute off of the next recess for each time she swears. A middle/junior high school student might owe one minute of the next passing period for the first incident and ten minutes in detention (during lunch or after school) for each subsequent incident. During the time the student owes, she should be required to sit and do nothing.

b. Each time you hear the student swear, inform her that she owes time, and record the incident on a monitoring sheet that you will review before the next recess (or before the class period ends). "Nellie, that's swearing. You owe another minute off of the next recess."

3. **Use reinforcement to encourage appropriate behavior.**

a. Give the student increased praise. Be especially alert for situations in which the student might have used a swear word and did not, and praise her for these demonstrations of her ability to use responsible language in school. "Nellie, I noticed that you dropped your books. What you did was gave a big sigh and said, 'This is not my day!' Great example of using responsible language at school."

If the student would be embarrassed by public praise, praise the student privately or even give the student a note. Remember that any time the student is refraining from swearing, you can praise her for using responsible language.

b. Give the student frequent attention (e.g., say "hello" to her as she enters the classroom, call on her frequently during class activities, and occasionally ask her to assist you with a class job that needs to be done) and praise her for other positive behaviors she exhibits. For example, you might comment about how effective she is with written communication, or about how friendly she has been in welcoming a new student to the classroom. This demonstrates to the student that you notice many positive things she does, not just the fact that she is refraining from swearing.

PLAN B

Some students are very skilled at gaining attention through their negative behavior. If you find yourself frequently nagging, reminding, or lecturing the student to stop swearing, it is possible that she is trying to gain adult attention through her misbehavior. Whether or not the student overtly seems to like the attention, you should make sure that she receives more frequent and more satisfying attention when she behaves appropriately than when she swears.

1. *Help the student identify replacement responses for her obscene language (see PLAN A).*

2. *Respond consistently to the inappropriate behavior.*

a. Implement time owed for each instance of swearing (see PLAN A).

b. If attention is reinforcing to this student, you'll want to keep the interaction as short and as nonengaging as possible. For example, each time the student swears, you might simply get her attention and say, "One minute." Then mark the incident on a recording sheet and resume instruction. Avoid lecturing, explaining, or justifying the consequence.

c. If the student tries to argue or negotiate, do not become involved in these discussions. Simply restate the consequence and tell the student what she needs to be doing. "When you swear it costs a minute. Right now you need to . . . ." If the student continues to argue, ignore her behavior.

3. *Use reinforcement to encourage appropriate behavior.*

a. Frequent praise and attention is the core of this plan. The student must see that she receives more frequent and more satisfying attention when she behaves appropriately than when she swears. Thus, whenever the student is not swearing (or otherwise misbehaving), make an effort to praise and spend time with her. "Nellie, I really appreciate the effort you are putting into remembering to use responsible language at school. Would you like to walk with me as we go to lunch today? I would like to find out about some of the things you enjoy doing outside of school."

b. You may also wish to use intermittent rewards to acknowledge the student's success. Occasional, and unexpected, rewards can motivate the student to demonstrate responsible behavior more often. The idea is to provide a reward when the student has had a particularly good period of not swearing.

Appropriate rewards might include reading a story to a younger class, receiving a note from the principal about her responsible use of language, or receiving a phone call from you at home to congratulate her. *(NOTE: A list of additional reinforcement ideas can be found in APPENDIX 1.)* Use intermittent rewards more frequently at the beginning of the intervention to encourage the student, and then less often as her behavior improves.

4. *Ensure a 3-1 ratio of positive to negative attention.*

a. When attention is a motivating force for the student, you want to be sure that you are giving the student *three times as much* positive as negative attention. One way to do this is to monitor your interactions with the student at least one day per week. Keep a card on a clipboard or in your pocket and record each interaction you have with the student as either positive or negative by writing a "+" or a "-", respectively, on the card.

To determine whether an interaction is positive or negative, ask yourself whether the student was swearing (or otherwise misbehaving) at the time the interaction occurred. Any interaction that stems from inappropriate behavior is negative, and all interactions that occur while the student is meeting classroom expectations are positive. Thus, assigning time owed is a negative interaction, but praising the student for using responsible language is positive. Greeting the student as she enters the room or asking her if she has any questions during independent work are also considered positive interactions. *(NOTE: Ignoring the student's behavior is not recorded at all, because it is not an interaction.)*

b. If you find that you are not giving the student three times as much positive as negative attention, try to increase the number of positive interactions you have with the student. Sometimes prompts can help. For example, you might decide that each time the student enters the classroom you will say "hello" to her, or that three times each morning and each afternoon you will

find a time to praise the student. You can also increase the ratio of positive to negative attention by ignoring more of the student's inappropriate behavior.

 (OPTIONAL)
Arrange for the student to receive positive attention from other adults.

If the student seems especially starved for attention, you might ask the principal, playground supervisors, and/or other teachers to give her lots of attention. If several adults make it a point to greet the student whenever they see her and make an effort to "catch" her when she is not swearing and provide praise, it may reduce the student's need to swear to gain attention both in class and in other school settings.

P L A N   C

Sometimes a student uses profanity as a way of demonstrating her personal power and/or as an attempt to impress her peers. If the student seems motivated by the reactions she gains from her peers, the intervention must involve reducing the power she achieves through swearing and helping her learn to wield her personal power in appropriate ways.

 Help the student identify replacement responses for her obscene language (see PLAN A).

(NOTE: It is especially critical to find replacement language that will not make the student look "uncool" in front of her peers.)

 Respond consistently to the inappropriate behavior.

a. Implement time owed for each instance of swearing (see PLAN A).

b. Demonstrate that the student's swearing has no power to influence you. This may be difficult if you are a person who finds profanity particularly offensive. However, if the student's motivation for swearing is, at least in part, power, any evidence that she can "push your buttons" (i.e., making you angry, flustered, or otherwise upset) is probably reinforcing the student's swearing. Your goal should be to remain perfectly calm whenever the student swears.

You might find it useful to mentally rehearse situations in which the student is swearing and imagine yourself calmly and consistently stating the consequence and resuming instruction. Tell yourself that any time the student sees she has the power to make you angry, it's the same as

if you had paid her $50.00 for behaving inappropriately.

c. If necessary, encourage the other students to ignore the student's swearing. If other students are reinforcing the student's swearing by either laughing or acting shocked, provide a gentle correction. "Nellie, one minute. And Harv and Teresita, when you react and make a big deal out of it, you encourage that kind of language. It would be better not to act like this is shocking. Just ignore Nellie's swearing."

3. **Acknowledge the student's power with her peers.**

a. During your initial meeting with the student (see SUGGESTED STEPS FOR DEVELOPING AND IMPLEMENTING A PLAN), let her know that you realize she has a great deal of influence over the other students and that you do not want to take that away from her. If appropriate, tell her that she is a natural leader. Also tell her that you do not expect her to become some "goody-goody" type of student, but that you believe that she can maintain, and even enhance, her powerful image with her peers while still using responsible language in school.

b. If the student is not well-liked by her peers, and is using swearing to gain status with them, you might suggest a peer model. That is, you could encourage her to watch a student she looks up to—a student who is powerful but uses language appropriately.

Have the student focus on the way her peer model handles personal power without needing to swear. "Nellie, one thing I would like to encourage you to do is to watch Lila. Do you think Lila is a goody-goody kind of person? No, I don't either. And yet, she consistently uses responsible language in school. I don't know if she swears when teachers aren't around, but the point is that she never swears in class. For the next few days, observe the way Lila interacts with me and with the other students. I think you might get some good ideas about how to use language that is responsible without feeling uncool."

(NOTE: It is very important not to imply that the peer model is somehow a better or more worthwhile person than the target student, just that he/she has a particular skill that is worth observing.)

4. **Give the student a high status job or responsibility.**

a. One of the most effective ways to teach a student how to wield personal power wisely is to put her in a position of power. Try to think of a job or responsibility that the student would enjoy and would be good at. For example, the student might tutor a younger student in math, work in the school's computer lab, or be a library assistant. The best job is one that happens regularly (e.g., daily or twice per week) and in which the student's "job supervisor" is someone other than yourself.

Be sure the student receives sufficient job training and that the supervisor explains all the expectations and consequences clearly at the beginning (with special emphasis placed on using appropriate language). Let the student know that there can be absolutely no swearing on the job. "Nellie, you are going to be tutoring a younger student and if you use swear words, she will probably start to use those words too. If during the tutoring sessions I hear you swear, you will get one warning. If it happens again, even three weeks later, you will lose your job, and the student you are tutoring will have to be given another tutor."

b. If the student is assigned a job that she would like to perform, she should be allowed to perform her job regardless of how well she is doing with the swearing in class. That is, just as you are expected to perform your job regardless of your language at home, so should the student be expected to perform her job. If the job is made contingent upon her language in your class, it will become simply one more power issue. The student is likely to think, "You can't make me stop swearing by threatening that I will not get to tutor."

5. **Use reinforcement to encourage appropriate behavior.**

a. Give the student frequent praise and attention for using responsible language (see PLAN A).

b. Also praise the student for being responsible about her assigned job. "Nellie, Ms. Diaz tells me that you have been a big help with your tutoring. I am proud of you—you should feel very good about how responsible you've been and what a good job you're doing. Keep it up!"

PLAN D

Whenever a student's problem behavior has become habitual and/or she does not seem to have a desire to reduce it, you may need to implement a system of external incentives (i.e., rewards and consequences) based on the student's behavior to motivate her to stop swearing and to substitute more responsible language.

1. **Help the student identify replacement responses for her obscene language (see PLAN A).**

2. **Respond consistently to the inappropriate behavior.**

a. Implement time owed for each instance of swearing (see PLAN A).

b. Record, and meet with the student each day to chart the number of minutes the student owed that day (i.e., the total number of times the student swore).

3. *Establish a structured system for reinforcing the reduction of swearing.*

a. With the student, create a list of reinforcers that she can earn. Although you might want to have some suggestions in mind, the system will be more effective if the student identifies most of the items or activities herself. *(NOTE: A list of reinforcement ideas can be found in APPENDIX 1.)*

b. Assign "prices" (in points) for each of the rewards on the list and have the student select the reward she would like to earn first.

The prices should be based on the instructional, personnel, and/or monetary costs of the items. Monetary cost is clear—the more expensive the item, the more points required to earn it. Instructional cost refers to the amount of instructional time lost or interfered with by a particular reward. Thus, an activity which causes the student to miss part of academic instruction should require more points than one the student can do on her own recess time. Personnel cost involves the time required by you and/or other staff to fulfill the reinforcer. Having lunch with the principal, therefore, would cost more points than spending five minutes of free time with a friend.

c. Have the student begin each day with a certain number of points. This number should equal the student's daily average of minutes owed, plus two. Thus, if she has owed an average of 13 minutes per day, she would begin each day with 15 points. Each time you record that she owes a minute for swearing, she loses a point. The points remaining at the end of each day are then added together to be applied toward the reinforcer the student is striving to earn.

(NOTE: A lottery system might be more effective with a primary level student. In this system, the student would begin each day with tickets in a jar instead of points. All the tickets would have prizes written on them—one would have a big prize, a couple would have moderate prizes, and the majority would have little prizes. Each

time you record that the student owes a minute, you remove one ticket from the jar—but neither you nor the student are allowed to see what is written on it. At the end of each day, the student would draw one ticket from those remaining in the jar, and receive that prize.)

d. When the student has accumulated enough points to earn the reward she has chosen, she "spends" the points necessary and the system begins again. That is, she selects another reward to earn and begins with zero points.

If the student is immature, and needs more frequent encouragement, you might consider letting her earn several "less expensive" rewards (e.g., five minutes of free time after 20 points) on the way to a bigger reward (e.g., one hour with you for 200 points). That is, the student receives the small rewards without spending points; they continue to accumulate toward the selected reward.

e. Once all the day's points (or tickets) are used up, the student will still owe one minute of time for each subsequent incident of swearing, but will not lose any more points. That is, if the student runs out of points (or tickets), do not take points that the student has earned on previous days away. If the student can lose already-earned points, she might develop an attitude of, "I am losing so many points, why should I even bother to try?"

4. *Use reinforcement to encourage appropriate behavior.*

a. Give the student increased praise and attention for using responsible language (see PLAN A).

b. In addition, show interest and enthusiasm about how the student is doing on the system. "Nellie, you have been doing such a nice job of remembering to use responsible language. You have not lost any points all morning. As a special thank you from me, I am adding three bonus points to those that you have saved, plus however many you have left at the end of today."

PLAN E

Sometimes an entire class will fall into a pattern of using inappropriate language. If the students do not seem to be aware of how frequently they are swearing, you might conduct a group problem-solving discussion in which the class generates a plan for dealing with the problem.

Keep a frequency count of the amount of swearing.

For at least two consecutive days, record every incidence of swearing. One way to do this is to write the name of the student who swore on a card you keep in your pocket or on a clipboard. This way you will obtain a class-wide total each day as well as a tally for each individual student.

An alternative form of record keeping is to keep handy a card or class list with all the students' names preprinted. This way, you can simply write a tally mark next to a student's name when he/she swears.

If the students ask what you are doing, be straightforward. Tell them, "I am just trying to figure out how often I hear swearing." However, if they do not ask, do not bring up the frequency count yourself.

 Schedule and conduct a class-wide discussion on the problem.

a. Let the students know one day in advance that there will be a class meeting to figure out ways to reduce the amount of swearing in the classroom. Shortly before the meeting, write an agenda (similar to the sample shown) on the chalkboard.

Agenda

1. Define swearing—Why is it a problem? (e.g., How is swearing perceived in the world of work?)

2. Define the problem from the students' perspective.

3. Brainstorm consequences for swearing.

4. Decide on a consequence for swearing.

5. Decide on a process for counting and charting the daily amount of swearing.

6. Brainstorm ideas for reducing the amount of swearing in the classroom.

7. Set a daily performance goal for reducing and eventually eliminating the swearing from the classroom.

8. Decide on a celebration activity to occur when the goal is met.

---

b. During the meeting, invite participation from as many class members as possible. Begin the meeting by clarifying the nature of the problem. Share with them the frequency count information you have been collecting. Explain that while swearing may be acceptable in some homes and other places, it is not acceptable in school and will not be acceptable in most work environments.

Work through the remaining steps on the agenda, placing special emphasis on Steps 3 and 6 (brainstorming consequences and ideas for reducing classroom swearing). During these brainstorming sessions, write down all of the students' suggestions. If any of the suggestions are clearly unreasonable (e.g., any student caught swearing will have his/her mouth washed out with soap by the class), eliminate them and explain why to the class. Have the class select (using voting, if appropriate) a couple of the consequences and a few of the suggestions for reducing the swearing. Keep the tone of the discussion positive, and communicate that you have a high expectation that the students can develop a successful plan.

 Each day, chart the number of swearing incidents and discuss the results with the class.

Count and chart the daily total of swearing incidents using the method decided upon during the brainstorming portion of the class meeting. Then have a brief (three to five minute) class discussion about how the day went in relation to the daily performance goal.

 Use reinforcement to encourage appropriate behavior.

a. Give the students increased praise and attention for using responsible language. (Adapt the suggestions in PLAN A for the class as a whole.)

b. As the group makes progress, reinforce the entire class. With middle/junior high school students it may be useful to identify the use of good responsible language as an example of good work place behavior. "Class, everyone should be very proud of how responsible you are being about your language. You have demonstrated that you could be successful with managing your language if you were to work in a setting where swearing would cause you problems."

PLAN F

In some cases, a few influential students seem "cool" or "tough" when they swear, and so other students try to emulate them. Soon many students are swearing in the classroom. In this case, the intervention should include a structural reinforcement system (i.e., rewards and consequences) to create mild peer pressure to reduce the swearing.

1. *Count and chart the daily total of swearing incidents (see PLAN E).*

2. *Establish a team competition and response cost lottery.*

a. Divide the class into four to six equal teams, making sure that the students with the greatest tendency to swear are distributed evenly amongst the teams.

b. Have the class brainstorm different reinforcers (i.e., items, privileges, or activities) that the teams might like to earn. From the students' brainstormed ideas, create a list of reinforcers that are possible to deliver. Reasonable possibilities might include extra computer time, leaving for lunch three minutes early, a ticket that a allows them to do only half of a daily homework assignment, etc. *(NOTE: A list of additional reinforcement ideas can be found in APPENDIX 1.)* Then have each team select the reinforcer that they would like to earn the first time their team wins.

c. Begin each day (or period) by giving each team a certain number of tickets (ten, for example) on which they would write their team name. Each time a student swears, that person's team would lose a ticket.

(NOTE: Do not count an incident of swearing unless you personally hear it. Do not encourage groups to "tell on" other groups.)

At the end of the day, each team would put their remaining tickets in a hat for a lottery drawing. The name of the team on the ticket drawn earns the reward they have chosen. (Obviously the more tickets a team has in the hat, the better their chance of winning, but even a team with only one ticket has a chance to win their selected reinforcer.)

3. *While implementing this reinforcement system, keep student attention focused on how much more pleasant the classroom atmosphere is as the amount of swearing is reduced.*

Tell the students, for example: "Class, each team has most of their tickets left in the drawing today, but more importantly, you are all helping this class be a place that we all will enjoy. Our room is a place we can all be proud of."

4. *Respond consistently to the inappropriate behavior.*

a. Each time a student swears, take a ticket from that student's team (see Step 2).

b. If it seems necessary, establish an additional consequence of time owed for each incident of swearing. That is, if a student is heard swearing, not only does his/her team lose a ticket, but he/she also owes time off of the next recess (or in detention). Note that the whole team does not owe the time, just the student who swore.

c. If one student is consistently ruining his/her team's chances, take that student off the team. Assign the student time owed for each incident of swearing, and do not allow the student to participate in any rewards his/her former teammates earn.

. . . .

Suggested Steps for Developing and Implementing a Plan

The following steps are designed to help you develop an appropriate intervention plan and implement it effectively, whether you choose to use one of the MODEL PLANS or create a customized plan of your own. The steps are, however, suggestions—they are not intended to be followed rigidly or in any particular order. Use your professional judgment and the knowledge of your particular situation to make them work for you.

1. *Make sure you have enough information about the situation.*

a. If you think a minimal intervention like PLAN A will be sufficient, you may already have enough information to proceed. However, when a more involved plan seems necessary, you should consider collecting additional objective information for a couple of days.

b. The easiest objective measure of the problem to take (and an objective way to monitor the student's progress) is to count the frequency of the swearing incidents. Simply keep a card in your pocket or on a clipboard and write a tally mark on the card each time the student swears.

You might also want to code the tallies to discern whether the behavior occurs more frequently during certain times, subjects, or activities (e.g., using an "A" or "P" to indicate that the incident happened in the morning or afternoon; or clustering the tallies by math or reading, teacher directed instruction or independent work, etc.).

c. If the student notices what you are doing and asks about it, be straightforward—tell her that you are collecting information to see whether her swearing is a problem that needs to be worked on.

d. The frequency information is fairly easy to summarize on a chart or graph. Seeing how often she swears may help the student and her parent(s) better understand your concern.

e. Continuing to collect frequency information and keeping the chart up-to-date while you implement a plan will help you to monitor whether the situation is getting worse, staying the same, or getting better.

2. *Identify a focus for the intervention and labels for referring to the appropriate and inappropriate behaviors.*

a. To be effective, the intervention must address more than just eliminating the student's inappropriate behavior—there must be a concurrent emphasis on increasing some positive behavior (e.g., using responsible language). Having a specific positive behavior in mind will make it easier for you to "catch" and reinforce the student for behaving appropriately, and the positive focus will help you to frame the situation more productively.

For example, if you simply say that "the student has a problem with swearing," you don't really provide any useful information, and may put the

student and her parent(s) on the defensive. However, when you explain that you want to help the student "learn to use responsible language," you present an important, and reasonable, goal for the student to work toward. You also clarify what it is the student needs to do to be successful.

b. Specifying labels for the appropriate and inappropriate behaviors (e.g., "using responsible language" and "swearing," respectively) will help you to use consistent vocabulary when discussing the situation with the student.

3. *Determine when and how to include the parent(s).*

a. While it is not necessary to contact the student's parent(s) if the problem has just begun, it might be a good idea to take advantage of any scheduled activities (e.g., conferences, weekly notes home) to let them know of your concern.

b. If the problem appears to be chronic (e.g., the student swears several times per day), you should contact the student's parent(s). Share with them any information you have collected about the behavior (i.e., the frequency count), and explain why you are concerned. Focus in particular on how the behavior can hinder the student academically and/or socially (e.g., it is a behavior that is likely to offend many teachers and future employers).

You might ask if the parent(s) have any insight into the situation and/or whether they have noticed similar behavior at home. Whether or not the parent(s) perceive a problem, explain that you want to help the student "learn to use responsible language at school," and invite them to join you for an initial meeting with the student to develop a plan. If the parent(s) are unable or unwilling to participate, let them know that you will keep them informed of the student's progress.

c. Once the parent(s) have been involved in any way, you should give them updates at least once per week while the plan is being implemented.

4. *Prepare for, then conduct, an initial meeting about the situation.*

a. Arrange a meeting to discuss your concerns with the student and anyone else who will be involved in the plan (e.g., the parent[s]). Although the specifics will vary depending upon the age of the student and the severity of the problem, there are some general guidelines to consider when scheduling the meeting.

First, meet at a neutral time (i.e., not immediately after a problem has occurred), when emotions are less likely to hamper communication. In general, a day's notice is appropriate, however a primary age student may worry excessively and/or forget what the meeting is about if it is scheduled more than an hour before it takes place.

Second, make the meeting appropriately private. With a primary student who has a mild problem, you might meet in the classroom while the other students are working independently. However, when dealing with a middle/junior high school student and the student's parent(s), you will need some place private (e.g., the counselor's office) to ensure that the discussion will not be overheard.

Third, try to make sure the meeting is scheduled for a time and place that it is not likely to be interrupted. Finally, if the parent(s) will be participating, they should be the ones to tell the student about the meeting.

b. Construct a preliminary plan. Decide whether you think you can use one of the MODEL PLANS or if you need to create a customized plan using components from various plans and/or of your own design. Although you will invite and encourage the student to help develop the plan during the initial meeting, having a proposed plan in mind before you meet can alleviate frustration and wasted time if the student is unwilling or unable to participate.

c. Review the information you have collected and think about how you want the student to behave. Then prepare a thorough description of the borderline between swearing and responsible language. The more specific you can be and the more concrete examples you have, the easier it will be to clarify (and for the student to understand) your expectations.

You do not have to review every word you consider to be swearing, but be sure to clarify for the student those words or phrases that you consider swearing that other people may not. "Nellie, although some people do not view it as inappropriate, I consider the use of 'God' and 'Jesus' as exclamations to be swearing. On the other hand, if we are discussing world religions in social studies and you mention something about the life of Jesus, it would not be swearing."

Be sure to consider the student's behavior in all relevant activities (e.g., independent work, teacher directed instruction, unstructured class times, recess and lunch, etc.).

d. Conduct the meeting in an atmosphere of collaboration. The following agenda is one way you might structure the meeting:

• **Share your concerns about the student's behavior.**

Briefly describe the problem behavior and explain why you consider swearing to be a problem. You might want to note that although swearing is not considered offensive by all people in all settings, it is not appropriate language for school. You could also tell the student that if she is allowed to swear at school, she may develop a habit that eventually she is unable to control. Finally, let the student know that there are jobs in which swearing is completely inappropriate, and that since one purpose of school is to prepare students for the world of work, you feel you need to help her learn to eliminate this behavior at school. If you wish, you can let the student know that you do not care if she chooses to use that sort of language in other settings; your focus is on school.

• **Discuss how you can work together to improve the situation.**

Tell the student that you would like to help her "learn to use responsible language at school," and describe your preliminary plan. Invite the student to give you input on the various aspects of the plan, and together work out any necessary details (e.g., time owed, use of the chart, etc.).

You may have to brainstorm different possibilities if the student is uncomfortable with the initial plan. Incorporating any of the student's suggestions that strengthen the plan is likely to increase her sense of "ownership" in and commitment to it.

• **Make sure the student understands what you mean by appropriate and inappropriate behavior.**

To ensure that you and the student are in agreement about the expectations, you might present hypothetical scenarios and have her identify whether the language used is responsible or swearing. Help the student to identify replacement language for use in the types of circumstances that generally lead to her swearing (e.g., "darn" for "damn" when she drops something).

- **Conclude the meeting.**

  Always end the meeting with words of encouragement. Let the student know that you are confident that she can be successful. Be sure to reinforce her for participating in the meeting.

 Give the student regular, ongoing feedback about her behavior.

It is important to meet with the student periodically to discuss her progress. In most cases, three to five minutes once per week should suffice. *(NOTE: PLANS D, E, and F suggest daily meetings.)* During the meetings, review any information that has been collected and discuss whether or not the situation is getting better. As much as possible, focus on the student's improvements, however, also address any new or continuing problems. As the situation improves, the meetings can be faded to once every other week and then to once per month.

 Evaluate the situation (and the plan).

Implement any plan for at least two weeks before deciding whether to change plans; to continue, modify, or fade the plan you are using; or to cease the intervention. Generally, if the student's behavior is clearly improving (based on the objective information that's been collected and/or the subjective perceptions of yourself, the student, and possibly the parent[s]), stick with what you are doing. If the situation has remained the same or worsened, some kind of change will be necessary. Always discuss any changes to the plan with the student first.

TALKING/EXCESSIVE NOISE IN CLASS

. . . .

DESCRIPTION

There are students in your class who engage in excessive talking or noise.

GOAL

The students will learn to manage their behavior so that the amount of talking and noise in the classroom stay within acceptable levels.

OVERVIEW OF PLANS

- PLAN A: For a situation in which the problem has just begun or occurs infrequently.
- PLAN B: For a problem that may stem from classroom management or organizational factors.
- PLAN C: For a problem that may stem from the students not knowing the line between reasonable and excessive talking/noise.
- PLAN D: For a problem that may stem from the students not realizing how often they engage in excessive talking/noise.
- PLAN E: For a situation in which the students simply aren't motivated to manage their excessive talking/ noise.

Alternative Problems

- **Beginning Class—Getting Students Settled Down**
- **Chaos/Classroom Out of Control**
- **Participation In Class, Lack of**
- **Talking Irresponsibly (Individual)**

General Considerations

- These five plans are geared for a situation in which quite a few students in the class have a problem with excessive talking/noise. If you are mainly concerned about the behavior of one or two individual students, see **Talking Irresponsibly (Individual)**.

- If the inappropriate behavior is resulting in the students avoiding or not completing their schoolwork, begin with a plan to increase the students' work completion (see **Work Completion—Daily Work**).Once the students are turning in completed work on a regular basis, you can consider an intervention for the excessive talking/noise, if the problem still exists.

Model Plans

PLAN A

If the problem has just begun and/or occurs only two or three times per day, it may not be necessary, or even beneficial, to use an involved plan. The following actions, along with making the students aware of your concerns, may resolve the situation.

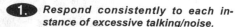 **Respond consistently to each instance of excessive talking/noise.**

Whenever you notice excessive talking/noise in the classroom, give the students a gentle correction. Tell the class that this is an example of excessive talking/noise, and provide information on what they should be doing instead. Be emotionally neutral and avoid talking too much while giving the correction—your goal is to impart information. "Class, this is too loud. It is okay to be talking in your groups, but use quieter voices."

Be consistent in correcting the students. The goal is to help the students learn the borderline between acceptable and excessive noise. Therefore, it is important that any time the group crosses that line, you impart information.

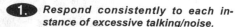 **Use reinforcement to encourage appropriate behavior.**

a. Praise individual students for meeting your expectations regarding managing the noise level. Keep an eye on those students who have had the greatest tendency to be excessively noisy. Whenever these students are not engaged in excessive talking/noise, praise them for demonstrating their ability to manage the noise level. "Rand, Melinda, and Rodney, you are doing a great job of managing the noise level there in the computer center. "

If the students would be embarrassed by public praise, praise them privately or even give the students a note.

b. In addition, occasionally praise those students who rarely or never have a problem with excessive talking/noise. Because these students have already mastered the positive expectations, they do not need positive feedback as often as the students who have had difficulty. However, you do not want them to feel that you take their positive behavior for granted. "You people at this work station consistently manage the noise level independently. I appreciate that I never need to give your reminders about too much noise."

c. Finally, when there has been a significant classwide improvement, praise the entire class. Remember that any time the students are refraining from excessive talking/noise, you can praise them for managing the noise level. "Class, throughout the day today everyone has worked on managing the noise level without my needing to nag you. Thanks for your help. I appreciate not having to play the role of 'Noise Police.'"

PLAN B

The way you organize your classroom and instruction has a significant impact on the degree to which students will engage in excessive talking/noise. Although a particular classroom organization may be fine for most groups of students, every now and again you may have a class that cannot handle your usual style of management and organization. Modifying organizational and instructional variables can reduce off-task talking/noise to tolerable levels.

1. **Examine your instructional practices, particularly the balance among teacher directed instruction, cooperative learning groups, and independent seatwork or projects.**

a. Too much time on any one of these activities is likely to bore the students, who may then become involved in excessive talking/noise and/or misbehavior. Regardless of the instructional activity, try to increase student participation and keep the pace lively so the students will remain engaged.

b. Pay special attention to independent seatwork periods. If you assign students to work independently for long periods, break up the time by interspersing short periods of guided practice in which you lead the class through parts of the activity together. Or, schedule an activity in the middle of the work period that allows the students to be out of their seats and moving around. This can even be as simple as a regularly scheduled two-minute exercise/stretch break.

2. **Examine the amount and difficulty level of the work you assign the students.**

a. When there is not enough work to keep the students occupied, they are more likely to engage in excessive talking/noise. Adjust the amount of work so that the students are occupied during the majority of each work period. In addition, develop "cushion activities" that can be done by students who have completed their assigned work. If the class activity calls for students to be working quietly and independently, the choices offered to students as cushion activities should be those that can also be done quietly and independently (e.g., write in a journal, read a book, study for a test, or even word searches/puzzles). Do not let the students engage in talking when they have completed their work because it impossible to tell if the students who *are* talking have completed their work or not.

b. On the other hand, too much work or work that is too difficult may be overwhelming to the students. When a significant number of students feel "swamped," some may decide it is hopeless and give up altogether (e.g., "I will never get all of this done, so I may as well not even try. I'll just spend the time talking to my neighbor.") If this is the case, you might want to lead the class through more of the work as guided practice—that is, complete a significant portion (e.g., 30%, 50%, or even 80%) of the assignment together as a class.

3. **Evaluate and modify, if necessary, the physical organization of your classroom.**

a. Adjusting the physical setting and/or seating arrangements in the classroom can reduce excessive talking/noise. Although there is no right or wrong way to arrange a classroom, when a group has a tendency to engage in excessive talking/noise, having the desks in a U-shape around the perimeter of the room may reduce the talking/noise significantly. If this is not possible because there are too many students, you might consider using a double row U-shape (however, be sure to include access points so that you can easily reach the students in the second row).

b. Rows of desks facing front prompt less talking than desks clustered together. However, if you want to encourage the students to work together, having their desks in clusters will be quieter than students trying to carry on conversations across rows.

c. Regardless of how the students' desks are arranged, be sure you have access from any point in the room to any other point in the room. For example, if there are rows facing front, ensure perpendicular access that allows you to reach any point in the room without having to walk all the way out to the end of the rows. If the desks are arranged in groups, be sure you can move easily around and between the groups of desks.

d. Free choice of seating may be fine for many classes, but in some cases the students make bad choices. If your class is excessively noisy, it may be better to use assigned seats and change the seat assignment every month or so.

4. *Increase your the level of direct supervision by increasing the frequency of visual scanning and physical proximity.*

a. During teacher directed instruction, present from different parts of the room. When supervising independent work periods or cooperative groups, move throughout the classroom in unpredictable ways. Spend more time near students with the greatest tendency to be noisy/talk excessively.

b. If moving amongst the students is not possible because you are teaching a small group or are presenting from the overhead projector, for example, make frequent visual contact with all parts of the room. The students are less likely to be noisy/talk excessively when they know that you will probably see them.

P L A N   C

If the students are not clear about the borderline between reasonable noise levels and excessive talking/noise, the intervention must include some way of teaching them this distinction.

1. *Clarify your communication expectations for each activity and transitions between activities.*

a. Identify your expectations for talking/noise for the different types of classroom activities. In the following example, all the classroom activities fall into one of three categories of communication expectations:

- Category A—No talking is acceptable, unless you have been called on by the teacher or have raised your hand and been called on.

- Category B—Quiet talking is acceptable, but only with people in your group and only about the assigned task.

- Category C—Quiet talking to someone near you about any topic is acceptable.

b. Decide which category of communication is appropriate for each activity in the schedule and for transitions between activities. For example, the expectation would be Category A during art while you are demonstrating and teaching new concepts—no talking is acceptable unless you have called on a student. However, once the students are working independently, it might be reasonable to allow quiet talking about any topic (Category C). During a cooperative learning activity, the students would be expected to follow the expectations for Category B—quiet talking, but only to group members about the assigned task. Finally, when transitioning from one activity to another, the students would be expected to follow Category C expectations—quiet talking to someone close by.

c. Teach the students the communication expectations for each classroom activity. With middle/junior high school students, this procedure can be as simple as telling the students the expectation immediately before the activity. With elementary school students, a visual representation of the expectations can be useful. For example, you might construct a three-sided sign out of cardboard, with each side at least 11" x 22". On each face of the sign, write or draw one of the categories of communication expectations (see the sample).

Stand the sign on your desk or in some other prominent location in the classroom. When you change activities and the communication expectations change, simply turn the sign (or ask a student to turn it) to the appropriate side. This will serve to prompt the students about what they need to do to be successful.

Quiet, independent work.

If you have a question, quietly raise your hand.

2. *Prompt appropriate behavior by clarifying the communication expectations right before each activity.*

a. Tell the class, for example, "Class, for the next 15 minutes you can work on your math assignment. Please note that no talking is acceptable unless you have a question you need to address to me." Or, "Class, we have five minutes before it is time for lunch. You can use this time to work, or if you want to relax and talk quietly, I am turning the sign to indicate that talking about things other than your work is okay."

b. For the first week or two, also take a few moments to determine if the students fully understand the expectations: "Terje, during the next activity, is any talking between students okay?"; "Claudette, talking is okay, but about what?"; "Julio, what would you do if you needed to talk to me?"

3. Respond consistently to all instances of excessive talking/noise.

a. Whenever you notice the students engaged in excessive talking/noise, gently correct them. Consider this correction a warning: "Helena and Brent, look at the sign. This is a 'no talking' period. This is your warning."; or "Bess and Samantha, now is a quiet talking period, but I can hear you clear across the room. This is your warning."

b. If you have to give more than one reminder to a student during a particular instructional activity, assign that student time owed. Elementary school students might owe one minute off of recess for each reminder given after the warn-

ing. At the middle/junior high school level, assign one minute after class for the first reminder after a warning and ten minutes in detention (during lunch or after school) for each subsequent reminder.

c. When using this system, you'll probably want to keep a class list near you at all times. Whenever you have to correct a student who is being noisy/talking excessively, simply write a tally mark next to that student's name. This will help you to monitor who is at the warning stage and who owes time (see the sample).

4. Use reinforcement to encourage appropriate behavior.

a. Praise individual students for meeting the expectations for managing talking/noise, and praise the entire class when overall improvement takes place (see PLAN A).

b. Make a special point of letting the students know (both individually and as a class) that you notice their efforts to use the strategies that you have discussed with the class. "Dani and Rick started talking, then looked up at the sign, realized it was a 'no talking' time and quit talking. Nice job of managing that situation without needing reminders from me."

Tally of Reprimands for Talking

Week of ___1/26___

Name	Mon.	Tues.	Wed.	Thurs.	Fri.	**TOTAL**
Abrams, Lise	ЛℋГ					
Adams, Jordan	/					
Behrens, Cherise	//					
(Etc.)						

PLAN D

Sometimes students do not seem to realize when and/or how frequently they engage in excessive talking/noise. In this case, the intervention should include some way of helping the students to become more aware of their own behavior.

1. Clarify your communication expectations for each activity and transitions between activities (see PLAN C).

2. Respond consistently to all instances of excessive talking/noise.

a. Implement a warning for the first incident per student, then time owed for each subsequent incident (see PLAN C).

b. In addition, whenever you correct an individual student, make sure the incident is recorded (see Step 3).

3. *Publicly monitor the number of incidents of excessive talking/noise.*

a. Record tallies of each incident of excessive talking/noise using a class list (see PLAN C).

b. Create and post a chart showing the daily cumulative totals of reminders given. *(NOTE: This should be a class total and not a report on individual students' behavior.)*

c. Each day, conduct a short class meeting to review that day's record. Have a student record the information on the chart (or do it yourself), and discuss with the class whether the day was better, worse, or about the same as previous days. If the day did not go well, encourage the students to talk about why and have them identify what they can do the next day to help them remember to manage their talking/noise. If the students behave inappropriately during the meeting, keep the review session very short. Just let the class know that you are sure tomorrow will be a better day.

4. *Use reinforcement to encourage appropriate behavior.*

a. Praise individual students for meeting your expectations for managing talking/noise, and praise the entire class when overall improvement takes place (see PLAN A).

b. During the daily review meetings, praise the students for being willing to look seriously at their cumulative record for the day. Even on a bad day, if the students are willing to discuss why it was a bad day, praise them. "Class, you are really handling this responsibly. Even though it was a rough day, you are willing to talk to about things you might do differently tomorrow. That is a real sign that we are making progress."

Regardless of how the day went, try to make the end-of-the-day meeting upbeat and encouraging—you want the students to look forward to the daily review sessions.

c. Use intermittent rewards to acknowledge the class' success. Occasional, and unexpected, rewards can motivate the students to demonstrate responsible behavior more often. The idea is to provide a reward when the class has had a particularly good period of managing their talking/noise.

Appropriate rewards might include talking quietly during an activity that is usually a "no talking" time, going to recess a few minutes early, or reducing the length of a regular homework assignment. *(NOTE: A list of additional reinforcement ideas can be found in APPENDIX 1.)*

Use intermittent rewards more frequently at the beginning of the intervention to encourage the students, and then less often as their behavior improves.

PLAN E

Sometimes an entire class falls into a pattern of excessive talking/noise. This can happen when the behavior becomes habitual and/or when a few influential students set a negative example for the rest of the class. In these cases it is often very difficult to change the students' behavior. You may need to implement a system of structured reinforcement (i.e., rewards and consequences) that creates mild peer pressure to motivate the students to behave appropriately.

1. *Respond consistently to all instances of excessive talking/noise with a warning for the first incident per student, and time owed for each subsequent incident (see PLAN C).*

2. *Publicly monitor the number of incidents of excessive talking/noise (see PLAN D).*

3. *Encourage the class to set a daily performance goal.*

Help the students to set a realistic goal (e.g., reducing the daily number of incidents from 40 to 32). Some students may want to set an overly challenging goal, such as reducing the number of incidents from 40 to zero per day. Explain that if the goal is no less than 32, for example, they can always reduce the number of incidents even more, but that they increase their chances of success. Then as the class experiences success, the target number should become progressively lower until there are no incidents of excessive talking/noise on most days.

4. *Establish a group reinforcement system.*

a. Have the students brainstorm a list of reinforcement ideas for the entire class, then eliminate from the list any items that are not possible (i.e., the suggestions are too expensive or could not be provided to all the students in the class).

b. Assign "prices" (in points) to the remaining items on the list. The prices should be based on the instructional, personnel, and/or monetary costs of the items. Monetary cost is clear—the more expensive the item, the more points required to earn it. Instructional cost refers to the amount of instructional time lost or interfered with by a particular reward. Thus, an activity which causes the class to miss part of academic instruction should require more points than one the class can do on their own free time. Personnel cost involves the time required by you and/or other staff to fulfill the reinforcer. Thus, earning an extra recess period in which extra supervision would need to be arranged would cost more than having music playing in class for 15 minutes.

c. Have the class vote on the reinforcers. The reinforcer that receives the most votes is the one the students will strive for first, and the items that come in second (and third) will be the next ones worked for.

d. Establish a sliding scale in which the class earns points for meeting its performance goal, and additional points when even fewer incidents of excessive talking/noise occur. For example, if the initial target number is 32, the following scale could be used.

e. If a class-wide system seems unlikely to be effective, an alternative strategy is to set up a

more than 32 reminders	= 0 points
25 to 31 reminders	= 1 point
18 to 24 reminders	= 2 points
10 to 17 reminders	= 3 points
4 to 9 reminders	= 5 points
0 to 3 reminders	= 7 points

team competition and response cost lottery. In this system, the class is divided into four to six equal teams. Design the teams to decrease the likelihood that the teammates will want to talk excessively (i.e., separate the frequent talkers).

In this system, each team would begin the day with a certain number of tickets, on which they would write the name of their team. Each time you have to remind a student about excessive talking/noise, that student's team would lose a ticket. *(NOTE: If the particular student requires any more warnings, he/she would also owe one minute off of recess for each subsequent incident.)* At the end of the day, each team would put all their remaining tickets in a hat for a lottery drawing. The team whose name is on the ticket drawn would earn the predetermined reward for that day.

5. *While implementing any reinforcement system, keep student attention focused on the concept that they are learning to manage their talking/noise.*

Tell the class, for example: "Class, you earned five points for the day, but more importantly, you are all helping this class be a place that we will all enjoy. Our class is a place we can all be proud of."

. . . .

Suggested Steps for Developing and Implementing a Plan

The following steps are designed to help you develop an appropriate intervention plan and implement it effectively, whether you choose to use one of the MODEL PLANS or create a customized plan of your own. The steps are, however, suggestions—they are not intended to be followed rigidly or in any particular order. Use your professional judgment and the knowledge of your particular situation to make them work for you.

1. *Make sure you have enough information about the situation.*

(NOTE: Documentation is probably not necessary if you think either PLAN A or PLAN B is appropriate to resolve your situation.)

a. You need to be able to explain what has led you to conclude that "the class has a problem with excessive talking/noise." Since talking or noise in and of themselves are not problem behaviors, you must identify the aspects of the students' talking/noise that make it inappropriate. Is it when the students talk? where? how loud they talk? for how long? For example, the students may be talking at a time when these interactions are acceptable, but doing so too loudly.

Anecdotal notes from actual incidents can help you define the problem behavior thoroughly. Simply keep a card in your pocket or on a clipboard and occasionally make notes on incidents of excessive talking/noise.

For each entry, briefly describe the circumstances—where and when the incident occurred, who was involved, what was said and/or done, and any other relevant observations (e.g., what prompted the behavior). You do not need to take notes every time there is a problem with talking/noise; the idea is to capture a range of examples so that you will be able to describe the behavior clearly and completely.

b. It may also be useful to document how often the excessive talking/noise occurs (i.e., a frequency count). This information will provide both a more objective measure of the problem and an objective way to monitor progress. You can use the same card on which you are collecting anecdotal notes to keep the frequency count—simply write a tally mark on the card each time there is a problem with excessive talking/noise. Or, you can record the tallies on a class list as described in PLAN C.

You might also want to code the tallies to discern whether the behavior occurs more frequently during certain times, subjects, or activities (e.g., using an "A" or "P" to indicate that the incident happened in the morning or afternoon; or clustering the tallies by math or reading, teacher directed instruction or independent work, etc.).

c. If a student one notices what you are doing and asks about it, be straightforward—say that you are collecting information to see whether the excessive talking/noise is a problem that the class needs to work on.

d. The frequency information is fairly easy to summarize on a chart or graph. Seeing how often the problem occurs may help the students better understand your concern.

e. Continuing to collect this type of information and keeping the chart up-to-date while you implement a plan will help you to monitor whether the situation is getting worse, staying the same, or getting better.

2. **Decide how to present the situation to the class.**

a. Depending upon your personal philosophy and whether or not you think a simple intervention such as PLAN A will be appropriate, you may choose to have an informal discussion with the class.

b. If you intend to use one of the other MODEL PLANS, you might want to schedule a class meeting. Wait for a time when you are calm (i.e., not right after an incident has occurred) and inform the students that you are finding their excessive talking/noise to be a problem. Then specifically define your expectations regarding talking and noise, and outline the procedures you intend to implement.

Give the students the opportunity to ask questions/make comments and end the session by thanking the students for listening. Let them know that you are confident they will make an effort to better manage their talking/noise in the future.

c. If you want the students to assume more ownership of the problem, you might want to conduct a class meeting in which the students participate in analyzing the situation and developing an action plan. In this case, before the meeting you will need to have clarified the nature/extent of the problem and your expectations for the students' behavior. You will also need to identify any aspects of the plan that you do not feel comfortable opening up to a group decision.

For example, you must decide ahead of time whether or not to give the class the opportunity to determine if there will be a consequence for the excessive talking/noise and/or what the consequence should be. If you firmly believe that there must be a consequence, then you should not seek student input on that particular issue.

3. **Conduct the class meeting.**

(NOTE: The following steps are a guide to helping the class generate a plan; although you may wish to suggest one or more procedures from the MODEL PLANS.)

a. Schedule the meeting for a neutral time, and allow enough time for a reasonable discussion. Inform the students in advance that the meeting will take place; this will give them time to think about the problem. "Class, this afternoon we are going to have a class meeting on the problem of excessive talking/noise. Please give some thought to this problem and what we might do as a class to solve it."

b. Use an agenda to structure the meeting. Shortly before the meeting, write the agenda on the chalkboard. Following is one possible agenda you may wish to use.

Agenda

1. Excessive talking/noise—Define the magnitude of the problem.

   (NOTE: Share your examples and the frequency data.)

2. Review the expectations regarding managing talking/noise.

3. Brainstorm ideas for improving the situation.

4. Select strategies that everyone agrees to.

5. Establish the consequences if students are engaged in excessive talking/noise.

---

c. Establish clear rules for both you and the students regarding the brainstorming phase of the meeting. For example:

1. Any idea is okay (but no obscenity).

2. Ideas will not be evaluated initially (i.e., no approval—"Good idea" or disapproval—"What a stupid idea," or "We couldn't do that" should be expressed during brainstorming).

3. All ideas will be written down and discussed at the conclusion of brainstorming.

At the conclusion of brainstorming, evaluate the ideas, and lead the class to consensus on any decisions that need to be made. Use voting as a decision-making process when appropriate.

4. *Determine when and how to include the parent(s).*

a. For a class-wide situation, contacting the parents of all the students who engage in excessive talking/noise is probably not appropriate or realistic (it isn't feasible for you to call five to ten parents every night). However, after discussing the problem with the students, it may be useful to send a memo to the parents (or include an item in the classroom newsletter, if you have one) explaining the class-wide focus on managing the noise level of the classroom.

b. If the situation involves only one or two students who have or continue to have a problem with excessive talking/noise, you should contact the parents of those individual students. Let them know the magnitude of the problem (i.e., how many times a day you are having to give reminders) and what steps you are taking to correct the situation. Frequent contact is not required, but whenever you intend to implement an individualized plan, the parent(s) should be informed prior to its implementation and should be given feedback about the student's progress every two to four weeks.

5. *Give the class regular, ongoing feedback about their behavior.*

Periodically meet with the students to discuss the situation. In most cases, three to five minutes once per week should suffice. *(NOTE: PLANS D and E suggest daily meetings.)* During the meetings, review any information that has been collected and discuss whether or not things are getting better.

As much as possible, focus on improvements, however, also address any new or continuing problems. As you discuss problems, acknowledge that there are individuals in the class who consistently behave appropriately. However, do not single out individuals when discussing problems or progress with the entire group. As the situation improves, the meetings can be faded to once every other week and then to once per month.

6. *Evaluate the situation (and the plan).*

Any plan should be implemented for at least two weeks before deciding whether or not it is effective. Generally, if the situation has improved (based on the objective information that's been collected and/or the subjective perceptions of yourself and the students), continue with what you have been doing. (Eventually you will want to fade, then eliminate, the plan.) If the problem remains the same or worsens, some kind of change (i.e., modifying the current plan or switching to another plan) will be necessary. Always discuss any change to the intervention with the class first.

TALKING IRRESPONSIBLY (INDIVIDUAL)

DESCRIPTION

You have a student who talks in class in an irresponsible manner (i.e., excessively or at inappropriate times).

GOAL

The student will eliminate the irresponsible aspects of his communication by learning to talk at appropriate times and in appropriate ways.

OVERVIEW OF PLANS

- PLAN A: For a situation in which the problem is relatively mild or has just begun.

- PLAN B: For a student who talks irresponsibly to gain attention from adults.

- PLAN C: For a student who does not realize when and/or how often he talks irresponsibly.

- PLAN D: For a student whose irresponsible talking has become habitual.

Alternative Problems

- **Blurting Out/Not Raising Hand**

- **Disruptive Behavior— Moderate**

- **Talking/Excessive Noise in Class**

....
General Considerations

- If the inappropriate behavior stems in any way from academic issues (e.g., the student talks irresponsibly to cover up the fact that he is unable to meet the academic expectations), concurrent efforts must be made to ensure his academic success (see **Academic Deficits, Determining**).

- If the student lacks the basic social skills to interact with his peers appropriately, it may be necessary to begin by teaching him those skills.

Social Skills, Lack of contains information on a variety of published social skills curricula.

- If the inappropriate behavior is resulting in the student avoiding or not completing his schoolwork, start with a plan to increase the student's work completion (see **Work Completion—Daily Work**). Once the student is turning in completed work on a regular basis, you can consider an intervention for irresponsible talking, if the problem still exists.

....
Model Plans

PLAN A

It is not always necessary, or even beneficial, to use an involved plan. If the problem has just begun and/or is relatively mild, the following actions, along with making the student aware of your concerns, may resolve the situation.

1. Respond consistently to the inappropriate behavior.

a. During your initial meeting with the student (see SUGGESTED STEPS FOR DEVELOPING AND IMPLEMENTING A PLAN), devise a non-embarrassing signal to cue him that he needs to "stop talking." You want the signal to be a fairly subtle one that only the student will recognize and understand in order to minimize the chance that he will be teased by his peers. Signal possibilities include putting the fingertips of your hands together, rubbing your neck, or even just direct eye contact and a head nod.

Tell the student that you may also need to quietly say his name to get his attention before you give the signal. You should be prepared to use the signal frequently and for a fairly long time, since it is likely that the behavior is, at least in part, an unconscious habit for the student.

b. Whenever the student is talking irresponsibly, give the signal. If the student does not stop talking, gently correct him. Let the student know that this is an example of irresponsible talking and give him direct information about whether he should be completely silent or if moderate talking is allowed. "Amelio, some talking while you are cleaning up is fine, but keep your attention focused on the job of putting things away." Because your goal is to impart information, you

want to be emotionally neutral while giving the correction.

2. Use reinforcement to encourage appropriate behavior.

a. Give the student increased praise. Be especially alert for situations in which the student is talking in an appropriate manner, and praise him for these demonstrations of his ability to communicate responsibly. "Amelio, I noticed that you talked with Joli Ann a couple of times while the two of you were working, but you kept your attention focused on your art project. You communicated responsibly and were very productive. May I look at what the two of you came up with?"

If the student would be embarrassed by public praise, praise the student privately or even give the student a note. You can also praise the student for being appropriately silent. "Amelio, I noticed that throughout the geography lesson you did not say a word. By saying nothing you were communicating responsibly, and the message you were sending is that you are a hard worker who can keep his attention focused."

Remember that any time the student refrains from talking or talks in moderation, you can praise him for communicating responsibly.

b. Privately praise the student for responding to the signal. "Amelio, three times this morning I gave you the signal that you were talking irresponsibly, and all three times you stopped talking. That was very responsible."

c. Give the student frequent attention (e.g., say "hello" to him as he enters the classroom, call on him frequently during class activities, and occasionally ask him to assist you with a class job that needs to be done) and praise him for other positive behaviors he exhibits. For example, you might comment about the accuracy of his work or his musical talent. This demonstrates to the student that you notice many positive things he does, not just the fact that he is refraining from talking irresponsibly.

PLAN B

Some students are very skilled at gaining attention through their negative behavior. If you find yourself frequently nagging, reminding, or coaxing your student to stop talking, it is possible that he is trying to gain adult attention through his irresponsible talking. Whether or not the student overtly seems to like the attention, you should make sure that he receives more frequent and more satisfying attention for behaving appropriately than for talking irresponsibly.

1. Respond consistently to the inappropriate behavior.

a. Identify a signal to let the student know when he needs to stop talking (see PLAN A).

b. Whenever the student is talking irresponsibly, give him the signal. If he does not stop talking, implement a consequence such as time owed off of recess or in after-school detention. (NOTE: Although it is important for the student to learn that he will not be able to prompt people to nag and pay attention to him with this behavior, since the talking itself is likely to be reinforcing you need to interrupt it rather than simply ignore this behavior.)

Whenever consequences will be part of the plan, the student should be told during the initial meeting (see SUGGESTED STEPS FOR DEVELOPING AND IMPLEMENTING A PLAN) what will happen when he continues to talk irresponsibly after being given the signal. Then, if you give the signal and the student continues to talk (or stops, but starts again within a few minutes) you can simply state, for example, "Amelio, you owe a minute off of recess for talking during silent reading." When you inform the student of the consequence, keep the interaction very short and avoid giving the student too much attention.

c. After two weeks or so, stop using the signal. However, first give the student a couple of days notice that he will not longer be given a warning signal. "Amelio, starting on Thursday, I am no longer going to provide the signal to remind you that you should stop talking. Beginning Thursday, if you are talking when you shouldn't or if you are talking too much, I will simply inform you that you owe a minute off of your next recess. Each time I have to remind you, it will cost an additional minute. You are going to have to try very hard to remember to communicate responsibly, because you won't have an advance warning signal anymore—but I am sure you can do it."

2. Use reinforcement to encourage appropriate behavior.

a. Frequent praise and attention is the core of this plan. The student must see that he receives more frequent and more satisfying attention when he behaves appropriately than when he talks irresponsibly. Thus, whenever the student is not engaging in irresponsible talking, make an effort to praise and spend time with him. "Amelio, you participated so well in today's lesson. You contributed, but only when it was your turn. This shows that you can listen to others. Would it be okay if I joined you and your group as you start this next task?"

b. You may also wish to use intermittent reinforcement. Occasional, and unexpected, rewards that acknowledge the student's success may motivate him to demonstrate responsible behavior more often. The idea is to provide a reward when the student has had a particularly good period of not talking irresponsibly.

Appropriate rewards may include letting the student play a game or help you in the classroom, congratulating him in front of the principal, or letting him choose a friend to play a game with. (NOTE: A list of additional reinforcement ideas can be found in APPENDIX 1.) If you use intermittent reinforcement, do so more frequently at the beginning of the intervention to encourage the student, and less often as the student's behavior improves over time.

 Ensure a 3-1 ratio of positive to negative attention.

a. Given that attention is a motivating force for this student, you want to be sure that you are giving the student *three times as much* positive as negative attention. One way to do this is to monitor your interactions with the student at least one day per week. Simply keep a card on a clipboard or in your pocket and record each interaction you have with the student as either positive or negative by writing a "+" or a "-", respectively, on the card.

To determine whether an interaction is positive or negative, ask yourself whether the student was talking irresponsibly (or otherwise misbehaving) at the time the interaction occurred. Any interactions that stem from inappropriate behavior are negative, while all interactions that occur while the student is meeting classroom expectations are positive. Thus, gently correcting the student or assigning time owed are both negative interactions, but praising the student for not needing the signal is positive. Greeting the student as he enters the room and asking him if he has any questions during independent work are also considered positive interactions.

b. If you find that you are not giving the student three times as much positive as negative attention, try to increase the number of positive interactions you have with the student. Sometimes prompts can help. For example, you might decide that each time the student enters the classroom you will say "hello" to him, that whenever you look at the clock you will find a time to praise the student, or that whenever a student uses the drinking fountain you will check the target student and as soon as possible praise some aspect of his behavior.

PLAN C

Some students are not really aware of when they are talking irresponsibly and/or how often they talk irresponsibly. If your student doesn't seem to recognize that he is talking too much or talking at the wrong time, the intervention should include some way of helping him become more aware of his own behavior.

 Respond consistently to the inappropriate behavior.

a. Use a signal to cue to the student that he is talking irresponsibly (see PLAN A), and implement a consequence such as time owed if he does not stop talking (see PLAN B).

b. Whenever you give the student the signal, make sure the incident is recorded (see Step 2).

c. Based both on the student's average behavior and your own tolerance, determine what you consider to be the maximum number of signals given that are reasonable per half day. Then explain to the student that when you have to signal him more times than the determined amount, he will have to spend the next half day in semi-isolation. As long as the number of signals stays under the agreed-upon amount, the student will be allowed to stay in proximity of the other students.

For example, if the student has a particularly bad morning (e.g., he needs the signal more than ten times), move his desk away from the rest of the class for the afternoon. If he has a bad afternoon, his desk would be moved the next morning. Only use the modified placement for a half day at a time.

 Implement a system for monitoring the frequency (and/or duration) of the student's irresponsible talking.

a. Determine what information will be monitored (e.g., a frequency count and/or the duration time—see SUGGESTED STEPS FOR DEVELOPING AND IMPLEMENTING A PLAN) and who will record the information. If the student talks for long periods of time, you may wish to monitor how much time the student spends talking irresponsibly. Otherwise, a frequency count is appropriate. Since the point of the intervention is for the student to become more aware of his own behavior, having him do the recording (i.e., self-monitoring) will be more effective than if you do it. However, if the student cannot or will not be accurate (or if he would be too embarrassed to self-monitor), you should do the recording.

If you record the information, remember that the idea is for the student to be made aware of each time he talks irresponsibly, and for him to know that each incident is being recorded. *(NOTE: Even when the student self-monitors, you should keep your own record approximately one day per week to verify the student's accuracy.)*

b. If the student is self-monitoring his own behavior, have him tape a card like the sample following to the inside cover of his notebook or in some other unobtrusive location. When frequency is being monitored, explain that whenever the student sees you give the signal, he should cross out one number on the card, beginning with number 1.

For duration time, you should note the difference (in minutes) between when you gave the

---

Name _Amelio Paquet_

Behavior to be Counted: _Each time I talk_

irresponsibly

MONDAY _3/3_

  1 2 3 4 5 6 7 8

  9 10 11 12 13 14 15 16

17 18 19 20 21 22 23 24

TUESDAY _3/4_

  1 2 3 4 5 6 7 8

  9 10 11 12 13 14 15 16

17 18 19 20 21 22 23 24

WEDNESDAY _3/5_

  1 2 3 4 5 6 7 8

  9 10 11 12 13 14 15 16

17 18 19 20 21 22 23 24

THURSDAY _3/6_

  1 2 3 4 5 6 7 8

  9 10 11 12 13 14 15 16

17 18 19 20 21 22 23 24

FRIDAY _3/7_

  1 2 3 4 5 6 7 8

  9 10 11 12 13 14 15 16

17 18 19 20 21 22 23 24

---

signal and when the student stopped talking irresponsibly, and then subtly slip the student a piece of paper on which this information is written. The student should then add this information to his card.

c. Each day, meet with the student for a few minutes to review that day's record. Have the student chart the information (or do it yourself), and talk with him about whether the day was better, worse, or about the same as previous days. *(NOTE: If you monitor both frequency and duration, chart them separately as one may improve faster than the other.)*

If the day did not go well, encourage the student to talk about why and have him identify what he can do to help himself remember to communicate responsibly the next day. If there seem to be specific situations in which the student is more likely to engage in irresponsible talking, work with him to develop strategies for avoiding or improving those situations. For example, if the student talks more when he is seated near a friend or if he is more tempted to talk when he is sitting next to a high traffic area such as the pencil sharpener, help him choose another location in the room to sit. Always end the daily meeting by letting the student know that you are sure tomorrow will be a better day.

3. *Use reinforcement to encourage appropriate behavior.*

a. Give the student increased praise and attention for communicating responsibly (see PLAN A).

b. In addition, during the end-of-the-day review meetings, praise the student for responding to the signal (if applicable), for accurately monitoring his own behavior (if applicable), and for being willing to look at his record for the day. Even on a bad day, if the student has recorded his behavior accurately, praise him. "Amelio, you are really handling this responsibly. It was a rough day, but you accurately recorded your behavior and are willing to talk to me about things you might do differently tomorrow. That is a real sign that you are growing up."

When the number of incidents is low because the student worked half of the day in semi-isolation, you can still praise him. "Amelio, the chart is going down. Working quietly at the side of the room this afternoon helped you to have only 11 incidents for the entire day. I wonder if you can keep it this low tomorrow without having to work by yourself. If you have less than ten signals in the morning, we'll have a chance to find out."

Regardless of how the day went, try to make the end-of-the-day meeting upbeat and encouraging—you want the student to look forward to these review meetings.

4. ***Encourage the student to use self-reinforcement.***

Whenever things are going well (i.e., less irresponsible talking than usual), prompt the student to

mentally reinforce himself. "Amelio, this has been a very successful morning. Silently tell yourself that you are really good at communicating responsibly." Encourage the student to use this sort of self-reinforcement intermittently throughout the day and during the end-of-the-day review meetings.

PLAN D

If the student's irresponsible talking has become habitual and/or he does not seem to have a desire to reduce it, you may need to implement a system of external incentives (i.e., rewards and consequences) based on his behavior to motivate the student to stop talking irresponsibly and to start communicating responsibly.

1. ***Use a signal to cue the student when he is talking irresponsibly (see PLAN A).***

2. ***Monitor the frequency (and/or duration) of the student's irresponsible talking (see PLAN C).***

3. ***Establish a structured system for reinforcing the appropriate behavior and providing a consequence for the inappropriate behavior.***

a. With the student, compile a list of several reinforcers that he can earn. Although you might want to have some suggestions in mind, the system will be more effective if the student identifies most of the items or activities himself. *(NOTE: A list of reinforcement ideas can be found in APPENDIX 1.)*

b. Assign a "price" (in points) for each of the reinforcers on the list, and have the student select the one he would like to work for first.

The prices should be based on the number of points the student can earn and the cost (instructional, personnel, and/or monetary) of the items. Monetary cost is clear—the more expensive the item, the more points required to earn it. Instructional cost refers to the amount of instructional time lost or interfered with by a particular reward. Thus, an activity that causes the student to miss part of academic instruction would require more points than one the student can do on his own free time. Personnel cost involves the time required by you and/or other staff to fulfill the reinforcer. Having lunch with the principal, therefore, would cost more points

than spending five minutes of free time with a friend.

c. Establish a response cost system. In this type of system, the student begins each day with a number of points equal to the average number of times per day the student has been talking irresponsibly, plus two. For example, if the student has talked irresponsibly an average of 13 times per day, he would begin each day with 15 points. Each time you have to give the signal that he is talking irresponsibly, the student loses one point. The points remaining at the end of each day are added together and applied toward the reward the student is trying to earn.

(NOTE: A lottery system might be more effective with a primary level student. In this type of system, the student would begin each day with tickets in a jar instead of points. All the tickets would have prizes written on them—one would have a big prize, a couple would have moderate prizes, and the majority would have small prizes. Each time you have to use the signal, you would remove one ticket from the jar—but neither you nor the student would be allowed to see what is written on it. At the end of each day, the student would draw one ticket from those remaining in the jar, and receives that prize.)

d. Determine a consequence (e.g., time owed off of recess or in after-school detention) for any incident that occurs after the student has lost all his points (or tickets) for the day. However, do not take away any previously earned points. Once the student has earned the points, he should not risk losing them or it may jeopardize the system. The student could develop an attitude of, "I am losing so many points, why should I even bother to try?"

(NOTE: When you monitor duration time instead of frequency, you can use a similar system, but you will have to decide how you will translate the number of minutes into points and when to implement consequences.)

 Use reinforcement to encourage appropriate behavior.

a. Give the student increased praise and attention for communicating responsibly (see PLAN A).

b. In addition, show interest and enthusiasm about how the student is doing on the system. "Amelio, we are half way through the day and you still have 12 points left. Your responsible behavior is decreasing the number of days that you will have to wait to have lunch with the counselor!"

. . . .

Suggested Steps for Developing and Implementing a Plan

The following steps are designed to help you develop an appropriate intervention plan and implement it effectively, whether you choose to use one of the MODEL PLANS or create a customized plan of your own. The steps are, however, suggestions—they are not intended to be followed rigidly or in any particular order. Use your professional judgment and the knowledge of your particular situation to make them work for you.

 Make sure you have enough information about the situation.

a. If you think a minimal intervention like PLAN A will be sufficient, you probably already have enough information to proceed. However, when a more involved plan seems necessary, you should consider collecting additional descriptive and/or objective information for a couple of days so that you can thoroughly describe the problem behavior and monitor any changes in the situation.

b. Descriptive information (e.g., anecdotal notes) can be critical to developing a clear definition of the problem behavior. That is, you must be able to specify what it is about the student's talking that makes it irresponsible. Is it that he talks for long periods of time? talks at the wrong time or in the wrong place? Even if you are sure what it is about the student's talking that concerns you, having notes on actual incidents will help you explain the problem clearly to the student and his parent(s).

To collect anecdotal notes, simply keep a card in your pocket or on a clipboard and occasionally make notes on specific incidents in which the student talks irresponsibly. For each entry, include a brief description of the setting (where and when the incident occurred), what the student did or said, and any other relevant observations you have about the situation (e.g., what prompted the behavior). You do not need to take notes every time the student talks irresponsibly; the idea is to capture a range of examples of the behavior so you will be able to describe it completely.

You should also make notes on times when the student communicates responsibly; this will help him realize that you are not only aware of his inappropriate behavior, but also when he behaves responsibly. In addition, when you meet with the student, these positive examples will help you clarify how you want the student to behave.

c. In addition to being able to describe what the irresponsible behavior looks like, it can also be useful to document how often it occurs and/or how much time is involved. This information provides both a more objective measure of the problem and an objective way to monitor the student's progress. The easiest measurement is to record how often the student talks irresponsibly (i.e., a frequency count). On the same card that you use for anecdotal notes, simply write a tally mark each time the student talks irresponsibly.

You might also want to code the tallies as a way of discerning whether the behavior occurs more frequently during certain times, subjects, or activities (e.g., using an "A" or "P" to distinguish incidents that happened in the morning or afternoon; or clustering the tallies by math or reading, teacher directed instruction or independent work, etc.).

(NOTE: If you are using a signal to cue the student, you can also monitor the student's behavior by recording a + whenever you need to give the student the signal. If the student does not respond to the signal, circle the +. In this way, you can tell how many times the student talked irresponsibly and how often he corrected his own behavior when signaled.)

If you are concerned about the amount of time the student spends talking irresponsibly, you may wish to also (or instead of a frequency count) document how many minutes the student talks irresponsibly (i.e., the duration time). To do this, each time the student talks irresponsibly mentally note the time when he begins and the time when he stops talking. Record the difference (in the number of minutes) next to (or in place of) the tally mark. At the end of the day, you will be able to calculate the total number of minutes spent talking irresponsibly.

d. If the student notices what you are doing and asks about it, be straightforward—tell him that you are collecting information to see whether his irresponsible talking is a problem that needs to be worked on.

The following example shows anecdotal notes and frequency information that has been collected on a student's irresponsible talking.

Amelio's Irresponsible Talking—3/1

Teacher Directed Instruction	Independent Work Periods	Cooperative Groups/ Labs
AAAAA AAAPP PPPPP	AAAAA PP	AAA

Notes:

10:05—When I reprimanded Amelio for talking during geography, he said he was just asking for help. Is this responsible or irresponsible talking???

1:15—During cooperative groups everyone is talking, however I had to remind Amelio three times that he should only be talking about the assignment.

---

e. Both the frequency count and duration time are fairly easy to summarize on a chart or graph. Seeing how often and/or how much time he spends talking irresponsibly may help the student and his parent(s) better understand your

concern. If you collect both frequency and duration time information, chart them separately as one may improve faster than the other. For example, the number of times the student talks irresponsibly may remain about the same while the number of minutes decreases dramatically. The distinction could be important when deciding whether the situation is improving, staying the same, or getting worse.

2. *Identify a focus for the intervention and labels for referring to the appropriate and inappropriate behaviors.*

a. To be effective, the intervention must address more than just reducing the student's irresponsible talking—there must be a concurrent emphasis on increasing some positive behavior or trait (e.g., communicating responsibly). Not only will having a specific positive behavior in mind make it easier to "catch" and reinforce the student for behaving appropriately, but a positive focus will allow you to frame the situation productively.

For example, if you describe the situation simply as "the student has a problem with talking irresponsibly," you not only offer little in the way of useful information, but you may put the student and his parent(s) on the defensive. However, if you explain your concern by saying that you want to "help the student learn to communicate responsibly," you present an important, and reasonable, goal for the student to work toward and clearly identify what the student needs to do to be successful.

b. Identifying labels for referring to the appropriate and inappropriate behaviors (e.g., "communicating responsibly" and "talking irresponsibly," respectively) will help you to use consistent vocabulary when discussing the situation with the student. If you sometimes refer to the inappropriate behavior as "talking," for example, and other times tell the student that he "is being irresponsible" he may not realize that you are talking about the same thing.

3. *Determine when and how to include the parent(s).*

a. You probably do not need to contact the student's parent(s) if the problem has just begun and is not interfering with the student's academic or social progress. You might, however, take advantage of any scheduled activities (e.g., conferences, weekly notes home) to let them know of your concern.

b. The parent(s) should be contacted whenever the student's irresponsible talking is affecting his academic performance or is alienating him from his peers. Share with them any information you have collected (e.g., anecdotal notes, frequency and/or duration information), and explain why you are concerned. Focus in particular on how the behavior is hindering the student academically and/or socially (e.g., other students are beginning to get annoyed with his constant talking and are beginning to avoid him).

You might ask if the parent(s) have any insight into the behavior and/or whether they have noticed similar behavior at home. Whether or not the parent(s) perceive a problem, invite them to join you for an initial meeting with the student to develop a plan. If the parent(s) are unable or unwilling to participate, let them know that you will keep them informed of the student's progress.

c. Once the parent(s) have been involved in any way, you should give them updates at least once per week while the plan is being implemented.

4. **Prepare for, then conduct, an initial meeting about the situation.**

a. Schedule a meeting to discuss your concerns with the student and anyone else who will be involved in the plan (e.g., the parent[s], the school psychologist). Although the specifics of the meeting will vary depending upon the age of the student and the severity of the problem, there are some general guidelines to consider when scheduling the meeting.

First, meet at a neutral time (i.e., not immediately after a problem has occurred), when emotions are less likely to hamper communication. In general, a day's notice is appropriate, however a primary age student may worry excessively and/or forget what the meeting is about if it is scheduled more than an hour before it takes place.

Second, make the meeting appropriately private. For example, with a primary student with a mild problem, you might meet in the classroom while the other students are working independently. However, if you are dealing with a middle/junior high school student and the student's parent(s), you will want a private room (e.g., the counselor's office) to ensure that the discussion will not be overheard.

Third, try to make sure the meeting is scheduled for a time and place that it is not likely to be interrupted. Finally, if the parent(s) will be participating, they should be the ones to tell their student about the meeting.

b. Construct a preliminary plan. Based on the information you have collected and the focus for the intervention that you have identified, you may decide to use one of the MODEL PLANS or to create a customized plan using components from various plans and/or of your own design. Although it is important to invite and encourage the student to be an active partner in developing the plan during the initial meeting, having a proposed plan in mind before you meet can alleviate frustration and wasted time if the student is unwilling or unable to participate.

c. Using the information you have collected, prepare thorough descriptions of the inappropriate behavior and the positive behavior/trait on which the student will be working. Be as specific as you can and add concrete examples whenever possible. This will make it easier for you to clarify (and for the student to understand) your expectations. Be sure to identify the appropriate and inappropriate behavior in all relevant activities (e.g., independent work, teacher directed instruction, unstructured class times, recess and lunch, etc.).

d. Conduct the meeting in an atmosphere of collaboration. The following agenda is one way you might structure the meeting:

- **Share your concerns about the student's behavior.**

    Briefly describe the problem behavior and, when appropriate, show him the chart(s) of how often/how much he engages in irresponsible talking. Then explain why you consider this behavior to be a problem. You might tell the student that his irresponsible talking is affecting how others feel about him.

- **Discuss how you can work together to improve the situation.**

    Explain that you would like to help the student "learn to communicate responsibly" and describe your preliminary plan. Invite the student to give you input on the plan, and together work out any necessary details (e.g., the signal, reinforcers and consequences). You may have to brainstorm different possibilities if the student is uncomfortable with the initial plan. Incorporating any of the student's suggestions that strengthen the plan is likely to increase his sense of "ownership" in and his commitment to it.

- **Make sure the student understands what you mean by appropriate and inappropriate behavior.**

  Use the descriptions you have prepared to define and clarify the problem behavior and the positive (desired) behavior as specifically and thoroughly as you can. To ensure that you and the student are in agreement about the expectations, you might present hypothetical scenarios and have him identify whether each is an example of communicating responsibly or talking irresponsibly. Or, you might present an actual situation that has occurred and ask the student to explain how he could have communicated responsibly in that situation.

- **Conclude the meeting.**

  Always end the meeting with words of encouragement. Let the student know that you are confident that he can be successful, and that he may actually find that he likes school more when he is communicating responsibly. Be sure to reinforce him for participating in the meeting.

5. *Give the student regular, ongoing feedback about his behavior.*

It is important to periodically discuss the student's progress with him. Unless the plan calls for daily meetings (i.e., PLANS C and D), a three to five minute meeting once per week should suffice. During the meetings, review any information that has been collected and discuss whether or not the situation is improving. As much as possible, focus on the student's improvements, however, also address any new or continuing problems. As the situation improves, the meetings can be faded to once every other week and then to once per month.

6. *Evaluate the situation (and the plan).*

Implement any plan for at least two weeks before deciding whether to change plans; to continue, modify, or fade the plan you are using; or to cease the intervention. Generally, if the student's behavior is clearly improving (based on the objective information that's been collected and/or the subjective perceptions of yourself, the student, and possibly the parent[s]), stick with what you are doing. If the situation has remained the same or worsened, some kind of change will be necessary. Always discuss any changes to the plan with the student first.

TANTRUMMING
(K OR 1ST GRADER)

DESCRIPTION

You have a student who tantrums (e.g., screaming, pounding and kicking the floor, sobbing) when things do not go her way or when faced with circumstances she views as unpleasant.

GOAL

The student will reduce and eventually eliminate her tantrumming behavior and learn to express her emotions and desires in a more mature and responsible way.

OVERVIEW OF PLANS

- PLAN A: For a situation in which the problem has just begun or occurs infrequently.

- PLAN B: For a student who lacks the skills or ability to mange her emotions and/or to communicate her feelings and needs in more responsible ways.

- PLAN C: For a student who uses tantrumming to escape unpleasant or difficult situations.

- PLAN D: For a student who uses tantrumming as a way to gain attention or power.

- PLAN E: For a student whose tantrumming behavior has become habitual and/or who is not motivated to reduce the frequency of this behavior.

Alternative Problems

- **Babyish Behavior**

- **Crying, Chronic**

- **Physically Dangerous Behavior—to Self or Others**

- **Self-Control Issues**

- **Spoiled Behavior**

· · · · · · · ·
General Considerations

- If the student's problem behavior stems in any way from academic issues (e.g., the student tantrums because she is unable to understand her schoolwork), concurrent efforts must be made to ensure her academic success (see **Academic Deficits, Determining**).

- If the student lacks the basic social skills to interact with her peers appropriately, it may be necessary to begin by teaching her those skills. **Social Skills, Lack of** contains information on a variety of published social skills curricula.

- If the student's tantrums are so severe that no other learning can occur, you may wish to incorporate the procedures for removing a student from the classroom that are outlined in the problem **Disruptive Behavior—Severe**.

- In some rare instances, the student might show an extreme fear of a particular activity, such as getting her hands wet, and tantrum to avoid this activity. If you believe this to be the case, discuss the situation with the student's parent(s). Then if the student's tantrums seem to be the result of a severe emotional problem or deep seated phobia, refer the problem to the school psychologist or other mental health professional.

- If the tantrums pose a physical danger to the student herself or the other students, coordinate the strategies provided here with those in **Physically Dangerous Behavior—to Self or Others**.

· · · · · · · ·
Model Plans

PLAN A

It is not always necessary, or even beneficial, to use an involved plan. If the inappropriate behavior has just begun and/or occurs infrequently (i.e., has only happened once or twice), the following actions, along with making the student aware of your concerns, may resolve the situation.

1. *Respond consistently to the inappropriate behavior.*

a. Whenever the student is beginning to get frustrated or angry, give the student a verbal cue that reminds her of a positive expectation. Use the same wording every time you give the student this verbal cue. For a student with a sophisticated vocabulary, the cue could be worded as, "Remember, stay relaxed, then quietly communicate what you are thinking or feeling." For a less sophisticated student, use a less complicated cue (e.g., "Remember, stay calm."). Give this cue one time as the student is beginning to become frustrated or angry.

b. If the student becomes increasingly angry or frustrated, instruct the student to go to a predetermined time-out ("cool down") location. This location could be as simple as a chair placed in a low traffic area of the classroom. When the student goes to time-out, she should have nothing to do—she should not be allowed to take books or other toys with her.

The amount of time the student must spend in time-out should be very short (e.g., one minute). However, the one minute should not begin until the student is settled in the time-out area and is quiet and under control. After the one minute in the time-out area, the student should be instructed to resume class activities. "Bonnie, you have calmed yourself down. Come join us here on the rug for our story time."

c. If the student does not go to time-out, begins to tantrum, or tantrums in the time-out area, ignore this behavior. Make no attempt to calm the student or try to stop her tantrum. When she is done with the tantrum, remind her that she needs to "go to the cool down area for one minute to show that she is calm and ready to be with the rest of the class."

2. *Use reinforcement to encourage appropriate behavior.*

a. Give the student increased praise. Be especially alert for situations in which the student remains calm when faced with a difficult or frustrating situation and praise her for these demonstrations of her ability to stay relaxed, then quietly communicate what she is thinking or feeling. "Bonnie, Vu Lee cut in front of you, but you stayed relaxed and quietly told her that you are the line leader today. Vu Lee, you need to go to the back of the line. Bonnie, that was a great example of calmly communicating what you were thinking."

Remember that any time the student is calmly communicating her thoughts or feelings, and/or simply remaining calm, you can praise her.

b. Praise the student for responding to the verbal reminder. "Wow, Bonnie. You were starting to get upset, but you listened to my reminder and you got yourself to relax. Now tell me what it is that concerns you."

c. Also praise the student if she goes directly to time-out when directed and remains calm while there. "Bonnie, you got upset, but you went to the 'cool down' area, calmed down, and you are now ready to join us. Excellent, you are learning to manage your angry feelings."

d. Give the student frequent attention (e.g., say "hello" to her as she enters the classroom, call on her frequently during class activities, and occasionally ask her to assist you with a class job that needs to be done) and praise her for other positive behaviors she exhibits. For example, you might comment about her participation in class or the creativity of her art projects. This demonstrates to the student that you notice many positive things she does, not just the fact that she is refraining from tantrumming.

PLAN B

Some students do not know how to stay relaxed, then calmly communicate what they are thinking or feeling. If your student does not seem to possess the necessary skills to communicate her thoughts or feelings in a responsible manner, then the intervention must include a way to teach her how to do so.

1. Respond consistently to the inappropriate behavior.

a. Whenever the student is beginning to become frustrated or angry, give her a consistent verbal cue that reminds her of a positive expectation. If she becomes increasingly frustrated or angry, instruct her to go to time-out (the "cool down" area) for one minute, and ignore any subsequent tantrumming (see PLAN A).

b. When you give the verbal cue, also suggest one of the calming strategies that the student has been practicing (see Step 2).

2. Conduct lessons to teach the student how to stay relaxed.

(NOTE: Some people may consider these lessons somewhat controversial. Be sure to check with your administrator and/or obtain parental permission before implementing this step.)

a. Identify one or more strategies the student might be able to use to remain calm. Possibilities include: counting backwards from ten; taking two slow, deep breaths; speaking in a quiet, calm voice; and/or unclenching her fists. *(NOTE: **Anxiety/Nervousness** provides procedures for teaching one or more of these strategies to the student.)*

b. During the lessons, use examples of situations that tend to make the student engage in tantrumming. For each situation, have the student describe, then role play, how she would normally feel in that situation. Introduce one or two of the calming strategies, and teach the student how to use those strategies when faced with the difficult situation.

Then have the student role play the situation again, this time using one of the calming strategies. Be sure to emphasize that the student may not always be able to get her own way by staying calm, but that there is a better chance than if she tantrums.

c. Conduct the lessons daily if possible, but at least twice per week, perhaps while the other students are at recess. The lessons needn't last more than three to five minutes, and it is important that they be handled in a matter-of-fact manner so the student does not feel that she is being ridiculed.

Continue the lessons until the student is consistently responding to the verbal cue to stay calm and/or is no longer tantrumming when confronted with a difficult situation.

3. *Use reinforcement to encourage appropriate behavior.*

a. Give the student increased praise and attention for remaining calm (see PLAN A).

b. In addition, make a special point of letting the student know that you notice her efforts to use the calming strategies that she has been learning/practicing. "Bonnie, I noticed that when I reminded you to stay calm, you took two slow, deep breaths; unclenched your fists; and talked to me in a quiet, calm voice. Nice job of doing what we have been practicing."

PLAN C

Some students use tantrumming as a strategy for avoiding unpleasant, difficult, or stressful situations. If it seems like your student is avoiding a particular location or activity (e.g., missing recess each day) through tantrumming, first determine whether the student really needs assistance with this location or activity. Then make sure that the student is not able to use tantrumming to avoid reasonable school expectations.

1. *Respond consistently to the inappropriate behavior.*

Whenever the student is beginning to become frustrated or angry, give her a consistent verbal cue that reminds her of a positive expectation. If she becomes increasingly frustrated or angry, instruct her to go to time-out (the "cool down" area) for one minute, and ignore any subsequent tantrumming (see PLAN A).

2. *Identify and analyze the type(s) of situations the student tries to avoid by tantrumming.*

a. Look for patterns in the tantrumming behavior to determine exactly what the student is trying to avoid (e.g., a location, activity, type of assignment, etc.).

b. For each identified situation, determine if there is any possibility that the student's fear or aversion to the situation is warranted. Usually this will not be the case, and a tantrum will be the result of something as simple as the student not wanting to put away the supplies she was using, for example. However, in some cases, the tantrumming behavior can mask a deeper problem. For example, a student who is falling behind in an academic task that she perceives other students as mastering—let's say participation in a reading group—may tantrum to avoid having to go to reading.

In these sorts of incidents, treating the problem exclusively as tantrumming would be a disservice to the student. Something must be done to remediate the student's skills, or change the student's placement so she can be successful. Similarly, a student who tantrums about going out to recess might not know how to deal with an unstructured situation like recess, or might be fearful of a particular student who has been bullying her (see **Victim—Student Who Is Always Picked On**).

3. *Construct a plan to ensure that the student is not able to avoid a reasonable school expectation through tantrumming.*

a. For each of the situations identified that involve a reasonable expectation, structure a way to ensure that, even if the student tantrums, she will have to engage in the activity or situation that she was trying to escape through tantrumming. The student must learn that while a tantrum may delay a particular activity, it will not successfully eliminate her participation.

For this to work, you will need to decide ahead of time how various situations will be handled and prepare yourself for the possibility that the student will tantrum for a fairly long time. For example, if the student tantrums when instructed to put away her materials, you can let the student know that she will not be allowed to participate in any other activity until the materials are put away.

If the student starts to tantrum shortly before lunch, you will need a contingency plan for supervising her while the rest of the class goes to lunch, which should include details such as how to make sure the student's lunch will be available as soon as she puts away her materials. If the student tantrums because she does not want to do an assigned academic task, determine how the student can be required to complete the assigned task prior to engaging in fun activities and/or, if possible, before she goes home.

Some plans may require parental participation and/or support. Work with the student's parent(s) on these plans—including being able to keep the student after school until the required tasks are performed. If you cannot obtain parental approval/support for keeping the student after school when necessary, make sure that upon arrival the next day, the student has to meet the expectations right away.

b. For each type of problematic situation, identify a strategy that will help give the student confidence that she can be successful (and maybe even have fun) in that situation. Privately meet with the student periodically to discuss and/or practice these strategies. For example, you might teach the student to use self-reinforcing strategies such as saying to herself, "I can do it! I know I can!" Or, you can spend a few minutes having the student actually practice the task that has been avoided. "Bonnie, today I would like us to spend time playing a game about math. Why don't you be the teacher and assign me to do some problems on this page." Then, after you model an appropriate way to begin the task through this game, trade roles and have the student practice the task.

 Prompt the student to remain calm by using precorrections.

Prior to situations in which the student is likely to tantrum, remind her that she will need to remember to stay calm. If time permits, you might have her identify how she can behave responsibly. "Bonnie, we are a few minutes from starting our math assignment. Start getting yourself ready to begin, the way we practiced yesterday. I'll bet you can do it. Are you ready for me to give the assignment to the class? What are you going to do to keep yourself calm?" If this type of discussion would embarrass the student, speak to the student privately.

 Use reinforcement to encourage appropriate behavior.

a. Give the student increased praise and attention for remaining calm (see PLAN A).

b. In addition, right before, during, and immediately after any problematic situation, provide the student frequent encouragement and support. Given that the situation is truly stressful for the student, knowing that you are there to support her will make it easier for the student to face the situation calmly.

PLAN D

Some students are very skilled at gaining attention and power through negative behavior. If you find yourself frequently nagging, reminding, or coaxing the student to stop tantrumming, and/or find yourself "walking on eggshells" with the student in order to avoid a tantrum, it is possible that this is the student's motivation. Whether or not the student overtly seems to like the attention, you should make sure that she receives more frequent and more satisfying attention when she behaves appropriately than when she tantrums.

 Respond consistently to the inappropriate behavior.

a. Whenever the student is beginning to become frustrated or angry, give her a consistent verbal cue that reminds her of a positive expectation. If she becomes increasingly frustrated or angry, instruct her to go to time-out (the "cool down" area) for one minute, and ignore any subsequent tantrumming (see PLAN A).

b. Realize that the student may be skilled at making you feel that it is your job to keep her from tantrumming, and be especially careful to avoid repeated reminders to the student to either stay calm or to go to time-out. If the student does not respond to the verbal cue and/or the instruction to go to time-out, ignore this misbehavior. Be

sure to give the student *absolutely no* attention while she is engaged in a tantrum.

Try to stay calm. Do not act disgusted or impatient with the student's behavior. Simply interact in positive ways with students who are behaving appropriately and meeting classroom expectations. As soon as the target student is no longer tantrumming, pay attention to her, but make no reference to her inappropriate behavior.

c. If other students give the target student attention when she is tantrumming (e.g., staring at her or trying to calm her down), gently correct them. "Mick and Jevona, Bonnie can take care of herself and she will join us when she calms down. It would be best to let her work it out on her own."

2. Use reinforcement to encourage appropriate behavior.

a. Frequent praise and attention is the core of this plan. The student must see that she receives more frequent and more satisfying attention when she behaves appropriately than when she tantrums. Thus, whenever the student is not tantrumming (or otherwise misbehaving), make an effort to praise and spend time with her. "Bonnie, you have been doing such a fine job this morning of staying relaxed. Would it be okay if I sat with you a moment and watched as you work on your drawing? This is a very interesting pattern. Tell me about this."

b. You may also wish to use intermittent rewards to acknowledge the student's success. Occasional, and unexpected, rewards can motivate the student to demonstrate responsible behavior more often. The idea is to provide a reward when the student has had a particularly good period of staying relaxed. Appropriate rewards might include taking a note to the principal so she can congratulate the student, sitting with the student during an assembly, or letting the student staple some papers for you. *(NOTE: A list of additional reinforcement ideas can be found in APPENDIX 1.)*

Use intermittent rewards more frequently at the beginning of the intervention to encourage the student, and then less often as her behavior improves.

3. Ensure a 3-1 ratio of positive to negative attention.

a. Given that attention is a motivating force for this student, you want to be sure that you are giving her *three times as much* positive as negative attention. One way to do this is to monitor your interactions with the student at least one day per week. Simply keep a card on a clipboard or in your pocket and record each interaction you have with the student as either positive or negative by writing a "+" or a "-", respectively, on the card.

To determine whether an interaction is positive or negative, ask yourself whether the student was beginning to tantrum (or otherwise misbehaving) at the time the interaction occurred. Any interaction that stems from inappropriate behavior is negative, and all interactions that occur while the student is meeting classroom expectations are positive. Thus, giving the verbal cue and instructing the student to go to time-out are both negative interactions, but praising the student for calming down after you give the verbal cue is positive. Greeting the student as she enters the room or asking her if she has any questions during independent work are also considered positive interactions. *(NOTE: Ignoring the student's tantrumming is not recorded at all, because it is not an interaction.)*

b. If you find that you are not giving the student three times as much positive as negative attention, try to increase the number of positive interactions you have with her. Sometimes prompts can help. For example, you might decide that each time the student enters the classroom you will say "hello" to her; that every time you give the verbal cue and the student calms down you will praise her; or that during transitions between instructional activities you will check the target student and, as soon as possible, praise some aspect of her behavior.

4. Encourage the student to use self-reinforcement.

Whenever things are going well (i.e., less tantrumming than usual), prompt the student to mentally reinforce herself. "Bonnie, this has been a very successful morning. Silently tell yourself that you are really good at staying relaxed." Prompt the student this way intermittently throughout the day.

PLAN E

If the student's tantrumming behavior has become habitual and/or she does not seem to have a desire to reduce it, you may need to implement a system of external incentives (i.e., rewards and consequences) based on her behavior to motivate her to stop tantrumming and to stay relaxed and quietly communicate her thoughts and feelings.

1. Respond consistently to the inappropriate behavior.

Whenever the student is beginning to become frustrated or angry, give her a consistent verbal cue that reminds her of a positive expectation. If she becomes increasingly frustrated or angry, instruct her to go to time-out (the "cool down" area) for one minute, and ignore any subsequent tantrumming (see PLAN A).

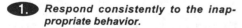

2. *Establish a structured system for reinforcing the appropriate behavior (i.e., the absence of tantrumming).*

a. With the student, create a list of reinforcers that she can earn. Although you might want to have some suggestions in mind, the system will be more effective if the student identifies most of the items or activities herself. *(NOTE: A list of reinforcement ideas can be found in APPENDIX 1.)*

b. Assign "prices" (in points) for each of the rewards on the list, and have the student choose the reward she would like to earn first.

The prices should be based on the instructional, personnel, and/or monetary costs of the items. Monetary cost is clear—the more expensive the item, the more points required to earn it. Instructional cost refers to the amount of instructional time lost or interfered with by a particular reward. Thus, an activity which causes the student to miss part of academic instruction should require more points than one the student can do at lunch time. Personnel cost involves the time required by you and/or other staff to fulfill the reinforcer. Having lunch with the principal, therefore, would cost more points than spending five minutes of free time with a friend.

c. Devise a way for the student to earn tokens (e.g., pieces of a special color of paper cut into 1" x 3" strips) for the absence of tantrumming. For example, the student might earn one token

for each hour in which there are no tantrums, and two tokens if she does not even have to go to time-out. At the end of each hour (or, if more appropriate, each instructional activity), take a minute to discuss with the student whether she earned zero, one, or two tokens for that hour.

d. When the student has accumulated enough points to earn the reward she has chosen, she "spends" the points necessary and the system begins again. That is, she selects another reward to earn and begins with zero points.

If the student needs more frequent encouragement, you might let her earn several "less expensive" rewards (e.g., five minutes of computer time after ten points) on the way to a bigger reward (e.g., one hour with you for 100 points) without spending her points. That way, she receives frequent, small rewards, but continues to accumulate points toward the selected reward.

 3. *Use reinforcement to encourage appropriate behavior.*

a. Give the student increased praise and attention for remaining calm (see PLAN A).

b. In addition, show interest and enthusiasm about how the student is doing on the system. "Bonnie, once again you have had another hour with no tantrums. You did need to go to time-out once, but even so you earn one token. Let's count how many you have saved already."

· · · · · · · ·
Suggested Steps for Developing and Implementing a Plan

The following steps are designed to help you develop an appropriate intervention plan and implement it effectively, whether you choose to use one of the MODEL PLANS or create a customized plan of your own. The steps are, however, suggestions—they are not intended to be followed rigidly or in any particular order. Use your professional judgment and the knowledge of your particular situation to make them work for you.

 1. *Make sure you have enough information about the situation.*

a. If you think a minimal intervention like PLAN A will be sufficient, you may already have enough information to proceed. However, when a more involved plan seems necessary, you should consider collecting additional descriptive and/or objective information for a couple of days.

b. You need to be able to explain what has led you to conclude that "the student has a problem with

tantrumming." Anecdotal notes on actual incidents should provide enough detail to define the problem behavior clearly and completely. To collect anecdotal notes, keep a card in your pocket or on a clipboard and make notes about instances when the student tantrums. For each entry, briefly describe where and when the tantrum occurred, what the student did or said, and any other relevant observations (e.g., what prompted the behavior).

You do not need to take notes every time the student tantrums; however, you want to capture a range of examples so that you will be able to thoroughly describe the behavior and recognize any patterns.

Also include some notes on times when the student handles difficult situations calmly. This will make it clear that you are not only aware of her problem behavior, but also recognize when she behaves appropriately. When you meet with the student, these positive examples will also help clarify how you want the student to behave.

c. In addition to information about what the student's tantrumming looks like, it can also be useful to document how often it occurs (i.e., a frequency count) and how long it lasts (i.e., the duration time). This will provide both a more objective measure of the problem and an objective way to monitor the student's progress.

You can use the same card on which you are collecting anecdotal notes to record frequency and duration data. Each time the student tantrums , mentally note the time when she begins and the time when she stops. Write the difference (in the number of minutes) on the card. At the end of the day, you will be able to determine the number of tantrums and calculate the total number of minutes spent tantrumming.

d. If the student notices what you are doing and asks about it, be straightforward—tell her that you are collecting information to see whether

her tantrumming is a problem that needs to be worked on.

e. Following is an example of anecdotal notes, frequency count, and duration time that have been collected on a student's tantrumming.

f. Frequency and duration time are fairly easy to summarize on a chart or graph. Seeing how often and/or how much time she spends tantrumming may help the student and her parent(s) better understand your concern. *(NOTE: If you collect both frequency and duration information, chart them separately as one may improve faster than the other. For example, the number of incidents may stay about the same, while the amount of time spent tantrumming decreases dramatically.)*

g. Continuing to collect this type of information and keeping the charts up-to-date while you implement a plan will help you to monitor whether the situation is getting worse, staying the same, or getting better.

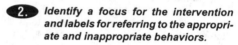 **2.** *Identify a focus for the intervention and labels for referring to the appropriate and inappropriate behaviors.*

a. To be effective, the intervention must address more than just reducing the student's tantrumming—there must be a concurrent emphasis on increasing some positive behavior or trait (e.g., staying relaxed and quietly communicating her thoughts and feelings). Having a specific positive behavior in mind will make it easier for you

---

Notes on Bonnie's Tantrums—10/17

Frequency & Time:

Morning	Afternoon
15 min.	18 min.
6 min.	
12 min.	

Notes:

9:50—I asked Bonnie to put away the books she was looking at and come over to the story area. She tantrummed for 15 minutes. She then put away the books, but she had missed the story. Should I make her do something to make up for missing the story? Today I did nothing; however, I should watch for a pattern.

11:15—When I instructed the class to put away the art supplies, she started again. Several other students were going to put her things away while she was crying on the floor. I thanked them for wanting to help, but I told them that she could put away her own things. She only lasted for six minutes. Progress???

---

to "catch" and reinforce the student for behaving appropriately, and the positive focus will frame the situation more productively.

For example, if you simply say that "the student has a problem with tantrumming," you don't really provide any useful information, and may put the student and her parent(s) on the defensive. However, when you explain that you want to help the student "learn to stay relaxed and quietly communicate her thoughts and feelings," you present an important, and reasonable, goal for the student to work toward and clearly identify what the student needs to do to be successful.

b. Specifying labels for the appropriate and inappropriate behaviors (e.g., " staying relaxed" and "tantrumming," respectively) will help you to use consistent vocabulary when discussing the situation with the student. If you sometimes refer to the inappropriate behavior as "getting angry," for example, and other times tell the student to "stop tantrumming," she may not realize that you are talking about the same behavior.

3. Determine when and how to include the parent(s).

a. With a tantrumming problem, the student's parent(s) should be contacted immediately. The parent(s) have a right to know that their child got very upset about something. Share with them any information you have about the behavior (e.g., anecdotal notes, frequency count, duration time), and explain why you are concerned. Focus in particular on how the behavior is hindering the student academically and/or socially (e.g., other students are avoiding her for fear of making her upset).

You might ask if the parent(s) have any insight into the tantrumming and/or whether they have experienced similar behavior at home. Whether or not the parent(s) perceive a problem, explain that you want to help the student "learn to stay relaxed and quietly communicate her thoughts and feelings," and invite them to join you for an initial meeting with the student to develop a plan. If the parent(s) are unable or unwilling to participate, let them know that you will keep them informed of the student's progress.

b. Once the parent(s) have been involved in any way, you should give them updates at least once per week while the plan is being implemented.

4. Prepare for, then conduct, an initial meeting about the situation.

a. Arrange a meeting to discuss your concerns with the student and anyone else who will be involved with the plan (e.g., the parent[s], the school psychologist). Although the specifics will vary depending upon the severity of the problem, there are some general guidelines to consider when scheduling the meeting.

First, meet at a neutral time (i.e., not immediately after a problem has occurred), when emotions are less likely to hamper communication. In general, a day's notice is appropriate, however a kindergarten or 1st grade student may worry excessively and/or forget what the meeting is about if it is scheduled more than an hour before it takes place.

Second, make the meeting appropriately private. Third, try to make sure the meeting is scheduled for a time and place that it is not likely to be interrupted (e.g., the counselor's office). Finally, if the parent(s) will be participating, let them be the ones to tell the student about the meeting.

b. Conduct a preliminary plan. Decide whether you think you can use one of the MODEL PLANS or if you need to create a customized plan using components from various plans and/or of your own design. Although you will invite and encourage the student to help develop the plan during the initial meeting, having a proposed plan in mind before you meet can alleviate frustration and wasted time if the student is unwilling or unable to participate.

c. After reviewing the information you have collected and thinking about how you want the student to behave, prepare thorough descriptions of both the inappropriate behavior and the positive behavior/trait on which the student will be working. The more specific you can be and the more concrete examples you have, the easier it will be to clarify (and for the student to understand) your expectations. Be sure to consider the student's behavior in all relevant activities (e.g., independent work, teacher directed instruction, unstructured class times, recess and lunch, etc.).

d. Conduct the meeting in an atmosphere of collaboration. The following agenda is one way you might structure the meeting:

- **Share your concerns about the student's behavior.**

  Briefly describe the problem behavior and, when appropriate, show the student the chart(s) of how often/how long she engages in tantrumming. Then explain why you consider this behavior to be a problem. You might tell the student that while she has a right to have strong feelings or ideas, she needs to learn to communicate them in more responsible ways.

- **Discuss how you can work together to improve the situation.**

  Tell the student that you would like to help her "learn to stay relaxed and quietly communicate her thoughts and feelings" and describe your preliminary plan. Invite the student to give you input on the various aspects of the plan, and together work out any necessary details (e.g., the verbal cue, use of time-out, rewards, etc.).

  You may have to brainstorm different possibilities if the student is uncomfortable with the initial plan. Incorporating any of the student's suggestions that strengthen the plan is likely to increase her sense of "ownership" in and commitment to it.

- **Make sure the student understands what you mean by appropriate and inappropriate behavior.**

  Use the descriptions you have prepared to define and clarify the problem behavior and the positive (desired) behavior as specifically and thoroughly as you can. To ensure that you and the student are in agreement about the expectations, you might present hypothetical scenarios and have her identify whether each is an example of tantrumming or staying relaxed. Or you might describe an

actual situation that has occurred and ask her to explain how she would stay relaxed, but still communicate what she was thinking or feeling (e.g., anger) in that situation.

- **Conclude the meeting.**

  Always end the meeting with words of encouragement. Let the student know that you are confident that she can be successful. Be sure to reinforce her for participating in the meeting.

5. *Give the student regular, ongoing feedback about her behavior.*

It is important to meet with the student periodically to discuss her progress. In most cases, three to five minutes once per week should suffice. *(NOTE: PLAN E requires that you meet with the student briefly every hour.)* During the meetings, review any information that has been collected and discuss whether or not the situation is getting better. As much as possible, focus on the student's improvements, however, also address any new or continuing problems. As the situation improves, the meetings can be faded to once every other week and then to once per month.

6. *Evaluate the situation (and the plan).*

Implement any plan for at least two weeks before deciding whether to change plans; to continue, modify, or fade the plan you are using; or to cease the intervention. Generally, if the student's behavior is clearly improving (based on the objective information that's been collected and/or the subjective perceptions of yourself, the student, and possibly the parent[s]), stick with what you are doing. If the situation has remained the same or worsened, some kind of change will be necessary. Always discuss any changes to the plan with the student first.

TARDINESS

Late to Class

DESCRIPTION

There are students in your class who are arriving after the official starting time (of school or class).

GOAL

The students will be in class on time.

OVERVIEW OF PLANS

- PLAN A: For a situation in which the problem occurs infrequently or has just begun.

- PLAN B: For a situation in which the students lack the motivation to arrive in class on time.

NOTE:

These two plans have been designed for a situation in which there are a number of students who tend to be tardy. However, each can easily be modified to intervene with only a few (one to three) students who have/continue to have a problem with tardiness.

Alternative Problems

- **Absenteeism**
- **Late Work**

General Considerations

- The use of consequences for tardiness (as described in PLAN A) may only be appropriate for students in grades four and above. For primary age students, use your professional judgment about consequences for tardiness. Given that tardiness with younger students may be more of a behavioral problem on the part of their *parents* (i.e., the parents consistently bring the students to school late), you should consider carefully whether it is reasonable to implement consequences for behavior that may be out of the students' control. However, it is reasonable to enact the positive components of either of the two plans in order to motivate students to get to school on time.

PLAN A

If the problem of tardy students has just begun and/or there are only one to three class-wide incidents of tardiness per week, it may not be necessary, or even beneficial, to use an involved plan. The following actions, along with making the students aware of your concerns, may resolve the situation.

1. Define what constitutes tardiness.

There is no one correct definition, but you should be clear and consistent in how *you* define tardiness. Consider: Are the students on time as long as they are in the room before the bell rings? or do they need to be in their seats? or in their seats with all their materials out and ready? A clear definition that has been taught to the students in advance eliminates the need to argue or negotiate with the student who says things like, "But I was almost in the room when the bell rang." If you are in a school without bells, a clear definition may be more difficult to clarify, but is probably even more important to establish.

2. Meet the students at the door and welcome them to the classroom.

a. Seeing you at the door and receiving a friendly greeting such as, "Good morning, William. It's nice to see you," is a very pleasant way to start the day (or class period). Standing at the door also indicates to the students that you are ready for them to arrive and for class to begin.

b. Begin class by thanking the students for being there on time and by giving them an overview of some of the interesting and worthwhile things that will happen that day or class period. (By the way, if you can't think of any, you need to reorganize your instructional priorities and/or methods.)

3. Respond consistently to each instance of tardiness.

If appropriate, you will want to assign, and consistently apply, consequences for tardiness. Following are three suggestions. If implemented, these consequences for tardiness should be tailored to the structure of your classroom and the developmental level of your students:

- Establish a system in which students who enter late are required to use a form that indicates the reason they are late. This form can be as simple as a small sheet of paper on which the students fill in blanks for name, date, time entering class, reason for being late, and if the tardiness is excused or unexcused. If the students have a parental or office excuse for being late, they can attach their excuse to the form.

Keep the forms in a pouch attached to the wall near the door. If a student enters late, he/she should pick up a form, go to his/her seat, and fill out the form. When the form is completed, the student should bring it to you. Take the form from the student without disrupting the flow of instruction, and clip it to your gradebook so you can file it later.

If a student neglects to pick up the form, or enters late and tries to disrupt the class by explaining the reason for lateness, simply point to the place on the wall where the forms are kept and resume instruction. One of the biggest advantages of this procedure is that students who are tardy are not allowed to disrupt instruction and/or get your attention and the attention of the entire class by standing in the front of the room explaining their tardiness.

In your gradebook, record that the student was tardy and code whether the tardy was excused or unexcused (e.g., write a small "te" or "tu"). Mark the gradebook at the time you take the form from the student. The student should see that you are recording the incident—even excused tardies. If the student asks what you are doing, be straightforward—explain that you keep track of both excused and unexcused tardies so that if a chronic problem develops, you have a record. This cumulative record in your gradebook will be useful for visually scanning the magnitude and nature of the problem and evaluating the effectiveness of any intervention plan.

Later during class, when the students are engaged in independent work or cooperative groups, talk to any student(s) who had unexcused tardies. Do not listen to or accept their excuses. Simply tell the student(s) that it was an unexcused tardy and give them information about their cumulative totals for the term. "Patrick, this was your third unexcused tardy for the term and it is only the third week of school. Arriving on time to this class is important, and I expect you to arrive on time." Be emotionally neutral while giving the correction—your goal is to impart information.

- Establish classroom-based consequences for unexcused tardiness. For example, for every three tardies a student accumulates the student owes time (e.g., 15 minutes) off recess or after school, plus you will make a parental contact. Time owed is a logical consequence because when students are late, they miss class time and therefore should make up that time.

- Follow through on school-wide consequences for tardiness. In most middle/junior high schools, all unexcused tardies must be reported to the office and repeated infractions result in time spent in detention or in-school suspension. Also, most schools require that tardiness be reported on report cards.

 4. *Use reinforcement to encourage appropriate behavior.*

a. Praise individual students for meeting your expectations about arriving on time. Keep a watchful eye on those students who have had the greatest tendency to be late. Whenever one of these students is not late, praise him/her for demonstrating the ability to be punctual. "Anti, it is nice to see you. You have arrived on time every day this week. I appreciate your punctuality." If the student would be embarrassed by public praise, praise the student privately, nonverbally (e.g., a nod and smile as the student enters the room), or even give the student a note.

b. In addition, occasionally praise those students who rarely or never have a problem with tardiness. Because these students have already mastered the positive expectations, they do not need positive feedback as often as the students who have had difficulty. However, you do not want them to feel that you take their positive behavior for granted. "Gwen, you consistently arrive on time. Punctuality is one of many successful habits you demonstrate."

c. Finally, when there has been a significant overall reduction in tardiness, praise the entire class. Remember that any time all the students arrive on time, you can mention the punctuality of the group.

PLAN B

Sometimes tardiness occurs because students have not been taught the importance of being punctual and, consequently, feel little incentive to arrive on time. When this is the case, the intervention may need to include a variety of incentives to motivate the students to arrive on time.

 1. *Clearly define what constitutes tardiness, greet the students at the door (those who are on time), and implement consistent consequences when the students are tardy (see PLAN A).*

2. *Always begin class right on time.*

a. If you have a casual attitude about the beginning of class, it may communicate to the students that the first few minutes of class are not important. Therefore, always set a precedent that class begins right on time.

Avoid lengthy attendance and "housekeeping" procedures at the beginning of class. If the first three minutes of the students' time is spent sitting doing nothing while you fill out forms, it will be very dull for them. Some students would rather be out wandering the halls or interacting with other students who are late to their classes. They might think, "After all, nothing is going on in class—I'm not missing anything." If your attendance and housekeeping procedures are monopolizing the beginning of class, discuss with other staff members how they begin their classes. There is an excellent chance that one or more of your colleagues will have figured out ways to accomplish administrative duties in a manner that allows them to begin instruction within seconds of the start of class.

b. Occasionally use the first minute or two of class for important new information. Reviewing previously taught concepts is important, but if this always happens in the first ten minutes of class, students who have mastered the content may think nothing important happens at the beginning of class. There is nothing instructionally wrong with beginning class by introducing some new information, and then reviewing the previously taught concepts as you integrate the new content.

c. Occasionally do something fun at the beginning of class. No one ever said that all fun activities have to occur at the end of class. Now and again let the students engage in favorite group activities (e.g., play a game, have music playing, etc.) during the first five minutes of class.

d. Occasionally do something unexpected at the beginning of class. If you are theatrical, you could do a humorous imitation of a historical figure. Or, now and again, you might give the students information in a conspiratorial manner (e.g., "Those of you who are here on time, don't tell anyone else, but on tomorrow's test three of the items will be on . . . so really study the end of the chapter.").

3. *Publicly post the percentage of students on time to class.*

(NOTE: Only use this procedure if several students have a problem with tardiness. If only one or two students have this problem, set up individualized plans to calculate their weekly percentage of punctuality.)

a. Once per week, calculate the percentage of students who were on time each day that week by dividing the number of students on time by the number of students present for each day.

b. Once per week, record (or have a student record) the information on a large chart that is visible to the entire class. *(NOTE: If you are a middle/junior high school teacher, create one transparency for each class, and only show any given class their own data.)* By recording the data weekly rather than daily, you reduce the chance that the posting will result in an individual receiving too much attention for having been late.

c. As the data is being posted, talk to the class about trends—is punctuality getting worse, staying the same, or getting better? If time permits, discuss strategies the students might use to arrive in class on time. For example, you might teach the students how to end a conversation with a friend in the hallway or how to organize their materials so it is not necessary to go back to their locker before each class.

d. While the data is being discussed, and at other times during the day (if appropriate), a "coach" for good attendance. In sports, an effective coach rallies the team's energies to meet a challenge. Frequently encourage the students to come to class on time. Use examples from employment situations, sports, the arts, etc. to emphasize that punctuality is a habit of successful people.

4. *Use reinforcement to encourage appropriate behavior.*

a. Praise individual students and the entire class for punctuality (see PLAN A).

b. You may also wish to use intermittent rewards to acknowledge the class' success. Occasional, and unexpected, rewards may motivate the students to demonstrate punctuality more often. The idea is to provide a reward when the class as a whole has made significant improvements in overall punctuality.

Appropriate rewards might include eliminating a homework assignment, congratulating the class in front of the principal, or even providing the class with an edible treat. *(NOTE: A list of additional group reinforcement ideas can be found in APPENDIX 1.)*

If you use intermittent rewards, do so more frequently at the beginning of the intervention to encourage the students, and then less often as the class' level of punctuality improves.

5. *(OPTIONAL)*
Establish a group reinforcement system.

a. Have the students brainstorm a list of reinforcement ideas for the entire class, and then eliminate any items that are not possible (i.e., the suggestions and too expensive or could not be provided to all the students in the class).

b. Assign "prices" (in points) to the remaining items on the list. The prices should be based on the instructional, personnel, and/or monetary costs of the items. Monetary cost is clear—the more expensive the item, the more points required to earn it. Instructional cost refers to the amount of instructional time lost or interfered with by a particular reward. Thus, an activity which causes the class to miss part of academic instruction should require more points than one the class can do during their free time. Personnel cost involves the time required by you and/or other staff to fulfill the reinforcer. Thus, earning an extra recess period in which extra supervision would need to be arranged would cost more than having music playing in class for 15 minutes.

c. Have the class vote on the list of reinforcers. The reinforcer that wins the most votes is the one they will work for first, and the items that come in second and third will be the next ones worked for.

d. On those days when the percentage of students on time is higher than the day before, the class earns five points toward the agreed-upon reward. Any day that the group has a record-breaking percentage (e.g., the highest percentage to date was 71%, and they have 73%), they earn ten points. And whenever 100% of the students are on time, the class earns 15 points.

e. During the weekly meeting to review and post the data, first share the data and determine Monday's points. Then share the data and calculate Tuesday's points, and so on for the remaining days of that week. When the students accumulate enough points, the class earns the agreed-upon reward and the system begins again.

. . . .
Suggested Steps for Developing and Implementing a Plan

The following information is designed to help you implement an appropriate and effective intervention plan, whether you choose to use one of the MODEL PLANS or create a customized plan of your own. The steps are, however, suggestions—they are not intended to be followed rigidly or in any particular order. Use your professional judgment and the knowledge of your particular situation to make them work for you.

1. *Discuss the situation with the class.*

a. If you plan to use one of the two MODEL PLANS as written, schedule a class meeting. Wait for a time when you are calm (i.e., not right after an incident has occurred) and inform the students that you are finding their tardiness to be a problem. Explain that punctuality is important in school, on a job, in sports, and even in personal relationships. Then specifically define your classroom expectations regarding punctuality and outline the procedures that will be implemented.

Give the students the opportunity to ask questions and make comments, and end the session by thanking the students for listening. Let them know that you are confident they will arrive on time in the future.

b. If you want the students to assume some ownership of the problem, you might wish to hold a class meeting in which the students participate in analyzing the situation and developing an action plan. In this case, before the meeting you will need to have clarified the nature/extent of the problem (use the information from your gradebook) and your expectations for punctuality.

You will also need to identify any aspects of the plan that you do not feel comfortable opening up to a group decision. For example, you must decide ahead of time whether or not to allow the class to determine *if* there will be a consequence for tardiness and/or what the consequence should be. If you firmly believe that there should be a consequence, then you should not seek student input on that particular issue.

. . . .

c. Schedule this meeting for a neutral time and allow enough time for a reasonable discussion. Inform the students in advance that the meeting will take place; this will give them time to think about the problem. "Class, this afternoon we are going to have a class meeting on the problem of tardiness. Please give some thought to this problem and what we might do as a class to solve it."

d. Use an agenda to structure the meeting. Shortly before the meeting, write the agenda on the chalkboard. Following is one example you may wish to use.

Agenda

1. Tardiness—Define the magnitude of the problem. *(NOTE: Share your data.)*

2. Review the expectations regarding on time behavior (punctuality).

3. Brainstorm ideas for improving the situation.

4. Select strategies that everyone agrees to.

5. Establish what will happen if a student is tardy (both excused and unexcused).

---

e. Establish clear rules for both you and the students regarding the brainstorming phase of the meeting. For example:

1. Any idea is okay (but no obscenity).

2. Ideas will not be evaluated initially (i.e., no approval—"Good idea" or disapproval—"What a stupid idea" or "We couldn't do that" should be expressed during brainstorming).

3. All ideas will be written down and discussed at the conclusion of brainstorming.

f. At the conclusion of brainstorming, evaluate the ideas, and lead the class to consensus on any decisions that need to be made. Use voting as a decision-making process when appropriate.

 Determine when and how to include the parent(s).

Any time an individual student has been tardy two or three times in a grading period, you should contact the student's parent(s). Let them know that their student is being tardy, and what steps you are taking to correct the situation. Frequent contact is not required, but as long as the problem continues you should keep the parent(s) informed of the behavior and the consequences that you are implementing at school.

 Give the class regular, ongoing feedback about their behavior.

Periodically meet with the students to discuss the situation. In most cases, three to five minutes once per week should suffice. *(NOTE: PLAN B includes a weekly meeting.)* During the meetings, review any information that has been collected (e.g., the gradebook, charted percentages) and discuss whether or not the situation is getting better. As much as possible, focus on improvements, however, also address any new or continuing problems.

As you discuss the problems, acknowledge that there are individuals in the class who consistently behave appropriately, however, do not single out individuals when discussing problems or progress with the entire group. As the situation improves, the meetings can be faded to once every other week and then to once per month.

Evaluate the situation (and the plan).

Any plan should be implemented for at least two weeks before deciding whether or not it is effective. Generally, if the situation has improved (based on the objective information that's been collected and/or the subjective perceptions of yourself and the students), continue with what you have been doing. (Eventually you will want to fade, then eliminate, the plan.) If the problem remains the same or worsens, some sort of change (e.g., modifying the current plan or switching to another plan) will be necessary. Always discuss any change in the intervention with the class first.

ATTLING

DESCRIPTION

There are students in your class who tell you every problem (from trivial to major) that takes place in the classroom and/or on the playground.

GOAL

The students will learn to discriminate between those situations that require adult intervention and those that do not, and will stop asking for your help with situations they can handle independently.

OVERVIEW OF PLANS

- PLAN A: For a situation in which the problem has just begun or occurs infrequently.
- PLAN B: For a problem that may stem from the students not understanding the difference between unnecessary tattling and social responsibility.
- PLAN C: For a problem that may stem from the students not realizing how often they are tattling unnecessarily.
- PLAN D: For a situation in which the students lack the motivation to stop tattling unnecessarily.
- PLAN E: For a situation in which the problem occurs/continues to occur with only one or two students.

Alternative Problems

- **Bothering/Tormenting Others**
- **Bullying Behavior/ Fighting**
- **Clinginess/ Dependency**
- **Cliques/Ganging Up**
- **Helplessness**
- **Victim—Student Who Is Always Picked On**

General Considerations

- The information presented in these five plans focuses on tattling about trivial issues (i.e., situations students should be able to handle on their own). However, it is important to be alert for those times when the students may truly need assistance.

- If the tattling frequently involves one particular student who torments or bullies others, it is probably more appropriate to deal with that individual student, rather than the problem of tattling. See **Bullying Behavior/Fighting** or **Bothering/Tormenting Others** for ideas.

- If only one student frequently tattles, determine whether that student is really being picked on. If so, see **Victim—Student Who Is Always Picked On** for ideas on helping this student who really needs help.

- If the students lack the basic social skills to interact with each other appropriately, it may be necessary to begin by teaching them those skills. **Social Skills, Lack of** contains information on a variety of published social skills curricula.

Model Plans

PLAN A

If the tattling has just begun and/or occurs only two to five times per week, it may not be necessary, or even beneficial, to use an involved plan. The following actions, along with making the students aware of your concerns, may resolve the situation.

1. Respond consistently to each instance of tattling.

a. Whenever a student tattles unnecessarily (i.e., reports a minor incident) about something that doesn't involve him/her, gently correct that individual in a way that acknowledges what the student said but provides little satisfaction for having tattled. For example, if a student is trying to get another student in trouble for a minor rule infraction (e.g., "Amory squirted water from the drinking fountain.") you might say something like, "I am glad that you know not to do that, and I will deal with Amory if I see him do it." Do not punish Amory based solely on the tattling, and do not bring Amory over for a "Yes you did"/"No I didn't" confrontation with the tattler.

Or, if a student reports on other students (e.g., "Rebecca and Eric are arguing over who gets to be first on the computer."), your response might be something like, "I am confident that Rebecca and Eric can handle that situation without your help."

b. If a student tattles about a minor infraction that someone committed against him/her (e.g., "Bryan and Antonio said I was a wimp."), you might want to respond with questions such as,

"I am sorry that happened. How did you handle it? How might you handle it if it happens again?"

Be aware, however, that if this type of correction is used too frequently, the students may not report serious incidents of bullying. Be sensitive to situations in which a student really needs help and tell him/her that if the problem keeps occurring, you are available for assistance. "That sounds like a great way to handle that sort of name calling. Give it a try, and let me know if it works. If the problem happens again and you need help, come and talk to me."

c. Whenever a student reports a serious incident (e.g., one student is threatening to beat up another student), investigate what the student told you. Although you should never implement a consequence based solely on one student's report, you can look into the situation. If you determine that the incident really did occur, then you can take action.

2. Use reinforcement to encourage appropriate behavior.

a. Praise individual students for meeting your expectations regarding unnecessary tattling. Keep an eye on those students who have had the greatest tendency to tattle. Whenever one of these students handles a situation without tattling, praise him/her for demonstrating independence. "Lucy, you have been doing a fine job of handling minor situations on the playground on your own. You know I am here if there is a big problem, but I really appreciate your independence in handling the smaller problems." If the student would be embarrassed by public praise, praise the student privately or even give the student a note.

b. Also, praise any student who reports a major incident that probably requires adult intervention for demonstrating social responsibility. Let that individual know that you do not consider his/her behavior to be tattling. "Phoenix, I appreciate you telling me your information about who did the graffiti. This report is socially responsible and not tattling. When it is a serious incident like this, we need people who have information to help us."

c. Occasionally praise students who rarely or never have a problem with unnecessary tattling. Because these students have already mastered the positive expectations, they do not need positive feedback as often as the students who have difficulty with tattling. However, you do not want them to feel that you take their positive behavior for granted. "Starla and Cameron, you are both independent and socially responsible. You help with big problems that require help, but you use excellent judgment about the things you can handle on your own."

d. When there has been a significant reduction in the amount of tattling, praise the entire class. Remember that any time the students are refraining from tattling, you can praise them for their independence. Additionally, whenever students report major incidents, you can praise them for their social responsibility.

PLAN B

It may be that the students do not actually know how to be independent and/or socially responsible. If you are not sure that your students possess the necessary knowledge or skills, the intervention must include a way of teaching them the difference between social responsibility and unnecessary tattling.

 Conduct lessons to teach the students the difference between unnecessary tattling and social responsibility.

a. Define for the students both social responsibility and tattling. The following definitions may be of some help. Social responsibility is someone getting help for themselves or another when help is really necessary. For example, seeing a store being broken into and calling 911 is social responsibility, not tattling, as the owner of the store is not there and cannot call the police herself.

Tattling, on the other hand, can be thought of as: (1) someone trying to get someone else in trouble, (2) someone trying to get someone else to solve the problem that that person can solve himself/herself, or (3) someone trying to get

help for someone else who is quite able to solve the problem himself/herself. When using definitions of this type, prepare lots of examples for each aspect of the definition.

b. During the lessons, use a T chart on the chalkboard with one or two examples filled in (see the sample shown). Have the students think of additional examples for each category, and write the examples in the chart. (NOTE: Some of the examples may need to be discussed to determine which side of the chart they should be written on.)

c. Once the students can discriminate between tattling and social responsibility, encourage them to reduce their tattling by being more independent. You may need to teach them how

Tattling	Social Responsibility
Someone called you a name once or twice.	Someone is hurt, and you get the playground supervisor.

to be independent and handle situations that would be tattling if they told an adult. To do so, review the examples on the lefthand side of the T chart and ask the students to generate ideas on how each situation could be handled independently.

End the lessons by reminding the students that the adults at school are there to help, and that they should not hesitate to ask for help about a situation that is really bothering them or is very serious.

d. These lessons needn't last more than 15 minutes, and should be conducted at least twice per week until the students really seem to understand the concepts of tattling, social responsibility, and independence. Continue the lessons until the students have reduced their tattling in practice, and are being socially responsible about reporting serious situations that legitimately require adult intervention.

2. *Respond consistently to each instance of tattling.*

Whenever a student tattles unnecessarily, provide a gentle verbal correction (see PLAN A).

3. *Use reinforcement to encourage appropriate behavior.*

a. Praise individual students for meeting your expectations regarding unnecessary tattling and praise the entire class when significant improvement takes place (see PLAN A).

b. In addition, make a special point of letting the students know (individually and as a class) that you notice their efforts to use the skills they have been learning/practicing. "Rose and Mercedes, you handled that problem independently. Nice job of doing what we have been discussing in the class lessons."

PLAN C

If the students do not seem to realize how frequently they are tattling unnecessarily, the intervention must include some way of helping them become more aware of their own behavior.

1. *Respond consistently to each instance of tattling.*

a. Whenever a student tattles unnecessarily, provide a gentle verbal correction. Be sure the student knows that this was an example of tattling—something he/she probably could have handled independently (see PLANS A and B).

b. In addition, whenever you correct an individual student, make sure the incident is recorded (see Step 2).

2. *Publicly monitor the frequency of unnecessary tattling.*

a. Create a space on the chalkboard or a wall chart to record how often students in the class tattle. You want a class-wide total rather than a record on individual students (you do not want to put undue peer pressure on individuals). Therefore, when there is an incident of tattling, gently correct the individual who tattled but write only a tally mark on the chart (not the individual student's name).

b. Each day, conduct a short class meeting to review that day's record. Have a student chart

the information (or do it yourself), and talk with the class about whether the day was better, worse, or about the same as previous days.

If the day did not go well, encourage the students to talk about why and have them identify what they can do the next day to help them remember to be independent rather than tattle. If the students behave inappropriately during the meeting, keep the review session very short. Simply let the class know that you are sure tomorrow will be a better day.

3. *Use reinforcement to encourage appropriate behavior.*

a. Praise individual students for meeting your expectations regarding unnecessary tattling and praise the entire class when significant improvement takes place (see PLAN A).

b. Let the class know that you are aware that some members of the class never have a problem with tattling, and that those individuals should be proud of themselves. However, do not identify specific individuals by name when discussing the situation with the class.

c. Praise the class if students are willing to look seriously at their daily total. Even on a bad day, if the students are able to discuss why it was a bad day, praise them. "Class, you are really handling this responsibly. Even though it was a rough day, you are willing to talk to about things you might do differently tomorrow. That is a real sign that we are making progress." Regardless of how the day went, try to make the end-of-the-day meeting upbeat and encouraging—you want the students to look forward to the daily review sessions.

PLAN D

When an entire classroom of students fall into a pattern of tattling, it can be very difficult to change their behavior. In this case, you may need to implement a structured system of external incentives (i.e., rewards and consequences) to create mild peer pressure and to motivate the students to behave appropriately.

1. *Respond consistently to each instance of tattling (see PLAN A).*

2. *Implement a procedure to publicly monitor the frequency of unnecessary tattling (see PLAN C).*

3. *Encourage the class to set daily performance goals.*

Each day, have the class set a goal for the maximum number of tattling incidents that will occur the next day. You may have to help the students set a realistic goal (some are likely to suggest that the class reduce the number of incidents from 40 per day to zero per day, for example). You should explain that by setting an attainable goal like 32, they can always have less tattling incidents, but that they increase their chances of success.

As the class does experience success, have them progressively lower the goal until the number of incidents is acceptable and comfortable. However, it is not necessary to ever set zero as a goal. The students should feel that they have some latitude as the line between tattling and social responsibility is slightly hazy, after all. Since the original problem was the excessive amount of tattling, success consists of reducing but not necessarily eliminating this behavior.

4. *Use reinforcement to encourage appropriate behavior.*

a. Praise individual students for meeting your expectations regarding unnecessary tattling and praise the entire class when significant improvement takes place (see PLAN A).

b. Use a system of group reinforcement. First have the class brainstorm reinforcement ideas that could be awarded to the entire class. Eliminate any items that are not possible (i.e., the suggestions are too expensive or could not be provided to all the students in the class) and assign "prices" (in points) to those that remain on the list.

The prices should be based on the instructional, personnel, and/or monetary costs of the items. Monetary cost is clear—the more expensive the item, the more points required to earn it. Instructional cost refers to the amount of instructional time lost or interfered with by a particular reward. Thus, an activity which causes the class to miss part of academic instruction should require more points than one the class can do on their own time. Personnel cost involves the time required by you and/or other staff to fulfill the reinforcer. Thus earning an extra recess period in which extra supervision would need to be arranged would cost more than having music playing in class for 15 minutes, for example.

c. Then have the class vote on the reinforcers. The one that earns the most votes is the reinforcer they will work for first. Those reinforcers earning the second and third most votes will be the second and third rewards the students will work for, respectively.

d. On days when the class has successfully kept their number of tattling incidents under the identified goal, the group earns a point toward the reward they are striving to earn.

e. Alternately, you may wish to implement a Mystery Motivator system (Rhode, Jenson, & Reavis, 1992). In this system, you mark an "X" on random days of a daily calendar, and then cover each daily space with a slip of paper. On days when the class is successful in meeting their goal, you remove the slips of paper from the appropriate day spaces. If there is an X, the class earns the reinforcer. Even on unsuccessful days you should uncover the space on the calendar so the students can see whether they would have received a reward if they had met their goal.

5. *(OPTIONAL)*
If a class-wide system does not seem likely to be effective, establish a team competition with a response cost lottery.

a. Divide the class into four to six teams (the teams should be made as equitable as possible). Each team begins the day with a certain number of tickets on which they write the name of their team. Whenever a student tattles, that student's team loses a ticket. At the end of the day, each team puts their remaining tickets in a hat for a lottery drawing. The team whose name is on the winning ticket receives a predetermined reward for that day.

b. This technique can be especially effective with tattling, because you can teach the students that whenever they think about "telling" the teacher something, they should talk it over with their team first. If their teammates agree that it is socially responsible to "tell," then they should go ahead and inform the teacher.

c. Give "bonus tickets" to teams whose members report serious incidents (i.e., who display social responsibility). "Renee, thank you for letting me know about the problems that have been occurring on the bus. I would like to give your team two bonus tickets for the drawing today. It was socially responsible of you to get help for those students who were being harassed."

6. *While implementing any reinforcement system, keep student attention focused on independence and social responsibility.*

Tell the class, for example: "Class, you earned your point for the day, but more importantly, you are all helping this class be independent and socially responsible. This room is a place we can all be proud of."

PLAN E

Some students are very skilled at gaining attention through their negative behavior. If there is an individual student (or couple of students) who has (or continues to have) a problem with unnecessary tattling, there is a good chance that the student is starved for adult attention. That is, if you find yourself frequently nagging, reminding, or coaxing the student to stop tattling, it is possible that she is trying to gain adult attention through the behavior. Whether or not the student overtly seems to like the attention, you should make sure that she receives more frequent and more satisfying attention when she behaves appropriately than when she tattles.

1. *Be sure the student understands the concepts of tattling, social responsibility, and independence (see PLAN B).*

2. *Respond consistently to each instance of tattling (see PLAN A).*

Be sure to keep your interactions with the student when she tattles very short. The less attention the student receives at the time of the tattling incident, the better.

3. *Use reinforcement to encourage appropriate behavior.*

a. Frequent praise and attention is the core of this plan. The student must see that she receives more frequent and more satisfying attention when she behaves independently than when she tattles. Thus, whenever the student is not tattling (or otherwise misbehaving), make an effort to praise and spend time with her. "Berkeley, you have been so independent today, and I am very proud of you. Would it be okay if I sat with you a moment and watched as you do the next step on this assignment?"

b. You may also wish to use intermittent rewards to acknowledge the student's success. Occasional, and unexpected, rewards can motivate the student to demonstrate responsible behavior more often. The idea is to provide a reward when the student has had a particularly good period of independence. Appropriate rewards might include any activity with you, such as playing a game or helping with a classroom job. *(NOTE: A list of additional reinforcement ideas can be found in APPENDIX 1.)* If you use intermittent rewards, do so more frequently at the beginning of the intervention to encourage the student, and then less often as the student's behavior improves over time.

 4. Ensure a 3-1 ratio of positive to negative attention.

a. When attention is a motivating force for the student, you want to be sure that you are giving the student *three times as much* positive as negative attention. One way to do this is to monitor your interactions with the student at least one day per week. Simply keep a card on a clipboard or in your pocket and record each interaction you have with the student as either positive or negative by writing a "+" or a "-", respectively, on the card.

To determine whether an interaction is positive or negative, ask yourself whether the student was tattling (or otherwise misbehaving) at the time the interaction occurred. Any interaction that stems from inappropriate behavior is negative, and all interactions that occur while the student is meeting classroom expectations are positive. Thus, providing a gentle correction is a negative interaction, but praising the student for being independent is positive. Greeting the student as she enters the room or asking her if she has any questions during independent work are also considered positive interactions.

b. If you find that you are not giving the student three times as much positive as negative attention, try to increase the number of positive interactions you have with the student. Sometimes prompts can help. For example, you might decide that each time the student enters the classroom you will say "hello" to her, or that you will interact positively with the student at least once during each instructional period.

Suggested Steps for Developing and Implementing a Plan

The following steps are designed to help you develop an appropriate intervention plan and implement it effectively, whether you choose to use one of the MODEL PLANS or create a customized plan of your own. The steps are, however, suggestions—they are not intended to be followed rigidly or in any particular order. Use your professional judgment and the knowledge of your particular situation to make them work for you.

 1. Make sure you have enough information about the situation.

a. You need to be able to explain exactly what you mean when you say that "the class has a problem with tattling." Anecdotal notes on actual incidents should help you define the problem behavior clearly and completely. To collect anecdotal notes, simply keep a card in your pocket or on a clipboard and occasionally when a student tattles, make notes on the circumstances.

For each entry, briefly describe where and when the tattling occurred, what was said or done, and any other relevant observations (e.g., what prompted the behavior). You do not need to take notes every time a student tattles; the idea is to capture a range of examples so that you will be able to describe the behavior thoroughly.

Also include some notes on times when a student appropriately reports something serious (i.e., an example of social responsibility). This will make it clear that you are not only aware of the problem behavior, but also recognize when the students behave appropriately. When you discuss your concerns with the class, these positive examples will also help you clarify how you want the students to behave.

b. It can also be useful to document just how often the unnecessary tattling occurs (i.e., a frequency count). This will provide both a more objective measure of the problem and an objective way to monitor the class' progress. Use the same card on which you are collecting anecdotal notes, and simply write a tally mark on the card each time a student tattles.

You might want to group the tallies to discern whether the behavior occurs more frequently during certain times, subjects, or activities (e.g., using "C" for classroom and "P" for playground as categories of where incidents occurred). Or, you might want to code the tallies as "U" for unnecessary tattling and "N" for reporting a situation that probably required adult intervention (i.e., a necessary display of social responsibility).

c. If a student notices what you are doing and asks about it, be straightforward—say that you are collecting information to see whether the class'

Tattling—9/17

Frequency:

Classroom	Playground
UUUUU UUUUU UU	UUNUN

Notes:

• During reading, Berkeley reported that Mona was bothering Liana.

• During math, Jonas report that Esteban was working on his science report and not his math assignment.

• Irene asked me if she should tell me about some 6th graders that were picking on 1st graders in the bathroom. (Great example of social responsibility and a good way to handle a situation she was not sure about—ask.)

• After recess, Christine reported that Ian had been climbing on the fence.

---

tattling is a problem that needs to be worked on. The following example shows anecdotal notes and a frequency count that have been collected on a class' tattling.

d. The frequency information is fairly easy to summarize on a chart or graph. Seeing how often the tattling occurs may help the students better understand your concern.

e. Continuing to collect this type of information (and keeping the chart up-to-date) while you implement a plan will help you to monitor whether the situation is getting worse, staying the same, or getting better.

2. *Identify a focus for the intervention and labels for referring to the appropriate and inappropriate behaviors.*

a. The intervention must address more than just reducing the students' tattling—to be effective, there must be a concurrent emphasis on increasing some positive behavior or trait. There are two behaviors that together comprise an appropriate opposite to tattling: "social responsibility," or getting help when necessary; and "independence," or handling things on one's own when possible. Be careful not to emphasize independence to the students without also explaining social responsibility, because some students might then assume that getting help for someone who is hurt, for example, would be tattling.

Having these positive behaviors in mind will make it easier for you to "catch" and reinforce the students for behaving appropriately, and will help you to explain your concerns more productively. For example, simply saying that "the class has a problem with tattling" doesn't really give the students any useful information (and may put them on the defensive). However, telling the students that you want to help them "learn to be independent and socially responsible" gives them important and reasonable goals to work toward and clarifies what they need to do to be successful.

b. Specifying labels for the appropriate and inappropriate behaviors (e.g., "independent"/"socially responsible" and "tattling," respectively) helps you to use consistent vocabulary whenever you talk about the situation. If you sometimes refer to the inappropriate behavior as "tattling," for example, and other times tell a student that "she needs to mind her own business," the student may not realize that you are talking about the same behavior.

3. *Present your concerns to the class.*

a. When you are calm (i.e., not right after a problem has occurred), discuss the problem with the class. Provide the students with information about why tattling is a problem. For example, you can explain that when school staff have to spend a lot of time responding to problems students can and should handle independently, it takes away from the time staff members have to deal with real problems that students have. You might also inform them that adults in the school are there to help whenever a student really needs help. However, as much as possible, the students should try to handle situations on their own.

In addition, define your expectations. Let the students know that if they see someone else being hurt, or if they really need help themselves, they should come and tell you or another adult. Give examples of socially responsible behavior. For example, telling a playground supervisor that a student is hurt is being socially responsible, not tattling. Telling you that an older student tried to sell drugs would be socially responsible.

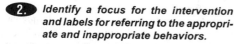

On the other hand, if the problem is a minor one, encourage the students to be independent and handle the situation on their own. Give examples of common situations they could try to handle independently. For example, if a student runs through a game they are playing at recess, they should try telling the student not to do that anymore.

b. Give the students the opportunity to ask questions regarding the problem and/or your expectations.

c. Thank the students for listening and let them know that you are confident that they will make an effort to be independent and socially responsible in the future.

4. *Determine when and how to include the parent(s).*

a. When a problem is class-wide, contacting the parents of individual students who tattled is probably neither appropriate nor realistic (it wouldn't be feasible for you to call five to ten parents every night). However, after establishing a plan with the students, you may wish to send a memo home (or include an item in your classroom newsletter, if you have one) explaining the focus of the intervention. If you do so, emphasize the importance of both independence and social responsibility.

b. If only one or two students have or continue to have a problem with tattling, you should contact the parent(s) of those individual student(s). Inform them that their student is frequently tattling and explain the steps you are taking to correct the situation. Frequent contact is not required,

but whenever you intend to implement an individualized plan, the parent(s) should be informed ahead of time and should be given feedback about the student's progress every two to four weeks.

5. *Give the class regular, ongoing feedback about their behavior.*

It is important to meet with the students periodically to discuss their progress. In most cases, three to five minutes once per week should suffice. *(NOTE: PLANS C and D suggest daily meetings to record information and/or determine points.)* During the meetings, review any information that has been collected and discuss whether or not the situation is getting better. As much as possible, focus on improvements, however, also address any new or continuing problems. As the situation improves, the meetings can be faded to once every other week and then to once per month.

6. *Evaluate the situation (and the plan).*

Implement any plan for at least two weeks before deciding whether to change plans; to continue, modify, or fade the plan you are using; or to cease the intervention. Generally, if the class' behavior is clearly improving (based on the objective information that's been collected and/or the subjective perceptions of yourself and the students), stick with what you are doing. If the situation has remained the same or worsened, some kind of change will be necessary. Always discuss any changes to the plan with the class first.

THREATENING OTHERS (STAFF OR STUDENTS)

Extortion

Intimidation

DESCRIPTION

You have a student who has, on at least one occasion, threatened a staff member or another student.

GOAL

The student will stop making threats and will learn both the serious nature and likely consequences of this type of behavior.

OVERVIEW OF PLANS

- PLAN A: For a situation in which the student has made only one or two threats, and you are quite sure that he is not serious.

- PLAN B: For a situation in which the student has repeatedly made threatening statements and/or you have reason to believe the student may be serious about his threat(s).

NOTE:

Although the following information specifically addresses threats of violence toward another person (e.g., "I am going to kill you."), it could easily be adapted and applied to a situation involving extortion (e.g., "Give me a dollar every day or I will beat you up.").

Alternative Problems

- **Aggression—Verbal and/or Physical**

- **Bossiness**

- **Bothering/Tormenting Others**

- **Bullying Behavior/ Fighting**

- **Cliques/Ganging Up**

....
General Considerations

- Take all threats seriously. Do not discount a threat just because it was made by a child. Assume the student meant what he said, and take whatever actions may be necessary to ensure all the students' physical safety.

- Be sure that the students in your class know that there are school personnel they can go to for help with tough situations. Periodically throughout the year, remind the students that they can come to you, the school counselor, the building principal, etc. Let them know that they should always ask for help from an adult if someone is threatening to hurt them or if they have any other problem they are unsure about how to solve. *(NOTE: It may even be advisable to implement a schoolwide plan to inform the students that the school personnel are available to help them with tough problems. Middle/junior high school staff, in particular, must make an effort to remind the students that asking for help is not the same as "ratting on someone.")*

- Follow building and district policies regarding the threatening behavior. If there is a school/district policy related to illegal actions, modify the plans suggested here so that they comply with the letter and the spirit of your policy. If you are unsure whether intervening is appropriate or within your policy, check with your building administrator before you proceed with a plan.

- These two MODEL PLANS are reactive in nature, designed to educate the student about the seriousness of his behavior. Neither attempts to address the root cause of the student's problem. To implement a more proactive plan, you may wish to consult one or more of the ALTERNATIVE PROBLEMS listed for additional information.

....
Model Plans

PLAN A

It is not always necessary, or even beneficial, to use an involved plan. If the student has made only one or two threats, and you are quite sure he was not serious (e.g., a first grade student who gets mad at someone he is playing with says, "I'm going to kill you."), the following actions, along with making the student and his parent(s) aware of your concerns, may resolve the situation.

 Respond immediately to any subsequent threats.

If the student makes another threat, tell him that his behavior was an example of a serious threat and that his parent(s) will be contacted. Record the incident in your anecdotal notes (see SUGGESTED STEPS FOR DEVELOPING AND IMPLEMENTING A PLAN), and be sure the student knows that you are doing so. Making the student aware that you are keeping a written record of these incidents may help communicate the serious nature of this behavior. If the student asks why you are writing the incident down, inform him that it is so you can be accurate in telling his parent(s) about the incident. If the student is in third grade or above,

you might also add that since he is threatening to do something illegal, you need an accurate record should it be necessary to involve the police. Do not present this as a threat, rather simply a piece of information about what you are doing and why.

 Use reinforcement to encourage appropriate behavior.

The student must see that you do not hold a grudge. Therefore, once you have discussed the issue of his making threats (see SUGGESTED STEPS FOR DEVELOPING AND IMPLEMENTING A PLAN), leave the problem behind and use praise and attention to let the student know that he is a valued member of the school community.

Watch for opportunities to praise the student for a wide variety of positive behaviors, but *not* for the absence of threatening behavior. (The only time to refer directly to his making threats is during follow-up meetings on his progress—see SUGGESTED

STEPS FOR DEVELOPING AND IMPLEMENTING A PLAN.)

In addition to praise, give the student frequent attention, such as talking to him before class begins and calling on him frequently during class.

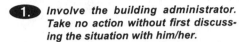

PLAN B

This plan is appropriate if the student has made repeated threats (i.e., three or more times) or one or two threats that seem truly dangerous (e.g., a seventh grade student who says he is going to bring his father's gun and "blow somebody away.").

1. Involve the building administrator. Take no action without first discussing the situation with him/her.

a. When you discuss the incident with your administrator, consider whether a school-based consequence (in addition to contacting the student's parent[s]) should be implemented. Possibilities include having the student write an apology; having the student investigate the legal consequences of the behavior described in the threat; restitution, such as cleaning the school grounds, etc.

b. In addition, if the threat was directed toward another student, you should address the following questions with your administrator:

- Should a student be accused of making threats based solely on the report of one other student? In general, if a student reports that he/she has been threatened, the report should be taken seriously and an investigation should be conducted. However, without corroboration that the threat actually occurred, do not assume that one student is right and the other is wrong. Together you and the administrator should arrange for an investigation that ensures student safety and avoids unjustly accusing a student of something that he/she may not have done.

- Should the students be encouraged to report threats? As noted in the GENERAL CONSIDERATIONS, the students need to know that if they really need help, school personnel are available. However, these assurances should be made in such a way that it does not encourage the students to "set up" particular students. That is, if the message is conveyed that you are inviting reports about one student specifically, a few other students who do not like that individual may fabricate reports of threats in an effort to get that individual student in trouble.

- Should documentation be kept about all reported threats? In general, you should probably keep detailed documentation on all threats, and the actions that were taken in response to the threats. Even if you have no proof that a reported threat took place, the documentation will be important for establishing any long-term patterns that may emerge and for demonstrating (should it ever become necessary) that the student who reported the threat was taken seriously and efforts were made to address the student's concern.

2. Gather information about the legal consequences of the student's behavior.

a. Contact your local district attorney's office and ask if making threats in and of itself is illegal behavior. If it is, ask what actions they would recommend school personnel take to ensure physical safety and to maintain compliance with the law.

b. In addition, ask about the legal consequences of the student carrying out the actions contained in his threats. For example, what would happen if the third grade student really did try to follow through on his repeated threats to kill the music teacher? Would he be taken from his home and placed in juvenile detention? How long would it probably take before there was a trial? If the student was found guilty, what type of sentence could be imposed

This information should be shared with the student and his parent(s) (see SUGGESTED STEPS FOR DEVELOPING AND IMPLEMENTING A PLAN). Although it may sound harsh, it is very important that the student know the real world consequences of his behavior. You might also consider having a police officer present during the meeting about this problem to make the message more real to the student and his parent(s).

3. *Use reinforcement to encourage appropriate behavior.*

Give the student increased praise and attention (see PLAN A).

4. *Respond immediately to any subsequent threats made by the student.*

a. Inform the student that what he just said was a threat and that you will meet with the building administrator to decide what further actions should be taken. Also, be sure to record the incident (see PLAN A).

b. In addition, you will need to design a proactive plan to help the student learn to interact with others in more positive ways and to eliminate the threatening behavior. Because this is primarily a reactive and punitive plan, it may not be sufficient in and of itself. At this point you need to consider implementing one or more of the proactive plans suggested elsewhere in this reference guide. For example, see **Self-Control Issues**, **Bullying Behavior/Fighting**, **Self-Concept Problems**, or any other relevant problems for ideas on proactive plans to help the student.

· · · · · · · ·
Suggested Steps for Developing and Implementing a Plan

The following steps are designed to help you develop an appropriate intervention plan and implement it effectively, whether you choose to use one of the MODEL PLANS or create a customized plan of your own. The steps are, however, suggestions—they are not intended to be followed rigidly or in any particular order. Use your professional judgment and the knowledge of your particular situation to make them work for you.

1. *Make sure you have enough information about the situation.*

It is vital to thoroughly document every instance of the student's threatening behavior. Use anecdotal notes to record specific details about the student's behavior. These notes will be crucial for discussing the situation with the student and his parent(s), the building administrator and/or school psychologist, and, if it becomes necessary, with the legal authorities.

To keep anecdotal notes, simply keep a card to write on in your pocket or on a clipboard. Begin the anecdotal notes with the first threatening incident, even if you think it will not happen again. If you do not, and subsequent incidents do occur, it may be very difficult to remember the details of the first incident. Following is an example of anecdotal notes begun a student's threatening behavior.

Luke's Threatening

9/5—Luke told the music teacher, Mrs. Bento, that he was going to kill her. At first Mrs. Bento thought he was making a joke, because Luke's comment seemed to come out of nowhere— besides he is only eight years old. When she asked him why he would say such a thing, he very seriously stated, "Because I really do plan to kill you."

---

2. *Determine when and how to include the parent(s).*

a. Any time the student makes a threat, contact his parent(s) immediately and inform them of exactly what the student did and said. Find out whether they have also heard the student make threats and/or whether they know if the student has ever attempted to carry out a threat. Let the parent(s) know that you take the situation seriously, and invite them to join you and the student for a meeting to discuss his behavior.

(NOTE: If the student's threats were directed toward another student, discuss with your administrator the procedures for contacting the parent[s] of that student to explain the situation to them. Those parent[s] should be informed of the threat, the actions that are being taken by the school personnel, and if there seems to be any imminent danger to their child.)

b. If the student's parent(s) seem to respond antagonistically or if they refuse to believe that their child has made threats, it would be prudent to have another professional (e.g., the principal or counselor) present during all further interactions with them. Whether or not the parent(s) are able or willing to participate, let them know that you will keep them informed of your intervention steps and the student's progress.

c. Once the parent(s) have been involved in any way, you should give them updates at least once per week while the plan is being implemented.

3. *Prepare for, then conduct, an initial meeting about the situation.*

a. Determine who should be present at the meeting. At the very least, the meeting should include the classroom teacher, the student, and his parent(s). In addition, it may be advisable to include the building administrator or school counselor, and even a representative of the police department. Discuss who should be invited to the meeting with your building administrator.

b. Conduct the meeting in an atmosphere of collaboration. Recognize that one major objective is to communicate to the student and his parent(s) that any threat made will be taken seriously. The following agenda is one way you might structure the meeting:

- **Explain to the student that you are concerned about his behavior.**

  Share your notes on the student's behavior and make sure the student and his parent(s) realize that all threats will be taken seriously. You might tell them that the school needs to ensure everyone's physical safety and that threats, even in jest, bring others' safety into question.

  You can explain that violent acts have been committed by children, and so any threat, no matter who makes it, will be treated seriously. Even if the student and his parent(s) think it is overreacting, let them know that if there are any more threats, it may become necessary to involve the legal authorities.

- **Discuss what can be done to improve the situation.**

  Tell the student that you want to help him cease making threats, and explain what the consequences are (if any) for having made or carried out any threat(s) to date, as well as what the consequences will be for any subsequent threats, whether the student means them seriously or not. In addition, if you intend to implement a proactive plan (e.g., from **Bullying Behavior/Fighting**), explain any relevant procedures from that plan.

- **Make sure the student understands exactly what constitutes a threat.**

  Use your notes to clarify for the student exactly what he does and/or says when he makes threats. Then describe as specifically as you can what he needs to do differently. Provide as much detail as you think is necessary for the student to clearly understand your expectations.

  To verify that the student understands the expectations, you might present hypothetical situations and have him identify whether they are threats or not, and if they are, how he might respond without making a threat.

- **Conclude the meeting.**

  End the meeting with words of encouragement. Let the student know that you are confident that he can be successful in eliminating threatening behavior.

4. *Give the student regular, ongoing feedback about his behavior.*

a. Periodically meet privately with the student to discuss the situation. Unless there are further incidents of threatening behavior, three to five minutes once per week will probably suffice. Let the student know that you are aware of his efforts to interact with others in nonthreatening ways. Tell the student he should be proud of his progress and his restraint. As the situation improves, the meetings can be faded to once every other week and then to once per month.

b. If there *are* subsequent incidents of threatening behavior, another planning meeting with the student, his parent(s), the building administrator, and any other relevant parties will be necessary. The purpose of this meeting will be to discuss the problem in more depth and to establish subsequent consequences should the problem continue. If the threats continue to occur after this meeting, then you may need to involve the legal authorities.

TOURETTE SYNDROME

DESCRIPTION

You have a student who has been identified as having Tourette Syndrome (TS), who exhibits inappropriate behavior(s) in your classroom that may or may not be related to the TS.

Because Tourette Syndrome is a medical condition, for which it is both inappropriate and impossible to "intervene" directly, there are no MODEL PLANS included with this problem. The purpose of the following information is to suggest an overall approach and some basic considerations for dealing with the inappropriate behavior(s) of a student who has Tourette Syndrome.

Alternative Problems

- **Aggression—Verbal and/or Physical**

- **Anxiety/Nervousness**

- **Blurting Out/Not Raising Hand**

- **Corrected, Student Gets Upset When**

- **Nose Picking/Oral Fetishes**

- **Physically Dangerous Behavior—to Self or Others**

- **Self-Control Issues**

- **Victim—Student Who Is Always Picked On**

· · · · · · · ·
General Information

- Tourette Syndrome (TS) is a genetic disorder characterized by the presence of both involuntary movements (i.e., motor tics) and involuntary vocalizations (i.e., vocal tics). The motor tics may include eye-blinking, grimacing, and/or jerky movements of the arms and legs, while the verbal tics may consist of coughing, hissing, sniffing, snorting, and/or verbal (often obscene) outbursts. In addition, TS may be associated with more global problems such as aggression, obsessive-compulsive behaviors, attention deficits, and learning problems.

- One of the most difficult aspects of assisting a student who has TS is determining which of the student's behavior(s) are appropriate for intervention and which are not. The issue has to do with the importance of helping the student assume responsibility for behaving appropriately when he/she can, and recognizing that there may be some behaviors over which the student has no control. Consider, for example, the metaphor of a student who is paraplegic and who is occasionally disrespectful to you. While it is completely inappropriate to attempt an intervention to motivate that student to walk, it is both appropriate and reasonable to intervene to help the student learn to treat adults with respect.

  In the case of a misbehaving student with TS, it is important that you discuss your concerns and any possible intervention with the student's parent(s) and/or the student's physician (if appropriate). You should rely on their guidance to help you determine which of the student's inappropriate behaviors are the direct result of the medical condition (and which, therefore, should be ignored when they occur), and which are reasonable to help the student learn to modify.

- Once you have identified a specific behavior that is appropriate for intervention, review the MODEL PLANS included for that particular behavior in this reference guide.

- If the student exhibits a number of different inappropriate behaviors, and you are not sure which poses the biggest problem, record anecdotal information about the student's behavior for a week or so. This type of documentation is fairly easy to collect—simply keep a card in your pocket or on a clipboard and, whenever the student does something (or doesn't do something) that creates a problem for himself or interferes with the smooth running of the class, make notes on the incident. For each entry, briefly describe the circumstances—where and when the misbehavior occurred, what was said and/or done, and any other relevant observations you may have about the situation (e.g., what prompted the behavior).

  After about a week, use the information you have collected to choose one specific behavior to address. It might be the misbehavior that occurs most often or the one that creates the biggest disruption for the class. Whatever your criteria, the important thing is to focus your intervention efforts on one problem behavior at a time. Often, as you work on one behavior (e.g., aggression), other problem behaviors (e.g., getting upset when corrected) seem to improve without specific intervention.

- As an educator, you should not attempt to diagnose Tourette Syndrome any more than you should attempt to diagnose diabetes, clinical depression, or any other medical/psychological disorder. If you have a student who exhibits behaviors that suggest the possibility of Tourette Syndrome, discuss your concerns with your building administrator, the school psychologist, and/or the school nurse. Then, depending upon the circumstances and your district's policy for addressing this type of situation, it may be appropriate to arrange for a meeting with the student's parent(s) and/or to suggest that the student be evaluated by a physician.

- For more information on Tourette Syndrome, contact:

  Tourette Syndrome Association (TSA)
  42-40 Bell Boulevard
  Bayside, NY 11361
  (718) 224-2999

TRANSITIONS, PROBLEMS WITH

Slow in Lining Up

DESCRIPTION

There are students in your class who are too slow during transitions (e.g., lining up, getting out books, etc.).

GOAL

The students will be efficient during transitions.

OVERVIEW OF PLANS

- PLAN A: For a situation in which the problem has just begun or occurs infrequently.

- PLAN B: For a problem that may stem from students not knowing how to be more efficient during transitions.

- PLAN C: For a situation in which the students lack the motivation to be more efficient.

> NOTE:
>
> *These three plans are geared for a situation in which quite a few students in the class have a problem being efficient during transitions. However, each can easily be modified to intervene with only a few (one to three) students, or more appropriate plans may be found in Dawdling.*

Alternative Problems

- **Beginning Class—Getting Students Settled Down**

- **Dawdling**

- **Cleaning Up, Problems With**

. . . .
General Considerations

- If you suspect that the students are being inefficient during transitions because they hope to delay/avoid the subsequent activities for some reason (e.g., they find the activities too difficult or unpleasant), you should analyze the activities carefully and modify them, as much as is reasonably possible, to make these activities less aversive for the students. However, it is still important to implement a plan to increase the students' transition efficiency.

. . . .
Model Plans

PLAN A

If this problem has just begun and/or occurs infrequently (e.g., only two to five times per week), it may not be necessary, or even beneficial, to use an involved plan. The following actions, along with making the students aware of your concerns, may to resolve the situation.

1. Immediately before each transition, obtain all the students' attention.

a. Do not give instructions for the transition until you have the full attention of the class.

b. Once you have student attention, define the transition task and specify approximately how long you think it should require. "Class, in a moment I am going to give an instruction to get ready for math. Please don't do anything yet. You need to get out your math book, blank notebook paper, and a pencil. Put your heading on the paper. I'll know you are ready when you put your pencil down. Let's see if everyone can finish and be ready in less than one minute. Get started now."

c. If a transition involves more than three steps, write the sequence of tasks on the chalkboard or on an overhead transparency.

2. Respond consistently to each instance of overly long transitions.

a. Whenever a transition takes too long, provide feedback on what the students could do differently. Be specific. "Class, next time we have this kind of transition, some of you need to work on not getting sidetracked. In fact, if someone tries to talk to you, just say, 'We need to be getting ready for math.'"

b. In addition, note how much longer the transition took than you had estimated. Record the time on a note card that you keep in your pocket or on a clipboard. Tell the students how much longer the transition required than you had set

as a goal. "That took us three minutes—two minutes longer than it should have. Let's work harder on these transitions."

3. Use reinforcement to encourage appropriate behavior.

a. Praise individual students for meeting your expectations regarding efficiency during transitions. Keep an eye on those students who have had the greatest tendency to dawdle or to otherwise waste time. Whenever one or more of these students meet the expectations, praise them for demonstrating the ability to be efficient. "Cynthia, Derrick, and Nola, thank you for being ready."

If the students would be embarrassed by public praise, praise the students privately, praise them nonverbally by simply making eye contact and giving a head nod as you begin instruction, or even give the students a note later.

b. In addition, occasionally praise those students who rarely or never have a problem with inefficient transitions. Because these students have already mastered the positive expectations, they do not need positive feedback as often as the students who have had difficulty. However, you do not want them to feel that you take their positive behavior for granted. "You people seated at this table are consistently efficient. I appreciate that I never need to give your reminders."

c. Finally, when there has been a significant overall improvement in the efficiency of classroom transitions, praise the entire class. Remember that any time the students are ready on time you can praise them for their cooperation and their efficiency.

PLAN B

If the students are not clear about how to be efficient during transitions, the intervention must include some way of teaching them efficient procedures.

 Identify five critical transitions to be the initial focus of the plan.

(NOTE: Other transitions can be added once the students are efficient with these.)

Choose transitions that have been particularly frustrating, and that happen daily. Do not include a transition in which the nature of the task is always different. Although putting things away after a field day may be a problem, for example, it would not be appropriate as one of the five initial focus transitions.

 For each of the identified transitions, directly teach the students to meet your expectations for efficiency.

a. Before the lessons, identify for yourself your expectations for student behavior during each transition. For each, prepare a written list of behavioral expectations on a poster or an overhead transparency. If there are problems that often require extra time for the students (e.g., not having a pencil, forgetting school books at home), develop "back-up" routines that specify what the students should do in those circumstances (e.g., "If you don't have your book . . .") Finally, decide on a time criterion—how long it should take to complete each transition.

b. Immediately before each identified transition, clarify your expectations for the students. Following is a sample of what the you might say as you show the list of instructions on the poster or the overhead transparency:

"When I give the instruction to put away your math and get out your spelling, quietly fold your math paper in half and put it in your book at the open page. Quietly, put your book in your desk. Get out your spelling book and a piece of paper. If you need to borrow paper, quietly ask your neighbor. If you do not have your book, look on with your neighbor, otherwise there is no need for talking. We should be able to do this in less than one minute. On some days, we have taken up to five minutes. That is a lot to remember, so let's review. What should you do first?"

c. After the review, ask the students if there are any questions. Prior to giving the instruction, ask the students if there is anything that would prevent them from being able to carry out the instruction. Now is the time to address issues such as a student who does not have the book and his/her neighbor does not have his/hers, either. There is no one correct way to deal with these problems, but work out the solutions with the students so that they know what to do if this situation happens in the future.

d. If the transition does not go well (e.g., students misbehave or some are inefficient), do it again. Repeat the transition until the whole class meets the reasonable criteria of efficiency. Be careful not to treat this practice time as a punishment. You might use a sports or musical example (e.g., when a basketball team is having trouble with a particular play, the coach sets up drills on that play).

 Respond consistently to inefficient transitions.

a. For the first week, if a transition does not go well, repeat the transition until it does. This may seem like a waste of time, but if practicing for five minutes one day saves two minutes per day for the rest of the year, large amounts of instructional time will be saved.

b. After approximately a week (possibly longer with primary level students), when you are sure that the students know and can meet the expectations for efficient transitions, tell the class that whenever a transition takes longer than the allotted time, the entire class will spend their recess time practicing that transition.

During recess, have the class practice each problem transition until they have been successful with it twice. If the problem occurs in a situation without recesses (e.g., in a middle/junior high school classroom, or an elementary school P.E. class), conduct the practice during class, and inform the students that the practice time will reduce the class time available for fun and/or independent activities. If the class took too long getting ready for math, for example, they would practice until they performed this transition successfully two times. This practice could take anywhere from two to 15 minutes. When the students have been successful twice, they can go out to recess for the remaining time.

c. It is very important that while implementing any of these procedures, you do not nag, coax, remind, or yell at the the students to be efficient. Your goal is to give clear instructions, but it is the students' job to be efficient.

4. **Use reinforcement to encourage appropriate behavior.**

a. Praise individual students for meeting the expectations regarding efficient transitions, and praise the entire class when improvement takes place (see PLAN A).

b. Make a special point of letting the students know (both individually and as a class) that you notice their efforts to use the skills they have been learning/practicing. "Watson and Ericka, you were very efficient in putting away your math and getting ready for spelling. Nice job of doing what we have been practicing."

c. You may also wish to use intermittent rewards to acknowledge student success. Occasional, and unexpected, rewards can motivate the class to demonstrate responsible behavior more often. The idea is to provide a reward when the students have been doing particularly well during transitions.

Appropriate rewards might include any class-wide activity, such as playing a game, extra recess, or free time in class. "Class, you have all been so efficient with our transitions, we have saved a lot of time this week. Because you have all helped to save time, let's take some time now to go out to recess early. I'll be with you until the other students and the playground supervisors arrive. *(NOTE: A list of additional reinforcement ideas can be found in APPENDIX 1.)* Use intermittent rewards more frequently at the beginning of the intervention to encourage the students, and then less often as their behavior improves.

PLAN C

Sometimes an entire class falls into a pattern of wasting time and not being ready during transitions. This can happen when the behavior becomes habitual and/or when a majority of students try to emulate a few influential students who act inefficient during transitions to look "cool" or "tough." In these cases, it can be very difficult to change the class' behavior, and you may need to implement a structured reinforcement system (i.e., rewards and consequences) that creates mild peer pressure to motivate the students to behave appropriately.

1. **Identify five key transitions and teach the students your expectations for these transitions (see PLAN B).**

2. **In addition, keep a record of time wasted during each transition (see PLAN A).**

3. **Respond consistently to all inefficient transitions.**

a. During recess, have the class practice any transition that is still taking too long (see PLAN B).

b. If only one or two students continue to have trouble with a transition, have just those students rather than the entire class stay in from recess to practice the transition.

c. Have middle/junior high school students stay after class for 30 seconds to one minute to discuss and/or practice the transition.

4. **Implement group reinforcement with a grab bag system.**

a. During the class meeting (see SUGGESTED STEPS FOR DEVELOPING AND IMPLEMENTING A PLAN), have the students brainstorm a number of reinforcement ideas for the entire class, then eliminate any items from the list that are not possible (i.e., the suggestions are too expensive or could not be provided to all the students in the class). Be sure there is a range from very minor reinforcement (e.g., a one-minute "talking" break during science) to major (e.g., renting a popular video and having popcorn one afternoon).

b. Make up a grab bag of the items that the class brainstormed. Write each of the acceptable items from the students' list on a separate slip of paper. In addition, write congratulatory phrases (e.g., "Great Job!" and "I am proud of this class!") on many slips of paper and include them in the grab bag as well. For example, if the students had identified 15 possible rewards, you would write each of those on a slip of paper for inclusion in the grab bag, along with, say, 45 slips of paper containing only a congratulatory message.

c. For each successful transition, allow a student to draw from the grab bag. The class receives the reinforcer on the slip of paper drawn. Because the "deck is stacked," so to speak, most of the time the paper will contain a congratulatory message, but occasionally the paper will specify a tangible reinforcer.

d. As the class is consistently more successful with their transitions, reduce the odds of them receiving an actual reinforcer by including more congratulatory messages in the grab bag.

e. If a class-wide reinforcement system seems unlikely to be effective, an alternative method is to implement a team competition and response cost lottery. In this type of system, the class is divided into four to six teams (designed to be as equitable as possible). Each team begins the day with a certain number of tickets (e.g., six) on which they write the name of their team. Whenever a student is not efficient during a transition, that student's team loses a ticket. At the end of the day, each team puts all their remaining tickets in a hat for a lottery drawing. The team whose name is on the ticket that is drawn receives the predetermined reward for that day.

5. *When implementing any of these reinforcement systems, focus student attention on the fact that efficient transitions mean more time for class activities.*

Tell the class, for example: "Class, you earned two chances at the grab bag today, but more importantly, there has been very little instructional time wasted. I appreciate your cooperation and efficiency."

. . . .
Suggested Steps for Developing and Implementing a Plan

The following information is designed to help you develop an appropriate intervention plan and implement it effectively, whether you choose to use one of the MODEL PLANS or create a customized plan of your own. The steps are, however, suggestions—they are not intended to be followed rigidly or in any particular order. Use your professional judgment and the knowledge of your particular situation to make them work for you.

1. *Decide how to present the situation to the class.*

a. When you think a simple intervention like PLAN A will be appropriate, you may choose to have an informal discussion with the students. Wait for a time when you are calm (i.e., not right after an incident has occurred) and inform the students that you are finding the time required for transitions to be a problem. Then specifically define your expectations.

Give the students the opportunity to ask questions or make comments and end the session by thanking the students for listening. Let the students know that you are confident that they will make an effort to be efficient during transitions in the future.

b. If you prefer to implement one of the more structured MODEL PLANS, schedule a class meeting for the purpose of clarifying all aspects of the plan and giving the students an opportunity to ask questions or make comments.

c. If you want the students to assume some ownership of the problem, you might want to hold a class meeting in which the students participate in analyzing the situation and developing an action plan. In this case, before the meeting clarify the nature/extent of the problem and your expectations for the students' behavior.

Also identify any aspects of the plan that you do not feel comfortable opening up to a group decision. For example, you must decide ahead of time whether or not to allow the class to determine *if* there will be a consequence for inefficient transitions and/or what the consequence should be. If you firmly believe that there must be a consequence, then you should not seek student input on that particular issue.

Conduct the class meeting to present your proposed plan or to have the students generate a plan.

(NOTE: Following is a guide to helping the class generate a plan; however, feel free to include one or more procedures from the MODEL PLANS.)

a. Schedule the meeting for a neutral time and allow enough time for a reasonable discussion. Inform the students in advance that the meeting will take place; this will give them time to think about the problem. "Class, this afternoon we are going to have a class meeting on the problem of time wasted during transitions. Please give some thought to this problem and what we might do as a class to solve it."

b. Use an agenda to structure the meeting. Shortly before the meeting, write the agenda on the chalkboard. Following is one possibility you may wish to use.

Agenda

1. Wasted time—Define the magnitude of the problem. (Share the data collected on cumulative time wasted during transitions.)

2. Review the expectations regarding different transitions.

3. Brainstorm ideas for improving the situation.

4. Select strategies that everyone in the class agrees to.

5. Clarify the consequences for one student wasting time and the consequences for lots of students in the class wasting time.

---

c. It is important to establish clear rules for both you and the students regarding the brainstorming phase of the meeting. For example:

- Any idea is okay (but no obscenity).

- Ideas will not be evaluated initially (i.e., no approval—"Good idea" or disapproval—"What a stupid idea" or "We couldn't do that" should be expressed during brainstorming).

- All ideas will be written down and discussed at the conclusion of brainstorming.

d. At the conclusion of brainstorming, evaluate the ideas, and lead the class to consensus on any decisions that need to be made. Use voting as a decision-making process when appropriate.

Determine when and how to include the parent(s).

a. Because this problem is more of a procedural than behavioral or motivational problem, involving the students' parents is not critical with a class-wide situation.

b. If the situation involves one or two students who have or continue to have a problem with transitions, you should contact the parents of those individual students. Let them know that their student is wasting time during transitions and what steps you are taking to correct the situation.

Frequent contact is not required, but whenever you intend to implement an individualized plan, the student's parent(s) should be informed prior to its implementation and should be given feedback about the student's progress every two to four weeks.

Give the class regular, ongoing feedback about their behavior.

Periodically meet with the students to discuss the situation. In most cases, three to five minutes once per week should suffice. During the meetings, review any information that has been collected and discuss whether or not things are getting better. As much as possible, focus on improvements, however, also address any new or continuing problems. As you discuss problems, acknowledge that there are individuals in the class who consistently behave appropriately. However, do not single out individuals when discussing problems or progress with the entire class. As the situation improves, the meetings can be faded to once every other week and then to once per month.

Evaluate the situation (and the plan).

Any plan should be implemented for at least two weeks before deciding whether or not it is effective. Generally, if the situation has improved (based on the objective information that's been collected and/or the subjective perceptions of yourself and the students), continue with what you have been doing. (Eventually you will want to fade, then eliminate, the plan.) If the problem remains the same or worsens, some kind of change (e.g., modifying the current plan or switching to another plan) will be necessary. Always discuss any change in the intervention plan with the class first.

V ANDALISM / DESTRUCTION OF PROPERTY

DESCRIPTION

Acts of vandalism (e.g., carving in desktops, graffiti, punching holes in walls) have occurred in your classroom, and you may or may not know the culprit.

GOAL

The acts of vandalism will stop and the perpetrator(s) will be identified (if unknown).

OVERVIEW OF PLANS

- PLAN A: For establishing basic procedures to help students report what they know without having to publicly "squeal," and for reducing the probability that your classroom will be vandalized in the future.

- PLAN B: For a situation in which you know the individual student(s) who was/were involved in the vandalism.

Alternative Problems

- **Stealing—Major Problem, Culprit Known**

- **Stealing—Major Problem, Culprit Unknown**

....
General Considerations

- If you know who the culprit is and suspect that the behavior stems in any way from academic issues (e.g., the student is angry and frustrated because he/she repeatedly experiences academic failure), concurrent efforts must be made to ensure the student's academic success (see **Academic Deficits, Determining**).

- If vandalism is a chronic school-wide problem, a proactive and preventative approach should be designed and implemented by the entire faculty. For specific information on vandalism, see:

  Mayer, G.R. & Sulzer-Azaroff, B. (1991). Interventions for vandalism. In G. Stoner, M.R. Shinn, & H.M. Walker (Eds.), *Interventions for achievement and behavior problems* (pp. 559-580). Silver Springs, MD: National Association of School Psychologists.

One of the primary recommendations by Mayer and Sulzer-Azaroff is that a school develop a positive and preventative school-wide discipline policy. For information on developing such a policy, see:

Sprick, R.S., Sprick, M.S., & Garrison, M. (1993). *Foundations: Establishing positive discipline policies.* Longmont, CO: Sopris West.

- Vandalism and destruction of property are illegal acts and should not be taken lightly. If you are faced with a situation of classroom vandalism, develop a proposed plan and then ask your school administrator for feedback and/or assistance with any changes that might need to be made to the plan.

....
Model Plans

PLAN A

When the individual student(s) responsible for the vandalism is/are not known, the most effective intervention may be to create a nonthreatening, private procedure for students to report any knowledge of the situation. In addition, you can involve the students in implementing strategies for preventing future acts of vandalism.

 Keep anecdotal notes on all incidents of vandalism.

Record what was damaged, when the vandalism probably occurred, the approximate cost of the damage, what actions you have taken (e.g., talking to the class, talking to your building administrator, etc.), and any other relevant information.

 Establish procedures that allow the students to report any information they may have about the vandalism in such a way that they will not be ostracized as a "squealer."

a. One simple procedure is to make yourself accessible. Tell the students specifically when and how they can communicate with you in confidence. Make it clear that any information shared will be confidential. To accommodate those who

would prefer to remain anonymous, you might invite the students to leave unsigned notes on your desk or in your box at the office. Also, remind the students about other adults (e.g., the school counselor, the principal, etc.) to whom they can talk confidentially about incidents of vandalism.

b. The following procedure is a slightly more direct way of encouraging the students to report what they know about a particular incident.

"Class, because of the severe damage done to the supply cabinet, this matter must be investigated further. I have put the following statement up on the chalkboard:

I have reason to suspect that _____ may know something about the damage to the supply cabinet.

"When I tell you to, I want each of you to copy this statement on an index card that I will be passing out to you. You do not need to sign your name. Everyone in the class, whether or not they know anything, must write and turn in this statement. If you do not know anyone who might know something about the vandalism, write 'John Doe' in the blank. (Write this name on the chalkboard.) I want you to understand that you are not accusing anyone of doing the vandalism, and that no one will be punished as a result of having their name written down. However, this will allow the principal and me to conduct a more thorough investigation of what really happened.

"For those of you who think that this is like 'ratting' on a classmate, I urge you to consider this: If you know something and do not report it, the person who did this damage is likely to get away with it and may decide to continue vandalizing. Your silence could actually be putting this person's future in serious trouble. When we find out who was responsible, there will be consequences, of course, but we can also help this person learn to stop vandalizing. So if you know anyone who might know something about this, please write that person's name in the blank.

"Please take the index card I am now passing out. Cover it so that no one can see what you are writing and copy the statement on the chalkboard. If you can think of anyone who might know something about this, fill in the name or names. Remember, write John Doe if you have no idea of anyone who might have direct knowledge."

c. Review the cards later, when the students are not present. If one or more names surface, share this information with your building administrator and get advice on how to proceed with interviewing those student(s). Ask the administrator to join you for the interview(s) and coordinate with the administrator on when and how to involve the parent(s) and/or the juvenile authorities.

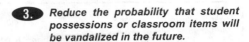 **3.** **Reduce the probability that student possessions or classroom items will be vandalized in the future.**

a. Hold a class meeting about the problem, and ask the students to brainstorm strategies for protecting their own possessions and strategies for protecting the classroom.

First establish clear rules for brainstorming that would apply both to you and the students. For example:

1. Any idea is okay (but no obscenity).

2. Do not evaluate any idea during brainstorming (i.e., no approval—"Good idea" or disapproval—"What a stupid idea" or "We couldn't do that" should be expressed).

3. All ideas will be written down and discussed at the conclusion of brainstorming.

b. Begin the brainstorming by writing down every suggestion made. Then lead the class in discussing the viability of each suggestion, and give the students the opportunity to ask questions about any of the ideas. For example, a student might say something like, "Never trust anybody." When discussing this suggestion, you might take the opportunity to talk about the value of trust, being trustworthy, what it feels like to have people you can trust, and what it feels like to have no one you can trust.

c. Encourage each student to set up a personal plan to protect his/her possessions, and then discuss with the class which of the strategies could be used to protect the classroom.

d. Implement a classroom plan incorporating the best of the brainstormed suggestions (contribute your own, if necessary).

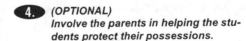 **4.** **(OPTIONAL)** **Involve the parents in helping the students protect their possessions.**

A note such as the sample shown following could be sent to the parents after a class discussion about the problem.

Dear Parents:

As you may already know, there has been a serious problem with vandalism in our classroom. Although efforts are being made to identify the culprit, thus far those steps have been unsuccessful. Therefore, I am asking all the students to be extra careful about protecting their own possessions.

During a class discussion, the students came up with the following ideas for doing so:

- "Don't bring valuable stuff to school."

- "Put things away in your desk or locker."

- "Don't bring any toys from home."

- "Keep your lunch box by the coats, not in the Activity Room."

Please review these suggestions with your child and discuss other things he/she might do to prevent the possibility of vandalism within the classroom.

In addition, if your child has reported anything to you that might help us identify who has been involved in the vandalism, please call me at school between 3:30 and 4:00, or call Ms. Strein (the counselor) or Ms. Wacker (the principal) at any time.

Thank you.

PLAN B

When you know which student or students did the vandalizing, the intervention must include implementing consequences for those acts, plus developing a proactive plan to help the student(s) refrain from such behavior in the future.

 1. Keep anecdotal records of all actions and circumstances related to the vandalism.

Make notes on evidence which supports that the student did the vandalism, notes on discussions about the problem with the student, notes on parental contacts, and any other relevant details. *(NOTE: Do not confront or accuse a student of vandalism unless you have substantiation.)*

 2. Determine how to include the student's parent(s).

Whenever a student has committed an act of vandalism, the parent(s) should be informed. If the damage was extensive and/or expensive, the student's parent(s) should be invited to participate in the initial discussion you have with the student (see Step 3). However, if the incident involved only minor damage, you may wish to have the student inform his parent(s) himself as part of the consequence.

 3. Discuss the situation with the student.

a. Schedule a meeting with the student (and the student's parent[s], if applicable). Depending upon the severity of the situation, you may also wish to invite to the meeting a building administrator, the counselor, or an outside authority (e.g., a police officer, a district attorney, or a representative of child protective services).

b. Explain that you have reason to believe that the student was the party responsible for the incident of vandalism (i.e., share the evidence you have noted). If the student denies involvement, take no further action. Without *proof* of the student's involvement, you should not make accusations—seek guidance from your administrator about how to proceed.

If the student admits involvement, you will need to work out some way for the student to assume responsibility for his actions. Depending upon the age of the student and the extent of the damage, this may include having the student do some or all of the following:

- Tell his parent(s) what he did.

- Tell the principal what he did.

- Repair the damage either by himself or with the custodian.

- Arranging for the repair/replacement of the damage.

- Paying for the repair/replacement of the damage by either working at home to earn the money or by working at school to earn the money.

(NOTE: If the vandalism is severe, district policy may necessitate a consequence such as suspension or legal action in lieu of/in addition to these "reparation-type" consequences.)

c. Throughout your interactions with the student about this situation, make sure to provide positive acknowledgment when the student is accepting responsibility for his actions. "Abraham, you are being responsible about working to repair the damage. You should be proud of your ability to learn from a mistake."

It is not necessary to demand, or even imply, that the student should act remorseful. The primary goal is for the student to be accountable for repairing or replacing what was damaged.

4. ***Try to determine the reason(s) the student engaged in the vandalism.***

Understanding why a student would choose to vandalize will help you develop a plan for reducing the probability that the student will do so again. Following is a brief list of possible reasons and ideas for appropriate/effective responses:

- The student did not know any better.

  Conduct lessons with the student, modeling and practicing care of different types of items.

- The student is angry and vengeful toward the school (see **Self-Control Issues**).

- The student was trying to impress his peers (see **Disrespectful Behavior** for plans that can be adapted for this problem).

- The student is involved in gang activity or is a gang member "wannabe" (see **Gang Involvement** for references pertaining to this very serious problem).

5. ***Decide whether to continue, fade, or change intervention plans.***

Continually evaluate the effectiveness of your intervention. If the student continues to vandalize, consider additional preventative tactics that might reduce the student's temptation to vandalize. For example, can a sign-in system be established so the student's whereabouts are constantly known? Can the student's movements about the school be limited? If more than one or two additional incidents of vandalism occur, consider setting up a coordinated plan involving law enforcement personnel.

VICTIM—STUDENT WHO IS ALWAYS PICKED ON

DESCRIPTION

There is one particular student in your class who tends to be the target of tormenting (i.e., teasing and/or bullying) by other students.

GOAL

The student who is picked on will learn skills and strategies for reducing the likelihood of being victimized and for effectively dealing with any tormenting that does occur.

OVERVIEW OF PLANS

- PLAN A: For a situation in which the problem has just begun or occurs infrequently.

- PLAN B: For a situation in which the student responds to the tormenting in a way that encourages further abuse.

- PLAN C: For a situation in which the student has a distinguishing feature (e.g., poor hygiene, an accent, a disability) that sets her apart from her peers.

- PLAN D: For a situation in which the student tends to provoke others into victimizing her.

NOTE:

If your particular problem is one in which several different students in your class are being victimized, you might consider obtaining a copy of an excellent resource from which many of the ideas and suggestions provided in this problem have been adapted with permission:

Garrity, C., Jens, K., Porter, W., Sager, N., & Short-Camilli, C. (1994). Bully-proofing your school: A comprehensive approach for elementary schools. Longmont, CO: Sopris West.

Alternative Problems

- **Bullying Behavior/ Fighting**

- **Cliques/Ganging Up**

- **Harassment— Racial/Sexual**

- **Hygiene Problems**

- **Name Calling/ Put-Downs**

- **Self-Concept Problems**

- **Tattling**

· · · · · · · ·
General Considerations

- If the student's problem stems in any way from academic issues (e.g., she stands out because she is academically unsuccessful), concurrent efforts should be made to ensure her academic success (see **Academic Deficits, Determining**).

- If the student lacks the basic social skills to interact with her peers appropriately, it may be necessary to begin by teaching her those skills. **Social Skills, Lack of** contains information on a variety of published social skills curricula.

- If you suspect that the student could be depressed, see **Depression**. This problem includes a set of questions to help you decide whether the student should be referred for counseling or pyschological services.

- If the tormenting tends to be done by one particular student (or group of students), concurrent efforts must be made to deal with the perpetrator(s). See **Bullying Behavior/Fighting** for ideas.

· · · · · · · ·
Model Plans

PLAN A

It is not always necessary, or even beneficial, to use an involved plan. If the problem has just begun or occurs only infrequently, the following actions may resolve the situation.

 Suggest strategies the student can use to reduce the probability that she will be victimized.

a. During your initial meeting with the student (see SUGGESTED STEPS FOR DEVELOPING AND IMPLEMENTING A PLAN), try to increase the student's awareness of ways she might control the occurrence of tormenting. You might, for example, help the student identify ways to avoid being in a position in which tormenting is likely to take place, such as:

- Sitting in a different location in the classroom.

- Making a point of not interacting with particular students.

- Trying to stay relatively close to the playground supervisors during recess.

b. You might also share with the student the following potentially effective strategies for responding to tormenting:

- Ignoring (i.e., simply pretending not to hear the comment).

- Using "I statements" (e.g., "I have a right to be treated with respect," or "It hurts my feelings to be treated that way. I want you to stop.").

- Staying calm—Using techniques like deep breathing, counting to ten, muscle relaxation, etc.

(NOTE: These suggestions represent only a few of the possibilities. Obviously, you should tailor the discussion to your student's particular situation. A more comprehensive list of ideas can be found in **Name Calling/Put-Downs***.)*

 Specify how the student should go about obtaining adult help when she really needs it.

There is a fine line between promoting unnecessary tattling and/or reliance upon adults and ensuring that a student has access to adult help when necessary. Since it is a fact that some students truly are victimized, you need to make sure that your student knows exactly *how* she could obtain adult assistance (from you or a playground supervisor, counselor, etc.) if necessary in a tormenting situation. By also making clear to the student *when* she should seek such assistance (i.e., the parameters of when that would be appropriate), you balance your responsibility for reassuring the student with the goal of encouraging her to handle her own problems.

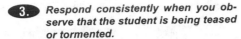

3. *Respond consistently when you observe that the student is being teased or tormented.*

a. During your initial meeting with the student (see SUGGESTED STEPS FOR DEVELOPING AND IMPLEMENTING A PLAN), establish a nonembarrassing signal that you can use to cue her that she needs to use one or more of the strategies for effectively responding to bullying. You want the signal to be a fairly subtle one that only the student will recognize and understand to minimize the chance that she will be the recipient of additional tormenting.

Possibilities include clasping your hands together in front of you, rubbing your neck, or even just direct eye contact and a head nod. Let the student know that you may also need to quietly say her name to get her attention before you give the signal.

b. Regardless of how the student being victimized responds, if the bullying continues, intervene and correct the tormentors. If it is a "first offense" for a particular student, provide a verbal reprimand. "Stop that now. In this school we treat everyone with respect. If you treat Opal or anyone else in this way again, there will be consequences."

If you have to correct the same student(s) for victimizing the target student more than once, implement consequences such as parental contact, having the student(s) stay in from recess or after school to write a short essay on treating others with respect, or having the stu-

dent(s) perform some sort of community service in the school.

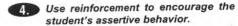

4. *Use reinforcement to encourage the student's assertive behavior.*

a. Give the student increased praise. Be especially alert for situations in which the student responds well to being teased or tormented and praise her for these demonstrations of her ability to be assertive. "Opal, I saw the way you dealt with Paula when she kept bumping into your desk. She was trying to get you upset, but you stayed calm and told her that she needed to stop and respect your space."

Since public praise may focus negative peer attention on the target student, praise the student privately or even give the student a note.

b. Praise the student privately for responding to the signal. "Opal, Brenda was trying to get you to react, I gave the signal, and you did a great job of ignoring."

c. Give the student frequent attention (e.g., say "hello" to her as she enters the classroom, call on her frequently during class activities, and occasionally ask her to assist you with a class job that needs to be done), and praise her for other positive behaviors she exhibits. For example, you might comment about her reading speed or how consistent she is about making entries in her journal. This demonstrates to the student that you notice many positive things she does. This student is going through a tough time, so provide her with lots of attention and support.

PLAN B

Some students do not know how to respond to teasing/bullying without encouraging the perpetrators. If you think your student is encouraging her tormentors by giving them what they want (e.g., by crying), the intervention must include teaching her more effective ways of responding.

1. *Try to increase the student's awareness of how she might control the occurrence of tormenting (see PLAN A).*

2. *Specify how the student should go about getting adult help when she really needs it (see PLAN A).*

3. *Respond consistently when you see the student being tormented (see PLAN A).*

4. *Conduct lessons to specifically teach the student effective ways of responding to tormenting so that the perpetrators are not encouraged to continue.*

a. If simply suggesting more effective ways of responding to the tormenting (as presented in PLAN A) is not sufficient, you should conduct more formal instruction (i.e., lessons that involve, among other things, role play and practice), and structured content (such as mnemonics for remembering to implement the strategies). Schedule at least two 15-minute lessons per week (daily lessons are better). *(NOTE: Given the probable amount of time involved, it may be necessary for someone else, such as the school counselor, to actually conduct the lessons.)*

b. During the lessons, first help the student identify what it is she is doing that is encouraging the tormentors. For example, does she cry? become angry? act scared? Then help her understand that her reactions make the tormentors feel like they have power over her, and so

actually increases the chances that she will be the victim of tormenting again.

Next, specifically teach the student a number of alternative responses to the tormenting and a method (or methods) to ensure that she will remember to implement the alternative responses. For example, one suggestion found in *Bully-Proofing Your School* (Garrity et al., 1994), involves the mnemonic "HA HA, SO." The following information as been adapted from that publication with permission.

The "HA HA, SO" Strategies

- **Help**—When and how to seek help from peers and/or an adult.

This strategy is best used in situations where help is available and willing, like at a "bully-proofed school." A victim can use this strategy during a bullying situation by calling to some other children, for example, "Could you help me ask Teddy to stop taking my books away from me?"; or by running to an adult, describing what is happening, and saying, "I need help." A victim can also use this strategy when anticipating a bullying situation by asking several other children to stay close. For example, "Sally and her friends have been bullying me at recess. Could you play with me today and help me figure out what to do if they come at me again?" The victim could also inform the teacher and ask for a watchful eye.

- **Assert Yourself**—When it would be wise to use assertiveness and when it would not.

This strategy is usually the best strategy for a victim to start with. But it should not be used with severe bullying or when the victim is very scared. To use this strategy, the victim looks the bully in the eye and says, for example, "I don't like how you are gossiping about me and trying to make me have no friends. It is mean and unfair. Stop doing it."

- **Humor**—How to use humor to deescalate a situation.

This strategy is fun for children and can be used in conjunction with the "Help" strategy by asking other children to help dream up humorous ways to deal with a certain bullying situation. Several children's books (many of which are listed in the Resource Guide provided in *Bully-Proofing Your School*) illustrate humor as a strategy for dealing with a bully (e.g., in the

book *Loudmouth George and the Sixth Grade Bully*, the victim, with the help of his friend, makes a horrific lunch with pickles in the sandwich and tabasco sauce in the thermos for a bully who was stealing his lunch). This strategy could also be used by the victim by writing a funny note or poem to the bully.

- **Avoid**—How to walk away in order to avoid a bullying situation.

This strategy may be best for situations when the victim is alone. One way for the victim to use the "Avoid" strategy is to avoid a bully physically. The victim can cross the street or can avoid the situation(s) where the bullying is occurring. The victim can also avoid a bully by being with others rather than alone, perhaps by asking to walk home from school with other children. Another way for the victim to use the "Avoid" strategy is to analyze the situation and to stop doing anything that might be provoking the bully. If the bullying is happening when the class lines up, and both the victim and the bully want to be at the front of the line, the victim can choose to be at the end of the line instead to avoid the bullying situation.

- **Self-Talk**—How to use self-talk to maintain positive self-esteem during a bullying situation.

A victim's self-esteem drops when he/she is being bullied. The "Self-Talk" strategy is used to keep feeling good about oneself. The strategy involves "putting on a record in one's mind" that says nice things to oneself, like: "I'm a good kid. I try my best at school and I'm nice to other kids. When Jason calls me dumb, it is not my fault. It is his problem that he is being mean. It is unfair. I don't have to accept his opinion of me. I can have my own opinion about me and like myself."

(continued)

(cont'd)

The "HA HA, SO" Strategies

- **Own It**—How to "own" the put-down or belittling comment in order to defuse it.

  This strategy can be combined with the "Humor" strategy with responses like, "I agree that this is an ugly dress; my mother made me wear

it." It can also be combined with the "Assert Yourself" strategy with responses like, "I do have slanted eyes and that is because I'm Korean. Korea is a really cool country. Do you want to hear some things about it?"

(sample student worksheet)

What I Can Do If I Am Being Bullied

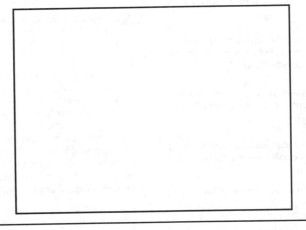

Directions:

    Draw or write about a good time to use a HA HA, SO strategy in the box below.

---

c. Use hypothetical situations (some of which can be based on actual incidents) to teach the student how and when to apply the six different response strategies included in HA HA, SO. First, present a scenario and have the student identify which of the six responses she might use in that situation. If the student's choice is appropriate, have her role play the scenario using that response. Follow this procedure with a couple of different scenarios during each lesson.

(NOTE: In addition to having the student role play/practice responding appropriately, you might occasionally have her assume the role of the perpetrator while you pose as a victim who responds in a way that encourages more tormenting so that she can see the effect of that type of response.)

d. You need to handle the lessons in a matter-of-fact manner and make sure that the student understands that you are not trying to embarrass her, but want her to see how others perceive her reaction. It is very important that the student not feel that she is being ridiculed.

e. Continue the lessons until the student has demonstrated that she can and does use appropriate responses both during the lessons and during actual tormenting situations.

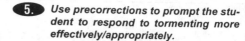 **Use precorrections to prompt the student to respond to tormenting more effectively/appropriately.**

Prior to any circumstances in which the student is likely to encounter tormenting, privately remind her of the HA HA, SO mnemonic and the fact that she should be prepared to use what she has been practicing in the lessons. If time permits, you might have her identify specifically how she would respond to a certain situation. "Opal, what are you planning on doing during recess today? Sounds fun. If someone starts to bother you, what will you remember to do? Excellent. Have a nice break and let me know how it goes."

PLAN C

Some students are picked on because something about them sets them apart from the other students. If this distinguishing feature is one that can and should be change (e.g., poor hygiene, bad breath, nose picking), the intervention should focus on helping the student make that change. If the distinguishing feature is one that cannot or should not be changed (e.g., a physical disability, race), the intervention should focus on helping the student recognize, accept, and even celebrate her uniqueness.

1. *Try to increase the student's awareness of how she might control the occurrence of tormenting (see PLAN A).*

2. *Specify how the student should go about getting adult help when she really needs it (see PLAN A).*

3. *Respond consistently when you see the student being tormented (see PLAN A).*

4. *Consider the student's distinguishing feature and decide on the focus of the intervention.*

a. It is not always easy to know whether to help the student learn to accept her uniqueness or to help her make a change. For example, say the student is picked on because she is from a poor family and has only one change of clothes for school. While it is reasonable to teach her to accept and like herself in spite of her families income level, it might also be reasonable to see about obtaining some additional clothing for the student. If you are not sure of the most appropriate focus of the intervention and/or the issue is a potentially sensitive one (e.g., the clothing situation), talk it over with your building administrator and the student's parent(s) before you take any action.

5. *Conduct lessons to specifically teach the student effective ways of responding to tormenting (see PLAN B).*

a. If the student needs to change a bad habit (e.g., nose picking), use the lesson time for teaching her how to do so in addition to giving her specific strategies for responding to her tormentors. You will have to decide what specific skills need to be taught and who will do the teaching. You will find additional information on specific bad habits and how to help a student cease them in one or more of the following problems in this reference guide: **Hygiene Problems**, **Nose Picking/Oral Fetishes**, **Babyish Behavior**, **Pouting**.

b. For a student who doesn't need to make a change, use the lesson time for helping the student learn ways to accept and celebrate her differences in addition to providing instruction in specific strategies for responding to tormentors. The following suggestions represent just a few of the possibilities you might use:

- Teach the student to use positive self-talk (see **Self-Concept Problems** for more details).

- Have the student read an age-appropriate story, novel, or biography about someone with a similar feature.

- Ask the student to write a report about her particular disability (which might later be shared with the class).

- Give the student a responsibility within the school that may help her take increased pride in herself and her uniqueness (see APPENDIX 2 for ideas).

(NOTE: Elementary teachers may want to provide or read to the student [or even the class as a whole] the children's book Different is Not Bad, Different is the World: A Book About Disabilities [Smith, 1994]. This outstanding resource focuses on various disabilities [both learning and physical] and reinforces the innate worth of children who have disabilities, while also helping children without disabilities learn to understand and empathize with those who are different from them—to respect and prize diversity.)

PLAN D

The *Bully-Proofing Your School* program refers to "provocative victims." These students can be characterized as being restless, irritating, easily angered, having the tendency to fight back (but usually losing), and/or not knowing when to stop bothering others. With this type of student, you may feel like she deserves whatever she gets. Nonetheless, the intervention should help the student identify specific bothersome behaviors she needs to change and help her learn that she can influence how frequently she is bullied by others.

1. *Try to increase the student's awareness of how she might control the occurrence of tormenting (see PLAN A).*

2. *Specify how the student should go about getting adult help when she really needs it (see PLAN A).*

3. *Respond consistently when you see the student being tormented (see PLAN A).*

4. *Identify the specific behavior(s) the student engages in that set her up for conflicts with her peers.*

Bothering/Tormenting Others contains ideas that may be useful for defining what your student

does that is bothersome, and plans for helping the student reduce those behaviors.

5. *Have the student self-monitor the frequency of her victimization.*

a. Establish a procedure for the student to record the number of times per day she is teased or tormented *and* how she responds. There are two advantages to this: when the bullying takes place, recording the incident will give the student something to do and reduce the likelihood of her reacting the way her tormentor hopes she will; and the record itself will give you (and/or the school counselor) specific information to discuss during daily review meetings (see Step 5b).

Following is a sample card the student might be taught to use for the self-monitoring.

Record of Teasing/Tormenting	
Name _____	Date _____
Make a ✓ for each incident of teasing.	Describe how you responded: Help, Assert Yourself, Humor, Avoid, Self-Talk, Own It, or another way.

b. Each day, meet with the student for a few minutes to review that day's record. You might also have the student chart the information (the number of "✓"s on the self-monitoring chart) on a graph (or do this yourself). Talk with the student about whether the day was better, worse, or about the same as previous days.

If the day did not go well, encourage the student to talk about why and have her identify strategies she can use the next day to help herself remember to bother others less and/or to respond differently to any teasing or tormenting that does occur. Make sure the student understands that reducing her bothersome behavior and modifying her responses will diminish and eventually eliminate the teasing/tormenting.

6. *Reinforce the student to encourage her cooperative yet assertive behavior.*

a. Give the student increased praise and attention for responding to teasing/tormenting in an assertive manner (see PLAN A).

b. Also look for opportunities to praise the student for reducing her bothersome behavior. Let the student know that her restraint will make it easier for others to like her and to stop teasing and tormenting her.

c. In addition, praise the student during the review meetings for accurate recording and for being willing to look at her own behavior that day. Even on a bad day, if the student is willing to discuss why it was a bad day, praise her. "Opal, you are really handling this responsibly. Even though it was a rough day, you are willing to talk to me about things you might do differently tomorrow. That is a real sign that you are growing up." Regardless of how the day went, try to make the end-of-the-day meeting upbeat and encouraging—you want the student to look forward to the review at the end of the day and feel supported during this difficult time for her.

d. Use intermittent reinforcement to encourage the student's efforts. Watch for times the student tries to respond to teasing or tormenting in productive ways (i.e., using one of the strategies discussed). If the student is being bullied and handles the situation well herself, go to her and let her know that she should be proud of herself. In addition, ask her if she would like to help you with a special job (or any other fun activity or reward).

. . . .
Suggested Steps for Developing and Implementing a Plan

The following steps are designed to help you develop an appropriate intervention plan and implement it effectively, whether you choose to use one of the MODEL PLANS or create a customized plan of your own. The steps are, however, suggestions—they are not intended to be followed rigidly or in any particular order. Use your professional judgment and the knowledge of your particular situation to make them work for you.

1. *Make sure you have enough information about the situation.*

a. If you think a minimal intervention like PLAN A will be sufficient, you may already have enough information to proceed. However, when a more involved plan seems necessary, you should consider collecting additional descriptive and/or objective information for a couple of days.

b. You need to be able to explain what has led you to conclude that the student has a problem with being victimized. Anecdotal notes on actual incidents should provide enough details to help you define the problem clearly and completely. To collect anecdotal notes, simply keep a card in your pocket or on a clipboard and take notes

on *every* instance in which you are aware that the student is being teased or tormented.

For each entry, briefly describe where and when the victimization occurred, the nature of the teasing/bullying, what the student did or said, whether an adult intervened or not, and any other relevant observations (e.g., what prompted the teasing or tormenting—whether the student was behaving provocatively).

You want as much information as possible as these notes will allow you to analyze the nature of the teasing/tormenting, the student's responses to the bullying, if the student is doing something to precipitate the bullying, and to determine if adults are giving too much or not enough help to the student being victimized. *(NOTE: Given the likelihood that many incidents may take place during recess, you might want to ask the playground supervisor[s] to take notes as well—or at least to fill you in on any incidents they see.)*

2. **Determine when and how to include the parent(s).**

a. The parent(s) of the student being picked on should be contacted as soon as you realize there is a problem. They need to know what their child is experiencing as well as what is being done to remedy the situation. Share with them any information you have collected about the problem (e.g., anecdotal notes), and explain why you are concerned. Focus in particular on how the behavior is affecting the student academically and/or socially (e.g., the student is being teased by many different students and is beginning to be afraid to go out to recess).

You might ask if the parent(s) have any insight into the situation and/or whether they have noticed similar occurrences with the children in their neighborhood. Explain to the parent(s) that you want to help the student "learn to deal with being teased," and invite them to join you for an initial meeting with the student to develop a plan. If the parent(s) are unable or unwilling to participate, let them know that you will keep them informed about the situation.

b. You should give the student's parent(s) updates at least once per week while the plan is being implemented.

3. **Prepare for, then conduct, an initial meeting about the situation.**

a. Arrange a meeting to discuss your concerns with the student and anyone else who will be involved (e.g., the parent[s], the school counselor, a playground supervisor). Although the specifics will vary depending upon the age of the student and the severity of the problem, there are some general guidelines to consider when scheduling the meeting.

First, meet at a neutral time (i.e., not immediately after victimization has occurred), when emotions are less likely to hamper communication. In general, a day's notice is appropriate, however a primary age student may worry excessively and/or forget what the meeting is about if it is scheduled more than an hour before it takes place.

Second, make the meeting appropriately private (e.g., the counselor's office) to ensure that the discussion will not be overheard by the student's peers.

Third, try to make sure the meeting is scheduled for a time and place that it is not likely to be interrupted. Finally, if the parent(s) will be participating, they should be the ones to tell the student about the meeting.

b. Construct a preliminary plan. Decide whether you think you can use one of the MODEL PLANS or if you need to create a customized plan using components from various plans and/or of your own design. Although you will invite and encourage the student to help develop the plan during the initial meeting, having a proposed plan in mind before you meet can alleviate wasted time if the student is unable to participate.

c. After reviewing the information you have collected and thinking about how you want the student to respond to the bullying, prepare thorough descriptions of the inappropriate strategies the student has used to respond to teasing/tormenting and the positive strategies on which the student will be working. The more specific you can be and the more concrete examples you have, the easier it will be to clarify (and for the student to understand) your expectations. Be sure to consider the student's responses in all relevant locations and activities (e.g., in class, during cooperative groups, during unstructured class times, at recess and lunch, etc.).

d. Conduct the meeting in an atmosphere of collaboration. The following agenda is one way you might structure the meeting:

- **Share your concerns about the situation.**

  Briefly describe the problem and review some of your anecdotal notes with the student. Explain why you consider her responses to be a problem. You might tell the student that everyone gets teased or tormented sometimes, but she needs to learn some new strategies so she does not give her tormentors what they want (i.e., a feeling of power over her).

- **Discuss how you can work together to improve the situation.**

  Tell the student that you would like to help her learn to "deal with being teased in ways that the teasers don't like," and describe your preliminary plan. Invite the student to give you input on the various aspects of the plan, and together work out any necessary details (e.g., the signal, lesson content, use of the self-monitoring form, etc.). You may have to brainstorm different possibilities if the student is uncomfortable with the initial plan. Incorporating any of the student's suggestions that strengthen the plan is likely to increase her sense of "ownership" in and commitment to it.

- **Conclude the meeting.**

Always end the meeting with words of encouragement. Let the student know that you are confident that she can be successful. Be sure to reinforce her for participating in the meeting.

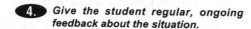 *Give the student regular, ongoing feedback about the situation.*

It is important to meet with the student periodically to discuss the situation. In most cases, three to five minutes once per week should suffice. *(NOTE:*

PLAN D requires daily meetings.) During the meetings, review any information that has been collected and discuss whether or not the situation is getting better. As much as possible, focus on the student's strengths, however, also address any increase in the severity of the victimization. As the situation improves, these meetings can be faded to once every other week and then to once per month.

5. *Evaluate the situation (and the plan).*

Implement any plan for at least two weeks before deciding whether to change plans; to continue, modify, or fade the plan you are using; or to cease the intervention. Generally, if the problem is clearly decreasing (based on the anecdotal notes and/or the subjective perceptions of yourself, the student, and possibly the parent[s]), stick with what you are doing. If the situation has remained the same or worsened, some kind of change will be necessary. Always discuss any changes to the plan with the student first.

WEAPONS

DESCRIPTION

There has been an incident involving weapons on your school campus. *(NOTE: Even if there has not yet been an incident at your school, there is a strong possibility that this could happen, given the increase in such occurrences nationwide.)*

The presence of weapons on school campuses is a growing problem in this country, however actual incidents must be handled according to individual school and district policies. Therefore, there are no MODEL PLANS provided for this problem. The purpose of the following information is to suggest some basic considerations for dealing with weapons at school.

Alternative Problems

- Aggression—Verbal and/or Physical

- Bullying Behavior/Fighting

- Cliques/Ganging Up

- Physically Dangerous Behavior—to Self or Others

- Threatening Others (Staff or Students)

- Self-Control Issues

········
General Information

- You should be able to answer the following questions concerning weapons at your school. If you are unsure about the answers to any of these questions, check with your building administrator or central office staff for clarification:

  - Are there school board policies or state laws related to weapons that all students should be informed of?

  - What is considered to be a weapon? Guns are obviously considered weapons, but what about knives? kitchen knives? pocket knives? What about "nunchuks," clubs/sticks, or metal knuckles?

  - What should you do if you hear a rumor that a student has a weapon?

  - What should you do if you have knowledge that a student has a weapon?

  - What should you do if an emergency happens (e.g., a student is threatening you or someone else with a knife)? Is there an adequate communication system to let the office know that an emergency exists? Is there a back-up plan? For example, what if you cannot get to the intercom? Is there a system for using a responsible student as an emergency messenger?

  - What sort of documentation are you supposed to keep on weapon-related incidents? Are anecdotal notes sufficient, or is there some form (e.g., an "Incident Report Form") that you are expected to fill out?

  - What requirements or expectations exist for parental involvement? If a student has been involved in or is suspected of a weapon-related incident, should *you* contact the parent(s) or should a building administrator?

- If one of your students is suspended from school because of a weapons-related incident, you might think about whether the student has a particular behavioral issue that would benefit from intervention. For example, if the student has the tendency to bully others and is caught threatening another student with scissors, just being suspended for that act is not likely to change the student's general bullying behavior. Thus, in addition to the suspension, you could review the information in **Bullying Behavior/Fighting** and develop a proactive plan for working with him specifically on his bullying behavior when he returns to school.

- Additional information on violence prevention in communities and schools can be found in the following excellent resource:

  Prothrow-Stith, D. & Weissman, M. (1991). *Deadly consequences: How violence is destroying our teenage population and a plan to begin solving the problem.* New York: Harper Collins.

WETTING/SOILING PANTS

Toiletting Problems

DESCRIPTION

You have a student who wets and/or soils her pants.

GOAL

The student will use the restroom rather than wetting or soiling her pants.

OVERVIEW OF PLANS

- PLAN A: For a situation in which the problem has only occurred once or twice.

- PLAN B: For a student who wets and/or soils her pants because she forgets about using the restroom until it is too late.

- PLAN C: For a student who wets and/or soils her pants to avoid something or to gain power.

NOTE:

The following information is not intended for a student who has not yet been toilet trained. If your student has not been toilet trained, work with her parent(s) and special education personnel to develop a long-range toilet training program.

Alternative Problems

- **Helplessness**
- **Hygiene Problems**
- **Self-Control Issues**
- **School Phobia**

. . . .
General Considerations

- If you have any reason to suspect a physiological basis for the student's behavior (e.g., the student might have a urinary tract infection), consult with your building administrator, school nurse, and/or school psychologist for advice on district procedures for following up on the situation.

- If the student's problem behavior stems in any way from academic issues (e.g., the student cannot do the schoolwork and wets or soils her pants to avoid it), concurrent efforts must be made to ensure her academic success (see **Academic Deficits, Determining**).

- If you suspect that the inappropriate behavior could be related to the student being depressed, see **Depression**. This problem includes a set of questions to help you decide whether the student should be referred for counseling or psychological services.

. . . .
Model Plans

P L A N   A

It is not always necessary, or even beneficial, to use an involved plan. If the problem has occurred only once (or has occurred twice, but with more than a month between incidents), the following actions, along with making the student aware of your concerns, may resolve the situation.

1. *Respond consistently to any incidents of wetting and/or soiling pants.*

a. Make any arrangements necessary for the student to be able to clean herself up. This will involve having a change of clothes available in a location where the student can change without fear of being ridiculed by other students. Many elementary schools keep several emergency sets of clothes (that could be used by any student) in the nurse's office for this type of situation, since the nurse is a logical person to help the student if she needs assistance.

b. When the student has an accident, deal with it as privately as possible. Tell the student to go to the nurse's office (or other prearranged location) and clean herself up. *(NOTE: A kindergarten or first grade student who has defecated in her pants may need assistance in getting clean.)*

2. *Develop a plan for dealing with any overt teasing that you observe from other students.*

If other students know that the student has had an accident, there is a high probability that someone will tease her. If this happens, gently correct the student(s) who do the teasing. If you have a classroom rule concerning respect or cooperation, refer to that rule, then change the subject and direct the attention of the class onto a classroom activity. "Timothy, one of our rules says to treat people with respect and the best way to do that is to mind your own business. Now class, the next thing we are going to do is . . . ."

When giving a correction, be very matter-of-fact. If you are at all emotional or harsh, it may increase the chance that some students will tease the target student when you are not around.

3. *Use reinforcement to encourage appropriate behavior.*

a. During the school day, identify and reinforce many different positive behaviors the target student exhibits, and do not refer to past toileting problems.

b. Also praise the other students for their positive behaviors as frequently as possible. By creating a positive and supportive atmosphere with your praise, you will help deflect attention from any toileting accident that may have occurred.

If you had to gently correct any student(s) for teasing the target student, try to "catch" those students doing something well later in the day and praise them. If you can make those students feel successful and responsible, you reduce the chance that they will tease the target student in unsupervised settings.

c. Be cautious about drawing too much attention to the target student on the day of the incident, but by the next day you should be giving her frequent attention (e.g., say "hello" to her as she enters the classroom, call on her frequently during class activities, and occasionally ask her to assist you with a class job) and praising her for other positive behaviors she exhibits.

PLAN B

Some students simply neglect to use the restroom until it is too late. For example, a student may be in such a rush to get out to recess that she forgets to go to the restroom and ends up wetting or soiling herself. If this has happened on more than two or three occasions, the intervention must include some way of reminding the student to use the restroom.

 Respond consistently to any incidents of wetting and/or soiling pants.

Arrange for the student to be able to clean herself up, and handle each instance as privately as possible (see PLAN A).

 Conduct lessons to teach the student strategies that will increase the likelihood of her using the restroom during those times in the school day that bathroom breaks occur.

a. Identify the bathroom breaks that occur during the school day and determine some techniques that will help the student remember to use the restroom at those times. For example, during the initial meeting with the student (see SUGGESTED STEPS FOR DEVELOPING AND IMPLEMENTING A PLAN) you might develop a signal that you can use to remind her that it is time to use the restroom. The signal should be an unobtrusive one that only the student will recognize and understand (e.g., when it's time to line up for recess, you make eye contact with her and give a head nod, then instruct the class to line up).

Or, you might arrange for the student to let you know that she used the restroom by saying a code word or phrase to you after the identified bathroom breaks. For instance, she might come up to you after recess and say, "Hello," which would be code for, "I did use the restroom during the break."

b. If the regularly scheduled bathroom breaks are not sufficient for the student (e.g., her physician has noted that she has a small bladder and needs to use the restroom every hour or so), you may need to find a way to prompt the student to use the restroom at times other than the breaks. For example, you might ask the student's parent(s) to give the student an inexpensive digital watch that beeps on the hour, and then teach the student go to the restroom whenever her watch beeps. If the parent(s) cannot or will not provide a watch, you could see if there is a school account from which you could make the purchase for the student.

c. Two or three times per week, conduct lessons in which you explain and have the student practice the strategies you have identified. The lessons needn't last more than three to five minutes, but should be continued until the student is using the strategies consistently.

It is important to handle the lessons in a matter-of-fact manner so the student does not feel ridiculed. Let the student know that you are not trying to embarrass her, but that you want to make sure that she has strategies to reduce the possibility that she will forget to use the restroom.

d. When the student fails to use the strategies, gently correct her. "Beth, could I see you for a moment? I heard your watch beep a couple of minutes ago. You need to go use the restroom now."

 Use reinforcement to encourage appropriate behavior.

a. Provide praise and attention to the student for positive behaviors unrelated to her toileting problem (see PLAN A).

b. Privately let the student know that she should be proud of herself for remembering to use the restroom.

PLAN C

Sometimes a student will develop a pattern of wetting or soiling her pants to avoid having to do something or as a way to exert control over or "get back at" an adult with whom she is angry. If it seems as if the student is trying to achieve something with her behavior, and there have been more than four or five incidents of the toileting problem, this plan may be useful in resolving the situation.

 Respond consistently to any incidents of wetting and/or soiling pants.

Arrange for the student to be able to clean herself up, and handle each instance as privately as possible (see PLAN A).

 Try to identify the student's goal and make sure that she cannot achieve that goal by wetting or soiling her pants.

a. If the student has been sent home after her accidents, it may be that she is trying to avoid being in school. Try to determine whether there are any specific aspects of school that the student wishes to escape (e.g., academic expectations, teasing or bullying by other students, etc.) and address those. For example, you may need to help the student be more successful academically or help her learn to deal with fearful situations.

If the student is not trying to avoid anything specific, but just wants to be at home, it is especially important to work with the student's parent(s) (see SUGGESTED STEPS FOR DEVELOPING AND IMPLEMENTING A PLAN)

and implement procedures that ensure that the student remains at school after her accidents.

b. If the student is using the toileting problem as a power struggle or to "get back at" adults, it is important to show no emotional response (e.g., anger, frustration, disappointment) when instructing the student to clean herself up (see Step 1). The student must not see any adult as trying to punish her or hurry her through the process of cleaning up after an accident. If the student is unable to clean herself (e.g., she is too young), the nurse should help her, but remain emotionally neutral while doing so.

c. If there are other specific problem(s) of the student's that you believe to be related to her toileting problem (e.g., work completion, tantrumming, etc.), you can look them up in this reference guide to see if one or more of those plans might also be appropriate for the student.

 Use reinforcement to encourage appropriate behavior.

Provide praise and attention to the student for her positive behaviors unrelated to the toileting problem (see PLAN A).

. . . .

Suggested Steps for Developing and Implementing a Plan

The following steps are designed to help you develop an appropriate intervention plan and implement it effectively, whether you choose to use one of the MODEL PLANS or create a customized plan of your own. The steps are, however, suggestions—they are not intended to be followed rigidly or in any particular order. Use your professional judgment and the knowledge of your particular situation to make them work for you.

 Make sure you have enough information about the situation.

With this problem, you should *document every incident*. Adequate information can provide a better idea about whether the behavior is accidental (i.e., the student forgets to use the bathroom until it is too late) or purposeful (i.e., the student is trying

to accomplish something by wetting and/or soiling her pants). This information will be useful for developing an intervention plan and/or, should it become necessary, to refer the problem to the school psychologist or other specialist.

Because wetting/soiling of pants tends to be a rather low incidence behavior, anecdotal notes will provide both descriptive and objective (i.e., frequency count) information. To collect anecdotal notes, simply keep a card or piece of notebook paper handy, and write a brief description of the circumstances (e.g., where and when the problem happened, possible precipitating events, etc.) each time the student wets or soils her pants.

 Identify a focus for the intervention and labels for referring to the appropriate and inappropriate behaviors.

a. To be effective, any intervention must address more than just eliminating the student's problem behavior—there must be a concurrent emphasis on some positive behavior or trait for which the student can be reinforced. In this case, the positive behavior should be unrelated to the toileting problem. That is, unless the student is just learning toileting skills (e.g., a student with developmental delays), praising her for not having a problem toileting could be more harmful than helpful. A comment such as, "For two days now you have not had a problem with wetting your pants," may just serve to remind the student of a recent embarrassing accident.

The reinforcement you use should focus on positive classroom traits or behaviors such as consistent on-task behavior, work completion, paying attention, following directions, etc.

b. You will also want to decide ahead of time how you will refer to the problem at the time of any accidents. Direct references to wetting or soiling her pants might be unnecessarily insulting to or embarrassing for the student. Simply noting that the student needs to "clean herself up" and/or "change clothes" may be sufficient. However, when talking to the parent(s), it is probably wise to be direct—for example, stating that the student wet her pants.

 Determine when and how to include the parent(s).

The parent(s) should be contacted and made active partners in any intervention for this problem. Even if the accident was a one time occurrence, the parent(s) should be informed so they can help their child deal with any embarrassment or teasing that may result. Share whatever information you have about the situation and ask if they have any insights into the problem. If they have noticed similar behavior at home, you might suggest that they discuss the situation with the student's pediatrician to rule out the possibility of a physiological problem.

If there have been more than two incidents of wetting/soiling pants, invite the parent(s) to join you for an initial meeting with the student to develop a plan. If the parent(s) are unable or unwilling to participate, let them know that you will keep them informed of the student's progress.

Once the parent(s) have been involved in any way, you should give them updates at least once per week while the plan is being implemented.

 Prepare for, then conduct, an initial meeting about the situation.

a. Unless you are fairly certain that an incident was only a one time problem, you should schedule a meeting to discuss your concerns with the student and her parent(s). The meeting should be held at a neutral time and in a place where the discussion will not be overheard. In addition, try to make sure the meeting is scheduled for a time and place that it is not likely to be interrupted. If the parent(s) will be participating, they should be the ones to tell the student about the meeting.

b. Construct a preliminary plan. Based on the information you have collected (e.g., anecdotal notes) and the focus you have determined, you may decide to use one of the MODEL PLANS or you might choose to create a customized plan using components from various plans and/or of your own design.

Although it is important to invite and encourage the student to be an active partner in developing the plan during the initial meeting, having a proposed plan in mind before you meet can alleviate frustration and wasted time if the student is unwilling or unable to participate.

c. Conduct the meeting in an atmosphere of collaboration. The following agenda is one way you might structure the meeting:

• **Share your concerns about the student's behavior.**

Explain why you perceive the situation to be a problem, and discuss any possible reasons for the problem.

• **Discuss how you can work together to improve the situation.**

Describe your preliminary plan. Invite the student to give you input on the plan, and together work out any necessary details (e.g., where the student will be able to clean herself up; the signal, etc.). You may have to brainstorm different possibilities if the student is uncomfortable with the initial plan. Incorporating any of the student's suggestions that strengthen the plan is likely to increase her sense of "ownership" in and commitment to it.

- **Conclude the meeting.**

Always end the meeting with words of encouragement. Let the student know that you are confident that she can be successful. Be sure to reinforce her for participating in the meeting.

 Determine whether/how to give the student feedback about her behavior.

It is important to continue to keep anecdotal notes on the situation; although they can be limited to the date, time, and place of any accident and occasional notes on how the plan is going. Use your judgment about whether follow-up meetings would help or hurt in this particular situation. If the problem is getting better or has been resolved, follow-up meetings would probably be counterproductive. However, if the situation is not improving, plan to meet with the student and her parent(s) at least once every two weeks.

 Evaluate the situation (and the plan).

Implement any plan for at least two weeks before deciding whether to change plans; to continue, modify, or fade the plan you are using; or to cease the intervention. If the situation has not improved after two weeks of using either PLAN B or C, consider referring the problem to the school psychologist for additional intervention suggestions. Always discuss any changes to the plan with the student (and in this case, her parent[s]) first.

WHINING

DESCRIPTION

You have a student who unnecessarily uses a whiny tone of voice.

GOAL

The student will reduce and eventually eliminate the whining, and learn to express himself in a mature and responsible manner.

OVERVIEW OF PLANS

- PLAN A: For a situation in which the problem is relatively mild or has just begun.

- PLAN B: For a student who lacks the skills or strategies for reducing his whining.

- PLAN C: For a student who uses whining as a way of gaining attention or of getting his own way.

- PLAN D: For a student who is unaware of when and/or how frequently he whines.

- PLAN E: For a student whose whining has become habitual.

Alternative Problems

- **Babyish Behavior**
- **Blaming Others/ Excuses for Everything**
- **Complaining**
- **Crying, Chronic**
- **Disrespectful Behavior**
- **Helplessness**
- **Hypochondria**
- **Pouting**
- **Tattling**

General Considerations

- If the student's problem behavior stems in any way from academic issues (e.g., he whines when he becomes frustrated with schoolwork that is beyond his ability), concurrent efforts must be made to ensure his academic success (see **Academic Deficits, Determining**).

- If the student lacks the basic social skills to interact with his peers appropriately, it may be necessary to begin by teaching him those skills.

Social Skills, Lack of contains information on a variety of published social skills curricula.

- If you have any reason to suspect a physiological basis for the student's behavior (e.g., the student is incapable of using anything other than a whiny voice), consult with your building or district speech/language specialist for advice on this type of situation.

Model Plans

PLAN A

It is not always necessary, or even beneficial, to use an involved plan. If the inappropriate behavior has just begun and/or is relatively mild (i.e., not interfering with the student's academic or social progress), the following actions, along with making the student aware of your concerns, may resolve the situation.

1. Respond consistently to the inappropriate behavior.

a. During your initial meeting with the student (see SUGGESTED STEPS FOR DEVELOPING AND IMPLEMENTING A PLAN), establish a nonembarrassing signal that you can use to cue him that he is not using a grown up voice (i.e., whining). You want the signal to be a fairly subtle one that only the student will recognize and understand in order to minimize the chance that he will be teased by his peers. Possibilities include placing your hand against your cheek, clasping your hands together and holding them in front of you, or even just direct eye contact and a head nod.

Let the student know that you may also need to quietly say his name to gain his attention before you give the signal. You should be prepared to use the signal frequently and for a fairly long time, since it is likely that the student's behavior is, at least in part, an unconscious habit for him.

b. Whenever the student whines, give him the signal. If the student does not stop whining, and other students are around, ignore the student's behavior. However, if an incident takes place when you and the student are alone, give the student a gentle, but direct, verbal correction. "Khegan, you need to use a slower and deeper voice. Take a slow, deep breath, then tell me

what you want to say." Because your goal is to impart information, you want to be emotionally neutral while giving the correction.

2. Use reinforcement to encourage appropriate behavior.

a. Give the student increased praise. Be especially alert for situations in which the student speaks without whining and praise him for demonstrating his ability to use a grown up voice (or with an older student, his ability to communicate responsibly). If the student would be embarrassed by public praise, praise the student privately or even give him a note. Remember that any time the student is not whining, you can praise him for using a grown up voice.

b. Praise the student privately for responding to the signal. "Khegan, three times this morning I gave you the signal, and you switched to a grown up voice each time. Nice job of paying attention to the signal we worked out together."

c. Give the student frequent attention (e.g., say "hello" to him as he enters the classroom, look at and comment about his work, and occasionally ask him to assist you with a class job that needs to be done) and praise him for other positive behaviors he exhibits. For example, you might comment about how helpful he is toward younger students or how consistent he is about making entries in his journal. This demonstrates to the student that you notice many positive things he does, not just the fact that he is refraining from using a whiny tone of voice

PLAN B

Some students have trouble using a grown up voice during times of excitement or stress. If your student tends to whine in specific situations, the intervention should focus on helping him with those times.

 Respond consistently to the inappropriate behavior.

When the student whines, give him a signal, then either ignore the behavior or gently correct the student, as appropriate (see PLAN A).

 Conduct a goal-setting conference with the student.

(NOTE: This step can be done as part of the initial planning—see SUGGESTED STEPS FOR DEVELOPING AND IMPLEMENTING A PLAN.)

a. Meet with the student, and perhaps the student's parent(s), to set a goal for using a more grown up voice. A goal contract (see the sample shown) can be established with the student or prepared in advance. Generally, if the student is involved in the process, he is more likely to strive to achieve the goal.

b. Identify one broad-based goal (e.g., "to use a grown up voice") and three specific ways that the student can demonstrate that he is working on the goal.

c. Finally, identify several things that you can do to support the student's efforts. A finished goal contract might look like the sample following.

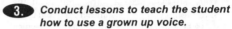 **Conduct lessons to teach the student how to use a grown up voice.**

a. You might consider using a tape recorder during the lessons so that the student will get the opportunity to hear the difference between his "grown up" voice and his "not grown up" voice. If you do plan to tape the student, be sure to ask the student's permission first. The point of these lessons is not to humiliate the student or to put him on the defensive, but to educate him about how different his "grown up" voice sounds from his "not grown up" voice.

Goal Contract

I, ___Khegan___ agree to work on _using_ a more grown up voice.

I can show that I am working on this goal by:

1. _Taking a deep breath before I speak_

2. _Using a low, not a high voice_

3. _Making "I statements"_

___Khegan Walker___
Student Signature

___Sept. 20___
Date

I, _Ms. Baldwin_ agree to help _Khegan_ achieve the goal by:

1. _Giving Khegan the signal that he needs to use a more grown up voice_

2. _Not commenting about "whining" if other students are near_

3. _Privately reminding Khegan if he does not respond to the signal_

___B. Baldwin___
Teacher Signature

___9/20___
Date

Decide whether there are any particular strategies that might help the student to use a grown up voice. For example:

- Taking a deep breath before speaking;

- Using a deeper voice;

- Speaking more slowly;

- Projecting more from his diaphragm; and/or

- Avoiding a sing-song rhythm.

b. During the lessons, have the student make a hypothetical request using a whiny voice, then repeat the request using a grown up voice. When appropriate, remind the student to use one or more of the identified strategies. Have the student repeat this procedure with several different statements.

You can also take a turn. That is, make a statements yourself—sometimes using a whiny voice and sometimes using your normal voice—and ask the student to identify whether you are using a "grown up" voice or "not grown up" voice each time. If he is accurate, praise him. If the student cannot seem to tell the difference, provide instruction on which voice is which.

If the student is comfortable with the tape recorder, record both you and the student making statements in whiny and grown up voices. Then replay the tape and have the student identify whether each sample is a "grown up" or "not grown up" voice.

c. Conduct the lessons at least twice per week. The lessons should involve just you and the student (perhaps while the other students are

at recess), and needn't last more than three to five minutes.

It is important that the lessons be handled in a matter-of-fact manner so the student does not feel that he is being ridiculed. You want to be very clear that you are not trying to embarrass him, but that you do want him to hear his voice the way others do. Continue the lessons until the student is no longer whining.

4. Prompt the student to behave appropriately by using precorrections.

Watch for circumstances in which the student is likely to whine and remind him that he will need to remember to use a grown up voice. For example, if the student tends to whine about things that have happened during recess, after recess provide a precorrection such as: "Khegan, before you tell me what you have to say, remember your goal. What is the goal? Right! To use a grown up voice. Now what did you want to tell me?"

5. Use reinforcement to encourage appropriate behavior.

a. Give the student increased praise and attention for using a grown up voice (see PLAN A).

b. In addition, make a special point of letting the student know that you notice his efforts to use the skills he has been learning/practicing. "Khegan, I noticed that you took a slow, deep breath before you told Rupert that you needed his help putting away the supplies you two used. You then used a nice deep voice. Good job doing what we have been practicing."

PLAN C

Some students are very skilled at gaining attention through their negative behavior. If you find yourself frequently nagging, reminding, or coaxing the student to stop whining, it is possible that he is trying to gain power or adult attention through his misbehavior. Whether or not the student overtly seems to like the attention, you should make sure that he receives more frequent and more satisfying attention when he uses a grown up voice than when he whines.

 Respond consistently to the inappropriate behavior.

a. Use a signal to cue the student that he is whining (see PLAN A). If the student then switches to a grown up voice, praise him.

b. In order for the student to learn that he will not be able to prompt people to nag and pay attention to him by whining, you must ignore any

subsequent whining that occurs after giving the student the signal. While ignoring, do not look at the student or talk to him. Do not act disgusted or impatient with his behavior. Simply interact in positive ways with students who are behaving appropriately and meeting classroom expectations. As soon as the target student is no longer whining, pay attention to him, but make no reference to his previous whining.

c. If other students give the target student attention when he is whining, gently correct them. "Noah and Vin Lu, Khegan can take care of himself and he can tell me what he has to say when he is ready to use a grown up voice. It would be best to let him work it out on his own."

2. Use reinforcement to encourage appropriate behavior.

a. Frequent praise and attention is the core of this plan. The student must see that he receives more frequent and more satisfying attention when he behaves appropriately than when he whines. Thus, whenever the student is not whining (or otherwise misbehaving), make an effort to praise and spend time with him. "Khegan, you have been remembering to use a grown up voice so well, would you like to help me organize the computer lab during recess today?"

b. You may also wish to use intermittent rewards to acknowledge the student's success. Occasional, and unexpected, rewards can motivate the student to demonstrate responsible behavior more often. The idea is to provide a reward when the student has had a particularly good period of remembering to use a grown up voice.

Appropriate rewards might include making an announcement over the school intercom, calling his parent(s) to report his success, or telling a story to the class or small group. *(NOTE: A list of additional reinforcement ideas can be found in APPENDIX 1.)* Use intermittent rewards more frequently at the beginning of the intervention to encourage the student, and then less often as his behavior improves.

3. Ensure a 3-1 ratio of positive to negative attention.

a. Since attention is a motivating force for this student, you want to be sure that you are giving the student *three times as much* positive as negative attention. One way to do this is to monitor your interactions with the student at least one day per week. Simply keep a card on a clipboard or in your pocket and record each interaction you have with the student as either positive or negative by writing a "+" or a "-", respectively, on the card.

To determine whether an interaction is positive or negative, ask yourself whether the student was whining (or otherwise misbehaving) at the time the interaction occurred. Any interaction that stems from inappropriate behavior is negative, and all interactions that occur while the student is meeting classroom expectations are positive. Thus, giving the student the signal or providing a verbal correction are both negative interactions, but praising the student for not needing the signal is positive. Greeting the student as he enters the room or asking him if he has any questions during independent work are also considered positive interactions. *(NOTE: Ignoring the student's whining is not recorded at all, because it is not an interaction.)*

b. If you find that you are not giving the student three times as much positive as negative attention, try to increase the number of positive interactions you have with the student. Sometimes prompts can help. For example, you might decide that each time the student enters the classroom you will say "hello" to him, that whenever he speaks directly to you you will praise him if he is not whining, or that whenever a student uses the pencil sharpener you will check the target student and, as soon as possible, praise some aspect of his behavior.

PLAN D

Some students do not seem to know when they are behaving inappropriately. If your student doesn't realize when and/or how frequently he whines, the intervention must include some way of helping the student become more aware of his own behavior.

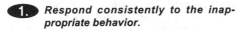 **Respond consistently to the inappropriate behavior.**

a. Use a signal to cue the student when he is whining (see PLAN A).

b. Each time you give the student the signal, make sure it is recorded (see Step 2).

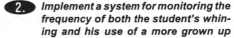 **Implement a system for monitoring the frequency of both the student's whining and his use of a more grown up voice.**

a. Determine who will record the behavior. Since the point is for the student to become more aware of his own behavior, having him record his own behavior (i.e., self-monitoring) will be more effective than if you do the recording. However, if the student cannot or will not be accurate (or if he would be too embarrassed to self-monitor), you should record the behavior yourself. If you do the recording, remember that the student should be aware that each time he speaks to you you will record the incident as either using a "grown up" voice or a "not grown up" voice. *(NOTE: Even when the student self-monitors, you should keep your own record approximately one day per week to verify the student's accuracy.)*

b. If the student is self-monitoring his own behavior, he can keep on his desk or in his notebook a form like the sample shown. Tell the student that each time he sees you give him the signal, he should circle a number on the form.

Khegan's Communication Card

Date _____

Grown Up Voice

1	2	3	4	5	6	7	8	9
10	11	12	13	14	15	16	17	18
19	20							

Not Grown Up Voice

1	2	3	4	5	6	7	8	9
10	11	12	13	14	15	16	17	18
19	20							

In addition, at various other times throughout the day, you should ask the student if he is using a grown up or not grown up voice. If he is whining, he should circle a number in the lower section of the card. If he is using a grown up voice, he should circle the next number in the upper section of the card.

c. Do not implement this procedure unless you are willing and able to make the effort to "catch" the student more often when he is communicating maturely than when he is whining—even when the student is having a bad day. In other words, you must structure success by asking the question more frequently when the student is being mature than when he is being whiny.

d. Be sure the student realizes that the goal is to have more "grown up voice" numbers circled by

the end of the day than "not grown up voice" numbers. Eventually the goal should be modified to one of reducing the number of "not grown up voice" numbers circled each day to zero.

e. Each day, meet with the student for a few minutes to review that day's record. Have the student chart the information on a graph (or do it yourself) by using two different colors of pen—one for the "not grown up voice" numbers and another for the "grown up voice" numbers.

Also talk with the student about whether the day was better, worse, or about the same as previous days. If the day did not go well, encourage the student to talk about why and have him identify strategies he can use the next day to help himself remember to use a grown up voice more often. If the student behaves inappropriately during the meeting, keep the interaction very short. Just let the student know that you are sure tomorrow will be a better day.

 Use reinforcement to encourage appropriate behavior.

a. Give the student increased praise and attention for using a grown up voice (see PLAN A).

b. In addition, praise the student during the daily review meetings for accurate recording (if applicable), and for being willing to look at his daily totals. Even on a bad day, if the student is willing to chart the data and discuss why it was a bad day, praise him. "Khegan, you are really handling this responsibly. Even though it was a rough day, you are willing to talk to me about things you might do differently tomorrow. That is a real sign that you are growing up."

Regardless of how the day went, try to make the meeting upbeat and encouraging—you want the student to look forward to the end-of-the-day review sessions.

4. **Encourage the student to use self-reinforcement.**

Whenever things are going well (i.e., less whining than usual), prompt the student to mentally reinforce himself. "Khegan, this has been a very successful morning. Silently tell yourself that you are using a grown up voice to communicate." Prompt the student in this manner intermittently throughout the day and during the end-of-the-day review meetings.

PLAN E

Whenever a student's problem behavior has become habitual and/or he does not seem to have a desire to reduce it, you may need to implement a structured system of external incentives (i.e., rewards and consequences) based on his behavior to motivate him to stop whining and to start using a more grown up voice.

1. Use a signal to cue the student when he is whining (see PLAN A).

2. Implement a system for monitoring the frequency of both the student's whining and his use of a more grown up voice (see PLAN D).

3. Establish a structured system for reinforcing the appropriate behavior and providing a consequence for the inappropriate behavior.

a. With the student, create a list of reinforcers that he can earn. Although you might want to have some suggestions in mind, the system will be more effective if the student identifies most of the items or activities himself. *(NOTE: A list of reinforcement ideas can be found in APPENDIX 1.)*

b. Assign "prices" (in points) for each of the rewards on the list and have the student select the reward he would like to earn first. The prices should be based on the instructional, personnel, and/or monetary costs of the items. Monetary cost is clear—the more expensive the item, the more points required to earn it. Instructional cost refers to the amount of instructional time lost or interfered with by a particular reward. Thus, an activity which causes the student to miss part of academic instruction should require more points than one the student can do on his own free time. Personnel cost involves the time required by you and/or other staff to fulfill the reinforcer. Having lunch with the principal, therefore, would cost more points than spending five minutes of free time with a friend.

c. Calculate the student's daily points by subtracting the "not grown up voice" total from the "grown up voice" total. If the student had more "not grown up voice" numbers circled, do not consider these negative points and take points earned on previous days away. The student would simply earn no points for that day. Add any points the student *did* earn to the points from previous days.

d. When the student has accumulated enough points to earn the reward he has chosen, he "spends" the points necessary and the system begins again. That is, selects another reward to earn and begins with zero points.

If the student is immature, and needs more frequent encouragement, you might consider letting him earn several "less expensive" rewards (e.g., five minutes of free time after 20 points) on the way to a bigger reward (e.g., one hour with you for 200 points). This way he receives the small rewards without spending points; they continue to accumulate toward the selected reward.

4. Use reinforcement to encourage appropriate behavior.

a. Give the student increased praise and attention for using a grown up voice (see PLAN A).

b. In addition, show interest and enthusiasm about how the student is doing on the system. "Khegan, today you have earned 14 points because there were no 'not grown up voice' marks that we needed to subtract. This is best day you have had yet!"

. . . .
Suggested Steps for Developing and Implementing a Plan

The following steps are designed to help you develop an appropriate intervention plan and implement it effectively, whether you choose to use one of the MODEL PLANS or create a customized plan of your own. The steps are, however, suggestions—they are not intended to be followed rigidly or in any particular order. Use your professional judgment and the knowledge of your particular situation to make them work for you.

 Make sure you have enough informa-tion about the situation.

a. If you think a minimal intervention like PLAN A will be sufficient, you may already have enough information to proceed. However, when a more involved plan seems necessary, you should consider collecting additional descriptive and/or objective information for a couple of days.

b. You need to be able to explain what you mean by "whiny." Anecdotal notes on actual incidents should provide enough detail to help you define the problem behavior clearly and completely. To collect anecdotal notes, simply keep a card in your pocket or on a clipboard and occasion-ally make notes on specific instances when the student whines.

For each entry, briefly describe the circum-stances and indicate what made the student's voice seem whiny. Was it the tone of voice, the pitch, or the rate of speech? You do not need to take notes every time the student whines; the idea is to capture a range of examples so that you can describe the behavior completely.

It is also important to include notes on times when the student uses a grown up voice. This will make it clear that you are not only aware of his problem behavior, but also recognize when he behaves appropriately. In addition, the posi-tive examples will help you clarify how you want the student to behave and sound.

c. Along with being able to describe the student's inappropriate behavior, it can also be useful to document how often it occurs (i.e., a frequency count). This information will provide both a more objective measure of the problem and an objec-tive way to monitor the student's progress. You can use the same card on which you are col-lecting anecdotal notes to keep a frequency count—simply write a tally mark on the card each time the student whines.

d. If the student notices what you are doing and asks about it, be straightforward—tell him that you are collecting information to see whether his tone of voice is a problem that needs to be worked on.

 Identify a focus for the intervention and labels for referring to the appropri-ate and inappropriate behaviors.

a. To be effective, the intervention must address more than just reducing the student's whining—there must be a concurrent emphasis on in-creasing some positive behavior or trait (e.g., "using a grown up voice" or, with an older stu-dent, "communicating responsibly"). Having a specific positive behavior in mind will make it easier for you to "catch" and reinforce the stu-dent for behaving appropriately, and the posi-tive focus will help you to frame the situation more productively.

For example, if you simply say that "the student has a problem with whining," you don't really provide any useful information, and may put the student and his parent(s) on the defensive. However, when you explain that you want to help the student "learn to use a grown up voice," you present an important, and reasonable, goal for the student to work toward and clearly iden-tify what the student needs to do to be success-ful.

b. Specifying labels for the appropriate and inap-propriate behaviors (e.g., "using a grown up voice" and "not using a grown up voice," respec-tively) will help you to use consistent vocabulary when discussing the situation with the student. Referring to the problem behavior as "whining" is probably less awkward, however it may be more *effective* to describe the behavior as "not using a grown up voice."

 Determine when and how to include the parent(s).

a. It is not necessary to contact the student's parent(s) if the problem has just begun and is not interfering with the student's academic or social progress. However, it might be a good idea to take advantage of any scheduled activities (e.g., conferences, weekly notes home) to let them know of your concern.

b. If the problem has gone on for a couple of weeks, you should contact the parent(s). Share with them any information you have collected about the behavior (e.g., anecdotal notes, frequency count), and explain why you are concerned. Focus in particular on how the behavior is hindering the student academically and/or socially (e.g., other students are unwilling to listen to him and take him seriously when he whines).

You might ask if the parent(s) have any insight into the situation and/or whether they have noticed similar behavior at home. Whether or not the parent(s) perceive a problem, explain that you want to help the student "learn to use a grown up voice," and invite them to join you for an initial meeting with the student to develop a plan. If the parent(s) are unable or unwilling to participate, let them know that you will keep them informed of the student's progress.

c. Once the parent(s) have been involved in any way, you should give them updates at least once per week while the plan is being implemented.

4. *Prepare for, then conduct, an initial meeting about the situation.*

a. Arrange a meeting to discuss your concerns with the student and anyone else who will be involved in the plan (e.g., the parent[s]). Although the specifics will vary depending upon the age of the student and the severity of the problem, there are some general guidelines to consider when scheduling the meeting.

First, meet at a neutral time (i.e., not immediately after a problem has occurred), when emotions are less likely to hamper communication. In general, a day's notice is appropriate, however a primary age student may worry excessively and/or forget what the meeting is about if it is scheduled more than an hour before it takes place.

Second, make the meeting appropriately private to ensure that the discussion will not be overheard. Third, try to make sure the meeting is scheduled for a time and place that it is not likely to be interrupted (e.g., the counselor's office). Finally, if the parent(s) will be participating, they should be the ones to tell the student about the meeting.

b. Construct a preliminary plan. Decide whether you think you can use one of the MODEL PLANS or if you need to create a customized plan using components from various plans and/or of your own design. Although you will invite and encourage the student to help develop the plan during the initial meeting, having a proposed plan in mind before you meet can alleviate frustration and wasted time if the student is unwilling or unable to participate.

c. After reviewing the information you have collected and thinking about how you want the student to behave, prepare thorough descriptions of the inappropriate behavior and the positive behavior/trait on which the student will be working. The more specific you can be and the more concrete examples you can have, the easier it will be to clarify (and for the student to understand) your expectations. Be sure to consider the student's behavior in all relevant activities (e.g., independent work periods, teacher directed instruction, unstructured class times, recess and lunch, etc.).

d. Conduct the meeting in an atmosphere of collaboration. The following agenda is one way you might structure the meeting:

• **Share your concerns about the student's behavior.**

Briefly describe the problem behavior and, when appropriate, show the student how often he engages in it. Then explain why you consider his whining to be a problem. You might tell the student that how one sounds has a big influence on how seriously others listen. To illustrate your point, without making fun of the student model two different types of speech and have him identify which would be taken more seriously.

• **Discuss how you can work together to improve the situation.**

Tell the student that you would like to help him "learn to use a grown up voice," and describe your preliminary plan. Invite the student to give you input on the various aspects of the plan, and together work out any necessary details (e.g., the signal, use of the self-monitoring form, etc.). You may have to brainstorm different possibilities if the student is uncomfortable with the initial plan. Incorporating any of the student's suggestions that strengthen the plan is likely to increase his sense of "ownership" in and commitment to it.

- **Make sure the student understands what you mean by appropriate and inappropriate behavior.**

Use the descriptions you have prepared to define and clarify the problem behavior and the positive (desired) behavior as specifically and thoroughly as you can. To ensure that you and the student are in agreement about the expectations, you might make a variety of statements, and have the student identify whether each is an example of using a grown up voice or a not grown up voice. They have the student demonstrate his own grown up voice, and coach or correct him as necessary.

- **Conclude the meeting.**

Always end the meeting with words of encouragement. Let the student know that you are confident that he can be successful. Be sure to reinforce him for participating in the meeting.

5. *Give the student regular, ongoing feedback about his behavior.*

It is important to meet with the student periodically to discuss his progress. In most cases, three to five minutes once per week should suffice. *(NOTE: PLANS D and E suggest daily meetings.)* During the meetings, review any information that has been collected and discuss whether or not the situation is getting better. As much as possible, focus on the student's improvements, however, also address any new or continuing problems. As the situation improves, the meetings can be faded to once every other week and then to once per month.

6. *Evaluate the situation (and the plan).*

Implement any plan for at least two weeks before deciding whether to change plans; to continue, modify, or fade the plan you are using; or to cease the intervention. Generally, if the student's behavior is clearly improving (based on the objective information that's been collected and/or the subjective perceptions of yourself, the student, and possibly the parent[s]), stick with what you are doing. If the situation has remained the same or worsened, some kind of change will be necessary. Always discuss any changes to the plan with the student first.

WORK COMPLETION—DAILY WORK

Not Turning in Assigned Work

DESCRIPTION

You have a student who fails to complete some portion of her academic assignments.

GOAL

The student will complete and turn in daily assigned work on a consistent basis.

OVERVIEW OF PLANS

- PLAN A: For a situation in which the problem has just begun or occurs infrequently.
- PLAN B: For a student with academic deficits who needs accommodations in the assigned work in order to complete her assignments.
- PLAN C: For a student who does not do her work in order to gain adult attention.
- PLAN D: For a student whose problem stems from not knowing how to keep organized, use self-reinforcement, and/or how to switch from one task to another.
- PLAN E: For a student who is able, but lacks the motivation, to do her daily work.
- PLAN F: For a situation in which several students in your class do not complete some portion of their daily work.

Alternative Problems

- **Apathetic Behavior**
- **Homework Issues**
- **Late Work**
- **Participation In Class, Lack of**
- **Sloppy Work**
- **Work Completion—Long-Term Projects**

········
General Considerations

- If the problem stems in any way from academic issues (e.g., the student is unable to meet the academic expectations and thus cannot do the work that is assigned), concurrent efforts must be made to ensure her academic success. PLAN B of this problem includes accommodations to help the student complete assignments, but not remediate skill deficits. See **Academic Deficits, Determining** for information on determining if assigned academic tasks represent a reasonable expectation for the student.

- If you think that the student's lack of work completion could be related to the student being depressed, see **Depression**. This problem includes a set of questions to help decide whether the student should be referred for counseling or psychological services.

········
Model Plans

PLAN A

It is not always necessary, or even beneficial, to use an involved plan. If the inappropriate behavior has just begun or is infrequent (e.g., the student completes her work 90% of the time), the following actions, along with making the student aware of your concerns, may resolve the situation.

1. Consider modifying the student's work environment.

a. If the student is having difficulty using her time wisely where she is currently sitting, discuss alternative locations or settings with the student. Jointly decide on an appropriate work setting in which it will be easier for the student to be responsible for completing her work. Possibilities include: working in a private study carrel, sitting at a desk placed far away from high traffic areas, being seated with/near a group of highly responsible students, etc.

b. If you can identify patterns in the student's work habits (e.g., the student works better in the morning than the afternoon), take these into account. For example, in the morning the student might work at her desk in its standard location with the other students, while in the afternoon she would work in a study carrel. However, do not use this procedure as a threat or punishment. These alternatives should simply be part of the plan to help the student be more responsible for her work completion.

2. Respond consistently to the inappropriate behavior.

a. During your initial meeting with the student (see SUGGESTED STEPS FOR DEVELOPING AND IMPLEMENTING A PLAN), establish a nonembarrassing signal that you can use to cue her that she is wasting time and that she needs to be responsible for her work. In most cases, you will need to give the student this signal during independent work periods. You want the signal to be a fairly subtle one that only the student will recognize and understand in order to minimize the chance that she will be teased by her peers.

Possibilities include a particular hand gesture, rubbing your neck, or even just direct eye contact and a head nod. Let the student know that you may also need to quietly say her name to get her attention before you give the signal. You should be prepared to use the signal frequently and for a fairly long time since it is likely that the behavior is, at least in part, an unconscious habit for the student.

b. Whenever the student is wasting time during independent work periods, give her the signal. Then, if the student does not focus her attention on her work, give a gentle verbal correction. Let the student know that this is an example of wasting time, and give her direct information about what she should be doing instead. "Thelma, you need to go to your seat and get started working on your math assignment." Because your goal is to impart information, you want to be emotionally neutral while giving the correction.

3. Develop specific procedures for addressing incomplete assignments.

a. Decide how you will handle the occurrence of incomplete assignments. If the student's parent(s) are willing and able to help, the incomplete work should go home as homework. If involving the student's parent(s) is not feasible, you will need an alternative. For example, will the student just receive an "F" in the gradebook or can you make arrangements for the student to get her work completed at school? Whenever possible, the student should know that she will be held accountable for completing the work.

b. If possible, establish a system so that if the student's work is not completed by a certain time, the student is restricted from privileges until the work is done. For example, the student might be told that if the current day's work is not completed by the end of that day, the student will have to stay after school until the work is completed.

If staying after school is not an option due to transportation or supervision issues, arrange for check points throughout the day. With check points, certain tasks will need to be completed by each point or the student will not receive privileges. For example, if the student does not have three assignments completed by lunch time, she will have to work through her lunch break (the student still eats her lunch, but does not receive a break or recess until she completes the required number of tasks). Then if the student does not finish another two assignments by the afternoon break, she would have to work through that break (or recess) time, until the tasks are completed. This would ensure a total of five assignments completed for the day.

4. Use reinforcement to encourage appropriate behavior.

a. Give the student increased praise. Be especially alert for situations in which the student demonstrates any behavior that represents an aspect of work completion (e.g., writing down an assignment, taking notes in class, heading a paper, staying on task, etc.). Praise the student for this demonstration of her ability to behave in a way that will help her to be responsible for completing her assignments. "Thelma, I noticed that you took notes as I was giving directions on the requirements for the short story assignment. That is a great example of being responsible for work completion. Those notes will really help you when you begin working on the assignment this afternoon."

If the student would be embarrassed by public praise, praise the student privately or even give the student a note. Remember that whenever the student exhibits any behavior that is a step toward work completion, you can reinforce her for being responsible.

b. Praise the student specifically for completed tasks, and for any increases in the overall percentage of work completion. "Thelma, since we had our talk, you have had two days with 100% work completion. You are doing a great job of learning to be responsible about completing your work."

c. Praise the student for responding to the signal. If the student focuses her attention on her work when you give her the signal, let her know that responding to the signal demonstrates an effort to be responsible for completing assignments. "Thelma, four times this morning I gave you the signal that you needed to get back to work, and every time you got right back to work. I don't mind giving the signal when I see you making such an effort to be responsible."

d. Give the student frequent attention (e.g., say "hello" to her as she enters the classroom, call on her frequently during class activities, and occasionally ask her to assist you with a class job that needs to be done) and praise her for other positive behaviors she exhibits. For example, you might comment upon how well the student works in cooperative groups or how skilled she is in P.E. This will show the student that you notice many positive things she does, not just the fact that she is working to be more responsible for completing her assignments.

P L A N   B

Sometimes a student fails to complete assigned tasks because the work is too difficult for her. In this case, accommodations may be necessary in the type or amount of work the student is assigned. This intervention plan outlines a few simple strategies for increasing student success with assigned work.

(NOTE: It is important to realize that accommodation is not the same as remediation. That is, if the student is a poor reader, accommodation in the assigned work may make it possible for the student to experience greater success with assignments in subjects requiring heavy reading, but will not help the student to read better. If the student has academic deficits, coordinate your efforts with the special education staff and/or school psychologist to remediate the student's academic deficits.)

1. Consider modifying the student's work environment (see PLAN A).

2. Establish a signal to cue the student when she is wasting time (see PLAN A).

3. Develop specific procedures for addressing incomplete assignments (see PLAN A).

4. Use any or all of the following suggested accommodations to help your student succeed.

a. **Reduce the size of assignments for the student.**

If the student's work completion is affected by her academic deficits, the amount of assigned work may have to be reduced. Asking the student to do the same amount of work as the other students could mean that she must spend up to three times as long working on it in some cases—a potentially unreasonable expectation. Cutting each assignment in half may help the student "see the light at the end of the tunnel."

b. **Correct the first part of the student's assignments.**

If the student is insecure about whether she is doing tasks correctly, she can become discouraged and cease working. However, when the student can bring her assignments to you at a predetermined point (e.g., when a quarter of the task is complete) for correction, the student can find out if she is on the right track before going too far on the assignment.

c. **Allow the student to work with a peer on the first portion of assignments.**

If the student has difficulty completing tasks correctly or frequently has lots of questions, allow her to work with a responsible peer until the first quarter (or even half) of an assignment

is completed. Then have the student complete the remainder of the assignment independently.

Different (willing) students could be designated to work with the target student on different tasks (e.g., Celia helps with math, Miles with science, etc.), thus reducing the chance that the tutoring will become too much of a burden/responsibility for any one student.

d. **Give the student textbooks in which the critical content has been identified with a highlighter pen.**

If the student has reading difficulties, she can be given the same textbooks (e.g., science, health, social studies, etc.) as the other students, but a copy in which the critical content of each chapter has been marked with a yellow highlighter pen. This effectively reduces the actual amount the student must read to a fraction of what the other students read for class. In addition, the time the student spends studying the text is targeted on the critical information.

e. **Allow the student to dictate rather than write her answers/assignments.**

If the student's problems stem from writing difficulties, allow the student to complete some (or all) of her daily assignments by dictating to another student or recording her responses into a tape recorder. This procedure can significantly reduce the laborious time the student spends writing.

f. **When assignments or questions require reading to find the information, provide page numbers.**

If the students must answer study questions or find particular vocabulary words in a textbook chapter, give the target student the same assignment as all the other students, but include the page numbers where the answers or vocabulary words can be found. This way, the student does not have to struggle through the entire chapter in order to find each answer—he can turn right to the pages where the answers will be found.

g. **Provide framed writing assignments.**

When assigning the students to write a story or an essay question to answer, give the target student information about how to provide the correct information. Following is a sample study question with a "framed" response that you can use as a model.

The Civil War

Directions:

Explain why the North and the South differed over the issue of slavery.

The North and South differed over the issue of slavery because _____

_____

_____

The North had _____

_____

while the South had _____

_____

The South needed _____

_____

(NOTE: For additional information on adapting instructional techniques to meet the needs of struggling students, see Intervention D: Academic Assistance in:

Sprick, R. Sprick, M., & Garrison, M. (1993). *Interventions: Collaborative planning for students at risk.* Longmont, CO: Sopris West.

PLAN C

Sometimes a student learns that passivity (i.e., sitting and doing nothing) leads to a lot of adult attention and/or to a feeling of power over adults (e.g., "Get to work now!"). If the student behaves in a way that seems to imply that it is your job to make her do her work, this plan will be appropriate. Whether or not the student overtly seems to like the attention, you should make sure that she receives more frequent and more satisfying attention when she behaves appropriately than when she is not getting her work done.

1. *Consider modifying the student's work environment (see PLAN A).*

2. *Respond consistently to the inappropriate behavior.*

a. Because you must teach the student that she will not be able to prompt people to nag and pay attention to her by doing nothing, most of the time you need to ignore the student when she is passively sitting (i.e., not being responsible for her assigned work). While ignoring, do not look at the student or talk to her. Do not act disgusted or impatient wither her behavior. Simply interact in positive ways with students who are working and meeting the classroom expectations. When the student begins working on the assigned task, make eye contact with her. Pay attention to her, but make no reference to her previous pasivity.

b. The only time not to ignore the student's behavior is when it is affecting other students. In this case you should use a consequence, such as time owed. In an elementary classroom, the student might owe one minute off of recess for each infraction. In middle/junior high school, the consequence could be one minute owed after class for the first infraction and ten minutes in after-school detention for each subsequent infraction. Thus, if the student is not working because she is roving around the room bothering others, you might state, "Thelma, return to your seat. You owe one minute off of recess for needing this reminder."

Make sure the student knows ahead of time what the consequence will be, and only use the consequence for situations in which the student's behavior is directly interfering with the other students—otherwise ignore the behavior.

(NOTE: For a student in kindergarten or first grade, time-out may be more appropriate than time owed. In this case, walk over to the student and, without saying anything or making eye contact, gently lead the student to a time-out chair for a one-minute time-out.)

c. Make sure you have procedures in place to ensure that the student completes her work prior to participating in any privileges and/or fun activities. The goal is for the student to see that she is accountable for getting her work done, and that the teacher will not nag and cajole her during independent work periods.

3. *Use reinforcement to encourage appropriate behavior.*

a. Frequent praise and attention are at the core of this plan. The student must see that she receives more frequent and more satisfying attention for behaving responsibly than for doing nothing. Therefore, whenever the student is engaged in any behavior associated with work completion, pay attention to the student.

If the student has been motivated by power issues (e.g., "You can't make me.") simple attention may be better than overt praise. "Thelma, how are things going? Do you have any questions? Well, let me know if you need any help." Overt praise for being on task or for getting work done may be too direct a reminder that the student is now "playing the game" the way the teacher wants it played.

b. You may also wish to use intermittent rewards to celebrate the student's success. Occasional, and unexpected, rewards can motivate the student to demonstrate responsible behavior more often. When the student has had a particularly good period of behaving responsibly and completing more work than usual, provide a reward. Do this more frequently at the beginning of the intervention to encourage the student, and then less often as her behavior improves over time.

Appropriate rewards might include giving the student a responsibility, such as reading to younger students; giving the student time to play a game or work on the computer with a peer

of her choice; or dismissing the student from class a few minutes early.

4. *Ensure a 3-1 ratio of positive to negative attention.*

a. If attention is a motivating force for the student, you want to be sure that you are giving the student *three times as much* positive as negative attention. One way to do this is to monitor your interactions with the student at least one day per week. Simply keep a card on a clipboard or in your pocket and record each interaction you have with the student as either positive or negative by writing a "+" or a "-", respectively, on the card.

To determine whether an interaction is positive or negative, ask yourself whether the student was off task (or otherwise misbehaving) at the time the interaction occurred. Interactions that are the result of the student behaving inappropriately are negative, and any interaction that occurs while the student is meeting the classroom expectations is positive. Thus, implementing time owed is a negative interaction, but asking the student, while she is working on her assignments, whether she has any questions is a positive interaction. Greeting the student as she enters the room is also considered a positive interaction. *(NOTE: Ignoring the student while she is sitting doing nothing is not recorded at all, because it is not an interaction.)*

b. If you find that you are not giving the student three times as much positive as negative attention, try to increase the number of positive interactions you have with the student. Sometimes prompts can help. For example, you might decide that each time the student enters the classroom you will say "hello" to her, that within the first five minutes of each work period you will interact with the student if she is on task, or that whenever a student uses the drinking fountain you will check the target student and as soon as possible praise some aspect of her behavior. You can also increase the ratio of positive to negative attention by ignoring more of the student's inappropriate behavior.

PLAN D

Sometimes a student may lack the organizational skills required for work completion. If your student is disorganized, often forgets to write down assignments, often forgets whether she has finished an assignment and/or whether she has handed an assignment in, the intervention plan must provide the student with a way to self-monitor these types of skills.

1. *Consider modifying the student's work environment (see PLAN A).*

2. *Establish a signal to cue the student when she is wasting time (see PLAN A).*

3. *Develop specific procedures for addressing incomplete assignments (see PLAN A).*

4. *Determine whether the student has organizational strategies for keeping her assignments organized.*

One such strategy might be the use of a notebook. If the student does not have an organizational strategy in place, work with her to obtain the necessary materials and teach the student to use them. The best choice is probably a notebook, but if in your school notebooks are considered "nerdy" by the students, identify what socially acceptable organizational tools the other students use.

5. *Help the student establish a self-monitoring system for work completion.*

a. One system might utilize a self-monitoring form with spaces for recording each assignment, when the student began working on the assignment, when she completes the assignment, and when she turns the assignment in (see the following sample form).

This sample form is appropriate for a middle/junior high school student who has separate periods for each subject; however, it can easily be modified for an elementary student with a variety of subjects during the day.

b. Teach the student how to use the system and why it can be beneficial. Walk the student through each subject (or each period) that has a daily assignment. Have the student identify where she would write her assignment down (e.g., the appropriate section of her notebook) and where she will mark on the "Work Completion Form" that she did in fact write down the assignment. Inform the student that keeping track of one's assignments strictly by memory is very difficult, which is the reason that most adults keep lists of things they have to do.

c. Show the student where on the form she should check off that she has started the assignment. The purpose here is two-fold. Checking off this section of the form reinforces the student for beginning the assignment, which is often the hardest part of a task. Making starting a task important enough to check off implies that starting is a major step on the road to completion. Also, seeing the check marks lets the student know at a glance whether or not a task has been begun. Thus, when the student comes back from lunch, for example, and is not sure where she is in completing her tasks, she could look at the sheet and see that she has started, but not completed, her reading assignment—and that this is where she should resume.

Then show the student where to check off work that has been completed, and work that has been turned in. Make sure the student realizes that these are separate things. Some students become responsible for completing their work, but continue to have become responsible for problems because they do not remember to hand in the work.

6. *Review the record daily with the student.*

a. Each day, meet with the student for a few minutes to examine her record. (For a middle/junior high school student, the best person to do this may be the school counselor or the student's "Advisory Teacher"). Have the student calculate and chart her daily percentage of work completed. Teach the student to calculate this percentage by dividing the number of assignments handed in by the total number due each day. Then discuss whether the day was better, worse, or about the same as previous days in terms of the percentage of work completion.

b. If the day did not go well, encourage the student to talk about why. Have the student identify things she can do the next day to help herself remember to be more responsible for her work. See if the two of you can identify what aspect of the process is causing the student the most difficulty. Is the student forgetting to write down her assignments? Does she begin her assignments, but get distracted and forget to finish them? If you do identify one or two specific areas that are giving the student trouble, work with her to come up with some techniques or strategies that might help (e.g., the student can check with you before she goes home each day to verify that all the assignments have been recorded).

Work Completion Form

Student _____ Week of _____

Period Subject	M	T	W	TH	F
I wrote down the assignment.					
I started the assignment.					
I finished the assignment.					
I handed in the assignment.					
Period **Subject**					
I wrote down the assignment.					
I started the assignment.					
I finished the assignment.					
I handed in the assignment.					
Period **Subject**					
I wrote down the assignment.					
I started the assignment.					
I finished the assignment.					
I handed in the assignment.					
Period **Subject**					
I wrote down the assignment.					
I started the assignment.					
I finished the assignment.					
I handed in the assignment.					
Period **Subject**					
I wrote down the assignment.					
I started the assignment.					
I finished the assignment.					
I handed in the assignment.					

I will put an "X" in any box where nothing was assigned or due during that subject/period.
When a box is successfully completed, I will initial that box.
I will meet with _____ each day to discuss my progress.
When/Where: _____

7. **Use reinforcement to encourage appropriate behavior.**

a. Give the student frequent praise and attention for work completion (see PLAN A).

b. Praise the student when you see her using the self-monitoring form. For example, as you are giving an assignment, if the student is writing down the assignment and then checks of the appropriate space on her form, make eye contact with the student, smile, and nod.

c. Praise the student during the daily review meetings for accurate monitoring/recording on the form (if applicable) and for being willing to review her progress. Even on a bad day, if the student is willing to chart the data and discuss why it was a bad day, praise her. "Thelma, you are really handling this responsibly. Even though it was not a very productive day, you are willing to talk to me about things you might do differently tomorrow. I will be interested to see if the ideas we came up with help you get more work done tomorrow."

8. **Encourage the student to use self-reinforcement.**

Inform the student that each time she checks off a task on the form, that she should tell herself that she is a responsible individual and that she is taking responsibility for getting her work completed. This self-reinforcement may need to be prompted by you. "Thelma, I noticed you marking that you are beginning the math assignment. What did you tell yourself as you marked that box?" Prompt the student privately if a public interaction would embarrass the student.

PLAN E

Once a behavior becomes habitual, it can be extremely difficult to change. If your student's work completion problem is long-standing and/or she does not seem to care about the fact that she is not completing her assigned tasks, you may need to implement a structured system of reinforcement (i.e., rewards and consequences) based on her behavior in order to motivate the student to turn in assigned work.

1. **Consider modifying the student's work environment (see PLAN A).**

2. **Establish a signal to cue the student when she is wasting time (see PLAN A).**

3. **Develop specific procedures for addressing incomplete assignments (see PLAN A).**

4. **Help the student establish a self-monitoring system for work completion (see PLAN D).**

5. **Combine a reinforcement system with the student's self-monitoring.**

a. With the student, create a list of reinforcers that she can earn. Although you might want to have some suggestions in mind, the system will be more effective if the student identifies most of the items or activities herself. *(NOTE: A list of reinforcement ideas can be found in APPENDIX 1.)*

b. Assign "prices" (in points) for each of the rewards on the list and have the student select the reward she would like to earn first.

The prices should be based on the instructional, personnel, and/or monetary costs of the items. Monetary cost is clear—the more expensive the item, the more points required to earn it. Instructional cost refers to the amount of instructional time lost or interfered with by a particular reward. Thus, an activity which causes the student to miss part of academic instruction should require more points than one the student can do on her own free time. Personnel cost involves the time required by you and/or other staff to fulfill the reinforcer. Having lunch with the principal, therefore, would cost more points than spending five minutes of free time with a friend.

c. Arrange for the student to earn points for each square on the "Work Completion Form" that is correctly filled in and completed. Structure the system so that the "I handed in the assignment" box is worth more points (e.g., three points) than the other boxes. For example, the "I wrote down the assignment," "I started the assignment," and "I finished the assignment" boxes would each be with one point.

In this way, each completed assignment that is successfully recorded on the sheet and has been handed in will be worth six points. These points accumulate toward the agreed-upon reward. If there was no assignment (marked with an "X" on the form), there are no points.

d. If the student is immature, and needs more frequent encouragement, you might consider letting her earn several "less expensive" rewards (e.g., five minutes of computer time after 20 points) on the way to a bigger reward (e.g., one hour with you for 200 points). That is, the student receives the small rewards without spending points; they continue to accumulate toward the selected reward.

6. *Use reinforcement to encourage appropriate behavior.*

a. Give the student frequent praise and attention for work completion (see PLAN A).

b. In addition, show interest and enthusiasm about how the student is doing on the system. "Thelma, we are half way through the day and you have already earned 24 points. I'll bet by the middle of the day tomorrow you will have enough points to earn the time on the computer."

PLAN F

In some cases, several students in a class will have a problem with work completion. If this is the case, a class-wide intervention plan will be appropriate.

Choose one or more of the following strategies to create a plan for the class as a whole:

a. Use direct teaching and guided practice through larger percentages of the assigned work. For example, if the science lesson includes 20 study questions to answer, lead the class through the first ten as a group, allowing the students to complete the first half of the assignment together as a class.

b. Conduct daily lessons to teach the entire class study and organizational skills that will assist them with their work completion. Many elementary and middle/junior high school students have never been taught specific organizational and study skills.

   (NOTE: An excellent program to assist with these lessons has been developed by Archer and Gleason [1990]. In only a few minutes per day, your entire class can learn many skills that will help them succeed in school and work settings.)

c. Have every student in the class keep a "Work Completion Form" (see PLAN D). All aspects of PLAN D can be easily modified for group instruction so that every student in the class keeps a record of each assigned task and the current status of those tasks.

d. Set up "On-Task Groups." Organize the students into equal groups of four. The members of each group are responsible for giving each other reminders and encouragement about staying on task and completing their assigned work. Help the students learn how to give other members of their group gentle reminders about

getting back on task. Also teach them how to reinforce and encourage each other for staying on task.

Optionally, you might give the groups the right to schedule some of their own breaks, thus giving the students a sense of control of their own work schedule. Tell each group that they are allowed a total of ten minutes for breaks during the day, but that all four members of each group must take their breaks together. Aside from the breaks, the students are expected to keep their own groups on task during independent work periods.

e. Set up group competitions:

   • Divide the class into teams of four to six students, making sure they are equitable in terms of students who do and do not have problems with work completion. Seat the team members together (e.g., at the same table or with their desks in clusters) and have each team give themselves a name you can use to refer to them. Encourage the teams to think of funny, but appropriate, names if they wish.

   • Have the class brainstorm ideas for the teams to earn as reinforcers. Possibilities include a free homework pass for each team member, dismissing team members a few minutes earlier than the rest of class, five minutes of extra recess, or a ticket for an ice cream in the cafeteria. Have the students identify at least six or seven different ideas, and rank them in order of perceived value.

   • Set up a grab bag system. Write the different reinforcers on individual pieces of paper and put these in a bag or box. "Weight" the box so that the most valuable items are included only once, while the more moderate reinforcers are each written on two or three slips of paper. This reduces the students' odds of winning the "biggest" reward—thus reducing how frequently you need to provide the big rewards.

After using the system successfully for a couple of weeks, increasingly add slips with congratulatory messages only (e.g., "You did great! But no prize today."). This way you can fade the system, but the students still have a chance of earning the big prize.

- At the end of each day, the group with the highest percentage of work completed and turned in (or all groups that achieved 100% work completion) can draw a slip of paper from the grab bag, and receive the reinforcer specified on the paper.

. . . .
Suggested Steps for Developing and Implementing a Plan

The following steps are designed to help you develop an appropriate intervention plan and implement it effectively, whether you choose to use one of the MODEL PLANS or create a customized plan of your own. The steps are, however, suggestions—they are not intended to be followed rigidly or in any particular order. Use your professional judgment and the knowledge of your particular situation to make them work for you.

 Make sure you have enough information about the situation.

a. Keep your gradebook current. If you think a minimal intervention like PLAN A will be sufficient, the gradebook will provide enough information to proceed. However, when a more involved plan seems necessary, you should consider collecting additional descriptive information for a couple of days.

b. You need to be able to help the student identify what may be causing her problem with work completion. Observe the student carefully during independent work periods and keep anecdotal notes on what the student does (or does not do). These notes should provide enough detail to help you define the problem behavior clearly and completely. Simply keep a card in your pocket or on a clipboard and occasionally make notes on what the student is doing when she should be working.

For each entry, briefly describe where and when the behavior occurred, what the student did or said, and any other relevant observations (e.g., what prompted the behavior). You do not need to take notes during every work period; the idea is to capture a range of examples (e.g., different subjects, different times of the day) to help you analyze the nature of the problem. For example, does the student sit and do nothing? does the student talk to other students or move about the room, playing with things? does the student work for a few minutes and then get distracted? does the student work well during the first part of a work period, but then have problems as the period progresses? does the student do better in the morning or the afternoon? does the student have trouble with organization?

c. If the student notices what you are doing and asks about it, be straightforward—tell her that you are collecting information to see whether her behavior during independent work periods is contributing to her work completion problem.

Following is an example of anecdotal notes that have been collected on a student with a work completion problem.

**Thelma's Behavior During
Work Periods—4/2**

10:00—During math, Thelma got started on the assignment but only worked for a couple of minutes, then just sat and played with her pencil and looked bored. I reminded her to get to work three or four times. Each time she would get to work for a few minutes, then stop. When I sat with her to see if she could do the work, she was able to.

2:00—During the afternoon period, the other students used the time to wrap up assignments. Thelma just frittered the time away: playing with her pencil, staring at the wall, wandering around the room. She never bothered anyone else though. It is almost as if she wants me to "make" her do the work?

---

d. Use the information from your gradebook to create a chart or graph of the student's work completion. One way to do this is to calculate a daily or weekly percentage of assignments that were completed and handed in. (Simply divide the number of assignments the student handed in by the total number of assignments that were due for that period.) Charting this information can be a very effective and efficient way of helping the student and the student's parent(s) to understand your concern.

e. Continuing to collect this type of information and keeping the work completion chart up-to-date while you implement a plan will help you to monitor whether the situation is getting worse, staying the same, or getting better.

2. Identify a focus for the intervention and labels for referring to the appropriate and inappropriate behaviors.

The focus of this intervention is, obviously, on increasing the student's work completion. However, specifying labels for the appropriate and inappropriate behaviors (e.g., "being responsible for completing assignments" and "not being responsible for completing assignments," respectively) will help you to use consistent vocabulary when discussing the situation with the student. If you sometimes refer to the inappropriate behavior as "wasting time," for example, and other times tell the student that "she is not getting anything done" she may not realize that you are talking about the same thing—not being responsible for completing assignments.

3. Determine when and how to include the parent(s).

a. Although it is not necessary to contact the student's parent(s) if the problem has just begun, contact the student's parent(s) immediately if the problem has gone on for more than a few days. Share any information you have collected about the behavior (e.g., gradebook records, anecdotal notes), and explain why you are concerned. Focus in particular on how the behavior represents a bad habit which could jeopardize the student's school success if allowed to continue.

You might ask if the parent(s) have any insight into the situation and/or whether they have noticed similar behavior at home (e.g., does the student follow through on home responsibilities such as daily chores?) Whether or not the parent(s) perceive a problem, explain that you want to help the student "learn to be responsible for

completing assignments," and invite them to join you for an initial meeting with the student to develop a plan. If the parent(s) are unable or unwilling to participate, let them know that you will keep them informed of the student's progress.

b. Once the parent(s) have been involved in any way, you should give them updates at least once per week (e.g., a phone call or note) while the plan is being implemented.

4. Prepare for, then conduct, an initial meeting about the situation.

a. Arrange a meeting to discuss your concerns with the student and anyone else who will be involved in the plan (e.g., the parent[s]). Make the meeting appropriately private, and schedule it for a time and place that it is not likely to be interrupted (e.g., the counselor's office). If the parent(s) will be participating, they should be the ones to tell the student about the meeting.

b. Construct a preliminary plan. Decide whether you think you can use one of the MODEL PLANS or if you need to create a customized plan using components from various plans and/or of your own design. Although you will invite and encourage the student to help develop the plan during the initial meeting, having a proposed plan in mind before you meet can alleviate frustration and wasted time if the student is unwilling or unable to participate.

c. After reviewing the information you have collected and thinking about how you want the student to behave, prepare thorough descriptions of the inappropriate behavior and the positive behavior/trait on which the student will be working. The more specific you can be and the more concrete examples you have, the easier it will be to clarify (and for the student to understand) your expectations.

d. Conduct the meeting in an atmosphere of collaboration. The following agenda is one way you might structure the meeting:

- **Share your concerns about the student's behavior.**

  Briefly describe the problem behavior and show the student the record of her missing assignments in your gradebook. Then explain why you consider her level of work completion to be a problem. You might tell the student that not completing assigned tasks will slow down the rate at which she learns, and will create bad work habits that may affect her in subsequent years in school and on a job.

- **Discuss how you can work together to improve the situation.**

Tell the student that you would like to help her "learn to be responsible for completing assignments," and describe your preliminary plan. Invite the student to give you input on the various aspects of the plan, and together work out any necessary details (e.g., the signal, use of the self-monitoring form, etc.).

You may have to brainstorm different possibilities if the student is uncomfortable with the initial plan. Incorporating any of the student's suggestions that strengthen the plan is likely to increase her sense of "ownership" in and commitment to it.

- **Make sure the student understands what you mean by appropriate and inappropriate behavior.**

Using your notes, make sure the student is aware of exactly what she does when she is not doing her work. Then, as specifically as you can, describe the positive behavior the student will be working on (e.g., What does the on-task behavior look like?).

Provide as much detail as necessary to make sure the student understands your expectations. Also verify that the student understands what will happen if her work is not completed (e.g., being kept after school or losing break time during lunch).

- **Conclude the meeting.**

Always end the meeting with words of encouragement. Let the student know that you are confident that she can be successful. Be sure to reinforce her for participating in the meeting.

 5. *Give the student regular, ongoing feedback about her behavior.*

It is important to meet with the student periodically to discuss her progress. In most cases, three to five minutes once per week should suffice. *(NOTE: PLANS D and E require daily meetings.)* During the meetings, review any information that has been collected and discuss whether or not the situation is getting better. As much as possible, focus on the student's improvements, however, also address any new or continuing problems. As the situation improves, the meetings can be faded to once every other week and then to once per month.

6. *Evaluate the situation (and the plan).*

Implement any plan for at least two weeks before deciding whether to change plans; to continue, modify, or fade the plan you are using; or to cease the intervention. Generally, if the student's behavior is clearly improving (based on your gradebook record and/or the subjective perceptions of yourself, the student, and possibly the parent[s]), stick with what you are doing. If the situation has remained the same or worsened, some kind of change will be necessary.

Always discuss any changes to the plan with the student first. If the problem continues for more than six to eight weeks, ask for assistance from your school counselor, school psychologist, Teacher Assistance Team, or any other person or team available to assist you with brainstorming additional strategies.

WORK COMPLETION— LONG-TERM PROJECTS

Procrastination

DESCRIPTION

There are students in your class who neglect long-term projects and/or "throw something together" at the last minute.

There are no MODEL PLANS included with this problem, however, the following information suggests some basic considerations and strategies for helping students learn to pace themselves and complete long-term projects in a timely fashion.

Alternative Problems

- **Late Work**
- **Participation In Class, Lack of**
- **Work Completion— Daily Work**

. . . .
Intervention Information

- If the problem behavior stems in any way from academic issues (e.g., the students are unable to successfully complete the projects), concurrent efforts must be made to remediate any academic deficits. (See **Academic Deficits, Determining** for information on evaluating academic competence and references for assisting students who are struggling academically.)

PROCEDURES

 1. *Design assignments so that the students clearly understand the expected outcome(s) of each long-term project.*

a. One of the best strategies for presenting the desired outcome(s) is to show the students actual models of completed projects. For example, if the assignment is to write a lengthy term paper, you could show the students finished samples of "excellent," "good," and "average" papers. Point out the differences in length, number of references, organization, neatness, use of graphics or maps, etc.—this gives students an idea of the "final destination" before they begin the "journey."

b. In addition, provide the criteria for the project to the students in writing. If the assignment is to design a timeline, for example, the written criteria might look like the sample following.

Timeline on Transportation From 1800
100 Points Possible
Due 9/3

Basic requirements—80 points possible

Before 1800	Show at least three methods of transportation. Write a one or two sentence description of each form.
1800 - 1825	Show the building of national roads. Write a one or two sentence description of road building in 1800-1825.
1825 - 1850	Show the building of canals. Write a one or two sentence description of canal building.
1860 and later	Show a steamboat. Write a one or two sentence description of the use of steamboats.

Excellence—20 points possible

Can be demonstrated by:

- Showing progress in transportation beyond the year 1860
- Neatness
- Originality
- Special design features
- Extra effort

Points will be deducted for:

- Late work (-5 points per day, up to two days)
- Incomplete work
- Incomplete sentences and incorrect use of capitals, end marks, spelling
- Sloppy work

If you want to do a different project, make notes on your idea and come and talk to me.

---

c. When you wish to give the students a variety of choices on how to construct the project (e.g., a timeline, diorama, multimedia presentation, simulation, writing a play, etc.), provide at least one example of what the students should do if they do not have an alternative idea. For this example, have a sample and the written criteria as described previously. Students who want to do something different can then be invited to negotiate with you directly.

 Construct timelines for assignments that include multiple checkpoints.

For example, if there are four weeks available for a project, provide the students with a timeline that gives them an idea of approximately how much they should have accomplished by the end of each week. Each checkpoint should include clear criteria regarding the expectations. At right is a sample timeline illustrating multiple checkpoints for a research paper.

 Consider making the procedures in Step 2 a requirement.

If you know that many students in your class are likely to have problems pacing themselves on a long-term project, do not give them the chance to procrastinate. Establish timeline checkpoints as requirements. Then set consequences for students who do not meet the checkpoint criteria. For example, you might specify that students who do not meet the first checkpoint requirements have to stay in from the first half of recess each day until they get caught up. In addition, you could pull together small groups of students who have fallen behind for teacher directed instruction to help them get caught up (this could occur while the other students are working independently on the next stages of their projects).

(NOTE: Students who are doing independent projects [i.e., students who negotiated alternatives to the basic project], may or may not need to be assigned a required system of multiple checkpoints.)

Timeline for Completion Research Paper Due 10/23	
By 10/2	Collect a minimum of 60 facts on cards. • Use at least two sources. • Begin sorting by major topic.
By 10/9	Collect a minimum or 20 more cards and develop an outline. • Outline should have at least four major topics. • Notecards should be sorted into major topic categories.
By 10/16	Write a rough draft. • Write an introduction. • Write body of report using major outline headings and note cards. • Write a conclusion.
10/18	Edit in class. • Check for complete sentences. • Check for capitals and end marks. • Check spelling.
By 10/23	Finish final draft and turn in.

The
Teacher's
Encyclopedia of
Behavior Management:
100 Problems/500 Plans

. . . .

ADDITIONAL
INFORMATION

REFERENCES/RESOURCES

Adams, M.J. (1990). *Beginning to read: Thinking and learning about print.* Cambridge, MA: MIT Press.

Alberg, J., Petry, C., & Eller, S. (1994). *The social skills planning guide.* Longmont, CO: Sopris West.

Albert, L. (1989). *A teacher's guide to cooperative discipline: How to manage your classroom and promote self-esteem.* Circle Pines, MN: American Guidance Service.

Alessi, N.E. (1993). Is your child or adolescent depressed? *Journal of Emotional and Behavioral Problems, 2*(2), 21.

Algozzine, B. & Ysseldyke, J. (1992). *Strategies and tactics for effective instruction.* Longmont, CO: Sopris West.

Archer, A. & Gleason, M. (1990). *Skills for school success.* North Billerica, MA: Curriculum Associates.

Barkley, R. (1987). *Defiant children: A clinician's manual for parent training.* New York: Guilford Press.

Barkley, R. (1990). *Attention deficit hyperactive disorder: A handbook for diagnosis and treatment.* New York: Guilford Press.

Barrett, T. (1987). *Youth in crisis: Seeking solutions to self-destructive behavior.* Longmont, CO: Sopris West.

Bender, W.N. & McLaughlin, P.J. (1994). *A.D.D. from A to Z: A comprehensive guide to attention deficit disorder.* Longmont, CO: Sopris West.

Colvin, G. (1992). *Managing acting-out behavior: A staff development program to prevent and manage acting-out behavior.* Longmont, CO: Sopris West.

Colvin, G. & Sugai, G. (1989). *Managing escalating behavior* (2nd ed.). Eugene, OR: Behavior Associates.

Davis, D. (1994). *Reaching out to children with FAS/FAE.* West Nyack, NY: The Center for Applied Research in Education.

Ellis, A. & Kraus, W.J. (1977). *Overcoming procrastination.* New York: Signet.

Emmer, E.T., Evertson, C.M., Sanford, J.P., Clements, B.S., & Worsham, M.E. (1984). *Classroom management for secondary teachers.* Englewood Cliffs, NJ: Prentice Hall.

Englemann, S. & Miller, S. (1980). *The cursive writing program.* Columbus, OH: Science Research Associates.

Evertson, C.M., Emmer, E.T., Clements, B.S., Sanford, J.P., & Worsham, M.E. (1984). *Classroom management for elementary teachers.* Englewood Cliffs, NJ: Prentice Hall.

Flatter, C.H. & McCormick, K. (1990). *Learning to live drug free: A curriculum model for prevention.* Washington, DC: U.S. Department of Education.

Garrity, C., Jens, K., Porter, W., Sager, N. & Short-Camilli, C. (1994). *Bully-proofing your school: A comprehensive approach for elementary schools.* Longmont, CO: Sopris West.

Goldfried, M.R. (1971). Systematic desensitization as training in self-control. *Journal of Consulting and Clinical Psychology, 37,* 228-234.

Goldstein, A.P. (1988). *The prepare curriculum.* Champaign, IL: Research Press.

Goldstein, A.P. (1991). *Delinquent gangs: A psychological perspective.* Champaign, IL: Research Press.

Goldstein, A.P. & Glick, B. (1987). *Aggression replacement training.* Champaign, IL: Research Press.

Goldstein, A.P. & Huff, C.R. (Eds.). (1993). *The gang intervention handbook.* Champaign, IL: Research Press.

Goldstein, A.P. & Keller, H. (1987). *Aggressive behavior: Assessment and intervention.* New York: Pergamon Press.

Goldstein, A.P., Sprafkin, R.P., Gershaw, N.J., & Klein, P. (1980). *Skillstreaming the adolescent: A structured learning approach to teaching prosocial skills.* Champaign, IL: Research Press.

Guevremont, D.C. (1991). Truancy and school absenteeism. In G. Stoner, M.R. Shinn, & H.M. Walker (Eds.), *Interventions for achievement and behavior problems* (pp. 581-591). Silver Spring, MD: National Association of School Psychologists.

Haines, A.T., Jackson, M.S., & Davidson, J. (1983). Children's resistance to the temptation to steal in real and hypothetical situations: A comparison of two treatment programs. *Australian Psycologogist, 18,* 229-303.

Hasbrouck, J.E. & Tindal, G. (1992). Curriculum-based oral reading fluency norms for students in grades 2 through 5. *Teaching Exceptional Children, 24*(3), 41-44.

Henderson, J. (1983). Follow-up of stealing behavior in 27 youths after a variety of treatment programs. *Journal of Behavior Therapy and Experimental Psychiatry, 14,* 331-337.

Hicks, B.B. (1990). *Youth suicide: A comprehensive manual for prevention and intervention.* Bloomington, IN: National Education Service.

Huggins, P. (1990). *Teaching cooperation skills.* Longmont, CO: Sopris West.

Huggins, P. (1993a). *Helping kids handle anger: Teaching self-control.* Longmont, CO: Sopris West.

Huggins, P. (1993b). *Teaching friendship skills: Intermediate version.* Longmont, CO: Sopris West.

Huggins, P. (1993c). *Teaching friendship skills: Primary version.* Longmont, CO: Sopris West.

Huggins, P. (1994). *Helping kids find their strengths.* Longmont, CO: Sopris West.

Jackson, N.F., Jackson, D.A., & Monroe, C. (1983). *Getting along with others: Teaching social effectiveness to children.* Champaign, IL: Research Press.

Jones, V.F. & Jones, L.S. (1986). *Comprehensive classroom management.* Boston: Allyn and Bacon.

Kameenui, E.J. & Simmons, D.C. (1990). *Designing instructional strategies: The prevention of academic learning problems.* Columbus, OH: Merrill/Macmillan.

Kanfer, F.H. (1970). Self-monitoring: Methodological limitations and clinical applications. *Journal of Consulting and Clinical Psychology, 35,* 143-152.

Kauffman, J.M., Hallahan, D.P., Mostert, M.P., Trent, S.C., & Nuttycombe, D.G. (1993). *Managing classroom behavior: A reflective case-based approach.* Boston: Allyn and Bacon.

Kerr, M.M. & Nelson, C.M. (1989). *Strategies for managing behavior problems in the classroom* (2nd ed.). New York: Macmillan.

Linn-Benton Educational Service District. (1993). *A principal's handbook.* Albany, OR: Author.

Long, N.J. & Brendtro, L.K. (Eds.). (1993). Rage and aggression. *Journal of Emotional and Behavioral Problems, 2*(1).

Mayer, G.R. & Sulzer-Azaroff, B. (1991). Interventions for vandalism. In G. Stoner, M.R. Shinn, & H.M. Walker (Eds.), *Interventions for achievement and behavior problems* (pp. 559-580). Silver Springs, MD: National Association of School Psychologists.

McGinnis, E., Goldstein, A.P., Sprafkin, R.P., & Gershaw, N.J. (1984). *Skillstreaming the elementary school child: A guide for teaching prosocial skills*. Champaign, IL: Research Press.

Meichenbaum, D.H. & Goodman, J. (1971a). *Cognitive-behavior modification: An integrative approach*. New York: Plenum.

Meichenbaum, D.H. & Goodman, J. (1971b). Training impulsive children to talk to themselves: A means of developing self-control. *Journal of Abnormal Psychology, 77*, 115-126.

Mercer, C.D. & Mercer, A.R. (1989). *Teaching students with learning problems* (3rd ed.). New York: Macmillan.

Miller, G.E. & Prinz, R.J. (1991). Designing interventions for stealing. In G. Stoner, M.R. Shinn, & H.M. Walker (Eds.), *Intervention for acheivement and behavior problems* (pp. 593-610). Silver Springs, MD: National Association of School Psychologists.

Morgan, D.P. & Jenson, W.R. (1988). *Teaching behaviorally disordered students*. Columbus, OH: Merrill.

O'Neill, R.E., Horner, R.H., Albin, R.W., Storey, K., & Sprague, J.R. (1990). *Fuctional analysis of problem behavior: A practical assessment guide*. Sycamore, IL: Sycamore Publishing.

Paine, S.C., Radicchi, J., Deutchman, L., Rosellini, L.C., & Darch, C.B. (1983). *Structuring your classroom for academic success*. Champaign, IL: Research Press.

Prothrow-Stith, D. & Weissman, M. (1991). *Deadly consequences: How violence is destroying our teenage population and a plan to begin solving the problem*. New York: Harper Collins.

Purkey, W. & Novak, J. (1984). *Inviting school success*. Belmont, CA: Wadsworth.

Reid, R., Maag, J.W., & Vasa, S.F. (1994). Attention deficit hyperactivity disorder as a disability catagory: A critique. *Exceptional Children, 60*(3), 198-214.

Rhode, G., Jenson, W.R., & Reavis, H.K. (1992). *The tough kid book: Practical classroom management strategies*. Longmont, CO: Sopris West.

Seligman, E.P. (1990). *Learned optimism: How to change your mind and your life*. New York: Simon and Schuster.

Shinn, M.R. (Ed.). (1989). *Curriculum-based measurement: Assessing special children*. New York: The Guilford Press.

Silvernail, D.L. (1987). *Developing positive student self-concept* (2nd ed.). Washington, DC: National Education Association.

Smith, S. (1994). *Different is not bad, different is the world: A book about disabilities*. Longmont, CO: Sopris West.

Sprick, R. (1981). *The solution book: A guide to classroom discipline*. Chicago: Science Research Associates.

Sprick, R. (1985). *Discipline in the secondary classroom: A problem by problem survival guide*. Englewood Cliffs, NJ: Prentice Hall.

Sprick, R. (1990). *Playground discipline: Positive techniques for playground supervision*. Eugene, OR: Teaching Strategies.

Sprick, R., Sprick, M., & Garrison, M. (1992). *Foundations: Establishing positive discipline policies*. Longmont, CO: Sopris West.

Sprick, R., Sprick, M., & Garrison, M. (1993). *Interventions: Collaborative planning for students at risk*. Longmont, CO: Sopris West.

Staff. (1990). *Student daily planner* [calendar]. Meredith, NH: Elan Publishing.

Staff. (1994, December). *Homeless children: What can teachers do? CONNECT, 4*(1), 4-5.

Stephans, R.D. (1993). School-based interventions: Safety and security. In A.P. Goldstein & C.R. Huff (Eds.), *The gang intervention handbook* (pp. 219-256). Champaign, IL: Research Press.

Walker, H.M. (in press). *The acting-out child: Coping with classroom disruption* (2nd ed.). Longmont, CO: Sopris West.

Walker, H.M., McConnel, S., Holmes, D., Todis, B., Walker, J., & Golden, N. (1983). *The ACCEPTS program: A curriculum for children's effective peer and teacher skills.* Austin, TX: Pro-Ed.

Walker, H.M. & Severson, H.H. (1990). *Systematic screening for behavior disorders (SSBD).* Longmont, CO: Sopris West.

Walker, H.M., Severson, H.H., & Feil, E.G. (1995). *Early screening project (ESP).* Longmont, CO: Sopris West.

Walker, H.M., Todis, B., Holmes, D., & Horton, D. (1988). *The ACCESS program: Adolescent coping curriculum for communication and effective social skills.* Austin, TX: Pro-Ed.

Walker, H. & Walker, J. (1991). *Coping with noncompliance in the classroom: A positive approach for teachers.* Austin, TX: Pro-Ed.

Wong, H.K. & Wong, R.T. (1991). *The first days of school: How to start school successfully.* Sunnyvale, CA: Harry K. Wong Publications.

Woods, M.L. & Moe, A.J. (1989). *Analytic reading inventory (ARI).* New York: Macmillan

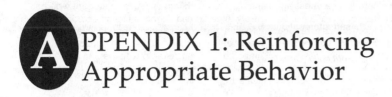

APPENDIX 1: Reinforcing Appropriate Behavior

Motivation can be either *intrinsic* (e.g., satisfaction in finishing a task, pride in one's work, the enjoyment that comes from reading a good book) or *extrinsic* (e.g., a paycheck, a college diploma, meaningful praise from someone you respect). Obviously, having intrinsically motivated students is the optimum for a teacher. However, because this is something over which a teacher has little control, it may be necessary to provide extrinsic reinforcement to motivate a student, especially in the early stages of learning a new skill or behavior.

There are three major forms of extrinsic reinforcement: (1) *interactional* reinforcement—praise, notes on papers, etc.; (2) *intermittent* reinforcement—spur-of-the-moment celebrations of success; and (3) *structured* reinforcement systems—point systems, token economies, etc. The three forms of extrinsic reinforcement could be said to exist on a continuum related to how far away they are from intrinsic motivation (see the following illustration).

When designing an intervention plan, the goal is to choose (and use) the weakest form of extrinsic reinforcement that will still effectively motivate the student to behave responsibly.

For some students, increased praise and approval may be sufficiently motivating. This is most likely when an improvement goal is easy or involves only a slight change in a student's behavior. Your praise and attention for responsible behavior may be enough to motivate such a student to demonstrate even more responsible actions in the future.

Intrinsic Motivation:
– Enjoyment of the task
– Satisfaction in doing a good job
– Feeling virtuous about working hard

Interactional Reinforcement:
– Praise
– Notes on a paper
– Smiles or other signs of approval

Intermittent Reinforcement:
– Work posted in the classroom
– Special privileges (e.g., bonus time on the computer)
– Parent(s) called about good behavior

Structured Reinforcement:
– Points earned toward predetermined rewards
– Grading systems
– High school diploma

The use of intermittent reinforcement is most applicable when the desired behavior change will be moderately difficult (e.g., a student needs to reduce infrequent, but annoying sarcasm; or the teacher is trying to get the whole class to increase their rate of work completion). This form of reinforcement involves giving a reward on some, but not all, occasions when a particular goal has been met or when behavior has been particularly appropriate (i.e., for an unusually long period of time or during an especially problematic activity).

You will want to use these "celebrations of success" more frequently in the early stages of an intervention to reinforce the student, and then decrease the frequency as the student's successful behavior becomes self-reinforcing over time. Another key is to avoid being too consistent in providing rewards—keeping things unpredictable is what will make a reward special.

For increasing and maintaining a student's motivation to meet an extremely difficult goal or to modify a deeply ingrained habit, a structured reinforcement system—analogous to a paycheck or contract—may be required. The longer the student has behaved irresponsibly, the greater the likelihood that you will need to use powerful extrinsic reinforcement techniques. Also, a student who has rarely experienced school success and/or the satisfaction that comes from responsible behavior may need the structure of systematic reinforcement (i.e., knowing exactly what he/she will receive in return for his/her positive behavior) to stay motivated.

Whichever form of extrinsic reinforcement you use, as the student experiences success in behaving appropriately, you should try to gradually fade the reinforcement to that of a more intrinsic nature.

Listed following are ideas for rewards to be used as either intermittent reinforcement or as part of a structured reinforcement system. The leftmost column includes suggestions for younger students, the middle column lists ideas for older students (although most will work with younger students as well), and the column on the right has recommendations for groups or classes as a whole. These lists should not be viewed as complete or comprehensive—for additional ideas, talk to colleagues, read other books, and/or even ask your students!

(NOTE: Examples of class and school jobs that can be used as intermittent reinforcers are presented in APPENDIX 2.)

Ideas for Younger Students (Pre K-4th Grade)	Ideas for Older Students (3rd-8th Grade)	Ideas for the Group
Let student choose a story	Let student teach a portion of the lesson	Let class listen to recorded music during an independent work period
Let student be first in line	Let student tell a joke to the class	Let class select a theme for one day, such as: – Dress-up day – Backward day – Opposite day – Hat day
Let student use piano, computer, etc.	Let student supervise or tutor younger students	Let class invite someone to come to class to see completed projects or assignments
Let student dictate a story that someone types and prints for the student to illustrate	Let student repair a broken desk or replace batteries in calculator	Let class work outside
Let student earn extra minutes of recess for entire class	Let student choose a modified or independent assignment	Let class redecorate classroom
Let student wear a sign or a badge	Let student choose a peer with whom to play a board game or computer game	Have a class party

Ideas for Younger Students (Pre K-4th Grade)	Ideas for Older Students (3rd-8th Grade)	Ideas for the Group
Let student work near a class pet or have hamster (or other caged pet) on desk for the day	Let student leave class a few minutes early	Give everyone in class food/beverage: – Popcorn – Fruit – Crackers – Juice
Let student sit in your chair	Give student a "Certificate of Achievement"	Go to recess or lunch with class
Let student perform for the class	Publicly congratulate (but be careful not to embarrass) student	Have class applaud for themselves
Have class give student applause	Congratulate student in front of another adult	Tell a joke to class
Identify student as "Special Student of the Day"	Give (or loan from the library) student a book that was special to you at the same age	Give class a new freedom or responsibility (e.g., increased freedom to move about the room)
Allow student to keep a special trophy or stuffed animal on desk for the day	Give student a job or responsibility (see APPENDIX 2 for specific ideas)	Give everyone in class a special pencil or other school-supply item
Give student a gift certificate for free ice cream or french fries	Give student a ticket to school dance or sporting event	Read to class
Congratulate student in front of class	Ask the principal or counselor to call student in and congratulate student on classroom success	Give class additional recess or break time
Take student's picture and post it	Send student or parent(s) a letter via the mail	Invite parents to come and watch class demonstrate a particular skill or competency
Draw stars on back of student's hand	Shake student's hand and congratulate in a very "adult-to-adult" manner	Set up a challenge or competition with another class
Invite student to eat in room with you	Give student a "Free Homework Pass"	Have a pizza delivered to classroom
Give student a paper crown to wear	Write a positive note to student	Teacher wears funny clothes to class
Post banner or poster with student's name and accomplishment	Call student at home to congratulate for classroom success	Schedule a field trip

Listed following are three of the most commonly expressed concerns about using extrinsic reinforcement; each accompanied by a brief explanation that addresses the particular issue raised:

1. *"Isn't this the equivalent of bribery?"* Absolutely not! Bribery is usually defined as "an inducement, usually monetary, to do something illegal or immoral." Extrinsic reinforcement is more accurately compared to a paycheck (when you meet certain conditions, rewards will be provided), or a merit bonus (because an employee does something special, a special monetary reward is occasionally provided).

2. *"Why should this problem student get a special contract and get to earn reinforcers that the other students—the good students—don't have access to?"* Students who are currently working successfully have sufficient reinforcers (intrinsic and/or extrinsic) to stay motivated. Perhaps they have parents who talk to them about daily successes in school, and/or who look at their work, and/or who talk to them about their success. Some students are adept at self-reinforcment—

taking pride in jobs well done and/or in always having good grades on their report cards.

On the other hand, some students have none of these. Such a student may need special incentives to get started experiencing success. While in some ways this may not seem fair, it is also not fair that some students have parents that look at every graded paper that comes home and celebrate success, while other students come from homes where no one even asks about school. When an individual student lacks motivation, one can either set up a special system or let the student continue to fail. Obviously, the former is in the student's best interest.

3. *"Won't this get the kid hooked on being reinforced all the time?"* Hopefully—the idea is to let the student have the experience of being successful and feeling empowered to meet a goal. The emphasis can always be shifted from extrinsic rewards to intrinsic motivation, but it is important to begin by getting the student "hooked on" success. One of the biggest problems in schools these days is that too many students are too comfortable with failure.

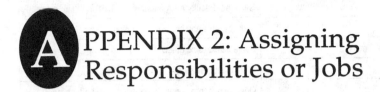

APPENDIX 2: Assigning Responsibilities or Jobs

Most people, adults and children alike, thrive on feeling needed and enjoy doing a job that is important and useful. For this reason, giving students responsibility at school is an excellent way to encourage responsible behavior and improve their self-esteem. It also capitalizes on the idea that most children want to be older and more powerful than they are. A primary grade student who is given a job that makes him/her feel influential receives a strong message about the faith others have in his/her ability. Similarly, an adolescent who is assigned a job that he/she feels is an adult-like responsibility is more likely to act maturely in other settings.

In some cases, a responsibility can be used as an intermittent reward. "Diane, you have been so responsible about getting your work done, would you like to be an assistant to Ms. Washington with an art project she is doing this afternoon with her kindergarten class?" In other cases, the responsibility can be a reinforcer within a structured system. "Allejandro, each day that your work is completed by 2:00, you get to spend the last half hour working with Ms. Terrence maintaining and repairing the computers in the lab."

There are also cases in which it is better for a student to have a daily job, regardless of other conditions. For example, a student into power struggles or one who is extremely discouraged is likely to benefit from having a job (not contingent upon behavior) to do everyday. "Erin, everyday, I would like to have your help. I want you to assist me in sorting through the announcements to determine which need to be read to the class. The way we will do this is . . . ."

Following is a list of specific ideas for jobs within both the classroom and the school.

Classroom Jobs	School-Wide Jobs
Staple papers	Tutor a younger student
Make a bulletin board	Read to a kindergarten class
File (nonconfidential) papers	Assist another teacher
Clean the room	Collect coffee cups from teachers at end of day
Organize a new learning center	Work in kitchen
Keep a computer area neat and organized	Assist custodial staff
Help teacher time length of transitions	Help raise the flag in the morning
Help teacher take attendance	Assist principal in organizing an assembly
Assist teacher with class calendar	Serve on task force with adults (e.g., What will be done about vandalism and graffiti)
Pass out papers	Get room ready for weekly teachers' meeting
Write notice for classroom newsletter	Be a messenger
Prepare materials for special class project	Work in office

Classroom Jobs	School-Wide Jobs
Lead a fund-raising effort	Serve as "Faculty Art Assistant"
Manage playground equipment	Make badges and banners on computer
Be in charge of audio-visual equipment	Serve as crossing guard
Clean the fish tank or pet cage	Work in student store
Track inventory and order supplies	Operate popcorn popper (if popcorn is sold after school)
Be in charge of classroom recycling	Serve as tour guide for visitors to the school (with the assistance of an adult, if necessary)

APPENDIX 3: Responding to Inappropriate Behavior

Because most teachers in the course of each day deal with more than one student who misbehaves (and often several students who exhibit more than one inappropriate behavior), it can be very difficult to decide how to respond to each misbehavior. Should you ignore the misbehavior? keep the student after school? talk to the student to see if something is bothering him/her? Should you honestly let the student know how mad the misbehavior makes you? Too often what happens is a spur-of-the-moment reaction to an incident of misbehavior that has just occurred—that is, emotion-based action rather than rational and purposeful responding. Deciding ahead of time how you will respond to misbehavior is more effective than unplanned reactions for several reasons.

First of all, on-the-spot decisions tend to result in inconsistency, which may actually reinforce misbehavior. When responses are not predictable, it can feel like a game to a student: "I wonder what the teacher will do now." Second, sometimes "teacher reaction" is exactly what the student is looking for. Most students who have trouble behaving appropriately have become very skilled at getting what they want. For example, the student who craves attention will behave in ways that will gain attention from his/her teacher and peers. This applies, as well, to the student who wants power or wishes to avoid something, and the student who tries to hurt someone's feelings or make someone angry. Finally, constantly having to make decisions about what to do when a student misbehaves can be exhausting and emotionally draining.

The goal of predetermining procedures for dealing with various misbehaviors is to know exactly what to do when each misbehavior occurs. For example, "When Carly makes noises, I will ignore them. If Ramone and Jessica talk during lessons, they will not get to sit together for the rest of the day. Whenever a student swears, he/she will lose two minutes off of recess." Having a plan not only helps you to be consistent, but also minimizes the possibility that you will inadvertently reinforce misbehavior.

The procedures should be determined, in part, by identifying what a student is trying to achieve with a particular misbehavior and then developing a response that *does not* give the student what he/she wants. (Remember, to be effective an intervention must also include providing plenty of positive reinforcement for appropriate behaviors.) Identifying responses to misbehaviors, before they occur, leaves more time and energy for the fun aspects of teaching—such as interacting with each student when he/she is behaving responsibly.

The following steps can help you to establish procedures for dealing with the misbehavior of a particular student:

1. *Define the problem behavior(s) the student exhibits.*

   Sit down with a blank piece of paper and think through a typical day, identifying problems that occur during various activities. Write down anything you would consider to be an example of inappropriate (or bordering on inappropriate) behavior. For example:

   - When the student first enters the classroom

     – Does he/she say or do anything that bothers you or is annoying?

     – Does he/she say or do anything that interferes with learning? disrupts the class? wastes class time?

   Progress through each activity of the day (e.g., attendance and opening activities, individual subjects like math or science, transitions, walking down the hall to the cafeteria, etc.), identifying and giving specific examples of as many typical misbehaviors as possible. Although not all the misbehaviors will be dealt with through one intervention plan, a complete list will help define the parameters of any intervention. Other questions to ask include:

- Does the student comply with instructions?
- Does the student get his/her work done? is it done satisfactorily?
- How does the student get along with the other students?
- Are there any other problems you've noticed?

2. *Categorize the various problem behaviors.*

Examine the list to see which behaviors might be clustered together. For example, pencil tapping, "screeching" the chair, and making animal noises might comprise the category "making noises." Or, telling everyone to pick up their things, telling the teacher to watch the clock, telling other students to sharpen their pencils, etc. could be combined under a category "bossiness."

The final list might look something like this sample:

Being Disrespectful	Making Noises at Desk
• Rude	• Pencil tapping
• Smart-aleck comments during lessons	• Screeching chair
• Puts down other students	• Making animal noises
Bothering Other Students	**Wasting Time**
• Tapping shoulders	• Frequently going for a drink of water
• Talking	• Frequently sharpening pencil
• Knocking things off desks	• Daydreaming

3. *Determine whether any categories require systematic definition.*

One important key to an effective intervention is clearly defining the inappropriate behavior, especially in those cases where the behavior might be open to interpretation (e.g., "being disrespectful" and "bothering other students"). This means making sure the student knows specifically, and the two of you agree upon, the

"borderline" (difference) between appropriate and inappropriate behavior.

It is especially important to define borderlines if there are going to be consequences for misbehavior. It is not reasonable to have consequences for disrespectful behavior, for example, unless the student understands the difference between respectful and disrespectful acts. Clearly defined borderlines will also increase the consistency with which you implement the consequences because you are more likely to follow through on a consequence if you are certain that the student knows his/her behavior is inappropriate.

On the other hand, when borderlines haven't been defined, consequences may occur more frequently on days when you are not feeling patient and less frequently on days when you are in a good mood. Such inconsistency can seem arbitrary and unfair to the student, and may result in his/her experimenting to find out what will happen today. "Hey, that is the same thing I said yesterday and you didn't nail me then. That's not fair."

Also, once borderlines have been clarified, it is not necessary to keep re-explaining the problem behavior. Each time the student misbehaves, simply state the misbehavior and the consequence. "Raina, we have discussed that disruptive behavior; You lose one of your lottery tickets." Explaining each time why a behavior is disruptive gives too much attention to the misbehavior.

4. *Define the borderlines for any behavior(s) requiring systematic definition.*

One way to establish the borderline between appropriate and inappropriate behavior is to use positive and negative examples of concepts such as respect/disrespect, polite/rude, supportively funny/cruelly sarcastic, etc. Carefully choosing and describing several examples of inappropriate behavior and several corresponding examples of alternative, appropriate behavior can both delineate the borderline and allow you to verify the student's understanding. "Jake, I am going to give you an example of how a student might handle a direction give by the teacher, and you tell me if it would be respectful or disrespectful."

This method of defining borderlines is always appropriate when teaching or clarifying a new concept. For example, if a student does not know what you mean by disruptive behavior, providing positive and negative examples will help him/her understand the difference between acceptable classroom noise and disruptive noise.

"T charts" can also help you to establish borderlines. The horizontal line of the "T" describes a particular situation that might lead to the inappropriate behavior. Below the horizontal line on the left are examples of inappropriate student actions, and on the right is a list of appropriate and/or desirable actions. By choosing situations and examples carefully, you can provide valuable information to the student about his/her behavior.

Sample T charts for several behaviors are shown following.

- For a problem with disrespect:

Situation—The teacher says, "Good morning, Carly."	
Examples of Disrespectful Behaviors	*Examples of Respectful Behaviors*
– Carly says in a mocking voice, "Good morning, Teacher."	– Carly says in a friendly or neutral voice, "Good morning" or "How are you?"
– Carly turns her back on the teacher.	– Carly responds with a smile or nod.
– Carly sarcastically compares the teacher to a TV character.	

- For a problem with inappropriate language:

Situation—Treat trips in the classroom.	
Examples of Inappropriate Responses	*Examples of Appropriate Responses*
– "Damn!"	– "Darn!"
– "Sh—!"	– "Oops!"

- For a problem with hitting (explanation for the student will involve physical examples):

Situation—Brianna wants someone's attention.	
Examples of Inappropriate Behaviors	*Examples of Appropriate Behaviors*
– "Hitting" or touching like this . . . (hit the wall to demonstrate)."	– "Tapping or touching like this . . . (tap the student's shoulder to demonstrate)."
– "Pushing or shoving like this . . . (push a chair to demonstrate)."	– Standing next to someone in line without touching or bumping into that person.

- For a problem with a student putting other students down:

Situation—Someone says something that the student already knows.	
Examples of Inappropriate Responses	*Examples of Appropriate Responses*
– "Isn't that obvious?"	– Nodding his/her head (demonstrate).
– "Bravo, aren't you smart!"	– "I noticed that, too."

The fuzzier a borderline is, the more important it is to include a number of different situations (along with corresponding examples of appropriate and inappropriate behaviors) so that both the teacher and the student will be able to generalize the borderline to classroom situations.

Another way to define the borderline is to set limits. Sometimes what makes a student's behavior problematic is how frequently it occurs rather than the behavior itself. In these cases, the borderline might be defined by letting the student know, specifically, how often exhibiting the behavior is acceptable and when it is too much.

For example, you may have a student who asks to have assignments clarified well beyond what is necessary. You might decide to limit the number of questions the student can ask. "Arthur, I want you to keep trying your best, but I've noticed that you often ask questions when you know the answers. To help you learn to be more independent and trust yourself more, I am going to give you eight tickets to use for questions each morning. Each time you ask a question, you will use a ticket. When you run out of tickets, I won't be able to answer your questions. This will help you think carefully about the questions you want to ask."

By limiting the number of questions, you begin to define the borderline between appropriate and inappropriate behavior. Limits tend to be especially useful for behaviors that must be reduced rather than eliminated altogether.

To determine a sensible limit, consider: (1) what would be acceptable from an average student; (2) what is reasonable for you to tolerate; and (3) whether the student can reasonably meet the expectation. When a major behavior change is required, begin with limits that are within the range of the student's potential for success and gradually shape the behavior. Setting limits also requires establishing a consequence for times the student exceeds the limit.

5. *Identify a procedural response for each category of misbehavior.*

You must decide whether it makes more sense to ignore, implement a consequence, or give information when a student exhibits a particular misbehavior. In general, *attention-getting behavior* is best ignored; *willful misbehavior* usually requires a consequence (e.g., time owed, time-out, a response cost lottery, etc.); and *misbehavior that stems from a student not knowing how to behave appropriately* should

result in the delivery of some form of information (e.g., a gentle verbal correction, a signal to cue the student, self-monitoring, self-evaluation, positive practice, redirection, etc.).

The following chart lists several misbehaviors and example procedural responses for each.

Misbehavior	Procedural Response
Being disrespectful – Being rude – Making smart-aleck comments – Putting down other students	Self-monitoring
Making noises at desk – Pencil tapping – Screeching the chair – Making animal noises	Ignore
Bothering other students – Tapping their shoulders – Talking – Knocking things off their desks	One minute owed off of recess per infraction
Not finishing work	No recess until work is finished; assigned as homework if not done by the end of the day
Wasting time – Frequently getting a drink of water – Frequently sharpening pencil – Daydreaming	Ignore

6. *Make sure the student is aware of how you will respond to the inappropriate behavior.*

Before you actually implement the intended procedural response, you need to explain to the student exactly how you plan to respond to his/her inappropriate behavior. Ask if he/she has any suggestions, and incorporate any that are reasonable so that the student feels he/she has a voice in the plan. Next, ask the student questions to verify that he/she understands. "Carly, if you go over and start tapping Nick on the shoulder while he is trying to work, what will I do? Right, I will tell you that you need to take your seat and that you owe a minute off of recess. If you . . . (etc.)."

During implementation of the plan, you may also wish to occasionally prompt the student. For example, if you have set a limit on a student who has a problem with asking too many questions, you might help the student evaluate whether to ask a question or not. "Debby, do you know the answer to that question? Are you sure you want to use one of your tickets for that question?" Providing verbal feedback when the student does ask a question can also help. "Debby, that was a good use of one of your question tickets. You needed that information to get started."; or "Debby, you just used a question ticket to get information that wasn't important. Think carefully before you ask your next question."

7. *Strive to be consistent in responding to the various misbehaviors.*

At least once per week, evaluate the consistency of your responses. Identify any procedures that are not working. For example, it may be that a student's noise making is so intrusive that you cannot ignore it—you may need to respond with an in-class consequence. Always inform the student prior to making any changes in the plan.

INDEX

J

K

L

Q

R

. . . .

S

. . . .

V

. . . .

W

ORDER FORM

☐ Same as Billing Address?

BILL TO: _____

_____

PHONE: (_____)_____

SHIP TO: _____

_____

PHONE: (_____)_____

QTY.	PRODUCT CODE	TITLE	UNIT PRICE*	SHIPPING/ UNIT**	TOTAL
	65ENC	*The Teacher's Encyclopedia of Behavior Management*	$ 39.50	$ 3.95	
	49MAN	*Interventions Procedural Manual* and 16 Intervention Booklets	$ 65.00	$ 6.50	
	49TAPE	*Interventions* Audio Tape Album	$ 59.00	$ 5.90	
	49MT	*Interventions* Kit (Manual, 16 Booklets, and Audio Tape Album)	$112.50	$11.25	
	37FOUND	*Foundations*	$495.00	(included)	
	73BUS	*Bus Discipline*	$299.00	$ 6.50	
	73LEGAL	*Legal Issues in School Transportation*	$199.00	$ 5.00	
	Order both programs and SAVE $50.00		$448.00	$10.00	
	73CD	*Cafeteria Discipline*	$249.00	$ 5.00	
	73PLAY	*Playground Discipline*	$249.00	$ 5.00	
	73STP	*STP: Stop, Think, Plan*	$249.00	$ 5.00	
	Order any two programs and SAVE $100.00		$348.00	$10.00	
	Order all three programs and SAVE $175.00		$572.00	$15.00	

* Prices subject to change without notice.
** Additional charges will be assessed for orders outside the continental United States or for rush delivery.

TOTAL AMOUNT DUE

Please send me the following FREE, no-obligation videotape preview(s):

☐ *Foundations* ☐ *Bus Discipline* ☐ *Legal Issues in School Transportation*
☐ *Cafeteria Discipline* ☐ *Playground Discipline* ☐ *STP: Stop, Think, Plan*

METHOD OF PAYMENT

☐ VISA ☐ MasterCard ☐ Check/Money Order
(Please make payable to Sopris West.)

☐ Purchase Order No. _____
(A copy of P.O. MUST be attached.)

Account No. __ __ __ __ __ __ __ __ __ __ __ __ __ __ __ __

Expiration Date: __ __ / __ __

Print exact name appearing on credit card.

Cardholder Signature

3 EASY WAYS TO ORDER

Phone Toll Free 1-800-547-6747   **MAIL** Sopris West • 1140 Boston Avenue • Longmont, CO 80501
FAX (303) 776-5934

. . . .
The Teacher's Encyclopedia of Behavior Management: 100 Problems/500 Plans

GIVE US FEEDBACK

Your Name_____

Title or Position _____

School or Organization _____

Address _____

_____

Phone_____

Problem(s) that are not included in this edition of *The Teacher's Encyclopedia of Behavior Management* that should be included in the next edition:

_____

_____

_____

A MODEL PLAN that I use for _____ that is not
(please specify *Encyclopedia* problem title)

included in this edition of the *The Encyclopedia* is:

_____

_____

_____

_____

(Attach additional sheets if necessary.)

If the plan you described above is used in the next edition of *The Encyclopedia*, please specify if you would like your name to be credited in the book:

❑ Yes, please include my name if the plan above is used in the next edition.

Authorization signature required_____

date_____

❑ No, include the suggested plan above, but do not use my name.

Return this completed form to:
Editor • Sopris West • 1140 Boston Avenue • Longmont, CO 80501